Infants, Children, and Adolescents

Third Edition

Laura E. Berk

ILLINOIS STATE UNIVERSITY

ALLYN AND BACON

BOSTON   LONDON   TORONTO   SYDNEY   TOKYO   SINGAPORE

TO MY HUSBAND, KEN,

AND MY SONS, DAVID AND PETER,

WITH LOVE

Vice President and Editor-in-Chief, Social Sciences and Education: Sean W. Wakely
Senior Development Editor: Sue Gleason
Development Editors: Barbara Brooks, Anne A. Reid
Series Editorial Assistant: Jessica Barnard
Vice President and Director of Field Marketing: Joyce Nilsen
Composition Buyer: Linda Cox
Manufacturing Buyer: Megan Cochran
Cover Administrator: Linda Knowles
Cover Designer: Susan Paradise
Photo Researcher: Sarah Evertson—ImageQuest
Editorial-Production Service: Thomas E. Dorsaneo, Publishing Consultants
Copy Editor: Betty Barr
Text Design and Electronic Composition: Seventeenth Street Studios

Copyright © 1999, 1996, 1993 by Allyn & Bacon
A Viacom Company
160 Gould Street
Needham Heights, MA 02494

Internet: www.abacon.com

Portions of this book are also published under the title *Infants and Children:
Prenatal Through Middle Childhood,* Third Edition, by Laura E. Berk, copyright
© 1999, 1996, 1994 by Allyn and Bacon

Library of Congress Cataloging-in-Publication Data

Berk, Laura E.
    Infants, children, and adolescents / Laura E. Berk. —3rd ed.
      p.   cm.
    Includes bibliographical references and index.
    ISBN 0-205-28504-X
     1. Child development. 2. Infants—development. 3. Adolescence.
   I. Title.
   RJ131.B387   1999
   305.231—dc21   98–25280
                                                CIP
                                              AC

Printed in the United States of America
10 9 8 7 6 5 4 3 2 1 VHP 02 01 00 99 98

ABOUT THE AUTHOR

Laura E. Berk is a distinguished professor of psychology at Illinois State University, where she teaches child development to both undergraduate and graduate students. She received her Bachelor's degree in psychology from the University of California, Berkeley, and her masters and doctoral degrees in early childhood development and education from the University of Chicago. She has been a visiting scholar at Cornell University, UCLA, Stanford University, and the University of South Australia. Berk has published widely on the effects of school environments on children's development and, more recently, on the development of private speech. Her research has been funded by the U.S. Office of Education and the National Institute of Child Health and Human Development. It has appeared in many prominent journals, including *Child Development, Developmental Psychology, Merrill-Palmer Quarterly, Journal of Abnormal Child Psychology,* and *Development and Psychopathology.* Her empirical studies have attracted the attention of the general public, leading to contributions to *Psychology Today* and *Scientific American.* Berk has served as research editor of *Young Children* and is currently consulting editor of *Early Childhood Research Quarterly.* She is author of the chapter on the extracurriculum of schooling for the American Educational Research Association's *Handbook of Research on Curriculum.* Her books include *Private Speech: From Social Interaction to Self-Regulation, Scaffolding Children's Learning: Vygotsky and Early Childhood Education,* and *Landscapes of Development, An Anthology of Readings.* In addition to *Infants, Children, and Adolescents,* she is author of the best-selling texts *Child Development* and *Development Through the Lifespan,* published by Allyn and Bacon.

BRIEF CONTENTS

LIST OF FEATURES

CONTENTS

I THEORY AND RESEARCH IN CHILD DEVELOPMENT

II FOUNDATIONS OF DEVELOPMENT

III INFANCY AND TODDLERHOOD: THE FIRST TWO YEARS

V MIDDLE CHILDHOOD: SIX TO ELEVEN YEARS

11 PHYSICAL DEVELOPMENT IN MIDDLE CHILDHOOD 408

12 COGNITIVE DEVELOPMENT IN MIDDLE CHILDHOOD 436

16 EMOTIONAL AND SOCIAL
DEVELOPMENT IN ADOLESCENCE   600

PREFACE FOR INSTRUCTORS

My decision to write *Infants, Children, and Adolescents* was inspired by a wealth of professional and personal experiences. First and foremost were the interests and needs of hundreds of students of child development with whom I have worked in twenty-eight years of college teaching. I aimed for a text that is intellectually stimulating, that provides depth as well as breadth of coverage, that portrays the complexities of child development with clarity and excitement, and that is relevant and useful in building a bridge from theory and research to children's everyday lives. Instructor and student enthusiasm for the book not only has been among my greatest sources of pride and satisfaction, but also has inspired me to rethink and improve each edition.

This third edition includes a great many changes that represent several major trends in the field:

■ *Inclusion of interdisciplinary research is expanded.* The contemporary move toward viewing the child's thoughts, feelings, and behavior as an integrated whole, affected by a wide array of influences in biology, social context, and culture, has motivated developmental researchers to strengthen their links with other fields of psychology and other disciplines. Topics and findings included in the text increasingly reflect the contributions of educational psychology, social psychology, health psychology, clinical psychology, neuropsychology, biology, pediatrics, sociology, anthropology, and other fields.

■ *Diverse pathways of change are highlighted.* Investigators have reached broad consensus that variations in biological makeup, everyday tasks, and the people who support children in mastery of those tasks lead to wide individual differences in children's skills. This edition pays more attention to variability in development and recent theories, including ecological, sociocultural, and dynamic systems, that attempt to explain it.

■ *The interconnected roles of biology and environment are given greater emphasis.* Accumulating evidence on development of the brain, motor skills, cognitive competencies, temperament, and developmental problems underscores the way biological factors emerge in, are modified by, and share power with experience. The interconnection between biology and environment is revisited throughout the text narrative and in a new Biology and Environment feature.

■ *The link between theory, research, and applications—a theme of this book since its inception—is strengthened.* As researchers intensify their efforts to generate findings that can be applied to real-life situations, I have placed greater weight on social policy issues and sound theory- and research-based practices.

TEXT PHILOSOPHY

The basic approach of this book has been shaped by my own professional and personal history as a teacher, researcher, and parent. It consists of six philosophical ingredients that I regard as essential for students to emerge from a course with a thorough understanding of child development:

1. An understanding of major theories and the strengths and shortcomings of each. The first chapter begins by emphasizing that only knowledge of multiple theories can do justice to the richness of child development. As I take up each age sector and aspect of development, I present a variety of theoretical perspectives, indicate how each approach highlights previously overlooked contributions to development, and discuss research that has been used to evaluate them. Consideration of contrasting theories also serves as the context for an evenhanded analysis of many controversial issues throughout the text.

2. Knowledge of both the sequence of child development and the processes that underlie it. Students are provided with a description of the organized sequence of development along with a discussion of processes of change. An understanding of process—how complex combinations of biological and environmental events produce development—has been the focus of most recent research. Accordingly, the text reflects this emphasis. But new information about the timetable of change has also emerged. In many ways, children have proved to be far more competent than they were believed to be in the past. Current evidence on the timing and sequence of development, along with its implications for process, is presented throughout the book.

3. An appreciation of the impact of context and culture on child development. A wealth of research indicates that children live in rich physical and social contexts that affect all aspects of development. In each chapter, the student travels to distant parts of the world as I review a growing body of cross-cultural evidence. The text narrative also discusses many findings on socioeconomically and ethnically diverse children within the United States. Besides highlighting the role of immediate settings, such as family, neighborhood, and school, I make a concerted effort to underscore the impact of larger social structures—societal values, laws, and government programs—on children's well-being.

4. An understanding of the joint contributions of biology and environment to development. The field recognizes more powerfully than ever before the joint roles of hereditary/constitutional and environmental factors—that these contributions to development combine in complex ways and cannot be separated in a simple manner. Numerous examples of how biological dispositions can be maintained as well as transformed by social contexts are presented throughout the book.

5. A sense of the interdependency of all aspects of development—physical, cognitive, emotional, and social. Every chapter takes an integrated approach to understanding children. I show how physical, cognitive, emotional, and social development are interwoven. Within the text narrative, students are referred to other sections of the book to deepen their grasp of relationships among various aspects of change.

6. An appreciation of the interrelatedness of theory, research, and applications. Throughout this book, I emphasize that theories of child development and the research stimulated by them provide the foundation for sound, effective practices with children. The link between theory, research, and applications is reinforced by an organizational format in which theory and research are presented first, followed by implications for practice. In addition, a current focus in the field—harnessing child development knowledge to shape social policies that support children's needs—is reflected in every chapter. The text addresses the current condition of children in the United States and around the world and shows how theory and research have sparked successful interventions.

TEXT ORGANIZATION

I have chosen a chronological organization for this text. The chronological approach has the advantage of enabling students to get to know children of a given age period very

well. It also eases the task of integrating the various aspects of development, since each is discussed in close proximity. At the same time, a chronologically organized book requires that theories covering several age periods be presented piecemeal. This creates a challenge for students, who must link the various parts together. To assist with this task, I remind students of important earlier achievements before discussing new developments. Also, chapters devoted to the same topic (for example, Cognitive Development in Early Childhood, Cognitive Development in Middle Childhood) are similarly organized, making it easier for students to draw connections across age periods and construct a continuous vision of developmental change.

NEW COVERAGE IN THE THIRD EDITION

In this edition, I continue to represent a rapidly transforming contemporary literature with theory and research from over 1,500 new citations. To make room for new coverage, I have condensed and reorganized some topics and eliminated others that are no longer as crucial in view of new evidence. The following is a sampling of major content changes in this edition, organized by part divisions of the book (a more complete description of changes can be found in the Annotated Instructor's Manual that accompanies the text):

■ **THEORY AND RESEARCH IN CHILD DEVELOPMENT**
Attention to new theoretical directions—the dynamic systems perspective—and new sections on psychophysiological methods and the microgenetic design (Chapter 1).

■ **FOUNDATIONS OF DEVELOPMENT**
Revised section on environmental contexts for development, with increased attention to ecological systems theory and consideration of the impact of individualist and collectivist values on child and family policies (Chapter 2). Current research on effects of prenatal nutrition on development, including a new Social Issues box on vitamin–mineral supplements, with special attention to the power of folic acid to prevent neural tube defects (Chapter 3). Expanded section on the transition to parenthood, including changes in the family system and parent interventions (Chapter 4).

■ **INFANCY AND TODDLERHOOD:**
THE FIRST TWO YEARS
Additional attention to brain growth, including a new Biology and Environment box on sensitive periods in brain development (Chapter 5). New sections on dynamic systems theory of motor development and on object perception (Chapter 5). Revised and updated research evaluating Piaget's theory of sensorimotor development,

including a new section on physical reasoning (Chapter 6). Expanded discussion of recent ideas about how early cognitive development takes place, including an introduction to and critique of the modular view of the mind (Chapter 6). Revised section on the impact of infant and toddler day care on mental development, with special attention to recent evidence on the quality of American day care (Chapter 6). New section on development of peer sociability in infancy and toddlerhood, and enhanced treatment of self-development, including the role of self-awareness in early emotional development (Chapter 7).

■ EARLY CHILDHOOD: TWO TO SIX YEARS

New evidence on infectious disease, including oral rehydration therapy as a life-saving treatment for diarrhea in developing countries; the status of childhood immunization in the United States and other industrialized nations; and the impact of otitis media on development (Chapter 8). New sections on development of spatial representation and on evaluating Vygotsky's theory (Chapter 9). Enhanced discussion of the young child's theory of mind, including diverse factors that contribute to an early understanding of mental life (Chapter 9). New sections on cultural variations in peer sociability, parental and sibling influences on early peer relations, and television as a source of gender stereotypes (Chapter 10). New research on the distinction between overt and relational aggression, including sex differences (Chapter 10).

■ MIDDLE CHILDHOOD: SIX TO ELEVEN YEARS

Current findings on the prevalence and causes of unintentional injury in middle childhood (Chapter 11). New sections on the impact of class size on academic achievement and on Vygotsky-inspired approaches to elementary education, including reciprocal teaching (Chapter 12). Special attention to variations in friendship quality between prosocial and aggressive children, and new sections on only children and on gay and lesbian families (Chapter 13).

■ ADOLESCENCE: THE TRANSITION TO ADULTHOOD

New research on biological contributions to homosexuality and a new Biology and Environment box on homosexual identity development, including coming out (Chapter 14). New sections on postformal thought, the role of metacognition in advanced cognitive development, and the impact of personality on vocational choice (Chapter 15). Updated coverage of sex differences in mental abilities, including single-sex secondary schools and a new Biology and Environment box on sex differences in spatial abilities (Chapter 15). New section on responses to hypothetical versus real-life moral dilemmas, highlighting factors beyond rationally weighing alternatives that influence moral judgment (Chapter 16). Special emphasis on bio-

logical and environmental contributions to adolescent problem behavior, as illustrated by depression, suicide, and delinquency, including a new Biology and Environment box on two routes to adolescent delinquency (Chapter 16).

■ INSTRUCTOR'S SUPPLEMENTS

A variety of teaching tools are available to assist instructors in organizing lectures, planning demonstrations and examinations, and ensuring student comprehension.

■ ANNOTATED INSTRUCTOR'S MANUAL (AIM)

This convenient teaching tool provides Learning Objectives, Test Bank Item numbers, references to Lecture Extensions and Learning Activities, answers to "Ask Yourself . . ." questions, and other instructor's annotations keyed to reduced versions of actual text pages. It also offers a chapter summary, list of new material, and Chapter-at-a-Glance grid for each chapter.

■ INSTRUCTOR'S RESOURCE MANUAL (IRM)

Prepared by Heather A. Bouchey, University of Denver, Laura E. Berk, Illinois State University, and Belinda M. Wholeben, Rockford College, this thoroughly revised IRM contains additional material to enrich your class presentations. For each chapter, the IRM provides a Brief Chapter Summary, detailed Lecture Outline, Lecture Extensions, Learning Activities, Suggested Readings, and Media Materials.

■ TEST BANK

Prepared by Carol Satterfield Tate, University of the South, the test bank contains over 2,000 multiple-choice questions, each of which is cross-referenced to a Learning Objective, page-referenced to chapter content, and classified by type (factual, applied, or conceptual); essay questions; and premade tests.

■ COMPUTERIZED TEST BANK

This computerized version of the test bank is available in Windows and Macintosh formats using ESATEST III, the best-selling test generation software.

■ TRANSPARENCIES

Over 200 full-color transparencies taken from the text and other sources are referenced in the margins of the Annotated Instructor's Manual for the most appropriate use in your classroom presentation.

■ SEASONS OF LIFE VIDEO SERIES

Illustrating the text's interdisciplinary focus, this five-video series explores a multitude of biological, psychological and social influences on development. Nearly 75 psychologists, biologists, sociologists, and anthropologists present theory, methods, and research. Your publisher's representative can provide you with details on class enrollment restrictions.

■ FILMS FOR THE HUMANITIES AND SCIENCES: CHILD DEVELOPMENT VIDEO AND VIDEODISC

Complementing the text's linkage of theory and research to application, both the video and the videodisc feature high-interest segments on topics such as learning disabilities, fetal alcohol syndrome, genetic counseling, and teen suicide.

■ "INFANTS, CHILDREN, AND ADOLESCENTS IN ACTION" OBSERVATION PROGRAM

In conjunction with the Illinois State University Television Production Studio, I have created this real-life videotape, containing hundreds of observation segments that illustrate the many theories, concepts, and milestones of child development. An Observation Guide helps students use the video in conjunction with the textbook to deepen their understanding of the material and apply what they have learned to everyday life. The videotape and Observation Guide are free to instructors who adopt the text and are available to students at a discount when packaged with the text.

■ WEBSITE

http://www.abacon.com/berk

Designed for students and faculty of Child Development and Human Development or Lifespan classes, this comprehensive website encourages online and interactive learning and also offers current links and information about development. It includes an Online Study Guide, a Teaching Aids section, biographical sketches of personalities from the text, and a variety of additional features.

ACKNOWLEDGMENTS

The dedicated contributions of a great many individuals have helped make this book a reality. An impressive cast of reviewers provided many helpful suggestions, constructive criticisms, and encouragement and enthusiasm for the organization and content of the book. I am grateful to each one of them.

■ REVIEWERS OF THE FIRST AND SECOND EDITIONS

Kathleen Bey, Palm Beach Community College
Donald Bowers, Community College of Philadelphia
Jerry Bruce, Sam Houston State College
Joseph J. Campos, University of California, Berkeley
Nancy Taylor Coghill, University of Southwest Louisiana
Jennifer Cook, Kent State University
Roswell Cox, Berea College
Sheridan DeWolf, Grossmont College
Constance DiMaria-Kross, Union County College
Kathleen Fite, Southwest Texas State University
Vivian Harper, San Joaquin Delta College
Janice Hartgrove-Freile, North Harris Community College
Vernon Haynes, Youngstown State University
Paula Hillmann, University of Wisconsin, Waukesha
Malia Huchendorf, Normandale Community College
Clementine Hansley Hurt, Radford University
John S. Klein, Castleton State College
Eugene Krebs, California State University, Fresno
Carole Kremer, Hudson Valley Community College
Gary W. Ladd, University of Illinois, Urbana-Champaign
Linda Lavine, State University of New York at Cortland
Gail Lee, Jersey City State College
Frank Manis, University of Southern California
Mary Ann McLaughlin, Clarion University of Pennsylvania
Cloe Merrill, Weber State University
Tizrah Schutzengel, Bergen Community College
Johnna Shapiro, Illinois Wesleyan University
Gregory Smith, Dickinson College
Thomas Spencer, San Francisco State University
Carolyn Spies, Bloomfield College
Judith Ward, Central Connecticut State University
Shawn Ward, Le Moyne College
Alida Westman, Eastern Michigan University
Sue Williams, Southwest Texas State University
Deborah Winters, New Mexico State University

■ REVIEWERS OF THE THIRD EDITION

Mark B. Alcorn, University of Northern Colorado
Michele Y. Breault, Truman State University
Diane Brothers Cook, Gainesville College
Zoe Ann Davidson, Alabama A & M University
Trisha Folds-Bennett, College of Charleston
Bert Hayslip, Jr., University of North Texas
Judith R. Levine, State University of New York at Farmingdale
Rich Metzger, University of Tennessee at Chattanooga
Jennifer Trapp Myers, University of Michigan
Peter V. Oliver, University of Hartford
Virginia Parsons, Carroll College
Alan Russell, Flinders University
Connie Steele, University of Tennessee, Knoxville
Janet Strayer, Simon Fraser University
Marcia Summers, Ball State University
Connie K. Varnhagen, University of Alberta

In addition, I thank the following individuals for responding to a survey that provided vital feedback for the new edition:

Karen L. Bauer, Edinboro University; Diane Clark, Shippensburg University; C. Timothy Dickel, Creighton University; Claire Etaugh, Bradley University; Robin L. Harwood, University of Connecticut; Mona Ibrahim, Michigan State University; Jacqueline Kikuchi, University of Rhode Island; Judith R. Levine, State University of New York at Farmingdale; Kathryn A. Markell, Cardinal Stritch College; Beatrice McChesney, Marshall University; Olivia Melroe, Moorehead State University; Martha L. Pott, Wellesley College; James Sottile, Marshall University; Marcia Summers, Ball State University; Connie K. Varnhagen, University of Alberta; Penelope Vinden, Clark University; and Dinah Volk, Cleveland State University.

I have been fortunate to work with an exceptionally capable editorial team at Allyn and Bacon. Sean Wakely, Vice President and Editor-in-Chief, has inspired and energized my work, bringing to bear a combination of qualities unmatched in my experience—keen awareness of instructors' and students' needs, balanced attention to the text's overall concept and to vital details, thorough manuscript reviewing, and a sense of enthusiasm, respect for scholarship, and vision that has prompted me to strive for greater heights. I have especially appreciated his forthrightness and day-to-day communication, through which he forges a true editor–author partnership. Sean's innovative approach to text editing led me to develop the Biology and Environment and Caregiving Concerns features for this edition. I look forward to working with him on future editions and other projects in the years to come.

I would like to express a heartfelt thank you to Joyce Nilsen, Vice President, Field Marketing, for the outstanding work she has done over the years in marketing my texts. Joyce has made sure that accurate and clear information about the texts and their ancillaries reached Allyn and Bacon's sales force and that the needs of prospective and current adopters were met. Each time I have watched Joyce teach others about my books, I have been impressed with both her knowledge of their content and the vitality with which she conveys her message. She cares deeply about my texts—and about the teaching of child development in colleges and universities. It is a privilege and pleasure to have her in command of marketing activities for the third edition of *Infants, Children, and Adolescents.*

Sue Gleason, Senior Development Editor, coordinated the complex development activities for the book and the preparation of text supplements. Her exceptional management skills, astute advice, and prompt and patient responses to my concerns and queries have enhanced every aspect of this edition. I am grateful to Barbara Brooks for a fresh look at the text narrative and for many recommendations for effective page and illustration layout. Annie Reid read the manuscript, offering a wealth of helpful suggestions for clarity and economy of expression. She has contributed immeasurably to the quality of the final product, as she has done for each of my texts over the past six years.

Elaine Ober, Editorial-Production Manager, assembled an outstanding production team. Tom Dorsaneo coordinated the complex production tasks that resulted in this beautiful third edition. His competence, courtesy, diplomatic problem solving, and interest in the subject matter as an involved grandfather of an energetic preschooler have made working with him a great delight. Betty Barr's meticulous, caring copy editing ensured accuracy and precision on every page. I thank Sarah Evertson for obtaining the exceptional photographs that so aptly illustrate the text narrative. Jessica Barnard, Editorial Assistant, graciously arranged for manuscript reviews and attended to a wide variety of pressing, last-minute details.

A final word of gratitude goes to my family whose love, patience, and understanding have enabled me to be wife, mother, teacher, researcher, and text author at the same time. My sons, David and Peter, grew up with my child development texts, passing from childhood to adolescence and then to young adulthood as successive editions were written. David has a special connection with the books' subject matter as an elementary school teacher; Peter is embarking on the study of law as the book goes to press. Both continue to enrich my understanding through reflections on events and progress in their own lives. This past year, David's reports of his first-year teaching experiences led me to think much more deeply about diversity in development as I wrote. My husband, Ken, willingly made room for this time-consuming endeavor in our life together and communicated his belief in its importance in a great many unspoken, caring ways.

Laura Berk

My twenty-eight years of teaching child development have brought me in contact with thousands of students like you—students with diverse college majors, future goals, interests, and needs. Some are affiliated with my own department, psychology, but many come from other child-related fields—education, sociology, anthropology, family studies, and biology, to name just a few. Each semester, my students' aspirations have proved to be as varied as their fields of study. Many look toward careers in applied work with children—teaching, caregiving, nursing, counseling, social work, school psychology, and program administration. Some plan to teach child development, and a few want to do research. Most hope someday to have children, whereas others are already parents who come with a desire to better understand and rear their own youngsters. And almost all arrive with a deep curiosity about how they themselves developed from tiny infants into the complex human beings they are today.

My goal in preparing this third edition of *Infants, Children, and Adolescents* is to provide a textbook that meets the instructional goals of your course as well as your own personal needs. To achieve these objectives, I have grounded this book in a carefully selected body of classic and current research brought to life with stories and vignettes about children and families, many of whom I have known personally. In addition, the text discussion highlights the joint contribution of biology and environment to development, explains how the research process helps solve real-world problems, and pays special attention to policy issues that are crucial for safeguarding children's well-being in today's world. I have also used a clear, engaging writing style and provided the following pedagogical program that will assist you in mastering information, integrating the various aspects of development, critically examining controversial issues, and applying what you have learned.

PEDAGOGICAL FEATURES

Maintaining a highly accessible writing style—one that is lucid and engaging without being simplistic—continues to be one of this text's goals. I will frequently converse with and encourage you to relate what you read to your own life. In doing so, I hope to make the study of child development involving and pleasurable.

■ **Stories and Vignettes About Children.** To help you construct a clear image of development and to enliven the text narrative, each chronological age division is unified by case examples woven throughout that set of chapters. For example, within the infancy and toddlerhood section, we'll sit in on periodic gatherings of three mothers and their babies, observe dramatic changes and striking individual differences in the children's capabilities, and address the impact of family background, child-rearing practices, and parents' and children's life experiences on development. Besides a set of main characters, many additional vignettes offer vivid examples of development and diversity among children. Student response to this feature has been so positive that I have made a special effort to enhance it in this edition.

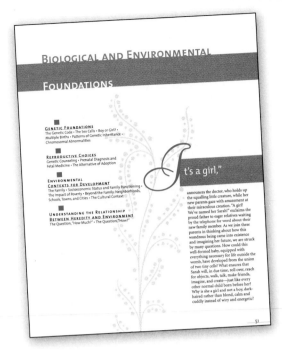

■ **Chapter Introductions and End-of-Chapter Summaries.** To provide you with a helpful preview of what you are about to read, I include an outline and overview of chapter content in each chapter introduction. Especially comprehensive end-of-chapter summaries, organized according to the major divisions of each chapter and highlighting important terms, will remind you of key points in the text discussion. Review questions are included in the summaries to encourage active study.

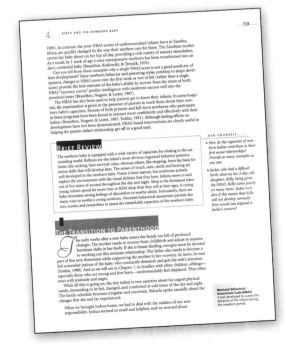

■ **Brief Reviews.** Interim summaries of text content appear at the end of most major sections in each chapter. They enhance retention by encouraging you to reflect on information you have just read before moving on to a new section.

■ **Ask Yourself . . .** Active engagement with the subject matter is also supported by critical thinking questions, which can be found in the margins at the end of major sections. The focus of these questions is divided between theory and applications. Many describe problematic situations faced by parents, teachers, and children and ask you to resolve them in light of what you have learned. In this way, the questions inspire deeper mastery of child development and new insights.

■ **Boxes.** Three types of boxes accentuate the philosophical themes of this book.

■ *Cultural Influences* boxes underscore the impact of context and culture on all aspects of development. They include such topics as Father–Infant Relationships among the Aka, a hunter–gatherer people of Central Africa, highlighting the importance of a warm marital bond for infant–father attachment; and the Impact of Ethnic and Political Violence on Children, emphasizing the role of parental and community support in preventing lasting negative consequences.

■ *Social Issues* boxes discuss the condition of children in the United States and around the world and emphasize the need for sensitive social policies to ensure their well-being. They include the U.N. Convention on the Rights of the Child, the first legally binding human rights treaty to recognize the civil, political, economic, social, and cultural rights of children; and Regulating Children's Television, addressing societal obstacles to controlling harmful TV and providing strategies parents can use to protect their children.

■ *Biology and Environment* boxes present a balanced, interconnected view of key biological and environmental influences on development. Examples are Resilient Children, addressing personal and experiential factors that help children spring back from adversity; and the Biology Basis of Shyness and Sociability, focusing on genetic and physiological contributions to temperament and the extent to which environment can modify a child's temperamental style.

■ **Caregiving Concerns Tables.** To accentuate the relationship of theory and research to practice woven throughout the text narrative, Caregiving Concerns tables provide easily accessible practical advice on the importance of caring for, protecting, and supporting the development of children of all ages. They include Ways Couples Can Ease the Transition to Parenthood; Building a Foundation for Good Eating Habits; Keeping Infants and Toddlers Safe; Supporting Early Language Learning; Fostering a Healthy Self-Image in Young Children; Encouraging Critical Thinking in School-Age Children; Fostering a Mastery Approach to Learning and Preventing Learned Helplessness; and Supporting Healthy Identity Development during Adolescence.

■ **Milestones Tables.** A Milestones table appears at the end of each chronological age division of the text. These tables summarize major physical, cognitive, language, and emotional and social developments of each age span. Entries in the Milestones tables are page-referenced to the text narrative to facilitate study and review.

■ **Additional Tables, Illustrations, and Photographs.** Additional tables are liberally included to help you grasp essential points in the text discussion, extend information on a topic, and consider applications. The many full-color illustrations throughout the book depict important theories, methods, and research findings. In this edition, the photo program has been extended. Each photo has been carefully selected to portray the text discussion and to represent the diversity of children in the United States and around the world.

■ **Marginal Glossary, End-of-Chapter Term List, and End-of-Book Glossary.** Mastery of terms that make up the central vocabulary of the field is promoted through a marginal glossary, an end-of-chapter term list, and an end-of-book Glossary. Important terms and concepts also appear in boldface type in the text narrative.

- **FYI ... For Further Information and Help.** Students in my own classes frequently ask where they can go to find out more about high-interest topics or to seek help in areas related to their own lives. To meet this need, I have included an annotated section at the end of each chapter that provides the names, phone numbers, and website addresses of organizations that disseminate information about child development and offer special services.

STUDY AIDS

Beyond the study aids found in this textbook, Allyn and Bacon offers a number of supplements for students. Ask your instructor or your bookstore about their availability. The website is open to all visitors to the Internet.

- **Study Guide.** Prepared by Jenny L. Churchill and Laura E. Berk, Illinois State University, this helpful guide offers Chapter Summaries, Learning Objectives, Study Questions organized according to major headings in the text, "Ask Yourself" questions that also appear in text margins, Suggested Readings, crossword puzzles for mastering important terms, and multiple-choice self-tests.

- **Practice Tests.** Twenty multiple-choice items per chapter plus an answer key with justifications are drawn from the test bank to assist you in preparing for course exams.

- **Website.** Visit *http://www.abacon.com/berk,* an easy-to-use website that features an interactive study guide, current links to information about development, biographical sketches of personalities from the text, and other learning aids.

I hope your experience learning about child development will be as rewarding as I have found it over the years. I would like to know what you think about both the field of child development and this book. I welcome your comments; please feel free to send them to me at Department of Psychology, Box 4620, Illinois State University, Normal, IL 61790, or care of the publisher, who will forward them to me.

Laura E. Berk

"Counting Leaves"
Chen Jie
6 years, China

As this child wanders through an autumn forest, captivated by the shapes, colors, and movement of falling leaves, she reminds us that development is complex, fascinating, and in many ways mystifying. As you read Chapter 1, it will open the door to a multiplicity of ways of thinking about and studying children.

History, Theory,
and Research Strategies

ot long ago, I left my midwestern home to live for a year near the small city in northern California where I spent my childhood years. One morning, I visited the neighborhood where I grew up—a place I had not seen since I was 12 years old.

I stood at the entrance to my old schoolyard. Buildings and grounds that looked large to me as a child now seemed strangely small from my grown-up vantage point. I peered through the window of my first-grade classroom. The desks were no longer arranged in rows but grouped in intimate clusters around the room. A computer rested against the far wall, near the spot where I once sat.

I walked my old route home from school, the distance shrunken by my larger stride. I stopped in front of my best friend Kathryn's house, where we once drew sidewalk pictures, crossed the street to play kickball, produced plays for neighborhood audiences in the garage, and traded marbles and stamps in the backyard. In place of the small shop where I had purchased penny candy stood a neighborhood day care center, filled with the voices and vigorous activity of toddlers and preschoolers.

As I walked, I reflected on early experiences that contributed to who and what I am today—weekends helping my father in his downtown clothing shop, the year my mother studied to become a high school teacher, moments of companionship and rivalry with my sister and brother, Sunday outings to museums and the seashore, and visits to my grandmother's house, where I became someone extra special.

As I passed the homes of my childhood friends, I thought of what I knew about their present lives. My close friend Kathryn, star pupil and president of our sixth-grade class—today a successful corporate lawyer and mother of two children. Shy, withdrawn Phil, cruelly teased because of his cleft lip—now owner of a thriving chain of hardware stores and member of the city council. Julio, immigrant from Mexico who joined our class in third grade—today director of an elementary school bilingual education program and single parent of an adopted Mexican boy. And finally, my next-door neighbor Rick, who picked fights at recess, struggled with reading, repeated fourth grade, dropped out of high school, and (so I heard) moved from one job to another over the following 10 years.

As you begin this course in child development, perhaps you, too, wondered about some of the same questions that crossed my mind during that nostalgic neighborhood walk:

- What determines the features that humans have in common and those that make each of us unique—in physical characteristics, mental capacities, interests, and behaviors?

- Is the infant and young child's perception of the world much the same as the adult's, or is it different in basic respects?

- Why do some of us, like Kathryn and Rick, retain the same styles of responding that characterized us as children, whereas others, like Phil, change in essential ways?

- How did Julio, transplanted to a foreign culture at 8 years of age, master its language and customs and succeed in its society, yet remain strongly identified with his ethnic community?

- In what ways are children's home, school, and neighborhood experiences the same today as they were in generations past, and in what ways are they different? How does generational change—employed mothers, day care, divorce, smaller families, and new technologies—affect children's characteristics and skills?

These are central questions addressed by **child development**, a field of study devoted to understanding all aspects of human growth and change from conception through adolescence. Child development is part of a larger discipline known as *developmental psychology*, or, in its interdisciplinary sense, *human development*, which includes all changes we experience throughout the lifespan. Great diversity characterizes the interests and concerns of the thousands of investigators who study child development. But all have a single goal in common: the desire to describe and identify those factors that influence the consistencies and transformations in young people during the first two decades of life.

THE FIELD OF CHILD DEVELOPMENT

*L*ook again at the questions about children just listed, and you will see that they are not just of scientific interest. Each is of *applied*, or practical, importance as well. In fact, scientific curiosity is just one factor that led child development to become the exciting field of study it is today. Research about development has also been stimulated by social pressures to better the

child development
A field of study devoted to understanding all aspects of human growth and change from conception through adolescence.

lives of children. For example, the beginning of public education in the early part of this century led to a demand for knowledge about what and how to teach children of different ages. The interest of pediatricians in improving children's health required an understanding of physical growth and nutrition. The social service profession's desire to treat children's anxieties and behavior problems required information about personality and social development. And parents have continually asked for advice about child-rearing practices and experiences that would promote the well-being of their child.

Our vast storehouse of information about child development is *interdisciplinary*. It has grown through the combined efforts of people from many fields of study. Because of the need for solutions to everyday problems concerning children, academic scientists from psychology, sociology, anthropology, and biology joined forces in research with professionals from a variety of applied fields, including education, home economics, medicine, and social service, to name just a few. Today, the field of child development is a melting pot of contributions. Its body of knowledge is not just scientifically important but practically relevant and useful.

A theory describes, explains, and predicts behavior. For example, a good theory of infant–caregiver attachment would explain why this crying 6-month-old seeks comfort and affection from her mother rather than from an unfamiliar adult. *(Frank Sitman/Stock Boston)*

BASIC ISSUES

Before scientific study of the child, questions about children were answered by turning to common sense, opinion, and belief. Research on children did not begin until the early part of the twentieth century. Gradually it led to the construction of theories of child development, to which professionals and parents could turn for understanding and guidance.

Although there are a great many definitions, for our purposes we can think of a **theory** as an orderly, integrated set of statements that describes, explains, and predicts behavior. For example, a good theory of infant–caregiver attachment would (1) *describe* the behaviors that lead up to babies' strong desire to seek the affection and comfort of a familiar adult around 6 to 8 months of age, (2) *explain* why infants have such a strong desire, and (3) *predict* what might happen if babies do not develop this close emotional bond.

Theories are vital tools in child development (and any other scientific endeavor) for two reasons. First, they provide organizing frameworks for our observations of children. In other words, they *guide and give meaning to* what we see. Second, theories that are verified by research often serve as a sound basis for practical action. Once a theory helps us *understand* development, we are in a much better position to know *what to do* in our efforts to improve the welfare and treatment of children.

As we will see later, theories are influenced by the cultural values and belief systems of their times. But theories differ in one important way from mere opinion and belief: a theory's continued existence depends on *scientific verification* (Scarr, 1985). This means that the theory must be tested by using a fair set of research procedures agreed on by the scientific community.

In the field of child development, there are many theories with very different ideas about what children are like and how they develop. The study of child development provides no ultimate truth, since investigators do not always agree on the meaning of what they see. In addition, children are complex beings; they grow physically, mentally, emotionally, and socially. As yet, no single theory has been able to explain all of these aspects. Finally, the existence of many theories helps advance knowledge, since researchers are continually trying to support, contradict, and integrate these different points of view.

This chapter introduces you to the major child development theories and the research strategies that have been used to test them. We will return to each theory in greater detail in later parts of this book. Although there are many theories, we can easily organize them, since almost all take a stand on three basic issues about childhood and child development. To help you remember these controversial issues, they are briefly summarized in Table 1.1 Let's take a close look at each.

theory
An orderly, integrated set of statements that describes, explains, and predicts behavior.

TABLE 1.1

Basic Issues in Child Development

ISSUE	QUESTION RAISED ABOUT DEVELOPMENT
View of the developing child; organismic versus mechanistic	Are children active beings with psychological structures that underlie and control development, or are they passive recipients of environmental inputs?
View of the course of development: continuous versus discontinuous	Is child development a matter of cumulative adding on of skills and behaviors, or does it involve qualitative, stagewise changes?
View of the determinants of development: nature versus nurture	Are genetic or environmental factors the most important determinants of development? If environment is crucial, to what extent do early experiences establish lifelong patterns of behavior? Can later experiences overcome early negative effects?

VIEWS OF THE DEVELOPING CHILD

Recently, the mother of a 16-month-old boy named Angelo reported to me with amazement that her young son pushed a toy car across the living room floor while making a motorlike sound, "Brmmmm, brmmmm," for the first time. "We've never shown him how to do that!" exclaimed Angelo's mother. "Did he make up that sound himself," she inquired, "or did he copy it from some other child at day care?" Angelo's mother has asked a puzzling question about the nature of children. It contrasts two basic perspectives: the organismic, or *active,* position with the mechanistic, or *passive,* point of view.

Organismic theories assume that change is stimulated from *within the organism*— more specifically, that psychological structures exist inside the child that underlie and control development. Children are viewed as active, purposeful beings who make sense of their world and determine their own learning (Dixon & Lerner, 1992). For an organismic theorist, the surrounding environment supports development, as Angelo's mother did when she provided him with stimulating toys. But since children invent their own ways of understanding and responding to events around them, the environment does not bring about the child's growth. Instead, the "organism selects, modifies, or rejects environmental influences pressing upon it" (White, 1976, p. 100).

In contrast, **mechanistic theories** focus on relationships between environmental inputs and behavioral outputs. The approach is called *mechanistic* because children's development is compared to the workings of a machine. Change is stimulated by the environment, which shapes the behavior of the child, who is a passive reactor (Miller, 1993). For example, when Angelo's playmate says, "Brmmmm," Angelo responds similarly. According to this view, new capacities result from external forces acting on the child. Development is treated as a straightforward, predictable consequence of events in the surrounding world.

VIEWS OF THE COURSE OF DEVELOPMENT

How can we best describe the differences in capacities and behavior among small infants, young children, adolescents, and adults? As Figure 1.1 illustrates, major theories recognize two possibilities.

On the one hand, babies and preschoolers may respond to the world in much the same way as adults. The difference between the immature and mature being may simply be one of *amount* or *complexity* of behavior. For example, little Angelo's thinking might be just as logical and well organized as our own. Perhaps (as his mother reports) Angelo

organismic theories
Theories that assume the existence of psychological structures inside the child that underlie and control development.

mechanistic theories
Theories that regard the child as a passive reactor to environmental inputs.

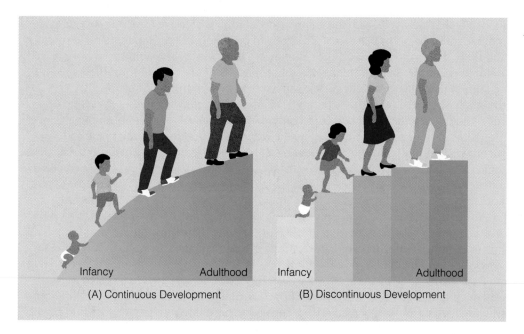

(A) Continuous Development   (B) Discontinuous Development

FIGURE 1.1

Is development continuous or discontinuous?
(a) Some theorists believe that development is a smooth, continuous process. Children gradually add more of the same types of skills. (b) Other theorists think that development takes place in discontinuous stages. Children change rapidly as they step up to a new level of development and then change very little for a while. With each new step, the child interprets and responds to the world in a qualitatively different way.

can sort objects into simple categories, recognize whether there are more of one kind than another, and remember where he left his favorite toy at day care the week before. Angelo's only limitation may be that he cannot perform these skills with as many pieces of information as we can. If this is true, then changes in Angelo's thinking must be **continuous**—a process that consists of gradually adding on more of the same types of skills that were there to begin with.

On the other hand, Angelo may have *unique ways of thinking, feeling, and behaving* that must be understood on their own terms—ones quite different from our own. If so, then development is a **discontinuous** process in which new ways of understanding and responding to the world emerge at particular time periods. From this perspective, Angelo is not yet able to organize objects or remember experiences in the same way as adults. Instead, he will move through a series of developmental steps, each of which has unique features, until he reaches a final transformation that marks the beginning of adulthood.

Theories that accept the discontinuous perspective include a vital developmental concept: the concept of stage. **Stages** are *qualitative changes* in thinking, feeling, and behaving that characterize specific time periods of development. In stage theories, development is much like climbing a staircase, with each step corresponding to a more mature, reorganized way of functioning than the one that came before. The stage concept also assumes that children undergo periods of rapid transformation as they step up from one stage to the next, followed by plateaus during which they stand solidly within a stage. In other words, change is fairly sudden rather than gradual and always ongoing. Finally, stages are assumed to be universal across children and cultures. That is, stage theories propose that children everywhere follow the same sequence of development.

Does development actually take place in a neat, orderly, stepwise sequence that is identical for all human beings? For now, let's note that this is a very ambitious assumption that has not gone unchallenged. We will review some very influential stage theories later in this chapter.

VIEWS OF THE DETERMINANTS OF DEVELOPMENT

In addition to describing the course of child development, each theory takes a stand on a major question about its underlying causes: Are genetic or environmental factors most important? This is the age-old **nature–nurture controversy.** By *nature,* we mean

continuous development
A view that regards development as a cumulative process of adding on more of the same types of skills that were there to begin with.

discontinuous development
A view in which new and different ways of interpreting and responding to the world emerge at specific time periods.

stage
A qualitative change in thinking, feeling, and behaving that characterizes a specific time period of development.

nature–nurture controversy
Disagreement among theorists about whether genetic or environmental factors are the most important determinants of development and behavior.

inborn biological givens—the hereditary information we receive from our parents at the moment of conception that signals the body to grow and affects all our characteristics and skills. By *nurture,* we mean the complex forces of the physical and social world that children encounter in their homes, neighborhoods, schools, and communities.

Although all theories grant at least some role to both nature and nurture, they vary in the emphasis placed on each. For example, consider the following questions: Is the older child's ability to think in more complex ways largely the result of an inborn timetable of growth? Or is it primarily influenced by the way parents and teachers stimulate and encourage the child? Do children acquire language because they are genetically predisposed to do so, or because parents intensively tutor them from an early age? And what accounts for the vast individual differences among children—in height, weight, physical coordination, intelligence, personality, and social skills? Is nature or nurture more influential?

Notice how a theory's stance on the nature–nurture controversy is related to its position on the previously discussed issues. An organismic theorist would never assume that nurture is more powerful than nature. And a mechanistic theorist would always stress the importance of nurture.

Furthermore, the position a theory takes on nature versus nurture is linked to its explanation of individual differences. Some theorists emphasize *stability*—that children who are high or low in a characteristic (such as verbal ability, anxiety, or sociability) will remain so at later ages. These theorists typically stress the importance of *heredity.* If they regard environment as crucial, they generally point to *early experience* as establishing a lifelong pattern of behavior. Powerful negative events in the first few years, they argue, cannot be fully overcome by later, more positive ones (Bowlby, 1980; Sroufe, Egeland, & Kreutzer, 1990). Other theorists are more optimistic. They believe that change is possible if new experiences support it (Chess & Thomas, 1984; Sampson & Laub, 1993; Werner & Smith, 1992).

Throughout this book, we will see that investigators disagree, often sharply, on the question of *stability versus change.* And the answers they provide are of great applied significance. If you believe that development is largely due to nature, then providing children with experiences aimed at stimulating change would seem to be of little value. If, on the other hand, you are convinced of the supreme importance of early experience, then you would intervene as soon as possible, offering high-quality stimulation and support to ensure that children develop at their best. Finally, if you think that environment has a profound impact throughout development, you would extend high-quality experiences into later years. In addition, you would provide assistance any time children or adolescents face difficulties, believing that they can recover from early negative events with the help of favorable life circumstances.

A BALANCED POINT OF VIEW

So far, we have discussed the basic issues of child development in terms of extremes—solutions on one side or the other. As we trace the unfolding of the field of child development in the rest of this chapter, you will see that the thinking of many theorists has softened. Modern theorists, especially, recognize the merits of both sides.

Some theories take an intermediate stand between an organismic versus mechanistic perspective. They regard both the child and the surrounding environment as active and as collaborating to produce development. Similarly, some contemporary researchers believe that both continuous and discontinuous changes characterize development and alternate with one another. Furthermore, investigators have moved away from asking whether heredity or environment is more important. Instead, they want to know precisely *how nature and nurture work together* to influence the child's traits and capacities.

Finally, as you will discover in later parts of this book, the relative impact of early and later experiences varies greatly from one aspect of development to another and even (as the Biology and Environment box on pages 10–11 indicates) across individuals! Because of the complex network of factors contributing to human change and the challenge of isolating the effects of each, many theoretical points of view have gathered research support. Although debate continues, this circumstance has also sparked more balanced visions of child development.

HISTORICAL FOUNDATIONS

*M*odern theories of child development are the result of centuries of change in Western cultural values, philosophical thinking about children, and scientific progress. To understand the field as it exists today, we must return to its early beginnings—to influences that long preceded scientific child study. We will see that many early ideas about children linger on as important forces in current theory and research.

MEDIEVAL TIMES

In medieval Europe (the sixth through the fifteenth centuries), little importance was placed on childhood as a separate phase of the life cycle. The idea accepted by many theories today, that the child's nature is unique and different from that of youths and adults, was much less common then. Instead, once children emerged from infancy, they were regarded as miniature, already formed adults, a view called **preformationism.** This attitude is reflected in the art, entertainment, and language of the times. Look carefully at medieval paintings, and you will see that children are depicted as immature adults. Before the sixteenth century, toys and games were not designed to amuse children but were for all people. And age, so central to modern personal identity, was unimportant in medieval custom and usage. People did not refer to it in conversation, and it was not recorded in family and civil records until the fifteenth and sixteenth centuries (Ariès, 1962).

Nevertheless, faint glimmerings of the idea that children are unique emerged during medieval times. Some laws recognized that children needed protection from people who might mistreat them, and medical works provided special instructions for their care. But even though in a practical sense there was some awareness of the vulnerability of children, as yet there were no theories about the uniqueness of childhood or separate developmental periods (Borstelmann, 1983; Sommerville, 1982).

In this medieval painting, the young child is depicted as a miniature adult. His dress, expression, and activities resemble those of his elders. Through the fifteenth century, little emphasis was placed on childhood as a unique phase of the life cycle. *(Giraudon/Art Resources)*

THE REFORMATION

In the sixteenth century, a revised image of childhood sprang from the religious movement that gave birth to Protestantism—in particular, the Puritan belief in original sin. According to Puritan doctrine, children were born evil and stubborn and had to be civilized toward a destiny of virtue and salvation (Ariès, 1962; Shahar, 1990).

Harsh, restrictive child-rearing practices were recommended to tame the depraved child. Children were dressed in stiff, uncomfortable clothing that held them in adultlike postures, and disobedient pupils were routinely beaten by their schoolmasters (Stone, 1977). Although these attitudes represented the prevailing child-rearing philosophy of the time, they probably were not typical of everyday practices in Puritan families. Recent evidence suggests that love and affection for their children made many Puritan parents reluctant to exercise extremely repressive measures (Moran & Vinovskis, 1986).

As the Puritans emigrated from England to the United States, they brought with them the belief that child rearing was one of their most important obligations. Although they continued to regard the child's soul as tainted by original sin, they tried to promote reason in their sons and daughters so they would be able to separate right from wrong. The Puritans were the first to devise special reading materials for children that instructed

preformationism
Medieval view of the child as a miniature adult.

BIOLOGY & ENVIRONMENT   RESILIENT CHILDREN

John and his best friend, Gary, grew up in a run-down, crime-ridden inner-city neighborhood. By age 10, each had experienced years of family conflict followed by parental divorce. Reared for the rest of childhood and adolescence in mother-headed households, John and Gary rarely saw their fathers. Both achieved poorly, dropped out of high school, and were in and out of trouble with the police.

Then John and Gary's paths of development diverged. By age 30, John had fathered two children with women he never married, had spent time in prison, was unemployed, and drank alcohol heavily. In contrast, Gary had returned to finish high school, had studied auto mechanics at a community college, and became manager of a gas station and repair shop. Married with two children, he had saved his earnings and bought a home. He was happy, healthy, and well adapted to life.

A wealth of evidence shows that environmental risks—poverty, nega-tive family interactions, parental divorce, job loss, mental illness, and drug abuse—predispose children to future problems. On the basis of these findings, we would have expected both John and Gary to develop serious psychological difficulties. Why did Gary "beat the odds" and come through unscathed?

New evidence on *resiliency*—the ability to spring back from adversity—is receiving increasing attention because investigators want to find ways to protect young people from the damaging effects of stressful life conditions (Cicchetti & Garmezy, 1993). This interest was inspired by several long-term studies on the rela-tionship of life stressors in childhood to competence and adjustment in adolescence and adulthood (Garmezy, 1993; Rutter, 1985, 1987; Werner & Smith, 1992). In each study, some chil-dren were shielded from negative out-comes, whereas others had lasting problems. Three broad factors seemed to offer protection from the damaging effects of stressful life events:

■ **PERSONAL CHARACTERISTICS OF CHILDREN.** A child's biologically endowed characteristics can reduce exposure to risk or lead to experiences that compensate for early stressful events. Temperament is particularly powerful. Children with calm, easy-going, sociable dispositions who are willing to take initiative have a special capacity to adapt to change and elicit positive responses from others. Chil-dren who are emotionally reactive and irritable often strain the patience of people around them (Gribble et al., 1993; Milgram & Palti, 1993; Smith & Prior, 1995; Wyman et al., 1992). For example, both John and Gary moved several times during their childhoods. Each time, John became anxious and angry, picking arguments with his parents, siblings, and peers. In con-trast, Gary was sad to leave his home but soon looked forward to making new friends and exploring new parts of the neighborhood. Intellectual abil-ity is another protective factor, it increases the chances of rewarding experiences in school that may offset

---

them in religious and moral ideals. As they trained their children in self-reliance and self-control, Puritan parents gradually adopted a moderate balance between discipline and indulgence, severity and permissiveness (Pollock, 1987).

PHILOSOPHIES OF THE ENLIGHTENMENT

The seventeenth-century Enlightenment brought new philosophies of reason and emphasized ideals of human dignity and respect. Conceptions of childhood appeared that were more humane than those of centuries past.

■ **JOHN LOCKE.** John Locke (1632–1704), a leading British philosopher, viewed the child as a **tabula rasa.** Translated from Latin, this means a "blank slate." According to this idea, children were, to begin with, nothing at all, and their characters could be shaped by all kinds of experiences during the course of growing up. Locke (1690/1892) described parents as rational tutors who could mold the child in any way they wished, through care-ful instruction, effective example, and rewards for good behavior. He was ahead of his time in recommending child-rearing practices that were eventually supported by twenti-eth-century research. For example, Locke suggested that parents not reward children with

tabula rasa
Locke's view of the child as a blank slate whose character is shaped by experience.

the impact of a stressful homelife (Dubow & Luster, 1990).

■ **A WARM PARENTAL RELATIONSHIP.** A close relationship with at least one parent who provides affection and assistance and introduces order and organization into the child's life fosters resilience. But note that this factor (as well as the next one) is not independent of children's personal characteristics. Children who are relaxed, socially responsive, and able to deal with change are easier to rear and more likely to enjoy positive relationships with parents and other people. At the same time, some children may develop more attractive dispositions as a result of parental warmth and attention (Luthar & Zigler, 1991; Smith & Prior, 1995).

■ **SOCIAL SUPPORT OUTSIDE THE IMMEDIATE FAMILY.** A person outside the immediate family—perhaps a grandparent, teacher, or close friend—who forms a special relationship with the child can promote resilience. Gary

may have overcome the effects of a stressful home life because of the support he received in adolescence from his grandfather, who listened to Gary's concerns and helped him solve problems constructively. In addition, Gary's grandfather had a stable marriage and work life and handled stressors skillfully. Consequently, he served as a model of effective coping (Zimmerman & Arunkumar, 1994).

Research on resiliency highlights the complex connections between heredity and environment. Armed with positive characteristics, which may stem from innate endowment, favorable rearing experiences, or both, children take action to reduce stressful situations. Nevertheless, when many risks pile up, they are increasingly difficult to overcome (Sameroff et al., 1993). Therefore, effective interventions need to reduce risks and enhance relationships at home, in school, and in the community that inoculate children against the negative effects of risk. This means

attending to both the person and the environment—building capacity as well as fixing problems.

This child's special relationship with her grandfather provides the social support she needs to cope with stress and solve problems constructively. A warm tie with a person outside the immediate family can promote resilience. *(Alan Hicks/Tony Stone Images)*

money or sweets but rather with praise and approval. He also opposed physical punishment: "The child repeatedly beaten in school cannot look upon books and teachers without experiencing fear and anger." Locke's philosophy led to a change from harshness toward children to kindness and compassion.

Look carefully at Locke's ideas, and you will see that he took a firm stand on each of the basic issues we discussed earlier in this chapter. As blank slates, children are viewed in passive, *mechanistic* terms. The course of growth is written upon them by the environment. Locke also regarded development as *continuous*. Adultlike behaviors are gradually built up through the warm, consistent teachings of parents. Finally, Locke was a champion of *nurture*—of the power of the environment to determine whether children become good or bad, bright or dull, kind or selfish.

■ **JEAN JACQUES ROUSSEAU.** In the eighteenth century, a new theory of childhood was introduced by the French philosopher of the Enlightenment, Jean Jacques Rousseau (1712–1778). Children, Rousseau (1762/1955) thought, were not blank slates and empty containers to be filled by adult instruction. Instead, they were **noble savages,** naturally endowed with a sense of right and wrong and with an innate plan for orderly, healthy growth. Unlike Locke, Rousseau thought children's built-in moral sense and unique ways

noble savage
Rousseau's view of the child as naturally endowed with an innate plan for orderly, healthy growth.

of thinking and feeling would only be harmed by adult training. His was a permissive philosophy in which the adult should be receptive to the child's needs at each of four stages of development: infancy, childhood, late childhood, and adolescence.

Rousseau's philosophy includes two vitally important concepts that are found in modern theories. The first is the concept of *stage,* which we discussed earlier in this chapter. The second is the concept of **maturation,** which refers to a genetically determined, naturally unfolding course of growth. If you accept the notion that children mature through a sequence of stages, then they cannot be preformed, miniature adults. Instead, they are unique and different from adults, and their development is determined by their own inner nature. Compared to Locke, Rousseau took a very different stand on basic developmental issues. He saw children as *organismic* (active shapers of their own destiny), development as a *discontinuous* stagewise process, and *nature* as having mapped out the path and timetable of growth.

DARWIN'S THEORY OF EVOLUTION

A century after Rousseau, another ancestor of modern child study—this time, of its scientific foundations—emerged. In the mid-nineteenth century, Charles Darwin (1809–1882), a British naturalist, joined an expedition to distant parts of the world, where he made careful observations of fossils and animal and plant life. Darwin (1859/1936) noticed the infinite variation among species. He also saw that within a species, no two individuals are exactly alike. From these observations, he constructed his famous theory of evolution.

The theory emphasized two related principles: *natural selection* and *survival of the fittest.* Darwin explained that certain species were selected by nature to survive in particular parts of the world because they had characteristics that fit with, or were adapted to, their surroundings. Other species died off because they were not as well suited to their environment. Individuals within a species who best met the survival requirements of the environment lived long enough to reproduce and pass their more favorable characteristics to future generations. Darwin's emphasis on the adaptive value of physical characteristics and behavior eventually found its way into important twentieth-century theories.

During his explorations, Darwin discovered that the early prenatal growth of many species was strikingly similar. This suggested that all species, including human beings, were descended from a few common ancestors. Other scientists concluded from Darwin's observation that the development of the human child, from conception to maturity, followed the same general plan as the evolution of the human species. Although this belief eventually proved to be inaccurate, efforts to chart parallels between child growth and human evolution prompted researchers to make careful observations of all aspects of children's behavior. Out of these first attempts to document an idea about development, the science of child study was born.

SCIENTIFIC BEGINNINGS

Scientific child study evolved quickly during the early part of the twentieth century. As we will see in the following sections, rudimentary observations of individual children were soon followed by improved methods and theories. Each advance contributed to the firm foundation on which the field rests today.

■ **THE BABY BIOGRAPHIES.** Imagine yourself as a forerunner of the field of child development, confronted with studying children for the first time. How might you go about this challenging task? Scientists of the late nineteenth and early twentieth century did what most of us would probably do in their place. They selected a child of their own or of a close relative. Then, beginning in early infancy, they jotted down day-by-day

maturation
A genetically determined, naturally unfolding course of growth.

descriptions and impressions of the youngster's behavior. Dozens of these baby biographies had been published by the early twentieth century. In the following excerpt from one of them, the author reflects on the birth of her young niece, whose growth she followed during the first year of life:

> Its first act is a cry, not of wrath, . . . nor a shout of joy, . . . but a snuffling, and then a long, thin, tearless á—á, with the timbre of a Scotch bagpipe, purely automatic, but of discomfort. With this monotonous and dismal cry, with its red, shriveled, parboiled skin. . . , squinting, cross-eyed, pot-bellied, and bow-legged, it is not strange that, if the mother . . . has not come to love her child before birth, there is a brief interval occasionally dangerous to the child before the maternal instinct is fully aroused.
>
> It cannot be denied that this unflattering description is fair enough, and our baby was no handsomer than the rest of her kind. . . . Yet she did not lack admirers. I have never noticed that women (even those who are not mothers) mind a few little aesthetic defects, . . . with so many counterbalancing charms in the little warm, soft, living thing. (Shinn, 1900, pp. 20–21)

Can you tell from this passage why the baby biographies have sometimes been upheld as examples of how *not* to study children? These first investigators tended to be emotionally invested in the infants they observed, and they seldom began with a clear idea of what they wanted to find out about the child. Not surprisingly, many of the records made were eventually discarded as biased. However, we must keep in mind that the baby biographers were like explorers first setting foot on alien soil. When a field is new, we cannot expect its theories and methods to be well formulated.

Nevertheless, the baby biographies were clearly a step in the right direction. In fact, two theorists of the nineteenth century, Darwin (1877) and German biologist William Preyer (1882/1888), contributed to these early records of children's behavior. Preyer, especially, set high standards for making observations. He recorded what he saw immediately, as completely as possible, and at regular intervals. And he checked the accuracy of his own notes against those of a second observer (Cairns, 1983). These are the same high standards that modern researchers use when observing children. As the result of the biographers' pioneering efforts, in succeeding decades the child became a common focus of scientific research.

■ **THE NORMATIVE PERIOD OF CHILD STUDY.** G. Stanley Hall (1846–1924), one of the most influential American psychologists of the early twentieth century, is generally regarded as the founder of the child study movement (Dixon & Lerner, 1992). Inspired by Darwin's work, Hall and his well-known student Arnold Gesell (1880–1961) developed theories based on evolutionary ideas. These early leaders regarded child development as a genetically determined series of events that unfolds automatically, much like a blooming flower (Gesell, 1933; Hall, 1904).

Hall and Gesell are remembered less for their one-sided theories than for their intensive efforts to describe all aspects of child development. Aware of the limitations of the baby biographies, Hall set out to collect a sound body of objective facts about children. This goal launched the **normative approach** to child study. In a normative investigation, measurements of behavior are taken on large numbers of children. Then age-related averages are computed to represent typical development. Using this method, Hall constructed elaborate questionnaires asking children of different ages almost everything they could tell about themselves—interests, fears, imaginary playmates, dreams, friendships, everyday knowledge, and more (White, 1992).

In the same tradition, Gesell devoted a major part of his career to collecting detailed normative information on the behavior of infants and children. His schedules of infant development were particularly complete, and revised versions continue to be used today (see Figure 1.2).

normative approach
An approach in which age-related averages are computed to represent typical development.

FIGURE 1.2

Sample milestones from the most recent revision of Gesell's schedules of infant development. Norms on hundreds of motor, mental, language, and social skills are included. *(Adapted from Knobloch, Stevens, and Malone, 1980.)*

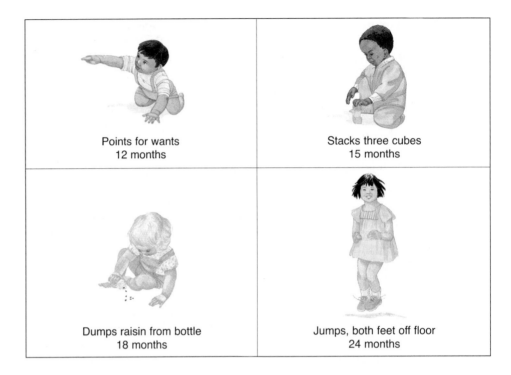

Points for wants
12 months

Stacks three cubes
15 months

Dumps raisin from bottle
18 months

Jumps, both feet off floor
24 months

Gesell was also among the first to make knowledge about child development meaningful to parents. He provided them with descriptions of motor achievements, personality characteristics, and social behaviors (Gesell & Ilg, 1943/1949, 1946/1949). Gesell hoped to relieve parents' anxieties by informing them of what to expect at each age. If, as he believed, the timetable of development is the product of millions of years of evolution, then children are naturally knowledgeable about their needs. His child-rearing advice, in the tradition of Rousseau, was a permissive approach that recommended sensitivity and responsiveness to children's cues (Thelen & Adolph, 1992).

■ **THE MENTAL TESTING MOVEMENT.** While Hall and Gesell were developing their theories and methods in the United States, French psychologist Alfred Binet (1857–1911) also took a normative approach to child development, but for a different reason. In the early 1900s, Binet and his colleague Theodore Simon were asked by Paris school officials to find a way to identify children with learning problems who needed to be placed in special classes. The first successful intelligence test, which they constructed for this purpose, grew out of practical educational concerns.

Previous attempts to create a useful test of intelligence had met with little success. But Binet's effort was unique in that he began with a well-developed theory. In contrast to earlier views, which reduced intelligence to simple elements of reaction time and sensitivity to physical stimuli, Binet captured the complexity of children's thinking (Siegler, 1992). He defined intelligence as good judgment, planning, and critical reflection. Then he selected test questions that directly measured these abilities, creating a series of age-graded items that permitted him to compare the intellectual progress of different children.

In 1916, at Stanford University, Binet's test was translated into English and adapted for use with American children. It became known as the *Stanford-Binet Intelligence Scale.* Besides providing a score that could successfully predict school achievement, the Binet test sparked tremendous interest in individual differences in development. The mental testing movement was in motion. Comparisons of the intelligence test scores of children who vary in sex, ethnicity, birth order, family background, and other characteristics became a major focus of research. Intelligence tests also rose quickly to the forefront of the controversy over nature versus nurture that continues today.

BRIEF REVIEW

The modern field of child development has deep historical roots. In medieval Europe, children were regarded as miniature adults. By the sixteenth century, childhood became a distinct phase of the life cycle. The Puritan belief in original sin fostered a harsh, authoritarian approach to child rearing. During the seventeenth-century Enlightenment, Locke's "blank slate" and Rousseau's "inherently good" child promoted more humane views of children. Darwin's evolutionary ideas inspired maturational theories and the first attempts to study the child directly, in the form of baby biographies and Hall and Gesell's normative investigations. Out of the normative tradition arose Binet's first successful intelligence test and a concern with individual differences among children.

ASK YOURSELF . . .

■ *If you could interview people of medieval Europe to find out whether they thought child development was a continuous or discontinuous process, how do you think they would respond?*

■ *Suppose we could arrange a debate between John Locke and Jean Jacques Rousseau on the nature–nurture controversy. Summarize the argument that each historical figure is likely to present.*

MID-TWENTIETH-CENTURY THEORIES

In the mid-twentieth century, the field of child development expanded. Specialized societies were founded, and research journals were launched. As child development attracted increasing interest, a variety of theories emerged, each of which continues to have followers today. In these theories, the European concern with the child's inner thoughts and feelings contrasts sharply with the focus of American academic psychology on scientific precision and concrete, observable behavior.

THE PSYCHOANALYTIC PERSPECTIVE

By the 1930s and 1940s, many parents whose children suffered from serious emotional stress and behavior problems sought help from psychiatrists and social workers. The earlier normative movement had answered the question, What are children like? But to treat children's difficulties, child guidance professionals had to address the question, How and why did children become the way they are? They turned for help to the **psychoanalytic perspective** on personality development because of its emphasis on understanding the unique developmental history of each child.

According to the psychoanalytic approach, children move through a series of stages in which they confront conflicts between biological drives and social expectations. The way these conflicts are resolved determines the person's ability to learn, to get along with others, and to cope with anxiety. Although many individuals contributed to the psychoanalytic perspective, two have been especially influential: Sigmund Freud, founder of the psychoanalytic movement, and Erik Erikson.

■ **FREUD'S THEORY.** Freud (1856–1939), a Viennese physician, saw patients in his practice with a variety of nervous symptoms, such as hallucinations, fears, and paralyses, that appeared to have no physical basis. Seeking a cure for these troubled adults, Freud found that their symptoms could be relieved by having patients talk freely about painful events of their childhood. Using this "talking cure," he carefully examined the unconscious motivations of his patients. Startling the straightlaced Victorian society in which he lived, Freud concluded that infants and young children were sexual beings and that the way they were permitted to express their impulses lay at the heart of their adult behavior. Freud constructed his **psychosexual theory** of development on the basis of adult remembrances. It emphasizes that how parents manage their child's sexual and aggressive drives in the first few years of life is crucial for healthy personality development.

psychoanalytic perspective An approach to personality development introduced by Freud that assumes children move through a series of stages in which they confront conflicts between biological drives and social expectations. The way these conflicts are resolved determines psychological adjustment.

psychosexual theory Freud's theory, which emphasizes that how parents manage children's sexual and aggressive drives during the first few years is crucial for healthy personality development.

TABLE 1.2

Freud's Psychosexual Stages

PSYCHOSEXUAL STAGE	PERIOD OF DEVELOPMENT	DESCRIPTION
Oral	Birth–1 year	The new ego directs the baby's sucking activities toward breast or bottle. If oral needs are not met appropriately, the individual may develop such habits as thumb sucking, fingernail biting, and pencil chewing in childhood and overeating and smoking in later life.
Anal	1–3 years	Young toddlers and preschoolers enjoy holding and releasing urine and feces. Toilet training becomes a major issue between parent and child. If parents insist that children be trained before they are ready or make too few demands, conflicts about anal control may appear in the form of extreme orderliness and cleanliness or messiness and disorder.
Phallic	3–6 years	Id impulses transfer to the genitals, and the child finds pleasure in genital stimulation. Freud's Oedipus conflict for boys and Electra conflict for girls take place. Young children feel a sexual desire for the opposite-sex parent. To avoid punishment, they give up this desire and, instead, adopt the same-sex parent's characteristics and values. As a result, the superego is formed. The relations between id, ego, and superego established at this time determine the individual's basic personality.
Latency	6–11 years	Sexual instincts die down, and the superego develops further. The child acquires new social values from adults outside the family and from play with same-sex peers.
Genital	Adolescence	Puberty causes the sexual impulses of the phallic stage to reappear. If development has been successful during earlier stages, it leads to marriage, mature sexuality, and the birth and rearing of children.

Erik Erikson expanded Freud's theory, emphasizing the psychosocial outcomes of development. At each psychosexual stage, a major psychological conflict is resolved. If the outcome is positive, individuals acquire attitudes and skills that permit them to contribute constructively to society.
(Olive Pierce/Black Star)

Three Parts of the Personality. In Freud's theory, three parts of the personality—id, ego, and superego—become integrated during a sequence of five stages of development. The *id*, the largest portion of the mind, is the source of basic biological needs and desires. The *ego*—the conscious, rational part of personality—emerges in early infancy to redirect the id's impulses so they are discharged on appropriate objects at acceptable times and places. For example, aided by the ego, the hungry baby of a few months of age stops crying when he sees his mother unfasten her clothing for breast-feeding or warm a bottle. And the more competent preschooler goes into the kitchen and gets a snack on her own.

Between 3 and 6 years of age, the superego, or conscience, develops from interactions with parents, who eventually insist that children conform to the values of society. Now the ego faces the increasingly complex task of reconciling the demands of the id, the external world, and conscience (Freud, 1923/1974). For example, when the ego is tempted to gratify an id impulse by hitting a playmate to get an attractive toy, the superego may warn that such behavior is wrong. The ego must decide which of the two forces (id or superego) will win this inner struggle or work out a reasonable compromise, such as asking for a turn with the toy. According to Freud, the relations established between id, ego, and superego during the preschool years determine the individual's basic personality.

Psychosexual Development. Freud (1938/1973) believed that over the course of childhood, sexual impulses shift their focus from the oral to the anal to the genital regions of the body. In each stage of development, parents walk a fine line between permitting too much or too little gratification of their child's basic needs. If parents strike an appropriate balance, then children grow into well-adjusted adults with the capacity for mature sexual behavior, investment in family life, and rearing of the next generation. Table 1.2 summarizes each of Freud's stages.

Freud's psychosexual theory highlighted the importance of family relationships for children's development. It was the first theory to stress the role of early experience. But Freud's perspective was eventually criticized for several reasons: First, the theory overem-

TABLE 1.3

Erikson's Psychosocial Stages, with Corresponding Psychosexual Stages Indicated

PSYCHOSOCIAL STAGE	PERIOD OF DEVELOPMENT	DESCRIPTION
Basic trust versus mistrust (Oral)	Birth–1 year	From warm, responsive care, infants gain a sense of trust, or confidence, that the world is good. Mistrust occurs when infants have to wait too long for comfort and are handled harshly.
Autonomy versus shame and doubt (Anal)	1–3 years	Using new mental and motor skills, children want to choose and decide for themselves. Autonomy is fostered when parents permit reasonable free choice and do not force or shame the child.
Initiative versus guilt (Phallic)	3–6 years	Through make-believe play, children experiment with the kind of person they can become. Initiative—a sense of ambition and responsibility—develops when parents support their child's new sense of purpose and direction. The danger is that parents will demand too much self-control, which leads to overcontrol, or too much guilt.
Industry versus inferiority diffusion (Latency)	6–11 years	At school, children develop the capacity to work and cooperate with others. Inferiority develops when negative experiences at home, at school, or with peers lead to feelings of incompetence.
Identity versus identity confusion (Genital)	Adolescence	The adolescent tries to answer the question, Who am I, and what is my place in society? Self-chosen values and vocational goals lead to a lasting personal identity. The negative outcome is confusion about future adult roles.
Intimacy versus isolation	Young adulthood	Young people work on establishing intimate ties to others. Because of earlier disappointments, some individuals cannot form close relationships and remain isolated from others.
Generativity versus stagnation	Middle adulthood	Generativity means giving to the next generation through child rearing, caring for other people, or productive work. The person who fails in these ways feels an absence of meaningful accomplishment.
Ego integrity versus despair	Old age	In this final stage, individuals reflect on the kind of person they have been. Integrity results from feeling that life was worth living as it happened. Old people who are dissatisfied with their lives fear death.

phasized the influence of sexual feelings in development. Second, because the theory was based on the problems of sexually repressed, well-to-do adults, it did not apply in cultures differing from nineteenth-century Victorian society. Finally, Freud's ideas were called into question because he did not study children directly.

■ **ERIKSON'S THEORY.** Several of Freud's followers took what was useful from his theory and stretched and rearranged it in ways that improved on his vision. The most important of these neo-Freudians for the field of child development was Erik Erikson (1902–1994).

Although Erikson (1950) accepted Freud's basic psychosexual framework, he expanded the picture of development at each stage. In his **psychosocial theory,** Erikson emphasized that the ego does not just mediate between id impulses and superego demands. It is also a positive force in development. At each stage, it acquires attitudes and skills that make the individual an active, contributing member of society. A basic psychological conflict, which is resolved along a continuum from positive to negative, determines healthy or maladaptive outcomes at each stage. As Table 1.3 shows, Erikson's first five stages parallel Freud's stages. However, Erikson did not regard important developmental tasks as limited to early childhood. He added three adult stages to Freud's model and was one of the first to recognize the lifespan nature of development.

Finally, unlike Freud, Erikson pointed out that normal development must be understood in relation to each culture's life situation. For example, among the Yurok Indians

psychosocial theory
Erikson's theory, which emphasizes that the demands of society at each Freudian stage not only promote the development of a unique personality but also ensure that individuals acquire attitudes and skills that help them become active, contributing members of their society.

(a tribe of fishermen and acorn gatherers on the Northwest coast of the United States), babies are deprived of breast-feeding for the first 10 days after birth and instead are fed a thin soup from a small shell. At age 6 months, infants are abruptly weaned—an event enforced, if necessary, by having the mother leave for a few days. These experiences, from our cultural vantage point, might seem cruel. But Erikson explained that the Yurok live in a world in which salmon fill the river just once a year, a circumstance that requires the development of considerable self-restraint for survival. In this way, he showed that child rearing can be understood only by making reference to the competencies valued and needed by the child's society.

■ **CONTRIBUTIONS AND LIMITATIONS OF PSYCHOANALYTIC THEORY.** A special strength of the psychoanalytic perspective is its emphasis on the individual's unique life history as worthy of study and understanding (Emde, 1992). Consistent with this view, psychoanalytic theorists accept the *clinical method,* which synthesizes information from a variety of sources into a detailed picture of the personality functioning of a single child. (We will discuss the clinical method further at the end of this chapter.) Psychoanalytic theory has also inspired a wealth of research on many aspects of emotional and social development, including infant–caregiver attachment, aggression, sibling relationships, child-rearing practices, morality, gender roles, and adolescent identity.

Despite its extensive contributions, the psychoanalytic perspective is no longer in the mainstream of child development research (Cairns, 1998; Miller, 1993). Psychoanalytic theorists may have become isolated from the rest of the field because they were so strongly committed to the clinical approach that they failed to consider other methods. In addition, many psychoanalytic ideas, such as Freud's Oedipus conflict and the psychosexual stages, are so vague and subject to interpretation that they are difficult or impossible to test empirically. Nevertheless, Erikson's broad outline of psychosocial change captures the essence of personality development during childhood and adolescence. Consequently, we will return to it in later chapters.

BEHAVIORISM AND SOCIAL LEARNING THEORY

As psychoanalytic theory gained in prominence, child study was also influenced by a very different perspective: **behaviorism,** a tradition consistent with Locke's image of the tabula rasa. American behaviorism began with the work of psychologist John Watson (1878–1958) in the early part of the twentieth century. Watson wanted to create an objective science of psychology. Unlike psychoanalytic theorists, he believed in studying directly observable events—stimuli and responses—rather than the unseen workings of the mind (Horowitz, 1992).

■ **TRADITIONAL BEHAVIORISM.** Watson was inspired by studies of animal learning carried out by famous Russian physiologist Ivan Pavlov. Pavlov knew that dogs release saliva as an innate reflex when they are given food. But he noticed that his dogs were salivating before they tasted any food—when they saw the trainer who usually fed them. The dogs, Pavlov reasoned, must have learned to associate a neutral stimulus (the trainer) with another stimulus (food) that produces a reflexive response (salivation). As a result of this association, the neutral stimulus by itself could bring about the response. Anxious to test this idea, Pavlov successfully taught dogs to salivate at the sound of a bell by pairing it with the presentation of food. He had discovered *classical conditioning.*

Watson wanted to find out if classical conditioning could be applied to children's behavior. In a historic experiment, he taught Albert, an 11-month-old infant, to fear a neutral stimulus—a soft white rat—by presenting it several times with a sharp, loud sound, which naturally scared the baby. Little Albert, who at first had reached out eagerly to touch the furry rat, soon cried and turned his head away when he caught

behaviorism
An approach that views directly observable events—stimuli and responses—as the appropriate focus of study and the development of behavior as taking place through classical and operant conditioning.

sight of it (Watson & Raynor, 1920). In fact, Albert's fear was
so intense that researchers eventually questioned the ethics of
studies like this one. On the basis of findings like these, Watson concluded that environment is the supreme force in development. According to the traditional behaviorist view, the
child is a passive being whom adults can mold by carefully
controlling stimulus–response associations. And development
is a continuous process, consisting of a gradual increase with
age in the number and strength of these associations.

After Watson, American behaviorism developed along several lines. The first was Clark Hull's *drive reduction theory.*
According to this view, children continually act to satisfy physiological needs and reduce states of tension. As *primary drives*
of hunger, thirst, and sex are met, a wide variety of stimuli
associated with them become *secondary,* or *learned, drives.* For
example, a Hullian theorist believes that infants prefer the
closeness and attention of adults who have given them food
and relieved their discomfort. To ensure adults' affection, children will acquire all sorts
of responses that adults desire of them—politeness, honesty, patience, persistence, obedience, and more.

Another form of behaviorism was B. F. Skinner's (1904–1990) *operant conditioning
theory.* Skinner rejected Hull's idea that primary drive reduction is the only way to get
children to learn. According to Skinner, a child's desirable behavior can be increased by
following it with a wide variety of *reinforcers* besides food and drink, such as praise, a
friendly smile, or a new toy. It can also be decreased through *punishment,* such as withdrawal of privileges, parental disapproval, or being sent to be alone in one's room. As a
result of Skinner's work, operant conditioning became a broadly applied learning principle in child psychology. We will consider these conditioning principles more fully when
we explore the infant's learning capacities in Chapter 5.

■ **SOCIAL LEARNING THEORY.** Psychologists quickly became interested in whether
behaviorism might offer a more direct and effective explanation of the development of
children's social behavior than did the less precise concepts of psychoanalytic theory. This
concern sparked the emergence of **social learning theory.** Social learning theorists
accepted the principles of conditioning and reinforcement, they also built on these principles, offering expanded views of how children and adults acquire new responses. By the
1950s, social learning theory became a major force in child development research.

Several kinds of social learning theory emerged. The most influential was devised by
Albert Bandura and his colleagues. Bandura (1977) demonstrated that *modeling,* otherwise
known as *imitation* or *observational learning,* is the basis for a wide variety of children's
behaviors. He recognized that children acquire many favorable and unfavorable responses
by watching and listening to people around them. The baby who claps her hands after her
mother does so, the child who angrily hits a playmate in the same way that he has been
punished at home, and the teenager who wears the same clothes and hairstyle as her
friends at school are all displaying observational learning.

Bandura's work continues to influence much research on children's social development. However, like changes in the field of child development as a whole, today his theory
stresses the importance of *cognition,* or thinking. Bandura has shown that children's ability to listen, remember, and abstract general rules from complex sets of observed behavior
affects their imitation and learning. In fact, the most recent revision of Bandura's (1986,
1989) theory places such strong emphasis on how children think about themselves and
other people that he calls it a *social-cognitive* rather than a social learning approach.
According to this view, children gradually become more selective in what they imitate.
From watching others engage in self-praise and self-blame and through feedback about

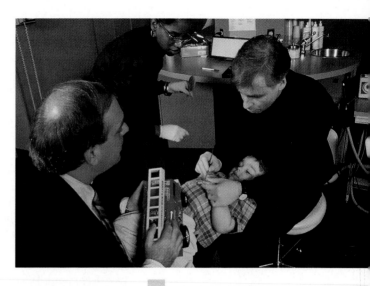

Applied behavior analysis
(see page 20) can be used to
reduce a child's anxious reactions during dental treatment.
This dentist engages in a
counting game to relax his
young patient before conducting an examination. While the
dentist works on the boy's
teeth, the boy's father will
distract him with a toy fire
engine. After the session is
over, the father will reinforce
the boy's cooperative behavior
by permitting him to play with
the toy. *(Jacques Chenet/
Woodfin Camp & Associates)*

social learning theory
An approach that emphasizes
the role of modeling, or observational learning, in the development of behavior. Its most
recent revision stresses the
importance of thinking in
social learning and is called
social-cognitive theory.

the worth of their own actions, children develop *personal standards* for behavior and a *sense of self-efficacy*—beliefs about their own abilities and characteristics—that guide their responses in specific situations (Bandura, 1997). For example, imagine a parent who often remarks, "I'm glad I kept working on that task, even though it was hard," who explains the value of persistence to her child, and who encourages it by saying, "I know you can do that homework very well!" As a result, the child starts to view himself as hard working and high achieving and, from the many people available in the environment, selects models with these characteristics to copy.

■ **CONTRIBUTIONS AND LIMITATIONS OF BEHAVIORISM AND SOCIAL LEARNING THEORY.** Like psychoanalytic theory, behaviorism and social learning theory have had a major impact on applied work with children. Yet the techniques used are decidedly different. **Applied behavior analysis** refers to procedures that combine conditioning and modeling to eliminate undesirable behaviors and increase socially acceptable responses. It has been used to relieve a wide range of serious developmental problems, such as persistent aggression, language delays, and extreme fears (Pierce & Epling, 1995; Wolpe & Plaud, 1997). But it is also effective in dealing with more common difficulties of childhood. For example, in one study, preschoolers' anxious reactions during dental treatment were reduced when the children received small toys (reinforcers) for answering questions about a story read to them while the dentist worked. Because the children could not listen to the story and kick and cry at the same time, their disruptive behaviors subsided (Stark et al., 1989).

Nevertheless, modeling and reinforcement do not provide a complete account of development (Horowitz, 1987). We will see in later sections that many theorists believe that behaviorism offers too narrow a view of important environmental influences. These extend beyond immediate reinforcement and modeled behaviors to the richness of children's physical and social worlds. Finally, in emphasizing cognition, Bandura is unique among theorists whose work grew out of the behaviorist tradition in granting children an active role in their own learning. Behaviorism and social learning theory have been criticized for underestimating children's contributions to their own development.

PIAGET'S COGNITIVE-DEVELOPMENTAL THEORY

If one individual has influenced the modern field of child development more than any other, it is Swiss cognitive theorist Jean Piaget (1896–1980). American investigators had been aware of Piaget's work since 1930. However, they did not grant it much attention until the 1960s, mainly because Piaget's ideas and methods of studying children were very much at odds with behaviorism, which dominated American psychology during the middle of the twentieth century (Beilin, 1992). Piaget did not believe that knowledge was imposed on a passive, reinforced child. According to his **cognitive-developmental theory,** children actively construct knowledge as they manipulate and explore their world, and their cognitive development takes place in stages.

■ **PIAGET'S STAGES.** Piaget's view of development was greatly influenced by his early training in biology. Central to his theory is the biological concept of *adaptation* (Piaget, 1971). Just as the structures of the body are adapted to fit with the environment, so the structures of the mind develop during childhood to better fit with, or represent, the external world. In infancy and early childhood, children's understanding is very different from adults'. For example, Piaget believed that young babies do not realize that an object hidden from view—a favorite toy or even the mother—continues to exist. He also concluded that preschoolers' thinking is full of faulty logic. Children younger than age 7 commonly say that the amount of milk or lemonade changes when it is poured into a differently shaped container. According to Piaget, children eventually revise these incorrect ideas in their ongoing efforts to achieve an *equilibrium,* or balance, between internal structures and information they encounter in their everyday worlds (Beilin, 1992; Kuhn, 1992).

Through careful observations of and clinical interviews with children, Jean Piaget developed his comprehensive theory of cognitive development. His work has inspired more research on children than any other single theory. *(Yves de Braine/Black Star)*

applied behavior analysis
A set of practical procedures that combine reinforcement, modeling, and the manipulation of situational cues to change behavior.

According to Piaget's theory, at first schemes are motor action patterns. As this 1-year-old takes apart, bangs, and drops these nesting cups, she discovers that her movements have predictable effects on objects and that objects influence one another in regular ways. *(Erika Stone)*

In Piaget's preoperational stage, preschool children represent their earlier sensorimotor discoveries with symbols. Language and make-believe play develop rapidly. These 4-year-olds create an imaginative play scene with dress-up clothes and the assistance of a very cooperative family pet. *(Tom McCarthy/Stock South)*

In Piaget's theory, children move through four broad stages of development, each of which is characterized by qualitatively distinct ways of thinking. Table 1.4 provides a brief description of Piaget's stages. In the *sensorimotor stage,* cognitive development begins with the baby's use of the senses and movements to explore the world. These action patterns evolve into the symbolic but illogical thinking of the preschooler in the *preoperational stage.* Then cognition is transformed into the more organized reasoning of the school-age child in the *concrete operational stage.* Finally, in the *formal operational stage,* thought becomes the complex, abstract reasoning system of the adolescent and adult.

■ **PIAGET'S METHODS OF STUDY.** Piaget devised special methods for investigating how children think. In the early part of his career, he carefully observed his three infant children and also presented them with little problems, such as an attractive object that could be grasped, mouthed, kicked, or searched for when hidden from view. From their reactions, Piaget derived his ideas about cognitive changes that take place during the first 2 years of life.

In studying childhood and adolescent thought, Piaget took advantage of children's ability to describe their thinking. He adapted the clinical method of psychoanalysis, conducting open-ended *clinical interviews* in which a child's initial response to a task served as the basis for the next question he would ask. We will look at an example of a Piagetian clinical interview, as well as the strengths and weaknesses of this technique, when we discuss research methods later in this chapter.

■ **CONTRIBUTIONS AND LIMITATIONS OF PIAGET'S THEORY.** Piaget's cognitive-developmental perspective convinced the field that children are active learners whose minds are inhabited by rich structures of knowledge. Besides investigating children's understanding of the physical world, Piaget explored their reasoning about the social world. As we will see in later chapters, his stages have sparked a wealth of research on children's conceptions of themselves, other people, and human relationships. Practically speaking, Piaget's theory encouraged the development of educational programs that emphasize children's discovery learning and direct contact with the environment.

cognitive-developmental theory
An approach introduced by Piaget that views the child as actively building psychological structures and cognitive development as taking place in stages.

TABLE 1.4

Piaget's Stages of Cognitive Development

STAGE	PERIOD OF DEVELOPMENT	DESCRIPTION
Sensorimotor	Birth–2 years	Infants "think" by acting on the world with their eyes, ears, and hands. As a result, they invent ways of solving sensorimotor problems, such as pulling a lever to hear the sound of a music box, finding hidden toys, and putting objects in and taking them out of containers.
Preoperational	2–7 years	Preschool children use symbols to represent their earlier sensorimotor discoveries. Development of language and make-believe play takes place. However, thinking lacks the logical qualities of the two remaining stages.
Concrete operational	7–11 years	Children's reasoning becomes logical. School-age children understand that a certain amount of lemonade or play dough remains the same even after its appearance changes. They also organize objects into hierarchies of classes and subclasses. However, thinking falls short of adult intelligence. It is not yet abstract.
Formal operational	11 years on	The capacity for abstraction permits adolescents to reason with symbols that do not refer to objects in the real world, as in advanced mathematics. They can also think of all possible outcomes in a scientific problem, not just the most obvious ones.

In Piaget's concrete operational stage, school-age children think in an organized and logical fashion about concrete objects. This 8-year-old boy understands that the hamster on one side of the balance scale is just as heavy as the metal weights on the other, even though the two types of objects look and feel quite different from each other. *(Tim Davis/Photo Researchers)*

Despite Piaget's overwhelming contribution to child development and education, in recent years his theory has been challenged. New evidence indicates that Piaget underestimated the competencies of infants and preschoolers. We will see in later chapters that when young children are given tasks scaled down in difficulty, their understanding appears closer to that of the older child and adult than Piaget believed. This discovery has led many investigators to conclude that the maturity of children's thinking may depend on their familiarity with the investigator's task and the kind of knowledge sampled. Finally, many studies show that children's performance on Piagetian problems can be improved with training. This finding raises questions about his assumption that discovery learning rather than adult teaching is the best way to foster development.

Today, the field of child development is divided over its loyalty to Piaget's ideas. Those who continue to find merit in Piaget's approach accept a modified view of his cognitive stages—one in which changes in children's thinking are not sudden and abrupt but take place much more gradually than Piaget believed (Case, 1992, 1998; Fischer & Pipp, 1984). Others have given up the idea of cognitive stages in favor of a continuous approach to development—information processing, which we will take up in the next section.

In Piaget's formal operational stage, adolescents can think logically and abstractly. These high school students solve a complex scientific problem by thinking of all possible outcomes, not just the most obvious. Then they systematically test each possibility to see if it occurs in the real world. *(Will Faller)*

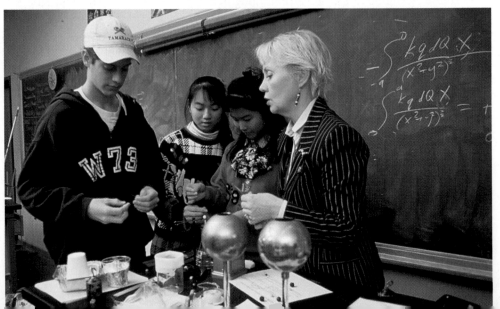

BRIEF REVIEW

Three theoretical perspectives dominated child development research in the middle of the twentieth century. Child guidance professionals turned to Freud's psychoanalytic approach, and Erikson's expansion of it, for help in understanding personality development and the origins of emotional difficulties. Behaviorism and social learning theory rely on conditioning and modeling to explain the appearance of new responses and to treat behavior problems. Piaget's stage theory of cognitive development revolutionized the field with its view of children as active beings who take responsibility for their own learning.

ASK YOURSELF . . .

■ *A 4-year-old becomes frightened of the dark and refuses to go to sleep at night. How would a psychoanalyst and a behaviorist differ in their views of how this problem developed?*

■ *What biological concept is emphasized in Piaget's cognitive-developmental approach? From which nineteenth-century theory did Piaget borrow this idea?*

RECENT THEORETICAL PERSPECTIVES

New ways of understanding the child are constantly emerging—questioning, building on, and enhancing the discoveries of earlier theories. Today, a burst of fresh approaches and research emphases, including information processing, ethology, ecological systems theory, Vygotsky's sociocultural theory, and the dynamic systems perspective, are broadening our understanding of children's development.

INFORMATION PROCESSING

During the 1970s, child development researchers became disenchanted with behaviorism as a complete account of children's learning and were disappointed in their efforts to fully verify Piaget's ideas. They turned to new trends in the field of cognitive psychology for ways to understand the development of children's thinking. Today, a leading perspective is **information processing,** a general approach that emerged with the design of digital computers that use mathematically specified steps to solve problems. These systems suggested to psychologists that the human mind might also be viewed as a symbol-manipulating system through which information flows (Klahr & MacWhinney, 1998). From presentation to the senses at *input* and behavioral responses at *output,* information is actively coded, transformed, and organized.

Information processing is often thought of as a field of scripts, frames, and flow charts. Diagrams are used to map the precise series of steps people use to solve problems and complete tasks, much like the plans devised by programmers to get computers to perform a series of "mental operations." Let's look at an example to clarify the usefulness of this approach. The top of Figure 1.3 shows the steps that Andrea, an academically successful 8-year-old, used to complete a two-digit subtraction problem. The bottom of the figure displays the faulty procedure of Jody, who arrived at the wrong answer. The flow-chart approach ensures that models of child and adult thinking will be very clear. For example, by comparing the two procedures shown in Figure 1.3, we know exactly what is necessary for effective problem solving and where Jody went wrong in searching for a solution. As a result, we can pinpoint Jody's difficulties and design an intervention to help her improve her reasoning.

A wide variety of information-processing models exist. Some (like the one in Figure 1.3) are fairly narrow in that they track children's mastery of one or a few tasks. Others describe the human information-processing system as a whole (Atkinson & Shiffrin, 1968; Craik & Lockhart, 1972). These general models are used as guides for asking questions about broad age changes in children's thinking. For example, does a child's ability to search the environment for information needed to solve a problem become more organized and

information processing
An approach that views the human mind as a symbol-manipulating system through which information flows and regards cognitive development as a continuous process.

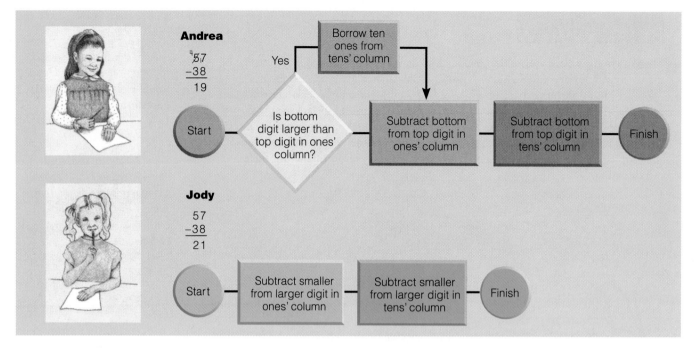

FIGURE 1.3

Information-processing flow charts showing the steps that two 8-year-olds used to solve a math problem. In this two-digit subtraction problem with a borrowing operation, you can see how Andrea's procedure is correct, whereas Jody's results in a wrong answer.

planful with age? How much new information can preschoolers hold in memory compared with older children and adults? To what extent does a child's current knowledge influence her ability to learn more?

The information-processing approach is also being used to clarify the processing of social information—for example, how children come to view themselves and others in gender-linked terms (Liben & Signorella, 1993; Ruble & Martin, 1998). If we can identify how rigid gender stereotypes arise in childhood, then we are in a good position to design interventions that promote more flexible conceptions of male and female role possibilities at an early age.

Like Piaget's theory, the information-processing approach regards children as active, sense-making beings who modify their own thinking in response to environmental demands (Klahr & MacWhinney, 1998). But unlike Piaget's theory, there are no stages of development. Rather, the thought processes studied—perception, attention, memory, planning strategies, categorization of information, and comprehension of written and spoken prose—are assumed to be similar at all ages but present to a lesser extent in children. Therefore, the view of development is one of continuous increase rather than abrupt, stagewise change.

Perhaps you can tell from what we have said so far that information-processing research has important implications for education (Geary, 1994; Siegler, 1998). But information processing has fallen short in some respects. Perhaps its greatest shortcoming stems from its central strength: By analyzing thinking into its components, information processing has difficulty putting them back together into a comprehensive theory of development. In addition, aspects of children's cognition that are not linear and logical, such as imagination and creativity, are all but ignored by this approach (Greeno, 1989). Furthermore, information-processing research has largely been conducted in artificial laboratory situations. Consequently, critics complain that it isolates children's thinking from important features of real-life learning situations. Recently, information-processing investigators have addressed this concern by focusing on more realistic materials and activities. Today, they study children's conversations, stories, memory for everyday events, and strategies for performing academic tasks.

Fortunately, since many child development theories exist, they encourage one another to attend to previously neglected dimensions of children's lives. A unique feature of the final three perspectives we will discuss is the emphasis they place on *contexts for develop-*

Konrad Lorenz was one of the founders of ethology and a keen observer of animal behavior. He developed the concept of imprinting. Here, young geese who were separated from their mother and placed in the company of Lorenz during an early, critical period show that they have imprinted on him. They follow him about as he swims through the water, a response that promotes survival. *(Nina Leen/LIFE Magazine © Time Warner)*

ment. The impact of context, or environment, can be examined at many levels. We will see that family, school, community, larger society, and culture all affect children's growth. In addition, human capacities have been shaped by a long evolutionary history during which our brains and bodies adapted to their surroundings. The next theory, ethology, emphasizes this biological side of development.

ETHOLOGY

Ethology is concerned with the adaptive, or survival, value of behavior and its evolutionary history (Dewsbury, 1992; Hinde, 1989). It was first applied to research on children in the 1960s but has become even more influential today. The origins of ethology can be traced to the work of Darwin. Two European zoologists, Konrad Lorenz and Niko Tinbergen, laid its modern foundations.

Watching the behaviors of diverse animal species in their natural habitats, Lorenz and Tinbergen observed behavior patterns that promote survival. The best known of these is *imprinting,* the early following behavior of certain baby birds that ensures that the young will stay close to the mother and be fed and protected from danger. Imprinting takes place during an early, restricted time period of development. If the mother goose is not present during this time, but an object resembling her in important features is, young goslings may imprint on it instead (Lorenz, 1952).

Observations of imprinting led to a major concept that has been widely applied in child development: the *critical period.* It refers to a time span during which the child is biologically prepared to acquire certain capacities but needs the support of an appropriately stimulating environment. Many researchers have conducted studies to find out whether complex cognitive and social behaviors must be learned during certain time periods. For example, if children are deprived of adequate food or physical and social stimulation during the early years of life, will their intelligence be impaired? If language is not mastered during the preschool years, is the child's capacity to acquire it reduced?

As we address these and other similar questions in later chapters, we will discover that the term *sensitive period* offers a better account of human development than does the strict notion of a critical period (Bornstein, 1989). A **sensitive period** is a time that is optimal for certain capacities to emerge and in which the individual is especially responsive to environmental influences. However, the boundaries of a sensitive period are less well defined than are those of a critical period. Development may occur later, but it is harder to induce at that time.

Inspired by observations of imprinting, British psychoanalyst John Bowlby (1969) applied ethological theory to the understanding of the human infant–caregiver relationship. He argued that attachment behaviors of babies, such as smiling, babbling, grasping,

ethology
An approach concerned with the adaptive, or survival, value of behavior and its evolutionary history.

sensitive period
A time span that is optimal for certain capacities to emerge and in which the individual is especially responsive to environmental influences.

and crying, are built-in social signals that encourage the parent to approach, care for, and interact with the baby. By keeping the mother near, these behaviors help ensure that the baby will be fed, protected from danger, and provided with the stimulation and affection necessary for healthy growth.

The development of attachment in human infants is a lengthy process involving changes in psychological structures that lead the baby to form a deep affectional tie with the caregiver (Bretherton, 1992). As we will see in Chapter 7, it is far more complex than imprinting in baby birds. But for now, note how the ethological view of attachment, which emphasizes the role of innate infant signals, differs sharply from the behaviorist drive reduction explanation we mentioned earlier—that the baby's desire for closeness to the mother is a learned response based on feeding.

Observations by ethologists have shown that many aspects of children's social behavior, including emotional expressions, aggression, cooperation, and social play, resemble those of our primate relatives. Today, efforts are also under way to apply an evolutionary perspective to children's cognition (Bjorklund, 1997; Geary, 1994). Researchers are returning to the central question posed by Piaget: How must children think to adapt to the environments in which they find themselves? We will explore some new answers in later chapters.

Although ethology emphasizes the genetic and biological roots of development, learning is also considered important because it lends flexibility and greater adaptiveness to behavior. The interests of ethologists are broad. They want to understand the entire organism–environment system (Hinde, 1989; Miller, 1993). The next contextual perspective we will discuss, ecological systems theory, serves as an excellent complement to ethology, since it shows how various aspects of the environment, from immediate human relationships to larger societal forces, work together to affect children's development.

ECOLOGICAL SYSTEMS THEORY

Urie Bronfenbrenner, an American psychologist, is responsible for an approach to child development that has risen to the forefront of the field over the past 2 decades. **Ecological systems theory** views the child as developing within a complex *system* of relationships affected by multiple levels of the surrounding environment. Since the child's biological dispositions join with environmental forces to mold development, Bronfenbrenner (1998) recently characterized his perspective as a *bioecological model.*

Before Bronfenbrenner's (1979, 1989, 1993) theory, most researchers viewed the environment fairly narrowly—as limited to events and conditions immediately surrounding the child. As Figure 1.4 shows, Bronfenbrenner expanded this view by envisioning the environment as a series of nested structures that includes but extends beyond home, school, and neighborhood settings in which children spend their everyday lives.

■ **THE MICROSYSTEM.** The innermost level of the environment is the **microsystem,** which refers to activities and interaction patterns in the child's immediate surroundings. Bronfenbrenner emphasizes that to understand child development at this level, we must keep in mind that all relationships are *bidirectional and reciprocal.* That is, adults affect children's behavior, but children's biologically and socially influenced characteristics—their physical attributes, personalities, and capacities—also influence the behavior of adults. For example, a friendly, attentive child is likely to evoke positive and patient reactions from parents, whereas a distractible youngster is more likely to be responded to with restriction and punishment (Danforth, Barkley, & Stokes, 1990). As these reciprocal interactions become well established and occur often over time, they have an enduring impact on development (Bronfenbrenner, 1995).

But whether parent–child (or other two-person) relationships enhance or undermine development is affected by *third parties.* If other individuals in the setting are supportive, then the quality of relationships is enhanced. For example, when parents encourage one another in their child-rearing roles, each engages in more effective parenting (Gottfried,

Urie Bronfenbrenner is the originator of ecological systems theory. He views the child as developing within a complex system of relationships affected by multiple levels of the surrounding environment, from immediate settings to broad cultural values, laws, and customs. *(Courtesy of Urie Bronfenbrenner, Cornell University)*

ecological systems theory
Bronfenbrenner's approach, which views the child as developing within a complex system of relationships affected by multiple levels of the environment, from immediate settings of family and school to broad cultural values and programs.

microsystem
In ecological systems theory, the activities and interaction patterns in the child's immediate surroundings.

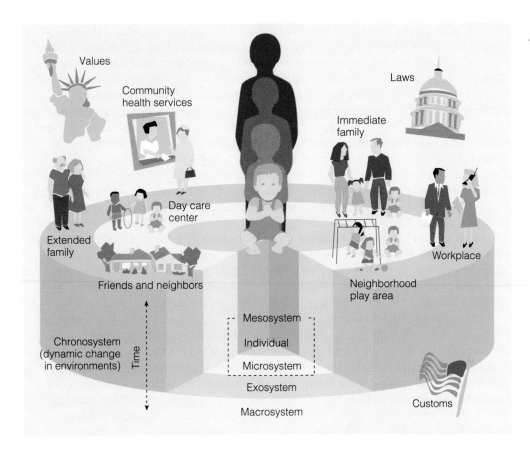

FIGURE 1.4

**Structure of the
environment in ecological
systems theory.**
The *microsystem* concerns
relations between the developing person and the immediate environment; the
mesosystem, connections
among immediate settings;
the *exosystem,* social settings
that affect but do not contain the child; and the
macrosystem, the values,
laws, customs, and resources
of the culture that affect
activities and interactions at
all inner layers. The
chronosystem is not a specific
context. Instead, it refers to
the dynamic, ever-changing
nature of the child's
environment.

Gottfried, & Bathurst, 1988; Simons et al., 1992). In contrast, marital conflict is associated with inconsistent discipline and hostile reactions toward children. In response, children typically become hostile, and their adjustment suffers (Davies & Cummings, 1994).

■ **THE MESOSYSTEM.** For children to develop at their best, child-rearing supports must also exist in the larger environment. The second level in Bronfenbrenner's theory is the **mesosystem.** It encompasses connections between microsystems, such as home, school, neighborhood, and day care center, that foster children's development. For exam-ple, a child's academic progress depends not just on activities that take place in class-rooms. It is also promoted by parental involvement in school life and the extent to which academic learning is carried over into the home (Grolnick & Slowiaczek, 1994). Simi-larly, parent–child interaction is likely to be affected by the child's relationships with caregivers at day care, and vice versa. Parent–child and caregiver–child relationships are each likely to support development when there are links, in the form of visits and exchange of information, between home and day care setting.

■ **THE EXOSYSTEM.** The **exosystem** refers to social settings that do not contain chil-dren but that affect their experiences in immediate settings. These may be formal organi-zations, such as the parents' workplace or health and welfare services in the community. For example, flexible work schedules, paid maternity and paternity leave, and sick leave for parents whose children are ill are ways that work settings can help parents in their child-rearing roles and, indirectly, enhance development. Exosystem supports can also be informal, such as parents' social networks—friends and extended family members who provide advice, companionship, and even financial assistance. Research confirms the neg-ative impact of a breakdown in exosystem activities. Families who are socially isolated because they have few personal or community-based ties or who are affected by unem-ployment show increased rates of conflict and child abuse (Garbarino & Kostelny, 1992).

mesosystem
In ecological systems theory,
connections between chil-
dren's immediate settings.

exosystem
In ecological systems theory,
settings that do not contain
children but that affect their
experiences in immediate settings. Examples are parents'
workplace and health and welfare services in the community.

■ **THE MACROSYSTEM.** The outermost level of Bronfenbrenner's model is the **macrosystem.** It is not a specific context. Instead, it consists of the cultural values, laws, customs, and resources. The priority that the macrosystem gives to children's needs affects the support they receive at inner levels of the environment. For example, in countries that require high-quality standards for day care and workplace benefits for employed parents, children are more likely to have favorable experiences in their immediate settings. As we will see in greater detail in later chapters, although most European nations have such programs in place, they are not yet widely available in the United States (Children's Defense Fund, 1998; Kamerman, 1993).

■ **AN EVER-CHANGING SYSTEM.** According to Bronfenbrenner, we must keep in mind that the environment is not a static force that affects people in a uniform way. Instead, it is ever-changing. Important life events, such as the birth of a sibling, entering school, moving to a new neighborhood, or parents' divorce, modify existing relationships between children and their environments, producing new conditions that affect development. In addition, the timing of environmental change affects its impact. The arrival of a new sibling has very different consequences for a homebound toddler than for a school-age child with many relationships and activities beyond the family.

Bronfenbrenner refers to the temporal dimension of his model as the **chronosystem** (the prefix *chrono-* means time). Changes in life events can be imposed on the child, as in the examples just given. But they can also arise from within the child, since as children get older they select, modify, and create many of their own settings and experiences. Therefore, in ecological systems theory, development is neither controlled by environmental circumstances nor driven by inner dispositions. Instead, children are both products and producers of their environments, both of which form a network of interdependent effects. Notice how our discussion of resilient children on pages 10–11 illustrates this idea. We will see many more examples in later chapters of this book.

CROSS-CULTURAL RESEARCH AND VYGOTSKY'S SOCIOCULTURAL THEORY

Ecological systems theory, as well as Erikson's psychosocial theory, underscores the connection between culture and development. In line with this emphasis, child development research has recently seen a dramatic increase in cross-cultural studies. Investigations that make comparisons across cultures, and among ethnic groups within cultures, provide insight into whether developmental theories apply to all children or are limited to specific conditions. In doing so, cross-cultural research helps us untangle the contributions of biological and environmental factors to the timing and order of appearance of children's behaviors (Greenfield, 1994).

In the past, cross-cultural studies focused on broad cultural differences in development—for example, whether children in one culture are more advanced in motor development or do better on intellectual tasks than do children in another. However, this approach can lead us to conclude—incorrectly—that one culture is superior in enhancing development, whereas another is deficient. In addition, it does not help us understand the precise experiences that contribute to cultural differences in children's behavior.

Today, more research is examining the relationship of *culturally specific practices* to child development. The contributions of Russian psychologist Lev Semenovich Vygotsky (1896–1934) have played a major role in this trend. Vygotsky's (1934/1987) perspective is called **sociocultural theory.** It focuses on how *culture*—the values, beliefs, customs, and skills of a social group—is transmitted to the next generation. According to Vygotsky, *social interaction*—in particular, cooperative dialogues between children and more knowledgeable members of society—is necessary for children to acquire the ways of thinking and behaving that make up a community's culture (Wertsch & Tulviste, 1992). Vygotsky believed that as adults and more expert peers help children master culturally meaningful activities, the communication between them becomes part of children's thinking. Once

According to Lev Semenovich Vygotsky, many cognitive processes and skills are socially transferred from more knowledgeable members of society to children. Vygotsky's sociocultural theory helps us understand the wide variation in cognitive competencies from culture to culture. Vygotsky is pictured here with his daughter. *(Courtesy of James V. Wertsch, Clark University)*

children internalize the essential features of these dialogues, they use the language within them to guide their own actions and acquire new skills. The young child instructing herself while working a puzzle or tying her shoes has started to produce the same kind of guiding comments that an adult previously used to help her master important tasks (Berk, 1994b).

Vygotsky's theory has been especially influential in the study of children's cognition. But Vygotsky's approach to cognitive development is quite different from Piaget's. Recall that Piaget did not regard direct teaching by adults as vital for cognitive development. Instead, he emphasized children's active, independent efforts to make sense of their world. Vygotsky agreed with Piaget that children are active, constructive beings. But unlike Piaget, he viewed cognitive development as a *socially mediated process*—as dependent on the support that adults and more mature peers provide as children try new tasks. Finally, Vygotsky did not regard all children as moving through the same sequence of stages. Instead, as soon as children acquire language, their enhanced ability to communicate with others leads to continuous, step-by-step changes in thought and behavior that can vary greatly from culture to culture.

A major finding of cross-cultural research is that cultures select different tasks for children's learning. In line with Vygotsky's theory, social interaction surrounding these tasks leads to knowledge and skills essential for success in a particular culture (Rogoff & Chavajay, 1995). For example, among the Zinacanteco Indians of southern Mexico, young girls become expert weavers of complex garments through the informal guidance of adults (Childs & Greenfield, 1982). In Brazil, child candy sellers with little or no schooling develop sophisticated mathematical abilities as the result of buying candy from wholesalers, pricing it in collaboration with adults and experienced peers, and bargaining with customers on city streets (Saxe, 1988).

Vygotsky's theory, and the research stimulated by it, reveals that children in every culture develop unique strengths that are not present in other cultures. A cross-cultural perspective reminds us that the majority of child development specialists reside in the United States, and their research includes only a small minority of humankind. We cannot assume that the developmental sequences observed in our own children are "natural" or that the experiences fostering them are "ideal" without looking around the world.

At the same time, Vygotsky's emphasis on culture and social experience led him to neglect biological contributions to development. Although he recognized the importance of maturation, he said little about the role of brain growth in cognitive change. Furthermore, Vygotsky's focus on social transmission of knowledge meant that he placed less emphasis than did other theorists on children's capacity to shape their own development. Modern followers of Vygotsky grant the individual and society more balanced roles (Rogoff, 1998; Wertsch & Tulviste, 1998).

NEW DIRECTIONS: DEVELOPMENT AS A DYNAMIC SYSTEM

Today, child development specialists recognize both consistency and variability in child development. But instead of merely describing consistencies, they want to do a better job of explaining variation.

A new wave of theorists has adopted a **dynamic systems perspective** on development (Fischer & Bidell, 1998; Thelen & Smith, 1998). According to this view, the child's mind, body, and physical and social worlds form an *integrated system* that guides mastery of new skills. The system is *dynamic,* or constantly in motion. A change in any part of it—from brain maturation to physical and social surroundings—disrupts the current organism–environment relationship. When this happens, the child actively reorganizes his or her behavior so the various components of the system work together again, but in a more complex and effective way.

Because children have similar brains and bodies and live in stimulating environments, certain broad outlines of development apply to many youngsters. But biological makeup, everyday tasks, and the people who collaborate with children on those tasks vary greatly,

This South American child candy seller is learning to solve arithmetic problems involving large currency values through everyday street vending activities. Her mathematical skills illustrate how culture and social experience influence cognitive development. *(David Bartruff/Stock Boston)*

macrosystem
In ecological systems theory, cultural values, laws, customs, and resources that influence experiences and interactions at inner levels of the environment.

chronosystem
In ecological systems theory, temporal changes in children's environments, which produce new conditions that affect development. These changes can be imposed externally or arise from within the child.

sociocultural theory
Vygotsky's theory, in which children acquire the ways of thinking and behaving that make up a community's culture through cooperative dialogues with more knowledgeable members of society.

dynamic systems perspective
A view that regards the child's mind, body, and physical and social worlds as a dynamic, integrated system. A change in any part of the system leads the child to reorganize his or her behavior so the system operates in a more complex and effective way.

These children are about the same age, but they vary widely in competencies and the precise ways they developed specific skills. The dynamic systems perspective aims to explain this variation. *(B. Daemmrich/The Image Works)*

leading to wide individual differences in specific skills. Even when children master the same skills, such as walking, talking, or adding and subtracting, they often do so in unique ways. And because children build competencies by engaging in real activities in real contexts, different skills vary in maturity within the same child. From this perspective, development is more like a web of fibers branching out in many directions than a single line of stagewise or continuous change (Fischer & Bidell, 1998).

The dynamic systems view has been inspired by similar ideas in other scientific disciplines (Thelen & Smith, 1994). In addition, it draws on information processing and contextual theories—ethology, ecological systems theory, and sociocultural theory. At present, dynamic systems research is in its early stages. The perspective has largely been applied to children's motor and cognitive skills, but some investigators think it might help explain emotional and social development as well. As the field of child development enters the twenty-first century, researchers are analyzing development in all its complexity, in search of an all-encompassing approach to understanding change.

ASK YOURSELF . . .

■ *What shortcoming of the information-processing approach is a strength of ethology, ecological systems theory, and Vygotsky's sociocultural theory?*

■ *Return to the Biology and Environment box on pages 10–11. How does the story of John and Gary illustrate bidirectional and reciprocal relationships within the microsystem, as described in Bronfenbrenner's model?*

■ *What features of Vygotsky's sociocultural theory distinguish it from Piaget's theory?*

BRIEF REVIEW

New child development theories are constantly emerging, questioning and building on earlier discoveries. Using computerlike models of mental activity, information processing has brought exactness and precision to the study of children's thinking. Ethology highlights the adaptive, or survival, value of children's behavior and its evolutionary history. Ecological systems theory stresses that adult–child interaction is a two-way street affected by a range of environmental influences, from immediate settings of home and school to broad cultural values and programs. Vygotsky's sociocultural theory takes a closer look at social relationships that foster development: Through cooperative dialogues with more mature members of society, children acquire unique, culturally adaptive competencies. In an effort to account for variation in development, researchers have begun to characterize development as a dynamic system.

COMPARING CHILD DEVELOPMENT THEORIES

In the previous sections, we reviewed theoretical perspectives that are major forces in modern child development research. They differ in many respects. First, they focus on different aspects of development. Some, such as the psychoanalytic perspective and ethology, emphasize children's emotional and social development. Others, such as Piaget's cognitive-developmental theory, information processing, and Vygotsky's sociocultural theory, stress important changes in children's thinking. The remaining approaches—behaviorism, social learning theory, and ecological systems theory—discuss factors assumed to affect all aspects of children's functioning.

Second, every theory contains a unique point of view about the nature of children and their development. As we conclude our review of theoretical perspectives, take a moment to identify the stand that each theory takes on the three controversial issues presented at the beginning of this chapter. Then check your own analysis of theories against Table 1.5. If you had difficulty classifying any of them, return to the relevant section of this chapter and reread the description of that theory.

TABLE 1.5

Stance of Major Theories on Three Basic Issues in Child Development

THEORY	VIEW OF THE DEVELOPING PERSON	VIEW OF THE COURSE OF DEVELOPMENT	VIEW OF THE DETERMINANTS OF DEVELOPMENT
Psychoanalytic perspective	*Organismic:* Relations among structures of the mind (id, ego, and superego) determine personality.	*Discontinuous:* Stages of psychosexual and psychosocial development are emphasized.	*Both nature and nurture:* Innate impulses are channeled and controlled through social experiences. *Early experiences* set the course of later development.
Behaviorism and social learning theory	*Mechanistic:* The person consists of connections established between stimulus inputs and behavioral responses.	*Continuous:* Quantitative increase in learned behaviors occurs with age.	*Emphasis on nurture:* Learning principles of conditioning and modeling determine development. *Both early and later experiences* are important.
Piaget's cognitive-developmental theory	*Organismic:* Psychological structures determine the child's understanding of the world. The child actively constructs knowledge.	*Discontinuous:* Stages of cognitive development are emphasized.	*Both nature and nurture:* Children's innate drive to discover reality is emphasized. However, it must be supported by a rich, stimulating environment. *Both early and later experiences* are important.
Information processing	*Both organismic and Mechanistic:* Active processing structures combine with a mechanistic, computerlike model of stimulus input.	*Continuous:* A quantitative increase in perception, attention, memory, and problem-solving skills takes place with age.	*Both nature and nurture:* Maturation and learning opportunities affect information-processing skills. *Both early and later experiences* are important.
Ethology	*Organismic:* The individual is biologically prepared with social signals that actively promote survival. Over time, psychological structures develop that underlie attachment and other adaptive behaviors.	*Both continuous and discontinuous:* Adaptive behaviors increase in quantity over time. But sensitive periods—restricted time periods in which qualitatively distinct capacities emerge fairly suddenly—are also emphasized.	*Both nature and nurture:* Biologically based, evolved behaviors are stressed, but an appropriately stimulating environment is necessary to elicit them. Also, learning can improve the adaptiveness of behavior. *Early experiences* set the course of later development.
Ecological systems theory	*Organismic:* Children's personality characteristics and capacities actively contribute to their development.	*Not specified*	*Both nature and nurture:* Children's characteristics and the reactions of others affect each other in a bidirectional fashion. Layers of the environment influence child-rearing experiences. *Both early and later experiences* are important.
Vygotsky's sociocultural theory	*Organismic:* Children internalize features of social dialogues, forming psychological structures that they use to guide their own behavior.	*Continuous:* Interaction with more expert members of society leads to step-by-step changes in thought and behavior.	*Both nature and nurture:* Maturation and opportunities to interact with more expert members of society affect the development of psychological structures and culturally adaptive skills. *Both early and later experiences* are important.
Dynamic systems perspective	*Organismic:* Children actively reorganize their behavior, yielding a more complex and effective dynamic system.	*Cotinuous:* Change in the system is always ongoing. Wide variation in the childs' skills leads development to resemble a web of fibers branching out in many directions.	*Both nature and nurture:* The childs' mind, body, and physical and social surroundings form an integrated system that guides mastery of new skills. *Both early and later experiences* are important.

Finally, we have seen that theories have strengths and weaknesses. This may remind you of an important point made earlier in this chapter—that no theory provides a complete account of development. Perhaps you found that you were attracted to some theories, but you had doubts about others. As you read more about child development research in later chapters of this book, you may find it useful to keep a notebook in which you test your own theoretical likes and dislikes against the evidence. Do not be surprised if you revise your ideas many times, just as theorists have done throughout this century. By the end of the course, you will have built your own personal perspective on child development. It might turn out to be a blend of several theories, because each viewpoint we have discussed has contributed in important ways to what we know about children. And like the field of child development as a whole, you will be left with some unanswered questions. I hope they will motivate you to continue your quest to understand children in the years to come.

STUDYING THE CHILD

In every science, theories, like those we've just reviewed, guide the collection of information, its interpretation, and its application to everyday life. In fact, research usually begins with a *hypothesis,* or prediction, drawn directly from a theory. But theories and hypotheses are only the beginning of the many activities that result in sound research on child development. Conducting research according to scientifically accepted procedures involves many important steps and choices. Investigators must decide which participants, and how many, to include. Then they must figure out what the participants will be asked to do and when, where, and how many times each will need to be seen. Finally, they must examine relationships and draw conclusions from their data.

In the following sections, we take a look at research strategies commonly used to study children. We begin with *research methods*—the specific activities of participants, such as taking tests, answering questionnaires, responding to interviews, or being observed. Then we turn to *research designs*—overall plans for research studies that permit the best possible test of the investigator's hypothesis. Finally, we discuss special ethical issues involved in doing research on children.

At this point, you may be wondering, Why learn about research strategies? Why not leave these matters to research specialists and concentrate on what is already known about the child and how this knowledge can be applied? There are two reasons. First, each of us must be wise and critical consumers of knowledge, not naive sponges who soak up facts about children. A basic appreciation of the strengths and weaknesses of research strategies becomes important in separating dependable information from misleading results. Second, individuals who work directly with children are sometimes in a position to carry out research studies, either on their own or with an experienced investigator. At other times, they may have to provide information on how well their goals for children are being realized to justify continued financial support for their programs and activities. Under these circumstances, an understanding of research strategies becomes essential practical knowledge.

COMMON METHODS USED TO STUDY CHILDREN

How does a researcher choose a basic approach to gathering information about children? Common methods in the field of child development include systematic observation, self-reports, psychophysiological measures, clinical or case studies of a single child, and ethnographies of the life circumstances of a specific group of children. As you read about these methods, you may find it helpful to refer to Table 1.6, which summarizes the strengths and limitations of each.

TABLE 1.6

Strengths and Limitations of Common Research Methods

METHOD	DESCRIPTION	STRENGTHS	LIMITATIONS
Systematic Observation			
Naturalistic ion observation	Observation of behavior in natural contexts	Observations reflect participants' everyday lives.	Conditions under which participants are observed cannot be controlled.
Structured observation	Observation of behavior in a laboratory	Conditions of observation are the same for all children.	Observations may not be typical of the way participants behave in everyday life.
Self-Reports			
Clinical interview	Flexible interviewing procedure in which the investigator obtains a complete account of the participant's thoughts	Comes as close as possible to the way participants think in everyday life; great breadth and depth of information can be obtained in a short time.	Pariticipants may not report information accurately; flexible procedure makes comparing individuals' responses difficult.
Structured interview, questionnaires, and tests	Self-report instruments in which each participant is asked the same questions in the same way	Standardized method of asking questions permits comparisons of participants' responses and efficient data collection and scoring.	Does not yield the same depth of information as a clinical interview; responses are still subject to inaccurate reporting.
Psychophysiological Methods	Methods that measure the relationship between physiological processes and behavior	Reveals which central nervous system structures contribute to development and individual differences in certain competencies. Helps identify the perceptions, thoughts, and emotions of infants and young children, who cannot report them clearly.	Cannot reveal with certainty how an individual processes stimuli. Many factors besides those of interest to the researcher can influence a physiological response.
Clinical Method (Case Study)	A full picture of a single individual's psychological functioning, obtained by combining interviews, observations, test scores, and sometimes psychophysiological assessments	Provides rich, descriptive insights into processes of development.	May be biased by researcher's theoretical preferences; findings cannot be applied to individuals other than the participant.
Ethnography	Understanding a culture or distinct social group through participant observation; by making extensive field notes, the researcher tries to capture the culture's unique values and social processes	Provides a more complete and accurate description than can be derived from a single observational visit, interview, or questionnaire.	May be biased by researcher's values and theoretical preferences; findings cannot be applied to individuals and settings other than the ones studied.

■ **SYSTEMATIC OBSERVATION.** To find out how children actually behave, a researcher may choose *systematic observation*. Observations of the behavior of children, and of the adults who are important in their lives, can be made in different ways. One approach is to go into the field, or natural environment, and observe the behavior of interest, a method called **naturalistic observation.**

A study of preschoolers' responses to their peers' distress provides a good example of this technique (Farver & Branstetter, 1994). Observing 3- and 4-year-olds in day care centers, the researchers recorded each instance of crying and the reactions of nearby children—whether they ignored, watched curiously, commented on the child's unhappiness,

naturalistic observation
A method in which the researcher goes into the natural environment to observe the behavior of interest.

scolded or teased, or shared, helped, or expressed sympathy. Caregiver behaviors, such as explaining why a child was crying, mediating conflict, or offering comfort, were noted to see if adult sensitivity was related to children's caring responses. A strong relationship emerged. The great strength of naturalistic observation in studies like this one is that investigators can see directly the everyday behaviors they hope to explain (Miller, 1998).

Naturalistic observation also has a major limitation: Not all individuals have the same opportunity to display a particular behavior in everyday life. In the study just mentioned, some children may have witnessed a child crying more often than did others or been exposed to more cues for positive social responses from caregivers. For this reason, they might have displayed more compassion.

Researchers commonly deal with this difficulty by making **structured observations** in a laboratory. In this approach, the investigator sets up a situation that evokes the behavior of interest so every participant has an equal opportunity to display the response. In one study, children's comforting behavior was observed by playing a tape recording of a baby crying in the next room. Using an intercom, children could either talk to the baby or push a button so they did not have to listen (Eisenberg et al., 1993). Notice how structured observation gives investigators more control over the research situation. But its great disadvantage is that people do not necessarily behave in the laboratory as they do in everyday life.

The procedures used to collect systematic observations vary considerably, depending on the purpose of the research. Some investigators need to describe the entire stream of behavior—everything said and done over a certain time period. The goal of one of my own studies was to find out how sensitive, responsive, and verbally stimulating caregivers were when they interacted with children in day care centers (Berk, 1985). In this case, everything each caregiver said and did—even the amount of time she spent away from the children, taking coffee breaks and talking on the phone—was important. In other studies, only one or a few kinds of behavior are needed, and it is not necessary to preserve the entire behavior stream. In these instances, researchers use more efficient observation procedures in which they record only certain events or mark off behaviors on checklists.

Systematic observation provides invaluable information on how children and adults actually behave, but it tells us little about the reasoning that lies behind their responses. For this kind of information, researchers must turn to another type of method: self-reports.

■ **SELF-REPORTS: INTERVIEWS AND QUESTIONNAIRES.** Self-reports are instruments that ask participants to answer questions about their perceptions, thoughts, abilities, feelings, attitudes, beliefs, and past experiences. They range from relatively unstructured clinical interviews, the method used by Piaget to study children's thinking, to highly structured interviews, questionnaires, and tests.

Let's look at an example of a **clinical interview** in which Piaget questioned a 5-year-old child about his understanding of dreams:

> Where does the dream come from?—*I think you sleep so well that you dream.*—Does it come from us or from outside?—*From outside.*—When you are in bed and you dream, where is the dream?—*In my bed, under the blanket. I don't really know. If it was in my stomach, the bones would be in the way and I shouldn't see it.*—Is the dream there when you sleep?—*Yes, it is in the bed beside me . . .*—You see the dream when you are in the room, but if I were in the room, too, should I see it?—*No, grownups don't ever dream.*—Can two people ever have the same dream?—*No, never.*—When the dream is in the room, is it near you?—*Yes, there!* (pointing to 30 cm. in front of his eyes). (Piaget, 1926/1930, pp. 97–98)

Notice how Piaget used a flexible, conversational style to encourage the child to expand his ideas. Prompts are given to obtain a fuller picture of the child's reasoning.

The clinical interview has two major strengths. First, it permits people to display their thoughts in terms that are as close as possible to the way they think in everyday life. Sec-

structured observation
A method in which the investigator sets up a situation that evokes the behavior of interest and observes it in a laboratory.

clinical interview
A method in which the researcher uses a flexible, conversational style to probe for the participant's point of view.

ond, the clinical interview can provide a large amount of information in a fairly brief period of time. For example, in an hour-long session, we can obtain a wide range of child-rearing information from a parent—much more than we could capture by observing parent–child interaction for the same amount of time.

A major limitation of the clinical interview has to do with the accuracy with which people report their thoughts, feelings, and experiences. Some participants, desiring to please the interviewer, may make up answers that do not represent their actual thinking. When asked about past events, they may have trouble recalling exactly what happened. And because the clinical interview depends on verbal ability and expressiveness, it may underestimate the capacities of individuals who have difficulty putting their thoughts into words.

The clinical interview has also been criticized because of its flexibility. When questions are phrased differently for each participant, responses may be due to the manner of interviewing rather than to real differences in the way people think about a certain topic. **Structured interviews,** in which each participant is asked the same set of questions in the same way, can eliminate this problem. In addition, these techniques are much more efficient. Answers are briefer, and researchers can obtain written responses from an entire class of children or group of parents at the same time. Also, when structured interviews use multiple-choice, yes–no, and true–false formats, as is done on many tests and questionnaires, responses can be tabulated by machine. However, we must keep in mind that these approaches do not yield the same depth of information as a clinical interview. And they can still be affected by the problem of inaccurate reporting.

■ **PSYCHOPHYSIOLOGICAL METHODS.** Researchers' desire to uncover the biological bases of children's cognitive and emotional responses has led to the use of **psychophysiological methods,** which measure the relationship between physiological processes and behavior. Investigators who rely on these methods want to find out which central nervous system structures contribute to development and individual differences. Another benefit of psychophysiological methods is that they help identify the perceptions, thoughts, and emotions of infants and young children, who cannot describe their psychological experiences clearly.

Involuntary activities of the autonomic nervous system—changes in heart rate, blood pressure, respiration, and pupil dilation—are among the most commonly used physiological measures because of their sensitivity to psychological state. For example, heart rate can be used to infer whether an infant is staring blankly at a stimulus (heart rate is stable) or attending to and processing information (heart rate slows during concentration) (Izard et al., 1991; Porges, 1991). Heart rate variations are also linked to certain emotional expressions, such as interest, anger, and sadness (Fox & Fitzgerald, 1990). And as Chapter 7 will reveal, distinct patterns of autonomic activity are related to aspects of temperament, such as shyness and sociability (Kagan, 1992, 1998).

Autonomic indicators of cognition and emotion have been enriched by measures of brain functioning. In an *electroencephalogram (EEG)*, researchers tape electrodes to the scalp to record the electrical activity of the brain. EEG waves are linked to different states of arousal, from deep sleep to alert wakefulness, permitting researchers to see how these states change with age. Investigators can also study EEG waves that accompany particular events. For example, a unique wave pattern appears when infants older than 4 months of age are re-exposed to a stimulus they saw earlier. This reaction seems to reflect babies' active efforts to search their memories (Nelson, 1993).

Using the clinical interview, this researcher asks a mother to describe her child's development. The method permits large amounts of information to be gathered in a relatively short period of time. However, a major drawback of this method is that subjects do not always report information accurately. *(Tony Freeman/Photo Edit)*

structured interview
A method in which each participant is asked the same questions in the same way.

psychophysiological methods
Methods that measure the relation between physiological processes and behavior. Among the most common are measures of autonomic nervous system activity (such as heart rate and respiration) and brain functioning (such as the EEG and fMRI).

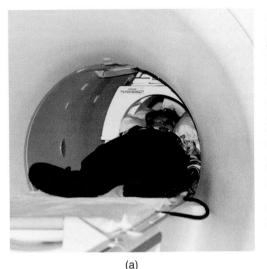

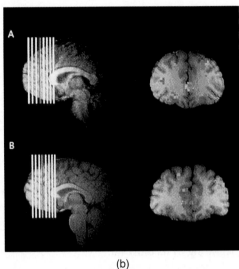

(a)   (b)

In functional magnetic resonance imaging (fMRI), the child looks up at a stimulus, and changes in blood flow within brain tissue are detected magnetically (a). The result is a computerized image of activated areas (b), permitting study of age-related changes in brain organization and the brain functioning of children with serious learning and emotional problems. *(B.J. Casey/UPMC)*

Functional brain-imaging techniques, which yield three-dimensional pictures of brain activity, provide the most precise information on which brain regions are specialized for certain functions, such as language or emotion. *Functional magnetic resonance imaging (fMRI)* is the most promising of these methods, since it does not depend on X-ray photography. Instead, when a child is shown a stimulus, changes in blood flow within the brain are detected magnetically, producing a computerized image of active areas. Currently, fMRI is being used to study age-related changes in brain organization and the brain functioning of children with serious learning and emotional problems (Schifter et al., 1994; Schultz et al., 1994).

Despite their virtues, psychophysiological methods have limitations. First, interpreting the results involves a high degree of inference. Even though a stimulus produces a consistent pattern of autonomic or brain activity, researchers cannot be sure that an infant or child has processed it in a certain way. Second, many factors besides those of interest can influence a physiological response, such as hunger, boredom, fatigue, or fear of the laboratory equipment and situation (Tyc et al., 1995).

■ **THE CLINICAL METHOD.** Earlier in this chapter, we discussed the **clinical method** (sometimes called the *case study approach*) as an outgrowth of psychoanalytic theory, which stressed the importance of understanding the individual. Recall that the clinical method brings together a wide range of information on a single child, including interviews, observations, and test scores. Today, psychophysiological measures are sometimes included as well (Haynes, 1991). The aim is to obtain as complete a picture as possible of a child's psychological functioning and the experiences that led up to it.

Although clinical studies are usually carried out on children with developmental problems, they sometimes focus on well-adjusted youngsters. In one recent investigation, the researchers wanted to find out what contributes to the accomplishments of children with extraordinary intellectual talents (Feldman, 1991). Among the six prodigies studied intensively was Adam, a boy who read, wrote, and composed musical pieces before he was out of diapers. Adam's parents provided a home rich in stimulation and raised him with affection, firmness, and humor. They searched for schools in which he could develop his abilities while forming rewarding social relationships. By age 4, Adam was intensively involved in mastering human symbol systems—BASIC for the computer, French, German, Russian, Sanskrit, Greek, ancient hieroglyphs, music, and mathematics.

Would Adam have realized his abilities without the chance combination of his special gift with nurturing, committed parents? Probably not, the investigators concluded.

clinical method
A method in which the researcher attempts to understand the unique individual child by combining interview data, observations, test scores, and sometimes psychophysiological measures.

ethnography
A method in which the researcher attempts to understand the unique values and social processes of a culture or a distinct social group by living with its members and taking field notes for an extended period of time.

Adam's case illustrates the unique strengths of the clinical method. It yields case narratives that are rich in descriptive detail and that offer valuable insights into development.

The clinical method is subject to the same problems as the clinical interview. Also, more than other methods, the theoretical preferences of the researcher can bias the interpretations of clinical data. Finally, investigators cannot assume that their conclusions apply to anyone other than the specific child studied. The insights drawn from clinical investigations need to be tested further with other research methods.

■ **ETHNOGRAPHY.** Because of a growing interest in the impact of culture, child development researchers have begun to rely increasingly on a method used often by anthropologists—**ethnography.** Like the clinical method, ethnographic research is a descriptive, qualitative technique. But instead of aiming to understand a single individual, it is directed toward understanding a culture or a distinct social group (Winthrop, 1991).

The ethnographic method achieves its goals through *participant observation.* Typically, the researcher lives within the cultural community for a period of months or years, participating in its daily life. Extensive field notes, which consist of a mix of observations, self-reports from members of the culture, and interpretations by the investigator are gathered. Later, these notes are put together into a description of the community that tries to capture its unique values and social processes.

Ethnographies of children from diverse cultures currently exist, and many more are being compiled. In some, investigators focus on many aspects of children's experience, as one researcher did in describing what it is like to grow up in a small American town (Peshkin, 1978). In other instances, the study is limited to one or a few settings, such as home or school life (Chang, 1992; LeVine et al., 1994). Because the ethnographic method is committed to trying to understand others' perspectives, it often overturns widely held stereotypes, as the Cultural Influences box on page 38 reveals.

Ethnographers try to minimize their influence on the culture being studied by becoming part of it. Nevertheless, at times their presence does alter the situation. In addition, as with clinical research, investigators' cultural values and theoretical commitments sometimes lead them to observe selectively or misinterpret what they see. Finally, the findings of ethnographic studies cannot be assumed to apply to people and settings other than those in which the research was originally conducted (Hammersley, 1992).

BRIEF REVIEW

Researchers use naturalistic observation to gather information on children's everyday behaviors. When it is necessary to control the conditions of observation, researchers often make structured observations in a laboratory. The flexible, conversational style of the clinical interview provides a wealth of information on the reasoning behind behavior. However, participants may not report their thoughts accurately, and comparing their responses is difficult. The structured interview is a more efficient method that questions each person in the same way, but it does not yield the same depth of information as a clinical interview. Psychophysiological methods are used to uncover the biological bases of children's behavior. However, they require a high degree of inference about the meaning of physiological responses. Clinical studies of individual children provide rich insights into the processes of development, but the information obtained is often unsystematic and subjective. In ethnographic research, an investigator tries to understand a distinct social group through participant observation. Like clinical studies, ethnographies can be affected by researchers' theoretical biases, and the findings may not generalize beyond the people studied.

ASK YOURSELF . . .

■ *Why is it important for students of child development and individuals who work directly with children to understand research strategies?*

■ *A researcher wants to study the thoughts and feelings of children who have experienced their parents' divorce. Which method is best suited for investigating this question?*

■ *What limitations do the clinical method and ethnography have in common?*

CULTURAL INFLUENCES

SCHOOL MATTERS IN MEXICAN-AMERICAN HOMES: AN ETHNOGRAPHIC STUDY

For many years, the poor school achievement of low-income minority children was attributed to "cultural deficits"—home environments that place little value on education. A recent ethnographic study of Mexican-American families challenges this assumption. Concha Delgado-Gaitan (1992, 1994) spent many months getting to know the residents of a Mexican-American community located in a small California city. There she collected extensive field notes on six families, each with a second-grade child. While in their homes, she carefully examined children's experiences related to education.

■ **HOME ENVIRONMENTS.** Although the Mexican-American parents had little schooling themselves, they regarded education as a great privilege and supported their children's learning in many ways. Their homes were cramped, one-bedroom apartments, occasionally shared with relatives. Still, parents did their best to create a stable environment that encouraged children to think positively about school. They offered material rewards for good grades (such as a new book or dinner at a favorite restaurant), set regular bedtime hours, and, where possible, provided a special place for doing schoolwork. And they frequently spoke to their children about their own educational limitations and the importance of taking advantage of the opportunity to study.

■ **SOCIAL SUPPORT.** During the week, many parent–child conversations revolved around homework. All parents did their best to help with assignments and foster behaviors valued in school. But how well they succeeded depended on social networks through which they could obtain information about educational matters. Some parents relied on relatives who had more experience dealing with the school system. Others sought out individuals at church or at work as advisers.

When social support was available, perplexing school problems were quickly resolved. For example, one parent, Mrs. Matias, received repeated reports from her son Jorge's teacher about his unruly behavior. Finally, a note arrived threatening suspension if Jorge did not improve. Mrs. Matias consulted one of her co-workers, who suggested that she ask for permission to leave during the lunch hour to talk with Jorge's teacher. After a conference revealed that Jorge needed to stay away from certain boys who were provoking him, his fighting subsided.

■ **LINKS BETWEEN HOME AND SCHOOL.** Despite sincere efforts, lack of familiarity with school tasks often hampered Mexican-American parents' ability to help their children. Mrs. Serna insisted that her poorly achieving daughter Norma do her homework at regularly scheduled times, and she checked to make sure that Norma completed her assignments. But when she tried to assist Norma, Mrs. Serna frequently misinterpreted the instructions. And she did not understand the school environment well enough to contact teachers for information about how to support her child. As a result, Norma's progress remained below average.

Discontinuity between Mexican cultural values and the requirements of the school was often at the heart of children's academic difficulties. At home, respect for elders was emphasized. Mexican-American children learned not to express verbal opinions (especially contrary opinions) to adults. Instead, they listened and followed directions. Yet in their classrooms, they were expected to ask questions and engage in verbal argument—behaviors in conflict with their parents' teachings.

Although the Mexican-American families had limited income and material resources, these deficits did not detract from their desire to create a home environment conducive to learning. As they became aware of cultural differences between home and school, the parents formed a community organization through which they could share knowledge about how to help their children succeed in the classroom. For example, parents began to accept their children's questions as necessary for academic progress. Gradually, the organization became a source of empowerment, opening lines of communication with teachers.

Delgado-Gaitan's ethnographic research shows that education of ethnic minority children can be promoted through informal social ties and community organizing. In this Mexican-American community, parents joined together as catalysts for cultural change, establishing vital links between home and school.

This Mexican-American mother tries to support her children's academic development by helping with homework and providing a quiet place for study. Ethnographic research reveals that how well she will succeed depends on access to information and resources from the school. *(Laura Dwight/PhotoEdit)*

GENERAL RESEARCH DESIGNS

In deciding on a research design, investigators choose a way of setting up a study that permits them to test their hypotheses with the greatest certainty possible. Two main designs are used in all research on human behavior: correlational and experimental.

■ **CORRELATIONAL DESIGN.** In a **correlational design,** researchers gather information on already existing groups of individuals without altering their experiences in any way. Suppose we want to answer such questions as, Does attending a day care center promote children's friendliness with peers? Do mothers' styles of interacting with children have any bearing on children's intelligence? How do child abuse and neglect affect children's feelings about themselves and relationships with peers? In these and many other instances, it is either very difficult or ethically impossible to arrange and control the conditions of interest.

The correlational design offers a way of looking at relationships between children's experiences or characteristics and their behavior or development. But correlational studies have one major limitation: We cannot infer cause and effect. For example, if we find in a correlational study that mothers' interaction does relate to children's intelligence, we would not know whether maternal behavior actually causes intellectual differences among children. In fact, the opposite is certainly possible. The behaviors of highly intelligent children may be so attractive that they cause parents to interact more favorably. Or a third variable that we did not even consider, such as amount of noise and distraction in the home, may be causing both maternal interaction and children's intelligence to change together in the same direction.

In correlational studies, and in other types of research designs, investigators often examine relationships by using a **correlation coefficient,** a number that describes how two measures, or variables, are associated with one another. We will encounter the correlation coefficient in discussing research findings throughout this book. So let's look at what it is and how it is interpreted. A correlation coefficient can range in value from +1.00 to −1.00. The *magnitude, or size, of the number* shows the *strength of the relationship.* A zero correlation indicates no relationship, but the closer the value is to +1.00 or −1.00, the stronger the relationship that exists. *The sign of the number* (+ or −) refers to the *direction of the relationship.* A positive sign (+) means that as one variable *increases,* the other also *increases.* A negative sign (−) indicates that as one variable *increases,* the other *decreases.*

Let's take some examples to illustrate how a correlation coefficient works. In one study, a researcher found that a measure of maternal language stimulation at 13 months was positively correlated with the size of children's vocabularies at 20 months, at +.50 (Tamis-LeMonda & Bornstein, 1994). This is a moderately high correlation, which indicates that the more mothers spoke to their infants, the more advanced their children were in spoken language during the second year of life. In another study, a researcher reported that the extent to which mothers ignored their 10-month-olds' bids for attention was negatively correlated with children's willingness to comply with parental demands 1 year later—at −.46 for boys and −.36 for girls (Martin, 1981). These moderate correlations reveal that the more mothers ignored their babies, the less cooperative their children were during the second year of life.

Both of these investigations found a relationship between maternal behavior in the first year and children's behavior in the second year. Although the researchers suspected that maternal behavior affected children's responses, in neither study could they really be sure about cause and effect. However, finding a relationship in a correlational study suggests that tracking down its cause—with a more powerful experimental research strategy, if possible—would be worthwhile.

■ **EXPERIMENTAL DESIGN.** Unlike correlational studies, an **experimental design** permits inferences about cause and effect. In an experiment, the events and behaviors of

correlational design
A research design in which the researcher gathers information without altering participants' experiences and examines relationships between variables. Does not permit inferences about cause and effect.

correlation coefficient
A number, ranging from +1.00 to −1.00, that describes the strength and direction of the relationship between two variables.

experimental design
A research design in which the investigator randomly assigns participants to treatment conditions. Permits inferences about cause and effect.

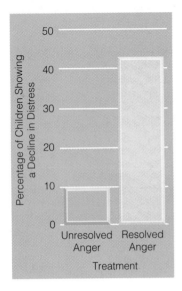

FIGURE 1.5

Does the way adults end their angry encounters affect children's emotional reactions? A laboratory experiment showed that when adults resolve their disputes by apologizing and compromising, children are more likely to decline in distress than when adults leave their arguments unresolved. Notice in this graph that only 10 percent of children in the unresolved-anger treatment declined in distress (see bar on the left), whereas 42 percent of children in the resolved-anger treatment did so (see bar on the right). *(Adapted from El-Sheikh, Cummings, & Reiter, 1996.)*

independent variable
The variable manipulated by the researcher in an experiment.

dependent variable
The variable the researcher expects to be influenced by the independent variable in an experiment.

interest are divided into two types: independent and dependent variables. The **independent variable** is the one anticipated by the investigator to cause changes in another variable. The **dependent variable** is the one the investigator expects to be influenced by the independent variable. Inferences about cause-and-effect relationships are possible because the researcher directly *controls* or *manipulates* changes in the independent variable. This is done by exposing participants to two or more treatment conditions and comparing their performance on measures of the dependent variable.

In one *laboratory experiment,* researchers explored the impact of adults' angry interactions on children's adjustment (El-Sheikh, Cummings, & Reiter, 1996). They hypothesized that the way angry encounters end (independent variable) affects children's emotional reactions (dependent variable). Four- and 5-year-olds were brought one at a time to a laboratory, accompanied by their mothers. One group was exposed to an *unresolved-anger treatment,* in which two adult actors entered the room and argued but did not work out their disagreements. The other group received a *resolved-anger treatment,* in which the adults ended their disputes by apologizing and compromising. As Figure 1.5 shows, during a follow-up adult conflict, more children in the resolved-anger treatment showed a decline in distress, such as anxious facial expressions, freezing in place, and seeking closeness to their mothers. The experiment revealed that anger resolution can reduce the stressful impact of adult conflict on children.

In experimental studies, investigators must take special precautions to control for unknown characteristics of participants that could reduce the accuracy of their findings. For example, in the study just described, if a greater number of children from homes high in parental conflict happened to end up in the unresolved-anger treatment, we could not tell whether the independent variable or children's background characteristics produced the results. *Random assignment* of participants to treatment conditions offers protection against this problem. By using an evenhanded procedure, such as drawing numbers out of a hat or flipping a coin, the experimenter increases the chances that children's characteristics will be equally distributed across treatment groups.

Sometimes researchers combine random assignment with another technique called *matching.* In this procedure, participants are measured before the experiment on the factor in question—in our example, parental conflict. Then children from homes high and low in parental conflict are assigned in equal numbers to each treatment condition. In this way, the experimental groups are deliberately matched, or made equivalent, on characteristics that are likely to distort the results.

■ **MODIFIED EXPERIMENTAL DESIGNS: FIELD AND NATURAL EXPERIMENTS.** Most experiments are conducted in laboratories, where researchers can achieve the maximum possible control over treatment conditions. But, as we have already indicated, findings obtained in laboratories may not apply to everyday situations. The ideal solution to this problem is to do experiments in the field as a complement to laboratory investigations. In *field experiments,* investigators capitalize on rare opportunities to randomly assign people to different treatments in natural settings. In the experiment we just considered, we can conclude that the emotional climate established by adults affects children's behavior in the laboratory. But does it also do so in daily life?

Another study helps answer this question. This time, the research was carried out in a day care center. A caregiver deliberately interacted differently with two groups of preschoolers. In one condition (the *nurturant treatment),* she modeled many instances of warmth and helpfulness. In the second condition (the *control,* since it involved no treatment), she behaved as usual, with no special emphasis on concern for others. Two weeks later, the researchers created several situations that called for helpfulness. For example, a visiting mother asked each child to watch her baby for a few moments, but the baby's toys had fallen out of the playpen. The investigators recorded whether or not each child returned the toys to the baby. Children exposed to the nurturant treatment behaved in a much more helpful way than those in the control condition (Yarrow, Scott, & Waxler, 1973).

TABLE 1.7

Strengths and Limitations of Research Designs

DESIGN	DESCRIPTION	STRENGTHS	LIMITATIONS
General			
Correlational	The investigator obtains information on already existing groups, without altering participants' experiences.	Permits study of relationships between variables.	Does not permit inferences about cause-and-effect relationships.
Experimental	The investigator manipulates an independent variable and looks at its effect on a dependent variable; can be conducted in the laboratory or natural environment.	Permits inferences about cause-and-effect relationships.	When conducted in the laboratory, findings may not apply to the real world; when conducted in the field, control over treatment is usually weaker than in the laboratory.
Developmental			
Longitudinal	The investigator studies the same group of participants repeatedly at different ages.	Permits study of common patterns and individual differences in development and relationships between early and later events and behaviors.	Age-related changes may be distorted because of dropout and test-wiseness of participants and cohort effects.
Cross-sectional	The investigator studies groups of participants differing in age at the same point in time.	More efficient than the longitudinal design.	Does not permit study of individual developmental trends. Age differences may be distorted because of cohort effects.
Longitudinal-sequential	The investigator studies two or more groups of participants born in different years repeatedly at different ages.	Permits both longitudinal and cross-sectional comparisons; reveals existence of cohort effects.	May have the same problems as longitudinal and cross-sectional strategies, but the design itself helps identify difficulties.
Microgenetic	The investigator tracks change from the time it begins until it stabilizes, as participants master an everyday or novel task.	Offers unique insights into the process of development.	Requires intensive study of participants' moment-by-moment behaviors; the time required for participants to change is difficult to anticipate; practice effects may distort developmental trends.

Often researchers cannot randomly assign participants and manipulate conditions in the real world, as these investigators were able to do. Sometimes researchers can compromise by conducting *natural experiments.* Treatments that already exist, such as different school environments, day care centers, and preschool programs, are compared. These studies differ from correlational research only in that groups of participants are carefully chosen to ensure that their characteristics are as much alike as possible. In this way, investigators rule out as best as they can alternative explanations for their treatment effects. But despite these efforts, natural experiments are unable to achieve the precision and rigor of true experimental research.

To help you compare the correlational and experimental designs we have discussed, Table 1.7 summarizes their strengths and limitations. It also includes an overview of designs for studying development, to which we now turn.

DESIGNS FOR STUDYING DEVELOPMENT

Scientists interested in child development require information about the way research participants change over time. To answer questions about development, they must extend correlational and experimental approaches to include measurements at different ages. Longitudinal and cross-sectional designs are special *developmental* research strategies. In each, age comparisons form the basis of the research plan.

■ **THE LONGITUDINAL DESIGN.** In a **longitudinal design,** a group of participants is studied repeatedly at different ages, and changes are noted as the participants mature. The time spanned may be relatively short (a few months to several years) or very long (a decade or even a lifetime).

The longitudinal approach has two major strengths. First, since it tracks the performance of each person over time, researchers can identify common patterns of development as well as individual differences in the paths children follow to maturity. Second, longitudinal studies permit investigators to examine relationships between early and later events and behaviors. Let's take an example to illustrate these ideas.

A group of researchers wondered whether children who display extreme personality styles—either angry and explosive or shy and withdrawn—retain the same dispositions when they become adults. In addition, they wanted to know what kinds of experiences promote stability or change in personality and what consequences explosiveness and shyness have for long-term adjustment. To answer these questions, the researchers delved into the archives of the Guidance Study, a well-known longitudinal investigation initiated in 1928 at the University of California, Berkeley, and continued over several decades (Caspi, Elder, & Bem, 1987, 1988).

Results revealed that the two personality styles were only moderately stable. Between ages 8 and 30, a good number of individuals remained the same, whereas others changed substantially. When stability did occur, it appeared to be due to a "snowballing effect," in which children evoked responses from adults and peers that acted to maintain their dispositions. In other words, explosive youngsters were likely to be treated with anger and hostility (to which they reacted with even greater unruliness), whereas shy children were apt to be ignored.

Persistence of extreme personality styles affected many areas of adult adjustment, but these outcomes were different for males and females. For men, the results of early explosiveness were most apparent in their work lives, in the form of conflicts with supervisors, frequent job changes, and unemployment. Since few women in this sample of an earlier generation worked after marriage, their family lives were most affected. Explosive girls grew up to be hotheaded wives and parents who were especially prone to divorce. Sex differences in the long-term consequences of shyness were even greater. Men who had been withdrawn in childhood were delayed in marrying, becoming fathers, and developing stable careers. Because a withdrawn, unassertive style was socially acceptable for females, women who had shy personalities showed no special adjustment problems.

■ **PROBLEMS IN CONDUCTING LONGITUDINAL RESEARCH.** Despite their many strengths, longitudinal investigations pose a number of problems. For example, participants may move away or drop out of the research for other reasons. This changes the original sample so it no longer represents the population to whom researchers would like to generalize their findings. Also, from repeated study, people may become "test-wise." Their performance may improve as a result of *practice effects*—better test-taking skills— not because of factors commonly associated with development.

The most widely discussed threat to the accuracy of longitudinal findings is cultural-historical change, or what are commonly called **cohort effects.** Longitudinal studies

longitudinal design
A research design in which one group of participants is studied repeatedly at different ages.

cohort effects
The effects of cultural-historical change on the accuracy of findings: Children born in one period of time are influenced by a particular set of cultural and historical conditions.

examine the development of *cohorts*—children born in the same time period who are influenced by a particular set of cultural and historical conditions. Results based on one cohort may not apply to children growing up at other times. For example, children's intelligence test performance has risen since the middle of the twentieth century and is still rising (Flynn, 1996; Neisser et al., 1996). Gains in nutrition, the stimulating quality of schooling and daily life, and parental attitudes toward fostering children's mental development may be involved. And in the study of personality styles described in the preceding section, we might ask whether the sex differences obtained are still true, in view of recent changes in gender roles in our society.

■ **THE CROSS-SECTIONAL DESIGN.** The length of time it takes for many behaviors to change, even in limited longitudinal studies, has led researchers to turn to a more convenient strategy for studying development. In the **cross-sectional design,** groups of people differing in age are studied at the same point in time.

A recent investigation provides a good illustration (Buhrmester & Furman, 1990). Children in grades 3, 6, 9, and 12 filled out a questionnaire asking about their sibling relationships. Findings revealed that sibling interaction was characterized by greater equality and less power assertion with age. Also, feelings of sibling companionship declined during adolescence. The researchers thought that these age changes were due to several factors. As later-born children become more competent and independent, they no longer need and are probably less willing to accept direction from older siblings. In addition, as adolescents move from psychological dependence on the family to greater involvement with peers, they may have less time and emotional need to invest in siblings These intriguing ideas about the impact of development on sibling relationships, as we will see in Chapter 16, have been confirmed in subsequent research.

■ **PROBLEMS IN CONDUCTING CROSS-SECTIONAL RESEARCH.** The cross-sectional design is a very efficient strategy for describing age-related trends. But when researchers choose it, they are shortchanged in the kind of information they can obtain about development. Evidence about change at the level at which it actually occurs—the individual—is not available. For example, in the study of sibling relationships that we just discussed, comparisons are limited to age-group averages. We cannot tell if important individual differences exist in the development of sibling relationships, some becoming more supportive and intimate and others becoming increasingly distant with age.

Cross-sectional studies that cover a wide age span have another problem. Like longitudinal research, they can be threatened by cohort effects. For example, comparisons of 5-year-old cohorts and 15-year-old cohorts—groups of children born and reared in different years—may not really represent age-related changes. Instead, they may reflect unique experiences associated with the different time periods in which the age groups were growing up.

■ **IMPROVING DEVELOPMENTAL DESIGNS.** Researchers have devised ways of building on the strengths and minimizing the weaknesses of longitudinal and cross-sectional approaches. Several modified developmental designs have resulted.

Combining Longitudinal and Cross-Sectional Designs.   Researchers merge longitudinal and cross-sectional strategies in the **longitudinal-sequential design.** It is called *sequential* because it is composed of two or more different age groups of participants, each of which is followed longitudinally for a number of years.

The design has three advantages: (1) It permits researchers to find out whether cohort effects are operating by comparing children of the same age who were born in different years. Using the example shown in Figure 1.6, we can compare the behaviors of the two samples at ages 6 and 9. If they do not differ, then we can rule out cohort effects. (2) It is possible to do both longitudinal and cross-sectional comparisons. If outcomes are similar

cross-sectional design
A research design in which groups of participants of different ages are studied at the same point in time.

longitudinal-sequential design
A research design with both longitudinal and cross-sectional components in which groups of participants born in different years are followed over time.

FIGURE 1.6

Example of a longitudinal-sequential design. Two samples of children, one born in 1982 and the other in 1985, are observed longitudinally from 3 to 12 years of age. The design permits the researcher to check for cohort effects by comparing children of the same age who were born in different years. Also, both longitudinal and cross-sectional comparisons can be made.

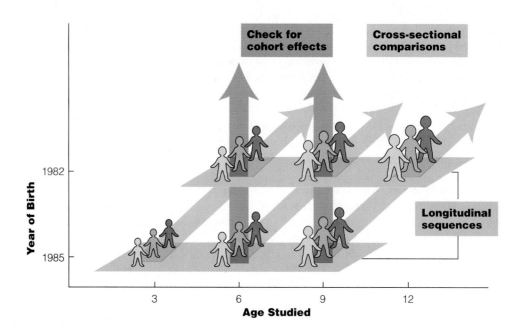

in both, then we can be especially confident about our findings. (3) The design is efficient. In the example shown in Figure 1.6, the researcher can find out about change over a 9-year period by following each cohort for just 6 years. Although the longitudinal-sequential design is used only occasionally, it provides researchers with a convenient way to profit from the strengths of both longitudinal and cross-sectional approaches.

What strategies does this child use to solve puzzles, and how does she become proficient at puzzle solving? Since a microgenetic design permits researchers to follow children's mastery of a challenging task, from the time change begins until it stabilizes, it is uniquely suited to answering these questions. *(Alex Bartel/The Picture Cube, Inc.)*

Studying Microcosms of Development. Notice how, in the examples of developmental research we have discussed, observations of children are fairly widely spaced. When we observe at ages 5, 10, and 15, we can describe development, but we have little opportunity to capture the processes that produce change. A recent modification of the longitudinal approach, called the **microgenetic design,** is becoming more popular because it offers unique insights into how development takes place. In microgenetic studies, researchers present children with a novel task and follow their mastery over a series of closely spaced sessions (Kuhn, 1995; Siegler & Crowley, 1991, 1992). Within this "microcosm" of development, they see how change occurs.

The microgenetic design is especially useful for studying cognitive development. For example, it has permitted researchers to examine the strategies children use to acquire new knowledge in reading, mathematics, and science (Kuhn et al., 1995; Siegler, 1996). As we will see in Chapter 5, it has also been used to trace infants' mastery of motor skills.

Nevertheless, microgenetic studies are very difficult to carry out. Researchers must pore over hours of videotaped records, analyzing each participant's behavior many times. In addition, the time required for children to change is hard to anticipate. It depends on a careful match between the child's capabilities and the demands of the task (Siegler & Crowley, 1991). Finally, as in other longitudinal research, practice effects can distort the findings of microgenetic studies. But when researchers overcome these challenges, they reap the benefits of seeing development as it takes place.

BRIEF REVIEW

A variety of research designs are commonly used to study children. In correlational research, information is gathered on existing groups of individuals. Investigators can examine relationships between variables, but they cannot infer cause and effect. Because experimental design involves random assignment of participants to treatment groups, researchers can find out if an independent variable causes change in a dependent variable. Field and natural experiments permit generalization to everyday life, but they sacrifice rigorous experimental control.

Longitudinal and cross-sectional designs are uniquely suited for studying development. Longitudinal research provides information on common patterns as well as individual differences in development and the relationship between early and later events and behaviors. The cross-sectional approach is more efficient, but comparisons are limited to age-group averages. The longitudinal-sequential approach permits researchers to reap the benefits of both longitudinal and cross-sectional strategies. A special longitudinal approach, the microgenetic design, offers unique insights into processes of development.

ETHICS IN RESEARCH ON CHILDREN

Research into human behavior creates ethical issues because, unfortunately, the quest for scientific knowledge can sometimes exploit people. When children take part in research, the ethical concerns are especially complex. Children are more vulnerable than adults to physical and psychological harm. In addition, immaturity makes it difficult or impossible for children to evaluate for themselves what participation in research will mean. For these reasons, special ethical guidelines for research on children have been developed by the federal government, by funding agencies, and by research-oriented associations such as the American Psychological Association (1992) and the Society for Research in Child Development (1993).

Table 1.8 presents a summary of children's basic research rights drawn from these guidelines. Once you have examined them, read the following research situations, each of which poses a serious ethical dilemma. What precautions do you think should be taken in each instance? Is either so threatening to children's well-being that it should not be carried out?

- To study the development of children's willingness to separate from their caregivers, an investigator decides to ask mothers of 1- and 2-year-olds to leave their youngsters alone for a brief time period in an unfamiliar playroom. The researcher knows that under these circumstances, some children become very upset.

- In a study of moral development, an investigator wants to assess children's ability to resist temptation by videotaping their behavior without their knowledge. Seven-year-olds are promised an attractive prize for solving some very difficult puzzles. They are also told not to look at a classmate's correct solutions, which are deliberately placed at the back of the room. If the researcher has to tell children ahead of time that cheating is being studied or that their behavior is being closely monitored, she will destroy the purpose of her study.

Did you find it difficult to decide on the best course of action in these examples? Virtually every committee that has worked on developing ethical principles for research has concluded that the conflicts raised by studies like these cannot be resolved with simple right-or-wrong answers. The ultimate responsibility for the ethical integrity of research lies with the investigator.

ASK YOURSELF . . .

- A researcher compares children who went to summer leadership camps with children who attended athletic camps. She finds that those who attended leadership camps are friendlier. Should the investigator tell parents that sending children to leadership camps will cause them to be more sociable? Why or why not?

- A researcher wants to find out if children who go to day care centers during the first few years of life do as well in school as those who are not in day care. Which developmental design, longitudinal or cross-sectional, is appropriate for answering this question? Explain why.

microgenetic design
A research design in which change is tracked from the time it begins until it stabilizes, as participants master a novel task.

TABLE 1.8

Children's Research Rights

RESEARCH RIGHT	DESCRIPTION
Protection from harm	Children have the right to be protected from physical or psychological harm in research. If in doubt about the harmful effects of research, investigators should seek the opinion of others. When harm seems possible, investigators should find other means for obtaining the desired information or abandon the research.
Informed consent	All research participants, including children, have the right to have explained to them, in language appropriate to their level of understanding, all aspects of the research that may affect their willingness to participate. When children are participants, informed consent of parents as well as others who act on the child's behalf (such as school officials) should be obtained, preferably in writing. Children, and the adults responsible for them, have the right to discontinue participation in the research at any time.
Privacy	Children have the right to concealment of their identity on all information collected in the course of research. They also have this right with respect to written reports and any informal discussions about the research.
Knowledge of results	Children have the right to be informed of the results of research in language that is appropriate to their level of understanding.
Beneficial treatments	If experimental treatments believed to be beneficial are under investigation, children in control groups have the right to alternative beneficial treatments if they are available.

Sources: American Psychological Association, 1992; Society for Research in Child Development, 1993.

However, researchers are advised or, in the case of federally funded research, required to seek advice from others. Special committees exist in colleges, universities, and other institutions for this purpose. These committees weigh the costs of the research to the participant in terms of time, stress, and inconvenience against its value for advancing knowledge and improving children's conditions of life. If there are any negative implications for the safety and welfare of participants that the worth of the research does not justify, then preference is always given to the interests of the research participant.

The ethical principle of *informed consent* requires special interpretation when the research participants are children. The competence of youngsters of different ages to make choices about their own participation must be taken into account. Parental consent is meant to protect the safety of children whose ability to make these decisions is not yet fully mature. Besides parental consent, researchers should obtain the agreement of other individuals who act on children's behalf, such as institutional officials when research is conducted in schools, day care centers, or hospitals. This is especially important when research includes special groups of children, such as abused youngsters, whose parents may not always represent their best interests (Fisher, 1993; Thompson, 1990b).

For children 7 years and older, their own informed consent should be obtained in addition to parental consent. Around age 7, changes in children's thinking permit them to better understand basic scientific principles and the needs of others. Researchers should respect and enhance these new capacities by providing school-age children with a full explanation of research activities in language they can understand (Fisher, 1993). Extra care must be taken when telling children that the information they provide will be kept confidential and that they can end their participation at any time. Children may not understand, and sometimes do not believe, these promises (Abramovitch et al., 1991, 1995).

Finally, young children rely on a basic faith in adults to feel secure in unfamiliar situations. For this reason, it is possible for some types of research to be particularly disturbing to them. All ethical guidelines advise that special precautions be taken in the use of deception and concealment, as occurs when researchers observe children from behind one-way mirrors, give them false feedback about their performance, or do not tell them the truth regarding what the research is about. When these kinds of procedures are used with adults, *debriefing*, in which the experimenter provides a full account and justification of the activities, occurs after the research session is over. Debriefing should also take place with children, but it does not always work as well. Despite explanations, children may come away from the research situation with their belief in the honesty of adults undermined. Ethical standards permit deception in research with children if investigators satisfy institutional committees that such practices are necessary. Nevertheless, since deception may have serious emotional consequences for some youngsters, many child development specialists believe that its use is always unethical and that researchers should come up with other research procedures when children are involved (Cooke, 1982).

THE CHRONOLOGICAL APPROACH OF THIS BOOK

With the completion of this overview of history, theory, and research, we are ready to chart the course of child development itself. In the following chapters, the story of childhood and adolescence unfolds in chronological sequence. We begin with a chapter on biological and environmental foundations—the basics of human heredity and how it combines with environmental influences to shape children's characteristics and skills. Then we turn to particular time spans of development:

- Prenatal development and birth

- Infancy and toddlerhood—the first 2 years

- Early childhood—2 to 6 years

- Middle childhood—6 to 11 years

- Adolescence—11 to 20 years

Within each age period, a separate chapter is devoted to the following aspects of development:

- *Physical development*—changes in body size and proportions, brain development, perceptual and motor capacities, and physical health

- *Cognitive development*—development of a wide variety of intellectual abilities, including attention, memory, academic and everyday knowledge, problem solving, imagination, creativity, and the uniquely human capacity to represent the world through language

- *Emotional and social development*—development of emotional communication and understanding, knowledge of the self and other people, social skills, and moral reasoning and behavior

You are already aware from reading this chapter that these aspects of development are not really distinct; they overlap and interact a great deal. As our discussion proceeds, we will continually point out relationships between all aspects of development.

Finally, it is my hope that the content, organization, and instructional features of this book will help meet the needs and interests of you, its readers. Perhaps you aspire to a career in applied work with children, want to teach child development or advance its knowledge base, plan someday to raise children, are already a parent, or are simply curious about how you yourself developed from a tiny infant into the complex adult you are today. Whichever goals happen to be yours, as you embark on the study of children, I wish you a stimulating and rewarding journey.

ASK YOURSELF . . .

- *An investigator decides to conduct a study of teacher–pupil interaction in a fourth-grade classroom. From whom should she seek informed consent for research participation?*

- *An investigator wants to assess the effectiveness of an intervention designed to promote independence and assertiveness in 10-year-olds. After the study is under way, several parents complain that in their ethnic group, it is not appropriate for children to behave in these ways. How should the researcher respond? What could he have done to avoid this problem?*

Summary

THE FIELD OF CHILD DEVELOPMENT

What is child development, and what factors stimulated expansion of the field?

- **Child development** is the study of human growth and change from conception through adolescence. It is part of a larger field known as developmental psychology, or human development, which includes all changes that take place throughout the lifespan. Research on child development has been stimulated by both scientific curiosity and social pressures to better the lives of children.

BASIC ISSUES

Identify three basic issues on which child development theories take a stand.

- Child development **theories** can be organized according to the stand they take on three controversial issues: (1) Is the child an **organismic** or **mechanistic** being? (2) Is development a **continuous** process, or does it follow a series of **discontinuous stages?** (3) Is development primarily determined by **nature** or **nurture?**

HISTORICAL FOUNDATIONS

Describe major historical influences on modern theories of child development.

- Modern theories of child development have roots extending far back into the past. In medieval times, children were thought of as miniature adults, a view called **preformationism.** By the sixteenth and seventeenth centuries, childhood became a distinct phase of the life cycle. However, the Puritan conception of original sin led to a harsh philosophy of child rearing.

- The Enlightenment brought new ideas favoring more humane child treatment. Locke's notion of the **tabula rasa** provided the basis for twentieth-century behaviorism, and Rousseau's idea of the **noble sav-**

age foreshadowed the concepts of stage and **maturation.** A century later, Darwin's theory of evolution stimulated scientific child study.

- Efforts to observe the child directly began in the late nineteenth and early twentieth centuries with the baby biographies. Soon after, Hall and Gesell introduced the **normative approach,** which produced a large body of descriptive facts about children. Binet and Simon constructed the first successful intelligence test, which initiated the mental testing movement.

MID-TWENTIETH-CENTURY THEORIES

What theories influenced child development research in the mid-twentieth century?

- In the 1930s and 1940s, child guidance professionals turned to the **psychoanalytic perspective** for help in understanding children with emotional problems. In Freud's **psychosexual theory,** children move through five stages, during which three portions of the personality—id, ego, and superego—become integrated. Erikson's **psychosocial theory** builds on Freud's theory by emphasizing the development of culturally relevant attitudes and skills and the lifespan nature of development.

- Academic psychology also influenced child study. From **behaviorism** and **social learning theory** came the principles of conditioning and modeling and practical procedures of **applied behavior analysis** with children.

- In contrast to behaviorism, Piaget's **cognitive-developmental theory** emphasizes an active child with a mind inhabited by rich structures of knowledge. According to Piaget, children move through five stages, beginning with the baby's sensorimotor action patterns and ending with the elaborate, abstract reasoning system of the adolescent. Piaget's work has stimulated a wealth of research on children's thinking and encouraged educational programs that emphasize discovery learning.

RECENT THEORETICAL PERSPECTIVES

Describe recent theoretical perspectives on child development.

- **Information processing** views the mind as a complex, symbol-manipulating system, operating much like a computer. This approach helps investigators achieve a detailed understanding of what children of different ages do when faced with tasks and problems.

- Three modern theories place special emphasis on contexts for development. **Ethology** stresses the evolutionary origins and adaptive value of behavior and inspired the **sensitive period** concept.

- In **ecological systems theory,** nested layers of the environment—**microsystem, mesosystem, exosystem,** and **macrosystem**—are seen as major influences on children's well-being. The **chronosystem** represents the dynamic, ever-changing nature of children and their experiences.

- Vygotsky's **sociocultural theory** has enhanced our understanding of cultural influences, especially in the area of cognitive development. Through cooperative dialogues with more mature members of society, children acquire culturally relevant knowledge and skills.

- Inspired by ideas in other sciences and recent perspectives in child development, a new wave of theorists has adopted a **dynamic systems perspective.** They want to account for wide variation in development.

STUDYING THE CHILD

Describe research methods commonly used to study children.

- **Naturalistic observations,** gathered in children's everyday environments, permit researchers to see directly the everyday behaviors they hope to explain. In contrast, **structured observations** take place in laboratories, where every participant has an equal opportunity to display the behaviors of interest.

■ Self-report methods, such as the **clinical interview,** can be flexible and open-ended. Alternatively, **structured interviews** and questionnaires, which permit efficient administration and scoring, can be given.

■ **Psychophysiological methods** measure the relation between physiological processes and behavior. They help researchers uncover the biological bases of children's cognitive and emotional responses.

■ Investigators use the **clinical method** when they desire an in-depth understanding of a single child. It involves synthesizing a wide range of information, including interviews, observations, test scores, and sometimes psychophysiological measures.

■ **Ethnography** uses participant observation to capture the unique values and social processes of a culture or distinct social group.

Distinguish correlational and experimental research designs, noting the strengths and limitations of each.

■ Two main types of designs are used in all research on human behavior. The **correlational design** examines relationships between variables as they happen to occur, without any intervention. The **correlation coefficient** is often used to measure the association between variables. Correlational studies do not permit statements about cause and effect. However, their use is justified when it is difficult or impossible to control the variables of interest.

■ An **experimental design** permits inferences about cause and effect. Researchers randomly assign participants to treatment conditions and manipulate an **independent variable.** Then they determine what impact this manipulation has on a **dependent variable.** To achieve high degrees of control, most experiments are conducted in laboratories, but their findings may not apply to everyday life. Field and natural experiments are strategies used to compare treatments in natural environments.

Describe designs for studying development, noting the strengths and limitations of each.

■ Longitudinal and cross-sectional designs are uniquely suited for studying development. The **longitudinal design** permits study of common patterns as well as individual differences in development and the relationship between early and later events and behaviors. The **cross-sectional design** offers an efficient approach to investigating development. However, it is limited to comparisons of age group averages. Findings of longitudinal and cross-sectional research can be distorted by **cohort effects.**

■ Modified developmental designs overcome some of the limitations of longitudinal and cross-sectional research. By combining the two approaches in the **longitudinal-sequential design,** investigators can test for cohort effects. In the **microgenetic design,** researchers track change as it occurs for unique insights into processes of development.

What special ethical concerns arise in doing research on children?

■ Because of their immaturity, children are more vulnerable to harm and often cannot evaluate the risks and benefits of research. Ethical guidelines help ensure that children's research rights are protected. Besides parental consent and the consent of others who work on children's behalf, researchers should seek the informed consent of children 7 years and older for research participation. The use of deception in research with children is especially risky, since it may undermine their basic faith in the trustworthiness of adults.

ℐmportant terms and concepts

"My Mom, My Dad, and My Siblings

Hector Duarte Salinas
6 years, Chile

This boy's portrayal of his mother, father, and siblings suggests unusually warm, close ties. Is family resemblance in personality, interests, and abilities partly responsible? Chapter 2 will introduce you to the complex blend of genetic and environmental influences that leads parents and children to be both alike and different.

Reprinted by permission from The International Museum of Children's Art, Oslo, Norway.

BIOLOGICAL AND ENVIRONMENTAL FOUNDATIONS

*I*t's a girl," announces the doctor, who holds up the squalling little creature, while her new parents gaze with amazement at their miraculous creation. "A girl! We've named her Sarah!" exclaims the proud father to eager relatives waiting by the telephone for word about their new family member. As we join these parents in thinking about how this wondrous being came into existence and imagining her future, we are struck by many questions. How could this well-formed baby, equipped with everything necessary for life outside the womb, have developed from the union of two tiny cells? What ensures that Sarah will, in due time, roll over, reach for objects, walk, talk, make friends, imagine, and create—just like every other normal child born before her? Why is she a girl and not a boy, dark-haired rather than blond, calm and cuddly instead of wiry and energetic?

What difference will it make that Sarah is given a name and place in one family, community, nation, and culture rather than another?

To answer these questions, this chapter takes a close look at the foundations of development: heredity and environment. Because nature has prepared us for survival, all humans have many features in common. Yet a brief period of time spent in the company of any child and his or her family reveals that each human being is unique.

Take a moment to jot down the most obvious similarities in physical characteristics and behavior for several children and parents whom you know well. Did you find that one child shows combined features of both parents, another resembles just one parent, whereas still a third is not like either parent? These directly observable characteristics are called **phenotypes.** They depend in part on the individual's **genotype**—the complex blend of genetic information transmitted from one generation to the next that determines our species and influences all our unique characteristics. Throughout life, phenotypes are also affected by the person's history of experiences in the environment.

We begin our discussion of development at the moment of conception, an event that establishes the hereditary makeup of the new individual. In the first section of this chapter, we review basic genetic principles that help explain similarities and differences among us in appearance and behavior. Next, we turn to a variety of aspects of the environment that play a powerful role in children's lives.

As our discussion proceeds, you will quickly see that both nature and nurture affect all aspects of development. In fact, some findings and conclusions in this chapter may surprise you. For example, many people believe that when children inherit unfavorable characteristics, not much can be done to help them. Others are convinced that when environments are harmful, the damage done to children can easily be corrected. We will see that neither of these assumptions is true. In the final section of this chapter, we take up the question of how nature and nurture *work together* to shape the course of development.

GENETIC FOUNDATIONS

Basic principles of genetics were unknown until the mid-nineteenth century, when the Austrian monk and botanist Gregor Mendel began a series of experiments with pea plants in his monastery garden. Recording the number of times white- and purple-flowered plants had offspring with white or purple flowers, Mendel found that he could predict the characteristics of each new generation. Mendel inferred the presence of genes, factors controlling the physical traits he studied. Although peas and humans may seem completely unrelated, today we know that heredity operates in similar ways among all forms of life. Since Mendel's ground-breaking observations, our understanding of how genetic messages are coded and inherited has vastly expanded.

THE GENETIC CODE

Each of us is made up of trillions of separate units called *cells.* Inside every cell is a control center, or *nucleus.* When cells are chemically stained and viewed through a powerful microscope, rodlike structures called **chromosomes** are visible in the nucleus. Chromosomes store and transmit genetic information. Their number varies from species to species—48 for chimpanzees, 64 for horses, 40 for mice, and 46 for human beings.

Chromosomes come in pairs (an exception is the XY pair in males, which we will discuss shortly). Each member of a pair corresponds to the other in size, shape, and the traits their genes regulate. One is inherited from the mother and one from the father. Therefore, in humans, we speak of 23 *pairs* of chromosomes residing in each human cell (see Figure 2.1).

phenotype
The individual's physical and behavioral characteristics, which are determined by both genetic and environmental factors.

genotype
The genetic makeup of an individual.

chromosomes
Rodlike structures in the cell nucleus that store and transmit genetic information.

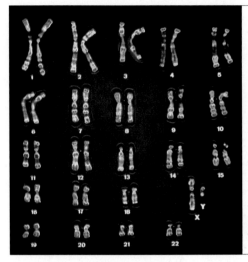
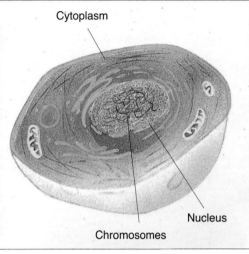

FIGURE 2.1

A karyotype, or photograph, of human chromosomes.
The 46 chromosomes shown on the left were isolated from a human cell, stained, greatly magnified, and arranged in pairs according to decreasing size of the upper "arm" of each chromosome. Note the twenty-third pair, XY, which reveals that the cell donor is a male. In females, the twenty-third pair would be XX. *(CNRI/ Science Photo Library/Photo Researchers)*

Each chromosome is made up of a chemical substance called **deoxyribonucleic acid, or DNA.** As Figure 2.2 shows, DNA is a long, double-stranded molecule that looks like a twisted ladder. Notice that each rung of the ladder consists of a specific pair of chemical substances called *bases,* joined together between the two sides. Although the bases always pair up in the same way across the ladder rungs—A with T and C with G—they can occur in any order along its sides. It is this sequence of base pairs that provides genetic instructions. A **gene** is a segment of DNA along the length of the chromosome. Genes can be of different lengths—perhaps 100 to several thousand ladder rungs long. Altogether, about 50,000 to 100,000 genes lie along the human chromosomes (Schuler et al., 1996).

Genes accomplish their task by sending instructions for making a rich assortment of proteins to the *cytoplasm,* the area surrounding the nucleus of the cell. Proteins, which trigger chemical reactions throughout the body, are the biological foundation on which our characteristics and capacities are built.

A unique feature of DNA is that it can duplicate itself. This special ability makes it possible for a single cell, formed at conception, to develop into a complex human being composed of a great many cells. This process of cell duplication is called **mitosis.** In mitosis, the DNA ladder splits down the middle, opening somewhat like a zipper (refer again to Figure 2.2). Then each base is free to pair up with a new mate from the area surrounding the nucleus of the cell. Notice how this process creates two identical DNA ladders, each containing one new side and one old side from the previous ladder. At the level of chromosomes, during mitosis each chromosome copies itself. As a result, each new body cell contains the same number of chromosomes and the identical genetic information.

THE SEX CELLS

If babies developed from the joining of two regular body cells (one from the mother and one from the father), they would have too many chromosomes to grow normally. Instead, new individuals are created when two special cells called **gametes,** or sex cells—the sperm and ovum—combine. Gametes are unique in that they contain only 23 chromosomes, half as many as a regular body cell. They are formed through a cell division process called **meiosis,** which halves the number of chromosomes normally present in body cells.

Meiosis takes place according to the steps in Figure 2.3. First, chromosomes pair up within the original cell, and each one copies itself. Then a special event called **crossing over** takes place. In crossing over, chromosomes next to each other break at one or more

deoxyribonucleic acid (DNA)
Long, double-stranded molecules that make up chromosomes.

gene
A segment of a DNA molecule that contains hereditary instructions.

mitosis
The process of cell duplication, in which each new cell receives an exact copy of the original chromosomes.

gametes
Human sperm and ova, which contain half as many chromosomes as a regular body cell.

meiosis
The process of cell division through which gametes are formed and in which the number of chromosomes in each cell is halved.

crossing over
Exchange of genes between chromosomes next to each other during meiosis.

FIGURE **2.2**

DNA's ladderlike structure.
The figure on the left shows
that the pairings of bases
across the rungs of the ladder
are very specific: adenine (A)
always appears with thymine
(T), and cytosine (C) always
appears with guanine (G).
Here, the DNA strand dupli-
cates by splitting down the
middle of its ladder rungs.
Each free base picks up a new
complementary partner from
the area surrounding the cell
nucleus. The photo on the right
shows a computer-generated
model of DNA. By simulating
and color-coding DNA's structure, scientists can rotate the
image and study it from different vantage points. *(Jean-
Claude Revy/Phototake)*

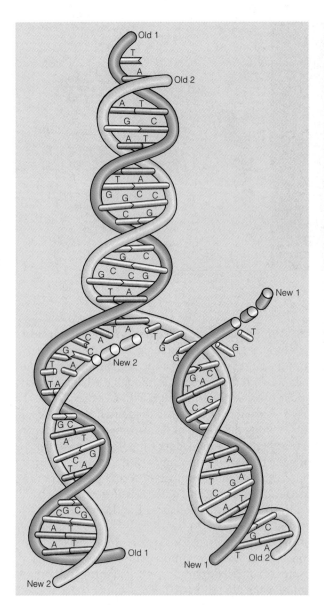

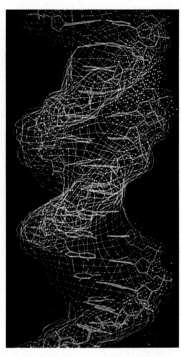

points along their length and exchange segments, so that genes from one are replaced by
genes from another. This shuffling of genes in crossing over creates new hereditary combinations. Next, the paired chromosomes separate into different cells, but chance determines which member of each pair will gather with others and eventually end up in the
same gamete. Finally, in the last phase of meiosis, each chromosome leaves its duplicate
and becomes part of a gamete containing 23 chromosomes instead of the usual 46.

In the male, four sperm are produced when meiosis is complete. Also, the cells from
which sperm arise are produced continuously throughout life. For this reason, a healthy
man can father a child at any age after sexual maturity. In the female, gamete production
is much more limited, since meiosis produces just one ovum. In addition, the female is
born with all her ova already present in her ovaries, and she can bear children for only
three to four decades. Most women stop ovulating between the ages of 45 and 53. Still,
there are plenty of female sex cells. About 1 to 2 million are present at birth, 40,000
remain at adolescence, and approximately 350 to 450 will mature during a woman's childbearing years (Moore & Persaud, 1993).

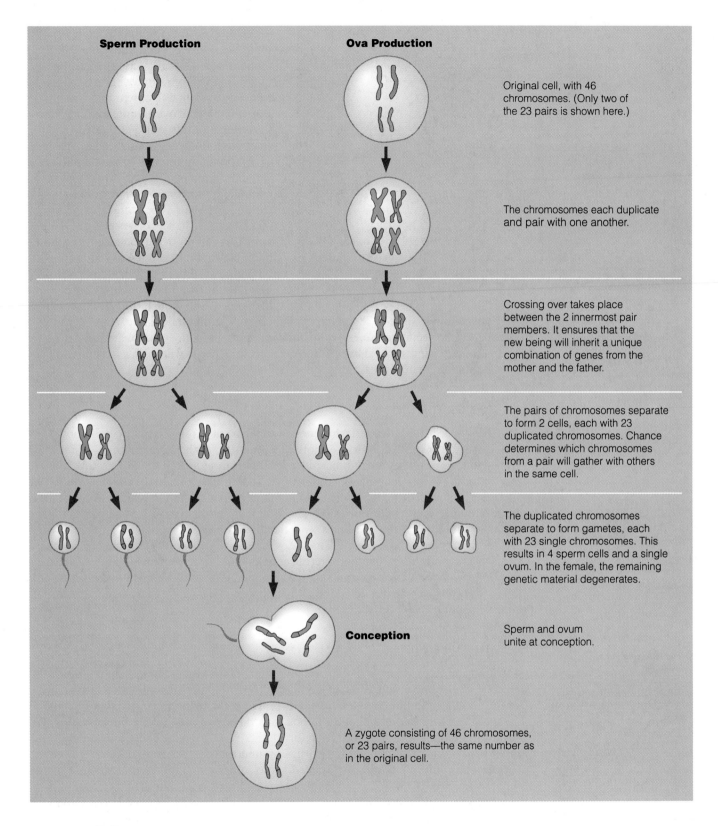

Original cell, with 46 chromosomes. (Only two of the 23 pairs is shown here.)

The chromosomes each duplicate and pair with one another.

Crossing over takes place between the 2 innermost pair members. It ensures that the new being will inherit a unique combination of genes from the mother and the father.

The pairs of chromosomes separate to form 2 cells, each with 23 duplicated chromosomes. Chance determines which chromosomes from a pair will gather with others in the same cell.

The duplicated chromosomes separate to form gametes, each with 23 single chromosomes. This results in 4 sperm cells and a single ovum. In the female, the remaining genetic material degenerates.

Sperm and ovum unite at conception.

A zygote consisting of 46 chromosomes, or 23 pairs, results—the same number as in the original cell.

Sperm Production

Ova Production

Conception

FIGURE 2.3

The cell division process of meiosis leading to gamete formation. (Here, original cells are depicted with 2 rather than the full complement of 23 pairs.) Meiosis creates gametes with only half the usual number of chromosomes. When sperm and ovum unite at conception, the first cell of the new individual (the zygote) has the correct, full number of chromosomes.

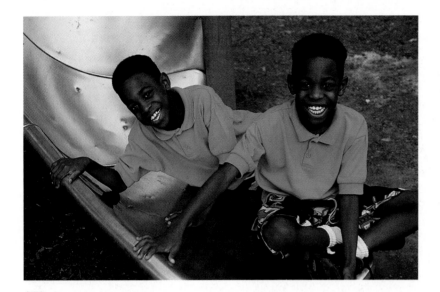

These identical, or monozygotic, twins were created when a duplicating zygote separated into two clusters of cells, and two individuals with the same genetic makeup developed. Identical twins look alike, and as we will see later in this chapter, tend to resemble each other in a variety of psychological characteristics. *(Reg Parker/FPG International)*

Look again at the steps of meiosis displayed in Figure 2.3, and notice how they ensure that a constant quantity of genetic material (46 chromosomes in each cell) is transmitted from one generation to the next. When sperm and ovum unite at conception, the cell that results, called a **zygote,** will again have 46 chromosomes.

Can you also see how meiosis leads to variability among offspring? Crossing over and random sorting of each member of a chromosome pair into separate sex cells mean that the chances of offspring of the same two parents being genetically the same is extremely slim—about 1 in 700 trillion (Gould & Keeton, 1996). Therefore, meiosis helps us understand why siblings differ from each other, even though they also have features in common, since their genotypes come from a common pool of parental genes. The genetic variability produced by meiosis is important in an evolutionary sense. It increases the chances that at least some members of a species will be able to cope with ever-changing environments and survive.

BOY OR GIRL?

Using special microscopic techniques, the 23 pairs of chromosomes in each human cell can be distinguished from one another. Twenty-two of them are matching pairs, called **autosomes.** They are numbered by geneticists from longest (1) to shortest (22) (refer back to Figure 2.1 on page 53). The twenty-third pair consists of **sex chromosomes.** In females, this pair is called XX; in males, it is called XY. The X is a relatively large chromosome, whereas the Y is short and carries less genetic material. When gametes form in males, the X and Y chromosomes separate into different sperm cells. In females, all gametes carry an X chromosome. The sex of the new organism is determined by whether an X-bearing or a Y-bearing sperm fertilizes the ovum. In fact, scientists have isolated a single gene on the Y chromosome that triggers male sexual development by switching on the production of male sex hormones. When that gene is absent, the fetus that develops is female (Goodfellow & Lovell, 1993).

MULTIPLE BIRTHS

Ruth and Peter, a couple I know well, tried for several years to have a child, without success. Ruth's doctor finally prescribed a fertility drug, and twins—Jeannie and Jason—were born. Jeannie and Jason are **fraternal,** or **dizygotic, twins,** the most common type of multiple birth. The drug that Ruth took caused two ova to be released from her ovaries, and both were fertilized. Therefore, Jeannie and Jason are genetically no more alike than ordinary siblings. Fertility drugs are only one cause of fraternal twinning (and occasionally more offspring). As Table 2.1 shows, other genetic and environmental factors are also involved.

There is another way that twins can be created. Sometimes a zygote that has started to duplicate separates into two clusters of cells that develop into two individuals. These are called **identical,** or **monozygotic, twins** because they have the same genetic makeup. The frequency of identical twins is unrelated to the factors listed in Table 2.1. It is the same around the world—about 3 of every 1,000 births (Tong, Caddy, & Short, 1997). Animal research has uncovered a variety of environmental influences that prompt this type of

zygote
The newly fertilized cell formed by the union of sperm and ovum at conception.

autosomes
The 22 matching chromosome pairs in each human cell.

sex chromosomes
The twenty-third pair of chromosomes, which determines the sex of the child. In females, called XX; in males, called XY.

fraternal, or dizygotic, twins
Twins resulting from the release and fertilization of two ova. They are genetically no more alike than ordinary siblings.

identical, or monozygotic, twins
Twins that result when a zygote, during the early stages of cell duplication, divides in two. They have the same genetic makeup.

TABLE 2.1

Maternal Factors Linked to Fraternal Twinning

FACTOR	DESCRIPTION
Ethnicity	About 8 per 1,000 births among whites, 12 to 16 per 1,000 among blacks, and 4 per 1,000 among Asians[a]
Age	Rises with maternal age, peaking at 35 years, and then rapidly falls
Nutrition	Occurs less often among women with poor diets; occurs more often among women who are tall and overweight or of normal weight as opposed to slight body build
Number of births	Chances increase with each additional birth
Fertility drugs and in vitro fertilization	Treatment of infertility with hormones and through in vitro fertilization (see page 68) increases the likelihood of multiple fraternal births, from twins to quintuplets

[a] Worldwide rates, with the effects of fertility drugs removed.

Source: Collins, 1994; Mange & Mange, 1994.

twinning, including temperature changes, variation in oxygen levels, and late fertilization of the ovum.

During their early years, children of single births are often healthier and develop more rapidly than do twins (Moilanen, 1989). Ruth and Peter's experience indicates why. Jeannie and Jason were born early (as are most twins)—3 weeks before Ruth's due date (Powers & Wampler, 1996). As we will see in Chapter 4, like other premature infants they required special care after birth. When the twins came home from the hospital, Ruth and Peter had to divide time between them, and neither baby got quite as much attention as the average single infant. As a result, Jeannie and Jason walked and talked several months later than other children their age, although both caught up in development by middle childhood.

PATTERNS OF GENETIC INHERITANCE

Jeannie has her parents' dark, straight hair, whereas Jason is curly-haired and blond. Patterns of genetic inheritance—the way genes from each parent interact—explain why this is the case. Recall that except for the XY pair in males, all chromosomes come in corresponding pairs. Two forms of each gene occur at the same place on the autosomes, one inherited from the mother and one from the father. Each different form of a gene is called an **allele.** If the alleles from both parents are alike, the child is **homozygous** and will display the inherited trait. If the alleles are different, then the child is **heterozygous,** and relationships between alleles determine the trait that will appear.

■ **DOMINANT–RECESSIVE RELATIONSHIPS.** In many heterozygous pairings, only one allele affects the child's characteristics. It is called *dominant;* the second allele, which has no effect, is called *recessive.* Hair color is an example of **dominant–recessive inheritance.** The allele for dark hair is dominant (we can represent it with a capital *D)*, whereas the one for blond hair is recessive (symbolized by a lowercase *b).* Children who inherit either a homozygous pair of dominant alleles *(DD)* or a heterozygous pair *(Db)* will be dark-haired, even though their genetic makeup is different. Blond hair (like Jason's) can result only from having two recessive alleles *(bb).* Still, heterozygous individuals with just one recessive allele *(Db)* can pass that trait to their children. Therefore, they are called **carriers** of the trait.

allele
Each of two forms of a gene located at the same place on the autosomes.

homozygous
Having two identical alleles at the same place on a pair of chromosomes.

heterozygous
Having two different alleles at the same place on a pair of chromosomes.

dominant–recessive inheritance
A pattern of inheritance in which, under heterozygous conditions, the influence of only one allele is apparent.

carrier
A heterozygous individual who can pass a recessive trait to his or her children.

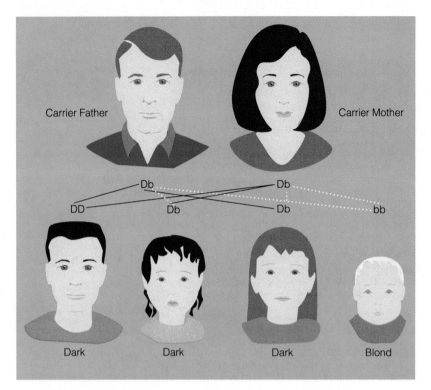

Carrier Father   Carrier Mother

Db   Db

DD   Db   Db   bb

Dark   Dark   Dark   Blond

FIGURE 2.4

Dominant–recessive model of inheritance as illustrated by hair color. By looking at the possible combinations of the parents' genes, we can predict that 25 percent of their children are likely to inherit two dominant genes for dark hair; 50 percent are likely to receive one dominant and one recessive gene, resulting in dark hair; and 25 percent are likely to receive two recessive genes for blond hair.

In dominant–recessive inheritance, if we know the genetic makeup of the parents, we can predict the percentage of children in a family who are likely to display a trait or be carriers of it. Figure 2.4 shows the pattern of inheritance for hair color. Note that for Jason to be blond, both Peter and Ruth must be carriers of a recessive allele *(b)*. The figure also indicates that if Peter and Ruth decide to have more children, most are likely to be dark-haired, like Jeannie. Peter and Ruth's children, whether dark- or blond-haired, may vary in precise shade of hair color. *Modifier genes* often act on alleles, slightly altering their effects.

Some human characteristics and disorders that follow the rules of dominant–recessive inheritance are given in Table 2.2 and in Table 2.3 on pages 60–61. As you can see, many disabilities and diseases are the product of recessive alleles. One of the most frequently occurring recessive disorders is *phenylketonuria,* or *PKU.* It affects the way the body breaks down proteins contained in many foods, such as cow's milk, bread, eggs, and fish. Infants born with two recessive alleles lack an enzyme that converts one of the basic amino acids that make up proteins (phenylalanine) into a by-product essential for body functioning (tyrosine). Without this enzyme, phenylalanine quickly builds to toxic levels that damage the central nervous system. Around 3 to 5 months of age, infants with untreated PKU start to lose interest in their surroundings. By 1 year, they are permanently retarded.

Despite its potentially damaging effects, PKU provides an excellent illustration of the fact that inheriting unfavorable genes does not always mean that the child's condition is untreatable. All U.S. states require that each newborn be given a blood test for PKU. If the disease is found, treatment involves placing the baby on a diet low in phenylalanine. Children who receive this treatment show delayed development of higher-order cognitive skills, such as planning and problem solving, in infancy and early childhood because even small amounts of phenylalanine interfere with brain functioning (Diamond et al., 1997). But as long as dietary treatment begins early and continues, children with PKU usually attain an average level of intelligence and have a normal lifespan (Mazzocco et al., 1994).

As Table 2.3 suggests, only rarely are serious diseases due to dominant alleles. Think about why this is so. Children who inherited the dominant allele would always develop the disorder. They would seldom live long enough to reproduce, and the harmful dominant allele would be eliminated from the family's heredity in a single generation. Some dominant disorders, however, do persist. One of them is *Huntington disease,* a condition in which the central nervous system degenerates. Why has this disorder endured in some families? The reason is that its symptoms usually do not appear until age 35 or later, after the person has passed the dominant gene to his or her children.

■ **CODOMINANCE.** In some heterozygous circumstances, the dominant–recessive relationship does not hold completely. Instead, we see **codominance,** a pattern of inheritance in which both alleles influence the person's characteristics.

The *sickle cell trait,* a heterozygous condition present in many black Africans, provides an example. *Sickle cell anemia* (see Table 2.3) occurs in full form when a child inherits two recessive alleles. They cause the usually round red blood cells to assume a sickle shape, a response that is especially great under low oxygen conditions. The sickled cells clog the blood vessels and block the flow of blood. Individuals who have the disorder suffer severe attacks involving intense pain, swelling, and tissue damage. They generally die in the first 20 years of life; few live past age 40. Heterozygous individuals are protected from the disease under most circumstances. However, when they experience oxygen deprivation—for example, at high altitudes or after intense physical exercise—the single recessive allele asserts itself, and a temporary, mild form of the illness occurs (Sullivan, 1987).

The sickle cell allele is common among black Africans for a special reason. Carriers of it are more resistant to malaria than are individuals with two alleles for normal red blood cells. In Africa, where malaria is common, these carriers have survived and reproduced more frequently than others, leading the gene to be maintained in the black population. In regions of the world where the risk of malaria is low, the frequency of the gene is steadily declining. For example, only 10 percent of African Americans carry it, compared to 20 percent of black Africans (Mange & Mange, 1994).

■ **X-LINKED INHERITANCE.** Males and females have an equal chance of inheriting recessive disorders carried on the autosomes, such as PKU and sickle cell anemia. But when a harmful allele is carried on the X chromosome, **X-linked inheritance** applies. Males are more likely to be affected because their sex chromosomes do not match. In females, any recessive allele on one X chromosome has a good chance of being suppressed by a dominant allele on the other X. But the Y chromosome is only about one-third as long and therefore lacks many corresponding alleles to override those on the X.

Red–green color blindness (a condition in which individuals cannot tell the difference between shades of red and green) is one example of an X-linked recessive trait. It affects males twice as often as females (Mange & Mange, 1994). In one 3-year-old boy I know, the problem was discovered when he had difficulty learning the names of colors at preschool. The boy's maternal grandfather was also color blind. Although his mother was unaffected, she was a carrier who had passed an X chromosome with the recessive allele to her son. Refer again to Table 2.3 and review the diseases that are X-linked. A well-known example is *hemophilia*, a disorder in which the blood fails to clot normally. Figure 2.5 on page 62 shows its greater likelihood of inheritance by male children whose mothers carry the abnormal allele.

Besides X-linked disorders, many sex differences reveal the male to be at a disadvantage. Rates of miscarriage and infant and childhood deaths are greater for males. Learning disabilities, behavior disorders, and mental retardation are also more common among boys (Halpern, 1997). It is possible that these sex differences can be traced to the genetic code. The female, with two X chromosomes, benefits from a greater variety of genes. Nature, however, seems to have adjusted for the male's disadvantage. Worldwide, about 106 boys are born for every 100 girls, and judging from miscarriage and abortion statistics, a still greater number of boys appear to be conceived (Shettles & Rorvik, 1984).

TABLE **2.2**

Examples of Dominant and Recessive Characteristics

DOMINANT	RECESSIVE
Dark hair	Blond hair
Normal hair	Pattern baldness
Curly hair	Straight hair
Nonred hair	Red hair
Facial dimples	No dimples
Normal hearing	Some forms of deafness
Normal vision	Nearsightedness
Farsightedness	Normal vision
Normal vision	Congenital eye cataracts
Normal color vision	Red–green color blindness
Pigmented skin	Albinism
Double-jointedness	Normal joints
Type A blood	Type O blood
Type B blood	Type O blood
Rh-positive blood	Rh-negative blood

Note. Many normal characteristics that were previously thought to be due to dominant– recessive inheritance, such as eye color, are now regarded as due to multiple genes. For the characteristics listed here, there still seems to be fairly common agreement that the simple dominant–recessive relationship holds. *Source:* McKusick, 1995.

codominance
A pattern of inheritance in which both alleles in a heterozygous combination are expressed.

X-linked inheritance
A pattern of inheritance in which a recessive gene is carried on the X chromosome. Males are more likely to be affected.

TABLE 2.3

Examples of Dominant and Recessive Diseases

DISEASE	DESCRIPTION	MODE OF INHERITANCE	INCIDENCE	TREATMENT	PRENATAL DIAGNOSIS	CARRIER IDENTIFICATION[a]
AUTOSOMAL DISEASES						
Cooley's anemia	Pale appearance, retarded physical growth, and lethargic behavior begin in infancy.	Recessive	1 in 500 births to parents of Mediterranean descent	Frequent blood transfusions; death from complications usually occurs by adolescence.	Yes	Yes
Cystic fibrosis	Lungs, liver, and pancreas secrete large amounts of thick mucus, leading to breathing and digestive difficulties.	Recessive	1 in 2,000 to 2,500 Caucasian births. 1 in 16,000 African-American births	Bronchial drainage, prompt treatment of respiratory infections, dietary management. Advances in medical care allow survival with good life quality into adulthood.	Yes	Yes
Phenylketonuria (PKU)	Inability to neutralize the harmful amino acid phenylalanine, contained in many proteins, causes severe central nervous system damage in the first year of life.	Recessive	1 in 8,000 births	Placing the child on a special diet results in average intelligence and normal life span. Subtle difficulties with planning and problem solving are often present.	Yes	Yes
Sickle cell anemia	Abnormal sickling of red blood cells causes oxygen deprivation, pain, swelling, and tissue damage. Anemia and susceptibility to infections, especially pneumonia, occur.	Recessive	1 in 500 African-American births	Blood transfusions, painkillers, prompt treatment of infections. No known cure; 50 percent die by age 20.	Yes	Yes
Tay-Sachs disease	Central nervous system degeneration, with onset at about 6 months, leads to poor muscle tone, blindness, deafness, and convulsions.	Recessive	1 in 3,600 births to Jews of European descent	None. Death by 3 to 4 years of age.	Yes	Yes

■ GENETIC IMPRINTING. More than 1,000 human characteristics follow the rules of dominant–recessive and codominant inheritance (McKusick, 1995). In these cases, regardless of which parent contributes a gene to the new individual, the gene responds in the same way. Geneticists, however, have identified some exceptions governed by a newly discovered mode of inheritance. In **genetic imprinting,** alleles are *imprinted*, or chemically *marked*, in such a way that one pair member (either the mother's or the father's) is activated, regardless of its makeup. The imprint is often temporary: it may be erased in the next generation, and it may not occur in all individuals (Cassidy, 1995).

Imprinting helps us understand the confusion in genetic inheritance for some disorders. For example, children are more likely to develop diabetes if their father, rather than their mother, suffers from it. And people with asthma or hay fever tend to have mothers, not

genetic imprinting
A pattern of inheritance in which alleles are imprinted, or chemically marked, in such a way that one pair member is activated, regardless of its makeup.

TABLE 2.3   CONTINUED

DISEASE	DESCRIPTION	MODE OF INHERITANCE	INCIDENCE	TREATMENT	PRENATAL DIAGNOSIS	CARRIER IDENTIFICATION[a]
Huntington disease	Central nervous system degeneration leads to muscular coordination difficulties, mental deterioration, and personality changes. Symptoms usually do not appear until age 35 or later.	Dominant	1 in 18,000 to 25,000 American births	None. Death occurs 10 to 20 years after symptom onset.	Yes	Not applicable
Marfan syndrome	Tall, slender build; thin, elongated arms and legs. Heart defects and eye abnormalities, especially of the lens. Excessive lengthening of the body results in a variety of skeletal defects.	Dominant	1 in 20,000 births	Correction of heart and eye defects sometimes possible. Death from heart failure in young adulthood common.	Yes	Not applicable
X-LINKED DISEASES						
Duchenne muscular dystrophy	Degenerative muscle disease. Abnormal gait, loss of ability to walk between 7 and 13 years of age.	Recessive	1 in 3,000 to 5,000 male births	None. Death from respiratory infection or weakening of the heart muscle usually occurs in adolescence.	Yes	Yes
Hemophilia	Blood fails to clot normally. Can lead to severe internal bleeding and tissue damage.	Recessive	1 in 4,000 to 7,000 male births	Blood transfusions. Safety precautions to prevent injury.	Yes	Yes
Diabetes insipidus	A form of diabetes present at birth caused by insufficient production of the hormone vasopressin. Results in excessive thirst and urination. Dehydration can cause central nervous system damage.	Recessive	1 in 2,500 male births	Hormone replacement.	Yes	No

[a]Carrier status detectable in prospective parents through blood test or genetic analyses.

Sources: Behrman & Vaughan, 1987; Cohen, 1984; Fackelmann, 1992; Gilfillan et al., 1992; Martin, 1987; McKusick, 1995; Simpson & Harding, 1993.

fathers, with the illness. Scientists do not yet know what causes this parent-specific genetic transmission. At times, it reveals itself in heart-breaking ways. Imprinting is involved in several childhood cancers and in *Praeder-Willi syndrome,* a disorder with symptoms of mental retardation and severe obesity. It may also explain why Huntington disease, when inherited from the father, tends to emerge at an earlier age and progress more rapidly (Day, 1993).

In these examples, genetic imprinting affects traits carried on the autosomes. It can also operate on the sex chromosomes, as *fragile X syndrome* reveals. In this disorder, an abnormal repetition of a sequence of DNA bases occurs in a special spot on the X chromosome, damaging a particular gene (Ryynänen et al., 1995; Turk, 1995). Fragile X syndrome is the most common inherited cause of mild to moderate mental retardation. It has also been linked to 2 to 3 percent of cases of infantile autism, a serious emotional disorder of early

FIGURE **2.5**

X-linked inheritance.
In the example shown here, the allele on the father's X chromosome is normal. The mother has one normal and one abnormal recessive allele on her X chromosomes. By looking at the possible combinations of the parents' alleles, we can predict that 50 percent of male children will have the disorder and 50 percent of female children will be carriers of it.

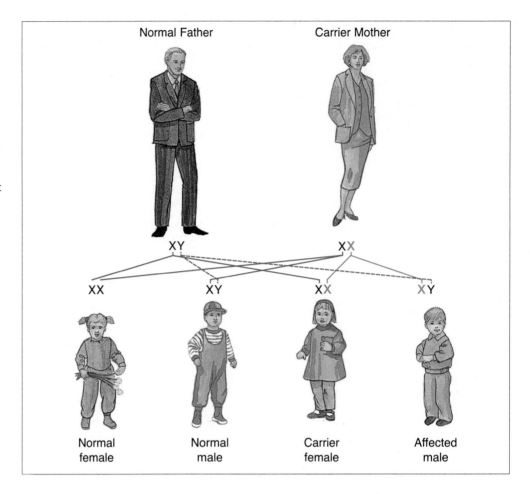

childhood involving bizarre, self-stimulating behavior and delayed or absent language and communication (Bailey et al., 1993; Hagerman, 1996). Recent research reveals that the defective gene at the fragile site is expressed only when it is passed from mother to child (Rose, 1995; Thapar et al., 1994).

■ **MUTATION.** At this point, you may be wondering, How are harmful genes created in the first place? The answer is **mutation,** a sudden but permanent change in a segment of DNA. A mutation may affect only one or two genes, or it may involve many genes, as is the case for the chromosomal disorders we will discuss shortly. Some mutations occur spontaneously, simply by chance. Others are caused by a wide variety of hazardous environmental agents that enter our food supply or are present in the air we breathe.

For many years, ionizing radiation has been known to cause mutations. Women who receive repeated doses of radiation before conception are more likely to miscarry and give birth to children with hereditary defects (Zhang, Cai, & Lee, 1992). Genetic abnormalities are also higher when fathers are exposed to radiation in their occupations. In one instance, men who worked at a reprocessing plant for nuclear fuel in England were fathers of an usually high number of children who developed cancer. Exposure to radiation at the plant is believed to have damaged chromosomes in the male sex cells, causing cancer in their children years later (Gardner et al., 1990). Does this mean that routine chest and dental X-rays are dangerous to future generations? Research indicates that infrequent and mild exposure to radiation does not cause genetic damage. Instead, high doses over a long period of time appear to be required.

Although only 3 percent of pregnancies result in the birth of a baby with a hereditary abnormality, these children account for about 40 percent of childhood deaths and 5 to 10

mutation
A sudden but permanent change in a segment of DNA.

polygenic inheritance
A pattern of inheritance in which many genes determine a characteristic.

percent of childhood hospital admissions (Shiloh, 1996). As these figures reveal, progress in preventing and treating genetic diseases still lags far behind that of non-genetic diseases. However, as we will see shortly, great strides are currently being made.

■ **POLYGENIC INHERITANCE.** So far, we have discussed patterns of inheritance in which people either display a particular trait or do not. These cut-and-dried individual differences are much easier to trace to their genetic origins than are characteristics that vary continuously among people. Many traits of interest to child development specialists, such as height, weight, intelligence, and personality, are of this type. People are not just tall or short, bright or dull, outgoing or shy. Instead, they show gradations between these extremes. Continuous traits like these are due to **polygenic inheritance,** in which many genes determine the characteristic in question. Polygenic inheritance is complex, and much about it is still unknown. In the final section of this chapter, we will pay special attention to this form of genetic transmission by examining ways that researchers infer the influence of heredity on human attributes when knowledge of precise patterns of inheritance is unavailable.

CHROMOSOMAL ABNORMALITIES

Besides inheriting harmful recessive alleles, abnormalities of the chromosomes are a major cause of serious developmental problems. Most chromosomal defects are the result of mistakes during meiosis, when the ovum and sperm are formed. A chromosome pair does not separate properly or part of a chromosome breaks off. Since these errors involve far more DNA than do problems caused by single genes, they usually produce disorders with many physical and mental symptoms.

■ **DOWN SYNDROME.** The most common chromosomal disorder, occurring in 1 out of every 800 live births, is *Down syndrome.* In most cases, it results from a failure of the twenty-first pair of chromosomes to separate during meiosis, so the new individual inherits three of these chromosomes rather than the normal two. For this reason, Down syndrome is sometimes called *trisomy 21.* In other less frequent forms, an extra broken piece of a twenty-first chromosome is present. Or an error occurs during the early stages of mitosis, causing some but not all body cells to have the defective chromosomal makeup (called a *mosaic* pattern). In these instances, since less genetic material is involved, symptoms of the disorder are less extreme (Epstein, 1993; Fishler & Koch, 1991).

The behavioral consequences of Down syndrome include mental retardation, speech problems, limited vocabulary, and slow motor development. Affected individuals also have distinct physical features—a short, stocky build, a flattened face, a protruding tongue, almond-shaped eyes, and an unusual crease running across the palm of the hand. In addition, infants with Down syndrome often are born with eye cataracts and heart and intestinal defects. Because of medical advances, fewer individuals with Down syndrome die in childhood today than in the past. Most live until middle adulthood (Baird & Sadovnick, 1987).

As Table 2.4 shows, the risk of a Down syndrome baby rises dramatically with maternal age (Halliday et al., 1995). Why is this so? Geneticists believe that the ova, present in the woman's body since her own prenatal period, weaken over time because of the aging process or increased exposure to harmful environmental agents. As a result, chromosomes do not separate properly during meiosis (Antonarakis, 1992). The mother's gamete, however, is not always the cause of a Down syndrome child. In about 20 percent of cases, the extra genetic material originates with the father. However, Down syndrome and other chromosomal abnormalities are not related to advanced paternal age. In these instances, the mutation occurs for other unknown reasons (Phillips & Elias, 1993).

The facial features and short, stocky build of the boy on the left are typical of Down syndrome. Although his intellectual development is impaired, he is doing well because he is growing up in a stimulating home where his speech needs are met and he is loved and accepted. *(Stephen Frisch/Stock Boston)*

TABLE 2.4

Risk of Giving Birth to a Down Syndrome Child by Maternal Age

MATERNAL AGE	RISK
20	1 in 1,900 births
25	1 in 1,200
30	1 in 900
33	1 in 600
36	1 in 280
39	1 in 130
42	1 in 65
45	1 in 30
48	1 in 15

Note. The risk of giving birth to a Down syndrome baby after age 35 has increased slightly over the past 20 years, due to improved medical interventions during pregnancy and consequent greater likelihood of a Down syndrome fetus surviving to be liveborn.
Source: Adapted from Halliday et al., 1995; Meyers et al., 1997.

■ **ABNORMALITIES OF THE SEX CHROMOSOMES.** Disorders of the autosomes other than Down syndrome usually disrupt development so severely that miscarriage occurs. When such babies are born, they rarely survive beyond early childhood. In contrast, abnormalities of the sex chromosomes usually lead to fewer problems. In fact, sex chromosome disorders often are not recognized until adolescence when, in some of the deviations, puberty is delayed. The most common problems involve the presence of an extra chromosome (either X or Y) or the absence of one X chromosome in females (see Table 2.5).

A variety of myths about individuals with sex chromosome disorders exist. For example, many people believe that males with *XYY syndrome* are more aggressive and antisocial than are XY males. Yet by examining Table 2.5, you will see that this is not true. Also, it is widely believed that children with sex chromosome disorders are retarded. Yet most are not. The intelligence of XYY syndrome boys is similar to that of normal children (Netley, 1986; Stewart, 1982). And the intellectual problems of children with *triple X, Klinefelter,* and *Turner syndromes* are very specific. Verbal difficulties (for example, with reading and vocabulary) are common among girls with triple X syndrome and boys with Klinefelter syndrome, each of whom inherits an extra X chromosome (Netley, 1986; Rovet et al., 1996). In contrast, Turner syndrome girls, who are missing an X, have trouble with spatial relationships. Their handwriting is poor, and they have difficulty telling right from left, following travel directions, and noticing changes in facial expressions (Money, 1993; Romans et al., 1997; Temple & Carney, 1995). These findings tell us that adding to or subtracting from the usual number of X chromosomes results in specific intellectual deficits. At present, geneticists do not know the reason why.

ASK YOURSELF . . .

■ *Two brothers, Todd and Blake, looks strikingly different. Todd is tall and thin; Blake is short and stocky. What events taking place during meiosis contributed to these differences?*

■ *Gilbert and Jan are planning to have children. Gilbert's genetic makeup is homozygous for dark hair; Jan's is heterozygous for blond hair. What color is Gilbert's hair? How about Jan's? What proportion of their children are likely to be dark haired?*

■ *Ashley and Harold both carry the defective gene for fragile X syndrome. Explain why Ashley's child inherited the disorder but Harold's did not.*

BRIEF REVIEW

Each individual is made up of trillions of cells. Inside each cell nucleus are chromosomes, which contain a chemical molecule called DNA. Genes are segments of DNA that determine our species and unique characteristics. Gametes, or sex cells, are formed through a special process of cell division called meiosis that halves the usual number of chromosomes in human cells. Then, when sperm and ovum unite at conception, each new being has the correct number of chromosomes. A different combination of sex chromosomes establishes whether a child will be a boy or a girl. Two types of twins—fraternal and identical—are possible. Fraternal twins are genetically no more alike than other siblings, whereas identical twins have the same genetic makeup.

Four patterns of inheritance—dominant–recessive, codominant, X-linked, and genetic imprinting—underlie many traits as well as disorders. Continuous characteristics, such as height and intelligence, result from the enormous complexities of polygenic inheritance, which involves many genes. Chromosomal abnormalities occur when meiosis is disrupted during gamete formation.

REPRODUCTIVE CHOICES

Two years after they were married, Ted and Marianne gave birth to their first child. Kendra appeared to be a healthy and lively infant, but by 4 months her growth had slowed. Diagnosed as having Tay-Sachs disease (see Table 2.3), Kendra died at 2 years of age.

TABLE 2.5

Sex Chromosomal Disorders

DISORDER	DESCRIPTION	INCIDENCE	TREATMENT
XYY syndrome	Inheritance of an extra Y chromosome. Typical characteristics are above-average height, large teeth, and sometimes severe acne. Intelligence, development of male sexual characteristics, and fertility are normal.	1 in 1,000 male births	No special treatment necessary.
Triple X syndrome (XXX)	Inheritance of an extra X chromosome. Impaired verbal intelligence. Affected girls are no different in appearance or sexual development from normal agemates, except for a greater tendency toward tallness.	1 in 500 to 1,250 female births	Special education to treat verbal ability problems.
Klinefelter syndrome (XXY)	Inheritance of an extra X chromosome. Impaired verbal intelligence. Afflicted boys are unusually tall, have a body fat distribution resembling females, and show incomplete development of sex characteristics at puberty. They are usually sterile.	1 in 900 male births	Hormone therapy at puberty to stimulate development of sex characteristics. Special education to treat verbal ability problems.
Turner syndrome (XO)	All or part of the second X chromosome is missing. Impaired spatial intelligence. Ovaries usually do not develop prenatally. Incomplete development of sex characteristics at puberty. Other features include short stature and webbed neck.	1 in 2,500 to 8,000 female births	Hormone therapy in childhood to stimulate physical growth and at puberty to promote development of sex characteristics. Special education to treat spatial ability problems.

Sources: Cohen, 1984; Money, 1993; Netley, 1986; Pennington et al., 1982; Ratcliffe, Pan, & McKie, 1992; Rovet et al., 1996; Schiavi et al., 1984.

Ted and Marianne were devastated by Kendra's death. Although they did not want to bear another infant who would endure such suffering, they badly wanted a child. When Ted and Marianne took walks in the neighborhood, they saw children in strollers, and tears came to their eyes. They began to avoid family get-togethers, where little nieces and nephews were constant reminders of the void in their lives.

In the past, many couples with genetic disorders in their families chose not to have children rather than risk the birth of an abnormal baby. Today, genetic counseling and prenatal diagnosis help people make informed decisions about conceiving, carrying a pregnancy to term, or adopting a child.

GENETIC COUNSELING

Genetic counseling is a communication process designed to help couples assess their chances of giving birth to a baby with a hereditary disorder and choose the best course of action in view of risks and family goals (Shiloh, 1996). Individuals likely to seek counseling are those who have had difficulties bearing children, such as repeated miscarriages, or who know that genetic problems exist in their families. In addition, women who delay childbearing past age 35 are candidates for genetic counseling. After this time, the overall rate of chromosomal abnormalities rises sharply, from 1 in every 190 to as many as 1 in every 10 pregnancies at age 48 (Meyers et al., 1997).

genetic counseling
A communication process designed to help couples assess their chances of giving birth to a baby with a hereditary disorder and choose the best course of action in view of risks and family goals.

If a family history of mental retardation, physical defects, or inherited diseases exists, the genetic counselor interviews the couple and prepares a *pedigree*, a picture of the family tree in which affected relatives are identified. The pedigree is used to estimate the likelihood that parents will have an abnormal child, using the same genetic principles we discussed earlier in this chapter. In the case of many disorders, blood tests or genetic analyses can reveal whether the parent is a carrier of the harmful gene. Turn back to pages 60–61, and you will see that carrier detection is possible for most of the diseases listed in Table 2.3. A carrier test has been developed for fragile X syndrome as well (Ryynänen et al., 1995).

When all the relevant information is in, the genetic counselor helps people consider appropriate options. These include "taking a chance" and conceiving, choosing from among a variety of reproductive technologies (see the Social Issues box on pages 68–69), or adopting a child.

PRENATAL DIAGNOSIS AND FETAL MEDICINE

prenatal diagnostic methods
Medical procedures that permit detection of developmental problems before birth.

If couples who might bear an abnormal child decide to conceive, several **prenatal diagnostic methods**—medical procedures that permit detection of problems before birth—are available (see Table 2.6). Women of advanced maternal age are prime candidates for *amniocentesis* or *chorionic villus sampling* (see Figure 2.6). Except for *ultrasound*

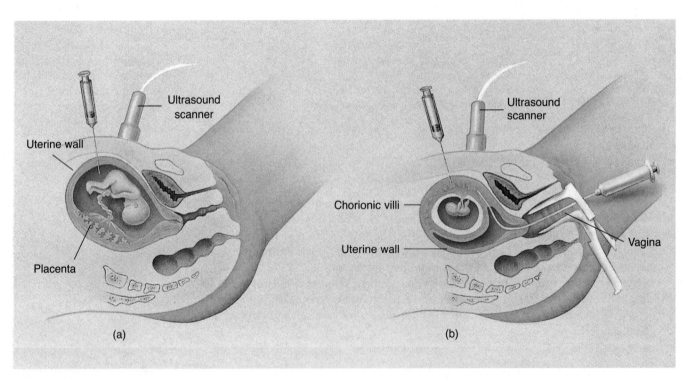

FIGURE 2.6

Amniocentesis and chorionic villi sampling. Today, several hundred defects and diseases can be detected before birth using these procedures. (a) In amniocentesis, a hollow needle is inserted through the abdominal wall into the uterus. Fluid is withdrawn and fetal cells are cultured, a process that takes about 1 to 2 weeks. (b) Chorionic villus sampling can be performed much earlier in pregnancy, at 6 to 8 weeks after conception, and results are available within 24 hours. Two approaches to obtaining a sample of chorionic villi are shown: inserting a thin tube through the vagina into the uterus or a needle through the abdominal wall. In both amniocentesis and chorionic villus sampling, an ultrasound scanner is used for guidance. (From K. L. Moore & T. V. N. Persaud, 1993, *Before We Are Born*, 4th ed., Philadelphia: Saunders, p. 89. Adapted by permission of the publisher and author.)

TABLE 2.6

Prenatal Diagnostic Methods

METHOD	DESCRIPTION
Amniocentesis	The most widely used technique. A hollow needle is inserted through the abdominal wall to obtain a sample of fluid in the uterus. Cells are examined for genetic defects. Can be performed by 11 to 14 weeks after conception; 1 to 2 more weeks are required for test results. Small risk of miscarriage.
Chorionic villus sampling	A procedure that can be used if results are desired or needed very early in pregnancy. A thin tube is inserted into the uterus through the vagina or a hollow needle is inserted through the abdominal wall. A small plug of tissue is removed from the end of one or more chorionic villi, the hairlike projections on the membrane surrounding the developing organism. Cells are examined for genetic defects. Can be performed at 6 to 8 weeks after conception, and results are available within 24 hours. Entails a slightly greater risk of miscarriage than does amniocentesis. Also associated with a small risk of limb deformities, which increases the earlier the procedure is performed.
Fetoscopy	A small tube with a light source at one end is inserted into the uterus to inspect the fetus for defects of the limbs and face. Also allows a sample of fetal blood to be obtained, permitting diagnosis of such disorders as hemophilia and sickle cell anemia as well as neural defects (see below). Usually performed between 15 and 18 weeks after conception, although can be done as early as 5 weeks. Entails some risk of miscarriage.
Ultrasound	High-frequency sound waves are beamed at the uterus; their reflection is translated into a picture on a videoscreen that reveals the size, shape, and placement of the fetus. By itself, permits assessment of fetal age, detection of multiple pregnancies, and identification of gross physical defects. Also used to guide amniocentesis, chorionic villi biopsy, and fetoscopy. When used five or more times, may increase the chances of low birth weight.
Maternal blood analysis	By the second month of pregnancy, some of the developing organism's cells enter the maternal blood stream. An elevated level of alpha-fetoprotein may indicate kidney disease, abnormal closure of the esophagus, or neural tube defects, such as anencephaly (absence of most of the brain) and spina bifida (bulging of the spinal cord from the spinal column). Isolated cells can be examined for genetic defects, such as Down syndrome.
Preimplantation genetic diagnosis	After in vitro fertilization and duplication of the zygote into a cluster of about eight cells, one cell is removed and examined for hereditary defects. Only if that cell is free of detectable genetic disorders is the fertilized ovum implanted in the woman's uterus.

Sources: Benacerraf et al., 1988; Burton, 1992; Canick & Saller, 1993; Holmes, 1993; Lissens & Sermon, 1997; Newnham et al., 1993; Quintero, Puder, & Cotton, 1993; Shurtleff & Lemire, 1995; Steele et al., 1996.

and *maternal blood analysis,* prenatal diagnosis should not be used routinely, since other methods have some chance of injuring the developing organism (Steele et al., 1996).

Improvements in prenatal diagnosis have led to new advances in fetal medicine. Today, some medical problems are being treated before birth. For example, by inserting a needle into the uterus, doctors can administer drugs to the fetus. Surgery has been performed to repair such problems as heart and lung malformations, urinary tract obstructions, and neural defects. Recently, a fetus with a hereditary immune deficiency received a bone marrow transplant from his father that succeeded in creating a normally functioning immune system (Flake et al., 1996).

Nevertheless, these practices remain controversial. Although some babies are saved, the techniques frequently result in complications, the most common being premature labor and miscarriage (Quinn & Adzick, 1997). Yet when parents are told that their unborn child has a serious defect, they may be willing to try almost any option, even if there is only a slim chance of success. Currently, the medical profession is struggling with how to help parents make informed decisions about fetal surgery. One suggestion is that the advice of an independent counselor be provided—a doctor or nurse who understands the risks but is not involved in doing research on or performing the procedure (Harrison, 1993).

Advances in *genetic engineering* also offer new hope for correcting hereditary defects. Genetic repair of the prenatal organism, once inconceivable, is a goal of today's genetic

SOCIAL ISSUES

THE PROS AND CONS OF REPRODUCTIVE TECHNOLOGIES

Some couples decide not to risk pregnancy because of a history of genetic disease. And many others—in fact, one-sixth of all couples who try to conceive—discover that they are sterile. Today, increasing numbers of individuals are turning to alternative methods of conception—technologies that, although fulfilling the wish of parenthood, have become the subject of heated debate.

■ **DONOR INSEMINATION AND IN VITRO FERTILIZATION.** For several decades, *donor insemination*—injection of sperm from an anonymous man into a woman—has been used to overcome male reproductive difficulties. In recent years, it has also permitted women without a heterosexual partner to bear children. In the United States alone, 30,000 children are conceived through donor insemination each year (Swanson, 1993).

In vitro fertilization is another reproductive technology that has become increasingly common. Since the first "test tube" baby was born in England in 1978, thousands of infants have been created this way. With in vitro fertilization, hormones are given to a woman, stimulating ripening of several ova. These are removed surgically and placed in a dish of nutrients, to which sperm are added. Once an ovum is fertilized and begins to duplicate into several cells, it is injected into the mother's uterus where, hopefully, it will implant and develop.

In vitro fertilization is usually used to treat women whose fallopian tubes are permanently damaged, and it is successful for 20 percent of those who try it. These results have been encouraging enough that the technique has been expanded. By mixing and matching gametes, pregnancies can be brought about when either or both partners have a reproductive problem. Fertilized ova and sperm can even be frozen and stored in embryo banks for use at some future time, thereby guaranteeing healthy zygotes should age or illness lead to fertility problems. For example, a childless widow conceived after in vitro fertilization with sperm donated by her husband before he received radiation treatment for testicular cancer, which left him sterile (Ahaja et al., 1997).

Children conceived through these methods may be genetically unrelated to one or both of their parents. In addition, most parents who have used in vitro fertilization do not tell their children about their origins, although health professionals now encourage them to do so (Cook et al., 1995). Does lack of genetic ties or secrecy surrounding these techniques interfere with parent–child relationships? Apparently not. A recent study found that quality of parenting was superior (warmer and more emotionally involved) for 4- to 8-year-olds conceived through in vitro fertilization or donor insemination than for naturally conceived children. A strong desire for parenthood among couples who have experienced reproductive problems seems to enhance family functioning (Golombok et al., 1995). Consistent with this interpretation, children of in vitro fertilization score just as well as, and sometimes better than, other children in cognitive and social skills (McMahon et al., 1995).

Clearly donor insemination and in vitro fertilization have many benefits. Nevertheless, serious questions have arisen about their use. Many states have no legal guidelines for these procedures. As a result, donors are not always screened for genetic or sexually transmitted diseases. In addition, few American doctors keep records of donor characteristics. Yet the resulting children may someday want to know their genetic background or need to know it for medical reasons (Nachtigall, 1993).

■ **SURROGATE MOTHERHOOD.** A more controversial form of medically assisted conception is *surrogate motherhood*. Typically in this procedure, sperm from a man whose wife is infertile are used to inseminate a woman, who is paid a fee for her childbearing services. In return, the surrogate agrees to turn the baby over to the man (who is the natural father). The child is then adopted by his wife.

Although most of these arrangements proceed smoothly, those that end up in court highlight serious risks for all concerned. In one case, both parties rejected the infant with severe disabilities that resulted from the pregnancy. In several others, the surrogate mother changed her mind and wanted to keep the baby. These children came into the world in the midst of family conflict that threatened to last for years to come.

Since surrogacy favors the wealthy as contractors for infants and the less economically advantaged as surrogates, it may promote exploitation of financially needy women (Sureau, 1997). In addition, most surrogates already have children of their own, who may be deeply affected by the pregnancy. Knowledge that their mother would give away a baby for profit may cause these youngsters to worry about the security of their own family circumstances.

■ **NEW REPRODUCTIVE FRONTIERS.** Reproductive technologies are evolving faster than societies can weigh the ethics of these procedures.

Doctors have used donor ova from younger women in combination with in vitro fertilization to help post-menopausal women become pregnant. Most recipients are in their 40s, but a 62-year-old has given birth in Italy and a 63-year-old in the United States (Beck, 1994; Kalb, 1997). Even though candidates for post-menopausal-assisted childbirth are selected on the basis of good health, serious questions arise about bringing children into the world whose parents may not live to see them reach adulthood. Based on U.S. life expectancy data, 1 in 3 mothers and 1 in 2 fathers having a baby at age 55 will die before their child enters college (Bowman & Saunders, 1994).

Currently, experts are debating other reproductive options. At donor banks, customers can select ova or sperm on the basis of physical characteristics and even the IQ of potential donors. Some worry that this practice is a dangerous step toward selective breeding of the human species.

Researchers have delivered baby mice using the transplanted ovaries of aborted fetuses (Hashimoto, Noguchi, & Nakatsuji, 1992). If the same procedure were eventually applied to human beings, it would create babies whose genetic mothers had never been born.

Finally, scientists have successfully cloned (made multiple copies of) fertilized ova in sheep, cattle, and monkeys, and they are working on effective ways to do so in humans (Haworth & Strosnider, 1997; Kolberg, 1993). By providing extra ova for injection, cloning might improve the success rate of in vitro fertilization. But it also opens the possibility of mass producing genetically identical people. Consequently, no federal grants are available for research on human cloning.

Although new reproductive technologies permit many barren couples to rear healthy newborn babies, laws are needed to regulate them. In Australia, New Zealand, and Sweden, individuals conceived with donated gametes have a right to information about their genetic origins (Daniels & Lewis, 1996). Pressure from those working in the field of assisted reproduction may soon lead to a similar policy in the United States.

In the case of surrogate motherhood, the ethical problems are so complex that 18 U.S. states have sharply restricted the practice, and Australia, Canada, and many European nations have banned it, arguing that the status of a baby should not be a matter of commercial arrangement, and that a part of the body should not be rented or sold (McGee, 1997). Recently, England, France, and Italy prohibited in vitro fertilization for women past menopause (Beck, 1994).

At present, nothing is known about the psychological consequences of being a product of these procedures. Research on how such children grow up, including what they know and how they feel about their origins, is important for weighing the pros and cons of these techniques.

Fourteen years after menopause, 63-year-old Arceli Keh gave birth to a baby using a donor ovum that was fertilized in vitro with her 61-year-old husband's sperm and injected into her uterus. Will baby Cynthia's parents live to see her reach adulthood? Post-menopausal childbearing is highly controversial. *(National Enquirer)*

engineers. As part of the Human Genome Project, researchers are mapping human chromosomes, finding the precise location of genes for specific traits and using this information to identify abnormal conditions with greater accuracy and to devise new, gene-based treatments. To find out about the project's progress, refer to the Biology and Environment box on pages 72–73.

THE ALTERNATIVE OF ADOPTION

Adults who cannot have children, who are likely to pass along a genetic disorder, or who are older and single but want a family are turning to adoption in increasing numbers. Adoption agencies try to find parents of the same ethnic and religious background as the child. Where possible, they also try to choose parents who are the same age as most natural parents. Because the availability of healthy babies has declined (since fewer young unwed mothers give up their babies than in the past), more people are adopting from foreign countries or taking children who are older or who have developmental problems.

Selection of adoptive parents is important, since sometimes adoptive relationships do not work out. The risk of adoption failure is greatest for children adopted at older ages and children with disabilities, but it is not high. More than 85 percent of these children do well in their adoptive homes. Of those who do not, 9 out of 10 are successfully placed with a new family (Churchill, 1984; Glidden & Pursley, 1989). The outcomes are good because of careful pairing of children with parents along with advice and guidance provided to adopting families by well-trained social service professionals.

Still, adopted children and adolescents—whether born in a foreign country or the country of their adoptive parents—have more learning and emotional difficulties than occur in the general child population (Brodzinsky, 1990; Verhulst & Versluis-Den Bieman, 1995). There are many reasons for this trend. The biological mother may have been unable to care for the child because of problems believed to be partly genetic, such as alcoholism or severe depression. She may have passed this tendency to her offspring. Or perhaps she experienced stress, poor diet, or inadequate medical care during pregnancy— factors that can affect the child (as we will see in Chapter 3). Finally, children adopted after infancy often have a history of conflict-ridden family relationships and lack of parental affection.

But despite these risks, most adopted children have happy childhoods and grow up to be well-adjusted, productive citizens. And young people who were transracially or transculturally adopted typically develop identities that are healthy blends of their birth and rearing backgrounds (Simon, Altstein, & Melli, 1994). However, this favorable outcome depends on parents' willingness to help their child learn about his or her heritage. In a longitudinal study of African-American children whose parents tended to avoid racial issues, ethnic identity was often weak at adolescence—a factor that contributed to adjustment problems (DeBerry, Scarr, & Weinberg, 1996).

As we conclude our discussion of reproductive choices, perhaps you are wondering how things turned out for Ted and Marianne. They were my next-door neighbors for many years, and I am glad to report that their story had a happy ending. Through genetic counseling, Marianne discovered a history of Tay-Sachs disease on her mother's side of the family. Ted had a distant cousin who died of the disorder. The genetic counselor explained that the chances of giving birth to another affected baby were 1 in 4. Ted and Marianne took the risk. Their son Douglas is now 12 years old. Although Douglas is a carrier of the recessive allele, he is a normal, healthy boy. In a few years,

This transracially adopted African-American baby plays with her Caucasian older sisters. Will she develop an identity that is a healthy blend of her birth and rearing backgrounds? The answer depends on the extent to which her adoptive parents expose her to her African-American heritage. *(Jim Pickerell/Stock Boston)*

CAREGIVING CONCERNS

Steps Prospective Parents Can Take before Conception to Increase the Chances of Having a Healthy Baby

SUGGESTION	RATIONALE
Arrange for a physical exam.	A physical exam before conception permits detection of diseases and other medical problems that might reduce fertility, be difficult to treat after the onset of pregnancy, or affect the developing organism.
Reduce or eliminate toxins under your control.	Since the developing organism is highly sensitive to damaging environmental agents during the early weeks of pregnancy (see Chapter 3), drugs, alcohol, cigarette smoke, radiation, pollution, chemical substances in the home and workplace, and infectious diseases should be avoided while trying to conceive. Furthermore, ionizing radition and some industrial chemicals are known to cause mutations.
Consider your genetic makeup.	Find out if anyone in your family has had a child with a genetic disease or disability. If so, seek genetic counseling before conception.
Consult a physician after 12 months of unsuccessful efforts at conception.	Long periods of infertility may be due to undiagnosed spontaneous abortions, which can be caused by genetic defects in either partner. If a physical exam reveals a healthy reproductive system, seek genetic counseling.

Ted and Marianne will tell Douglas about his genetic history and explain the importance of genetic counseling and testing before he has children of his own. The Caregiving Concerns table above summarizes steps that prospective parents can take before conception to increase their chances of having a healthy baby.

BRIEF REVIEW

Genetic counseling helps couples who have a family history of reproductive problems or hereditary defects make informed decisions about bearing a child. For those who decide to conceive, prenatal diagnostic methods permit early detection of fetal problems. Reproductive technologies, such as donor insemination, in vitro fertilization, and surrogate motherhood, are also available, but they raise serious ethical concerns. Although learning and emotional problems are more common among adopted children than among children in general, careful selection of adoptive parents and family support services make adoption successful in the large majority of cases.

ASK YOURSELF . . .

■ *A woman over age 35 has just learned that she is pregnant. Although she would like to find out as soon as possible whether her child has a chromosomal disorder, she wants to minimize the risk of injury to the developing organism. Which prenatal diagnostic method is she likely to choose?*

■ *Describe the ethical pros and cons of fetal surgery, surrogate motherhood, and postmenopausal-assisted childbearing.*

ENVIRONMENTAL CONTEXTS FOR DEVELOPMENT

Just as complex as the heredity that sets the stage for development is the child's environment—a many-layered set of influences that combine with one another to help or hinder the course of growth. Take a moment to think back to your own childhood, and jot down a brief description of the first 10 memories that come to mind. When I ask my students to do this, about half the events they list involve their families. This emphasis on the family is not surprising, since it is the child's first and longest-lasting context for development. But other settings turn out to be important as well. Friends, neighbors, school, workplace, scouting troops, religious organizations, and successes and disappointments at school generally make the top ten.

BIOLOGY & ENVIRONMENT   THE HUMAN GENOME PROJECT

Begun in 1990, the Human Genome Project is an ambitious, international research program aimed at deciphering the chemical makeup of human genetic material (genome) and identifying all 50,000 to 100,000 human genes. Its main goals are to provide powerful new approaches for understanding human evolution and the development of genetic disorders, so they can be prevented and treated. An additional goal is to examine the ethical, legal, and social implications of genetic technologies and to educate the public about them.

The research is an enormous undertaking. The human genome contains 3 billion chemical building blocks, or base pairs (see page 54), enough to fill a thousand 1000-page telephone books if each base pair is represented by a single letter. Given the size of the project, researchers have had to develop methods for DNA analysis that can process large amounts of information relatively quickly and accurately. Even with these procedures, scientists will have worked for more than a decade before they attain their goal, at a cost of billions of dollars.

■ **MAPPING AND SEQUENCING DNA.** The Human Genome Project yields three main research tools, which enable scientists to identify specific genes (Lander, 1996). Each tool is a major phase of the research.

1. *Genetic map.* A genetic map consists of thousands of *markers,* or short, distinctive pieces of DNA, spaced along the chromosomes. Just as finding a landmark in your city is easier if you can narrow its location between two nearby points, so researchers first try to limit their search for a particular gene to a small segment of a chromosome. Genetic mapping begins with collection of blood or tissue samples from families in which a trait or disorder is common. After extracting DNA from these samples, researchers look for sequences of bases shared among affected family members, which mark the location of the gene.

2. *Physical map.* To further pinpoint the gene, researchers create a physical map, made up of overlapping DNA fragments that span the marked regions of a chromosome. Using various methods, the chromosome is snipped into pieces. These are cloned, stored in the order in which they originally occurred along the chromosome, and used for further studies aimed at finding the specific gene. The fragments can then be analyzed to discover the base-by-base sequence of DNA.

3. *Sequence map.* The most challenging task is the creation of a sequence map of all 3 billion DNA bases of the human genome. Now that the genetic and physical maps are largely complete, the sequence map is being constructed, which allows scientists to find specific genes. Sequencing is expected to be accomplished by the year 2005.

To make all the information available to researchers worldwide, computer methods for easy storage, retrieval, and analysis of data are being devised. Also, since valuable information about human genes and their functions can be obtained by comparing them with corresponding genes in other species, mapping is being carried out on several other organisms—the mouse, the rat, the fruit fly, the roundworm, yeast, and the common intestinal bacterium E. coli.

■ **APPLICATIONS.** The detailed genetic, physical, and sequence maps produced by the Human Genome Project are vital for understanding disorders due to single genes and those that result from a complex interplay of

Think back to Bronfenbrenner's ecological systems theory, discussed in Chapter 1. It emphasizes that environments extending beyond the microsystem, or the immediate settings just illustrated, powerfully affect development. Indeed, there is one very important context my students rarely mention. Its impact is so pervasive that we seldom stop to think about it in our daily lives. This is the broad social climate of society—its values and programs that support and protect children's development. All families need help in rearing their children—safe neighborhoods, well-equipped parks and playgrounds, good schools, affordable health services, and more. And some families, because of poverty or special tragedies, need considerably more help than others.

In the following sections, we take up these contexts for development. Since they affect every age period and aspect of change, we will return to them in later chapters. For now,

multiple genes and environmental factors, including heart disease, many forms of cancer, and mental illnesses, such as depression and alcoholism. As of 1998, more than 38,000 human genes had been mapped or identified, including those for hundreds of inherited disorders, such as cystic fibrosis, Huntington disease, Duchenne muscular dystrophy, and some forms of cancer (Human Genome Program, 1998).

Discovery of disease-associated genes is leading to rapid advances in genetic counseling and prenatal diagnosis as additional tests for detecting abnormal genes become available. The Human Genome Project is also providing the basis for a new, molecular medicine. Gene-based treatments are being developed for hereditary disorders, cancer, and AIDS. Among these experimental procedures is *gene splicing*—delivering DNA carrying a functional gene to the patient's cells, thereby correcting a genetic abnormality.

Although inserting a gene into its proper place in a patient's genome is an immense challenge, one successful experiment reveals its potential. Four-year-old Ashanthi and 9-year-old Cynthia, each born with an inherited defect of the immune system, had experienced one life-threatening infection after another until researchers found a way to inject a normal, disease-fighting gene into their white blood cells. Because the body constantly replaces these cells, the procedure is not a cure; it must be repeated regularly. But today, Ashanthi and Cynthia are leading healthy, active lives (Bodmer & McKie, 1997).

■ **ETHICAL, LEGAL, AND SOCIAL CONCERNS.** As the Human Genome Project transforms biological research and medical practice, it has sparked concerns about how its tools will be applied. A major controversy involves testing children and adults who are at risk for genetic diseases but who do not yet show symptoms. Delay between the availability of diagnostic tests and effective intervention means that affected people must live with the anxiety of a future illness they cannot prevent. And some have encountered discrimination because of their heredity; they have lost their health insurance and even their jobs. As a result, guidelines for responsible use of genetic technologies are being drawn up, and ethical principles have been devised to ensure the privacy of genetic information and protection against genetic discrimination (Marshall, 1996).

The Human Genome Project is making invaluable contributions to our knowledge of the hereditary basis

A technician examines a DNA fingerprinting, or visual image of the sequence of bases in a particular region of a chromosome. Sequence mapping of all human DNA bases in the Human Genome Project permits meaningful interpretation of sequence variations between people, which can reveal who is healthy and who is susceptible to or stricken by certain diseases. *(Peter Menzel/Stock Boston)*

of human biology and disease—information that offers great promise for improving human health. As its maps and sequences become broadly available to the scientific community, investigators continue to debate the best ways to protect the public interest while reaping the project's monumental rewards.

our discussion emphasizes that besides heredity, environments can enhance growth or create risks for children. And when a vulnerable child—a youngster with physical or psychological problems—is exposed to unfavorable child-rearing contexts, then development is seriously threatened.

THE FAMILY

In power and breadth of influence, no context for development equals the family. The family introduces children to the physical world through the opportunities it provides for play and exploration of objects. It also creates unique bonds between people. The attachments children form with parents and siblings usually last a lifetime, and they

The family is a complex social system in which each person's behavior influences the behavior of others, in both direct and indirect ways. The positive mealtime atmosphere in this family is probably a product of many forces, including parents who respond to children with warmth and patience, aunts and uncles who support parents in their child-rearing roles, and children who have developed cooperative dispositions. *(Michal Heron/Woodfin Camp & Associates)*

serve as models for relationships in the wider world of neighborhood and school. Within the family, children experience their first social conflicts. Discipline by parents and arguments with siblings provide important lessons in compliance and cooperation and opportunities to learn how to influence the behavior of others. Finally, within the family, children learn the language, skills, and social and moral values of their culture.

When child development specialists first studied the family in the middle part of this century, they investigated it in a very limited way. Most studies focused on the mother-child relationship and emphasized one-way effects of child-rearing practices on children's behavior. Today, investigators recognize that children are not mechanically shaped by the inputs of others. Instead, recall from ecological systems theory that *bidirectional influences* exist in which the behaviors of each family member affect those of others (Bronfenbrenner, 1989, 1995). The very term *system* implies that the responses of all family members are related. These system influences operate in both *direct* and *indirect* ways.

■ **DIRECT INFLUENCES.** Keep a sharp lookout the next time you pass through the checkout counter at your local supermarket. Recently, I witnessed the following two episodes, in which parents and children directly affected each other:

■ Little Danny stood next to tempting rows of candy as his mom lifted groceries from the cart onto the counter. "Pleeeeease, can I have it, Mom?" begged Danny, holding up a large package of bubble gum. "Do you have a dollar? Just one?"

"No, not today," his mother answered softly. "Remember, we picked out your special cereal. That's what I need the dollar for." Danny's mother handed him the cereal while gently taking the bubble gum from his hand and returning it to the shelf. "Here, let's pay the man," she said, as she lifted Danny into the empty grocery cart where he could see the cash register.

■ Three-year-old Meg sat in the cart while her mom transferred groceries to the counter. Meg turned around, grabbed a bunch of bananas, and started to pull them apart.

"Stop it, Meg!" shouted her mom, who snatched the bananas from Meg's hand. Meg reached for a chocolate bar from a nearby shelf while her mother wrote the check. "Meg, how many times have I told you, DON'T TOUCH!" Loosening the candy from Meg's tight little grip, Meg's mother slapped her hand. Meg's face turned red with anger as she began to wail. "Keep this up, and you'll get it when we get home," threatened Meg's mom as they left the store.

These observations fit with a wealth of research on the family system. Many studies show that when parents are warm but patient (like Danny's mom), children tend to comply with their requests. And when children cooperate, their parents are likely to be warm and gentle in the future (Baumrind, 1983; Lewis, 1981). In contrast, parents who discipline with harshness and impatience (like Meg's mom) have children who refuse and rebel. And because children's misbehavior is stressful for parents, they may increase their use of punishment, leading to more unruliness by the child (Dodge, Pettit, & Bates, 1994; Patterson, Reid, & Dishion, 1992). In these examples, the behavior of one family member helps sustain a form of interaction in another that either promotes or undermines children's well-being.

■ **INDIRECT INFLUENCES.** The impact of family relationships on child development becomes even more complicated when we consider that interaction between any two members is affected by others present in the setting. Ecological systems theory calls these indirect influences the effect of *third parties* (see Chapter 1, page 26). Researchers have become intensely interested in how a range of relationships—mother with father, parent with sibling, grandparent with parent—modifies the child's direct experiences in the family.

Third parties can serve as effective supports for child development. For example, when parents' marital relationship is warm and considerate, mothers and fathers praise and stimulate their children more and nag and scold them less. In contrast, when a marriage is tense and hostile, parents are likely to criticize and punish (Cox et al., 1989; Howes & Markman, 1989; Simons et al., 1992). Yet even when children's adjustment is strained by arguments between their parents, other family members may help restore effective interaction. Grandparents are a case in point. They can promote children's development in many ways—both directly, by responding warmly to the child, and indirectly, by providing parents with child-rearing advice, models of child-rearing skill, and even financial assistance (Cherlin & Furstenberg, 1986). Of course, like any indirect influence, grandparents can sometimes be harmful. When quarrelsome relations exist between parents and grandparents, parent–child communication may suffer.

■ **ADAPTING TO CHANGE.** Think back to the *chronosystem* in Bronfenbrenner's theory (see page 28). To make matters even more complicated, the interplay of forces within the family must constantly adapt to the development of its members, since each changes throughout the lifespan.

For example, as children acquire new skills, parents adjust the way they treat their more competent youngsters. When you next have a chance, notice the way that a parent relates to a tiny baby as opposed to a walking, talking toddler. During the first few months of life, much time is spent in caregiving—feeding, changing, bathing, and cuddling the infant. Within a year, things change dramatically. The 1-year-old points, shows, names objects, and makes his way through the household cupboards. In response, parents spend less time in physical care and more in talking and playing games (Campos, Kermoian, & Zumbahlen, 1992). These new ways of interacting encourage the child's expanding cognitive, language, and motor skills.

Parents' development affects children as well. In Chapter 14, we will see that the mild increase in parent-child conflict that often occurs in early adolescence is not solely due to teenagers' striving for independence and desire to explore new values and goals. Most parents of adolescents have reached middle age and are reconsidering their own commitments. They are very conscious that their youngsters will soon leave home and establish their own lives (Grotevant, 1997; Hill & Holmbeck, 1987). Consequently, while the adolescent presses for greater autonomy, the parent may press for more togetherness. This imbalance promotes friction that is gradually resolved as parent and teenager accommodate to changes in one another (Collins, 1997).

Finally, historical time period contributes to a dynamic family system. In recent decades, a variety of societal changes have had a profound impact on families. These include a declining birth rate, increased participation of women in the work force, and a high divorce rate, resulting in a dramatic rise in single parents, remarried parents, employed mothers, and dual earner families. In addition, more couples are postponing parenthood until a later age. Clearly families in industrialized nations have become more pluralistic than ever before. In later chapters we will take up these and other diverse family forms, emphasizing how each affects family relationships and, ultimately, children's development.

Despite the family's flexible and changing nature, child development specialists have discovered some general rules about good parenting practices. As we will see in later chapters, parental *responsiveness* is repeatedly associated with better development. In infancy, responsive parents sensitively adapt their own behaviors to those of the baby. They hold the infant tenderly, wait until she is ready for the next spoonful of food, and gaze into her eyes, smile, and talk softly when she indicates she is ready for social stimulation. Babies who receive such care are likely to develop into especially competent toddlers and preschoolers, both cognitively and socially (Frankel & Bates, 1990; Thompson, 1998).

During childhood and adolescence, responsive parents communicate in a warm, affectionate manner and listen patiently to their youngster's point of view. And when they combine this sensitivity with another crucial feature of effective parenting—*reasonable demands for mature behavior*—their children tend to be socially active and responsible and to achieve well in school (Baumrind, 1971, 1991). In fact, research examining parenting in more than 180 societies indicates that a style that is warm but moderately demanding is a common pattern around the world (Rohner & Rohner, 1981).

Nevertheless, consistent differences in parenting practices do exist. In Chapter 10, we will see that the balance of parental warmth and control often varies with ethnicity—in ways that reflect family values and life circumstances (Parke & Buriel, 1998). And in the United States and other Western nations, a major source of variation in parenting is socioeconomic status.

SOCIOECONOMIC STATUS AND FAMILY FUNCTIONING

People in industrialized nations are stratified on the basis of what they do at work and how much they earn for doing it—factors that determine their social position and economic well-being. Researchers assess a family's standing on this continuum through an index called **socioeconomic status (SES).** It combines three interrelated, but not completely overlapping, variables: (1) years of education and (2) the prestige of and skill required by one's job, both of which measure social status; and (3) income, which measures economic status. As socioeconomic status rises and falls, parents and children face changing circumstances that profoundly affect family functioning.

When asked about qualities they would like to encourage in their children, parents who work in skilled and semiskilled manual occupations (for example, machinists, truck drivers, and custodians) tend to place a higher value on external characteristics, such as obedience, neatness, and cleanliness. In contrast, parents in white-collar and professional occupations tend to emphasize inner psychological traits, such as curiosity, happiness, and self-control. These differences in values are reflected in parents' behaviors. Parents higher in SES talk to and stimulate their infants more and grant them greater freedom to explore (Luster, Rhoades, & Haas, 1989). When their children are older, they use more explanations and verbal praise. In contrast, commands, such as "You do that because I told you to," as well as criticism and physical punishment occur more often in low-SES households (Dodge, Pettit, & Bates, 1994; Hoff-Ginsberg & Tardiff, 1995).

These differences in child rearing can be understood in terms of the life conditions of families. Low-SES parents often feel a sense of powerlessness and lack of influence in their relationships beyond the home. For example, at work they must obey the rules of others in positions of power and authority. When they get home, their parent–child interaction seems to duplicate these experiences, only with them in the authority roles. In contrast, higher-SES parents have a greater sense of control over their own lives. At work, they are used to making independent decisions and convincing others of their point of view. At home, they teach these same skills to their children (Greenberger, O'Neil, & Nagel, 1994).

Education also contributes to SES differences in child rearing. Higher-SES parents' interest in developing their children's inner characteristics is supported by years of schooling, during which they learned to think about abstract, subjective ideas. In research carried out in Mexico, where female school enrollment has recently increased, the more years of education a mother had, the more she stimulated her young child through face-to-face conversation (Richman, Miller, & LeVine, 1992; Uribe, LeVine, & LeVine, 1994).

Furthermore, the greater economic security of higher-SES parents frees them from the burden of having to worry about making ends meet on a daily basis. They can devote more energy and attention to their own inner characteristics and those of their children.

socioeconomic status (SES)
A measure of a family's social position and economic well-being that combines three interrelated, but not completely overlapping, variables: (1) years of education and (2) the prestige of and skill required by one's job, both of which measure social status; and (3) income, which measures economic status.

And they can also provide many more experiences—from toys to special outings to after-school lessons—that encourage these characteristics.

As early as the second year of life, SES is positively correlated with cognitive and language development. And throughout childhood and adolescence, higher-SES children do better in school (Brody, 1997; Walker et al., 1994). Child development specialists believe that SES variations in parenting practices have much to do with these outcomes.

THE IMPACT OF POVERTY

When families slip into poverty, effective parenting and children's development are seriously threatened. Shirley Brice Heath (1990), an anthropologist who has spent many years studying children and families of poverty, describes the case of Zinnia Mae, who grew up in Trackton, a close-knit black community located in a small southeastern American city. As unemployment struck Trackton in the 1980s and citizens moved away, 16-year-old Zinnia Mae caught a ride to Atlanta. Two years later, Heath visited her there. By then, Zinnia Mae was the mother of three children—a 16-month-old daughter named Donna and 2-month-old twin boys. She had moved into a high-rise public housing project, one of eight concrete buildings surrounding a dirt plot scattered with broken swings, see-saws, and benches. Describing her life to Heath, Zinnia Mae said,

> "My days, you know, I just do what I can, can't get away much . . . . I can't haul [Donna] up and down those six flights of steps to get her out with them other kids, and the place here is too cramped as it is; . . . so me and Donna, we pretty much stay in here with the babies by ourselves 'cept when I get the neighbor girl to come in so I can go get some food for us to eat . . . ." (p. 504)

Each of Zinnia Mae's days was much the same. She watched TV and talked with girlfriends on the phone. The children had only one set meal (breakfast) and otherwise ate whenever they were hungry or bored. Their play space was limited to the living room sofa and a mattress on the floor. Toys consisted of scraps of a blanket, spoons and food cartons, a small rubber ball, a few plastic cars, and a roller skate abandoned in the building. Zinnia Mae's most frequent words were "I'm so tired." She worried about how to get papers to the welfare office, where to find a baby-sitter so she could go to the laundry or grocery, and what she would do if she located the twins' father, who had stopped sending money. She rarely had enough energy to spend time with her children.

Over the past 25 years, economic changes in the United States have caused the poverty rate to climb substantially. Today, nearly 37 million people—14.5 percent of the population—are affected. Those hit hardest are parents under age 25 with young children and elderly people who live alone. Poverty is also magnified among ethnic minorities and women. For example, nearly 22 percent of American children are poor, a rate that climbs to 40 percent for Hispanic children and 47 percent for African-American children. For single mothers with preschool children, the poverty rate is over 60 percent (U.S. Bureau of the Census, 1997).

Since the 1970s, poverty has been more widespread among children than any other age group. Parental unemployment, a high divorce rate, a high rate of adolescent childbearing, and (as we will see later) inadequate government programs to meet family needs are responsible for these disheartening statistics. The condition of American children is particularly worrisome because the earlier poverty begins and the longer it lasts, the more devastating is its effect on children's physical and mental health and school achievement (Chase-Lansdale & Brooks-Gunn, 1994; McLeod & Shanahan, 1996).

The constant stresses that accompany poverty gradually weaken the family system. Poor families have many daily hassles—bills to pay, the car breaking down, loss of welfare and unemployment payments, something stolen from the house, to name just a few. When daily crises arise, parents become irritable and distracted, hostile interactions

Homelessness in the United States has risen over the past 15 years. Families like this one travel from place to place in search of employment and a safe and secure place to live. At night, they sleep in the family car. Because of constant stresses, homeless children are usually behind in development, have frequent health problems, and show poor psychological adjustment. *(Rick Browne/Stock Boston)*

between family members increase, and children's development suffers (Conger et al., 1992; Garrett, Ng'andu, & Ferron, 1994). These outcomes are especially severe in families that must live in poor housing and dangerous neighborhoods—conditions that make everyday existence even more difficult while reducing social supports that assist in coping with economic hardship (Duncan, Brooks-Gunn, & Klebanov, 1994; McLoyd et al., 1994).

Besides poverty, another problem—one that was quite uncommon 20 years ago—has reduced the life chances of poor children in the United States: homelessness. On any given night, approximately 735,000 people have no place to live (Wright, 1997). Homelessness has increased more among families with children than any other group. Nearly 40 percent of America's homeless population is made up of families, and 1 in every 4 homeless individuals is a child. The rise in child homelessness is due to a number of factors, the most important of which is a dramatic decline in the availability of government-supported low-cost housing (Children's Defense Fund, 1998).

Most homeless families consist of women on their own with young children—usually under age 5. These children suffer from developmental delays and serious emotional stress (DiBiase & Waddell, 1995; Oberg, Bryant, & Bach, 1995). Homeless youngsters also have many health problems due to inadequate diets, living outdoors or in crowded public shelters, and lack of immunization against childhood diseases (McNamee, Bartek, & Lynes, 1994).

An estimated 25 to 50 percent of homeless children who are old enough do not attend school. Some have difficulty enrolling because they lack a permanent address or prior school records (Rafferty, 1995). Others do not have transportation, a change of clothes, or school supplies. And still others stay away because they are embarrassed about having no home or find it difficult to adjust to new teachers and classmates every few months. Because of poor school attendance and health and emotional problems, homeless children who do go to school achieve less well than other poor children, and they are more likely to repeat a grade (Vostanis, Grattan, & Cumella, 1997).

BEYOND THE FAMILY: NEIGHBORHOODS, SCHOOLS, TOWNS, AND CITIES

In ecological systems theory, the mesosystem and the exosystem underscore that ties between family and community are vital for children's well-being. From our discussion of child poverty, perhaps you can see why this is so. In poverty-stricken urban areas, community life is usually disrupted. Families move often, parks and playgrounds are in disarray, and community centers providing organized leisure time activities do not exist (Wilson, 1991). Research indicates that child abuse and neglect are greatest where residents are dissatisfied with their community, describing it as a socially isolated place to live. In contrast, when family ties to the community are strong—as indicated by regular church attendance and frequent contact with friends and relatives—family stress and child adjustment problems are reduced (Garbarino & Kostelny, 1993).

■ NEIGHBORHOODS. Let's take a closer look at the functions that communities serve in the lives of children by beginning with the neighborhood. What were your childhood experiences like in the yards, streets, and parks surrounding your home? How did you spend your time, whom did you get to know, and how important were these moments to you?

Neighborhoods differ in the extent to which they encourage play and exploration among children. In one study, researchers compared the impact of several neighborhoods in the same large American city on children's social lives. One of them was Monterey, a well-to-do, hilly area with homes set back on large lots and streets without sidewalks. The arrangement of this neighborhood restricted children's freedom to move about and gather. In contrast, the flat, densely populated city neighborhood of Yuba provided rich social experiences. Children played often in large groups, used the sidewalks and streets for spontaneous games, built secret hideaways in empty lots, and traveled together to make purchases in nearby shops (Berg & Medrich, 1980).

The resources offered by neighborhoods play an important part in children's development. In one study, the more varied children's neighborhood experiences—group memberships (such as scouting and 4-H), contact with adults of their grandparents' generation, visits to parents' workplace, and places to go off by themselves or with friends (a treehouse, a fort, or a neighbor's garage)—the better their social and emotional adjustment (Bryant, 1985).

Neighborhood resources have a greater impact on young people growing up in economically disadvantaged than well-to-do neighborhoods—an effect that strengthens with age (McLeod & Shanahan, 1996). Families residing in affluent sections of cities and in suburbs are not as dependent on their immediate surroundings for social supports and leisure pursuits. They can afford to reach beyond the streets near their home, transporting their children to lessons and entertainment in distant parts of the community (Elliott et al., 1996). In low-income areas, neighborhood organization and informal social activity predict many aspects of adolescents' psychological functioning, including self-confidence, school performance, and educational aspirations (Gonzales et al., 1996).

In areas riddled with unemployment, crime, urban renewal, and population turnover, social ties that link families to one another and to other institutions are weak or absent, since relationships are constantly changing. Consequently, informal social controls over young people's behavior weaken, giving rise to substance abuse and delinquent gangs. In disintegrating neighborhoods, stronger parental supervision and control are needed to prevent children from becoming involved in antisocial activities. When lack of neighborhood organization combines with little or no parent involvement, youth antisocial activity is especially high (Elliott et al., 1996).

The resources offered by neighborhoods are important for development and well-being at all ages. This city park permits residents to gather for weekend picnics and festivals, where the opportunity to get to know neighbors in a relaxed, safe atmosphere fosters pleasurable interaction and social support. *(Jeff Dunne/The Picture Cube)*

■ **SCHOOLS.** Unlike the informal worlds of family and neighborhood, school is a formal institution designed to transmit knowledge and skills that children need to become productive members of their society. Children spend many long hours in school—6 hours a day, 5 days a week, 36 weeks a year—totaling, altogether, about 15,000 hours by graduation from high school. In fact, if we consider that during the first 5 years of life, many more children are entering day care centers and preschools that are "school-like," then the impact of schooling begins earlier and is even more powerful than these figures suggest.

Schools themselves are complex social systems bringing together a wide variety of factors that affect many aspects of development. Schools differ in the quality of their physical environments—size of the student body, number of children per class, and how much space is available for work and play. They also vary in their educational philosophies—whether teachers regard children as passive learners to be molded by adult instruction; as active, curious beings who determine their own learning; or as collaborative partners in acquiring new skills. Finally, social life varies from school to school—for example, in the degree to which pupils are cooperative or competitive; in the extent to which children of different ethnic groups spend time together; and in whether classrooms, hallways, and play yards are safe, humane settings or riddled with violence. We will discuss each of these aspects of schooling in later chapters.

Consistent with the mesosystem in ecological systems theory, regular contact between families and teachers supports children's development at all ages. In childhood and adolescence, parents who are involved in school activities and who attend parent–teacher conferences have children who show superior academic achievement (Grolnick & Slowiaczek, 1994; Stevenson & Baker, 1987). Phone calls and visits to school are common

Regular contact between parents and teachers supports children's development. This mother visits her child's classroom and looks on as the teacher explains how second graders are learning to tell time. As a result, the mother finds out how to foster her daughter's mastery of an important skill. Notice how the younger brother benefits as well! *(Will Hart)*

among higher-SES parents, whose backgrounds and values are similar to those of teachers. In contrast, low-SES and ethnic minority parents often feel uncomfortable about coming to school (Delgado-Gaitan, 1992, 1994; Heath, 1989). Contact between parents and teachers is also more frequent in small towns, where most citizens know each other and schools serve as centers of community life (Peshkin, 1994). Extra steps must be taken with low-income, poverty-stricken, and minority families and in large urban areas to build supportive ties between families and schools.

■ **TOWNS AND CITIES.** Besides family–school contact, other aspects of life are different for children growing up in small towns than in large cities. A well-known study examined the kinds of community settings children entered and the roles they played in a midwestern town with a population of 700 (Barker, 1955). Many settings existed, in which children were granted important responsibilities. For example, they helped stock shelves at Kane's Grocery Store, played in the town band, and operated the snow plow when help was short. As children joined in these activities, they did so alongside adults, who taught them the skills they needed to become responsible members of the community.

Of course, children in small towns cannot visit aquariums, take rides on subways and buses, enjoy a variety of ethnic foods, or attend professional baseball games and orchestra concerts on a regular basis. The variety of settings is somewhat reduced compared to large cities. In small towns, however, children's active involvement in the community is likely to be greater. In addition, public places in small towns are relatively safe and secure. Streets and people are familiar, and responsible adults are present in almost all settings to keep an eye on children—a situation hard to match in today's urban environments.

Think back to the case of Zinnia Mae and her three young children, described on page 77. It reveals that community life is especially undermined in high-rise urban housing projects. In these dwellings, social contact is particularly important, since many residents have been uprooted from neighborhoods where they felt a strong sense of cultural identity and belonging. Typically, high rises are heavily populated with young, single mothers who are separated from family and friends by the cost and inconvenience of cross-town transportation. They report intense feelings of loneliness in the small, cramped apartments.

At Heath's (1990) request, Zinnia Mae agreed to tape-record her interactions with her children over a two-year period. In 500 hours of tape, (other than simple directions or questions about what the children were doing) Zinnia Mae started a conversation with Donna and the boys only 18 times. Cut off from community ties, Zinnia Mae found it difficult to join in activities with her children. As a result, Donna and her brothers experienced a barren, understimulating early environment—one very different from the home and community in which Zinnia Mae herself had grown up.

THE CULTURAL CONTEXT

Our discussion in Chapter 1 emphasized that child development can only be fully understood when viewed in the larger cultural context in which it takes place. The following sections expand on this theme by taking up the role of the macrosystem in children's development. First, we discuss ways in which cultural values and life conditions affect the environments in which children grow up. Second, we consider how children are deeply influenced by the political and economic conditions of their nation. We will see that healthy development depends on laws and government programs that shield children from harm and foster their well-being.

■ **CULTURAL VALUES AND PRACTICES.** Cultures shape family interaction, school experiences, and community settings beyond the home—in short, all aspects of the child's daily life. Many of us remain blind to aspects of our own cultural heritage until we see them in relation to the practices of others (Rogoff & Morelli, 1989).

Each semester, I ask my students to think about the question; Who should be responsible for rearing young children? Here are some typical answers: "If parents decide to have a baby, then they should be ready to care for it." "Most people are not happy about others intruding into family life." These statements reflect a widely held opinion in the United States—that the care and rearing of young children, and paying for that care, are the duty of parents, and only parents (Rickel & Becker, 1997; Scarr, 1996; Shweder & Haidt, 1993).

This autonomous view of the family has a long history—one in which independence, self-reliance, and the privacy of family life emerged as central American values. It is one reason, among others, that the American public has been slow to accept the idea of publicly supported family benefits, such as health insurance and day care (Hayghe, 1990). It has also contributed to the large number of American families that remain poor, despite the fact that their members are gainfully employed (Chase-Lansdale & Vinovskis, 1995).

Although many Americans value independence and privacy, cooperative structures can be found in the United States. In large industrialized nations like ours, not all citizens share the same values. **Subcultures** exist—groups of people with beliefs and customs that differ from those of the larger culture. The values and practices of many ethnic minority groups help protect their members from the harmful effects of poverty. A case in point is the African-American family. As the Cultural Influences box on page 82 indicates, the black cultural tradition of **extended-family households,** in which parent and child and their nearest kin (for example, grandparents, aunts, or uncles) live together, is a vital feature of black family life that has enabled its members to survive, despite a long history of prejudice and economic deprivation. Active and involved extended families also characterize Asian-American, Native-American, and Hispanic subcultures (Harrison et al., 1994).

Consider our discussion so far, and you will see that it reflects a broad dimension on which cultures and subcultures differ: the extent to which *individualism versus collectivism* is emphasized. In **collectivist societies,** people define themselves as part of a group and stress group over individual goals. In **individualistic societies,** people think of themselves as separate entities and are largely concerned with their own personal needs (Triandis, 1989; Triandis et al., 1988). Although individualism tends to increase as cultures become more complex, cross-national differences remain. The United States is more individualistic than most other industrialized nations. As we will see in the next section, collectivist versus individualistic values have a powerful impact on a nation's approach to protecting children's development and well-being.

■ **PUBLIC POLICIES AND CHILD DEVELOPMENT.** When widespread social problems arise, such as poverty, homelessness, hunger, and disease, nations attempt to solve them by developing **public policies**—laws and government programs designed to improve the condition of children and families. For example, when poverty increases and families become homeless, a country might decide to build more low-cost housing, raise the minimum wage, and increase welfare benefits. When reports indicate that many children are not achieving well in school, federal and state governments might grant more tax money to school districts and make sure that help reaches children who need it most.

The United States is among the wealthiest of nations and has the broadest knowledge base for intervening effectively in children's lives. Still, American public policies safeguarding children and youths have lagged behind those in other developed nations. As Table 2.7 reveals, the United States does not rank among the top countries on any key measure of children's health and well-being.

The problems of American children and youths extend beyond the indicators in the table. For example, 20 percent have no health insurance, making them the largest segment of the uninsured population (Children's Defense Fund, 1998). Furthermore, the

subculture
A group of people with beliefs and customs that differ from those of the larger culture.

extended-family household
A household in which parent and child live with one or more adult relatives.

collectivist societies
Societies in which people define themselves as part of a group and stress group over individual goals.

individualistic societies
Societies in which people think of themselves as separate entities and are largely concerned with their own personal needs.

public policies
Laws and government programs designed to improve current conditions.

CULTURAL INFLUENCES

THE AFRICAN-AMERICAN EXTENDED FAMILY

The African-American extended family can be traced to the African heritage of most black Americans. In many African societies, newly married couples do not start their own households. Instead, they marry into a large extended family that assists its members with all aspects of daily life. This tradition of a broad network of kinship ties traveled to the United States during the period of slavery. Since then, it has served as a protective shield against the destructive impact of poverty and racial prejudice on African-American family life (McAdoo, 1993). Today, more black than white adults have relatives other than their own children living in the same household. African-American parents also see more kin during the week and perceive them as more important figures in their lives, respecting the advice of relatives and caring deeply about what they think is important (Wilson et al., 1995).

By providing emotional support and sharing income and essential resources, the African-American extended family helps reduce the stress of poverty and single parenthood. In addition, extended-family members often help with child rearing (Pearson et al., 1990). The presence of grandmothers in the households of many African-American teenagers and their infants protects babies from the negative influence of an overwhelmed and inexperienced mother. In one study, black grandmothers displayed more sensitive interaction with the babies of their teenage daughters than did the teenage mothers themselves. The grandmothers also provided basic information about infant development to these young mothers (Stevens, 1984). Furthermore, black adolescent mothers living in extended families are more likely to complete high school and get a job and less likely to be on welfare than are mothers living on their own—factors that return to benefit children's well-being (Trent & Harlan, 1994).

For single mothers who were very young at the time of their child's birth, extended-family living continues to be associated with more positive mother–child interaction during the preschool years. Otherwise, establishing an independent household with the help of nearby relatives is related to improved child rearing. Perhaps this arrangement permits the more mature mother who has developed effective parenting skills to implement them (Chase-Lansdale, Brooks-Gunn, & Zamsky, 1994). In families with adolescents, kinship support increases the likelihood of effective parenting, which, in turn, is related to self-reliance, emotional well-being, and reduced delinquency (Taylor & Roberts, 1995).

Finally, the African-American extended family plays an important role in transmitting black cultural values to children. Compared to African Americans who live in nuclear family households (which include only parents and their children), extended-family arrangements place more emphasis on cooperation and moral and religious values (Tolson & Wilson, 1990). Older black adults, such as grandparents and great-grandparents, are also more likely to possess a strong ethnic identity and to regard educating children about their African heritage as an important part of socialization (Thornton & Taylor, 1988). These influences strengthen family bonds, protect children's development, and increase the chances that the extended-family lifestyle will carry over to the next generation.

Strong bonds with extended-family members have helped to protect the development of many African-American children growing up under conditions of poverty and single parenthood. *(Karen Kasmauski/Woodfin Camp & Associates)*

TABLE 2.7

How Does the United States Compare to Other Nations on Indicators of Child Health and Well-Being?

INDICATOR	U.S. RANK	SOME COUNTRIES THE UNITED STATES TRAILS
Childhood poverty[a]	8th (among 8 industrialized nations considered)	Australia, Canada, Germany, Great Britain, Norway, Sweden, Switzerland
Infant deaths in the first year of life	22nd (worldwide)	Hong Kong, Ireland, Singapore, Spain
Low-birth-weight newborns	20th (worldwide)	Bulgaria, Egypt, Greece, Iran, Jordan, Kuwait, Paraguay, Romania, Saudi Arabia
Percentage of young children immunized against measles	43rd (worldwide)	Chile, Czechoslovakia, Jordan, Poland, Romania
Expenditures on education as percentage of gross national product[b]	14th (among 16 industrialized nations considered)	Canada, France, Great Britain, the Netherlands, Sweden
Teenage pregnancy rate	11th (among 11 industrialized nations considered)	Australia, Canada, Czech Republic, France, New Zealand, Sweden

[a]The U.S. child poverty rate of nearly 22 percent is more than twice that of any of these nations. For example, the rate is 9 percent in Australia, 9.3 percent in Canada, 4.6 percent in France, and 1.6 percent in Sweden.

[b]Gross national product is the value of all goods and services produced by a nation during a specified time period. It serves as an overall measure of a nation's wealth.

Sources: Bellamy, 1997; Central Intelligence Agency, 1996; Children's Defense Fund, 1998; Harris, 1997; Sivard, 1996.

United States has been slow to move toward national standards and funding for day care. According to recent evidence, much day care is substandard in quality (Helburn, 1995; Phillips et al., 1994). In families affected by divorce, weak enforcement of child support payments heightens poverty in mother-headed families. By the time American young people finish high school, many do not have the educational preparation they need to contribute fully to society. Non-college-bound youths generally lack vocational skills required for well-paid jobs. And about 13 percent of adolescents leave high school without a diploma. If they do not return to finish their education, they are at risk for lifelong poverty (Children's Defense Fund, 1998).

Why has the United States not yet created conditions that protect the development of its youngest citizens? As noted earlier, the American ideals of self-reliance and privacy have made government hesitant to become involved in family matters. In addition, there is less consensus among Americans than citizens of Western European nations on issues of child and family policy (Wilensky, 1983). Finally, good social programs are expensive, and they must compete for a fair share of a country's economic resources. Children can easily remain unrecognized in this process, since they cannot vote or speak out to protect their own interests, as adult citizens do. Instead, they must rely on the good will of others to become an important government priority.

■ **CONTEMPORARY PROGRESS IN MEETING CHILDREN'S NEEDS.** Public policies aimed at fostering children's development can be justified on two important grounds. The first is humanitarian—children's basic rights as human beings (Huston, 1991). In 1989, the United Nations' General Assembly drew up the Convention on the Rights of the Child, an international treaty written in the form of a legal agreement among nations. It commits each participating country to work toward guaranteeing children environments that foster their development and protect them from harm. To find out more about the Convention, refer to the Social Issues box on page 84. Second, child-oriented policies can be justified on the basis that children are the parents, workers, and citizens of tomorrow. Investing in them can yield valuable returns to a

SOCIAL ISSUES · THE U.N. CONVENTION ON THE RIGHTS OF THE CHILD

The U.N. Convention on the Rights of the Child is the first legally binding human rights treaty to recognize the civil, political, economic, social, and cultural rights of children. Many nations helped draft it, making it a rich blend of views that affirm children's rights to protection from harm, to environments that support their development, and to participation and self-determination in their community (Murphy-Berman & Weisz, 1996).

When a nation's legislature ratifies the Convention, it agrees to meet or work toward meeting an extensive list of obligations to children. Each reflects the Convention's basic themes—that children's best interests be primary in any actions concerning them, that they be accorded rights in a manner consistent with their capacities, and that their dignity be respected. (See the Caregiving Concerns table below for examples.)

To accomplish its goals, the Convention established an international committee of experts to monitor participating nations' progress toward guaranteeing children's rights. Within 2 years of ratifying the Convention and every 5 years thereafter, each country must submit a report to the committee on the measures it has taken. It must also make that report widely available to its citizens. In this way, the Convention tries to create a constructive dialogue aimed at improving children's condition.

Since its initiation in 1989, the Convention has been ratified by more than 180 nations. Although the United States played a crucial role in drawing up the document, it is one of the very few countries that has not yet ratified it. American individualism has stood in the way. Opponents maintain that the Convention's provisions will shift the burden of child rearing from the family to the state (Levesque, 1996;

Limber & Wilcox, 1996). Supporters counter that this belief is unfounded, since the Convention stresses parents' responsibilities while also recognizing that society must actively support children and families.

Yet another frequently voiced reservation is that the Convention will do little to change the lives of American children and families. But many experts disagree, arguing that an international consensus on children's rights can energize change—and has already done so in many parts of the world (Limber & Flekkøy, 1995). At present, the United States is in compliance with many aspects of the Convention but falls far short of its total expectations. Even in the absence of ratification, the Convention offers lawmakers and child advocates a valuable guide for devising policies that ensure children safety, personhood, and favorable environments for development.

CAREGIVING CONCERNS

A Sampling of Childrens' Rights Specified in the U.N. Convention on the Rights of the Child

CATEGORY OF RIGHTS	EXAMPLES
Protection from harm	Protection from all forms of abuse and neglect
	Protection from participation in armed conflict
Survival and development	The highest attainable standard of health
	A standard of living adequate for physical, mental, spiritual, moral, and social development
	A happy, understanding, and loving family environment
	Free and compulsory education that develops physical abilities, the intellect, personality, and respect for one's cultural identity, one's homeland, other civilizations, and the environment
	Rest, leisure, and age-appropriate play and recreational activities; participation in cultural activities and the arts
Community participation and self-determination	Freedom to seek, receive, and impart information and ideas of all kinds, subject to respect for the rights of others, public health, and morals
	Freedom to express personal opinions in all matters affecting the child
	Protection against interference with privacy, family, home, and correspondence
	Freedom of thought, conscience, and religion, subject to appropriate parental guidance and national law and in a manner consistent with the child's developing capacities

nation's quality of life. In contrast, failure to invest in children can result in "economic inefficiency, loss of productivity, shortages in needed skills, high health care costs, growing prison costs, and a nation that will be less safe, less caring, and less free" (Hernandez, 1994, p. 20).

To be sure, a wide variety of government-sponsored child and family programs do exist in the United States, and we will see many examples in later chapters. But they are largely crisis oriented, aimed at handling the most severe family difficulties rather than preventing problems before they happen. Furthermore, funding for these efforts has waxed and waned and been seriously threatened at various times. In most cases, only a minority of needy children and youths are helped (Harris, 1996).

Nevertheless, new policy initiatives are under way that promise to improve the status of American children. For example, extra federal dollars have been allocated for child care for children of low-income employed parents (although the amount granted is still far short of the need). A new federal law increases the ease with which payroll deductions can be made when a noncustodial parent fails to make child support payments after divorce. Furthermore, public health insurance coverage for low-income pregnant women and their children has recently expanded. And beginning in 1994, all medically uninsured children were guaranteed free vaccinations, a policy that sparked a dramatic rise in the percentage of 2-year-olds fully immunized (Still, as Table 2.7 shows, the U.S. immunization rate falls behind that of many other nations.) (Children's Defense Fund, 1998).

Child-related professional organizations are also taking a strong leadership role. In the absence of federal guidelines for high-quality day care, the National Association for the Education of Young Children (NAEYC, a 100,000-member organization of early childhood educators) established a voluntary accreditation system for preschool and day care centers. It grants special professional recognition to programs that meet its rigorous standards of quality. Efforts like this are serving as inspiring models for the nation as a whole.

Finally, child development specialists are joining with concerned citizens to become advocates for children's causes. Over the past two decades, several influential interest groups with children's well-being as their central purpose have emerged in the United States. One of the most vigorous is the Children's Defense Fund, a private nonprofit organization founded by Marion Wright Edelman in 1973. It engages in research, public education, legal action, drafting of legislation, congressional testimony, and community organizing. Each year, it publishes *The State of America's Children*, which provides a comprehensive analysis of the current condition of children, government-sponsored programs serving them, and proposals for improving child and family programs. As efforts like these continue, there is every reason to expect increased responsiveness to children's needs in the years to come.

In 1973, Marion Wright Edelman founded the Children's Defense Fund, a private, nonprofit organization that provides a strong, effective voice for American children, who cannot vote, lobby, or speak for themselves. Edelman continues to serve as president of the Children's Defense Fund today. (Westenberger /Liaiso, USA)

ASK YOURSELF . . .

■ *On one of your trips to the local shopping center, you see a father getting very angry at his young son. Using ecological systems theory, list as many factors as you can that might account for the father's behavior.*

■ *Links between family and community are essential for children's well-being. Provide examples and research findings from our discussion that support this idea.*

■ *Check your local newspaper and one or two national news magazines to see how often articles appear on the condition of children and families. Why is it important for researchers to communicate with the general public about children's needs?*

BRIEF REVIEW

Just as complex as heredity are the environments in which children grow up. First and foremost is the family—a system of mutually influencing relationships that changes over time. Child rearing in families is modified by socioeconomic status, and it is seriously threatened by poverty and homelessness. A variety of additional contexts—neighborhoods that offer worthwhile activities and frequent contact with peers and adults, high-quality schools that establish ties with families, and communities in which children participate actively—support development. Cultural values and practices—in particular, the extent to which collectivism versus individualism is emphasized—have a substantial impact on environmental contexts for development. In the complex world in which we live, favorable public policies are essential for protecting children's development and well-being.

UNDERSTANDING THE RELATIONSHIP BETWEEN HEREDITY AND ENVIRONMENT

So far in this chapter, we have discussed a wide variety of hereditary and environmental influences, each of which has the power to alter the course of development. Yet many examples exist in which children born into the same family (and who therefore share genes and environments) are quite different in characteristics. We also know that some children are affected more than others by their environments. Cases exist in which a child provided with all the advantages in life does poorly, whereas a second child exposed to the worst of rearing conditions does well. How do scientists explain the impact of heredity and environment when they seem to work in so many different ways?

All child development specialists agree that both heredity and environment are involved in every aspect of development. There is no real controversy on this point because an environment is always needed for genetic information to be expressed. But for polygenic traits (due to many genes) such as intelligence and personality, scientists are a long way from knowing the precise hereditary influences involved. They must study the impact of genes on these characteristics indirectly, and the nature–nurture controversy remains unresolved because researchers do not agree on how heredity and environment influence these complex characteristics.

Some believe that it is useful and possible to answer the question of *how much* each factor contributes to differences among children. These researchers use special methods to find out which factor plays the major role. A second group of investigators regards the question of which factor is more important as neither useful nor answerable. They believe that heredity and environment do not make separate contributions to behavior. Instead, they are always related, and the real question we need to explore is *how* they work together. Let's consider each of these two positions in turn.

THE QUESTION, "HOW MUCH?"

Two methods—heritability estimates and concordance rates—are used to infer the importance of heredity in complex human characteristics. Let's look closely at the information these procedures yield, along with their limitations.

■ **HERITABILITY.** **Heritability estimates** measure the extent to which individual differences in complex traits, such as intelligence and personality, are due to genetic factors. They are obtained from **kinship studies,** which compare the characteristics of family members. The most common type of kinship study compares identical twins, who share all their genes, with fraternal twins, who share only some. If people who are genetically more alike are also more similar in intelligence and personality test scores, then the researcher assumes that heredity plays an important role.

Kinship studies of intelligence provide some of the most controversial findings in the field of child development. Some experts claim a strong role for heredity, whereas others believe that genetic factors are barely involved. Currently, most researchers support a moderate role for heredity. When many twin studies are examined, correlations between the scores of identical twins are consistently higher than those of fraternal twins. In a summary of more than 30 such investigations, the correlation for intelligence was .86 for identical twins and .60 for fraternal twins (Bouchard & McGue, 1981).

Researchers use a complex statistical procedure to compare these correlations, arriving at a heritability estimate ranging from 0 to 1.00. The value for intelligence is about .50, which indicates that half the variation in intelligence among children can be explained by differences in their genetic makeup (Plomin, 1994a). The fact that the intelligence of adopted children is more strongly related to the scores of their biological parents than to

heritability estimate
A statistic that measures the extent to which individual differences in complex traits, such as intelligence or personality, are due to genetic factors.

kinship studies
Studies comparing the characteristics of family members to determine the importance of heredity in complex human characteristics.

those of their adoptive parents offers further support for the role of heredity (Horn, 1983; Scarr & Weinberg, 1983).

Heritability research also reveals that genetic factors are important in personality. In fact, for personality traits that have been studied a great deal, such as sociability, emotional expressiveness, and activity level, heritability estimates are at about the same moderate level as that reported for intelligence (Braungart et al., 1992; Loehlin, 1992).

■ CONCORDANCE. A second measure that has been used to infer the contribution of heredity to complex characteristics is the **concordance rate.** It refers to the percentage of instances in which both twins show a trait when it is present in one twin. Researchers typically use concordance to study the contribution of heredity to emotional and behavioral disorders, which can be judged as either present or absent.

A concordance rate ranges from 0 to 100 percent. A score of 0 indicates that if one twin has the trait, the other twin never has it. A score of 100 means that if one twin has the trait, the other one always has it. When a concordance rate is much higher for identical twins than for fraternal twins, then heredity is believed to play a major role. As Figure 2.7 reveals, twin studies of schizophrenia (a disorder involving delusions and hallucinations, difficulty distinguishing fantasy from reality, and irrational and inappropriate behaviors) and severe depression show this pattern of findings. Look carefully at the figure, and you will see that the evidence for heredity is less convincing for delinquency and criminality. In that case, the difference between concordance rates for identical and fraternal twins is not great enough to support a strong genetic role (Plomin, 1994a). Once again, adoption studies lend support to these results. Biological relatives of schizophrenic and depressed adoptees are more likely to share the disorder than are adoptive relatives (Loehlin, Willerman, & Horn, 1988).

Taken together, concordance and adoption research suggests that the strong tendency for schizophrenia and depression to run in families is partly due to genetic factors. However, we also know that environment is involved, since the concordance rate for identical twins would have to be 100 percent if heredity were the only influence operating. Already we have seen that environmental stresses, such as poverty, family conflict, and a disorganized home and neighborhood life, are often associated with emotional and behavior problems. We will encounter many more examples of this relationship in later chapters.

■ LIMITATIONS OF HERITABILITY AND CONCORDANCE. Although heritability estimates and concordance rates provide evidence that genetic factors contribute to complex human characteristics, questions have been raised about their accuracy. Both measures are heavily influenced by the range of environments to which twin pairs are exposed. For example, identical twins reared together under highly similar conditions have more strongly correlated intelligence test scores than those reared apart in very different environments. When the former are used to compute heritability estimates, the higher correlation causes the importance of heredity to be overestimated (Hoffman, 1994).

To overcome this difficulty, researchers try to find twins who have been reared apart in adoptive families. But few separated twin pairs are available for study, and when they are, social service agencies often place them in advantaged homes that are alike in many ways (Eisenberg, 1998). Because the environments of most twin pairs do not represent the broad range of environments found in the general population, it is often difficult to generalize heritability and concordance findings to the population as a whole.

Heritability estimates are controversial measures because they can easily be misapplied. For example, high heritabilities have been used to suggest that ethnic differences in

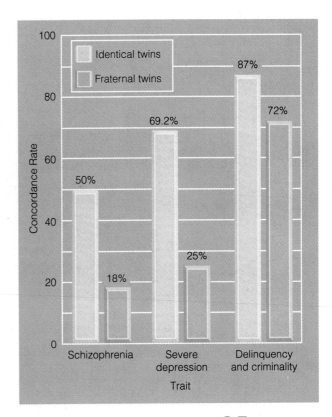

FIGURE **2.7**

Concordance rates for schizophrenia, severe depression, and delinquency and criminality. Heredity plays some role in schizophrenia and is even more influential in severe depression, since the concordance rate is much higher for identical than fraternal twins. Heredity contributes much less to delinquency and criminality, since the difference in concordance rates for identical and fraternal twins is relatively small. *(From Gottesman, 1991; Gottesman, Carey, & Hanson, 1983; McGuffin & Sargeant, 1991.)*

concordance rate
The percentage of instances in which both members of a twin pair show a trait when it is present in one pair member. Used to study the role of heredity in emotional and behavioral disorders, which can be judged as either present or absent.

Identical twins Jim Lewis and Jim Springer were separated 4 weeks after birth, grew up in different homes, and led separate adult lives until, at age 39, they were reunited. The two Jims discovered they were alike in many ways. Both drove the same model car, chain smoked, chewed their fingernails, and vacationed at the beach. On personality tests, they scored almost exactly the same. The study of identical twins reared apart reveals that heredity contributes to many psychological characteristics. Nevertheless, not all separated twins match up as well as this pair, and generalizing from twin evidence to the population as a whole is controversial. *(D. Gordon/*Time *Magazine)*

intelligence, such as the poorer performance of black compared to white children, have a genetic basis (Jensen, 1969, 1985b). Yet this line of reasoning is widely regarded as incorrect. Heritabilities computed on mostly white twin samples do not tell us what is responsible for test score differences between ethnic groups. We have already indicated that large economic and cultural differences are involved. As we will see in Chapter 12, research shows that when black children are adopted into economically advantaged homes at an early age, their scores are well above average and substantially higher than those of children growing up in impoverished families.

Perhaps the most serious criticism of heritability estimates and concordance rates has to do with their usefulness. Although they are interesting statistics that tell us that heredity is undoubtedly involved in complex traits such as intelligence and personality, they give us no precise information about how these traits develop or how children might respond when exposed to environments designed to help them develop as far as possible (Bronfenbrenner & Ceci, 1994; Wachs, 1994). Investigators who conduct heritability research argue that their studies are a first step. As more evidence accumulates to show that heredity underlies important human characteristics, then scientists can begin to ask better questions—about the specific genes involved, the way they affect development, and how their impact is modified by environmental factors.

THE QUESTION, "HOW?"

According to a second perspective, heredity and environment cannot be divided into separate influences. Instead, behavior is the result of a dynamic interplay between these two forces. How do heredity and environment work together to affect development? Several important concepts shed light on this complex question.

■ **REACTION RANGE.** The first of these ideas is **range of reaction** (Gottesman, 1963). It emphasizes that each person responds to the environment in a unique way because of his or her genetic makeup. Let's explore this idea by taking a look at Figure 2.8. Reaction range can apply to any characteristic; here it is illustrated for intelligence. Notice that when environments vary from extremely unstimulating to highly enriched, Ben's intelligence increases steadily, Linda's rises sharply and then falls off, and Ron's begins to increase only after the environment becomes modestly stimulating.

Reaction range highlights two important points about the relationship between heredity and environment. First, it shows that because each of us has a unique genetic makeup, we respond quite differently to the same environment. Look carefully at Figure 2.8, and notice how a poor environment results in similarly low scores for all three children. But Linda is by far the best-performing child when environments provide an intermediate level of stimulation. And when environments are highly enriched, Ben does best, followed by Ron, both of whom now exceed Linda. Second, sometimes different

range of reaction
Each person's unique, genetically determined response to a range of environmental conditions.

canalization
The tendency of heredity to restrict the development of some characteristics to just one or a few outcomes.

genetic–environmental correlation
The idea that heredity influences the environments to which individuals are exposed.

genetic–environmental combinations can make two children look the same! For example, if Linda is reared in a minimally stimulating environment, her score will be about 100—average for children in general. Ben and Ron can also obtain this score, but to do so they must grow up in a fairly enriched home.

The concept of range of reaction tells us that children differ in their range of possible responses to the environment. And it illustrates the meaning of the phrase *heredity and environment interact,* since it shows that unique blends of heredity and environment lead to both similarities and differences in behavior (Wahlsten, 1994).

■ **CANALIZATION.** The concept of canalization provides another way of understanding how heredity and environment combine. **Canalization** is the tendency of heredity to restrict the development of some characteristics to just one or a few outcomes. A behavior that is strongly canalized follows a genetically set growth plan, and only strong environmental forces can change it (Waddington, 1957). For example, infant perceptual and motor development seems to be strongly canalized, since all normal human babies eventually roll over, reach for objects, sit up, crawl, and walk. It takes extreme conditions to modify these behaviors or cause them not to appear. In contrast, intelligence and personality are less strongly canalized, since they respond easily to changes in the environment.

Recently, scientists expanded the notion of canalization to include environmental influences. We now know that environments can also limit development (Gottlieb, 1991). For example, when children are exposed to harmful environments early in life, there may be little that later experiences can do to change characteristics (such as intelligence) that were quite flexible to begin with. In Chapter 3, we will see that this is the case for babies exposed prenatally to high levels of alcohol, radiation, or oxygen deprivation. And later in this book, we will find that it is also true for children who spend many years living in extremely deprived homes and institutions (Turkheimer & Gottesman, 1991).

Using the concept of canalization, we learn that genes restrict the development of some characteristics more than others. And over time, even very flexible behaviors can become fixed and canalized, depending on the environments to which children were exposed.

■ **GENETIC–ENVIRONMENTAL CORRELATION.** Nature and nurture work together in still another way. Sandra Scarr and Kathleen McCartney (1983) point out that a major problem in trying to separate heredity and environment is that they are often correlated. According to the concept of **genetic–environmental correlation,** our genes influence the environments to which we are exposed. In support of this idea, a recent study showed that the greater the genetic similarity between pairs of adolescents, the more alike they were in child rearing experiences, including parental discipline, affection, conflict, and monitoring of the young person's activities (Plomin et al., 1994).

These findings indicate that children's heredity plays a role in molding their experiences. The way this happens changes with development.

Passive and Evocative Correlation.   At younger ages, two types of genetic–environmental correlation are common. The first is called *passive* correlation because the child has no control over it. Early on, parents provide environments that are influenced by their

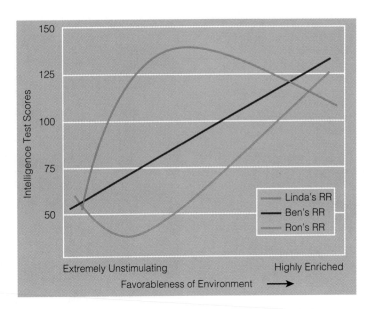

FIGURE 2.8

Intellectual ranges of reaction (RR) for three children in environments that vary from extremely unstimulating to highly enriched. Each child, due to his or her genetic makeup, responds differently as quality of the environment changes. Ben's intelligence increases steadily, Linda's rises sharply and then falls off, and Ron's begins to increase only after the environment becomes modestly stimulating. *(Adapted from Wahlsten, 1994.)*

This father is an accomplished ice skater who exposes his son to a stimulating ice-skating environment. In addition, the boy may have inherited his father's talent for ice skating. When heredity and environment are correlated, they jointly foster the same capacities, and the influence of one cannot be separated from the influence of the other. (Le Duc/ Monkmeyer Press)

own heredity. For example, parents who are good athletes are likely to emphasize outdoor activities and enroll their children in swimming and gymnastics lessons. Besides getting exposed to an "athletic environment," the children may have inherited their parents' athletic ability. As a result, they are likely to become good athletes for both genetic and environmental reasons.

The second type of genetic–environmental correlation is *evocative*. A child evokes responses from others that are influenced by the child's heredity, and these responses strengthen the child's original style of responding. For example, an active, friendly baby is likely to receive more social stimulation from those around her than is a passive, quiet infant. And a cooperative, attentive preschooler will probably receive more patient and sensitive interactions from parents than an inattentive, distractible child.

Active Correlation.   At older ages, *active* genetic–environmental correlation becomes common. As children extend their experiences beyond the immediate family to school, neighborhood, and community and are given the freedom to make more of their own choices, they play an increasingly active role in seeking out environments that fit with their genetic tendencies. The well-coordinated, muscular child spends more time at after-school sports, the musically talented youngster joins the school orchestra and practices his violin, and the intellectually curious child is a well-known visitor at her local library.

This tendency to actively choose environments that complement our heredity is called **niche-picking** (Scarr & McCartney, 1983). Infants and young children cannot do much niche-picking, since adults select environments for them. In contrast, older children and adolescents are much more in charge of their own environments. The niche-picking idea explains why pairs of identical twins reared apart during childhood and later reunited often find, to their great surprise, that they have similar hobbies, food preferences, friendship choices, and vocations (Bouchard et al., 1990; Plomin, 1994a). It also helps us understand some curious longitudinal findings indicating that identical twins become somewhat more similar and fraternal twins and adopted siblings less similar from infancy to adolescence (Scarr & Weinberg, 1983; Wilson, 1983). The influence of heredity and environment is not constant but changes over time. With age, genetic factors may become more important in determining the environments we experience and choose for ourselves.

A major reason child development researchers are interested in the nature–nurture issue is that they want to find ways to improve environments to help children develop as far as possible. The concepts of range of reaction, canalization, and niche-picking remind us that development is best understood as a series of complex exchanges between nature and nurture. When a characteristic is strongly determined by heredity, it can still be modified. However, children cannot be changed in any way we might desire. The success of any attempt to improve development depends on the characteristics we want to change, the genetic makeup of the child, and the type and timing of our intervention.

ASK YOURSELF . . .

■ *A researcher wants to know whether genetic factors contribute to bedwetting in middle childhood. Which method of inferring the importance of heredity in complex human characteristics could help answer this question?*

■ *Bianca's parents are both accomplished musicians. Bianca began taking piano lessons when she was 4 years old and was accompanying her school choir by age 10. When she reached adolescence, she asked her parents if she could attend a special music high school. Explain how genetic and environmental factors work together to promote Bianca's talent.*

niche-picking
A type of genetic–environmental correlation in which individuals actively choose environments that complement their heredity.

Summary

GENETIC FOUNDATIONS

What are genes, and how are they transmitted from one generation to the next?

- Each individual's **phenotype,** or directly observable characteristics, is a product of both **genotype** and environment.

- **Chromosomes,** rodlike structures within the cell nucleus, contain our hereditary endowment. Along their length are **genes,** segments of **DNA** that make us distinctly human and influence our development and characteristics.

- **Gametes,** or sex cells, are produced by the process of cell division known as **meiosis. Crossing over** and independent assortment of chromosomes ensure that each zygote receives a unique set of genes from each parent. Once sperm and ovum unite, the resulting **zygote** starts to develop into a complex human being through cell duplication, or **mitosis.**

- If the fertilizing sperm carries an X chromosome, the child will be a girl; if it contains a Y chromosome, a boy will be born. **Fraternal,** or **dizygotic, twins** result when two ova are released from the mother's ovaries and each is fertilized. In contrast, **identical,** or **monozygotic, twins** develop when a zygote divides in two during the early stages of cell duplication.

Describe various patterns of genetic inheritance.

- **Dominant–recessive** and **codominant** relationships are patterns of inheritance that apply to many traits controlled by single genes. In dominant-recessive inheritance, **heterozygous** individuals with one recessive **allele** are **carriers** of the recessive trait.

- When recessive disorders are **X-linked** (carried on the X chromosome), males are more likely to be affected. **Genetic imprinting** is a pattern of inheritance in which one parent's allele is activated, regardless of its makeup.

- Unfavorable genes arise from **mutations,** which can occur spontaneously or be induced by hazardous environmental agents.

- Human traits that vary continuously, such as intelligence and personality, are **polygenic,** or influenced by many genes. Since the genetic principles involved are unknown, scientists must study the influence of heredity on these characteristics indirectly.

Describe major chromosomal abnormalities, and explain how they occur.

- Most chromosomal abnormalities are due to errors in meiosis. The most common chromosomal disorder is **Down syndrome,** which results in physical defects and mental retardation.

- Disorders of the **sex chromosomes** are milder than defects of the **autosomes.** Contrary to popular belief, males with XYY syndrome are not prone to aggression. Studies of children with triple X, Klinefelter, and Turner syndromes reveal that adding to or subtracting from the usual number of X chromosomes leads to specific intellectual problems.

REPRODUCTIVE CHOICES

What procedures are available to assist prospective parents in having healthy children?

- **Genetic counseling** helps couples at risk for giving birth to children with genetic abnormalities decide whether or not to conceive. **Prenatal diagnostic methods** make early detection of genetic problems possible. Although reproductive technologies, such as donor insemination, in vitro fertilization, and surrogate motherhood, permit many individuals to become parents who otherwise would not, they raise serious legal and ethical concerns.

- Many parents who cannot conceive or who have a high likelihood of transmitting a genetic disorder decide to adopt. Although adopted children have more learning and emotional problems than children in general, in the long run most fare quite well.

ENVIRONMENTAL CONTEXTS FOR DEVELOPMENT

Describe family functioning from the perspective of ecological systems theory, along with aspects of the environment that support family well-being and children's development.

- Just as complex as heredity are the environments in which children grow up. The family is the child's first and foremost context for development. Ecological systems theory emphasizes that the behaviors of each family member affect those of others. The family system is also dynamic, constantly adjusting to the development of its members and to societal change.

- Two aspects of parenting promote effective development at all ages: (1) responsiveness, and (2) reasonable demands for mature behavior. Although warm, moderately demanding child rearing is a common pattern around the world, it is affected by ethnicity and **socioeconomic status (SES).** Effective parenting, along with all aspects of children's development, is seriously undermined by poverty and homelessness.

- Children profit from supportive ties between the family and the surrounding environment. Neighborhoods that provide constructive leisure time activities, high-quality schools that communicate often with parents, and communities that promote children's active participation alongside adults enhance child development.

- The values and life conditions of cultures and **subcultures** mold the environments in which children grow up. **Extended-family households,** in which parent and

Summary (continued)

child live with one or more adult relatives, are common among ethnic minorities. They protect children's development under conditions of high life stress.

- In the complex world in which we live, children's well-being depends on favorable **public policies.** Effective social programs are influenced by many factors, including cultural values that stress **collectivism** over **individualism,** a nation's economic resources, and organizations and individuals that work for children's causes.

UNDERSTANDING THE RELATIONSHIP BETWEEN HEREDITY AND ENVIRONMENT

Explain the various ways in which heredity and environment may combine to influence complex traits.

- Scientists do not agree on how heredity and environment influence complex characteristics, such as intelligence and personality. Some believe that it is useful and possible to determine "how much" each factor contributes to individual differences. These investigators compute heri-

tability estimates and **concordance rates** from **kinship studies.** Although these measures show that genetic factors contribute to such traits as intelligence and personality, questions have been raised about their accuracy and usefulness.

- Other scientists believe that the important question is "how" heredity and environment work together. The concepts of **range of reaction, canalization,** and **genetic–environmental correlation** remind us that development is best understood as a series of complex exchanges between nature and nurture.

Important terms and concepts

allele (p. 57)
autosomes (p. 56)
canalization (p. 88)
carrier (p. 57)
chromosomes (p. 52)
codominance (p. 59)
collectivist societies (p. 81)
concordance rate (p. 87)
crossing over (p. 53)
deoxyribonucleic acid (DNA) (p. 53)
dominant–recessive inheritance (p. 57)
extended-family household (p. 81)
fraternal, or dizygotic, twins (p. 56)
gametes (p. 53)

gene (p. 53)
genetic counseling (p. 65)
genetic imprinting (p. 60)
genetic–environmental correlation (p. 88)
genotype (p. 52)
heritability estimate (p. 86)
heterozygous (p. 57)
homozygous (p. 57)
identical, or monozygotic, twins (p. 56)
individualistic societies (p. 81)
kinship studies (p. 86)
meiosis (p. 53)

mitosis (p. 53)
mutation (p. 62)
niche-picking (p. 90)
phenotype (p. 52)
polygenic inheritance (p. 62)
prenatal diagnostic methods (p. 66)
public policies (p. 81)
range of reaction (p. 88)
sex chromosomes (p. 56)
socioeconomic status (SES) (p. 76)
subculture (p. 81)
X-linked inheritance (p. 59)
zygote (p. 56)

FOR FURTHER INFORMATION AND HELP

GENETICS AND GENETIC DISORDERS

Human Genome Project
*Website: www.ornl.gov/TechResources/
Human_Genome/home/html</1>*

*A website providing comprhehensive informa-
tion about the international Human Genome
Project. Describes project goals and current
status, including progress in DNA sequence
mapping to date and ethical, legal and social
concerns.*

March of Dimes Birth Defects Foundation
(914) 428-7100
Website: www.modimes.org

*Works to prevent genetic disorders and other
birth defects through public education and
community service programs.*

PKU Parents
(415) 457-4632

*Provides support and education for parents of
children with PKU.*

Sickle Cell Disease Association of America
(800) 421-8453

*Provides information and assists local groups
that serve individuals with sickle cell anemia.*

National Down Syndrome Congress
(312) 823-7550
Website: www.carol.net/ndsc

*Assists parents in finding solutions to the
needs of children with Down syndrome. Local
groups exist across the United States.*

INFERTILITY

Resolve, Inc.
(617) 623-0744
Website: www.resolve.org

*Offers counseling referral and support to
persons with fertility problems.*

ADOPTION

National Adoption Information
Clearinghouse
(800) 332-6347
Website: www.naicinfo.com

*Provides information on all aspects of adop-
tion, including children from other countries,
children with special needs, and state and federal adoption laws.*

PUBLIC POLICY

Children's Defense Fund
(800) 424-9602
Website: www.childrensdefense.org

*An active child advocacy organization.
Provides information on the condition of
children and government-sponsored programs serving them.*

National Center for Children in Poverty
(212) 304-7100
Website: cpmcnet.columbia.edu/dept/nccp

*Aims to identify and promote strategies that
reduce the number of young children living in
poverty in the United States. Seeks to achieve
this goal through disseminating information
about early education and maternal and child
health and by proposing new initiatives to
lawmakers.*

"Mother and Child"

Jessica Charlton
5 years, United States

This painting captures the physical and psychological bonds that form as expectant parents await the arrival of a new being. How is the one-celled organism gradually transformed into a baby with the human capacity to play, dream, and create? What factors support or undermine this earliest phase of development? Chapter 3 provides answers to these questions.

PRENATAL

DEVELOPMENT

After months of wondering if the time in their lives was right, Yolanda and Jay decided to have a baby. I met them one fall in my child development class, when Yolanda was just 2 months pregnant. Both were full of questions: "How does the baby grow before birth? When are different organs formed? Has its heart begun to beat? Can it hear, feel, or sense our presence in other ways?" Already, Yolanda and Jay had scanned the shelves of the public library and local bookstores, picking up a dozen or more sources on pregnancy, childbirth, and caring for the newborn.

Most of all, Yolanda and Jay wanted to do everything possible to make sure their baby would be born healthy. At one time, they believed that the developing organism was completely shielded by the uterus from any dangers in the environment. All babies born with problems, they thought, had unfavorable genes. After browsing through several pregnancy books, Yolanda and Jay realized that they were wrong. Yolanda started to wonder about her diet and whether she should keep up her daily aerobics routine. And she asked me whether an aspirin for a headache, a sleeping pill before bedtime, a glass of wine at dinnertime, or a few cups of coffee during study hours might be harmful.

In this chapter, we answer Yolanda and Jay's questions, along with a great many more that scientists have asked about the events before birth. We begin our discussion during the time period before pregnancy with these puzzling questions: Why is it that generation after generation, most couples who fall in love and marry want to become parents? And how do they decide whether to have just one child or more than one?

Then we trace prenatal development—the 9-month period before birth. Our discussion pays special attention to environmental supports that are necessary for healthy growth, as well as damaging influences that threaten the child's health and survival. Finally, the prenatal period marks an important transitional phase in the lives of expectant parents—one that creates challenges as well as opportunities for personal growth. We look at ways in which couples prepare psychologically for the arrival of the baby and how a new sense of self as mother or father begins to emerge.

MOTIVATIONS FOR PARENTHOOD

s part of her semester project for my class, Yolanda interviewed her grandmother, asking why she wanted to have children and how she settled on a particular family size. Yolanda's grandmother, whose children were born in the early 1940s, replied,

> We didn't think much about whether or not to have children in those days. We just had them—everybody did. It would have seemed odd not to! I was 22 years old when I had the first of my four children, and I had four because—well, I wouldn't have had just one since we all thought children needed brothers and sisters, and only children could end up spoiled and selfish. Life is more interesting with children, you know. And now that we're older, we've got family we can depend on and grandchildren to enjoy.

WHY HAVE CHILDREN?

In some ways, the reasons given by Yolanda's grandmother for wanting children are like those of modern parents. In other ways, they are very different. In the past, the issue of whether to have children was, for many adults, "a biological given or unavoidable cultural demand" (Michaels, 1988, p. 23). Today, in Western industrialized nations, it is a matter of true individual choice. Effective birth control techniques permit adults who do not want to become parents to avoid having children in most instances. And changing social values allow people to remain childless with much less fear of social criticism and rejection than was the case a generation or two ago.

When modern American couples are asked about their desire to have children, they mention a variety of advantages and disadvantages, which are listed in Table 3.1. Take a moment to consider which ones are most important to you. Although some ethnic and regional differences exist, reasons for having children that are most important to all groups include the desire for a warm, affectionate relationship and the stimulation and fun that children provide. Also frequently mentioned are growth and learning experiences that children bring into the lives of adults, the desire to have someone carry on after one's own death, and feelings of accomplishment and creativity that come from helping children grow (Cowan & Cowan, 1992; Michaels, 1988).

TABLE 3.1

Advantages and Disadvantages of Parenthood Mentioned by American Couples

ADVANTAGES	DISADVANTAGES
Giving and receiving warmth and affection	Loss of freedom, being tied down
Experiencing the stimulation and fun that children add to life	Financial strain
Being accepted as a responsible and mature member of the community	Worries over children's health, safety, and well-being
Experiencing new growth and learning opportunities that add meaning to life	Interference with mother's employment opportunities
Having someone carry on after one's own death	Risks of bringing up children in a world plagued by crime, war, and pollution
Gaining a sense of accomplishment and creativity from helping children grow	Reduced time to spend with husband or wife
Learning to become less selfish and to sacrifice	Loss of privacy
Having offspring who help with parents' work or add their own income to the family's resources	Fear that children will turn out badly, through no fault of one's own

Source: Cowan & Cowan, 1992.

Most young adults are also aware that having children means years of extra burdens and responsibilities. When asked about the disadvantages of parenthood, they mention "loss of freedom" most often, followed by "financial strain." Indeed, the cost of child rearing is a major factor in modern family planning. According to a conservative government estimate, today's new parents will spend about $240,000 to rear a child from birth through 4 years of college. Finally, many adults worry greatly about bringing children into a troubled world—one filled with crime, war, and pollution (Michaels, 1988).

Careful weighing of the pros and cons of having children was rare in Yolanda's grandmother's time, yet it is increasingly common today. This means that many more couples are making informed and personally meaningful choices about becoming parents—a trend that should increase the chances that they are ready to have children and that their own lives will be enriched by their decision.

HOW LARGE A FAMILY?

In contrast to her grandmother, Yolanda plans to have no more than two children. And she and Jay are talking about whether to limit their family to a single child. In 1960, the average number of children in an American family was 3.1. Today, it is 2.1, a downward trend expected to continue. In other developed countries, the birth rate is already less than two children per family—for example, 1.9 in Australia and Canada; 1.6 in Austria and the Netherlands; 1.5 in Japan; and 1.3 in Germany (Bellamy, 1997). In addition to more effective birth control, a major reason that family size has declined in industrialized nations is that many women are experiencing the economic and personal rewards of a career. A family size of one or two children is certainly more compatible with a woman's decision to divide her energies between work and family.

Research also indicates that modern children benefit from growing up in small families. Parents who have fewer children are more patient and less punitive. They also have more time to devote to each child's activities, schoolwork, and other special needs. Furthermore, in smaller families, siblings are more likely to be widely spaced (born more than 2 years apart), which adds to the attention and resources parents can invest in each child. Together, these findings may account for the fact that children who grow up in small families are healthier, have somewhat higher intelligence test scores, do better in

SOCIAL ISSUES

A GLOBAL PERSPECTIVE ON FAMILY PLANNING

Approximately one-fifth of the world's population—one billion people in all—live in extreme poverty, the majority in slums and shantytowns of developing countries. If current trends in population growth continue, the number of poor will quadruple within the next 60 to 70 years. Poverty and rapid population growth are intertwined: Poverty leads to high birthrates, and rising birthrates heighten poverty and deprivation. Why is this so?

There are many reasons. First, in poor regions of the world where child death rates are high, parents have more children to compensate for the fact that some will certainly die. Second, lack of status, education, and opportunities for women, characteristic of most nonindustrialized societies, restrict life choices to early marriage and prolonged childbearing. Third, in regions where few basic services and labor-saving technologies exist, families often depend on children to help in the fields and at home. Fourth, poverty is associated with absence of family planning services, which causes birthrates to remain high even when people begin to realize the advantages of smaller families. And finally, lack of hope in the future is a major obstacle to life planning in general and family planning in particular (Bellamy, 1996; Grant, 1994).

As a country's population grows, poverty worsens. The labor force expands more quickly than available work, and a new generation of unemployed or underemployed parents emerges. Basic resources, including food, water, land, and fuel, are in shorter supply, and health and educational services are increasingly strained. As a result, overcrowding in urban areas—along with malnutrition, disease, illiteracy, and hopelessness—spreads. A circuit forms through which poverty and high birthrates perpetuate one another.

Two interrelated strategies are especially effective for intervening in this cycle:

■ Making family planning information and services available to all who want them, in ways that are compatible with each country's cultural and religious traditions. Over the last 35 years, the proportion of married women in the developing world using birth control has increased from 10 to 50 percent,

demonstrating that substantial change in practices can be brought about in a relatively short period of time (Grant, 1994). Still, in almost all developing countries, the unmet demand for family planning remains high.

■ Emphasizing education and literacy, particularly for girls. As Figure 3.1 shows, education is a strong determinant of smaller family size. Because women with more years of education have better life opportunities, they are more likely to marry at a later age and take advantage of family planning services. As a result, they have fewer, more widely spaced, and healthier children (Bellamy, 1996).

Family planning combined with education leads to substantial declines in birthrates and resulting improvements in quality of life for both mothers and children. These benefits carry over to future generations.

FIGURE **3.1**

Number of births per mother by years of education in Africa, Latin America, and Asia. Educated women have considerably fewer children. (From Black, 1993.)

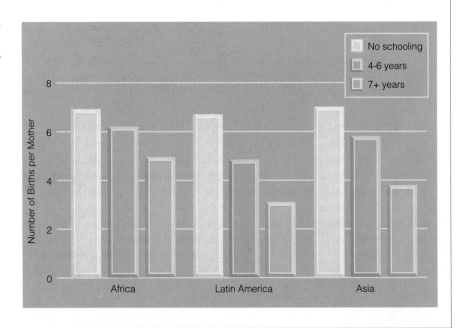

school, and attain higher levels of education (Blake, 1989; Grant, 1994; Powell & Steelman, 1993).

However, recall from Chapter 1 that a correlation between family size and children's characteristics does not tell us for sure about causation. Large families are usually less well off economically than smaller ones. Factors associated with low income—crowded housing, poor nutrition, and parental stress—may be responsible for the negative relationship between family size and children's well-being. Indeed, evidence supports this idea. When children grow up in large, well-to-do families, the unfavorable outcomes typically associated with large family size are reduced, but they are not eliminated (Powell & Steelman, 1993). As the Social Issues box on the previous page indicates, family planning is a major consideration in improving the quality of children's lives, especially in poverty-stricken regions of the world.

Is Yolanda's grandmother right that parents who have just one child are likely to end up with a spoiled, selfish youngster? As we will see in Chapter 13, a great deal of research indicates that this commonly held belief is not correct. Only children are just as well adjusted as are children with siblings. Still, the one-child family has both pros and cons, as does every family lifestyle. In a survey in which only children and their parents were asked what they liked and disliked about living in a single-child family, each mentioned a set of advantages and disadvantages, which are summarized in Table 3.2. The list is a useful one for parents to consider when deciding how many children would best fit their personal and family life plans.

A doctor explains birth control options to two women visiting a clinic in Nepal. Family planning combined with education helps limit rising birthrates in developing countries. Smaller families mean an enhanced quality of life for both mothers and children. *(Takeshi Takahara/Photo Researchers, Inc.)*

IS THERE A BEST TIME DURING ADULTHOOD TO HAVE A CHILD?

Yolanda's grandmother had her first child in her early twenties, shortly after she was married. Yolanda is pregnant for the first time at age 28. Many people believe that giving birth during the twenties is ideal, not only because the risk of having a baby with a chromosomal disorder is reduced (see Chapter 2) but also because younger parents have more energy to keep up with active children.

However, as Figure 3.2 reveals, first births to women in their thirties have increased greatly over the past two decades. Many more couples are putting off childbearing until

TABLE 3.2

Advantages and Disadvantages of a One-Child Family

ADVANTAGES		DISADVANTAGES	
Mentioned by Parents	Mentioned by Children	Mentioned by Parents	Mentioned by Children
Having time to pursue one's own interests and career	Avoiding sibling rivalry	Walking a "tightrope" between healthy attention and overindulgence	Not getting to experience the closeness of a sibling relationship
Less financial pressure	Having more privacy		
Not having to worry about "playing favorites" among children	Enjoying greater affluence	Having only one chance to "make good" as a parent	Feeling too much pressure from parents to succeed
	Having a closer parent–child relationship	Being left childless in case of the child's death	Having no one to help care for parents when they get old

Source: Hawke & Knox, 1978.

FIGURE 3.2

First births to American women of different ages in 1970 and 1995. The birthrate decreased over this time period for women 20–24 years of age, whereas it increased for women 25 years and older. For women in their thirties, the birthrate more than doubled. *(Adapted from Ventura, 1989; U.S. Department of Health and Human Services, 1997.)*

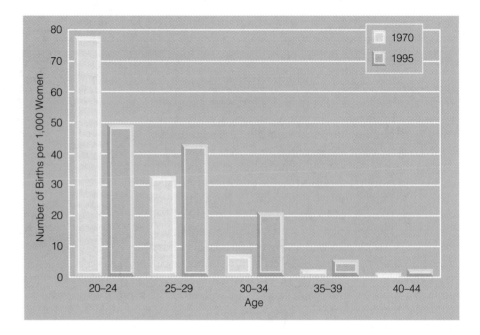

their careers are well established and they know they can support a child (Dion, 1995). Older parents may be somewhat less energetic than they were at earlier ages, but they are financially better off and more mature emotionally. For these reasons, they may be better able to invest in parenting. In support of this idea, when individuals who grew up with older parents are asked to reflect back on their childhoods, they often mention emotional stability as a distinct advantage (Yarrow, 1991).

Nevertheless, adult children of older parents do mention drawbacks. Some felt jealous of childhood friends because their parents seemed more active, playful, and fun loving. In addition, as they reached young adulthood, a great many began to worry about losing their parents. They had to come to terms with the fact that they would probably live much of their lives without their mothers and fathers (Yarrow, 1991).

Finally, fertility problems among women increase from age 15 to 50, with a sharp rise in the mid-thirties. Between ages 30 and 34, nearly 15 percent are affected, a figure that climbs to 28 percent for 35- to 39-year-olds (Catanzarite et al., 1995; McFalls, 1990). Age also affects male reproductive capacity. Concentration of sperm in each ejaculation gradually declines after age 40 (Murray & Meacham, 1993). Although there is no best time during adulthood to begin rearing children, individuals who decide to put off childbirth until well into their thirties or early forties do risk the possibility that they may not have children at all.

ASK YOURSELF . . .

■ *In what ways are couples' reasons for having children the same today as they were in Yolanda's grandmother's time? In what ways has the decision to have children changed?*

■ *Rhonda and Mark are career-oriented, 35-year-old parents of an only child. They are thinking about having a second baby. What factors should they keep in mind as they decide whether to add to their family at this time in their lives?*

BRIEF REVIEW

In industrialized nations today, more couples weigh the pros and cons of parenthood before deciding to have children than was the case in the past. The current trend toward smaller families fits with the greater career commitment of modern women, and it also has benefits for children. Contrary to popular belief, parents who limit their families to a single child are just as likely to raise a well-adjusted youngster as are families with several children. Like all family lifestyles, the decision to postpone childbearing to a later age has both advantages and disadvantages.

PRENATAL DEVELOPMENT

*T*he sperm and ovum that unite to form the new individual are uniquely suited for the task of reproduction. The ovum is a tiny sphere, measuring ¹⁄₁₇₅ inch in diameter, that is barely visible to the naked eye as a dot the size of a period at the end of this sentence. But in its microscopic world, it is a giant—the largest cell in the human body. The ovum's size makes it a perfect target for the much smaller sperm, which measure only ¹⁄₅₀₀ inch.

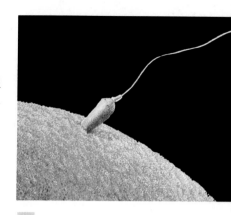

In this photograph of fertilization taken with the aid of a powerful microscope, a tiny sperm completes its journey and starts to penetrate the surface of an enormous-looking ovum, the largest cell in the human body. *(Francis Leroy, Biocosmos/Science Photo Library/Photo Researchers)*

CONCEPTION

About once every 28 days, in the middle of a woman's menstrual cycle, an ovum bursts from one of her *ovaries*, two walnut-sized organs located deep inside her abdomen (see Figure 3.3). Surrounded by thousands of nurse cells that will feed and protect it along its path, the ovum is drawn into one of two *fallopian tubes*—long, thin structures that lead to the hollow, soft-lined uterus. While the ovum is traveling, the spot on the ovary from which it was released, now called the *corpus luteum*, begins to secrete hormones that prepare the lining of the uterus to receive a fertilized ovum. If pregnancy does not occur, the corpus luteum shrinks, and the lining of the uterus is discarded 2 weeks later with menstruation.

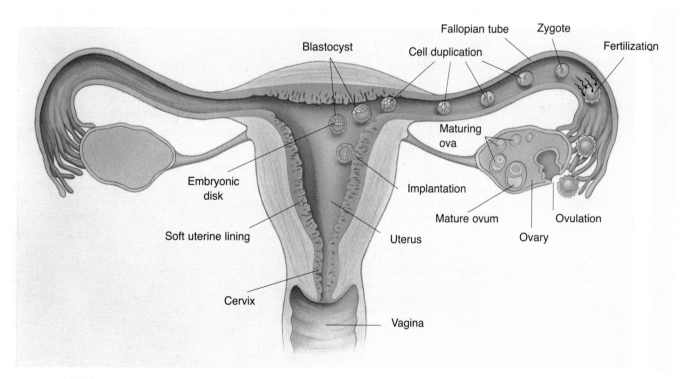

FIGURE 3.3

Female reproductive organs, showing fertilization, early cell duplication, and implantation. As the zygote moves down the fallopian tube, it begins to duplicate, at first slowly and then more rapidly. By the fourth day, it forms a hollow, fluid-filled ball called a blastocyst. The inner cells will become the new organism; the outer cells will provide protective covering. At the end of the first week, the blastocyst begins to implant in the uterine lining. *(From K. L. Moore and T. V. N. Persaud, 1993, Before We Are Born, 4th ed., Philadelphia: Saunders, p. 33. Reprinted by permission of the publisher and the author.)*

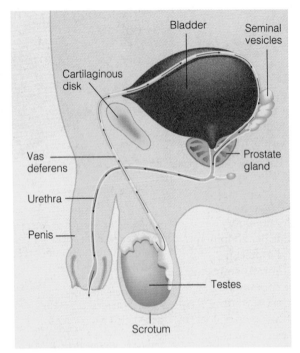

FIGURE 3.4

Male reproductive organs, showing the path of sperm during sexual intercourse. Sperm produced in the testes move through the vas deferens, where they are mixed with semen from the prostate gland and seminal vesicles. At sexual climax they are released through the urethra in the penis.

The male produces sperm in vast numbers—an average of 300 million a day—in the *testes,* two glands located in the *scrotum,* sacs that lie just behind the penis (see Figure 3.4). In the final process of maturation, each sperm develops a tail that permits it to swim long distances. During sexual intercourse, about 360 million sperm move through the *vas deferens,* a thin tube in which they are bathed in a protective fluid called *semen.* At sexual climax, semen is ejaculated from the penis into the woman's vagina.

Immediately, the sperm begin to swim upstream in the female reproductive tract, through the *cervix* (opening of the uterus), and into the *fallopian tube,* where fertilization usually takes place (refer again to Figure 3.3). The journey is difficult, and many sperm die. Only 300 to 500 reach the ovum, if one happens to be present. Sperm live for up to 6 days and can lie in wait for the ovum, which survives for only 1 day after being released into the fallopian tube. However, most conceptions result from intercourse during a 3-day period—on the day of the 2 days preceding ovulation (Wilcox, Weinberg, & Baird, 1995).

With conception, the story of prenatal development begins to unfold. The vast changes that take place during the 38 weeks of pregnancy are usually divided into three phases: (1) the period of the zygote, (2) the period of the embryo, and (3) the period of the fetus. As we look at what happens in each, you may find it useful to refer to Table 3.3, which summarizes major milestones of prenatal development.

THE PERIOD OF THE ZYGOTE

The period of the zygote lasts about 2 weeks, from fertilization until the tiny mass of cells drifts down and out of the fallopian tube and attaches itself to the wall of the uterus. The zygote's first cell duplication is long and drawn out; it is not complete until about 30 hours after conception. Gradually, new cells are added at a faster rate. By the fourth day, 60 to 70 cells exist that form a hollow, fluid-filled ball called a **blastocyst.** The cells on the inside, called the **embryonic disk,** will become the new organism; the outer ring will provide protective covering.

Period of the zygote: seventh to ninth day. During the period of the zygote, the fertilized ovum begins to duplicate at an increasingly rapid rate, forming a hollow ball of cells, or blastocyst, by the fourth day after fertilization. Here the blastocyst, magnified thousands of times, burrows into the uterine lining between the seventh and ninth day. (© *Lennart Nilsson,* A Child Is Born/*Bonniers*)

blastocyst
The zygote 4 days after fertilization, when the tiny mass of cells forms a hollow, fluid-filled ball.

embryonic disk
A small cluster of cells on the inside of the blastocyst, from which the embryo will develop.

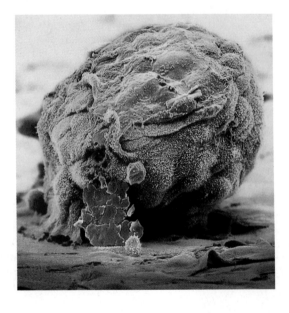

TABLE 3.3

Major Milestones of Prenatal Development

TRIMESTER	PERIOD	WEEKS	LENGTH AND WEIGHT	MAJOR EVENTS
First	Zygote	1		The one-celled zygote multiplies and forms a blastocyst.
		2		The blastocyst burrows into the uterine lining. Structures that feed and protect the developing organism begin to form—amnion, chorion, yolk sac, placenta, and umbilical cord.
	Embryo	3–4	1/4 inch	A primitive brain and spinal cord appear. Heart, muscles, backbone, ribs, and digestive tract begin to develop.
		5–8	1 inch; 1/7 ounce	Many external body structures (for example., face, arms, legs, toes, fingers) and internal organs form. The sense of touch begins to develop, and the embryo can move.
	Fetus	9–12	3 inches; less than 1 ounce	Rapid increase in size begins. Nervous system, organs, and muscles become organized and connected, and new behavioral capacities (kicking, thumb sucking, mouth opening, and rehearsal of breathing) appear. External genitals are well formed, and the fetus's sex is evident.
Second		13–24	12 inches; 1.8 pounds	The fetus continues to enlarge rapidly. In the middle of this period, fetal movements can be felt by the mother. Vernix and lanugo keep the fetus's skin from chapping in the amniotic fluid. All of the neurons that will ever be produced in the brain are present by 24 weeks. Eyes are sensitive to light, and the fetus reacts to sound.
Third		25–38	20 inches; 7.5 pounds	The fetus has a chance of survival if born around this time. Size continues to increase. Lungs gradually mature. Rapid brain development causes sensory and behavioral capacities to expand. In the middle of this period, a layer of fat is added under the skin. Antibodies are transmitted from mother to fetus to protect against disease. Most fetuses rotate into an upside-down position in preparation for birth.

Sources: Moore & Persaud, 1993; Nilsson & Hamberger, 1990.

■ **IMPLANTATION.** Sometime between the seventh and ninth days, **implantation** occurs: the blastocyst burrows deep into the uterine lining. Surrounded by the woman's nourishing blood, now it starts to grow in earnest. At first, the protective outer layer multiplies fastest. A membrane, called the **amnion,** is formed that encloses the developing organism in **amniotic fluid.** It helps keep the temperature of the prenatal world constant and provides a cushion against any jolts caused by the woman's movement. A *yolk sac* also appears. It produces blood cells until the developing liver, spleen, and bone marrow are mature enough to take over this function (Moore & Persaud, 1993).

The events of these first 2 weeks are delicate and uncertain. As many as 30 percent of zygotes do not make it through this phase. In some, the sperm and ovum do not join properly. In others, for some unknown reason, cell duplication never begins. By preventing

implantation
Attachment of the blastocyst to the uterine lining 7 to 9 days after fertilization.

amnion
The inner membrane that forms a protective covering around the prenatal organism.

amniotic fluid
The fluid that fills the amnion, helping to keep temperature constant and to provide a cushion against jolts caused by the mother's movement.

FIGURE **3.5**

Cross-section of the uterus showing the placenta. The mother's blood circulates in spaces surrounding the chorionic villi. A membrane between the two blood supplies permits food and oxygen to be delivered and waste products to be carried away. The two blood supplies do not mix directly. *(From K. L. Moore and T. V. N. Persaud, 1993, Before We Are Born, 4th ed., Philadelphia: Saunders, p. 98. Reprinted by permission of the publisher and the author.)*

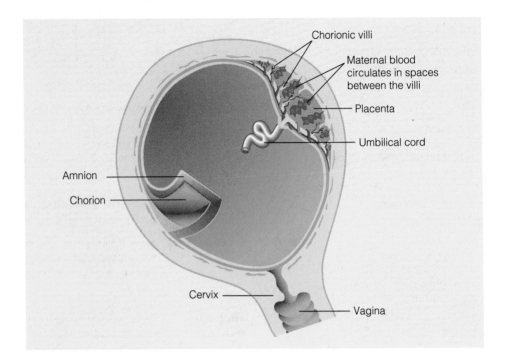

chorion
The outer membrane that forms a protective covering around the prenatal organism. It sends out tiny, fingerlike villi, from which the placenta begins to emerge.

placenta
The organ that separates the mother's bloodstream from the embryo or fetal bloodstream but permits exchange of nutrients and waste products.

umbilical cord
The long cord connecting the prenatal organism to the placenta that delivers nutrients and removes waste products.

embryo
The prenatal organism from 2 to 8 weeks after conception, during which time the foundations of all body structures and internal organs are laid down.

implantation in these cases, nature eliminates most prenatal abnormalities in the very earliest stages of development (Sadler, 1995).

■ **THE PLACENTA AND UMBILICAL CORD.** By the end of the second week, another protective membrane, called the **chorion,** surrounds the amnion. From the chorion, tiny fingerlike *villi,* or blood vessels, begin to emerge.[1] As these villi burrow into the uterine wall, a special organ called the **placenta** starts to develop. By bringing the mother's and embryo's blood close together, the placenta will permit food and oxygen to reach the developing organism and waste products to be carried away. A special membrane forms that allows these substances to be exchanged but prevents the mother's and embryo's blood from mixing directly (see Figure 3.5).

The placenta is connected to the developing organism by the **umbilical cord.** In the period of the zygote, it first appears as a primitive body stalk, but during the course of pregnancy, it grows to a length of 1 to 3 feet. The umbilical cord contains one large vein that delivers blood loaded with nutrients and two arteries that remove waste products. The force of blood flowing through the cord keeps it firm, much like a garden hose, so it seldom tangles while the embryo, like a space-walking astronaut, floats freely in its fluid-filled chamber (Moore & Persaud, 1993).

By the end of the period of the zygote, the developing organism has found food and shelter in the uterus. Already, it is a very complex being. These dramatic beginnings take place before all but the most sensitive mother knows she is pregnant.

THE PERIOD OF THE EMBRYO

The period of the **embryo** lasts from implantation through the eighth week of pregnancy. During these brief 6 weeks, the most rapid prenatal changes take place as the groundwork for all body structures and internal organs is laid down. Because all parts of

---

[1]Recall from Chapter 2 that chorionic villus sampling, in which tissue from the ends of the villi are removed and examined for genetic abnormalities, is the prenatal diagnostic method that can be performed earliest, by 6 to 8 weeks after conception.

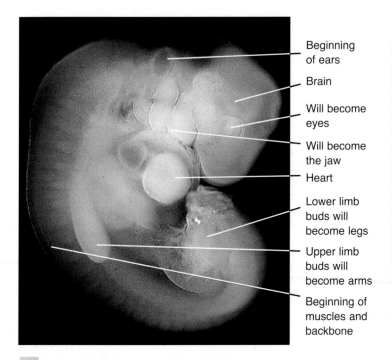

Beginning
of ears

Brain

Will become
eyes

Will become
the jaw

Heart

Lower limb
buds will
become legs

Upper limb
buds will
become arms

Beginning of
muscles and
backbone

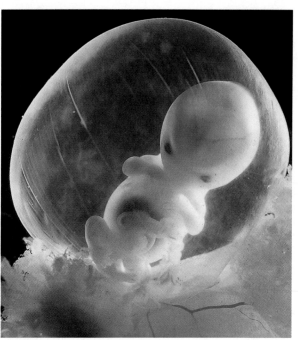

Period of the embryo: fourth week. In actual size, this
4-week-old embryo is only 1/4-inch long, but many
body structures have begun to form. The primitive tail
will disappear by the end of the embryonic period.
(© Lennart Nilsson, A Child Is Born/*Bonniers)*

Period of the embryo: seventh week. At 7 weeks, the
embryo's posture is more upright. Body structures—eyes,
nose, arms, legs, and internal organs—are more distinct. An
embryo of this age responds to touch. It can also move,
although at less than an inch long and an ounce in weight,
it is still too tiny to be felt by the mother. *(© Lennart Nilsson,*
A Child Is Born/*Bonniers)*

the body are forming, the embryo is especially vulnerable to interference with healthy
development. But the fact that embryonic growth takes place over a fairly short time span
helps limit opportunities for serious harm to occur.

■ **LAST HALF OF THE FIRST MONTH.** In the third week after conception, the
embryonic disk folds over to form three layers of cells: (1) the *ectoderm,* which will
become the nervous system and skin; (2) the *mesoderm,* from which will develop the
muscles, skeleton, circulatory system, and other internal organs; and (3) the *endoderm,*
which will become the digestive system, lungs, urinary tract, and glands. These three layers give rise to all parts of the body.

At first, the nervous system develops fastest. The ectoderm folds over to form a **neural
tube,** or primitive spinal cord. At 3½ weeks, the top swells to form a brain. Production of
neurons (brain cells that store and transmit information) begins deep inside the neural
tube. Once formed, neurons travel along tiny threads to their permanent locations, where
they will form the major parts of the brain (Casaer, 1993).

While the nervous system is developing, the heart begins to pump blood around the
embryo's circulatory system, and muscles, backbone, ribs, and digestive tract start to
appear. At the end of the first month, the curled embryo consists of millions of organized
groups of cells with specific functions, although it is only one-fourth inch long.

■ **THE SECOND MONTH.** In the second month, growth continues rapidly. The eyes,
ears, nose, jaw, and neck form. Tiny buds become arms, legs, fingers, and toes. Internal
organs are more distinct: the intestines grow, the heart develops separate chambers, and
the liver and spleen take over production of blood cells so that the yolk sac is no longer
needed. Changing body proportions cause the embryo's posture to become more upright.

neural tube
The primitive spinal cord that
develops from the ectoderm,
the top of which swells to form
the brain.

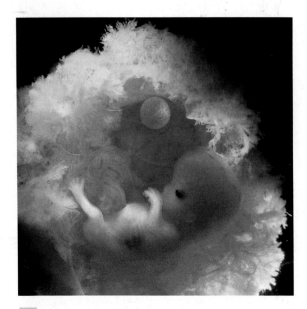

Period of the fetus: eleventh week. During the period of the fetus, the organism increases rapidly in size, and body structures are completed. At 11 weeks, the brain and muscles are better connected. The fetus can kick, bend its arms, open and close its hands and mouth, and suck its thumb. Notice the yolk sac, which shrinks as pregnancy advances. The internal organs have taken over its function of producing blood cells. (© Lennart Nilsson, A Child Is Born/Bonniers)

Now an inch long and one-seventh of an ounce in weight, the embryo can already sense its world. It responds to touch, particularly in the mouth area and on the soles of the feet. And it can move, although its tiny flutters are still too light to be felt by the mother (Nilsson & Hamberger, 1990).

THE PERIOD OF THE FETUS

Lasting until the end of pregnancy, the period of the **fetus** is the "growth and finishing" phase. During this longest prenatal period, the developing organism begins to increase rapidly in size. The rate of body growth is extraordinary, especially from the ninth to the twentieth week (Moore & Persaud, 1993).

■ **THE THIRD MONTH.** In the third month, the organs, muscles, and nervous system start to become organized and connected. The brain signals, and in response, the fetus kicks, bends its arms, forms a fist, curls its toes, opens its mouth, and even sucks its thumb. The tiny lungs begin to expand and contract in an early rehearsal of breathing movements. By the twelfth week, the external genitals are well formed, and the sex of the fetus is evident. Using ultrasound, Yolanda's doctor could see that she would have a boy (although Yolanda and Jay asked not to be told the fetus's sex). Other finishing touches appear, such as fingernails, toenails, tooth buds, and eyelids that open and close. The heartbeat is now stronger and can be heard through a stethoscope.

Prenatal development is sometimes divided into **trimesters,** or three equal periods of time. At the end of the third month, the first trimester is complete. Two more must pass before the fetus is fully prepared to survive outside the womb.

■ **THE SECOND TRIMESTER.** By the middle of the second trimester, between 17 and 20 weeks, the new being has grown large enough that its movements can be felt by the mother. If we could look inside the uterus, we would find the fetus completely covered with a white cheeselike substance called **vernix.** It protects the skin from chapping during the long months spent bathing in the amniotic fluid. A white, downy hair covering called **lanugo** also appears over the entire body, helping the vernix stick to the skin.

At the end of the second trimester, many organs are quite well developed. And a major milestone is reached in brain development, in that all the neurons are now in place. No more will be produced in the individual's lifetime. However, *glial cells,* which support and feed the neurons, continue to increase at a rapid rate throughout the remaining months of pregnancy, as well as after birth (Nowakowski, 1987).

Brain growth means new behavioral capacities. The 20-week-old fetus can be stimulated by sounds. And if a doctor has reason to look inside the uterus using fetoscopy (see Chapter 2, page 67), fetuses try to shield their eyes from the light with their hands, indicating that the sense of sight has begun to emerge (Nilsson & Hamberger, 1990). Still, a fetus born at this time cannot survive. Its lungs are quite immature, and the brain has not yet developed enough to control breathing movements and body temperature.

■ **THE THIRD TRIMESTER.** During the final trimester, a fetus born early has a chance for survival outside the womb. The point at which the baby can first survive is called the **age of viability.** It occurs sometime between 22 and 26 weeks (Moore & Persaud, 1993). If born between the seventh and eighth months, a baby would still have trouble breathing, and oxygen assistance would be necessary. Although the respiratory center of the brain is now mature, tiny air sacs in the lungs are not yet ready to inflate and exchange carbon dioxide for oxygen.

The brain continues to make great strides during the last 3 months. The *cerebral cortex,* the most highly evolved part of our brain and the seat of human intelligence, enlarges

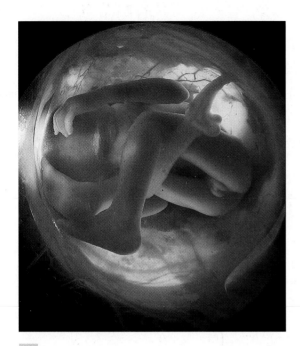

Period of the fetus: twenty-second week. At 22 weeks, this fetus is almost a foot long and slightly over a pound in weight. Its movements can be easily felt by the mother and by other family members who place a hand on her abdomen. If born at this time, a baby has a slim chance of surviving. *(© Lennart Nilsson, A Child Is Born/Bonniers)*

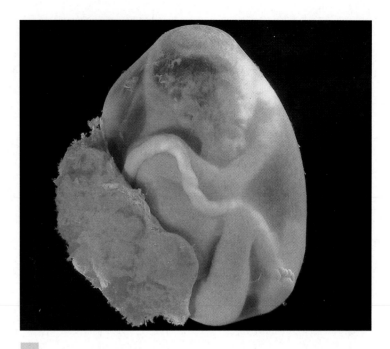

Period of the fetus: thirty-sixth week. This 36-week-old fetus fills the uterus. To support its need for nourishment, the umbilical cord and placenta have grown very large. Notice the vernix (cheeselike substance) on the skin, which protects it from chapping. The fetus has accumulated a layer of fat to assist with temperature regulation after birth. In another 2 weeks, it would be full term. *(© Lennart Nilsson, A Child Is Born/Bonniers)*

(see Figure 3.6). As neurological organization improves, the fetus spends more time awake. At 20 weeks, heart rate variability reveals no periods of alertness. But by 28 weeks, fetuses are awake about 11 percent of the time, a figure that rises to 16 percent just before birth (DiPietro et al., 1996a). Around 24 weeks, the fetus can first feel pain, so after this time painkillers should be used in any surgical procedures (Royal College of Obstetricians and Gynecologists, 1997).

The third trimester also brings greater responsiveness to external stimulation. Yolanda told me that one day when she turned on an electric mixer, the fetus reacted with a forceful startle. By 28 weeks, fetuses blink their eyes in reaction to nearby sounds (Birnholz & Benacerraf, 1983; DiPietro et al., 1996a). And in the last weeks of pregnancy, they learn to prefer the tone and rhythm of their mother's voice. In one clever study, mothers were asked to read aloud Dr. Seuss's lively poem *The Cat in the Hat* to their unborn babies for the last 6 weeks of pregnancy. After birth, their infants were given a chance to suck on nipples that turned on recordings of the mother reading this poem or different rhyming stories. The infants sucked hardest to hear *The Cat in the Hat,* the sound they had come to know while still in the womb (DeCasper & Spence, 1986).

During the final 3 months, the fetus gains more than 5 pounds and grows 7 inches. As it fills the uterus, it gradually moves less often. In addition to reduced space, brain maturation, which permits the organism to inhibit behavior, may also contribute to a decline in physical activity (DiPietro et al., 1996a).

In the eighth month, a layer of fat is added under the skin to assist with temperature regulation. The fetus also receives antibodies from the mother's blood to protect against illnesses, since the newborn's own immune system will not work well until several months after birth. In the last weeks, most fetuses assume an upside-down position, partly because of the shape of the uterus and partly because of gravity: the head is heavier than the feet. Growth of the fetus slows, and birth is about to take place.

fetus
The prenatal organism from the beginning of the third month to the end of pregnancy, during which time completion of body structures and dramatic growth in size takes place.

trimesters
Three equal time periods in prenatal development, each of which lasts 3 months.

vernix
A white, cheeselike substance that covers the fetus and prevents the skin from chapping due to constant exposure to amniotic fluid.

lanugo
A white, downy hair that covers the entire body of the fetus, helping the vernix stick to the skin.

age of viability
The age at which the fetus can first survive if born early. Occurs sometime between 22 and 26 weeks.

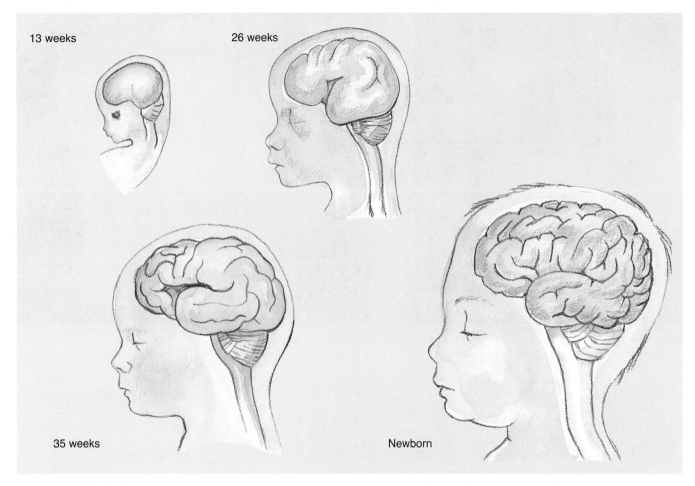

13 weeks

26 weeks

35 weeks

Newborn

FIGURE **3.6**

Growth of the brain during the prenatal period, shown half the actual size. The *cerebral cortex,* the outer layer of gray matter, is responsible for higher brain functions, including sensation, voluntary movement, and thought. At 13 weeks, its surface is smooth. By 26 weeks (beginning of the third trimester), grooves and convolutions start to appear. These permit a dramatic increase in surface area without extensive increase in head size. As a result, maximum prenatal brain growth takes place while still permitting the full-term baby's head to pass through the birth canal. As cortical folds become more apparent (35 weeks), fetal sensory and behavioral capacities expand. The fetus spends more time awake, responds to external stimulation, and moves more vigorously (although less often as it fills the uterus). It also learns to prefer familiar sounds, such as the tone and rhythm of the mother's voice. *(Adapted from Moore, Persaud, & Shiota, 1994.)*

ASK YOURSELF . . .

■ *Amy, who is 2 months pregnant, wonders how the embryo is being fed and what parts of the body have formed. Amy imagines that very little development has yet taken place. How would you answer Amy's questions? Will she be surprised at your response?*

■ *How does brain maturation relate to fetal behavior during the third trimester?*

BRIEF REVIEW

The vast changes that take place during pregnancy are usually divided into three periods. In the period of the zygote, the tiny one-celled fertilized ovum begins to duplicate and implants itself in the uterine lining. Structures that will feed and protect the developing organism begin to form. During the period of the embryo, the foundations for all body tissues and organs are rapidly laid down. The longest prenatal phase, the period of the fetus, is devoted to growth in size and completion of body systems. Turn back to Table 3.3 on page 103 to review the specific changes that take place during the 9 months before birth.

PRENATAL ENVIRONMENTAL INFLUENCES

lthough the prenatal environment is far more constant than the world outside the womb, a great many factors can affect the embryo and fetus. Yolanda and Jay learned that there was much they could do to create a safe environment for development before birth.

TERATOGENS

The term **teratogen** refers to any environmental agent that causes damage during the prenatal period. It comes from the Greek word *teras,* meaning "malformation" or "monstrosity." This label was selected because scientists first learned about harmful prenatal influences from cases in which babies had been profoundly damaged.

Yet the harm done by teratogens is not always simple and straightforward. It depends on the following factors:

■ *Dose.* We will see as we discuss particular teratogens that larger doses over longer time periods usually have more negative effects.

■ *Heredity.* The genetic makeup of the mother and the developing organism plays an important role. Some individuals are better able to withstand harmful environments.

■ *Other negative influences.* The presence of several negative factors at once, such as poor nutrition, lack of medical care, and additional teratogens, can worsen the impact of a single harmful agent.

■ *Age of the prenatal organism.* The effects of teratogens vary with the age of the organism at time of exposure.

We can best understand this last idea if we think of prenatal development in terms of the *sensitive period* concept introduced in Chapter 1. Recall that a sensitive period is a limited time span in which a part of the body or a behavior is biologically prepared to develop rapidly. During that time, it is especially vulnerable to its surroundings. If the environment is harmful, then damage occurs that would not have otherwise happened, and recovery is difficult and sometimes impossible.

Figure 3.7 on page 110 summarizes sensitive periods during prenatal development. Look carefully at it, and you will see that some parts of the body, such as the brain and eye, have long sensitive periods that extend throughout the prenatal phase. Other sensitive periods, such as those for the limbs and palate, are much shorter. Figure 3.7 also indicates that we can make some general statements about the timing of harmful influences. During the period of the zygote, before implantation, teratogens rarely have any impact. If they do, the tiny mass of cells is usually so completely damaged that it dies. The embryonic period is the time when serious defects are most likely to occur, since the foundations for all body parts are being laid down. During the fetal period, damage caused by teratogens is usually minor. However, some organs, such as the brain, eye, and genitals, can still be strongly affected.

The effects of teratogens are not limited to immediate physical damage. Although deformities of the body are easy to notice, important psychological consequences are harder to identify. Some may not show up until later in development. Others may occur as an indirect effect of physical damage. For example, a defect resulting from drugs the mother took during pregnancy can change reactions of others to the child as well as the child's ability to move about the environment. Over time, parent–child interaction, peer relations, and opportunities to explore may suffer. These experiences, in turn, can have far-reaching consequences for cognitive, emotional, and social development (Friedman, 1996).

teratogen
Any environmental agent that causes damage during the prenatal period.

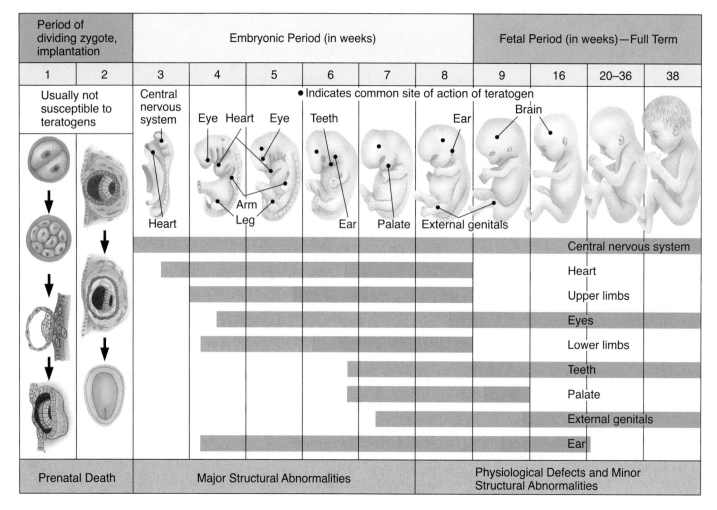

Period of dividing zygote, implantation		Embryonic Period (in weeks)						Fetal Period (in weeks)—Full Term			
1	2	3	4	5	6	7	8	9	16	20–36	38

FIGURE 3.7

Sensitive periods in prenatal development. Each organ or structure has a sensitive period during which its development may be disturbed. Gray horizontal lines indicate highly sensitive periods. Pink horizontal lines indicate periods that are somewhat less sensitive to teratogens, although damage can occur. *(From K. L. Moore & T. V. N. Persaud, 1993, Before Are Born, 4th ed., Philadelphia: Saunders, p. 130. Reprinted by permission of the publisher and the author.)*

Notice how an important idea about development that we discussed in earlier chapters is at work here—that of *bidirectional influences* between child and environment. Now let's take a look at what scientists have discovered about a variety of teratogens.

■ **PRESCRIPTION AND NONPRESCRIPTION DRUGS.** Just about any drug taken by the mother can enter the embryonic or fetal bloodstream. In the early 1960s, the world learned a tragic lesson about drugs and prenatal development. At that time, a sedative called **thalidomide** was widely available in Canada, Europe, and South America. Although the embryos of test animals were not harmed by it, in humans it had drastic effects. When taken by mothers between the fourth and sixth weeks after conception, thalidomide produced gross deformities of the embryo's developing arms and legs. About 7,000 infants around the world were affected (Moore & Persaud, 1993). As children exposed to thalidomide grew older, a large number of them scored below average in intelligence. Perhaps the drug damaged the central nervous system directly. Or the child-rearing conditions of these severely deformed youngsters may have impaired their intellectual development (Vorhees & Mollnow, 1987).

thalidomide
A sedative widely available in Europe, Canada, and South America in the early 1960s. When taken by mothers between the fourth and sixth weeks after conception, it produced gross deformities of the embryo's arms and legs.

Despite the bitter lesson of thalidomide, many pregnant women continue to take over-the-counter drugs without consulting their doctors. Aspirin is one of the most common. Several studies suggest that repeated use of aspirin is linked to low birth weight, infant death around the time of birth, poor motor development, and lower intelligence test scores in early childhood (Barr et al., 1990; Streissguth et al., 1987). Other research, however, has failed to confirm these findings (see, for example, Hauth et al., 1995).

Another frequently consumed drug is caffeine, contained in coffee. Heavy caffeine intake (more than 3 cups of coffee per day) is associated with low birth weight, prematurity, miscarriage, and newborn withdrawal symptoms, such as irritability and vomiting (Dlugosz & Bracken, 1992; Eskenazi, 1993). Some researchers report dose-related effects: The more caffeine consumed, the greater the likelihood of negative outcomes (Fortier, Marcoux, & Beaulac-Baillargeon, 1993; Infante-Rivard et al., 1993).

Because children's lives are involved, we must take findings like these quite seriously. At the same time, it is important to note that we cannot yet be sure that these drugs actually cause the problems just mentioned. Imagine how difficult it is to study the effects of many substances on the unborn! Often mothers take more than one kind of drug. If the prenatal organism is injured, it is hard to tell which drug might be responsible or if other factors correlated with drug taking are really at fault. Until we have more information, the safest course of action is the one that Yolanda took: Cut down on or avoid these drugs entirely.

■ **ILLEGAL DRUGS.** The use of highly addictive mood-altering drugs, such as cocaine and heroin, has become more widespread, especially in poverty-stricken inner-city areas, where they provide a temporary escape from a daily life of hopelessness. The number of "cocaine babies" born in the United States has reached crisis levels in recent years. About 100,000 to 375,000 infants are affected annually, a figure expected to climb to more than 500,000 within a few years (Barton, Harrigan, & Tse, 1995; Landry & Whitney, 1996). Here is a brief account of what two of these hospitalized newborns looked like:

> Guillermo . . . has spent his whole short life crying. He is jittery and goes into spasms when he is touched. His eyes don't focus. He can't stick out his tongue, or suck. Born a week ago to a cocaine addict, Guillermo is described by his doctors as an addict himself. Nearby, . . . Paul lies motionless in an incubator, feeding tubes riddling his tiny body. He needs a respirator to breathe and a daily spinal tap to relieve fluid buildup on his brain. Only one month old, he has already suffered two strokes. (Barol, 1986, p. 56)

Babies born to users of cocaine, heroin, or methadone (a less addictive drug used to wean people away from heroin) are at risk for a wide variety of problems, including prematurity, low birth weight, physical defects, breathing difficulties, and death around the time of birth (Allen et al., 1991; Burkett et al., 1994; Handler et al., 1994; Kandall et al., 1993; Miller, Boudreaus, & Regan, 1995). In addition, these infants arrive drug addicted. Guillermo and Paul were feverish and irritable at birth. They had trouble sleeping, and their cries were abnormally shrill and piercing—a common symptom among stressed newborns that we will discuss in Chapter 4 (Delaney-Black et al., 1996; Friedman, 1996; Martin et al., 1996). When mothers with many problems of their own must take care of these babies, who are difficult to calm down, cuddle, and feed, behavior problems are likely to persist.

Throughout the first year, heroin- and methadone-exposed infants are less attentive to the environment, and their motor development is slow. After infancy, some children get better, whereas others remain jittery and inattentive. Researchers believe that the kind of parenting these youngsters receive may explain why there are lasting problems for some but not for others (Lane, 1996).

This baby, whose mother took crack during pregnancy, was born many weeks premature. He breathes with the aid of a respirator. His central nervous system may be seriously damaged. Researchers do not yet know if these outcomes are actually caused by crack or by the many other high-risk behaviors of drug users. *(Chuck Nacke/Woodfin Camp & Associates)*

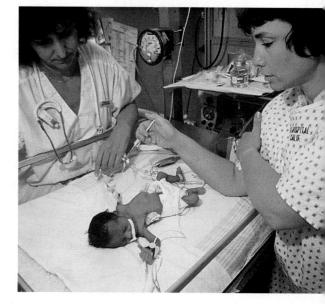

Unlike findings on heroin and methadone, growing evidence on cocaine suggests that large numbers of prenatally exposed babies have lasting difficulties. Cocaine constricts the blood vessels, causing oxygen delivered to the developing organism to fall dramatically for 15 minutes following a high dose. It also alters the chemical balance in the fetus's brain (Dow-Edwards, 1995). These effects may contribute to a specific set of cocaine-linked physical defects, including eye, bone, genital, urinary tract, kidney, and heart deformities, as well as brain hemorrhages and seizures (Fox, 1994; Holzman & Paneth, 1994; Moroney & Allen, 1994).

Babies born to mothers who smoke crack (a cheap form of cocaine that delivers high doses quickly through the lungs) seem to be worst off in terms of low birth weight and damage to the central nervous system. Visual, motor, and language problems are present during the preschool years (Bender et al., 1995; Richardson et al., 1996). Fathers may contribute to these outcomes. Research suggests that cocaine can attach itself to sperm, "hitchhike" its way into the zygote, and cause birth defects (Yazigi, Odem, & Polakoski, 1991).

Still, it is difficult to isolate the precise damage caused by cocaine, since users often take several drugs and engage in other high-risk behaviors (Lester, Freier, & LaGasse, 1995). For example, the majority of cocaine users smoke cigarettes and drink alcohol (Landry & Whitney, 1996). The joint impact of these substances may be responsible for the negative outcomes just described.

Another illegal drug, marijuana, is used more widely than cocaine and heroin. Studies examining its relationship to low birth weight and prematurity reveal mixed findings (Fried, 1993). Several researchers have linked prenatal marijuana exposure to newborn startles, an abnormally high-pitched cry, and reduced visual attention to the environment (Dahl et al., 1995; Lester & Dreher, 1989). These outcomes certainly put newborn babies at risk for future problems, even though long-term effects have not been established.

■ **TOBACCO.** Although smoking has recently declined in the United States, an estimated one-fourth to one-third of adults are regular cigarette users. The rate of tobacco use is especially high among women younger than 25 years of age—30 to 40 percent (Birenbaum-Carmeli, 1995; U.S. Bureau of the Census, 1997). The most well-known effect of smoking during pregnancy is low birth weight. But the likelihood of other serious consequences, such as prematurity, impaired breathing during sleep, miscarriage, infant death, and cancer later in childhood, is also increased. The more cigarettes a mother smokes, the greater the chances that her baby will be affected. If a pregnant woman decides to stop smoking at any time, even during the last trimester, she can help her baby. She immediately reduces the chances that the infant will be born underweight and suffer from future problems (Ahlsten, Cnattingius, & Lindmark, 1993; Kahn et al., 1994; Li, Windsor, & Perkins, 1993).

Even when a baby of a smoking mother appears to be born in good physical condition, slight behavioral abnormalities may threaten the child's development. Newborns of smoking mothers are less attentive to sounds and display more muscle tension (Fried & Makin, 1987). An unresponsive, restless baby may not evoke the kind of interaction from adults that promotes healthy psychological development. Some long-term studies report that prenatally exposed children have shorter attention spans and poorer mental test scores in early childhood, even after many other factors have been controlled (Fergusson, Horwood, & Lynskey, 1993; Fried & Watkinson, 1990). But other researchers have not been able to replicate these findings, so lasting effects remain uncertain (Barr et al., 1990; Streissguth et al., 1989).

Exactly how can smoking harm the fetus? Nicotine, the addictive substance in tobacco, causes the placenta to grow abnormally. As a result, transfer of nutrients is reduced, and the fetus gains weight poorly. Also, smoking raises the concentration of carbon monoxide in the bloodstreams of both mother and fetus. Carbon monoxide displaces oxygen from red blood cells. It damages the central nervous system and reduces birth weight in the fetuses of laboratory animals. Similar effects may occur in humans (Cotton, 1994; Friedman, 1996).

Smoking during pregnancy is associated with low birth weight, prematurity, miscarriage, infant death and childhood cancer. During childhood, youngsters who were prenatally exposed to nicotine may be at risk for attentional and learning problems. This mother can still protect her child by giving up smoking immediately. *(Innervisions)*

Finally, from one-third to one-half of nonsmoking pregnant women are "passive smokers" because their husbands, relatives, and co-workers use cigarettes. Passive smoking is also related to low birth weight, infant death, and possible long-term impairments in attention and learning (Fortier, Marcoux, & Brisson, 1994; Makin, Fried, & Watkinson, 1991). Consequently, Jay made a special effort to give up cigarettes when Yolanda became pregnant.

■ **ALCOHOL.** In *The Broken Cord,* Michael Dorris (1989), a Dartmouth University anthropology professor, described what it was like to raise his adopted son Adam, whose biological mother drank heavily throughout pregnancy and died of alcohol poisoning shortly after his birth. A Sioux Indian, Adam was 3 years old when he came into Dorris's life. He was short and underweight and had a vocabulary of only 20 words. But Dorris was sure that with extra care and attention, Adam would overcome these problems.

Unfortunately, Adam's difficulties did not go away. Although he ate well, Adam grew slowly and remained painfully thin. He was prone to infection and had repeated brain seizures. His vocabulary did not expand like that of normal preschoolers. When he was 7, special testing revealed that Adam's intelligence was below average and that he had trouble concentrating. At age 12, he could not add, subtract, or identify the town in which he lived.

Fetal alcohol syndrome (FAS) is the scientific name for Adam's condition. Mental retardation, poor attention and memory, and overactivity are typical of children with the disorder. Distinct physical symptoms also accompany it. These include slow physical growth and a particular pattern of facial abnormalities: widely spaced eyes, short eyelid openings, a small upturned nose, and a thin upper lip. The small heads of these children indicate that the brain has been prevented from reaching full development. Other defects—of the eyes, ears, nose, throat, heart, genitals, urinary tract, or immune system— may also be present. In all babies born with FAS, the mother drank heavily through most or all of her pregnancy (Streissguth, 1997).

Sometimes children do not display all the abnormalities just described—only some of them. In these cases, the child is said to suffer from **fetal alcohol effects (FAE).** Usually, the mothers of these children drank alcohol in smaller quantities. The particular defects of FAE children vary with timing and length of alcohol exposure during pregnancy (Streissguth, 1997).

Even when provided with enriched diets, FAS babies fail to catch up in physical size during infancy or childhood. Mental impairment is also permanent: In his teens and twenties, Adam's intelligence remained below average, and he had trouble concentrating and keeping a routine job. He also suffered from poor judgment. For example, he would buy something and not wait for change, or he would wander off in the middle of a task. The more alcohol consumed by a woman during pregnancy, the poorer the child's motor coordination, speed of information processing, reasoning, and intelligence and achievement test scores during the preschool and school years (Hunt et al., 1995; Jacobson et al., 1993; Streissguth et al., 1994). In adolescence, FAS is associated with disrupted school experiences, trouble with the law, inappropriate sexual behavior, alcohol and drug abuse, and lasting mental health problems (Streissguth, Bookstein, & Barr, 1996).

How does alcohol produce its devastating effects? Researchers believe it does so in two ways. First, alcohol interferes with cell duplication and migration in the primitive neural tube. Psychophysiological measures, including fMRI and EEGs, reveal structural damage and abnormalities in brain functioning, including electrical and chemical activity involved in transferring messages from one part of the brain to another (Mattson & Riley, 1995; Swayze et al., 1997). Second, large quantities of oxygen are required to metabolize alcohol. When pregnant women drink heavily, they draw oxygen away from the embryo or fetus that is vital for cell growth in the brain and other parts of the body (Vorhees & Mollnow, 1987).

Like heroin and cocaine, alcohol abuse is higher in poverty-stricken sectors of the population (Streissguth, 1997). On the reservation where Adam was born, many children show symptoms of prenatal alcohol exposure. Unfortunately, when girls with FAS or FAE later become pregnant, the poor judgment caused by the syndrome often prevents them

The mother of the severely retarded boy above drank heavily during pregnancy. His widely spaced eyes, thin upper lip, and short eyelid openings are typical of fetal alcohol syndrome. The adolescent girl below also has these physical symptoms. The brain damage caused by alcohol before she was born is permanent. It has made learning in school and adapting to everyday challenges extremely difficult. *(George Steinmetz)*

fetal alcohol syndrome (FAS)
A set of defects that results when women consume large amounts of alcohol during most or all of pregnancy. Includes mental retardation, slow physical growth, and facial abnormalities.

fetal alcohol effects (FAE)
The condition of children who display some but not all the defects of fetal alcohol syndrome. Usually their mothers drank alcohol in smaller quantities during pregnancy.

from understanding why they should avoid alcohol themselves. Thus, the tragic cycle is likely to repeat itself in the next generation.

At this point, you may be wondering: How much alcohol is safe during pregnancy? Is it all right to have a drink or two, either on a daily basis or occasionally? A recent study found that as little as 2 ounces of alcohol a day, taken very early in pregnancy, was associated with FAS-like facial features (Astley et al., 1992). But recall that other factors—both genetic and environmental—can make some fetuses more vulnerable to teratogenic effects. Therefore, because a precise dividing line between safe and dangerous drinking levels cannot be established, it is best for pregnant women to avoid alcohol entirely.

■ **HORMONES.** In Chapter 2, we saw that the Y chromosome causes male sex hormones (called *androgens*) to be secreted prenatally, leading to formation of male reproductive organs. In the absence of male hormones, female structures develop. Hormones are released as part of a delicately balanced system. If their quantity or timing is off, then defects of the genitals as well as of other organs can occur.

Between 1945 and 1970, a synthetic hormone called **diethylstilbestrol (DES)** was widely used to prevent miscarriages in women who had a history of pregnancy problems. As the daughters of these mothers reached adolescence and young adulthood, they showed an unusually high rate of vaginal cancer and malformations of the uterus. When they tried to have children, their pregnancies more often resulted in prematurity, low birth weight, and miscarriage than did those of non-DES-exposed women. Young men whose mothers took DES prenatally were also affected. They showed an increased risk of genital abnormalities and cancer of the testes (Linn et al., 1988; Stillman, 1982). Because of these findings, pregnant women are no longer treated with DES. But many individuals whose mothers took it are now of childbearing age, and they need to be carefully monitored by their doctors.

■ **RADIATION.** In Chapter 2, we saw that ionizing radiation can cause mutation, damaging the DNA in ova and sperm. When mothers are exposed to radiation during pregnancy, additional harm can come to the embryo or fetus. Defects due to radiation were tragically apparent in the children born to pregnant Japanese women who survived the bombing of Hiroshima and Nagasaki during World War II. Miscarriage, slow physical growth, an underdeveloped brain, and malformations of the skeleton and eyes were common (Michel, 1989). Even when an exposed child appears normal at birth, the possibility of later problems cannot be ruled out. For example, research suggests that even low-level radiation, as the result of industrial leakage or medical X-rays, can increase the risk of childhood cancer (Smith, 1992). Women need to tell their doctors and dentists before having X-ray examinations if they are pregnant or trying to become pregnant. In addition, they should avoid work environments in which they might be exposed to X-rays.

■ **ENVIRONMENTAL POLLUTION.** Yolanda and Jay like to refinish antique furniture in their garage, and Jay is an enthusiastic grower of fruit trees in the backyard. When Yolanda became pregnant, they postponed work on several pieces of furniture, and Jay did not spray the fruit trees in the fall and spring of that year. Continuing to do so, they learned, might expose Yolanda and the embryo or fetus to chemical levels thousands of times greater than judged safe by the federal government.

An astounding number of potentially dangerous chemicals are released into the environment in industrialized nations. In the United States, 100,000 are in common use, and 1,000 new ones are introduced each year (Samuels & Samuels, 1996). Although many chemicals cause serious birth defects in laboratory animals, the impact on the human embryo and fetus is known for only a small number of them.

Mercury and Lead. Among metallic elements, mercury and lead are established teratogens. In the 1950s, an industrial plant released waste containing high levels of mercury into a bay providing food and water for the town of Minimata, Japan. Many children born

diethylstilbestrol (DES)
A synthetic hormone widely used between 1945 and 1970 to prevent miscarriage. Children whose mothers took the hormone during pregnancy had an increased chance of developing genital tract abnormalities and cancer of the vagina and testes in adolescence and young adulthood.

at the time were mentally retarded and showed other serious symptoms, including abnormal speech, difficulty in chewing and swallowing, and uncoordinated movements. Autopsies of those who died revealed widespread brain damage (Vorhees & Mollnow, 1987).

Pregnant women can absorb lead from car exhaust, lead-based paint flaking off the walls in old houses and apartment buildings, and other materials used in industrial occupations. High levels of lead exposure are consistently linked to prematurity, low birth weight, brain damage, and a wide variety of physical defects (Dye-White, 1986). Even a very low level of prenatal lead exposure seems to be dangerous. Affected babies show slightly poorer mental development during the first 2 years (Bellinger et al., 1987).

Polychlorinated Biphenyls (PCBs).   For many years, polychlorinated biphenyls (PCBs) were used to insulate electrical equipment. In 1977, they were banned by the U.S. government after research showed that like mercury, they found their way into waterways and entered the food supply. In one study, newborn babies of women who frequently ate PCB-contaminated fish caught in Lake Michigan were compared with newborns whose mothers ate little or no fish. The PCB-exposed babies had a variety of problems, including slightly-lower-than-average birth weight, smaller heads (suggesting brain damage), and less interest in their surroundings (Jacobson et al., 1984). When studied again at 7 months of age, infants whose mothers ate fish during pregnancy did more poorly on memory tests (Jacobson et al., 1985). A follow-up at 4 years of age showed persisting memory difficulties and lower verbal intelligence test scores (Jacobson, Jacobson, & Humphrey, 1990; Jacobson et al., 1992).

■ **MATERNAL DISEASE.**   On her first prenatal visit, Yolanda's doctor asked if she and Jay had already had measles, mumps, and chicken pox, as well as other illnesses. In addition, Yolanda was checked for the presence of several infections, and for good reason. As you can see in Table 3.4, certain diseases during pregnancy are major causes of miscarriage and birth defects.

Viruses.   Five percent of women catch a virus of some sort while pregnant. Most of these illnesses, such as the common cold and various strains of the flu, appear to have no impact on the embryo or fetus. However, a few can result in extensive damage.

The best known of these is **rubella** (3-day or German measles). In the mid-1960s, a worldwide epidemic of rubella led to the birth of over 20,000 American babies with serious defects. Consistent with the sensitive period concept, the greatest damage occurs when rubella strikes during the embryonic period. More than 50 percent of infants whose mothers became ill during that time show heart defects; eye cataracts; deafness; genital, urinary, and intestinal abnormalities; and mental retardation. Infection during the fetal period is less harmful, but low birth weight, hearing loss, and bone defects may still occur (Eberhart-Phillips, Frederick, & Baron, 1993; Samson, 1988).

Since 1966, infants and young children have been routinely vaccinated against rubella, so the number of prenatal cases today is much less than it was a generation ago. Still, 10 to 20 percent of American women of childbearing age lack the rubella antibody, so new outbreaks of the disease are still possible (Lee et al., 1992).

The *human immunodeficiency virus (HIV),* which leads to **acquired immune deficiency syndrome (AIDS),** a disease that destroys the immune system, is infecting increasing numbers of newborn babies. The percentage of AIDS victims who are women has risen dramatically over the past decade—from 6 to 13 percent in the United States and to more than 50 percent in Africa. When they become pregnant, about 20 to 30 percent of the time they pass the deadly virus to the developing organism (Grant, 1995; Provisional Committee on Pediatric AIDS, 1995).

In older children and adults, AIDS symptoms take years to emerge. In contrast, the disease proceeds rapidly in infants. By 6 months, weight loss, diarrhea, and repeated respiratory illnesses are common. The virus also causes brain damage, as indicated by seizures, a gradual loss in brain weight, and delayed mental and motor development. Most prenatal

Rubella
Three-day German measles. Causes a wide variety of prenatal abnormalities, especially when it strikes during the embryonic period.

acquired immune deficiency syndrome (AIDS)
A relatively new viral infection that destroys the immune system and is spread through transfer of body fluids from one person to another. It can be transmitted prenatally.

TABLE 3.4

Effects of Some Infectious Diseases during Pregnancy

+ = established finding   o = no present evidence,   ? = possible effect that is not clearly established.

DISEASE	MISCARRIAGE	PHYSICAL MALFORMATIONS	MENTAL RETARDATION	LOW BIRTH WEIGHT AND PREMATURITY
Viral				
Acquired immune deficiency syndrome (AIDS)	o	?	+	?
Chicken pox	o	+	+	+
Cytomegalovirus	+	+	+	+
Herpes simplex 2 (genital herpes)	+	+	+	+
Mumps	+	?	o	o
Rubella (German measles)	+	+	+	+
Bacterial				
Syphilis	+	+	+	?
Tuberculosis	+	?	+	+
Parasitic				
Malaria	+	o	o	+
Toxoplasmosis	+	+	+	+

Sources: Chatkupt et al., 1989; Cohen, 1993; Peckham & Logan, 1993; Qazi et al., 1988; Samson, 1988; Sever, 1983; Vorhees, 1986.)

AIDS babies survive for only 5 to 8 months after the appearance of these symptoms (Chamberlain, Nichols, & Chase, 1991). The antiviral drug AZT reduces prenatal AIDS transmission by 75 percent, but it can also cause birth defects (Chadwick & Yogev, 1995).

As Table 3.4 reveals, the developing organism is especially sensitive to the family of herpes viruses, for which there is no vaccine or treatment. Among these, *cytomegalovirus* (the most frequent prenatal infection, transmitted through respiratory or sexual contact) and *herpes simplex 2* (which is sexually transmitted) are especially dangerous. In both, the virus invades the mother's genital tract. Babies can be infected either during pregnancy or at birth.

Bacterial and Parasitic Diseases.   Table 3.4 also includes several bacterial and parasitic diseases. Among the most common is **toxoplasmosis,** caused by a parasite found in many animals. Pregnant women may become infected from eating raw or undercooked meat or from contact with the feces of infected cats. About 40 percent of women who have the disease transmit it to the developing organism. If it strikes during the first trimester, it is likely to cause eye and brain damage. Later infection is linked to mild visual and cognitive impairments (Peckham & Logan, 1993). Expectant mothers can avoid toxoplasmosis by making sure that the meat they eat is well cooked, having pet cats checked for the disease, and turning over care of litter boxes to other family members. Outdoor areas that cats may frequent should be avoided as well.

OTHER MATERNAL FACTORS

Besides avoiding teratogens, expectant parents can support the development of the embryo or fetus in other ways. Regular exercise, good nutrition, and emotional well-being of the mother are crucially important. Blood type differences between mother and fetus can create preventable difficulties. Finally, many expectant parents wonder how a

toxoplasmosis
A parasitic disease caused by eating raw or undercooked meat or coming in contact with the feces of infected cats. During the first trimester, it leads to eye and brain damage.

mother's age and previous births affect the course of pregnancy. We examine each of these factors in the following sections.

■ **EXERCISE.** Yolanda continued her half-hour of aerobics three times a week into the third trimester, although her doctor cautioned her to avoid bouncing, jolting, and jogging movements that might subject the fetus to too many shocks and startles. In healthy, physically fit women, regular moderate exercise, such as walking, swimming, biking, and aerobics, is related to increased birth weight (Hatch et al., 1993). However, very frequent, vigorous exercise (working up a sweat four or more times a week) predicts the opposite outcome—lower birth weight than in healthy, non-exercising controls (Bell, Palma, & Lumley, 1995). Hospital-sponsored childbirth education programs frequently offer exercise classes and suggest appropriate routines that help prepare for labor and delivery. Exercises that strengthen the back, abdominal, pelvic, and thigh muscles are emphasized, since the growing fetus places some strain on these parts of the body (Nilsson & Hamberger, 1990).

During the last trimester, when the abdomen grows very large, mothers find it difficult to move freely and often must cut back on exercise. In most cases, a mother who has remained fit during the earlier months is likely to experience fewer of the physical discomforts that arise at this time, such as back pain, upward pressure on the chest, and difficulty breathing.

Finally, pregnant women with health problems, such as circulatory difficulties or a history of miscarriages, should consult their doctors before beginning or continuing a physical fitness routine. For these mothers, exercise (especially the wrong kind) can endanger the pregnancy.

■ **NUTRITION.** Children grow more rapidly during the prenatal period than at any other phase of development. During this time, they depend totally on the mother for nutrients to support their growth.

Mild, regular exercise keeps a mother fit during pregnancy and helps her prepare for the hard physical work of labor and delivery. It is also related to increased birth weight. *(Mike Malyszko/Stock Boston)*

Consequences of Prenatal Malnutrition.   During World War II, a severe famine occurred in the Netherlands, giving scientists a rare opportunity to study the impact of nutrition on prenatal development. Findings revealed that the sensitive period concept operates with nutrition, just as it does with the teratogens discussed earlier in this chapter. Women affected by the famine during the first trimester were more likely to have miscarriages or give birth to babies with physical defects. When women were past the first trimester, fetuses were more likely to survive, but many were born underweight and had small heads (suggesting an underdeveloped brain) (Stein et al., 1975).

We now know that prenatal malnutrition can damage the central nervous system and other parts of the body. Autopsies of malnourished babies who died at or shortly after birth reveal fewer brain cells and a brain weight that is as much as 36 percent below average. The poorer the mother's diet, the greater the loss in brain weight, especially if malnutrition occurred during the last trimester. During that time, the brain is growing rapidly in size, and a maternal diet high in all the basic nutrients is necessary for it to reach its full potential (Morgane et al., 1993). An inadequate diet during pregnancy can distort the structure of other organs, including the pancreas, liver, and blood vessels, thereby increasing the risk of heart disease and diabetes in adulthood (Barker et al., 1993).

Prenatally malnourished babies enter the world with serious problems. They frequently catch respiratory illnesses, since poor nutrition suppresses development of the immune system (Chandra, 1991). In addition, these infants are irritable and unresponsive to stimulation around them. Like drug-addicted newborns, they have a high-pitched cry that is particularly distressing to their caregivers. The effects of poor nutrition quickly combine with an impoverished, stressful home life. With age, low intelligence test scores and serious learning problems become more apparent (Lozoff, 1989).

SOCIAL ISSUES

VITAMIN–MINERAL SUPPLEMENTS PREVENT BIRTH DEFECTS

Many women of childbearing age do not consume major nutrients in sufficient quantity to meet recommended daily allowances. Levels are particularly low for women who are young or poverty stricken—groups least likely to take vitamin–mineral supplements on a regular basis to make up for their dietary inadequacies (Block & Abrams, 1993; Keen & Zidenberg-Cherr, 1994).

The impact of vitamin–mineral intake on pregnancy outcomes was strikingly revealed when iodine was added to commonly eaten foods, such as table salt. (Iodine is an essential component of thyroxine, a thyroid hormone necessary for central nervous system development and body growth.) As a result, iodine-induced cretinism, involving mental retardation, short stature, and bone deterioration, was virtually eradicated (Dunn, 1993).

Other vitamins and minerals also have established benefits. For example, enriching pregnant women's diets with calcium helps prevent maternal high blood pressure and premature births (Repke, 1992). Magnesium and zinc reduce the incidence of many prenatal and birth complications (Facchinetti et al., 1992; Jameson, 1993; Spätling & Spätling, 1988). And a multivitamin supplement taken around the time of conception protects against cleft lip and palate (Tolarova, 1986).

Recently, the power of folic acid to prevent abnormalities of the neural tube, such as anencephaly and spina bifida (see Table 2.6 on page 67), has captured the attention of medical and public health experts. This member of the vitamin B complex group can be found in green vegetables, fresh fruit, liver, and yeast. In a British study of nearly 2,000 women in seven countries who had previously given birth to a baby with a neural tube defect, half were randomly selected to receive a folic acid supplement around the time of conception and half a mixture of other vitamins or no supplement. As Figure 3.8 on the opposite page reveals, the folic acid group showed 72 percent fewer neural tube defects (MCR Vitamin Study Research Group, 1991). In addition, adequate folate intake during the last 10 weeks of pregnancy cuts the risk of premature delivery and low birth weight in half (Scholl et al., 1996).

Because the average American woman gets less than half the recommended amount of folic acid from her diet, the U.S. Food and Drug Administration proposed that it be added to flour, bread, and other grain products (Hopkins-Tanne, 1994). Yet even under these conditions, we cannot be sure that pregnant women will get enough folic acid. Therefore, an intensive media campaign is under way to get all women of childbearing age to consume at least 0.4 mg but not more than 1 mg of folic acid per day through taking a regular vitamin–mineral supplement. Special emphasis is being placed on folic acid enrichment around the time of conception and during the early weeks of pregnancy, when the neural tube is forming.

However, recommending vitamin–mineral supplements for all potential childbearing women is con-

Prevention and Treatment.   Many studies show that providing pregnant women with adequate food has a substantial impact on the health of their newborn babies. Yet the growth demands of the prenatal period require more than just increasing the quantity of a typical diet. As the Social Issues box above reveals, finding ways to optimize maternal nutrition through vitamin–mineral enrichment as early as possible—even before conception—is crucial.

When poor nutrition is allowed to continue throughout pregnancy, infants often require more than dietary enrichment. Their tired, restless behavior leads mothers to be less sensitive and stimulating, and in response, babies become even more passive and withdrawn. Successful treatment must break this cycle of apathetic mother–baby interaction. Some programs do so by teaching parents how to interact effectively with their infants, whereas others focus on stimulating infants to promote active engagement with their physical and social surroundings (Grantham-McGregor et al., 1994; Zeskind & Ramey, 1978, 1981).

Although prenatal malnutrition is highest in poverty-stricken regions of the world, it is not limited to developing countries. Each year, about 80,000 to 120,000 American infants are born seriously undernourished. The federal government provides food packages to impoverished pregnant women through its Special Supplemental Food Program for

troversial. The greatest concern is that a national supplement program might lead some people to consume dangerously high levels of certain nutrients because they believe, incorrectly, that more is always better. For example, excessive daily intake of vitamins A and D (by taking even two or three multivitamin pills) can result in birth defects (Rosa, 1993; Rothman et al., 1995). Furthermore, if people conclude that taking a supplement means they need not worry about eating a well-balanced diet, a supplement program could reduce consumption of essential nutrients not provided in the supplement (Keen & Zidenberg-Cherr, 1994).

Experts agree that encouraging all women of childbearing age to take an appropriate vitamin–mineral supplement is vital for preventing birth defects. But without a public education campaign that emphasizes the dangers of excessive vitamin–mineral consumption and the importance of maintaining a high-quality diet, a national supplement program poses grave risks.

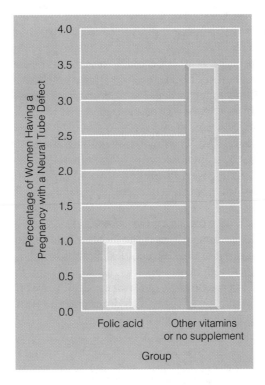

FIGURE 3.8

Percentage of pregnancies with a neural tube defect in folic-acid-supplemented women versus other-vitamins or no-supplement controls. Folic acid taken around the time of conception dramatically reduced the incidence of neural tube defects—a finding confirmed by other large-scale studies. Note, however, that folic acid did not eliminate all neural tube defects. These abnormalities, like many others, have multiple origins in the embryo's genetic disposition and factors in the environment. *(Adapted from MCR Vitamin Study Research Group, 1991.)*

Finally, a supplement policy should complement, not replace, economic programs designed to improve maternal diets during pregnancy. For women with low incomes who do not get enough food or adequate variety of foods, multivitamin tablets are a necessary, but not sufficient, intervention.

Women, Infants, and Children (WIC). Unfortunately, because of funding shortages, the program serves only 70 percent of those who are eligible (Children's Defense Fund, 1998).

At this point, it is important to note that the fetuses of some middle- and high-SES expectant mothers are also poorly nourished. Pregnancy is not the time for a woman to worry about her figure! A weight gain of 25 to 30 pounds is normal and helps ensure the health of both mother and baby. Yet in the United States, where thinness is the feminine ideal, women often feel uneasy about gaining this much weight, and they may try to limit their food intake. When they do so, they risk their infant's development in all of the ways just described.

■ **EMOTIONAL STRESS.** When women experience severe emotional stress during pregnancy, their babies are at risk for a wide variety of difficulties. Intense anxiety is associated with a higher rate of miscarriage, prematurity, low birth weight, and newborn respiratory illness. It is also related to certain physical defects, such as cleft palate and pyloric stenosis (tightening of the infant's stomach outlet, which must be treated surgically) (Hoffman & Hatch, 1996; Omer & Everly, 1988).

How can maternal stress affect the developing organism? To understand this process, think back to how your own body felt the last time you were under considerable stress.

When we experience fear and anxiety, stimulant hormones are released into our bloodstream. These cause us to be "poised for action." Large amounts of blood are sent to parts of the body involved in the defensive response—the brain, the heart, and muscles in the arms, legs, and trunk. Blood flow to other organs, including the uterus, is reduced. As a result, the fetus is deprived of a full supply of oxygen and nutrients. Stress hormones also cross the placenta, leading the fetus's heart rate and activity level to rise dramatically. In fact, long-term exposure to these hormones might be responsible for the irritability and digestive disturbances observed in babies of highly stressed mothers after birth. Finally, women who experience long-term anxiety are more likely to smoke, drink, eat poorly, and engage in other behaviors that harm the embryo and fetus. These factors probably contribute to the negative outcomes just described.

But women under severe emotional stress do not always give birth to babies with problems. The risks are greatly reduced when mothers have husbands, other family members, and friends to whom they can turn for emotional support (Nuckolls, Cassel, & Kaplan, 1972). The link between social support and positive pregnancy outcomes is particularly strong for low-income women (Hoffman & Hatch, 1996). These results suggest that finding ways to enhance isolated expectant mothers' supportive social networks during pregnancy can help prevent prenatal complications.

■ **RH BLOOD INCOMPATIBILITY.** When inherited blood types of mother and fetus differ, in some instances the incompatibility can cause serious problems. The most common cause of these difficulties involves a blood protein called the **Rh factor.** When the mother is Rh negative (lacks the protein) and the father is Rh positive (has the protein), the baby may inherit the father's Rh-positive blood type. (Recall from Table 2.2 on page 59 that Rh-positive blood is dominant and Rh-negative blood is recessive, so the chances are good that a baby will be Rh positive.)

During the third trimester and at the time of birth, some maternal and fetal blood cells usually cross the placenta, in small enough amounts to be quite safe. But if even a little of the baby's Rh-positive blood passes into a mother's Rh-negative bloodstream, she begins to form antibodies to the foreign Rh protein. If these enter the baby's system, they destroy red blood cells, reducing the supply of oxygen. Mental retardation, damage to the heart muscle, and infant death can occur.

Since it takes time for the mother to produce Rh antibodies, first-born children are rarely affected. The danger increases with each additional pregnancy. Fortunately, the harmful effects of Rh incompatibility can be prevented in most cases. After the birth of each Rh-positive baby, Rh-negative mothers are routinely given a vaccine called RhoGam, which prevents the buildup of antibodies in the mother's system. However, sometimes errors are made in maternal blood typing, and the mother's production of antibodies is not controlled. In these cases, if the baby is in danger, blood transfusions can be performed immediately after birth or, if necessary, even before the baby is born (Larson, 1996).

■ **MATERNAL AGE AND PREVIOUS BIRTHS.** Earlier we indicated that women who delay having children until their thirties or forties face a greater risk of infertility, miscarriage, and babies born with chromosomal defects. Are other pregnancy problems more common for older mothers?

For many years, scientists thought that aging and repeated use of the mother's reproductive organs increased the likelihood of a wide variety of pregnancy complications. Recently, this idea has been questioned. When women without serious health difficulties are considered, even those in their forties do not experience more prenatal problems than those in their twenties (Ales, Druzin, & Santini, 1990; Dildy et al., 1996; Spellacy, Miller, & Winegar, 1986). And a large study of over 50,000 pregnancies showed no relationship between number of previous births and pregnancy complications (Heinonen, Slone, & Shapiro, 1977).

In the case of teenage mothers, does physical immaturity cause prenatal problems? Again, research indicates that it does not. A teenager's body is large enough and strong enough to support pregnancy. In fact, as we will see in Chapter 14, young adolescent girls

Rh factor
A protein that, when present in the fetus's blood but not in the mother's, can cause the mother to build up antibodies. If these return to the fetus's system, they destroy red blood cells, reducing the oxygen supply to organs and tissues.

grow taller and heavier and their hips broaden (in preparation for child-bearing) *before* their menstrual periods begin. Nature tries to ensure that once a girl can conceive, she is physically ready to carry and give birth to a baby. Infants of teenagers are born with a higher rate of problems for quite different reasons. Many adolescents do not have access to medical care or are afraid to seek it. In addition, most pregnant teenagers come from low-income backgrounds where stress, poor nutrition, and health problems are common (Chase-Lansdale & Brooks-Gunn, 1994).

THE IMPORTANCE OF PRENATAL HEALTH CARE

Yolanda had her first prenatal appointment 3 weeks after her first missed menstrual period. After that, she visited the doctor's office once a month until she was 7 months pregnant, then twice during the eighth month. As birth grew near, Yolanda's appointments increased to once a week. The doctor kept track of Yolanda's general health, weight gain, and the capacity of her uterus and cervix to support the fetus. The fetus's growth was also carefully monitored. During these visits, Yolanda had plenty of opportunity to ask questions, pick up literature in the waiting room, get to know the person who would deliver her baby, and plan the kind of birth experience she and Jay desired.

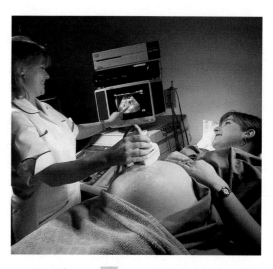

During a routine prenatal visit, this doctor uses ultrasound to show an expectant mother an image of her fetus and to evaluate its development. All pregnant women should receive early and regular prenatal care—to protect their own health and the health of their babies. *(Deep Light Productions/Science Photo Library/Photo Researchers, Inc.)*

Yolanda's pregnancy, like most others, was free of complications. But unexpected difficulties can arise, especially if mothers have health problems to begin with. For example, women with diabetes need careful monitoring during pregnancy. The presence of extra sugar in the diabetic mother's bloodstream causes the fetus to grow larger than average, although it is physically less mature than the fetus of a nondiabetic mother. As a result, problems at birth are common for both mother and infant.

Another pregnancy risk is **toxemia** (sometimes called *eclampsia*). In the 5 to 10 percent of women who develop this illness in the latter half of their pregnancies, blood pressure increases sharply and the face, hands, and feet swell. If untreated, serious harm can result, including convulsions in the mother and death of the fetus. Usually, toxemia can be brought under control through hospitalization, bed rest, and drugs to bring blood pressure down. If not, the baby must be delivered at once (Carlson, Eisenstat, & Ziporyn, 1996).

Unfortunately, 10 percent of pregnant women in the United States wait until after the first trimester to seek prenatal care, and 4 percent delay until the end of pregnancy or never get any at all. Most of these mothers are adolescents, unmarried, or poverty stricken. Their infants are far more likely to be born underweight and to die before birth or during the first year of life than are the babies of mothers who receive early medical attention (Children's Defense Fund, 1998).

Financial problems are a major barrier to early prenatal care. Most American women who delay going to the doctor do not receive health insurance as a fringe benefit of their jobs. Others have no insurance because they are unemployed. Although the very poorest of these mothers are eligible for government-sponsored health services, many women who have low incomes and need benefits do not qualify. In Europe, where affordable health care is universally available, the percentage of late-care pregnancies is greatly reduced. Some countries offer special financial incentives. For example, in France, every expectant mother who maintains a regular schedule of prenatal visits throughout pregnancy receives a monetary allowance (Buekens et al., 1993).

Besides financial hardship, there are other reasons that some mothers do not seek prenatal care. When researchers asked women who first went to the doctor late in pregnancy why they waited so long, they mentioned a wide variety of personal problems, including psychological stress, the demands of taking care of other young children, lack of transportation, ambivalence about the pregnancy, and family crises. Many were also engaging in high-risk behaviors, such as smoking and drug abuse (Melnikow & Alemagno, 1993).

toxemia
An illness of the last half of pregnancy in which the mother's blood pressure increases sharply and her face, hands, and feet swell. If untreated, it can cause convulsions in the mother and death of the fetus.

CAREGIVING CONCERNS

Do's and Don'ts for a Healthy Pregnancy

DO	DON'T
Do make sure that you have been vaccinated against infectious diseases dangerous to the embryo and fetus, such as rubella, before you get pregnant. Most vaccinations are not safe during pregnancy.	Don't take any drugs without consulting your doctor.
Do see a doctor as soon as you suspect that you are pregnant—within a few weeks after a missed menstrual period.	Don't smoke. If you have already smoked during part of your pregnancy, you can protect your baby by cutting down or (better yet) quitting at any time. If other members of your family are smokers, ask them to quit or smoke outside.
Do continue to get regular medical checkups throughout pregnancy.	
Do obtain literature from your doctor, local library, and bookstore about prenatal development and care. Ask questions about anything you do not understand.	Don't drink alcohol from the time you decide to get pregnant. If you find it difficult to give up alcohol, ask for help from your doctor, local family service agency, or nearest chapter of Alcoholics Anonymous.
Do eat a well-balanced diet and take vitamin–mineral supplements as prescribed by your doctor. On the average, a woman should increase her intake by 300 calories a day over her usual needs—less at the beginning and more at the end of pregnancy. Gain 25 to 30 pounds gradually.	Don't engage in activities that might expose your baby to environmental hazards, such as radiation or chemical pollutants. If you work in an occupation that involves these agents, ask for a safer assignment or a leave of absence.
Do keep physically fit through mild exercise. If possible, join a special exercise class for expectant mothers.	Don't engage in activities that might expose your baby to harmful infectious diseases, such as childhood illnesses and toxoplasmosis.
Do avoid emotional stress. If you are a single parent, find a relative or friend on whom you can count for emotional support.	Don't choose pregnancy as a time to go on a diet.
Do get plenty of rest. An overtired mother is at risk for pregnancy complications.	Don't overeat and gain too much weight during pregnancy. A very large weight gain is associated with complications.
Do enroll in a prenatal and childbirth education class along with the baby's father. When parents know what to expect, the 9 months before birth can be one of the most joyful times of life.	

ASK YOURSELF . . .

■ *Why is it difficult to determine the effects of some environmental agents, such as over-the-counter drugs and pollution, on the embryo and fetus?*

■ *Nora, who is expecting for the first time at age 40, wonders whether she is likely to have a difficult pregnancy because of her age. How would you respond to Nora's concern?*

■ *Trixie has just learned she is pregnant. Since she has always been healthy and feels good right now, she cannot understand why the doctor wants her to come in for checkups so often. Why is early and regular prenatal care important for Trixie?*

These women, who had no medical attention for most of their pregnancies, were among those who needed it most!

Clearly, public education about the importance of early prenatal care and medical services that reach all pregnant women, especially those who are young, single, and poor, are badly needed. The Caregiving Concerns table above provides a summary of "do's and don'ts" for a healthy pregnancy, based on our discussion of the prenatal environment.

BRIEF REVIEW

Teratogens—cigarettes, alcohol, certain drugs, radiation, environmental pollutants, and diseases—can seriously harm the embryo and fetus. The effects of teratogens are complex. They depend on amount and length of exposure, the genetic makeup of mother and baby, and the presence of other harmful environmental agents. Teratogens operate according to the sensitive period concept. In general, greatest damage occurs during the embryonic phase, when all parts of the body are forming. Poor maternal nutrition, severe emotional stress, and Rh blood incompatibility can also endanger the developing organism. As long as they are in good health, teenagers, women in their thirties and forties, and women who have given birth to several children have a high likelihood of problem-free pregnancies. Regular medical checkups are important for all expectant mothers, and they are crucial for women with a history of health difficulties.

PREPARING FOR PARENTHOOD

Although we have discussed a great many ways that development can be thrown off course during the prenatal period, over 90 percent of pregnancies in industrialized nations result in normal newborn babies. For most expectant parents, the prenatal period is not a time of medical hazard. Instead, it is a period of major life change accompanied by excitement, anticipation, and looking inward. The 9 months before birth not only permit the fetus to grow but also give men and women time to develop a new sense of themselves as mothers and fathers.

This period of psychological preparation is vital. Many young people say they do not feel ready to deal with the demands and responsibilities of parenthood (Cowan & Cowan, 1992). How effectively individuals construct a new parental identity during pregnancy has important consequences for the parent–infant relationship. A great many factors contribute to the personal adjustments that take place.

SEEKING INFORMATION

We know most about how mothers adapt to the psychological challenges of pregnancy, although some evidence suggests that fathers use many of the same techniques (Colman & Colman, 1991). One common strategy is to seek information, as Yolanda and Jay did when they read books on pregnancy and childbirth and enrolled in my class. In fact, expectant mothers regard books as an extremely valuable source of information, rating them as second in importance only to their doctors. And the more a pregnant woman seeks information—by reading, accessing relevant websites, asking friends, consulting her own mother, or attending a prenatal class—the more confident she tends to feel about her own ability to be a good mother (Cowan & Cowan, 1992; Deutsch et al., 1988).

Why does information seeking promote adjustment during pregnancy? First, when people gather information about an unfamiliar event, it often becomes less threatening. Second, pregnant women who learn a great deal about what they are about to experience start to imagine themselves engaging in the activities of motherhood. For example, when they read about breast-feeding, they see themselves nursing their own baby. Expectant mothers who imagine themselves as competent caregivers make better adjustments after birth and report greater satisfaction in caring for their babies (Deutsch et al., 1988).

THE BABY BECOMES A REALITY

At the beginning of pregnancy, the baby seems far off in the future. Except for a missed period and some morning sickness (nausea that most women experience during the first trimester), the woman's body has not changed much. But gradually, her abdomen enlarges, and the baby starts to become more of a reality. A major turning point occurs when expectant parents are presented with concrete proof that a fetus is, indeed, developing inside the uterus. For Yolanda and Jay, this happened 13 weeks into the pregnancy. Jay went with Yolanda to the doctor, who showed them an ultrasound image of the fetus. As Jay described this experience, "We saw it, these little hands and feet waving and kicking. It had the cord and everything. It's really a baby in there!" Sensing the fetus's movements for the first time can be just as thrilling. Of course, the mother feels these "kicks" first, but soon after, the father (and any siblings) can participate by touching her abdomen.

Mothers begin to get to know the child as an individual through these signs of life. From the vigor of its movements and its daily cycles of activity and rest, the fetus takes on the beginnings of a personality (see the Biology and Environment box on page 124). Both parents start to dream of a relationship with the baby, to talk about names, and to make plans to welcome the newcomer into their lives.

BIOLOGY & ENVIRONMENT

TEMPERAMENT IN THE WOMB

As Yolanda rested one afternoon, 3 weeks before her due date, she felt several bursts of fetal activity, interspersed with quiet periods. "Hey, little one," she whispered, looking down at her large abdomen as it bulged after a foot kick, "you're on the move again. You always do this when I try to take a nap!" Then Yolanda wondered, "Can the fetus's behavior tell us anything about what he or she will be like after birth?"

Yolanda's question is at the heart of current efforts to determine whether individual differences in temperament have genetic origins. The earlier in development that predictors of temperamental traits can be identified, the greater the likelihood that heredity contributes to those traits.

Until recently, limited access to the fetus made it hard to study the relationship between fetal measures and temperament after birth. Today, sophisticated equipment for monitoring fetal responses permits researchers to address this issue.

In the most extensive study to date, 31 volunteer women, whose newborns were delivered healthy and full term, were monitored periodically during the prenatal period, from 20 weeks to just before birth (DiPietro et al., 1996b). During each session, the mothers lay quietly while a variety of fetal measures, including heart rate and activity level, were recorded. Then, at 3 and 6 months after birth, the mothers were asked to rate various aspects of their baby's temperament, including fussiness, adaptability to new persons and situations, activity level, and regularity of eating and sleeping.

Findings revealed that pattern of fetal activity in the last few weeks of pregnancy was the best predictor of infant temperament. Fetuses (like Yolanda's) who cycled between quiet and active periods tended to become calm babies with predictable sleep–waking schedules. In contrast, fetuses who were highly active for long stretches were more likely to become difficult, unpredictable babies—fussy, especially when confronted with new people and situations; irregular in eating and sleeping; constantly wriggling and squirming; and waking often during the night (see Figure 3.9).

But we must keep in mind that these links between prenatal measures and infant characteristics are only modest. In Chapter 7, we will see that sensitive care can modify a difficult baby's temperamental style. Furthermore, researchers have yet to determine whether fetal activity predicts *actual* infant behavior, not just *maternal judgments* of that behavior.

But if the relationships just described hold up, then parents whose fetuses are very active can prepare for extra caregiving challenges. Recognizing that their baby-to-be may have a fussy, difficult disposition, they can take extra steps to provide a sympathetic environment as soon as the baby is born.

FIGURE 3.9

Temperament scores 6 months after birth of highly active fetuses versus other fetuses. Fetuses who were very active in the last weeks of pregnancy developed into 6-month-old babies who were fussier, more unadaptable to new people and situations, more irregular in eating and sleeping, and more active, as judged by their mothers. They also woke more often at night (not shown in the graph). *(Adapted from DiPietro et al., 1996b.)*

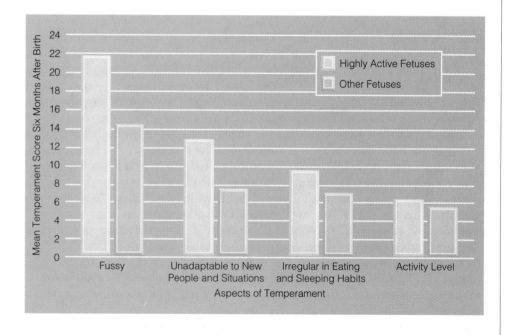

MODELS OF EFFECTIVE PARENTHOOD

As pregnancy proceeds, expectant parents think about important models of parenthood in their own lives—for the woman, her mother, and for the man, his father. Research indicates that when men and women have had good relationships with their own parents, they are more likely to develop positive images of themselves as parents during pregnancy (Deutsch et al., 1988). These images, in turn, predict favorable relationships with children during infancy and early childhood (Cowan et al., 1994; Fonagy, Steele, & Steele, 1991; van IJzendoorn et al., 1991).

If their own parental relationships are mixed or negative, expectant mothers and fathers may have trouble building a healthy picture of themselves as parents. Some adults handle this problem constructively, by seeking out other examples of effective parenthood. One father named Roger shared these thoughts with his wife and several expectant couples who met regularly with a counselor to talk about their concerns during pregnancy:

> I rethink past experiences with my father and my family and am aware of how I was raised. I just think I don't want to do that again, I want to change that; I don't want to be like my father in that way. I wish there had been more connection and closeness and a lot more respect for who I was. For me, my father-in-law combines spontaneity, sincerity, and warmth. He is a mix of empathy and warmth plus stepping back and being objective that I want to be as a father. (Colman & Colman, 1991, p. 148)

A warm, secure relationship with their own parents is helpful to adults in developing an optimistic view of themselves as parents, but it is not a necessity. Like Roger, many people come to terms with negative experiences in their own childhoods, recognize that other options are available to them as parents, and build healthier and happier relationships with their children (Cox et al., 1992). Roger achieved this understanding after he participated in a special intervention program designed to help expectant mothers and fathers prepare for parenthood. Couples who take part in such programs feel better about themselves and their marital relationships, regard the demands of caring for the new baby as less stressful, and adapt more easily when family problems arise (Duncan & Markman, 1988).

PRACTICAL CONCERNS

When women first learn they are pregnant, they often wonder how long they will be able to continue their usual activities. Culture has a major impact on answers to this question. In the United States, women in good health often work and travel until the very end of their pregnancies, without any apparent harm to the fetus. And as long as the pregnancy has gone well, American health professionals advise that sexual intercourse can be continued through most or all of the 9 months before birth (Boston Women's Health Book Collective, 1992; Samuels & Samuels, 1996).

In contrast, when a Japanese woman learns that she is pregnant, she changes her daily life considerably, out of a belief that this is necessary to protect the health of her baby. Nancy Engel (1989), an American nurse, described her experience of becoming pregnant for the first time while living in Japan:

> When I announced my pregnancy it was assumed that I would quit my teaching position and drop out of language school. My teacher told me that language study was stressful, and the increased [hormone levels] it caused were harmful to the baby. Similarly, I was advised that the noise of train travel, typing, or using a sewing machine should be avoided. My colleagues at college . . . were particularly concerned when I revealed plans to go to Thailand on vacation during the fourth month. They told me

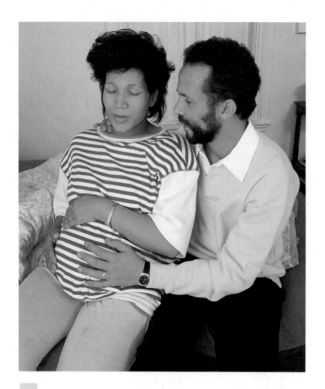

As this man and woman share the thrill of sensing the fetus's movements, parenthood starts to become more of a reality. Mother and father begin to get to know their child. *(Carol Palmer/Picture Cube)*

ASK YOURSELF . . .

- *Muriel, who is expecting her first child, recalls her own mother as cold and distant. Muriel is worried about whether she will be effective at caring for her new baby. What factors during pregnancy affect the quality of Muriel's maternal behavior?*

that airplane travel would cause miscarriage, and they cited numerous examples. . . . My doctor assumed that I would not engage in sexual activity, to ensure a healthy newborn. (p. 83)

As the seventh or eighth month of pregnancy approaches, the Japanese woman returns to her mother's home, where she rests until birth and recuperates for several months afterward.

Although Engel could not accept these practices for herself, she realized that they were based on cultural values that hold the maternal role in high esteem and place the safety of the infant first. This investment in the child's well-being makes Japan an excellent place to have a baby. It has one of the lowest rates of pregnancy and birth complications in the world (Bellamy, 1997).

THE PARENTAL RELATIONSHIP

The most important preparation for parenthood takes place in the context of the parents' relationship. Expectant couples who are unhappy in their marriages during pregnancy continue to be dissatisfied after the baby is born (Cowan & Cowan, 1992). Deciding to have a baby in hopes of improving a troubled relationship is a serious mistake. There is good evidence that pregnancy adds to rather than subtracts from family conflict if a marriage is in danger of falling apart (Belsky & Kelly, 1994).

When a couple's relationship is faring well and both partners want and planned for the baby, the excitement of a first pregnancy may bring husband and wife closer together. At the same time, pregnancy does change a marriage. Expectant parents do not just add parenting to their existing responsibilities. They must adjust their established roles to make room for children. Women start to plan how they will juggle the demands of work and child rearing. Men reconsider the adequacy of their jobs and the size of the family bank account.

In addition, each partner is likely to develop new expectations of the other. Women look for greater demonstrations of affection, interest in the pregnancy, and help with household chores from their husbands. They see these behaviors as important signs of the husband's continued acceptance of his wife, the pregnancy, and the baby to come. Similarly, men are particularly sensitive to expressions of warmth from their pregnant wives. These reassure the husband that he will continue to occupy a central place in the new mother's emotional life after the baby is born (Cowan & Cowan, 1992).

When a relationship rests on a solid foundation of love and respect, parents are well equipped to master the challenges of pregnancy. They are also prepared to handle the much more demanding changes that will take place in the family as soon as the baby is born.

Summary

MOTIVATIONS FOR PARENTHOOD

List the advantages and disadvantages of parenthood, and explain the impact of family size and parental age on child rearing and child development.

■ Today, adults in Western industrialized nations are more likely to weigh the advantages and disadvantages of becoming parents than they were a generation or two ago. Parents are also having smaller families, a trend that has positive consequences for children's development.

■ When couples limit their families to just one child, their youngsters are just as socially well adjusted as are children with siblings. Many adults are waiting until later in their lives to have children, when their careers are well established and they are emotionally more mature.

PRENATAL DEVELOPMENT

List the three phases of prenatal development, and describe the major milestones of each.

■ Prenatal development is usually divided into three phases. The period of the zygote lasts about 2 weeks, from fertilization until the **blastocyst** becomes deeply **implanted** in the uterine lining. During this time, structures that will support prenatal growth begin to form. The **embryonic disk** is surrounded by the **amnion,** which is filled with **amniotic fluid.** From the **chorion,** villi emerge that burrow into the uterine wall, and the **placenta** starts to develop. The developing organism is connected to the placenta by the **umbilical cord.**

■ The period of the **embryo** lasts from 2 to 8 weeks, during which the foundations for all body structures are laid down. In the first week of this period, the **neural tube** forms, and the nervous system starts to develop. Other organs follow and grow

rapidly. At the end of this phase, the embryo responds to touch and can move.

■ The period of the **fetus,** lasting until the end of pregnancy, involves a dramatic increase in body size and completion of physical structures. It is the longest prenatal phase and includes the second and third **trimesters.** By the middle of the second trimester, the mother can feel movement. The fetus becomes covered with **vernix,** which protects the skin from chapping. White, downy hair called **lanugo** helps the vernix stick to the skin. At the end of the second trimester, the production of neurons in the brain is complete.

■ The **age of viability** occurs at the beginning of the final trimester, sometime between 22 and 26 weeks. The brain continues to develop rapidly, and new sensory and behavioral capacities emerge. Gradually the lungs mature, the fetus fills the uterus, and birth is near.

PRENATAL ENVIRONMENTAL INFLUENCES

What factors influence the impact of teratogens on the developing organism?

■ **Teratogens** are environmental agents that cause damage during the prenatal period. Their effects conform to the sensitive period concept. The developing organism is especially vulnerable during the embryonic period, since all essential body structures are rapidly emerging.

■ The impact of teratogens differs from one case to the next, due to amount and length of exposure, the genetic makeup of mother and fetus, and the presence or absence of other harmful agents. The effects of teratogens are not limited to immediate physical damage. Serious psychological consequences may appear later in development. Some are indirectly caused by physical defects through bidirectional exchanges between child and environment.

List agents known or suspected of being teratogens, and discuss evidence supporting the harmful impact of each.

■ Drugs, cigarettes, alcohol, hormones, radiation, environmental pollution, and infectious diseases are teratogens that can endanger the developing organism. **Thalidomide,** a sedative widely available in the early 1960s, showed without a doubt that drugs could cross the placenta and cause serious damage. Babies whose mothers took heroin, methadone, or cocaine during pregnancy have withdrawal symptoms after birth and are jittery and inattentive. Cocaine is especially risky, since it is associated with physical defects and central nervous system damage.

■ Infants of parents who use tobacco are often born underweight and may have attention and learning problems in early childhood. When mothers consume alcohol in large quantities, **fetal alcohol syndrome (FAS),** a disorder involving mental retardation, poor attention, overactivity, slow physical growth, and facial abnormalities, often results. Smaller amounts of alcohol may lead to some of these problems—a condition known as **fetal alcohol effects (FAE).**

■ A hormone called **diethylstilbestrol (DES)** has a delayed impact. Children whose mothers took this drug during pregnancy have an increased chance of developing genital tract abnormalities and cancer of the vagina and testes in adolescence and young adulthood. Radiation, mercury, and lead can result in a wide variety of problems, including physical malformations and severe brain damage. PCBs have been linked to decreased responsiveness to the environment and memory difficulties during infancy, and poorer memory and verbal intelligence in early childhood.

■ Many diseases can harm the embryo and fetus. **Rubella** causes a wide variety of abnormalities, which vary with its time of

Summary (continued)

occurrence during pregnancy. **Acquired immune deficiency syndrome (AIDS)** can be transmitted prenatally and is linked to brain damage, delayed development, and early death. **Toxoplasmosis** in the first trimester may lead to eye and brain damage.

Describe the impact of additional maternal factors on prenatal development.

- Other maternal factors can either support or complicate prenatal development. In healthy, physically fit women, regular moderate exercise contributes to an expectant woman's general health and readiness for childbirth and is related to increased birth weight. When the mother's diet is inadequate, low birth weight and brain damage are major concerns.

- Severe emotional stress is linked to many pregnancy complications, although its impact can be reduced by providing the mother with emotional support.

- If the mother's blood is Rh negative, or lacks the **Rh factor,** and the fetus's blood is Rh positive, special precautions must be taken to ensure that antibodies to the Rh protein do not pass from mother to fetus.

- Aside from the risk of chromosomal abnormalities, older women in good health do not experience more prenatal problems than do younger women. Poor health and environmental risks associated with poverty are the strongest predictors of pregnancy complications in teenagers and older women.

Why is early and regular health care vital during the prenatal period?

- Early and regular prenatal health care is important for all pregnant women. Unexpected difficulties, such as **toxemia,** can arise, especially when mothers have health problems to begin with. Prenatal care is especially crucial for women unlikely to seek it—in particular, those who are young, single, or poor.

PREPARING FOR PARENTHOOD

What factors contribute to preparation for parenthood during the prenatal period?

- Pregnancy is an important period of psychological transition. Mothers and fathers prepare for their new role by seeking information from books and other sources and becoming acquainted with the movements and daily cycles of the fetus. They also rely on effective models of parenthood as they build images of themselves as mothers and fathers.

- The most important preparation for parenthood takes place in the context of the couple's relationship. During the 9 months preceding birth, parents adjust their various roles and expectations of one another as they prepare to welcome the baby into the family.

Important terms and concepts

acquired immune deficiency syndrome (AIDS) (p. 115)
age of viability (p. 107)
amnion (p. 103)
amniotic fluid (p. 103)
blastocyst (p. 102)
chorion (p. 104)
diethylstilbestrol (DES) (p. 114)
embryo (p. 104)

embryonic disk (p. 102)
fetal alcohol effects (FAE) (p. 113)
fetal alcohol syndrome (FAS) (p. 113)
fetus (p. 107)
implantation (p. 103)
lanugo (p. 107)
neural tube (p. 105)
placenta (p. 104)
Rh factor (p. 120)

rubella (p. 115)
teratogen (p. 109)
thalidomide (p. 110)
toxemia (p. 121)
toxoplasmosis (p. 116)
trimesters (p. 107)
umbilical cord (p. 104)
vernix (p. 107)

PRENATAL HEALTH

National Center for Education in Maternal and Child Health
(703) 524-7802
Website: www.ncemch.georgetown.edu

Government-sponsored agency that provides information on all aspects of maternal and child health.

ALCOHOL ABUSE

National Clearinghouse for Alcohol and Drug Information
(301) 468-2600
Website: www.health.org

Government-sponsored agency that provides information on all aspects of alcohol and drug abuse.

Alcoholics Anonymous
(212) 870-3400
Website: www.alcoholics-anonymous.org

An international organization aimed at helping people recover from alcoholism. Local chapters exist in many countries.

BIRTH DEFECTS

National Easter Seal Society
(312) 726-6200
Website: www.seals.com

Provides information on birth defects. Works with other agencies to help individuals with disabilities.

National Information Center for Children and Youth with Disabilities
(800) 695-0285
Website: www.social.com/health/nhic/ data/hr2000/hr2002.html

Provides information to parents and educators on services for children with disabilities.

March of Dimes Birth Defects Foundation
(914) 428-7100
Website: www.modimes. org

Works to prevent birth defects through public education and community service programs.

Parents Helping Parents
(612) 827-2966
Website: www.pacer.org/textonly/parent/parent.htm

Offers a wide variety of services and educational programs to help parents rear children with special needs, including those with birth defects.

"Our Planet"
Sameh Mortaz Herjri
9 years, Iran

This idyllic scene depicts an infant who has successfully made the transition to life outside the womb with the help of loving parents. As the artist emphasizes, for children to develop at their best, they need the protection and support of their physical and social worlds. Chapter 4 explores the birth process and the marvelous competencies of newborn babies.

BIRTH AND THE

NEWBORN BABY

Although Yolanda

and Jay completed my course 3 months before their baby was born, they returned the following spring to share their reactions to birth and new parenthood with my next class. Two-week-old Joshua came along as well. Yolanda and Jay's story revealed that the birth of a baby is one of the most dramatic and emotional events in human experience. Jay was present throughout Yolanda's labor and delivery. Yolanda explained,

> By morning, we knew I was in labor. It was Thursday, so we went in for my usual weekly appointment. The doctor said, yes, the baby was on the way, but it would be a while. He told us to go home and relax or take a leisurely walk and come to the hospital in 3 or 4 hours. We checked in at 3 in the afternoon; Joshua arrived at 2 o'clock the next morning. When, finally, I was ready to deliver,

it went quickly; a half hour or so and some good hard pushes, and there he was! His body had stuff all over it, his face was red and puffy, and his head was misshapen, but I thought, "Oh! he's beautiful. I can't believe he's really here!"

Jay was also elated by Joshua's birth. "I wanted to support Yolanda and to experience as much as I could. It was awesome, indescribable," he said, holding little Joshua over his shoulder and patting and kissing him gently. "For me, it meant everything to be there."

In this chapter, we explore the experience of childbirth, from both the parents' and the baby's point of view. As recently as 30 years ago, the birth process was treated more like an illness than a natural and normal part of life. Fortunately, childbirth is rarely like this today. Women in industrialized nations have many more choices about where and how they give birth than ever before, and modern hospitals often go to great lengths to make the arrival of a new baby a rewarding, family-centered event.

Joshua reaped the benefits of Yolanda and Jay's careful attention to his needs during pregnancy. He was strong, alert, and healthy at birth. Nevertheless, the birth process does not always go smoothly. We will pay special attention to the problems of infants who are born underweight or too early. Our discussion will also examine the pros and cons of medical interventions, such as pain-relieving drugs and surgical deliveries, designed to ease a difficult birth and protect the health of mother and baby.

Finally, Yolanda and Jay spoke candidly about how, since Joshua's arrival, life at home had changed. "It's exciting and wonderful," reflected Yolanda, "but the adjustments are enormous. I wasn't quite prepared for the intensity of Joshua's 24-hour-a-day demands." In the last part of this chapter, we take a close look at the remarkable ability of newborn babies to adapt to the external world and to communicate their needs. We also consider how parents adjust to the realities of everyday life with a new baby.

THE STAGES OF CHILDBIRTH

It is not surprising that childbirth is often referred to as *labor*. It is the hardest physical work that a woman may ever do. A complex series of hormonal changes initiates the process. Yolanda's whole system, which for 9 months supported and protected Joshua's growth, now turned toward a new goal: getting him safely out of the uterus.

The events that lead to childbirth begin slowly in the ninth month of pregnancy and gradually pick up speed. Several signs indicate that labor is near:

- Yolanda felt the upper part of her uterus contract once in a while. These contractions are often called *false labor* or *prelabor,* since they remain brief and unpredictable for several weeks.

- About 2 weeks before birth, an event called *lightening* occurred; Joshua's head dropped down low into the uterus. The reason was that Yolanda's cervix had begun to soften, thin, and open in preparation for delivery. As a result, it no longer supported Joshua's weight so easily. Lightening relieved some of the breathing and abdominal discomfort that Yolanda felt toward the end of pregnancy, although it brought other symptoms, such as low backache and difficulty in walking.

- A sure sign that labor is only hours or days away is the *bloody show*. As the cervix widens more, the plug of mucus that sealed it during pregnancy is released, producing a reddish discharge (Samuels & Samuels, 1996). Soon after this happens, contractions of the uterus become more frequent, and mother and baby have entered the first of three stages of labor (see Figure 4.1).

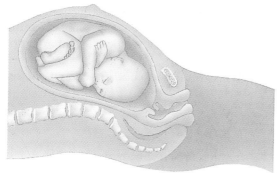

(a) Dilation and Effacement of the Cervix

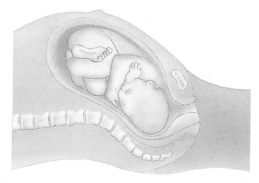

(b) Transition

Stage 1

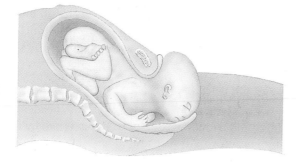

(c) Pushing

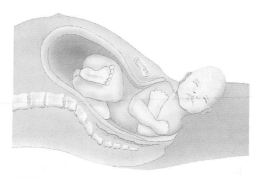

(d) Birth of the Baby

Stage 2

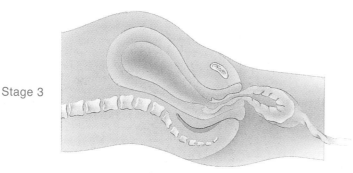

(e) Delivery of the Placenta

Stage 3

FIGURE **4.1**

The three stages of labor. Stage 1: (a) Contractions of the uterus cause dilation and effacement of the cervix. (b) Transition is reached when the frequency and strength of the contractions are at their peak and the cervix opens completely. Stage 2: (c) The mother pushes with each contraction, forcing the baby down the birth canal, and the head appears. (d) Near the end of Stage 2, the shoulders emerge and are followed quickly by the rest of the baby's body. Stage 3: (e) With a few final pushes, the placenta is delivered.

STAGE 1: DILATION AND EFFACEMENT OF THE CERVIX

Stage 1 is the longest, lasting an average of 12 to 14 hours with a first baby and 4 to 6 hours with later births. **Dilation and effacement of the cervix** take place—that is, the cervix widens and thins to nothing. As a result, a clear channel from the uterus into the birth canal, or vagina, is formed. Uterine contractions that open the cervix are forceful and regular, starting out 10 to 20 minutes apart and lasting about 15 to 20 seconds. Gradually, they get closer together, occurring every 2 to 3 minutes. In addition, they become more powerful, continuing for as long as 60 seconds.

During this stage, there was nothing Yolanda could do to speed up the process. She was urged to relax; Jay held her hand, provided sips of juice and water, and helped her get comfortable. Throughout the first few hours, Yolanda walked, stood, or sat upright. As the contractions became more intense, she leaned against pillows or lay on her side.

dilation and effacement of the cervix Widening and thinning of the cervix during the first stage of labor.

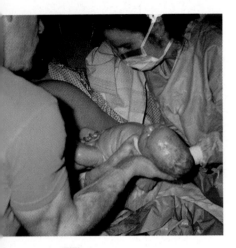

This newborn baby is held by his mother's birthing coach (on the left) and midwife (on the right) just after delivery. The umbilical cord has not yet been cut. Notice how the infant's head is molded from being squeezed through the birth canal for many hours. It is also very large in relation to his body. As the infant takes his first few breaths, his body turns from blue to pink. He is wide awake and ready to get to know his new surroundings. *(Courtesy of Dakoda Brandon Dorsaneo)*

transition
Climax of the first stage of labor, in which the frequency and strength of contractions are at their peak and the cervix opens completely.

episiotomy
A small incision made during childbirth to increase the size of the vaginal opening.

Apgar Scale
A rating used to assess the newborn baby's physical condition immediately after birth.

The climax of Stage 1 is a brief period called **transition,** in which the frequency and strength of contractions are at their peak and the cervix opens completely. Although transition is the most uncomfortable part of childbirth, it is especially important that the mother relax during this time. If she tenses or bears down with her muscles before the cervix is completely dilated and effaced, she is likely to bruise the cervix and slow the progress of labor.

STAGE 2: DELIVERY OF THE BABY

In Stage 2, which lasts about 50 minutes for a first baby and 20 minutes in later births, the infant is born. Strong contractions of the uterus continue, but the mother also feels a natural urge to squeeze and push with her abdominal muscles. As she does so with each contraction, she forces the baby down and out.

Yolanda dozed lightly between contractions. As each new wave came, "I pushed with all my might," she said. In the meantime, the doctor performed an **episiotomy,** or small incision that increases the size of the vaginal opening, permitting the baby to pass without tearing the mother's tissues.

When the doctor announced that the baby's head was *crowning*—the vaginal opening had stretched around the entire head—Yolanda felt renewed energy; she knew that soon the baby would arrive. Quickly, with several more pushes, Joshua's forehead, nose, and chin emerged, then his upper body and trunk. The doctor held him up, wet with amniotic fluid and still attached to the umbilical cord. Air rushed into his lungs, and Joshua cried. When the umbilical cord stopped pulsing, it was clamped and cut. Joshua was placed on Yolanda's chest, where she and Jay could see, touch, and gently talk to him. Then he was wrapped snugly to help with temperature regulation.

STAGE 3: BIRTH OF THE PLACENTA

Stage 3 brings labor to an end with a few final contractions and pushes. These cause the placenta to separate from the wall of the uterus and be delivered in about 5 to 10 minutes. Yolanda and Jay were surprised at the large size of the thick 1½-pound red–gray organ that had taken care of Joshua's basic needs for the previous 9 months.

THE BABY'S ADAPTATION TO LABOR AND DELIVERY

Consider, for a moment, what childbirth must be like for the baby. Joshua, after being squeezed and pushed for many hours, was forced from Yolanda's dark, warm, protective uterus into a cold, brightly lit external world. The strong contractions exposed his head to a great deal of pressure, and they repeatedly squeezed the placenta and the umbilical cord. Each time, Joshua's supply of oxygen was temporarily reduced.

At first glance, these events may strike you as a dangerous ordeal. Fortunately, healthy babies are well equipped to withstand the trauma of childbirth. The force of the contractions causes the infant to produce high levels of stress hormones. Recall from Chapter 3 that during pregnancy, the effects of maternal stress can endanger the baby. In contrast, during childbirth the infant's production of stress hormones is adaptive. It helps the baby withstand oxygen deprivation by sending a rich supply of blood to the brain and heart. In addition, it prepares the baby to breathe effectively by causing the lungs to absorb excess liquid and by expanding the bronchial tubes (passages leading to the lungs). Finally, stress hormones arouse the infant into alertness at birth. Joshua was born wide awake, ready to interact with the surrounding world (Emory & Toomey, 1988; Lagercrantz & Slotkin, 1986).

THE NEWBORN BABY'S APPEARANCE

What do babies look like after birth? Jay smiled when my students asked this question. "Yolanda and I are probably the only people in the world who thought Joshua was beautiful!" The average newborn is 20 inches long and 7½ pounds in weight; boys tend to be slightly longer and heavier than girls. Body proportions contribute to the baby's strange appearance. The head is very large in comparison to the trunk and legs, which are short and bowed. In fact, if your head were as large as that of a newborn infant, you would be balancing something about the size of a watermelon between your shoulders! As we will see in later chapters, the combination of a big head (with its well-developed brain) and a small body means that human infants learn quickly in the first few months of life. But unlike most mammals, they cannot get around on their own until much later.

Even though newborn babies may not match the idealized image many parents created in their minds during pregnancy, some features do make them attractive. Their round faces, chubby cheeks, large foreheads, and big eyes are just those characteristics that make adults feel like picking them up and cuddling them (Berman, 1980; Lorenz, 1943). The skin is also soft and smooth, although temporary rashes may appear on the face, which result from hormonal changes or plugged skin ducts. These clear up without treatment.

ASSESSING THE NEWBORN'S PHYSICAL CONDITION: THE APGAR SCALE

Infants who have difficulty making the transition to life outside the uterus must be given special help at once. To quickly assess the newborn's physical condition, doctors and nurses use the **Apgar Scale.** As Table 4.1 shows, a rating of 0, 1, or 2 on each of five characteristics is made at 1 and 5 minutes after birth. An Apgar score of 7 or better indicates that the infant is in good physical condition. If the score is between 4 and 6, the baby requires assistance in establishing breathing and other vital signs. If the score is 3 or below, the infant is in serious danger, and emergency medical attention is needed. Two Apgar ratings are given, since some babies have trouble adjusting at first but are doing quite well after a few minutes (Apgar, 1953).

After looking at Table 4.1, you may be wondering how infants like Joshua, who is dark-skinned, can be rated on color, the last of the five Apgar signs. Color is the least dependable of the Apgar ratings. The skin tone of nonwhite babies cannot be judged easily for pinkness and blueness. However, all newborns can be rated for a rosy glow that results from the flow of oxygen through body tissues once the baby starts to breathe, since skin tone is usually lighter at birth than the baby's inherited pigmentation.

TABLE 4.1

The Apgar Scale

SIGN[a]	SCORE		
	0	1	2
Heart rate	No heartbeat	Under 100 beats per minute	100 to 140 beats per minute
Respiratory effort	No breathing for 60 seconds	Irregular, shallow breathing	Strong breathing and crying
Reflex irritability (sneezing, coughing, and grimacing)	No response	Weak reflexive response	Strong reflexive response
Muscle tone	Completely limp	Weak movements of arms and legs	Strong movements of arms and legs
Color	Blue body, arms, and legs	Body pink with blue arms and legs	Body, arms, and legs completely pink

[a]To remember these signs, you may find it helpful to use a technique in which the original labels are reordered and renamed as follows: color = Appearance, heart rate = Pulse, reflex irritability = Grimace, muscle tone = Activity, and respiratory effort = Respiration. Together, the first letters of the new labels spell Apgar.

Source: Apgar, 1953.

ASK YOURSELF . . .

■ *What factors help newborn babies withstand the trauma of labor and delivery?*

■ *Explain why first-time parents are often surprised at the appearance of the new-born baby.*

BRIEF REVIEW

The hard work of labor takes place in three stages. In the first and longest stage, the cervix dilates and effaces to permit the baby to pass out of the uterus. In the second stage, the mother assists by pushing with each contraction, and the baby is born. In the third stage, the placenta is delivered. Stress hormones help the infant withstand the trauma of childbirth, and breathing generally starts easily and automatically. The Apgar Scale provides a quick rating of the baby's physical condition immediately after birth.

APPROACHES TO CHILDBIRTH

Childbirth practices, like other aspects of family life, are molded by the society of which mother and baby are a part. The extent to which birth is affected by culture is brought into bold relief when we look at the very different approaches to childbirth around the world (see the Cultural Influences box on the following page). Even in large Western nations, childbirth customs have changed dramatically over the centuries.

Before the late 1800s, birth took place at home and was a family-centered event. Relatives, friends, and children were often present. As a result, when young people had children of their own, they knew just what to expect and were supported by family members. The industrial revolution brought greater crowding to cities along with new health problems. As a result, childbirth began to move from home to hospital, where the health of mothers and babies could be protected. Once the responsibility for childbirth was placed in the hands of doctors, women's knowledge about it was reduced, and relatives and friends were no longer welcome to participate (Borst, 1995).

By the 1950s and 1960s, women started to question the medical procedures that had come to be used routinely during labor and delivery. Many felt that frequent use of strong drugs and delivery instruments had robbed them of a precious experience and were often not necessary or safe for the baby. Gradually, a natural childbirth movement arose in Europe and spread to the United States. Its purpose was to make hospital birth as comfortable and rewarding for mothers as possible. Today, most hospitals carry this theme further by offering birth centers that are family centered in approach and homelike in appearance. *Freestanding birth centers,* which operate independently of hospitals and offer less in the way of backup medical care, also exist. And a small but growing number of American women are rejecting institutional birth entirely by choosing to have their babies at home.

Each of these places of childbirth—hospital delivery room, birth center, and home—has advantages and disadvantages that an expectant mother should consider before deciding where to have her baby. Hospitals are best equipped to handle patients with complications, since emergency medical equipment is readily available. However, hospitals usually have rigid rules that grant mothers little control over birth and post-birth experiences.

Birth centers are less likely than traditional hospitals to use unnecessary medical procedures, have less rigid rules, and encourage early contact between parents and baby. Their informal, homelike birth settings are less expensive than hospital delivery rooms, but they are more expensive than home deliveries.

Mothers who decide to give birth at home are in a familiar environment best suited to early parent–infant contact. But training of birth attendants can vary widely, and routine medical procedures, if needed, are usually not available. In case of emergency, mother and baby must be transported to a hospital, delaying necessary intervention.

CULTURAL INFLUENCES

CHILDBIRTH PRACTICES IN TRIBAL AND VILLAGE SOCIETIES

In cultures everywhere, birth is regarded as a special event, often magical and mysterious and cause for celebration. When we look at how tribal and village societies handle childbirth, we become aware of the wide range of ways babies can be ushered into the world.

Cultures vary greatly in whether they consider birth to be an illness or a natural body function. Among the Cuna Indians of Panama, childbirth is regarded as so abnormal that the pregnant mother visits the medicine man daily for drugs to help her. Throughout labor, she is constantly medicated. Cuna children are kept ignorant about the facts of life as long as possible. They are told that babies miraculously appear in the forest between deers' horns or are put on the beach by dolphins.

In contrast, the Jarara of South America and the Pukapukans of the Pacific Islands treat birth as a normal part of life. The Jarara mother gives birth in a passageway or shelter in full view of the entire community, including small children. The Pukapukan girl is so familiar with the events of labor and delivery that she can frequently be seen playing at it. Using a coconut to represent the baby, she stuffs it inside her dress, imitates the mother's pushing, and lets the nut fall at the proper moment.

In most cultures, women are assisted during childbirth, usually by two or more helpers. The type of support given varies, but in many cases, the mother is physically held from behind. Among the Mayans of the Yucatán, she is propped up by the body and arms of a woman called the "head helper," who sits in back. The helper supports the mother's weight and pushes and breathes with her during each contraction.

The majority of non-Western cultures have the mother give birth in a vertical position—sometimes on the knees, at other times, sitting, squatting, or standing. The Siriono of South America are an exception. The mother lies in a hammock slung low to the ground. A crowd of women keeps her company, standing by or sitting in nearby hammocks. Unlike the Mayan helpers, these women do not actively take part. The mother delivers the baby herself, and the infant, once born, is allowed to slide off the hammock onto the soft earth below. The mild jolt of falling a few inches is enough to stimulate the baby's first breath.

Sensory and physical stimulation is often provided during labor. The Laotians of Indochina and the Navaho of North America play special music for the mother. The Punjab of India rub melted butter across the mother's abdomen. Among the Comanche, warmed rocks are placed on the mother's back. The Tübatulabel Indians of California dig a trench, in which they build a fire. The trench is covered with slabs of stone, layers of earth, and mats. There, the mother lies down and gives birth.

When expectant mothers in our culture know something about the great variety of birth practices, they become more aware of their own alternatives. As a result, they may be more likely to explore childbirth options and choose ones that best fit with their own life circumstances and personal needs.

Sources: Jordan, 1993; Mead & Newton, 1967.

Among the !Kung of Botswana, Africa, a mother gives birth in a sitting position, and she is surrounded by women who encourage and help her. *(Shostak/Anthro-Photo)*

Let's take a closer look at two childbirth approaches that have grown in popularity in recent years: natural childbirth and home delivery.

NATURAL, OR PREPARED, CHILDBIRTH

Yolanda and Jay chose **natural, or prepared, childbirth**. Although there are many natural childbirth techniques, all try to overcome the idea that birth is a painful ordeal that requires extensive medical intervention. Most programs draw on methods developed by Grantly Dick-Read (1959) in England and Ferdinand Lamaze (1958) in France. These physicians emphasized that cultural attitudes had taught women to fear the birth experience. An anxious, frightened woman in labor tenses her muscles, turning the mild pain that sometimes accompanies strong contractions into a great deal of pain.

Yolanda and Jay enrolled in a typical natural childbirth program offered by a hospital birth center. The program consisted of three parts:

- *Classes.* Yolanda and Jay attended classes in which they learned about the anatomy and physiology of labor and delivery. Knowledge about the birth process reduces a mother's fear.

- *Relaxation and breathing techniques.* After each lecture, Yolanda was taught relaxation and breathing exercises aimed at counteracting any pain she might feel during uterine contractions.

- *Labor coach.* While Yolanda mastered breathing and relaxation techniques, Jay was taught to be a "labor coach." He learned how to help Yolanda during childbirth—by reminding her to relax and breathe, massaging her back, supporting her body during labor and delivery, and offering words of encouragement and affection.

■ **POSITIONS FOR DELIVERY.** When natural childbirth is combined with delivery in a birth center or at home, mothers often give birth in the upright, sitting position shown in Figure 4.2 rather than lying flat on their backs with their feet in stirrups (which is the traditional hospital delivery room practice). In Europe, women are typically encouraged to give birth on their sides because it reduces the need for an episiotomy, since pressure of the baby's head against the vaginal opening is less intense (Bobak, Jensen, & Zalar, 1989).

Research findings favor the sitting position. When mothers are upright, labor is shortened because pushing is easier and more effective. The baby benefits from a richer supply of oxygen because blood flow to the placenta is increased (Davidson et al., 1993). Furthermore, since the mother can see the delivery, she can track the effectiveness of each contraction in pushing the baby out of the birth canal. This helps her work with the doctor or midwife to ensure that the baby's head and shoulders emerge slowly, which reduces the chances of tearing the vaginal opening (Samuels & Samuels, 1996).

■ **CONSEQUENCES OF NATURAL CHILDBIRTH.** Studies comparing mothers who experience natural childbirth with those who do not reveal many benefits. Because mothers feel more in control of labor and delivery, their attitudes toward the childbirth experience are more positive (Green, Coupland, & Kitzinger, 1990; Mackey, 1995). They also feel less pain. As a result, they require less medication—very little or none at all (Hetherington, 1990).

Research suggests that social support is important to the success of natural childbirth techniques. In Guatemalan and American hospitals that routinely isolated patients during childbirth, some mothers were randomly assigned a companion who stayed with them throughout labor, talking to them, holding their hands, and rubbing their backs to promote relaxation. These mothers had fewer birth complications, and their labors were sev-

FIGURE **4.2**

Sitting position often used for delivery in a birth center or at home. It facilitates pushing during the second stage of labor; increases blood flow to the placenta, which grants the baby a richer supply of oxygen; and permits the mother to see the delivery.

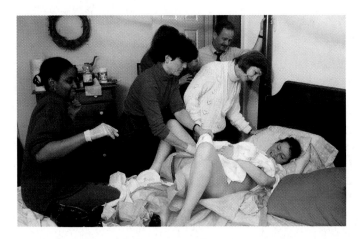

Women who choose home birth want to share the joy of childbirth with family members, avoid unnecessary medical procedures, and exercise greater control over their own care and that of their babies. When assisted by a well-trained doctor or midwife, healthy women can give birth at home safely. *(Franck Logue/ Stock South)*

eral hours shorter than those of women who did not have supportive companionship. Guatemalan mothers who received social support were more likely to respond to their babies in the first hour after delivery by talking, smiling, and gently stroking (Kennell et al., 1991; Sosa et al., 1980).

HOME DELIVERY

Home birth has always been popular in certain industrialized nations, such as England, the Netherlands, and Sweden. The number of American women choosing to have their babies at home has increased in recent years, although it is still small, amounting to about 1 percent. These mothers want birth to be an important part of family life. In addition, most want to avoid unnecessary medical procedures and exercise greater control over their own care and that of their babies than most hospitals permit (Bastian, 1993). Although some home births are attended by doctors, many more are handled by certified *nurse-midwives* who have degrees in nursing and additional training in childbirth management.

The joys and perils of home delivery are well illustrated by the story that Don, who painted my house as I worked on this book, told me as we took several coffee breaks together. Don is the father of four children, two of whom were born at home. "Our first child was delivered in the hospital," he said. "Even though I was present, Kathy and I found the whole atmosphere to be rigid and insensitive. We wanted a warmer, more personal environment in which to have our children." Don and Kathy's second child, Cindy, was born at their farmhouse, three miles out of town. A nurse-midwife was present. She coached Don, and he delivered Cindy himself. When, 3 years later, Kathy was in labor with Marnie, a heavy snowstorm prevented the midwife from getting to the house on time. Don delivered the baby alone, but the birth was difficult. Marnie failed to breathe for several minutes; with great effort, Don managed to revive her.

The frightening memory of Marnie's limp, blue body convinced Don and Kathy to return to the hospital to have their last child. By then, the hospital's birth practices had changed greatly. Don and Kathy got to know their doctor well, and he learned that Don had delivered Cindy and Marnie. When the baby's head crowned, the doctor stepped aside and permitted Don to bring his youngest child into the world himself.

Don and Kathy's experience raises the question of whether it is just as safe to give birth at home as in a hospital. For healthy women who are assisted by a well-trained doctor or midwife, it seems so, since complications rarely occur (Olsen, 1997; Remez, 1997). However, when attendants are not carefully trained and prepared to handle emergencies, the rate of infant death is high (Mehlmadrona & Madrona, 1997). When mothers are at risk for any kind of complication, the appropriate place for labor and delivery is the hospital, where life-saving treatment is available should it be needed.

natural, or prepared, childbirth
An approach designed to reduce pain and medical intervention and to make childbirth a rewarding experience for parents.

MEDICAL INTERVENTIONS

Medical interventions during childbirth are practiced in much smaller, simpler cultures as well as in industrialized nations. For example, some preliterate tribal and village societies have discovered drugs that stimulate labor and have developed surgical techniques to deliver babies. Yet, more so than anywhere else in the world, childbirth in the United States is a medically monitored and controlled event (Jordan, 1993; Notzon, 1990). What medical techniques are doctors likely to use during labor and delivery? When are they justified, and what dangers do they pose to mothers and babies? These are questions we take up in the following sections.

FETAL MONITORING

Fetal monitors are electronic instruments that track the baby's heart rate during labor. An abnormal heartbeat pattern may indicate that the baby is in distress due to lack of oxygen and needs to be delivered immediately. Fetal monitors are required in almost all American hospitals. Two types are in common use. The most popular kind is strapped across the mother's abdomen throughout labor (see Figure 4.3). A second more accurate method involves threading a recording device through the cervix and placing it directly under the baby's scalp.

Fetal monitoring is a safe medical procedure that has been shown to save the lives of many babies when mothers have a history of pregnancy and birth complications. Nevertheless, the practice is controversial. In mothers who have had healthy pregnancies, fetal monitoring does not reduce the rate of infant brain damage or death (Rosen & Dickinson, 1992; Sheth & Malpani, 1997). Most infants have some heartbeat irregularities during labor, which makes these recordings hard to interpret. Critics worry that use of fetal monitors identifies many babies as in danger who, in fact, are not. Fetal monitoring is linked to an increase in the number of emergency cesarean (surgical) deliveries, a practice we will discuss shortly (Samuels & Samuels, 1996).

There is another reason that fetal monitors are controversial. Some women complain that the devices are uncomfortable, prevent them from moving easily, and interfere with the normal course of labor. Still, it is likely that fetal monitors will continue to be used routinely, even though they might not be necessary in most cases. Today, doctors can be sued for malpractice if an infant dies or is born with problems and they cannot show that they did everything possible to protect the baby (Chez, 1997; Springer & van Weel, 1996). And despite lack of evidence, some doctors firmly believe that fetal monitoring contributes to healthy outcomes in all types of mothers.

LABOR AND DELIVERY MEDICATION

Some form of medication is used in 80 to 95 percent of births in the United States (Korte & Scaer, 1992). **Analgesics** are drugs used to relieve pain. When given during labor, the dose is usually mild and intended to help a mother relax. **Anesthetics** are a stronger type of painkiller that blocks sensation. General anesthesia, which puts the mother to sleep, is rarely used during childbirth today. More common are regional painkillers injected into the spinal column to numb the lower half of the body.

In complicated deliveries, pain-relieving drugs are essential because they permit life-saving medical interventions to be carried out. But when used routinely, they can cause problems. Anesthesia interferes with the mother's ability to feel contractions during the

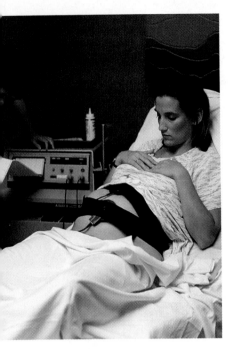

FIGURE 4.3

External fetal monitor, which is attached to the mother's abdomen and records fetal heart rate using ultrasound. This type of fetal monitoring is used routinely in American hospitals. When mothers have a history of pregnancy and birth complications, fetal monitoring saves many lives. But it may also lead to an increase in unnecessary cesarean (surgical) deliveries. And some women complain that the monitors are uncomfortable and restrict their freedom of movement. *(George White)*

fetal monitors
Electronic instruments that track the baby's heart rate during labor.

analgesic
A mild pain-relieving drug.

anesthetic
A strong pain-killing drug that blocks sensation.

second stage of labor. As a result, she may not push effectively, increasing the likelihood of an instrument delivery (see next section).

Labor and delivery medication rapidly crosses the placenta. When given in fairly large doses, it produces a depressed state in the newborn baby that may last for days. The infant is sleepy and withdrawn, sucks poorly during feedings, and is likely to be irritable when awake (Brazelton, Nugent, & Lester, 1987).

Does the use of medication during childbirth have a lasting impact on physical and mental development? Some researchers claim so (Brackbill, McManus, & Woodward, 1985), but their findings have been challenged, and contrary results exist (Broman, 1983). Anesthesia may be related to other risk factors that could account for the long-term consequences in some studies, and more research is needed to sort out these effects. In the meantime, the negative impact of these drugs on the early infant–mother relationship supports the current trend to limit their use.

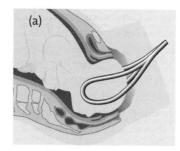 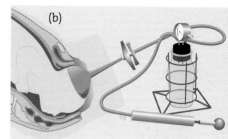

FIGURE 4.4

Instrument delivery. (a) The pressure that must be applied to pull the infant from the birth canal with forceps involves risk of injury to the baby's head. (b) An alternative method, the vacuum extractor, is not used as often in North America. Although vacuum extraction is less likely than forceps to injure the mother, it is just as risky for the infant. Scalp injuries are common.

INSTRUMENT DELIVERY

Forceps, metal clamps placed around the baby's head to pull the infant from the birth canal, have been used since the sixteenth century to speed up delivery (see Figure 4.4). A more recent instrument, the **vacuum extractor,** consists of a plastic cup (placed on the baby's head) attached to a suction tube. Instrument delivery is appropriate if the mother's pushing during the second stage of labor does not move the baby through the birth canal in a reasonable period of time.

In the United States, forceps or vacuum extractors are used in about 12 percent of births. In contrast, they are used less than 5 percent of the time in Europe (National Center for Health Statistics, 1997). These figures suggest that instruments may be applied too freely in American hospitals. When a doctor uses forceps to pull the baby through most or all of the birth canal, deliveries are associated with higher rates of brain damage. As a result, forceps are seldom used this way today.

Low-forceps delivery (carried out when the baby is most of the way through the vagina) is not associated with poorer intellectual functioning in childhood and adolescence (Seidman et al., 1991; Wesley, van den Berg, & Reece, 1993). Still, some risk of injury to the baby's head remains. Vacuum extractors are less likely to tear the mother's tissues than are forceps, but the chances of harming the infant are just as great (Hanigan et al., 1990; Johanson et al., 1993). For these reasons, neither method should be used when the mother can still be encouraged to deliver normally and there is no special reason to hurry the birth.

INDUCED LABOR

An **induced labor** is one that is started artificially. This is usually done by breaking the amnion, or bag of waters (an event that usually takes place naturally in the first stage of labor), and giving the mother synthetic oxytocin, a hormone involved in stimulating contractions.

Are there good reasons to induce labor? Yes, when continuing the pregnancy threatens the well-being of mother or baby. Too often, though, labors are induced for the doctor's or

forceps
Metal clamps placed around the baby's head, used to pull the infant from the birth canal.

vacuum extractor
A plastic cup attached to a suction tube, used to deliver the baby.

induced labor
A labor started artificially by breaking the amnion and giving the mother a hormone that stimulates contractions.

the patient's convenience. In a healthy mother, the onset of labor should not be scheduled like her doctor's appointment. An induced labor often proceeds differently from a naturally occurring one. The contractions are longer, harder, and closer together, increasing the possibility of inadequate oxygen supply to the baby. In addition, mothers often find it more difficult to stay in control of an induced labor, even when they have been coached in natural childbirth techniques. As a result, labor and delivery medication is likely to be used in larger amounts, and there is a greater chance of instrument delivery (Brindley & Sokol, 1988).

Occasionally, induction is performed before the mother is physically ready to give birth, and the procedure fails. When this happens, a cesarean delivery is necessary (Xenakis et al., 1997).

CESAREAN DELIVERY

A **cesarean delivery** is a surgical birth; the doctor makes an incision in the mother's abdomen and lifts the baby out of the uterus. It received its name from the belief that Roman emperor Julius Caesar was born this way.

Thirty years ago, cesarean delivery was rare in the United States, performed only when the life of mother or baby was in immediate danger. In 1970, 3 percent of babies were born in this way. Over the next quarter-century, the cesarean rate climbed steadily. In 1993, the practice accounted for 24 percent of American births. Recently, the incidence dropped slightly—to 22 percent (U.S. Bureau of the Census, 1997; Young, 1997). Still, it is the highest in the world, far surpassing Canada, the second-ranked nation at 14 percent. Countries such as Japan and the Netherlands have cesarean rates of less than 7 percent (Samuels & Samuels, 1996). Yet, as we will see later, these nations have considerably lower infant death rates than does the United States.

Birth complications that lead to cesarean deliveries are summarized in Table 4.2. Cesareans have always been warranted by the serious medical emergencies noted in the last entry of the table. In contrast, there is growing evidence that surgical delivery is not always needed to deal with the first four problems listed, which account for 87 percent of cesarean births.

The two most common reasons for cesareans are a failure of labor to progress normally and a previous history of cesarean birth (Samuels & Samuels, 1996). Many physicians take the position "once a cesarean, always a cesarean" because the uterine scar might rupture if the mother is permitted to deliver vaginally in a later birth. However, the surgical technique used today—a small horizontal cut in the lower part of the uterus—makes this possibility unlikely. Even when it does occur, it is not life threatening to mother or baby (Korte, 1997).

As mentioned earlier, fetal monitoring increases the likelihood of cesarean delivery because some infants may be falsely identified as distressed. Cesareans are also routinely performed when babies are in **breech position,** or turned so that the buttocks or feet would be delivered first (about 1 in every 25 births). The breech position increases the possibility that the umbilical cord may be squeezed as the large head moves through the birth canal, depriving the infant of oxygen. Head injuries are also more likely. Cesareans are justified in many of these cases (Cheng & Hannah, 1993). However, the exact positioning of the infant (which can be felt by the doctor) makes a difference. Certain breech babies fare just as well with a normal delivery as they do with a cesarean (Flamm & Quilligan, 1995). Sometimes the doctor can gently turn a breech baby into a head-down position during the early part of labor.

Because many unnecessary cesareans are performed in the United States, pregnant women should ask questions about the procedure before choosing a doctor. When a mother does have a cesarean, she and her baby need extra support. The operation itself is quite safe, but it requires more time for recovery. Since anesthesia may have crossed the placenta, cesarean newborns are more likely to be sleepy and unresponsive and to have

cesarean delivery
A surgical delivery in which the doctor makes an incision in the mother's abdomen and lifts the baby out of the uterus.

breech position
A position of the baby in the uterus that would cause the buttocks or feet to be delivered first.

TABLE 4.2

Common Reasons for Cesarean Delivery

REASON	PERCENTAGE OF CESAREANS IN THE U.S.
Previous cesarean	36
Abnormal labor	31
Baby in breech position	10
Infant distress due to oxygen deprivation	10
Other emergencies Serious maternal illness—diabetes, heart disease, or infection (such as herpes simplex 2) that can be transmitted to the fetus during vaginal delivery. Medical emergencies, such as premature separation of the placenta from the uterus or Rh incompatibility.	13

Source: Samuels & Samuels, 1996.

breathing difficulties. (Cox & Schwartz, 1990). These factors can negatively affect the early mother–infant relationship.

BRIEF REVIEW

In industrialized nations, a woman can choose to have her baby in a traditional hospital setting, a birth center, or at home. Natural, or prepared, childbirth programs are widely available. Home births are safe for healthy women, provided attendants are well trained. Medical interventions during childbirth are more likely to be used in the United States than anywhere else in the world. Although often justified, these procedures can cause problems. In some instances, fetal monitoring may mistakenly identify babies as distressed. Pain-relieving drugs can cross the placenta, producing a withdrawn state in the infant. Because induced labors are more difficult, they are associated with greater use of medication. Instrument deliveries involve some risk of head injury. Cesarean births require extra recovery time for the mother, and babies tend to be less alert and more likely to have breathing difficulties.

ASK YOURSELF . . .

■ *Use of any single medical intervention during childbirth increases the likelihood that others will also be used. Provide as many examples as you can to illustrate this idea.*

■ *Sharon, a heavy smoker, has just arrived at the hospital in labor. Which one of the medical interventions discussed in the preceding sections is her doctor justified in using? (For help in answering this question, return to the discussion of prenatal effects of tobacco in Chapter 3, pages 112–113.)*

BIRTH COMPLICATIONS

We have seen that some babies—in particular, those whose mothers are in poor health, do not receive good medical care, or have a history of pregnancy problems—are especially likely to experience birth complications. Inadequate oxygen, a pregnancy that ends too early, and a baby who is born underweight are serious complications that we have mentioned many times. Another risk factor is a pregnancy in which the baby remains in the uterus too long. Let's look at the impact of each of these complications on later development.

OXYGEN DEPRIVATION

Some years ago, I got to know 2-year-old Melinda and her mother, Judy, both of whom participated in a special program for infants with disabilities at our laboratory school. Melinda has **cerebral palsy,** which is a general term for a variety of problems that result from brain damage before, during, or just after birth. Difficulties in muscle coordination are always involved, such as a clumsy walk, uncontrolled movements, and unclear speech. The disorder can range from very mild tremors to severe crippling and mental retardation. One out of every 500 children born in the United States has cerebral palsy. Twenty-two percent of these youngsters experienced **anoxia,** or inadequate oxygen supply, during labor and delivery (Mecham, 1996; Torfs et al., 1990).

Melinda walks with a halting, lumbering gait, and she has difficulty keeping her balance. "Some mothers don't know how the palsy happened," confided Judy, "but I do. I got pregnant accidentally, and my boyfriend didn't want to have anything to do with it. I was frightened and alone most of the time. I arrived at the hospital at the last minute. Melinda was breech, and the cord was wrapped around her neck."

Squeezing of the umbilical cord, as in Melinda's case, is one cause of anoxia. Another cause is *placenta abruptio,* or premature separation of the placenta, a life-threatening event that requires immediate delivery. Although the reasons for placenta abruptio are not well understood, teratogens that cause abnormal development of the placenta, such as cigarette smoking, are strongly related to it (Handler et al., 1994). In still other instances, the birth seems to go along all right, but the baby fails to start breathing within a few minutes. Newborns can survive periods without oxygen longer than adults, but there is risk of brain damage if breathing is delayed for more than 3 minutes (Stechler & Halton, 1982). Can you think of other possible causes of oxygen deprivation that you learned about as you studied prenatal development and birth?

How do children who experience anoxia during labor and delivery fare as they get older? Melinda's physical disability was permanent, but otherwise she did well. The same is true for most oxygen-deprived newborns. These infants remain behind their agemates in intellectual and motor progress throughout early childhood. But by the school years, most catch up in development (Corah et al., 1965; Graham et al., 1962).

When problems do persist, the oxygen deprivation was probably extreme. Perhaps it was caused by prenatal damage to the baby's respiratory system, or it may have happened because the infant's lungs were not yet mature enough to breathe. For example, infants born more than 6 weeks early commonly have **respiratory distress syndrome** (also called *hyaline membrane disease*). Their tiny lungs are so poorly developed that the air sacs collapse, causing serious breathing difficulties and sometimes death. Today, mechanical ventilators keep many such infants alive. In spite of these measures, some babies suffer permanent damage from lack of oxygen, and in other cases their delicate lungs are harmed by the treatment itself (Vohr & Garcia-Coll, 1988). Respiratory distress syndrome is only one of many risks for babies born too soon, as we will see in the following section.

PRETERM AND LOW-BIRTH-WEIGHT INFANTS

Janet, almost 6 months pregnant, and her husband, Rick, boarded a flight in Hartford, Connecticut, on their way to a vacation in Hawaii. The plane was scheduled to make two stops before the long journey across the Pacific Ocean. During a stopover in San Francisco, Janet told Rick she was bleeding. They realized she was in trouble. Rushed to a hospital, she gave birth to Keith, who weighed less than 1½ pounds. Delivered 23 weeks after conception, he barely reached the age of viability (see Chapter 3, page 106).

During Keith's first month, he experienced one crisis after another, all of which are common in very premature infants. Three days after birth, an ultrasound scan suggested that fragile blood vessels feeding Keith's brain had hemorrhaged, a complication that can cause brain damage. Within three weeks, Keith had surgery to close a valve in his heart that seals automatically in full-term babies. Keith's immature immune system made infections difficult to contain. Repeated illnesses and the drugs used to treat them caused permanent hearing loss. He also had respiratory distress syndrome and was attached to a ventilator. Soon there was evidence of lung damage, and Keith's vision was threatened

cerebral palsy
A general term for a variety of problems, all of which involve muscle coordination, that result from brain damage before, during, or just after birth.

anoxia
Inadequate oxygen supply.

respiratory distress syndrome
A disorder of preterm infants in which the lungs are so immature that the air sacs collapse, causing serious breathing difficulties.

because of constant exposure to oxygen. It took over 3 months of hospitalization for Keith's rough course of complications and treatment to ease (Turiel, 1991a).

Babies born 3 weeks or more before the end of a full 38-week pregnancy or who weigh less than 5½ pounds (2,500 grams) have for many years been referred to as "premature." A wealth of research indicates that premature babies are at risk for many problems. Birth weight is the best available predictor of infant survival and healthy development. Many newborns who weigh less than 2⅕ pounds (1,000 grams) experience difficulties that are not overcome, an effect that becomes stronger as birth weight decreases (Novy, McGregor, & Iams, 1995). Frequent illness, inattention, overactivity, low intelligence test scores, and deficits in motor coordination and school learning are some of the problems that extend into the childhood years (Hack et al., 1994, 1995; Liaw & Brooks-Gunn, 1993; McCormick, Gortmaker, & Sobol, 1990).

About 1 in 14 infants in the United States is born underweight. The problem can strike unexpectedly, as it did for Janet and Rick. It is highest among low-income pregnant women, especially ethnic minorities (Children's Defense Fund, 1998). These mothers, as we indicated in Chapter 3, are more likely to be undernourished and to be exposed to other harmful environmental influences—factors strongly linked to low birth weight. In addition, they often do not receive the prenatal care necessary to protect their vulnerable babies.

You may recall from Chapter 2 that prematurity is also common when mothers are carrying twins. Twins are usually born about 3 weeks early, and because of restricted space inside the uterus, they gain less weight after the twentieth week of pregnancy than do singleton babies.

■ **PRETERM VERSUS SMALL FOR DATE.** Although low-birth-weight infants face many obstacles to healthy development, individual differences exist in how well they do. Over half go on to lead normal lives—even some who weighed only a couple of pounds at birth (Vohr & Garcia-Coll, 1988). To better understand why some of these babies do better than others, researchers have divided them into two groups. The first is called **preterm.** These infants are born several weeks or more before their due date. Although small in size, their weight may still be appropriate for the amount of time they spent in the uterus. The second group is called **small for date.** These babies are below their expected weight when length of the pregnancy is taken into account. Some small-for-date infants are actually full term. Others are preterm infants who are especially underweight.

Of the two types of babies, small-for-date infants usually have more serious problems. During the first year, they are more likely to die, catch infections, and show evidence of brain damage. By middle childhood, they have lower intelligence test scores, are less attentive, achieve more poorly in school, and are socially immature (Copper et al., 1993; Schothorst & van Engeland, 1996). Small-for-date infants probably experienced inadequate nutrition before birth. Perhaps their mothers did not eat properly, the placenta did not function normally, or the babies themselves had defects that prevented them from growing as they should.

■ **CHARACTERISTICS OF PRETERM INFANTS: CONSEQUENCES FOR CAREGIVING.** Imagine a scrawny, thin-skinned infant whose body is only a little larger than the size of your hand. You try to play with the baby by stroking and talking softly, but he is sleepy and unresponsive. When you feed him, he sucks poorly. He is usually irritable during the short, unpredictable periods in which he is awake.

Unfortunately, the appearance and behavior of preterm babies can lead parents to be less sensitive and responsive in caring for them. Compared to full-term infants, preterm babies—especially those who are very ill at birth—are less often held close, touched, and talked to gently. At times, mothers of these infants are overly intrusive, engaging in interfering pokes and verbal commands in an effort to obtain a higher level of response from a baby who is a passive, unrewarding social partner (Patteson & Barnard, 1990).

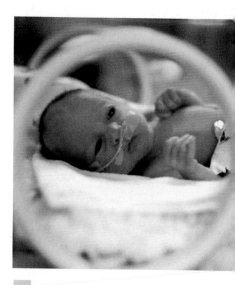

This is 1-day-old Kenneth Robert, who at 3 pounds 4 ounces was the largest of the McCaughey septuplets, born in DeMoine, Iowa, on November 19, 1997. Like other multiple births, Kenneth, his three brothers, and his three sisters were preterm; they arrived about 9 weeks before their due date. Yet all the babies benefited from excellent prenatal care and were in good health. They are believed to be the world's first surviving set of septuplets. *(Reuters/Blank Children's Hospital Archives)*

preterm
Infants born several weeks or more before their due date. Although small in size, their weight may still be appropriate for the time they spent in the uterus.

small for date
Infants whose birth weight is below normal when length of pregnancy is taken into account.

Some parents may step up these intrusive acts when faced with continuing ungratifying infant behavior. This may explain why preterm babies as a group are at risk for child abuse. When these infants are born to isolated, poverty-stricken mothers who have difficulty managing their own lives, the chances for unfavorable outcomes are increased. In contrast, parents with stable life circumstances and social supports can usually overcome the stresses of caring for a preterm infant. In these cases, even sick preterm babies have a good chance of catching up in development by middle childhood (Liaw & Brooks-Gunn, 1993).

These findings suggest that how well preterm babies develop has a great deal to do with the kind of relationship established between parent and child, to which both partners contribute. If a good relationship between parent and baby can help prevent the negative effects of early birth, then intervention programs directed at supporting this relationship should help these infants recover.

■ **INTERVENING WITH PRETERM INFANTS.** A preterm baby is cared for in a special bed called an *isolette*. It is a plexiglass-enclosed box in which temperature is carefully controlled, since these infants cannot yet regulate their own body temperature effectively. Air is filtered before it enters the isolette to help protect the baby from infection.

When a preterm infant is fed through a stomach tube, breathes with the aid of a respirator, and receives medication through an intravenous needle, the isolette can be very isolating indeed! Physical needs that otherwise would lead to close contact and other forms of stimulation from an adult are met mechanically. At one time doctors believed that stimulating such a fragile baby could be harmful. Now we know that certain kinds of stimulation in proper doses can help preterm infants develop.

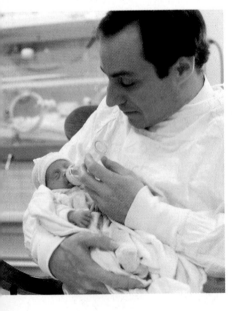

This father feeds his preterm baby in a hospital intensive care nursery. A good parent–infant relationship, the stimulation of touch, and a soft, gentle voice are likely to help this infant recover and catch up in development. *(Joseph Nettis/Photo Researchers)*

Special Infant Stimulation.   In some intensive care nurseries, preterm babies can be seen rocking in suspended hammocks or lying on waterbeds—interventions designed to replace the gentle motion they would have received while being carried in the mother's uterus. Other forms of stimulation have also been used—for example, an attractive mobile or a tape recording of a heartbeat, soft music, or the mother's voice. Many studies show that these experiences promote faster weight gain, more predictable sleep patterns, and greater alertness during the weeks after birth (Beckwith & Sigman, 1995).

Touch is an especially important form of stimulation for preterm newborns. In studies of baby animals, touching the skin releases certain brain chemicals that support physical growth. These effects are believed to occur in humans as well (Schanberg & Field, 1987). In one study, preterm infants who were gently massaged several times each day in the hospital gained weight faster and, at the end of the first year, were advanced in mental and motor development over preterm babies not given this stimulation (Field et al., 1986).

In developing countries where hospitalization is not always possible, skin-to-skin "kangaroo baby care," in which the preterm infant is tucked between the mother's breasts and peers over the top of her clothing, is encouraged. The technique is used often in Europe as a supplement to hospital intensive care. It fosters oxygenation of the baby's body, temperature regulation, improved feeding, and infant survival (Anderson, 1991; Hamelin & Ramachandran, 1993).

Some very small or sick babies are too weak to handle much stimulation. The noise, bright lights, and constant medical monitoring of the intensive care nursery are already quite overwhelming for them. And much like full-term infants, preterm infants differ in how excited and irritable they get when exposed to sights and sounds (Korner, 1996). Doctors and nurses need to carefully adjust the amount and kind of stimulation to fit the baby's individual needs.

Training Parents in Infant Caregiving Skills.   When effective stimulation helps preterm babies develop, parents are likely to feel good about their infant's growth and interact with the baby more effectively. Interventions that support the parenting side of this relationship generally teach parents about the infant's characteristics and promote caregiving skills.

For parents with the economic and personal resources to care for a preterm infant, just a few sessions of coaching in recognizing and responding to the baby's needs is helpful. Infants of mothers randomly selected to receive this training during home visits in the months after hospital discharge, compared to infants of mothers who were not, gained steadily in mental test performance over the childhood years until their scores equaled those of full-term youngsters (Achenbach et al., 1990).

When preterm infants live in stressed, low-income households, long-term, intensive intervention is required to reduce developmental problems. In a recent study, preterm babies born into poverty received a comprehensive intervention that combined medical follow-up, weekly parent training sessions, and cognitively stimulating day care from 1 to 3 years of age. As Figure 4.5 shows, compared to controls receiving only medical follow-up, nearly four times as many intervention children were within normal range at age 3 in intelligence, psychological adjustment, and physical growth (Bradley et al, 1994).

Yet by age 5, the intervention children had lost ground. And by age 8, group differences were no longer present for children who had been very low-birth-weight (Brooks-Gunn et al., 1994; McCarton et al., 1997). To sustain gains in development in these very vulnerable children, high-quality intervention is needed well beyond age 3—even into the school years.

What happened to Keith, the very sick baby whom you met at the beginning of this section? Because of advanced medical technology and new ways of helping parents, many preterm infants survive and eventually catch up in development, but Keith was not one of the lucky ones. Even with the best of care, from 30 to 70 percent of babies born as early as Keith either die or end up with serious disabilities. Six months after he was born, Keith died without ever having left the hospital (Turiel, 1991b).

Keith's premature birth was unavoidable, but the high rate of underweight babies in the United States—one of the worst in the industrialized world—could be greatly reduced by improving the health and social conditions described in the Social Issues box on page 148. Fortunately, today we can save many preterm babies, but an even better course of action would be to prevent this serious threat to infant survival and development before it happens.

POSTTERM INFANTS

The normal length of pregnancy is 38 weeks. Infants born after 42 weeks are **postterm.** About 10 percent fall into this category. Most of these late-arriving newborns are quite normal. However, a small number start to lose weight at the end of pregnancy because the placenta no longer functions properly. As the baby becomes more overdue, the amount of amniotic fluid drops sharply. This increases the chances that the infant's movements in the uterus will squeeze the umbilical cord. Also, since postterm infants grow larger during the extra weeks spent in the uterus, they may have difficulty moving through the birth canal. All these factors increase the possibility of oxygen deprivation and head injuries in a postterm birth (Rosen & Dickinson, 1992).

Since the likelihood of birth complications and infant death rises steeply as a pregnancy continues past 42 weeks, doctors usually induce labor in these mothers (Resnick, 1988). Once born, most postterm babies do well. Their mental development may be slightly behind during infancy and early childhood, but it generally evens out by school entry (Shime, 1988).

UNDERSTANDING BIRTH COMPLICATIONS

In the preceding sections, we considered a variety of birth complications that threaten children's well-being. Now let's try to put the evidence together. Are there any

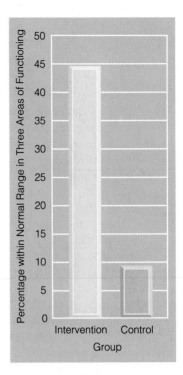

FIGURE 4.5

Percentage of preterm infants born into poverty and assigned to an intensive intervention or a control group who were developing normally at age 3. Children who experienced the intervention, consisting of medical follow-up, parent training, and cognitively stimulating day care, were nearly four times more likely than medical-follow-up-only controls to be within normal range in intelligence, psychological adjustment, and physical growth. Without continued intervention, however, these gains are not sustained. (Adapted from Bradley et al., 1994.)

postterm
Infants who spend a longer than average time in the uterus—more than 42 weeks.

ISSUES

A CROSS-NATIONAL PERSPECTIVE ON INFANT MORTALITY

Infant mortality is an index used around the world to assess the overall health of a nation's children. It refers to the number of deaths in the first year of life per 1,000 live births. How do you think the United States compares to other industrialized nations in infant mortality? The information in Figure 4.6 may surprise you.

Although the United States has the most up-to-date health care technology in the world, it has made less progress than many other countries in reducing infant deaths. Over the past three decades, it slipped down in the international rankings, from seventh in the 1950s to twentieth in the mid-1990s. Members of America's poor ethnic minorities, African-American babies especially, are at greatest risk. Black infants are more than twice as likely as white infants to die in the first year of life. Their infant mortality rate is about the same as in developing nations with poor economies, such as Trinidad and Tobago (Bellamy, 1997; Children's Defense Fund, 1998).

Neonatal mortality, the rate of death within the first month of life, accounts for 67 percent of the high infant death rate in the United States. Two factors are largely responsible for neonatal mortality. The first is serious physical defects, most of which cannot be prevented. The percentage of babies born with physical defects is about the same in all ethnic and income groups. The second leading cause of neonatal mortality is low birth weight, which is largely preventable. Black babies are more than four times more likely to die because they are born early and underweight than are white infants. On an international scale, the number of under-weight babies born in the United States is alarmingly high. It is greater than that of 22 other countries (Bellamy, 1997).

Why are American babies more likely to be born underweight and to die than infants in so many other nations? Experts agree that widespread poverty and weak health care programs for mothers and young children are responsible. Except for the United States, each country listed in Figure 4.6 provides all its citizens with government-sponsored health care benefits. And each takes extra steps to make sure that pregnant mothers and babies have access to good nutrition, high-quality medical care, and social and economic supports that promote effective parenting.

For example, all Western European nations guarantee women a certain number of prenatal visits at very low or no cost. A health professional routinely visits the home after a baby is born to provide counseling about infant care and to arrange continuing medical services. Home assistance is especially extensive in the Netherlands. For a token fee, each mother is granted the services of a specially trained maternity helper, who assists with infant care, shopping, housekeeping, meal preparation, and the care of other children during the 10 days after delivery (Kamerman, 1993).

In countries with low infant mortality rates, expectant mothers need not wonder how or where they will get health care assistance or who will pay for it. The clear link between high-quality maternal and infant health services and reduced infant mortality provides strong justification for implementing similar programs in the United States.

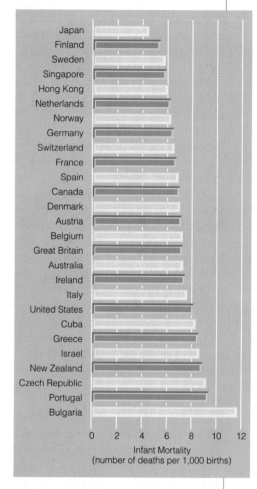

FIGURE **4.6**

Infant mortality in 27 nations. Despite its advanced health care technology, the United States ranks poorly. It is twentieth in the world, with a death rate of 8 infants per 1,000 births. *(Adapted from Central Intelligence Agency, 1996.)*

general principles that might help us understand how infants who survive a traumatic birth are likely to develop? A landmark study carried out in Hawaii provides answers to this question.

In 1955, Emmy Werner began to follow nearly 700 infants on the island of Kauai who experienced either mild, moderate, or severe birth complications. Each was matched, on the basis of SES and ethnicity, with a healthy newborn (Werner & Smith, 1982).

Findings revealed that the likelihood of long-term difficulties increased if birth trauma was severe. But among mildly to moderately stressed children, the best predictor of how well they did in later years was the quality of their home environments. Children growing up in stable families did almost as well on measures of intelligence and psychological adjustment as did those with no birth difficulties. Those exposed to poverty, family disorganization, and mentally ill parents often developed serious learning difficulties, behavior problems, and emotional disturbance during childhood and adolescence.

The Kauai study tells us that as long as birth injuries are not overwhelming, a supportive home environment can restore children's growth. But the most intriguing cases in this study were the handful of exceptions to this rule. A few youngsters with both fairly serious birth complications and very troubled families grew into competent adults who fared as well as controls in career attainment and psychological adjustment.

Werner found that these children relied on factors outside the family and within themselves to overcome stress. Some had especially attractive personalities that caused them to receive positive responses from relatives, neighbors, and peers. In other cases, a grandparent, aunt, uncle, or baby-sitter established a warm relationship with the child and provided the needed emotional support (Werner, 1989; Werner & Smith, 1992).

Do these outcomes remind you of the characteristics of resilient children, discussed in Chapter 1? The Kauai study reveals that as long as the overall balance of life events tips toward the favorable side, children with serious birth problems can develop successfully. When negative factors outweigh positive ones, even a sturdy newborn baby can become a lifelong casualty.

BRIEF REVIEW

Birth complications can threaten children's development. Oxygen deprivation, when extreme, causes lasting brain damage. Preterm and small-for-date babies are at risk for many problems. Providing these infants with special stimulation and teaching parents how to care for and interact with them helps restore favorable growth. The longer a postterm infant remains in the uterus, the greater the likelihood of birth difficulties. When newborns with serious complications grow up in positive social environments, they have a good chance of catching up in development.

PRECIOUS MOMENTS AFTER BIRTH

Yolanda and Jay's account of Joshua's birth revealed that the time spent holding and touching him right after delivery was a memorable period filled with intense emotion. A mother given her infant at this time will usually stroke the baby gently, look into the infant's eyes, and talk softly (Klaus & Kennell, 1982).

Fathers respond similarly. Most are overjoyed at the birth of the baby; characterize the experience as "awesome," "indescribable," or "unforgettable"; and display intense interest and involvement in their newborn child (Bader, 1995). Regardless of SES or participation

ASK YOURSELF . . .

■ *Explain how the long-term outcomes reported for oxygen-deprived and preterm babies fit with findings of the Kauai study.*

■ *Sensitive care can help preterm infants recover, but unfortunately they are less likely to receive such care than are full-term newborns. Explain why.*

infant mortality
The number of deaths in the first year of life per 1,000 live births.

neonatal mortality
The number of deaths in the first month of life per 1,000 live births.

This father displays intense interest in and involvement with his newborn child. Parents typically express their elation at the baby's arrival by stroking the infant gently, looking into the baby's eyes, and talking softly. *(Erika Stone)*

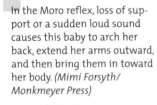

In the Moro reflex, loss of support or a sudden loud sound causes this baby to arch her back, extend her arms outward, and then bring them in toward her body. *(Mimi Forsyth/ Monkmeyer Press)*

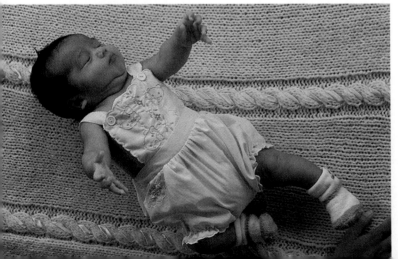

in childbirth classes, fathers touch, look at, talk to, and kiss their newborn infants just as much as mothers do. When they hold the baby, sometimes they exceed mothers in stimulation and affection (Parke & Tinsley, 1981).

Immediately after birth, many nonhuman animals engage in specific caregiving behaviors that are critical for survival of the young. For example, a mother cat licks her newborn kittens and then encircles them with her body (Schneirla, Rosenblatt, & Tobach, 1963). Rats, sheep, and goats engage in similar licking behaviors. But if the mother is separated from the young during the period following delivery, her responsiveness declines until finally she rejects the infant (Poindron & Le Neindre, 1980; Rosenblatt & Lehrman, 1963).

Do human parents also require close physical contact with their babies in the hours after birth for **bonding,** or feelings of affection and concern for the infant, to develop? A few investigators used to think so, but current evidence indicates that the parent–infant relationship does not depend on a precise period of togetherness in human beings (Eyer, 1992; Lamb, 1994).

Some parents report sudden, deep feelings of affection on first holding their babies. For others, these emotions emerge gradually, over the first few weeks of life (MacFarlane, Smith, & Garrow, 1978). In adoptive parents, a warm, affectionate relationship can develop quite successfully even if the child enters the family months or years after birth (Dontas et al., 1985; Hodges & Tizard, 1989). Taken together, these findings indicate that human bonding is a complex process that depends on many factors, not just what happens during a short sensitive period.

Still, contact with the infant after birth might be one of several factors that helps build a good relationship between parent and baby. Research shows that mothers learn to discriminate their own newborn baby from other infants on the basis of touch, smell, and sight (a photograph) after as little as one hour of contact (Kaitz et al., 1987, 1988; Kaitz et al., 1993a, 1993b). This early recognition probably facilitates responsiveness to the infant. Realizing this, today hospitals offer an arrangement called **rooming in,** in which the infant stays in the mother's hospital room all or most of the time. If parents choose not to take advantage of this option or cannot do so for medical reasons, there is no evidence that their competence as caregivers will be compromised or that the baby will suffer emotionally (Lamb, 1994).

THE NEWBORN BABY'S CAPACITIES

As recently as the mid-twentieth century, scientists considered the newborn baby to be a passive, disorganized being who could see, hear, feel, and do very little. Today, we know that this image of an incompetent newborn is wrong. Newborn babies have a remarkable set of capacities that are crucial for survival and for evoking parental attention and care. In relating to the physical world and building their first social relationships, babies are active from the very start.

NEWBORN REFLEXES

A **reflex** is an inborn, automatic response to a particular form of stimulation. Reflexes are the newborn baby's most obvious organized patterns of behavior. Human infants come into the world with dozens of them. As Jay put Joshua down on a table in my classroom, we saw several. When Jay bumped the side of the table, Joshua reacted by flinging his arms wide and bringing them back toward his body. As Yolanda stroked Joshua's cheek, he turned his head in her direc-

TABLE 4.3

Some Newborn Reflexes

REFLEX	STIMULATION	RESPONSE	AGE OF DISAPPEARANCE	FUNCTION
Eye blink	Shine bright light at eyes or clap hand near head	Infant quickly closes eyelids	Permanent	Protects infant from strong stimulation
Rooting	Stroke cheek near corner of mouth	Head turns toward source of stimulation	3 weeks (becomes voluntary head turning at this time)	Helps infant find the nipple
Sucking	Place finger in infant's mouth	Infant sucks finger rhythmically	Permanent	Permits feeding
Swimming	Place infant face down in pool of water	Baby paddles and kicks in swimming motion	4–6 months	Helps infant survive if dropped into body of water
Moro	Hold infant horizontally on back and let head drop slightly, or produce a sudden loud sound against surface supporting infant	Infant makes an "embracing" motion by arching back, extending legs, throwing arms outward, and then bringing them in toward the body	6 months	In human evolutionary past, may have helped infant cling to mother
Palmar grasp	Place finger in infant's hand and press against palm	Spontaneous grasp of adult's finger	3–4 months	Prepares infant for voluntary grasping
Tonic neck	Turn baby's head to one side while lying awake on back	Infant lies in a "fencing position." One arm is extended in front of eyes on side to which head is turned, other arm is flexed	4 months	May prepare infant for voluntary reaching
Stepping	Hold infant under arms and permit bare feet to touch a flat surface	Infant lifts one foot after another in stepping response	2 months	Prepares infant for voluntary walking
Babinski	Stroke sole of foot from toe toward heel	Toes fan out and curl as foot twists in	8–12 months	Unknown

Sources: Knobloch & Pasamanick, 1974; Prechtl & Beintema, 1965.

tion. When she put her finger in the palm of Joshua's hand, he grabbed on tightly. Jay held Joshua upright with his feet touching the table, and he made little stepping movements. Table 4.3 provides a description of the major newborn reflexes. See if you can name the ones that Joshua displayed. Then let's look at the meaning and purpose of these curious behaviors.

■ **SURVIVAL VALUE OF REFLEXES.** Some reflexes have survival value. The rooting reflex helps a breast-fed baby find the mother's nipple. And if sucking were not automatic, our species would be unlikely to survive for a single generation! The swimming reflex helps a baby who is accidentally dropped into a body of water stay afloat, increasing the chances of retrieval by the caregiver.

bonding
Parents' feelings of affection and concern for the newborn baby.

rooming in
An arrangement in which the newborn baby stays in the mother's hospital room all or most of the time.

reflex
An inborn, automatic response to a particular form of stimulation.

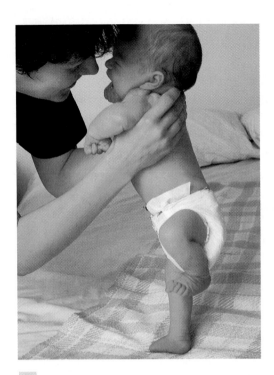

When held upright under the arms, newborn babies show reflexive stepping movements. *(Innervisions)*

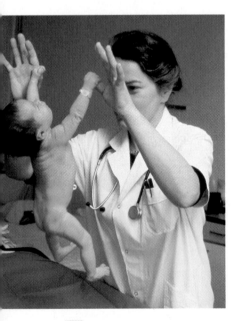

The palmar grasp reflex is so strong during the first week after birth that many infants can use it to support their entire weight. *(J. da Cunha/ Petit Format/Photo Researchers)*

Other reflexes probably helped babies survive during our evolutionary past. For example, the Moro or "embracing" reflex is believed to have helped infants cling to their mothers when babies were carried about all day. If the baby happened to lose support, the reflex caused the infant to embrace and, along with the grasp reflex, regain its hold on the mother's body (Kessen, 1967; Prechtl, 1958).

■ **REFLEXES AND THE DEVELOPMENT OF MOTOR SKILLS.** A few reflexes form the basis for complex motor skills that will develop later. For example, the tonic neck reflex may prepare the baby for voluntary reaching. When infants lie on their backs in this "fencing position," they naturally gaze at the hand in front of their eyes. The reflex may encourage them to combine vision with arm movements and, eventually, reach for objects (Knobloch & Pasamanick, 1974).

The stepping reflex looks like a primitive walking response. In infants who gain weight quickly in the weeks after birth, the stepping reflex drops out because thigh and calf muscles are not strong enough to lift the baby's increasingly chubby legs. However, if the lower part of the infant's body is dipped in water, the reflex reappears, since the buoyancy of the water lightens the load on the baby's muscles (Thelen, Fisher, & Ridley-Johnson, 1984). When the stepping reflex is exercised regularly, babies display more spontaneous stepping movements and are likely to walk several weeks earlier than if it is not practiced (Zelazo, 1983; Zelazo et al., 1993). However, there is no special need for parents to get their infants to use the stepping reflex, since all normal babies walk in due time.

■ **REFLEXES AND EARLY SOCIAL RELATIONSHIPS.** A baby who searches for and successfully finds the nipple, sucks easily during feedings, and grasps when the hand is touched encourages parents to respond lovingly and feel competent as caregivers. Reflexes also can help parents comfort the baby, since they permit infants to control distress and amount of stimulation to some degree themselves. For example, on short trips with Joshua to the grocery store, Yolanda brought along a pacifier. If he became fussy, sucking helped quiet him until she could feed, change, or hold and rock him.

The next time you have a chance to watch a young baby nursing, look carefully. You will see that the baby's sucking behavior is highly organized. Bursts of sucks are separated by pauses, a style of feeding that is unique to the human species. Some researchers believe that this burst–pause rhythm is an evolved behavior pattern that helps parents and infants establish satisfying interaction as soon as possible. Notice what most mothers do during the baby's pause: they jiggle the infant to encourage more sucking. In response, newborn babies learn to expect and wait for their mother's jiggle. This early sequence of interaction during feeding resembles the turn taking of human conversation. Using the primitive sucking reflex, the young baby participates as an active, cooperative partner (Kaye & Wells, 1980).

■ **THE IMPORTANCE OF ASSESSING NEWBORN REFLEXES.** Look at Table 4.3 again, and you will see that most newborn reflexes disappear during the first 6 months of life. Researchers believe this is due to a gradual increase in voluntary control over behavior as the cortex of the brain matures.

Pediatricians test reflexes carefully, especially if a newborn has experienced birth trauma, since reflexes provide one way of assessing the health of the baby's nervous system. In brain-damaged infants, reflexes may be weak or absent, or in some cases exaggerated and overly rigid. Brain damage may also be indicated when reflexes persist past the point in development when they should normally disappear. However, individual differences in reflexive responses exist that are not cause for concern. Newborn reflexes must be observed along with other characteristics of the baby to accurately distinguish normal from abnormal central nervous system functioning (Touwen, 1984).

SENSORY CAPACITIES

What can babies perceive with the senses at birth? On his visit to my class, Joshua looked wide-eyed at my bright pink blouse and turned to the sound of his mother's voice. During feedings, he lets Yolanda know by the way he sucks that he prefers the taste of breast milk to a bottle of plain water. Clearly, Joshua has some well-developed sensory capacities. In the following sections, we explore the newborn baby's responsiveness to touch, taste, smell, sound, and visual stimulation. Table 4.4 summarizes these remarkable abilities.

This baby shows Babinski reflex. When an adult strokes the sole of the foot, the toes fan out. Then they curl as the foot twists in. *(Innervisions)*

■ **TOUCH.** In our discussion of preterm infants, we indicated that touch helps stimulate early physical growth, and as we will see in Chapter 7, it is important for emotional development as well. Therefore, it is not surprising that sensitivity to touch is well developed at birth. Return once more to the reflexes listed in Table 4.3. They reveal that the newborn baby responds to touch, especially around the mouth, on the palms of the hands, and on the soles of the feet. During the prenatal period, these areas, along with the genitals, are the first to become sensitive to touch, followed by other regions of the body (Humphrey, 1978).

Reactions to temperature change are also present at birth. When Yolanda and Jay undress Joshua, he often expresses his discomfort by crying and becoming more active. Newborn babies are more sensitive to stimuli that are colder than body temperature than to those that are warmer (Humphrey, 1978).

At birth, infants are quite sensitive to pain. If male newborns are circumcised, anesthetics are usually not used because of the risk of giving pain-relieving drugs to a very young infant. Babies often respond with an intense, high-pitched, stressful cry (Hadjistavropoulos et al., 1994). In addition, heart rate and blood pressure rise, irritability increases, and sleep is disturbed for hours afterward (Anand, 1990). Recent research aimed at developing safe pain-relieving drugs for newborns promises to ease the stress of such procedures. One helpful approach is to offer a nipple that delivers a sugar solution, which quickly reduces crying and discomfort in young babies, preterm and full-term alike

TABLE 4.4

The Newborn Baby's Sensory Capacities

SENSE	FUNCTIONING IN THE NEWBORN
Touch	Responsive to touch, temperature change, and pain
Taste	Prefers sweetness; can distinguish sweet, salty, sour, and bitter tastes
Smell	Reacts to the smell of certain foods in the same way as adults; can identify the location of an odor and turn away from unpleasant odors; prefers the smell of a lactating woman (if breast fed, can distinguish own mother's breast odor)
Hearing	Prefers complex sounds to pure tones; can distinguish some sound patterns; recognizes differences among almost all human speech sounds; turns in the general direction of a sound; prefers high-pitched, expressive voices with rising intonation and the sound of own mother's voice
Vision	Least well-developed sense at birth; focusing ability and visual acuity limited; scans visual field and attempts to track moving objects; color vision not yet well developed

(Smith & Blass, 1996). Doctors are becoming more aware that small infants, just like older children and adults, must not be treated as if they are insensitive to pain.

■ **TASTE.** All babies come into the world with the ability to communicate their taste preferences to caregivers. When given a sweet liquid instead of water, Joshua uses longer sucks with fewer pauses, indicating that he prefers sweetness and tries to savor the taste of his favorite food (Crook & Lipsitt, 1976). If water is made salty, Joshua shortens his sucking bursts, as if to avoid an unpleasant taste (Crook, 1978).

Facial expressions also reveal that infants can distinguish between several tastes. Much like adults, newborn babies relax their facial muscles in response to sweetness, purse their lips when the taste is sour, and show a distinct archlike mouth opening when it is bitter (Steiner, 1979). These reactions are important for survival, since (as we will see in Chapter 5) the food that is ideally suited to support the infant's early growth is the sweet-tasting milk of the mother's breast.

■ **SMELL.** Like taste, the newborn baby's responsiveness to the smell of certain foods is surprisingly similar to that of adults, suggesting that some odor preferences are innate. For example, the smell of bananas or chocolate causes a relaxed, pleasant facial expression, whereas the odor of rotten eggs makes the infant frown (Steiner, 1979). Newborns can also identify the location of an odor and, if it is unpleasant, defend themselves. When a whiff of ammonia is presented to one side of the baby's nostrils, infants less than 6 days old quickly turn their heads in the other direction (Reiser, Yonas, & Wikner, 1976).

In many mammals, the sense of smell plays an important role in eating and protecting the young from predators by helping mothers and babies recognize each other. Although smell is less well developed in humans than in other mammals, traces of its survival value are still present. Mothers can identify their own baby by smell shortly after birth, and the baby responds in kind. The ability to recognize the mother's smell occurs only in breast-fed newborns (Cernoch & Porter, 1985). However, bottle-fed babies prefer the smell of any lactating (milk-producing) woman to the smell of a non-lactating woman. And when given a choice between the smell of the lactating breast and their familiar formula, once again they choose the former (Makin & Porter, 1989; Porter et al., 1992). Newborn infants' attraction to the odor of the lactating breast probably helps them locate an appropriate food source and, in the process, learn to identify their own mother.

■ **HEARING.** Newborn infants can hear a wide variety of sounds, but they are more responsive to some than to others. For example, they prefer complex sounds, such as noises and voices, to pure tones (Bench et al., 1976). In the first few days of life, infants can already tell the difference between a few sound patterns—a series of tones arranged in ascending versus descending order, utterances with two versus three syllables, and the stress patterns of words, such as <u>ma</u>ma versus ma<u>ma</u> (Bijeljac-Babic, Bertoncini, & Mehler, 1993; Sansavini, Bertoncini, & Giovanelli, 1997).

These capacities, as well as others, indicate that the newborn baby is marvelously prepared for the awesome task of acquiring language. Tiny infants are especially sensitive to the sounds of human speech. They can make fine-grained distinctions among a wide variety of speech sounds—"ba" and "ga," "ma" and "na," and the short vowel sounds "ah" and "eh," to name just a few. For example, when given a nipple that turns on the "ba" sound, babies suck vigorously for a period of time, and then sucking slows down. When the sound switches to "ga," sucking picks up again, indicating that infants can detect this subtle sound difference. Using this method, researchers have found that there are only a few speech sounds that newborns cannot discriminate, and their ability to perceive sounds not found in their language environment is more precise than an adult's (Jusczyk, 1995). Infants seem to come into the world biologically prepared to respond to the sounds of any human language.

Responsiveness to sound supports the newborn baby's visual exploration of the environment. Infants as young as 3 days turn their eyes and head in the general direction of a sound. The ability to identify the precise location of a sound will improve greatly over the first 6 months and show further gains into the second year (Ashmead et al., 1991; Hillier, Hewitt, & Morrongiello, 1992).

Listen carefully to yourself the next time you talk to a young baby. You will probably speak in a high-pitched, expressive voice and use a rising tone at the ends of phrases and sentences. Adults probably communicate this way with infants because they notice that babies are more attentive when they do so. Indeed, newborns prefer speech with these characteristics (Aslin, Jusczyk, & Pisoni, 1997). They will also suck more on a nipple to hear a recording of their own mother's voice than that of an unfamiliar woman, and to hear their native language as opposed to a foreign language (Moon, Cooper, & Fifer, 1993; Spence & DeCasper, 1987). These preferences probably developed from hearing the muffled sounds of the mother's voice before birth.

Infants' special responsiveness to speech encourages parents to talk to the baby. As they do so, both readiness for language and the emotional bond between parent and child are strengthened.

(a) Newborn View

■ **VISION.** Humans depend on vision more than any other sense for active exploration of the environment. Yet vision is the least mature of the newborn baby's senses. Visual structures in both the eye and the brain continue to develop after birth. For example, the muscles of the *lens,* the part of the eye that permits us to adjust our focus to varying distances, are weak. Also, cells in the *retina,* the membrane lining the inside of the eye that captures light and transforms it into messages that are sent to the brain, are not as mature or densely packed as they will be in several months (Banks & Bennett, 1988). Furthermore, the optic nerve and other pathways that relay these messages, along with cells in the cortex that receive them, will not be adultlike for several years (Hickey & Peduzzi, 1987).

Because of these factors, newborn babies cannot focus their eyes very well. In addition, their **visual acuity,** or fineness of discrimination, is limited. When you have your vision tested, the doctor provides an estimate of your visual acuity, which indicates how finely you perceive stimuli in comparison to an adult with normal vision. Applying this same index to newborn babies, researchers have found that they perceive objects at a distance of 20 feet about as clearly as adults do at 600 feet (Courage & Adams, 1990; Held, 1993). Furthermore, unlike adults (who see nearby objects most clearly), newborn babies see equally unclearly across a wide range of distances (Banks, 1980). As a result, images such as the parent's face, even from close up, look much like the blur shown in Figure 4.7.

Although newborn infants cannot yet see well, they actively explore their environment with the limited visual abilities that they have. They scan the visual field for interesting sights and try to track moving objects. However, their eye movements are slow and inaccurate (Aslin, 1993).

Joshua's captivation with my pink blouse reveals that he is attracted to bright objects. Nevertheless, once newborns focus on an object, they tend to look only at a single feature—for example, the corner of a triangle instead of the entire shape. Although newborn babies prefer to look at colored rather than gray stimuli, they are not yet good at discriminating colors. It will take a month or two for color vision to improve (Adams, 1987; Adams, Courage, & Mercer, 1994).

NEWBORN STATES

Throughout the day and night, newborn infants move in and out of five different **states of arousal,** or degrees of sleep and wakefulness, described in Table 4.5. During the first month, these states alternate frequently. Quiet alertness is the most fleeting. It usually moves toward fussing and crying relatively quickly. Much to the relief of their fatigued

(b) Adult View

FIGURE 4.7

The newborn baby's limited focusing ability and poor visual acuity lead the mother's face, even when viewed from close up, to look much like the fuzzy image in part (a) rather than the clear image in part (b).

visual acuity
Fineness of visual discrimination.

states of arousal
Different degrees of sleep and wakefulness.

TABLE 4.5

Infant States of Arousal

STATE	DESCRIPTION	DAILY DURATION IN NEWBORN
Regular sleep	The infant is at full rest and shows little or no body activity. The eyelids are closed, no eye movements occur, the face is relaxed, and breathing is slow and regular.	8–9 hours
Irregular sleep	Gentle limb movements, occasional stirring, and facial grimacing occur. Although the eyelids are closed, occasional rapid eye movements can be seen beneath them. Breathing is irregular.	8–9 hours
Drowsiness	The infant is either falling asleep or waking up. The body is less active than in irregular sleep but more active than in regular sleep. The eyes open and close; when open, they have a glazed look. Breathing is even but somewhat faster than in regular sleep.	Varies
Quiet alertness	The infant's body is relatively inactive, with eyes open and attentive. Breathing is even.	2–3 hours
Waking activity and crying	The infant shows frequent bursts of uncoordinated body activity. Breathing is very irregular. Face may be relaxed or tense and wrinkled. Crying may occur.	1–4 hours

Source: Wolff, 1966.

parents, newborns spend the greatest amount of time asleep—on the average, about 16 to 18 hours a day.

Although sleep is the dominant state in all newborns, striking individual differences in daily rhythms exist that affect parents' attitudes toward and interactions with the baby. A few infants sleep for long periods at an early age, increasing the rest their parents get and the energy they have for sensitive, responsive care. Babies who cry a great deal require that parents try harder to soothe them. If these efforts are not successful, parents' positive feelings for the infant and sense of competence may suffer. Babies who spend more time alert are likely to receive more social stimulation. And since this state provides opportunities to explore the environment, infants who favor it may have a slight advantage in cognitive development (Moss et al., 1988).

Of the five states listed in Table 4.5, the two extremes—sleep and crying—have been of greatest interest to researchers. Each tells us something about normal and abnormal early development.

■ **SLEEP.** One day, Yolanda and Jay watched Joshua while he slept and wondered why his eyelids and body twitched and his rate of breathing varied, speeding up at some points and slowing down at others. "Is this how babies are supposed to sleep?" they asked, somewhat worried. "Indeed, it is," I responded.

Sleep is made up of at least two states. Irregular, or **rapid-eye-movement (REM) sleep,** is the one that Yolanda and Jay happened to observe. The expression "sleeping like a baby" was probably not meant to describe this state! During REM sleep, the brain and parts of the body are highly active. Electrical brain wave activity is remarkably similar to that of the waking state. The eyes dart beneath the lids; heart rate, blood pressure, and breathing are uneven; and slight body movements occur. In contrast, during regular, or **non-rapid-eye movement (NREM) sleep,** the body is quiet, and heart rate, breathing, and brain wave activity are slow and regular (Dittrichova et al., 1982).

Like children and adults, newborns alternate between REM and NREM sleep. However, they spend far more time in the REM state than they ever will again. REM sleep accounts for 50 percent of the newborn baby's sleep time. It declines steadily to 20 percent between 3 and 5 years of age, which is about the same percentage it consumes in adulthood (Roffwarg, Muzio, & Dement, 1966).

rapid-eye-movement (REM) sleep
An "irregular" sleep state in which brain wave activity is similar to that of the waking state; eyes dart beneath the lids; heart rate, blood pressure, and breathing are uneven; and slight body movements occur.

non-rapid-eye movement (NREM) sleep
A "regular" sleep state in which the body is quiet and heart rate, breathing, and brain wave activity are slow and regular.

Why do young infants spend so much time in REM sleep? In older children and adults, the REM state is associated with dreaming. Babies probably do not dream, at least not in the same way we do. Young infants are believed to have a special need for the stimulation of REM sleep because they spend little time in an alert state, when they can get input from the environment. REM sleep seems to be a way in which the brain stimulates itself. Sleep researchers believe that this stimulation is vital for growth of the central nervous system. In support of this idea, the percentage of REM sleep is especially great in the fetus and in preterm babies, who are even less able to take advantage of external stimulation than are full-term newborns (DiPietro et al., 1996a; Parmelee et al., 1967).

Because the normal sleep behavior of the newborn baby is organized and patterned, observations of sleep states can help identify central nervous system abnormalities. In infants who are brain damaged or who have experienced serious birth trauma, disturbed REM–NREM sleep cycles often are present (Whitney & Thoman, 1993).

■ **CRYING.** Crying is the first way that babies communicate, letting parents know that they need food, comfort, and stimulation. During the weeks after birth, all babies seem to have some fussy periods when they are difficult to console. But most of the time, the nature of the cry helps guide parents toward its cause. The baby's cry is actually a complex stimulus that varies in intensity, from a whimper to a message of all-out distress (Gustafson & Harris, 1990). As early as the first few weeks of life, infants can be identified by the unique vocal "signature" of their cry, which helps parents locate their baby from a distance (Gustafson, Green, & Cleland, 1994).

Newborn infants usually cry because of physical needs. Hunger is the most common cause, but young infants may also cry in response to temperature change when undressed, a sudden loud sound, or a painful stimulus. Interestingly, newborn crying can also be caused by the sound of another crying baby. Some researchers believe this response reflects an inborn capacity to react to the suffering of others (Hoffman, 1988; Martin & Clark, 1982).

The next time you hear a baby cry, notice your own mental and physical reaction. A crying baby stimulates strong feelings of arousal and discomfort in just about anyone—men and women and parents and nonparents alike (Boukydis & Burgess, 1982; Murray, 1985). The powerful effect of the infant's cry is probably innately programmed in all human beings to make sure that babies receive the care and protection they need to survive.

Although parents do not always interpret their baby's cry correctly, experience quickly improves their accuracy. As the baby gets older, parents respond to more subtle cues in the cry—not just intensity, but whimpering and calling sounds—to detect anxiety in their infant (Thompson & Leger, 1998).

Even when parents are fairly certain about the cause of the cry, the baby may not always calm down. Fortunately, as the Caregiving Concerns table on page 158 indicates, there are many ways to soothe a crying newborn when feeding and diaper changing do not work. The technique that Western parents usually try first, lifting the baby to the shoulder, is also the one that works the best. Among the Quechua, who live in the cold, high-altitude desert regions of Peru, young babies are dressed in several layers of clothing and blankets. Then a cloth belt is tightly wound around the body, over which are placed additional blankets that cover the head and face and serve as a carrying cloth. The result—a nearly sealed, warm pouch placed on the mother's back that moves rhythmically as she walks—reduces crying and promotes sleep. As a result, the baby conserves energy for early growth in the harsh Peruvian highlands (Tronick, Thomas, & Daltabuit, 1994).

Like reflexes and sleep patterns, the infant's cry offers a clue to central nervous system distress. The cries of brain-damaged

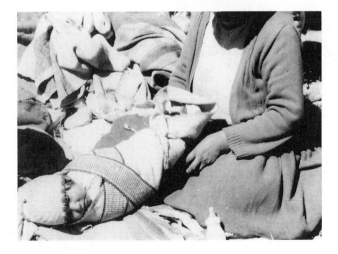

This Quechua mother dresses her infant in several layers of clothing and blankets and winds a cloth belt tightly around the body, over which will be placed additional blankets. The resulting sealed, warm pouch placed on the mother's back reduces crying and promotes sleep, conserving energy for early growth in the harsh Peruvian highlands. *(Edward Tronick)*

CAREGIVING CONCERNS

Ways of Soothing a Crying Newborn

METHOD	EXPLANATION
Lift the baby to the shoulder and rock or walk.	This provides a combination of physical contact, upright posture, and motion. It is the most effective soothing technique, causing young infants to become quietly alert.
Swaddle the baby.	Restricting movement and increasing warmth often soothes a young infant.
Offer a pacifier.	Sucking helps babies control their own level of arousal.
Talk softly or play rhythmic sounds.	Continuous, monotonous, rhythmic sounds, such as a clock ticking, a fan whirring, or peaceful music, are more effective than intermittent sounds.
Take the baby for a short car ride or walk in a baby carriage; swing the baby in a cradle.	Gentle, rhythmic motion of any kind helps lull the baby to sleep.
Massage the baby's body.	Stroke the baby's torso and limbs with continuous, gentle motions. This technique is used in some non-Western cultures to relax the baby's muscles.
Combine several of the methods just listed.	Stimulating several of the baby's senses at once is often more effective than stimulating only one.
If these methods do not work, let the baby cry for a short period of time.	Occasionally, a baby responds well to just being put down and will, after a few minutes, fall asleep.

Sources: Campos, 1989; Heinl, 1983; Lester, 1985; Reisman, 1987.

Similar to women in the Zambian culture, this Inuit mother of Northern Canada carries her baby about all day, providing close physical contact and a rich variety of stimulation. *(Eastcott/Momatiak; Woodfin Camp & Associates)*

babies and those who have experienced prenatal and birth complications often are shrill and piercing (Huntington, Hans, & Zeskind, 1990; Lester, 1987). Most parents try to respond to a sick baby's call for help with extra care and attention. In some cases, however, the cry is so unpleasant and the infant so difficult to soothe that parents become frustrated, resentful, and angry. Research reveals that preterm and sick babies are more likely to be abused by their parents than are healthy infants. Often these parents mention a high-pitched, grating cry as one factor that caused them to lose control and harm the baby (Frodi, 1985).

NEONATAL BEHAVIORAL ASSESSMENT

The many capacities described in the preceding sections have been put together into tests that permit doctors, nurses, and researchers to assess the behavior of the infant during the newborn period. The most widely used of these tests is T. Berry Brazelton's **Neonatal Behavioral Assessment Scale (NBAS)** (Brazelton & Nugent, 1995). With it, the examiner can look at the baby's reflexes, state changes, responsiveness to physical and social stimuli, and other reactions.

The NBAS has been given to many infants around the world. As a result, researchers have learned a great deal about individual and cultural differences in newborn behavior and how a baby's reactions can be maintained or changed by child-rearing practices. For example, NBAS scores of Asian and Native American babies reveal that they are less irritable than Caucasian infants. Mothers in these cultures often encourage their babies' calm dispositions through swaddling, close physical contact, and nursing at the first signs of discomfort (Chisholm, 1989; Freedman & Freedman, 1969; Murrett-Wagstaff & Moore,

1989). In contrast, the poor NBAS scores of undernourished infants born in Zambia, Africa, are quickly changed by the way their mothers care for them. The Zambian mother carries her baby about on her hip all day, providing a rich variety of sensory stimulation. As a result, by 1 week of age a once unresponsive newborn has been transformed into an alert, contented baby (Brazelton, Koslowski, & Tronick, 1976).

Can you tell from these examples why a single NBAS score is not a good predictor of later development? Since newborn behavior and parenting styles combine to shape development, *changes in NBAS scores* over the first week or two of life (rather than a single score) provide the best estimate of the baby's ability to recover from the stress of birth. NBAS "recovery curves" predict intelligence with moderate success well into the preschool years (Brazelton, Nugent, & Lester, 1987).

The NBAS has also been used to help parents get to know their infants. In some hospitals, the examination is given in the presence of parents to teach them about their newborn baby's capacities. Parents of both preterm and full-term newborns who participate in these programs have been found to interact more confidently and effectively with their babies (Brazelton, Nugent, & Lester, 1987; Tedder, 1991). Although lasting effects on development have not been demonstrated, NBAS-based interventions are clearly useful in helping the parent–infant relationship get off to a good start.

BRIEF REVIEW

The newborn baby is equipped with a wide variety of capacities for relating to the surrounding world. Reflexes are the infant's most obvious organized behavior patterns. Some, like sucking, have survival value, whereas others, like stepping, form the basis for motor skills that will develop later. The senses of touch, taste, smell, and hearing are well developed in the newborn baby. Vision is least mature, but newborns actively explore the environment with the visual abilities that they have. Infants move in and out of five states of arousal throughout the day and night. Sleep is the dominant state; young infants spend far more time in REM sleep than they will at later ages. A crying baby stimulates strong feelings of discomfort in nearby adults. Fortunately, there are many ways to soothe a crying newborn. Neonatal behavioral assessment permits doctors, nurses, and researchers to assess the remarkable capacities of the newborn baby.

THE TRANSITION TO PARENTHOOD

The early weeks after a new baby enters the family are full of profound changes. The mother needs to recover from childbirth and adjust to massive hormone shifts in her body. If she is breast-feeding, energies must be devoted to working out this intimate relationship. The father also needs to become a part of this new threesome while supporting the mother in her recovery. At times, he may feel somewhat jealous of the baby, who constantly demands and gets his wife's attention (Jordan, 1990). And as we will see in Chapter 7, in families with other children, siblings—especially those who are young and first born—understandably feel displaced. They often react with jealously and anger.

While all this is going on, the tiny infant is very assertive about his urgent physical needs, demanding to be fed, changed, and comforted at odd times of the day and night. The family schedule becomes irregular and uncertain. Yolanda spoke candidly about the changes that she and Jay experienced:

When we brought Joshua home, we had to deal with the realities of our new responsibility. Joshua seemed so small and helpless, and we worried about

ASK YOURSELF . . .

■ *How do the capacities of newborn babies contribute to their first social relationships? Provide as many examples as you can.*

■ *Jackie, who had a difficult birth, observes her 2-day-old daughter, Kelly, being given the NBAS. Kelly scores poorly on many items. Jackie wonders if this means that Kelly will not develop normally. How would you respond to Jackie's concern?*

Neonatal Behavioral Assessment Scale (NBAS)
A test developed to assess the behavior of the infant during the newborn period.

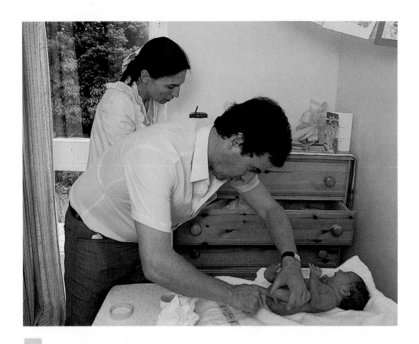

The demands of new parenthood, from baby care to added financial responsibilities, often lead to a mild decline in marital satisfaction. This father's involvement can limit marital unhappiness by reducing his feelings of being an "outsider" and freeing up time for the couple to spend together. *(Nancy Durrell McKenna/Photo Researchers, Inc.)*

whether we would be able to take proper care of him. It took us 20 minutes to change the first diaper. I rarely feel rested because I'm up two to four times every night, and I spend a good part of my waking hours trying to anticipate Joshua's rhythms and needs. If Jay weren't so willing to help by holding and walking Joshua, I think I'd find it much harder.

CHANGES IN THE FAMILY SYSTEM

The demands of new parenthood—disrupted sleep schedules, less time for husband and wife to devote to each other, and new financial responsibilities—often lead to a mild decline in a couple's marital happiness. In addition, entry of the baby into the family usually causes the roles of husband and wife to become more traditional (Cowan & Cowan, 1992; Huston & Vangelisti, 1995). This is even true for couples like Yolanda and Jay, who are strongly committed to gender equality and were used to sharing household tasks. Yolanda took a leave of absence from work, whereas Jay's career life continued just as it had before. As a result, Yolanda spent much more time at home with the baby, whereas Jay focused more on his provider role.

This movement toward traditional roles is hardest on new mothers who have been used to active involvement in a career. The larger the difference in men's and women's responsibilities, the greater the rise in conflict and decline in marital satisfaction and mental health after childbirth, especially for women (Hawkins et al., 1993; Levy-Shiff, 1994). Overall, women experience a more difficult transition to parenthood than do men. (See the Biology and Environment box on the following page).

Violated expectations about jointly caring for a new baby contribute to the decline in marital happiness. Women, especially, count on far more help from their partners than they usually get (Hackel & Ruble, 1992). Postponing childbearing until the late twenties or thirties, as Yolanda and Jay did, eases the transition to parenthood. Waiting permits couples to pursue occupational goals and gain life experience. Under these circumstances, men are more enthusiastic about becoming fathers and therefore more willing to participate. And women whose careers are under way are more likely to encourage their husbands to share housework and child care (Coltrane, 1990).

Men who view themselves as especially caring show less decline in marital satisfaction after the birth of a baby, probably because they are better at meeting the needs of their wives and infants. The father's involvement can reduce his feelings of being an "outsider" and free up time for partners to spend together. Also, men's participation enhances the marital relationship because women tend to see it as a loving act toward themselves (Levy-Shiff, 1994).

PARENT INTERVENTIONS

Special interventions exist to ease the transition to parenthood. For parents who are not at high risk for problems, couples' groups led by counselors are highly effective (Cowan & Cowan, 1995). In one program, first-time expectant couples gathered once a week for 24 weeks, with their babies joining the group as they were born. Sessions focused on partners' dreams for the family and changes in relationships sparked by the baby's

BIOLOGY & ENVIRONMENT

POSTPARTUM DEPRESSION AND THE PARENT–CHILD RELATIONSHIP

For as many as 50 to 80 percent of first-time mothers, the excitement of the baby's arrival gives way to an emotional letdown during the first week after delivery known as the *postpartum* (or after-birth) *blues*. The blues are temporary. They die down as new mothers adjust to hormonal changes following childbirth, gain confidence in caring for the baby, and are reassured by their husbands, family members, and friends. However, as many as 10 percent of women do not bounce back from childbirth so easily. They experience **postpartum depression,** mild to severe feelings of sadness and withdrawal that continue for weeks or months.

Stella was one of these women. Her genetic makeup may have predisposed her to develop postpartum depression, since the best predictor of depression after childbirth is depression before the baby is born (Hock et al., 1995). Yet Stella's case shows that social and cultural factors are also involved.

During Stella's pregnancy, her husband Kyle's lack of interest in the baby caused her to worry that having a child might be a mistake. Shortly after Lucy was born, Stella's mood plunged. She was anxious and weepy, overwhelmed by Lucy's needs, and angry that she no longer had control over her own schedule. When Stella approached Kyle about her own fatigue and his unwillingness to help with the baby, he snapped that she overreacted to every move he made. Stella's friends, who did not have children, stopped by once to see Lucy and did not call again.

Stella's depressed mood quickly affected her relationship with the baby. As Lucy started to spend more time awake and alert, Stella rarely smiled and talked to her. Lucy responded to Stella's sad, vacant gaze by turning away, crying, and often looking sad or angry herself (Campbell, Cohen, & Meyers, 1995; Murray & Cooper, 1997). Each time this happened, Stella felt guilty and inadequate as a mother, and her depression deepened. By 6 months of age, Lucy showed emotional symptoms common in babies of depressed mothers—a negative, irritable mood and attachment difficulties (Teti et al., 1995).

When maternal depression persists, parent–child relationship problems worsen. Depressed parents use inconsistent discipline—sometime lax, at other times too forceful—a pattern that reflects their disengaged as well as hostile behavior (Zahn-Waxler et al., 1990a). As we will see in later chapters, children exposed to these parenting practices often have serious adjustment difficulties. To avoid their parent's insensitivity, they sometimes withdraw into a depressive mood themselves. Or they may mimic their parent's anger and become impulsive and antisocial (Conger, Patterson, & Ge, 1995). Children of depressed parents may inherit a tendency to develop emotional and behavior problems. But clearly, quality of parenting plays a major role

Early treatment of maternal depression is vital to prevent the disorder from doing harm to children. Stella described her tearfulness, fatigue, and inability to comfort Lucy to her doctor. He referred her to a special program for depressed mothers and their babies. A counselor worked with the family, helping Stella and Kyle with their marital problems and encouraging them to be more sensitive and patient with Lucy. At times, antidepressant medication is prescribed. In most cases of postpartum depression, treatment is successful (Cooper & Murray, 1997). When depressed mothers do not respond easily to treatment, a warm relationship with the father or another caregiver can safeguard children's development.

arrival. Eighteen months after the program ended, participating fathers described themselves as more involved with their child than did fathers assigned to a no-intervention condition. Perhaps because of their partners' caregiving assistance, participating mothers maintained their prebirth satisfaction with family and work roles. Three years after the birth, the marriages of all participating couples were still intact and just as happy as they had been before parenthood. In contrast, 13 percent of couples receiving no intervention had divorced (Cowan & Cowan, 1992).

For high-risk parents struggling with poverty or the birth of a child with disabilities, interventions must be more intensive. Programs in which a trained intervener visits the

postpartum depression
Feelings of sadness and withdrawal that appear shortly after childbirth and that continue for weeks or months.

CAREGIVING CONCERNS
Ways Couples Can Ease the Transition to Parenthood

STRATEGY	DESCRIPTION
Devise a plan for sharing household tasks.	As soon as possible in the relationship, talk about division of household responsibilities. Decide who does a particular chore on the basis of who has the needed skill and time, not gender. Schedule regular times to rediscuss your plan to fit changing family circumstances.
Begin sharing child care right after the baby's arrival.	For fathers, strive to spend equal time with the baby early. For mothers, refrain from imposing your standards on your partner. Instead, share the role of "child-rearing expert" by discussing parenting values and concerns often. Attend a new-parenthood course together.
Talk over conflicts about decision making and responsibilities.	Face conflict through communication. Clarify your feelings and needs and express them to your partner. Listen and try to understand your partner's point of view. Then be willing to negotiate and compromise.
Establish a balance between work and parenting.	Critically evaluate the time you devote to work in view of new parenthood. If it is too much, try to cut back.
Press for workplace and public policies that assist parents in rearing children.	Difficulties faced by new parents are partly due to lack of workplace and societal supports. Encourage your employer to provide benefits that help combine work and family roles, such as paid employment leave; flexible work hours; and onsite high-quality, affordable day care. Communicate with lawmakers and other citizens about improving policies for children and families.

ASK YOURSELF . . .

■ *Louise has just given birth to her first child. Because her husband works long hours and is seldom available to help, she feels overwhelmed by the pressures of caring for a new baby. Why does Louise's 4-week maternity leave pose a risk to her mental health?*

home and focuses on enhancing social support and the parent–child relationship have resulted in improved parent–infant interaction and benefits for children's cognitive and social development up to 5 years after the intervention (Meisels, Dichtelmiller, & Liaw, 1993).

A vital macrosystem, or societal, intervention is paid parental employment leave. It is widely available in Western Europe, where it typically ranges from 2 to 12 months. In Sweden, a couple has the right to 15 months of paid leave to share between them. Even less-developed nations often provide this benefit. For example, in the People's Republic of China, a new mother is granted 3 months' leave at regular pay (Hyde, 1995). Yet in the United States, the federal government mandates only 12 weeks of *unpaid* leave.

When a couple's relationship is stressed by the baby's arrival or a woman's job is overly demanding, a short employment leave (6 weeks or less) is linked to maternal anxiety and depression and negative interactions with the baby. Longer leaves of 12 weeks or more predict favorable maternal mental health and sensitive, responsive caregiving (Clark et al., 1997; Hyde et al., 1995). Single women and their babies are most hurt by the absence of a national paid leave policy. These mothers are usually the sole source of support for their family and can least afford to take time from their jobs.

The Caregiving Concerns table above lists strategies that foster adjustment to parenthood. When favorable workplace policies exist and couples try to support each other's needs, the stress caused by the birth of a baby stays at manageable levels. Family relationships and infant care are worked out after a few months. Nevertheless, as one pair of counselors who have worked with many new parents point out, "As long as children are dependent on their parents, those parents find themselves preoccupied with thoughts of their children. This does not keep them from enjoying other aspects of their lives, but it does mean that they never return to being quite the same people they were before they became parents" (Colman & Colman, 1991, p. 198).

Summary

THE STAGES OF CHILDBIRTH

Describe the three stages of childbirth, the baby's adaptation to labor and delivery, and the newborn baby's appearance.

■ Childbirth takes place in three stages. In the first stage, **dilation and effacement of the cervix** occur as uterine contractions increase in strength and frequency. This stage culminates in **transition,** a brief period in which contractions are strongest and closest together and the cervix opens completely. In the second stage, the mother feels an urge to bear down with her abdominal muscles, and the baby is born. Often an **episiotomy** is performed to permit the baby to pass without tearing the mother's tissues. In the final stage, the placenta is delivered.

■ During labor, infants produce high levels of stress hormones, which help them withstand oxygen deprivation and arouse them into alertness at birth. Newborn infants have large heads, small bodies, and facial features that make adults feel like picking them up and cuddling them. The **Apgar Scale** is used to assess the newborn baby's physical condition at birth.

APPROACHES TO CHILDBIRTH

Describe natural childbirth and home delivery, noting any benefits and concerns associated with each.

■ **Natural, or prepared, childbirth** involves classes in which prospective parents learn about labor and delivery, instruction of the mother in relaxation and breathing techniques, and a companion who serves as a coach during childbirth. The method helps reduce stress and pain during labor and delivery. As a result, most mothers require little or no medication, and they feel more positively about the birth experience.

■ As long as mothers are healthy and assisted by a well-trained doctor or mid-wife, it is just as safe to give birth at home as in a hospital.

MEDICAL INTERVENTIONS

List common medical interventions during childbirth, circumstances that justify their use, and any dangers associated with each.

■ Medical interventions during childbirth are more common in the United States than anywhere else in the world. When women have a history of pregnancy and birth complications, **fetal monitors** help save the lives of many babies. However, when used routinely, they may identify infants as in danger who, in fact, are not.

■ **Analgesics** and **anesthetics** are necessary in complicated deliveries. When given in large doses, these drugs produce a depressed state in the newborn that affects the early mother–infant relationship. They also increase the likelihood of an instrument delivery. **Forceps** or **vacuum extractors** are appropriate if the mother's pushing does not cause the infant to move through the birth canal in a reasonable period of time, but they can cause head injuries.

■ Since **induced labors** are more difficult than naturally occurring ones, they should not be scheduled for reasons of convenience. **Cesarean deliveries** are justified in cases of medical emergency and serious maternal illness and sometimes when babies are in **breech position.** Many unnecessary cesareans are performed in the United States.

BIRTH COMPLICATIONS

What risks are associated with oxygen deprivation, preterm and low birth weight, and postterm birth, and what factors can help infants who survive a traumatic birth develop?

■ Although most births proceed normally, serious complications can occur. A major cause of **cerebral palsy** is lack of oxygen during labor and delivery. As long as **anoxia** is not extreme, most oxygen-deprived newborns catch up in development by the school years. **Respiratory distress syndrome,** which can cause permanent damage due to lack of oxygen, is common in infants who are more than 6 weeks premature.

■ Premature births are high among low-income pregnant women and mothers of twins. Compared to **preterm** babies whose weight is appropriate for time spent in the uterus, **small-for-date** infants are more likely to develop poorly. The fragile appearance and unresponsive, irritable behavior of preterm infants affects the kind of care they receive.

■ Some interventions provide special stimulation in the intensive care nursery. Others teach parents how to care for and interact with their babies. A major cause of **neonatal** and **infant mortality** is low birth weight.

■ **Postterm** infants are at risk for serious birth complications. Therefore, doctors usually induce labor in mothers whose pregnancies have continued for more than 42 weeks.

■ When babies experience birth trauma, a supportive home environment can help restore their growth. Even infants with severe birth complications can recover with the help of favorable life events.

PRECIOUS MOMENTS AFTER BIRTH

Is close parent–infant contact shortly after birth necessary for bonding to occur?

■ Human parents do not require close physical contact with the baby immediately after birth for **bonding** and effective parenting behavior to occur. Nevertheless, most parents find early contact with the infant especially meaningful. Hospital practices that promote parent–infant closeness, such as **rooming in,** may help

*S*ummary (continued)

parents build a good relationship with their baby.

THE NEWBORN BABY'S CAPACITIES

Describe the newborn baby's reflexes and sensory capacities.

- Infants begin life with remarkable skills for relating to their physical and social worlds. **Reflexes** are the newborn baby's most obvious organized patterns of behavior. Some have survival value, whereas others provide the foundation for voluntary motor skills that will develop later.

- The senses of touch, taste, smell, and sound are well developed at birth. Newborns are especially responsive to high-pitched expressive voices, and they prefer the sound of their mother's voice. They can distinguish almost all speech sounds in human languages.

- Vision is the least mature of the newborn's senses. At birth, focusing ability and **visual acuity** are limited. In exploring the visual field, newborn babies are attracted to bright objects, but they limit their looking to single features. The newborn infant has difficulty discriminating colors.

Describe newborn states of arousal, including sleep characteristics and ways to soothe a crying baby.

- Although newborns alternate frequently among five different **states of arousal,** they spend most of their time asleep. Sleep consists of at least two states: **rapid-eye-movement (REM)** and **non-rapid-eye movement (NREM) sleep.** REM sleep is greater during the newborn period than at any later age. It provides young infants with stimulation essential for central nervous system development.

- A crying baby stimulates strong feelings of discomfort in nearby adults. The intensity of the cry and the experiences that led up to it help parents tell what is wrong. Once feeding and diaper changing have been tried, lifting the baby to the shoulder is the most effective soothing technique. Many other soothing methods are helpful.

Why is neonatal behavioral assessment useful?

- The most widely used instrument for assessing the behavior of the newborn infant is Brazelton's **Neonatal Behavioral Assessment Scale (NBAS).** The NBAS has helped researchers understand individual and cultural differences in newborn behavior. Sometimes it is used to teach parents about their baby's capacities.

THE TRANSITION TO PARENTHOOD

Describe typical changes in the family after the birth of a new baby.

- The new baby's arrival is exciting but stressful. The demands of new parenthood often lead to a slight drop in marital happiness, and family roles become more traditional.

- About 10 percent of women experience **postpartum depression.** If not treated early, it can have serious consequences for children's development.

- Couples' groups for low-risk parents and intensive home intervention for high-risk parents can ease the transition to parenthood. Employment leaves of at least 12 weeks reduce adjustment problems. Single women and their babies are the group most affected by the absence of a national paid leave policy in the United States.

*I*mportant terms and concepts

analgesic (p. 140)
anesthetic (p. 140)
anoxia (p. 144)
Apgar Scale (p. 134)
bonding (p. 151)
breech position (p. 142)
cerebral palsy (p. 144)
cesarean delivery (p. 142)
dilation and effacement of the cervix
 (p. 133)
episiotomy (p. 134)
fetal monitors (p. 140)

forceps (p. 141)
induced labor (p. 141)
infant mortality (p. 148)
natural, or prepared, childbirth
 (p. 139)
Neonatal Behavioral Assessment Scale
 (NBAS) (p. 159)
neonatal mortality (p. 148)
non-rapid-eye-movement (NREM)
 sleep (p. 156)
postpartum depression (p. 161)
postterm (p. 147)

preterm (p. 145)
rapid-eye-movement (REM) sleep
 (p. 156)
reflex (p. 151)
respiratory distress syndrome (p. 144)
rooming in (p. 151)
small for date (p. 145)
states of arousal (p. 155)
transition (p. 134)
vacuum extractor (p. 141)
visual acuity (p. 155)

*F*yi... FOR FURTHER INFORMATION AND HELP

GENERAL CHILDBIRTH INFORMATION

National Association of Parents and
Professionals for Safe Alternatives in
Childbirth
(573) 238-2010

*Provides information on all aspects of child-
birth. Places special emphasis on choosing safe
childbirth alternatives.*

Childbirth.Org

*Through an informative website, offers a
wealth of information on all aspects of
childbirth.*
 Website: www.childbirth.org

NATURAL CHILDBIRTH

American Society for Psychoprophylaxis
in Obstetrics (ASPO)
(202) 857-1128
Website: www.lamaze-childbirth.com

*Trains and certifies instructors in the Lamaze
method of natural childbirth. Provides information to expectant parents.*

American Academy of Husband-Coached
Childbirth
(800) 423-2397
Website: www.bradleybirth.com

*Certifies instructors in the Bradley method of
natural childbirth, which emphasizes coaching by the husband.*

MIDWIVES

American College of Nurse-Midwives
(202) 728-9860
Website: www.acnm.org

*Certifies nurse-midwives and provides refer-
rals to expectant parents.*

CESAREAN DELIVERY

Cesareans/Support, Education, and Concern, Inc. (C/Sec, Inc.)
(508) 877-8266

*Provides information on and support for
cesarean mothers, including vaginal birth
after cesarean.*

CEREBRAL PALSY

United Cerebral Palsy Association
(800) 872-5827
Website: www.ucpa.org

*Provides assistance to people with cerebral
palsy and their families. Local and state
chapters offer medical, therapeutic, and
social services.*

"The Night of the
Lantern Festival"

Giao Shan

6 years, China

The delighted expressions and
animated behavior of children
in this scene suggest a strong
drive to explore, understand,
and gain control of their world.
Immediately after birth, infants
display these tendencies. During
the first year, they grow quickly,
move on their own, and make
sense of complicated sights and
sounds. Chapter 5 traces these
awesome achievements.

PHYSICAL DEVELOPMENT IN

INFANCY AND TODDLERHOOD

BODY GROWTH
Changes in Body Size • Changes in Body Proportions • Changes in Muscle–Fat Makeup • Early Skeletal Growth • Appearance of Teeth

BRAIN DEVELOPMENT
Development of Neurons • Development of the Cerebral Cortex

FACTORS AFFECTING EARLY PHYSICAL GROWTH
Heredity • Nutrition • Malnutrition • Emotional Well-Being

CHANGING STATES OF AROUSAL

MOTOR DEVELOPMENT
The Sequence of Motor Development • Motor Skills as Dynamic Systems • Dynamic Motor Systems in Action • Cultural Variations in Motor Development • Fine Motor Development: Voluntary Reaching and Grasping • Bowel and Bladder Control

LEARNING CAPACITIES
Classical Conditioning • Operant Conditioning • Habituation and Dishabituation • Imitation

PERCEPTUAL DEVELOPMENT
Hearing • Vision • Object Perception • Intermodal Perception

UNDERSTANDING PERCEPTUAL DEVELOPMENT

Within a two-day period, Lisa, Beth, and Felicia each gave birth to their first child at the same hospital. Over the next 2 years, the mothers permitted me to sit in as they met once a month to talk over questions and concerns about the development of their babies—Byron, Rachel, and April. I watched and listened as the three lap babies became cruising 1-year-olds, and, finally, walking, talking toddlers.

As the infants grew, the mothers' conversations changed. At first they worried most about physical care— breast-feeding, how soon to introduce solid foods, and when the babies sleep–waking schedules would become more predictable. Between 2 and 3 months, each mother noticed that her baby's daily rhythms had become more organized and patterned, and all three youngsters were much more alert. "Two months seems like a real turning point," commented Felicia. "Life is easier now that I can anticipate April's feedings and naptimes. She seems like more of a little person, and she's much more interested in the world around her."

As the infants' motor skills developed, the home setting in which the mothers gathered changed as well. By the second half of the first year, mothers and babies no longer sat quietly in pairs on the sofa. Instead, the floor was covered with toys, and all three infants crawled about while their mothers kept a watchful eye for coffee table corners, lamp cords, and electric sockets.

Soon crawling became walking. This marked the beginning of *toddlerhood*—a period that spans the second year of life. At first, the youngsters did, indeed, "toddle" with an awkward gait, rocking from side to side and tipping over frequently. But their faces reflected the thrill of being upright, and they explored enthusiastically. As their 2-year-old birthdays approached, Lisa reflected, "Byron is nearly twice as tall and four times as heavy as when he was born. He's starting to look more like a little boy than a baby."

This chapter traces physical growth during the first 2 years—one of the most remarkable and busiest times of development. We will see how rapid changes in the infant's body and brain support new motor skills, learning mechanisms, and perceptual capacities. Byron, Rachel, and April will join us along the way, to illustrate individual differences and environmental influences on physical development.

BODY GROWTH

The next time you have a chance, briefly observe several infants and toddlers while walking in your neighborhood or at a nearby shopping center. You will see that their capabilities are vastly different. One reason for the change in what children can do over the first 2 years is that their bodies change enormously—so much so that relatives who visit just after a baby is born and return again a year or two later often remark that the child does not seem like the same individual.

CHANGES IN BODY SIZE

To parents, the most obvious signs of physical growth are changes in the overall size of the child's body. During the first 2 years, these changes are rapid—faster than they will be at other times of life. As Figure 5.1 shows, by the end of the first year a typical infant's height is 50 percent greater than it was at birth, and by 2 years of age it is 75 percent greater. Weight shows similar dramatic gains. By 5 months of age, birth weight has doubled, at 1 year it has tripled, and at 2 years it has quadrupled.

Researchers who have carefully tracked height changes in infancy and toddlerhood report that rather than steady gains, little growth spurts occur. In one study, children followed over the first 21 months of life went for periods of 7 to 63 days with no growth and then added as much as a half-inch in a 24-hour period. Almost always, parents described their babies as irritable, restless, and very hungry on the day before the spurt (Lampl, 1993; Lampl, Veldhuis, & Johnson, 1992).

As in all aspects of development, differences among children in body size exist. In infancy, girls are slightly shorter and lighter than boys. This small sex difference continues throughout early and middle childhood and will be greatly magnified at adolescence. Ethnic differences in body size are apparent as well. Look again at Figure 5.1, and you will see that Rachel, a Japanese-American child, is below the growth norms (height and weight averages) for children her age. In contrast, April is slightly above average, as African-American children tend to be (Tanner, 1990).

These Brazilian Indian infants and toddlers in an Amazon rubber trapper's home range from 6 months to 2 years of age. Throughout the world, children grow quickly during the first 2 years—faster than at other times of life. Height increases by 75 percent, and weight quadruples. *(Randall Hyman/Stock Boston)*

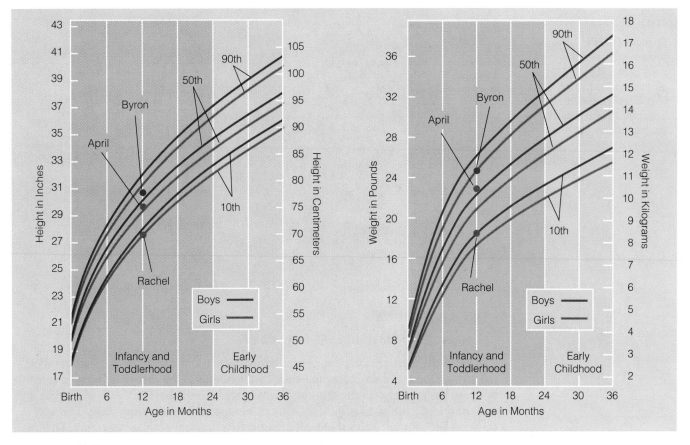

FIGURE 5.1

FIGURE 5.1

Gains in height and weight during infancy and toddlerhood among North American children. The steep rise in these growth curves shows that children grow rapidly from birth to 2 years. At the same time, wide individual differences in body size exist. Infants and toddlers who fall at the 50th percentile are average in height and weight. Those who fall at the 90th percentile are taller and heavier than 90 percent of their agemates. Those who fall at the 10th percentile are taller and heavier than only 10 percent of their peers. Notice that girls are slightly shorter and lighter than boys. As children move into early childhood, rate of growth slows.

CHANGES IN BODY PROPORTIONS

As the child's overall size increases, different parts of the body grow at different rates. Recall from Chapter 3 that during the prenatal period, the head develops first from the primitive embryonic disk, followed by the lower part of the body. After birth, the head and chest continue to have a growth advantage, but the baby's trunk and legs gradually pick up speed. This organized pattern of physical growth is called the **cephalocaudal trend,** which, translated from Latin, means "head to tail." You can see it depicted in Figure 5.2. At birth, the head makes up one-fourth of total body length, the legs only one-third. Notice how the lower portion of the body catches up by age 2. At that time, the head accounts for only one-fifth and the legs for nearly one-half of total body length.

A second growth pattern describes changes in body proportions. It is called the **proximodistal trend,** meaning that growth proceeds, literally, from "near to far," or from the center of the body outward. Again, this is what happened during the prenatal period. The head, chest, and trunk grew first, followed by the arms and legs, and finally the hands and feet. During infancy and childhood, the arms and legs continue to grow somewhat ahead of the hands and feet. As we will see later, motor development follows these same developmental trends.

cephalocaudal trend
An organized pattern of physical growth and motor control that proceeds from head to tail.

proximodistal trend
An organized pattern of physical growth and motor control that proceeds from the center of the body outward.

FIGURE 5.2

Changes in body proportions from the early prenatal period to adulthood. This figure illustrates the cephalocaudal trend of physical growth. The head gradually becomes smaller, and the legs longer, in proportion to the rest of the body.

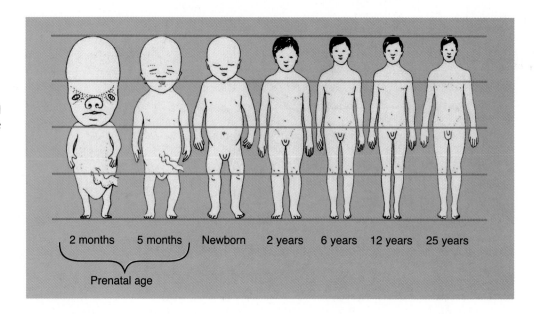

CHANGES IN MUSCLE–FAT MAKEUP

One of the most obvious changes in Byron, Rachel, and April's appearance was their transformation into round, plump babies by the middle of the first year. Body fat (most of which lies just beneath the skin) begins to increase in the last few weeks of prenatal life and continues to do so after birth, reaching a peak at about 9 months of age. This very early rise in "baby fat" helps the small infant keep a constant body temperature. Then, during the second year, most toddlers start to slim down, a trend that continues into middle childhood (Tanner, 1990).

Muscle tissue grows according to a different plan than fat. It increases very slowly during infancy and childhood and will not reach a peak until adolescence. Babies are not very muscular creatures, and their strength and physical coordination are limited.

As with body size, slight differences between boys and girls in muscle–fat makeup exist. From the beginning, girls have a higher ratio of fat to muscle than do boys, a difference that will increase in middle childhood and become very large during adolescence (Malina & Bouchard, 1991).

EARLY SKELETAL GROWTH

Children of the same age differ in *rate* of physical growth. In other words, some make faster progress toward a mature body size than others. We cannot tell how quickly a child's physical growth is moving along just by looking at current body size. For example, Byron is slightly larger and heavier than Rachel and April, but he is not physically more mature. In a moment, you will see why.

■ **GENERAL SKELETAL GROWTH.** The best way of estimating a child's physical maturity is to use **skeletal age,** a measure of development of the bones of the body. The embryonic skeleton is first formed out of soft, pliable tissue called *cartilage.* Then, beginning in the sixth week of pregnancy, cartilage cells gradually harden into bone, a very gradual process that continues throughout childhood and adolescence (Moore & Persaud, 1993).

Once bones have taken on their basic shape, special growth centers called **epiphyses** appear just before birth (see Figure 5.3). In the long bones of the body, the epiphyses emerge at the two extreme ends of each bone. There, new cartilage cells are produced and

skeletal age
An estimate of physical maturity based on development of the bones of the body.

epiphyses
Growth centers in the bones where new cartilage cells are produced and gradually harden.

gradually harden. As growth continues, the epiphyses get thinner and disappear. When this occurs, no more bone growth is possible. Skeletal age can be estimated by X-raying the bones and seeing how many epiphyses there are and the extent to which they are fused. These X-rays are compared to norms established for bone maturity based on large numbers of children (Malina & Bouchard, 1991).

When the skeletal ages of infants and children are examined, they reveal that African-American children tend to be slightly ahead of Caucasian children at all ages. And girls are considerably ahead of boys—the reason Byron's skeletal age lags behind that of April and Rachel. At birth, the difference between the sexes amounts to about 4 to 6 weeks, a gap that widens over infancy and childhood and is responsible for the fact that girls reach their full body size several years before boys. Girls are advanced in development of other organs of the body as well. Their greater physical maturity may contribute to the fact that they are more resistant to harmful environmental influences throughout development. As we pointed out in Chapter 2, girls experience fewer developmental problems than do boys, and infant and childhood mortality for girls is also lower (Tanner, 1990).

■ **GROWTH OF THE SKULL.** Doctors routinely measure children's head sizes between birth and 2 years of age. Skull growth is especially rapid during the first 2 years because of large increases in brain size. At birth, the bones of the skull are separated by six gaps, or "soft spots," called **fontanels** (see Figure 5.4). The gaps permit the bones to overlap as the large head of the baby passes through the mother's narrow birth canal. You can easily feel the largest gap, the anterior fontanel, at the top of a baby's skull. It is slightly more than an inch across. It gradually shrinks and is filled in during the second year. The other fontanels are smaller and close more quickly. As the skull bones come in contact with one another, they form *sutures*, or seams. These permit the skull to expand easily as the brain grows during the first few years of life.

APPEARANCE OF TEETH

On the average, an African-American baby's first tooth appears at about 4 months, a Caucasian baby's around 6 months, although there are wide individual differences. April already had a tooth when she was born; a few infants do not get their first tooth until 1 year of age. After the first tooth erupts, new ones appear every month or two. By age 2, the

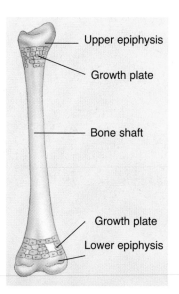

FIGURE 5.3

Diagram of a long bone showing upper and lower epiphyses. Cartilage cells are produced at the growth plates and gradually harden into bone. *(From J. M. Tanner, Foetus into Man (2nd ed.), Cambridge, MA: Harvard University Press, p. 32. Copyright © 1990 by J. M. Tanner. All rights reserved. Reprinted by permission of the publisher and author.)*

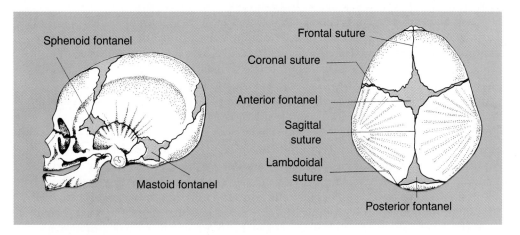

FIGURE 5.4

The skull at birth, showing the fontanels and sutures. The fontanels gradually close during the first 2 years, forming sutures that permit the skull to expand easily as the brain grows. (From P. M. Hill & P. Humphrey, 1982, *Human Growth and Development Throughout Life: A Nursing Perspective,* Delmar Publishers, Inc., p. 42. Copyright 1982. Reprinted by permission.)

fontanels
Six soft spots that separate the bones of the skull at birth.

average child has 20 teeth. Dental development provides a rough clue to overall rate of skeletal development. A child who gets teeth early is likely to be advanced in physical maturity (Mott, James, & Sperhac, 1990).

Teething is often accompanied by the baby's first illnesses, but it does not cause them. Around the time that the teeth appear, antibodies the baby received from the mother during the prenatal period begin to decline. As a result, infants are somewhat less resistant to infection, although breast-feeding affords extra immunity.

BRAIN DEVELOPMENT

At birth, the brain is nearer to its adult size than any other physical structure, and it continues to develop at an astounding pace throughout infancy and toddlerhood. To best understand brain growth, we need to look at it from two vantage points: (1) the microscopic level of individual brain cells, and (2) the larger level of the cerebral cortex, the most complex brain structure and the one responsible for the highly developed intelligence of our species.

DEVELOPMENT OF NEURONS

The human brain has 100 to 200 billion **neurons,** or nerve cells, that store and transmit information, many of which have thousands of direct connections with other neurons. Neurons differ from other body cells in that they are not tightly packed together. There are tiny gaps, or **synapses,** between them where fibers from different neurons come close together but do not touch. Neurons release chemicals that cross the synapse, thereby sending messages to one another.

The basic story of brain growth concerns how neurons develop and form this elaborate communication system. Recall from Chapter 3 that neurons are produced in the primitive neural tube of the embryo. From there, they travel to form the major parts of the brain. By the end of the second trimester of pregnancy, this process is complete; no more neurons will ever again be produced. After birth, the neurons form complex networks of synaptic connections. As Figure 5.5 shows, during infancy and toddlerhood, growth of neural fibers and synapses increases at an astounding pace.

Once neurons form connections, a new factor becomes important in their survival: *stimulation.* Neurons that are stimulated by input from the surrounding environment continue to establish new synapses. Those that are seldom stimulated soon die off (Huttenlocher, 1994). This suggests that appropriate stimulation of the child's brain is critically important during periods in which the formation of synapses is at its peak (Greenough et al., 1993). Research in which animals have been deprived of stimulation during the early weeks and months of life supports this idea. And as the Biology and Environment box on pages 174–175 indicates, there seem to be periods in which rich and varied stimulation is essential for the human brain to reach its potential as well.

Perhaps you are wondering; If no more neurons are produced after the prenatal period, what causes the dramatic increase in brain size during the first 2 years? About half the brain's volume is made up of **glial cells,** which do not carry messages. Instead, their most important function is **myelinization,** a process in which neural fibers are coated with an insulating fatty sheath (called *myelin)* that improves the efficiency of message transfer. Glial cells multiply dramatically from the fourth month of pregnancy through the second year of life, after which their rate of production slows down (Casaer, 1993). Myelinization is responsible for the rapid gain in overall size of the brain. At birth, the brain is nearly 30 percent of its adult weight; by the time toddlerhood is complete, it reaches 70 percent.

neurons
Nerve cells that store and transmit information.

synapses
The gaps between neurons, across which chemical messages are sent.

glial cells
Cells that serve the function of myelinization.

myelinization
A process in which neural fibers are coated with an insulating fatty sheath (called myelin) that improves the efficiency of message transfer.

cerebral cortex
The largest structure of the human brain that accounts for the highly developed intelligence of the human species. Surrounds the rest of the brain, much like a half-shelled walnut.

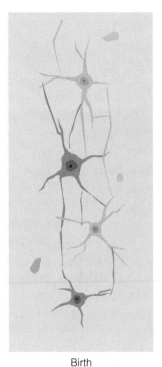 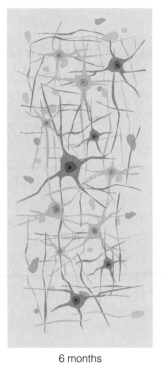 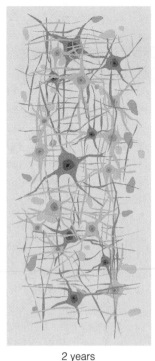

Birth   6 months   2 years

FIGURE 5.5

Development of neurons. Growth of neural fibers takes place rapidly from birth to 2 years. During this time, new synapses are formed at an astounding pace, supporting the emergence of many new capacities. Stimulation is vitally important for maintaining and increasing this complex communication network. *(From J. L. Conel,* The Postnatal Development of the Human Cerebral Cortex. *Cambridge, MA: Harvard University Press. Copyright © 1959 by the President and Fellows of Harvard College. All rights reserved.)*

DEVELOPMENT OF THE CEREBRAL CORTEX

The **cerebral cortex** is the largest structure of the human brain, accounting for 85 percent of its weight and containing the greatest number of neurons and synapses. The cortex surrounds the rest of the brain, much like a half-shelled walnut. Of all brain structures, the cerebral cortex is the last to stop growing. For this reason, it is believed to be much more sensitive to environmental influences than any other part of the brain.

■ **REGIONS OF THE CORTEX.** As Figure 5.6 shows, different regions of the cerebral cortex have specific functions, such as receiving information from the senses, instructing the body to move, and thinking. The order in which cortical regions develop corresponds to the order in which various capacities emerge in the infant and growing child. For example, among areas responsible for body movement, neurons that control the head, arms, and chest mature ahead of those that control the trunk and legs. Do you recognize a familiar developmental trend? Language areas of the cortex display dramatic gains from late infancy into the preschool years—the same period in which young children acquire language rapidly (Thatcher, 1991).

One of the last regions of the cortex to develop and myelinate are the *frontal lobes,* which are responsible for thought and consciousness. From age 2 months onward, this area functions more effectively, and it continues to grow for years, well into the second and third decades of life (Fischer & Rose, 1994, 1995).

■ **LATERALIZATION AND PLASTICITY OF THE CORTEX.** Figure 5.6 shows only one *hemisphere,* or side, of the cortex. If you could turn the brain around, you would see that it has two hemispheres—left and right. Although the hemispheres look alike, they do not have precisely the same functions. Some tasks are done

FIGURE 5.6

The left side of the human brain, showing the cerebral cortex. The cortex is divided into different lobes, each of which contains a variety of regions with specific functions. Some major ones are labeled here.

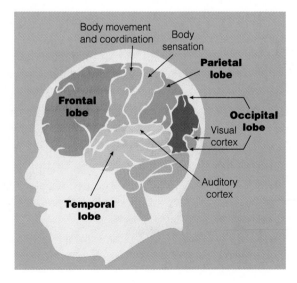

BIOLOGY & ENVIRONMENT

SENSITIVE PERIODS IN BRAIN DEVELOPMENT

The existence of sensitive periods in development of the cortex has been amply demonstrated in studies of animals exposed to extreme forms of sensory deprivation. For example, there seems to be a time when visual experiences must occur for the visual centers of the brain to develop normally. If a month-old kitten is deprived of light for as brief a time as 3 or 4 days, these areas start to degenerate. If the kitten is kept in the dark for as long as 2 months, the damage is permanent. Severe stimulus deprivation also affects overall brain growth. When animals reared as pets are compared to animals reared in isolation, the brains of the pets are heavier and thicker and contain as many as 25 percent more synapses per neuron (Greenough & Black, 1992).

Because we cannot ethically expose children to such experiments, researchers interested in identifying sensitive periods for human brain development must rely on naturally occurring circumstances or less direct evidence. They have found some close parallels with the animal findings just described. For example, without early

corrective surgery, babies born with *strabismus* (a condition in which one eye does not focus because of muscle weakness) show permanent impairments in depth perception (which depends on blending visual images from both eyes), visual acuity, and perception of the spatial layout of the environment (Birch, 1993).

Focusing on the cortex as a whole, investigators have identified intermittent brain growth spurts from infancy to early adulthood, based on gains in brain weight and skull size as well as changes in electrical activity of the cortex, as measured by the EEG (Epstein, 1980; Hudspeth & Pribram, 1992; Thatcher, 1991, 1994). These spurts coincide with peaks in children's intelligence test performance and major gains in cognitive competence. For example, as Figure 5.7 shows the findings of a Swedish study, in which EEGs were measured during a quiet, alert state in individuals ranging from 1 to 21 years of age. The first EEG energy spurt occurred around age $1\frac{1}{2}$ to 2, a period in which representation and language flourish. The next three spurts, at ages 9, 12, and 15, probably reflect the emergence and

From infancy to early adulthood, several brain growth spurts occur that coincide with peaks in intelligence test performance and major gains in cognitive competence. How brain development can best be supported through stimulation during each of these periods is a challenging question for future research. *(John Yurka/The Picture Cube)*

---

mostly by one hemisphere and some by the other. For example, each hemisphere receives sensory information from and controls only one side of the body—the one opposite to it.[1] For most of us, the left hemisphere is responsible for verbal abilities (such as spoken and written language) and positive emotion (for example, joy), whereas the right hemisphere handles spatial abilities (judging distances, reading maps, and recognizing geometric shapes) and negative emotion (such as distress). This pattern may be reversed in left-handed people, but more often, the cortex of left-handers is less clearly specialized than that of right-handers.

Specialization of the two hemispheres is called **lateralization**. Few topics in child development have stimulated more interest than the question of when brain lateralization occurs. Scientists are interested in this issue because they want to know more about **brain plasticity.** A highly *plastic* cortex is still adaptable because many areas are not yet commit-

lateralization
Specialization of functions of the two hemispheres of the cortex.

brain plasticity
The ability of other parts of the brain to take over functions of damaged regions. Disappears when hemispheres of the cortex lateralize.

---

[1] The eyes are an exception. Messages from the right half of each retina go to the left hemisphere; messages from the left half of each retina go to the right hemisphere. Thus, visual information from *both* eyes is received by *both* hemispheres.

refinement of abstract thinking. Another spurt, around age 18 to 20, may signal the capacity for mature, reflective thought (Fischer & Rose, 1995; Kitchener et al., 1993).

New connections between brain growth spurts and mental and motor development are continually being discovered. For example, several surges in EEG activity in the frontal lobe, which gradually spread to other cortical regions, occur during the first years of life: at 3 to 4 months, when infants typically engage in voluntary reaching; around 8 months, when they begin to crawl and search for hidden objects; and around 12 months, when they walk and display more advanced object-search behaviors (Bell & Fox, 1994, 1998; Fischer & Bidell, 1997).

Massive production of synapses may underlie the earliest brain growth spurts. Development of more complex and efficient neural networks, due to myelinization and long-distance connections between the frontal lobe and other cortical regions, may account for the later ones. Researchers are convinced that what "wires" a child's brain during each of these periods is experience. Yet exactly

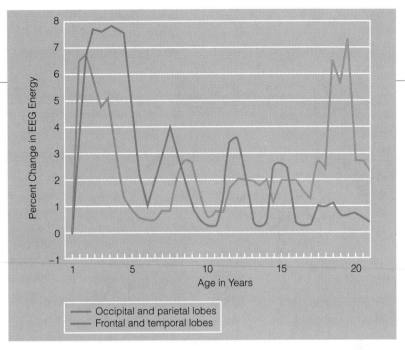

FIGURE 5.7

Brain growth spurts, based on findings of a Swedish cross-sectional study in which EEGs were measured in individuals 1 to 21 years of age. EEG energy peaks indicate periods of rapid growth. These occurred around 1½ to 2, 9, 12, 15, and 18 to 20 years of age in all lobes of the cortex (frontal, temporal, occipital, and parietal). The spurts coincide with peaks in children's intelligence test performance and major gains in cognitive competence. *(From K. W. Fischer & S. P. Rose, 1995, Concurrent Cycles in the Dynamic Development of Brain and Behavior. Newsletter of the Society for Research in Child Development, p. 16. Reprinted by permission of the authors.)*

how brain and behavioral development might best be supported by stimulation during each growth spurt is still a question for future research.

Once we have such information, it will have major implications for child-rearing and educational practices.

ted to specific functions. If a part of the brain is damaged, other parts can take over tasks that would have been handled by the damaged region. But once the hemispheres lateralize, damage to a specific region means that the abilities controlled by it will be lost forever.

Researchers used to think that lateralization of the cortex did not begin until after 2 years of age (Lenneberg, 1967). Today we know that the hemispheres have already started to specialize at birth. For example, most newborns favor the right side of the body in their reflexive reactions (Grattan et al., 1992). And EEG brain-wave recordings taken as infants react to different kinds of stimulation reveal that like adults, they show greater electrical activity in the left hemisphere while listening to speech sounds. In contrast, their right hemisphere reacts more strongly to nonspeech sounds as well as stimuli (such as a sour-tasting fluid) that evoke negative emotion (Davidson, 1994; Fox & Davidson, 1986; Hahn, 1987).

Brain lateralization begins early in life, but it takes years to complete. Research on preterm infants who have experienced brain hemorrhages provides dramatic evidence for early plasticity. Although hemorrhaging caused brain damage, it did not predict mental and motor development at 2 years of age. As infants gained perceptual, cognitive, and motor experiences, other stimulated brain structures seemed to compensate for the injured areas (Sostek et al., 1987).

Another illustration of how early experience can mold brain organization comes from studies of deaf adults who, as infants and children, learned to communicate through sign language. EEG recordings reveal that compared to hearing adults, these individuals depend more on the right hemisphere for language processing (Mills, Coffey-Corina, & Neville, 1994).

Finally, research on toddlers shows that 20-month-olds advanced in vocabulary development show greater left-hemispheric specialization for language than do their more slowly developing agemates (Neville, 1991). Apparently, the very process of acquiring spoken language promotes lateralization.

During the first few years, the brain is more plastic than at any later time of life, perhaps because many of its synapses are not yet firmly established. The cortex is programmed from the start for hemispheric specialization, but the rate and success of this genetic program are influenced greatly by experience (Fox, Calkins, & Bell, 1994). A lateralized brain is certainly adaptive. It permits a much greater variety of talents to be represented in the two hemispheres than if both sides of the cortex served exactly the same functions.

ASK YOURSELF . . .

- *When Joey was born, the doctor found that his anterior fontanel had started to close prematurely. Joey had surgery to open the fontanel when he was 3 months old. From what you know about the function of the fontanels, why was early surgery necessary?*

- *Felicia commented that at age 2 months, April's daily schedule seemed more predictable, and she was much more alert. What aspects of brain development might be responsible for this change?*

BRIEF REVIEW

The infant's body increases rapidly in overall size during the first 2 years of life. Different parts of the body grow at different rates, following cephalocaudal and proximodistal trends. During the first year, body fat increases much faster than muscle. The skull expands rapidly as the brain grows. Around 4 to 6 months, the first teeth emerge. The human brain grows faster early in development than any other organ of the body. During the first 2 years, synapses, or connections between neurons, are rapidly laid down. Myelinization is responsible for efficient communication among neurons and a dramatic increase in brain weight. The cerebral cortex is the last part of the brain to stop growing. It is also the structure most affected by stimulation. Although the cortex is genetically programmed to lateralize, early experience has a profound impact on hemispheric specialization. The brain retains considerable plasticity during the first few years of life.

FACTORS AFFECTING EARLY PHYSICAL GROWTH

Physical growth, like other aspects of development, results from the continuous and complex interplay between heredity and environment. April, who has tall parents, is likely to be tall herself. Although Byron, Rachel, and April are growing up in homes with plenty of food, love, and stimulation, many infants are not so fortunate. Heredity, nutrition, and emotional well-being all affect early physical growth.

HEREDITY

Since identical twins are much more alike in height and weight than are fraternal twins, we know that heredity is important in physical growth. When diet and health are adequate, height and rate of physical growth (as measured by skeletal age) are largely determined by heredity. In fact, as long as negative environmental influences such as poor nutrition or illness are not severe, children and adolescents typically show *catch-up growth*—a return to a genetically determined growth path. Physical growth is a strongly canalized process (see Chapter 2, page 89).

Genetic makeup also affects body weight, since the weights of adopted children correlate more strongly with those of their biological than adoptive parents (Stunkard et al.,

1986). However, as far as weight is concerned, environment—in particular, nutrition—plays an especially important role.

NUTRITION

Good nutrition is important at any time of development, but it is especially critical in infancy because the baby's brain and body are growing so rapidly. Pound for pound, a young baby's energy needs are twice as great as those of an adult. This is because 25 percent of the infant's total caloric intake is devoted to growth, and extra calories are needed to keep rapidly developing organs of the body functioning properly (Pipes, 1996).

Babies not only need enough food, they need the right kind of food. In early infancy, breast milk is especially suited to their needs, and bottled formulas try to imitate it. Later, infants require well-balanced solid foods. If a baby's diet is deficient in either quantity or quality, growth can be permanently stunted.

■ **BREAST- VERSUS BOTTLE-FEEDING.** For thousands of years, all human babies were fed the ultimate human health food: breast milk. Only within the last hundred years has bottle-feeding been available. As formulas became easier to prepare, breast-feeding declined from the 1940s into the 1970s when more than 75 percent of American infants were bottle-fed. Partly as a result of the natural childbirth movement (see Chapter 4), breast-feeding became more common in the 1970s and 1980s, especially among well-educated, middle-SES women.

Today, nearly two-thirds of American mothers breast-feed. Unfortunately, most do so for only a short time. Although breast milk is a complete food for babies until 6 months of age, by 4 months only one-fourth of mothers are still nursing (National Center for Health Statistics, 1997). The Caregiving Concerns table below summarizes the major nutritional and health advantages of breast-feeding.

CAREGIVING CONCERNS
Nutritional and Health Advantages of Breast-Feeding

ADVANTAGE	DESCRIPTION
Correct balance of fat and protein	Compared to the milk of other mammals, human milk is higher in fat and lower in protein. This balance, as well as the unique proteins and fats contained in human milk, is ideal for a rapidly myelinating nervous system.
Nutritional completeness	A mother who breast-feeds need not add other foods to her infant's diet until the baby is 6 months old. The milks of all mammals are low in iron, but the iron contained in breast milk is much more easily absorbed by the baby's system. Consequently, bottle-fed infants need iron-fortified formula.
Protection against disease	Through breast-feeding, antibodies and other infection-fighting agents are transferred from mother to child. As a result, breast-fed babies have far fewer respiratory and intestinal illnesses and allergic reactions than do bottle-fed infants. Components of human milk that protect against disease can be added to formula, but breast-feeding provides superior immunity.
Protection against faulty jaw development and tooth decay	Breast-feeding helps avoid malocclusion, a condition in which the upper and lower jaws do not meet properly. It also protects against tooth decay due to sweet liquid remaining in the mouths of infants who fall asleep while sucking on a bottle.
Digestibility	Since breast-fed babies have a different kind of bacteria growing in their intestines than do bottle-fed infants, they rarely become constipated or have diarrhea.
Smoother transition to solid foods	Breast-fed infants accept new solid foods more easily than do bottle-fed infants, perhaps because of their greater experience with a variety of flavors, which pass from the maternal diet into the mother's milk.

Sources: Bruerd & Jones, 1996; Pickering et al., 1998; Räihä & Axelsson, 1995; Raloff, 1995; Sullivan & Birch, 1994.

Breast-feeding is especially important in developing countries, where infants are at risk for malnutrition and early death due to widespread poverty. This baby of Rajasthan, India, is likely to grow normally during the first year because his mother decided to breast-feed. *(Jane Schreirman/Photo Researchers)*

marasmus
A disease usually appearing in the first year of life that is caused by a diet low in all essential nutrients. Leads to a wasted condition of the body.

kwashiorkor
A disease usually appearing between 1 and 3 years of age that is caused by a diet low in protein. Symptoms include an enlarged belly, swollen feet, hair loss, skin rash, and irritable, listless behavior.

Because of these benefits, breast-fed babies in poverty-stricken regions of the world are much less likely to be malnourished and 6 to 14 times more likely to survive the first year of life. Breast-feeding exclusively for the first 6 months would save the lives of one million infants annually. And breast-feeding for just a few weeks would offer some protection against respiratory and intestinal infections that are devastating to young children in developing countries. Furthermore, because a mother is less likely to get pregnant while she is nursing, breast-feeding helps increase spacing between siblings, a major factor in reducing infant and childhood deaths in economically depressed populations (Grant, 1995). (Note, however, that breast-feeding is not a reliable method of birth control.)

Yet many mothers in the developing world do not know about the benefits of breast-feeding. Consequently, they give their babies low-grade nutrients, such as rice water, highly diluted cow's and goat's milk, or commercial formula. These foods often lead to illness because they are contaminated due to poor sanitation. The United Nations has encouraged all hospitals and maternity units in developing countries to promote breast-feeding—a campaign that has been highly successful. For example, of over 70 countries that previously allowed free or subsidized formula to be distributed to new mothers, all but one banned the practice (Grant, 1995).

In industrialized nations, most women who choose breast-feeding find it to be an emotionally satisfying experience, but breast-feeding is not for everyone. Some mothers simply do not like it, or they are embarrassed by it. A few others, for physiological reasons, are unable to produce enough milk. Occasionally, medical reasons prevent a mother from nursing. If she is taking certain drugs, they can be transmitted to the baby through the milk. If she has a serious viral or bacterial disease, such as AIDS or tuberculosis, she runs the risk of infecting her baby (Kuhn & Stein, 1997).

Breast milk is so easily digestible that a breast-fed infant becomes hungry quite often—every 1½ to 2 hours in comparison to the 3- to 4-hour schedule of the bottle-fed baby. This makes breast-feeding inconvenient for many employed women. Not surprisingly, mothers who return to work sooner wean their babies from the breast earlier (Visness & Kennedy, 1997). However, a mother who cannot be with her baby all the time can still breast-feed or combine it with bottle-feeding. For example, Lisa returned to her job part time when Byron was 2 months old. Each morning, she pumped her milk into a bottle for later feeding by his caregiver (Hills-Banczyk et al., 1993).

The same technique can be used for infants who are hospitalized. Preterm infants, especially, benefit from the antibodies and easy digestibility of breast milk. The breast milk produced for a preterm baby is different from that produced for a full-term infant. It is higher in protein and certain minerals and specially adapted to the preterm infant's growth needs (Gross, Geller, & Tomarelli, 1981).

Some women who cannot or do not want to breast-feed worry that they might be harming the baby's emotional development. As we will see in Chapter 7, emotional well-being is affected by the warmth and sensitivity that accompanies infant feeding, not by the type of milk offered. Regardless of the feeding method a mother chooses, she can respond promptly to her hungry baby and hold and stroke the infant gently. Research reveals that breast- and bottle-fed youngsters do not differ in psychological development (Fergusson, Horwood, & Shanon, 1987).

■ ARE CHUBBY BABIES AT RISK FOR LATER OVERWEIGHT AND OBESITY?

Byron was an enthusiastic eater from early infancy. He nursed vigorously and gained weight quickly. By 5 months, he began reaching for solid food from his parents' plates. Lisa wondered: Was she overfeeding Byron and increasing his chances of being permanently overweight?

Only a slight correlation exists between fatness in infancy and obesity at older ages (Roche, 1981). Most chubby infants thin out during toddlerhood and the preschool years, as weight gain slows and they become more active. Infants and toddlers can eat nutritious foods freely, without risk of becoming too fat.

When infants are first given solid foods, iron-fortified cereal mixed with whole milk satisfies their needs. Between 6 and 12 months, mashed and minced fruits, vegetables, starches, and meats should gradually be added. Around 1 year, most infants have enough teeth to make the transition to chopped table foods, which should include all the basic food groups.

Although a baby's food intake should not be limited, concerned parents can prevent their infants from becoming overweight children and adults in other ways. One way is to encourage good eating habits. Candy, soft drinks, French fries, and other high-calorie foods loaded with sugar, salt, and saturated fats should be avoided. When given such foods regularly, young children start to prefer them (Birch & Fisher, 1995). Physical exercise also guards against excessive weight gain. Once toddlers learn to walk, climb, and run, parents should encourage their natural delight at being able to control their bodies by providing opportunities for energetic play.

MALNUTRITION

Osita is an Ethiopian 2-year-old whose mother has never had to worry about his gaining too much weight. When she weaned him at 1 year, there was little for him to eat besides starchy rice flour cakes. Soon his belly enlarged, his feet swelled, his hair began to fall out, and a rash appeared on his skin. His bright-eyed, curious behavior vanished, and he became irritable and listless.

In developing countries and war-torn areas where food resources are limited, malnutrition is widespread. Recent evidence indicates that 40 to 60 percent of the world's children do not get enough to eat (Bellamy, 1997; Bread for the World Institute, 1994). Among the 4 to 7 percent who are severely affected, malnutrition leads to two dietary diseases: marasmus and kwashiorkor.

Marasmus is a wasted condition of the body that usually appears in the first year of life. It is caused by a diet that is low in all essential nutrients. The disease often occurs when a malnourished mother cannot produce enough breast milk and bottle-feeding is also inadequate. Her starving baby becomes painfully thin and is in danger of dying.

Osita has **kwashiorkor.** It is due to an unbalanced diet that is very low in protein. Kwashiorkor usually strikes after weaning, between 1 and 3 years of age. It is common in areas of the world where children get just enough calories from starchy foods, but protein resources are scarce. The child's body responds by breaking down its own protein reserves. This causes the swelling and other symptoms that Osita experienced.

Children who manage to survive these extreme forms of malnutrition grow to be smaller in all body dimensions (Galler, Ramsey, & Solimano, 1985a). In addition, the brain is seriously affected. One long-term study of marasmic children revealed that an improved diet led to some catch-up growth in height, but the children failed to catch up in head size (Stoch et al., 1982). The malnutrition probably interfered with myelinization, causing a permanent loss in brain weight. By middle childhood, these youngsters score low on intelligence and achievement tests, show poor fine motor coordination, and have difficulty paying attention in school (Galler et al., 1984, 1990; Galler, Ramsey, & Solimano, 1985b).

Recall from our discussion of prenatal malnutrition in Chapter 3 that the passivity and irritability of malnourished children make the impact of poor diet even worse. These behaviors appear even when protein-calorie deprivation is only mild to moderate (Ricciuti, 1993). They reduce the child's ability to pay

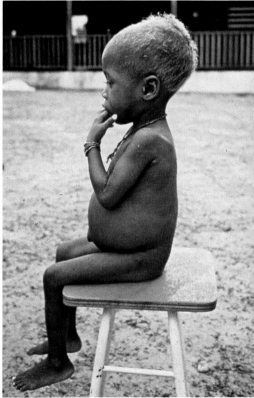

The swollen abdomen and listless behavior of this child are classic symptoms of kwashiorkor, a nutritional illness that results from a diet very low in protein. *(CNRI/Phototake)*

attention, explore, and evoke sensitive caregiving from parents, whose lives are already disrupted by poverty and stressful living conditions (Wachs et al., 1992). For this reason, interventions for malnourished children must improve the family situation as well as the child's nutrition.

Even better are efforts at prevention—providing food and medical care before the effects of early malnutrition are allowed to run their course. Research in Guatemala, where dietary deficiencies are common, underscores the importance of early nutritional intervention. Children receiving food supplements prenatally and during the first 2 years of life scored higher on a variety of mental tests in adolescence than did children given supplements only after their second birthday (Pollitt et al., 1993). Other longitudinal findings from Egypt, Kenya, and Mexico reveal that quality of food (protein, vitamin, and mineral content) is far more important than quantity of food in contributing to the favorable outcomes just described (Sigman, 1995).

Like prenatal malnutrition, malnutrition after birth is not confined to developing countries. Recent surveys indicate that over 12 percent of American children go to bed hungry. Although few of these children have marasmus or kwashiorkor, their physical growth and ability to learn in school are still affected (Children's Defense Fund, 1998; Wach, 1995). Malnutrition is clearly a national and international crisis—one of the most serious problems confronting the human species today.

EMOTIONAL WELL-BEING

We are not used to thinking of affection and stimulation as necessary for healthy physical growth, but they are just as vital to infants as food. **Nonorganic failure to thrive** is a growth disorder resulting from lack of parental love that is usually present by 18 months of age. Infants who have it show all the signs of marasmus, described in the previous section. Their bodies look wasted, and they are withdrawn and apathetic. However, no organic (or biological) cause can be found for the baby's failure to grow. Enough food is offered, and the infant does not have a serious illness.

Lana, an observant nurse, noticed signs of failure to thrive in Melanie, whose mother brought her to a public health clinic at 8 months of age. Melanie was three pounds lighter than she had been 2 months earlier. Her mother claimed to feed her often and could not understand why she did not grow. Lana took a close look at Melanie's behavior. Unlike most infants her age, she did not mind separating from her mother. Lana tried offering Melanie a toy, but she showed little interest. Instead, she kept her eyes on adults in the room, anxiously watching their every move. When Lana tried to interact with Melanie by looking into her eyes and smiling, Melanie turned her head away (Black et al., 1994; Leonard, Rhymes, & Solnit, 1986).

The family circumstances surrounding failure to thrive help explain these typical reactions. During feeding and diaper changing, Melanie's mother sometimes acted cold and distant, at other times impatient and hostile. Melanie tried to protect herself by keeping track of her mother's whereabouts and, when her mother approached, avoiding her gaze. Often an unhappy marriage and parental psychological disturbance contribute to these serious caregiving problems (Drotar, Pallotta, & Eckerle, 1994; Duniz et al., 1996). In Melanie's case, her mother was severely depressed, her father was an alcoholic who was out of work, and her parents argued constantly. Her mother had little energy to meet the psychological needs of Melanie and her three siblings. Sometimes the baby displays abnormal feeding behaviors, such as poor sucking or vomiting, that stress the parent–child relationship further (Ramsay, Gisel, & Boutry, 1993).

When treated early, by helping parents or placing the baby in a caring foster home, failure-to-thrive infants show quick catch-up growth. But if the disorder is not corrected in infancy, most children remain small and show lasting cognitive and emotional difficulties (Heffner & Kelley, 1994).

nonorganic failure to thrive
A growth disorder usually present by 18 months of age that is caused by lack of affection and stimulation.

BRIEF REVIEW

Heredity, nutrition, and emotional well-being all contribute to early physical growth. Studies of twins show that height and weight are affected by genetic makeup. Breast-feeding provides babies with the ideal nutrition between birth and 6 months of age and protects many poverty-stricken infants against malnutrition, disease, and early death. However, bottle- and breast-fed babies do not differ in psychological development. A mother who feeds her baby nutritious foods need not worry about a chubby infant becoming an overweight child. Malnutrition is a serious global problem. When marasmus and kwashiorkor are allowed to persist, physical size, brain growth, and ability to learn are permanently affected. Nonorganic failure to thrive reminds us of the close connection between sensitive, loving care and how children grow.

ASK YOURSELF . . .

■ *Explain why breast-feeding offers babies protection against disease and early death in poverty-stricken regions of the world.*

■ *Ten-month-old Shaun is below average in height and painfully thin. He has one of two serious growth disorders. Name them, and indicate what clues you would look for to tell which one Shaun has.*

CHANGING STATES OF AROUSAL

Between birth and 2 years, the organization of sleep and wakefulness changes substantially, and fussiness and crying also decline. Recall from Chapter 4 that the newborn baby takes round-the-clock naps that add up to about 16 hours of sleep. The decline in total sleep time from birth to 2 years is not great; the average 2-year-old still needs 12 to 13 hours. Instead, short periods of sleep and wakefulness are gradually put together. Although from birth babies tend to sleep more at night than during the day, this pattern increases steadily with age (Whitney & Thoman, 1994). By 4 months, the nightly sleep period of many babies reared in Western nations resembles that of the parents in that it is 8 hours; by 6 months, it is 10 to 12 hours. And over time, infants remain awake for longer daytime periods and need fewer naps—by the second year, only one or two (Blum & Carey, 1996).

These changes in arousal patterns are due to brain maturation, but they are affected by the social environment as well. In the United States and other Western nations, many parents try to get their babies to sleep through the night as soon as possible—usually by offering an evening feeding before putting them down in a separate, quiet room. In this way, they push young infants to the limits of their neurological capacities. Not until the middle of the first year is the secretion of *melatonin,* a hormone within the brain that promotes drowsiness, much greater at night than during the day (Sadeh, 1997).

As the Cultural Influences box on the following page reveals, the practice of isolating infants to promote sleep is rare throughout most of the world. Influenced by Japanese child-rearing customs, Beth held Rachel close for much of the day. At night, she lay in her mother's bed, sleeping and waking to nurse at will. For infants experiencing this type of care, the average sleep period remains constant at 3 hours, from 1 to 8 months of age. Only at the end of the first year do these babies move in the direction of an adultlike sleep–waking schedule (Super & Harkness, 1982).

Even after infants sleep through the night, they continue to wake occasionally for the next few years. In studies carried out in Great Britain, Israel, and the United States, about 30 percent of children between ages 1 and 4 awoke during the night at least once a week (Beltramini & Hertzig, 1983; Johnson, 1991; Scher et al., 1995). Night wakings peaked between 18 months and 2 years and then declined. As Chapter 7 will reveal, the emotional and social challenges of this period—ability to range further from the familiar caregiver and awareness of the self as separate from others—often prompt anxiety in toddlers, evident in increased clinginess and disturbed sleep. When parents offer comfort and support, these behaviors gradually subside.

CULTURAL INFLUENCES

CULTURAL VARIATION IN INFANT SLEEPING ARRANGEMENTS

While awaiting the birth of a new baby, middle-SES, Caucasian-American parents typically furnish a special room as the infant's sleeping quarters. At first, young babies may be placed in a bassinet or cradle in the parents' bedroom for reasons of convenience, but most are moved by 3 to 6 months of age. Many adults in the United States regard this nighttime separation of baby from parent as perfectly natural. Throughout this century, child-rearing advice from experts has strongly encouraged it. For example, in each edition of *Baby and Child Care* from 1945 to the present, Benjamin Spock states with authority, "I think it is a sensible rule not to take a child into the parents' bed for any reason" (Spock & Rothenberg, 1992, p. 213).

Yet parent–infant "cosleeping" is common around the globe, in industrialized and nonindustrialized countries alike. Japanese children usually lie next to their mothers throughout infancy and early childhood and continue to sleep with a parent or other family member until adolescence (Takahashi, 1990). Cosleeping is also frequent in some American subcultures. African-American children are more likely than Caucasian-American children to fall asleep with parents and to remain with them for part or all of the night (Lozoff et al., 1995). Appalachian children of eastern Kentucky typically sleep with their parents for the first 2 years of life (Abbott, 1992). Among the Maya of rural Guatemala, mother–infant cosleeping is interrupted only by the birth of a new baby, at which time the older child is moved beside the father or to another bed in the same room (Morelli et al., 1992).

Available household space plays a minor role in infant sleeping arrangements. Dominant child-rearing beliefs are much more important. In one study, researchers interviewed Caucasian-American mothers and Guatemalan Mayan mothers about their sleeping practices. American mothers frequently mentioned the importance of early independence training, preventing bad habits, and protecting their own privacy. In contrast, Mayan mothers explained that cosleeping helps build a close parent–child bond, which is necessary for children to learn the ways of people around them. When told that American infants sleep by themselves, Mayan mothers reacted with shock and disbelief, stating that it would be painful for them to leave their babies alone at night (Morelli et al., 1992).

Infant sleeping practices affect other aspects of family life. Sleep problems are not an issue for Mayan parents. Babies doze off in the midst of ongoing social activities and are carried to bed by their mothers. In the United States, getting young children ready for bed often requires an elaborate ritual that takes a good part of the evening. Many infants and preschoolers insist on taking security objects to bed with them—a blanket or teddy bear that recaptures the soft, tactile comfort of physical closeness to the mother. In societies in which caregivers are continuously available to babies, children seldom develop these object attachments (Wolf & Lozoff, 1989). Perhaps bedtime struggles, so common in American homes but rare elsewhere in the world, are related to the stress young children feel when they are required to fall asleep without assistance (Kawasaki et al., 1994).

Infant sleeping arrangements, like other parenting practices, are meant to foster culturally valued characteristics in the young. Caucasian-American parents view babies as dependent beings who must be urged toward independence, and so they usually require them to sleep alone. In contrast, Japanese, Mayan, and Appalachian parents regard young infants as separate beings who need to establish an interdependent relationship with the community to survive.

This Cambodian father and child sleep together—a practice common in their culture and around the globe. When children fall asleep with their parents, sleep problems are rare during the early years. And many parents who practice cosleeping believe that it helps build a close parent–child bond. *(Stephen L. Raymer/ National Geographic Image Collection)*

MOTOR DEVELOPMENT

Lisa, Beth, and Felicia each kept baby books, filling them with proud notations about when the three children held up their heads, reached for objects, sat by themselves, and walked alone. Parents' enthusiasm for these achievements makes perfect sense. They are, indeed, milestones of development. With each new motor skill, babies master their bodies and the environment in a new way. For example, sitting alone grants infants an entirely different perspective on the world compared to lying on their backs and stomachs. Voluntary reaching permits babies to find out about objects by acting on them. And when infants can move on their own, their opportunities for exploration are multiplied.

Babies' motor achievements have a powerful effect on their social relationships. April was the first of the three babies to master crawling. In response, Felicia began to restrict April's movements by saying no, expressing mild anger and impatience, and picking her up and moving her—strategies that were unnecessary when, placed on a blanket, she would stay there! When April started walking, first "testing of wills" occurred (Biringen et al., 1995). Despite her mother's warnings, she sometimes continued to pull items off shelves that were "off limits." "Oh, April, I said not to do that!" Felicia would remark as she took April by the hand and redirected her activities.

At the same time, expressions of affection and playful activities expanded as April sought her parents out for greetings, hugs, and a gleeful game of hide-and-seek around the living room sofa (Campos, Kermoian, & Zumbahlen, 1992). Soon after, April turned the pages of a cardboard picture book and pointed while Felicia named the objects. April's expressions of delight—laughing, smiling, and babbling—as she worked on new motor competencies triggered pleasurable reactions in others, which encouraged her efforts further (Mayes & Zigler, 1992). Motor skills, social competencies, cognition, and language were developing together and supporting one another.

THE SEQUENCE OF MOTOR DEVELOPMENT

Gross motor development refers to control over actions that help infants get around in the environment, such as crawling, standing, and walking. In contrast, *fine motor development* has to do with smaller movements, such as reaching and grasping. Figure 5.8 shows the average age at which a variety of gross and fine motor skills are achieved during infancy and toddlerhood. Most (but not all) children follow this sequence.

Notice that Figure 5.7 also presents the age ranges during which the majority of babies accomplish each skill. These indicate that although the sequence of motor development is fairly uniform across children, there are large individual differences in the rate at which motor development proceeds. Also, a baby who is a late reacher is not necessarily going to be a late crawler or walker. We would be concerned about a child's development only if many motor skills were seriously delayed.

Look at Figure 5.8 once more, and you will see that there is organization and direction to the infant's motor achievements. The *cephalocaudal trend* discussed earlier in this chapter is clearly evident. Motor control of the head comes before control of the arms and trunk, and control of the arms and trunk is mastered before control of the legs. The *proximodistal trend* can also be seen in that head, trunk, and arm control is advanced over coordination of the hands and fingers. During the prenatal period, infancy, and childhood, physical growth follows these same trends. This physical–motor correspondence suggests a genetic contribution to the pattern of motor development.

However, we must be careful not to think of motor skills as isolated, unrelated accomplishments that follow a fixed maturational timetable. Earlier in this century, researchers

Head erect and steady	Elevates self by arms	Rolls from side to back	Grasps cube
6 weeks 3 weeks–4 months	2 months 3 weeks–4 months	2 months 3 weeks–5 months	3 months, 3 weeks 2–7 months
Rolls from back to side	**Sits alone**	**Crawls**	**Pulls to stand**
4½ months 2–7 months	7 months 5–9 months	7 months 5–11 months	8 months 5–12 months
Plays pat-a-cake	**Stands alone**	**Walks alone**	**Builds tower of 2 cubes**
9 months, 3 weeks 7–15 months	11 months 9–16 months	11 months, 3 weeks 9–17 months	13 months, 3 weeks 10–19 months
Scribbles vigorously	**Walks up stairs with help**	**Jumps in place**	**Walks on tiptoe**
14 months 10–21 months	16 months 12–23 months	23 months, 2 weeks 17–30 months	25 months 16–30 months

FIGURE 5.8

Gross and fine motor skills achieved during the first 2 years. The average age at which each skill is attained is presented, followed by the age range during which 90 percent of infants master the skill. *(From Bayley, 1969, 1993.)*

made this mistake. Today, we know that each skill is a product of earlier motor attainments and a contributor to new ones. Furthermore, children acquire motor skills in highly individual ways. For example, most babies crawl before they pull to a stand and walk. Yet Rachel, who disliked being placed on her tummy but enjoyed sitting and being held upright, pulled to a stand and walked before she crawled!

Many influences—both internal and external to the child—combine to support the vast transformations in motor competencies of the first 2 years. The *dynamic systems* perspective, a new theoretical approach introduced in Chapter 1 (see page 29), helps us understand how motor development takes place.

MOTOR SKILLS AS DYNAMIC SYSTEMS

According to **dynamic systems theory of motor development,** mastery of motor skills involves acquiring increasingly complex *systems of action.* When motor skills work as a *system,* separate abilities blend together, each cooperating with others to produce more effective ways of exploring and controlling the environment. For example, control of the head and upper chest are combined into sitting with support. Kicking, rocking on all fours, and reaching are gradually put together into crawling. Then crawling, standing, and stepping are united into walking alone (Hofsten, 1989; Pick, 1989; Thelen, 1989).

Each new skill is a joint product of the following factors: (1) central nervous system development; (2) movement possibilities of the body; (3) the task the child has in mind; and (4) environmental supports for the skill. Change in any of these factors leads to loss of stability in the system, and the child starts to explore and select new, more effective motor patterns.

The factors that induce change vary with age. In the early weeks of life, brain and body growth are especially important as infants achieve postural control over the head, shoulders, and upper torso. Later, the tasks the baby wants to accomplish (getting a toy or crossing the room) and environmental supports (parental encouragement, objects in the infants' everyday setting) play a greater role. The broader physical world also has a profound impact on motor skills. For example, had Byron, Rachel, and April been reared in the moon's reduced gravity, they would have found it more efficient to jump rather than walk or run!

When a skill is first acquired, it is tentative and uncertain. Infants must practice and refine it so it becomes smooth and accurate. For example, when April began to crawl, she often collapsed on her tummy and ended up moving backward instead of forward. As she experimented with muscle patterns and observed the consequences of her movements, she perfected the crawling motion (Thelen & Smith, 1998). These efforts fostered the growth of new synaptic connections in the brain that govern motor activity.

Look carefully at dynamic systems theory, and you will see why motor development cannot be a genetically prewired process. Since it is motivated by exploration and the desire to master new tasks, it can be mapped out by heredity only at a very general level. Each skill is acquired by revising and combining earlier accomplishments into a more complex system that permits the child to reach a desired goal. Consequently, different paths to the same motor skill exist.

DYNAMIC MOTOR SYSTEMS IN ACTION

To study infants' mastery of motor milestones, researchers have conducted *microgenetic studies* (see Chapter 1, page 44), following babies from their first attempts at a skill until it becomes smooth and effortless. Using this research strategy, Esther Thelen (1994) illustrated how infants acquire motor skills by modifying what the body can already do to fit a new task. She placed 3-month-old babies under an attractive mobile, attaching one foot to it with a long cord. To produce the dazzling sight of the dancing mobile, infants quickly learned to kick with one foot or two feet in alternation.

dynamic systems theory of motor development
A theory that views new motor skills as reorganizations of previously mastered skills that lead to more effective ways of exploring and controlling the environment. Each new skill is a product of central nervous system development, movement possibilities of the body, the task the child has in mind, and environmental supports.

FIGURE **5.9**

A 3-month-old infant in the mobile experiment, with legs linked together by an elastic ankle cuff. Consistent with dynamic systems theory, the baby revised previously learned motor acts into a more effective motor system for activating the mobile. In response to the cuff, he replaced single- and alternate-leg kicking with simultaneous kicks. *(Courtesy of Esther Thelen, Indiana University)*

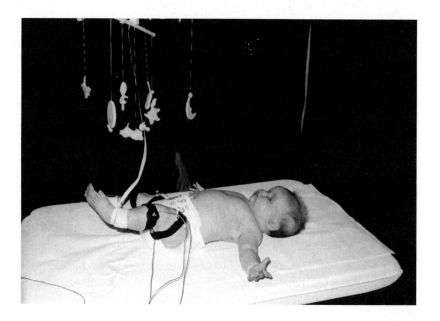

Then Thelen changed the movement environment; she linked the babies' legs together with a soft piece of elastic attached to ankle cuffs (see Figure 5.9). Although this permitted single- or alternate-leg kicking, it made kicking both legs in unison much more effective for activating the mobile. When the elastic was in place, infants gradually discovered the new motion. They began with a few tentative simultaneous kicks and, seeing the effects, replaced earlier movements with this new form. When the elastic was removed, infants quickly gave up the simultaneous kicking pattern in favor of their previous behavior.

Thelen's findings show that infants are active in acquiring motor skills. They readily experiment, revising motor actions to fit changing conditions of a task. Development occurs through their own problem-solving activity.

CULTURAL VARIATIONS IN MOTOR DEVELOPMENT

Cross-cultural research demonstrates how early movement opportunities and a stimulating environment contribute to motor development. Several decades ago, Wayne Dennis (1960) observed infants in Iranian orphanages who were deprived of the tantalizing surroundings that motivate infants in most homes to acquire motor skills. The Iranian babies spent their days lying on their backs in cribs, without toys to play with. As a result, most did not move about on their own until after 2 years of age. When they finally did move, the constant experience of lying on their backs led them to scoot in a sitting position rather than crawl on their hands and knees. As a result, walking was delayed. Since babies who scoot come up against objects such as furniture with their feet, not their hands, they are far less likely to pull themselves to a standing position in preparation for walking. Indeed, only 15 percent of the Iranian orphans walked alone by 3 to 4 years of age.

Cultural variations in infant-rearing practices also affect motor development. Take a quick survey of several parents you know, asking these questions: Can babies profit from training? Should sitting, crawling, and walking be deliberately encouraged? Answers vary widely from culture to culture. Japanese mothers, for example, believe such efforts are unnecessary and unimportant. Among the Zinacanteco Indians of southern Mexico, rapid motor progress is actively discouraged. Babies who walk before they know enough to keep away from cooking fires and weaving looms are viewed as dangerous to themselves and disruptive to others (Greenfield, 1992).

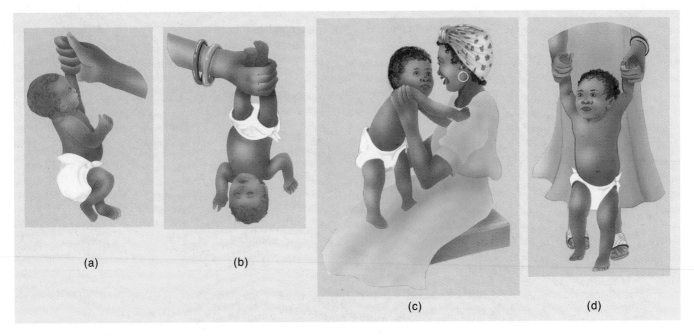

(a)   (b)   (c)   (d)

FIGURE 5.10

West Indian mothers use a formal handling routine with their babies. Exercises practiced in the first few months include (a) holding the infant upside-down by the ankles and (b) grasping the baby's head on both sides, lifting upward, and stretching the neck. Later in the first year, the baby is (c) "walked" up the mother's body and (d) encouraged to take steps on the floor while supported. *(Adapted from B. Hopkins & T. Westra, 1988), "Maternal Handling and Motor Development: An Intracultural Study,"* Genetic, Social and General Psychology Monographs, *14, pp. 385, 388, 389. Reprinted with permission of the Helen Dwight Reid Educational Foundation. Published by Heldref Publications, 1319 Eighteenth Street, N.S., Washington, DC 20036-1802. Copyright © 1988.)*

In contrast, among the Kipsigis of Kenya and the West Indians of Jamaica, babies hold their heads up, sit alone, and walk considerably earlier than do North American infants. Kipsigi parents deliberately teach these motor skills. In the first few months, babies are seated in holes dug in the ground, and rolled blankets are used to keep them upright. Walking is promoted by frequently bouncing babies on their feet (Super, 1981). Unlike the Kipsigis, the West Indians of Jamaica do not train their infants in specific skills. Instead, beginning in the first few weeks of life, babies experience a highly stimulating, formal handling routine (see Figure 5.10). Asked why they use this routine, West Indian mothers refer to the traditions of their culture and the need to help babies grow up strong, healthy, and physically attractive (Hopkins & Westra, 1988).

Putting together the evidence we have discussed so far, we must conclude that early motor skills, like other aspects of development, are due to complex transactions between nature and nurture. As dynamic systems theory suggests, heredity establishes the broad outlines of change, but experience contributes to the precise sequence of motor milestones and the rate at which they are reached.

FINE MOTOR DEVELOPMENT: VOLUNTARY REACHING AND GRASPING

Of all motor skills, voluntary reaching is believed to play the greatest role in infant cognitive development, since it opens up a whole new way of exploring the environment (Bushnell & Boudreau, 1993). By grasping things, turning them over, and seeing what happens when they are released, infants learn a great deal about the sights, sounds, and feel of objects.

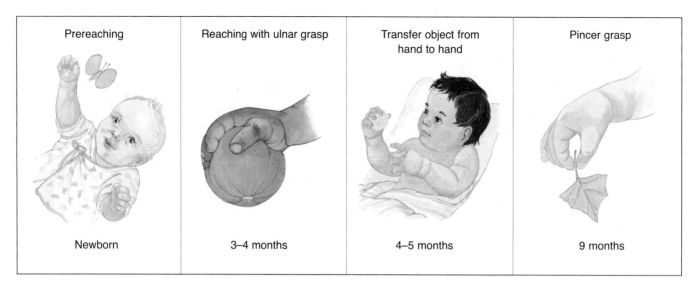

Prereaching	Reaching with ulnar grasp	Transfer object from hand to hand	Pincer grasp
Newborn	3–4 months	4–5 months	9 months

FIGURE **5.11**

Some milestones of voluntary reaching. The average age at which each skill is attained is given. *(Ages from Bayley, 1969; Rochat, 1989)*

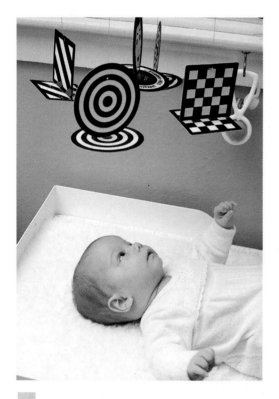

This 3-month-old baby looks at patterns hung over his crib that match his level of visual development. Research shows that a moderate amount of stimulation, tailored to the young baby's needs, results in earlier development of reaching. Either very little or excessive stimulation yields slower motor progress. *(Julie O'Neil/The Picture Cube)*

The development of reaching and grasping, shown in Figure 5.11, provides an excellent example of how motor skills start out as gross, diffuse activity and move toward mastery of fine movements. Newborns make poorly coordinated swipes or swings, called **prereaching,** toward an object dangled in front of them. Because they cannot control their arms and hands, they are rarely successful in contacting the object. Like the reflexes we discussed in Chapter 4, prereaching eventually drops out, around 7 weeks of age.

■ **DEVELOPMENT OF VOLUNTARY REACHING AND GRASPING.** At about 3 months, voluntary reaching appears and gradually improves in accuracy (Bushnell, 1985; Hofsten, 1984). Infants of this age reach just as effectively for an unseen, sounding object in the dark as for an object they can see in the light. This indicates that early reaching does not require visual guidance of the arms and hands. Instead, it is controlled by *proprioception,* our sense of movement and location in space, arising from stimuli within the body (Clifton et al., 1994). From the start, vision is freed from the basic act of reaching so it can focus on more complex adjustments, such as fine-tuning actions to fit the distance and shape of objects.

Improvements in reaching are largely a matter of controlling arm and hand movements. At first, infants reach too fast or too slowly and often miss their mark. Individual differences in movement styles affect how the skill is perfected (Thelen, Corbetta, & Spencer, 1996). For example, Brian's motions were large and forceful; he had to make them less vigorous to reach for a toy successfully. In contrast, Rachel's quiet, gentle actions became faster and more energetic as she moved toward smoothly executed reaching (Thelen et al., 1993). Each infant builds the act of reaching uniquely by exploring the match between current movements and those demanded by the task (Thelen & Smith, 1998).

Once infants can reach, they start to modify their grasp. When the grasp reflex of the newborn period weakens, it is replaced by the **ulnar grasp,** a clumsy motion in which the fingers close against the palm (Halverson, 1931). Around 4 to 5 months, when infants begin to master sitting, they no longer need their arms to maintain body balance. This frees both hands to become coordinated in exploring objects. Babies of this age can hold an object in one hand while the other scans it with the tips of the fingers, and they frequently transfer objects from hand to hand (Rochat, 1992; Rochat & Goubet, 1995). By the latter part of the first year, infants use the thumb and index finger opposably in a well-coordinated **pincer grasp.** Then the ability to manipulate objects expands greatly. The 1-year-old can pick up raisins and blades of grass, turn knobs, and open and close small boxes.

Between 8 and 11 months, reaching and grasping are well practiced. As a result, attention is released from coordinating the motor skill itself to events that occur before and after obtaining the object. As we will see in Chapter 6, around this time infants can first solve simple problems involving reaching, such as searching for and finding a hidden toy.

■ **EARLY EXPERIENCE AND VOLUNTARY REACHING.** Like other motor milestones, voluntary reaching is affected by early experience. In a well-known study, Burton White and Richard Held (1966) found that institutionalized babies provided with a moderate amount of visual stimulation—at first, simple designs and later, a mobile hung over their crib—reached for objects 6 weeks earlier than did infants given nothing to look at. A third group of babies provided with massive stimulation—patterned crib bumpers and mobiles at an early age—also reached sooner than unstimulated babies. But this heavy dose of enrichment took its toll. These infants looked away and cried a great deal, and they were not as advanced in reaching as the moderately stimulated group. White and Held's findings remind us that more stimulation is not necessarily better. Trying to push infants beyond their current readiness to handle stimulation can undermine the development of important motor skills.

As infants' and toddlers' motor skills permit them to manipulate objects and move about the environment, caregivers must devote more energy to protecting them from harm. Refer to the Caregiving Concerns table on page 190 for a variety of suggestions for keeping infants and toddlers safe. In Chapter 8, we will consider the topic of unintentional injuries in greater detail.

BOWEL AND BLADDER CONTROL

More than any other aspect of early muscular development, parents wonder about bowel and bladder control. Lisa admitted that she once tried sitting Byron on a child-size potty at 15 months. "That lasted for about two seconds," she said. "Byron is so absorbed in walking and exploring right now that he doesn't have the patience to sit there, waiting for something to happen."

Two or three generations ago, many mothers tried to toilet train small infants. However, they did not really succeed in teaching anything. They only caught the baby's urine or bowel movement at a convenient moment. Toilet training is best delayed until the end of the second or the beginning of the third year. Not until then can toddlers consistently identify the signals from a full bladder or rectum and wait until they are in the right place to permit these muscles to open. Research indicates that mothers who postpone training until age 2 succeed in having infants who are fully trained within 4 months. Starting earlier does not produce a more reliably trained preschooler; the whole process just takes longer (Brazelton, 1997). In addition, as we will see in Chapter 7, pressuring too much in this area, as well as in others, can negatively affect the toddler's emotional well-being.

Toddlers are not ready for toilet training until around age 2, when they can control bladder and rectal muscles consistently. The parents of this 2-year-old girl bought a small toilet on which she can sit comfortably, and they make toileting a pleasant experience. She is likely to be fully trained within a few months. *(Elizabeth Crews)*

prereaching
The poorly coordinated, primitive reaching movements of newborn babies.

ulnar grasp
The clumsy grasp of the young infant, in which the fingers close against the palm.

pincer grasp
The well-coordinated grasp emerging at the end of the first year, involving thumb and forefinger opposition.

CAREGIVING CONCERNS
Keeping Infants and Toddlers Safe

STRATEGY	DESCRIPTION
Provide safe toys	Match all toys to the child's age and abilities (see the Caregiving Concerns table in Chapter 6, page 223).
	Inspect all toys for small parts that can be swallowed, sharp edges that can cut, and materials that can shatter.
	Avoid cord-activated toys and toys intended to be attached to a crib or playpen; the infant's neck can become entangled in the cord or clothing can catch on a part of the toy, resulting in strangulation.
	Remove crib mobiles and crib gyms when the baby begins to push up on hands and knees; although researchers often use such toys to investigate infant capacities, the risk of becoming entangled is high.
	Do not let young children play with balloons, which can be inhaled if the child tries to blow them up.
Child-proof all rooms	Keep lids of toilets closed and buckets of water used for cleaning away from infants and toddlers; a curious toddler who tries to play in the water can fall in and drown.
	Keep all medicines, cosmetics, cleaners, paints, glues, and other toxic substances out of reach, preferably in locked cabinets; make sure that medicine bottles have child-resistant safety caps.
	Put safety plugs in all unused electrical outlets.
	Unplug all appliances or remove dials when not in use so the child cannot turn them on.
	Keep cords for window blinds and curtains out of reach.
	Remove unstable furniture, such as tall floor lamps and freestanding bookshelves.
	When the infant starts to crawl, install safety gates at top and bottom of stairs.
Continuously monitor the infant or toddler in situations that pose any risk of injury	Never leave a young child alone in the bath or on a changing table, even for a moment.
	At mealtimes, strap the infant or toddler into a high chair, and do not leave the child unattended.
Use a federally approved car seat	When driving, always strap the young child into the car seat. Never permit an infant or toddler to ride on your lap; in an accident, your body could crush the child as you are thrown forward.
Report any unsafe toys and equipment	If you discover any toys or equipment that seem unsafe, report them to the Consumer Product Safety Commission, (800) 638-2772. It keeps a record of complaints and initiates recalls of dangerous products.

Source: American Academy of Pediatrics, 1993.

ASK YOURSELF . . .

■ *Rosanne read in a magazine that infant motor development could be speeded up through exercise and visual stimulation. She hung mobiles and pictures all over her newborn baby's crib, and she massages and manipulates his body daily. Is Rosanne doing the right thing? Why or why not?*

BRIEF REVIEW

The overall sequence of motor development follows the cephalocaudal and proximodistal trends. However, motor development is not programmed into the brain. According to dynamic systems theory, it is energized by the baby's exploration and desire to master new tasks and jointly influenced by central nervous system maturation, movement possibilities of the body, and environmental supports for the skill. Microgenetic studies reveal how previously learned acts are reorganized into new motor attainments. Cross-cultural research underscores the contribution of movement opportunities, a stimulating environment, and infant-rearing practices to motor progress.

Voluntary reaching plays a vital role in infant cognitive development. It begins with the uncoordinated prereaching of the newborn baby and gradually evolves into a refined pincer grasp by the end of the first year. Once reaching and grasping are well practiced, infants integrate these behaviors into increasingly elaborate motor systems.

Toddlers are not ready for toilet training until the end of the second or the beginning of the third year. Before this time, they cannot control the muscles that retain and release urine and bowel movements.

LEARNING CAPACITIES

L
earning refers to changes in behavior as the result of experience. Babies come into the world with built-in learning capacities that permit them to profit from experience immediately. Infants are capable of two basic forms of learning, which were introduced in Chapter 1: classical and operant conditioning. In addition, they learn through their natural preference for novel stimulation. Finally, newborn babies have a remarkable ability to imitate the facial expressions and gestures of adults.

CLASSICAL CONDITIONING

Newborn reflexes, discussed in Chapter 4, make **classical conditioning** possible in the young infant. In this form of learning, a new stimulus is paired with a stimulus that leads to a reflexive response. Once the baby's nervous system makes the connection between the two stimuli, then the new stimulus by itself produces the behavior.

Recall from Chapter 1 that Russian physiologist Ivan Pavlov first demonstrated classical conditioning in some famous research he conducted with dogs (see page 18). Classical conditioning is of great value to human infants, as well as other animals, because it helps them recognize which events usually occur together in the everyday world. As a result, they can anticipate what is about to happen next, and the environment becomes more orderly and predictable (Rovee-Collier, 1987). Let's take a closer look at the steps of classical conditioning.

As Beth settled down in the rocking chair to nurse Rachel, she often gently stroked Rachel's forehead. Soon Beth noticed that each time Rachel's forehead was stroked, she made active sucking movements. Rachel had been classically conditioned. Here is how it happened (see Figure 5.12):

1.   Before learning takes place, an **unconditioned stimulus (UCS)** must consistently produce a reflexive, or **unconditioned, response (UCR).** In Rachel's case, the stimulus of sweet breast milk (UCS) resulted in sucking (UCR).

2.   To produce learning, a *neutral stimulus* that does not lead to the reflex is presented at about the same time as the UCS. Ideally, the neutral stimulus should occur just before the UCS. Beth stroked Rachel's forehead as each nursing period began. Therefore, the stroking (neutral stimulus) was paired with the taste of milk (UCS).

3.   If learning has occurred, the neutral stimulus by itself produces the reflexive response. The neutral stimulus is then called a **conditioned stimulus (CS),** and the response it elicits is called a **conditioned response (CR).** We know that Rachel has been classically conditioned because stroking her forehead outside the feeding situation (CS) results in sucking (CR).

If the CS is presented alone enough times, without being paired with the UCS, the CR will no longer occur. In other words, if Beth strokes Rachel's forehead again and again without feeding her, Rachel will gradually stop sucking in response to stroking. This is referred to as **extinction.** In a classical conditioning experiment, the occurrence of responses to the CS during the extinction phase shows that learning has taken place.

Young babies can be classically conditioned most easily when the association between two stimuli has survival value. Rachel learned quickly in the feeding situation, since learning which stimuli regularly accompany feeding improves the infant's ability to get food and survive (Blass, Ganchrow, & Steiner, 1984). In contrast, some responses are very difficult to condition in young babies. Fear is one of them. Until infants have the motor skills to escape unpleasant events, they do not have a biological need to form these associations. But between 8 and 12 months, the conditioning of fear is easily accomplished, as seen in

classical conditioning
A form of learning that involves associating a neutral stimulus with a stimulus that leads to a reflexive response.

unconditioned stimulus (UCS)
In classical conditioning, a stimulus that leads to a reflexive response.

unconditioned response (UCR)
In classical conditioning, a reflexive response that is produced by an unconditioned stimulus (UCS).

conditioned stimulus (CS)
In classical conditioning, a neutral stimulus that through pairing with an unconditioned stimulus (UCS) leads to a new response (CR).

conditioned response (CR)
In classical conditioning, an originally reflexive response that is produced by a conditioned stimulus (CS).

extinction
In classical conditioning, decline of the conditioned response (CR) as a result of presenting the conditioned stimulus (CS) enough times without the unconditioned stimulus (UCS).

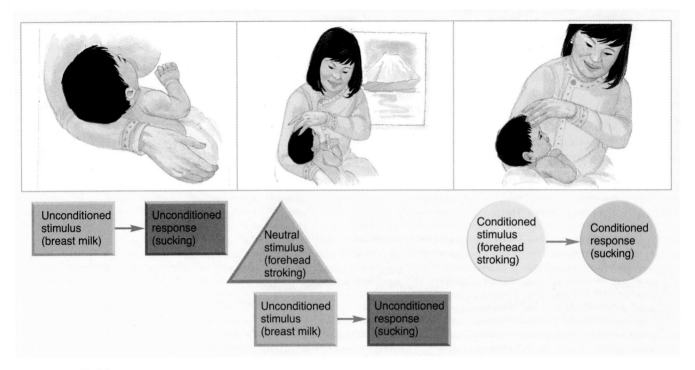

Unconditioned stimulus (breast milk) → Unconditioned response (sucking)	Neutral stimulus (forehead stroking) Unconditioned stimulus (breast milk) → Unconditioned response (sucking)	Conditioned stimulus (forehead stroking) → Conditioned response (sucking)

FIGURE 5.12

The steps of classical conditioning. The example here shows how Rachel was classically conditioned to make sucking movements when her forehead was stroked. After breast milk (which reflexively produced sucking) was repeatedly paired with forehead stroking, Rachel sucked when her forehead was stroked in the absence of breast milk.

the famous example of little Albert, conditioned by John Watson to withdraw and cry at the sight of a furry white rat. Return to Chapter 1, page 18, to review this well-known experiment. Then test your knowledge of classical conditioning by identifying the UCS, UCR, CS, and CR in Watson's study. In Chapter 7, we will discuss the development of fear, as well as other emotional reactions, in detail.

OPERANT CONDITIONING

In classical conditioning, babies build expectations about stimulus events in the environment, but their behavior does not influence the stimuli that occur. **Operant conditioning** is quite different. In this form of learning, infants act (or operate) on the environment, and stimuli that follow their behavior change the probability that the behavior will occur again.

Recall from Chapter 4 that newborn babies take longer sucks when a nipple delivers sweet liquid as opposed to plain water. If they are given a sour-tasting fluid, they purse their lips and stop sucking entirely. When you read about this research, you were actually studying operant conditioning. A stimulus that increases the occurrence of a response is called a **reinforcer.** Removing a desirable stimulus or presenting an unpleasant one to decrease the occurrence of a response is called **punishment.** In the example just described, sweet liquid *reinforces* the sucking response, whereas a sour-tasting fluid *punishes* it.

Because the young infant can control only a few behaviors, successful operant conditioning is limited to sucking and head-turning responses. However, many stimuli besides food can serve as reinforcers. For example, researchers have created special laboratory conditions in which the baby's rate of sucking on a nipple produces a variety of interest-

operant conditioning
A form of learning in which a spontaneous behavior is followed by a stimulus that changes the probability that the behavior will occur again.

reinforcer
In operant conditioning, a stimulus that increases the occurrence of a response.

punishment
In operant conditioning, removing a desirable stimulus or presenting an unpleasant one to decrease the occurrence of a response.

ing sights and sounds. Newborns will suck faster to see visual designs or to hear music and human voices (Rovee-Collier, 1987).

Even preterm babies will seek reinforcing stimulation. In one study, they increased their contact with a soft teddy bear that "breathed" quietly at a rate reflecting the infant's respiration, whereas they decreased their contact with a nonbreathing bear (Thoman & Ingersoll, 1993). As these findings suggest, operant conditioning has become a powerful tool for finding out what stimuli babies can perceive and which ones they prefer.

As infants get older, operant conditioning expands to include a wider range of responses and stimuli. Turn back to page 188 to see the special mobile, attached to the baby's foot with a long cord, that moves with each kick. Under these conditions, it takes only a few minutes for 2- to 6-month-olds to start kicking vigorously (Rovee-Collier & Hayne, 1987; Shields & Rovee-Collier, 1992).

Operant conditioning soon modifies parents' and babies' reactions to each other. As the infant gazes into the adult's eyes, the adult looks and smiles back, and then the infant looks and smiles again. The behavior of each partner reinforces the other, and both continue their pleasurable interaction. In Chapter 7, we will see that this kind of contingent responsiveness plays a role in the development of infant–caregiver attachment.

Recall from Chapter 1 that classical and operant conditioning originated with behaviorism, an approach that views the child as a relatively passive responder to environmental stimuli. If you look carefully at the findings just described, you will see that young babies are not passive. Instead, they use any means they can to explore and control their surroundings. In fact, when infants' environments are so disorganized that their behavior does not lead to predictable outcomes, serious developmental problems, ranging from intellectual retardation to apathy and depression, can result (Cicchetti & Aber, 1986; Seligman, 1975). In addition, as the Social Issues box on page 194 reveals, problems in brain functioning may prevent some babies from actively learning certain life-saving responses; and the absence of such responses may lead to sudden infant death syndrome, a major cause of infant mortality.

HABITUATION AND DISHABITUATION

Take a moment to walk through the rooms of the library, your home, or wherever you happen to be reading this book. What did you notice? Probably those things that are new and different caught your attention first, such as a recently purchased picture on the wall or a piece of furniture that has been moved.

The human brain is set up to be attracted to novelty. **Habituation** refers to a gradual reduction in the strength of a response due to repetitive stimulation. Looking, heart rate, and respiration may all decline, indicating a loss of interest. Once this has occurred, a new stimulus—some kind of change in the environment—causes responsiveness to return to a high level. This recovery is called **dishabituation**. Habituation and dishabituation enable us to focus our attention on those aspects of the environment we know least about. As a result, learning is more efficient.

By studying the stimuli that infants of different ages habituate and dishabituate to, researchers can tell much about their understanding of the world. For example, a baby who first habituates to a visual pattern (e.g., a 2×2 checkerboard) and then dishabituates to a new one (a 4×4 checkerboard) clearly remembers the first stimulus and perceives the second one as new and different from it. This method of studying infant perception and cognition, which is illustrated in Figure 5.13 on page 195, can be used with newborn babies, including those who are preterm. It has even been used to study the fetus's sensitivity to external stimuli—for example, by measuring changes in fetal heart rate to repeated presentations of various sounds (Hepper, 1997).

Habituation is evident as early as the third trimester of pregnancy. As fetuses and babies get older, they habituate to stimuli more quickly, indicating that their processing

habituation
A gradual reduction in the strength of a response as the result of repetitive stimulation.

dishabituation
Increase in responsiveness after stimulation changes.

SOCIAL   ISSUES

THE MYSTERIOUS TRAGEDY OF SUDDEN INFANT DEATH SYNDROME

Before they went to bed, Millie and Stuart looked in on 3-month-old Sasha. She was sleeping soundly, her breathing no longer as labored as it had been 2 days before when she caught her first cold. There had been reasons to worry about Sasha at birth. She was born 3 weeks early, and it took more than a minute before she started breathing. "Sasha's muscle tone seems a little weak," Millie remembered the doctor saying. "She just needs to get busy and gain a little weight, and then she'll be well on her way."

Millie awoke with a start the next morning and looked at the clock. It was 7:30, and Sasha had missed her night waking and early morning feeding. Wondering if she was all right, Millie tiptoed into the room. Sasha lay still, curled up under her blanket. She had died silently during her sleep.

Sasha was a victim of **sudden infant death syndrome (SIDS),** the unexpected death, usually during the night, of an infant under 1 year of age that remains unexplained after thorough investigation. In industrialized nations, SIDS is the leading cause of infant mortality between 1 week and 12 months of age. It accounts for more than one-third of these deaths in the United States (Cadoff, 1995). Millie and Stuart's grief was especially hard to bear because no one could give them a definite answer about why Sasha died. They felt guilty and under attack by relatives, and their 5-year-old daughter Jill reacted with sorrow that lasted for months.

Although the precise cause of SIDS is not known, infants who die of it usually show physical problems from the very beginning. Early medical records of SIDS babies reveal higher rates of prematurity and limp muscle tone. Abnormal heart rate, cry patterns, and respiration as well as disturbances in sleep–waking activity are also associated with the disorder (Corwin et al., 1995; Malloy & Hoffman, 1995). At the time of death, over half of SIDS babies have a mild respiratory infection. This seems to increase the chances of respiratory failure in an already vulnerable baby (Cotton, 1990).

One hypothesis about the cause of SIDS is that problems in brain functioning prevent these infants from learning how to respond when their survival is threatened—for example, when respiration is suddenly interrupted (Lipsitt, 1990). Between 2 and 4 months of age, when SIDS is most likely to occur, reflexes decline and are replaced by voluntary, learned responses. Respiratory and muscular weaknesses of SIDS babies may stop them from acquiring behaviors that replace defensive reflexes. As a result, when breathing difficulties occur during sleep, they do not wake up, shift the position of their bodies, or cry out for help. Instead, they simply give in to oxygen deprivation and death.

In an effort to reduce the occurrence of SIDS, researchers are studying environmental factors related to it. Although babies of poverty-stricken, ethnic minority mothers are at greater risk, these findings may be due to mistaking other causes of infant death for SIDS. When SIDS diagnoses are "certain" rather than "questionable," family background closely resembles that of the general population (Taylor & Sanderson, 1995). In contrast, maternal cigarette smoking, both during and after pregnancy, as well as smoking by other caregivers is strongly predictive of the disorder. Babies exposed to cigarette smoke are 2 to 3 times more likely to die of SIDS than are non-exposed infants (Klonoff-Cohen et al., 1995; Poets et al., 1995).

Other consistent findings are that SIDS babies are more likely to sleep on their stomachs or sides than their backs and are often wrapped very warmly in clothing and blankets (Fleming et al., 1996; Irgens et al., 1995). Why are these factors associated with SIDS? Scientists think that smoke and excessive body warmth (which can be encouraged by putting babies down on their stomachs or their sides, since they often roll from side to stomach) place a strain on the respiratory control system in the brain. In an at-risk baby, the respiratory center may stop functioning. In other cases, healthy babies sleeping face down in soft bedding may die from continually breathing their own exhaled breath (Kemp & Thach, 1993).

Research confirms that quitting smoking, changing an infant's sleeping position, and removing a few bedclothes can reduce the incidence of SIDS. For example, if women refrained from smoking while pregnant, an estimated 30 percent of SIDS would be prevented. Public education campaigns that discourage parents from putting babies down on their stomachs have led to dramatic reductions in SIDS in Australia, Great Britain, New Zealand, and the United States (American Academy of Family Physicians, 1997; Taylor, 1991; Wigfield et al., 1992).

When SIDS does occur, surviving family members require a great deal of help to overcome a sudden and unexpected infant death. Parent support groups exist in many communities. As Millie commented 6 months after Sasha's death, "It's the worst crisis we've ever been through. What's helped us most are the comforting words of others who've experienced the same tragedy."

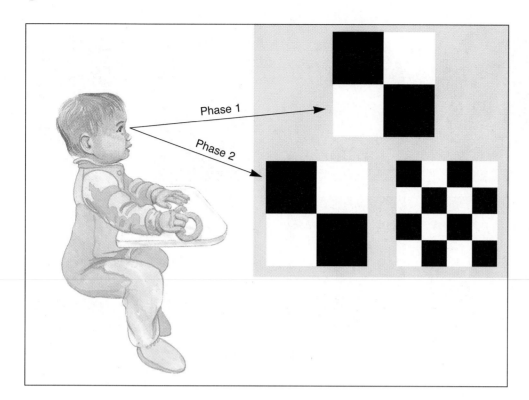

FIGURE **5.13**

Example of how the habituation–dishabituation sequence can be used to study infant perception and cognition. In Phase 1, an infant is permitted to look at (habituate to) a 2 × 2 checkerboard. In phase 2, the baby is again shown the 2 × 2 checkerboard, but this time it appears alongside a new, 4 × 4 checkerboard. If the infant dishabituates to (spends more time looking at) the 4 × 4 checkerboard, then we know the baby remembers the first stimulus and can tell that the second one is different from it.

of information is becoming more efficient. Yet a fascinating exception to this trend exists. Two-month-old babies actually take longer to habituate to novel visual forms than do newborns and older infants (Hood et al., 1996; Slater et al., 1996). Later, we will see that 2 months is also a time of dramatic gains in visual perception. Perhaps when young babies are first able to perceive certain information, they require more time to take it in (Johnson, 1996).

The habituation–dishabituation sequence provides researchers with a marvelous window into early mental development. We will return to it in this chapter, when we discuss perception, and in Chapter 6, when we consider attention, memory, and other aspects of infant cognition.

IMITATION

For many years, researchers believed that **imitation**—learning by copying the behavior of another person—was beyond the capacity of very young infants. They were not expected to imitate until several months after birth. Then a growing number of studies began to report that newborn babies come into the world with the ability to imitate the behavior of their caregivers.

Figure 5.14 shows examples of responses obtained in two of the first studies of newborn imitation (Field et al., 1982; Meltzoff & Moore, 1977). As you can see, babies from 2 days to several weeks old imitated a variety of adult facial expressions. Since then, the newborn's capacity to imitate has been demonstrated in many ethnic groups and cultures (Meltzoff & Kuhl, 1994).

Explanations of the response are more controversial. Imitation is more difficult to induce in babies 2 to 3 months old than just after birth. Some investigators regard the capacity as little more than an automatic response to particular stimuli. But Andrew Meltzoff (1990) points out that newborns model diverse facial expressions and head movements, and they do so even after short delays—when the adult is no longer demonstrating the behavior. This suggests that they imitate in much the same way we do—by actively trying to match body movements they "see" with ones they "feel" themselves

sudden infant death syndrome (SIDS)
The unexpected death, usually during the night, of an infant under 1 year of age that remains unexplained after thorough investigation.

imitation
Learning by copying the behavior of another person. Also called modeling or observational learning.

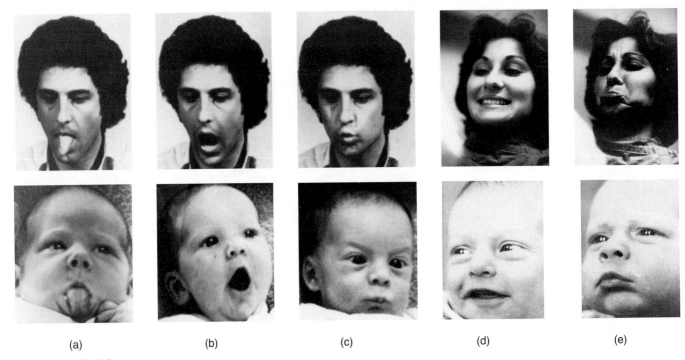

(a)   (b)   (c)   (d)   (e)

FIGURE **5.14**

Photographs from two of the first studies of newborn imitation. Those on the left show 2- to 3-week-old infants imitating tongue protrusion (a), mouth opening (b), and lip protrusion (c) of an adult experimenter. Those on the right show 2-day-old infants imitating happy (d) and sad (e) adult facial expressions. (*From A. N. Meltzoff & M. K. Moore, 1977, "Imitation of Facial and Manual Gestures by Human Neonates,"* Science, 198, *p. 75; and T. M. Field et al., 1992, "Discrimination and Imitation of Facial Expressions by Neonates,"* Science, 218, *p. 180. Copyright 1977 and 1982, respectively, by the AAAS. Reprinted by permission.*)

ASK YOURSELF . . .

■ *Nine-month-old Byron has a toy with large, colored push buttons on it. Each time he pushes a button, he hears a nursery tune. Which learning capacity is the manufacturer of this toy taking advantage of?*

■ *Recall that infants with nonorganic failure to thrive are unlikely to smile at a friendly adult. Also, they keep track of nearby adults in an anxious, fearful way. Explain these reactions using the learning capacities discussed in the preceding sections.*

■ *Return to the section on intervening with preterm infants on page 146 of Chapter 4. Why might a preterm baby seek contact with a soft, "breathing" teddy bear, as reported in our discussion of operant conditioning on page 193?*

make. Later in this chapter, we will encounter evidence that young babies are surprisingly good at coordinating information across sensory systems. Taken together, these findings support a view of newborn imitation as a flexible, voluntary capacity (Meltzoff & Moore, 1992).

As we will see in Chapter 6, a baby's ability to imitate improves greatly over the first 2 years. But however limited it is at birth, imitation is a powerful means of learning. Using imitation, young infants begin to explore their social world, getting to know people by matching behavioral states with them. In the process, babies notice similarities between their own actions and those of others, and they start to find out about themselves. Furthermore, through imitation, adults can get young infants to express desirable behaviors, and once they do, adults can encourage these further. Finally, caregivers take great pleasure in a baby who imitates their facial gestures and actions. Newborn imitation seems to be one of those capacities that helps get the infant's relationship with parents off to a good start.

BRIEF REVIEW

Young babies are marvelously equipped to learn. Through classical conditioning, infants acquire stimulus associations that have survival value. Operant conditioning permits them to control events in the surrounding world. Habituation and dishabituation reveal that infants, much like adults, are naturally attracted to novel stimulation. Finally, newborns' amazing ability to imitate the facial expressions and gestures of adults helps them get to know their social world.

PERCEPTUAL DEVELOPMENT

*I*n Chapter 4, you learned that the senses of touch, taste, smell, and hearing are remarkably well developed at birth. Now let's turn to a related question: How does perception change over the first year of life?

Our discussion will focus on infant hearing and vision because almost all research addresses these two aspects of perceptual development. Unfortunately, we know little about how touch, taste, and smell develop after birth. Also, in Chapter 4 we used the word *sensation* to talk about these capacities. Now we are using the word *perception*. The reason is that sensation suggests a fairly passive process—what the baby's receptors detect when they are exposed to stimulation. In contrast, perception is much more active. When we perceive, we organize and interpret what we see.

As we look at the perceptual achievements of infancy, you will probably find it hard to tell where perception leaves off and thinking begins. Thus, the research we are about to discuss provides an excellent bridge to the topic of Chapter 6—cognitive development during the first 2 years.

HEARING

On Byron's first birthday, Lisa bought several tapes of nursery songs, and she turned one on each afternoon at naptime. Soon Byron let her know his favorite tune. If she put on the tape with "Twinkle, Twinkle," he stood up in his crib and whimpered until she replaced it with "Jack and Jill." Byron's behavior illustrates the greatest change that takes place in hearing over the first year of life: Babies start to organize sounds into complex patterns. If two melodies differing only slightly are played, 1-year-olds can tell that they are not the same (Morrongiello, 1986).

As we will see in the next chapter, throughout the first year babies are preparing to acquire language. Recall from Chapter 4 that newborns can distinguish between almost all sounds in human languages, and they prefer listening to their native tongue. As infants continue to listen actively to the talk of people around them, they learn to focus on meaningful sound variations in their own language. By 6 months of age, they "screen out" sounds that are not useful in their language community (Kuhl et al., 1992; Polka & Werker, 1994).

In the second half of the first year, infants focus on larger speech units that are crucial for making sense of what they hear. They recognize familiar words in spoken passages (Jusczyk & Aslin, 1995; Jusczyk & Hohne, 1997). Older infants can also detect clauses and phrases in sentences (Aslin, Jusczyk, & Pisoni, 1997). In one study, researchers recorded two versions of a mother telling a story. In the first, she spoke naturally, with pauses occurring between clauses, like this: "Cinderella lived in a great big house [pause], but it was sort of dark [pause] because she had this mean stepmother." In the second version, the mother inserted pauses in unnatural places—in the middle of clauses: "Cinderella lived in a great big house, but it was [pause] sort of dark because she had [pause] this mean stepmother." Like adults, 7-month-olds clearly preferred speech with natural breaks (Hirsh-Pasek et al., 1987).

By 9 months, infants extend this rhythmic sensitivity to individual words. They listen much longer to speech with stress patterns and sound sequences common in their own language, and they use these cues to divide the speech stream into wordlike segments (Jusczyk, Cutler, & Redanz, 1993; Morgan & Saffran, 1995).

Taken together, these findings reveal that between 6 and 9 months, infants have begun to analyze the internal structure of sentences and words. This information will be vital for linking speech units with their meanings in the second year.

VISION

If you had to choose between hearing and vision, which would you select? Most people decide on vision, for good reason. More than any other sense, humans depend on vision for active exploration of the environment. Although at first the baby's visual world is fragmented, it undergoes extraordinary changes during the first 7 to 8 months of life.

Visual development is supported by rapid maturation of the eye and visual centers in the cortex. Recall from Chapter 4 that the newborn baby's focusing ability and color perception are poor. By 2 months, infants can discriminate colors across the entire spectrum, and at 3 months they can focus on objects just as well as adults can (Banks, 1980; Brown, 1990). Visual acuity (fineness of discrimination) improves steadily throughout the first year. In Chapter 4, we noted that newborns see about as clearly at 20 feet as adults do at 600 feet. By 6 months, their acuity is about 20/100. At 11 months, it reaches a near-adult level (Courage & Adams, 1990). Over the first 6 months, the ability to track moving objects becomes more accurate (Hainline, 1993).

As infants see more clearly and explore their visual field more adeptly, they work on figuring out the characteristics of objects and how they are arranged in space. We can best understand how they do so by examining the development of three aspects of vision: depth, pattern, and object perception.

■ **DEPTH PERCEPTION.** *Depth perception* is the ability to judge the distance of objects from one another and from ourselves. It is important for understanding the layout of the environment and for guiding motor activity. To reach for objects, babies must have some sense of depth. Later, when infants crawl, depth perception helps prevent them from bumping into furniture and falling down staircases. However, as we will see shortly, parents are unwise to trust the baby's judgment entirely in these situations!

The earliest studies of depth perception used a well-known apparatus called the *visual cliff* (see Figure 5.15). Devised by Eleanor Gibson and Richard Walk (1960), it consists of a glass-covered table with a platform at the center. On one side of the platform (the shallow side) is a checkerboard pattern just under the surface of the glass. On the other side (the deep side), the checkerboard is several feet beneath the glass. The researchers placed crawling infants on the platform and asked their mothers to entice them across both the deep and shallow sides by calling to them and holding out a toy. Although the babies readily crossed the shallow side, all but a few reacted with fear to the deep side. The researchers concluded that around the time that infants crawl, most distinguish deep from shallow surfaces and avoid drop-offs that look dangerous.

Gibson and Walk's research shows that crawling and avoidance of drop-offs are linked, but it does not tell us how they are related or when depth perception first appears. To better understand the development of depth perception, recent research has looked at babies' ability to detect specific depth cues, using methods that do not require that they crawl.

Emergence of Depth Perception.   How do we know when an object is near rather than far away? Try these exercises to find out. Look toward the far wall while moving your head from side to side. Notice that objects close to your eye move past your field of vision more quickly than those far away. Next, pick up a small object (such as your cup) and move it toward and away from your face. Did its image grow larger as it approached and smaller as it receded?

Motion provides us with a great deal of information about depth, and it is the first type of depth cue to which infants are sensitive. Babies 3 to 4 weeks of age blink their eyes defensively when an object moves toward their face as if it is going to hit (Nánez, 1987; Nánez & Yonas, 1994). As they are carried about and people and things turn and move before their eyes, infants learn more about depth. For example, by 3 months, motion has

FIGURE **5.15**

The visual cliff. By refusing to cross the deep side and showing a preference for the shallow surface, this infant demonstrates the ability to perceive depth. (William Vandivert/ Scientific American)

helped them figure out that objects are not flat shapes but are instead three dimensional (Arterberry, Craton, & Yonas, 1993).

Binocular depth cues arise because our two eyes have slightly different views of the visual field. The brain registers and combines these two images. Researchers have used ingenious methods to find out if infants are sensitive to binocular cues. One approach is similar to a 3-D movie. The experimenter projects two overlapping images before the baby, who wears special goggles to ensure that each eye receives one of them. If babies use binocular cues, they see and visually track an organized form rather than random dots. Results reveal that binocular sensitivity emerges between 2 and 3 months and gradually improves over the first half year (Birch, 1993). Infants quickly make use of binocular depth perception in their reaching, adjusting arm and hand movements to match the distance of objects from the eye.

Pictorial depth cues are the same ones that artists use to make a painting look three dimensional. Examples are lines that create the illusion of perspective, changes in texture (nearby textures are more detailed than ones far away), and overlapping objects (an object partially hidden by another object is perceived to be more distant). Investigators have explored infants' sensitivity to pictorial cues by covering one eye (so the baby cannot rely on binocular vision), presenting stimuli with certain cues, and seeing which ones babies reach for. These experiments show that 7-month-old babies are sensitive to a variety of pictorial cues, but 5-month-olds are not (Yonas et al., 1986). Thus, pictorial depth perception is last to develop, emerging around the middle of the first year.

Table 5.1 summarizes the infant's developing sensitivity to depth. Why does perception of depth cues emerge in the order just described? Researchers speculate that motor development is involved. For example, control of the head during the early weeks of life may help babies notice motion cues. Improved focusing ability at 3 months may permit detection of binocular cues. And around 5 to 6 months, the ability to turn, poke, and feel the surface of objects may promote perception of pictorial cues as infants pick up information about size, texture, and shape (Bushnell & Boudreau, 1993).

The close correspondence between depth perception and action reveals that these two aspects of development support one another (Bertenthal & Clifton, 1998). Indeed, as we will see next, research shows that one aspect of motor progress—the baby's ability to move about independently—plays a vital role in refinement of depth perception.

Independent Movement and Depth Perception.   Just before she reached the 6-month mark, April started crawling. "She's like a fearless daredevil," exclaimed Felicia to the other mothers. "If I put her down in the middle of our bed, she crawls right over the edge. Several times I stopped her just before she went overboard The same thing's also happened by the stairs."

Will April become more wary of the side of the bed and the staircase as she becomes a more experienced crawler? Research suggests that she will. In one study, infants with more crawling experience (regardless of when they started to crawl) were far more likely to refuse to cross the deep side of the visual cliff (Bertenthal, Campos, & Barrett, 1984). Avoidance of heights, the investigators concluded, is "made possible by independent loco-motion" (Bertenthal & Campos, 1987, p. 563).

Independent movement contributes to other aspects of three-dimensional under-standing as well. For example, crawling infants are better at remembering object locations and finding hidden objects than are their noncrawling agemates. And the more crawling experience they have, the better their performance on these tasks (Bai & Bertenthal, 1992; Campos & Bertenthal, 1989).

Why does crawling make such a difference? Compare your own experience of the environment when you are driven from one place to another as opposed to when you walk or drive yourself. When you move on your own, you are much more aware of land-marks and routes of travel, and you take more careful note of what things look like from different points of view. The same is true for infants. In fact, researchers believe that crawling is so important in structuring babies' experience of the world that it may pro-mote a new level of brain organization by strengthening certain synaptic connections in the cortex (Fox, Calkins, & Bell, 1994).

Many American parents place babies who are not yet crawling in "walkers." Consisting of a seat with a frame on castors, these devices permit babies to move around independently by pushing with their feet. Do walkers help stimulate development in the ways just described? Research suggests that they do (Kermoian & Campos, 1988). However, there is no evidence that walkers have lasting effects on development, and they can be dangerous. Infants frequently tip over in them and careen down staircases, perhaps because the frame and seat provide a false sense of security. In the United States, walkers account for over 20,000 infant injuries annually (American Academy of Pediatrics, 1995). For safety's sake, it is best not to put babies in these devices. The reorganization of experience linked to independent movement eventually takes place for all normal infants.

■ PATTERN PERCEPTION. Are young babies sensitive to the pattern, or form, of things they see, and do they prefer some patterns to others? Early research revealed that even newborns prefer to look at patterned as opposed to plain stimuli—for example, a drawing of the human face or one with scrambled facial features rather than a black-and-white oval (Fantz, 1961).

Since then, many studies have shown that as infants get older, they prefer more com-plex patterns. For example, when shown black-and-white checkerboards, 3-week-old

TABLE 5.1

Development of Depth Perception

AGE	PERCEPTUAL CAPACITY
3 weeks–3 months	Sensitivity to motion cues appears and improves.
3–6 months	Sensitivity to binocular cues appears and improves.
6–7 months	Sensitivity to pictorial cues appears.
6–11 months	Wariness of heights develops and is encouraged by the ability to move about independently.

Two checkerboards differing in contrast

Appearance of checkerboards to very young infants

FIGURE 5.16

The way two checkerboards differing in complexity look to infants in the first few weeks of life. Because of their poor vision, very young infants cannot resolve the fine detail in the more complex checkerboard. It appears blurred, like a gray field. The large, bold checkerboard appears to have more contrast, so babies prefer to look at it. *(Adapted from M. S. Banks & P. Salapatek, 1983, "Infant Visual Perception," in M. M. Haith & J. J. Campos (Eds.),* Handbook of Child Psychology: Vol. 2. Infancy and Developmental Psychobiology *(4th ed.), New York: Wile, p. 504. Copyright © 1983 by John Wiley & Sons. Reprinted by permission.)*

infants look longest at ones with a few large squares, whereas 8- and 14-week-olds prefer those with many squares (Brennan, Ames, & Moore, 1966). Infant preferences for many other patterned stimuli have been tested—curved versus straight lines, connected versus disconnected elements, and whether a pattern is organized around a central focus (as in bull's eye), to name just a few.

Contrast Sensitivity.   For many years, researchers did not understand why babies of different ages find certain patterns more attractive than others. Then, a general principle was discovered that accounts for early pattern preferences. It is called **contrast sensitivity** (Banks & Ginsburg, 1985). *Contrast* refers to the difference in amount of light between adjacent parts of a pattern. If babies *are sensitive to* (can detect) the contrast in two or more patterns, they prefer the one with more contrast.

To understand this idea, look at the two checkerboards in the top row of Figure 5.16. To the mature viewer, the one with many small squares has more contrasting elements. Now look at the bottom row, which shows how these checkerboards appear to infants in the first few weeks of life. Because of their poor vision, young babies cannot resolve the small features in more complex patterns. To them, the large, bold checkerboard has more contrast, so they prefer to look at it. By 2 months of age, detection of fine-grained detail has improved considerably. As a result, infants become sensitive to the greater contrast in complex patterns and spend much more time looking at them (Dodwell, Humphrey & Muir, 1987).

Combining Pattern Elements.   In the early weeks of life, infants respond to the separate parts of a pattern. For example, when shown drawings of human faces, 1-month-olds limit their visual exploration to the border of the stimulus, and they stare at single high-contrast features, such as the hairline or chin (see Figure 5.17). At about 2 months, when

contrast sensitivity
A general principle accounting for early pattern preferences, which states that if babies can detect a difference in contrast between two or more patterns, they will prefer the one with more contrast.

FIGURE **5.17**

Visual scanning of the pattern of the human face by 1- and 2-month-old infants. One-month-olds limit their scanning to single features on the border of the stimulus, whereas 2-month-olds explore internal features. *(From P. Salapatek, 1975, "Pattern Perception in Early Infancy," in L. B. Cohen & P. Salapatek (Eds.),* Infant Perception: From Sensation to Cognition, *New York: Academic Press, p. 201. Reprinted by permission.)*

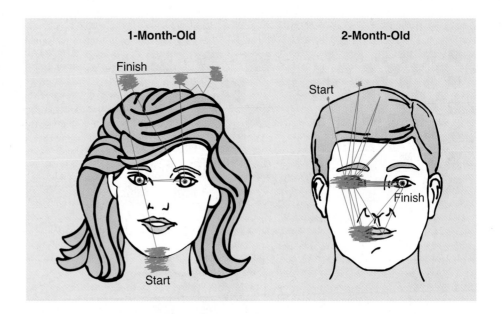

FIGURE **5.18**

Subjective boundaries in a visual pattern. Do you perceive a square in the middle of this figure? By 4 months of age, infants do, too. *(Adapted from Ghim, 1990.)*

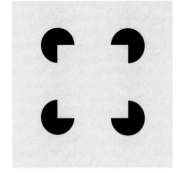

scanning ability and contrast sensitivity have improved, infants start to thoroughly explore a pattern's internal features by moving their eyes quickly around the figure and pausing briefly to look at each salient part (Bronson, 1991).

Once babies can detect all aspects of a pattern, they combine pattern elements, integrating them into a unified whole. By 4 months, they are so good at detecting pattern organization that they even perceive subjective boundaries that are not really present. For example, look at Figure 5.18. Four-month-old babies perceive a square in the center of this pattern, just as you do (Ghim, 1990).

Older infants carry this responsiveness to subjective form even further. Nine-month-olds can detect the organized, meaningful pattern in a series of moving lights that resemble a human being walking, in that they look much longer at this display than they do at upside-down or disorganized versions. Although 3- to 5-month-olds can tell the difference between these patterns, they do not show a special preference for one with both an upright orientation and a humanlike movement pattern (Bertenthal et al., 1985, 1987).

As these findings reveal, over time infants' knowledge of familiar objects and actions increasingly governs pattern perception (Bertenthal, 1993). We will see additional examples of this trend in the development of face perception.

Perception of the Human Face. Do babies have an innate tendency to respond to human faces? Some researchers think so, since newborns will track a facelike pattern moving across their visual field farther than they will track other stimuli (Morton & Johnson, 1991). This behavior is believed to be a built-in, adaptive capacity to orient toward members of one's own species, just as many other newborn creatures do.

But all agree that infants younger than 2 months cannot discriminate the features of the human face from other, equally complex patterns, largely because (as we noted earlier) 1-month-olds do not inspect the internal features of a stimulus.[2] At 2 to 3 months, when infants explore an entire stimulus, they do prefer a face to other stimulus arrange-

---

[2] Perhaps you are wondering how newborns can display the remarkable imitative capacities described earlier in this chapter if they do not scan the internal features of a face. The facial expressions in newborn imitation research were not static poses but live demonstrations. Their dynamic quality probably caused infants to notice them.

TABLE 5.2

Development of Pattern and Face Perception

	BIRTH–1 MONTH	2–3 MONTHS	4–10 MONTHS
Pattern perception	Preference for patterns with large elements. Visual exploration limited to the border of a stimulus and single features	Preference for patterns with fine details Visual exploration of entire stimulus, including internal features Combining pattern elements into an organized whole	Detection of increasingly complex, meaningful patterns
Face perception	Absence of preference for the human facial pattern	Preference for a facial pattern over other, equally complex patterns Recognition of the mother's face in a photo	More fine-grained discrimination of faces, including the ability to perceive emotional expressions as organized wholes

ments (Dannemiller & Stephens, 1988). Infants' recognition of faces follows the same sequence of development as sensitivity to other patterned stimuli.

The baby's tendency to search for structure in a patterned stimulus is quickly applied to face perception. By 3 months of age, infants make fine distinctions among the features of different faces. For example, they can tell the difference between the photos of two strangers, even when the faces are moderately similar. Around this time, babies first recognize their mother's facial features, since they look longer at a photo of her face than at a photo of a stranger's face (Morton, 1993). Between 7 and 10 months, infants start to perceive emotional expressions as organized wholes. They treat positive faces (happy and surprised) as different from negative ones (sad and fearful), even when these expressions are demonstrated in slightly varying ways by different people (Ludemann, 1991).

In Chapter 7 we will see that as face perception improves, infants recognize and respond to the expressive behavior of others. Like many other early capacities, perception of the human face plays an important role in infants' earliest social relationships.

The development of pattern perception in general, and face perception in particular, is summarized in Table 5.2. Note the close parallels between them. The table shows that several important developments in pattern perception take place around 2 months of age. Recall that 2 months also is a time when the frontal lobes of the cerebral cortex function more effectively and when babies become more alert and interested in the world around them. Brain growth supports the baby's improved ability to make sense of patterned stimuli.

OBJECT PERCEPTION

Research on pattern perception involves only two-dimensional stimuli, but our environment is made up of stable, three-dimensional objects. Do young infants perceive a world of independently existing objects—knowledge essential for distinguishing the self, other people, and things?

■ **SIZE AND SHAPE CONSTANCY.** As we move around the environment, the images objects cast on our retina are constantly changing in size and shape. To perceive objects as stable and unchanging, we must translate these varying retinal images into a single representation.

Size constancy—perception of an object's size as the same, despite changes in its retinal image size—is evident in the first week of life. To test for it, researchers capitalized on the habituation–dishabituation response using the procedure described and illustrated in

size constancy
Perception of an object's size as the same, despite changes in the size of its retinal image.

FIGURE **5.19**

Testing newborns for size constancy. (a) First, infants were habituated to a small black-and-white cube at varying distances from the eye. In this way, the researchers hoped to desensitize the baby to changes in the cube's retinal image size and direct their attention to its actual size. (b) Next, the small cube and a new, large cube were presented together, but at different distances so they cast the same size retinal image. All babies dishabituated to (looked much longer at) the novel large cube, indicating that they distinguish objects on the basis of actual size, not retinal image size. *(Adapted from Slater, Mattock, & Brown, 1990.)*

Figure 5.19. Perception of an object's shape as stable, despite changes in the shape projected on the retina, is called **shape constancy.** Habituation–dishabituation research reveals that it, too, is present within the first week of life, long before babies can actively rotate objects with their hands and view them from different angles (Slater, 1996).

In sum, both size and shape constancy seem to be innate capacities that assist babies in detecting a coherent world of objects. Yet they provide only a partial picture of young infants' object perception.

■ **PERCEPTION OF OBJECTS AS DISTINCT, BOUNDED WHOLES.** When Lisa dangled a colorful rattle in front of 6-month-old Byron, he grabbed it eagerly. But when she placed the rattle on top of a book, Byron no longer reached for it. Instead, he reached for the larger, supporting object. Byron's behavior suggests that he did not perceive the boundary between two objects created by their different sizes, shapes, and textures. Rather, he treated two objects close together as a single unit.

Research reveals that it is the movement of objects relative to one another and to their background that gradually enables infants to construct a visual world of separate objects. In one series of studies, 3- to 5-month-olds viewed two objects. Sometimes the objects touched each other; at other times they were separated. Also, sometimes the objects were stationary; at other times they moved independently or together. When objects touched and either stood still or moved in the same direction, infants reached for them as a whole. When they were separated or moved in opposite directions, infants acted as if the objects were distinct and reached for only one of them (Hofsten & Spelke, 1985; Spelke, Hofsten, & Kestenbaum, 1989).

These findings indicate that at first, motion and spatial arrangement determine infants' identification of objects (Kellman, 1993). Indeed, young babies are fascinated by moving objects. They almost always prefer to look at a moving stimulus instead of an identical stationary one. As infants track moving objects, they pick up additional information about an object's boundaries, such as consistent distance of all its parts from their eye and distinct shape, color, and texture. Babies over 6 months of age rely on these cues to identify objects as separate units, just as adults do (Johnson, 1997; Spelke, Gutheil, & Van de Walle, 1995).

INTERMODAL PERCEPTION

When we take in information from the environment, we often use **intermodal perception.** That is, we combine stimulation from more than one *modality,* or sensory system, at

shape constancy
Perception of an object's shape as the same, despite changes in the shape of its retinal image.

intermodal perception
Perception that combines information from more than one sensory system.

differentiation theory
The view that perceptual development involves the detection of increasingly fine-grained, invariant features in the environment.

invariant features
In differentiation theory of perceptual development, features that remain stable in a constantly changing perceptual world.

a time. For example, we know that the shape of an object is the same whether we see it or touch it, that lip movements are closely coordinated with the sound of a voice, and that dropping a rigid object on a hard surface will cause a sharp, banging sound. Recent evidence reveals that from the start, babies perceive the world in an intermodal fashion (Meltzoff, 1990; Spelke, 1987).

Recall that newborns turn in the general direction of a sound, and they reach for objects in a primitive way. These behaviors suggest that infants expect sight, sound, and touch to go together. In one study, 1-month-old babies were given a pacifier to suck with either a smooth surface or a surface with nubs on it. After exploring it in their mouths, the infants were shown two pacifiers—one smooth and one nubbed. They preferred to look at the shape they had sucked, indicating that they could match touch and visual stimulation without much experience seeing and feeling objects (Meltzoff & Borton, 1979).

Within a few months, infants make impressive intermodal matches. Three- and 4-month-olds can relate the shape and tempo of an adult's moving lips to the corresponding sounds in speech. And 7-month-olds can link a happy or angry voice with the appropriate face of a speaking person (Pickens et al., 1994; Soken & Pick, 1992).

Of course, a great many intermodal associations, such as the way a train sounds or a teddy bear feels, must be based on experience. Infants acquire these relationships remarkably quickly, often after just one exposure to a new situation. In addition, when researchers try to teach intermodal matches by pairing sights and sounds that do not naturally go together, babies will not learn them (Bahrick, 1992). Intermodal perception is yet another capacity that helps infants build an orderly, predictable perceptual world.

BRIEF REVIEW

During the first year, infants gradually organize sounds into more complex patterns, and they become sensitive to the sound patterns of their own language. Changes in visual abilities are striking. Depth perception improves as infants detect motion, binocular, and pictorial depth cues. Experience in independent movement plays an important role in avoidance of heights as well as other aspects of three-dimensional understanding. The principle of contrast sensitivity accounts for young babies' pattern preferences. As vision improves, infants perceive the parts of a pattern as an organized whole.

Size and shape constancy are present at birth. At first, infants distinguish objects by attending to their motion and spatial arrangement. Only later do they respond to other features that signal an object's boundaries, such as distinct shape, color, and texture. Face perception follows the same sequence of development as pattern perception in general. Young infants have a remarkable ability to combine information across different sensory modalities.

UNDERSTANDING PERCEPTUAL DEVELOPMENT

Now that we have reviewed the development of infant perceptual capacities, how can we put together this diverse array of amazing achievements? Do any general principles account for perceptual development? Eleanor and James Gibson's **differentiation theory** provides widely accepted answers. According to the Gibsons, infants actively search for **invariant features** of the environment—those that remain stable—in a constantly changing perceptual world. For example, in pattern perception, at first babies are confronted with a confusing mass of stimulation. But very quickly, they search for features that stand out along the border of a

ASK YOURSELF . . .

■ Five-month-old Tyrone sat in his infant seat, passing a teething biscuit from hand to hand, moving it up close to his face and far away, and finally dropping it overboard on the floor below. What aspect of visual development is Tyrone probably learning about? Explain your answer.

■ Diane put up bright wallpaper with detailed pictures of animals in Jana's room before she was born. During the first 2 months of life, Jana hardly noticed the wallpaper. Then, around 2 months, she showed keen interest. What new visual abilities probably account for this change?

FIGURE **5.20**

Acting on the environment plays a major role in perceptual differentiation. The crawling infant on the left plunges headlong down a steeply sloping surface. He has not yet learned that it *affords* the possibility of falling. The walking toddler on the right approaches the slope more cautiously. Experience in trying to remain upright but frequently tumbling over has made him more aware of the consequences of his actions in this situation. He perceives the incline differently than he did at a younger age. (Courtesy of Karen Adolph, Emory University.)

stimulus. Then they explore its internal features, noticing stable relationships among those features. As a result, they detect patterns, such as squares and faces. The development of intermodal perception also reflects this principle. Babies seem to seek out invariant relationships, such as a similar tempo in an object's motion and sound, that unite information across different modalities.

The Gibsons use the word *differentiation* (meaning analyze or break down) to describe their theory because over time, the baby makes finer and finer distinctions among stimuli. In addition to pattern perception, differentiation applies to depth and object perception. Recall how in each, sensitivity to motion precedes awareness of detailed cues. So one way of understanding perceptual development is to think of it as a built-in tendency to search for order and stability in the surrounding world, a capacity that becomes increasingly fine-tuned with age (Gibson, 1970; Gibson, 1979).

Acting on the environment plays a major role in perceptual differentiation. Think back to the links between motor milestones and perceptual development discussed in this chapter. According to the Gibsons, infants and toddlers constantly look for ways in which the environment *affords* opportunities for action (Gibson, 1988). As adults, we know when we can execute particular actions—when an object can be touched or a surface is appropriate for sitting or walking. Infants and toddlers build these associations as they act on their world. For example, when they move from crawling to walking, toddlers first realize that a steeply sloping surface *affords the possibility of falling,* since they hesitate to go down it (see Figure 5.20). Experience in trying to remain upright but frequently tumbling over on various surfaces seems to make new walkers more aware of the consequences of their actions in different situations. As a result, they perceive surfaces in new ways and act more competently when confronted with them (Adolph, 1997; Adolph, Eppler, & Gibson, 1993). Can you think of other links between motor milestones and perceptual development described in this chapter?

At this point, it is only fair to note that some researchers believe that babies do not just make sense of experience by searching for invariant features. Instead, they impose *meaning* on what they perceive, constructing categories of objects and events in the surrounding environment. We have already seen the glimmerings of this cognitive point of view in some of the evidence reviewed in this chapter. For example, older babies *interpret* a familiar face as a source of pleasure and affection and a pattern of blinking lights as a moving human being. We will save our discussion of infant cognition for the next chapter, acknowledging for now that the cognitive perspective also has merit in understanding the achievements of infancy. In fact, many researchers combine these two positions, regarding infant development as proceeding from a perceptual to a cognitive emphasis over the first year of life (Haith & Benson, 1998; Mandler, 1998).

Summary

BODY GROWTH

Describe major changes in body size, proportions, muscle–fat makeup, and skeletal growth over the first 2 years.

■ Changes in height and weight are rapid during the first 2 years. Physical growth of parts of the body follows **cephalocaudal** and **proximodistal trends.** Body fat is laid down quickly during the first 9 months, whereas muscle development is slow and gradual.

■ **Skeletal age,** a measure based on the number of **epiphyses** and the extent to which they are fused, is the best way to estimate the child's overall physical maturity. At birth, infants have six **fontanels,** which permit the skull bones to expand as the brain grows. The first tooth emerges around 4 to 6 months of age.

BRAIN DEVELOPMENT

Describe brain development during infancy and toddlerhood, at the level of individual brain cells and at the level of the cerebral cortex.

■ Early in development the brain grows faster than any other organ of the body. During infancy, **neurons** form **synapses,** or complex communication networks, at a rapid rate. Stimulation determines which neurons will survive and which will die off. **Glial cells,** which are responsible for **myelinization,** multiply dramatically through the second year and result in large gains in brain size.

■ Changes in electrical activity of the cortex, along with gains in brain weight and skull size, indicate that brain growth spurts occur intermittently from infancy through adolescence. These may be sensitive periods in brain development.

■ The development of different regions of the **cerebral cortex** corresponds to the order in which various capacities emerge in the infant and child. **Lateralization** refers to specialization of the hemispheres of the cortex. During the first few years, before many regions have taken on specialized roles, there is high **brain plasticity.** However, some brain specialization already exists at birth.

FACTORS AFFECTING EARLY PHYSICAL GROWTH

Cite evidence indicating that heredity, nutrition, and affection and stimulation contribute to early physical growth.

■ Physical growth results from a continuous and complex interplay between heredity and environment. Twin and adoption studies reveal that heredity contributes to body size and rate of physical maturation.

■ Breast milk is ideally suited to the growth needs of young babies and offers protection against disease. Breast-feeding prevents malnutrition and infant death in poverty-stricken areas of the world. Breast-fed and bottle-fed babies do not differ in psychological development.

■ Although overweight and obesity are widespread problems in industrialized nations, chubby babies are not at risk for becoming overweight adults. Providing nutritious food and encouraging good eating habits and physical exercise guard against excess fat.

■ **Marasmus** and **kwashiorkor** are dietary diseases caused by malnutrition that affect many children in developing countries. If allowed to continue, body growth and brain development can be permanently stunted. **Nonorganic failure to thrive** illustrates the importance of affection and stimulation for normal physical growth.

CHANGING STATES OF AROUSAL

How does the organization of sleep and wakefulness change over the first 2 years?

■ During infancy, short periods of sleep and wakefulness are put together and coincide with a night and day schedule. Changing arousal patterns are affected by brain development, but the social environment also plays a role. Infants in Western nations sleep through the night much earlier than do babies throughout most of the world.

MOTOR DEVELOPMENT DURING THE FIRST TWO YEARS

Describe the general course of motor development during the first 2 years, along with factors that influence it.

■ Like physical development, motor development follows the cephalocaudal and proximodistal trends. According to **dynamic systems theory of motor development,** new motor skills are a matter of combining existing skills into increasingly complex systems of action. Each new skill develops as a joint product of central nervous system maturation, movement possibilities of the body, environmental supports for the skill, and the child's motivation to accomplish a task.

■ Experience profoundly affects motor development, as shown by research on infants raised in deprived institutions. Stimulation of infant motor skills accounts for cross-cultural differences in motor development.

■ During the first year, infants gradually perfect their reaching and grasping. The poorly coordinated **prereaching** of the newborn period eventually drops out. Once voluntary reaching appears, the clumsy **ulnar grasp** is gradually transformed into a refined **pincer grasp.**

■ Young children are not physically and psychologically ready for toilet training until the end of the second or beginning of the third year of life.

Summary (continued)

LEARNING CAPACITIES

Describe infant learning capacities, the conditions under which they occur, and the unique value of each.

■ Infants can be **classically conditioned** when the pairing of an **unconditioned stimulus (UCS)** and **conditioned stimulus (CS)** has survival value. Young babies are easily conditioned in the feeding situation. Classical conditioning of fear is difficult before 8 to 12 months.

■ **Operant conditioning** of infants has been demonstrated in many studies. In addition to food, interesting sights and sounds serve as effective **reinforcers** by increasing the occurrence of a response. **Punishment** involves removing a desirable stimulus or presenting an unpleasant one to decrease the occurrence of a response.

■ **Habituation** and **dishabituation** reveal that at birth, babies are attracted to novelty. Newborn infants also have a primitive ability to **imitate** the facial expressions and gestures of adults, a capacity that may promote social understanding and the early parent–infant relationship.

PERCEPTUAL DEVELOPMENT

What changes in perception of speech sounds, depth and pattern perception, and intermodal perception take place during infancy?

■ Over the first year, infants organize sounds into more complex patterns. They also become more sensitive to the speech sounds and clause, phrase, and word units of their own language.

■ Rapid development of the eye and visual centers in the brain supports the development of focusing, color discrimination, and visual acuity during the first half-year. The ability to track a moving object also improves.

■ Research on depth perception reveals that responsiveness to motion develops first, followed by sensitivity to binocular and then pictorial cues. Experience in moving about independently promotes babies' three-dimensional understanding, including avoidance of edges and drop-offs (such as the deep side of the visual cliff) and memory for object locations.

■ **Contrast sensitivity** accounts for babies' early pattern preferences. At first, infants look at the border of a stimulus and at single features. Around 2 months of age, they explore the internal features of a pattern and start to detect pattern organization. Over time, they discriminate increasingly complex and meaningful patterns. Perception of the human face follows the same sequence of development as sensitivity to other patterned stimuli.

■ At birth, **size** and **shape constancy** assist babies in building a coherent world of objects. At first, infants depend on motion and spatial arrangement to identify objects. After 6 months of age, they rely on other features that signal an object's boundaries, such as distinct shape, color, and texture.

■ Infants have a remarkable, built-in capacity to engage in **intermodal perception.** They quickly combine information across sensory modalities, often after just one exposure to a new situation.

UNDERSTANDING PERCEPTUAL DEVELOPMENT

Explain differentiation theory of perceptual development.

■ The Gibsons' **differentiation theory** is a widely accepted account of perceptual development. Over time, infants detect increasingly fine-grained, **invariant features** in a constantly changing perceptual world. Acting on the world plays a major role in perceptual differentiation.

Important terms and concepts

brain plasticity (p. 174)
cephalocaudal trend (p. 169)
cerebral cortex (p. 172)
classical conditioning (p. 191)
conditioned response (CR) (p. 191)
conditioned stimulus (CS) (p. 191)
contrast sensitivity (p. 201)
differentiation theory (p. 204)
dishabituation (p. 193)
dynamic systems theory of motor
    development (p. 185)
epiphyses (p. 170)
extinction (p. 191)
fontanels (p. 171)

glial cells (p. 172)
habituation (p. 193)
imitation (p. 195)
intermodal perception (p. 204)
invariant features (p. 204)
kwashiorkor (p. 178)
lateralization (p. 174)
marasmus (p. 178)
myelinization (p. 172)
neurons (p. 172)
nonorganic failure to thrive (p. 180)
operant conditioning (p. 192)
pincer grasp (p. 188)
prereaching (p. 188)

proximodistal trend (p. 169)
punishment (p. 192)
reinforcer (p. 192)
shape constancy (p. 204)
size constancy (p. 203)
skeletal age (p. 170)
sudden infant death syndrome
    (SIDS) (p. 195)
synapses (p. 172)
ulnar grasp (p. 188)
unconditioned response (UCR)
    (p. 191)
unconditioned stimulus (UCS)
    (p. 191)

FYI... FOR FURTHER INFORMATION AND HELP

PHYSICAL GROWTH AND HEALTH

Healthy Mothers, Healthy Babies
(202) 863-2458
Website: www.hmhb.org

A coalition of national and state organizations concerned with maternal and child health. Serves as a network through which information on nutrition, injury prevention, and infant mortality is shared.

United Nations Children's Fund
(UNICEF)
(212) 326-7000
Website: www.unicef.org

International organization dedicated to addressing the problems of children around the world. Develops and implements health and nutrition programs, campaigns to have children vaccinated against disease, and coordinates delivery of food and other aid to disaster-stricken areas.

World Health Organization (WHO)
(212) 791-2111
Website: www.unicef.org

International health agency of the United Nations that seeks to obtain the highest level of health care for all people. Promotes prevention and treatment of disease and strives to eliminate poverty. Places special emphasis on the health needs of developing countries.

BREAST-FEEDING

La Leche League International
(708) 455-7730
Website: www.lalecheleague.org

Provides information and support to breast-feeding mothers. Local chapters exist in many cities.

MALNUTRITION

Food Research and Action Center
(202) 986-2200
Website: www.iglou.com/why/resource/
1100.htm

Provides assistance to community organizations trying to make federal food programs more responsive to the needs of millions of hungry Americans. Seeks to enhance public awareness of the problems of hunger and poverty in the United States.

SUDDEN INFANT DEATH SYNDROME (SIDS)

National Sudden Infant Death Syndrome Foundation
(410) 964-8000
Website: www.sidsnetwork.org

Provides assistance to parents who have lost a child to SIDS. Works with families and health professionals in caring for infants at risk due to heart and respiratory problems.

"Happy Spring"
Soledad Urán
11 years, Argentina

Wide-eyed with amazement, a newly walking toddler watches as his older sister plays with the family puppy. In Chapter 6, you will see that a stimulating environment combined with the guidance of more mature members of their culture ensures that young children's cognition will develop at its best.

COGNITIVE DEVELOPMENT IN INFANCY AND TODDLERHOOD

When Byron, Rachel, and April were brought together by their mothers at age 18 months, the room was alive with activity. The three spirited explorers were bent on discovery. Rachel dropped shapes through holes in a plastic box that Beth held and adjusted so the harder ones would fall smoothly into the container. Once a few shapes were inside, Rachel grabbed and shook the box, squealing with delight as the lid fell open and the shapes scattered around her. The clatter attracted Byron, who picked up a shape, carried it to the railing at the top of the basement steps, and dropped it overboard, then followed with a teddy bear, a ball, his shoe, and a spoon. In the meantime, April pulled open a drawer, unloaded a set of wooden bowls, stacked them in a pile, knocked it over, then banged two bowls together like cymbals. With each action, the children seemed to be asking, "What's out here in this world? Which behavior leads to which consequence? What events can I control?"

As the toddlers experimented, I could see the beginnings of language—a whole new way of influencing the world. April was the most vocal of the three youngsters. "All gone baw!" she exclaimed as Byron tossed the bright red ball down the basement steps. "Bye-bye, baw," Rachel chimed in, waving as the ball disappeared from sight. A close look at Rachel revealed that the capacity to represent experience through words and gestures had opened up a new realm of play possibilities. Rachel could pretend. "Night-night," she said as she put her head down and closed her eyes, ever so pleased that in make-believe, she could decide for herself when and where to go to bed.

Over the first 2 years, the small, reflexive newborn baby becomes a self-assertive, purposeful being who solves simple problems and has started to master the most amazing of human abilities—language. "How does all this happen so quickly?" asked Felicia, turning to me. In this chapter, we take up three perspectives on early cognitive development: Piaget's *cognitive-developmental theory, information processing*, and Vygotsky's *sociocultural theory*. We will also consider the usefulness of tests that measure intellectual progress during this earliest phase of development.

Our discussion concludes with the beginnings of language. We will see how toddlers' first words build on early cognitive achievements. But very soon, new words and expressions greatly increase the speed and flexibility of human thinking. Throughout development, cognition and language mutually support one another.

PIAGET'S COGNITIVE-DEVELOPMENTAL THEORY

The Swiss theorist Jean Piaget is the twentieth-century giant of cognitive development. His work led researchers all over the world to view children as busy, motivated explorers whose thinking develops as they act directly on the environment. Influenced by his background in biology, he believed that the child's mind forms and modifies psychological structures to achieve a better adaptive fit with external reality. In the following sections, we will first describe development as Piaget saw it. Then we will consider evidence indicating that the cognition of young infants is more advanced than Piaget imagined it to be.

KEY PIAGETIAN CONCEPTS

According to Piaget, between infancy and adolescence, children move through four stages of development. As the name **sensorimotor stage** implies, Piaget believed that infants and toddlers "think" with their eyes, ears, hands, and other sensorimotor equipment. They cannot yet carry out many activities inside their heads. But by the end of toddlerhood, children can solve practical, everyday problems and represent their experiences in speech, gesture, and play. To understand Piaget's view of how these vast changes take place, let's look at Piaget's ideas about *what changes with development*, and *how cognitive change takes place*.

■ **WHAT CHANGES WITH DEVELOPMENT.** Piaget believed that *psychological structures*—the child's organized ways of making sense of experience—change with age. He referred to specific structures as **schemes**. At first, schemes are motor action patterns. For example, at age 6 months, Byron dropped objects in a fairly rigid way, simply by letting go of a rattle or teething ring and watching with interest. By age 18 months, his "dropping scheme" had become much more deliberate and creative. Byron tossed all sorts of objects down the basement stairs, throwing some up in the air, bouncing others off walls, releasing some gently and others forcefully. Soon Byron's schemes will move from an *action-based level* to a *mental level*. Instead of just acting on objects, he will show evidence of thinking before he acts. This change, as we will see later, marks the transition from sensorimotor to preoperational thought.

Behaviors that create work for caregivers can be important learning experiences for infants and toddlers. This 14-month-old experiments with his "pouring scheme." As milk drips out of his overturned bottle, he looks with interest, and his sensorimotor understanding of the world expands. (Laura Dwight)

sensorimotor stage
Piaget's first stage, during which infants and toddlers "think" with their eyes, ears, hands, and other sensorimotor equipment. Spans the first 2 years of life.

scheme
In Piaget's theory, a specific structure, or organized way of making sense of experience, that changes with age.

■ **HOW COGNITIVE CHANGE TAKES PLACE.** In Piaget's theory, two processes account for changes in schemes: *adaptation* and *organization*.

Adaptation.   The next time you have a chance, notice how infants and toddlers tirelessly repeat actions that lead to interesting effects. **Adaptation** involves building schemes through direct interaction with the environment. It consists of two complementary activities: *assimilation* and *accommodation*. During **assimilation,** we use our current schemes to interpret the external world. For example, when Byron dropped objects, he was assimilating them all into his sensorimotor dropping scheme. In **accommodation,** we create new schemes or adjust old ones after noticing that our current ways of thinking do not fit the environment completely. When Byron dropped objects in different ways, he modified his dropping scheme to take account of the varied properties of objects.

According to Piaget, the balance between assimilation and accommodation varies over time. When children are not changing very much, they assimilate more than they accommodate. Piaget called this a state of cognitive *equilibrium,* implying a steady, comfortable condition. During times of rapid cognitive change, however, children are in a state of *disequilibrium,* or cognitive discomfort. They realize that new information does not match their current schemes, so they shift away from assimilation toward accommodation. Once they have modified their schemes, they move back toward assimilation, exercising their newly changed structures until they are ready to be modified again.

Each time this back-and-forth movement between equilibrium and disequilibrium occurs, more effective schemes are produced. They take in a wider range of aspects of the environment, and there is less and less to throw them out of balance (Piaget, 1985). Because the times of greatest accommodation are the earliest ones, the sensorimotor stage is Piaget's most complex period of development.

Organization.   Schemes change through a second process called **organization.** It takes place internally, apart from direct contact with the environment. Once children form new structures, they start to rearrange them, linking them with other schemes to create a strongly interconnected cognitive system. For example, eventually Byron will relate "dropping" to "throwing" and to his developing understanding of "nearness" and "farness." According to Piaget, schemes reach a true state of equilibrium when they become part of a broad network of structures that can be jointly applied to the surrounding world (Piaget, 1936/1952).

THE SENSORIMOTOR STAGE

The difference between the newborn baby and the 2-year-old child is so vast that the sensorimotor stage is divided into six substages. Piaget's observations of his own three children served as the basis for this sequence of development. Although this is a very small sample, Piaget watched carefully and also presented his son and two daughters with everyday problems (such as hidden objects) that helped reveal their understanding of the world. In the following sections, we will first describe infant development as Piaget saw it. Then we will consider evidence that the cognitive competence of babies is more advanced than Piaget believed it to be.

■ **THE CIRCULAR REACTION.** At the beginning of the sensorimotor stage, infants know so little about their world that they cannot purposefully explore it. The **circular reaction** provides them with a special means of adapting their first schemes. It involves stumbling onto a new experience caused by the baby's own motor activity. The reaction is "circular" because the infant tries to repeat the event again and again. As a result, a sensorimotor response that first occurred by chance becomes strengthened into a new scheme. Consider Rachel, who at age 2 months accidentally made a smacking sound after a feeding. The sound was new and intriguing, so Rachel tried to repeat it until, after a few days, she became quite expert at smacking her lips.

adaptation
In Piaget's theory, the process of building schemes through direct interaction with the environment. Made up of two complementary processes: assimilation and accommodation.

assimilation
That part of adaptation in which the external world is interpreted in terms of current schemes.

accommodation
That part of adaptation in which new schemes are created and old ones adjusted to produce a better fit with the environment.

organization
In Piaget's theory, the internal rearrangement and linking together of schemes so that they form a strongly interconnected cognitive system.

circular reaction
In Piaget's theory, a means of building schemes in which infants try to repeat a chance event caused by their own motor activity.

TABLE 6.1

Summary of Cognitive Development During the Sensorimotor Stage

SENSORIMOTOR SUBSTAGE	TYPICAL ADAPTIVE BEHAVIORS
1. Reflexive schemes (birth to 1 month)	Newborn reflexes (see Chapter 4, page 151)
2. Primary circular reactions (1–4 months)	Simple motor habits centered around the infant's own body; limited anticipation of events
3. Secondary circular reactions (4–8 months)	Actions aimed at repeating interesting effects in the surrounding world; imitation of familiar behaviors
4. Coordination of secondary circular reactions (8–12 months)	Intentional, or goal-directed action sequences; improved anticipation of events; imitation of behaviors slightly different from those the infant usually performs; ability to find a hidden object in the first location in which it is hidden (object permanence).
5. Tertiary circular reactions (12–18 months)	Exploration of the properties of objects by acting on them in novel ways; imitation of unfamiliar behaviors; ability to search in several locations for a hidden object (AB search)
6. Mental combinations (18 months–2 years)	Internal representation of objects and events, as indicated by sudden solutions to sensorimotor problems, ability to find an object that has been moved while out of sight, deferred imitation, and make-believe play

During the first 2 years, the circular reaction changes in several ways. At first, it centers around the infant's own body. Later, it turns outward, toward manipulation of objects. Finally, it becomes experimental and creative, aimed at producing novel effects in the environment. Piaget considered these revisions in the circular reaction so important that he named the sensorimotor substages after them. As you read about each substage, you may find it helpful to refer to the summary in Table 6.1.

■ **SUBSTAGE 1: REFLEXIVE SCHEMES (BIRTH TO 1 MONTH).** Piaget regarded newborn reflexes as the building blocks of sensorimotor intelligence. At first, babies suck, grasp, and look in much the same way, no matter what experiences they encounter (see Figure 6.1). Beth reported an amusing example of Rachel's indiscriminate sucking at 2 weeks of age. She lay on the bed next to her father while he took a nap. Suddenly, he awoke with a start. Rachel had latched on and begun to suck on his back!

■ **SUBSTAGE 2: PRIMARY CIRCULAR REACTIONS—THE FIRST LEARNED ADAPTATIONS (1 TO 4 MONTHS).** Infants start to gain voluntary control over their actions by repeating chance behaviors that lead to satisfying results. Consequently, they develop some simple motor habits, such as sucking their fists or thumbs and opening and closing their hands (see Figure 6.2). Babies of this substage also begin to vary their behavior in response to environmental demands. For example, they open their mouths differently for a nipple than for a spoon. Young infants also begin to anticipate events. At age 3 months, when Byron awoke from his nap, he cried out with hunger. But as soon as Lisa entered the room and moved toward his crib, Byron's crying stopped. He knew that feeding time was near.

Piaget called the first circular reactions *primary,* and he regarded them as quite limited. Notice how, in the examples just given, infants' adaptations are oriented toward their own bodies and motivated by basic needs. According to Piaget, babies of this age are not yet very concerned with the effects of their actions on the external world.

Piaget believed that first efforts at imitation appear during this substage, but they are limited to copying someone else's imitation of the baby's actions. However, recall from Chapter 5 that newborns can imitate, so imitation seems to be an area in which Piaget misjudged the young baby's competence.

FIGURE 6.1

The newborn baby's schemes consist of reflexes, which will gradually be modified as they are applied to the surrounding environment.

■ **SUBSTAGE 3: SECONDARY CIRCULAR REACTIONS—MAKING INTERESTING SIGHTS LAST (4 TO 8 MONTHS).** Between 4 and 8 months, infants sit up and become skilled at reaching for, grasping, and manipulating objects. These motor achievements play a major role in turning their attention outward toward the environment. Using the *secondary* circular reaction, they try to repeat interesting effects in the surrounding world that are caused by their own actions. In the following illustration, Piaget dangles several dolls in front of his 4-month-old son, Laurent. After accidentally knocking them and producing a fascinating swinging motion, Laurent gradually builds the sensorimotor scheme of "hitting" (see Figure 6.3):

> At 4 months 15 days, with another doll hung in front of him, Laurent tries to grasp it, then shakes himself to make it swing, knocks it accidentally, and then tries simply to hit it. . . . At 4 months 18 days, Laurent hits my hands without trying to grasp them, but he started by simply waving his arms around, and only afterwards went on to hit my hands. The next day, finally, Laurent immediately hits a doll hung in front of him. (Piaget, 1936/1952, pp. 167–168)

FIGURE 6.2

At 2 months, Byron sees his hand open and close and tries to repeat this action, in a primary circular reaction.

Improved control over their own behavior permits infants of this substage to imitate the behavior of others more effectively. However, they cannot adapt flexibly and quickly enough to imitate very novel behaviors (Kaye & Marcus, 1981). Therefore, although 4- to 8-month-olds enjoy watching an adult demonstrate a game of pat-a-cake or peekaboo, they are not yet able to participate.

■ **SUBSTAGE 4: COORDINATION OF SECONDARY CIRCULAR REACTIONS (8 TO 12 MONTHS).** Now infants start to organize schemes. They combine secondary circular reactions into new, more complex action sequences. As a result, two landmark cognitive changes take place.

First, babies can engage in **intentional,** or **goal-directed, behavior.** Before this substage, actions that led to new schemes had a random, hit-or-miss quality to them—*accidentally* bringing the thumb to mouth or *happening* to hit the doll. But by 8 months, infants have had enough practice with a variety of schemes that they coordinate them deliberately to solve sensorimotor problems. The clearest example is provided by Piaget's object-hiding tasks, in which he shows the baby an attractive toy and then hides it behind his hand or under a cover. Infants of this substage can find the object. In doing so, they coordinate two schemes—"pushing" aside the obstacle and "grasping" the toy. Piaget regarded these *means–end action sequences* as the first sign that babies appreciate **physical causality** (the causal action one object exerts on another through contact) and as the foundation for all later problem solving.

FIGURE 6.3

At 4 months, Piaget's son Laurent accidentally hits a doll hung in front of him. He tries to recapture the interesting effect of the swinging doll. In doing so, he builds a new "hitting scheme" through the secondary circular reaction.

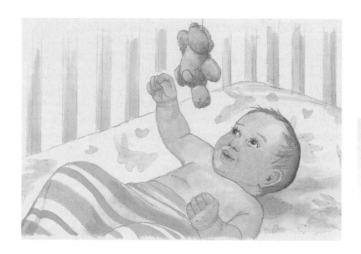

intentional, or **goal-directed, behavior**
A sequence of actions in which schemes are deliberately combined to solve a problem.

physical causality
The causal action one object exerts on another through contact.

FIGURE 6.4

Around 8 months, infants combine schemes deliberately in the solution of sensorimotor problems. They show the beginnings of object permanence, since they can find an object in the first place in which it is hidden.

FIGURE 6.5

At 18 months, Byron dropped a variety of objects down the basement stairs, throwing some up in the air, bouncing others off the wall, releasing some gently and others forcefully, in a deliberately experimental approach. Byron displayed a tertiary circular reaction.

The fact that infants can retrieve hidden objects reveals that they have begun to attain a second cognitive milestone: **object permanence,** the understanding that objects continue to exist when they are out of sight (see Figure 6.4). But awareness of object permanence is not yet complete. If an object is moved from one hiding place (A) to another (B), babies will search for it only in the first hiding place (A). Because 8- to 12-month-olds make this **AB search error,** Piaget concluded that they do not have a clear image of the object as persisting when hidden from view.

Substage 4 brings additional advances. First, infants are better at anticipating events, so they sometimes use their new capacity for intentional behavior to try to change those events. At 10 months, Byron crawled after Lisa when she put on her coat, whimpering to keep her from leaving. Second, babies can imitate behaviors slightly different from those they usually perform. After watching someone else, they try to stir with a spoon, push a toy car, or drop raisins in a cup. Once again, they draw on their capacity for intentional behavior, purposefully modifying schemes to fit an observed action (Piaget, 1945/1951).

■ **SUBSTAGE 5: TERTIARY CIRCULAR REACTIONS—DISCOVERING NEW MEANS THROUGH ACTIVE EXPERIMENTATION (12 TO 18 MONTHS).** At this substage, the circular reaction—now called *tertiary*—becomes experimental and creative. Toddlers repeat behaviors *with variation,* provoking new effects. Recall how Byron dropped objects over the basement steps, trying this, then that, and then another action (see Figure 6.5). Because they approach the world in this deliberately exploratory way, 12- to 18-month-olds are far better sensorimotor problem solvers than they were before. For example, Rachel figured out how to fit a shape through a hole in a container by turning and twisting it until it fell through, and she discovered how to use a stick to get toys that were out of reach.

According to Piaget, this new capacity to experiment leads to a more advanced understanding of object permanence. Toddlers look in not just one, but several locations to find a hidden toy; they no longer make the AB search error. Their more flexible action patterns also permit them to imitate many more behaviors, such as stacking blocks, scribbling on paper, and making funny faces.

■ **SUBSTAGE 6: MENTAL REPRESENTATION—INVENTING NEW MEANS THROUGH MENTAL COMBINATIONS (18 MONTHS TO 2 YEARS).** Substage 5 is the last truly *sensorimotor* stage, since Substage 6 brings with it the ability to create **mental representations** of reality—internal images of absent objects and past events. As a result, the older toddler can solve problems symbolically instead of by trial-and-error behavior. One sign of this new capacity is that children arrive at solutions to sensorimotor problems suddenly, suggesting that they experiment with actions inside their heads. For example, at 19 months, April received a new push toy. As she played with it for the first time, she rolled it over the carpet and ran into the sofa. She paused for a moment, as if to "think," and then immediately turned the toy in a new direction. Had she been in Substage 5, she would have pushed, pulled, and bumped it in a random fashion until it was free to move again.

With the capacity to represent, toddlers arrive at a more advanced understanding of object permanence—that objects can move or be moved when out of sight. Try the following object-hiding task with an 18- to 24-month-old as well as a younger child: Put a small toy inside a box and the box under a cover. Then, while the box is out of sight, dump the toy out and show the toddler the empty box. The Substage 6 child finds the hidden toy easily. Younger toddlers are baffled by this situation.

Mental representation also brings with it the capacity for **deferred imitation**—the ability to remember and copy the behavior of models who are not immediately present. A famous and amusing example is Piaget's daughter Jacqueline's imitation of another child's temper tantrum:

> Jacqueline had a visit from a little boy . . . who, in the course of the afternoon, got into a terrible temper. He screamed as he tried to get out of a playpen and pushed it backwards, stamping his feet. Jacqueline stood watching him in amazement . . . . The next day, she herself screamed in her playpen and tried to move it, stamping her foot lightly several times in succession. (Piaget, 1936/1952, p. 63)

Finally, the sixth substage leads to a major change in the nature of play. Throughout the first year and a half, infants and toddlers engage in **functional play**—pleasurable motor activity with or without objects through which they practice sensorimotor schemes. At the end of the second year, children's growing capacity to represent experience permits them to engage in **make-believe play,** or pretend, in which they act out everyday and imaginary activities. Like Rachel's pretending to go to sleep at the beginning of this chapter, the make-believe of the toddler is very simple (see Figure 6.6). However, make-believe expands greatly in early childhood, and it is so important for psychological development that we will return to it again.

FIGURE 6.6

When Rachel engaged in make-believe by pretending to go to sleep, she created a mental representation of reality. With the capacity for mental representation, the sensorimotor stage draws to a close.

RECENT RESEARCH ON SENSORIMOTOR DEVELOPMENT

Many researchers have tried to confirm Piaget's observations of sensorimotor development. Their findings show that infants display a wide array of cognitive capacities much sooner than Piaget believed. Think back to the challenge posed by studies of newborn imitation, mentioned in our discussion of Substage 2 (see page 214). You have already read about other conflicting evidence as well. Recall the operant conditioning research reviewed in Chapter 5, in which newborns sucked vigorously on a nipple to gain access to a variety of interesting sights and sounds. This behavior, which closely resembles Piaget's secondary circular reaction, shows that babies try to explore and control the external world long before 4 to 8 months. In fact, they do so as soon as they are born.

Piaget may have underestimated infant capacities because he did not have the sophisticated experimental techniques for studying early cognitive development that are available today. As we consider recent research on infants' reasoning about the physical world, we will see that operant conditioning and the habituation–dishabituation sequence have been used ingeniously to find out what the young baby knows.

■ **REASONING ABOUT THE PHYSICAL WORLD.** Piaget concluded that not until 8 to 12 months of age do infants appreciate important regularities of their physical world— that objects continue to exist when out of sight and influence one another in predictable ways. Yet as the following findings reveal, even very young babies are knowledgeable about object characteristics.

Object Permanence.   Before 8 months, do babies really believe that an object spirited out of sight no longer exists? In a series of studies in which babies did not have to engage in active search, Renée Baillargeon (1987; Baillargeon & DeVos, 1991) found evidence for object permanence as early as 3½ months of age! One investigation is described in Figure 6.7.

If 3½-month-olds grasp the idea of object permanence, then what explains Piaget's finding that much older infants (who are quite capable of voluntary reaching) do not try to search for hidden objects? One explanation is that, just as Piaget's theory suggests, they cannot yet put together the separate schemes—pushing aside the obstacle and grasping

object permanence
The understanding that objects continue to exist when they are out of sight.

AB search error
The error made by 8- to 12-month-olds after an object is moved from hiding place A to hiding place B. Infants in Piaget's Substage 4 search for it only in the first hiding place (A).

mental representation
An internal image of an absent object or a past event.

deferred imitation
The ability to remember and copy the behavior of models who are not immediately present.

functional play
A type of play involving pleasurable motor activity with or without objects. Enables infants and toddlers to practice sensorimotor schemes.

make-believe play
A type of play in which children pretend, acting out everyday and imaginary activities.

FIGURE 6.7

Testing infants for object permanence.
(a) First, infants were habituated to two events: a short carrot and a tall carrot moving behind a yellow screen, on alternate trials. Next the researchers presented two test events. The color of the screen was changed to help infants notice its window. (b) In the possible event, the carrot shorter than the window's lower edge moved behind the blue screen and reappeared on the other side. (c) In the *impossible event,* the carrot taller than the window's lower edge moved behind the screen, did not appear in the window, but then emerged intact on the other side. Infants as young as 3½ months dishabituated to (looked longer at) the impossible event, suggesting that they understood object permanence. *(Adapted from R. Baillargeon & J. DeVos, 1991, "Object Permanence in Young Infants: Further Evidence,"* Child Development, *62, p. 1230. © The Society for Research in Child Development. Reprinted by permission.)*

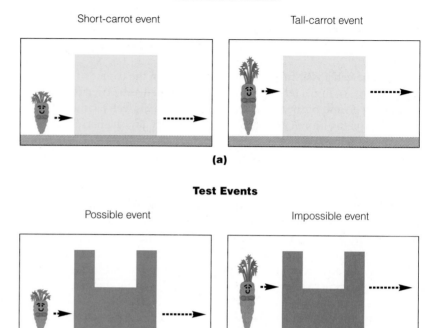

Habituation Events

Short-carrot event   Tall-carrot event

(a)

Test Events

Possible event   Impossible event

(b)   **(c)**

the object—necessary to retrieve a hidden toy. In other words, what they *know* about object permanence is not yet *evident* in their searching behavior (Baillargeon et al., 1990).

Searching for Objects Hidden in More Than One Location. Once 8- to 12-month-olds actively search for a hidden object, they make the AB search error. For some years, researchers thought that babies had trouble remembering an object's new location after it was hidden in more than one place. But recent findings reveal that poor memory cannot fully account for infants' unsuccessful performance, since between 5 and 12 months babies increasingly *look* at the correct location while *reaching* incorrectly (Hofstadter & Reznick, 1996).

Why don't infants reach for the right place when given an opportunity? Once again, before 12 months, infants seem to have difficulty translating what they know about an object moving from one place to another into a successful search strategy. This ability to integrate knowledge with action coincides with rapid development of the frontal lobes of the cortex at the end of the first year (Bell & Fox, 1992; Diamond, 1991; Nelson, 1995).

Other Aspects of Physical Reasoning. Habituation–dishabituation research reveals that young infants are aware of many object properties and the rules governing their behavior. For example, 3- to 4-month-olds are sensitive to object substance and physical limits on object motion. They realize that one solid object cannot move through another solid object and that an object much larger than an opening cannot pass through it (Spelke et al., 1992). Babies of this age are also sensitive to the effects of gravity. They look intently, as if surprised, when a moving object stops in midair without support (Sitskoorn & Smitsman, 1995).

In the next few months, infants apply these understandings to a wider range of circumstances. Read the description of the research depicted in Figure 6.8, and you will see that around the middle of the first year, babies realize that an object placed on top of another object will fall unless a large portion of its bottom surface contacts the lower object (Baillargeon, 1994a; Baillargeon, Needham, & DeVos, 1992).

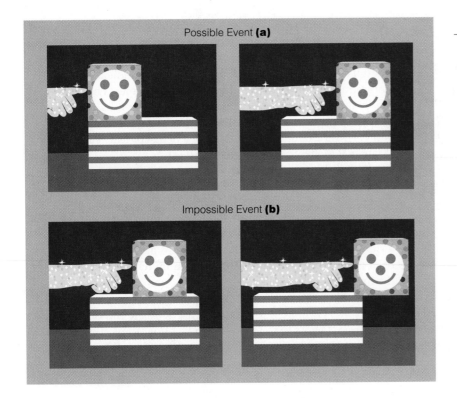

Possible Event **(a)**

Impossible Event **(b)**

FIGURE 6.8

Testing infants' understanding of object support. First, infants were habituated to an event in which a hand pushed an attractive box partway across a long platform (not shown). Next, the researchers presented two test events in which the hand pushed the box across a shorter platform. (a) In the *possible* event, the hand pushed the box until its leading edge reached the end of the platform, so it remained fully supported. (b) In the *impossible event*, the hand pushed the box until only 15 percent of its bottom surface remained on the platform. Results indicated that 5½-month-olds looked equally at the two test events. In contrast, 6½-month-olds dishabituated to the impossible event, suggesting that they expect the object to fall unless a large portion of its bottom surface lies on the platform. *(From R. Baillargeon, A. Needham, & J. DeVos, 1992, "The Development of Young Infants' Intuitions About Support,"* Early Development and Parenting, *1, p. 71. Reprinted by permission.)*

A beginning grasp of physical causality is also present very early, as dishabituation to other impossible events reveals. When a moving object (such as a rolling ball) collides with a stationary object, babies as young as 2½ months expect the stationary object to be displaced. By 5½ to 6½ months, they figure out that a larger moving object can cause the stationary object to travel farther (Baillargeon, 1994b). Gradually, infants extend their understanding of physical causality to more complex collision conditions. For example, after watching a blue ball disappear behind a screen and a red ball appear on the other side, 10-month-olds conclude that the first object must have launched the second while out of their sight (Oakes, 1994; Oakes & Cohen, 1995).

Clearly, infants have a rich appreciation of the regularities of their physical world. Basic understandings—that objects continue to exist when hidden from view, cannot move through the space occupied by other solid objects, fall without support, and move along continuous paths—are present long before 8 to 12 months, when infants can engage in the means–end action sequences of Piaget's Substage 4 (Haith & Benson, 1998). These notions are gradually refined over the first year.

■ **DEFERRED IMITATION.** In Piaget's theory, infants lead purely sensorimotor lives. They cannot represent experience until about 18 months of age. Yet new studies of deferred imitation reveal that the transition to mental representation takes place much earlier.

Andrew Meltzoff and Keith Moore (1994) brought 6-week-olds into the laboratory and deliberately tried to induce deferred imitation of facial expressions. Infants who watched an adult demonstrate mouth opening or tongue protrusion imitated the facial gesture when exposed to the same adult 24 hours later. These findings show that deferred imitation, a form of representation, is present by the second month of life. Perhaps young babies use it as a way to identify and communicate with persons they have seen before.

As motor capacities improve, infants start to copy adults' actions on objects. In one study, Meltzoff (1988) showed 9-month-olds how to manipulate three novel toys—an L-shaped piece of wood that could be bent, a box with a button that could be pushed, and a

Pots, pans, and other kitchen utensils are fascinating toys during infancy and toddlerhood. This 9-month-old is anxious to try his grandfather's novel action. If given the spoon and colander a day later, he is likely to repeat the banging gesture. Already he can engage in deferred imitation. *(Laura Dwight)*

plastic egg filled with metal nuts that could be shaken. When tested after a 24-hour delay, infants who saw these actions were far more likely to reproduce them than were babies exposed to the objects but not shown how they work. By 14 months, toddlers use deferred imitation skillfully to enrich their range of schemes. They retain highly unusual modeled behaviors for several months, copy the actions of peers as well as adults, and imitate across a change in context—for example, enact at home a behavior learned at day care (Hanna & Meltzoff, 1993; Meltzoff, 1994).

Around 18 months, toddlers imitate not only an adult's behavior, but the actions he or she *tries* to produce, even if these actions are not fully realized (Meltzoff, 1995). On one occasion, Lisa attempted to pour some raisins into a small paper bag but missed, spilling them onto the counter. A moment later, Byron climbed on a stool and began dropping the raisins into the bag. By age 2, children mimic entire social roles, such as mommy, daddy, or baby, during make-believe play.

In sum, deferred imitation does not conclude sensorimotor development, as Piaget believed. Nevertheless, it becomes far more flexible and complex by the end of toddlerhood, moving beyond specific behaviors to mimicking people's intentions and perspectives. This advance permits young children to better understand and predict others' behaviors.

EVALUATION OF THE SENSORIMOTOR STAGE

Table 6.2 summarizes the remarkable cognitive attainments we have just considered. Compare this table with the description of Piaget's sensorimotor substages on page 214. You will see that on the one hand, infants anticipate events, actively search for hidden objects, flexibly vary their sensorimotor schemes, and engage in make-believe play within Piaget's time frame. Yet on the other hand, many other capacities—including secondary circular reactions, understanding of object permanence and physical causality, and deferred imitation—emerge much earlier than Piaget expected.

Notice, also, that the cognitive attainments of infancy do not develop in the neat, stepwise fashion predicted by Piaget's substages. Consider deferred imitation, which requires that infants *remember a past event*. It is not as difficult a skill as finding an object that has been moved while out of sight. To do this, infants must *imagine an event they have not seen* (Rast & Meltzoff, 1995). Yet Piaget assumed that both representational capacities emerge at the same time, in Substage 6! Findings like these are among a rapidly accumulating body of evidence that questions Piaget's stagewise view of development.

Disagreements between Piaget's observations and those of recent research raise controversial questions about how early cognitive development takes place. Consistent with Piaget's ideas, motor development facilitates the construction of some types of knowledge. For example, in Chapter 5, we noted that crawling babies are better than noncrawling peers at perceiving depth on the visual cliff and finding hidden objects. Yet we have also seen that infants comprehend a great deal before they are capable of the motor behaviors Piaget assumed led to those understandings. How can we account for babies' amazing cognitive accomplishments? At present, there are many speculations. Let's explore three prominent ideas.

■ **A PERCEPTUAL VIEW.** Some researchers believe that important schemes develop through perceptual means—by looking and listening—rather than just through acting on the world. At the same time, they preserve Piaget's belief that the baby *constructs* new understandings.

Renée Baillargeon (1994b, 1995) argues that infants come to understand their physical world by first making all-or-none distinctions, which they add to as they are exposed to

TABLE 6.2

Some Cognitive Attainments of Infancy

AGE	TYPICAL ADAPTIVE BEHAVIORS	PHYSICAL REASONING	IMITATION
Birth–1 month	Newborn reflexes Exploration using limited motor skills, such as head turning and sucking	Size and shape constancy (see Chapter 5)	Imitation of adult facial expressions and gestures (see Chapter 4)
1–4 months	Exploration using more advanced motor skills, such as kicking, reaching, and grasping Limited anticipation of events	Awareness of object permanence Awareness of object solidity and certain effects of gravity and object collision (physical causality) Use of motion and spatial layout to identify objects as separate units (see Chapter 5)	Deferred imitation of adult facial expressions
4–8 months	Exploration using improved reaching and grasping, swiping, banging, and throwing	Improved understanding of the effects of gravity and object collision (physical causality) Use of shape, texture, and color to identify objects as separate units (see Chapter 5)	Imitation of adults' actions on objects, but limited to behaviors the infant has practiced many times
8–12 months	Intentional, or goal-directed, behavior Improved anticipation of events	Ability to retrieve an object from the first location in which it is hidden Understanding of more complex object collision conditions	Imitation of behaviors slightly different from ones the infant usually performs Deferred imitation of adults' actions on objects over a short time interval (24 hours)
12–18 months	Exploration of objects by acting on them in novel ways Trial-and-error solutions to sensorimotor problems	Ability to search in several locations for a hidden object (AB search)	Imitation of adults' and peers' novel behaviors Deferred imitation of behaviors over longer time intervals (up to 1 week) Deferred imitation across a change in context (for example, from day care to home)
18 months–2 years	Sudden solutions to sensorimotor problems, suggesting internal representation Beginnings of make-believe play	Ability to find an object that has been moved while out of sight	Imitation of actions an adult tries to produce, even if these are not fully realized Imitation of entire social roles in make-believe play

relevant information. At 3 months, April realized that an object will fall when released in midair and stop falling when it contacts a surface because she had seen adults drop toys in baskets and clothes in hampers many times. But not until the middle of the first year, when she could sit independently and put objects on surfaces herself, did she have a chance to observe that an object will fall unless much of its bottom surface is supported.

According to Lisa Oakes and Leslie Cohen (1995), an appreciation of physical causality develops similarly. As object perception improves (see Chapter 5) and infants have many opportunities to watch objects contacting one another, they detect the rules of object collision.

■ **A NATIVIST VIEW.** Other researchers take a *nativist* (meaning inborn) view. They are convinced that infants' remarkable cognitive skills are based on innate knowledge. Development is a matter of these built-in, core understandings becoming more elaborate as they come in contact with new information.

Elizabeth Spelke (1994) believes that infants know at birth that objects move on continuous paths, do not change shape or pass through one another as they move, and cannot act on one another until they come into contact. Later-emerging schemes are direct extensions of these innate structures, which channel infants' attention to relevant features of the environment. This gets their physical reasoning "off the ground" quickly (Spelke & Newport, 1998).

A growing number of researchers believe that innate knowledge also guides other aspects of development—for example, mastery of number concepts, language, and social understanding. They assume that development is uneven because each type of knowledge has its own *module,* or genetically prewired neural system in the brain, and timetable of maturation. Consequently, this perspective has been called the **modular view of the mind**.

Think about this alternative to Piaget's theory. Since so much is laid down in advance, the child is a far less active participant in constructing schemes than Piaget assumed. Critics complain that in emphasizing innate knowledge, the modular view sidesteps vital questions about development. Return to the opening of this chapter, and you will see that as Byron, Rachel, and April explore their physical and social worlds, they perform entirely new acts. Yet how these arise from built-in structures is not clear (Fischer & Bidell, 1998; Haith & Benson, 1998). Furthermore, the more predetermined we assume the child's mind to be, the less individual variability in thinking we would expect. Yet throughout this book, we will see many examples of wide individual differences in development.

Finally, according to the modular approach, we should be able to identify brain regions that govern specific types of knowledge at an early age. Yet research supports substantial brain plasticity in the early years and growth spurts across many areas of the cortex at once rather than in separate regions (see Chapter 5, pages 174–175). At present, neurological support for a separate brain/mind module is strongest for language. Later in this chapter, we will take up a nativist view of language development.

■ **A COMPROMISE POSITION.** How can we make sense of these clashing viewpoints? The future is likely to bring compromises between them. Clearly, there must be some built-in mental equipment for making sense of experience, since the young baby is not knowledge free. But this initial equipment might best be viewed as a set of biases, or learning procedures. Each grants infants a means for constructing and flexibly adapting certain types of knowledge, some of which are acquired more easily than others (Haith & Benson, 1998; Karmiloff-Smith, 1992). Consequently, infant cognitive skills emerge gradually, depending on biological makeup and specific experiences encountered. These ideas—that adultlike capacities are present during infancy in primitive form, that cognitive development is gradual and continuous, and that it is uneven because of the challenges of different types of tasks' and children's varying exposure to those tasks—serve as the basis for a major competing approach to Piaget's theory: information processing, which we take up next.

But before we turn to this alternative view, let's conclude our discussion of the sensorimotor stage by recognizing Piaget's enormous contributions. Although not all of his conclusions were correct, Piaget's work inspired a wealth of new research on infant cognition, including studies that eventually challenged his ideas. In addition, Piaget's observations have been of great practical value. Teachers and caregivers continue to look to the sensorimotor stage for guidelines on how to create developmentally appropriate

Did this toddler figure out that one container can rest on top of another through rich, constructive interaction with objects, as Piaget assumed? Or did he begin life with innate knowledge that enables him to grasp the regularities of his physical world with very little hands-on exploration? The future is likely to bring compromises between these clashing viewpoints. *(Elizabeth Crews)*

modular view of the mind
A nativist view that regards the mind as a collection of separate modules, or genetically prewired neural systems in the brain, each equipped with structures for making sense of a certain type of knowledge.

CAREGIVING CONCERNS

Play Materials that Support Infant and Toddler Cognitive Development

FROM 2 MONTHS	FROM 6 MONTHS	FROM 1 YEAR
Crib mobile	Squeeze toys	Large dolls
Rattles and other hand-held sound-making toys, such as a bell on a handle	Nesting cups	Toy dishes
	Clutch and texture balls	Toy telephone
Adult-operated music boxes, records, tapes, and CDs with gentle, regular rhythms, songs, and lullabies	Stuffed animals and soft-bodied dolls	Hammer and peg toy
	Filling and emptying toys	Pull and push toys
	Large and small blocks	Cars and trucks
	Pots, pans, and spoons from the kitchen	Rhythm instruments for shaking and banging, such as bells, cymbals, drums
	Simple, floating objects for the bath	Simple puzzles
	Picture books	Sandbox, shovel, and pail
		Shallow wading pool and water toys

Note. Return to the Caregiving Concerns table in Chapter 5, page 190, to review safety concerns related to toys for infants and toddlers.

Source: Bronson, 1995.

environments for infants and toddlers. Now that you are familiar with some milestones of infant and toddler development, consider what types of playthings would support the building of sensorimotor and representational schemes. Prepare your own list of infant and toddler toys, and justify it by making reference to the cognitive attainments of the first 2 years. Then compare your suggestions to the ones given in the Caregiving Concerns table above.

BRIEF REVIEW

According to Piaget, children actively build psychological structures, or schemes, as they manipulate and explore their world. Two processes, adaptation (which combines assimilation and accommodation) and organization, account for the development of schemes. The vast changes that take place during the sensorimotor stage are divided into six substages. The circular reaction, a special means that infants use to adapt schemes, changes from being oriented toward the infant's own body, to being directed outward toward objects, to producing novel effects in the surrounding world. During the last three substages, infants make strides in intentional behavior and understanding object permanence. By Substage 6, they start to represent reality and show the beginnings of make-believe play.

Recent research reveals that secondary circular reactions, understanding of object permanence and physical causality, and deferred imitation are present much earlier than Piaget believed. These findings raise questions about Piaget's claim that babies construct all aspects of their world through motor activity and that early cognitive development is best characterized as a purely sensorimotor stage. Modern researchers regard infants as having more built-in equipment for making sense of experience than did Piaget, but they differ on whether infants have built-in biases, or learning procedures, for constructing schemes or substantial innate knowledge.

ASK YOURSELF . . .

■ *At 14 months, Tony pushed his toy bunny through the slats of his crib onto a nearby table. Using his "pulling scheme," he tried to retrieve it, but it would not fit back through the slats. Next Tony tried jerking, turning, and throwing the bunny. What kind of circular reaction is Tony demonstrating? How would Tony have approached this problem a few months earlier?*

■ *Seven-month-old Mimi banged her rattle on the tray of her highchair. Then she dropped the rattle, which fell out of sight on her lap, but Mimi did not try to retrieve it. Does Mimi know that the rattle still exists? Why doesn't she search for it? Use research findings to explain your answer.*

INFORMATION PROCESSING

*I*nformation-processing theorists agree with Piaget that children are active, inquiring beings, but otherwise the information-processing view of human thinking is decidedly different. Unlike Piaget, the information-processing approach does not provide a single, unified theory of cognitive development. Instead, it focuses on many different aspects of thinking, from attention, memory, and categorization skills to complex problem solving.

In Chapter 1, we saw that the information-processing approach relies on scripts, frames, and flowcharts to describe the human cognitive system. Often the steps of thinking are likened to the operations a computer performs when it stores, interprets, and responds to incoming information. The computer model of human thinking is very attractive because it is explicit and precise. Information-processing researchers find it useful because they are not satisfied with global concepts, such as assimilation and accommodation, to describe how children think. Instead, they want to know exactly what individuals of different ages do when faced with a task or problem (Klahr & MacWhinney, 1998; Siegler, 1998).

THE STRUCTURE OF THE INFORMATION-PROCESSING SYSTEM

Most general models of the human information-processing system divide the mind into three basic parts: the *sensory register; working,* or *short-term, memory;* and *long-term memory* (see Figure 6.9). As information flows through each, we can operate on and transform it using **mental strategies.** Strategies increase the efficiency of thinking and the chances we will retain information for later use. They also permit us to think flexibly, adapting information to changing circumstances. To understand this more clearly, let's take a brief look at each aspect of the mental system.

First, information enters the **sensory register.** Here, sights and sounds are represented directly but cannot be held for long. For example, look around you, and then close your eyes. An image of what you saw probably persists for a few seconds, but then it decays or disappears, unless you use mental strategies to preserve it. For example, you can *attend* to some information more carefully than others, increasing the chances that it will transfer to the next step of the information-processing system.

The second part of the mind is **working,** or **short-term, memory.** This is the conscious part of our mental system, where we actively "work" on a limited amount of information. For example, if you are studying this book effectively, you are constantly applying mental strategies. Perhaps you are attending to certain information that seems most important. Or you may be using a variety of memory strategies, such as taking notes, repeating information to yourself, or grouping pieces of information together—a strategy much like Piaget's notion of organization.

Organization is an especially effective way to remember the many new concepts flowing into your working memory at the moment. If you permit information to remain piecemeal and disconnected, you can hold very little in your working memory at once, since you must focus on each item separately. But organize it, and you will not just improve your memory. You will increase the chances that information will be transferred to the third, and largest, storage area of your system.

Unlike the sensory register and working memory, the amount of information that can be held in **long-term memory,** our permanent knowledge base, is limitless. In fact, so much is stored in long-term memory that we sometimes have problems in *retrieval,* or getting information back from the system. To aid retrieval, we apply strategies in long-term memory just as we do in working memory. For example, think about how information in your long-term memory is arranged. It is *categorized* according to a master plan

mental strategies
In information processing, procedures that operate on and transform information, thereby increasing the efficiency and flexibility of thinking and the chances that information will be retained.

sensory register
In information processing, that part of the mental system in which sights and sounds are held briefly before they decay or are transferred to working, or short-term, memory.

working, or short-term, memory
In information processing, the conscious part of the mental system, where we actively "work" on a limited amount of information to ensure that it will be retained.

long-term memory
In information processing, the part of the mental system that contains our permanent knowledge base.

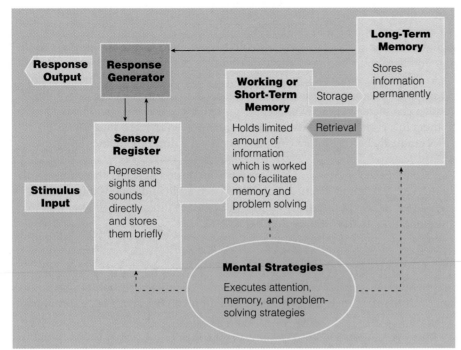

FIGURE **6.9**

Structure of the human information-processing system. Information flows through three parts of the mental system: the sensory register; working, or short-term memory; and long-term memory. In each, mental strategies can be used to manipulate information, increasing the efficiency of thinking and the chances that information will be retained. Strategies also permit us to think flexibly, adapting information to changing circumstances.

based on contents, much like a library shelving system based on the contents of books. When information is filed in this way, it can be retrieved quite easily by following the same network of associations used to store it in the first place.

Information-processing researchers believe that the basic structure of the human mental system is similar throughout life. However, the *capacity* of the system—the amount of information that can be processed at once and the speed with which it can be processed—increases, making possible more complex forms of thinking with age (Case, 1992; Halford, 1993). Gains in information-processing capacity are partly due to brain maturation. But they are largely the result of improvements in strategies, such as attending to information and categorizing it effectively. The development of these strategies is already under way in the first 2 years of life.

ATTENTION

Think back to the discussion of perceptual development in Chapter 5, and you will discover that you already know something about how attention develops in early infancy. Recall that between 1 and 2 months of age, infants shift from attending to a single high-contrast feature of their visual world to exploring objects and patterns more thoroughly.

Besides attending to more aspects of the environment, infants gradually become more efficient at managing their attention, taking information into their mental systems more quickly. Habituation–dishabituation research reveals that preterm and newborn babies require a long time to habituate and dishabituate to novel visual stimuli—about 3 or 4 minutes. But by 4 or 5 months, infants require as little as 5 to 10 seconds to take in a complex new visual stimulus and recognize that it is different from a previous one (Slater et al., 1996).

One reason that very young babies' habituation times are so long is that they sometimes have difficulty disengaging their attention from very bright, patterned stimuli, even when they try to do so (Posner et al., 1997). Once, Felicia held a doll dressed in red-and-white checked overalls in front of 2-month-old April, who stared intently until, unable to break her gaze, she burst into tears. Just as important as attending to a stimulus is the ability to shift attention from one stimulus to another. By 4 months, infants' attention becomes more flexible—a change believed to be due to maturation of brain structures controlling eye movements (Hood et al., 1996).

Throughout the first year, infants attend to novel and eye-catching events. With the transition to toddlerhood, children become increasingly capable of intentional behavior (refer back to Piaget's Substage 4). Consequently, attraction to novelty declines (but does not disappear) and *sustained attention* improves, especially when children play with toys. When a toddler can plan a play activity even in a very limited way, such as stacking blocks or putting them in a container, attention must be maintained to reach the goal. As plans and activities gradually become more complex, so does the duration of attention (Ruff & Lawson, 1990).

With age, infants and toddlers also become more interested in what others are attending to. Later we will see that this joint attention between adult and child is important in language development. By 18 months, toddlers are skilled at directing their attention to both partners and toys in play (Ruff & Rothbart, 1996).

MEMORY

Habituation does not just tell us about the efficiency of infant attention. It also provides a window into infant memory. For example, infants can be exposed to a stimulus until they habituate. Then they can be shown the same stimulus at a later time. If habituation takes place more rapidly on the second occasion, this indicates that babies recognize they have seen the stimulus before. Using this method, studies show that by 3 months, infants remember a visual stimulus for 24 hours; by the end of the first year for several days; and in the case of very familiar stimuli, such as a photo of the human face, even weeks (Fagan, 1973; Martin, 1975).

Note that habituation–dishabituation research tells us how long babies retain a new stimulus in the context of the laboratory, but it underestimates their ability to remember real-world events they can actively control. Recall the operant conditioning research discussed in Chapter 5, in which babies learned to make a mobile move by kicking. In a series of studies, Carolyn Rovee-Collier showed that 3-month-olds remember how to activate the mobile 1 week after training and, with a reminder (the experimenter briefly rotates the mobile for the baby), as long as 4 weeks. By 6 months of age, retention has increased to 6 weeks (Rovee-Collier & Bhatt, 1993; Rovee-Collier & Shyi, 1992). Much like older children and adults, babies seem to remember best when experiences take place in familiar contexts and when they participate actively.

So far, we have discussed only **recognition,** the simplest form of memory because all babies have to do is indicate (by looking or kicking) whether a new stimulus is identical or similar to one previously experienced. **Recall** is more challenging, since it involves remembering something not present. To recall, you must generate an image of the absent stimulus. Can infants engage in recall? By the middle of the first year, they can. Felicia reported that one day when her husband telephoned, 7-month-old April listened to him speak through the receiver and immediately crawled to the front door. April seemed to be *recalling* times when she had heard her father's muffled voice through the door as he arrived home from work (Ashmead & Perlmutter, 1980).

By the end of toddlerhood, recall for people, places, and objects is excellent (Bauer, 1996). For example, at age 2, Byron recalled a friend whom he had not seen for several months when he passed the friend's house. Yet a puzzling finding is that as adults, we no longer recall our earliest experiences. The Biology and Environment box on the following page explains why.

CATEGORIZATION

As infants gradually remember more information, they store it in a remarkably orderly fashion. Babies categorize information at such an early age that categorization is

recognition
A type of memory that involves noticing whether a stimulus is identical or similar to one previously experienced.

recall
A type of memory that involves remembering a stimulus that is not present.

autobiographical memory
Representations of special, one-time events that are long lasting because they are imbued with personal meaning.

BIOLOGY & ENVIRONMENT

INFANTILE AMNESIA

f toddlers remember many aspects of their everyday lives, then what explains infantile amnesia—the fact that practically none of us can retrieve events that happened to us before age 2 or 3? Forgetting cannot be due to the passage of time, since we can recall many events that happened long ago. At present, there are several explanations of infantile amnesia.

One possibility is that brain development during early childhood accounts for it. Growth of the frontal lobes of the cortex along with other structures may be necessary before experiences can be stored in ways that permit them to be retrieved many years later (Boyer & Diamond, 1992). Consistent with this view, some researchers believe that two levels of memory exist: one operates unconsciously and automatically, whereas the other is conscious, intentional, and verbal (Newcombe & Fox, 1994).

Yet the idea of vastly different approaches to remembering in younger and older individuals has been questioned, since even toddlers can describe memories verbally and retain them for extensive periods. A growing number of researchers believe that rather than a radical change in the way experience is represented, the offset of infantile amnesia requires the emergence of a special form of recall—**autobiographical memory,** or representations of special, one-time events that are long lasting because they are imbued with personal meaning. For example, perhaps you recall the day a sibling was born, the first time you took an airplane, or a move to a new house.

For memories to become autobiographical, two developments are necessary. First, the child must have a well-developed image of the self. Yet in the first few years, the sense of self is not yet mature enough to serve as an anchor for one-time events (Howe & Courage, 1993, 1997). Second, autobiographical memory requires that children integrate personal experiences into a meaningful life story. Recent evidence reveals that preschoolers learn to structure memories in story-like form by talking about them with adults, who expand on their recollections by explaining what happened when, where, and with whom (Nelson, 1993).

The developments just described— in self-image and using language to talk about the past—have a common bond. Both require mental representation. Turn back to Chapter 5, page 174, and note that around 1½ to 2 years, a major spurt in brain development occurs. Even researchers who point to evidence of young infants' representational abilities acknowledge that dramatic advances in representation occur at this time. Soon after, the period of infantile amnesia ends and autobiographical memory emerges.

The offset of infantile amnesia probably represents a change to which biology and social experience jointly contribute. One speculation is that vital changes in the brain during toddlerhood pave the way for an *explicit memory* system—one in which children remember deliberately and consciously rather than *implicitly,* without conscious awareness (Nelson, 1995). In Chapters 8 and 12, we will see that deliberate recall of information and experiences improves greatly during childhood, which undoubtedly supports autobiographical memory.

When he gets older, this toddler won't recall the exciting party that took place on his second birthday. According to recent evidence, the offset of infantile amnesia after age 3 is due to the emergence of autobiographical memory. For this special form of recall to develop, young children must have a well-developed image of the self and the language skills to talk about personal experiences with adults, who assist them in constructing a meaningful life story. *(Jeff Greenberg/ The Picture Cube)*

This 3-month-old infant discovered that by kicking, she could shake a mobile made of small blocks with the letter A on them. After a delay, the baby continued to kick vigorously only if the mobile she saw was labeled with the same form (the letter A). She did not kick when given a mobile with a different form (the number 2). The infant's behavior shows that she groups similar stimuli into categories and can distinguish the category A from the category 2. *(Courtesy of Carolyn Rovee-Collier/Rutgers University)*

among the strongest evidence that babies' brains are set up from the start to structure experience in adultlike ways (Mandler, 1998).

Some creative variations of the operant conditioning research described earlier have been used to find out about infant categorization. This time, 3-month-olds were taught to kick to make a mobile move that was made of a uniform set of stimuli—for example, small blocks, all with the letter *A* on them. After a delay, kicking returned to a high level only if the babies were given a mobile whose elements were labeled with the same form (the letter *A*). If the form was changed (from *A*s to *2*s), infants no longer kicked vigorously. While learning to make the mobile move, the babies had grouped together its perceptual features, associating the kicking response with the category "A" and, at later testing, distinguishing it from the category "2" (Bhatt, Rovee-Collier, & Weiner, 1994; Hayne, Rovee-Collier, & Perris, 1987).

Habituation–dishabituation research also has been used to study infant categorization. For example, infants can be shown a series of pictures belonging to one category (such as hot dog, piece of bread, slice of salami). Then the investigator observes whether they look longer at, or dishabituate to, a picture that is not a member of the category (chair) than one that is (apple). Findings of such studies reveal that 6- to 12-month-olds structure objects into an impressive array of meaningful categories—food items, furniture, birds, animals, vehicles, spatial location ("above" and "below"), and more (Mandler & McDonough, 1993; Oakes, Coppage, & Dingel, 1997; Quinn & Eimas, 1996; Younger, 1985, 1993).

Besides organizing the physical world, infants of this age also categorize their emotional and social worlds. For example, they sort people and their voices into male and female (Francis & McCroy, 1983; Poulin-DuBois et al., 1994), have begun to distinguish emotional expressions, and can separate the natural movements of people from other motions (see Chapter 5, page 201). Consider these findings and you will see that older infants have moved beyond *perceptual* categorization, based on objects' similar appearance. By the end of the first year, many categories are *conceptual*—based on function and behavior.

In the second year, children become active categorizers during their play. Try giving a toddler a set of objects that differ in shape and color (such as small blocks). See if the child spontaneously categorizes them. Research shows that around 12 months, toddlers merely touch objects that belong together, without grouping them. A little later, they form single categories. For example, when given four balls and four boxes, a 16-month-old will put all the balls together but not the boxes. And finally, around 18 months, toddlers can sort objects correctly into two classes.

Interestingly, this advanced object-sorting behavior appears at about the same time that toddlers show a "naming explosion," or a sharp rise in vocabulary in which they label many more objects (Gopnik & Meltzoff, 1987, 1992). Language development seems to facilitate as well as build on improved categorization. In support of this idea, adult labeling of objects helps direct toddlers' attention to object categories (Waxman, 1995). Korean children, who learn a language in which object names are often omitted from sentences, develop object-grouping skills later than do their English-speaking counterparts (Gopnik & Choi, 1990).

EVALUATION OF INFORMATION-PROCESSING FINDINGS

Information-processing research underscores the *continuity* of human thinking from infancy into adult life. In attending to the environment, remembering everyday events, and categorizing objects, Byron, Rachel, and April think in ways that are remarkably similar to our own, even though they are far from being the proficient mental processors we are. Findings on infant memory and categorization join with other research in challenging Piaget's view of early cognitive development as taking place in discrete stages. If 3-month-olds can hold events in memory for as long as 2 weeks and categorize stimuli, then they must have some ability to mentally represent their experiences.

Information processing has contributed greatly to our view of infants and toddlers as sophisticated cognitive beings. Still, its greatest drawback stems from its central strength: By analyzing cognition into its components (such as perception, attention, and memory), information processing has had difficulty putting them back together into a broad, comprehensive theory.

During the past two decades, several attempts have been made to overcome this weakness. One approach has been to combine Piaget's theory with the information-processing approach (Case, 1985, 1992; Fischer & Pipp, 1984). We will discuss these efforts in Chapter 12. A more recent trend has been the application of a dynamic systems view to early cognition. Researchers analyze each new attainment to see how it is a product of a complex system of prior accomplishments and the child's current activities and goals, seeking common patterns of change (Smith & Katz, 1996; Thelen & Smith, 1998). These ideas have yet to be fully tested, but they may be moving the field closer to a more powerful view of how the mind of the infant and child develops.

THE SOCIAL CONTEXT OF EARLY COGNITIVE DEVELOPMENT

Take a moment to review the short episode at the beginning of this chapter, in which Rachel dropped shapes into a container. Notice that Rachel is not a solitary explorer who discovers how to use the toy on her own. Instead, she learns about it with her mother's help. With Beth's support, Rachel will gradually become better at matching shapes to openings and dropping them into the container. Then she will be able to perform the activity (and others like it) on her own.

Vygotsky's sociocultural theory has brought researchers to the realization that children live in rich social and cultural contexts that affect the way their cognitive world is structured (Rogoff, 1998; Wertsch & Tulviste, 1992). Vygotsky (1930–1935/1978) believed that complex mental functions, such as voluntary attention, deliberate memory, and problem solving, have their origins in social interaction. Through joint activities with more mature members of their society, children come to master activities and think in ways that have meaning in their culture.

A special Vygotskian concept, the **zone of proximal** (or potential) **development,** explains how this happens. It refers to a range of tasks that the child cannot yet handle alone but can accomplish with the help of more skilled partners. To understand this idea, think of a sensitive teacher or parent (such as Beth) who introduces a child to a new activity. The adult picks a task that the child can master but one challenging enough that the child cannot do it by herself. Or the adult capitalizes on an activity that the child has chosen. Such a task is especially suited for spurring development forward. Then the adult guides and supports, breaking the task into manageable units and calling the child's attention to specific features. By joining in the interaction, the child picks up mental strategies, and her competence increases. When this happens, the adult steps back, permitting the child to take over more responsibility for the task.

As we will see in Chapters 9 and 12, Vygotsky's ideas have mostly been applied at older ages, when children are more skilled in language and social communication. But recently, Vygotsky's theory has been extended to infancy and toddlerhood. Recall that babies are equipped with capabilities that ensure that caregivers will interact with them. Then adults adjust the environment and their communication in ways that promote learning.

A study by Barbara Rogoff and her collaborators (1984) illustrates this process. The researchers watched how several adults played with Rogoff's son and daughter over the first 2 years, while a jack-in-the-box toy was nearby. In the early months, adults tried to focus the baby's attention by working the toy and as the bunny popped out, saying something like "My, what happened?" By the end of the first year (when the baby's cognitive and motor skills had improved), interaction centered on how to use the jack-in-the-box. When the infant reached for the toy, adults guided the baby's hand in turning the crank

This mother assists her baby in making a music box work. By presenting a task within the child's zone of proximal development and fine-tuning her support to the infant's momentary needs, the mother promotes her son's cognitive development. *(Erika Stone)*

zone of proximal development
In Vygotsky's theory, a range of tasks that the child cannot yet handle alone but can do with the help of more skilled partners.

CULTURAL INFLUENCES

SOCIAL ORIGINS OF MAKE-BELIEVE PLAY

One of my husband Ken's shared activities with our two sons when they were young was to bake pineapple upside-down cake, a favorite treat. I remember well one Sunday afternoon when a cake was in the making. Little Peter, then 21 months old, stood on a chair at the kitchen sink, busy pouring water from one cup to another.

"He's in the way, Dad!" complained 4-year-old David, trying to pull Peter away from the sink.

"Maybe if we let him help, he'll give us some room," Ken suggested. As David stirred the batter, Ken poured some into a small bowl for Peter, moved his chair to the side of the sink, and handed him a spoon.

"Here's how you do it, Petey," instructed David, with an air of superiority. Peter watched as David stirred, then tried to copy his motion. When it was time to pour the batter, Ken helped Peter tip the small bowl so its contents flowed into the pan.

"Time to bake it," said Ken.

"Bake it, bake it," repeated Peter, as he watched Ken slip the pan into the oven.

Several hours later, we observed one of Peter's earliest instances of make-believe play. He got his pail from the sandbox and, after filling it with a handful of sand, carried it into the kitchen and put it down on the floor in front of the oven. "Bake it, bake it," Peter called to Ken. Together, father and son lifted the pretend cake inside the oven.

Until recently, most researchers studied make-believe play apart from the social environment in which it occurs, while children played alone.

Probably for this reason, Piaget and his followers concluded that toddlers discover make-believe independently, as soon as they are capable of representational schemes. Vygotsky's theory has challenged this view. He believed that society provides children with opportunities to represent culturally meaningful activities in play. Make-believe, like other mental functions, is initially learned under the guidance of expert partners (Garvey, 1990). In the example just described, Peter's capacity to represent daily events was extended when Ken drew him into the baking task and helped him act it out in play.

New evidence supports the idea that early make-believe is the combined result of children's readiness to engage in it and social experiences that promote it. In one observational study of middle-SES American toddlers, 75 to 80 percent of make-believe involved mother–child interaction. At 12 months, make-believe was fairly one-sided; almost all play episodes were initiated by caregivers. By the end of the second year, caregivers and children displayed mutual interest in getting make-believe started; half of pretend episodes were initiated by each. At all ages, caregivers elaborated on the child's contribution, resulting in joint activity in which both partners participated actively in an imaginative dialogue. Over time, the adult gradually released responsibility to the child for creating and guiding the fantasy theme (Haight & Miller, 1993).

When adults participate in toddlers' make-believe, it is more elaborate and advanced (O'Reilly & Bornstein, 1993). For example, play

themes are more varied. And toddlers are more likely to combine schemes into complex sequences, as Peter did when he put the sand in the bucket ("making the batter"), carried it into the kitchen, and (with Ken's help) put it in the oven ("baking the cake").

In many cultures, adults do not spend much time playing with young children. Instead, older siblings take over this function. For example, in Indonesia and Mexico, where extended-family households and sibling caregiving are common, make-believe is more frequent as well as complex with older siblings than with mothers. As early as 3 to 4 years of age, children provide rich, challenging stimulation to their younger brothers and sisters. The fantasy play of these toddlers is just as well developed as that of their middle-SES American counterparts (Farver, 1993; Farver & Wimbarti, 1995; Gaskins, 1994).

As we will see in Chapter 9, make-believe is a major means through which children extend their cognitive skills and learn about important activities in their culture. Vygotsky's theory, and the findings that support it, tell us that providing a stimulating environment is only part of what is necessary to promote early cognitive development. In addition, toddlers must be invited and encouraged by their elders to become active participants in the social world around them.

and putting the bunny back in the box. As the youngsters became toddlers, adults helped from a distance. They used verbal instructions and gestures, such as rotating a hand in a turning motion near the crank, while the child tried to make the toy work.

Research suggests that this fine-tuned support is related to cognitive competence. Infants whose mothers gently direct their attention and (as they get older) encourage them to manipulate the environment are advanced in play, language, and problem-solving skills during the second year (Bornstein et al., 1992b; Tamis-LeMonda & Bornstein, 1989).

Earlier in this chapter, we saw how infants create new schemes by acting on the physical world (Piaget) and how certain prewired skills become better developed as infants and toddlers represent their experiences in more efficient and meaningful ways (information processing). Vygotsky adds a third dimension to our understanding by emphasizing that important aspects of cognitive development are socially mediated. The Cultural Influences box on the previous page presents additional evidence for this idea. And we will see even more in the next section, as we look at individual differences in mental development during the first 2 years.

BRIEF REVIEW

Most general models of the information-processing system divide it into three parts: the sensory register; working, or short-term, memory; and long-term memory. Mental strategies operate on information as it flows through the system, increasing the likelihood that the information will be retained and adapting it to changing circumstances. Mental strategies gradually improve with age. Infants attend to more aspects of the environment, manage their attention more efficiently and flexibly, and remember information over longer periods. By the end of toddlerhood, sustained attention improves, and recall for people, places, and objects is excellent. Findings on categorization support the view that infants' brains are set up to structure experience in adultlike ways. Although information processing has helped us appreciate the remarkable cognitive abilities of infants, it has not yet provided a way of linking these diverse skills together. According to Vygotsky's sociocultural theory, early cognitive development is socially mediated as adults help infants and toddlers master tasks within the zone of proximal development.

INDIVIDUAL DIFFERENCES IN EARLY MENTAL DEVELOPMENT

*A*s he neared age 2, Byron had only a handful of words in his vocabulary, continued to play in a less mature way than Rachel and April, and seemed restless and overactive. Worried about Byron's progress, Lisa decided to take him to a psychological clinic, where he was given one of many tests available for assessing the mental development of infants and toddlers.

The mental testing approach is different from the cognitive theories we have just discussed, which try to explain the *process* of development—how children's thinking changes over time. In contrast, designers of mental tests are much more concerned with cognitive *products*. Their aim is to measure behaviors that reflect mental development and to arrive at scores that predict future performance, such as later intelligence, school achievement, and adult vocational success.

This concern with prediction arose nearly a century ago, when French psychologist Alfred Binet designed the first successful intelligence test, which predicted school achievement (see Chapter 1). It inspired the design of many new tests, including ones that measure intelligence at very early ages. If ways could be found to identify infants and toddlers at risk for developing poorly, then special help could be provided early in life, when there is greatest hope of preventing later problems.

ASK YOURSELF . . .

■ *Rachel played with toys in a far more intentional, goal-directed way as a toddler than as an infant. What impact is Rachel's more advanced toy play likely to have on the development of attention?*

■ *When Byron was 18 months old, his father stood behind him, helping him throw a large rubber ball into a box. When Byron showed that he could throw the ball, his father stepped back and let him try on his own. Using Vygotsky's ideas, explain how Byron's father is supporting his cognitive development.*

INFANT INTELLIGENCE TESTS

As you can probably imagine, accurately measuring the intelligence of infants is a challenge. Babies cannot answer questions or follow directions. All we can do is present them with stimuli, coax them to respond, and observe their behavior. As a result, most infant tests consist of perceptual and motor responses along with some tasks that tap early language and problem-solving abilities. One commonly used infant test is the *Bayley Scales of Infant Development,* for children between 1 month and 3½ years. It is made up of two scales: (1) the Mental Scale, which includes such items as turning to a sound, looking for a fallen object, building a tower of cubes, and naming pictures; and (2) the Motor Scale, which assesses gross and fine motor skills, such as grasping, sitting, drinking from a cup, and jumping (Bayley, 1993).

■ **COMPUTING INTELLIGENCE TEST SCORES.** Intelligence tests for infants, children, or adults are scored in much the same way. When a test is constructed, it is given to a large, representative sample of individuals. Performances of people at each age level form a *normal* or *bell-shaped curve* in which most scores fall near the center (the mean or average) and progressively fewer fall out toward the extremes. On the basis of this distribution, the test designer computes *norms,* or standards against which future test takers can be compared. For example, the number of items that Byron passes at age 2 will be compared with that of 2-year-olds in general. If Byron does better than 50 percent of his age-mates, his score will be 100, an average test score. If he exceeds most children his age, his score will be much higher. If he does better than only a small percentage of 2-year-olds, his score will be much lower.

Scores computed in this way are called **intelligence quotients,** or **IQs,** a term you have undoubtedly heard before. Table 6.3 describes the meaning of a range of IQ scores. Notice how the IQ offers a way of finding out whether a child is ahead, behind, or on time (average) in mental development in relation to other children of the same age. The great majority of individuals (96 percent) have IQs that fall between 70 and 130; only a very few achieve higher or lower scores.

■ **PREDICTING LATER PERFORMANCE FROM INFANT TESTS.** Many people assume, incorrectly, that IQ is a measure of inborn ability that does not change with age. Despite the careful construction of many infant tests, they predict later intelligence poorly. In one longitudinal study, most youngsters' scores changed considerably between toddlerhood and adolescence (McCall, Appelbaum, & Hogarty, 1973). In fact, the average

intelligence quotient, or IQ
A score that permits an individual's performance on an intelligence test to be compared to the performances of other individuals of the same age.

_TABLE **6.3**

Meaning of Different IQ Scores

SCORE	PERCENTILE RANK (CHILD DOES BETTER THAN . . . PERCENT OF SAME-AGE CHILDREN)	
70	2	
85	16	
100 (average IQ)	50	
115	84	
130	98	

IQ shift was as great as 28.5 points, and high scorers during the early years were not necessarily high scorers later.

Because infants and toddlers are especially likely to become distracted, fatigued, or bored during testing, their scores often do not reflect their true abilities. In addition, the perceptual and motor tasks on infant tests are quite different from the test questions given to older children, which emphasize verbal, conceptual, and problem-solving skills. Because of concerns that infant test scores do not tap the same dimensions of intelligence measured at older ages, they are conservatively labeled **developmental quotients,** or **DQs,** rather than IQs. Not until age 6 do IQ scores become stable, serving as reasonably good predictors of later performance (Hayslip, 1994).

It is important to note that infant tests do show somewhat better long-term prediction for extremely low-scoring babies (Colombo, 1993). Today, infant tests are used largely for *screening*—helping to identify for further observation and intervention babies whose very low scores mean that they are likely to have developmental problems in the future (Kopp, 1994).

Because infant tests do not predict later IQ for most children, researchers have turned to the information-processing approach for new ways to assess early mental functioning. Their findings show that habituation and dishabituation to visual stimuli are the best available infant predictors of childhood intelligence. Correlations between the speed of these responses and 3- to 11-year-old IQ consistently range from the .30s to the .60s (McCall & Carriger, 1993; Rose & Feldman, 1995). The habituation–dishabituation sequence seems to be an especially effective early index of intelligence because it assesses quickness of thinking, a characteristic of bright individuals. It also taps basic cognitive processes—attention, memory, and response to novelty—that underlie intelligent behavior at all ages (Colombo, 1995; Rose & Feldman, 1997).

The *Fagan Test of Infant Intelligence* is made up entirely of habituation–dishabituation items. To take it, the infant sits on the mother's lap and views a series of pictures. After the infant's exposure to each one, the examiner records looking time toward a novel picture that is paired with the familiar one. Besides predicting childhood IQ, the Fagan test is highly effective in identifying babies who (without intervention) will soon show serious delays in intellectual development (Fagan & Detterman, 1992).

Like habituation–dishabituation, Piagetian object permanence tasks predict later IQ better than traditional infant tests, perhaps because they, too, reflect a basic intellectual process—problem solving (Wachs, 1975). The consistency of these findings has prompted designers of the most recent edition of the Bayley test to include several items that tap higher-order cognitive skills, such as preference for novel stimuli, categorization, and ability to find hidden objects.

EARLY ENVIRONMENT AND MENTAL DEVELOPMENT

In Chapter 2, we indicated that intelligence is a complex blend of hereditary and environmental influences. Many studies have examined the relationship of environmental factors to infant and toddler mental test scores. As we consider this evidence, you will encounter findings that highlight the role of genetic factors as well.

■ **THE HOME ENVIRONMENT.** From what you have learned so far in this chapter, what aspects of young children's home experiences would you expect to influence early mental development? To answer this question, Robert Bradley, Bettye Caldwell, and their collaborators developed the **Home Observation for Measurement of the Environment (HOME),** a checklist for gathering information about the quality of children's home lives through observation and parental interview (Caldwell & Bradley, 1994). The Caregiving Concerns table on page 234 lists factors measured by HOME during the first 3 years. Each is positively related to toddlers' mental test performance. In addition, high HOME scores are associated with IQ gains between 1 and 3 years of age, whereas low HOME scores predict declines as large as 15 to 20 points (Bradley et al., 1989).

developmental quotient, or DQ
A score on an infant intelligence test, based primarily on perceptual and motor responses. Computed in the same manner as an IQ.

Home Observation for Measurement of the Environment (HOME)
A checklist for gathering information about the quality of children's home lives through observation and parental interview.

Home Observation for the Measurement of the Environment (HOME): Infancy and Toddler Subscales

SUBSCALE	SAMPLE ITEM
Emotional and verbal responsiveness of the parent	Parent caresses or kisses child at least once during observer's visit.
Parental acceptance of the child	Parent does not interfere with child's actions or restrict child's movements more than three times during observer's visit.
Organization of the physical environment	Child's play environment appears safe and free of hazards.
Provision of appropriate play materials	Parent provides toys or interesting activities for child during observer's visit.
Parental involvement with the child	Parent tends to keep child within visual range and to look at child often during observer's visit.
Variety in daily stimulation	Child eats at least one meal per day with mother and/or father, according to parental report.

Source: Elardo & Bradley, 1981.

When researchers look at different SES and ethnic groups, the findings on early home environment are much the same. An organized, stimulating physical setting and parental encouragement, involvement, and affection repeatedly predict infant and early childhood IQ, no matter what the child's background (Bradley & Caldwell, 1982; Bradley et al., 1989). The extent to which parents talk to infants and toddlers is particularly important. As the final section of this chapter will reveal, it contributes strongly to early language progress. Language competence, in turn, predicts intelligence and academic achievement in elementary school (Hart & Risley, 1995).

Yet we must be cautious in interpreting these correlational findings. In the research just mentioned, all the children were reared by their biological parents, with whom they share not just a common environment but also a common heredity. Parents who are genetically more intelligent might provide better experiences as well as give birth to genetically brighter children. In addition, brighter children may evoke more stimulation from their parents. Note that these hypotheses refer to *genetic–environmental correlation* (see Chapter 3, page 89).

Indeed, there is support for a genetic contribution to the HOME–mental development relationship. The correlation is not as strong for adopted children as it is for biological children (Cherny, 1994). Yet heredity does not account for all of the association between home environment and mental tests scores. Family living conditions continue to predict children's IQ beyond the contribution of parental IQ, which highlights the importance of environment (Luster & Dubow, 1992; Sameroff et al., 1993).

Can the research summarized so far help us understand Lisa's concern about Byron's development? Indeed, it can. Andrew, the psychologist who tested Byron, found that he scored slightly below average but well within normal range. Andrew also interviewed Lisa about her child-rearing practices and watched her play with Byron. He noticed that Lisa, anxious about how well Byron was doing, tended to pressure him a great deal. She constantly bombarded him with questions and instructions that were not related to his ongoing actions.

Andrew explained that when parents are intrusive in these ways, infants and toddlers are likely to be distractible, show less mature forms of play, and do poorly on mental tests (Bradley et al., 1989; Fiese, 1990). He coached Lisa in how to establish a sensitive give-and-take in the way she played with Byron. At the same time, he assured her that Byron's current performance need not forecast his future development, since warm, responsive parenting that builds on toddlers' current capacities is a much better indicator of how they will do later than is an early mental test score.

■ **INFANT AND TODDLER DAY CARE.** Home environments are not the only influential settings in which young children spend their days. Today, more than 60 percent of mothers with a child under age 2 are employed (U.S. Bureau of the Census, 1997). Day care for infants and toddlers is common, and its quality has a major impact on mental development.

Research consistently shows that infants and young children exposed to poor-quality day care, regardless of whether they come from middle- or low-income homes, score lower on measures of cognitive and social skills. In one American study, children who entered poor-quality day care during their first year and remained there during early childhood were rated by kindergarten teachers as distractible, low in task involvement, and inconsiderate of others (Howes, 1990).

In contrast, good day care can reduce the negative impact of a stressed, poverty-stricken home life, and it sustains the benefits of growing up in an economically advantaged family (Burchinal et al., 1996; Lamb, 1998). In Swedish longitudinal research, entering high-quality day care in infancy and toddlerhood was associated with cognitive, emotional, and social competence in middle childhood and adolescence (Andersson, 1989, 1992; Broberg et al., 1997).

Arrange to visit some day care settings, and take notes on what you see. In contrast to reports from most European countries, where day care is nationally regulated and liberally funded to ensure its quality, reports on American day care are cause for deep concern. Standards are set by the states, and they vary greatly across the nation. In some places, caregivers need no special training in child development, and one adult is permitted to care for as many as 6 to 12 babies at once (Children's Defense Fund, 1997). Large numbers of infants and toddlers attend unlicensed day care homes, where no one checks to see that minimum health and safety standards are met.

In a study of several hundred randomly selected day care centers in California, Colorado, Connecticut, and North Carolina, researchers judged that only 1 in 7 provided a level of care sufficient to promote healthy psychological development. As Figure 6.10 shows, the quality of infant/toddlerhood programs was abysmal; the large majority were either mediocre or poor (Helburn, 1995). Similar conclusions have been reached about family care homes (Galinsky et al., 1994).

This caregiver works in a day-care center that meets rigorous, professionally established standards of quality. A generous caregiver-child ratio, a limited number of children in each room, and training in child development enable him to respond to infants' and toddlers' needs to be held, comforted, and stimulated. *(Laura Berk)*

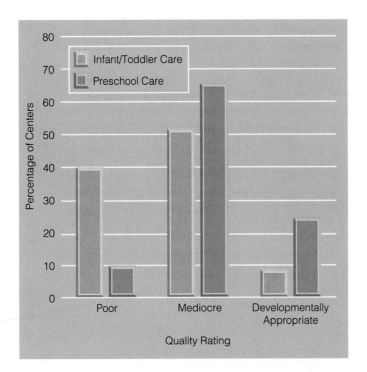

FIGURE 6.10

Quality ratings of day-care for infants, toddlers, and preschoolers in the United States. Visits were made to 400 randomly selected day care centers in California, Colorado, Connecticut, and North Carolina. Centers were classified as (1) *inadequate*—children's needs for health and safety are not met, and there is no warmth, support, and encouragement of learning; (2) *mediocre*—children's health and safety needs are met, and there is minimal to moderate warmth, support, and encouragement of learning; or (3) *developmentally appropriate*—children's health and safety needs are met, and warmth, support, and encouragement of learning are plentiful. *(From Cost, Quality, and Outcomes Study Team, 1995, "Cost, Quality, and Child Outcomes in Child Care Centers: Key Findings and Recommendations," Young Children, 50(4), p. 41 © National Association for the Education of Young Children. Adapted by permission.)*

CAREGIVING CONCERNS

Signs of Developmentally Appropriate Infant and Toddler Day Care

PROGRAM CHARACTERISTIC	SIGNS OF QUALITY
Physical setting	Indoor environment is clean, in good repair, well lighted, and well ventilated. Fenced outdoor play space is available. Setting does not appear overcrowded when children are present.
Toys and equipment	Play materials are appropriate for infants and toddlers and stored on low shelves within easy reach. Cribs, highchairs, infant seats, and child-sized tables and chairs are available. Outdoor equipment includes small riding toys, swings, slide, and sandbox.
Caregiver–child ratio	In day care centers, caregiver–child ratio is no greater than 1 to 3 for infants and 1 to 5 for toddlers. Group size (number of children in one room) is no greater than 6 infants with 2 caregivers and 12 toddlers with 2 caregivers. In day care homes, caregiver is responsible for no more than 6 children; within this group, no more than 2 are infants and toddlers. Staffing is consistent, so infants and toddlers can form relationships with particular caregivers.
Daily activities	Daily schedule includes times for active play, quiet play, naps, snacks, and meals. It is flexible rather than rigid, to meet the needs of individual children. Atmosphere is warm and supportive, and children are never left unsupervised.
Interactions among adults and children	Caregivers respond promptly to infants' and toddlers' distress; hold, talk to, sing, and read to them; and interact with them in a contingent manner that respects the individual child's interests and tolerance for stimulation.
Caregiver qualifications	Caregiver has some training in child development, first aid, and safety.
Relationships with parents	Parents are welcome any time. Caregivers talk daily with parents about children's behavior and development.
Licensing and accreditation	Day care setting, whether a center or home, is licensed by the state. Accreditation by the National Academy of Early Childhood Programs or the National Association for Family Child Care is evidence of an especially high-quality program.

Sources: Bredekamp & Copple, 1997; National Association for the Education of Young Children, 1991.

developmentally appropriate practice
A set of standards devised by the National Association for the Education of Young Children that specify program characteristics that meet the developmental and individual needs of young children of varying ages, based on current research and the consensus of experts.

Unfortunately, children most likely to have inadequate day care come from low-income and poverty-stricken families, where parents cannot afford to pay for the services their youngsters need (Phillips et al., 1994). As a result, these children receive a double dose of vulnerability, both at home and in the day care environment. The Caregiving Concerns table above lists signs of high-quality programs that can be used in choosing a day care setting for an infant or toddler, based on standards for **developmentally appropriate practice** devised by the National Association for the Education of Young Children (Bredekamp & Copple, 1997). These standards specify program characteristics that meet the developmental and individual needs of young children of varying ages, based on current research and the consensus of experts.

Of course, for parents to select day care that is developmentally appropriate, there must be enough of it available. Day care in the United States is affected by a macrosystem of individualistic values (see Chapter 2, page 81) and weak government regulation and funding. Furthermore, many parents think their children's day care experiences are higher in quality than they really are (Helburn, 1995). Inability to identify good care means that many parents do not demand it. Yet communities and nations that invest in day care have selected a highly cost-effective means of protecting the well-being of all children. Day care can also serve as effective early intervention for children whose development is at risk, much like the programs we are about to consider in the next section.

EARLY INTERVENTION FOR AT-RISK INFANTS AND TODDLERS

Many studies indicate that children living in poverty are likely to show gradual declines in intelligence test scores and to achieve poorly when they reach school age

(Brody, 1992). These problems are largely due to home environments that, from the earliest ages, undermine children's ability to learn and increase the chances that they will remain poor throughout their lives. A variety of intervention programs have been developed to break this tragic cycle of poverty. Although most begin during the preschool years (we will discuss these in Chapter 9), a few start during infancy and continue through early childhood.

Some interventions are center based. The Carolina Abecedarian Project, described in the Social Issues box on page 238, is a well-known example. Others are home based. A skilled adult visits the home and works with parents, teaching them how to stimulate a very young child's development. In most intervention programs, participating youngsters score higher on mental tests than do untreated controls by age 2—gains that persist as long as the program lasts and occasionally longer. The more intense the intervention (for example, full-day, year-round, high-quality day care plus support services for parents), the greater children's cognitive and academic performance when they reach school age (Barnett, 1995; Campbell & Ramey, 1995).

Without some form of early intervention, large numbers of children born into economically disadvantaged families will not reach their full potential. Recognition of this reality recently led the United States Congress to provide limited funding for intervention services directed at infants and toddlers who already have serious developmental problems or who are at risk for them because of poverty. At present, available programs are not nearly enough to meet the need. Nevertheless, the ones that exist are a promising beginning in a new effort aimed at preventing the serious learning difficulties of millions of poverty-stricken children by starting to help them at a very early age.

BRIEF REVIEW

The mental testing approach arrives at IQ scores that compare a child's performance to that of same-age children. Infant intelligence tests consist largely of perceptual and motor responses, and they predict later intelligence poorly. Consequently, scores on these tests are conservatively labeled DQs rather than IQs. Speed of habituation and dishabituation to visual stimuli and object permanence show better prediction. Factors in the home environment—stimulation provided by the physical setting and parental encouragement, involvement, affection, and verbal responsiveness—are consistently related to early test scores. High-quality day care supports mental development, whereas poor-quality day care undermines it. Intensive early intervention for poverty-stricken infants and toddlers has been successful in producing improvements in intelligence test scores and school performance.

LANGUAGE DEVELOPMENT

As perception and cognition improve during infancy, they pave the way for an extraordinary human achievement—language. On the average, children say their first word at 12 months of age, with a range of about 8 to 18 months. Once words appear, language develops rapidly. Sometime between 1½ and 2 years, toddlers combine two words. Soon their utterances increase in length and complexity (Bloom, 1998). By age 6, children have a vocabulary of about 10,000 words, speak in elaborate sentences, and are skilled conversationalists.

To appreciate what an awesome task this is, think about the many abilities involved in your own flexible use of language. When you speak, you must select words that match the underlying concepts you want to convey. Then you must combine them into phrases and sentences using a complex set of grammatical rules. Next, you must pronounce these

ASK YOURSELF . . .

■ *Fifteen-month-old Joey's developmental quotient (DQ) is 115. His mother wants to know exactly what this means and what she should do at home to support his mental development. How would you respond to her questions?*

■ *Using what you learned about brain development in Chapter 5, explain why intensive intervention for poverty-stricken children beginning in the first 2 years has a greater impact on IQ than intervention at a later age?*

SOCIAL ISSUES

THE CAROLINA ABECEDARIAN PROJECT: A MODEL OF EARLY INTERVENTION

In the 1970s, an experiment was begun to find out if educational enrichment starting at a very early age could prevent the declines in mental development that affect children born into extreme poverty. The Carolina Abecedarian Project identified over a hundred infants at serious risk for school failure, based on parent education and income, a history of poor school achievement among older siblings, and other family problems. Shortly after birth, the babies were randomly assigned to either a treatment or a control group.

Between 3 weeks and 3 months of age, infants in the treatment group were enrolled in a full-time, year-round day-care program, where they remained until they entered school. During the first 3 years, the children received stimulation aimed at pro-

moting motor, cognitive, language, and social skills. After age 3, the goals of the program expanded to include prereading and math concepts.

At all ages, special emphasis was placed on adult–child communication. Teachers were trained to engage in informative, helpful, and nondirective interaction with the children, who were talked to and read to daily. Both treatment and control children received nutrition and health services. The primary difference between them was the day-care experience, designed to support the treatment group's mental development.

Intelligence test scores were gathered on the children regularly, and (as Figure 6.11 indicates) by 12 months the performance of the two groups began to diverge. Treatment children scored higher than controls throughout the preschool years. Although the high-

risk backgrounds of both groups led their IQs to decline over middle childhood, follow-up testing at ages 8, 12, and 15 revealed that treatment children maintained their advantage in IQ over controls (see Figure 6.11). In addition, at ages 12 and 15, treatment youngsters were achieving considerably better, especially in reading and mathematics (Campbell & Ramey, 1991, 1994, 1995).

When the Carolina Abecedarian children entered elementary school, the researchers conducted a second experiment to compare the impact of early and later intervention. From kindergarten through second grade, half the treatment and half the control group were provided with a special resource teacher. She introduced supplementary educational activities into the home, addressing the child's specific learning needs. School-age intervention had little impact on IQ (refer again to Figure 6.11). And although it enhanced children's academic achievement, the effects were much weaker than the impact of very early intervention (Campbell & Ramey, 1994, 1995). The Carolina Abecedarian Project shows that providing children with continuous, high-quality enrichment from infancy through the preschool years is an effective way to reduce the devastating impact of poverty on children's mental development.

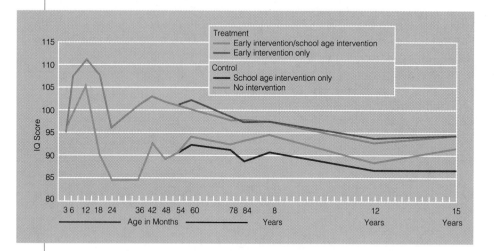

FIGURE 6.11

IQ scores of treatment and control children from 6 months to 15 years in the Carolina Abecedarian Project. To compare the impact of early and later intervention, half the treatment and half the control group were provided with supplementary educational activities suited to their learning needs from kindergarten through second grade. School-based intervention had little impact on age-related changes in IQ; the effects of early intervention were far more powerful. *(From F. A. Campbell & C. T. Ramey, 1995, "Cognitive and School Outcomes for High-Risk African-American Students at Middle Adolescence: Positive Effects of Early Intervention," American Educational Research Journal, 32, p. 757. Reprinted by permission of the American Educational Research Association)*

Infants are communicative beings from the start, as this interchange between a 3-month-old and her grandfather indicates. How will this child accomplish the awesome task of becoming a fluent speaker of her native tongue during the first few years of life? Theorists disagree sharply on answers to this question. *(Sotographs/ Liason International)*

utterances correctly, or you will not be understood. Finally, you must follow the rules of everyday conversation. For example, if you do not take turns, make comments that are relevant to what your partner just said, and use an appropriate tone of voice, then no matter how clear and correct your language, others may refuse to listen to you.

Infants and toddlers make remarkable progress in getting these skills under way. How do they manage to do so? There are several theories of how early language development takes place. Let's examine and evaluate each, based on what we know about the beginnings of language in the first 2 years.

THREE THEORIES OF LANGUAGE DEVELOPMENT

In the 1950s, researchers did not take seriously the idea that very young children might be able to figure out important properties of the language they hear, just as they organize the world of objects into meaningful units. As a result, the first two theories of how children acquire language were extreme views. One, *behaviorism,* regarded language development as entirely due to environmental influences—in particular, intensive training by parents. The second, *nativism,* assumed that children are prewired to master the intricate rules of their language.

■ **THE BEHAVIORIST PERSPECTIVE.** Well-known behaviorist B. F. Skinner (1957) proposed that language, just like any other behavior, is acquired through *operant conditioning* (see Chapter 5, pages 192–193). As the baby makes sounds, parents reinforce those that are most like words with smiles, hugs, and speech in return. For example, at 12 months, my older son, David, could often be heard babbling something like this: "book-a-book-a-dook-a-dook-a-book-a-nook-a-book-aaa." One day while he babbled away, I held up his picture book and said, "Book!" Very soon David was saying "book-aaa" in the presence of books.

Some behaviorists rely on *imitation* to explain how children rapidly acquire complex utterances, such as whole phrases and sentences (Whitehurst & Vasta, 1975). And imitation can combine with reinforcement to promote language, as when the parent coaxes, "Say 'I want a cookie,'" and delivers praise and a treat after the toddler responds, "Wanna cookie!"

Although reinforcement and imitation contribute to early language development, they are best viewed as supporting rather than fully explaining it. As Felicia remarked one day, "It's amazing how creative April is with language. She combines words in ways she's never heard before, such as 'needle it' when she wants me to sew up her teddy bear and 'allgone outside' when she has to come in from the backyard." Felicia's observations reveal that young children say a great many things that are not directly taught.

■ **THE NATIVIST PERSPECTIVE.** Linguist Noam Chomsky (1957) was the first to recognize that even small children assume much responsibility for their own language learning. His nativist theory regards the young child's amazing language skill as etched into the structure of the human brain.

Focusing on grammar, Chomsky believed that the rules of sentence organization are much too complex to be directly taught to or independently discovered by a young child. Instead, he argued, all children have a **language acquisition device (LAD),** a biologically based innate system that contains a set of rules common to all languages. It permits children, no matter which language they hear, to speak in a rule-oriented fashion as soon as they have picked up enough words.

Are children biologically primed to acquire language? Proponents point out that children the world over reach major language milestones in a similar sequence—evidence that fits with the idea of a biologically determined language program (Gleitman & Newport, 1996). Results of efforts to teach nonhuman primates language and the existence of language areas in the brain are also consistent with Chomsky's view that humans are prepared for language in specialized ways.

Nim, a chimp taught American Sign Language, built a vocabulary of more than one hundred signs over several years of training. In addition, his two-sign combinations, such as "groom me," "hug Nim," and "Nim book," were similar to those of human toddlers. But for sign strings longer than two, Nim's productions showed little resemblance to human grammar. *(Susan Kuklin/Photo Researchers)*

language acquisition device (LAD)
In Chomsky's theory, a biologically based innate system for picking up language that permits children, as soon as they have learned enough words, to combine them into grammatically consistent expressions and to understand the meaning of sentences they hear.

Broca's area
A language structure located in the frontal lobe of the cerebral cortex that controls language production.

Wernicke's area
A language structure located in the temporal lobe of the cerebral cortex that is responsible for interpreting language.

Can Great Apes Acquire Language? Many attempts have been made to teach language to chimpanzees, who are closest to humans in the evolutionary hierarchy. In some instances, researchers created artificial languages in which plastic tokens or computer keyboards are used to generate strings of visual symbols representing sentences. In other cases, chimps were trained in American Sign Language, a gestural communication system used by the deaf that is as elaborate as any spoken language.

Findings reveal that the ability of chimps to acquire a humanlike language system is limited. Many months and sometimes years of training and reinforcement are necessary to get them to master a basic vocabulary. And although their two-sign combinations resemble the two-word utterances of human toddlers, there is no convincing evidence that they can master complex grammatical forms (Berko Gleason, 1997).

Recently, researchers began to study pygmy chimps, who are more intelligent and sociable than common chimps. When taught to comprehend many expressions before producing them (a form of language learning like that of human children), pygmy chimps show more rapid vocabulary development and better comprehension of novel sentences than ever before attained by nonhuman primates (Savage-Rumbaugh et al., 1993). Still, even pygmy chimps require several extra years of experience to attain the basic grammatical understandings of human 2- and 3-year-olds.

Language Areas in the Brain. Humans have evolved specialized regions in the brain that support language skills. Recall from Chapter 5 that for most people, language is housed in the left hemisphere of the cortex. Within it are two language-specific structures (see Figure 6.12). **Broca's area,** located in the frontal lobe, controls language production. **Wernicke's area,** located in the temporal lobe, is responsible for interpreting language.

As children acquire language, the brain becomes increasingly specialized for language processing. When researchers recorded EEGs while 20-month-olds listened to words they

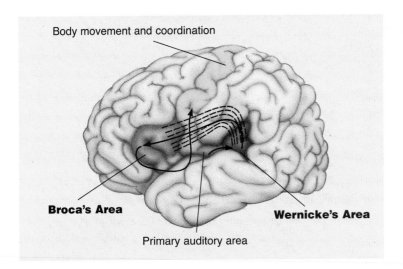

FIGURE 6.12

Language-specific structures in the left hemisphere of the cortex. *Broca's area* controls language production by creating a detailed program for speaking, which it sends to the face area of the cortical region that controls body movement and coordination. *Wernicke's area* interprets language by receiving impulses from the primary auditory area, where sensations from the ears are sent. To produce a verbal response, Wernicke's area communicates with Broca's area through a bundle of nerve fibers, represented by dotted lines in the figure.

already knew, toddlers advanced in language development showed electrical activity concentrated in certain regions of the left hemisphere. Those less advanced displayed a more widely distributed response (Mills, Coffey-Corina, & Neville, 1993). This relationship between brain lateralization and language competence is certainly consistent with the idea that an LAD exists in a specific part of the brain.

■ **LIMITATIONS OF THE NATIVIST PERSPECTIVE.** Chomsky's theory has had a major impact on current views of language development. It is now widely accepted that humans have a unique, biological predisposition to acquire language. At the same time, Chomsky's account of development has been challenged.

First, researchers have had great difficulty identifying the single system of grammar that Chomsky believes underlies all languages. Even simple grammatical distinctions, such as the use of *the* versus *a,* are made in quite different ways around the world. For example, several African languages rely on tone patterns to express these articles. In Japanese and Chinese, they are inferred entirely from sentence context. Critics of Chomsky's theory doubt the existence of an LAD that can account for such varied approaches to conveying the same meaning (Maratsos, 1998; Tomasello, 1995).

Second, language acquisition is no longer regarded as accomplished quite as quickly as nativist theory suggests. Although extraordinary strides are made during the early years, children's progress in mastering many sentence constructions is not immediate, but steady and gradual. As we will see in Chapter 12, complete mastery of some grammatical forms is not achieved until well into middle childhood (Tager-Flusberg, 1997). This suggests that more learning and discovery are involved in language development than Chomsky assumed.

■ **THE INTERACTIONIST PERSPECTIVE.** In recent years, new ideas about language development have arisen, emphasizing *interactions* between inner capacities and environmental influences. Although several interactionist theories exist, all stress the social context of language learning. An active child, well endowed for acquiring language, observes and participates in social exchanges. From these experiences, children gradually build a communication system that relates the form and content of language to its social meaning. According to this view, native capacity, a strong desire to interact with others, and a rich language and social environment combine to assist children in discovering the functions and regularities of language (Bohannon & Bonvillian, 1997).

Although all interactionists regard children as active, communicative beings, debate continues over the precise nature of their innate language abilities. Some theorists accept a modified view of Chomsky's position. They believe that children are primed to acquire

TABLE 6.4

Milestones of Language Development During the First Two Years

APPROXIMATE AGE	MILESTONE
2 months	Infants coo, making pleasurable vowel sounds.
4 months on	Infants and parents establish joint attention, and parents often verbally label what the baby is looking at.
6–14 months	Infants babble, adding consonants to the sounds of the cooing period and repeating syllables. By 7 months, babbling of hearing infants starts to include many sounds of mature spoken languages. Deaf babies exposed to sign language babble with their hands.
6–14 months	Infants become capable of playing simple games, such as pat-a-cake and peekaboo. These provide practice in conversational turn-taking and also highlight the meaning and function of spoken words.
8–12 months	Infants begin using preverbal gestures, such as showing and pointing, to influence the behavior of others. Word comprehension first appears.
12 months	Infants say their first recognizable word.
18–24 months	Vocabulary expands from about 50 to 200 words.
20–26 months	Toddlers combine two words.

language but form and refine hypotheses about its structure based on language experience (Slobin, 1985). Other theorists are impressed by the remarkable cognitive capacities of infants and preschoolers. They believe that children make sense of their complex language environments by applying powerful strategies of a general cognitive kind rather than ones specifically tuned to language (Bates, 1995; MacWhinney, 1996).

As we chart the course of early language growth, we will come across a great deal of evidence that supports the interactionist position. But we must keep in mind that none of these theories has yet been fully tested. In reality, biology, cognition, and social experience may operate in different balances with respect to various aspects of language— vocabulary, grammar, and communication skills. And to complicate matters further, their relative contributions may change with age. Table 6.4 provides an overview of early language milestones that we will take up in the next few sections.

GETTING READY TO TALK

Before babies say their first word, they are preparing for language in many ways. They listen attentively to human speech, and they make speechlike sounds. As adults, we can hardly help but respond.

■ **COOING AND BABBLING.** Around 2 months, babies begin to make vowel-like noises, called **cooing** because of their pleasant "oo" quality. Gradually, consonants are added, and around 6 months **babbling** appears, in which infants repeat consonant–vowel combinations in long strings, such as "bababababa" or "nanananana."

The timing of early babbling seems to be due to maturation, since babies everywhere (even those who are deaf) start babbling at about the same age and produce a similar range of early sounds (Stoel-Gammon & Otomo, 1986). But for babbling to develop further, infants must be able to hear human speech. Around 7 months, babbling starts to include the sounds of mature spoken languages. However, if a baby's hearing is impaired, these speechlike sounds are greatly delayed, and, in the case of deaf infants, are totally absent (Eilers & Oller, 1994; Oller & Eilers, 1988). When deaf infants are exposed to sign language from birth, they babble with their hands in much the same way hearing infants do through speech (Petitto & Marentette, 1991).

cooing
Pleasant vowel-like noises made by infants, beginning around 2 months of age.

babbling
Repetition of consonant–vowel combinations in long strings, beginning around 6 months of age.

This 15-month-old delights in playing peekaboo with her mother. As she participates, she practices the turn-taking pattern of human conversation. *(Tony Freeman/PhotoEdit)*

When a baby coos or babbles and gazes at you, what are you likely to do? One day while I was standing in line at the post office, a mother and her 7-month-old daughter entered. As we waited, the baby babbled, and three adults—myself and two people standing beside me—started to talk to the infant. We cooed and babbled ourselves, imitating the baby, and also said such things as "My, you're a big girl, aren't you? Out to help Mommy mail letters today?" Then the baby smiled and babbled all the more.

As infants listen to spoken language, babbling increases. By the end of the first year, it reflects the consonant–vowel and intonation patterns of the infant's language community, some of which are transferred to their first words (Boysson-Bardies & Vihman, 1991). Listen to an older baby babble, and you are likely to notice that certain sounds appear in particular contexts—for example, when exploring objects, looking at books, and walking upright (Blake & Boysson-Bardies, 1992). Through babbling, babies experiment with both the sound system and the meaning of language before they speak in conventional ways.

■ **BECOMING A COMMUNICATOR.** Adults interact with infants not only when they coo and babble, but in many other situations. By age 4 months, infants start to gaze in the same direction adults are looking, and adults follow the baby's line of vision as well. When this happens, parents often comment on what the infant sees. In this way, the environment is labeled for the baby. Researchers believe that this joint attention may be quite important for early language development. Infants and toddlers who often experience it talk earlier and show faster vocabulary development (Dunham & Dunham, 1992; Dunham, Dunham, & Curwin, 1993).

Around 6 months, interaction between parent and baby begins to include give-and-take. Turn-taking games, such as pat-a-cake and peekaboo, appear. At first, the parent starts the game and the baby is an amused observer. But by 12 months, babies actively participate, exchanging roles with the parent. As they do so, they practice the turn-taking pattern of human conversation, and they also hear words paired with the actions they perform (Ratner & Bruner, 1978).

At the end of the first year, as infants become capable of intentional behavior, they use preverbal gestures to influence the behavior of others (Bates, 1979; Fenson et al., 1994). For example, they hold up a toy to show it or point to the cupboard to ask for a cookie. When adults respond to babies' gestures and also label them ("Oh, you want a cookie!"), infants learn that using language quickly leads to desired results. Soon toddlers utter words along with these reaching and pointing gestures, the gestures recede, and spoken language is under way (Goldin-Meadow & Morford, 1985).

FIRST WORDS

Ask several parents of toddlers to tell you which words appeared first in their children's vocabularies. You will quickly see that early language builds on the sensorimotor foundations Piaget described and on categories children construct during the first 2 years. First words refer to important people ("Mama," "Dadda"), objects that move or can be acted on ("ball," "car," "cat," "shoe"), familiar actions ("bye-bye," "more," "up"), or outcomes of familiar actions ("dirty," "hot," "wet"). In their first 50 words, toddlers rarely name things that just *sit there*, like table or vase (Nelson, 1973). Sensorimotor contributions to early language are also supported by evidence that hearing children exposed to both signed and spoken words are slightly advanced in learning signed symbols (Goodwyn & Acredolo, 1993).

Some early words are linked to specific cognitive achievements. For example, use of disappearance words, like "all gone," occurs at about the same time toddlers master advanced object permanence problems. And success and failure expressions, such as "there!" and "uh-oh!" appear when toddlers can solve sensorimotor problems suddenly, in Piaget's Substage 6. As one pair of researchers concluded, "Children seem to be motivated to acquire words that are relevant to the particular cognitive problems they are working on at the moment" (Gopnik & Meltzoff, 1986, p. 1057).

Besides cognition, emotion influences early word learning. At first, toddlers' talk focuses on people, objects, and events that their feelings are about rather than on the feelings themselves. When acquiring a word, Byron, Rachel, and April said it rather neutrally; they needed to listen carefully to learn, and strong emotion drew attention away from this process. As the word became better learned, they integrated talking and expressing feelings (Bloom, 1998). "Shoe!" April said with an enthusiastic grin as Felicia tied April's shoelaces before an outing. In the last half of the second year, toddlers begin to label their emotions with words like "happy," "mad," and "sad"—a development we will consider further in Chapter 7.

Toddlers often do not use a new word in just the way we do. Sometimes they apply it too narrowly, an error called **underextension.** For example, at 16 months, April used the word "doll" only to refer to the worn and tattered doll that she carried around with her much of the day. A more common error is **overextension**—applying a word to a wider collection of objects and events than is appropriate. For example, Rachel used the word "car" for buses, trains, trucks, and fire engines.

Toddlers' overextensions reflect a remarkable sensitivity to categorical relations. They do not overextend randomly. Instead, they apply a new word to a group of similar experiences, such as "dog" to refer to furry, four-legged animals and "open" to mean opening a door, peeling fruit, and untying shoelaces (Behrend, 1988; Naigles & Gelman, 1995). This suggests that children sometimes overextend deliberately because they have difficulty recalling or have not acquired a suitable word. In addition, when a word is hard to pronounce, toddlers are likely to substitute a related one they can say (Elsen, 1994). As their vocabularies enlarge, children start to make finer distinctions, and overextensions gradually disappear.

THE TWO-WORD UTTERANCE PHASE

Young toddlers add to their vocabularies slowly, at a rate of 1 to 3 words a month. Over time, the number of words learned accelerates. Between 18 and 24 months, a spurt in vocabulary usually takes place. Many children add 10 to 20 new words a week, an increase that occurs at about the same time their understanding of categories accelerates (Fenson et al., 1994; Reznick & Goldfield, 1992). An improved ability to retrieve words from memory also contributes to this "naming explosion" (Gershkoff-Stowe & Smith, 1997).

As vocabulary size moves toward 200 words, toddlers combine two words, such as "Mommy shoe," "go car," and "more cookie," and "my truck," in **telegraphic speech.** Like

underextension
An early vocabulary error in which a word is applied too narrowly, to a smaller number of objects and events than is appropriate.

overextension
An early vocabulary error in which a word is applied too broadly, to a wider collection of objects and events than is appropriate.

telegraphic speech
Toddlers' two-word utterances that, like a telegram, leave out smaller and less important words.

a telegram, they focus on high-content words and leave out smaller and less important ones, such as "can," "the," and "to." For children learning languages that emphasize word order (such as English and French), endings like "-s" and "-ed" are not yet present. In languages in which word order is flexible and small grammatical markers are stressed, children's first sentences include them from the start (de Villiers & de Villiers, 1992).

Even though the two-word utterance is very limited, toddlers the world over use it to express an impressive variety of meanings. In doing so, are they already applying a consistent grammar? At least to some extent they are, since children rarely engage in gross violations of the structure of their language. For example, April said "Daddy eat" rather than "eat Daddy" and "my chair" rather than "chair my" (Bloom, 1990). Yet two-word sentences are largely based on simple formulas, such as "want X" and "more X," in which toddlers insert many different words in the X position. And many early word combinations do not follow adult grammatical rules (Maratsos & Chalkley, 1980). At 20 months, Rachel said "more hot" and "more read," expressions not acceptable in English grammar.

These findings tell us that in learning to talk, toddlers are absorbed in figuring out the meanings of words and using their limited vocabularies in whatever way possible to get their thoughts across to others. Some of their expressions match adult rules, whereas others reflect their own ideas about particular word combinations (Owens, 1996). But it does not take long for children to figure out the basic structure of their language. As we will see in Chapter 9, the beginnings of grammar are in place by age 2½.

COMPREHENSION VERSUS PRODUCTION

So far, we have focused on language **production**—the words and word combinations children use. What about **comprehension**—the language children understand? At all ages, comprehension develops ahead of production. For example, the 8-month-old whose mother says "Where's the doggie?" is likely to look around the room for the family's pet dog. And toddlers follow many simple directions, such as "Bring me your book" or "Don't touch the lamp," even though they cannot yet express all these words in their own speech.

Why is language comprehension ahead of production? Think back to the distinction made earlier in this chapter between two types of memory—recognition and recall. Comprehension requires only that children recognize the meaning of a word, whereas production demands that they recall, or actively retrieve from their memories, the word as well as the concept for which it stands (Kuczaj, 1986). Language production is clearly a more difficult task. Failure to say a word does not mean that toddlers do not understand it. When we evaluate a child's language development, we need to keep both of these processes in mind. If we rely only on what children say, we will underestimate their knowledge of language.

INDIVIDUAL AND CULTURAL DIFFERENCES IN EARLY LANGUAGE DEVELOPMENT

We have discussed steps in language development that characterize children everywhere. But as we have seen with Byron, Rachel, and April, great individual differences exist in how quickly language learning proceeds. Each child's progress results from a complex blend of biological and environmental influences.

Recall that Byron's spoken language was delayed, in part because Lisa pressured him a great deal. But Byron is also a boy, and many studies show that girls are slightly ahead of boys in early vocabulary growth (Fenson et al., 1994). The most common biological explanation is girls' faster rate of physical maturation, believed to promote earlier development of the left cerebral hemisphere, where language is housed. But mothers also talk much more to toddler-age girls than boys (Leaper, Anderson, & Sanders, 1998). Besides the child's sex, temperament makes a difference. Toddlers who are very reserved and cautious often wait until they understand a great deal before trying to speak. When they finally do speak, their vocabularies grow rapidly (Nelson, 1973).

production
In language development, the words and word combinations that children use.

comprehension
In language development, the words and word combinations that children understand.

This Nepalese mother speaks to her baby daughter in short, clearly pronounced sentences with high-pitched, exaggerated intonation. Adults in many countries use this form of language, called child-directed speech, with infants and toddlers. It eases the task of early language learning. *(David Austen/Stock Boston)*

referential style
A style of early language learning in which toddlers use language mainly to label objects.

expressive style
A style of early language learning in which toddlers use language mainly to talk about the feelings and needs of themselves and other people. Initial vocabulary emphasizes pronouns and social formulas.

child-directed speech (CDS)
A form of language adults use to speak to infants and toddlers that consists of short sentences with high-pitched, exaggerated expression, clear pronunciation, and distinct pauses between speech segments.

Listen closely to what toddlers say, and you are likely to observe some unique styles of early language learning. April (like most toddlers) used a **referential style;** her vocabulary consisted of many words that referred to objects. In contrast, Rachel used an **expressive style.** She produced many more pronouns and social formulas, such as "stop it," "thank you," and "I want it," which she uttered as compressed phrases, much like single words (as in "Iwannit"). Toddlers who use these styles have different early ideas about the functions of language. April thought words were for naming objects, whereas Rachel believed they were for talking about the feelings and needs of herself and other people. April's vocabulary grew faster, since all languages contain many more object labels than social phrases (Bates, Bretherton, & Snyder, 1988; Bates et al., 1994).

What accounts for a toddler's choice of a particular language style? Once again, both biological and environmental factors seem to be involved. April had an especially active interest in exploring objects and parents who eagerly responded with names of things to her first attempts to talk. She also freely imitated words she heard others say, a strategy that supports swift vocabulary growth because it helps children retain new labels in memory (Masur, 1995). Rachel's personality was more social, and she listened carefully as her parents used verbal routines ("How are you?" "It's no trouble") designed to support social relationships (Goldfield, 1987).

The two language styles are also linked to culture. When speaking to infants and toddlers, American mothers label objects more frequently than do Japanese mothers. In contrast, Japanese mothers more often engage young children in social routines, perhaps because their culture stresses the importance of membership in the social group (Fernald & Morikawa, 1993). Similarly, African mothers of Mali, Mauritania, and Senegal respond verbally to their infant's glances and vocalizations to other people, not to the baby's exploration of objects (Jamin, 1994).

Sheer amount of parental speech is related to variations in early word learning. The more words caregivers use, the greater the number that toddlers pick up. And words parents say very often tend to be acquired earliest (Hart, 1991; Huttenlocher et al., 1991). Whereas object words (nouns) are particularly common in the vocabularies of English-speaking toddlers, action words (verbs) are more numerous among early Korean and Mandarin Chinese speakers. When caregivers' speech is examined in each culture, it reflects these very differences (Choi & Gopnik, 1995; Tardif, 1996).

At what point should parents be concerned if their child does not talk or says very little? If a toddler's language is greatly delayed when compared to the norms given in Table 6.4, then parents should consult the child's doctor or arrange for an evaluation by a speech and language therapist. Some toddlers who do not follow simple directions could have a hearing problem. A child over age 2 who has great difficulty putting thoughts into words may have a serious language disorder that requires immediate and intensive treatment (Ratner, 1997).

SUPPORTING EARLY LANGUAGE DEVELOPMENT

There is little doubt that children are biologically prepared for acquiring language, since no other species can develop as flexible and creative a capacity for communication as we can. At the same time, a great deal of evidence fits with the interactionist approach—that a rich social environment builds on young children's natural readiness to speak their native tongue. The Caregiving Concerns table on the following page summarizes ways that caregivers can consciously support early language learning. They also do so unconsciously—through a special style of speech.

Adults in many countries speak to young children in **child-directed speech (CDS),** a form of language made up of short sentences with high-pitched, exaggerated expression, clear pronunciation, and distinct pauses between speech segments (Fernald et al., 1989). CDS also contains many simplified words, such as "night-night," "bye-bye," and "tummy," that are easy for toddlers to pronounce. In addition, speakers of CDS often repeat

CAREGIVING CONCERNS

Supporting Early Language Learning

SUGGESTION	CONSEQUENCE
Respond to coos and babbles with speech sounds and words	Encourages experimentation with sounds that can later be blended into first words. Provides experience with turn-taking pattern of human conversation.
Establish joint attention and comment on what child sees	Predicts earlier onset of language and faster vocabulary development.
Play social games, such as pat-a-cake and peekaboo	Provides experience with with turn-taking pattern of human conversation. Permits pairing of words with actions they represent.
Engage toddlers in joint make-believe play	Promotes all aspects of conversational dialogue.
Engage toddlers in frequent conversations	Predicts faster early language development and academic competence during the school years.
Read to toddlers often, engaging them in dialogues about picture books	Provides exposure to many aspects of language, including vocabulary, grammar, communicative conventions, and information about written symbols and story structures.

Sources: Berk, 1994; Dunham & Dunham, 1992; Dunham, Dunham, & Curwin, 1993; Hart & Risley, 1995; Ratner & Bruner, 1978; Walker et al., 1994.

phrases, ask questions, and give directions, perhaps as a way of checking to see if their message has been properly received. Deaf parents use a similar style of communication when signing to their babies (Masataka, 1992). Here is an example of Felicia using CDS with 18-month-old April as together they get ready to leave for home:

April: "Go car."

Felicia: "Yes, time to go in the car. Where's your jacket?"

April: (looks around, walks to the closet) "Dacket!" (pointing to her jacket)

Felicia: "There's that jacket! Let's put it on. (She helps April into the jacket.) On it goes! Let's zip up. (Zips up the jacket.) Now, say bye-bye to Byron and Rachel."

April: "Bye-bye, By-on."

Felicia: "What about Rachel? Bye to Rachel?"

April: "Bye-bye, Ta-tel (Rachel)."

Felicia: "Where's your doll? Don't forget your doll."

April: (looks around)

Felicia: "Look by the sofa. See? Go get the doll. By the sofa." (April gets the doll.)

Parents do not seem to be deliberately trying to teach children to talk when they use CDS, since many of the same speech qualities appear when adults communicate with foreigners. CDS probably arises from adults' unconscious desire to keep young children's attention and ease their task of understanding, and it works effectively in these ways. From birth on, children prefer to listen to CDS over other kinds of adult talk (Cooper & Aslin, 1994). By 5 months, they are more emotionally responsive to it and can discriminate the tone quality of CDS with different meanings—for example, approving from soothing utterances (Moore, Spence, & Katz, 1997; Werker, Pegg, & McLeod, 1994).

Dialogues about picture books are an especially effective way of stimulating young children's language development. As this father talks about the pictures with his 2-year-old daughter, he exposes her to great breadth of language and literacy knowledge. *(Tony Freeman/PhotoEdit)*

Parents constantly fine-tune CDS to fit with children's needs. Notice how Felicia used an utterance length that was just ahead of April's, creating a sensitive match between the stimulation she provided and what April was capable of understanding and producing. In a study carried out in four cultures, American, Argentinean, French, and Japanese mothers tended to speak to 5-month-olds in emotion-laden ways, emphasizing greetings, repeated sounds, and affectionate names. At 13 months, when toddlers began to understand as well as respond, more maternal speech was information-laden—concerned with giving directions, asking questions, and describing what was happening at the moment (Bornstein et al., 1992b).

CDS contains many features that support early language development. For example, parents who frequently repeat part of their own or the child's previous utterance and use simple questions have 2-year-olds who make faster language progress (Hoff-Ginsberg, 1986). But this does not mean that we should deliberately load our speech to toddlers with repetitions, questions, and other characteristics of CDS! These qualities occur naturally as adults draw young children into dialogues in which their attempts to talk are accepted as meaningful and worthwhile. Conversational give-and-take between parent and toddler is one of the best predictors of early language development and academic competence during the school years. It provides many examples of speech just ahead of the child's current level and a sympathetic environment in which children pick up many new cognitive skills (Huttenlocher et al., 1991; Walker et al., 1994).

As early as the second year, reading to children facilitates language progress. Adult–toddler story reading is related to language ability and a variety of reading readiness measures during the preschool years (Crain-Thoreson & Dale, 1992). When caregivers engage children in dialogues about books and respond contingently to their verbalizations, reading exposes them to great breadth of language knowledge, from vocabulary, grammar, and communicative conventions to information about written symbols and story structures. Reading picture and story books is especially helpful for low-income toddlers at risk for later language and literacy problems. Two- and 3-year-olds who participate in daily reading experiences in day care or at home, compared with those who do not, are greatly advanced in language comprehension and production (Valdez-Menchaca & Whitehurst, 1992; Whitehurst et al., 1994).

Do social experiences that promote language development remind you of ones discussed earlier in this chapter that strengthen cognitive development in general? Notice how parent–child conversation and CDS that is a part of it create a *zone of proximal development* in which children's language expands. In the next chapter, we will see that the very same sensitivity to children's needs and capacities that supports cognition and language is at the heart of their emotional and social development as well.

ASK YOURSELF . . .

■ *Erin's first words included "see," "give," and "thank you," and her vocabulary grew slowly during the second year. What style of early language learning did she display, and what factors might explain it?*

■ *Cognition and language are interrelated. Cite examples of how cognitive development fosters language progress. Next, cite examples of how language development fosters cognitive advances.*

ummary

PIAGET'S COGNITIVE-DEVELOPMENTAL THEORY

According to Piaget, how do schemes change over the course of development?

■ Influenced by his background in biology, Piaget viewed cognitive development as an adaptive process. By acting directly on the environment, children move through four stages in which internal structures achieve a better fit with external reality.

■ In Piaget's theory, psychological structures, or **schemes,** change in two ways. The first is through **adaptation,** which is made up of two complementary activities—**assimilation** and **accommodation.** The second is through **organization,** the internal rearrangement of schemes so that they form a strongly interconnected cognitive system.

Describe the major cognitive achievements of the sensorimotor stage.

■ Piaget's **sensorimotor stage** is divided into six substages. Through the **circular reaction,** the newborn baby's reflexes are gradually transformed into the more flexible action patterns of the older infant and finally into the representational schemes of the 2-year-old child. During Substage 4, infants develop **intentional,** or **goal-directed, behavior** and begin to understand **physical causality** and **object permanence.** Substage 5 brings a more exploratory approach to **functional play** and infants no longer make the **AB search error.** By Substage 6, toddlers can **mentally represent** reality, as shown by **deferred imitation** and **make-believe play.**

What does recent research have to say about the accuracy of Piaget's sensorimotor stage?

■ Piaget underestimated the capacities of young infants. Secondary circular reactions, physical reasoning (including object permanence and physical causality), and deferred imitation are present earlier than Piaget believed.

■ Today, researchers believe that newborns have more built-in equipment for making sense of their world than Piaget assumed. Some speculate that infants build important schemes through perceptual learning. Others advocate a nativist, **modular view of the mind** that grants newborns substantial built-in knowledge. The future is likely to bring compromises between these views.

INFORMATION PROCESSING

Describe the information-processing view of cognitive development and the general structure of the information-processing system.

■ Unlike Piaget's stage theory, information processing regards development as a continuous process; the cognitive approach of children and adults is assumed to be much the same. Information-processing researchers study many different aspects of thinking. They want to know exactly what individuals of different ages do when faced with a task or problem.

■ Most general models of the information-processing system divide the mind into three parts: the **sensory register; working,** or **short-term, memory;** and **long-term memory.** As information flows through each, **mental strategies** operate on it to increase the efficiency of thinking as well as the chances that information will be retained.

What changes in attention, memory, and categorization take place over the first 2 years?

■ With age, infants attend to more aspects of the environment, take information into their mental systems more quickly, and flexibly shift their attention from one stimulus to another. In the second year, attention to novelty declines and sustained attention improves, especially during play with toys.

■ As infants get older, they remember experiences longer. Young infants are capable of **recognition** memory; by 7 months, they can **recall** stimuli that are not pre-

sent. By the end of toddlerhood, recall for people, places, and objects is excellent. Both biology and social experience probably contribute to the emergence of **autobiographical memory.**

■ Infants remember information in a remarkably orderly fashion. During the first year, they group stimuli into increasingly complex and meaningful categories. In the second year, they become active categorizers, spontaneously sorting objects during their play.

Describe the contributions and limitations of the information-processing approach to our understanding of early cognitive development.

■ Information processing has contributed greatly to our view of young infants as sophisticated cognitive beings. It challenges Piaget's view of early cognitive development as taking place in discrete stages. However, it has not yet provided a broad, comprehensive theory of children's thinking.

THE SOCIAL CONTEXT OF EARLY COGNITIVE DEVELOPMENT

How does Vygotsky's concept of the zone of proximal development expand our understanding of early cognitive development?

■ According to Vygotsky's sociocultural theory, complex mental functions have their origins in social interaction. By engaging in joint activities with more skilled partners, infants master tasks within the **zone of proximal development**—ones just ahead of their current capacities. Through the support and guidance of others, cognitive competence increases.

INDIVIDUAL DIFFERENCES IN EARLY MENTAL DEVELOPMENT

Describe the mental testing approach, the meaning of intelligence test scores, and the extent to which infant tests predict later performance.

Summary (continued)

■ The mental testing approach measures intellectual development in an effort to predict future performance. **Intelligence quotients, or IQs,** are scores on mental tests that compare a child's performance to that of same-age children. Infant tests consist largely of perceptual and motor responses; they predict later intelligence poorly. As a result, scores on infant tests are called **developmental quotients, or DQs,** rather than IQs. The habituation–dishabituation sequence and object permanence, which tap basic cognitive processes, show better predictability.

Discuss environmental influences on early mental development, including home, day care, and early intervention for at-risk infants and toddlers.

■ Research with the **Home Observation for Measurement of the Environment (HOME)** reveals that stimulation provided by the home environment and parental encouragement, involvement, affection, and verbal responsiveness repeatedly predict early mental test scores, no matter what the child's background. Although the HOME–IQ relationship is partly due to heredity, family living conditions do affect mental development.

■ The quality of infant and toddler day care has a major impact on cognitive and social skills. Standards for **developmentally appropriate practice** specify program characteristics that meet the developmental needs of young children. Intensive early intervention is required to prevent the gradual declines in intelligence so often experienced by poverty-stricken children.

LANGUAGE DEVELOPMENT

Describe three theories of language development, and indicate the emphasis each places on innate abilities and environmental influences.

■ Three theories provide different accounts of how young children develop language. According to the behaviorist perspective, parents train children in language skills by relying on operant conditioning and imitation. Behaviorism has difficulty accounting for children's novel, rule-based utterances.

■ Chomsky's nativist view regards children as naturally endowed with a **language acquisition device (LAD).** Consistent with this perspective, a complex language system is unique to humans, and language-specific structures—**Broca's** and **Wernicke's areas**—can be found in the left hemisphere of the cortex. However, vast diversity among languages and children's gradual mastery of many constructions have raised questions about Chomsky's theory.

■ New interactionist theories offer a compromise between these extreme views, stressing that innate abilities and social contexts combine to promote language development.

Describe major milestones of language development in the first 2 years, individual differences, and ways in which adults support infants' and toddlers' emerging capacities.

■ During the first year, a great deal of preparation for language takes place. Infants begin **cooing** at 2 months and **babbling** around 6 months. When adults respond to infants' coos and babbles, play turn-taking games with them, and acknowledge their preverbal gestures, they encourage language progress.

■ Around 12 months, toddlers say their first word. When picking up new words, young children make errors involving **underextension** and **overextension.** Between 18 and 24 months, a spurt in vocabulary typically occurs, and two-word utterances called **telegraphic speech** appear. At all ages, language **comprehension** develops ahead of **production**.

■ Individual differences in early language development exist. Girls show faster progress than boys, and reserved, cautious toddlers may wait for a period of time before trying to speak. Most toddlers use a **referential style** of language learning, in which early words consist largely of names for objects. A few use an **expressive style,** in which social formulas are common and vocabulary grows more slowly. Temperament, culture, and language environment distinguish referential- from expressive-style toddlers.

■ Adults in many cultures speak to young children in **child-directed speech (CDS),** a simplified form of language that is well suited to children's learning needs. CDS occurs naturally when caregivers engage toddlers in conversations that accept and encourage their early efforts to talk.

Important terms and concepts

AB search error (p.217)
accommodation (p. 213)
adaptation (p. 213)
assimilation (p. 213)
autobiographical memory (p. 226)
babbling (p. 242)
Broca's area (p. 240)
child-directed speech (CDS) (p. 246)
circular reaction (p. 213)
comprehension (p. 245)
cooing (p. 242)
deferred imitation (p. 217)
developmental quotient, or DQ
  (p. 233)
developmentally appropriate practice
  (p. 236)
expressive style (p. 246)

functional play (p. 217)
Home Observation for Measurement
  of the Environment, (HOME)
  (p. 233)
intelligence quotient, or IQ (p. 232)
intentional, or goal-directed, behavior
  (p. 215)
language acquisition device (LAD)
  (p. 240)
long-term memory (p. 224)
make-believe play (p. 217)
mental representation (p. 217)
mental strategies (p. 224)
modular view of the mind (p. 222)
object permanence (p. 217)
organization (p. 213)
overextension (p. 244)

physical causality (p. 215)
production (p. 245)
recall (p. 226)
recognition (p. 226)
referential style (p. 246)
scheme (p. 212)
sensorimotor stage (p. 212)
sensory register (p. 224)
telegraphic speech (p. 244)
underextension (p. 244)
Wernicke's area (p. 240)
working, or short-term, memory
  (p. 224)
zone of proximal development
  (p. 229)

FYI... FOR FURTHER INFORMATION AND HELP

INFANT AND TODDLER CARE, DEVELOPMENT, AND EDUCATION

Association for Childhood Education
International (ACEI)
(301) 942-2443
Website: www.udel.edu/bateman/acei

Organization interested in promoting sound educational practice from infancy through early adolescence. Student membership is available and includes a subscription to Childhood Education, *a bimonthly journal covering research, practice, and public policy issues.*

National Association for the Education of
Young Children (NAEYC)
(800) 424-2460
Website: www.naeyc.org/naeyc

Organization open to all individuals interested in acting on behalf of young children's needs, with primary focus on educational services. Student membership is available. Membership and includes a subscription to Young Children, *a bimonthly journal covering theory, research, and practice in infant and early childhood development and education.*

National Association for
Family Child Care
(800) 359-3817
Website: www.assoc-mgmt.com/users.nafcc

Organization open to caregivers, parents, and other individuals involved or interested in family day care. Serves as a national voice that promotes high-quality day care.

EARLY INTERVENTION

High/Scope Educational Research
Foundation
(313) 485-2000
Website: www//highscope.org

Devoted to improving development and education from infancy through the high school years. Has designed a parent–infant education program. Conducts longitudinal research to determine the effects of early intervention on development.

"Kite Flying"
Chen Xiao
5 years, China

When parents care for infants and toddlers with love and sensitivity, their competence in relating to peers builds quickly, as this scene of young kite fliers reveals. The importance of early family relationships for emotional and social development is a major theme of Chapter 7.

EMOTIONAL AND SOCIAL DEVELOPMENT

IN INFANCY AND TODDLERHOOD

*L*isa, Beth, and

Felicia's monthly conversations often focused on the emotional and social sides of their infants' development. As the babies reached 8 months of age, Beth noticed some important changes: "For some reason, Rachel's become more fearful in the last few weeks. I took her to the airport to meet my parents, who recently arrived from Japan. When they stepped off the plane and tried to hug her, she didn't return their enthusiasm, as she would have a month or two ago. Instead, she turned her head away and buried it against my shoulder. Several days later, I left Rachel with my parents for several hours—the first time I'd been away from her since she was born. She wailed as soon as she saw me head for the door. And when I returned, Rachel seemed angry. She insisted on being held but also pushed me away and continued to cry. It took 5 or 10 minutes before I was able to calm her down."

Lisa and Felicia also reported an increasing wariness of strangers in Byron and April, and a strong desire to remain close to familiar adults. At the same time, each baby seemed more willful. An object removed from the hand at 5 months produced little response, but at 8 months Byron actively resisted when Lisa took away a table knife he had managed to reach. And he could not be consoled by the toys she offered in its place. Taken together, these reactions reflect two related aspects of personality that begin to develop during the first 2 years: *close ties to others* and *a sense of self*—an awareness of one's own separateness and uniqueness.

Our discussion begins with major theories that provide an overall picture of personality development during infancy and toddlerhood. Then we take a look at factors that contribute to these changes. First, we chart the general course of emotional development. As we do so, we will discover why fear and anger became more apparent in Byron, Rachel, and April's range of emotions by the end of the first year. Second, our attention turns to individual differences in temperament and personality. We will examine biological and environmental contributions to these differences and their consequences for future development.

Next, we take up attachment to the caregiver, the child's first affectional tie that develops over the course of infancy. We will see how the feelings of security that grow out of this important bond provide a vital source of support for the child's exploration, sense of independence, and expanding social relationships.

Finally, we focus on early self-development. By the end of toddlerhood, April recognized herself in mirrors and photographs, labeled herself as a girl, and showed the beginnings of self-control. "Don't touch!" she instructed herself one day as she resisted the desire to pull a lamp cord out of its socket. Cognitive advances combine with social experiences to produce these changes during the second year.

THEORIES OF INFANT AND TODDLER PERSONALITY

*I*n Chapter 1, we pointed out that psychoanalytic theory is no longer in the mainstream of child development research. But one of its lasting contributions has been its ability to capture the essence of personality development during each phase of life. Recall from Chapter 1 that Sigmund Freud, founder of the psychoanalytic movement, believed that psychological health and maladjustment could be traced to the early years—in particular, to the quality of the child's relationships with parents.

Return to page 16 of Chapter 1 and reread the brief description of Freud's *psychosexual stages*. Freud's limited concern with the channeling of instincts and his neglect of important experiences beyond infancy and early childhood came to be heavily criticized. But the basic outlines of his theory were accepted and elaborated by several noted psychoanalysts who came after him. The leader of these neo-Freudians is Erik Erikson, whose *psychosocial theory* was also introduced in Chapter 1.

In the following sections, we take a closer look at the emotional and social tasks of infancy and toddlerhood, as Erikson and a second well-known psychoanalyst—Margaret Mahler—saw them. Although each emphasized somewhat different features of early experience as central to development, we will see that the two theories have much in common.

ERIK ERIKSON: TRUST AND AUTONOMY

Erikson (1950) characterized each stage of development as an inner conflict, which is resolved positively or negatively, depending on the child's experiences with caregivers. When parenting supports the child's needs, the first year leads to feelings of trust in others and the next 2 years to a sense of personal autonomy. These early attitudes provide the foundation for healthy emotional and social development throughout life.

According to Erikson, basic trust grows out of the quality of the mother's relationship with the baby. A mother who relieves her infant's discomfort promptly and holds the baby tenderly, especially during feedings, promotes basic trust. *(Jeffrey W. Myers/Stock Boston)*

■ **BASIC TRUST VERSUS MISTRUST.** Freud called the first year the *oral stage* and regarded gratification of the infant's need for food and oral stimulation as vital. Erikson accepted Freud's emphasis on the importance of feeding, but he expanded and enriched Freud's view. A healthy outcome during infancy, Erikson believed, does not depend on the *amount* of food or oral stimulation offered, but rather on the *quality* of the caregiver's behavior. A mother who supports her baby's development relieves discomfort promptly and sensitively. For example, she holds the infant gently during feedings, patiently waits until the baby has had enough milk, and weans when the infant shows less interest in the breast or bottle and sucking.

Erikson recognized that it is impossible to be constantly and perfectly in tune with the baby's needs. Many factors affect maternal responsiveness—feelings of personal happiness, momentary life conditions (for example, whether she has one or several small children to care for), and culturally valued child-rearing practices. But when the *balance of care* is sympathetic and loving, then the psychological conflict of the first year—**basic trust versus mistrust**—is resolved on the positive side. The trusting infant expects the world to be good and gratifying, so he feels confident about venturing out and exploring it. The mistrustful baby cannot count on the kindness and compassion of others, so he protects himself by withdrawing from people and things around him.

■ **AUTONOMY VERSUS SHAME AND DOUBT.** During Freud's *anal stage,* instinctual energies shift to the anal region of the body. He viewed toilet training, in which children must bring their impulses in line with social requirements, as crucial for personality development. (Return to Chapter 5, page 189, to review how adults can best support toddlers' attainment of bladder and bowel control.)

Erikson agreed that the parent's manner of toilet training is essential for psychological health. But he regarded it as only one of a broad range of important experiences encountered by newly walking, talking toddlers. Their familiar refrains—"No!" and "Do it myself!"—reveal that they want to decide for themselves with all their powers, not just in toileting, but in other situations as well. The great conflict of this stage, **autonomy versus shame and doubt,** is resolved favorably when parents provide young children with suitable guidance and reasonable choices. A self-confident, secure 2-year-old has been encouraged not just to use the toilet but also to eat with a spoon and to help pick up his toys. His parents do not criticize or attack him when he fails in these new skills. And they meet his assertions of independence with tolerance and understanding. For example, they grant him an extra 5 minutes to finish his play before leaving for the grocery store and wait patiently while he tries to zip his jacket.

basic trust versus mistrust
In Erikson's theory, the psychological conflict of infancy, which is resolved positively if caregiving, especially during feeding, is sympathetic and loving.

autonomy versus shame and doubt
In Erikson's theory, the psychological conflict of toddlerhood, which is resolved positively if parents provide young children with suitable guidance and appropriate choices.

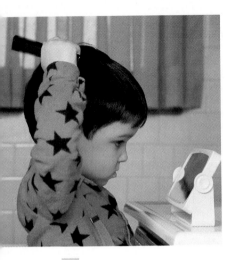

This 2-year-old is intent on combing his hair. Toddlers who are allowed to decide and do things for themselves in appropriate situations develop a sense of autonomy—the feeling that they can control their bodies and act competently on their own. *(Brent Jones/Stock Boston)*

According to Erikson, the parent who is over- or undercontrolling in toileting is likely to be so in other aspects of the toddler's life. The outcome is a child who feels forced and shamed and who doubts his ability to control his impulses and act competently on his own.

MARGARET MAHLER: SEPARATION–INDIVIDUATION

Erikson's theory describes how sensitive channeling of the baby's drives leads to positive attitudes toward others (trust) and to good feelings about the self (autonomy). Mahler carries this theme further, focusing on how the infant's early relationship with the mother provides the foundation for a sense of self that emerges in the second year (Mahler, Pine, & Bergman, 1975). According to Mahler, awareness of the self as separate and unique results from events in two phases of development: symbiosis and separation–individuation.

■ **SYMBIOSIS.** The phase of **symbiosis**—the blending of two people into an intimate, harmonious relationship—begins in early infancy. Gradually, young babies become more alert and interested in sights and sounds around them (see Chapter 5). But unlike the older child and adult, they do not realize that these events exist outside themselves. Instead, the self and surrounding world (including the person they depend on most for survival—the mother) are completely fused.

According to Mahler, this oneness with the mother is a necessary first step on the way to developing a sense of self. It is promoted by her responsiveness to infant emotional signals. As the baby cries, coos, and smiles, the mother reacts promptly and with positive emotional tone. The more she does so, the more confidently and easily the infant will separate from her during the next phase. In contrast, infants handled harshly and impatiently are likely to have great difficulty distancing themselves from their mothers.

■ **SEPARATION–INDIVIDUATION.** In Mahler's second phase, **separation–individuation,** the baby's capacity to move away from the mother triggers *individuation,* or self-awareness. The process of separating from the mother begins around 4 to 5 months, when the infant, held in his mother's arms, leans away from her body to scan the environment. But the decisive events of this phase are crawling and then walking.

Newly crawling 8- to 10-month-olds venture only a short distance from the mother. They look back frequently for reassurance and return to the mother's side to re-experience the safety and security of close body contact. Yet as crawling babies come and go, they experience the mother from a new, distant vantage point and become dimly aware of their own separateness.

Walking brings a dramatic advance in individuation. As toddlers enjoy greater freedom of movement and delight in exploration, they become even more conscious that the mother and the self are distinct beings. Around 18 months, this realization is full-blown, and at first it is frightening. Older toddlers may engage in all kinds of behaviors aimed at resisting and undoing this separateness—following and clinging to the mother, filling her lap with objects retrieved from the surrounding environment, and darting away in hopes of being chased, caught, and reminded of her continuing commitment. According to Mahler, the temper tantrums that often occur around this time—called the "terrible twos" by many parents—are signs of the new self's desire to assert itself, mixed with feelings of helpless dependence at not being able to manage all the challenges of the environment.

The mother's patience and reassurance eventually help toddlers surmount this temporary crisis. Between 2 and 3 years of age, children whose caregiving experiences have been gratifying and supportive emerge with a sturdy sense of themselves as separate people. They are affectionate, caring, and cooperative; play energetically; and can cope with mild frustration. And gains in representation and language (see Chapter 6) enable children to create a positive inner image of the mother that they can rely on in her absence, making separations easier.

symbiosis
In Mahler's theory, the baby's intimate sense of oneness with the mother, encouraged by warm, physical closeness and gentle handling.

separation–individuation
In Mahler's theory, the process of separating from the mother and becoming aware of the self, which is triggered by crawling and walking.

SIMILARITIES BETWEEN ERIKSON'S AND MAHLER'S THEORIES

As you read about Erikson's and Mahler's theories, undoubtedly you noticed several common themes. Each regards warm, sensitive parenting as vital for personality development. In addition, each theorist views toddlerhood as a time of budding selfhood. For Erikson, it is a stage when children achieve autonomous control over basic impulses; for Mahler, it is a period during which they learn to separate confidently from the parent. Both theorists also agree that when children emerge from the first few years without sufficient trust in caregivers and a healthy sense of individuality, the seeds are sown for adjustment problems. Adults who have difficulty establishing intimate ties to others, who are overly dependent on a loved one, or who continually doubt their own ability to meet new challenges may not have fully mastered the tasks of trust, autonomy, and individuation during infancy and toddlerhood.

BRIEF REVIEW

Erikson's and Mahler's psychoanalytic theories provide an overview of the emotional and social tasks of infancy and toddlerhood. According to Erikson, basic trust and autonomy grow out of warm, supportive parenting and reasonable expectations for impulse control during the second year. Mahler's theory suggests that sensitive exchange of emotional signals between mother and baby leads to a symbiotic bond, which provides the foundation for a confident sense of self as infants crawl and then walk on their own. Both theorists agree that the development of trust and individuality during infancy and toddlerhood have lasting consequences for personality development.

EMOTIONAL DEVELOPMENT

In the previous chapter, I suggested that you observe several infants and parents, noting babies' increasingly effective schemes for controlling the environment and ways that adults support cognitive and language development. Now focus on another aspect of infant and caregiver behavior: the expression and exchange of emotions. While you observe, note the various emotions the infant displays, the cues you rely on to interpret the baby's emotional state, and how the caregiver responds.

Researchers have conducted many such observations to find out how effectively infants and toddlers communicate their emotions and interpret those of others. They have discovered that emotions play a powerful role in organizing the developments that Erikson and Mahler regarded as so important during the early years—relationships with caregivers, exploration of the environment, and discovery of the self.

Think back to dynamic systems theory, introduced in Chapters 1 and 4. As you read about early emotional development in the sections that follow, notice how emotions are an essential part of young children's *dynamic systems of action* (Saarni, Mumme, & Campos, 1998). In other words, emotions energize development. At the same time, they are an aspect of the system that develops, becoming more varied and complex as children reorganize their behavior to achieve a better fit with their physical and social surroundings.

DEVELOPMENT OF SOME BASIC EMOTIONS

Do infants come into the world with the ability to express a wide variety of emotions? Some investigators believe that all the **basic emotions**—those that can be directly inferred

ASK YOURSELF . . .

■ *Derek's mother fed him in a warm and loving manner during the first year. But when he became a toddler, she kept him in a playpen for many hours because he got into too much mischief while exploring freely. Use Erikson's theory to evaluate Derek's early experiences.*

■ *Around 18 months, Betina became clingy and dependent. She followed her mother around the house and asked to be held often. How would Mahler account for Betina's behavior? How should Betina's parents respond?*

basic emotions
Emotions that can be directly inferred from facial expressions, such as happiness, interest, surprise, fear, anger, sadness, and disgust.

FIGURE **7.1**

Which emotions are these babies displaying? The MAX (Maximally Discriminative Facial Movement) System is a widely used method for classifying infants' emotional expressions. Facial muscle movements are carefully rated to determine their correspondence with basic feeling states, since people around the world associate different facial gestures with emotions in the same way. For example, cheeks raised and corners of the mouth pulled back and up signal happiness (a). Eyebrows raised, eyes widened, and mouth opened with corners pulled straight back denote fear (b). *(From Izard, 1979)*

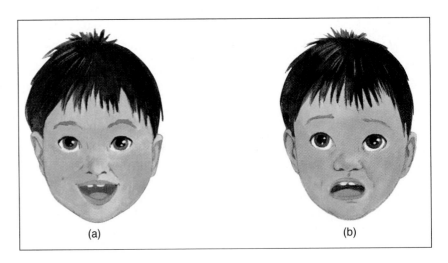

(a)   (b)

from facial expressions, such as happiness, interest, surprise, fear, anger, sadness, and disgust—are present in the first few weeks of life (Campos et al., 1983; Izard, 1991). Others regard the emotional life of the newborn baby as quite limited. For example, according to one view, separate emotions gradually emerge over the first year out of two global arousal states: the newborn baby's tendency to approach pleasant and withdraw from unpleasant stimulation (Fox, 1991; Sroufe, 1979).

Still, most researchers agree, on the basis of commonly used methods for analyzing babies' facial expressions (see Figure 7.1), that signs of almost all the basic emotions are present in infancy (Izard et al., 1995; Malatesta-Magai, Izard, & Camras, 1991). Around 6 months, face, gaze, voice, and posture form distinct patterns that are clearly related to social events. For example, April typically responded to her mother's playful interaction with a joyful face, pleasant cooing, and a relaxed posture, as if to say, "This is fun!" In contrast, an unresponsive mother is likely to evoke a sad face, fussy sounds, and a tense body (sending the message, "I'm overwhelmed") or an angry face, crying, and "pick-me-up" gestures (stating, "Change this unpleasant event!"). In sum, by the middle of the first year, emotional expressions are well organized and specific—and therefore able to tell us a great deal about the infant's internal state (Weinberg & Tronick, 1994, 1996).

Three basic emotions—happiness, anger, and fear—have received the most research attention. Refer to Table 7.1 for an overview of changes during the first 2 years in these emotions as well as others we will take up in this chapter.

This 1-year-old smiles and laughs as she masters new motor skills. Her exuberance leads caregivers to return her joy and encourage her efforts. As a result, she approaches her surroundings with enthusiasm. *(John Coletti/The Picture Cube)*

social smile
The smile evoked by the stimulus of the human face. First appears between 6 and 10 weeks.

■ **HAPPINESS.** Happiness—first in terms of blissful smiles and later through exuberant laughter—contributes to many aspects of development. Infants smile and laugh when they conquer new skills, expressing their delight in cognitive and motor mastery. The smile also encourages caregivers to be affectionate as well as stimulating, so the baby will smile even more. Happiness binds parent and baby into a warm, supportive relationship that fosters the infant's developing competence.

During the early weeks, newborn babies smile when full, during sleep, and in response to gentle touches and sounds, such as stroking of the skin, rocking, and the mother's soft, high-pitched voice. By the end of the first month, infants start to smile at interesting sights, but these must be dynamic, eye-catching events, such as a bright object jumping suddenly across the baby's field of vision. Between 6 and 10 weeks, the human face evokes a broad grin called the **social smile,** which is soon accompanied by pleasurable cooing (Sroufe & Waters, 1976). By 3 months, infants smile most often when interacting with people, indicating that they identify humans as having unique social qualities (Ellsworth, Muir, & Hains, 1993). Perhaps you can already tell that early changes in smiling parallel the development of infant perceptual capacities—in particular, babies' increasing sensitivity to visual patterns, including the human face—that we discussed in Chapter 5.

TABLE 7.1

Milestones of Emotional Development during the First Two Years

APPROXIMATE AGE	MILESTONE
Birth	Infants show signs of almost all the basic emotions.
2–3 months	Infants engage in social smiling and respond in kind to adults' facial expressions.
3–4 months	Infants begin to laugh at very active stimuli.
6–8 months	Emotional expressions are well organized and clearly related to social events. Infants start to become angry more often and in a wider range of situations.
	Fear, especially stranger anxiety, begins to arise. Attachment to the familiar caregiver is clearly evident, and separation anxiety appears. Infants use caregivers as a secure base for exploration.
8–12 months	Infants perceive facial expressions as organized patterns, and meaningful understanding of them improves. Social referencing appears. Infants laugh at subtle elements of surprise.
18–24 months	Self-conscious emotions of shame, embarrassment, and pride appear. A vocabulary for talking about feelings develops rapidly. Toddlers begin to appreciate that others' emotional reactions may differ from their own. Emotional self-regulation improves. First signs of empathy appear.

Laughter, which appears around 3 to 4 months, reflects faster processing of information than smiling. But like smiling, the first laughs occur in response to very active stimuli, such as the parent saying playfully, "I'm gonna get you!" and kissing the baby's tummy. As infants understand more about their world, they laugh at events that contain more subtle elements of surprise. At 10 months, Byron chuckled as Lisa played a silent game of peekaboo. At 1 year, he laughed heartily as she crawled on all fours and then walked like a penguin (Sroufe & Wunsch, 1972).

Around the middle of the first year, infants smile and laugh more often when interacting with familiar people, a preference that supports and strengthens the parent–child bond. During the second year, the smile becomes a deliberate social signal. Toddlers break their play with an interesting toy to turn around and communicate their delight to an attentive adult (Jones & Raag, 1989).

■ **ANGER AND FEAR.** Newborn babies respond with generalized distress to a variety of unpleasant experiences, including hunger, painful medical procedures, changes in body temperature, and too much or too little stimulation (see Chapter 4). During the first 2 months, fleeting expressions of anger appear as babies cry. These gradually increase in frequency and intensity from 4 to 6 months into the second year. Older infants also show anger in wider range of situations—for example, when an interesting object or event is removed, their arms are restrained, the caregiver leaves for a brief time, or they are put down for a nap (Camras et al., 1992; Stenberg & Campos, 1990).

Like anger, fear rises during the second half of the first year. Older infants hesitate before playing with a new toy that they would have grasped immediately at an earlier age. And, as we saw in Chapter 5, research with the visual cliff reveals that they start to show fear of heights around this time. But the most frequent expression of fear is to unfamiliar adults, a response called **stranger anxiety.** Many infants and toddlers are quite wary of strangers, although the reaction does not always occur. It depends on several factors: the infant's temperament (some babies are generally more fearful), past experiences with strangers, and the situation in which baby and stranger meet (Thompson & Limber, 1991).

To understand these influences, let's return to Rachel's fearful withdrawal from her grandparents, described at the beginning of this chapter. From birth, Rachel's mother cared for her continuously. She had little opportunity to get to know strange adults. Also, she met her grandparents for the first time in an unfamiliar environment (a crowded airport), and they rushed over and tried to hold her. Under these conditions, babies are most

stranger anxiety
The infant's expression of fear in response to unfamiliar adults. Appears in many babies after 6 months of age.

As this Israeli family ventures from their kibbutz home to spend time with relatives in Jerusalem, their toddler cries in response to new people and places. Frequent terrorist attacks have led to widespread wariness of strangers among kibbutz residents—emotional reactions that are communicated to young children. Stranger anxiety is especially high among kibbutz babies. *(Alan Oddie/PhotoEdit)*

likely to display fearful reactions. Later, at home, Rachel watched with interest and approached as her grandmother sat quietly on the sofa, smiling and holding out a teddy bear. A familiar setting, the opportunity to become acquainted from a distance, and warmth and friendliness on the part of the stranger reduced Rachel's fear (Horner, 1980).

What is the significance of this rise in anger and fear after 6 months of age? Researchers believe that these emotions have special survival value as infants begin to move on their own. Older babies can use the energy mobilized by anger to defend themselves or overcome obstacles. And fear keeps babies' enthusiasm for exploration in check, making it more likely that they will remain close to the caregiver and be careful about approaching unfamiliar people and objects. Anger and fear are also strong social signals that motivate caregivers to comfort a suffering infant.

Cognitive development plays an important role in infants' angry and fearful reactions, just as it does in their expressions of happiness. Between 8 and 12 months, when (as Piaget pointed out) babies grasp the notion of intentional behavior, they have a better understanding of the cause of their frustrations. Therefore, they know whom or what to get angry at. In the case of fear, improved memory permits older infants to distinguish familiar from strange events better than they could before.

Finally, culture can modify these emotions through infant-rearing practices. Maternal mortality is very high among the Efe hunters and gatherers of Zaire, Africa. To ensure infant survival, a collective caregiving system exists in which Efe babies are passed from one adult to another—relatives and nonrelatives alike. Consequently, Efe infants show little stranger anxiety (Tronick, Morelli, & Ivey, 1992). In contrast, in Israeli kibbutzim (cooperative agricultural settlements), frequent terrorist attacks have led to widespread wariness of strangers. By the end of the first year, when (as we will see later) infants look to others for cues about how to respond emotionally, kibbutz babies display far greater stranger anxiety than do their city-reared counterparts (Saarni, Mumme, & Campos, 1998).

UNDERSTANDING AND RESPONDING TO THE EMOTIONS OF OTHERS

Infants' emotional expressions are closely tied to their ability to interpret the emotional cues of others. Already we have seen that in the first few months, babies match the feeling tone of the caregiver in face-to-face communication. Early on, babies detect others' emotions through a fairly automatic process of *emotional contagion,* just as we tend to smile, laugh, or feel sad when we sense these emotions in others.

Between 7 and 10 months, infants perceive facial expressions as organized patterns, and they can match the emotion in a voice with the appropriate face of a speaking person (see Chapter 5). Responding to emotional expressions as organized wholes indicates that these signals have become meaningful to babies. Soon they realize that an emotional expression not only has meaning but is a meaningful reaction to a specific object or event (Bornstein & Lamb, 1992).

Once these understandings are in place, infants engage in **social referencing,** in which they actively seek information about a trusted person's feelings in an uncertain situation. Beginning at 8 to 10 months, when infants start to evaluate events with regard to their safety and security, social referencing occurs often. Many studies show that a caregiver's facial and vocal emotional signals (happy, angry, or fearful) influence whether a 1-year-old will be wary of strangers, play with an unfamiliar toy, or cross the deep side of the visual cliff (Mumme, Fernald, & Herrera, 1996; Rosen, Adamson, & Bakeman, 1992; Sorce et al., 1985).

Social referencing provides infants with a powerful means of learning about the world through indirect experience. By recognizing and responding to caregivers' emotional cues, babies can avoid harmful situations (such as a shock from an electric outlet or a fall

social referencing
Relying on a trusted person's emotional reaction to decide how to respond in an uncertain situation.

down a steep staircase) without first experiencing their unpleasant consequences. And parents can capitalize on social referencing to teach their youngster, whose capacity to explore is rapidly expanding, how to react to a great many novel events.

Social referencing also permits toddlers to compare their own assessments of events with those of others. By the middle of the second year, they begin to appreciate that others' emotional reactions may differ from their own. In recent study, an experimenter showed 14- and 18-month-olds broccoli and crackers. In one condition, she acted delighted with the taste of broccoli but disgusted with the taste of crackers. In the other condition, she showed the reverse preference. When asked to share the food, 14-month-olds offered only the type of food they themselves preferred—usually crackers. In contrast, 18-month-olds gave the experimenter whichever food they saw she liked, regardless of their own preferences (Repacholi & Gopnik, 1997).

In sum, with the transition from infancy to toddlerhood, children move beyond simply reacting to others' emotional messages. They use those signals to find out about others' internal states and preferences and to guide their own actions (Saarni, Mumme, & Campos, 1998).

EMERGENCE OF SELF-CONSCIOUS EMOTIONS

Besides basic emotions, humans are capable of a second, higher-order set of feelings, including shame, embarrassment, guilt, envy, and pride. These are called **self-conscious emotions** because each involves injury to or enhancement of our sense of self. For example, when we are ashamed or embarrassed, we feel negatively about ourselves. In contrast, pride reflects delight in the self's achievements (Campos et al., 1983).

Self-conscious emotions appear at the end of the second year, as the sense of self emerges. Between 18 and 24 months, children can be seen feeling ashamed and embarrassed as they lower their eyes, hang their heads, and hide their faces with their hands. Pride also emerges around this time, and envy and guilt are present by age 3 (Lewis et al., 1989; Sroufe, 1979). Besides self-awareness, self-conscious emotions require an additional ingredient: adult instruction in *when* to feel proud, ashamed, or guilty. Parents begin to provide this tutoring early, when they say to the toddler and preschooler, "My, look at how far you can throw that ball!" or "Shame on you for grabbing that toy from Billy!"

As these comments indicate, self-conscious emotions help children acquire socially valued behaviors and goals. The situations in which adults encourage children to experience these feelings vary from culture to culture. In most of the United States, children are taught to feel pride over personal achievement—throwing a ball the farthest, winning a game, and (later on) getting good grades. Among the Zuni Indians, shame and embarrassment occur in response to purely personal success, whereas pride is evoked by generosity, helpfulness, and sharing (Benedict, 1934b). In Japan, violating cultural standards of concern for others—a parent, a teacher, or an employer—is cause for intense shame (Lewis, 1992b).

Self-conscious emotions appear at the end of the second year. This Guatemalan 2-year-old undoubtedly feels a sense of pride as she helps care for her elderly grandmother—an activity highly valued in her culture. *(Celia Roberts/Earth Images)*

BEGINNINGS OF EMOTIONAL SELF-REGULATION

Besides expanding their range of emotional reactions, infants and toddlers begin to find ways to manage their emotional experiences. **Emotional self-regulation** refers to the strategies we use to adjust our emotional state to a comfortable level of intensity so we can accomplish our goals (Eisenberg et al., 1995; Thompson, 1994). If you drank a cup of coffee to wake up this morning, reminded yourself that an anxiety-provoking event would be over soon, or decided not to see a scary horror movie, you were engaging in emotional self-regulation.

self-conscious emotions
Emotions that involve injury to or enhancement of the sense of self. Examples are shame, embarrassment, guilt, envy, and pride.

emotional self-regulation
Strategies for adjusting our emotional state to a comfortable level of intensity.

In the early months of life, infants have only a limited capacity to regulate their emotional states. Although they can turn away from unpleasant stimulation and mouth and suck when their feelings get too intense, they are easily overwhelmed by internal and external stimuli. As a result, they depend on the soothing interventions of caregivers—lifting the distressed infant to the shoulder, rocking, and talking softly—for help in adjusting their emotional reactions.

Rapid development of the cerebral cortex (see Chapter 5) gradually increases the baby's tolerance for stimulation. Between 2 and 4 months, caregivers start to build on this capacity by initiating face-to-face play and attention to objects. In these interactions, parents arouse pleasure in the baby while adjusting the pace of their own behavior so the infant does not become overwhelmed and distressed. As a result, the baby's tolerance for stimulation increases further (Field, 1994). By the end of the first year, crawling and walking enable infants to regulate emotions more effectively by approaching or retreating from various stimuli.

As caregivers help infants regulate their emotional states, they contribute to the child's style of emotional self-regulation. For example, a parent who waits to intervene until an infant has become extremely agitated reinforces the baby's rapid rise to intense distress (Thompson, 1990a). This makes it harder for the parent to soothe the baby in the future—and for the baby to learn to calm him- or herself.

Parents' interventions also provide lessons in socially approved ways of expressing feelings. The unrestrained expression of negative emotion is not acceptable in most cultures because it interferes with successful social interaction. Beginning in the first few months, mothers match their baby's positive feelings far more often than the negative ones. In this way, they encourage happiness and discourage anger and sadness. Interestingly, boys get much more training in hiding their unhappiness than do girls. The well-known sex difference—females as emotionally expressive and males as emotionally controlled—is promoted at a very tender age (Malatesta & Haviland, 1982; Malatesta et al., 1986).

By the second year, growth in representation and language leads to new ways of regulating emotions. A vocabulary of words for talking about feelings, such as "happy," "love," "surprised," "scary," "yucky," and "mad," develops rapidly after 18 months (Dunn, Bretherton, & Munn, 1987). Although children of this age often succeed at redirecting their attention for short periods when they are distressed, they are not yet good at using language to comfort themselves (Grolnick, Bridges, & Connell, 1996). But by describing their emotions, toddlers can guide caregivers in ways that will help them feel better. For example, while listening to a story about monsters, Rachel whimpered "Mommy, scary." Beth put the book down and gave Rachel a comforting hug.

Toddlers' use of words to label feelings shows that they already have a remarkable understanding of themselves and others as emotional beings. As we will see in later chapters, development of the ability to think about feelings leads emotional self-regulation to improve greatly during early and middle childhood.

BRIEF REVIEW

Changes in infants' ability to express emotion and respond to the emotions of others reflect their developing cognitive capacities and serve social as well as survival functions. The social smile appears between 6 and 10 weeks, laughter around 3 to 4 months. In the middle of the first year, anger and fear start to increase. Young infants match the feeling tone of their caregivers' facial expressions. At 8 to 10 months, they begin to engage in social referencing, actively seeking information about the caregiver's feelings in an uncertain situation. Self-conscious emotions, such as shame, embarrassment, and pride, emerge at the end of the second year as toddlers develop self-awareness. Emotional self-regulation is supported by brain maturation, improvements in cognition and language, and sensitive child-rearing practices.

TEMPERAMENT AND DEVELOPMENT

As I got to know Byron, Rachel, and April well, their unique patterns of emotional responding became apparent. Byron was constantly in motion. As early as the first few weeks of life, he wriggled about in his crib and squirmed vigorously on the diaper table. When he crawled and walked, his parents found themselves chasing after him as he dropped one toy, moved on to the next, and climbed on chairs and tables. Lisa envied Beth's calm, relaxed experience with Rachel. At 7 months, she sat through a lengthy family celebration at a restaurant, contented in her high chair for almost 2 hours. And April's sociability was unmistakable to everyone who met her. She smiled and laughed at adults and was especially at ease in the company of other children, whom she readily approached during the second year.

When we describe one person as cheerful and "upbeat," another as active and energetic, and still others as calm, cautious, or prone to angry outbursts, we are referring to **temperament**—stable individual differences in quality and intensity of emotional reaction, activity level, attention, and emotional self-regulation (Rothbart & Bates, 1998). Researchers have become increasingly interested in temperamental differences among infants and children, since the psychological traits that make up temperament are believed to form the cornerstone of the adult personality.

The New York Longitudinal Study, initiated in 1956 by Alexander Thomas and Stella Chess, is the longest and most comprehensive study of temperament to date. A total of 141 children were followed from the first few months of life over a period that now extends well into adulthood. Results showed that temperament is a major factor in increasing the chances that a child will experience psychological problems or, alternatively, be protected from the effects of a highly stressful home life. However, Thomas and Chess (1977) also found that temperament is not fixed and unchangeable. Parenting practices can modify children's emotional styles considerably.

These findings inspired a growing body of research on temperament, including its stability, its biological roots, and its interaction with child-rearing experiences. Let's begin to explore these issues by looking at the structure, or makeup, of temperament and how it is measured.

THE STRUCTURE OF TEMPERAMENT

Thomas and Chess's nine dimensions, listed in Table 7.2, served as the first influential model of temperament, inspiring all others that followed. When detailed descriptions of infants' and children's behavior obtained from parental interviews were rated on these dimensions, certain characteristics clustered together, yielding three types of children:

- The **easy child** (40 percent of the sample). This child quickly establishes regular routines in infancy, is generally cheerful, and adapts easily to new experiences.

- The **difficult child** (10 percent of the sample). This child is irregular in daily routines, is slow to accept new experiences, and tends to react negatively and intensely.

- The **slow-to-warm-up child** (15 percent of the sample). This child is inactive, shows mild, low-key reactions to environmental stimuli, is negative in mood, and adjusts slowly to new experiences.

Note that 35 percent of the children did not fit any of these categories. Instead, they showed unique blends of temperamental characteristics.

Of the three temperamental types, the difficult pattern has sparked the most interest, since it places children at high risk for adjustment problems. In the New York Longitudinal Study, 70 percent of young preschoolers classified as difficult developed behavior problems by school age, whereas only 18 percent of easy children did (Thomas, Chess, &

temperament
Stable individual differences in quality and intensity of emotional reaction, activity level, attention, and emotional self-regulation.

easy child
A child whose temperament is such that he or she quickly establishes regular routines in infancy, is generally cheerful, and adapts easily to new experiences.

difficult child
A child whose temperament is such that he or she is irregular in daily routines, is slow to accept new experiences, and tends to react negatively and intensely.

slow-to-warm-up child
A child whose temperament is such that he or she is inactive, shows mild, low-key reactions to environmental stimuli, is negative in mood, and adjusts slowly when faced with new experiences.

TABLE **7.2**

Two Models of Temperament

THOMAS AND CHESS		ROTHBART AND MAURO	
DIMENSION	DESCRIPTION AND EXAMPLE	DIMENSION	DESCRIPTION
Activity level	Proportion of active periods to inactive ones. Some babies are always in motion. Others move about very little.	Activity level	Level of gross motor activity
Rhythmicity	Regularity of body functions. Some infants fall asleep, wake up, get hungry, and have bowel movements on a regular schedule, whereas others are much less predictable.	Rhythmicity	Regularity of functions, such as sleep, wakefulness, hunger, and excretion
Distractibility	Degree to which stimulation from the environment alters behavior. Some hungry babies stop crying temporarily if offered a pacifier or a toy to play with. Others continue to cry until fed.	Attention span/persistence	Duration of orienting or interest
Approach/withdrawal	Response to a new object or person. Some babies accept new foods and smile and babble at strangers, whereas others pull back and cry on first exposure.	Fearful distress	Wariness and distress in response to intense or novel stimuli, including time taken to adjust to new situations
Adaptability	Ease with which the child adapts to changes in the environment. Although some infants withdraw when faced with new experiences, they quickly adapt, accepting the new food or person on the next occasion. Others continue to fuss and cry.	Irritable distress	Fussing, crying, and showing distress when desires are frustrated
Attention span and persistence	Amount of time devoted to an activity. Some babies watch a mobile or play with a toy for a long time, whereas others lose interest after a few minutes.	Positive affect	Frequency of expression of happiness and pleasure
Intensity of reaction	Intensity or energy level of response. Some infants laugh and cry loudly, whereas others react only mildly.		
Threshold of responsiveness	Intensity of stimulation required to evoke a response. Some babies startle at the slightest change in sound or lighting. Others take little notice of these changes in stimulation.		
Quality of mood	Amount of friendly, joyful behavior as opposed to unpleasant, unfriendly behavior. Some babies smile and laugh frequently when playing and interacting with people. Others fuss and cry often.		

Sources: Rothbart & Mauro, 1990; Thomas & Chess, 1977.

inhibited, or shy, child
A child whose temperament is such that he or she reacts negatively to and withdraws from novel stimuli. Resembles slow-to-warm-up child.

uninhibited, or sociable, child
A child whose temperament is such that he or she displays positive emotion to and approaches novel stimuli.

Birch, 1970). And other longitudinal findings indicate that as early as infancy, difficultness predicts defiant, aggressive behavior in early and middle childhood (Bates et al., 1991).

Unlike difficult children, slow-to-warm-up children do not present many problems in the early years. They encounter special challenges later, after they enter school and peer groups in which they are expected to respond actively and quickly. Thomas and Chess found that by middle childhood, 50 percent of these children began to show adjustment difficulties (Chess & Thomas, 1984).

A second model of temperament is also shown in Table 7.2 (Rothbart & Mauro, 1990). It combines dimensions of Thomas and Chess and other researchers that overlap. For example, "distractibility" and "attention span and persistence" are considered opposite ends of the same dimension and simply called "attention span/persistence." It also includes a dimension not identified by Thomas and Chess—"irritable distress"—that emphasizes emotional self-regulation. Overall, the temperamental characteristics shown in Table 7.2 provide a fairly complete picture of the traits most often studied.

MEASURING TEMPERAMENT

Researchers measure temperament in diverse ways. Typically, they select from a variety of methods that assess children's behavior. But new techniques are focusing on physiological reactions in an effort to identify biological processes at the heart of temperamental styles.

■ **ASSESSMENTS OF BEHAVIOR.** Temperament is often assessed through interviews or questionnaires given to parents, although behavior ratings by pediatricians, teachers, and others familiar with the child, as well as direct observations by researchers, have also been used. Parental reports have been emphasized because of their convenience and parents' depth of knowledge about the child.

At the same time, information from parents has been criticized for being biased and subjective. For example, parents' prebirth expectations for their infant's temperament affect their reports after the infant arrives (Diener, Goldstein, & Mangelsdorf, 1995). And mothers who are anxious, depressed, and low in self-esteem tend to regard their babies as more difficult (Mebert, 1991; Vaughn et al., 1987). Nevertheless, parental ratings are moderately related to observations of children's behavior (Rothbart & Bates, 1998). And parent perceptions are useful for understanding the way parents view and respond to their child.

■ **ASSESSMENTS OF PHYSIOLOGICAL REACTIONS.** To explore the biological basis of temperament, researchers are turning to psychophysiological measures. Most efforts have focused on **inhibited, or shy, children,** who react negatively to and withdraw from novel stimuli (much like Thomas and Chess's slow-to-warm-up children), and **uninhibited, or sociable, children,** who display positive emotion to and approach novel stimuli. As the Biology and Environment box on pages 266–267 reveals, heart rate, hormone levels, and EEG waves in the frontal region of the cortex differentiate children with inhibited and uninhibited temperamental styles.

Investigators do not yet know how or when these diverse psychophysiological measures become interrelated—information that would shed light on the integrated role of various brain structures in shyness and sociability. And, as we will see in the following sections, more research is needed to clarify how brain mechanisms combine with experience to support consistency and change in children's temperamental styles.

STABILITY OF TEMPERAMENT

It would be difficult to claim that something like temperament really exists if children's emotional styles were not stable over time. Indeed, the findings of many studies provide support for the long-term stability of temperament. Infants and young children who score low or high on attention span, irritability, sociability, or shyness are likely to respond similarly when assessed again a few years later and, occasionally, even into the adult years (Caspi, Elder, & Bem, 1987, 1988; Goldsmith & Gottesman, 1981; Kochanska & Radke-Yarrow, 1992; Pedlow et al., 1993; Riese, 1987; Ruff et al., 1990). The temperamental styles identified in the New York Longitudinal Study are also fairly stable. Compared to easy children, difficult preschoolers are more likely to show problems in concentrating and getting along with peers after they enter school. And slow-to-warm-up youngsters often are overwhelmed by demands that they adapt quickly to new experiences in school, a circumstance that may intensify their withdrawal in middle childhood (Chess & Thomas, 1984; Thomas, Chess, & Korn, 1982).

Beginning at birth, Chinese infants are calmer, more easily soothed when upset, and better at quieting themselves than are Caucasian infants. These differences are probably hereditary, but cultural variations in child rearing support them. *(Alan Oddie/PhotoEdit)*

BIOLOGY & ENVIRONMENT

BIOLOGICAL BASIS OF SHYNESS AND SOCIABILITY

At age 4 months, Larry and Mitch were brought by their mothers to the laboratory of Jerome Kagan , who observed their reactions to a variety of unfamiliar experiences. When exposed to new sights and sounds, such as a moving mobile decorated with colorful toys, Larry tensed his muscles, moved his arms and legs with agitation, and began to cry. Mitch's body remained relaxed and quiet, and he smiled and cooed pleasurably at the excitement around him.

Larry and Mitch returned to the laboratory as toddlers. This time, each experienced a variety of procedures designed to induce uncertainty. For example, electrodes were placed on their bodies and blood pressure cuffs on their arms to measure heart rate; highly stimulating toy robots, animals, and puppets moved before their eyes; and unfamiliar people entered and behaved in atypical ways or wore novel costumes. Larry whimpered and

quickly withdrew, seeking his mother's protection. Mitch watched with interest, laughed at the strange sights, and approached the toys and strangers when invited to do so.

On a third visit, at age 4½ years, Larry barely talked or smiled during an interview with an unfamiliar adult. In contrast, Mitch spontaneously asked questions, commented on the procedures, and communicated his pleasure at each intriguing activity. In a playroom with two unfamiliar peers, Larry pulled back, keeping an anxious eye on the other children. Mitch made friends quickly.

In longitudinal research on several hundred Caucasian children, Kagan (1998) found that about 20 percent of 4-month-old babies were easily upset by novelty (like Larry) , whereas 40 percent were comfortable, even delighted, with new experiences (like Mitch). About 30 percent of these extreme groups retained their temperamental styles as they grew older. Those resembling Larry tended to

become fearful, inhibited toddlers and preschoolers; those resembling Mitch developed into outgoing, uninhibited youngsters.

■ **PHYSIOLOGICAL CORRELATES OF SHYNESS AND SOCIABILITY.** Kagan believes that individual differences in arousal of the *amygdala,* an inner brain structure that controls avoidance reactions, contribute to these contrasting temperamental styles. In shy, inhibited children, novel stimuli easily excite the amygdala and its connections to the cerebral cortex and sympathetic nervous system, which prepares the body to act in the face of threat. The same level of stimulation evokes minimal neural excitation in highly sociable, uninhibited children. In support of this theory, several physiological responses of shy infants and children resemble those of highly timid animals and are known to be mediated by the amygdala:

■ **Heart Rate.** As early as the first few weeks of life, the heart rates of

When the evidence as a whole is examined carefully, however, temperamental stability from one age period to the next is usually modest. Although quite a few children remain the same, a good number have changed when assessed again as soon as a year or two later. In fact, some characteristics, such as shyness and sociability, are stable over the long term only in children at the extremes—those who are very inhibited or very outgoing to begin with (Kerr et al., 1994; Robinson et al., 1992).

The fact that early in life, children show marked individual differences in temperament, some of which are related to physiological reactions, indicates that biological factors play an important role. At the same time, the changes shown by many children suggest that temperament can be modified by experience (although children rarely change from one extreme to another—that is, a shy toddler practically never becomes highly sociable). Let's take a close look at genetic and environmental contributions to temperament in the following sections.

GENETIC INFLUENCES

To what extent are temperament and personality heritable? To answer this question, many studies have compared individuals varying in genetic relationship to one another. The most common approach is to compare identical with fraternal twins.

shy children are consistently higher than those of sociable youngsters, and they speed up further in response to unfamiliar events (Snidman et al., 1995).

■ **Cortisol.** Saliva concentration of cortisol, a hormone that regulates blood pressure and is involved in resistance to stress, tends to be higher in shy than sociable children (Gunnar & Nelson, 1994; Kagan & Snidman, 1991).

■ **Pupil dilation and blood pressure.** Compared with sociable children, shy children show greater pupil dilation and rise in blood pressure when faced with novelty and challenge (Kagan, 1994).

Yet another physiological correlate of approach–withdrawal to people and objects is the pattern of EEG waves in the frontal region of the cerebral cortex. Recall from Chapter 5 that the left cortical hemisphere is specialized to respond with positive emotion, the right hemisphere with negative emotion. Shy infants and preschoolers show greater right than left frontal brain wave activity; their sociable counterparts show the opposite pattern (Calkins, Fox, & Marshall, 1996; Fox, Bell, & Jones, 1992; Fox, Calkins & Bell, 1994). Neural activity in the amygdala is transmitted to the frontal lobe and may influence these patterns.

■ **LONG-TERM CONSEQUENCES.** According to Kagan (1998), children who are extremely shy or sociable inherit a physiology that biases them toward a particular temperamental style. Among Caucasians, shy children are more likely to have certain physical traits—blue eyes, thin faces, and hay fever—known to be affected by heredity (Arcus & Kagan, 1995; Kagan, Reznick, & Snidman, 1988). The genes controlling these characteristics may also influence the excitability of the amygdala.

Yet heritability research indicates that genes make only a modest contribution to shyness and sociability. They share power with experience. When early inhibition persists into middle childhood, adolescence, and adulthood, it can lead to adjustment difficulties, such as excessive cautiousness, social withdrawal, and loneliness (Caspi & Silva, 1995; Rubin, Stewart, & Coplan, 1995). At the same time, many inhibited infants and young children cope with novelty more effectively as they get older.

Child-rearing practices affect the chances that an emotionally reactive baby will become a fearful child. When parents protect infants who dislike novelty from minor stresses, they make it harder for the child to overcome an urge to retreat from unfamiliar events. In contrast, parents who make appropriate demands for their baby to approach new experiences help the child overcome fear (Park et al., 1997; Rubin et al., 1997). In sum, for children to develop at their best, parenting must be tailored to their temperaments—a theme we will encounter again in this and later chapters.

Findings reveal that identical twins are more similar than fraternal twins across a wide range of temperamental traits (activity level, sociability, shyness, irritability, intensity of emotional reaction, attention span, and persistence) and personality measures (introversion, extroversion, anxiety, agreeableness, and impulsivity) (Caspi, 1998; DiLalla, Kagan, & Reznick, 1994; Emde et al., 1992; Goldsmith, Buss, & Lemery, 1997; Saudino & Eaton, 1991). In Chapter 2, we indicated that heritability estimates derived from twin studies suggest a moderate role for genetic factors in temperament and personality: About half of the individual differences among us can be traced to differences in our genetic makeup.

Consistent ethnic and sex differences in early temperament exist, again implying a role for heredity. Compared to Caucasian infants, Chinese and Japanese babies tend to be less active, irritable, and vocal, more easily soothed when upset, and better at quieting themselves (Kagan et al., 1994; Lewis, Ramsay, & Kawakami, 1993). Rachel's capacity to remain contentedly seated in her high chair through a long family dinner certainly fits with this evidence. And Byron's high rate of activity is consistent with sex differences in emotional styles. From an early age, boys tend to be more active and daring and girls more anxious and timid—a difference reflected in boys' higher unintentional injury rates throughout childhood and adolescence (Richardson, Koller, & Katz, 1986).

ENVIRONMENTAL INFLUENCES

Although genetic influences on temperament are clear, no study has shown that infants maintain their early emotional styles in the absence of environmental supports. Instead, heredity and environment combine to strengthen the stability of temperament, since (as we saw in Chapter 2), the child's approach to the world affects the experiences to which she is exposed. To see how this works, let's take a second look at ethnic and sex differences in temperament.

As I watched Beth care for Rachel as a 3-month-old baby, her calm, soothing manner and use of gentle rocking and touching contrasted with Lisa and Felicia's stimulation of their infants through lively facial expressions and talking. These differences in caregiving appear repeatedly in studies comparing Caucasian with Asian infant–mother pairs (Fogel, Toda, & Kawai, 1988; Otaki et al., 1986). The findings suggest that some differences in early temperament are encouraged by cultural beliefs and practices. When asked about their approach to child rearing, Japanese mothers respond that babies come into the world as independent beings who must learn to rely on their mothers through close physical contact. American mothers are likely to believe just the opposite—that they must wean the baby away from dependence into autonomy (Kojima, 1986). As a result, Japanese mothers do more comforting and American mothers more stimulating—behaviors that enhance early temperamental differences between their infants.

A similar process seems to contribute to sex differences in temperament. Within the first 24 hours after birth (before they could have had much experience with the baby), parents already perceive male and female newborns differently. Sons are rated as larger, better coordinated, more alert, and stronger. Daughters are viewed as softer, more awkward, weaker, and more delicate (Stern & Karraker, 1989; Vogel et al., 1991). Gender-stereotyped beliefs carry over into the way parents treat their infants and toddlers. For example, parents more often encourage their young sons to be physically active and their daughters to seek help and physical closeness (Fagot, 1978). These practices promote and sustain temperamental differences between boys and girls.

In families with several children, an additional influence on temperament is at work. Parents often look for and emphasize each child's unique characteristics (Plomin, 1994c). You can see this in the comments parents make after the birth of a second baby: "He's so much calmer," "She's a lot more active," or "He's more sociable." Research shows that when one child in a family is viewed as easy, another is likely to be perceived as difficult, even though the second child might not be very difficult when compared with children in general (Schachter & Stone, 1985). Each child, in turn, evokes responses from caregivers that are consistent with parental views and with the child's actual temperamental style.

Besides different experiences within the family, siblings have unique experiences with peers, teachers, and others in their community that can profoundly affect development (Caspi, 1998). These findings demonstrate that temperament and personality can be understood only in terms of complex interdependencies between genetic and environmental factors.

TEMPERAMENT AND CHILD REARING: THE GOODNESS-OF-FIT MODEL

goodness-of-fit model
Thomas and Chess's model, which states that an effective match, or "good fit," between child-rearing practices and a child's temperament leads to favorable development and psychological adjustment. A "poor fit" leads to adjustment problems.

We have already indicated that the temperaments of many children do change over time. This suggests that environments do not always act in the same direction as a child's temperament. In fact, if a child's disposition interferes with learning or getting along with others, it is important for adults to gently but consistently counteract the child's maladaptive behavior.

Thomas and Chess (1977) proposed a **goodness-of-fit model** to explain how temperament and environmental pressures can work together to produce favorable outcomes.

Goodness of fit involves creating child-rearing environments that recognize each child's temperament while helping the youngster achieve more adaptive functioning. In short, children with different temperaments have unique child-rearing needs.

Goodness of fit helps explain why children with difficult temperaments are at high risk for later behavior problems. These children, at least in many Western middle-SES families, frequently experience parenting that fits poorly with their dispositions. As infants, they are far less likely to receive sensitive caregiving (van den Boom & Hoeksma, 1994). By the second year, parents of difficult children often resort to angry, punitive discipline. In response, the child reacts with defiance and disobedience. Then parents often behave inconsistently, rewarding the child's noncompliant behavior by giving in to it, although they initially resisted (Lee & Bates, 1985). The difficult child's temperament combined with harsh, inconsistent child rearing forms a poor fit that maintains and even increases the child's irritable, conflict-ridden style. In contrast, when parents are positive and establish a happy, stable home life despite their child's negative, unpredictable behavior, infant difficultness declines (Belsky, Fish, & Isabella, 1991).

According to the goodness-of-fit model, caregiving is not just responsive to the child's temperament. It also depends on life conditions and cultural values. During a famine in Africa, difficult infant temperament was associated with survival—probably because difficult babies demanded and received more maternal attention and food (deVries, 1984). In low-SES Puerto Rican families, difficult children are treated with sensitivity and patience; they are not at risk for adjustment problems (Gannon & Korn, 1983). Although Westerners usually regard shy, withdrawn children as socially incompetent, Chinese adults evaluate such children positively—as advanced in social maturity and understanding (Chen, Rubin, & Li, 1995). Expectations for restrained, persistent child behavior are so strong in Thailand that Thai teachers regard children as inattentive and unmotivated who would be seen as quite normal in the United States (Weisz et al., 1995).

In cultures where particular temperamental styles are linked to adjustment problems, an effective match between rearing conditions and child temperament is best accomplished early, before unfavorable temperament–environment relationships have had a chance to produce maladjustment that is hard to undo. Both difficult and shy children benefit from warm, accepting parenting that makes firm but reasonable demands for mastering new experiences. In the case of reserved, inactive toddlers, research shows that highly stimulating maternal behavior (frequent questioning, instructing, and pointing out objects) fosters exploration of the environment. Yet these same parental behaviors inhibit exploration in very active toddlers (Gandour, 1989). Recall from Chapter 6 that Lisa often behaved in a highly stimulating, intrusive way with Byron. A "poor fit" between her behavior and Byron's active temperament may have contributed to his tendency to move from one activity to the next with little involvement.

The goodness-of-fit model reminds us that babies come into the world with unique dispositions that adults need to accept. Children cannot be molded in ways that do not blend with their basic styles. This means that parents can neither take full credit for their children's virtues nor be blamed for all their faults. But parents can turn an environment that exaggerates a child's problems into one that builds on the youngster's strengths, helping each child master the challenges of development.

In the following sections, we will see that goodness of fit is also at the heart of infant–caregiver attachment. This first intimate relationship grows out of interaction between parent and baby, to which the emotional styles of both partners contribute.

This mother is perplexed because her 1-year-old baby is not responding to her efforts to help him calm down. Difficult children react negatively and intensely to many new experiences. When parents are patient and provide opportunities for gradual, repeated exposure to new situations, difficultness often subsides. *(Nubar Alexanian/Stock Boston)*

ASK YOURSELF . . .

- *Rachel, like many Asian infants, is calm and easily soothed when upset. What factors contribute to her temperamental style?*

- *At age 18 months, highly active Byron climbed out of his highchair long before his meal was finished. Exasperated with Byron's behavior, his father made him sit at the table until he had eaten all his food. Soon Byron's behavior escalated into a full-blown tantrum. Using the concept of goodness of fit, suggest another way of handling Byron.*

BRIEF REVIEW

Children's unique temperamental styles are apparent in early infancy. However, the stability of temperament is only modest; some children retain their original dispositions, while others change over time. Heredity influences early temperament, but child-rearing experiences determine whether an infant or toddler's style of responding is sustained or modified over time. A good fit between parenting practices and child temperament helps children whose temperaments predispose them to adjustment problems function more adaptively. The adaptiveness of different temperamental styles is powerfully affected by culture.

DEVELOPMENT OF ATTACHMENT

Attachment is the strong, affectional tie we feel for special people in our lives that leads us to feel pleasure and joy when we interact with them and to be comforted by their nearness during times of stress. By the end of the first year, infants have become attached to familiar people who have responded to their need for physical care and stimulation. Watch babies of this age, and notice how parents are singled out for special attention. A whole range of responses are reserved just for them. For example, when the mother enters the room, the baby breaks into a broad, friendly smile. When she picks him up, he pats her face, explores her hair, and snuggles against her body. When he feels anxious or afraid, he crawls into her lap and clings closely.

EARLY THEORIES OF ATTACHMENT

Freud first suggested that the infant's emotional tie to the mother provides the foundation for all later relationships. We will see shortly that research on the consequences of attachment is consistent with Freud's idea. But attachment has also been the subject of intense theoretical debate. Turn back to the description of Freud's and Erikson's theories at the beginning of this chapter, and notice how *psychoanalytic theory* regards feeding as the central context in which caregivers and babies build this close emotional bond. *Behaviorism,* too, emphasizes the importance of feeding, but for different reasons. According to a well-known behaviorist *drive reduction explanation,* as the mother satisfies the baby's hunger *(primary drive),* her presence becomes a *secondary or learned drive* because it is paired with tension relief. As a result, the baby prefers to prefer all kinds of stimuli that accompany feeding, including the mother's soft caresses, warm smiles, and tender words of comfort (Sears, Maccoby, & Levin, 1957).

Although feeding is an important context in which mothers and babies build a close relationship, attachment does not depend on hunger satisfaction. In the 1950s, a famous experiment showed that rhesus monkeys reared with terrycloth and wire mesh "surrogate mothers" spent their days clinging to the terrycloth substitute, even though the wire mesh "mother" held the bottle and infants had to climb on it to be fed. (Harlow & Zimmerman, 1959). Observations of human infants also reveal that they become attached to family members who seldom if ever feed them, including fathers, siblings, and grandparents. And perhaps you have noticed that toddlers in Western cultures who sleep alone and experience frequent daytime separations from their parents sometimes develop strong emotional ties to cuddly objects, such as blankets or teddy bears. (Passman, 1987). Yet such objects have never played a role in infant feeding!

attachment
The strong, affectional tie that humans feel toward special people in their lives.

Another problem with drive reduction and psychoanalytic accounts of attachment is that a great deal is said about the mother's contribution to the attachment relationship. But much less attention is given to the importance of the infant's characteristics and behavior.

BOWLBY'S ETHOLOGICAL THEORY

Today, **ethological theory of attachment** is the most widely accepted view of the infant's emotional tie to the caregiver. Recall from Chapter 1 that according to ethology, many human behaviors have evolved over the history of our species because they promote survival. John Bowlby (1969), who first applied this idea to the infant–caregiver bond, was originally a psychoanalyst. In his theory, he retained the psychoanalytic idea that quality of attachment to the caregiver has profound implications for the child's feelings of security and capacity to form trusting relationships.

At the same time, Bowlby was inspired by Konrad Lorenz's studies of imprinting in baby geese (see Chapter 1). He believed that the human infant, like the young of other animal species, is endowed with a set of built-in behaviors that help keep the parent nearby, increasing the chances that the infant will be protected from danger. Contact with the parent also ensures that the baby will be fed, but Bowlby was careful to point out that feeding is not the basis for attachment. Instead, the attachment bond has strong biological roots. It can best be understood within an evolutionary framework in which survival of the species is of utmost importance.

According to Bowlby, the infant's relationship to the parent begins as a set of innate signals that call the adult to the baby's side. Over time, a true affectional bond develops, which is supported by new emotional and cognitive capacities as well as a history of warm, sensitive care. The development of attachment takes place in four phases:

1. *The preattachment phase* (birth to 6 weeks). A variety of built-in signals—grasping, smiling, crying, and gazing into the adult's eyes—help bring newborn babies into close contact with other humans. Once an adult responds, infants encourage her to remain nearby, since they are comforted when picked up, stroked, and talked to softly. Babies of this age can recognize their own mother's smell and voice (see Chapter 4). However, they are not yet attached to her, since they do not mind being left with an unfamiliar adult.

2. *The "attachment in the making" phase* (6 weeks to 6–8 months). During this phase, infants start to respond differently to a familiar caregiver than to a stranger. For example, at 4 months, Byron smiled, laughed, and babbled more freely when interacting with his mother and quieted more quickly when she picked him up. As infants engage in face-to-face interaction with the parent and experience relief from distress, they learn that their own actions affect the behavior of those around them. They begin to develop a sense of trust—the expectation that the caregiver will respond when signaled. But babies still do not protest when separated from the parent, despite the fact that they can recognize and distinguish her from unfamiliar people.

3. *The phase of "clear-cut" attachment* (6–8 months to 18 months–2 years). Now, attachment to the familiar caregiver is evident. Babies of this phase display separation anxiety, in that they become upset when the adult whom they have come to rely on leaves. **Separation anxiety** appears universally around the world after 6 months of age, increasing until about 15 months (see Figure 7.2). Its appearance suggests that infants have a clear understanding that the caregiver continues to exist when not in view. Consistent with this idea, babies who have not yet mastered Piagetian object permanence usually do not become anxious when separated from their mothers (Lester et al., 1974).

Baby monkeys reared with "surrogate mothers" from birth preferred to cling to a soft terry cloth "mother" instead of a wire mesh "mother" that held a bottle. These findings reveal that the drive reduction explanation of attachment, which assumes that the mother–infant relationship is based on feeding. *(Martin Rogers/Stock Boston)*

ethological theory of attachment
A theory formulated by Bowlby, which views the infant's emotional tie to the caregiver as an evolved response that promotes survival.

separation anxiety
An infant's distressed reaction to the departure of the familiar caregiver.

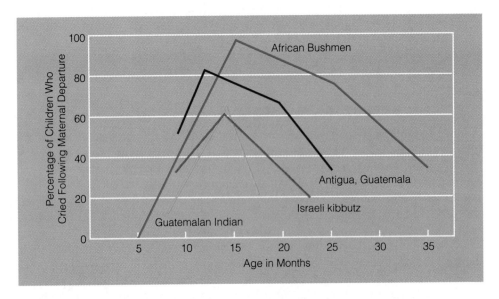

Besides protesting the parent's departure, older infants and toddlers act more deliberately to maintain her presence. They approach, follow, and climb on her in preference to others. And they use her as a **secure base** from which to explore, venturing into the environment and then returning for emotional support.

4. *Formation of a reciprocal relationship* (18 months–2 years and on). By the end of the second year, rapid growth in representation and language permits toddlers to understand some of the factors that influence the parent's coming and going and to predict her return. As a result, separation protest declines. Now children start to negotiate with the caregiver, using requests and persuasion to alter her goals rather than crawling after and clinging to her. For example, at age 2 April asked Felicia to read a story before leaving her with a baby-sitter. The extra time with her mother, along with a better understanding of where Felicia was going ("to a movie with Daddy") and when she would be back ("right after you go to sleep"), helped April withstand her mother's absence.

According to Bowlby (1980), out of their experiences during these four phases, children construct an inner representation of the parent–child bond that becomes a vital part of their personality. It serves as an **internal working model,** or set of expectations about the availability of attachment figures, their likelihood of providing support during times of stress, and the self's interaction with those figures. This image becomes the model, or guide, for all future close relationships—through childhood and adolescence and into adult life (Bretherton, 1992).

MEASURING THE SECURITY OF ATTACHMENT

Although virtually all family-reared babies become attached to a familiar caregiver by the second year, the quality of this relationship differs greatly from child to child. Some infants appear especially relaxed and secure in the presence of the caregiver; they know they can count on her for protection and support. Others seem more anxious and uncertain.

A widely used technique for measuring the quality of attachment between 1 and 2 years of age is the **Strange Situation**. In designing it, Mary Ainsworth and her colleagues (1978) reasoned that if the development of attachment has gone well, infants and toddlers should use the parent as a secure base from which to explore an unfamiliar playroom. In addition, when the parent leaves for a brief period of time, the child should show separation anxiety, and an unfamiliar adult should be less comforting than the parent. As summarized in Table 7.3, the Strange Situation takes the baby through eight short episodes in which brief separations from and reunions with the parent occur.

secure base
The use of the familiar caregiver as a base from which the infant confidently explores the environment and returns for emotional support.

internal working model
A set of expectations derived from early caregiving experiences concerning the availability of attachment figures and their likelihood of providing support during times of stress. Becomes a model, or guide, for all future close relationships.

Strange Situation
A procedure involving short separations from and reunions with the parent that assesses the quality of the attachment bond.

TABLE 7.3

Episodes in the Strange Situation

EPISODE	EVENTS	ATTACHMENT BEHAVIOR OBSERVED
1	Experimenter introduces parent and baby to playroom and then leaves.	
2	Parent is seated while baby plays with toys.	Parent as a secure base
3	Stranger enters, is seated, and talks to parent.	Reaction to unfamiliar adult
4	Parent leaves room. Stranger responds to baby and offers comfort if upset.	Separation anxiety
5	Parent returns, greets baby, and if necessary offers comfort. Stranger leaves room.	Reaction to reunion
6	Parent leaves room.	Separation anxiety
7	Stranger enters room and offers comfort.	Ability to be soothed by stranger
8	Parent returns, greets baby, if necessary offers comfort, and tries to reinterest baby in toys.	Reaction to reunion

Note: Episode 1 lasts about 30 seconds; the remaining episodes each last about 3 minutes. Separation episodes are cut short if the baby becomes very upset. Reunion episodes are extended if the baby needs more time to calm down and return to play.
Source: Ainsworth et al., 1978.

Observing the responses of infants to these episodes, researchers have identified a secure attachment pattern and three patterns of insecurity (Ainsworth et al., 1978; Main & Solomon, 1990). Which of the following patterns do you think Rachel displayed in the incident described at the beginning of this chapter?

- **Secure attachment.** These infants use the parent as a secure base from which to explore. When separated, they may or may not cry, but if they do, it is due to the parent's absence, since they show a strong preference for her over the stranger. When the parent returns, they actively seek contact, and their crying is reduced immediately. About 65 percent of American infants show this pattern.

- **Avoidant attachment.** These babies seem unresponsive to the parent when she is present. When she leaves, they usually are not distressed, and they react to the stranger in much the same way as the parent. During reunion, they avoid or are slow to greet the parent, and when picked up, they often fail to cling. About 20 percent of American infants show this pattern.

- **Resistant attachment.** Before separation, these infants seek closeness to the parent and often fail to explore. When she returns, they display angry, resistive behavior, sometimes hitting and pushing. In addition, many continue to cry after being picked up and cannot be comforted easily. About 10 to 15 percent of American infants show this pattern.

- **Disorganized/disoriented attachment.** This pattern reflects the greatest insecurity. At reunion, these infants show a variety of confused, contradictory behaviors. For example, they might look away while being held by the parent or approach her with a flat, depressed gaze. Most of these babies communicate their disorientation with a dazed facial expression. A few cry out unexpectedly after having calmed down or display odd, frozen postures. About 5 to 10 percent of American infants show this pattern.

Infants' reactions in the Strange Situation closely resemble their use of the parent as a secure base and their response to separation at home (Blanchard & Main, 1979). For this reason, the procedure is a powerful tool for assessing attachment security.

Recently, an alternative, more efficient method has become popular: the **Attachment Q-Sort.** It is suitable for children between 1 and 5 years of age. An observer—the parent or an expert informant—sorts a set of 90 descriptors of attachment-related behaviors (such as "Child greets mother with a big smile when she enters the room" and "If mother

secure attachment
The quality of attachment characterizing infants who are distressed by parental separation and easily comforted by the parent when she returns.

avoidant attachment
The quality of insecure attachment characterizing infants who are usually not distressed by parental separation and who avoid the parent when she returns.

resistant attachment
The quality of insecure attachment characterizing infants who remain close to the parent before departure and display angry, resistive behavior when she returns.

disorganized/disoriented attachment
The quality of insecure attachment characterizing infants who respond in a confused, contradictory fashion when reunited with the parent.

Attachment Q-Sort
An efficient method for assessing the quality of the attachment bond in which a parent or an expert informant sorts a set of 90 descriptors of attachment-related behaviors on the basis of how descriptive they are of the child. A score is then computed that permits children to be assigned to securely or insecurely attached groups.

moves very far, child follows along") into nine categories, ranging from highly descriptive to not at all descriptive of the child. Then a score is computed that permits children to be assigned to securely or insecurely attached groups (Waters et al., 1995). Q-Sort responses of expert observers correspond well with Strange Situation attachment classifications. And when mothers are carefully trained and supervised, their responses are reasonably consistent with those of expert observers (Seifer et al., 1996; Teti & McGourty, 1996).

STABILITY OF ATTACHMENT AND CULTURAL VARIATIONS

For middle-SES infants experiencing stable life conditions, quality of attachment to the caregiver is fairly stable. Indeed, evidence from Germany and the United States reveals that many such children continue to respond to the parent in a similar fashion when reobserved in a laboratory reunion situation at age 6 (Main & Cassidy, 1988; Wartner et al., 1994). However, when families experience major life changes, such as a shift in employment or marital status, the quality of attachment often changes—sometimes positively and at other times negatively (Thompson, 1998). This is expected, since family transitions affect parent–child interaction, which influences the attachment bond.

Nevertheless, cross-cultural evidence indicates that attachment patterns may have to be interpreted differently in other cultures. For example, as Figure 7.3 reveals, German infants show considerably more avoidant attachment than American babies. But German parents encourage their infants to be nonclingy and independent, so the baby's behavior may be an intended outcome of cultural beliefs and practices (Grossmann et al., 1985). Did you classify Rachel's attachment behavior as resistant? An unusually high number of Japanese infants display a resistant response, but the reaction may not represent true insecurity. Japanese mothers rarely leave their babies in the care of strange people, so the Strange Situation probably creates far greater stress for them than it does for infants who frequently experience maternal separations (Miyake, Chen, & Campos, 1985; Takahashi, 1990).

Despite these cultural variations, the secure pattern is still the most common attachment classification in all societies studied to date (van IJzendoorn & Kroonenberg, 1988). And when the Attachment Q-Sort is used to assess conceptions of the ideal child, mothers in diverse cultures—China, Germany, Israel, Japan, Norway, and the United States—prefer that their young children express their feelings of attachment by using the mother as a secure base for exploration (Posada et al., 1995).

FACTORS THAT AFFECT ATTACHMENT SECURITY

What factors might influence attachment security? First, simply having an opportunity to establish a close relationship with one or a few caregivers should be crucially important. Second, warm, responsive parenting should lead to greater attachment security. Third, since babies actively contribute to the attachment relationship, an infant's characteristics should make a difference in how well it proceeds. And finally, because children and parents are embedded in larger contexts, family circumstances and parents' internal working models should influence attachment quality. In the following sections, we examine each of these factors.

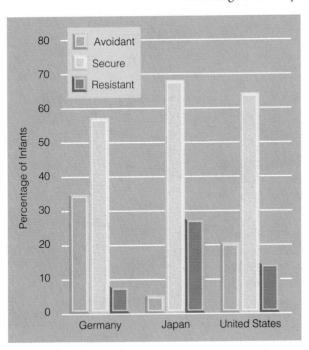

FIGURE 7.3

A cross-cultural comparison of infants' reactions in the Strange Situation. A high percentage of German babies seem avoidantly attached, whereas a substantial number of Japanese infants appear resistantly attached. Note that these responses may not reflect true insecurity. Instead, they are probably due to cultural differences in rearing practices. *(Adapted from van IJzendoorn & Kroonenberg, 1988.)*

sensitive caregiving
Caregiving involving prompt, consistent, and appropriate responding to infant signals.

interactional synchrony
A sensitively tuned "emotional dance," in which the caregiver responds to infant signals in a well-timed, appropriate fashion and both partners match emotional states, especially the positive ones.

■ **MATERNAL DEPRIVATION.** The powerful effect of the baby's affectional tie to the familiar caregiver is most evident when it is absent. In a series of landmark studies, René Spitz (1945, 1946) observed institutionalized infants who had been given up by their mothers between the third month and the end of the first year. The babies were placed on a large ward where they shared a nurse with at least seven other babies. In contrast to the happy, outgoing behavior they had shown before separation, they wept and withdrew from their surroundings, lost weight, and had difficulty sleeping. If a caregiver whom the baby could get to know did not replace the mother, the depression deepened rapidly.

These institutionalized infants experienced emotional difficulties because they were prevented from forming a bond with one or a few adults (Rutter, 1996). A more recent study of maternally deprived children supports this conclusion. Researchers followed the development of infants reared in an institution that offered a good caregiver–child ratio and a rich selection of books and toys. However, staff turnover was so rapid that the average child had a total of 50 different caregivers by the age of 4½! Many of these children became "late adoptees" who were placed in homes after age 4. Most developed deep ties with their adoptive parents, indicating that a first attachment bond can develop as late as 4 to 6 years of age.

But throughout childhood and adolescence, these youngsters were more likely to display emotional and social problems, including an excessive desire for adult attention, "overfriendliness" to unfamiliar adults and peers, and few friendships (Hodges & Tizard, 1989; Tizard & Hodges, 1978; Tizard & Rees, 1975). Although follow-ups into adulthood are necessary to be sure, these results leave open the possibility that fully normal development depends on establishing close bonds with caregivers during the first few years of life.

This Romanian institutionalized baby, orphaned shortly after birth, spends most of his days lying on his back, with little stimulation and no opportunity to form an emotional bond with a familiar caregiver. If he is not adopted soon, his development will suffer permanently. *(Pascal Scatence/Gamma-Liaison)*

■ **QUALITY OF CAREGIVING.** What kind of parental behavior promotes attachment? Research reveals that **sensitive caregiving** distinguishes securely from insecurely attached infants. Examining 66 studies involving over 4,000 mother–infant pairs, investigators reported that the extent to which mothers responded promptly, consistently, and appropriately to infant signals and held their babies tenderly and carefully was moderately related to attachment security (De Wolff & van IJzendoorn, 1997). In contrast, insecurely attached infants tend to have mothers who engage in less physical contact, handle them awkwardly, behave in a "routine" manner, and are sometimes negative, resentful, and rejecting (Ainsworth et al., 1978; Belsky, Rovine, & Taylor, 1984; Isabella, 1993; Pederson & Moran, 1996).

Exactly what is it that mothers of securely attached babies do to support their infants' feelings of trust? In several studies, a special form of communication called **interactional synchrony** separated the experiences of secure from insecure babies (Isabella, Belsky, & von Eye, 1989; Isabella & Belsky, 1991). It is best described as a sensitively tuned "emotional dance," in which caregiver–infant interaction appears to be mutually rewarding. The caregiver responds to infant signals in a well-timed, appropriate fashion, and both partners match emotional states, especially the positive ones. Watching Felicia interact with April in this way, I saw her respond to April's excited shaking of a rattle with an enthusiastic "That-a-girl!" When April babbled and looked at her mother, Felicia smiled and spoke expressively in return. When she fussed and cried, Felicia soothed with gentle touches and soft words.

But more evidence is needed to document the link between interactional synchrony and secure attachment. Other research reveals that only 30 percent of the time are exchanges between mothers and their babies perfectly "in sync" with one another. The remaining 70 percent of the time, interactive errors occur (Tronick, 1989). Perhaps warm, sensitive caregivers become especially skilled at repairing these errors and returning to a

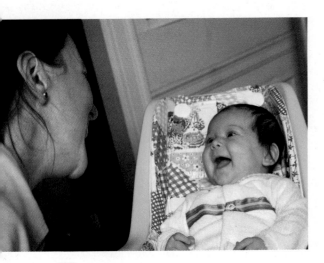

This mother and baby engage in a sensitively tuned form of communication called interactional synchrony in which they match emotional states, especially the positive ones. Interactional synchrony may support the development of secure attachment, but it does not characterize mother-infant interaction in all cultures. *(Julie O'Neil/The Picture Cube)*

synchronous state. Nevertheless, finely tuned, coordinated interaction does not characterize mother–infant interaction everywhere. Among the Gusii people of Kenya, mothers rarely cuddle, hug, and interact playfully with their babies, although they are very responsive to their infants' needs (LeVine et al., 1994). This suggests that secure attachment depends on attentive caregiving, but its association with moment-by-moment contingent interaction is probably limited to certain cultures.

Compared to securely attached infants, avoidant babies tend to receive overstimulating and intrusive care. Their mothers might, for example, talk energetically to a baby who is looking away or falling asleep. By avoiding the mother, these infants appear to be escaping from overwhelming interaction. Resistant infants often experience inconsistent care. Their mothers are minimally involved in caregiving and unresponsive to infant signals. Yet when the baby begins to explore, these mothers interfere, shifting the infant's attention back to themselves. As a result, the baby shows exaggerated dependence as well as anger and frustration at the mother's lack of involvement (Cassidy & Berlin, 1994; Isabella & Belsky, 1991).

When caregiving is extremely inadequate, it is a powerful predictor of disruptions in attachment. Child abuse and neglect (topics we will consider in Chapter 10) are associated with all three forms of attachment insecurity. Among maltreated infants, the most worrisome classification—disorganized/disoriented attachment—is especially high (Lyons-Ruth & Block, 1996). Infants of depressed mothers also show the uncertain behaviors of this pattern, mixing closeness, resistance, and avoidance while looking very sad and depressed themselves (Lyons-Ruth et al., 1990; Teti et al., 1995).

■ **INFANT CHARACTERISTICS.** Since attachment is the result of a *relationship* that builds between two partners, infant characteristics should affect how easily it is established. In Chapters 3 and 4, we saw that prematurity, birth complications, and newborn illness make caregiving more taxing for parents. In poverty-stricken, stressed families, these difficulties are linked to attachment insecurity (Wille, 1991). But when parents have the time and patience to care for a baby with special needs and the infant is not very sick, at-risk newborns fare quite well in the development of attachment (Pederson & Moran, 1995).

Infants also vary considerably in temperament, but its role in attachment security has been intensely debated. Some researchers believe that infants who are irritable and fearful may simply react to brief separations with intense anxiety, regardless of the parent's sensitivity to the baby (Kagan, 1989, 1998). Consistent with this view, proneness to distress in early infancy is moderately related to later insecure attachment (Seifer et al., 1996; Vaughn et al., 1992).

But other evidence argues for only a modest influence of temperament. First, quality of attachment to the mother and the father is often similar—a resemblance that could be due to parents' tendency to react similarly to their baby's temperament (Fox, Kimmerly, & Schafer, 1991; Rosen & Rothbaum, 1993). Yet quite a few infants establish distinct attachment relationships with each parent and with their professional caregivers (Goossens & van IJzendoorn, 1990). If temperament were very powerful, we would expect attachment quality to be more constant across familiar adults than it is.

Second, caregiving seems to be involved in the relationship between irritability and attachment insecurity. In one study, distress-prone infants who became insecurely attached tended to have rigid, controlling mothers who probably had trouble altering their immediate plans to comfort a baby who often cried (Mangelsdorf et al., 1990). And in another study, an intervention that taught mothers how to respond sensitively to their irritable 6-month-olds led to gains in maternal responsiveness and in children's attachment security, exploration, cooperativeness, and sociability that were still present at 3½ years of age (van den Boom, 1995).

Finally, other evidence confirms that caregiving can override the impact of infant characteristics on attachment security. When researchers combined data from over 34 studies including more than a thousand mother–infant pairs, they found that maternal problems—such as mental illness, teenage parenthood, and child abuse—were associated with a sharp rise in attachment insecurity (see Figure 7.4). In contrast, infant problems—ranging from prematurity and developmental delays to serious physical disabilities and psychological problems—had little impact on attachment quality (van IJzendoorn et al., 1992).

Clearly, temperament can influence how a baby responds in the Strange Situation. But a major reason that temperament and other infant characteristics do not show strong relationships with attachment security may be that their influence depends on goodness of fit. From this perspective, *many* child attributes can lead to secure attachment as long as the caregiver sensitively adjusts her behavior to fit the baby's needs (Seifer & Schiller, 1995; Sroufe, 1985). But when a parent's capacity to do so is strained—for example, by her own personality or stressful living conditions—then difficult infants are at greater risk for attachment problems.

■ **FAMILY CIRCUMSTANCES.** Around April's first birthday, Felicia's husband, Lonnie, lost his job, and constant arguments with Felicia over how they would pay the monthly bills caused him to leave the family for a time. Although Felicia tried not to let these worries affect her caregiving, April sensed the tension in the air. Several times, Felicia left April at Beth's house while she looked for employment. April, who had previously taken such separations quite well, cried desperately on her mother's departure and clung for a long time after she returned.

April's behavior reflects a repeated finding in the attachment literature: In families where there is stress and instability, insecure attachment is especially high. Job loss, a failing marriage, financial difficulties, and other stressors may undermine attachment by interfering with the sensitivity of parental care. Or they may affect babies' sense of security directly, by exposing them to angry adult interactions or unfavorable child-care arrangements (Owen & Cox, 1997; Thompson, 1998). The availability of social supports, especially assistance in caregiving, reduces stress and fosters attachment security. As Felicia and Lonnie resolved their difficulties, April's clinginess declined.

■ **PARENTS' INTERNAL WORKING MODELS.** Parents bring to the family context a long history of attachment experiences, out of which they construct internal working models that they apply to the bonds established with their babies. Lisa remembered her mother as tense and preoccupied and expressed regret that they had not had a closer relationship. Felicia recalled her mother as deeply affectionate and caring but much too controlling. Her mother's strictness, she explained, was probably influenced by the dangerous inner-city neighborhood in which the family lived. Do these images of parenthood affect the quality of Byron and April's attachments to their mothers?

To answer this question, researchers have assessed adults' internal working models by having them recall and evaluate childhood attachment experiences. Parents who show objectivity and balance in discussing their childhoods, regardless of whether they were positive or negative, tend to have securely attached infants. In contrast, parents who

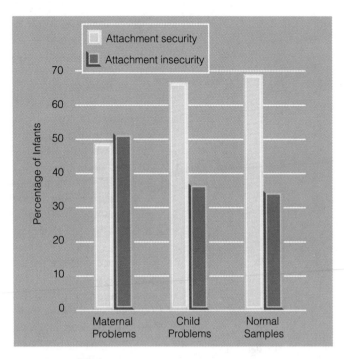

FIGURE 7.4

Comparison of the effects of maternal and child problem behaviors on the attachment bond. Maternal problems were associated with a sharp rise in attachment insecurity. In contrast, child problems had little impact on the rate of attachment security and insecurity, which resembled that of normal samples. *(Adapted from van IJzendoorn et al., 1992.)*

dismiss the importance of early relationships or describe them in angry, confused ways usually have insecurely attached babies (Steele, Steele, & Fonagy, 1996; van IJzendoorn, 1995a). Caregiving behavior helps explain these associations. Mothers with secure inner representations are warmer, more supportive of their children, and more likely to encourage learning and mastery. Their children, in turn, are more affectionate and comfortably interactive with them (Cox et al., 1992).

These findings indicate, in line with both psychoanalytic and ethological theories, that parents' childhood experiences are transferred to the next generation by way of their internal working models. This does not mean that adults with unhappy upbringings are destined to become insensitive parents. Instead, the way parents *view* their childhoods—their ability to integrate new information into their working models, to come to terms with negative events, and to look back on their own parents in an understanding, forgiving way—appears to be much more influential in how they rear their children than the actual history of care they received (van IJzendoorn, 1995b).

■ **ATTACHMENT IN CONTEXT.** Felicia eventually took a job; Lisa had returned to work many months before. When mothers divide their time between work and parenting and place their infants in day care, is the quality of attachment affected? The Social Issues box on the following page reviews the controversy over whether infant day care threatens attachment security.

After reading the box on day care and attachment, take a moment to consider each of the factors that influence the development of attachment. These include infant and parent characteristics, quality of the marital relationship, outside-the-family stressors such as employment status, the availability of social supports, parents' views of their own attachment history, and child care arrangements. Although attachment builds within the warmth and intimacy of caregiver–infant interaction, it can only be fully understood from an ecological systems perspective (Cowan, 1997; Thompson, 1997). Return to Chapter 1, page 26, to review Bronfenbrenner's ecological systems theory. Notice how the research we have reviewed confirms the importance of each level of the environment for attachment security.

MULTIPLE ATTACHMENTS

We have already indicated that babies develop attachments to a variety of familiar people—not just mothers, but fathers, siblings, grandparents, and professional caregivers. Although Bowlby (1969) made room for multiple attachments in his theory, he believed that infants are predisposed to direct their attachment behaviors to a single special person, especially when they are distressed. For example, when an anxious, unhappy 1-year-old is permitted to choose between the mother and the father as a source of comfort and security, the infant usually chooses the mother (Lamb, 1997). This preference typically declines over the second year of life. An expanding world of attachments enriches the emotional and social lives of many babies.

■ **FATHERS.** Like mothers', fathers' sensitive caregiving predicts secure attachment—an effect that becomes stronger the more time they spend with their babies (Cox et al., 1992; van IJzendoorn & De Wolff, 1997). Also, fathers of 1- to 5-year-olds enrolled in full-time day care report feeling just as much anxiety about separating from their child and just as much concern about the impact of these daily separations on the child's welfare as do mothers. Today, many fathers seem to "share anxieties that mothers have traditionally borne alone" (Deater-Deckard et al., 1994, p. 346).

As infancy progresses, mothers and fathers from a variety of cultures—Australia, India, Israel, Italy, Japan, and the United States—relate to babies in different ways. Mothers devote more time to physical care, such as changing, bathing, and feeding. In contrast, fathers spend more time in playful interaction (Lamb, 1987; Roopnarine et al., 1990).

SOCIAL ISSUES

IS INFANT DAY CARE A THREAT TO ATTACHMENT SECURITY?

Recent research suggests that American infants placed in full-time day care before 12 months of age are more likely than home-reared babies to display insecure attachment—especially avoidance—in the Strange Situation. Does this mean that babies who experience daily separations from their employed mothers and early placement in day care are at risk for developmental problems? Some researchers think so (Belsky, 1989, 1992; Sroufe, 1988), whereas others disagree (Clarke-Stewart, 1992; Scarr, Phillips, & McCartney, 1990). Yet a close look at the evidence reveals that we should be cautious about concluding that day care is harmful to infants.

First, in studies reporting a day care–attachment association, the rate of insecurity among day care infants is somewhat higher than that of non-day care infants (36 versus 29 percent), but it nevertheless resembles the overall rate of insecurity reported for children in industrialized countries around the world (Lamb, Sternberg, & Prodromidis, 1992). In fact, most infants of employed mothers are securely attached! Furthermore, not all investigations report a difference in attachment quality between day care and home-reared infants (NICHD Early Child Care Research Network, 1997; Roggman et al., 1994).

Second, we have seen that family conditions affect attachment security. Many employed women find the pressures of handling two full-time jobs (work and motherhood) stressful. Some respond less sensitively to their babies because they are fatigued and harried, thereby risking the infant's security (Stifter, Coulehan, & Fish, 1993). Other employed mothers proba-

bly value and encourage their infant's independence. Or their babies are unfazed by brief separations in the Strange Situation because they are used to separating from their parents. In these cases, avoidance in the Strange Situation may represent healthy autonomy rather than insecurity (Lamb, 1998). As yet, there is no evidence that "avoidant" day-care infants show problems in development as they get older.

Third, poor-quality day care may contribute to a higher rate of insecure attachment among infants of employed mothers. In a recent study of over 1,500 infants and their mothers, day care alone did not contribute to attachment insecurity. But when babies were exposed to several risk factors, including insensitive care at home and in day care, long hours in day care, and more than one day-care arrangement, the rate of insecurity increased (NICHD Early Child Care Research Network, 1996).

Finally, when young children first enter day care, they must adjust to new routines and daily separations from the parent. Under these conditions, signs of distress are expected. But after a few months, infants and toddlers enrolled in high-quality programs become more comfortable. They smile, play actively, seek comfort from sensitive caregivers they have come to know well, and begin to interact with agemates (Barnas & Cummings, 1994; Fein, Gariboldi, & Boni, 1993).

These findings reveal that assessing attachment security during the period of adaptation to day care may not provide an accurate picture of its impact on early emotional adjustment. Indeed, having the opportunity to form a warm bond with a stable

professional caregiver seems to be particularly helpful to infants whose relationship with one or both parents is insecure. When followed into the preschool and early school years, such children show higher self-esteem and socially skilled behavior than their insecurely attached agemates who did not attend day care (Egeland & Hiester, 1995).

Taken together, research suggests that some infants may be at risk for attachment insecurity due to inadequate day care and the joint pressures of full-time employment and parenthood experienced by their mothers. However, using this as evidence to justify a reduction in infant day care services is inappropriate. When family incomes are limited or mothers who want to work are forced to stay at home, children's emotional security is not promoted.

Instead, it makes sense to increase the availability of high-quality day care and to educate parents about the vital role of sensitive caregiving in early emotional development. Return to Chapter 6, page 236, to review signs of developmentally appropriate day care for infants and toddlers. To foster attachment security, the infant and toddler's relationship with the professional caregiver is vital. When caregiver–child ratios are generous, group sizes are small, and caregivers are educated about child development and child rearing, caregivers' interactions are more positive (NICHD Early Child Care Research Network, 1996). Day care with these characteristics can become part of an ecological system that relieves rather than intensifies parental and child stress, thereby promoting healthy attachment and development.

CULTURAL INFLUENCES

FATHER–INFANT RELATIONSHIPS AMONG THE AKA

Among the Aka hunters and gatherers of Central Africa, fathers devote more time to infants than in any other known society. Observations reveal that Aka fathers are within arm's reach of their infants more than half the day. They pick up and cuddle their babies at least five times more often than do fathers in other African hunting-and-gathering societies in Africa and elsewhere in the world.

Why are Aka fathers so involved with their babies? Research shows that when husband and wife help each other with many tasks, fathers assist more with infant care. The relationship between Aka husband and wife is unusually cooperative and intimate. Throughout the day, they share hunting, food preparation, and social and leisure activities. Babies are brought along on hunts, and mothers find it hard to carry them long distances. This explains, in part, why fathers spend so much time holding their infants. But when the Aka return to the campground, fathers continue to devote many hours to infant caregiving. The more Aka parents are together, the greater the father's interaction with his baby (Hewlett, 1992).

This Aka father spends much time in close contact with his baby. In Aka society, husband and wife share many tasks of daily living and have an unusually cooperative and intimate relationship. Infants are usually within arms reach of their fathers, who devote many hours to caregiving. *(Barry Hewlett)*

Also, mothers and fathers tend to play differently with babies. Mothers more often provide toys, talk to infants, and initiate conventional games like pat-a-cake and peekaboo. In contrast, fathers tend to engage in more exciting, highly physical bouncing and lifting games, especially with their infant sons (Yogman, 1981). In view of these differences, it is not surprising that babies tend to look to their mothers when distressed and to their fathers for playful stimulation.

However, this picture of "mother as caregiver" and "father as playmate" has changed in some families due to the revised work status of women. Employed mothers tend to engage in more playful stimulation of their babies than do unemployed mothers, and their husbands are somewhat more involved in caregiving (Cox et al., 1992). When fathers are the primary caregivers, they retain their arousing play style (Lamb & Oppenheim, 1989). Such highly involved fathers are less gender stereotyped in their beliefs; have sympathetic, friendly personalities; and regard parenthood as an especially enriching experience (Lamb, 1987; Levy-Shiff & Israelashvili, 1988).

A warm, gratifying marital relationship supports both parents' involvement with babies, but it is particularly important for fathers (Belsky, 1996). See the Cultural Influences box above for cross-cultural evidence that supports this conclusion.

■ **SIBLINGS.** Despite a declining family size, 80 percent of American children still grow up with at least one sibling. The arrival of a baby brother or sister is a difficult experience for most preschoolers, who quickly realize that now they must share their parents' attention and affection. They often become demanding and clingy for a time and engage in deliberate naughtiness. And their security of attachment typically declines, more so if they are over age 2 (old enough to feel threatened and displaced) and the mother is under stress due to marital or psychological problems (Teti et al., 1996).

Yet resentment is only one feature of a rich emotional relationship that starts to build between siblings after a baby's birth. The older child can also be seen kissing, patting, and calling out when the baby cries, "Mom, he needs you"—signs of growing caring and affection. By the time the baby is about 8 months old, siblings typically spend much time together, with the preschooler helping, sharing toys, imitating, and expressing friendliness in addition to anger and ambivalence (Dunn & Kendrick, 1982). Infants of this age are comforted by the presence of their preschool-age brother or sister during short absences of the mother (Stewart, 1983). And during the second year, they often imitate and join in play with the older child (Dunn, 1989).

Nevertheless, individual differences in the quality of sibling relationships appear shortly after a baby's birth and persist through early childhood (Dunn, 1992). Temperament plays an important role. For example, conflict increases when one sibling is emotionally intense or highly active (Brody, Stoneman, & McCoy, 1994; Dunn, 1994). Parental behavior also makes a difference. Secure infant–mother attachment and warmth toward both children are related to positive sibling interaction, whereas coldness is associated with sibling friction (Volling & Belsky, 1992).

Still, when a mother is very positive and playful with a new baby, her preschool-age child is likely to feel slighted and act in a less friendly way toward the infant. This does not mean that parents should limit the attention they give to infants, but it does indicate the importance of setting aside special times to devote to the older child. In addition, mothers who often discuss the baby's feelings and intentions have preschoolers who are more likely to comment on the infant as a person with special wants and needs. And such children behave in an especially considerate and friendly manner when interacting with the baby (Howe & Ross, 1990).

The Caregiving Concerns table below suggests way to promote positive relationships between babies and their preschool siblings. Research on brothers and sisters as

Although the arrival of a baby brother or sister is a difficult experience for most preschoolers, a rich emotional relationship quickly builds between siblings. This toddler is already actively involved in play with his 4-year-old brother, and both derive great pleasure from the interaction. *(Erika Stone/Photo Researchers, Inc.)*

CAREGIVING CONCERNS

Encouraging Affectional Ties Between Infants and Their Preschool Siblings

SUGGESTION	DESCRIPTION
Spend extra time with the older child.	To minimize feelings of being deprived of affection and attention, set aside time to spend with the older child. Fathers can be especially helpful in this regard, planning special outings with the preschooler and taking over care of the baby so the mother can be with the older child.
Handle sibling misbehavior with patience.	Respond patiently to the older sibling's misbehavior and demands for attention, recognizing that these reactions are temporary. Give the preschooler opportunities to feel proud of being more grown-up than the baby. For example, encourage the older child to assist with feeding, bathing, dressing, and offering toys, and show appreciation for these efforts.
Discuss the baby's wants and needs.	Discuss the baby's feelings and intentions with the preschooler, such as, "He's so little that he just can't wait to be fed" or "He's trying to reach his rattle and can't." By helping the older sibling understand the baby's point of view, parents can promote friendly, considerate behavior.

Sources: Dunn & Kendrick, 1982; Howe & Ross, 1990.

attachment figures reminds us of the complex, multidimensional nature of the infant's social world. Siblings offer a rich social context in which children learn and practice a wide range of skills, including affectionate caring, conflict resolution, and control of hostile and envious feelings.

FROM ATTACHMENT TO PEER SOCIABILITY

In cultures where agemates have regular contact during the first year of life, peer sociability begins early. By 6 months of age, Byron, Rachel, and April occasionally looked, reached, smiled, and babbled when they saw one another. These isolated social acts increased until by the end of the first year, an occasional reciprocal exchange occurred in which the children grinned, gestured, or otherwise imitated a playmate's behavior (Vandell & Mueller, 1995; Vandell, Wilson, & Buchanan, 1980).

Between 1 and 2 years, coordinated interaction occurs more often, largely in the form of mutual imitation involving jumping, chasing, or banging a toy. These imitative, turn-taking games mark an advance in social awareness. They indicate that the toddler is not only interested in the playmate but aware of the playmate's interest in him or her. And they create joint understandings that aid verbal communication. Around age 2, toddlers begin to use words to talk about and influence a peer's behavior, as when Rachel said to April, "Let's play chase," and after the game got going, "Hey, good running!" (Eckerman & Didow, 1996; Howes & Matheson, 1992). Reciprocal play and positive emotion are especially frequent in toddlers' interactions with familiar agemates, suggesting that they are building true peer relationships (Ross et al., 1992).

The beginnings of peer sociability emerge in infancy, in the form of reaches, smiles, and babbles that gradually develop into coordinated interaction in the second year. Early peer sociability is fostered by a warm, sensitive caregiver–child bond. *(Laura Dwight)*

Although quite limited, peer sociability is present in the first 2 years, and it is fostered by the early caregiver–child bond. From interacting with sensitive adults, babies learn how to send and interpret emotional signals in their first peer associations. Consistent with this idea, infants with a warm parental relationship engage in more extended peer exchanges (Vandell & Wilson, 1987). And for toddlers in day care, a secure attachment to a stable professional caregiver predicts advanced peer and play behavior (Howes & Hamilton, 1993).

ATTACHMENT AND LATER DEVELOPMENT

According to psychoanalytic and ethological theories, the inner feelings of affection and security that result from a healthy attachment relationship support not only peer sociability but all aspects of psychological development. Consistent with this view, many researchers have addressed the link between infant–mother attachment and cognitive, emotional, and social development.

In the most extensive longitudinal study of this kind, Alan Sroufe and his collaborators reported that preschoolers who were securely attached as babies showed more elaborate make-believe play and greater enthusiasm, flexibility, and persistence in problem solving by 2 years of age. At age 4, such children were rated by their preschool teachers as high in self-esteem, socially competent, cooperative, popular, and empathic. In contrast, their avoidantly attached agemates were viewed as isolated and disconnected, and those who were resistantly attached were regarded as disruptive and difficult. Studied again at age 11 in summer camp, children who were secure as infants had more favorable relationships with peers, closer friendships, and better social skills, as judged by camp counselors (Elicker, Englund, & Sroufe, 1992; Frankel & Bates, 1990; Matas, Arend, & Sroufe, 1978).

These findings have been taken by some researchers to mean that secure attachment in infancy causes improved cognitive, emotional and social competence during later years. Yet more evidence is needed before we can be certain of this conclusion. Longitudinal studies spanning only a few years yield a mixed picture; secure infants do not always show more favorable development than their insecure counterparts (Belsky & Cassidy, 1994).

Why is research on the long-term consequences of attachment quality as yet unclear? Michael Lamb and his colleagues (1985) suggest that *continuity of caregiving* determines whether attachment security is linked to later development. When parents respond sensitively not just in infancy but during later years, children are likely to develop favorably. In contrast, children of parents who react insensitively for a long time are at increased risk for maladjustment. In support of this interpretation, a closer look at Sroufe's longitudinal study reveals that in the few instances in which securely attached infants did develop later behavior problems, their mothers became less positive and supportive in early childhood. Similarly, the handful of insecurely attached babies who became well-adjusted preschoolers had mothers who were sensitive and provided their young children with clear structure and guidance (Egeland et al., 1990; Thompson, 1998).

Do these findings remind you of our discussion of *resiliency* in Chapter 1? A child whose parental caregiving improves or who has compensating affectional ties outside the immediate family can bounce back from adversity. In sum, efforts to create warm, responsive environments are not just important in infancy and toddlerhood; they are also worthwhile at later ages, as we will see in subsequent chapters.

BRIEF REVIEW

Drive reduction (behaviorist) and psychoanalytic theories have been criticized for overemphasizing feeding and paying little attention to the baby's active role in establishing an attachment bond. According to ethological theory, infant–caregiver attachment has evolved because it promotes survival. In early infancy, babies' innate signals help keep the parent nearby. By 6 to 8 months, separation anxiety and use of the mother as a secure base indicate that a true attachment has formed. Representation and language help toddlers tolerate brief separations from the parent.

Research on infants deprived of a consistent caregiver suggests that fully normal development depends on establishing a close affectional bond in the first few years of life. Caregiving that is responsive to babies' needs supports the development of secure attachment; insensitive caregiving is linked to attachment insecurity. Infant illness and irritable and fearful temperamental styles make attachment security harder to achieve, but good parenting can override the impact of infant characteristics. Family conditions and parents' internal working models also contribute to attachment quality.

Besides mothers, fathers and siblings are influential attachment figures. A warm parental relationship fosters early peer sociability. Research on the relationship of attachment to later development reveals a mixed picture. When attachment security predicts cognitive, emotional, and social competence, continuity of caregiving may be largely responsible.

SELF-DEVELOPMENT

Infancy is a rich, formative period for the development of physical and social understanding. In Chapter 6, you learned that infants develop an appreciation of the permanence of objects—that they continue to exist when no longer in view. And in this chapter, we have seen that over the first year, infants recognize and respond appropriately to others' emotions and distinguish familiar people from strangers. The fact that both objects and people achieve an independent,

ASK YOURSELF . . .

■ *Recall from Chapter 6 that Lisa tended to overwhelm Byron with questions and instructions that were not related to his ongoing actions. How would you expect Byron to respond in the Strange Situation? Explain your answer.*

■ *Maggy works full time and leaves her 14-month-old son, Roberto, at a day care center. When she arrives to pick him up at the end of the day, Roberto keeps on playing and ignores her. Maggy wonders whether Roberto is securely attached. Is Maggy's concern warranted?*

■ *List factors that affect the development of attachment security. Show how each level of the environment in ecological systems theory influences the development of attachment.*

This infant notices the correspondence between his own movements and the movements of the image in the mirror, a cue that helps him figure out that the grinning baby is really himself. *(Paul Damien/ Tony Stone Worldwide)*

stable existence for the infant implies that knowledge of the self as a separate, permanent entity emerges around this time.

SELF-AWARENESS

After her daily bath, Felicia often held April in front of the bathroom mirror. As early as the first few months, April smiled and returned friendly behaviors to her image. At what age did she realize that the charming baby gazing and grinning back was really herself?

■ **EMERGENCE OF THE I-SELF AND ME-SELF.** To answer this question, researchers have conducted clever laboratory observations in which they expose infants and toddlers to images of themselves in mirrors, on videotapes, and in photos. When shown a videotaped image of their own next to that of a peer, 3-month-olds look longer at the peer's image. This suggests that at least for babies with access to mirrors, discrimination of self from others is under way in the first few months of life (Bahrick, Moss, & Fadil, 1996).

Researchers agree that the earliest aspect of the self to emerge is the **I-self**—a sense of self as *subject*, or *agent*, who is separate from but attends to and acts on objects and other people. How do infants develop this awareness? According to many theorists, the beginnings of the I-self lie in infants' recognition that their own actions cause objects and people to react in predictable ways (Harter, 1998). Parents who encourage babies to explore and who respond to their signals consistently and sensitively help them construct a sense of self as agent (Pipp, Easterbrooks, & Brown, 1993).

Then, as infants act on the environment, they notice different effects that may help them sort out self from other people and objects. For example, batting a mobile and seeing it swing in a pattern different from the infant's own actions informs the baby about the relation between self and physical world. Smiling and vocalizing at a caregiver who smiles and vocalizes back helps specify the relation between self and social world. And watching the movements of one's own hand provides still another kind of feedback—one under much more direct control than other people or objects. The contrast between these experiences may help infants build an image of self as separate from external reality (Case, 1991; Lewis, 1991, 1994).

During the second year, toddlers start to construct a second aspect of self: the **me-self**, a reflective observer that treats the self as an object of knowledge and evaluation. Consequently, they become consciously aware of the self's features. In one study, 9- to 24-month-olds were placed in front of a mirror. Then, under the pretext of wiping the baby's face, each mother was asked to rub red dye on her child's nose. Younger infants touched

I-self
A sense of self as subject, or agent, who is separate from but attends to and acts on objects and other people.

me-self
A reflective observer that treats the self as an object of knowledge and evaluation.

the mirror as if the red mark had nothing to do with any aspect of themselves. But by 15 months, toddlers began to rub their strange-looking little red noses. They were keenly aware of their unique visual appearance (Lewis & Brooks-Gunn, 1979). By age 2, almost all children use their name or a personal pronoun ("I" or "me") to label their image or refer to themselves.

■ **SELF-AWARENESS AND EARLY EMOTIONAL AND SOCIAL DEVELOPMENT.** Self-awareness quickly becomes a central part of children's emotional and social lives. Earlier you learned that self-conscious emotions depend on toddlers' emerging sense of self. Self-awareness also leads to the child's first efforts to understand another's perspective. For example, it is associated with the beginnings of self-conscious behavior. It also precedes the appearance of sustained, mutual peer imitation (recall that such imitation indicates that the toddler realizes a playmate is interested in him or her) (Asendorpf, Warkentin, & Baudonniere, 1996). And self-awareness is accompanied by the first signs of **empathy**—the ability to understand another's emotional state and *feel for* that person, or respond emotionally in a similar way. For example, toddlers start to give to others what they themselves find comforting—a hug, a reassuring comment, or a favorite doll or blanket (Bischof-Köhler, 1991; Zahn-Waxler et al., 1992).

Along with an increase in empathic behavior comes a much clearer awareness of how to upset and frustrate other people (Dunn, 1989). One 18-month-old heard her mother comment to another adult, "Anny (sibling) is really frightened of spiders. In fact, there's a particular toy spider that we've got that she just hates" (p. 107). The innocent-looking toddler ran to get the spider out of the toy box, returned, and pushed it in front of Anny's face!

CATEGORIZING THE SELF

Once children have a me-self, they use their representational and language capacities to create a mental image of themselves. One of the first signs of this change is that toddlers begin to compare themselves to other people. Between 18 and 30 months, children label themselves and others on the basis of age ("baby," "boy," or "man"), sex ("boy" or "girl" and "lady" or "man"), physical characteristics ("big," "strong"), and even goodness and badness ("I good girl." "Tommy mean!"). They also start to refer to the self's competencies ("Did it!" "I can't") (Stipek, Gralinski, & Kopp, 1990).

Toddlers' understanding of these social categories is quite limited. But as soon as they categorize themselves, they use this knowledge to organize their own behavior. For example, toddlers' ability to label their own gender is associated with a sharp rise in gender-stereotyped responses (Fagot & Leinbach, 1989). As early as 18 months, children select and play in a more involved way with toys that are stereotyped for their own gender—dolls and tea sets for girls, trucks and cars for boys. Then parents encourage these preferences further by responding more positively when toddlers display them (Fagot, Leinbach, & O'Boyle, 1992). As we will see in Chapter 10, gender-typed behavior increases dramatically over early childhood.

EMERGENCE OF SELF-CONTROL

Self-awareness also provides the foundation for **self-control,** the capacity to resist an impulse to engage in socially disapproved behavior. Self-control is essential for morality, another dimension of the self that will flourish during childhood and adolescence. To behave in a self-controlled fashion, children must have some ability to think of themselves as separate, autonomous beings who can direct their own actions. And they must also have the representational and memory capacities to recall a caregiver's directive (such as "April, don't touch that light socket!") and apply it to their own behavior (Kopp, 1987).

empathy
The ability to understand another's emotional state and *feel for* that person, or respond emotionally in a similar way.

self-control
The capacity to resist an impulse to engage in socially disapproved behavior.

CAREGIVING CONCERNS

Helping Toddlers Develop Compliance and Self-Control

SUGGESTION	RATIONALE
Respond to the toddler warmly and sensitively.	Toddlers who experience warmth and sensitivity are far more compliant and cooperative than negative and resistant.
Provide advance notice when the toddler must stop an enjoyable activity.	Toddlers find it more difficult to stop a pleasant activity already under way than to wait before engaging in a desired action.
Offer many prompts and reminders.	Toddlers' ability to remember and comply with rules is limited; they need continuous adult oversight.
Respond to self-controlled behavior with verbal and physical approval.	Praise and hugs reinforce appropriate behavior, increasing its likelihood of occurring again.
Support language development.	Early language development is related to self-control. During the second year, children begin to use language to remind themselves about adult expectations.
Gradually increase rules in accord with the toddler's developing capacities.	As cognition and language improve, toddlers can follow more rules related to safety, respect for people and property, family routines, manners, and simple chores.

ASK YOURSELF . . .

■ *Nine-month-old Harry turned his cup upside down and spilled juice all over the tray of his highchair. His mother said sharply, "Harry, put your cup back the right way!" Can Harry comply with his mother's request? Why or why not?*

compliance
Voluntary obedience to adult requests and commands.

As these abilities appear, the first glimmerings of self-control emerge in the form of **compliance.** Between 12 and 18 months, children start to show clear awareness of care-givers' wishes and expectations and can voluntarily obey simple requests and commands (Kaler & Kopp, 1990). And, as every parent knows, they can also decide to do just the opposite! One way toddlers assert their sense of autonomy is by resisting adult directives. But among toddlers who experience warm, sensitive caregiving and reasonable expectations for mature behavior, opposition is far less common than eager, willing compliance (Kochanska, Aksan, & Koenig, 1995). Compliance quickly leads to toddlers' first morally relevant verbalizations—for example, correcting the self by saying "no, can't" before touching a light socket or jumping on the sofa (Kochanska, 1993).

Around 18 months, the capacity for self-control appears, and it improves steadily into early childhood. In one study, toddlers were given three tasks that required them to resist temptation. In the first, they were asked not to touch an interesting toy telephone that was within arm's reach. In the second, raisins were hidden under cups, and they were instructed to wait until the experimenter said it was all right to pick up a cup and eat a raisin. In the third, they were told not to open a gift until the experimenter had finished her work. On all three problems, the ability to wait increased steadily between 18 and 30 months of age. Toddlers who were especially self-controlled were also advanced in language development. In fact, some used verbal techniques, such as singing and talking to themselves, to keep from touching the desired objects (Vaughn, Kopp, & Krakow, 1984).

As self-control improves, mothers increase the rules they require toddlers to follow, from safety and respect for property and people to family routines, manners, and simple chores (Gralinski & Kopp, 1993). Still, toddlers' control over their own actions is very fragile. It depends on constant oversight and reminders by parents. To get April to stop playing to go on an errand, several prompts ("Remember, we're going to go in just a minute") and gentle insistence were usually necessary. The Caregiving Concerns table above summarizes effective ways of helping toddlers develop compliance and self-control.

As the second year of life drew to a close, Lisa, Beth, and Felicia were delighted with their youngsters' new-found capacity for compliance and self-control. It signaled that the three toddlers were ready to learn the rules of social life. As we will see in Chapter 10, advances in cognition and language, along with parental warmth and reasonable maturity demands, lead children to make tremendous strides in this area during the early childhood years.

Summary

THEORIES OF INFANT AND TODDLER PERSONALITY

Explain Erikson's and Mahler's theories of infant and toddler personality.

■ The psychoanalytic theories of Erikson and Mahler capture salient features of personality development during the first 2 years. According to Erikson, warm, responsive caregiving leads infants to resolve the psychological conflict of **basic trust versus mistrust** on the positive side. During toddlerhood, the conflict of **autonomy versus shame and doubt** is resolved favorably when parents provide appropriate guidance and reasonable choices.

■ According to Mahler, sensitive, loving care fosters **symbiosis,** which provides the foundation for **separation–individuation** during toddlerhood. The capacity to move away from the mother, by crawling and then walking, leads to self-awareness. Gains in representation and language help create a positive, inner image of the mother that can be relied on for emotional support in her absence.

EMOTIONAL DEVELOPMENT

Describe changes in happiness, anger, and fear over the first year, noting the adaptive function of each.

■ Signs of almost all the **basic emotions** are present in infancy, each of which becomes more recognizable with age. The **social smile** appears between 6 and 10 weeks, laughter around 3 to 4 months. Happiness strengthens the parent–child bond and reflects as well as supports physical and cognitive mastery. Anger and fear, especially in the form of **stranger anxiety,** increase in the second half of the first year. These reactions have survival value as infants' motor capacities improve.

Summarize changes in understanding others' emotions, expression of self-conscious emotions, and emotional self-regulation during the first 2 years.

■ The ability to understand the feelings of others expands over the first year as babies perceive facial expressions as organized patterns. Around 8 to 10 months, **social referencing** appears; infants actively seek emotional information from caregivers in uncertain situations. By the middle of the second year, infants begin to appreciate that others' emotional reactions may differ from their own.

■ During toddlerhood, self-awareness and adult instruction provide the foundation for **self-conscious emotions,** such as shame, embarrassment, and pride. Caregivers help infants with **emotional self-regulation** by relieving distress, engaging in stimulating play, and discouraging negative emotion. During the second year, growth in representation and language leads to more effective ways of regulating emotion.

TEMPERAMENT AND DEVELOPMENT

What is temperament, and how is it measured?

■ Infants differ greatly in **temperament,** or quality and intensity of emotion, activity level, attention, and emotional self-regulation. On the basis of parental descriptions of children's behavior, three patterns of temperament—the **easy child,** the **difficult child,** and the **slow-to-warm-up child**—were identified in the New York Longitudinal Study. Difficult children, especially, are likely to display adjustment problems.

■ Psychophysiological measures distinguish **inhibited,** or **shy, children** from **uninhibited,** or **sociable, children.** These youngsters may inherit a physiology that biases them toward a particular temperamental style.

Discuss the role of heredity and environment in the stability of temperament, including the goodness-of-fit model.

■ Many temperamental characteristics show moderate stability over time. Temperament has biological roots, but child rear-

ing has much to do with whether a child's emotional style remains the same or changes over time. Ethnic and sex differences in temperament are due to the combined influence of heredity and child rearing.

■ The **goodness-of-fit model** describes how temperament and environment work together to affect later development. Parenting practices that create a good fit with the child's temperament help difficult, shy, and highly active children achieve more adaptive functioning.

DEVELOPMENT OF ATTACHMENT

What are the unique features of ethological theory of attachment in comparison to drive reduction and psychoanalytic views?

■ The development of **attachment,** infants' strong affectional tie to familiar caregivers, has been the subject of intense theoretical debate. Although psychoanalytic and **drive reduction** (behaviorist) explanations exist, the most widely accepted perspective is **ethological theory.** It views babies as biologically prepared to contribute actively to ties established with their caregivers, which promote survival.

■ In early infancy, a set of built-in behaviors encourages the parent to remain close to the baby. Around 6 to 8 months, **separation anxiety** and use of the parent as a **secure base** indicate that a true attachment bond has formed. As representation and language develop, toddlers try to alter the mother's coming and going through requests and persuasion rather than following and clinging. Out of early caregiving experiences, children construct an **internal working model** that serves as a guide for all future close relationships.

Cite the four attachment patterns assessed by the Strange Situation and the Attachment Q-Sort, and discuss factors that affect attachment security.

■ A widely used technique for measuring the quality of attachment between 1 and 2

Summary (continued)

years of age is the **Strange Situation**. A more efficient method is the **Attachment Q-Sort.** Four attachment patterns have been identified: **secure, avoidant, resistant,** and **disorganized/disoriented.** Cultural conditions must be considered in interpreting reactions in the Strange Situation.

■ A variety of factors affect the development of attachment. Infants deprived of affectional ties with one or a few adults show lasting emotional and social problems. **Sensitive caregiving** is moderately related to secure attachment. **Interactional synchrony** also separates the experiences of secure from insecure babies, but its importance is probably limited to certain cultures.

■ Even sick infants or infants with irritable or fearful temperaments are likely to become securely attached if parents adapt their caregiving to suit the baby's needs. Family conditions, including stress and instability, influence caregiving behavior and attachment security. Parents' internal working models also predict the quality of infants' attachment bonds. The development of attachment clearly takes place within a complex ecological system.

Discuss infants' attachments to fathers and siblings, and indicate how attachment paves the way for early peer sociability.

■ Besides attachments to mothers, infants develop strong ties to fathers, usually through stimulating, playful interaction. Early in the first year, infants begin to build rich emotional relationships with siblings that mix affection and caring with rivalry and resentment. Individual differences in the quality of sibling relationships are influenced by temperament and parenting practices.

■ Peer sociability begins in infancy with isolated social acts that are gradually replaced by reciprocal exchanges, largely in the form of mutual imitation, in the second year of life. Sensitive parental and professional caregiver relationships foster the development of early peer sociability.

Describe and interpret the relationship between secure attachment in infancy and cognitive, emotional, and social competence in childhood.

■ At present, evidence for the impact of early attachment on cognitive, emotional, and social competence in later years is

mixed. Continuity of parental care may be the crucial factor that determines whether attachment security is linked to later development.

SELF-DEVELOPMENT

Describe the development of self-awareness in infancy and toddlerhood, along with the emotional and social capacities it supports.

■ The earliest aspect of the self to emerge is the **I-self,** a sense of self as subject, or agent. Its beginnings lie in infants' recognition that their own actions cause objects and people to react in predictable ways. During the second year, toddlers start to construct the **me-self,** a reflective observer that treats the self as an object of knowledge and evaluation.

■ Self-awareness permits toddlers to compare themselves to others. Social categories based on age, sex, physical characteristics, and goodness and badness are evident in toddlers' language. Self-awareness also provides the foundation for self-conscious emotions, **empathy, compliance,** and **self-control.**

*I*mportant terms and concepts

*F*yi... FOR FURTHER INFORMATION AND HELP

MENTAL HEALTH

American Academy of Child
and Adolescent Psychiatry
(202) 966-2891
Website: www.aacap.org

An organization of medical professionals dedicated to treating and improving quality of life for infants, children, and adolescents with emotional or behavior disorders. Distributes Facts for Families, *an information sheet on childhood mental health that can be accessed through its website. Also disseminates scholarly research through its monthly journal.*

American Academy of Pediatrics
(847) 228-5005
Website: www.aap.org

An organization of over 50,000 pediatricians dedicated to the physical and mental health of infants, children, and adolescents. Disseminates a wide variety of health-related information to professionals and parents through its publications, which include Pediatrics, *a monthly scholarly journal;* Healthy Kids *magazine; and child-care books and brochures.*

Milestones

AGE	PHYSICAL	COGNITIVE	LANGUAGE	EMOTIONAL/SOCIAL
Birth–6 months	■ Rapid height and weight gain. (168) ■ Reflexes decline. (152) ■ Sleep organized into a day-night schedule. (181) ■ Holds head up, rolls over, and reaches for objects. (184) ■ Can be classically and operantly conditioned. (191–192) ■ Habituates to unchanging stimuli; dishabituates to novel stimuli. (193) ■ Hearing well developed; by the end of this period, displays greater sensitivity to speech sounds of own language. (197) ■ Sensitive to motion and binocular depth cues. (198–199) ■ Perceives stimuli as organized patterns; recognizes and prefers pattern of human face. (201–203)	■ Engages in deferred imitation of adults' facial expressions. (219) ■ Repeats chance behaviors leading to pleasurable and interesting results. (214–215) ■ Aware of object permanence and other object properties in habituation–dishabituation task. (218) ■ Attention becomes more efficient and flexible. (255) ■ Recognition memory for people, places, and objects improves. (226) ■ Forms perceptual categories, based on objects' similar features. (228) 	■ Engages in cooing and, by the end of this period, babbling. (242) ■ Established joint attention with caregiver, who labels objects and events. (243) 	■ Shows signs of almost all basic emotions (happiness, interest, surprise, fear, anger, sadness, disgust). (258) ■ Social smile and laughter emerge. (258–259) ■ Matches adults' emotional expressions during face-to-face interaction. (258) ■ I-self emerges. (284) ■ If infant has access to mirrors, begins to distinguish own image from that of others. (284)
7–12 months	■ Sits alone, crawls, walks. (184) ■ Shows refined pincer grasp. (189) ■ Perceives larger speech units crucial to understanding meaning. (197) ■ Sensitive to pictorial depth cues. (199) ■ Organizes many stimuli into meaningful patterns. (201) ■ Relies on shape, color, and texture to distinguish objects from their surroundings. (204)	■ Combines sensorimotor schemes. (215) ■ Engages in intentional, or goal-directed, behavior. (215) ■ Finds objects hidden in one place. (216) ■ Understanding of object properties and physical causality expands. (218) ■ Engages in deferred imitation of adults' actions on objects. (220) ■ Recall memory for people, places, and objects improves. (226)	■ Babbling expands to include sounds of spoken languages and the child's language community. (242–243) ■ Uses preverbal gestures (showing, pointing) to communicate. (243) 	■ Anger and fear increase in frequency and intensity. (259) ■ Stranger anxiety and separation anxiety appear. (259, 271) ■ Uses caregiver as a secure base for exploration. (272) ■ Engages in social referencing. (260) ■ Shows "clear-cut" attachment to familiar caregivers. (271)

AGE	PHYSICAL	COGNITIVE	LANGUAGE	EMOTIONAL/SOCIAL
13–18 months	■ Height and weight gain rapid but not as great as in first year. (169) ■ Walking better coordinated. (184) ■ Manipulates small objects with improved coordination. (189)	■ Experiments with objects in a trial-and-error fashion. (216) ■ Finds object hidden in more than one place. (216) ■ Sorts objects into categories. (228) ■ Imitates actions across a change in context—for example, in the home imitates a behavior learned at day care. (220) ■ Sustained attention improves. (226)	■ Actively takes turns in games, such as pat-a-cake and peekaboo. (243) ■ Says first words. (241) ■ Makes errors of underextension and overextension. (244)	■ Joins in play with familiar adults and siblings. (280–281) ■ Recognizes image of self in mirrors. (285) ■ Begins to realize others' emotional reactions may differ from one's own. (261) ■ Shows signs of empathy. (285) ■ Complies with simple directives. (286) ■ Engages in imitative, turn-taking games with playmates. (282)

19–24 months	■ Jumps, runs, and climbs. (184) ■ Manipulates small objects with good coordination. (189)	■ Solves sensorimotor problems through representation. (216) ■ Finds object moved while out of sight. (216) ■ Engages in deferred imitation of actions an adult tries to produce, even if not fully realized. (220) ■ Engages in make-believe play. (217) ■ Sorts objects into categories more effectively. (228) ■ Recall memory for people, places, and objects improves further. (226)	■ Vocabulary increases to 200 words. (244) ■ Combines two words. (244)	■ Self-conscious emotions (shame, embarrassment, and pride) emerge . (261) ■ Acquires a vocabulary of emotional terms. (262) ■ Starts to use language to assist with emotional self-regulation. (262) ■ Begins to tolerate caregiver's absences more easily. (272) ■ Starts to use words to influence a playmate's behavior. (282) ■ Uses own name or personal pronoun to label image of self. (285) ■ Categorizes the self and others on the basis of age, sex, and goodness and badness. (285) ■ Shows gender-stereotyped toy choices. (285)

Note: Numbers in parenthesis indicate the page on which each milestone is discussed.

■ Self-control appears. (286)

8

"Swimming"
Cheng Ping
5 years, China

A transformed body and explosion of new motor skills contribute to an expanding sense of competence in early childhood, vigorously captured in this image of eager, confident young swimmers. Chapter 8 highlights the close link between early childhood physical growth and other aspects of development.

PHYSICAL DEVELOPMENT

in EARLY CHILDHOOD

*F*or more than a decade, my fourth-floor office window overlooked the preschool and kindergarten play yard of our university laboratory school. Sitting at my desk, I spent many fascinating moments watching young children at play. On mild fall and spring mornings, the doors of the preschool and kindergarten swung open, and sand table, woodworking bench, easels, and large blocks spilled out into a small, fenced courtyard. Around the side of the building was a grassy area with jungle gyms, swings, a small playhouse, and a flower garden planted by the children. Beyond it, I could see a circular path lined with tricycles and wagons. Each day the setting was alive with activity.

As I looked on from my distant vantage point, the physical changes of early childhood were clearly evident. Children's bodies were longer and leaner than they had been a year or two earlier. The awkward gait of toddlerhood had disappeared in favor of more refined movements that included climbing, jumping, galloping, and skipping. Throughout the morning, children scaled the jungle gym, searched for imaginary pirates behind trees and bushes, chased one another across the play yard, and peddled tricycles vigorously over the pavement.

Just as impressive as these gross motor achievements were gains in fine motor skills. At the sand table, children built hills, valleys, caves, and roads and prepared trays of pretend cookies and cupcakes. Nearby, blocks of wood were hammered into small sculptures. And as children grew older, the paintings that hung out to dry took on greater form and detail as family members, houses, trees, birds, sky, monsters, and letterlike forms appeared in the colorful creations.

The years from 2 to 6 are often called "the play years," and aptly so, since play blossoms during this time and supports every aspect of development. We begin our consideration of early childhood by tracing the physical achievements of this period—growth in body size, improvements in motor coordination, and refinements in perception. Our discussion pays special attention to biological and environmental factors that support these changes, as well as to their intimate connection with cognitive, emotional, and social development. The preschoolers whom I came to know well, first by watching from my office window and later by observing at close range in their classrooms, will provide us with many examples of developmental trends and individual differences.

BODY GROWTH

Although Darryl visited the doctor only once a year during early childhood, his parents continued to measure his growth every 3 months in a corner of the kitchen, where they recorded his height on the wall. Each new mark became a special event. Darryl backed up with shoulders straight and head held high, eagerly awaiting the results. On his fifth birthday, the family took an overall look at how he'd grown. Compared to the earliest marks, those of the preschool years were closer together and more evenly spaced.

CHANGES IN BODY SIZE AND PROPORTIONS

Look at Figure 8.1, and you will see that the rapid increase in body size in infancy tapers off into a slower pattern of growth during early childhood. On the average, 2 to 3 inches in height and about 5 pounds in weight are added each year. Boys continue to be slightly larger than girls.

At the same time, the "baby fat" that began to decline in toddlerhood drops off further. The child gradually becomes thinner, although girls retain somewhat more body fat, and boys are slightly more muscular. As the torso lengthens and widens, internal organs tuck neatly inside, and the spine straightens. By age 5, the top-heavy, bowlegged, potbellied toddler has become a more streamlined, flat-tummied, longer-legged child with body proportions similar to those of adults (Tanner, 1990). Consequently, posture and balance improve—changes that support the gains in motor coordination that we will take up later in this chapter.

Individual differences in body size are even more apparent during early childhood than in infancy and toddlerhood. Looking down at the play yard one day, I watched 5-year-old Darryl speed around the bike path. At 48 inches tall and 55 pounds, he towered over his kindergarten classmates and was, as his mother put it, "off the growth charts" at the doctor's office (the average American 5-year-old boy is 43 inches tall and weighs 42 pounds). Priti, an Asian-Indian child, was unusually small due to hereditary factors linked to her cultural background. Lynette and Hallie, two Caucasian children with impoverished home lives, were well below average for reasons we will discuss shortly.

Toddlers and 5-year-olds have very different body shapes. During early childhood, body fat declines, the torso enlarges to better accommodate the internal organs, and the spine straightens. Compared to her younger brother, this girl looks more streamlined. Her body proportions resemble those of an adult. *(Bob Daemmrich/Stock Boston)*

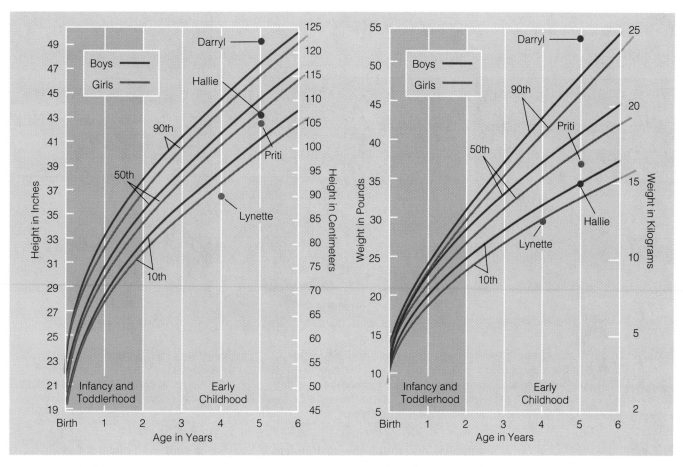

FIGURE 8.1

Gains in height and weight during early childhood among North American children. Compared to the first 2 years of life, growth is slower. Girls continue to be slightly shorter and lighter than boys. Wide individual differences in body size exist, as the percentiles on these charts reveal. Darryl, Priti, Lynette, and Hallie's heights and weights differ greatly.

The existence of cultural variations in body size reminds us that growth norms for one population (those in Figure 8.1 apply to North American children) are not good standards for many youngsters around the world. Consider the Efe of Zaire, an African people who normally grow to an adult height of less than 5 feet. Between 1 and 6 years, the growth of Efe children tapers off to a greater extent than that of American preschoolers. By age 5, the average Efe child is shorter than over 97 percent of 5-year-olds in the United States. For genetic reasons, the hormones controlling body size have less effect on Efe youngsters than they do on other children (Bailey, 1990). We would be mistaken to take the Efe youngster's small stature as a sign of serious growth or health problems, although this concern is warranted for an extremely slow-growing Caucasian child, such as Lynette, who falls below the tenth percentile for her age.

SKELETAL GROWTH

Skeletal changes under way in infancy continue throughout early childhood. Between ages 2 and 6, approximately 45 new *epiphyses* (growth centers in which cartilage is produced and hardens into bone) emerge in various parts of the skeleton. Others will appear in middle childhood. Figure 8.2, which shows X-rays of a girl's hand at three ages, illustrates changes in the epiphyses over time. Such X-rays permit doctors to estimate children's *skeletal age,* the best available measure of progress toward physical maturity (see Chapter 5, page 170). During early and middle childhood, information about skeletal age

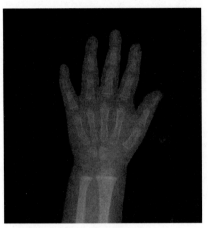
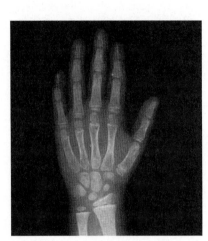
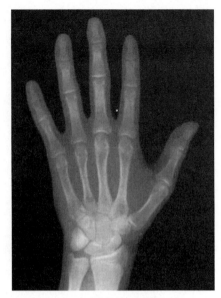

2½ years   6½ years   14½ years

FIGURE 8.2

X-rays of a girl's hand, showing skeletal maturity at three ages. Notice how, at age 2½, wide gaps exist between the wrist bones and at the ends of the finger and arm bones. By age 6½, these have filled in considerably. At age 14½ (when this girl reached her adult size), the wrist and long bones are completely fused. *(From J. M. Tanner, R. H. Whitehouse, N. Cameron, W. A. Marshall, M. J. R. Healy, & H. Goldstein, 1983,* Assessment of Skeletal Maturity and Prediction of Adult Height [TW2 Method], *2nd ed., Academic Press [London, Ltd.], p. 86. Reprinted by permission.)*

is helpful in diagnosing growth disorders. It also provides a rough estimate of children's chronological age in areas of the world where birth dates are not customarily recorded.

Parents and children are especially aware of another aspect of skeletal growth. By the end of the preschool years, Darryl's mother noticed that his face had become larger and its features more distinct as the jaw widened to make room for permanent teeth (Shelov, 1993). The age at which children lose their primary or "baby" teeth varies considerably and is heavily influenced by genetic factors. Girls, who are ahead of boys in physical development, lose them sooner. Cultural heritage also makes a difference. For example, American children typically get their first secondary (permanent) tooth at 6½ years, children in Ghana at just over 5 years, and children in Hong Kong around the sixth birthday. Environmental influences, especially prolonged malnutrition, can delay the age at which children cut their permanent teeth (Mott, James, & Sperhac, 1990).

Even though preschoolers will eventually lose their primary teeth, care of them is important, since diseased baby teeth can affect the health of permanent teeth. Consistent brushing, avoiding sugary foods, drinking fluoridated water, and getting topical fluoride treatments during regular dental visits prevent tooth cavities. Unfortunately, childhood tooth decay remains high, especially among low-SES children. An estimated 60 percent of American poverty-stricken 3- to 5-year-olds have at least some tooth decay. Their cavities advance at an especially rapid pace, affecting an average of 2.5 tooth surfaces each year. By the time American youngsters graduate from high school, five out of six have decayed teeth. Poor diet, lack of fluoridation in some communities, and inadequate health care are responsible (Edelstein & Douglass, 1995).

ASYNCHRONIES IN PHYSICAL GROWTH

From what you have learned so far in this chapter and in Chapter 5, can you come up with a single overall description of early physical growth? If you found yourself answering no to this question, you are correct. Figure 8.3 shows that physical growth is an *asynchronous process*. Different body systems have their own unique, carefully timed patterns of maturation.

Notice the **general growth curve,** which refers to change in overall body size as measured by height and weight. It takes its name from the fact that outer dimensions of the body as well as a variety of internal organs follow the same pattern—rapid growth during infancy, slower gains in early and middle childhood, and rapid growth again during adolescence.

Figure 8.3 also depicts some important exceptions to this trend. The genitals develop slowly from birth to age 4, change little throughout middle childhood, and then grow rapidly during adolescence. In contrast, the lymph tissue (small clusters of glands found throughout the body) grows at an astounding pace in infancy and childhood, but its growth declines in adolescence. The lymph system fights infection and assists in the absorption of nutrients, thereby supporting children's health and survival (Malina & Bouchard, 1991).

Figure 8.3 illustrates another growth trend with which you are familiar: During the first few years, the brain grows faster than any other part of the body. It develops especially rapidly during infancy and toddlerhood and continues to enlarge throughout early childhood, increasing from 70 percent of its adult weight at age 2 to 90 percent by age 6 (Tanner, 1990). Let's look at some highlights of brain development during early childhood.

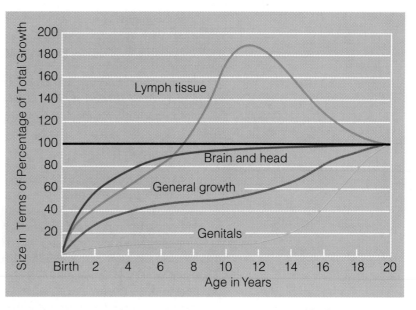

FIGURE **8.3**

Growth of three different organ systems and tissues contrasted with the body's general growth. Growth is plotted in terms of percentage of change from birth to 20 years. Notice how the lymph tissue rises to nearly twice its adult level by the end of childhood. Then it declines. *(Reprinted by permission of the publisher from J. M. Tanner, 1990, Foetus into Man, 2nd ed., Cambridge, MA: Harvard University Press, p. 16. Copyright © 1990 by J. M. Tanner. All rights reserved.)*

BRAIN DEVELOPMENT

Between ages 2 and 6, children gain in physical coordination, perception, attention, memory, language, logical thinking, and imagination. Virtually all theorists agree that brain development contributes importantly to these changes. During early childhood, neural fibers in the brain continue to form *synapses* and *myelinate*, as they did during infancy and toddlerhood.

SYNAPTIC GROWTH AND PRUNING

Neuroimaging studies reveal that brain metabolism reaches a peak around 4 years of age, when it is well above what it will be in adulthood. Researchers speculate that by this time, many cortical regions have actually overproduced synapses, resulting in a very high energy need (Johnson, 1998). The overabundance of synaptic connections is believed to play a role in the *plasticity* of the young brain. Many synapses serve identical functions, helping to ensure that the child will acquire certain abilities, even if some areas are damaged.

Next, a process called **synaptic pruning** occurs: Neurons seldom stimulated lose their connective fibers, and the number of synapses is reduced. Synaptic pruning is adaptive. It returns neurons not needed at the moment to an uncommitted state so they can support the development of future skills.

As the connective structures of active neurons become more elaborate, they require additional space. To make room for them, many surrounding neurons die (Huttenlocher,

general growth curve
A curve that represents overall changes in body size—rapid growth during infancy, slower gains in early and middle childhood, and rapid growth once more during adolescence.

synaptic pruning
Loss of connective fibers by seldom-stimulated neurons, thereby returning them to an uncommitted state so they can support the development of future skills.

1994). Consequently, a surprising feature of brain development is that rapid bursts of synaptic growth are accompanied by high rates of cell death. Fortunately, during the prenatal period, the neural tube produces an excess of neurons—far more than the brain will ever need.

As these changes occur, plasticity of the brain is reduced. By age 8 to 10, energy consumption of most cortical regions declines to near-adult levels, and the cerebral cortex has only a very limited capacity to recover functions following injury (Chugani, 1994).

LATERALIZATION

In Chapter 5, we saw that the cerebral cortex is made up of two *hemispheres* with distinct functions. In one study, EEG measures of the electrical activity of various cortical regions were taken at different ages. Results revealed that the two hemispheres develop at different rates. For most children, the left hemisphere is especially active between 3 and 6 years and then levels off. In contrast, activity in the right hemisphere increases steadily throughout early and middle childhood, with a slight spurt between ages 8 and 10 (Thatcher, Walker, & Giudice, 1987).

These findings fit nicely with what we know about several aspects of cognitive development. Language skills (typically housed in the left hemisphere) increase at an astonishing pace in early childhood. In contrast, spatial skills (such as finding one's way from place to place, drawing pictures, and recognizing geometric shapes) develop very gradually over childhood and adolescence. Differences in rate of development of the two hemispheres suggest that they are continuing to *lateralize* (specialize in functions). Let's take a closer look at brain lateralization during early childhood by focusing on the development of handedness.

HANDEDNESS

One morning on a visit to the preschool, I watched 3-year-old Moira as she drew pictures, worked puzzles, joined in snack time, and played outside. Unlike most of her classmates, Moira does most things—drawing, eating, and zipping her jacket—with her left hand. But she also uses her right hand for a few activities, such as throwing a ball. By age 2, hand preference is fairly stable, and it strengthens during early and middle childhood.

A strong hand preference reflects the greater capacity of one side of the brain—often referred to as the individual's **dominant cerebral hemisphere**—to carry out skilled motor action. Other abilities located on the dominant side may be superior as well. In support of this idea, for right-handed people, who make up 90 percent of the population, language is housed with hand control in the left hemisphere. For the remaining 10 percent who are left-handed, language is often shared between the hemispheres, rather than located in only one. This indicates that the brains of left-handers tend to be less strongly lateralized than those of right-handers (Hiscock & Kinsbourne, 1987). Consistent with this idea, many left-handed individuals (like Moira) are also *ambidextrous*. Although they prefer their left hand, they sometimes use their right hand skillfully as well (McManus et al., 1988).

Is handedness and, along with it, specialization of brain functions hereditary? Although researchers disagree on this issue, certain findings argue against a genetic explanation. Twins—whether identical or fraternal—are more likely than ordinary siblings to display opposite-handedness. Yet we would expect identical twins to be more alike if heredity played a powerful role. The hand preference of each twin is related to body position during the prenatal period (twins usually lie in opposite orientations) (Derom et al., 1996; Perelle & Ehrman, 1994). According to one theory, lateralization can be traced to prenatal events. The way most fetuses lie in the uterus—turned toward the left—may promote greater postural control by the right side of the body (Previc, 1991).

dominant cerebral hemisphere
The hemisphere of the brain responsible for skilled motor action. The left hemisphere is dominant in right-handed individuals. In left-handed individuals, the right hemisphere may be dominant, or motor and language skills may be shared between the hemispheres.

cerebellum
A brain structure that aids in balance and control of body movements.

reticular formation
A brain structure that maintains alertness and consciousness.

What about children whose hand use suggests an unusual organization of brain functions? Do these youngsters develop normally? Perhaps you have heard that left-handedness is more frequent among severely retarded and mentally ill people than it is in the general population. Although this is true, recall that when two variables are correlated, this does not mean that one causes the other. Atypical lateralization is probably not responsible for the problems of these individuals. Instead, they may have suffered early damage to the left hemisphere, which caused their disabilities and also led to a shift in handedness. In support of this idea, left-handedness is associated with prenatal and birth difficulties that can result in brain damage, including prolonged labor, prematurity, Rh incompatibility, and breech delivery (Coren & Halpern, 1991; Powls et al., 1996).

Twins typically lie in the uterus in opposite orientations during the prenatal period, which may explain why they are more often opposite-handed than are ordinary siblings. Although left-handedness is associated with developmental problems, the large majority of left-handed children are completely normal. *(Laura Dwight)*

Keep in mind, however, that only a small number of left-handers show developmental problems of any kind. The great majority, like Moira, are normal in every respect. In fact, the unusual lateralization of left-handed children may have certain advantages. Left- and mixed-handed youngsters are more likely than their right-handed agemates to develop outstanding verbal and mathematical talents (Flannery & Liederman, 1995). More even distribution of cognitive functions across both hemispheres may be responsible for this trend.

OTHER ADVANCES IN BRAIN DEVELOPMENT

Besides the cerebral cortex, several other areas of the brain make strides during early childhood. Figure 8.4 shows where each of these structures is located. As we look at these changes, you will see that they all involve establishing links between different parts of the brain, increasing the coordinated functioning of the central nervous system.

At the rear and base of the brain is the **cerebellum,** a structure that aids in balance and control of body movement. Fibers linking the cerebellum to the cerebral cortex begin to myelinate after birth, but they do not complete this process until about age 4 (Tanner, 1990). This change undoubtedly contributes to dramatic gains in motor control, so that by the end of the preschool years children can play hopscotch, pump a swing, and throw a ball with a well-organized set of movements.

The **reticular formation,** a structure in the brain stem that maintains alertness and consciousness, myelinates throughout early childhood, continuing its growth into adolescence. Neurons in the reticular formation send out fibers to other areas of the brain.

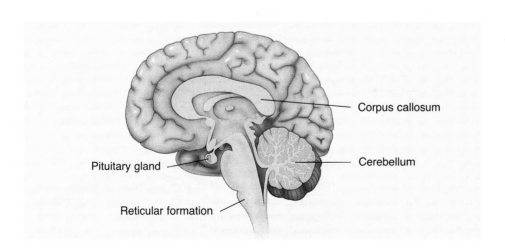

Corpus callosum

Cerebellum

Pituitary gland

Reticular formation

FIGURE 8.4

Cross section of the human brain, showing the location of the cerebellum, the reticular formation, and the corpus callosum. These structures undergo considerable development during early childhood. Also shown is the pituitary gland, which secretes hormones that control body growth (see page 300).

Many go to the frontal lobe of the cortex, contributing to improvements in sustained, controlled attention (McGuinness & Pribram, 1980).

A final brain structure that undergoes major changes during early childhood is the **corpus callosum.** It is a large bundle of fibers that connects the two hemispheres so they can communicate directly. Myelinization of the corpus callosum does not begin until the end of the first year of life. By age 4 to 5, its development is fairly advanced, supporting gains in the efficiency of thinking (Witelson & Kigar, 1988).

ASK YOURSELF . . .

- *After graduating from dental school, Norm worked in an inner-city public health clinic. He found that many poverty-stricken children had extensive tooth decay. In contrast, the young patients of his dental school friends in affluent suburbs had much less. What factors probably account for the difference?*

- *Explain why brain growth in early childhood involves not only an increase in neural connections but loss of synapses and cell death.*

- *Crystal noticed that her 4-year-old daughter Shana prefers her left hand for many activities. Crystal has heard that left-handedness is a sign of developmental problems, so she is worried about Shana. How would you respond to Crystal's concern?*

BRIEF REVIEW

Compared to infancy, gains in body size take place more slowly during early childhood, and the child's body becomes more streamlined. The skeleton adds new epiphyses, and by the end of the preschool years children start to lose their primary teeth. Physical growth is an asynchronous process; different parts of the body have their own carefully timed patterns of maturation. During early childhood, the brain continues to grow more rapidly than the rest of the body. Many cortical regions have overproduced synapses, and brain metabolism is at its peak. As synaptic pruning and neuronal death occur, brain plasticity is reduced. Hand preference strengthens, a sign of increasing brain lateralization. Although left-handedness is sometimes associated with developmental abnormalities, the large majority of left-handed children show no developmental problems of any kind. The cerebellum, the reticular formation, and the corpus callosum undergo considerable development during early childhood, contributing to connections between different parts of the brain.

FACTORS AFFECTING GROWTH AND HEALTH

As in the prenatal period and infancy, physical growth and health in early childhood result from the continuous and complex interplay of heredity and environment. In the following sections, you will see that in addition to genetic makeup, good nutrition, relative freedom from disease, and restful sleep affect the body's development. And as the Social Issues box on the following page illustrates, environmental pollutants can threaten healthy growth. The extent to which low-level lead—one of the most common—undermines children's physical and mental well-being is currently the subject of intensive research and debate. Finally, like infant mortality, childhood mortality is largely preventable. Unintentional injuries are the leading cause of death during the preschool years.

HEREDITY AND HORMONES

The impact of heredity on physical growth is evident throughout childhood. Children's physical size and rate of growth (as measured by skeletal age) are related to their parents'. Genes influence growth by controlling the body's production of hormones, especially two that are released by the **pituitary gland,** located near the base of the brain (return to Figure 8.4).

The first is **growth hormone (GH),** the only pituitary secretion produced continuously throughout life. It affects the development of all body tissues except the central nervous system and the genitals. Although GH does not seem to affect prenatal growth, it is necessary for physical development from birth on. Children who lack it reach an average mature height of only 4 feet, 4 inches, although they are normal in physical proportions and healthy in all other respects. When treated with injections of GH starting at an early

corpus callosum
The large bundle of fibers that connects the two hemispheres of the brain.

pituitary gland
A gland located near the base of the brain that releases hormones affecting physical growth.

growth hormone (GH)
A pituitary hormone that affects the development of all body tissues except the central nervous system and the genitals.

SOCIAL ISSUES

SHOULD CHILDREN BE TREATED FOR LOW-LEVEL LEAD EXPOSURE?

Four-year-old Desonia lives in an old, dilapidated tenement in a slum area of a large American city. Layers of paint applied over the years can be seen flaking off the inside walls and the back porch. The oldest paint chips are lead based. As an infant and young preschooler, Desonia picked them up and put them in her mouth. The slightly sweet taste of the leaded flakes encouraged her to nibble more. Soon Desonia became listless and irritable, and her appetite dropped off. When she complained of constant headaches, began to walk with an awkward gait, and experienced repeated convulsions (involuntary muscle contractions), her parents took her to a nearby public health clinic. Blood tests showed that she had severe lead poisoning, a condition that results in permanent brain damage and, if allowed to persist, early death (McDonald & Potter, 1996).

Severe lead poisoning like Desonia's has declined over the past 20 years in the United States, following passage of laws restricting use of lead-based paint. But lead already present in

homes is difficult to remove. And children can also absorb lead through residues in dust and soil, especially in inner-city industrial areas. Because of these dangers, until age 6 all children should be assessed for risk of excessive lead exposure.

The persistence of lead in the environment has sparked a broader concern: Is lead contamination a "silent epidemic"? Do children exposed to even small quantities show impaired intellectual functioning? To answer this question, seven longitudinal studies—three in the United States, two in Australia, one in Costa Rica, and one in Yugoslavia—were completed during the past decade. In each, lead exposure during the second year of life (when blood levels peak) was used to predict later mental development. Other factors, such as poverty, poor nutrition, and stressful home environments, that might account for the lead–IQ relationship were carefully controlled.

Only one of these investigations found a pervasive influence of low-level lead—not just on mental test scores, but on academic performance

and educational attainment as well (Needleman et al., 1990). These associations occurred at very low blood concentrations—amounts found in 20 percent of all American children and 60 percent of African-American children in urban areas (Berlin, 1997).

Alarmed by these findings, in 1991 the U.S. Public Health Service lowered the official "level of concern" for lead and required all children who met it to be followed up with efforts to reduce their exposure immediately. Although widespread agreement exists about controlling environmental lead, the new policy has sparked controversy. Supporters regard the more stringent standard as a necessary precaution. Critics point out that the majority of longitudinal studies show no effects of low-level lead exposure. They also worry that expensive, time-consuming monitoring of children for low blood lead will divert attention away from far more powerful causes of intellectual impairment, such as poverty and poor nutrition (Wolf, Jimenez, & Lozoff, 1994).

age, such children show catch-up growth and then grow at a normal rate. Consult the Biology and Environment box on page 302 for a current controversy surrounding GH treatment—whether it should be used for short children who are not GH deficient.

The second pituitary hormone affecting children's growth is **thyroid-stimulating hormone (TSH).** It stimulates the thyroid gland (located in the neck) to release *thyroxine,* which is necessary for normal development of the nerve cells of the brain and for GH to have its full impact on body size. Infants born with a deficiency of thyroxine must receive it at once or they will be mentally retarded. At later ages, children with too little thyroxine grow at a below-average rate. However, the central nervous system is no longer affected, since the most rapid period of brain development is complete. With prompt treatment, such children catch up in body growth and eventually reach normal size (Tanner, 1990).

EMOTIONAL WELL-BEING

In childhood as in infancy, emotional well-being can have a profound effect on growth and health. Preschoolers with very stressful home lives (due to divorce, financial difficul-

thyroid-stimulating hormone (TSH)
A pituitary hormone that stimulates the thyroid gland to release thyroxine, which is necessary for normal brain development and body growth.

BIOLOGY & ENVIRONMENT

TREATING SHORT CHILDREN WITH GROWTH HORMONE

Through childhood and adolescence, Stephen was among the shortest 3 percent of his age group. He recalls being teased and tormented by insensitive peers and called shrimp, pea, midget, squirt, and a dozen other insults. He looks back on these experiences calmly, perhaps because a late growth spurt led him to reach a final height of 5 feet 6 inches (Hall, 1996). But now, as he awaits the birth of his first child, he wonders, "Would treatment with GH have relieved the pain I experienced? Would it have added to or merely accelerated my growth? If my child is short, should I have him or her treated with a powerful drug to avoid psychological pain induced by society's prejudices?"

Genetically engineered GH has been available since 1985, permitting successful treatment of short stature for children with GH deficiency. Since then, research has been conducted on unusually short, normal-GH children to see if they, too, might benefit from hormone injections. Thousands of concerned parents have sought GH therapy for their children.

■ **ARE SHORT, NORMAL-GH CHILDREN MALADJUSTED?** A major justification for treating short, non-GH-deficient children is to improve their psychological functioning. Frequently reported problems include social stigma due to deviant appearance, poor social skills, social isolation, low self-esteem, and poor academic achievement. But most studies include only GH-deficient children (Meyer-Bahlburg, 1990). Do these negative outcomes apply to short, normal-GH children as well?

Recent findings are mixed. In a British investigation comparing very short with average-stature children on self-esteem, social behavior, and academic achievement, differences between the two groups were minimal on some measures and nonexistent on others (Vance, 1994). An American study found very short 4- to 18-year-old boys, but not girls, to have an above-average incidence of parent-reported emotional and behavior problems. But when boys themselves—not their parents—were asked, they reported good self-esteem as well as athletic competence. They seemed to find their niche in certain sports in which height is not essential (Sandberg, Brook, & Campos, 1994).

In sum, research suggests that a biological height deficit by itself does not lead to poor psychological adjustment. Family attitudes and social experiences that sensitize children to their short stature appear to be very powerful.

■ **DOES GH TREATMENT LEAD TO HEIGHT GAINS?** Many studies show that GH-deficient children benefit from GH therapy; their final height is considerably greater than it would have been without treatment. But the verdict is not yet in for short, normal-GH children. Several follow-ups of American and Canadian boys who began treatment in late childhood or early adolescence reveal faster initial growth—an outcome that may be emotionally beneficial for some youngsters. But most did not exceed their previously predicted adult height (Kaplowitz, 1995; Loche et al., 1994). As yet, no carefully controlled studies have followed treated children to their final stature.

Both biological and social forces influence a doctor's decision to prescribe GH for a short but otherwise normal child. On the biological side, doctors are more likely to treat an extremely short child who is growing very slowly yet has a normal skeletal age—a combination of factors that increases the chances of becoming a very short adult. On the social side, family wishes clearly influence medical recommendations. When the child's parents strongly desire treatment, the child is more likely to get it (Cuttler et al., 1996).

Yet until more evidence is in, great caution should be exercised in prescribing GH for short, GH-normal children (Bercu, 1996; Diller, 1996). The estimated cost is staggering—$15,000 to $30,000 annually for a regimen that must continue until the child reaches near-adult height. Potential side effects include allergy, diabetic-like symptoms, fluid retention, and—for genetically susceptible individuals—curvature of the spine and leukemia.

Because "heightism" exists in society, treatment of short children may be warranted in some instances. But doctors and parents should recognize the unjust social values that lead them to consider intervening in a condition that results from biologically normal human diversity.

ties, or a change in their parents' employment status) suffer more respiratory and intestinal illnesses as well as unintentional injuries (Beautrais, Fergusson, & Shannon, 1982).

Extreme emotional deprivation can interfere with the production of GH and lead to **deprivation dwarfism,** a growth disorder observed between 2 and 15 years of age. Lynette, the very small 4-year-old mentioned earlier in this chapter, was diagnosed this condition. She had been placed in foster care after child welfare authorities discovered that she spent most of the day at home alone, unsupervised. She may also have been physically abused. To help her recover, Lynette was enrolled in our laboratory preschool. She showed the typical characteristics of deprivation dwarfism—very short stature (she was no taller than an average 2½-year-old), weight in proportion to her height, immature skeletal age, and decreased GH secretion.

When such children are removed from their emotionally inadequate environments, their GH levels quickly return to normal, and they grow rapidly. But if treatment is delayed, the dwarfism can be permanent (Oates, Peacock, & Forrest, 1985).

SLEEP HABITS AND PROBLEMS

Sleep contributes to body growth, since GH is released during the child's sleeping hours. A well-rested child is better able to play, learn, and contribute positively to family functioning. By disrupting parental sleep, a child who sleeps poorly can cause significant family stress—a major reason that sleep difficulties are among the most common concerns parents raise with their preschooler's doctor (Whyte & Shaefer, 1995).

On the average, total sleep declines from 12 to 13 hours at ages 2 and 3 to 10 to 11 hours at ages 4 to 6. Younger preschoolers typically take a 1- to 2-hour nap in the early afternoon, although their daytime sleep needs vary widely. Some continue to take two naps, as they did in toddlerhood; others give up napping entirely. Unless a child routinely becomes irritable and overtired from lack of sleep, there is no need to force a nap on a preschooler (Shelov, 1993). Around age 4, most children no longer require any daytime sleep, although a quiet play period or rest after lunch helps them rejuvenate for the rest of the day.

Western preschoolers often become rigid about bedtime routines, such as using the toilet, listening to a story, getting a drink of water, taking a security object to bed, and hugging and kissing before turning off the light. These rituals, which typically take as long as 30 minutes, help young children adjust to feelings of uneasiness at being left by themselves in a darkened room. Difficulty falling asleep—calling to the parent or asking for another drink of water—is generally due to lingering separation anxiety (Lansky, 1991). A night light and a favorite blanket or stuffed animal tucked in with the child can ease these feelings.

Night waking continues to occur in early childhood, although less often than before. Almost all children begin to have a few nightmares between ages 3 and 6. When preschoolers awaken from a frightening dream, they need parental reassurance that "it's only a dream" and comfort until they calm down and fall back asleep. Sometimes scary television shows prompt nightmares, and parents need to monitor their child's TV watching more carefully—an issue we take up in Chapter 10.

About 15 percent of preschoolers experience frequent difficulty falling and staying asleep. Since persistent sleep problems may be a sign of illness, parents should consult the child's doctor. Family stress can also prompt childhood sleep disturbances. Preschoolers who sleep poorly are more likely to have mothers who are depressed or who recently changed schedules and are away at times the child had become used to the parent's presence (Kerr & Jowett, 1994). Intense bedtime struggles may result from inconsistent discipline, which often accompanies family turmoil. In these cases, addressing family problems is the key to improving children's sleep.

Western preschoolers often demand a bedtime routine, such as listening to a story, taking a security object to bed, and hugging and kissing before turning off the light. These rituals help them adjust to sleeping alone in a darkened room. (Tony Freeman/PhotoEdit)

deprivation dwarfism
A growth disorder observed between 2 and 15 years of age. Characterized by very short stature, weight that is usually appropriate for height, immature skeletal age, and decreased GH secretion. Caused by emotional deprivation.

NUTRITION

Early childhood often brings a dramatic change in the quantity and variety of foods that children will eat. Suddenly, appetite becomes unpredictable. Preschoolers may eat well at one meal and barely touch their food at the next. Many become picky eaters. One father I know wistfully recalled his son's eager sampling of the cuisine at a Chinese restaurant during toddlerhood. "He ate rice, chicken chow mein, egg rolls, and more. Now, at age 3, the only thing he'll try is the ice cream!"

This decline in the appetite is normal. It occurs because growth has slowed. And preschoolers' wariness of new foods may be adaptive. By sticking to familiar foods, young children are less likely to swallow dangerous substances when adults are not around to protect them (Birch & Fisher, 1995). Parents need not worry about variations in amount eaten from meal to meal. Over the course of a day, preschoolers' food intake is fairly constant. They compensate for a meal in which they ate little with a later one in which they eat more (Birch et al., 1991).

Even though they eat less, preschoolers need a high-quality diet. They require the same foods that make up a healthy adult diet—only smaller amounts. Milk and milk products, meat or meat alternatives (such as eggs, dried peas or beans, and peanut butter), vegetables and fruits, and breads and cereals should be included. Fats, oils, and salt are needed but should be kept to a minimum because of their early link to high blood pressure and heart disease in adulthood (Fisher, Van Horn, & McGill, 1997). Foods high in sugar should also be avoided. In addition to causing tooth decay, sugary cereals, cookies, cakes, soft drinks, and candy are high-energy items with little nutritional value. They lessen young children's appetite for healthy foods and increase their risk of overweight and obesity—a topic we will take up in Chapter 11.

The wide variety of foods eaten in cultures around the world indicates that the social environment has a powerful impact on young children's food preferences. For example, Mexican preschoolers enthusiastically eat chili peppers, whereas American children quickly reject them. What accounts for this difference? Children tend to imitate the food choices of people they admire—peers as well as adults. In Mexico, children often see family members delighting in the taste of peppery foods (Birch, Zimmerman, & Hind, 1980).

Repeated exposure to a new food (without any direct pressure to eat it) also increases children's acceptance. In one study, preschoolers were given one of three versions of a food they had never eaten before (sweet, salty, or plain tofu). After 8 to 15 exposures, they readily ate the food. But they preferred the version they had already tasted. For example, children in the "sweet" condition liked sweet tofu best, and those in the "plain" condition liked plain tofu best (Sullivan & Birch, 1990). These findings reveal that children's tastes are trained by foods they encounter repeatedly. Adding sugar or salt in hopes of increasing a young child's willingness to eat healthy foods simply teaches the child to like a sugary or salty taste.

The emotional climate at mealtimes has a powerful impact on children's eating habits. Many parents worry about how well their preschoolers eat, so meals become unpleasant and stressful. Sometimes parents bribe their children, saying, "Finish your vegetables, and you can have an extra cookie." Unfortunately, this practice causes children to like the healthy food less and the treat more (Birch, Johnson, & Fisher, 1995). The Caregiving Concerns table on the following page offers some suggestions for promoting healthy, varied eating in young children.

Finally, as we indicated in earlier chapters, many children in the United States and in developing countries are deprived of diets that support healthy growth. Five-year-old Hallie was bused to our laboratory preschool from a poor neighborhood. His mother's welfare check barely covered her rent, let alone food. Hallie's diet was deficient in protein as well as vitamins and minerals essential for healthy body growth and functioning—iron (to prevent anemia), calcium (to support development of bones and teeth), vitamin C (to facilitate iron absorption and wound healing), and vitamin A (to help maintain eyes, skin, and a variety of internal organs). These are the

Unpredictable appetites and picky eating are common during early childhood. At dinnertime, this 3-year-old girl seems more interested in playing than eating. Fortunately, her parents are sensitive to her nutritional needs. They offer a well-balanced meal and put only a small portion on her plate. *(Joel Gordon)*

CAREGIVING CONCERNS

Encouraging Good Nutrition in Early Childhood

SUGGESTION	DESCRIPTION
Offer a varied, healthy diet.	Provide a well-balanced variety of nutritious foods that are colorful and attractively served. Avoid serving sweets and "junk" foods as a regular part of meals and snacks.
Offer predictable meals as well as several snacks each day.	Preschoolers' stomachs are small, and they may not be able to eat enough in three meals to satisfy energy requirements. They benefit from extra opportunities to eat.
Offer small portions, and permit the child to ask for seconds.	When too much food is put on the plate, preschoolers may be overwhelmed and not even try to eat.
Offer new foods early in meal and over several meals, and respond with patience if the child rejects the food.	Introduce new foods before the child's appetite is satisfied. Let children see you eating and enjoying the new food. If the child rejects it, accept the refusal and serve it again at another meal. As foods become more familiar, they are more readily accepted.
Keep mealtimes pleasant, and include the child in mealtime conversations.	A pleasant, relaxed eating environment helps children develop positive attitudes about food. Avoid confrontations over disliked foods and table manners.
Avoid using food as a reward.	Saying, "No dessert until you clean your plate," tells children that they must eat regardless of how hungry they are and that dessert is the best part of the meal.

Sources: Birch, Johnson, & Fisher, 1995; Kendrick, Kaufmann, & Messenger, 1991.

most common dietary deficiencies of the preschool years. Not surprisingly, Hallie was thin, pale, and tired. By age 7, low-SES children in the United States are, on the average, about 1 inch shorter than their economically advantaged counterparts (Yip, Scanlon, & Trowbridge, 1993).

INFECTIOUS DISEASE

Two weeks into the school year, I looked outside my window and noticed that Hallie was absent from the play yard. Several weeks passed; still I did not see him. When I asked Leslie, his preschool teacher, what had happened, she explained, "Hallie's been hospitalized with the measles. He's had a difficult time recovering—lost weight when there wasn't much to lose in the first place." In well-nourished children, ordinary childhood illnesses have no effect on physical growth. But when children are undernourished, disease interacts with malnutrition in a vicious spiral, and the consequences for physical growth can be severe.

■ **INFECTIOUS DISEASE AND MALNUTRITION.** Hallie's reaction to the measles is commonplace among children in developing nations, where a large proportion of the population lives in poverty. In these countries, many children do not receive a program of immunizations. Illnesses such as measles and chicken pox, which typically do not appear until after age 3 in industrialized nations, occur much earlier. This is because poor diet depresses the body's immune system, making children far more susceptible to disease.

Disease, in turn, is a major cause of malnutrition and, through it, affects physical growth. Illness reduces appetite, and it limits the body's ability to absorb foods. These outcomes are especially severe among children with intestinal infections. In developing countries, diarrhea is widespread and increases in early childhood due to unsafe water and contaminated foods, leading to several million childhood deaths each year (Grant, 1995). Research in poverty-stricken Guatemalan villages showed that 7-year-olds who had been relatively free of diarrhea since birth were significantly heavier than their frequently ill peers (Martorell, 1980).

Most growth retardation and deaths due to diarrhea can be prevented with nearly cost-free **oral rehydration therapy (ORT)**, in which sick children are given a glucose, salt, and water solution that quickly replaces fluids the body loses. Since 1990, public health workers have taught nearly half of families in the developing world how to administer ORT. As a result, the lives of more than 1 million children are being saved annually (Bellamy, 1997).

■ **IMMUNIZATION.** In industrialized nations, childhood diseases have declined dramatically during the past half-century, largely due to widespread immunization of infants and young children. Hallie got the measles because, unlike his classmates from more advantaged homes, he did not receive a full program of immunizations during his first 2 years of life. Although the majority of preschoolers in the United States are immunized, some do not receive full protection until 5 or 6 years of age, when it is required for school entry (Children's Defense Fund, 1997).

To remedy this problem, in 1994 all medically uninsured American children were guaranteed free immunizations. As a result, immunization rates in the United States improved, but they continue to lag behind those of other Western nations. For example, 29 percent of American preschoolers are not fully immunized, a rate that rises to 40 percent for poverty-stricken children (U.S. Department of Health and Human Services, 1997). In contrast, fewer than 10 percent of preschoolers lack immunizations in Denmark and Norway, less than 7 percent in the Netherlands and Sweden (Bellamy, 1997; de Winter, Balleduz, & de Mare, 1997).

How is it that these countries have managed to achieve high rates of immunization, whereas the United States' record is so poor? In earlier chapters, we noted that many children in the United States do not have access to the medical care they need. The Cultural Influences box on the following page examines child health care in the United States and other Western nations.

Inability to pay for vaccines, however, is only one cause of lower immunization rates in the United States. Misconceptions about safe medical practices also contribute. American parents often report that they delay bringing their child in for a vaccination because they fear that their child might have an adverse reaction (Abbotts & Osborn, 1993; Shalala, 1993). Public education programs directed at increasing parental knowledge about the importance and safety of timely immunizations are badly needed.

■ **DAY CARE AND INFECTIOUS DISEASE.** A final point regarding communicable disease in early childhood deserves mention. Research in Europe and the United States indicates that childhood illness rises with day care attendance. On the average, a day care infant becomes sick 9 to 10 times a year, a day care preschool child 6 to 7 times. Diseases that spread most rapidly are diarrhea and respiratory infections—the most frequent illnesses suffered by young children (Thacker et al., 1992).

By age 3, over 70 percent of children in day care have had respiratory infections that resulted in at least one bout of **otitis media,** or middle ear infection; 33 percent have had repeated bouts. Some episodes are painful, but as many as half are accompanied by few or no symptoms. Parents learn of them only on routine visits to the doctor. Although antibiotics eliminate the bacteria responsible for otitis media, they do not reduce fluid buildup in the middle ear, which causes mild to moderate hearing loss that can last for weeks or months (Feagans & Proctor, 1994).

The incidence of otitis media is greatest between 6 months and 3 years, when children are first acquiring language. Low-SES children have especially high rates, perhaps because they are more likely to experience the health risks of crowded living conditions and poor-quality day care (Froom & Culpepper, 1991). Research indicates that frequent otitis media predicts delayed language progress and social isolation in early childhood and poorer academic performance after school entry. Difficulties in hearing speech sounds, particularly in noisy settings, may be responsible (Feagans & Proctor, 1994; Teele et al., 1990; Vernon-Feagans, Manlove, & Volling, 1996).

oral rehydration therapy (ORT)
A treatment for diarrhea in which sick children are given a glucose, salt, and water solution that quickly replaces fluids the body loses.

otitis media
Middle ear infection.

CULTURAL INFLUENCES

CHILD HEALTH CARE IN THE UNITED STATES AND OTHER WESTERN NATIONS

*H*istorically, Americans have been strongly committed to the idea that parents should assume total responsibility for the care and rearing of children. This belief, in addition to powerful economic interests in the medical community, has prevented government-sponsored health services from being offered to all children.

American health insurance is an optional, employment-related fringe benefit. Many businesses that rely on low-wage and part-time help do not insure their employees. If they do, they often do not cover other family members, including children. Although a variety of public health programs are available in the United States, they reach only the most needy individuals. This leaves nearly 10 million children from poor, low-income, and moderate-income families uninsured and, therefore, without affordable medical care (Children's Defense Fund, 1998).

Because of the high cost of medical treatment, American uninsured, low-SES children see a doctor only half as often as insured, higher-SES children with similar illnesses (Newacheck, Hughes, & Stoddard, 1996). Consequently, an estimated 60 percent of

children under age 5 who come from poverty-stricken families are in less-than-excellent health (Children's Defense Fund, 1992). Furthermore, most employed parents have no adequate solution to the problem of providing child care when their child becomes ill. Currently, only one-third to one-half of American employees receive paid sick leave of any kind (Giebink, 1993).

The inadequacies of American child health care stand in sharp contrast to services provided in other industrialized nations, where medical insurance is government sponsored and available to all citizens, regardless of income. Let's look at two examples.

In the Netherlands, every child receives free medical examinations from birth through adolescence. During the early years, health care also includes parental counseling in nutrition, disease prevention, and child development. The Netherlands achieves its extraordinarily high childhood immunization rate by giving parents of every newborn baby a written schedule that shows exactly when and where the child should be immunized. If the child is not brought in at the specified time, a public health nurse calls the family. In instances of

repeated missed appointments, the nurse goes to the home to ensure that the child receives the recommended immunizations (Verbrugge, 1990a, 1990b).

In Norway, federal law requires that well baby and child clinics be established in all communities and that examinations by doctors take place three times during the first year and at ages 2 and 4. Specialized nurses see children on additional occasions, monitoring their growth and development, providing immunizations, and counseling parents on physical and mental health. Although citizens pay a small fee for routine medical visits, hospital services are free of charge. Parents with a seriously ill child are given leave from work with full salary, a benefit financed by the government (Lie, 1990; Scarr et al., 1993).

In Australia, Canada, Europe, and other industrialized nations, child health care is regarded as a fundamental human right, no different from the right to education. Currently, many organizations, government officials, and concerned citizens committed to improving child health are working to find ways to guarantee every American child necessary medical care.

Widespread, government-sponsored immunization of infants and young children is a cost-effective means of supporting healthy growth by dramatically reducing the incidence of childhood diseases. Although this boy finds a routine inoculation painful, it will offer him life-long protection. *(Russell D. Curtis/Photo Researchers)*

CAREGIVING CONCERNS

Controlling the Spread of Infectious Disease in Day Care

STRATEGY	DESCRIPTION
Follow good personal hygiene.	Illness rates decline when adults and children routinely wash their hands—before touching food, after toileting, and after touching clothing or objects contaminated with body secretions.
Clean the day care environment regularly.	Regular cleaning reduces the spread of illness. Because infants and young children frequently put toys in their mouths, these objects should be rinsed frequently with a disinfectant solution.
Arrange the day care environment to minimize infection.	Food preparation and toileting areas should be physically separated. Spacious, well-ventilated rooms and small group sizes limit the spread of illness.
Make sure all children have a full program of infant and early childhood immunizations.	A schedule of diphtheria-tetanus-pertussis (DPT); polio; measles-mumps-rubella (MMR); hepatitis B; and haemophilus B (meningitis) immunizations should be given over the first 2 years. Follow-up immunizations—DPT and polio—should be given between 4 and 6 years.
Isolate children with communicable diseases that spread rapidly.	An isolation area should be provided for children who come down with a rapidly spreading infection or illness at day care. As long as good personal hygiene is followed, children with mild respiratory infections, such as the common cold, can continue to attend day care with little impact on the health of other youngsters.

Sources: American Academy of Pediatrics, 1998; Bredekamp & Copple, 1997; Shelov, 1993.

These serious consequences make frequent screening for otitis media vital. Plastic tubes that drain the ears are a common treatment, although their effectiveness remains controversial. Another way to reduce developmental problems associated with the disease is through high-quality day care. When caregivers are verbally stimulating and keep noise to a minimum, children have more opportunities to hear spoken language. Under these conditions, bouts of otitis media have few, if any, negative effects (Feagans, Kipp, & Blood, 1994; Roberts, Burchinal, & Campbell, 1994). The Caregiving Concerns table above summarizes strategies for controlling the spread of infectious disease in day care.

CHILDHOOD INJURIES

Three-year-old Tory caught my eye as I visited the preschool classroom one day. More than any other child, he had trouble sitting still and paying attention at story time. Outside, I saw him dart from one place to another, spending little time at a single activity. On a field trip to our campus museum, Tory ignored Leslie's directions and ran across the street without holding his partner's hand. Later in the year, I read in our local newspaper that Tory had narrowly escaped serious injury when he put his mother's car in gear while she was outside scraping its windows. The vehicle rolled through a guardrail and over the side of a 10-foot concrete overpass. There it hung until rescue workers arrived. Tory's mother was charged with failing to use a restraint seat for children under age 5.

Today, the greatest threat to children's physical health comes from a large collection of unintentional injuries—auto collisions, pedestrian accidents, drownings, firearm wounds, burns, falls, poisoning, swallowing of foreign objects, and others. Taken together, these events account for 40 to 50 percent of deaths in early and middle childhood and as many as 75 percent during adolescence. Approximately 22,000 youngsters die from these incidents each year. And for each death, thousands of other injured children survive but suffer pain, brain damage, and permanent physical disabilities. Overall, about one-fourth of American children experience at least one injury requiring medical treatment annually (Scheidt et al., 1995).

As Figure 8.5 shows, auto and traffic accidents, drownings, and burns are the most common injuries during the early childhood years. Motor vehicle collisions are by far the most frequent source of injury at all ages. They are the leading cause of death among children older than 1 year of age.

■ **FACTORS RELATED TO CHILD-HOOD INJURIES.** We are used to thinking of childhood injuries as "accidental," a word that encourages us to believe that chance is responsible for them and that they cannot be prevented (Kronenfeld & Glik, 1995). But a close look at childhood injuries reveals that a variety of individual, family, community, and societal factors are related to them. As with other aspects of development, they take place within a complex *ecological system.* This suggests that meaningful causes underlie childhood injuries, and we can, indeed, do something about them.

As Tory's case suggests, individual differences exist in the safety level of children's everyday behaviors. Because of their higher activity level and greater willingness to take risks during play, boys are more likely to be injured than girls. Temperamental characteristics—irritability, inattentiveness, and negative mood—are also related to childhood injuries. As we saw in Chapter 7, children with these traits present special child-rearing challenges. They are likely to protest when placed in auto seat restraints, refuse to take a companion's hand when crossing the street, and disobey after repeated instruction and discipline (Matheny, 1991). Adults must be especially vigilant and firm with them about safety.

At the same time, families whose preschoolers get injured tend to have characteristics that increase the likelihood of exposure to danger. Poverty and low parental education are strongly associated with injury deaths. Parents who must cope with many daily stresses often have little time and energy to monitor the safety of their youngsters. And the homes and neighborhoods of such families pose further risks. Noise, crowding, and confusion characterize these environments, and they tend to be located in run-down, inner-city neighborhoods with few safe places to play (Kronenfeld & Glik, 1995).

Broad societal conditions also affect childhood injury. Among Western industrialized nations, the United States ranks among the highest in childhood injury mortality. Furthermore, although injury deaths have declined steadily in nearly all developed countries during the past 30 years, they have dropped only minimally in the United States (U.S. Department of Health and Human Services, 1997).

What factors account for this worrisome picture? Widespread poverty, a shortage of high-quality day care (to supervise children in their parents' absence), and high rate of births to teenagers (who are neither psychologically nor financially ready to raise a child) are believed to play important roles. But children from advantaged families are also at somewhat greater risk for injury in the United States than they are in European nations (Williams & Kotch, 1990). This indicates that besides reducing poverty and teenage pregnancy and upgrading the status of day care, additional steps must be taken to ensure the safety of American children.

■ **PREVENTING CHILDHOOD INJURIES.** Childhood injuries have many causes, so a variety of approaches are needed to control them. Laws prevent a great many injuries by requiring car safety seats, child-resistant caps on medicine bottles, flame-proof clothing, and fenced-in backyard swimming pools (the site of 90 percent of early childhood drownings).

Communities can help by modifying their physical environments. For example, inexpensive and widely available public transportation can reduce the time that children spend in cars. Playgrounds, an especially common site of injury for children under age 5, can be covered with protective surfaces, such as rubber matting, sand, and wood chips

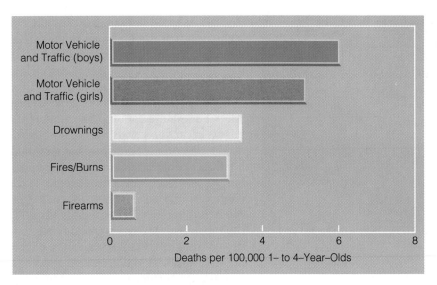

FIGURE 8.5

Rate of injury mortality in the United States for children between 1 and 4 years of age by type of injury. Between 1 and 4 years of age, motor vehicle and traffic fatalities are greater for boys than girls. For other injuries depicted here, death rates for boys and girls are similar until age 5, when boys begin to outdistance girls in all categories. (From U.S. Department of Health and Human Services, 1997)

This mother insists that her daughter ride properly restrained in a child car seat in the back seat of the car. In doing so, she reduces her preschooler's chances of injury and teaches good safety practices. *(Richard Hutchings/PhotoEdit)*

(Lillis & Jaffe, 1997). Free, easily installed window guards can be given to families living in high-rise apartment buildings to prevent falls. And public education—in the form of widespread media campaigns and information distributed in doctors' offices, schools, and day care centers—can inform parents and children about safety issues.

Nevertheless, many dangers cannot be eliminated from the environment. And even though they know better, many parents and children behave in ways that compromise safety. For example, about 15 percent of parents (like Tory's mother) fail to place their infants in car safety seats, and many others do not use the seats correctly (Kronenfeld & Glik, 1995). Adults often leave caps off medicine bottles, neglect to replace batteries in home smoke detectors, and leave handguns within reach of children. How can we change human behavior? A variety of programs based on *applied behavior analysis* (modeling and reinforcement) have improved the safety practices of adults and children alike. In one, counselors helped parents identify dangers in the home—fire hazards, objects that young children might swallow, poisonous substances, firearms, and others. Then they demonstrated specific ways to eliminate the dangers (Tertinger, Greene, & Lutzker, 1984). Several interventions reward parents and children with prizes if the child arrives at day care or school each morning properly restrained in a car seat (Roberts, Alexander, & Knapp, 1990; Roberts, Fanurik, & Wilson, 1988). Still other programs teach parents how to supervise their children properly and train preschoolers in safety skills (Peterson & Mori, 1985; Roberts & Turner, 1986).

Efforts like these have been remarkably successful, yet their focus is fairly narrow—on decreasing specific environmental risks and risky behaviors (Peterson & Brown, 1994). Attention must also be paid to family conditions that can prevent child injury, such as relieving crowding and chaos in the home, providing social supports to ease parental stress, and teaching parents to use effective discipline—a topic we take up in Chapter 10. Refer to the Caregiving Concerns table below for ways to reduce unintentional injuries in early childhood.

CAREGIVING CONCERNS

Reducing Unintentional Injuries in Early Childhood

SUGGESTION	DESCRIPTION
Provide age-appropriate supervision and safety instruction.	Despite increasing self-control, preschoolers need nearly constant supervision. Establish and enforce safety rules, explain the reasons behind them, and praise children for following them, thereby encouraging the child to remember, understand, and obey.
Know the child's temperament.	Children who are unusually active, distractible, and curious have more than their share of injuries and need extra monitoring.
Eliminate the most serious dangers from the home.	Examine all spaces for safety. For example, in the kitchen, store dangerous products in high cabinets out of sight, and keep sharp implements in a latched drawer. Always accompany young preschoolers to the bathroom, and keep all medicines in containers with safety caps.
During automobile travel, always restrain the child properly in the back seat of the car.	Use an age-appropriate, properly installed car seat, and strap the child in correctly every time. Children should always ride in the back seat; passenger-side air bags in the front seat deploy so forcefully that they can cause injury or death to a child.
Select safe playground equipment and sites.	Make sure sand, wood chips, or rubberized matting has been placed under swings, seesaws, and jungle gyms. Check yards for dangerous plants. Always supervise outdoor play.
Be extra cautious around water.	Constantly observe children during water play; even shallow, inflatable pools can be sites of drownings. While swimming, young children's heads should not be immersed in water; they may swallow so much that they develop water intoxication, which can lead to convulsions and death.
Practice safety around animals.	Wait to get a pet until the child is mature enough to handle and care for it—usually around age 5 or 6. Never leave a young child alone with an animal; bites often occur during playful roughhousing. Model and teach humane pet treatment.

Source: Shelov, 1993.

BRIEF REVIEW

Heredity influences physical growth by regulating the production of hormones. Two pituitary hormones, growth hormone (GH) and thyroid-stimulating hormone (TSH), play important roles in children's growth. Many environmental factors affect growth and health in early childhood. Extreme emotional deprivation can interfere with the production of GH, resulting in deprivation dwarfism. Total sleep decreases by an hour or two over the preschool years; around age 4, most children no longer need a daytime nap. Persistent sleep problems may result from illness or family stress.

Although preschoolers' appetites decline and they resist new foods, good nutrition remains important in early childhood. The emotional climate of mealtimes influences the quality and range of foods that young children will eat. Disease can interact with malnutrition to seriously undermine children's growth, an effect that is especially common in developing countries. Unintentional injuries are the leading cause of childhood mortality. Injury rates are related to child, family, and community characteristics as well as to broad societal conditions. Consequently, a variety of approaches are needed to prevent them.

ASK YOURSELF . . .

■ One day, Leslie prepared a new snack to serve at preschool: celery stuffed with ricotta cheese and pineapple. The first time she served it, few of the children touched it. What techniques can Leslie use to encourage her pupils to accept the snack? What methods should she avoid?

■ Using ecological systems theory, suggest ways to reduce childhood injuries by intervening in the microsystem, mesosystem, and macrosystem. Why are interventions at each of these levels necessary?

MOTOR DEVELOPMENT

Visit a playground at a neighborhood park, preschool, or day-care center, and observe several 2- to 6-year-olds. Jot down descriptions of their activities and movements, paying special attention to differences between the younger and older children. You will see that an explosion of new motor skills occurs in early childhood. Each builds on the simpler movement patterns of toddlerhood.

The same principle that governs motor development during the first 2 years of life continues to operate during the preschool years. Children integrate previously acquired skills into more complex *dynamic systems of action*. (Return to Chapter 5, page 185, to review this concept.) Then they revise each new skill as their bodies become larger and stronger, their central nervous systems become better developed, and their environments present new challenges. This means that although the motor skills of early childhood tend to appear in a regular sequence, they are not simply due to a genetically determined, maturational pattern (Clark, Phillips, & Petersen, 1989). Instead, a variety of factors—both genetic and environmental—combine to produce these accomplishments. Let's look closely at young children's gross and fine motor skills to illustrate this idea.

GROSS MOTOR DEVELOPMENT

As children's bodies become more streamlined and less top-heavy, their center of gravity shifts downward, toward the trunk. As a result, balance improves greatly, paving the way for new motor skills involving large muscles of the body (Ulrich & Ulrich, 1985). By age 2, preschoolers' gaits become smooth and rhythmic—secure enough that soon they leave the ground, at first by running and later by jumping, hopping, galloping, and skipping.

As children become steadier on their feet, their arms and torsos are freed to experiment with new skills—throwing and catching balls, steering tricycles, and swinging on horizontal bars and rings. Then upper and lower body skills combine into more refined actions. Five- and 6-year-olds simultaneously steer and peddle a tricycle and flexibly move their whole body when hopping and jumping. By the end of the preschool years, all skills are performed with greater speed and endurance. Table 8.1 provides an overview of gross motor development in early childhood.

TABLE 8.1

Changes in Gross Motor Skills During Early Childhood

AGE	WALKING AND RUNNING	JUMPING AND HOPPING	THROWING AND CATCHING	PEDALING AND STEERING
2–3 years	Walks more rhythmically; feet are not as widely spaced; opposite arm–leg swing appears. Hurried walk changes to true run.	Jumps down from step. Jumps several inches off floor with both feet, no arm action. Hops 1 to 3 times on same foot with stiff upper body and nonhopping leg held still.	Throws ball with forearm extension only; feet remain stationary. Awaits thrown ball with rigid arms outstretched.	Pushes riding toy with feet; little steering.
3–4 years	Walks up stairs, alternating feet. Walks down stairs, leading with one foot. Walks straight line.	Jumps off floor, with coordinated arm action. Broad jumps about 1 foot. Hops 4 to 6 times on same foot, flexing upper body and swinging nonhopping leg.	Throws ball with slight body rotation but little or no transfer of weight with feet. Flexes elbows in preparation for catching; traps ball against chest.	Pedals and steers tricycle.
4–5 years	Walks down stairs, alternating feet. Walks circular line. Walks awkwardly on balance beam. Runs more smoothly. Gallops and skips with one foot.	Jumps upward and forward more effectively; travels greater distance. Hops 7 to 9 times on same foot; improved speed of hopping.	Throws ball with increased body rotation and some transfer of weight forward. Catches ball with hands; if unsuccessful, may still trap ball against chest.	Rides tricycle rapidly, steers smoothly.
5–6 years	Walks securely on balance beam. Increases speed of run. Gallops more smoothly. Engages in true skipping.	Jumps off floor about 1 foot. Broad jumps 3 feet. Hops 50 feet on same foot in 10 seconds. Hops with rhythmic alternation (2 hops on one foot and 2 on the other).	Has mature throwing and catching pattern. Moves arm more and steps forward during throw. Awaits thrown ball with relaxed posture, adjusting body to path and size of ball.	Rides bicycle with training wheels.

Sources: Cratty, 1986; Getchell & Roberton, 1989; Newborg, Stock, & Wnek, 1984; Roberton, 1984.

Changes in ball skills provide an excellent illustration of preschoolers' gross motor progress. Play a game of catch with a 2- or 3-year-old, and watch the child's body carefully. Young preschoolers stand still facing the target, throwing with their arm thrust forward. At first appearance of the skill, other parts of the body are not involved. Catching is equally awkward. Two-year-olds extend their arms and hands rigidly, using them as a single unit to trap the ball. By age 3, children flex their elbows enough to trap the ball against the chest. But if the ball arrives too quickly, younger preschoolers cannot adapt, and it may simply bounce off the child's body (Roberton, 1984).

Gradually, children call on the shoulders, torso, trunk, and legs to support throwing and catching. By age 4, the body rotates as the child throws, and at 5 years preschoolers begin to shift their weight forward, stepping as they release the ball. As a result, the ball travels faster and farther. When the ball is returned, older preschoolers predict its place of landing by moving forward, backward, or sideways. Then they catch it with their hands and fingers, "giving" with arms and body to absorb the force of the ball (see Figure 8.6).

FINE MOTOR DEVELOPMENT

Like gross motor development, fine motor skills take a giant leap forward during early childhood (refer to Table 8.2). Because control of the hands and fingers improves, young children at play put puzzles together, build structures out of small blocks, cut and paste, and string beads. To parents, the fine motor progress of the preschool years is most

5-6 Years

2 Years

3 Years

FIGURE **8.6**

Changes in catching during early childhood. At age 2, children extend their arms rigidly, and the ball tends to bounce off the body. At age 3, they flex their elbows in preparation for catching, trapping the ball against the chest. By ages 5 and 6, children involve the entire body, catching with the hands and fingers.

apparent in two areas: (1) children's increasing ability to care for their own bodies, and (2) the drawings and paintings that fill the walls at home, day care, and preschool.

■ **SELF-HELP SKILLS.** During early childhood, children gradually become self-sufficient at dressing and feeding. Two-year-olds put on and take off simple items of clothing. By age 3, they do so well enough to take care of toileting needs by themselves. Between age 4 and 5, children can dress and undress without supervision. At mealtimes, young preschoolers use a spoon well, and they can serve themselves. By age 4, they are adept with a fork, and around 5 to 6 years they can use a knife to cut soft foods. Roomy clothing with large buttons and zippers and child-sized eating utensils help children master these skills.

Preschoolers get great satisfaction from managing their own bodies. They are proud of their independence, and their new skills also make life easier for adults. But parents need to be patient about these abilities. When tired and in a hurry, young children often revert to eating with their fingers. And the 3-year-old who dresses himself in the morning sometimes ends up with his shirt on inside out, his pants on backward, and his left snow boot on his right foot!

Perhaps the most complex self-help skill of early childhood is shoe tying, which children master around age 6. Success requires a longer attention span, memory for an intricate series of hand movements, and the dexterity to perform them. Shoe tying illustrates the close connection between cognitive and motor development. We will see additional examples of this relationship as we look at the development of young children's drawing and writing.

■ **DRAWING AND WRITING.** When given crayon and paper, even young toddlers scribble in imitation of others, but their scrawls seem like little more than random tangles of lines. As the young child's ability to mentally represent the world expands, marks on the page take on definite meaning.

From Scribbles to Pictures. A variety of factors combine with fine motor control in the development of children's artful representations. These include cognitive advances, such as gains in planning skills and spatial understanding (a move from a focus on separate objects to a broader visual perspective), and exposure to pictorial images in their

Putting on and fastening clothing is challenging but rewarding to preschoolers. Young children enjoy a new sense of independence when they can dress themselves. *(Elizabeth Zuckerman/PhotoEdit)*

TABLE 8.2

Changes in Fine Motor Skills During Early Childhood

AGE	DRESSING	FEEDING	OTHER
2–3 years	Puts on and removes simple items of clothing. Zips and unzips large zippers.	Uses spoon effectively.	Opens door by turning knob. Strings large beads.
3–4 years	Fastens and unfastens large buttons.	Serves self food without assistance.	Uses scissors to cut paper. Copies vertical line and circle.
4–5 years	Dresses and undresses without assistance.	Uses fork effectively.	Cuts with scissors, following line. Copies triangle, cross, and some letters.
5–6 years		Uses knife to cut soft food.	Ties single overhand knot; around age 6, ties shoes. Draws person with six parts. Copies some numerals and simple words.

Sources: Furuno et al., 1987; Newborg, Stock, & Wnek, 1984.

environment (Golomb, 1992). Typically, drawing progresses through the following three-stage sequence:

1. *Scribbles.* Western children begin to draw during the second year. At first, action rather than the resulting scribble contains the intended representation. For example, one 18-month-old took her crayon and hopped it around the page, explaining as she made a series of dots, "Rabbit goes hop-hop" (Winner, 1986).

2. *First representational shapes and forms.* By age 3, children's scribbles start to become pictures. Often this happens after they make a gesture with the crayon, notice that they have drawn a recognizable shape, and then decide to label it. In one case, a 2-year-old made some random marks on a page and then, realizing the resemblance between his scribbles and noodles, named the creation "chicken pie and noodles" (Winner, 1986).

   A major milestone in children's drawing occurs when they begin to use lines to represent the boundaries of objects. This permits them to draw their first picture of a person by age 3 or 4. Look at the tadpole image—a circular shape with lines attached—on the left in Figure 8.7. It is a universal one in which fine motor and cognitive limitations lead the preschooler to reduce the figure down to the simplest form that still looks like a human being. Gradually, preschoolers add features, such as eyes, nose, mouth, hair, fingers, and feet.

3. *More realistic drawings.* Unlike many adults, young children do not demand that a drawing be realistic. But as cognitive and fine motor skills improve, they learn to desire greater realism. As a result, they create more complex drawings, like the one on the right in Figure 8.7, made by a 6-year-old child. Within these, more conventional figures, in which the body is differentiated from the arms and legs, appear. (Look closely at the human and animal figures in the 6-year-old's drawing.) Over time, children improve the proportions of the head, trunk, and extremities and add more details.

   Still, children of this age are not very particular about mirroring reality. Their drawings contain perceptual distortions, since only gradually do they figure out how to represent depth. The missing third dimension helps make the preschool child's artwork look fanciful and inventive. Accomplished artists, who also try to represent reality freely, often must work hard to do deliberately what they did without effort as 5- and 6-year-olds (Winner, 1986).

FIGURE 8.7

Examples of young children's drawings. The universal tadpolelike shape that children use to draw their first picture of a person is shown on the left. The tadpole soon becomes an anchor for greater detail as arms, fingers, toes, and facial features sprout from the basic shape. By the end of the preschool years, children produce more complex, differentiated pictures like the one on the right, drawn by a 6-year-old child. *(Tadpole drawings from H. Gardner, 1980,* Artful Scribbles: The Significance of Children's Drawings, *New York: Basic Books, p. 64. Reprinted by permission of Basic Books, a division of HarperCollins Publishers, Inc. Six-year-old's picture from E. Winner, August 1986, "Where Pelicans Kiss Seals,"* Psychology Today, *20[8], p. 35. Reprinted by permission of the author.)*

Cultural Variations in Development of Drawing.   Children's drawings are greatly influenced by the art of their society and by schooling. Children in cultures with little interest in art produce simpler forms. In cultures that emphasize artistic expression, children's drawings reflect the conventions of their culture and are more sophisticated. For example, the women of Walbiri, an Aboriginal group in Australia, draw symbols in sand to illustrate stories for preschoolers. When their children go to preschool or school, these symbols often are mixed with more realistic images. In one instance, a child drew a semi-circle on a chair to represent a seated person (Wales, 1990).

Schooling provides opportunities to draw and write, see pictures, and grasp the notion that artistic forms have meanings that are shared by others (Cox, 1993). The Jimi Valley is a remote region of Papua New Guinea with no indigenous pictorial art. Many children do not go to school and therefore have little opportunity to develop drawing skills. When a Western researcher asked nonschooled Jimi 10- to 15-year-olds to draw a human figure for the first time, most produced nonrepresentational scribbles and shapes or simple "stick" or "contour" images (see Figure 8.8). Compared to the Western tadpole image, Jimi figures emphasize the body, hands, and feet over the head and face—a different view of what is salient in the human form (Martlew & Connolly, 1996).

When young children experiment with crayons and paint, they not only develop fine motor skills but acquire the artistic traditions of their culture. This Australian Aboriginal 4-year-old creates a dot painting. To Westerners, it looks abstract. To the child, it expresses a "dreamtime" story about the life and land of his ancestors. If asked about the painting, he might respond, "Here are the boulders on the creek line, the hills with kangaroos and emus, and the campsites." *(Laura Berk)*

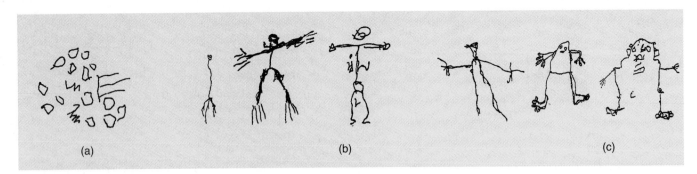

(a)   (b)   (c)

FIGURE 8.8

Drawings produced by nonschooled 10- to 15-year-old children of the Jimi Valley of Papua New Guinea when asked to draw a human figure for the first time. Many produced nonrepresentational scribbles and shapes (a), "stick" figures (b), or "contour" figures (c). Compared to the Western tadpole form, the Jimi "stick" and "contour" figures emphasize the hands and feet over the head and face. Otherwise, the drawings of these older children, who had little opportunity to develop drawing skills, resemble those of young preschoolers. *(From M. Martlew & K. J. Connolly, 1996, "Human Figure Drawings by Schooled and Unschooled Children in Papua New Guinea,"* Child Development, *67, pp. 2750–2751. © The Society for Research in Child Development, Inc. Adapted by permission.)*

Preschool boys are slightly ahead of girls in motor skills that emphasize force and power. Although only a small difference in physical capacity exists, this gap in performance widens as boys are given balls and encouraged to use them. (Tony Freeman/PhotoEdit)

No Jimi child enrolled in school produced nonrepresentational scribbles and shapes. Most drew Jimi-style contour images with greater detail or well-proportioned human figures with differentiated heads and bodies. That older Jimi children with no schooling often produce nonrepresentational forms suggests that this is a universal beginning stage in drawing. Once children realize that lines on the page must evoke human features, they find solutions to figure drawing that vary somewhat from culture to culture but, overall, follow the three-stage sequence described earlier.

Early Printing.   As young children experiment with lines and shapes, notice print in storybooks, and observe the writing of others, they try to print letters and, later, words. Often the first word printed is the child's name. Initially, it may be represented by a single letter. *"How do you make a D?"* my older son David asked at 3 years of age. When I printed a large uppercase *D* for him, he tried to copy. *"D for David,"* he said as he wrote, quite satisfied with his backward, imperfect creation. A year later, David added several additional letters, and around age 5, he wrote his name clearly enough that others could read it.

In addition to gains in fine motor control, advances in perception contribute to the ability to form letters and words. Like many children, David continued to reverse letters in his printing until well into second grade. When we take up early childhood perceptual development in the last section of this chapter, you will discover why these letter reversals are so common.

INDIVIDUAL DIFFERENCES IN MOTOR SKILLS

We have largely discussed motor milestones in terms of the average age at which children reach them in Western nations, but, of course, there are wide individual differences. Body build influences gross motor abilities. Compared to a short, stocky youngster, a tall, muscular child tends to move more quickly and acquire certain skills earlier. Researchers believe that body build contributes to the superior performance of African American over Caucasian-American children in running and jumping. African-American youngsters tend to have longer limbs, so they have better leverage (Lee, 1980; Wakat, 1978).

Sex differences in motor skills are also evident in early childhood. Boys are slightly ahead of girls in skills that emphasize force and power. By age 5, they can jump slightly farther, run slightly faster, and throw a ball much farther (about 5 feet beyond the distance covered by girls). At the same time, girls have an edge in fine motor skills and in certain gross motor skills that require a combination of good balance and foot movement, such as hopping and skipping. Boys' greater muscle mass and (in the case of throwing) their slightly longer forearms may contribute to their skill advantages. And in Chapter 5, we indicated that girls are ahead of boys in overall physical maturity. This difference may be partly responsible for girls' better balance and precision of movement.

From an early age, boys and girls are usually encouraged into different physical activities. For example, fathers often play catch in the backyard with their sons, but they seldom do so with their daughters. Baseballs and footballs are purchased for boys, jump ropes, hula hoops, and jacks for girls. As children get older, differences in motor skills between boys and girls get larger, yet sex differences in physical capacity remain small until adolescence (Thomas & French, 1985). These trends suggest that social pressures for boys to be active and physically skilled and for girls to play quietly at fine motor activities may exaggerate small, genetically based differences that are there in the first place .

When play spaces are properly designed and equipped for preschoolers, young children respond eagerly to motor challenges and develop new skills through informal play. *(Richard Hutchings/PhotoEdit)*

ENHANCING EARLY CHILDHOOD MOTOR DEVELOPMENT

Today, many parents provide preschoolers with early training in motor skills in the form of gymnastics, tumbling, and other lessons. These experiences offer excellent opportunities for physical exercise and social interaction. But aside from throwing (where direct instruction seems to make some difference), there is no evidence that preschoolers exposed to formal lessons are ahead in motor development. Instead, children seem to master the motor skills of early childhood naturally, as part of their everyday play (Roberton, 1984).

Does this mean that adults can do little to promote motor development? The physical environment in which informal play takes place can make a difference in children's mastery of complex motor skills. When children have play spaces and equipment appropriate for running, climbing, jumping, and throwing, along with encouragement to use them, they respond eagerly to these challenges. But if balls are too large and heavy to be properly grasped and thrown, or jungle gyms, ladders, and horizontal bars are suitable for only the largest and strongest youngsters, then children's motor skills are likely to be poorly learned. Preschools, day care centers, and city playgrounds need to accommodate a wide range of physical abilities by offering a variety of pieces of equipment that differ in size or that can be adjusted to fit the needs of individual children.

Similarly, fine motor development can be supported through daily routines, such as pouring juice and dressing, and play involving puzzles, construction sets, drawing, painting, sculpting, cutting, and pasting. Exposure to artwork of their own and other cultures enhances children's awareness of the creative possibilities of artistic media. Preschoolers should be encouraged represent their own ideas and feelings rather than coloring in pre-drawn forms.

Finally, the social climate created by adults can enhance or dampen preschoolers' motor skills. When parents and teachers criticize a child's performance, push specific motor skills, or promote a competitive attitude, they risk undermining young children's self-confidence and, in turn, their motor progress (Kutner, 1993). The appropriate goal of adult involvement in preschoolers' motor development should be fun rather than winning a game or perfecting the "correct" technique.

PERCEPTUAL DEVELOPMENT

Think back to our discussion of infant perceptual development in Chapter 5. The most striking changes occurred in vision, the sense on which humans depend most for obtaining information from the environment. For infants, the initial perceptual task is one of figuring out how the space around them is organized. Once objects are located in space, infants begin to sort them out. For example, they start to discriminate faces as well as other visual patterns. Recall that Eleanor and James Gibson's *differentiation theory* helped us understand this process. Over time, infants search for invariant features (those that remain stable in a changing perceptual world), making finer and finer distinctions between stimuli (to review this theory, return to page 205).

During early childhood, the trends in perceptual development that began in infancy continue. Brain maturation contributes to better integration between the visual and motor systems. As a result, older preschoolers can visually track a thrown ball while moving to a nearby point to catch it. And besides recognizing several geometric shapes and letters of the alphabet, 4- to 6-year-olds can copy them with reasonable accuracy.

Researchers have been especially interested in how detection of the fine-grained structure of visual patterns improves during early childhood, since it helps us understand how children go about the awesome task of discriminating written symbols as they learn to read. Eleanor Gibson has applied differentiation theory to this process. Her research shows that preschoolers begin by recognizing letters as a set of items. By age 3 or 4, they can tell writing from nonwriting (scribbling and pictures), even though they cannot yet identify many letters of the alphabet. Then they go about discriminating particular letters. Those that are alike in shape are most difficult to tell apart. For example, because the invariant features of *C* and *G, E* and *F,* and *M* and *W* are very subtle, many preschoolers confuse these letter pairs (Gibson, 1970).

Letters that are mirror images of one another, such as *b* and *d* and *p* and *q,* are especially hard for young children to tell apart. This finding may remind you of a point made earlier in our discussion of preschoolers' writing. Until age 7 or 8, children print many letters backward. One reason is that until they learn to read, children do not find it especially useful to notice the difference between mirror image forms. In everyday life, left–right reversals occur only when objects are twin aspects of the same thing. For example, two cups, one with a handle on the left and one with a handle on the right, are identical to young preschoolers. In contrast, children easily discriminate a cup turned upside down, one placed right side up, and one turned over on its side, since they have many daily experiences in which objects must be placed right side up to be used effectively (Bornstein, 1992). Research reveals that the ability to tune in to mirror images, as well as to scan a printed line from left to right, depends in part on experience with reading materials (Casey, 1986). Thus, the very activity of learning to read helps children notice the distinctive features of each letter of the alphabet.

Of course, becoming a skilled reader is a very long process, entailing much more than discriminating visual forms. Children must combine letters into words and sentences and use a variety of information-processing strategies to decipher their meaning, including sustained attention, memory, comprehension, and inference making. But perceptual skills do seem to be essential, since children with advanced visual abilities tend to read at higher levels (Fisher, Bornstein, & Gross, 1985; Kavale, 1982). We will consider other aspects of early literacy development in the next chapter.

ASK YOURSELF . . .

- *Mabel and Chad want to do everything they can to support their 3-year-old daughter's athletic development. What advice would you give them?*

- *When 4-year-old Terry sees the magnetic alphabet letters on the refrigerator, he likes to name the ones he knows. But he often confuses g with p. Explain why Terry makes this perceptual error.*

Summary

BODY GROWTH

Describe changes in body size, proportions, and skeletal maturity during early childhood.

■ Compared to infancy, gains in body size taper off into a slower pattern of growth in early childhood. Body fat also declines, and children become longer and leaner. New epiphyses appear in the skeleton, where cartilage gradually hardens into bone. Individual differences in body size and rate of physical growth become even more apparent during the preschool years.

■ By the end of early childhood, children start to lose their primary teeth. Care of primary teeth is important, since diseased baby teeth can affect the health of permanent teeth. Childhood tooth decay remains high, especially among low-SES children.

What makes physical growth an asynchronous process?

■ Physical growth is an asynchronous process. Different parts of the body grow at different rates. The **general growth curve** describes change in overall body size—rapid during infancy, slower during early and middle childhood, rapid again during adolescence. Exceptions to this trend include the genitals, the lymph tissue, and the brain.

BRAIN DEVELOPMENT

Describe brain development during early childhood, including synaptic growth and pruning, lateralization of the cortex, and changes in structures that establish links between different parts of the brain.

■ During early childhood, neural fibers in the brain continue to form synapses and myelinate. By this time, many cortical regions have overproduced synapses, and **synaptic pruning** occurs. To make room for the connective structures of active neurons, many surrounding neurons die, and plasticity of the brain is reduced.

■ The left cerebral hemisphere grows more rapidly than the right, supporting young children's rapidly expanding language skills.

■ Hand preference is fairly stable by age 2 and increases during early and middle childhood, indicating that lateralization strengthens during this time. Handedness indicates an individual's **dominant cerebral hemisphere.** Left-handers tend to be less strongly lateralized than right-handers. Although left-handedness is associated with developmental problems, the great majority of left-handed children are normal in every respect. Left- and mixed-handed youngsters are more likely to display outstanding verbal and mathematical talents.

■ During early childhood, connections are established between different brain structures. Fibers linking the **cerebellum** to the cerebral cortex myelinate, enhancing balance and motor control. The **reticular formation,** responsible for alertness and consciousness, and the **corpus callosum,** which connects the two cerebral hemispheres, also myelinate rapidly.

FACTORS AFFECTING GROWTH AND HEALTH

Explain how heredity influences physical growth.

■ Heredity influences physical growth by controlling the release of hormones from the **pituitary gland.** The most important pituitary hormones for childhood growth are **growth hormone (GH)** and **thyroid-stimulating hormone (TSH).**

Describe the effects of emotional well-being, restful sleep, nutrition, and infectious disease on physical growth and health in early childhood.

■ Emotional well-being continues to influence body growth in early childhood. An emotionally inadequate home life can lead to **deprivation dwarfism.**

■ Restful sleep in early childhood contributes to body growth and positive family functioning. Bedtime routines help Western children, who generally sleep alone, fall asleep. Almost all preschoolers awaken occasionally because of nightmares. Persistent sleep problems often are due to illness or family stress.

■ Preschoolers' slower growth rate causes their appetite to decline, and often they become picky eaters. Young children's social environments have a powerful impact on food preferences. Modeling by others, repeated exposure to new foods, and a positive emotional climate at mealtimes can promote healthy, varied eating in young children.

■ Malnutrition can combine with infectious disease to undermine healthy growth. In developing countries, diarrhea is widespread and claims millions of young lives. Teaching families how to administer **oral rehydration therapy (ORT)** can prevent most of these deaths.

■ Immunization rates are lower in the United States than in other industrialized nations because many economically disadvantaged children do not have access to the medical care they need. In addition, parental misconceptions about safe immunization practices are not always corrected through public education.

■ Childhood illness rises with day-care attendance. **Otitis media,** or middle ear infection, is especially common. Frequent bouts predict delayed language progress and social isolation in early childhood and poorer academic performance after school entry. Screening for the disease and high-quality day care can prevent these negative outcomes.

What factors increase the risk of unintentional injuries, and how can childhood injuries be prevented?

■ Unintentional injuries are the leading cause of childhood mortality. Injury victims are more likely to be boys; to be

Summary (continued)

temperamentally irritable, inattentive, and negative in mood; and to be growing up in stressed, poverty-stricken, inner-city families.

■ A variety of approaches are needed to prevent childhood injuries. These include reducing poverty, teenage childbearing, and other sources of family stress; upgrading the quality of day care; passing laws that promote child safety; creating safer home, travel, and play environments; improving public education; and changing parent and child behaviors.

MOTOR DEVELOPMENT

Cite major milestones of gross and fine motor development in early childhood.

■ During early childhood, children continue to integrate previously acquired motor skills into more complex dynamic systems of action. Body growth causes the child's center of gravity to shift toward the trunk, and balance improves, paving the way for an explosion of gross motor milestones.

■ Preschoolers' gaits become smooth and rhythmic, and they run, jump, hop, gallop, and eventually skip. These abilities, as well as throwing and catching, become better coordinated as movements of the entire body support each new skill.

■ Gains in control of the hands and fingers lead to dramatic changes in fine motor skills. Preschoolers gradually become self-sufficient at dressing themselves and using a fork and knife at mealtime.

■ By age 3, children's scribbles become pictures. Their drawings increase in complexity and realism with age and are greatly influenced by the art of their society and by schooling. Young children try to print letters of the alphabet and, later, words, an ability that improves with gains in fine motor control and perception.

Describe individual differences in preschoolers' motor skills and ways to enhance motor development in early childhood.

■ Body build, ethnicity, and sex influence early childhood motor development. Differences in motor skills between boys and girls are partly genetic, but environmental pressures exaggerate them.

■ Children master the motor skills of early childhood through informal play experiences. Richly equipped play environments that accommodate a wide range of physical abilities are important during the preschool years.

PERCEPTUAL DEVELOPMENT

Summarize perceptual development in early childhood, paying special attention to discrimination of written symbols.

■ During early childhood, brain maturation contributes to improvements in integrating the visual and motor systems. The Gibsons' differentiation theory helps explain how children discriminate written symbols as they learn to read.

■ Because preschoolers have little need to distinguish mirror image forms in everyday life, left–right letter reversals are common in early childhood. Exposure to reading materials increases the variety of perceptual cues to which children are sensitive.

Important terms and concepts

cerebellum (p. 298)
corpus callosum (p. 300)
deprivation dwarfism (p. 303)
dominant cerebral hemisphere (p. 298)

general growth curve (p. 297)
growth hormone (GH) (p. 300)
oral rehydration therapy (ORT) (p. 306)
otitis media (p. 306)

pituitary gland (p. 300)
reticular formation (p. 298)
synaptic pruning (p. 297)
thyroid-stimulating hormone (TSH) (p. 301)

INFECTIOUS DISEASES IN CHILDHOOD

American Academy of Pediatrics
(847) 228-5005
Website: www.kidsdoc@aap.org

Provides public education on a variety of childhood health issues. Among the many pamphlets and publications available are written guidelines for effective control of infectious disease.

Child Care Information Exchange
(206) 883-9394
Website: www.wolfene.com/ccie

A bimonthly publication written especially for day care directors that addresses the practical issues of running a center. Articles discussing health and safety often are included.

U. S. Centers for Disease Control Entry
(301) 443-2610
Website: www.cdc.gov

Surveys national disease trends and environmental health problems. Has organized an agency network to address problems of infectious disease in day care. Through its website, offers information to day care staff on techniques that prevent the spread of infection.

CHILDHOOD INJURY CONTROL

U. S. Consumer Product
Safety Commission
(800) 638-2772
Website: www.cpsc.gov

Establishes and enforces product safety standards. Operates a hotline providing information on safety issues and recall of dangerous consumer products.

National SAFE KIDS Campaign
(202) 662-0600
Website: www.jnj.com

A national organization dedicated to the prevention of unintentional injuries in childhood. The campaign comprises all 50 states. Links to each are available through the SAFE KIDS website.

"Self Portrait"
Roy
6 years, Australia

This bold, cheerful self-portrait by a budding young artist portrays the most striking cognitive achievement of early childhood. As Chapter 9 reveals, mental representation takes a giant leap forward.

COGNITIVE DEVELOPMENT

IN EARLY CHILDHOOD

ne rainy morning,

as I observed in our laboratory
preschool, Leslie, the children's teacher,
joined me at the back of the room to
watch for a moment herself.
"Preschoolers' minds are such a curious blend of logic, fantasy, and faulty
reasoning," Leslie reflected. "Every day,
I'm startled by the maturity and originality of many things they say and do.
Yet at other times, their thinking seems
limited and inflexible."

Leslie's comments sum up the puzzling contradictions of early childhood
cognition. Over the previous week, I
had seen many examples in 3-year-old
Sammy. That day, I found him at the
puzzle table, moments after a loud
clash of thunder outside. Sammy
looked up, startled, then said to Leslie,
"The man turned on the thunder!"
Leslie patiently explained that people
can't turn thunder on or off. But
Sammy persisted. "Then a lady did it,"
he stated with certainty.

In other respects, Sammy's cognitive skills seemed surprisingly advanced. At snack time, he accurately counted, "One, two, three, four!" and then got four cartons of milk, giving one to each child at his table. Sammy's keen memory and ability to categorize were also evident. As he sat in the reading corner, he recited by heart *The Very Hungry Caterpillar* (Carle, 1969), a story he had heard many times before. Sammy's favorite picture books were about animals, and he could name and group together dozens of them.

Still, Sammy's cognitive skills seemed fragile and insecure. When more than four children joined his snack group, Sammy's counting broke down. And some of his notions about quantity seemed as fantastic as his understanding of thunder. Across the snack table, Priti dumped out her raisins, and they scattered in front of her. "How come you got lots, and I only got this little bit?" asked Sammy, failing to realize that he had just as many; they were simply all bunched up in a tiny red box.

In this chapter, we explore the many facets of early childhood cognition, drawing from three theories with which you are already familiar. We begin with Piaget's preoperational stage, which, for the most part, emphasizes preschool children's deficits rather than their strengths. Recent research along with two additional perspectives—Vygotsky's sociocultural theory and information processing—extends our understanding of preschoolers' cognitive competencies. Then we turn to a variety of factors that contribute to individual differences in mental development—the home environment, the quality of preschool and day care, and the many hours young children spend watching television. Our chapter concludes with language development, the most awesome achievement of early childhood.

PIAGET'S THEORY: THE PREOPERATIONAL STAGE

As children move from the sensorimotor to the **preoperational stage,** the most obvious change is an extraordinary increase in representational, or symbolic, mental activity. Recall that infants and toddlers have some ability to mentally represent the world. Between the ages of 2 and 7, this capacity blossoms.

ADVANCES IN MENTAL REPRESENTATION

As I looked around the preschool classroom, signs of developing representation were everywhere—in the children's drawings and paintings, in their re-creations of family life in the housekeeping area, and in their delight at story time. Especially impressive were strides in language skill. During free play, a hum of chattering voices rose from the classroom.

Piaget acknowledged that language is our most flexible means of mental representation. By detaching thought from action, it permits cognition to be far more efficient than it was during the sensorimotor stage. When we think in words, we overcome the limits of our momentary perceptions. We can deal with the past, present, and future all at once, combining images of the world in unique ways, as when we think about a hungry caterpillar eating bananas or monsters flying through the forest at night (Miller, 1993).

Despite the power of language, Piaget did not believe that it plays a major role in cognitive development. According to Piaget, language does not give rise to representational thought. Instead, sensorimotor activity provides the foundation that makes language possible, just as it leads to deferred imitation and make-believe play. Can you think of evidence that supports Piaget's view? Recall from Chapter 6 that the first words toddlers use have a strong sensorimotor basis. In addition, toddlers acquire an impressive range of cognitive categories long before they use words to label them (see pages 226–228). Still, other theorists regard Piaget's account of the link between language and thought as incomplete, as we will see later in this chapter.

preoperational stage
Piaget's second stage, in which rapid growth in representation takes place. However, thought is not yet logical. Spans the years from 2 to 7.

MAKE-BELIEVE PLAY

Make-believe play provides another excellent example of the development of representation during the preoperational stage. Like language, it increases dramatically during early childhood. Piaget believed that through pretending, young children practice and strengthen newly acquired representational schemes. Drawing on Piaget's ideas, several investigators have traced changes in make-believe play during the preschool years.

■ **DEVELOPMENT OF MAKE-BELIEVE PLAY.** One day, Sammy's 18-month-old brother Dwayne came to visit the classroom. Dwayne wandered around, picked up the receiver of a toy telephone, said, "Hi, Mommy," and then dropped it. In the housekeeping area, he found a cup, pretended to drink, and toddled off again.

In the meantime, Sammy joined a group of children in the block area for a space shuttle launch. "That can be our control tower," he suggested to Vance, pointing to a corner by a bookshelf.

"Wait, I gotta get it all ready," said Lynette, who was still arranging the astronauts (two dolls and a teddy bear) inside a circle of large blocks, which represented the rocket.

"Countdown!" Sammy announced, speaking into a small wooden block, his pretend walkie-talkie.

"Five, six, two, four, one, blastoff!" responded Vance, commander of the control tower.

Lynette made one of the dolls push a pretend button and reported, "Brrrm, brrrm, they're going up!"

A comparison of Dwayne's pretend with that of Sammy and his classmates illustrates three important advances in make-believe. Each reflects the preschool child's growing symbolic mastery:

1. *Over time, play becomes increasingly detached from the real-life conditions associated with it.* In early pretending, toddlers use only realistic objects—for example, a toy telephone to talk into or a cup to drink from. Around age 2, they use less realistic toys, such as a block for a telephone receiver, more frequently. Sometime during the third year, children can imagine objects and events without support from the real world, as when Sammy invented the control tower in a corner of the room. We can see that children's mental representations are becoming more flexible, since a play symbol no longer has to resemble the object for which it stands (Corrigan, 1987; O'Reilly, 1995).

2. *The way the "child as self" participates in play changes with age.* When make-believe first appears, it is directed toward the self—for example, Dwayne pretends to feed only himself. A short time later, children direct pretend actions toward other objects, as when the child feeds a doll. And early in the third year, they use objects as active agents, and the child becomes a detached participant who makes a doll feed itself or (in Lynette's case) push a button to launch a rocket. Make-believe gradually becomes less self-centered, as children realize that agents and recipients of pretend actions can be independent of themselves (Corrigan, 1987; McCune, 1993).

3. *Make-believe gradually includes more complex scheme combinations.* For example, Dwayne can pretend to drink from a cup, but he does not yet combine drinking with pouring. Later on, children combine pretend schemes with those of peers in **sociodramatic play,** the make-believe with others that is underway by age 2½ (Haight & Miller, 1993; Howes & Matheson, 1992). Already, Sammy and his classmates can create and coordinate several roles in an elaborate plot. By 4 years of age, children have a sophisticated understanding of role relationships and story lines (Göncü, 1993).

sociodramatic play
The make-believe play with others that is under way by age 2½.

The appearance of complex sociodramatic play signals a major change in representation. Children do not just represent their world; they begin to display *awareness* that make-believe is a representational activity—an understanding that increases steadily from 4 to 8 years of age (Jarrold et al., 1994; Lillard, 1998). Listen closely to preschoolers as they jointly create an imaginary scene. You will hear them assign roles and negotiate make-believe plans: "*You pretend to be* the astronaut, *I'll act like* I'm operating the control tower! "Wait, *I gotta set up* the spaceship." In communicating about pretend, children think about and manipulate their own and others' fanciful representations. This indicates that they have started to reason about people's mental activities, a topic we will return to later in this chapter.

■ **ADVANTAGES OF MAKE-BELIEVE PLAY.** Today, Piaget's view of make-believe as mere practice of representational schemes is regarded as too limited. Research indicates that play not only reflects but contributes to children's cognitive and social skills (Nicolopoulou, 1993; Singer & Singer, 1990). Sociodramatic play has been studied most thoroughly. In comparison to social nonpretend activities (such as drawing or putting puzzles together), during social pretend preschoolers' interactions last longer, show more involvement, draw larger numbers of children into the activity, and are more cooperative (Creasey, Jarvis, & Berk, 1998).

When we consider these findings, it is not surprising that preschoolers who spend more time at sociodramatic play are advanced in general intellectual development and seen as more socially competent by their teachers (Burns & Brainerd, 1979; Connolly & Doyle, 1984). And many studies reveal that make-believe strengthens a wide variety of mental abilities, including memory, logical reasoning, language and literacy, imagination, creativity, and the ability to reflect on one's own thinking and take another's perspective (Dias & Harris, 1990; Ervin-Tripp, 1991; Kavanaugh & Engel, 1998; Newman, 1990).

What about children who spend much time in solitary make-believe creating *imaginary companions*—invisible characters with whom they form a special relationship, converse, and act out play scenes over an extended time period, usually several months. In the past, imaginary companions were viewed as a sign of maladjustment, but recent research challenges this assumption. About 65 percent of preschoolers have them, and those who do display more complex pretend play, are advanced in mental representation, and are actually more (not less) sociable with peers (Taylor, Cartright, & Carlson, 1993).

The Caregiving Concerns table on the following page offers suggestions for enhancing make-believe at home and in preschool and daycare. We will return to the topic of play in Chapter 10.

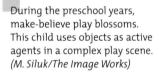

During the preschool years, make-believe play blossoms. This child uses objects as active agents in a complex play scene. *(M. Siluk/The Image Works)*

CAREGIVING CONCERNS
Enhancing Make-Believe in Early Childhood

STRATEGY	DESCRIPTION
Provide sufficient space, materials, and equipment.	Crowding large numbers of children into small spaces, especially when play materials and equipment are limited, limits play options and leads to conflict.
Supervise and support children's play without controlling it.	Respond to, guide, and elaborate on preschoolers' play themes when they indicate a need for assistance. Excessive adult control destroys the creativity and joy of children's play.
Offer a wide variety of realistic materials and materials without clear functions.	Children use realistic materials, such as trucks, dolls, tea sets, dress-up clothes, and toy scenes (house, farm, garage, airport) to act out culturally relevant roles. Materials without clear functions, such as blocks, cardboard cylinders, paper bags, and sand, inspire fantastic role play, such as pirate and creature from outer space.
Ensure that children have many rich, real-world experiences to inspire positive fantasy play.	Opportunities to participate in real-world activities with adults and to observe adult roles in the community provide children with rich social knowledge to integrate into make-believe. Restricting television viewing, especially programs with violent content, limits the degree to which violent themes and aggressive behavior become part of children's play. (See Chapter 10, pages 386–387.)
Help children solve social conflicts constructively.	Cooperation is essential for sociodramatic play. Guide children toward effective relations with agemates, using techniques that help them learn how to resolve disagreements. (For example, ask, "What could you do if you want a turn?" If the child cannot think of possibilities, suggest some options and assist the child in implementing them.)

Sources: Berk, 1994a; File, 1993; Frost, Shin, & Jacobs, 1998; Vandenberg, 1998.

SPATIAL REPRESENTATION

Leslie set up a doll house, replete with tiny furnishings, in a corner of the classroom. Sammy often arranged the furniture to match his real-world living room, kitchen, and bedroom. Spatial representations, like Sammy's, are powerful cognitive tools. When we understand that a photograph, model, or map corresponds to circumstances in everyday life, we can use it to acquire information about objects and places we have not experienced.

When do children realize that a spatial symbol stands for a specific state of affairs in the real world? In one study, 2½- and 3-year-olds watched as an adult hid a small toy (little Snoopy) in a scale model of a room. Then they were asked to find a larger toy (big Snoopy) hidden in the room that the model represented. Not until age 3 could most children find big Snoopy. By then, they realized that the model is not just a toy room but a symbol of another room (DeLoache, 1987; Uttal et al., 1998).

These findings reveal that spatial understanding improves rapidly over the third year of life. How do children grasp the meaning of spatial symbols? Insight into one type of symbol–real world relation seems to help preschoolers understand others. For example, they understand photographs very early, by age 2, since a photo's primary purpose is to stand for something. It is not an interesting object in its own right. Using a photograph to show where big Snoopy is hidden helps 2½-year-olds do better on the model task (DeLoache, 1991). And 3-year-olds who pass the model task readily transfer their understanding to a new spatial medium—using a simple map to locate big Snoopy (Marzolf & DeLoache, 1994).

Granting young children many opportunities to learn about the functions of diverse symbols—picture books, photographs, models, maps, drawings, and make-believe—enhances their understanding that one object or event can stand for another (DeLoache, 1995). As a result, the door is opened to new realms of knowledge.

Is this preschooler aware that the doll house is not just an interesting object in its own right, but can stand for a real house—that is, serve as a spatial symbol? Not until age 3 do most children grasp the representational meaning of models. *(Paul Gish/Monkmeyer Press)*

FIGURE **9.1**

Piaget's three-mountains problem. A child is permitted to walk around a display of three mountains. Each is distinguished by its color and by its summit. One has a red cross, another a small house, and the third a snow-capped peak. Then the child stands on one side, and a doll is placed at various locations around the display. The child must choose a photograph that shows what the display looks like from the doll's perspective. Before age 6 or 7, most children select the photo that shows the mountains from their own point of view.

LIMITATIONS OF PREOPERATIONAL THOUGHT

Aside from the development of representation, Piaget described preschool children in terms of what they *cannot,* rather than *can,* understand (Beilin, 1992). He compared them to older, more capable children in the concrete operational stage, as the term "*pre*operational" suggests. According to Piaget, young children are not capable of **operations**—mental actions that obey logical rules. Instead, their thinking is rigid, limited to one aspect of a situation at a time, and strongly influenced by the way things appear at the moment.

■ **EGOCENTRIC AND ANIMISTIC THINKING.** For Piaget, the most serious deficiency of preoperational thinking, the one that underlies all others, is **egocentrism.** He believed that when children first begin to mentally represent the world, they are unaware of any symbolic viewpoints other than their own, and they believe that everyone else perceives, thinks, and feels the same way they do (Piaget, 1950).

Piaget's most convincing demonstration of egocentrism involves a task called the *three-mountains problem,* described in Figure 9.1. Egocentrism, Piaget pointed out, shows up in other aspects of children's reasoning as well. Recall Sammy's firm insistence that someone must have turned on the thunder, in much the same way that he uses a switch to turn on a light or radio. Similarly, Piaget regarded egocentrism as responsible for preoperational children's **animistic thinking**—the belief that inanimate objects have lifelike qualities, such as thoughts, wishes, feelings, and intentions, just like themselves. The 3-year-old who charmingly explains that the sun is angry at the clouds and has chased them away is demonstrating this kind of reasoning. According to Piaget, because young children egocentrically assign human purposes to physical events, magical thinking is especially common during the preschool years.

Piaget argued that egocentrism is responsible for the rigidity and illogical nature of preoperational thought. Young children's thinking proceeds so strongly from their own point of view that they do not *accommodate,* or revise their thinking, in response to feedback from the physical and social world. Egocentric thought is not reflective thought, which critically examines itself. But to fully appreciate these shortcomings of the preoperational stage, let's consider some additional tasks that Piaget presented to children.

■ **INABILITY TO CONSERVE.** Piaget's famous conservation tasks reveal a variety of deficiencies of preoperational thinking. **Conservation** refers to the idea that certain physical characteristics of objects remain the same, even when their outward appearance

operations
Mental representations of actions that obey logical rules.

egocentrism
The inability to distinguish the symbolic viewpoints of others from one's own.

animistic thinking
The belief that inanimate objects have lifelike qualities, such as thoughts, wishes, feelings, and intentions.

conservation
The understanding that certain physical characteristics of objects remain the same, even when their outward appearance changes.

changes. At snack time, Sammy had difficulty with conservation of number. He and Priti had identical boxes of raisins, but after Priti spread hers out on the table, Sammy was convinced that she had more.

Another type of conservation task involves liquid. In this problem, the child is presented with two identical tall glasses of water and asked if they contain equal amounts. Once the child agrees, the water in one glass is poured into a short, wide container, changing the appearance of the water but not its amount. Then the child is asked whether the amount of water is still the same or whether it has changed. Preoperational children think that the quantity of water is no longer the same. They explain, "There is less now because the water is way down here" (that is, its level is so low in the short, wide container) or "There is more water now because it is all spread out." In Figure 9.2 on page 330, you will find other conservation tasks that you can try with children.

Preoperational children's inability to conserve highlights several related aspects of their thinking. First, their understanding is *centered,* or characterized by **centration.** In other words, they focus on one aspect of a situation and neglect other important features. In the case of conservation of liquid, the child centers on the height of the water in the two containers, failing to realize that all changes in height are compensated by changes in width. Second, their thinking is **perception bound.** They are easily distracted by the concrete, perceptual appearance of objects. It *looks like* there is less water in the short, wide container, so there *must be* less water. Third, children focus on **states rather than transformations**. In the conservation of liquid problem, they treat the initial and final *states* of the water as completely unrelated events, ignoring the *dynamic transformation* (pouring of water) between them.

The most important illogical feature of preoperational thought is its **irreversibility.** Children of this stage cannot mentally go through a series of steps and then reverse direction, returning to the starting point. *Reversibility* is part of every logical operation. Notice how Sammy cannot reverse after Priti spills her raisins. He does not think to himself, "I know that Priti doesn't have more raisins than I do. She just poured them out of that little red box, and if we put them back in again, her raisins and my raisins would look just the same."

■ **TRANSDUCTIVE REASONING.** Reversible thinking is flexible and well organized. Because preoperational children are not capable of it, Piaget concluded that their causal reasoning often consists of disconnected facts and contradictions. He called young children's incorrect explanations **transductive reasoning,** which means reasoning from particular to particular. In other words, preschoolers link together two events that occur close in time and space in a cause-and-effect fashion. Sometimes this leads to some fantastic connections, as in the following interview that Piaget conducted with a young child about why the clouds move:

> You have already seen the clouds moving along? What makes them move?—*When we move along, they move along too.*—Can you make them move?—*Everybody can, when they walk.*—When I walk and you are still, do they move?—*Yes.*—And at night, when everyone is asleep, do they move?—*Yes.*—But you tell me that they move when somebody walks.—*They always move. The cats, when they walk, and then the dogs, they make the clouds move along.* (Piaget, 1926/1929, p. 62)

■ **LACK OF HIERARCHICAL CLASSIFICATION.** Because preoperational children are not yet capable of logical operations, they cannot organize objects into classes and subclasses on the basis of similarities and differences between the groups. Piaget illustrated this difficulty with **hierarchical classification** in his famous *class inclusion problem,* described in Figure 9.3 on page 331. Preoperational children tend to center on the overriding perceptual feature of yellow and do not think reversibly by moving from the whole class (flowers) to the parts (yellow and blue) and back again.

centration
The tendency to focus on one aspect of a situation and neglect other important features.

perception bound
Being easily distracted by the concrete, perceptual appearance of objects.

states rather than transformations
The tendency to treat the initial and final states in a problem as completely unrelated.

irreversibility
The inability to mentally go through a series of steps in a problem and then reverse direction, returning to the starting point.

transductive reasoning
Reasoning from one particular event to another particular event, instead of from general to particular or particular to general.

hierarchical classification
The organization of objects into classes and subclasses on the basis of similarities and differences between the groups.

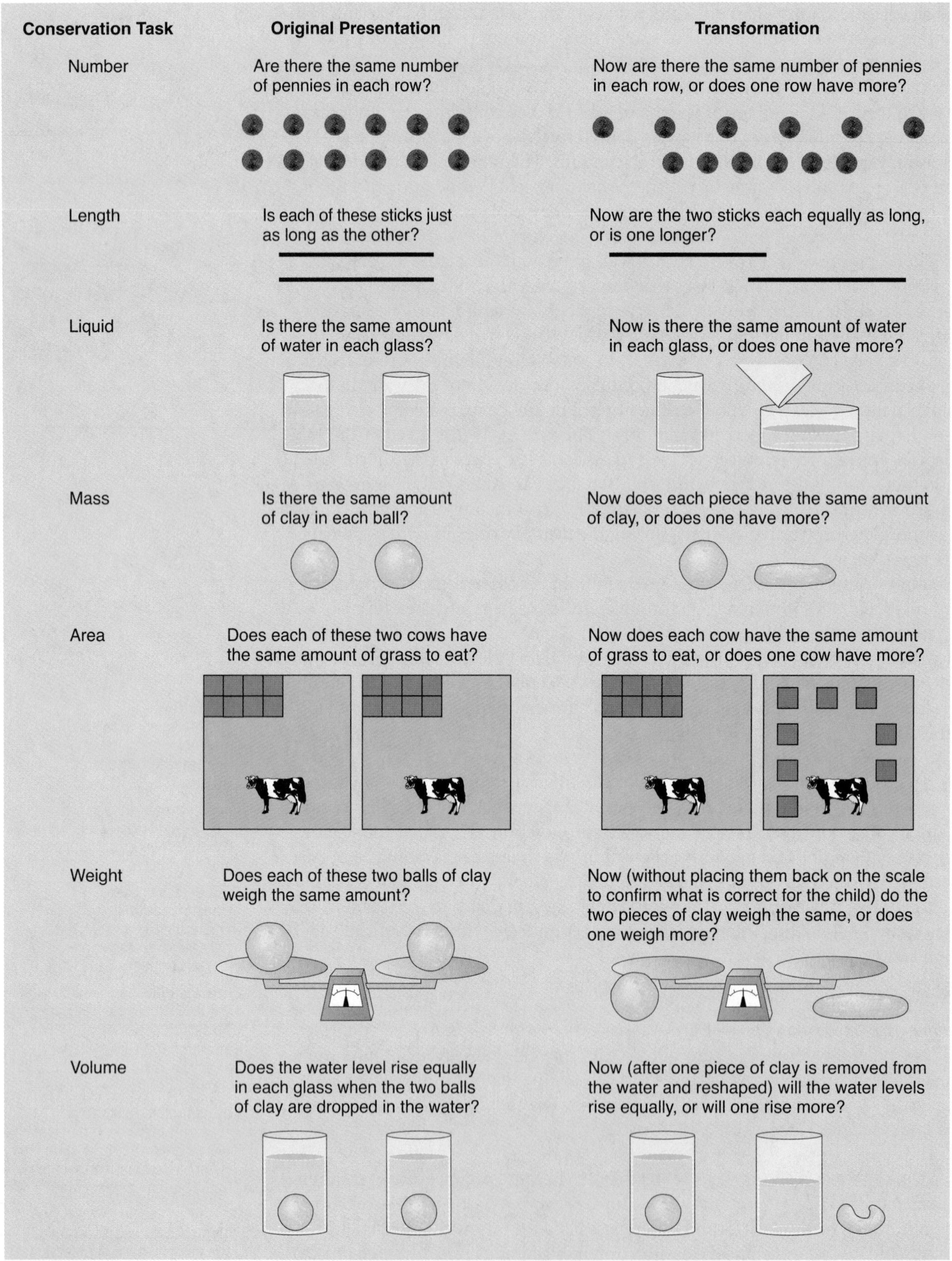

Conservation Task	Original Presentation	Transformation
Number	Are there the same number of pennies in each row?	Now are there the same number of pennies in each row, or does one row have more?
Length	Is each of these sticks just as long as the other?	Now are the two sticks each equally as long, or is one longer?
Liquid	Is there the same amount of water in each glass?	Now is there the same amount of water in each glass, or does one have more?
Mass	Is there the same amount of clay in each ball?	Now does each piece have the same amount of clay, or does one have more?
Area	Does each of these two cows have the same amount of grass to eat?	Now does each cow have the same amount of grass to eat, or does one cow have more?
Weight	Does each of these two balls of clay weigh the same amount?	Now (without placing them back on the scale to confirm what is correct for the child) do the two pieces of clay weigh the same, or does one weigh more?
Volume	Does the water level rise equally in each glass when the two balls of clay are dropped in the water?	Now (after one piece of clay is removed from the water and reshaped) will the water levels rise equally, or will one rise more?

FIGURE 9.2

Some Piagetian conservation tasks. Children at the preoperational stage cannot yet conserve.

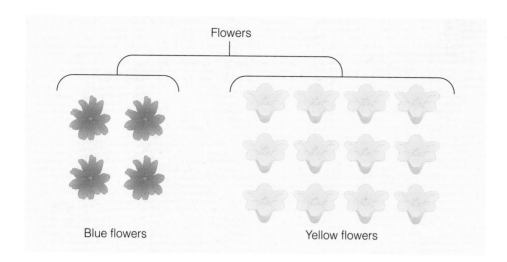

Flowers

Blue flowers

Yellow flowers

FIGURE **9.3**

A Piagetian class inclusion problem. Children are shown 16 flowers, 4 of which are blue and 12 of which are yellow. Asked whether there are more yellow flowers or more flowers, the preoperational child responds, "More yellow flowers," failing to realize that both yellow and blue flowers are included in the category of "flowers."

RECENT RESEARCH ON PREOPERATIONAL THOUGHT

Over the past two decades, Piaget's account of a cognitively deficient preschool child has been seriously challenged. If researchers give his tasks in just the way that he originally designed them, indeed they find that preschoolers do perform poorly. But a close look at Piagetian problems reveals that many of them contain confusing or unfamiliar elements or too many pieces of information for young children to handle at once. As a result, preschoolers' responses do not reflect their true abilities. Piaget also missed many naturally occurring instances of preschoolers' effective reasoning. Let's look at some examples that illustrate these points.

■ **EGOCENTRIC, ANIMISTIC, AND MAGICAL THINKING.** Are young children really so egocentric that they believe a person standing in a different location in a room sees the same thing they see? When researchers change the nature of Piaget's three-mountains problem to include familiar objects and use methods other than picture selection (which is difficult even for 10-year-olds), 4-year-olds show clear awareness of others' vantage points (Borke, 1975; Newcombe & Huttenlocher, 1992).

Nonegocentric responses also appear in young children's conversations. For example, preschoolers adapt their speech to fit the needs of their listeners. Sammy uses shorter, simpler expressions when talking to his little brother Dwayne than to agemates or adults (Gelman & Shatz, 1978). Also, in describing objects, children do not use such words as "big" and "little" in a rigid, egocentric fashion. Instead, they *adjust* their descriptions, taking account of context. By age 3, children judge a 2-inch shoe as small when seen by itself (because it is much smaller than most shoes) but as big when asked about its appropriateness for a very tiny 5-inch doll (Ebeling & Gelman, 1994).

Recent studies indicate that Piaget overestimated preschoolers' animistic beliefs because he asked children about objects with which they have little direct experience, such as the clouds, sun, and moon. Children as young as 3 rarely think that very familiar inanimate objects, like rocks and crayons, are alive. They do make errors when questioned about certain vehicles, such as trains and airplanes. But these objects appear to be self-moving, a characteristic of almost all living things. And they also have some lifelike features—for example, headlights that look like eyes and animate-like movement patterns (Poulin-Dubois & Héroux, 1994; Richards & Siegler, 1986). Children's animistic responses result from incomplete knowledge about objects, not from a rigid belief that inanimate objects are alive.

The same is true for other fantastic beliefs of the preschool years. Most 3- and 4-year-olds believe in the supernatural powers of fairies, goblins, and other enchanted creatures that appear in storybooks, movies, and holiday legends. But they deny that magic can

CULTURAL INFLUENCES

YOUNG CHILDREN'S UNDERSTANDING OF DEATH

Five-year-old Miriam arrived at preschool the day after her dog Pepper died. Instead of running to play with the other children, she stayed close by Leslie's side. Leslie noticed Miriam's discomfort and asked, "What's wrong?"

"Daddy said Pepper had a sick tummy. He fell asleep and died." For a moment, Miriam looked hopeful, "When I get home, Pepper might be up."

Leslie answered directly, "No, Pepper won't get up again. He's not asleep. He's dead, and that means he can't sleep, eat, run, or play anymore."

Miriam wandered off. Later, she returned to Leslie and confessed, "I chased Pepper too hard," tears streaming from her eyes.

Leslie put her arm around Miriam. "Pepper didn't die because you chased him. He was very old and very sick," she explained.

Over the next few days, Miriam asked many more questions: "When I go to sleep, will I die?" "Can a tummy ache make you die?" "Does Pepper feel better now?" "Will Mommy and Daddy die?"

■ **DEVELOPMENT OF THE DEATH CONCEPT.** A realistic understanding of death is based on three ideas:

1. *Permanence:* Once a living thing dies, it cannot be brought back to life.
2. *Universality:* All living things eventually die.
3. *Nonfunctionality:* All living functions, including thought, feeling, movement, and body processes, cease at death.

Without clear explanations, young children rely on egocentric and magical thinking to make sense of death. They may believe, as Miriam did, that they are responsible for a relative or pet's death. And they can easily arrive at incorrect conclusions—in Miriam's case, that sleeping or having a stomachache can cause someone to die.

Preschoolers grasp the three components of the death concept in the order just given, with most mastering them by age 7. *Permanence* is the first and most easily understood idea. When Leslie explained that Pepper would not get up again, Miriam accepted this fact quickly, perhaps because she had seen it in other, less emotionally charged situations, such as the dead butterflies and beetles that she picked up and inspected while playing outside (Furman, 1990). Appreciation of *universality* comes slightly later. At first, children think that certain people do not die, especially those with whom they have close emotional ties or who are like themselves—other children. Finally, *nonfunctionality* is the most difficult component of death for children to grasp. Many preschoolers view dead things as retaining living capacities. When they first comprehend nonfunctionality, they do so in terms of its most visible aspects, such as heartbeat and breathing. Only later do they understand that thinking, feeling, and dreaming cease (Lazar & Torney-Purta, 1991; Speece & Brent, 1992, 1996).

■ **CULTURAL INFLUENCES.** Although a mature appreciation of death is usually reached by the end of early childhood, ethnic variations suggest that religious teachings affect children's understanding. A comparison of four ethnic groups in Israel revealed that Druse and Moslem children's death concepts lagged behind those of Christian and Jewish children (Florian & Kravetz,

---

alter their everyday experiences—for example, turn a picture into a real object or living being (Subbotsky, 1994). Instead, they think magic accounts for events that violate their expectations and that they cannot otherwise explain. Between 4 and 8 years, as familiarity with physical events increases and scientific explanations are taught in school, magical beliefs decline. Children figure out who is really behind the activities of Santa Claus and the Tooth Fairy! They also realize that the antics of magicians are due to trickery, not special powers (Phelps & Woolley, 1994; Rosengren & Hickling, 1994).

The importance of knowledge and experience can be seen in preschoolers' grasp of other natural concepts. Refer to the Cultural Influences box above to find out about young children's developing understanding of death.

■ **ILLOGICAL CHARACTERISTICS OF THOUGHT.** Many studies have re-examined the illogical characteristics of the preoperational stage. Results show that when tasks are simplified and made relevant to their everyday lives, preschoolers do better than Piaget might have expected.

1985). The Druze emphasis on reincarnation and the greater religiosity of both the Druze and Moslem groups may underlie these findings. Religious teachings seem to have an especially strong impact on children's grasp of the permanence of death. For example, children of Southern Baptist families, who believe in an afterlife, are less likely to endorse permanence than are children from Northern Unitarian families, who focus on the here and now—peace and justice in today's world (Candy-Gibbs, Sharp, & Petrun, 1985).

In another study, Israeli Jewish children had a more advanced understanding of the permanence of death than did American children (Schonfeld & Smilansky, 1989). Variations in death-related experiences are probably responsible, since at the time of the research, Israel was at war. Some Israeli children had relatives who died in battle, and conversations about death at home and in classrooms were common.

■ **ENHANCING CHILDREN'S UNDER-STANDING.** Preschoolers' incompletely formed ideas about death are important to keep in mind when the death of a pet or relative occurs. Simple, direct explanations help children understand. Although parents often worry that discussing death with children will fuel their fears, this is not the case. Instead, children who have a good grasp of the facts of death have an easier time accepting it (Essa & Murray, 1994). When preschoolers ask very difficult questions—"Will I die?" "Will you die?"—parents can be truthful as well as comforting by taking advantage of children's sense of time. They can say something like "Not for many, many years. First I'm going to enjoy you as a grown-up and be a grandparent."

Discussions with children about death should also be culturally sensitive. Rather than presenting scientific evidence as counteracting religious beliefs, parents and teachers can assist children in blending the two sources of knowledge. As children get older, their grasp of permanence, universality, and nonfunctionality is often integrated with spiritual and philosophical views, which offer solace during times of bereavement (Cuddy-Casey & Orvaschel, 1997). Open, honest, and respectful communication with children contributes not only to their cognitive appreciation of the

Examining this dead mouse will help these children understand the permanence of death. Appreciation of two additional components of the death concept—universality and nonfunctionality—will come later. *(A. Carey/ The Image Works)*

death concept but also to their emotional well-being.

For example, when a conservation-of-number task is scaled down to include only three items instead of six or seven, preschoolers perform well (Gelman, 1972). And when they are asked carefully worded questions about what happens to substances (such as sugar) after they are dissolved in water, they give very accurate explanations. Most 3- to 5-year-olds know that the substance is conserved—that it continues to exist, can be tasted, and makes the liquid heavier, even though it is invisible in the water. (Au, Sidle, & Rollins, 1993; Rosen & Rozin, 1993). These findings indicate that preschoolers notice transformations, reverse their thinking, and understand causality in familiar contexts.

Indeed, a close look at 3- and 4-year-olds' descriptions of the world reveals that they use causal terms, such as "if–then" and "because," with the same degree of accuracy as adults do (McCabe & Peterson, 1988). Transductive reasoning seems to occur only when preschoolers grapple with unfamiliar topics. Consistent with this idea, recall that preschoolers are reluctant to resort to magical explanations unless they are faced with an extraordinary event. This supports the conclusion that they have a good understanding of causal principles that govern their everyday experiences.

■ **HIERARCHICAL CLASSIFICATION.** Even though preschoolers have difficulty with Piagetian class inclusion tasks, their everyday knowledge is organized into nested categories at an early age. By the second year, children have formed a variety of global categories, such as kitchen utensils, bathroom objects, animals, vehicles, plants, and furniture (Mandler, 1998; Mandler, Bauer, & McDonough, 1991; Mandler & McDonough, 1993). Consider these object groupings, and you will see that they challenge Piaget's assumption that young children's thinking is always perception bound. For example, the category of "kitchen utensils" includes objects that differ widely in appearance but that go together because of their common function and place of use.

Over the preschool years, these global categories differentiate. Children form many *basic-level categories*—ones at an intermediate level of generality, such as "chairs," "tables," "dressers," and "beds." Performance on object-sorting tasks indicates that by age 3 or 4, children can easily move back and forth between basic-level categories and *general categories,* such as "furniture." They also break down the basic-level categories into *subcategories,* such as "rocking chairs" and "desk chairs"—a development fostered by children's rapidly expanding vocabularies and adult labeling of these categories (Mervis, 1987; Mervis, Johnson, & Mervis, 1994). Preschoolers' category systems are not yet very complex, but the capacity to classify hierarchically is present in early childhood.

■ **APPEARANCE VERSUS REALITY.** So far, we have seen that preschoolers show some remarkably advanced reasoning when presented with familiar situations and simplified problems. Yet in certain situations, young children are easily tricked by the outward appearance of things, just as Piaget suggested.

John Flavell and his colleagues took a close look at children's ability to distinguish appearance from reality. They presented children with objects that were disguised in various ways and asked what the items were "really and truly." At age 3, children had some ability to separate the way an object appeared to feel from the way it truly felt. For example, they understood that even though an ice cube did not feel cold to their gloved finger, it "really and truly" was cold (Flavell, Green, & Flavell, 1989). In this task, the real and apparent object states were present at the same time, and children could easily compare them.

Preschoolers have more difficulty with problems involving sights and sounds, but not because (as Piaget suggested) they always confuse appearance and reality. Instead, these tasks require them to recall the real image of an object in the face of a second, contradictory representation. When asked whether a white piece of paper placed behind a blue filter is "really and truly blue" or whether a can that sounds like a baby crying when turned over is "really and truly a baby," preschoolers often respond "Yes!" Not until 6 to 7 years do children do well on these problems (Flavell, Green, & Flavell, 1987).

How do children go about mastering distinctions between appearance and reality? Make-believe play may be important. Preschoolers can tell the difference between pretend play and real experiences long before they answer many appearance–reality tasks correctly (Golomb & Galasso, 1995; Wellman & Woolley, 1990). Experiencing the contrast between everyday and playful use of objects may help children refine their understanding of what is real and what is unreal in the surrounding world.

EVALUATION OF THE PREOPERATIONAL STAGE

Table 9.1 provides an overview of the cognitive attainments of early childhood we have just considered. Take a moment to compare them with Piaget's description of the preoperational child on pages 324–329. How can we make sense of the contradictions between Piaget's conclusions and the findings of recent research?

The evidence as a whole indicates that Piaget was partly wrong and partly right about young children's cognitive capacities. When given simple tasks based on familiar experiences, preschoolers show the beginnings of logical operations long before the concrete operational stage. But their reasoning is not as well developed as that of school-age children, since they fail Piaget's three-mountains, conservation, and class inclusion tasks and have difficulty separating appearance from reality.

TABLE **9.1**

Some Cognitive Attainments of the Preschool Years

APPROXIMATE AGE	COGNITIVE ATTAINMENTS
2–4 years	Shows a dramatic increase in representational activity, as reflected in the development of language, make-believe play, and understanding of spatial symbols (such as photographs, models, and simple maps)
	Takes the perspective of others in simplified, familiar situations and in everyday, face-to-face communication
	Distinguishes animate beings from inanimate objects; denies that magic can alter everyday experiences
	Categorizes objects on the basis of common function and kind of thing, not just perceptual features
	Classifies familiar objects hierarchically
4–7 years	Replaces magical beliefs about fairies, goblins, and events that violate expectations with plausible explanations
	Notices transformations, reverses thinking, and explains events causally in familiar contexts
	Shows improved ability to distinguish appearance from reality

That preschoolers have some logical understanding suggests that they attain logical operations gradually. Over time, children rely on increasingly effective mental as opposed to perceptual approaches to solving problems. For example, research shows that children who cannot use counting to compare two sets of items do not conserve number (Sophian, 1995). Once preschoolers acquire this counting strategy, they apply it to conservation-of-number tasks with only a few items. As counting improves, they extend the strategy to problems with more items. By age 6, they have formed a mental understanding that a number remains the same after a transformation. Consequently, they no longer need to use counting to verify their answer (Siegler & Robinson, 1982). This sequence indicates that children pass through several phases of understanding, although (as Piaget indicated) they do not fully grasp conservation until the early school years.

Evidence that preschool children can be trained to perform well on Piagetian problems, such as conservation and class inclusion, also supports the idea that operational thought is not absent at one point in time and present at another. It makes sense that children who possess part of a capacity will benefit from training, unlike those with no understanding at all. A variety of training methods are effective, including having children interact with more capable peers, explain an adult's correct reasoning, or measure a transformed quantity (for example, determine how many ladles of liquid are in two differently shaped glasses) (Beilin, 1978; Roazzi & Bryant, 1997; Siegler, 1995).

That logical operations develop gradually poses a serious challenge to Piaget's stage concept, which assumes sudden and abrupt change toward logical reasoning around 6 or 7 years of age. Does a preoperational stage of development really exist? Some researchers no longer think so. They believe that children work out their understanding of each type of task separately. Their thought processes are regarded as basically the same at all ages—just present to a greater or lesser extent. Recall from earlier chapters that the idea that cognitive development is continuous is the basis for an alternative approach: *information processing*, which we take up shortly.

Other experts think the stage concept is still valid, but it must be modified. For example, some theorists combine Piaget's stage approach with the information-processing emphasis on task-specific change (Case, 1992; Fischer & Farrar, 1987; Halford, 1993). They believe that Piaget's strict stage definition needs to be transformed into a less tightly knit concept, one in which a related set of competencies develops over an extended time period, depending on biological maturity and specific experiences. These investigators point to findings indicating that as long as the complexity of different types of tasks is carefully controlled, children approach them in similar, stage-consistent ways (Case et al., 1992; Marini & Case, 1989, 1994).

In sum, although Piaget's description of the preoperational child is no longer fully accepted, researchers are a long way from consensus on how to modify or replace it. Yet they continue to draw inspiration from his quest to understand how children acquire new cognitive capacities.

PIAGET AND EDUCATION

Piaget's theory has had a major impact on education, especially during early childhood. Leslie was greatly influenced by Piaget's work, which she studied in college. Three educational principles derived from his theory have become realities in her classroom:

1. *An emphasis on discovery learning.* In a Piagetian classroom, children are encouraged to discover for themselves through spontaneous interaction with the environment. Leslie has equipped her classroom with a rich variety of materials and play areas designed to promote exploration and discovery—art, puzzles, table games, dress-up clothing, building blocks, reading corner, woodworking, and more. For most of the morning, children choose freely among these activities.

2. *Sensitivity to children's readiness to learn.* A Piagetian classroom does not try to speed up development. Instead, Piaget believed that appropriate learning experiences build on children's current thinking. Leslie watches and listens to her pupils, introducing experiences that permit them to practice newly discovered schemes and that are likely to challenge their incorrect ways of viewing the world. But she does not impose new skills before children indicate they are interested and ready, since this leads to superficial acceptance of adult formulas rather than true understanding (Johnson & Hooper, 1982).

3. *Acceptance of individual differences.* Piaget's theory assumes that all children go through the same sequence of development, but at different rates. Leslie plans activities for individual children and small groups rather than just for the total class (Ginsburg & Opper, 1988). In addition, she evaluates educational progress by comparing each child to his or her own previous course of development. She is less interested in how children measure up to normative standards or to the average performance of same-age peers.

Educational applications of Piaget's theory, like his stages, have met with criticism. Perhaps the greatest challenge has to do with his insistence that young children learn only through acting on the environment. In the next section, we will see that they also use language-based routes to knowledge, which Piaget de-emphasized. In any case, Piaget's influence on education has been powerful. He gave teachers new ways to observe, understand, and enhance young children's development and offered strong theoretical justification for child-oriented approaches to classroom teaching and learning.

BRIEF REVIEW

During Piaget's preoperational stage, mental representation flourishes, as indicated by growth in language, make-believe play, and understanding of spatial symbols, such as photographs, models, and simple maps. Aside from representation, Piaget's theory emphasizes the young child's cognitive limitations. Egocentrism underlies a variety of illogical features of preoperational thought, including animism, an inability to pass conservation tasks, transductive reasoning, and lack of hierarchical classification. Recent research reveals that when tasks are simplified and made relevant to children's everyday experiences, preschoolers show the beginnings of logical reasoning. These findings indicate that operational thought is not absent during early childhood, and they challenge Piaget's notion of stage. Piaget's theory has had a powerful influence on education, promoting discovery learning, sensitivity to children's readiness to learn, and acceptance of individual differences.

ASK YOURSELF . . .

■ *Two-year-old Brooke's father decided to shave off his thick beard and mustache. When Brooke saw him, she was very upset. Using Piaget's theory, explain why Brooke was distressed by her father's new appearance.*

■ *At home, 4-year-old Will understands very well that his tricycle isn't alive and can't move by itself. Yet when Will went fishing with his family and his father asked, "Why do you think the river is flowing along?" Will responded, "Because it's alive and wants to." What explains this contradiction in Will's reasoning?*

■ *Jason returned to preschool after several days of illness due to the flu. Leslie said, "Jason, I'm so glad you're back. Why were you sick?" "I was sick because I threw up," replied Jason. What kind of reasoning is Jason demonstrating, and why did he reason this way in response to Leslie's question?*

VYGOTSKY'S SOCIOCULTURAL THEORY

*P*iaget's de-emphasis on language as an important source of cognitive development brought on yet another challenge, this time from Vygotsky's sociocultural theory. We have seen that Vygotsky stressed the social context of cognitive development. In his theory, the child and the social environment collaborate to mold cognition in culturally adaptive ways.

According to Vygotsky, rapid growth in language broadens preschoolers' ability to participate in social dialogues while engaged in culturally important tasks. Soon children start to communicate with themselves in much the same way they converse with others. This greatly enhances the complexity of their thinking and their ability to control their own behavior. Let's see how this happens.

CHILDREN'S PRIVATE SPEECH

Watch preschoolers as they go about their daily activities, and you will see that they frequently talk out loud to themselves as they play and explore the environment. For example, as Sammy worked a puzzle one day, he said, "Where's the red piece? I need the red one. Now, a blue one. No, it doesn't fit. Try it here." On another occasion, while sitting next to another child, he blurted out, "It broke," without explaining what or when.

■ **PIAGET'S VIEW.** Piaget (1923/1926) called these utterances *egocentric speech,* a term expressing his belief that they reflect the preoperational child's inability to imagine the perspectives of others. For this reason, Piaget said, young children's talk is often "talk for self" in which they run off thoughts in whatever form they happen to occur, regardless of whether they are understandable to a listener.

Piaget believed that cognitive maturity and certain social experiences—namely, disagreements with peers—eventually bring an end to egocentric speech. Through arguments with agemates, children repeatedly see that others hold viewpoints different from their own. As a result, egocentric speech gradually declines and is replaced by social speech, in which children adapt what they say to their listeners.

■ **VYGOTSKY'S VIEW.** Vygotsky (1934/1987) voiced a powerful objection to Piaget's conclusion that young children's language is egocentric and nonsocial. He reasoned that children speak to themselves for self-guidance and self-direction. Because language helps children think about their own behavior and select courses of action, Vygotsky viewed it as the foundation for all higher cognitive processes, including controlled attention, deliberate memorization and recall, categorization, planning, problem solving, and self-reflection. As children get older and tasks become easier, their self-directed speech declines and is internalized as silent, inner speech—the verbal dialogues we carry on with ourselves while thinking and acting in everyday situations.

Over the past two decades, researchers have carried out many studies to determine which of these two views—Piaget's or Vygotsky's—is correct. Almost all the findings have sided with Vygotsky. As a result, children's "speech to self" is now referred to as **private speech** instead of *egocentric speech.* Research shows that children use more of it when tasks are difficult, after they make errors, or when they are confused about how to proceed (Berk, 1992a; 1994b). Also, just as Vygotsky predicted, private speech goes underground with age, changing into whispers and silent lip movements (Berk & Landau, 1993; Bivens & Berk, 1990). Finally, children who use private speech freely during a challenging activity are more attentive and involved and show greater improvement in task performance than their less talkative agemates (Behrend, Rosengren, & Perlmutter, 1992; Berk & Spuhl, 1995).

During the preschool years, children frequently talk to themselves as they play and explore the environment. Research supports Vygotsky's theory that children use private speech to guide their behavior when faced with challenging tasks. With age, private speech is transformed into silent, inner speech, or verbal thought. *(Kopstein/Monkmeyer Press)*

private speech
Self-directed speech that children use to plan and guide their own behavior.

SOCIAL ORIGINS OF EARLY CHILDHOOD COGNITION

Where does private speech come from? Vygotsky's answer to this question highlights the social orgins of cognition, his main difference of opinion with Piaget. Recall from Chapter 6 that Vygotsky believed children's learning takes place within the *zone of proximal development*—a range of tasks too difficult for the child to do alone but possible to accomplish with the help of others. During infancy, communication in the zone of proximal development is largely nonverbal. In early childhood, verbal dialogues are added as adults and more skilled peers help children master challenging activities. Consider the way Sammy's mother helped him put a difficult puzzle together:

Sammy: "I can't get this one in." (tries to insert a piece in the wrong place)

Mother: "Which piece might go down here?" (points to the bottom of the puzzle)

Sammy: "His shoes." (looks for a piece resembling the clown's shoes but tries the wrong one)

Mother: "Well, what piece looks like this shape?" (pointing again to the bottom of the puzzle)

Sammy: "The brown one." (tries it, and it fits; then attempts another piece and looks at his mother)

Mother: "Try turning it just a little." (gestures to show him)

Sammy: "There!" (puts in several more pieces. His mother watches.)

Eventually, children take the language of these dialogues, make it part of their private speech, and use this speech to organize their independent efforts in the same way.

■ **EFFECTIVE SOCIAL INTERACTION.** To promote cognitive development, social interaction must have certain features. The first is **intersubjectivity,** the process whereby two participants who begin a task with different understandings arrive at a shared understanding (Newson & Newson, 1975). Intersubjectivity creates a common ground for communication as each partner adjusts to the perspective of the other. Adults try to promote it when they translate their own insights in ways that are within the child's grasp. As the child stretches to understand the interpretation, he is drawn into a more mature approach to the situation (Rogoff, 1998).

A second feature of social experience that fosters development is **scaffolding** (Bruner, 1983; Wood, 1989). It refers to a changing quality of social support over the course of a teaching session. Adults who offer an effective scaffold for children's independent mastery adjust the assistance they provide to fit the child's current level of performance. Sammy's mother offers help at just the right moment and in the right amount. As Sammy becomes better at the task, his mother permits him to take over her guiding role and apply it to his own activity.

■ **RESEARCH ON SOCIAL INTERACTION AND COGNITIVE DEVELOPMENT.** Is there evidence to support Vygotsky's ideas on the social origins of cognitive development? In two studies, mothers who used patient, sensitive communication in teaching their preschoolers how to solve a challenging puzzle had children who used more private speech and were more successful in doing a similar puzzle by themselves (Behrend, Rosengren, & Perlmutter, 1992; Berk & Spuhl, 1995).

Other research indicates that although young children benefit from working on tasks with same-age peers, their planning and problem solving show more improvement when their partner is either an "expert" peer (especially capable at the task) or an adult (Azmi-

intersubjectivity
The process whereby two participants who begin a task with different understandings arrive at a shared understanding.

scaffolding
A changing quality of support over the course of a teaching session in which the adult adjusts the assistance provided to fit the child's current level of performance. As competence increases, the adult permits the child to take over her guiding role and apply it to his own activity.

tia, 1988; Radziszewska & Rogoff, 1988). Also, conflict and disagreement (the feature of peer interaction emphasized by Piaget) does not seem to be as important in fostering cognitive development as the extent to which children achieve intersubjectivity—by resolving differences of opinion, sharing responsibilities, and engaging in cooperative dialogues (Cannella, 1993; Forman & McPhail, 1993; Tudge, 1992).

VYGOTSKY AND EDUCATION

Today, educators are eager to use Vygotsky's ideas. Piagetian and Vygotskian classrooms clearly have features in common, such as opportunities for active participation and acceptance of individual differences in cognitive development. Yet a Vygotskian classroom goes beyond independent discovery learning. It promotes *assisted discovery*. Teachers guide children's learning with explanations, demonstrations, and verbal prompts, carefully tailoring their efforts to each child's zone of proximal development. Assisted discovery is helped along by *peer collaboration*. Teachers arrange *cooperative learning* experiences, grouping together classmates with varying abilities who teach and help one another (Forman, Minick, & Stone, 1993).

Vygotsky (1935/1978) saw make-believe play as the ideal social context for fostering cognitive development in early childhood. In make-believe, he explained, children learn to follow internal ideas and social rules rather than their immediate impulses. For example, a child pretending to go to sleep follows the rules of bedtime behavior. Another child imagining himself to be a father and a doll to be a child conforms to the rules of parental behavior. Yet a third child playing astronaut observes the rules of shuttle launch and space walk.

According to Vygotsky, make-believe play is a unique, broadly influential zone of proximal development in which children try out a wide variety of challenging activities and acquire many new competencies (Smolucha & Smolucha, 1998). Much evidence fits with this conclusion. Preschoolers' thinking about the pretend world seems to be more flexible and advanced than their thinking about the real world as they reason imaginatively about characters, events, and places (Lillard, 1993). Turn back to page 326 to review findings that make-believe play enhances a diverse array of cognitive and social skills.

EVALUATION OF VYGOTSKY'S THEORY

Some of Vygotsky's ideas, like Piaget's, have been challenged. As Barbara Rogoff (1990, 1998) notes, verbal communication may not be the only means, or even the most important means, through which children learn in some cultures. For example, the young child learning to sail a canoe in Micronesia or weave a garment on a foot loom in Guatemala may gain more from direct observation and practice accompanied by nonverbal communication (a gaze, a change in posture, or a sensitive touch) than from verbal guidance.

In a recent study, Rogoff and her collaborators (1993) asked caregivers to help young children with challenging tasks (getting dressed and operating novel toys) in four communities—two middle-SES urban areas, one in Turkey and one in the United States; a Mayan town in Guatemala; and a tribal village in India. In the middle-SES communities, parents assumed much responsibility for getting children involved in the tasks. They often verbally instructed, conversed, and interacted playfully with the child. Their communication resembled the teaching that takes place in school, where their children will spend years preparing for adult life. In contrast, in the Mayan and Indian communities, adults expected children to take greater responsibility for acquiring new skills through keen observation. As the child showed interest, caregivers often responded nonverbally, demonstrating with gestures. This style of interaction appeared well suited to conditions in which young children learn by participating in daily activities with adults.

In cultures everywhere, caregivers guide children's mastery of the practices of their community. Yet the type of assistance offered varies greatly, depending on the tasks that must be mastered to become a contributing member of society. Thus, we are reminded once again that children learn in a great many ways, and as yet, no single theory provides a complete account of cognitive development.

ASK YOURSELF . . .

■ *Tanisha sees her 5-year-old son, Toby, talking out loud to himself while he plays. She wonders whether she should discourage this behavior. Use Vygotsky's theory to explain why Toby talks to himself. How would you advise Tanisha?*

BRIEF REVIEW

Piaget and Vygotsky disagreed on the meaning of preschoolers' self-directed speech. Piaget regarded these utterances as egocentric and nonsocial. In contrast, Vygotsky viewed private speech as communication with the self for self-guidance and self-direction. According to Vygotsky, language provides the foundation for all higher cognitive processes. As adults and more skilled peers offer verbal guidance in the zone of proximal development, children incorporate these dialogues into their private speech and use them to guide their own behavior. Research supports Vygotsky's ideas. A Vygotskian early childhood classroom emphasizes teacher- and peer-assisted discovery and make-believe play. Although Vygotsky stressed the importance of verbal communication in cognitive development, it may not be the only means, or even the most important means, through which children learn in some cultures.

INFORMATION PROCESSING

Return for a moment to the model of information processing discussed on page 225 of Chapter 6. Recall that information processing focuses on *mental strategies* that children use to operate on stimuli flowing into their mental systems, increasing the chances that information will be retained and adapted to the situation at hand. During early childhood, advances in representation and children's ability to guide their own behavior lead to more efficient and flexible ways of manipulating information and solving problems. In the following sections, we look at attention and memory, children's growing awareness of their own mental life, and literacy and mathematical skills.

ATTENTION

Recall from Chapter 6 that sustained attention improves in toddlerhood, a trend that continues over the preschool years, and fortunately so, since children will rely on this capacity greatly once they enter school. In one study, 1- to 4-year-olds were seated at a table with toys. Their capacity to engage in complex play supported focused engagement with objects. Children became increasingly attentive as the session progressed, and concentrated involvement rose steadily with age (Ruff & Lawson, 1990). Nevertheless, parents and teachers are quick to notice that compared to school-age children, preschoolers spend relatively short times involved in tasks and are easily distracted.

During early childhood, attention also becomes more *planful*. By age 4, children search for a lost object in a play yard systematically and exhaustively, looking only in locations between where they last saw the object and where they discovered it missing (Wellman, Somerville, & Haake, 1979). Still, planful attention has a long way to go. When given detailed pictures or written materials, preschoolers fail to search thoroughly. And on complex tasks with many steps, they rarely make decisions about what to do first and what to do next in an orderly fashion. Even when young children do plan, they often fail to implement important steps (Prevost, Bronson, & Casey, 1995; Scholnick, 1995). Clearly planning places heavy demands on the information-processing system. As we will see in Chapter 12, it improves greatly during middle childhood.

MEMORY

Unlike infants and toddlers, preschoolers have the language skills to describe what they remember, and they can follow directions on simple memory tasks. As a result, memory development becomes easier to study in early childhood.

■ **RECOGNITION AND RECALL.** Try showing a young child a set of 10 pictures or toys. Then mix them up with some unfamiliar items and ask the child to point to the ones in the original set. You will find that preschoolers' *recognition* memory (ability to tell whether a stimulus is the same as or similar to one they have seen before) is remarkably good. It becomes even more accurate by the end of early childhood. In fact, 4- and 5-year-olds perform nearly perfectly.

Now, give the child a more demanding task. While keeping the items out of view, ask the child to name the ones she saw. This requires *recall*—that the child generate a mental image of an absent stimulus. One of the most obvious features of young children's memories is that their recall is much poorer than their recognition. At age 2, they can recall no more than one or two of the items, at age 4 only about three or four (Perlmutter, 1984).

Of course, recognition is much easier than recall for adults as well, but in comparison to adults, children's recall is quite deficient. The reason is that young children are less effective at using **memory strategies,** deliberate mental activities that improve our chances of remembering. For example, when you want to retain information, you might *rehearse,* or repeat the items over and over again. Or you might *organize* it, intentionally grouping together items that are alike so that you can easily retrieve them by thinking of their similar characteristics.

Preschoolers do show the beginnings of memory strategies. For example, when circumstances permit, they arrange items in space to aid their memories. In a study of 2- to 5-year-olds, an adult placed either an M&M or a wooden peg in each of 12 identical containers and handed them one by one to the child, who was asked to remember where the candy was hidden. By age 4, children put the candy containers in one place on the table and the peg containers in another, a strategy that almost always led to perfect recall (DeLoache & Todd, 1988). But preschoolers do not yet rehearse or organize items into *categories* (for example, all the vehicles together, all the animals together) when asked to recall a set of items. Even when trained to do so, their memory performance may not improve, and they rarely apply these strategies in new situations (Gathercole, Adams, & Hitch, 1994; Lange & Pierce, 1992).

Why do young children use memory strategies so rarely? Perhaps they see little need to remember information simply for its own sake. In support of this explanation, preschoolers use memory strategies most effectively when recall leads to a desired goal—for example, an M&M to eat, as in the research just described (Wellman, 1988a). Yet another reason that memory strategies are rarely used in early childhood and (when they are) usually do not lead to memory gains is that they tax young children's limited working memories (Bjorklund & Coyle, 1995). Preschoolers have difficulty holding on to the to-be-learned information and applying a strategy at the same time.

■ **MEMORY FOR EVERYDAY EXPERIENCES.** Think about the difference in your recall of the listlike information discussed in the previous section and your memory for everyday experiences, or what researchers call **episodic memory.** In remembering lists, you recall isolated pieces and bits of information, and you try to reproduce them exactly as you originally learned them. In remembering everyday experiences, you recall complex,

Children's memory for everyday experiences improves greatly during early childhood. This girl cannot remember the details of what she did on a particular day when she washed her hands at preschool. Instead, she recalls the event in script form—in terms of what typically occurs when you get ready for lunch. Her account will become more elaborate with age. Scripts help us predict what will happen on similar occasions in the future. *(Will Faller)*

memory strategies
Deliberate mental activities that improve the likelihood of remembering.

episodic memory
Memory for everyday experiences

meaningful events. Episodic memory involves selecting experiences, relating them to one another, and interpreting them on the basis of previous knowledge. Do children remember everyday experiences in these ways? The answer is clearly yes.

Memory for Familiar Events. Like adults, preschoolers remember familiar events—what you do when you get up in the morning, go to day care, or get ready for bed—in terms of **scripts,** general descriptions of what occurs and when it occurs in a particular situation. For very young children, scripts begin as a general structure of main acts. For example, when asked to tell what happens when you go to a restaurant, a 3-year-old might say, "You go in, get the food, eat, and then pay." Although children's first scripts contain only a few acts, as long as events in a situation take place in logical order, they are almost always recalled in correct sequence (Fivush, Kuebli, & Clubb, 1992). This is true even for 1- and 2-year-olds, who cannot yet verbally describe events but who act them out with toys (Bauer & Dow, 1994; Bauer & Mandler, 1992). With age, children's scripts become more elaborate, as in the following restaurant account given by a 5-year-old child: "You go in. You can sit in the booths or at a table. Then you tell the waitress what you want. You eat. If you want dessert, you can have some. Then you pay and go home" (Farrar & Goodman, 1992; Hudson, Fivush, & Kuebli, 1992).

Once formed, a script can be used to predict what will happen on similar occasions in the future. In this way, scripts are a basic means through which children organize and interpret repeated events. For example, children rely on scripts when listening to and telling stories. They recall more events from stories that are based on familiar event sequences than on unfamiliar ones (Hudson & Nelson, 1983). They also use script structures for the stories they act out in play. Listen carefully to preschoolers' make-believe. You will hear everyday scripts reflected in their dialogues as they pretend to put the baby to bed, go on a trip, or play school.

Memory for One-Time Events. In Chapter 6, we considered a second type of episodic memory—*autobiographical memory,* or representations of one-time events that are particularly meaningful in terms of the life story each of us creates about ourselves. Recall that autobiographical memory emerges as young children's sense of self becomes more firmly established and as they talk with adults about the past (see page 227). As 3- to 6-year-olds' cognitive and conversational skills improve, their descriptions of special, one-time events become better organized, detailed, and related to the larger context of their lives. As a result, children enter into the history of their family and community (Fivush, 1995; Fivush, Haden, & Adam, 1995).

Adults can enhance preschoolers' autobiographical memory by the way they talk about everyday events with children. Leslie often gathered the children on the rug to discuss special experiences—a field trip, a child's birthday celebration, the meaning of a national holiday, and the day Priti's parents became U.S. citizens. Research shows that mothers who converse about the past often, ask many questions, and provide a great deal of elaborative information have children who recount past events and stories in a more organized fashion and in greater detail (Fivush, 1991; Hudson, 1990). In line with Vygotsky's ideas, these findings indicate that early social experiences aid in the development of memory skills.

THE YOUNG CHILD'S THEORY OF MIND

As their representation of the world and ability to remember and solve problems improve, children start to reflect on their own thought processes. They begin to construct a *theory of mind,* or set of ideas about mental activities. This understanding often is called **metacognition.** The prefix "meta-," meaning beyond or higher, is applied to the term because the central meaning of metacognition is "thinking about thought."

As adults, we have a complex appreciation of our inner mental worlds. For example, you can tell the difference between believing, knowing, remembering, guessing, forget-

scripts
General descriptions of what occurs and when it occurs in a particular situation. A basic means through which children organize and interpret familiar experiences.

metacognition
Thinking about thought; awareness of mental activities.

ting, and imagining, and you are aware of a great many factors that influence these cognitive activities. We rely on these understandings to interpret our own and others' behavior as well as to improve our performance on various tasks. How early are preschoolers aware of their mental lives, and how complete and accurate is their knowledge?

■ **PRESCHOOLERS' UNDERSTANDING OF MENTAL LIFE.** Listen closely to the conversations of young children, and you will find evidence that awareness of mental activity emerges remarkably early. Such words as "think," "remember," and "pretend" are among the first verbs in children's vocabularies. After age 2½, they use them appropriately to refer to internal states (Wellman, 1990). For example, one day, while looking for crayons and paper, Sammy said, "I *thought* they were in the drawer, 'cept they weren't."

What is the young child's view of mental life like, and how does it change with age? Despite a vocabulary of mentalistic terms, 2-year-olds have only a beginning grasp of the distinction between mental life and behavior. They think that people always behave in ways consistent with their desires and do not understand that beliefs affect their actions (Wellman & Woolley, 1990).

Between ages 3 and 4, children figure out that both *beliefs* and *desires* determine behavior. In one instance, Sammy put a blanket over his head and, pretending to be a ghost, stumbled into Dwayne, who fell and began to cry. "I couldn't see him! The blanket was over my face," Sammy pleaded, trying to alter his mother's belief about his motive and, thereby, ward off any desire on her part to punish him. From early to middle childhood, efforts to alter others' beliefs increase, suggesting that children's grasp of the power of belief to influence action becomes more firmly established.

A dramatic illustration of preschoolers' developing theory of mind comes from games in which they are asked to mislead an adult. By age 4, children realize that people can hold *false beliefs* that combine with desire to determine behavior (Perner, 1991). In one study, 2½- to 4-year-olds were asked to hide the driver of a toy truck underneath one of five cups in a sandbox so an adult, who was out of the room, could not find it (see Figure 9.4). An experimenter showed the child how the truck left telltale tracks in the sand as a sign of where it had been. Most 2- and 3-year-olds needed explicit prompts to hide the evidence—smoothing over the tracks and returning the truck to its starting place. In contrast, 4-year-olds thought of doing these things on their own. They were also more likely

FIGURE 9.4

Game used to assess young children's understanding of false belief. Children between age 2½ and 4 were asked to hide the driver of a toy truck underneath one of five cups in a sandbox so an adult, who was out of the room, could not find it. The experimenter pointed out that the truck leaves telltale tracks in the sand as a sign of where it has been. Most 2- and 3-year-olds needed explicit prompts to hide the evidence—smoothing over the tracks and returning the truck to its starting place. In contrast, 4-year-olds thought of doing these things on their own. They were also more likely to trick the adult by laying false tracks or giving incorrect information about where the driver was hidden. *(Adapted from Sodian et al., 1991.)*

to trick the adult by laying false tracks or giving incorrect information about where the driver was hidden (Sodian et al., 1991). Other research confirms that children's understanding of false belief strengthens over the preschool years, becoming more secure between ages 4 and 6 (Flavell & Miller, 1998).

■ **WHERE DOES A THEORY OF MIND ORIGINATE?** How do children manage to develop a theory of mind at such a young age? Various speculations and findings suggest that social experience is profoundly important:

■ *Early forms of communication.* Perhaps an understanding of others' beliefs originates in certain early forms of communication, such as joint attention and social referencing, which require a beginning ability to represent another's mental state (Sigman & Kasari, 1995).

■ *Imitation.* Imitation may also contribute to an early grasp of mental life. Infants' primitive plan to copy an action, located inside the body, has much of the character of mental states. At the same time, imitation teaches infants that other people are like themselves. Perhaps this prompts them to conclude that others are also mental beings (Meltzoff & Gopnik, 1993).

■ *Make-believe play.* Make-believe play provides another possible foundation for thinking about the mind. As children play at various roles and use one object to represent another, they notice that the mind can change what objects mean. These experiences may trigger an awareness that belief influences behavior. In support of this idea, preschoolers who engage in extensive fantasy play are more advanced in their understanding of false belief and other aspects of the mind (Astington & Jenkins, 1995; Taylor & Carlson, 1997).

Since their language lacks mental state terms, these Quechua children of the Peruvian Highlands hear adults refer to "think" and "believe" indirectly. For example, a Quechua speaker typically uses a phrase that translates, "What would he say?" for "What would he think?" Without a mental-state vocabulary, Quechua children are delayed in development of a theory of mind. *(Vinden)*

■ *Language.* Understanding the mind requires the ability to reflect on thoughts, which is made possible by language. A grasp of false belief is related to language ability equivalent to that of an average 4-year-old or higher (Jenkins & Astington, 1996).

In addition, a mental-state vocabulary is necessary. Among the Quechua of the Peruvian highlands, adults refer to mental states such as "think" and "believe" indirectly, since their language lacks mental state terms. Quechua children have difficulty with false belief tasks for years after children in industrialized nations have mastered them (Vinden, 1996).

■ *Social interaction.* Preschoolers with older siblings are advanced in performance on false-belief tasks. And those with several older siblings do better than those with only one (Ruffman et al., 1998). Having older siblings may allow for more interactions that highlight the influence of beliefs on behavior—through teasing, trickery, make-believe play, and discussing feelings.

Besides siblings, interacting with more mature members of society enhances mental understanding. In a study of Greek preschoolers with large networks of extended family and neighbors, daily contact with many adults and older children predicted mastery of false belief (Lewis et al., 1996). These encounters probably provide young children with extra opportunities to observe different points of view and talk about inner states.

Many researchers believe that to profit from the social experiences just described, children must be biologically prepared to develop a theory of mind. Consistent with this assumption, children with *infantile autism,* who are indifferent to other people and display poor knowledge of social rules, seem to be impaired

BIOLOGY & ENVIRONMENT

"MINDBLINDNESS" AND INFANTILE AUTISM

Sidney stood at the water table in Leslie's classroom, repeatedly filling a plastic cup and dumping out its contents. Dip–splash, dip–splash, dip–splash he went, until Leslie came over and redirected his actions. Without looking at Leslie's face, Sidney moved to a new repetitive pursuit: pouring water from one cup into another and back again. As other children entered the play space and conversed, Sidney hardly noticed. He rarely spoke, and when he did, he usually used words to get things he wanted, not to exchange ideas with other people.

Sidney has *infantile autism*, the most severe behavior disorder of childhood. The term autism means "absorbed in the self," an apt description of Sidney. Like other children with the disorder, Sidney is impaired in emotional and gestural (nonverbal) behaviors required for successful social interaction. In addition, his language is delayed and stereotyped; some autistic children do not speak at all. Sidney's interests, which focus on the physical world, are narrow and overly intense. For example, one day he sat for more than an hour making a toy ferris wheel go round and round. When Leslie showed the children a movie about wild animals, Sidney watched the projector, not the screen.

Austism is highly heritable; its concordance is much greater for identical than fraternal twins. Researchers agree that the disorder stems from abnormal brain functioning, although psychophysiological research has not yet pinpointed a specific brain region (Bailey et al., 1995).

A growing body of evidence suggests that one psychological factor involved in autism is a severely deficient or absent theory of mind. Long after they reach the intellectual level of an average 4-year-old, autistic children have great difficulty with false-belief tasks. Most cannot attribute mental states to others or themselves. Such words as "think," "believe," "know," and "pretend" are rarely part of their vocabularies (Happé, 1995; Tager-Flusberg & Sullivan, 1994; Yirmiya, Solomonica-Levi, & Shulman, 1996).

As early as the second year, autistic children show deficits in capacities believed to contribute to an understanding of mentality. For example, they less often establish joint attention, engage in social referencing, or imitate an adult's novel behaviors than do other children (Charman et al., 1997). Furthermore, they are relatively insensitive to a speaker's gaze as a cue to what he or she is talking about. Instead, autistic children often assume that an adult's verbal label refers to what they themselves are attending to—a possible reason that they use many nonsensical expressions (Baron-Cohen, Baldwin, & Crowson, 1997). Finally, autistic children engage in much less make-believe play than do age- and mental-ability matched comparison groups—both normal children and children with other developmental problems (Hughes, 1998).

Do these findings indicate that autism is due to a specific cognitive impairment that leaves the child "mindblind" and therefore unable to engage in human sociability? Some researchers think so (Baron-Cohen, 1993). But others disagree. A second speculation is that infantile autism results from a deficit in comprehending emotion, which is essential for understanding others. In support of this view, autistic children have trouble interpreting emotional stimuli, such as facial expressions (Hobson, 1993).

Yet a third conjecture is that autism is due to a general memory deficit, which makes it hard to retain the parts of complex tasks (Bennetto, Pennington, & Rogers, 1996). Perhaps this explains autistic children's preoccupation with simple, repetitive acts. It may also account for their difficulty with problems, such as conservation, that require them to integrate several contexts at once (before, during, and after the transformation of a substance) (Yirmiya & Shulman, 1996). A memory deficit would also interfere with understanding the social world, since social interaction takes place quickly and requires integration of information from various sources.

At present, it is not clear which of these hypotheses is correct. Perhaps several biologically based deficits underlie the tragic social isolation of children like Sidney.

in mental understanding and in the early capacities believed to underlie it. See the Biology and Environment box above to find out more about the biological basis of reasoning about the mind.

■ **LIMITATIONS OF THE YOUNG CHILD'S THEORY OF MIND.** Although surprisingly advanced, preschoolers' awareness of mental activities is far from complete. For example, without strong situational cues (a challenging task and a thoughtful expression),

3- and 4-year-olds deny that a person is thinking. They indicate that the minds of people waiting, looking at pictures, listening to stories, or reading books are "empty of thoughts and ideas." They do not realize that people are constantly talking to themselves and engaged in thought (Flavell, Green, & Flavell, 1993, 1995; Flavell et al., 1997).

Furthermore, preschoolers pay little attention to the *process* of thinking but, instead, focus on outcomes of thought. For example, 3-year-olds use the words "know" to refer to acting successfully (finding a hidden toy) and "forget" to refer to acting unsuccessfully (not finding the toy), even when a person is guessing the toy's location (Lyon & Flavell, 1994; Perner, 1991). And children younger than age 6 have difficulty recalling what they were thinking just moments before. In one study, right after being taught a new fact, 4- and 5-year-olds claimed they had known it for a long time (Taylor, Esbensen, & Bennett, 1994). Finally, preschoolers believe that all events must be directly observed to be known. They do not understand that *mental inferences* can be a source of knowledge (Carpendale & Chandler, 1996).

How, then, should we describe the difference between the young child's theory of mind and that of the older child? Preschoolers know that people have an internal mental life. But they seem to view the mind as a passive container of information. They believe that physical experience determines mental experience. Consequently, they greatly underestimate the amount of mental activity that goes on in people and are poor at inferring what people know or are thinking about. In view of their limited awareness of the process of thinking, it is not surprising that preschoolers rarely plan or use memory strategies.

In contrast, older children view the mind as an active, constructive agent that selects and transforms information and affects how the world is perceived (Pillow, 1988; Wellman, 1990). We will consider this change further in Chapter 12 when we take up metacognition in middle childhood.

EARLY LITERACY AND MATHEMATICAL DEVELOPMENT

Researchers have begun to study how children's information-processing capacities affect the development of basic reading, writing, and mathematical skills that prepare them for school. The study of how preschoolers start to master these complex activities provides us with additional information on their cognitive strengths and limitations. In addition, we can use this knowledge to find ways to foster early literacy and mathematical development.

Preschoolers often congregate in the book corner in this literacy-rich early childhood classroom. The more informal literacy-related experiences young children have, the better prepared they will be for the complex tasks involved in becoming skilled readers and writers after they enter elementary school. *(Will Faller)*

■ **EARLY CHILDHOOD LITERACY.** One week, Leslie's pupils brought empty food boxes from home to place on special shelves in the classroom. Soon a make-believe grocery store opened. Children labeled items with prices, made shopping lists, and wrote checks at the cash register. A sign at the entrance announced the daily specials: "APLS BNS 5¢" ("apples bananas 5¢").

As their grocery store play reveals, preschoolers understand a great deal about written language long before they learn to read and write in conventional ways. This is not surprising when we consider that children in industrialized nations live in a world filled with written symbols. Each day, they observe and participate in activities involving storybooks, calendars, greeting cards, lists, and signs, to name just a few. As part of these experiences, children try to figure out how written symbols convey meaningful information. Their active efforts to construct literacy knowledge through informal experiences are called **emergent literacy.**

Young preschoolers search for units of written language as they "read" memorized versions of stories and recognize familiar signs, such as "ON" and "OFF" on light switches and "PIZZA" at their favorite fast food counter. But their early ideas about how written language is related to meaning are quite different from our own. For example, many

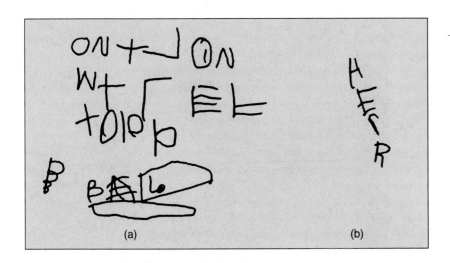

FIGURE **9.5**

A story (a) and a grocery list (b) written by a 4-year-old child. This child's writing has many features of real print. It also reveals an awareness of different kinds of written expression. *(From L. M. McGee & D. J. Richgels, 1996,* Literacy's Beginnings *(2nd ed.),* Boston: Allyn and Bacon, p. 81. Reprinted by permission.)*

preschoolers think that a single letter stands for a whole word or that each letter in a person's signature represents a separate name. Often they believe that letters (just like pictures) look like the meanings they represent. One child explained that the word *deer* begins with the letter *O* because it is shaped like a deer; then he demonstrated by drawing an *O* and adding a set of antlers to it (Dyson, 1984; Sulzby, 1985).

Gradually children revise these ideas as their perceptual and cognitive capacities improve, as they encounter writing in many different contexts, and as adults help them with various aspects of written communication. Soon preschoolers become aware of some general characteristics of written language. As a result, they create symbols in their own writing that have many features of real print. Figure 9.5 shows a story and grocery list written by a 4-year-old. This child understands that stories are written from left to right, that print appears in rows, that letters have certain features, and that stories look different from shopping lists (McGee & Richgels, 1996).

By the end of early childhood, children make other discoveries. In their own writing, they combine letters. However, their first ideas about how letters contribute to larger units usually are incorrect. Children often think that each letter represents a syllable. For example, a child named Santiago wrote his name with three letters ("SIO"), which he read, "San-tia-go." At the same time, he had clearly taken an important step in recognizing that letters are parts of words. Soon children realize that letters and sounds are linked in systematic ways. You can see this in the invented spellings that are typical between ages 5 and 7. At first, children rely heavily on the names of letters: "ADE LAFWTS KRMD NTU A LAVATR" ("eighty elephants crammed into a[n] elevator"). Over time, they will switch to conventional spelling (Gentry, 1981; McGee & Richgels, 1996).

Literacy development builds on a broad foundation of spoken language and knowledge about the world. The more literacy-related experiences young children have in their everyday lives, the better prepared they are to tackle the complex tasks involved in becoming skilled readers and writers. Adults can provide literacy-rich physical environments and encourage literacy-related play (Roskos & Neuman, 1998; Snow, 1993). Storybook reading with caregivers, especially, is related to preschoolers' language and reading readiness scores, which predict success in school (see Chapter 6, page 248). In early childhood, parents and teachers need not be overly concerned about the correctness of children's interpretations of written language. Instead, they can help most by accepting preschoolers' ideas and supporting their active efforts to revise and extend their knowledge.

■ **YOUNG CHILDREN'S MATHEMATICAL REASONING.** Mathematical reasoning, like literacy, builds on informal acquired knowledge. Habituation–dishabituation research shows that young infants are sensitive to the difference in the size of small sets—two or three items (Starkey, Spelke, & Gelman, 1990). Around 16 months, toddlers display a

emergent literacy
Young children's active efforts to construct literacy knowledge through informal experiences.

FIGURE 9.6

Sequence of body parts used for counting by the Oksapmin of Papua New Guinea. In the Oksapmin language, there are no terms for numbers aside from the body part names themselves (for example, "nose" represents "fourteen"). Children begin to use this system in the preschool years. Instead of counting on fingers, they can often be seen pointing to body parts. With age, they adapt the technique to handle more complex computation. *(From G. B. Saxe, 1985, "Effects of schooling on arithmetical understanding: Studies with Oksapmin children in Papua New Guinea,"* Journal of Educational Psychology, 77, p. 505. Copyright © 1985 by the American Psychological Association. Reprinted by permission of the publisher and author.)

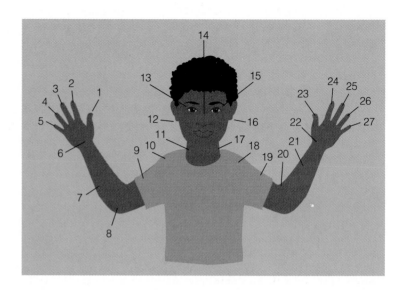

beginning grasp of **ordinality,** or order relationships between quantities, such as three is more than two and two is more than one (Strauss & Curtis, 1984). This remarkably early numerical sensitivity serves as the basis for more complex understandings.

In the early preschool period, children start to attach verbal labels (such as *lots, little, big,* and *small)* to different amounts and sizes. And between ages 2 and 3, many begin to count. At first, counting is little more than a memorized routine. Often numbers are recited in an unbroken string like this: "Onetwothreefourfivesix!" Or children repeat a few number words while vaguely pointing toward objects (Fuson, 1988).

Very soon, however, counting strategies become more precise. Most 3- to 4-year-olds have established an accurate one-to-one correspondence between a short sequence of number words and the items they represent (Gallistel & Gelman, 1992; Geary, 1994). Three-year-olds may not yet have memorized the appropriate number labels. For example, one child counted a sequence of three items by saying, "1, 6, 10." But her general method of counting was correct—she used only as many verbal tags as there were items to count.

Sometime between ages 4 and 5, children grasp the vital principle of **cardinality.** They understand that the last number in a counting sequence indicates the quantity of items in the set (Bermejo, 1996). At the beginning of this chapter, Sammy showed an appreciation of cardinality when he counted out milk cartons for his snack group. Mastery of cardinality increases the efficiency of children's counting. By the late preschool years, they no longer need to start counting with the number "one." Instead, knowing that there are six items in one pile and some additional ones in another, they begin with the number "six" and *count on* to determine the total quantity. Eventually, they generalize this strategy and *count down* to find out how many items remain after some are taken away. Once they master these procedures, children start to manipulate numbers without requiring that countable objects be physically present (Fuson, 1988). At this point counting on fingers becomes an intermediate step on the way to automatically doing simple addition and subtraction.

Cross-cultural research suggests that the basic arithmetic knowledge just described emerges universally around the world, although ways of representing numbers vary. For example, among the Oksapmin, an agricultural society of Papua New Guinea, counting is mapped onto 27 body parts, which serve as number terms. To count as the Oksapmin do, follow the directions in Figure 9.6. Using this system, Oksapmin children keep track of quantities, measure, and play number games. Instead of counting on fingers, they point to body parts as they expand their calculation skills (Saxe, 1985).

Depending on the extent to which informal counting experiences are available in their everyday lives, children may acquire early number understandings at different rates. In

ordinality
A principle specifying order (more-than and less-than) relationships between quantities.

cardinality
A principle stating that the last number in a counting sequence indicates the quantity of items in the set.

homes and preschools where adults provide many occasions for counting, children construct these basic concepts sooner (Geary, 1994). Then they are solidly available as supports for the wide variety of mathematical skills they will be taught once they enter

BRIEF REVIEW

With age, preschoolers sustain attention for longer periods of time and search planfully for missing objects in familiar environments. By the end of early childhood, recognition memory is highly accurate. In contrast, recall improves slowly because preschoolers rarely use memory strategies. Like adults, young children remember everyday experiences in terms of scripts, which become more elaborate with age. Autobiographical memory emerges and becomes better organized and detailed. Preschoolers begin to construct a theory of mind. By age 4, it includes an understanding of false belief. Young children develop a basic understanding of written symbols and mathematical concepts through informal experiences.

INDIVIDUAL DIFFERENCES IN MENTAL DEVELOPMENT

Preschoolers differ markedly in intellectual progress, just as they vary in physical growth and motor skills. Psychologists and educators typically measure how well preschoolers are developing cognitively by giving them intelligence tests. Scores are computed in the same way as they are for infants and toddlers (return to Chapter 6, page 232, to review). But instead of emphasizing perceptual and motor responses, tests for preschoolers sample a wide range of verbal and nonverbal cognitive abilities.

Child development specialists are interested in young children's mental test scores because by age 5 to 6, they become good predictors of later intelligence and academic achievement (Hayslip, 1994). In addition, understanding the link between early childhood experiences and intelligence test performance gives us ways to intervene in children's lives to support their cognitive growth.

EARLY CHILDHOOD INTELLIGENCE TESTS

Five-year-old Hallie, whom we introduced in Chapter 8, sat in a small, strange testing room while Sarah, an adult he met only a short while ago, gave him an intelligence test. Some of the questions Sarah asked were *verbal*. For example, she held out a picture of a shovel and said, "Tell me what this shows?"—an item measuring vocabulary. Then she tested his memory by asking him to repeat sentences and lists of numbers back to her. Hallie's quantitative knowledge was probed by seeing if he could count and solve simple addition and subtraction problems. Other tasks Sarah gave were *nonverbal* and largely assessed spatial reasoning. Hallie copied designs with special blocks, figured out the pattern in a series of shapes, and indicated what a piece of paper folded and cut would look like when unfolded (Thorndike, Hagen, & Sattler, 1986).

Before Sarah began the test, she took special steps to ensure that Hallie's responses would accurately reflect his knowledge. Sarah was aware that Hallie came from an economically disadvantaged family. When low-SES and ethnic minority preschoolers are faced with an unfamiliar adult who bombards them with questions, they sometimes become anxious and afraid. Also, such children may not define the testing situation in achievement terms. Often they look for attention and approval from the examiner rather

ASK YOURSELF . . .

■ *Piaget believed that preschoolers' egocentrism prevents them from reflecting on their own mental activities. What evidence in the preceding sections contradicts this assumption?*

■ *Lena notices that her 4-year-old son Gregor can recognize his name in print and count to twenty. She wonders why Gregor's preschool teacher permits him to spend so much time playing instead of teaching him academic skills. Gregor's teacher responds, "I am teaching him academics— through play." Explain why play is the best way to foster academic development in early childhood.*

than focusing on the test questions themselves. As a result, they may settle for lower levels of performance than their abilities allow. Sarah spent time playing with Hallie before she began testing. In addition, she praised and encouraged him while the test was in progress. When testing conditions like these are used, low-SES preschoolers improve in performance (Zigler & Finn-Stevenson, 1992).

Note that the questions Sarah asked Hallie tap knowledge and skills that not all children have had equal opportunity to learn. The issue of *cultural bias* in intelligence testing is a hotly debated topic that we will take up in Chapter 12. For now, keep in mind that intelligence tests do not sample the full range of human abilities, and performance is affected by cultural and situational factors. Nevertheless, test scores remain important because they predict school achievement, and this, in turn, is strongly related to vocational success in complex industrialized societies. Let's see how the environments in which children spend their days—home, preschool, and day care—affect mental test performance in early childhood.

HOME ENVIRONMENT AND MENTAL DEVELOPMENT

A special version of the *Home Observation for Measurement of the Environment (HOME)*, covered in Chapter 6, assesses aspects of 3- to 6-year-olds' home lives that support intellectual growth (see the Caregiving Concerns table below). In agreement with the theories of both Piaget and Vygotsky, physical surroundings and child-rearing practices play important roles. Preschoolers who develop well intellectually have homes rich in toys and books. Their parents are warm and affectionate, stimulate language and academic knowledge, and arrange outings to places where there are interesting things to see and do. They also make reasonable demands for socially mature behavior—for example, that the child perform simple chores and behave courteously toward others. And when conflicts arise, these parents use reason to resolve them instead of physical force and punishment (Bradley & Caldwell, 1979, 1982).

As we saw in Chapter 2, these characteristics are less likely to be found in poverty-stricken families where parents lead highly stressful lives (Garrett, Ng'andu, & Ferron, 1994). When low-income parents manage, despite daily pressures, to obtain high HOME scores, their youngsters do substantially better on intelligence and achievement tests (Bradley & Caldwell, 1979, 1981). These findings, as well as others we will discuss in Chapter 12, suggest that the home plays a major role in the generally poorer intellectual performance of low-SES children in comparison to their higher-SES peers.

CAREGIVING CONCERNS

Home Observation for the Measurement of the Environment (HOME): Early Childhood Subscales

SUBSCALE	SAMPLE ITEM
Stimulation through toys, games, and reading material	Home includes toys to learn colors, sizes, and shapes.
Language stimulation	Parent teaches child about animals through books, games, and puzzles.
Organization of the physical environment	All visible rooms are reasonably clean and minimally cluttered.
Pride, affection, and warmth	Parent spontaneously praises child's qualities or behavior twice during observer's visit.
Stimulation of academic behavior	Child is encouraged to learn colors.
Modeling and encouragement of social maturity	Parent introduces interviewer to child.
Variety in daily stimulation	Family member takes child on one outing at least every other week (picnic, shopping).
Avoidance of physical punishment	Parent neither slaps nor spanks child during observer's visit.

Source: Bradley & Caldwell, 1979.

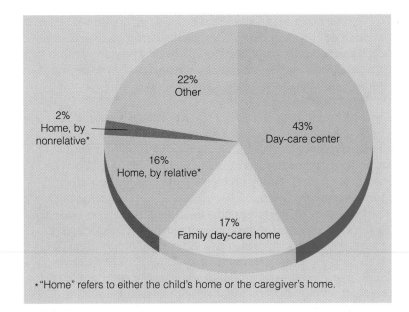

FIGURE 9.7

Who's minding America's preschoolers? The chart refers to settings in which 3- and 4-year-olds spend most time while their parents are at work. The "other" category consists mostly of children cared for by their mothers during working hours, while the mother works at home or in another workplace. Over one-fourth of 3- and 4-year-olds actually experience more than one type of child care, a fact not reflected in the chart. *(Adapted from B. Willer, S. L. Hofferth, E. E. Kisker, P. Divine-Hawkins, E. Farquhar, & F. B. Glantz, 1991,* The Demand and Supply of Child Care in 1990: Joint Findings from the National Child Care Survey 1990 and A Profile of Child Care Settings, *Washington, DC: National Association for the Education of Young Children. Reprinted by permission.)*

PRESCHOOL AND DAY CARE

Children between the ages of 2 and 6 spend even more time away from their homes and parents than infants and toddlers do. Over the last 30 years, the number of young children enrolled in preschool or day care has steadily increased. This trend is largely due to the dramatic rise in women participating in the labor force. Currently, 64 percent of preschool children have mothers who are employed (U.S. Bureau of the Census, 1997). Figure 9.7 shows where preschoolers spend their days while their parents are at work.

A *preschool* is a half-day program with planned educational experiences aimed at enhancing the development of 2- to 5-year-olds. In contrast, *day care* identifies a variety of arrangements for supervising children of employed parents, ranging from care in someone else's or the child's own home to some type of center-based program. The line between preschool and day care is a fuzzy one. As Figure 9.7 indicates, parents often select a preschool as a child care option. Many preschools (and public school kindergartens as well) have increased their hours to full days in response to the needs of employed parents (U.S. Department of Education, 1996). At the same time, today we know that good day care is not simply a matter of keeping children safe and adequately fed. It should provide the same high-quality educational experiences that an effective preschool does, the only difference being that children attend for an extended day.

■ **TYPES OF PRESCHOOL.** Preschool programs come in great variety, ranging along a continuum from child-centered to teacher-directed. In **child-centered preschools,** teachers provide a wide variety of activities from which children select, and most of the day is devoted to free play. In contrast, in **academic preschools**, teachers structure the program. Children are taught letters, numbers, colors, shapes, and other academic skills through repetition and drill, and play is de-emphasized.

Despite grave concern over the appropriateness of the academic approach, preschool teachers have felt increased pressure to stress formal academic training. The trend is motivated by a widespread belief that providing academic instruction at earlier ages will improve the ultimate achievement of American youths. Yet research shows that emphasizing formal academic training in early childhood undermines motivation and other aspects of emotional well-being. A recent study revealed that compared to children in teacher-directed classrooms, 3- to 6-year-olds in child-centered classrooms perceived their abilities to be higher, more often preferred challenging problems and had higher expectations for success on them, and were less likely to seek adult approval or worry about school (Stipek et al., 1995).

child-centered preschools
Preschools in which teachers provide a wide variety of activities from which children select, and most of the day is devoted to free play.

academic preschools
Preschools in which teachers structure the program, training children in academic skills through repetition and drill.

These economically disadvantaged 4-year-olds benefit from the comprehensive early intervention services of Project Head Start. A rich, stimulating preschool experience is an essential part of the program. As parents like this classroom volunteer participate, they improve their own life circumstances as well as their children's development. *(Elizabeth Crews)*

Furthermore, in countries that outperform the United States in math and science achievement, such as Japan and Korea, children have a relaxed early childhood. They are not hurried into academic work during the preschool years (Song & Ginsburg, 1987; Tobin, Wu, & Davidson, 1989).

■ **EARLY INTERVENTION FOR AT-RISK PRESCHOOLERS.** In the 1960s, when the United States launched a "war on poverty," a wide variety of intervention programs for economically disadvantaged preschoolers were initiated. They were based on the assumption that learning problems are best treated early, before formal schooling begins.

Project Head Start, begun by the federal government in 1965, is the most extensive of these experiments. A typical Head Start program provides children with a year or two of preschool, along with nutritional and medical services. Parent involvement is central to the Head Start philosophy. Parents serve on policy councils and contribute to program planning. They also work directly with children in classrooms, attend special programs on parenting and child development, and receive services directed at their own social, emotional, and vocational needs. Currently, over 1,300 Head Start centers located around the country enroll about 720,000 children each year (Currie & Thomas, 1997).

Benefits of Preschool Intervention. Over two decades of research establishing the long-term benefits of preschool intervention helped Head Start survive. The most important of these studies was coordinated by the Consortium for Longitudinal Studies, a group of investigators who combined data from seven university-based interventions. Results showed that children who attended the programs scored higher in IQ and school achievement than controls during the first 2 to 3 years of elementary school. After that time, differences in test scores declined (Lazar & Darlington, 1982).

Nevertheless, children who received intervention remained ahead on measures of real-life school adjustment into adolescence. As Figure 9.8 shows, they were less likely to be placed in special education classes or retained in grade, and a greater number graduated from high school. There were also lasting benefits in attitudes and motivation. Children who attended the programs were more likely to give achievement-related reasons (such as school or job accomplishments) for being proud of themselves, and their mothers held higher vocational aspirations. A separate report on one program suggests benefits lasting into young adulthood. It was associated with a reduction in delinquency and teenage pregnancy and a greater likelihood of employment (Berrueta-Clement et al., 1984).

Do these findings on the impact of outstanding university-based programs generalize to Head Start centers located in American communities? As long as programs are of high quality, the outcomes are much the same (Zigler & Styfco, 1994). In fact, as the Social Issues box on the following page indicates, initial mental test score gains are much greater for children in Head Start than for those in other types of preschools. A major reason these scores eventually decline is that former Head Start attendees enter public schools that are very low in quality.

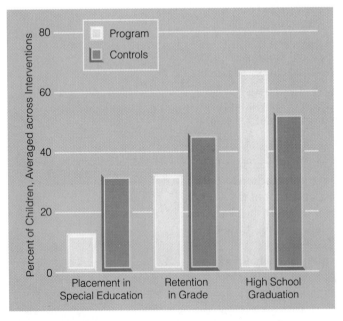

FIGURE 9.8

Benefits of preschool intervention programs. Low-income children who received intervention fared better than controls on real-life indicators of school adjustment. *(Adapted from Royce, Darlington, & Murray, 1983.)*

SOCIAL ISSUES

HEAD START: A SOCIAL POLICY SUCCESS STORY

The impact of Project Head Start on the lives of preschoolers has been questioned many times since the program began. Yet research reporting only minimal benefits is often biased by one very important factor: Because not all poor children can be served, Head Start typically enrolls the most economically disadvantaged. Controls to whom they are compared often do not come from such extremely impoverished families. A study of Head Start programs in two large cities took this into account. It also looked carefully at the effectiveness of Head Start by comparing it to other preschool alternatives as well as to no preschool at all.

Results showed that Head Start children, compared to "other preschool" and "no preschool" groups, had less educated mothers, came from more crowded households, and were more likely to be growing up in single-parent homes. Before entering preschool, they scored well below the other groups on mental tests. Yet a year later, Head Start children showed *greater gains* than both comparison groups (Lee, Brooks-Gunn, & Schnur, 1988; Lee et al., 1990).

These findings indicate that Head Start's unique model of combining high-quality education with parent involvement leads to impressive improvements in test scores. At the same time, Head Start children do not emerge from the program with cognitive skills equal to those of children from advantaged backgrounds. We must keep in mind that it is unrealistic to expect a single year of Head Start to make up for the early experiences of these youngsters.

Furthermore, former Head Start attendees enter public schools substantially lower in quality than do their "no preschool" counterparts. This difference is even greater when Head Start graduates are compared to "other-preschool" peers (Lee & Loeb, 1995). Improvements in mental test scores due to Head Start fade especially rapidly for African-American children; they are more likely to be sustained for Caucasian-American and Mexican-American children. This discouraging outcome is at least partly due to black children's higher likelihood of enrolling in inferior, inner-city schools (Currie & Thomas, 1995, 1997). The benefits of Head Start

are easily undermined when children do not have access to high-quality educational supports throughout the school years.

Yet the fact remains that a short-term Head Start experience can have lasting effects on children's ability to meet basic school requirements (refer to Figure 9.8). The success of Head Start has inspired another federal program that has enhanced American early intervention services. By 1991, public schools were required to offer preschool intervention for 3- to 5-year-olds who either have or are at risk for serious developmental problems. In addition, each state has taken steps to extend intervention downward to infants with delays in development (Richmond & Ayoub, 1993). Like Head Start, programs must ensure that parents participate in the education of their children, since involving and supporting parents increases the likelihood that program effects will be sustained.

The Future of Preschool Intervention. Although over one-fifth of American preschoolers are eligible for Head Start by virtue of their poverty level, at present the program serves only about one-third of these children. Yet Head Start and other interventions like it are highly cost effective. Program expenses are far less than the funds required to provide special education, treat delinquency, and support welfare dependency. Because of its demonstrated returns to society, a move is currently under way to expand Head Start and strengthen its impact.

Researchers believe that positive outcomes of high-quality preschool intervention may be largely due to changes in the attitudes, behaviors, and life circumstances of parents, who create better rearing environments for their children (Reynolds, 1992). Therefore, new interventions are being conceived as *two-generation models* that include developmental goals for *both* parents and children (Smith, 1995). A parent helped to move out of poverty with education, vocational training, and other social services is likely to gain in psychological well-being and planning for the future. When combined with child-centered intervention, these gains may translate into exceptionally strong benefits for children (Zigler & Styfco, 1994, 1995).

Project Head Start
A federal program that provides low-income children with a year or two of preschool education before school entry, along with nutritional and medical services, and that encourages parent involvement in children's development.

At present, the two-generation approach is too new to have yielded much research on long-term benefits (McLoyd, 1998). But one pioneering effort, Project Redirection, is cause for optimism. In it, teenage mothers received a variety of services for themselves and their babies, including education, employment, family planning, life management, parent education, and child health care. A five-year follow-up revealed that participants obtained higher HOME scores, were less likely to be on welfare, and had higher family earnings than controls receiving less intensive intervention. In addition, program children were more likely to have enrolled in Head Start, and they had higher verbal IQs (Polit, Quint, & Riccio, 1988).

■ **DAY CARE.** We have seen that high-quality early intervention can enhance the development of economically disadvantaged children. However, as we noted in Chapter 6, much day care in the United States is not of this high quality (see Figure 6.10 on page 235). Preschoolers exposed to poor-quality day care, regardless of whether they come from middle- or low-income homes, score lower on measures of cognitive and social skills (Howes, 1988, 1990; Lamb, 1998; Phillips et al., 1994).

What are the ingredients of high-quality day care in early childhood? Large-scale studies of center- and home-based care reveal that the following factors are important: group size (number of children in a single space), caregiver–child ratio, caregiver's educational preparation, and caregiver's personal commitment to learning about and caring for children. When these characteristics are favorable, adults are more verbally stimulating and sensitive to children's needs, and children do especially well on measures of intelligence, language, and social development (Galinski et al., 1994; Helburn, 1995; Howes, Phillips, & Whitebook, 1992). Other research shows that spacious, well-equipped environments and a rich variety of activities also contribute to positive outcomes (Howes, 1988). The Caregiving Concerns table below summarizes characteristics of high-quality early childhood programs, based on standards for developmentally appropriate practice devised by the National Association for the Education of Young Children. Together, they offer a set of

CAREGIVING CONCERNS

Signs of Developmentally Appropriate Early Childhood Programs

PROGRAM CHARACTERISTIC	SIGNS OF QUALITY
Physical setting	Indoor environment is clean, in good repair, and well ventilated. Classroom space is divided into richly equipped activity areas, including make-believe play, blocks, science, math, games and puzzles, books, art, and music. Fenced outdoor play space is equipped with swings, climbing equipment, tricycles, and sandbox.
Group size	In preschools and day care centers, group size is no greater than 18 to 20 children with 2 teachers.
Caregiver–child ratio	In day care centers, teacher is responsible for no more than 8 to 10 children. In family day care homes, caregiver is responsible for no more than 6 children.
Daily activities	Most of the time, children work individually or in small groups. Children select many of their own activities and learn through experiences relevant to their own lives. Teachers facilitate children's involvement, accept individual differences, and adjust expectations to children's developing capacities.
Interactions among adults and children	Teachers move among groups and individuals, asking questions, offering suggestions, and adding more complex ideas. They use positive guidance techniques, such as modeling and encouraging expected behavior and redirecting children to more acceptable activities.
Teacher qualifications	Teachers have college-level specialized preparation in early childhood development, early childhood education, or a related field.
Relationships with parents	Parents are encouraged to observe and participate. Teachers talk frequently with parents about children's behavior and development.
Licensing and accreditation	Program is licensed by the state. If a preschool or day care center, accreditation by the National Academy of Early Childhood Programs is evidence of an especially high quality program. If a day care home, accreditation by the National Association for Family Child Care is evidence of high-quality experiences for children.

Sources: Bredekamp & Copple, 1997; National Association for the Education of Young Children, 1991.

worthy goals as our nation strives to expand and upgrade day care and educational services for young children.

EDUCATIONAL TELEVISION

Besides home and preschool, young children spend a great deal of time in another learning environment: television. The average 2- to 6-year-old watches TV from 1½ to 3 hours a day—a very long time in the life of a young child (Comstock, 1993). However, large individual differences in TV viewing exist. In early and middle childhood, boys watch slightly more than girls. Low-SES, ethnic minority children are also more frequent viewers, perhaps because their families are less able to pay for out-of-home entertainment or their neighborhoods provide few alternative activities. And if parents tend to watch a lot of TV, their children usually do so as well (Huston & Wright, 1998).

Each afternoon, Sammy looked forward to certain educational programs; the well-known "Sesame Street" was his favorite. Find a time to watch an episode of "Sesame Street." The program was originally designed for the same population served by Head Start—low-SES children who enter school academically behind their more economically advantaged peers. It uses fast-paced action, lively sound effects, and humorous puppet characters to stress letter and number recognition, counting, vocabulary, and basic concepts. Today, more than 75 percent of American preschool children and 60 percent of kindergartners watch Sesame Street at least once a week, and it is broadcast in more than 40 countries around the world (Zill, Davies, & Daly, 1994).

Research shows that "Sesame Street" works well as an academic tutor. The more children watch, the higher they score on tests designed to measure the program's learning goals (Rice et al., 1990; Wright & Huston, 1995; Zill, Davies, & Daly, 1994). In other respects, however, the rapid-paced format of "Sesame Street" and other children's programs has been criticized. When different types of programs are compared, ones with slow-paced action and easy-to-follow story lines lead to more elaborate make-believe play. Those presenting quick, disconnected bits of information do not (Huston-Stein et al., 1981; Tower et al., 1979).

Some experts argue that because television presents such complete data to the senses, in heavy doses it encourages passive thinking. Too much television also takes up time children would otherwise spend reading, playing, and interacting with adults and peers (Singer & Singer, 1990). But television can support cognitive development as long as children's viewing is not excessive and programs meet their developmental needs. We will consider the impact of television on young children's emotional and social development in the next chapter.

BRIEF REVIEW

By 5 to 6 years of age, IQ scores become good predictors of school achievement. A stimulating home environment, warm parenting, and reasonable demands for mature behavior are positively related to mental test scores. Formal academic training, however, undermines motivation and other aspects of preschoolers' emotional well-being. Project Head Start, an intervention for low-income children that combines preschool education with parental support, results in immediate gains in IQ and achievement. Although these decline over time, children show lasting benefits in real-life indicators of school adjustment. Two-generation models are currently being tried to see if they can produce more powerful long-term outcomes. High-quality day care can serve as effective early intervention, whereas poor-quality day care undermines the development of children from all economic backgrounds. Preschoolers who watch "Sesame Street" score higher on tests of academic knowledge, but too much TV watching takes time away from many cognitively stimulating, worthwhile activities.

ASK YOURSELF . . .

■ *Senator Smith heard that IQ gains resulting from Head Start do not last, so he plans to vote against funding for the program. Write a letter to Senator Smith explaining why he should support Head Start.*

LANGUAGE DEVELOPMENT

Language is intimately related to virtually all the cognitive changes discussed in this chapter. Through it, children express a wide variety of cognitive skills, and it also extends many aspects of cognitive development. Between the years of 2 and 6, advances in language are awesome and momentous. Preschoolers' remarkable achievements, as well as their mistakes along the way, indicate that they master their native tongue in an active, rule-oriented fashion.

VOCABULARY DEVELOPMENT

At age 2, Sammy had a vocabulary of 200 words. By age 6, he will have acquired around 10,000 words. To accomplish this extraordinary feat, Sammy will learn an average of 5 new words each day (Anglin, 1993).

■ **RAPID GAINS IN VOCABULARY.** How do children build their vocabularies so quickly? Researchers have discovered that they can connect a new word with an underlying concept after only a brief encounter, a process called **fast mapping.** In one study, an adult presented preschoolers with a novel nonsense word, "koob," in a game in which the object for which it stood (an oddly shaped plastic ring) was labeled only once. Children as young as 2 picked up the meaning of the word (Dollaghan, 1985). Even toddlers comprehend new labels remarkably quickly, but they need more repetitions than preschoolers, who are better at remembering and categorizing speech-based information (Gathercole et al., 1992; Woodward, Markman, & Fitzsimmons, 1994).

Once children fast map a word, they often have to refine their first guess about its meaning. For example, Sammy heard Leslie announce to the children they would soon take a field trip. He excitedly told his mother at noon, "We're going on a field trip!" When she asked where the class would go, Sammy responded matter-of-factly, "To a field, of course."

Sammy's error suggests that young children fast map some words more easily than others. About a third of children's very early vocabularies consist of labels for objects. Children acquire these words because they refer to concrete items children already know a great deal about, and caregivers' speech often emphasizes names for things (Bloom, 1998; Menyuk, Liebergott, & Schultz, 1995). Words for actions are soon added in large numbers ("go," "run," "broke"), as well as modifiers that refer to features of objects and people ("red," "round" "sad"). If modifiers are related to one another in meaning, they take somewhat longer to learn. For example, 2-year-olds grasp the general distinction between "big" and "small," but not until age 3 to 5 are more refined differences between "tall" and "short," "high" and "low," and "long" and "short" understood. Similarly, children acquire "now–then" before "yesterday–today–tomorrow" (Clark, 1983; Stevenson & Pollitt, 1987).

■ **STRATEGIES FOR WORD LEARNING.** One way preschoolers figure out the meanings of new words is to contrast them with ones they already know. But exactly how they discover which concept each word picks out is not yet fully understood. Ellen Markman (1989, 1992) believes that in the early phases of vocabulary growth, children adopt a **principle of mutual exclusivity.** They assume that words refer to entirely separate (nonoverlapping) categories. The principle of mutual exclusivity works well as long as available referents are perceptually very distinct. For example, when 2-year-olds are told the names of two very different novel objects (a clip and a horn), they assign each label correctly, to the whole object and not a part of it (Waxman & Senghas, 1992).

But mutual exclusivity cannot account for what young children do when adults call a single object by more than one name. Under these conditions, they look for cues in the adult's behavior to determine whether the new word refers to a higher- or lower-order

Compared to when she was younger, this 5-year-old has a better grasp of modifying words that are related to one another in meaning. Rather than using the generic terms "big" and "small," she speaks with more precision. For example, she is likely to say that a "tall" person, not a "short" person, can reach the apples on the tree. *(Murray/Monkmeyer Press)*

fast mapping
Connecting a new word with an underlying concept after only a brief encounter.

principle of mutual exclusivity
The assumption by children in the early stages of vocabulary growth that words mark entirely separate (nonoverlapping) categories.

category or to particular features, such as a part of the object, its shape, its color, or a proper name (Hall, 1996; Tomasello & Barton, 1994; Waxman & Hatch, 1992). When no such cues are available, children as young as 2 demonstrate remarkable flexibility in their word learning strategies. They abandon the mutual exclusivity principle and treat the new word as a second name for the object (Mervis, Golinkoff, & Bertrand, 1994).

Although these findings tell us something about how children master object labels, they say little about principles used for other types of words (Bloom, Tinker, & Margulis, 1993). Children seem to draw on other components of language for help in these instances. According to one proposal, children deduce many word meanings by observing how words are used in *syntax*, or the structure of sentences—a hypothesis called **syntactic bootstrapping** (Gleitman, 1990; Naigles & Hoff-Ginsberg, 1995). Consider the sentence, "Please *give* me the doll." Notice how *give* is followed by an indirect object *(me)* and then a direct object *(doll)*. This is a strong cue that it is a verb of transfer, since transfer involves an object transferred and a person to whom it is transferred.

Once preschoolers have a sufficient vocabulary, they use words creatively to fill in for ones they have not yet learned. As early as age 2, children coin new words, and they do so in systematic ways. For example, Sammy said "plant-man" for gardener (created a compound word) and "crayoner" for a child using crayons (added the ending "-er") (Clark, 1995). Children's ability to invent these expressions is evidence for a remarkable, rule-governed approach to language at an early age.

Preschoolers also extend language meanings through metaphor. For example, one 3-year-old used the expression "fire engine in my tummy" to describe a stomachache (Winner, 1988). Not surprisingly, the metaphors preschoolers use and understand involve concrete, sensory comparisons, such as "clouds are pillows" and "leaves are dancers." Once their vocabulary and knowledge of the world expand, they start to appreciate nonsensory comparisons as well, such as "Friends are like magnets" (Karadsheh, 1991; Keil, 1986). Metaphors permit young children to communicate in especially vivid and memorable ways.

GRAMMATICAL DEVELOPMENT

Grammar refers to the way we combine words into meaningful phrases and sentences. Between ages 2 and 3, children adopt the word order of the adult speech to which they are exposed. English-speaking children use simple sentences that follow a subject–verb–object word order. This shows that they have a beginning grasp of the grammar of their language (de Villiers & de Villiers, 1992).

■ **FROM SIMPLE SENTENCES TO COMPLEX GRAMMAR.** As young children conform to word-order rules, they begin to make the small additions and changes in words that enable us to express meanings flexibly and efficiently—for example, adding "-s" to express plural (as in "cats"), applying prepositions (such as "in" and "on"), and forming various tenses from the verb "to be" ("is," "are," "were," "has been," "will"). All English-speaking children master these grammatical markers in a regular sequence, starting with the ones that involve the simplest meanings and the fewest structural changes (Brown, 1973; de Villiers & de Villiers, 1973). For example, children master the plural form "-s" before they learn tenses of the verb "to be."

By age 3½, children have acquired a great many grammatical rules, and they apply them so consistently that they overextend the rules to words that are exceptions, a type of error called **overregularization.** "My toy car *breaked*," "I *runned* faster than you," and "We each got two *feets*," are expressions that start to appear between 2 and 3 years of age. Overregularization occurs only occasionally—in about 5 to 8 percent of instances in which children use irregular forms, a rate that remains constant into middle childhood. It shows that children apply grammatical rules creatively, since they do not hear mature speakers use these overregularized forms (Marcus, 1995; Marcus et al., 1992).

syntactic bootstrapping
Figuring out word meanings by observing how words are used in the structure of sentences.

overregularization
Application of regular grammatical rules to words that are exceptions.

Between 3 and 6 years, children master even more complex grammatical structures, although they make predictable errors along the way. In asking questions, preschoolers are reluctant to let go of the "subject–verb–object" sequence that is so basic to the English language. At first, they form questions by using rising intonation and failing to invert the subject and verb, as in "Mommy baking cookies?" and "What you doing, Daddy?" (Stromswold, 1995; Tyack & Ingram, 1977). Other errors also occur because children tend to cling to a consistent word order. For example, some passive sentences give them trouble. When told, "The car was pushed by the truck," preschoolers often make a toy car push a truck. By age 5, they understand expressions like these, but full mastery of the passive form is not complete until the end of middle childhood (Horgan, 1978; Lempert, 1989).

Even though they make errors, preschoolers' grasp of grammar is impressive. By age 4 to 5, they form embedded sentences ("I think *he will come*"), tag questions ("Dad's going to be home soon, *isn't he?*"), and indirect objects ("He showed *his friend* the present"). As the preschool years draw to a close, children use most of the grammatical constructions of their language competently (Tager-Flusberg, 1997).

■ **STRATEGIES FOR ACQUIRING GRAMMAR.** Evidence that grammatical development is a gradual process has raised questions about Chomsky's language acquisition device (LAD), which assumes that children have innate, built-in knowledge of grammatical rules (see Chapter 6, page 240). Some experts believe that grammar is largely a product of general cognitive development—children's tendency to search the environment for consistencies and patterns of all sorts (Maratsos, 1998). Yet among these theorists, there is intense debate about how children acquire the structure of their language.

According to one view, young children rely on *semantics,* or word meanings, to figure out grammatical rules—an approach called **semantic bootstrapping.** For example, children might begin by grouping together words with "object qualities" as nouns and words with "action qualities" as verbs. Then they merge these categories with observations of how particular words are used in sentences (Bates & MacWhinney, 1987; Pinker, 1984). Others take the view that children acquire grammar through direct observations of the structure of language. That is, they notice which words appear in the same positions in sentences and are combined in the same way with other words. Over time, they group them into the same grammatical category (Braine, 1994).

Still other theorists agree with the essence of Chomsky's position that children's brains are specially tuned for acquiring grammar. For example, Dan Slobin (1985) proposes that children do not start with an innate knowledge of grammatical rules. But they do have a special **language-making capacity**—a set of procedures for analyzing the language they hear that supports discovery of grammatical regularities. Studying children acquiring more than 40 different native tongues, Slobin found common patterns suggesting that a basic set of strategies exists. Nevertheless, controversy continues over whether there is a universal, built-in language-processing device or whether children in different parts of the word develop unique strategies that are influenced by the specific language they hear (de Villiers & de Villiers, 1992).

BECOMING AN EFFECTIVE CONVERSATIONALIST

Besides acquiring vocabulary and grammar, children must learn to use language successfully in social contexts. For a conversation to go well, participants must take turns, stay on the same topic, state their messages clearly, and conform to cultural rules that govern how individuals are supposed to interact. This practical side of language is called **pragmatics,** and preschoolers make considerable headway in mastering it.

At the beginning of early childhood, children are already skilled conversationalists. In face-to-face interaction, they often initiate verbal exchanges, respond appropriately to their partner's remarks, take turns, and maintain a topic over time (Bloom et al., 1996;

semantic bootstrapping
Figuring out grammatical rules by relying on word meanings.

language-making capacity
A built-in set of procedures for analyzing language that supports the discovery of grammatical regularities.

pragmatics
The practical, social side of language that is concerned with how to engage in effective and appropriate communication with others.

Podrouzek & Furrow, 1988). The number of turns over which children can sustain interaction increases with age, but even 2-year-olds are capable of effective conversation. These surprisingly advanced abilities probably grow out of early interactive experiences with adults and siblings (see Chapter 7).

Indeed, the presence of an older sibling seems to provide a language environment that is especially conducive for acquiring the pragmatics of language. Younger children closely monitor conversations between their older siblings and parents. They often try to join in, and when they do, verbal exchanges last longer, with each participant taking more turns. To be successful at participating, younger children must understand the other speakers' topic and think of a way to add to it (Barton & Tomasello, 1991). And as they listen to conversations, they are exposed to models of important skills, such as use of personal pronouns ("I" versus "you"), which are more common in the early vocabularies of younger than older siblings (Pine, 1995).

By age 4, children already know a great deal about culturally accepted ways of adjusting their speech to fit the age, sex, and social status of their listeners. In one study, 4- to 7-year-olds were asked to act out different roles with hand puppets. Children of all ages used more commands when playing high-status and "masculine" roles, such as teacher, doctor, and father. In contrast, they spoke more politely and used more indirect requests when acting out lower-status and "feminine" roles, such as pupil, patient, and mother (Anderson, 1984). Older preschoolers also adjust their speech on the basis of how well they know their conversational partner. They give fuller explanations to a stranger than to someone with whom they share common experiences, such as a family member or friend (Menig-Peterson, 1975).

Preschoolers' conversational skills occasionally do break down. For example, have you tried talking on the telephone with a preschooler lately? Here is an excerpt of one 4-year-old's telephone conversation with his grandfather:

Grandfather: "How old will you be?"

John: "Dis many." (Holding up four fingers)

Grandfather: "Huh?"

John: "Dis many." (Again holding up four fingers)

(Warren & Tate, 1992, pp. 259–260)

John used gestures that his grandfather could not see, and when his grandfather signaled that he could not understand ("Huh?"), John did not revise his message. In fact, John's communication resembles the egocentric speech identified by Piaget, discussed earlier in this chapter. But children rarely use egocentric speech in informal, face-to-face interaction. Their speech is most likely to become egocentric in highly demanding situations. While on the telephone, children cannot see their listeners' reactions or rely on typical conversational aids, such as toys and objects to talk about. Not until middle childhood do children interact effectively without these supports.

These findings indicate that preschoolers' communication does vary considerably across contexts. When talking face-to-face with familiar people about topics they know well, preschoolers make sophisticated language adjustments. Their conversations appear less mature when they cannot use gestures and other concrete props to help overcome the limits of their current knowledge, vocabulary, and memory. Recall the many examples we have seen in which preschoolers' cognitive capacities depend on the difficulty of the task. Research on children's conversational skills echoes this familiar theme.

The presence of an older sibling seems to foster preschoolers' grasp of the pragmatics of language. To join in family conversations, young children must understand the other speakers' topic and think of a way to add to it. *(Charles Gupton/Stock Boston)*

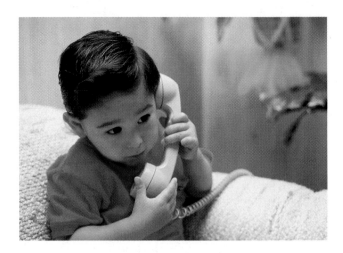

In highly demanding situations, preschool children's conversational skills can break down. This 3-year-old is likely to have trouble communicating clearly on the telephone because he lacks the supports available in face-to-face interaction, such as visual access to his partner's reaction and to objects that are topics of conversation. *(Tony Freeman/ PhotoEdit)*

SUPPORTING LANGUAGE LEARNING IN EARLY CHILDHOOD

From what you have learned so far, what experiences do you think would foster preschoolers' language acquisition? Interaction with more skilled speakers, which is so important during toddlerhood, remains vital during early childhood. Conversational give-and-take with adults, either at home or in preschool, is consistently related to language progress (Hart & Risley, 1995; McCartney, 1984).

Sensitive, caring adults use special techniques that promote preschoolers' language skills. When children use words incorrectly or communicate unclearly, such adults give helpful, explicit feedback, such as "There are several balls over there, and I can't tell exactly which one you want. Do you mean a large or small one or a red or green one?" (Robinson, 1981). At the same time, they do not overcorrect, especially when children make grammatical mistakes, because criticism discourages children from actively experimenting with language rules in ways that lead to new skills.

Instead, adults provide subtle, indirect feedback about grammar by using two strategies, often in combination: **expansions** and **recasts**. For example, a parent hearing a child say, "I gotted new red shoes," might respond, "Yes, you got a pair of new red shoes," *expanding* the complexity of the child's statement as well as *recasting* its incorrect features into appropriate form. Parents and nonparents alike are far more likely to respond in these ways after children make errors. When sentences are well formed, adults tend either to continue the topic of conversation or repeat exactly what the child just said (Bohannon & Stanowicz, 1988).

Nevertheless, some investigators question whether expansions and recasts are as important in children's mastery of grammar as is mere exposure to a rich language environment. Adults do not use these strategies very often, and they are not provided to children in all cultures (Marcus, 1993; Valian, 1993). Furthermore, whereas some studies report that parents' reformulations have a corrective effect, others show no impact on children's use of grammar (Farrar, 1990; Morgan, Bonama, & Travis, 1995). Rather than eliminating errors, perhaps expansions and recasts serve the broader purpose of modeling grammatical alternatives and encouraging children to experiment with them.

Do the findings just described remind you once again of Vygotsky's theory? In language as in other aspects of intellectual growth, parents and teachers seem to interact with young children in ways that gently prompt them to take the next developmental step forward. Children strive to master language because they want to attain social connectedness to other people. Adults, in turn, respond to children's natural desire to become competent speakers by listening attentively, elaborating on what they say, modeling correct usage, and stimulating them to talk further. In the next chapter we will see that this special combination of warmth and encouragement of mature behavior is at the heart of early childhood emotional and social development as well.

ASK YOURSELF . . .

■ *One day, Jason's mother explained to him that the family would take a vacation in Miami. The next morning, Jason emerged from his room with belongings spilling out of a suitcase and remarked, "I gotted my bag packed. When are we going to Your-ami?" What do Jason's errors reveal about his approach to mastering language?*

■ *What can adults do to support language development in early childhood? Provide a list of recommendations, noting research that supports each.*

expansions
Adult responses that elaborate on a child's utterance, increasing its complexity.

recasts
Adult responses that restructure children's incorrect speech into a more appropriate form.

Summary

PIAGET'S THEORY: THE PREOPERATIONAL STAGE

Describe advances in mental representation and limitations of thinking during the preoperational stage.

- Rapid advances in mental representation, notably language and make-believe play, mark the beginning of the **preoperational stage.** With age, make-believe becomes increasingly complex, evolving into **sociodramatic play** with others. Preschoolers' make-believe supports many aspects of cognitive and social development.

- Spatial understanding improves rapidly over the third year of life. Children realize that photographs, models, and simple maps correspond to circumstances in the real world. Insight into one type of symbol–real world relation helps preschoolers understand others.

- Aside from representation, Piaget described the young child in terms of deficits rather than strengths. Preoperational children are not yet capable of **operations** because they are **egocentric**—unable to imagine the perspectives of others and reflect on their own thinking. Egocentrism leads to a variety of illogical features of thought.

- According to Piaget, preschoolers engage in **animistic thinking,** and their cognitions are **centered, perception-bound,** focused on **states rather than transformations,** and **irreversible.** In addition, preoperational children engage in **transductive reasoning** rather than truly causal reasoning. Because of these difficulties, they fail **conservation** and **hierarchical classification** tasks.

What are the implications of recent research for the accuracy of the preoperational stage?

- When young children are given simplified problems relevant to their everyday lives, their performance appears more mature than Piaget assumed. Operational thinking develops gradually over the preschool years, a finding that challenges Piaget's concept of stage.

What educational principles can be derived from Piaget's theory?

- Piaget's theory has had a major impact on educational programs for young children. A Piagetian classroom promotes discovery learning, sensitivity to children's readiness to learn, and acceptance of individual differences.

VYGOTSKY'S SOCIOCULTURAL THEORY

Describe Vygotsky's perspective on the origins and significance of children's private speech.

- Whereas Piaget believed that language does not play a major role in cognitive development, Vygotsky regarded it as the foundation for all higher cognitive processes. According to Vygotsky, **private speech,** or self-directed language, emerges out of social communication as adults and more skilled peers help children master challenging tasks within the zone of proximal development. Eventually private speech is internalized as inner, verbal thought. **Intersubjectivity** and **scaffolding** are features of social interaction that promote transfer of cognitive processes to children.

Describe applications of Vygotsky's theory to education.

- A Vygotskian classroom emphasizes assisted discovery. Verbal guidance from teachers and peer collaboration are vitally important. According to Vygotsky, make-believe play is a unique, broadly influential zone of proximal development in early childhood.

INFORMATION PROCESSING

How do attention and memory change during early childhood?

- Attention gradually becomes more sustained and planful during early childhood. Nevertheless, compared to older children, preschoolers spend relatively short periods of time involved in tasks and are less systematic about planning.

- Young children's recognition memory is remarkably good and becomes even more accurate by the end of early childhood. In comparison to older children and adults, preschoolers' recall for listlike information is poor because they use **memory strategies** less effectively.

- **Episodic memory,** or memory for everyday experiences, is well developed in early childhood. Like adults, preschoolers remember familiar experiences in terms of **scripts,** which become more elaborate with age. As adults talk to children about the past, autobiographical memory becomes better organized, detailed, and related to the larger context of children's lives.

Describe the young child's theory of mind.

- Preschoolers begin to construct a theory of mind, indicating that they are capable of **metacognition,** or thinking about thought. Between ages 3 and 4, they understand that both beliefs and desires can influence behavior and that people can hold false beliefs.

- Many factors appear to contribute to young children's understanding of mental life, including early forms of communication, such as joint attention and social referencing; imitation; make-believe play; language development; and social interaction. Children may also be biologically primed to develop a theory of mind.

- Preschoolers' awareness of mental activities is far from complete. They regard the mind as a passive container of information rather than an active, constructive agent.

Summarize children's literacy and mathematical knowledge during early childhood.

- **Emergent literacy** reveals that young children understand a great deal about written language long before they read and write in conventional ways. Preschoolers gradually revise incorrect ideas about the meaning of written symbols as their perceptual and cognitive capacities improve, as they encounter writing in many different contexts, and as adults help them make sense of written information.

Summary (continued)

- Mathematical reasoning also builds on a foundation of informal knowledge. Toddlers display a beginning grasp of **ordinality,** which serves as the basis for more complex understandings. As children experiment with counting strategies, they discover additional mathematical principles, including **cardinality**. Gradually, counting becomes more flexible and efficient.

INDIVIDUAL DIFFERENCES IN MENTAL DEVELOPMENT

Describe the content of early childhood intelligence tests and testing conditions that affect children's performance.

- Intelligence tests in early childhood include a wide variety of verbal and non-verbal items that assess vocabulary, memory, quantitative knowledge, spatial reasoning, and other cognitive skills. When taking an intelligence test, low-income and ethnic minority children, especially, benefit from time to get to know the examiner and generous praise and encouragement.

Describe the impact of home, preschool and day care, and educational television on mental development in early childhood.

- Children growing up in warm, stimulating homes with parents who make reasonable demands for mature behavior score higher on mental tests. Home environment plays a major role in the poorer intellectual performance of low-income children in comparison to their more economically advantaged peers.

- Preschool programs come in great variety. **Child-centered preschools** emphasize free play. In **academic preschools,** teachers train academic skills through repetition and drill. Formal academic instruction, however, is inconsistent with young children's developmental needs and undermines their emotional well-being.

- **Project Head Start** is the largest federally funded preschool program for low-income children in the United States. High-quality preschool intervention results in immediate test score gains and long-term improvements in school adjustment for economically disadvantaged children. To strengthen the impact of intervention, new two-generation models are being tried.

- Poor-quality day care disrupts the development of children from all walks of life. When group size, caregiver–child ratio, caregiver educational preparation, and caregiver commitment to the childcare field are favorable, preschoolers are advantaged in cognitive and social development.

- Children pick up many cognitive skills from educational television programs like "Sesame Street." Programs with slow-paced action and easy-to-follow story lines foster make-believe play.

LANGUAGE DEVELOPMENT

Trace the development of vocabulary, grammar, and conversational skills in early childhood.

- Supported by **fast mapping,** children's vocabularies grow dramatically during early childhood. Preschoolers figure out the meaning of new words by contrasting them with ones they already know. The **principle of mutual exclusivity** explains children's acquisition of some, but not all, early words.

- Children also look for cues in the adult's behavior to figure out word meanings. In addition, they engage in **syntactic bootstrapping**—observing how words are used in the structure of sentences. Once preschoolers have a sufficient vocabulary, they extend language meanings, coining new words and creating metaphors.

- Between ages 2 and 3, children adopt the basic word order of their language. As they master additional grammatical constructions, they occasionally **overregularize,** or apply the rules to words that are exceptions. By the end of the preschool years, children have acquired a wide variety of complex grammatical forms.

- Some experts believe that grammar is a product of general cognitive development. According to one view, children engage in **semantic bootstrapping,** relying on word meanings to figure out grammatical rules. Others agree with the essence of Chomsky's theory that children's brains are specially tuned for acquiring grammar. One speculation is that children have a **language-making capacity** that supports the discovery of grammatical regularities.

- **Pragmatics** refers to the practical, social side of language. In face-to-face interaction with peers, young preschoolers are already skilled conversationalists. By age 4, they adapt their speech to their listeners in culturally accepted ways. Preschoolers' communicative skills appear less mature in highly demanding contexts, such as the telephone.

Cite factors that support language learning in early childhood.

- Conversational give-and-take with more skilled speakers fosters preschoolers' language skills. Adults often provide explicit feedback on the clarity of children's utterances. They give indirect feedback about grammer through **expansions** and **recasts.** However, the impact of these strategies on grammatical development has been challenged. For this aspect of language, exposure to a rich language environment may be sufficient.

Important terms and concepts

academic preschool (p. 351)
animistic thinking (p. 328)
cardinality (p. 348)
centration (p. 329)
child-centered preschools (p. 351)
conservation (p. 328)
egocentrism (p. 328)
emergent literacy (p. 347)
episodic memory (p. 341)
expansions (p. 360)
fast mapping (p. 356)
hierarchical classification (p. 329)
intersubjectivity (p. 338)

irreversibility (p. 329)
language-making capacity (p. 358)
memory strategies (p. 341)
metacognition (p. 342)
operations (p. 328)
ordinality (p. 348)
overregularization (p. 357)
perception bound (p. 329)
pragmatics (p. 358)
preoperational stage (p. 324)
principle of mutual exclusivity
   (p. 356)
private speech (p. 337)

Project Head Start (p. 353)
recasts (p. 360)
scaffolding (p. 338)
scripts (p. 342)
semantic bootstrapping (p. 358)
sociodramatic play (p. 325)
states rather than transformations
   (p. 329)
syntactic bootstrapping (p. 357)
transductive reasoning (p. 329)

Fyi . . .   FOR FURTHER INFORMATION AND HELP

EARLY CHILDHOOD DEVELOPMENT AND EDUCATION

Association for Childhood Education International (ACEI)
(301) 942-2443
Website: www.udel.edu/bateman/acei

Organization interested in promoting sound educational practice from infancy through early adolescence. Student membership is available and includes a subscription to Childhood Education, a bimonthly journal covering research, practice, and public policy issues.

National Association for the Education of Young Children (NAEYC)
(800) 424-2460
Website: www.naeyc.org/naeyc

Organization open to all individuals interested in acting on behalf of young children's needs, with primary focus on educational services. Student membership is available and includes a subscription to Young Children, a bimonthly journal covering theory, research, and practice in infant and early childhood development and education.

LITERACY

U.S. Department of Education
Helping Your Child Learn to Read
Website: www.ed.gov/pubs/parents/Reading/index.html

A Website with suggested strategies and activities for fostering literacy development from infancy through age 10.

The Children's Literature Web Guide
Website: www.acs.ucalgary.ca/~dkbrown/index.html

A Website that categorizes the growing number of books for children and young adults. Also provides information on authors and illustrators of children's books, and movies and television programs based on children's stories.

PRESCHOOL INTERVENTION

High/Scope Educational Research Foundation
(313) 485-2000
Website: www.highscope.org

Organization devoted to improving development and education from infancy through adolescence. Conducts longitudinal research to determine the effects of early intervention on development.

DAY CARE

National Association for Child Care Resource and Referral Agencies
(202) 393-5201

Organization that works for high-quality day care and provides information on available services to parents seeking day care for young children.

National Association for Family Child Care
(800) 359-3817
Website: www.assoc-mgmt.com/users.nafcc

Organization open to caregivers, parents, and other individuals involved or interested in family day care. Serves as a national voice that promotes high-quality family day care.

National Network for Child Care
(515) 294-0363
Website: www.exnet.iastate.edu/Pages/families/nncc

Organization that offers a website with extensive information on day care and child development, an e-mail listserve permitting communication with others concerned about day-care quality, and newsletters for center-based, home-based, and school-age daycare providers.

"Children at Play"
Group Collage
6 & 7 years, South Australia

This scene of young children engaged in outdoor play depicts the expanding peer activities and first friendships of early childhood. Chapter 10 describes these emotional and social capacities.

ACCESS ARTS Mural Project. Flagstaff Hill Junior Primary Schlool. Adelaide. South Australia. Reprinted by permission of Access Arts.

EMOTIONAL AND SOCIAL DEVELOPMENT
IN EARLY CHILDHOOD

*A*s the children in Leslie's classroom moved through the preschool years, their personalities took on clearer definition. By age 3, they voiced firm likes and dislikes as well as new ideas about themselves. "Stop bothering me," Sammy said to Mark as he aimed a beanbag toward the mouth of a large clown face. "See, I'm great at this game," Sammy announced with confidence, an attitude that kept him trying, even though he missed most of the throws.

The children's conversations also revealed their first notions about morality. Often they combined statements about right and wrong they had heard from adults with forceful attempts to defend their own desires. "You're 'posed to share," stated Mark while he grabbed a beanbag out of Sammy's hand.

"I was here first! Gimme it back," demanded Sammy, who pushed Mark while reaching for the beanbag. The two boys continued to struggle until Leslie intervened, provided an extra set of beanbags, and showed them how they could both play at once.

As Sammy and Mark's interaction reveals, preschoolers are quickly becoming complex social beings. Although arguments and aggression take place among all young children, cooperative exchanges are far more frequent. Between the years of 2 and 6, first friendships emerge in which children converse, act out complementary roles, and learn that their own desires for companionship and toys are best met when they consider the needs and interests of others.

Individual differences in sociability are also evident, becoming a distinct part of preschoolers' personalities. Sammy was an assertive, outgoing child who organized many episodes of make-believe play with his classmates. In contrast, Shirley spent so much time by herself working puzzles and painting pictures that one day her mother asked Leslie if this behavior was normal. Robbie's impulsive and distractible temperament made it difficult for him to make friends. He screamed and hit when he didn't get his way, and Leslie worked hard at showing him how to join play groups and settle conflicts successfully.

The children's play highlighted their developing understanding of their social world. This was especially apparent in the attention they gave to the dividing line between male and female. While Lynette and Karen cared for a sick baby doll in the housekeeping area, Sammy, Vance, and Mark transformed the block corner into a busy intersection. "Green light, go!" shouted police officer Sammy as Vance and Mark pushed large wooden cars and trucks across the floor. Already, the children preferred same-sex peers, and their play themes mirrored the gender stereotypes of their cultural community.

This chapter is devoted to the many facets of emotional and social development in early childhood. The theory of Erik Erikson provides an overview of personality change during the preschool years. Then we consider children's concepts of themselves, their insights into their social and moral worlds, and their increasing ability to manage their emotional and social behaviors. In the final sections of this chapter, we answer the question, What is effective child rearing? We also consider the complex conditions that support good parenting or lead it to break down. Today, child abuse and neglect rank among America's most serious national problems.

ERIKSON'S THEORY: INITIATIVE VERSUS GUILT

Erikson (1950) described early childhood as a period of "vigorous unfolding" (p. 255). Once children have a sense of autonomy and feel secure about separating from parents, they become more relaxed and less contrary than they were as toddlers. Their energies are freed for tackling the critical psychological conflict of the preschool years: **initiative versus guilt.** The word *initiative* means spirited, enterprising, and ambitious. It suggests that the young child has a new sense of purposefulness. Preschoolers are eager to tackle new tasks, join in activities with peers, and discover what they can do with the help of adults.

Erikson regarded play as a central means through which young children find out about themselves and their social world. Play permits preschoolers to try out new skills with little risk of criticism and failure. It also creates a small social organization of children who must cooperate to achieve common goals. Make-believe, especially, offers unique opportunities for developing initiative. In cultures around the world, children act out family scenes and highly visible occupations—police officer, doctor, and nurse in our society, rabbit hunter and potter among the Hopi Indians, and hut builder and spear maker among the Baka of West Africa (Garvey, 1990; Roopnarine et al., 1998). In this way, make-believe provides children with important insights into the link between self and wider society.

initiative versus guilt
In Erikson's theory, the psychological conflict of early childhood, which is resolved positively through play experiences that foster a healthy sense of initiative and through development of a superego, or conscience, that is not overly strict and guilt ridden.

This boy displays a sense of initiative when he joins his father in harvesting watermelons. Preschoolers are eager to tackle new tasks and discover what they can do with the help of adults. *(Ariel Skelley/The Stock Market)*

Recall that Erikson's theory builds on Freud's psychosexual stages. Freud's *phallic stage* of early childhood is a time when sexual impulses transfer to the genitals, and the well-known *Oedipus conflict* arises. The young boy wishes to have his mother all to himself and feels hostile and jealous of his father. Freud described a similar *Electra conflict* for girls, who want to possess their fathers and who envy their mothers.

Freud believed that these feelings soon lead to intense anxiety, since children fear they will lose their parents' love and be punished for their unacceptable wishes. To master the anxiety, avoid punishment, and maintain the affection of parents, children form a *superego*, or conscience, through **identification** with the same-sex parent. They take the parent's characteristics into their personality, and as a result, adopt the moral and gender-role standards of their society. Each time the child disobeys standards of conscience, painful feelings of guilt occur.

For Erikson, the negative outcome of early childhood is an overly strict superego, one that causes children to feel too much guilt because they have been threatened, criticized, and punished excessively by adults. When this happens, preschoolers' exuberant play and bold efforts to master new tasks break down. Their self-confidence is shattered, and they approach the world timidly and fearfully.

Although Freud's Oedipus and Electra conflicts are no longer regarded as satisfactory explanations of children's emotional, moral, and gender-role development, Erikson's image of initiative captures the diverse changes in young children's emotional and social lives. The preschool years are, indeed, a time when children develop a confident self-image, more effective control over emotions, new social skills, the foundations of morality, and a clear sense of themselves as boy or girl. Now let's take a close look at each of these aspects of development.

SELF-DEVELOPMENT

Children emerge from toddlerhood with a firm awareness of their separateness from others. During the preschool years, new powers of representation through language enable them to reflect on themselves. Language permits children to talk about the *I-self*—their own subjective experience of being (Harter, 1998). In Chapter 9, we noted that preschoolers quickly acquire a vocabulary for talking about their inner mental lives, begin to refine their understanding of mental states, and form an autobiographical memory through talking about the past with adults.

identification
In psychoanalytic theory, the process leading to the formation of conscience, in which children take the same-sex parent's characteristics into their personality, thereby adopting the moral and gender-role standards of their society.

As the I-self becomes more firmly established, children focus more intently on the *me-self*—knowledge and evaluation of the self's characteristics. They start to develop a **self-concept,** the set of attributes, abilities, attitudes, and values that an individual believes defines who he or she is. Let's see what children's earliest self-descriptions are like.

FOUNDATIONS OF SELF-CONCEPT

Ask a 3- to 5-year-old to tell you about him- or herself, and you are likely to hear something like this:

> I'm Tommy. See, I got this new red T-shirt. I'm 4 years old. I can brush my teeth, and I can wash my hair all by myself. I have a new Tinkertoy set, and I made this big, big tower.

As these statements indicate, preschoolers' self-concepts, like other aspects of their thinking, are very concrete. Usually they mention observable characteristics, such as their name, physical appearance, possessions, and everyday behaviors (Harter, 1996; Watson, 1990).

By age 3½, children also describe themselves in terms of typical beliefs, emotions, and attitudes, as in "I'm happy when I play with my friends" or "I don't like being with grown-ups" (Eder, 1989). And when asked to tell whether statements are true of themselves (a much easier task than producing a self-description), 3½-year-olds often respond consistently. For example, a child who says that she "doesn't push in front of other people in line" is also likely to indicate that she "feels like being quiet when angry" and "usually does what Mommy or the teacher says," as if she recognizes that she is high in self-control (Eder, 1990). This suggests that young children have a beginning understanding of their unique psychological characteristics.

Nevertheless, preschoolers cannot yet combine their separate self-descriptions into an integrated self-portrait. And they do not yet make explicit reference to psychological dispositions, such as "I'm helpful," "I'm friendly," or I'm usually truthful." Furthermore, they are not yet aware that a person can have opposing characteristics—for example, be both "nice" and "mean" or "good" and "bad." These understandings must wait for the greater cognitive maturity of middle childhood (Griffin, 1992).

In fact, very young preschoolers' concepts of themselves are so bound up with specific possessions and actions that they spend much time asserting their rights to objects, as Sammy did in the beanbag incident at the beginning of this chapter. The stronger the child's self-definition, the more possessive he or she tends to be about objects, claiming them as "Mine!" (Levine, 1983). These findings indicate that rather than a sign of selfishness, early struggles over objects seem to be a positive sign of developing selfhood, an effort to clearly mark off boundaries between self and others.

A firmer sense of self also permits children to cooperate for the first time in resolving disputes over objects, playing games, and solving simple problems (Brownell & Carriger, 1990; Caplan et al., 1991). Adults might take both of these capacities into account when trying to promote friendly peer interaction. For example, teachers and parents can accept the young child's possessiveness as a sign of self-assertion ("Yes, that's your toy") and then encourage compromise ("but in a little while, can you give someone else a turn?"), rather than simply insisting on sharing.

UNDERSTANDING INTENTIONS

As children learn more about themselves by reflecting on their own behavior, they start to distinguish actions that are deliberate and intentional from those that are accidental. By age 2, preschoolers already say "gonna," "hafta," and "wanna" to announce actions they are about to perform. Soon they use this grasp of purposefulness to defend them-

self-concept
The set of attributes, abilities, attitudes, and values that an individual believes defines who he or she is.

selves. After being scolded for bumping into a playmate or spilling a glass of milk, they often exclaim, "It was an accident!" or "I didn't do it on purpose!" (Astington, 1993).

By 2½ to 3 years, this understanding extends to others. Preschoolers become sensitive to cues that help them tell if another person is acting intentionally. At first, they focus on whether a person's desires are fulfilled. If a person says he is going to do something and then does it, 3-year-olds judge the behavior as deliberate. If statements and actions do not match, then the behavior was not intended (Astington, 1991, 1993). They do not yet appreciate that a person's intentions can remain unrealized or that a desired outcome can happen accidentally (Bartsch & Wellman, 1995).

By the end of the preschool years, children use a much wider range of information to judge intentionality. For example, 5-year-olds note whether a person is concentrating on what she is doing, whether her action leads to positive or negative outcomes (negative ones are usually not intended), and whether some external cause can account for the person's behavior (Smith, 1978). How do preschoolers acquire this knowledge? Adults' differing responses to intended and unintended acts probably play an important role. And over time, children undoubtedly notice that their own thoughts and feelings are very different when they intend to do something than when they do not (Flavell & Miller, 1998).

EMERGENCE OF SELF-ESTEEM

Another aspect of self-concept emerges in early childhood: **self-esteem,** the judgments we make about our own worth and the feelings associated with those judgments. Self-esteem ranks among the most important aspects of self-development, since evaluations of our own competencies affect emotional experiences, future behavior, and long-term psychological adjustment. Take a moment to think about your own self-esteem. Besides a global appraisal of your worth as a person, you have a variety of separate self-judgments. For example, you may regard yourself as well liked by others, very good at schoolwork, but only so-so at sports.

Preschoolers' sense of self-esteem is not as well defined as that of older children and adults. Young children distinguish how well others like them (social acceptance) from how "good" they are at doing things (competence). But before age 7, they are not very good at discriminating competence at different activities. When asked how well they can do something, they usually rate their own ability as extremely high and often underestimate task difficulty (Harter, 1990, 1998). Sammy's announcement that he was great at beanbag throwing despite his many misses is a typical self-evaluation during early childhood.

Preschoolers' high sense of self-esteem is adaptive during a period in which they must master so many new skills, and it contributes greatly to their sense of initiative. Young children's belief in their own capacities is supported by the patience and encouragement of adults. Most parents realize that their preschool youngsters are developing rapidly. They know that a child who has trouble riding a tricycle or cutting with scissors at age 3 will be able to do so a short time later. Preschoolers, too, know that they are growing bigger and stronger, and they see that failure on one occasion often precedes into success on another. When they cannot do something, they are usually eager and willing to try again later.

Nevertheless, by age 4 some children give up easily when faced with a challenge, such as working a hard puzzle or building a tall block tower. They conclude that they cannot do the task and are discouraged after failure (Cain & Dweck, 1995; Smiley & Dweck, 1994). When these young nonpersisters are asked to act out with dolls an adult's reaction to failure, they often respond, "He's punished because he can't do [the puzzle]" or "Daddy's gonna be very mad and spank her" (Burhans & Dweck, 1995, p. 1727). They also are likely to report that their parents would berate them for making small mistakes (Heyman, Dweck, & Cain, 1992). The Caregiving Concerns table on the following page suggests ways to avoid these self-defeating reactions and foster a healthy self-image in young children.

Most preschoolers have a high sense of self-esteem, a quality that encourages them to persist at tasks during a period in which many new skills must be mastered. *(Miro Vintoniv/Stock Boston)*

self-esteem
The aspect of self-concept that involves judgments about one's own worth and the feelings associated with those judgments.

CAREGIVING CONCERNS

Fostering a Healthy Self-Image in Young Children

SUGGESTION	DESCRIPTION
Build a positive relationship.	Indicate that you want to be with the child by arranging times to be fully available. Listen without being judgmental, and express some of your own thoughts and feelings. Mutual sharing helps children feel valued.
Nurture success.	Adjust expectations appropriately, and provide assistance when asking the child to do something beyond his or her current limits. Accentuate the positive in the child's work or behavior. Promote self-motivation by emphasizing praise over concrete rewards. Instead of simply saying, "That's good," mention effort and specific accomplishments. Display the child's artwork and other products, pointing out increasing skill.
Foster the freedom to choose.	Choosing gives children a sense of responsibility and control over their own lives. Where children are not yet capable of deciding on their own, involve them in some aspect of the choice, such as when and in what order a task will be done.
Acknowledge the child's emotions.	Accept the child's strong feelings, and suggest constructive ways to handle them. When a child's negative emotion results from an affront to his or her self-esteem, offer sympathy and comfort along with a realistic appraisal of the situation so the child feels supported and secure.
Use a warm, rational approach to child rearing.	The strategies discussed on pages 379 and 396 (induction and authoritative child rearing) promote self-confidence and self-control

EMOTIONAL DEVELOPMENT

Gains in mental representation, language, and self-concept support emotional development in early childhood. Between the ages of 2 and 6, children achieve a better understanding of their own and others' feelings, and their ability to regulate the expression of emotion improves. Self-development also contributes to a rise in *self-conscious emotions*—shame, embarrassment, guilt, envy, and pride.

UNDERSTANDING EMOTION

Preschoolers' vocabulary for talking about emotion expands rapidly, and they use it skillfully to reflect on their own and others' behavior. Here are some excerpts from everyday conversations in which 2-year-olds and 6-year-olds commented on emotionally charged experiences:

Two-year-old: (After father shouted at child, she became angry, shouting back) "I'm mad at you, Daddy. I'm going away. Good-bye."

Two-year-old: (Commenting on another child who refused to nap and cried) "Mom, Annie cry. Annie sad."

Six-year-old: (In response to mother's comment, "It's hard to hear the baby crying") "Well, it's not as hard for me as it is for you." (When mother asked why) "Well, you like Johnny better than I do! I like him a little, and you like him a lot, so I think it's harder for you to hear him cry."

Six-year-old: (Trying to comfort a small boy in church whose mother had gone up to communion) "Aw, that's all right. She'll be right back. Don't be afraid. I'm here." (Bretherton et al., 1986, pp. 536, 540, 541)

■ **COGNITIVE DEVELOPMENT AND EMOTIONAL UNDERSTANDING.** As the examples just given show, early in the preschool years, children refer to causes, consequences, and behavioral signs of emotion, and over time their understanding becomes more accurate and complex. By age 4 to 5, children correctly judge the causes of many basic emotional reactions. When asked why a nearby playmate is happy, sad, or angry, they describe events similar to those identified by adults, such as "He's happy because he's swinging very high" or "He's sad because he misses his mother." However, they are likely to emphasize external factors over internal states as explanations—a balance that changes with age (Fabes et al., 1991; Levine, 1995). Preschoolers are also good at predicting what a playmate expressing a certain emotion might do next. For example, they know that an angry child might hit someone and that a happy child is more likely to share (Russell, 1990). They are even aware that a lingering mood can affect a person's behavior for some time in the future (Bretherton et al., 1986).

If you look carefully at the examples just given, you will see that young children use emotional language not only to comment on and explain the reactions of others, but also to guide and influence a companion's behavior. Preschoolers also come up with effective ways to relieve others' negative feelings. For example, they suggest physical comfort, such as hugging, to reduce sadness and giving a desired object to a playmate to reduce anger (Fabes et al., 1988). Overall, preschoolers have an impressive ability to interpret, predict, and change others' feelings.

At the same time, there are limits to young children's emotional understanding. In situations with conflicting cues about how a person is feeling, preschoolers have difficulty making sense of what is going on. For example, when asked what might be happening in a picture showing a happy-faced child with a broken bicycle, 4- and 5-year-olds tended to rely only on the emotional expression ("He's happy because he likes to ride his bike"). Older children more often reconciled the two cues ("He's happy because his father promised to help fix his broken bike") (Gnepp, 1983). Furthermore, preschoolers do not realize that people can experience more than one emotion at a time—in other words, that they can have "mixed feelings" (Wintre & Vallance, 1994). As in their approach to Piagetian tasks, young children focus on the most obvious aspect of a complex emotional situation to the neglect of other relevant information.

■ **SOCIAL EXPERIENCE AND EMOTIONAL UNDERSTANDING.** Although cognitive development leads to gains in emotional understanding, social experience also contributes. Preschoolers growing up in families that frequently talk about feelings are better at judging the emotions of others when tested at later ages (Denham, Zoller, & Couchoud, 1994; Dunn et al., 1991). Discussions in which family members disagree about their feelings are particularly helpful. These dialogues seem to help children step back from the experience of emotion and reflect on its causes and consequences.

Furthermore, make-believe play, particularly with siblings, is related to advanced emotional understanding (Youngblade & Dunn, 1995). The intense nature of the sibling relationship, combined with frequent acting out of feelings, makes pretending an excellent context for early learning about emotions.

Emotional knowledge helps children greatly in their efforts to get along with others. As early as 3 to 5 years of age, it is related to friendly, considerate behavior, willingness to make amends after harming another, and peer acceptance (Cassidy et al., 1992; Dunn, Brown, & Maguire, 1995; Garner, Jones, & Miner, 1994).

EMOTIONAL SELF-REGULATION

Language also contributes to preschoolers' improved *emotional self-regulation*, or ability to control the expression of emotion. By age 3 to 4, children verbalize a variety of strategies for adjusting their emotional arousal to a more comfortable level. For example, they know that emotions can be blunted by restricting sensory input (covering your eyes or ears to block out a scary sight or sound), talking to yourself ("Mommy said she'll be back soon"), or changing your goals (deciding that you don't want to play anyway after being excluded from a game) (Thompson, 1990a).

Children's increasing awareness and use of these strategies means that emotional outbursts become less frequent over the preschool years. In fact, by age 3 children can even pose an emotion they do not feel, although these emotional "masks" are largely limited to the positive feelings of happiness and surprise. Children of all ages (and adults as well) find it more difficult to act sad, angry, or disgusted than to seem pleased (Lewis, Sullivan, & Vasen, 1987). Undoubtedly this is because most cultures encourage their members to communicate positive feelings and inhibit unpleasant ones as a way of promoting good interpersonal relations, and young children try hard to conform to this rule.

Temperament affects the development of emotional self-regulation. Children who experience negative emotion very intensely have greater difficulty inhibiting their feelings and shifting their focus of attention away from disturbing events. As early as the preschool years, they are more likely to respond with irritation to others' distress and get along poorly with peers (Eisenberg et al., 1996, 1997a, 1997b).

At the same time, the social environment powerfully affects children's capacity to cope with stress. By watching adults handle their own feelings, children pick up strategies for regulating emotion. When parents have difficulty controlling anger and hostility, children have problems as well (Cummings & Davies, 1994a).

Adults' conversations with children also provide information about cultural expectations for emotional control and techniques for regulating feelings. When parents prepare children for difficult experiences by describing what to expect and ways to handle anxiety, they offer coping strategies that children can apply. Preschoolers' vivid imaginations combined with their difficulty in separating appearance from reality make fears common in early childhood. The Caregiving Concerns below lists ways that parents can help young children manage them.

CAREGIVING CONCERNS

Helping Children Manage Common Fears of Early Childhood

FEAR	SUGGESTION
Monsters, ghosts, and darkness	Reduce exposure to frightening stories in books and on TV until the child is better able to sort out appearance from reality. Make a thorough "search" of the child's room for monsters, showing him or her that none are there. Leave a night-light burning, sit by the child's bed until he or she falls asleep, and tuck in a favorite toy for protection.
Preschool or day care	If the child resists going to preschool but seems content once there, then the fear is probably separation. Under these circumstances, provide a sense of warmth and caring while gently encouraging independence. If the child fears being at preschool, try to find out what is frightening—the teacher, the children, or perhaps a crowded, noisy environment. Provide extra support by accompanying the child at the beginning and lessening the amount of time you are present.
Animals	Do not force the child to approach a dog, cat, or other animal that arouses fear. Let the child move at his or her own pace. Demonstrate how to hold and pet the animal, showing the child that when treated gently, the animal reacts in a friendly way. If the child is bigger than the animal, emphasize this: "You're so big. That kitty is probably afraid of *you!*"
Very intense fears	If a child's fear is very intense, persists for a long time, interferes with daily activities, and cannot be reduced in any of the ways just suggested, it has reached the level of a *phobia*. Sometimes phobias are linked to family problems, and special counseling is needed to reduce them. At other times, phobias diminish without treatment.

SELF-CONSCIOUS EMOTIONS

One morning in Leslie's classroom, a group of children crowded around for a bread-baking activity. Leslie asked them to wait patiently while she got a baking pan. In the meantime, Sammy reached to feel the dough, but the bowl tumbled over the side of the table. A chorus of "Uh-ohs!" arose from the children. When Leslie returned, Sammy looked at her for a moment, covered his eyes with his hands, and said, "I did something bad." He was feeling ashamed and guilty.

As children's self-concepts become better developed, they become increasingly sensitive to praise and blame or (as in Sammy's case) the pos-sibility of such feedback. As a result, they experience *self-conscious emotions* more often—feelings that involve injury to or enhancement of their sense of self (see Chapter 7). By age 3, self-conscious emotions are clearly linked to self-evaluation (Lewis, 1995; Lewis, Alessandri, & Sullivan, 1992).

The presence of an audience seems to be necessary for young children to experience self-conscious emotions. As this mother offers praise, her daughter learns about cultural-ly approved standards of excel-lence and reacts with pride, an emotion that fosters further achievement. *(Mike Mahyszko/ FPG International)*

As Sammy's reaction indicates, preschoolers do not yet label self-conscious emotions precisely. And they experience them under somewhat different conditions than do older children and adults. For example, young children are likely to feel guilty for any act that can be described as wrongdoing, even if it was accidental (Graham, Doubleday, & Guarino, 1984). Also, the presence of an audience seems to be necessary for preschoolers to experi-ence self-conscious emotions. In the case of pride, children depend on external recogni-tion, such as a parent or teacher saying, "That's a great picture you drew" or "You did a good job picking up your toys today." And they are likely to experience guilt and shame only if their misdeeds are observed or detected by others (Harter & Whitesell, 1989).

Self-conscious emotions play an important role in children's achievement-related and moral behavior. Since preschoolers are still developing standards of excellence and con-duct, they depend on instruction, feedback, and example from adults to know when to feel pride, guilt, and shame. As children develop guidelines for good behavior, the pres-ence of others will no longer be necessary to evoke these emotions. In addition, they will be limited to situations in which children feel personally responsible for an outcome (Stipek, Recchia, & McClintic, 1992; Stipek, 1995).

EMPATHY

Another emotional capacity—*empathy*—becomes more common in early childhood, and continues to serve as an important motivator of positive social behavior. Young chil-dren who react with empathy are more likely to share and to help when they notice another person in distress (Eisenberg & Fabes, 1998).

Compared to toddlers, preschoolers rely more on words to console others, a change that indicates a more reflective level of empathy. A 6-year-old said this to his mother after noticing she was distressed at not being able to find a motel after a long day's travel: "You're pretty upset, aren't you, Mom. You're pretty sad. Well, I think, it's going to be all right. I think we'll find a nice place and it'll be all right" (Bretherton et al., 1986, p. 540). As children's ability to take the perspective of others gradually improves, empathic responding increases.

The development of empathy depends on cognitive and language development, but it is also supported by temperament and social experiences. Preschoolers who are sociable, assertive, and good at regulating emotion are more likely to respond empathically (Eisen-berg et al., 1992, 1996). Child rearing also has a profound impact. Parents who are warm and encouraging, who show a sensitive, empathic concern for their children, and who teach about the importance of kindness have preschoolers who are more likely to react in a concerned way to the distress of others (Zahn-Waxler & Radke-Yarrow, 1990).

In contrast, harsh, punitive parenting disrupts the development of empathy at an early age. In one study, researchers observed physically abused preschoolers at a day care center to see how they reacted to other children's distress. Compared to nonabused youngsters, they rarely showed any signs of empathy. Instead, they responded with fear, anger, and physical attacks (Klimes-Dougan & Kistner, 1990). The children's reactions resembled the behavior of their parents, since both responded insensitively to the suffering of others.

BRIEF REVIEW

Erikson's stage of initiative versus guilt provides an overview of the personality changes early childhood. During the preschool years, children develop a self-concept made up of observable characteristics and typical beliefs, emotions, and attitudes. They also distinguish actions that are intentional from those that are accidental. Preschoolers' high sense of self-esteem supports their enthusiasm for mastering new skills.

Language for talking about emotion grows rapidly. Young children have an accurate grasp of the causes and consequences of basic emotional states. Increasing awareness of strategies for controlling emotion along with adult modeling and encouragement promotes gains in emotional self-regulation. As self-awareness increases, children become more sensitive to the praise and criticism of others, and they experience self-conscious emotions more often. Cognition, language, improvements in emotional self-regulation, and warm, sensitive parenting support the development of empathy in early childhood.

PEER RELATIONS

As children become increasingly self-aware, more effective at communicating, and better at understanding the thoughts and feelings of others, their social skills improve rapidly. Nowhere is this more apparent than in their increasingly social play with peers. Peer interaction provides young children with learning experiences they can get in no other way. Because peers interact with one another on an equal footing, they must assume greater responsibility for keeping a conversation going, cooperating, planning, and setting goals for a play theme than with adults or older siblings. With peers, children form friendships—special relationships marked by attachment and common interests. Let's look at how peer interaction changes over the preschool years.

ADVANCES IN PEER SOCIABILITY

Early in this century, Mildred Parten (1932) observed young children in nursery school and noticed a dramatic rise with age in joint, interactive play. She concluded that social development proceeds in a three-step sequence. It begins with **nonsocial activity**—unoccupied, onlooker behavior and solitary play. Then it shifts to a limited form of social participation called **parallel play,** in which a child plays near other children with similar materials but does not try to influence their behavior. At the highest level, preschoolers engage in two forms of true social interaction. The first is **associative play,** in which children engage in separate activities, but they interact by exchanging toys and commenting on one another's behavior. The second is **cooperative play**—a more advanced type of interaction in which children orient toward a common goal, such as acting out a make-believe theme or working on the same product, for example, a sand castle or painting.

nonsocial activity
Unoccupied, onlooker behavior and solitary play.

parallel play
A form of limited social participation in which the child plays near other children with similar materials but does not interact with them.

associative play
A form of true social participation, in which children are engaged in separate activities, but they interact by exchanging toys and commenting on one another's behavior.

cooperative play
A form of true social participation, in which children's actions are directed toward a common goal.

These children are engaged in parallel play. Although they sit side by side and use similar materials, they do not try to influence one another's behavior. Parallel play remains frequent and stable over the preschool years, accounting for about one-fifth of children's play time. *(George Doodwin/ Monkmeyer Press)*

As these preschoolers trade toys and comment on each other's activities at the sand table, they engage in a form of true social interaction called associative play. *(Mary Kate Denny/ PhotoEdit)*

■ **RECENT EVIDENCE ON PEER INTERACTION.** Find a time to observe young children of varying ages and note how long they spend in each of these types of play. You will probably discover that the play forms just described emerge in the order suggested by Parten, but they do not form a developmental sequence in which later-appearing ones replace earlier ones (Howes & Matheson, 1992). Instead, all types coexist during the preschool years. Furthermore, although nonsocial activity declines with age, it is still the most frequent form of behavior among 3- to 4-year-olds. Even among kindergartners it continues to take up as much as a third of children's free-play time. Also, solitary and parallel play remain fairly stable from 3 to 6 years, accounting for as much of the young child's play as highly social, cooperative interaction.

We now understand that it is the *type*, rather than the amount, of solitary and parallel play that changes during early childhood. In studies of preschoolers' play in Taiwan and the United States, researchers rated the *cognitive maturity* of nonsocial, parallel, and cooperative play by applying the categories shown in Table 10.1. Within each of Parten's play types, 5-year-olds engaged in more cognitively mature behavior than did 4-year-olds (Pan, 1994; Rubin, Watson, & Jambor, 1978).

These findings are helpful in responding to the concerns of Shirley's mother, raised at the beginning this chapter. Often parents wonder if a preschooler who spends large

TABLE 10.1

Developmental Sequence of Cognitive Play Categories

PLAY CATEGORY	DESCRIPTION	EXAMPLES
Functional play	Simple, repetitive motor movements with or without objects. Especially common during the first 2 years of life.	Running around a room, rolling a car back and forth, kneading clay with no intent to make something
Constructive play	Creating or constructing something. Especially common between 3 and 6 years.	Making a house out of toy blocks, drawing a picture, putting together a puzzle
Make-believe play	Acting out everyday and imaginary roles. Especially common between 2 and 6 years.	Playing house, school, or police officer; acting out storybook or television characters

Source: Rubin, Fein, & Vandenberg, 1983.

These Chinese girls demonstrate an intricate hand-clapping game in which they must respond quickly and in unison. Preschoolers in the People's Republic of China frequently perform such games for classmates and parents. Their play reflects the value their culture places on group harmony. *(Jeff Greenberg/PhotoEdit)*

amounts of time playing alone is developing normally. Only *certain types* of nonsocial activity—aimless wandering, hovering near peers, and functional play involving immature, repetitive motor action—are cause for concern (Coplan et al., 1994; Rubin & Coplan, 1998). Most nonsocial play of preschoolers is not of this kind. Instead, it is positive and constructive, and teachers encourage it when they set out art materials, puzzles, and building toys during free play. Children like Shirley, who spend much time in these activities, are not maladjusted. Instead, they are bright youngsters who, when they do play with peers, show socially skilled behavior.

As we noted in Chapter 9, *sociodramatic play* (or make-believe with peers) becomes especially common during the preschool years. It supports both cognitive and social development. In joint make-believe, preschoolers act out and respond to one another's pretend feelings. Their play is rich in references to emotional states. Young children also explore and gain control of fear-arousing experiences when they play doctor or dentist or pretend to search for monsters in a magical forest. As a result, they are better able to understand the feelings of others and regulate their own. Finally, to collectively create and manage complex plots, preschoolers must resolve their disputes through negotiation and compromise—experiences that contribute greatly to their ability to get along with others (Garvey, 1990; Howes, 1992).

■ **CULTURAL VARIATIONS.** Culture shapes children's interaction and play activities. In collectivist societies that stress group harmony, peer sociability takes different forms than in individualistic cultures like the United States. For example, children in India generally play in large groups that require high levels of cooperation. Much of their behavior during sociodramatic play and early games is imitative, occurs in unison, and involves close physical contact. In a game called Atiya Piatiya, children sit in a circle, join hands, and swing while they recite a jingle. In Bhatto Bhatto, they act out a script about a trip to the market, touching each other's elbows and hands as they pretend to cut and share a tasty vegetable (Roopnarine et al., 1994).

Cultural beliefs about the importance of play also affect early peer associations. Caregivers who view play as mere entertainment are less likely to provide props and encourage pretend than are those who value its cognitive and social benefits (Farver & Wimbarti, 1995). Korean-American parents, who emphasize task persistence as the means to academic success, have preschoolers who spend less time at joint make-believe and more time unoccupied and in parallel play than do their Caucasian-American counterparts. A cultural de-emphasis on self-expression may also contribute to Korean-American children's reduced involvement in social pretending (Farver, Kim, & Lee, 1995).

FIRST FRIENDSHIPS

As preschoolers interact, first friendships form that serve as important contexts for emotional and social development. Take a moment to jot down what the word *friendship* means to you. You probably thought of a mutual relationship involving companionship, sharing, understanding of thoughts and feelings, and caring for and comforting one another in times of need. In addition, mature friendships endure over time and survive occasional conflicts.

Interviews with preschoolers show that they already understand something about the uniqueness of friendship. They know that a friend is someone "who likes you" and with whom you spend a lot of time playing (Youniss, 1980). Yet their ideas about friendship are far from mature. We have already seen that young children typically describe themselves in concrete, activity-based terms. Their notion of friendship is much the same. Four- to 7-year-olds regard friendship as pleasurable play and sharing of toys. As yet, friendship does not have a long-term, enduring quality based on mutual trust (Damon, 1977; Selman, 1980). Indeed, Sammy declared, "Mark's my best friend" on days when the boys got along well. But he would state just the opposite—"Mark, you're not my friend!"—when a dispute was not quickly settled.

Nevertheless, interactions between friends already have unique features. Preschoolers give twice as much reinforcement, in the form of greetings, praise, and compliance, to children whom they identify as friends, and they also receive more from them. Friends are also more emotionally expressive, talking, laughing, and looking at each other more often than nonfriends (Hartup, 1996). Although preschool friends get into more conflicts than other peers do, they are more likely to resolve these disputes cooperatively (Hartup & Laursen, 1991). Apparently, spontaneity, intimacy, and sensitivity characterize friendships very early, although children are not able to say until much later that these qualities are essential to a good friendship.

PARENTAL AND SIBLING INFLUENCES ON EARLY PEER RELATIONS

Outside of preschool and day care, young children are limited in their ability to find playmates. They depend on parents to help them establish rewarding peer associations. Parents who frequently arrange informal peer play activities tend to have preschoolers with larger peer networks and who are more socially skilled (Ladd, LeSieur, & Profilet, 1993). In providing opportunities for peer play, parents show children how to initiate their own peer contacts and encourage them to be good "hosts" who are concerned about their playmates' needs.

Parents also influence their children's social relations by offering advice, guidance, and effective examples of how to act toward others. In one study, parents who phrased their directives positively and politely ("Please . . ." or "Why don't you try . . . " instead of "Don't" or "No, you can't") had preschoolers who were more successful in influencing peers (Kochanska, 1992). And children whose parents are warm and responsive and who help them regulate negative emotion get along especially well with agemates (Gottman, Katz, & Hooven, 1996; Harrist et al., 1994; Kochanska, 1992).

Sibling and peer relationships are also linked, although not always in a straightforward way. Socially competent children seem to adapt to the demands of each type of relationship, behaving in a more hierarchical fashion with siblings and a more reciprocal way with peers. In contrast, children with stressful home lives often generalize their negative sibling interactions to peers (Dunn, 1993).

As early as the preschool years, some children have great difficulty getting along with agemates. In Leslie's classroom, Robbie was one of them. His demanding, aggressive behavior caused other children to dislike him. Wherever he happened to be, such comments as "I don't want to sit next to Robbie," "Robbie ruined our block tower," and "Robbie hit me for no reason" could be heard. You will learn more about how Robbie's family environment contributed to his problems as we take up moral development in the next section.

BRIEF REVIEW

Beginning in early childhood, peer interaction provides an important context for the development of social skills. Over the preschool years, cooperative play becomes common, although solitary and parallel play are also frequent. Although preschoolers do not have a mature understanding of friendship, interactions between friends are already more positive, emotionally expressive, and rewarding. Parents influence children's peer relations by providing opportunities for peer play, offering advice and guidance, and modeling competent social behavior. Children in stressful homes who get along poorly with siblings tend to have peer difficulties as well.

ASK YOURSELF . . .

■ *Three-year-old Bart lives in the country, where there are no other preschoolers nearby. His parents wonder whether it is worth driving Bart into town once a week to play with his 3-year-old cousin. What advice would you give Bart's parents, and why?*

FOUNDATIONS OF MORALITY

*P*reschoolers' first concepts of morality emerge in interactions with adults and peers. If you watch young children's behavior and listen in on their conversations, you will find many examples of their developing moral sense. By age 2, children show great concern with deviations from the way objects should be and people should act. They point to destroyed property, such as spots on furniture or broken toys, with an expression of discomfort, often exclaiming, "Uh-oh!" In addition, they typically react with alarm to behaviors that are aggressive or that might otherwise harm someone. And their language includes clear references to standards of conduct, such as "broken," "dirty," or "boo-boo," and evaluations of their own and others' actions as "good" or "bad" (Kochanska, Casey, & Fukumoto, 1995; Lamb, 1991).

Throughout the world, adults take note of this budding capacity to distinguish right from wrong. Some cultures have special terms for it. The Utku Indians of Hudson Bay say the child develops *ihuma* (reason). The Fijians believe that *vakayalo* (sense) appears. In response, parents hold children more responsible for their behavior (Kagan, 1989). By the end of early childhood, children can state a great many moral rules, such as "You're not supposed to take things without asking" or "Tell the truth!" In addition, they argue over matters of justice, as when they say, "You sat there last time, so it's my turn" or "It's not fair. He got more!"

All theories of moral development recognize that conscience begins to take shape during the preschool years. And most agree on the general direction of moral growth. At first, the child's morality is *externally controlled* by adults. Gradually, it becomes regulated by *inner standards.* That is, truly moral individuals do not do the right thing just when authority figures are around. Instead, they have developed *principles of good conduct,* which they follow in a wide variety of situations, regardless of the presence of others.

Although points of agreement exist among major theories, there are also important differences. Each emphasizes a different aspect of moral functioning. Psychoanalytic theory stresses the *emotional side* of conscience development—in particular, identification and guilt as motivators of good conduct. Social learning theory focuses on *moral behavior* and how it is learned through reinforcement and modeling. And the cognitive-developmental perspective emphasizes *thinking*—children's ability to reason about justice and fairness.

In addition, theories differ in the extent to which they view children as actively contributing to their own moral development. Think back to Chapter 1 and see if you can predict which perspective regards the child as an active moral being who wonders about right and wrong and searches for moral truth.

THE PSYCHOANALYTIC PERSPECTIVE

From our discussion of psychoanalytic theory earlier in this chapter, you already know something about this approach to moral development. To briefly review, in Freud's Oedipus and Electra conflicts, children desire to possess the parent of the other sex, but they give up this wish because they fear punishment and loss of parental love. Instead, they form a *superego,* or conscience, by *identifying* with the same-sex parent, whose moral standards they adopt. Children obey the superego to avoid *guilt,* a painful emotion that arises each time they are tempted to misbehave. According to Freud, moral development is largely complete by 5 to 6 years of age.

Today, most researchers disagree with Freud's account of conscience development. Notice how discipline promoting fear of punishment and loss of parental love is assumed to motivate young children to behave morally (Kochanska, 1993). Yet research shows that children whose parents frequently use threats, commands, or physical force usually feel little guilt after harming others. In the case of love withdrawal—for example, when a parent refuses to speak to or actually states a dislike for the child—children often respond with high levels of self-blame after misbehaving. They might think to themselves, "I'm no good, and nobody loves me." Eventually, these youngsters may protect themselves from overwhelming feelings of guilt by denying the emotion when they do something wrong. So they, too, develop a weak conscience (Kochanska, 1991; Zahn-Waxler et al., 1990b).

In contrast, a special type of discipline called **induction** supports conscience formation. It involves pointing out the effects of the child's misbehavior on others, by saying such things as "If you keep pushing him, he'll fall down and cry" or "She feels so sad because you won't give back her doll" (Hoffman, 1988). Induction works with children as early as 2 years of age. In one study, mothers who used inductive reasoning had children who were more likely to make up for their misdeeds. They also showed more **prosocial, or altruistic, behavior**—actions that benefit another person without any expected reward for the self. For example, they spontaneously gave hugs, toys, and verbal sympathy to others in distress (Zahn-Waxler, Radke-Yarrow, & King, 1979).

Why is induction so effective? The reason is that it tells children how to behave so they can call on this information in future situations. Also, by pointing out the impact of the child's actions on others, parents encourage preschoolers to empathize, which promotes prosocial behavior (Krevans & Gibbs, 1996). In contrast, discipline that relies too heavily on threats of punishment or love withdrawal produces such high levels of fear and anxiety that children cannot think clearly enough to figure out what they should do. These practices may stop unacceptable behavior temporarily, but they do not get children to internalize moral rules. At times, however, mild warnings and disapproval are necessary to get children to listen to the inductive message.

Although there is little support for Freudian ideas about conscience development, Freud was correct that guilt is an important motivator of moral action. Around age 3, guilt reactions are clearly evident, and internalization of the parent's moral voice has begun, as this typical preschooler's statement reveals, "Didn't you hear my mommy? We'd better not play with these toys" (Emde & Buchsbaum, 1990). But contrary to what Freud believed, guilt is not the only force that compels us to act morally. And moral development is not an abrupt event that is virtually complete by the end of early childhood. Instead, it is a much more gradual process, beginning in the preschool years and extending into adulthood.

Finally, Freud's theory places a heavy burden on parents to ensure that children develop an internalized conscience. The research we have reviewed indicates that parental discipline is vitally important. Yet in earlier chapters we emphasized that children's characteristics can affect the success of certain parenting techniques. Turn to the Biology and Environment box on page 380 for recent findings on the role of temperament in early conscience development.

BEHAVIORISM AND SOCIAL LEARNING THEORY

According to the traditional behaviorist view, *operant conditioning* is regarded as an important way in which children pick up new responses. From this perspective, children start to behave in accord with adult moral standards because parents and teachers follow up "good behavior" with *positive reinforcement* in the form of approval, affection, and other rewards.

■ **THE IMPORTANCE OF MODELING.** Operant conditioning is not enough for children to acquire moral responses. Recall from Chapter 5 that for a behavior to be reinforced, it must first occur spontaneously. Yet many prosocial behaviors, such as sharing, helping, or comforting an unhappy playmate, do not occur often enough at first for reinforcement to explain their rapid development in early childhood. Instead, social learning theorists believe that children largely learn to act morally through *modeling*—by observing and imitating models who demonstrate appropriate behavior (Bandura, 1977;

Is this mother using threats, commands, and physical force to discipline her young daughter? When parents rely on these techniques, they model aggressive behavior, induce high levels of anxiety in children, and encourage them to avoid the punitive adult. Frequent use of harsh punishment interferes with conscience development. *(D. Ogust The Image Works)*

induction
A type of discipline in which the effects of the child's misbehavior on others are communicated to the child.

prosocial, or altruistic, behavior
Actions that benefit another person without any expected reward for the self.

BIOLOGY & ENVIRONMENT

TEMPERAMENT AND CONSCIENCE DEVELOPMENT IN YOUNG CHILDREN

When her mother reprimanded her sharply for pouring water on the floor as she played in her bath, 3-year-old Katherine burst into tears. An anxious, sensitive child, Katherine was so distressed that it took her mother 10 minutes to calm her down. Outside in the front yard the next day, Katherine's mother watched as her next-door neighbor patiently asked her 3-year-old son, who was about to pick the first tulips to blossom in the garden, not to touch the flowers. Alex, an active, adventurous child, paid no attention. As he pulled at another tulip, Alex's mother grabbed him, scolded him harshly, and carried him inside. Alex responded by kicking, hitting, and screaming, "Let me down, let me down!"

What explains Katherine and Alex's very different reactions to firm parental discipline? Grazyna Kochanska (1993, 1995) points out that children's biologically based temperaments affect the parenting practices that best promote responsibility and concern for others. She found that for temperamentally inhibited 2- and 3-year-olds, maternal gentle discipline—reasoning, polite requests, suggestions, and distractions—predicted later conscience development, measured in terms of not cheating in some games and completing stories about moral issues with prosocial themes (saying "sorry," not taking someone else's toys, helping a child who is hurt). In contrast, for relatively fearless, impulsive children, mild disciplinary tactics showed no relationship to moral internalization. Instead, a secure attachment bond with the mother predicted a mature conscience (Kochanska, 1997).

According to Kochanska, inhibited children like Katherine, who are prone to anxiety, are easily overcome by intense psychological discipline. Mild, patient tactics are sufficient to motivate them to internalize parental messages. But impulsive children, such as Alex, may not respond to gentle interventions with enough discomfort to promote internalization. Yet frequent use of power-assertive methods is not effective either, since these techniques spark anger and resentment, which interfere with the child's processing of parental messages.

Why is secure attachment predictive of conscience development in nonanxious children? Kochanska suggests that when children are so low in anxiety that typically effective disciplinary practices fail, a close bond with the caregiver provides an alternative foundation for conscience formation. It motivates children unlikely to experience negative emotion to internalize rules as a means of preserving a spirit of affection and cooperation with the parent.

To foster early moral development, parents must tailor their child-rearing strategies to their child's temperament. In Katherine's case, a soft-spoken correction would probably be effective. For Alex, taking extra steps to build a warm, caring relationship during times when he behaves well is likely to promote moral internalization. Although Alex's parents need to use firmer and more frequent discipline than Katherine's do, emphasizing power assertion is counterproductive for both children. Do these findings remind you of the notion of *goodness of fit*, discussed in Chapter 7? Return to page 268 to review this idea.

Grusec, 1988). Once children acquire a moral response, such as sharing or telling the truth, reinforcement in the form of praising the act ("That was a very nice thing to do") and the child's character ("You're a very kind and considerate boy") increases its frequency (Mills & Grusec, 1989).

Many studies show that models who behave helpfully or generously increase young children's prosocial responses. The model's characteristics affect children's willingness to imitate in the following ways:

1. *Warmth and responsiveness.* Preschoolers are more likely to copy the prosocial actions of an adult who is warm and responsive rather than one who is cold and distant (Yarrow, Scott, & Waxler, 1973). Warmth seems to make children more attentive and receptive to the model. Also, warm, affectionate behavior is an example of altruism, and part of what children may be imitating is this aspect of the model's behavior.

2. *Competence and power.* Children admire and therefore tend to select competent, powerful models to imitate—the reason they are especially willing to copy the behavior of older peers and adults (Bandura, 1977).

3. *Consistency between assertions and behavior.* When models say one thing and do another—for example, announce that "it's important to help others" but rarely engage in helpful acts—children generally choose the most lenient standard of behavior that adults demonstrate (Mischel & Liebert, 1966).

Models exert their most powerful effect during the preschool years. At the end of early childhood, children with a history of consistent exposure to caring adults tend to behave prosocially regardless of whether a model is present. By that time, they have internalized prosocial rules from repeated observations and encouragement by others (Mussen & Eisenberg-Berg, 1977).

■ **EFFECTS OF PUNISHMENT.** Most parents are aware of the limited usefulness of *punishment,* such as scolding, criticism, and spankings, and apply it sparingly. Using sharp reprimands or physical force to restrain or move a child from one place to another is justified when immediate obedience is necessary—for example, when a 3-year-old is about to run into the street. In fact, parents are most likely to use forceful techniques under these conditions. When they are interested in fostering long-term goals, such as acting kindly toward others, they tend to rely on warmth and reasoning (Kuczynski, 1984).

Indeed, a great deal of research shows that punishment promotes only momentary compliance, not lasting changes in children's behavior. For example, Robbie's parents punished often—spanking, shouting, and criticizing when he did something wrong. Robbie usually stopped misbehaving when his mother and father were around, but he displayed the behavior again as soon as they were out of sight and he thought he could get away with it. As a result, Robbie was especially unmanageable in settings away from home, such as preschool (Strassberg et al., 1994).

Harsh punishment also has undesirable side effects. First, when parents spank, they often do so in response to children's aggression (Holden, Coleman, & Schmidt, 1995). Yet the punishment itself models aggression! Second, children who are frequently punished soon learn to avoid the punishing adult. When Robbie's parents came into the room, Robbie braced himself for something unpleasant and kept his distance. Consequently, they had little opportunity to teach him desirable behaviors. Finally, as punishment "works" to stop children's misbehavior temporarily, it offers immediate relief to adults, and they are reinforced for using coercive discipline. For this reason, a punitive adult is likely to punish with greater frequency over time, a course of action that can spiral into serious abuse.

■ **ALTERNATIVES TO HARSH PUNISHMENT.** Alternatives to criticism, slaps, and spankings can reduce the side effects of punishment. A technique called **time out** involves removing children from the immediate setting—for example, by sending them to their rooms—until they are ready to act appropriately. Time out is useful when a child is out of control and other effective methods of discipline cannot be applied at the moment (Betz, 1994). It usually requires only a few minutes to change behavior, and it also offers a "cooling off" period for angry parents. Another approach is *withdrawal of privileges,* such as playing outside or going to the movies. Removing privileges often generates some resentment in children, but it allows parents to avoid harsh techniques that could easily intensify into violence.

When parents do decide to use punishment, they can increase its effectiveness in several ways:

1. *Consistency.* Punishment that is unpredictable is related to especially high rates of disobedience in children. When parents permit children to act inappropriately on

One alternative to harsh punishment is time out, in which children are removed from the immediate setting until they are ready to act appropriately. Time out is useful when a child is out of control and other effective methods of discipline cannot be applied at the moment. But the best way to motivate good conduct is to let children know ahead of time how to act and praise them when they behave well. Then time out will seldom be necessary. *(Photo courtesy: Goodman/ Monkmeyer Press)*

time out
A form of mild punishment in which children are removed from the immediate setting until they are ready to act appropriately.

some occasions but scold them on others, children are confused about how to behave, and the unacceptable act persists.

2. *A warm parent–child relationship.* Children of involved and caring parents find the interruption in parental affection that accompanies punishment to be especially unpleasant. As a result, they want to regain the warmth and approval of parents as quickly as possible.

3. *Explanations.* Explanations help children recall the misdeed and relate it to expectations for future behavior.

Finally, parenting practices that encourage and reward good conduct are the most effective forms of discipline. Instead of waiting for children to misbehave, parents can serve as good examples, let children know ahead of time how to act, and praise children when they behave well (Zahn-Waxler & Robinson, 1995). Adults can also reduce opportunities for misbehavior. For example, on a long car trip, parents can bring along back-seat activities that relieve children's restlessness and boredom. At the supermarket, where there are a great many exciting temptations, they can engage preschoolers in conversation and encourage them to assist with shopping (Holden, 1983; Holden & West, 1989). When adults help children acquire acceptable behaviors that they can use to replace forbidden acts, the need for punishment is greatly reduced.

THE COGNITIVE-DEVELOPMENTAL PERSPECTIVE

The psychoanalytic and behaviorist approaches to morality focus on how children acquire ready-made standards of good conduct from adults. The cognitive-developmental perspective is different. It regards children as *active thinkers* about social rules. As early as the preschool years, children make moral judgments, deciding what is right or wrong on the basis of concepts they construct about justice and fairness (Gibbs, 1991).

Piaget's (1932/1965) work served as the original inspiration for the cognitive-developmental approach to morality. We will consider his theory of moral development in Chapter 16 because it has implications for adolescent moral understanding. Today, we know that Piaget underestimated young children's moral reasoning, just as he overlooked their ability to think about many aspects of their physical world (see Chapter 9). Preschoolers already have some well-developed ideas about morality. For example, 3-year-olds respond that a child who intentionally knocks a playmate off a swing is worse than one who does so accidentally (Yuill & Perner, 1988). By age 4, children can tell the difference between truthfulness and lying (Bussey, 1992). And 4-year-olds also say that disobeying *moral rules,* such as being kind to others and not taking someone else's possessions, is much more serious than violating *social conventions,* such as not saying "please" or "thank you" or eating messy food with fingers (Smetana & Braeges, 1990; Turiel, 1983).

How do young children come to make these distinctions? According to cognitive-developmental theorists, not through direct teaching, modeling, and reinforcement, since adults insist that children conform to social conventions just as often as they press for obedience to moral rules. Instead, children *actively make sense* of their experiences in moral and social-conventional situations. They observe that people respond differently to violations of moral rules than to breaks with social convention. When a moral offense occurs, children react emotionally, describe their own injury or loss, tell another child to stop, or retaliate. An adult who intervenes is likely to call attention to the rights and feelings of the victim. In contrast, children are less likely to react to violations of social convention. And in these situations, adults tend to demand obedience without explanation, as when they state, "Say the magic word!" or "Don't eat with your fingers" (Smetana, 1995b; Turiel, Smetana, & Killen, 1991).

Young preschoolers are clearly off to a good start in appreciating that moral rules are important because they protect the rights and welfare of people. Their developing cognition and language supports this understanding. But social experiences are also vital. Disputes over rights, possessions, and property usually occur when children interact with peers and siblings, providing important opportunities to work out first ideas about justice and fairness (Killen & Nucci, 1995). The way parents handle violations of rules and discuss moral issues also helps children reason about morality. Children who are advanced in moral thinking and prosocial behavior have parents who adapt their communications about fighting, honesty, and ownership to what their children can understand, respect the child's opinion, and gently stimulate the child to think further, without being hostile or critical (Janssens & Dekovic, 1997; Walker & Taylor, 1991a).

Preschoolers who are disliked by peers because of their aggressive approach to resolving conflict show difficulties with moral reasoning. They have trouble distinguishing moral rules from social conventions, and they violate both kinds often (Sanderson & Siegal, 1988). Without special help, such children show long-term disruptions in moral development.

An occasional expression of aggression is normal in early childhood. This preschooler displays instrumental aggression as he pushes a playmate to get an attractive toy. Instrumental aggression declines with age as children learn how to compromise and share. *(Crews/The Image Works)*

THE OTHER SIDE OF MORALITY: DEVELOPMENT OF AGGRESSION

Beginning in late infancy, all children display aggression from time to time as they become better at identifying sources of anger and frustration. By the early preschool years, two general types of aggression emerge. The most common is **instrumental aggression.** In this form, children want an object, privilege, or space, and in trying to get it, they push, shout at, or otherwise attack a person who is in the way. The other type, **hostile aggression,** is meant to hurt another person.

Hostile aggression comes in two varieties. The first is **overt aggression,** which harms others through physical injury or the threat of such injury—for example, hitting, kicking, or threatening to beat up a peer. The second is **relational aggression,** which damages another's peer relationships, as in social exclusion or rumor spreading. "Go away, I'm not going to be your friend anymore!" and "Don't play with Margie, she's a nerd" are examples of relational aggression.

For most preschoolers, instrumental aggression declines with age as they learn to compromise over possessions. In contrast, overt aggression increases between 4 and 7, although it is rare compared to friendly interactions (Shantz, 1987). This slight rise in overtly hostile encounters occurs as children become better at detecting others' intentions. Older preschoolers are more likely to recognize when another child is being deliberately malicious and to try to get even by attacking in return.

Although children of both sexes show this general pattern of development, on the average boys are more overtly aggressive than girls, a trend that appears in many cultures (Whiting & Edwards, 1988b). The sex difference is, in part, due to biology—in particular, to male sex hormones, or androgens. In humans, androgens contribute to boys' higher rate of physical activity, possibly increasing their opportunities for physically aggressive encounters (Collaer & Hines, 1995). At the same time, gender typing (a topic we will take up shortly) is also important. As soon as 2-year-olds become dimly aware of gender stereotypes—that males and females are expected to behave differently—overt aggression drops off in girls but is maintained in boys (Fagot & Leinbach, 1989).

But preschool and school-age girls are not less aggressive than boys! Instead, they are likely to express their hostility differently—through relational aggression (Crick, Casas, & Mosher, 1997; Crick & Grotpeter, 1995). When trying to harm a peer, children seem to do so in ways especially likely to thwart that child's social goals. Boys more often attack physically to block the dominance goals that are typical of boys. Girls resort to relational aggression because it interferes with the close, intimate bonds especially important to girls.

instrumental aggression
Aggression aimed at obtaining an object, privilege, or space with no deliberate intent to harm another person.

hostile aggression
Aggression intended to harm another person.

overt aggression
A form of hostile aggression that harms others through physical injury or the threat of such injury—for example, hitting, kicking, or threatening to beat up a peer.

relational aggression
A form of hostile aggression that does damage to another's peer relationships, as in social exclusion or rumor spreading.

An occasional aggressive exchange between young children is normal and to be expected. As we saw earlier, preschoolers sometimes assert their developing sense of self through these encounters, which become important learning experiences as adults intervene and teach alternative ways of satisfying desires. But some preschoolers show abnormally high rates of aggression. Researchers have traced their problems to strife-ridden families, poor parenting practices, and exposure to television violence—factors that often can be found together.

■ **THE FAMILY AS TRAINING GROUND FOR AGGRESSIVE BEHAVIOR.** "I can't control him, he's impossible," complained Nadine, Robbie's mother, to Leslie one day. When Leslie asked what might be going on at home that made it hard to handle Robbie, she discovered that Robbie's parents fought constantly. Their conflict led to high levels of family stress and a "spillover" of hostile communication into child rearing that stimulated and perpetuated Robbie's aggression.

Observations in families like Robbie's reveal that anger and punitiveness can quickly spread from one family member to another, creating a conflict-ridden family atmosphere and an "out of control" child. The pattern begins with forceful discipline, which is made more likely by stressful life experiences (such as economic hardship or an unhappy marriage), a parent's own personality, or a temperamentally difficult child (Coie & Dodge, 1998; Dodge, Pettit, & Bates, 1994). Once the parent threatens, criticizes, and punishes, then the child whines, yells, and refuses until the parent "gives in." This sequence is likely to be repeated, since at the end of each exchange, both parent and child get relief from stopping the unpleasant behavior of the other. The next time the child misbehaves, the parent is even more coercive and the child more defiant, until one member of the pair "begs off." As these cycles become more frequent, they generate anxiety and irritability among other family members, who soon join in the hostile interactions (Patterson, 1995; Patterson, Reid, & Dishion, 1992).

Aggressive children who are products of these family processes soon learn to view the world from a violent perspective. Because they expect others to react with anger and physical force, they see hostile intent where it does not exist (Dodge & Somberg, 1987; Quiggle et al., 1992). As a result, they make many unprovoked attacks, which contribute to the aggressive cycle.

For at least two reasons, boys are more likely than girls to become involved in family interactions that promote aggressive behavior. First, parents more often use commands and physical punishment with sons. Harsh physical discipline in the absence of warm, caring parental guidance is a strong predictor of later antisocial behavior (Deater-Deckard & Dodge, 1997). Second, parents are less likely to interpret fighting as aggressive when it occurs among boys, so they may overlook it more than they do with girls (Condry & Ross, 1985). In line with this idea, by middle childhood boys expect less parental disapproval and report feeling less guilty over overt aggression than do girls (Perry, Perry, & Weiss, 1989).

Unfortunately, highly aggressive children often have serious adjustment problems. Because of their hostility and poor self-control, they tend to be rejected by peers, to fail in school, and to form relationships with deviant peers, which lead them toward delinquency and adult criminality (see Chapter 16).

■ **TELEVISION AND AGGRESSION.** Televised violence also encourages childhood aggression. A recent large-scale survey of TV violence in the United States concluded that violence pervades American TV (see Figure 10.1). The majority of programs between 6 A.M. and 11 P.M. contain violent scenes, often in the form of repeated aggressive acts against a victim that go unpunished. In fact, most violent portrayals do not show victims experiencing any serious physical harm, and few condemn violence or depict alternative ways of solving problems. To the contrary, many violent TV scenes are embedded in humor. Violent content is 9 percent above average in children's programming, and cartoons are the most violent TV fare of all (Mediascope, 1996).

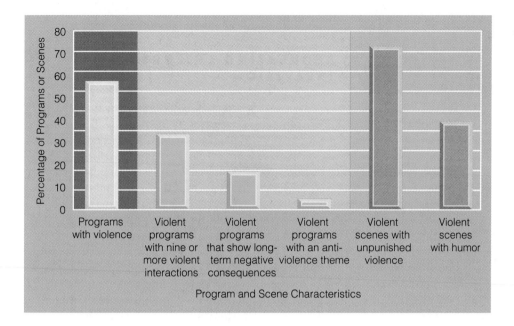

The y-axis is labeled "Percentage of Programs or Scenes" with values 0, 10, 20, 30, 40, 50, 60, 70, 80. The x-axis is labeled "Program and Scene Characteristics" with categories: Programs with violence; Violent programs with nine or more violent interactions; Violent programs that show long-term negative consequences; Violent programs with an anti-violence theme; Violent scenes with unpunished violence; Violent scenes with humor.

FIGURE 10.1

Violent characteristics of American television, based on a large representative sample of over 3,000 programs broadcast between 6 A.M. and 11 P.M. Violence occurs in the majority of programs. It often consists of repeated aggressive acts that go unpunished and that are embedded in humor. Only rarely do programs show long-term negative consequences of violence or present it in the context of an antiviolence theme. *(Adapted from Mediascope, 1996.)*

Young children are especially likely to be influenced by television. One reason is that before age 8, children fail to understand a great deal of what they see on TV. Because they have difficulty connecting separate scenes into a meaningful story line, they do not relate the actions of a TV character to motives or consequences (Collins et al., 1978). A villain who gets what he wants by punching, shooting, and killing may not be a "bad guy" to a preschooler, who fails to notice that the character was brought to justice in the end. Young children also find it hard to separate true-to-life from fantasized television content. Four-year-olds consider human actors "real" and cartoon characters "unreal." Five-year-olds make more accurate distinctions, saying that news and documentaries depict real events and that fictional programs are "just for TV." But not until age 7 do children fully grasp the unreality of TV fiction—that characters do not retain their roles in real life and that their behavior is scripted (Wright et al., 1994). These misunderstandings increase young children's willingness to uncritically accept and imitate what they see on TV.

Reviewers of thousands of studies have concluded that television provides children with "an extensive how-to course in aggression" (Comstock & Paik, 1994; Huston et al., 1992; Slaby et al., 1995, p. 163). The case is strengthened by the fact that research using a wide variety of research designs, methods, and participants has yielded similar findings. In addition, the relationship of TV violence to hostile behavior remains the same after many factors that might otherwise account for this association are controlled.

Violent programming creates both short-term and long-term difficulties in parent and peer relations. Longitudinal research reveals that highly aggressive children have a greater appetite for violent TV. As they watch more, they become increasingly likely to resort to hostile ways of solving problems, a spiraling pattern of learning that contributes to serious antisocial acts by adolescence and young adulthood (Huesmann, 1986; Huesmann & Miller, 1994). Television violence also "hardens" children to aggression, making them more willing to tolerate it in others. Heavy TV viewers begin to see the world as a mean, scary, and dangerous place where aggressive acts are a normal and acceptable means for solving problems (Donnerstein, Slaby, & Eron, 1994).

The ease with which television can manipulate the beliefs and behavior of children has resulted in strong public pressures to improve its content. As the Social Issues box on page 386 indicates, these efforts have not been very successful. At present, it is up to parents to regulate their children's exposure—a heavy burden, given that children find TV so attractive.

SOCIAL

ISSUES

REGULATING CHILDREN'S TELEVISION

Exposure to television is almost universal in the United States and other Western industrialized nations. Ninety-eight percent of American homes have at least one television set, and a TV is switched on in a typical household for a total of 7.1 hours a day. TV enters the lives of children at an early age, becoming a major teacher of undesirable attitudes and behavior.

Parents who watch TV with their children can help them interpret and evaluate televised messages. They can also encourage children to build on TV content in constructive ways—for example, through active play or a trip to the library to gather more information. *(Robert Brenner/PhotoEdit)*

Yet television has as much potential for good as it does for ill. If the content of television were changed, it could promote prosocial attitudes and behavior and convey information about nonviolent aspects of the world, such as history, science, literature, fine arts, and other cultures (Graves, 1993).

Unfortunately, recent changes in the media world have increased children's exposure to harmful messages. Over 60 percent of American families are cable subscribers, and about 80 percent own VCRs—rates that are rapidly increasing (Huston & Wright, 1998). Children with cable or VCR access can see films with far more graphic violence and sexual content than are shown on commercial TV (Huston et al., 1992).

Many organizations concerned with the well-being of children and families have recommended government regulation of TV. But the First Amendment right to free speech has made the U.S. federal government reluctant to place limits on television content. Today, there are fewer restrictions than there once were on program content and advertising for children.

For example, 15 years ago, characters in children's programs were not permitted to sell products. Now they

commonly do—a strategy that greatly increases children's desire to buy (Kunkel, 1993). Since preschoolers (and many older children as well) innocently believe that the promises of TV ads are true, they ask for products that they see, including toys and sugary foods, which make up about 80 percent of advertising aimed at children.

Professionals and committed public officials have sought ways to counteract the negative impact of television that are consistent with the First Amendment. Their efforts have led to limited successes. The U.S. federal government now requires broadcasters to provide at least 3 hours per week of educational programming for children. In addition, television manufacturers must include a "V-chip" that allows consumers to block programs with particular ratings. Most parents regard the rating system as helpful. Yet some people argue that labeling a program as violent or sexual increases its attraction to young audiences—a hypothesis supported for boys (Cantor & Harrison, 1996).

Sometimes it takes a tragedy to mobilize action to protect children. In 1992, a Canadian teenager, who believed that TV violence contributed to his sister's rape and murder,

■ **HELPING CHILDREN AND PARENTS CONTROL AGGRESSION.** Treatment for aggressive children must begin early, before their antisocial behavior becomes so well practiced that it is difficult to change. Breaking the cycle of hostilities between family members and replacing it with effective interaction styles is crucial.

Leslie suggested that Robbie's parents see a family therapist, who observed their inept practices, demonstrated alternatives, and had Nadine and her husband practice them. They learned not to give in to Robbie, to pair commands with reasons, to replace verbal insults and spankings with more effective punishments (such as time out and withdrawal of privileges), and to limit his access to TV with violent content (Patterson, 1982). The therapist also encouraged Robbie's parents to be warmer and more supportive and to give him attention and approval for prosocial acts. The coercive cycles of parents and aggressive children are so persistent that these children often get punished when they do behave appropriately (Strassberg, 1995).

CAREGIVING CONCERNS

Regulating Children's TV Viewing

STRATEGY	DESCRIPTION
Limit TV viewing.	Avoid using TV as a baby-sitter. Provide clear rules that limit what children can watch—for example, an hour a day and only certain programs—and stick to the rules.
Refrain from using TV as a reinforcer.	Do not use television to reward or punish children, a practice that increases its attractiveness.
Encourage child-appropriate viewing.	Encourage children to watch programs that are child-appropriate, informative, and prosocial.
Explain televised information to children.	As much as possible, watch with children, helping them understand what they see. When adults express disapproval of on-screen behavior, raise questions about the realism of televised information, and encourage children to discuss it, they teach children to evaluate TV content rather than accept it uncritically.
Link televised content to everyday learning experiences.	Build on TV programs in constructive ways, encouraging children to move away from the set into active engagement with their surroundings. For example, a program on animals might spark a trip to the zoo, a visit to the library for books about animals, or new ways of observing and caring for the family pet.
Model good viewing practices.	Avoid excess television viewing, especially violent programs, yourself. Parental viewing patterns influence children's viewing patterns.
Use a warm, rational approach to child rearing.	Respond to children with warmth and reasonable demands for mature behavior. Children who experience these practices prefer programs with prosocial content and are less attracted to violent TV.

Source: Slaby et al., 1995.

organized a petition to reduce violent TV programming. More than 1 million people signed it (Dubow & Miller, 1996). The Canadian television industry responded with a voluntary code that bans gratuitous violence (unnec-essary to the plot) and that requires the consequences of violence to be shown in children's programs. Still, programs from the United States that violate the code slip through on Canadian cable TV.

Parents face an awesome task in monitoring and controlling children's TV viewing, given the extent of harmful messages on the screen. The Caregiving Concerns table above lists some strategies they can use.

At the same time, Leslie began teaching Robbie more successful ways of relating to peers. As opportunities arose, she encouraged Robbie to talk about a playmate's feelings and express his own. This helped Robbie take the perspective of others and empathize. Soon he showed greater willingness to share and cooperate (Feshbach & Feshbach, 1982). Robbie also participated in **social problem-solving training**. Over several months, he met with Leslie and a small group of preschoolers. The children used puppets to act out common conflicts, discussed effective and ineffective ways of resolving them, and tried out successful strategies. Such training leads to gains in social competence that are still present a year after the intervention (Feis & Simons, 1985; Spivack & Shure, 1974). Effective social problem solving also provides children with a sense of mastery and self-worth in the face of stressful life events. It reduces the risk of adjustment difficulties in children from low-SES and troubled families (Downey & Walker, 1989; Goodman, Gravitt, & Kaslow, 1995).

social problem-solving training
Training in which children are taught how to resolve social conflicts through discussing and trying out successful strategies.

Finally, Robbie's parents got help with their marital problems. This, in addition to their improved ability to manage Robbie's behavior, greatly reduced tension and conflict in the household.

ASK YOURSELF . . .

■ *Alice and Wayne want their two young children to develop a strong, internalized conscience and to become generous, caring individuals. List as many parenting practices as you can that would promote these goals.*

■ *Nanette told her 3-year-old son Darren not to go into the front yard without asking, since the house faces a very busy street. Darren disobeyed several times, and now Nanette thinks it's time to punish him. How would you recommend that Nanette discipline Darren, and why?*

BRIEF REVIEW

The young child's morality gradually shifts from externally controlled responses to internalized standards. Contrary to predictions from Freudian theory, parental power assertion and love withdrawal do not promote the development of conscience. Instead, induction is far more successful. Behaviorism and social learning theory have shown that modeling combined with reinforcement in the form of praise is effective in encouraging prosocial acts. In contrast, harsh punishment promotes temporary compliance, not lasting changes in children's behavior. According to cognitive-developmental theory, children actively think about justice and fairness. During the preschool years, they recognize that intentionally hurting someone is worse than doing so accidentally. They also distinguish truthfulness from lying and moral rules from social conventions. Hostile family atmospheres, poor parenting practices, and heavy television viewing promote childhood aggression, which can spiral into serious antisocial activity.

GENDER TYPING

The process of developing *gender roles,* or gender-linked preferences and behaviors valued by the larger society, is called **gender typing.** Early in the preschool years, gender typing is well under way. In Leslie's classroom, children tended to play and form friendships with peers of their own sex. Girls spent more time in the housekeeping, art, and reading corners, whereas boys gathered more often in blocks, woodworking, and active play spaces.

The same three theories that provide accounts of morality have been used to explain gender-role development. According to *psychoanalytic theory,* gender-stereotyped beliefs and behaviors are adopted in the same way as other social standards—through identification with the same-sex parent in early childhood. Recall that Freud's ideas worked poorly in the area of morality. They also have difficulty accounting for gender typing. Research shows that the same-sex parent is only one of many influences in gender-role development. Other-sex parents, peers, siblings, teachers, and the broader social environment are important as well.

Social learning theory, with its emphasis on modeling and reinforcement, and *cognitive-developmental theory,* with its focus on children as active thinkers about their social world, are major current approaches to explaining children's gender typing. We will see that neither has proved adequate by itself. Consequently, a third perspective that combines elements of both, called *gender schema theory,* has gained favor. In the following sections, we consider the early development of gender typing, along with genetic and environmental contributions to it.

PRESCHOOLERS' GENDER-STEREOTYPED BELIEFS AND BEHAVIORS

Recall from Chapter 7 that around age 2, children begin to label their own sex and that of other people. As soon as basic gender categories are established, children start to sort out what they mean in terms of activities and behaviors. A wide variety of gender stereotypes are quickly mastered.

gender typing
The process of developing gender roles, or gender-linked preferences and behaviors valued by the larger society.

Preschoolers associate many toys, articles of clothing, tools, household items, games, occupations, behaviors, and even colors (pink and blue) with one sex or the other (Ruble & Martin, 1998). And their actions fall in line with their beliefs—not only in play preferences, but in personality traits as well. We have already seen that boys tend to be more active, assertive, and overtly aggressive. In contrast, girls tend to be more fearful, dependent, compliant, considerate, emotionally sensitive, and relationally aggressive (Brody & Hall, 1993; Eisenberg & Fabes, 1998; Feingold, 1994; Saarni, 1993).

Over the preschool years, children's gender-stereotyped beliefs become stronger—so much so that they operate like blanket rules rather than flexible guidelines (Biernat, 1991a; Martin, 1989). Once, when Leslie showed the children a picture of a Scottish bagpiper wearing a kilt, they insisted, "Men don't wear skirts!" During free play, they often exclaimed that girls don't drive fire engines and can't be police officers and boys don't take care of babies and can't be the teacher.

These one-sided judgments are a joint product of gender stereotyping in the environment and preschoolers' cognitive limitations—in particular, their difficulty coordinating conflicting sources of information. Most preschoolers do not yet realize that characteristics *associated* with gender—activities, toys, occupations, hairstyle, and clothing—do not *determine* whether a person is male or female. They have trouble understanding that males and females can be different in terms of their bodies yet similar in many other ways.

GENETIC INFLUENCES ON GENDER TYPING

The sex differences just described appear in many cultures around the world (Whiting & Edwards, 1988a). Some—the preference for same-sex playmates as well as male activity level and overt aggression—are widespread among animal species as well (Beatty, 1992). So it is reasonable to ask whether gender typing might be influenced by genetic factors. We have already indicated that there is good evidence that aggression is indirectly linked to sex hormones in human children. That is, androgens promote active play among boys, increasing the likelihood of hostile encounters.

Eleanor Maccoby (1990) argues that hormonal differences between males and females have important consequences for gender typing. Early on, hormones affect play styles,

During the preschool years, children seek out playmates of their own sex. Sex hormones affect children's play styles, leading to rough, noisy movements among boys and calm, gentle actions among girls. Then preschoolers naturally choose same-sex partners who share their interests and behavior. Social pressures for "gender-appropriate" play are also believed to promote gender segregation. *(Left, Michael Newman/PhotoEdit; right, Merritt Vincent/PhotoEdit)*

leading to rough, noisy movements among boys and calm, gentle actions among girls. Then, as children begin to interact with peers, they choose same-sex partners whose interests and behaviors are compatible with their own. By age 2, girls already appear overwhelmed by boys' rambunctious behavior. When paired with a boy in a laboratory play session, the girl is likely to stand idly by while he explores the toys (Jacklin & Maccoby, 1978). Nonhuman primates react similarly. When a male juvenile initiates rough, physical play, male peers join in, whereas females withdraw (Beatty, 1992).

Over the preschool years, girls increasingly seek out other girls and like to play in pairs because of a common preference for quieter activities. And boys come to prefer larger-group play with other boys, who respond positively to one another's desire to run, climb, play-fight, and build up and knock down. At age 4, children already spend three times as much time with same-sex as other-sex playmates. By age, 6, this ratio climbs to 11 to 1 (Benenson, 1993; Maccoby & Jacklin, 1987).

However, we must be careful not to overemphasize the contribution of heredity to gender typing. As we will see in the next section, a wide variety of environmental forces build on hereditary influences to promote children's awareness of and conformity to gender roles.

ENVIRONMENTAL INFLUENCES ON GENDER TYPING

A wealth of evidence reveals that family influences, encouragement by teachers and peers, and examples in the broader social environment combine to promote the vigorous gender typing of early childhood.

■ **THE FAMILY.** Beginning at birth, parents hold different perceptions and expectations of their sons and daughters (see Chapter 7), a trend that continues into the preschool years. Many parents state that they want their children to play with "gender-appropriate" toys, and they also believe that boys and girls should be reared differently. When asked about their child-rearing values, parents are likely to describe achievement, competition, and control of emotion as important for sons and warmth, "ladylike" behavior, and closely supervised activities as important for daughters (Brooks-Gunn, 1986; McGuire, 1988; Turner & Gervai, 1995).

These beliefs carry over into actual parenting practices. Mothers and fathers are far more likely to purchase guns, cars, and footballs for sons and dolls, tea sets, and jump ropes for daughters—toys that promote very different play styles. In addition, parents actively reinforce many gender-stereotyped behaviors. For example, they react more positively when a young son as opposed to a young daughter plays with cars and trucks, demands attention, or tries to take toys from others, thereby rewarding his active and assertive behavior (Fagot & Hagan, 1991; Leaper et al., 1995). In contrast, they more often direct play activities, provide help, and discuss emotions with a daughter, encouraging her dependency and emotional sensitivity (Kuebli, Butler, & Fivush, 1995; Lytton & Romney, 1991).

In most aspects of differential treatment of boys and girls, fathers are the ones who discriminate the most. In Chapter 7 we saw that fathers tend to engage in more physically stimulating play with their infant sons than daughters, whereas mothers tend to play in a quieter way with infants of both sexes. In childhood, fathers more than mothers encourage "gender-appropriate" behavior, and they place more pressure to achieve on sons than daughters (Gervai, Turner, & Hinde, 1995; Lytton & Romney, 1991).

These factors are major influences in gender-role learning, since parents who hold nonstereotyped values and apply them in their daily lives have less gender-typed children (Turner & Gervai, 1995; Weisner & Wilson-Mitchell, 1990). Other family members also contribute to gender typing. For example, preschoolers with older, other-sex siblings have many more opportunities to imitate and participate in "cross-gender" play (Stoneman, Brody, & MacKinnon, 1986).

In any case, of the two sexes, boys are clearly the more gender typed. One reason is that parents—particularly fathers—are less tolerant of "cross-gender" behavior in their sons than daughters (Lytton & Romney, 1991). They are more concerned if a boy acts like a "sissy" than if a girl acts like a "tomboy."

■ **TEACHERS.** Besides parents, teachers encourage children to conform to gender roles. Several times, Leslie caught herself responding in ways that furthered sex segregation and stereotyping in her classroom. One day when the class was preparing to leave for a field trip, she called out, "Will the girls line up on one side and the boys on the other?" Then, as the class became noisy with excitement, she pleaded, "Boys, I wish you'd quiet down like the girls!"

As in their experiences at home, girls get more encouragement to participate in adult-structured activities at preschool. They can frequently be seen clustered around the teacher, following directions in an activity. In contrast, boys more often choose areas of the classroom where teachers are minimally involved or entirely absent (Carpenter, 1983). As a result, boys and girls engage in very different social behaviors. Compliance and bids for help occur more often in adult-structured contexts, whereas assertiveness, leadership, and creative use of materials appear more often in unstructured pursuits.

■ **PEERS.** Children's same-sex peer relationships are powerful environments for strengthening stereotyped beliefs and behavior. By age 3, same-sex peers positively reinforce one another for gender-typed play by praising, imitating, or joining in the activity of an agemate. Similarly, when preschoolers engage in "gender-inappropriate" activities—for example, when boys play with dolls or girls with woodworking tools—they receive criticism from peers. Boys are especially intolerant of "cross-gender" play in their male companions (Carter & McCloskey, 1984; Fagot, 1984). A boy who frequently crosses gender lines is likely to be ignored by other boys even when he does engage in "masculine" activities!

Children also develop different styles of social influence in sex-segregated peer groups. To get their way with male peers, boys more often rely on commands, threats, and physical force. In contrast, girls learn to use polite requests and persuasion—strategies that succeed with other girls but not with boys, who start to ignore girls' gentle tactics by the end of early childhood (Borja-Alvarez, Zarbatany, & Pepper, 1991; Leaper, 1991). Consequently, an additional reason that girls may stop interacting with boys is that they do not find it very rewarding to communicate with an unresponsive social partner.

■ **TELEVISION.** Television is yet another powerful source of children's gender stereotypes. In TV programs, women appear less often than men, filling only one-fourth to one-third of character roles. Compared to a decade ago, women are more often shown as involved in careers (Allan & Coltrane, 1996). But overall, they continue to be portrayed as young, attractive, caring, emotional, victimized, and in romantic and family contexts. In contrast, men are depicted as dominant and powerful (Signorielli, 1993; Zillman, Bryant, & Huston, 1994).

Gender roles are especially stereotypic in entertainment programs for children and youths. For example, male cartoon characters are usually problem solvers, whereas females are sweet, childlike followers (Huston et al., 1992). Music television (MTV), designed for teenagers but also viewed by many children, includes males twice as often as females. When women appear, they tend to be dressed in revealing clothing and to be the object of sexual advances (Sommers-Flanagan, Sommers-Flanagan, & Davis, 1993).

■ **THE BROADER SOCIAL ENVIRONMENT.** Although American society has changed to some degree, children's everyday social environments contain many examples of traditional gender-role behavior—in occupations, leisure activities, and achievements of men and women (Ruble & Martin, 1998). As we will see in the next section, young children do not just imitate the many gender-linked responses they observe. They also start to view themselves and their environment in gender-biased ways, a perspective that can seriously limit their interests and skills.

GENDER IDENTITY

As adults, each of us has a **gender identity**—an image of oneself as relatively masculine or feminine in characteristics. By middle childhood, researchers can measure gender identity by asking children to rate themselves on personality traits, since at that time self-concepts begin to emphasize psychological attributes over concrete behaviors.

Individuals differ considerably in the way that they respond to these questionnaires. A child or adult with a "masculine" identity scores high on traditionally masculine items (such as self-sufficient, ambitious, and forceful) and low on traditionally feminine ones (such as affectionate, soft-spoken, and cheerful). Someone with a "feminine" identity does just the reverse. Although the majority of individuals view themselves in gender-typed terms, a substantial minority (especially females) have a type of gender identity called **androgyny.** They score high on *both* masculine and feminine personality characteristics (Boldizar, 1991).

Gender identity is a good predictor of psychological adjustment. Masculine and androgynous children and adults have a higher sense of self-esteem, whereas feminine individuals often think poorly of themselves, perhaps because many feminine traits are not highly valued in our society (Alpert-Gillis & Connell, 1989; Boldizar, 1991). In line with their flexible self-definitions, androgynous individuals are more adaptable in behavior—for example, able to show masculine independence or feminine sensitivity, depending on the situation (Taylor & Hall, 1982). Research on androgyny shows that it is possible for children to acquire a mixture of positive qualities traditionally associated with each gender—an orientation that may best help them realize their potential.

■ **EMERGENCE OF GENDER IDENTITY.** How do children develop gender identities that consist of varying mixtures of masculine and feminine characteristics? Both social learning and cognitive-developmental answers to this question exist. According to *social learning theory,* behavior comes before self-perceptions. Preschoolers first acquire gender-typed responses through modeling and reinforcement. Only later do they organize these behaviors into gender-linked ideas about themselves.

In contrast, *cognitive-developmental theory* regards the direction of development as the other way around. Over the preschool years, children first acquire a cognitive appreciation of their own gender. They develop **gender constancy,** the understanding that their sex is a permanent characteristic that remains the same even if clothing, hairstyle, and play activities change. Then children use this idea to guide their behavior (Kohlberg, 1966).

Research indicates that gender constancy is not present in most children until the end of the preschool years, when they pass Piagetian conservation tasks (De Lisi & Gallagher, 1991). Shown a doll whose hairstyle and clothing are transformed before their eyes, a child younger than age 6 is likely to insist that the doll's sex has changed as well (McConaghy, 1979). And when asked such questions as "When you (a girl) grow up, could you ever be a daddy?" or "Could you be a boy if you wanted to?" young children freely answer yes (Slaby & Frey, 1975).

Yet cognitive immaturity is not the only reason for preschoolers' poor performance on gender constancy tasks, as cognitive-developmental theory assumes. It also results from limited social experience—in particular, lack of opportunity to learn about genital differences between the sexes. In many households in Western societies, young children do not see members of the other sex naked. Therefore, they distinguish males and females using the only information they do have—the way each gender dresses and behaves. Children as

gender identity
An image of oneself as relatively masculine or feminine in characteristics.

androgyny
A type of gender identity in which the person scores high on both traditionally masculine and traditionally feminine personality characteristics.

gender constancy
The understanding that sex remains the same even if clothing, hairstyle, and play activities change.

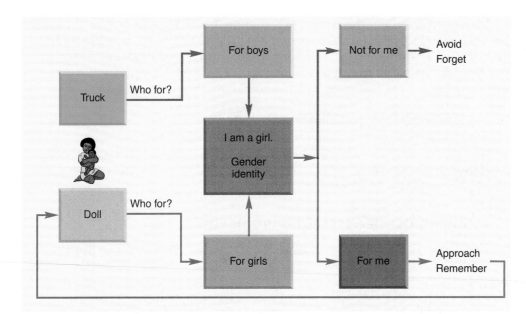

FIGURE 10.2

Effect of gender schemas on gender-stereotyped preferences and behavior. Mandy's network of gender schemas leads her to approach and explore "feminine" toys, such as dolls, and to avoid "masculine" ones, such as trucks. *(From C. L. Martin & C. F. Halverson, 1981, "A Schematic Processing Model of Sex Typing and Stereotyping in Children,"* Child Development, *52, p. 1121.* © *The Society for Research in Child Development, Inc. Adapted by permission.)*

young as 3 who are aware of genital differences usually answer gender constancy questions correctly (Bem, 1989).

Is cognitive-developmental theory correct that gender constancy is responsible for children's gender-typed behavior? Perhaps you have already concluded that evidence for this assumption is weak. "Gender-appropriate" behavior appears so early in the preschool years that modeling and reinforcement must account for its initial appearance, as social learning theory suggests. At present, researchers disagree on just how gender constancy contributes to gender-role development (Bussey & Bandura, 1992; Lutz & Ruble, 1995). But they do know that once children begin to reflect on gender roles, they form basic gender categories that strengthen gender-typed self-images and behavior. Yet another theoretical perspective shows how this happens.

■ **GENDER SCHEMA THEORY.** **Gender schema theory** is an information-processing approach to gender typing that combines social learning and cognitive-developmental features. It emphasizes that both environmental pressures and children's cognitions work together to shape gender-role development (Bem, 1984, 1993; Martin, 1993; Martin & Halverson, 1987).

At an early age, children respond to instruction from others, picking up gender-stereotyped preferences and behaviors. At the same time, they start to organize their experiences into *gender schemas,* or masculine and feminine categories, that they use to interpret their world. A young child who says, "Only boys can be doctors" or "Cooking is a girl's job" already has some well-formed gender schemas. As soon as preschoolers can label their own sex, they begin to select gender schemas that are consistent with it, applying those categories to themselves. As a result, self-perceptions become gender typed and serve as additional gender schemas that children use to process information and guide their own behavior.

Let's look at the example in Figure 10.2 to see exactly how this network of gender schemas strengthens gender-typed preferences and behavior. Three-year-old Mandy has been taught that "dolls are for girls" and "trucks are for boys." She also knows that she is a girl. Mandy uses this information to make decisions about how to behave. Because her schemas lead her to conclude that "dolls are for me," when given a doll she approaches it, explores it, and learns more about it. In contrast, on seeing a truck, she uses her gender schemas to conclude that "trucks are not for me" and responds by avoiding the "gender-inappropriate" toy (Martin & Halverson, 1981).

gender schema theory
An information-processing approach to gender typing that combines social learning and cognitive-developmental features to explain how environmental pressures and children's cognitions work together to shape gender-role development.

In research examining this pattern of reasoning, 4- and 5-year-olds were shown gender-neutral toys varying in attractiveness. An experimenter labeled some as boys' toys and others as girls' toys and left a third group unlabeled. The children engaged in gender-based reasoning, preferring toys labeled for their gender. Highly attractive toys, especially, lost their appeal in the "other-gender" category (Martin, Eisenbud, & Rose, 1995).

Gender schemas are so powerful that when children see others behaving in "gender-inconsistent" ways, they often cannot remember the behavior or distort their memory to make it "gender consistent" (Liben & Signorella, 1993). As a result, they increase their knowledge of "things for me" that fit with their gender schemas, but they learn much less about "cross-gender" activities and behaviors.

REDUCING GENDER STEREOTYPING IN YOUNG CHILDREN

How can we help young children avoid developing rigid gender schemas that restrict their behavior and learning opportunities? As the Cultural Influences box on the following page illustrates, when a nation makes a concerted effort to promote gender equality through its child and family policies, gender stereotyping is substantially reduced.

In cultures where values are slower to change, gender-linked associations are usually so pervasive that parents and teachers must work especially hard to prevent young children from absorbing them (Bem, 1993). Adults can begin by eliminating gender stereotyping from their own behavior and from the alternatives they provide for children. For example, mothers and fathers can take turns making dinner, bathing children, and driving the family car. They can provide sons and daughters with both trucks and dolls and pink and blue clothing. And teachers can make sure that all children spend some time each day in both adult-structured and unstructured activities. Also, efforts can be made to shield children from television and other media presentations that indicate males and females differ in what they can do.

Once children notice the vast array of gender stereotypes in their society, parents and teachers can point out exceptions. For example, they can arrange for children to see men and women pursuing nontraditional careers. And they can reason with children, explaining that interests and skills, not gender, should determine a person's occupation and activities. Research shows that such reasoning is very effective in reducing children's tendency to view the world in a gender-biased fashion (Bigler & Liben, 1990, 1992). And, as we will see in the next section, a rational approach to child rearing promotes healthy, adaptable functioning in many other areas as well.

ASK YOURSELF . . .

■ *Geraldine cut her 3-year-old daughter Fern's hair very short for the summer. When Fern looked in the mirror, she said, "I don't wanna be a boy," and began to cry. Why is Fern upset about her short hairstyle, and what can Geraldine do to help?*

■ *When 4-year-old Roger was in the hospital, he was cared for by a male nurse named Jared. After Roger recovered, he told his friends about Dr. Jared. Using gender schema theory, explain why Roger remembered Jared as a doctor, not a nurse.*

BRIEF REVIEW

During the preschool years, children develop a wide variety of gender-typed beliefs, personality traits, and behaviors. Although heredity contributes to several aspects of gender typing, environmental forces play an especially powerful role. Parents view and treat boys and girls differently, and traditional gender-role learning receives further support from teachers, same-sex peers, television, and the wider social environment. Children gradually develop a gender identity, a view of themselves as masculine, feminine, or androgynous in characteristics. Neither the cognitive-developmental nor the social learning account of gender identity provides a complete explanation. Gender schema theory is an information-processing approach that shows how environmental pressures and children's cognitions work together to sustain gender-typed preferences and behavior.

CULTURAL INFLUENCES

SWEDEN'S COMMITMENT TO GENDER EQUALITY

Of all nations in the world, Sweden is unique in its valuing of gender equality and its social programs that translate this commitment into action. Over a century ago, Sweden's ruling political party adopted equality as a central goal. One social class was not to exploit another, nor one gender another. In the 1960s, Sweden's expanding economy required that women enter the labor force in large numbers. When the question arose as to who would help sustain family life, the Swedish people called on the principle of equality and answered: fathers, just like mothers.

The Swedish "equal roles family model" maintains that husband and wife should have the same opportunity to pursue a career and be equally responsible for housework and child care. To support this goal, day care centers had to be made available outside the home. Otherwise, a class of less privileged women might be

exploited for caregiving and domestic work—an outcome that would contradict the principle of equality. And since full-time employment for both parents often strains a family with young children, Sweden mandated that mothers and fathers with children under age 8 could reduce the length of their working day to 6 hours, with a corresponding reduction in pay but not in benefits (Sandqvist, 1992).

According to several indicators, Sweden's family model is very successful. Maternal employment is extremely high; over 80 percent of mothers with infants and preschoolers work outside the home. Day care centers are numerous, of high quality, and heavily subsidized by the government (Kallós & Broman, 1997). And although Swedish fathers do not yet share housework and child care equally with mothers, they are more involved than fathers in North America and other Western European nations.

Has Sweden's progressive family policy affected the gender beliefs and

behaviors of its youths? A study of Swedish and American adolescents found that the "masculine" role was more highly valued than the "feminine" role in both countries. However, this difference was less pronounced in Sweden, where young people regarded each gender as a blend of instrumental and expressive traits. Furthermore, Swedish girls felt considerably better about their gender—a difference that might be due to greater equalization in men's and women's pay scales and a widespread attitude in Sweden that "feminine" work is important to society. Finally, compared to American adolescents, Swedish young people more often viewed gender roles as a matter of learned tasks and domains of expertise rather than inborn traits or rights and duties (Intons-Peterson, 1988).

Traditional gender typing is not eradicated in Sweden. But great progress has been made as a result of steadfastly pursuing a program of gender equality for several decades.

Sweden places a high value on gender equality. Swedish parents try especially hard to be sensitive and empathic, to ensure participation in decision making, and to spend most of their free time with their children. Compared to fathers in North America and other Western European nations, Swedish fathers are more involved in housework and child care. *(Bo Zaunders/ The Stock Market)*

CHILD REARING AND EMOTIONAL AND SOCIAL DEVELOPMENT

Throughout this chapter and the previous one, we have discussed many ways in which parents can foster children's development—by serving as warm models and reinforcers of mature behavior, by using reasoning, explanation, and inductive discipline, by avoiding harsh punishment, and by encouraging children to master new skills. Now let's put these elements together into an overall view of effective parenting.

STYLES OF CHILD REARING

In a series of landmark studies, Diana Baumrind gathered information on child-rearing practices by watching parents interact with their preschoolers. Two broad dimensions of child rearing emerged. The first is *demandingness.* Some parents establish high standards for their children and insist that their youngsters meet those standards. Other parents demand very little and rarely try to influence their child's behavior. The second dimension is *responsiveness.* Some parents are accepting of and responsive to their children. They frequently engage in open discussion and verbal give-and-take. Others are rejecting and unresponsive.

As Figure 10.3 shows, the various combinations of demandingness and responsiveness yield four styles of child rearing. Baumrind's research focused on three of them: authoritative, authoritarian, and permissive. The fourth type, the uninvolved style, has been studied by other researchers.

■ **AUTHORITATIVE CHILD REARING.** The **authoritative style** is the most adaptive approach to child rearing. Authoritative parents make reasonable demands for maturity, and they enforce them by setting limits and insisting that the child obey. At the same time, they express warmth and affection, listen patiently to their child's point of view, and encourage participation in family decision making. Authoritative child rearing is a rational, democratic approach that recognizes and respects the rights of both parents and children.

Baumrind's findings revealed that children of these parents were developing especially well. They were lively and happy in mood, self-confident in their mastery of new tasks, and self-controlled in their ability to resist engaging in disruptive behavior (Baumrind,

FIGURE 10.3

A two-dimensional classification of child-rearing styles. The various combinations of demandingness and responsiveness yield four styles of child rearing: authoritative, authoritarian, permissive, and uninvolved.

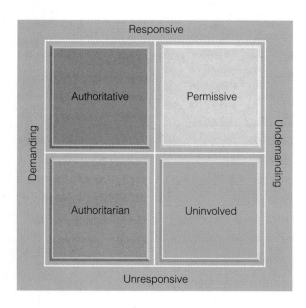

authoritative style
A child-rearing style that is demanding and responsive. A rational, democratic approach in which parents' and children's rights are respected.

1967). These children also seemed less gender typed. Girls scored particularly high in independence and desire to master new tasks and boys in friendly, cooperative behavior (Baumrind & Black, 1967).

■ **AUTHORITARIAN CHILD REARING.** Parents who use an **authoritarian style** are also demanding, but they place such a high value on conformity that they are unresponsive—even outright rejecting—when children are unwilling to obey. "Do it because I said so!" is the attitude of these parents. As a result, they engage in very little give-and-take with children, who are expected to accept their parent's word for what is right in an unquestioning manner. If they do not, authoritarian parents resort to force and punishment.

Baumrind found that preschoolers with authoritarian parents were anxious, withdrawn, and unhappy. When interacting with peers, they tended to react with hostility when frustrated (Baumrind, 1967). Boys, especially, showed high rates of anger and defiance. Girls were dependent and lacking in exploration, and they retreated from challenging tasks (Baumrind, 1971).

■ **PERMISSIVE CHILD REARING.** The **permissive style** of child rearing is nurturant and accepting, but it avoids making demands or imposing controls of any kind. Permissive parents allow children to make many of their own decisions at an age when they are not yet capable of doing so. They can eat meals and go to bed when they feel like it and watch as much television as they want. They do not have to learn good manners or do any household chores. Although some permissive parents truly believe this approach is best, many others lack confidence in their ability to influence their child's behavior and are disorganized and ineffective in running their households.

Baumrind found that children of permissive parents were very immature. They had difficulty controlling their impulses and were disobedient and rebellious when asked to do something that conflicted with their momentary desires. They were also overly demanding and dependent on adults, and they showed less persistence at tasks in preschool than did children of parents who exerted more control. The link between permissive parenting and dependent, nonachieving behavior was especially strong for boys (Baumrind, 1971).

■ **UNINVOLVED CHILD REARING.** The **uninvolved style** combines undemanding with indifferent, rejecting behavior. Uninvolved parents show little commitment to their role as caregivers beyond the minimal effort required to feed and clothe the child. Often they are emotionally detached and depressed and so overwhelmed by the many stresses in their lives that they have little time and energy to spare for children (Maccoby & Martin, 1983).

At its extreme, uninvolved parenting is a form of child maltreatment called *neglect*. It is likely to characterize depressed parents with many stresses in their lives, such as marital conflict, little or no social support, and poverty. Especially when it begins early, it disrupts virtually all aspects of development, including attachment, cognition, play, and social and emotional skills (Cummings & Davies, 1994b). Even when parental disengagement is less extreme, children display many problems—low tolerance for frustration, poor emotional control, school achievement difficulties, and delinquency in adolescence (Kurdek & Fine, 1994; Lamborn et al., 1991).

WHAT MAKES AUTHORITATIVE CHILD REARING EFFECTIVE?

Since Baumrind's early work, a great many studies have confirmed her findings. Throughout childhood and adolescence, authoritative parenting is associated with task persistence, social maturity, high self-esteem, internalized moral standards, and superior academic achievement (Denham, Renwick, & Holt, 1991; Parke & Buriel, 1998; Steinberg, Darling, & Fletcher, 1995).

authoritarian style
A child-rearing style that is demanding but low in responsiveness to children's rights and needs. Conformity and obedience are valued over open communication with the child.

permissive style
A child-rearing style that is responsive but undemanding. An overly tolerant approach to child rearing.

uninvolved style
A child-rearing style that is both undemanding and unresponsive. Reflects minimal commitment to parenting.

Why does this approach to parenting work so well? There are several reasons. First, control that appears fair and reasonable to the child, not abrupt and arbitrary, is far more likely to be complied with and internalized. Second, nurturant parents who are secure in the standards they hold for their children provide models of caring concern as well as confident, assertive behavior. Finally, parents who are authoritative make demands that are reasonable in terms of their child's developing capacities. By adjusting expectations to fit children's ability to take responsibility for their own behavior, these parents let children know that they are competent individuals who can do things successfully for themselves. As a result, high self-esteem and mature, independent behavior are fostered (Kuczynski et al., 1987).

CULTURAL VARIATIONS

Despite broad agreement on the advantages of authoritative child rearing, ethnic groups often have distinct child-rearing beliefs and practices. Some involve variations in warmth and demandingness that are adaptive when viewed in light of cultural values and family circumstances.

For example, compared to Caucasian Americans, Chinese adults describe their own parenting techniques and those they experienced as children as more demanding (Berndt et al., 1993). This greater emphasis on control continues to characterize Chinese parents who have immigrated to the United States. But control in Chinese families does not have the same meaning as authoritarian child rearing in Western culture. Instead, it reflects the Confucian belief in self-discipline, respect for elders, and socially desirable behavior, taught by parents who are deeply concerned and involved in the lives of their children (Chao, 1994; Lin & Fu, 1990).

In Hispanic and Asian Pacific Island families, firm insistence on respect for parental authority, particularly that of the father, is paired with unusually high maternal warmth. As in Chinese families, this combination reflects parental commitment rather than authoritarianism. It is believed to promote compliance, identification with parents and close relatives, and strong feelings of family loyalty (Fracasso & Busch-Rossnagel, 1992; Harrison et al., 1994).

Although wide variation exists among African Americans, research suggests that black mothers (especially those who are younger, less educated, and single) often rely on an adult-centered approach in which they expect immediate obedience from children (Kel-

Asked about their child-rearing practices, the grandparents and mother in this Chinese family would probably describe themselves as quite demanding. Yet clearly, the control they exert occurs in the context of high responsiveness— warmth, acceptance and involvement with the child. *(Ira Kirschenbaum/Stock Boston)*

ley, Power, & Wimbush, 1992; Kelly, Sanchez-Hucies, & Walker, 1993). Strict demands for compliance, however, make sense under certain conditions. When parents have few social supports and live in dangerous neighborhoods, forceful discipline may be necessary to protect children from becoming victims of crime or involved in antisocial activities. Consistent with this view, low-SES, ethnic minority parents who use more controlling strategies tend to have better-adjusted young children (Baldwin, Baldwin, & Cole, 1990; O'Neil & Parke, 1997). And in one recent study, physical discipline in early childhood predicted aggression and other conduct problems during the school years only for Caucasian-American children, not for African-American children (Deater-Deckard et al., 1996). This does not mean that slaps and spankings are effective strategies. But it does suggest the possibility of ethnic group differences in how children view parental behavior that can modify it consequences.

CHILD-REARING STYLES IN CONTEXT

The cultural variations we have just considered are a reminder that child-rearing styles can be fully understood only in their larger ecological context. As we have seen in earlier chapters, a great many factors contribute to parents' capacity to be appropriately warm, consistent, and demanding. These include personal characteristics of child and parent, socioeconomic well-being, access to extended family and community supports, cultural values and practices, and public policies that assist parents in their child-rearing roles (Parke & Buriel, 1998).

As we turn to the topic of child maltreatment, our discussion will underscore, once again, that effective child rearing is sustained not just by the desire of mothers and fathers to be good parents. Almost all want to be. Unfortunately, when vital supports for good parenting break down, children as well as their parents can suffer terribly.

CHILD MALTREATMENT

Child abuse is as old as the history of humankind, but only recently has there been widespread acceptance that the problem exists and research aimed at understanding it. Perhaps the increase in public concern is due to the fact that child maltreatment is especially common in large, industrialized nations. It occurs so often in the United States that a recent government committee called it "a national emergency." A total of 3.1 million cases were reported to juvenile authorities in 1996, an increase of 132 percent over the previous decade (U.S. Department of Health and Human Services, 1997). The true figure is surely much higher, since most cases go unreported.

Child maltreatment takes the following forms:

- *Physical abuse:* assaults on children that produce pain, cuts, welts, bruises, burns, broken bones, and other injuries

- *Sexual abuse:* sexual comments, fondling, intercourse, and other forms of exploitation

- *Physical neglect:* living conditions in which children do not receive enough food, clothing, medical attention, or supervision

- *Emotional neglect:* failure of caregivers to meet children's needs for affection and emotional support

- *Psychological abuse:* actions, such as ridicule, humiliation, scapegoating, or terrorizing, that damage children's emotional, social, or cognitive functioning

Although all experts recognize that these five types exist, they do not agree on how frequent and intense an adult's actions must be to be called maltreatment. The greatest problems arise in the case of subtle, ambiguous behaviors (Barnett et al., 1993; Cicchetti & Toth, 1998a). All of us can agree that broken bones, cigarette burns, and bite marks are abusive, but the decision is harder to make in instances in which an adult touches or makes degrading comments to a child.

Some investigators regard psychological and sexual abuse as the most destructive forms. The rate of psychological abuse may be the highest, since it accompanies most other types. More than 200,000 cases of child sexual abuse are reported each year (U.S. Department of Health and Human Services, 1997). Yet this statistic greatly underestimates the actual number, since affected children may feel frightened, confused, and guilty and are usually pressured into silence. Although children of all ages are targets, the largest number of sexual abuse victims are identified in middle childhood. We will pay special attention to this form of maltreatment in Chapter 13.

■ **ORIGINS OF CHILD MALTREATMENT.** Early findings suggested that child maltreatment was rooted in adult psychological disturbance (Kempe et al., 1962). The first studies indicated that adults who abused or neglected their children usually had a history of maltreatment in their own childhoods, unrealistic expectations that children satisfy their own emotional needs, and poor control of aggressive impulses. It soon became clear that although child abuse was more common among disturbed parents, a single "abusive personality type" did not exist. Sometimes even "normal" parents harmed their children! Also, parents who were abused as children did not always repeat the cycle with their own youngsters (Simons et al., 1991).

For help in understanding child maltreatment, researchers turned to *ecological systems theory* (see Chapters 1 and 2). They discovered that child abuse and neglect are affected by many interacting variables—at the family, community, and cultural levels. Table 10.2 summarizes factors associated with child maltreatment. The more of these risks that are present, the greater the likelihood that abuse will occur. Let's examine each set of influences in turn.

The Family. Within the family, certain children—those whose characteristics make them more of a challenge to rear—are more likely to become targets of abuse. These include premature or very sick babies and children who are temperamentally difficult, are inattentive and overactive, or have other developmental problems. But whether such children actually are maltreated depends on characteristics of parents (Belsky, 1993). In one study, temperamentally difficult youngsters who were physically abused had mothers who believed that they could do little to control the child's behavior. Instead, they attributed the child's unruliness to a stubborn or bad disposition, a perspective that led them to move quickly toward physical force when the child misbehaved (Bugental, Blue, & Cruzcosa, 1989).

TABLE 10.2

Factors Related to Child Maltreatment

FACTOR	DESCRIPTION
Parent characteristics	Psychological disturbance; alcohol and drug abuse; history of abuse as a child; belief in harsh, physical discipline; desire to satisfy unmet emotional needs through the child; unreasonable expectations for child behavior; young age (most under 30); low educational level
Child characteristics	Premature or very sick baby; difficult temperament; inattentiveness and overactivity; other developmental problems
Family characteristics	Low income; poverty; homelessness; marital instability; social isolation; physical abuse of mother by husband or boyfriend; frequent moves; large families with closely spaced children; overcrowded living conditions; disorganized household; lack of steady employment; other signs of high life stress
Community	Characterized by social isolation; few parks, day care centers, preschool programs, recreation centers, and churches to serve as family supports
Culture	Approval of physical force and violence as ways to solve problems

Sources: Belsky, 1993; Cicchetti & Toth, 1998a.

Once child abuse gets started, it quickly becomes part of a self-sustaining family relationship. The small irritations to which abusive parents react—a fussy baby, a preschooler who knocks over a glass of milk, or a child who will not mind immediately—soon become bigger ones. Then the harshness of parental behavior increases. By the preschool years, abusive and neglectful parents seldom interact with their children. When they do, they rarely express pleasure and affection; the communication is almost always negative (Trickett et al., 1991).

Most parents, however, have enough self-control not to respond to their children's misbehavior with abuse, and not all children with developmental problems are mistreated. Other factors must combine with these conditions to prompt an extreme parental response. Unmanageable parental stress is strongly associated with all forms of maltreatment. Abusive parents respond to stressful situations with high emotional arousal. At the same time, such factors as low income, unemployment, marital conflict, overcrowded living conditions, frequent moves, and extreme household disorganization are common in abusive homes (Howes & Cicchetti, 1993). These personal and situational conditions increase the chances that parents will be so overwhelmed that they cannot meet basic child-rearing responsibilities or will vent their frustrations by lashing out at their children.

The Community. The majority of abusive parents are isolated from both formal and informal social supports in their communities. There are at least two causes of this social isolation. First, because of their own life histories, many of these parents have learned to mistrust and avoid others. They do not have the skills necessary for establishing and maintaining positive relationships with friends and relatives (Polansky et al., 1985). Second, abusive parents are more likely to live in neighborhoods that provide few links between family and community, such as parks, day care centers, preschool programs, recreation centers, and churches (Coulton et al., 1995; Garbarino & Kostelny, 1993). For these reasons, they lack "lifelines" to others and have no one to turn to for help during particularly stressful times.

The Larger Culture. One final set of factors—cultural values, laws, and customs—profoundly affects the chances that child maltreatment will occur when parents feel overburdened. Societies that view violence as an appropriate way to solve problems set the stage for child abuse. These conditions exist in the United States. Although all 50 states have laws designed to protect children from maltreatment, strong support still exists for the use of physical force with children. For example, during the past 30 years, the United States Supreme Court has twice upheld the right of school officials to use corporal punishment to discipline children. Crime rates have risen in American cities, and television sets beam graphic displays of violence into family living rooms.

In view of the widespread acceptance of violent behavior in American culture, it is not surprising that over 90 percent of American parents report using slaps and spankings at one time or another to discipline their children (Staub, 1996). In countries where physical punishment is not accepted, such as China, Japan, Luxembourg, and Sweden, child abuse is rare (Zigler & Hall, 1989a).

■ **CONSEQUENCES OF CHILD MALTREATMENT.** The family circumstances of maltreated children impair the development of emotional self-regulation, self-concept, and social skills. Over time, these youngsters show serious learning and adjustment problems, including difficulties with peers, academic failure, severe depression, substance abuse, and delinquency (Cicchetti & Toth, 1998).

How do these damaging consequences occur? Think back to our earlier discussion of the effects of hostile cycles of parent–child interaction, which are especially severe for abused children. Indeed, a family characteristic strongly associated with child abuse is domestic violence, in which mothers are repeatedly brutalized (physically and psychologically) by their partners (McCloskey, Figueredo, & Koss, 1995). Clearly, the home lives of abused children overflow with opportunities to learn to use aggression as a way of solving problems.

Children learn by repetition.

You don't have to hit to hurt.

San Francisco Child Abuse Council
(415) 668-0494

Public service announcements help prevent child abuse by educating people about the problem and informing them of where to seek help. This poster reminds adults that degrading remarks can hit as hard as a fist. *(Courtesy San Francisco Child Abuse Council)*

ASK YOURSELF . . .

■ *Earlier in this chapter, we discussed induction as an especially effective form of discipline. Which child-rearing style is most likely to be associated with use of induction, and why?*

■ *Chandra heard a news report that ten severely neglected children, living in squalor in an inner-city tenement, were discovered by Chicago police. Chandra thought to herself, "What could possibly lead parents to mistreat their children so badly?" How would you answer Chandra's question?*

Furthermore, demeaning parental messages, in which children are ridiculed, humiliated, rejected, or terrorized, result in low self-esteem, high anxiety, self-blame, and efforts to escape from extreme psychological pain—at times severe enough to lead to attempted suicide in adolescence (Sternberg et al., 1993; Toth & Cicchetti, 1996). At school, maltreated children are serious discipline problems. Their noncompliance, poor motivation, and cognitive immaturity interfere with academic achievement—an outcome that further undermines their chances for life success (Eckenrode, Laird, & Doris, 1993).

Finally, the trauma of repeated abuse can lead to psychophysiological changes, including abnormal EEG activity and altered production of stress hormones (Hart, Gunnar, & Cicchetti, 1995; Pollack et al., 1997). These effects on brain functioning increase the chances that adjustment problems will endure.

■ **PREVENTING CHILD MALTREATMENT.** Since child maltreatment is embedded in families, communities, and society as a whole, efforts to prevent it must be directed at each of these levels. Many approaches have been suggested, including interventions that teach high-risk parents effective child-rearing and disciplinary strategies, high school child development courses that include direct experience with children, and broad social programs aimed at bettering economic conditions for low-SES families.

In early parts of this book, we saw that providing social supports to families is very effective in easing parental stress. This approach sharply reduces child maltreatment as well. Research indicates that a trusting relationship with another person is the most important factor in preventing mothers with childhood histories of abuse from repeating the cycle with their own youngsters (Caliso & Milner, 1992; Egeland, Jacobvitz, & Sroufe, 1988). Parents Anonymous, a national organization that has as its main goal helping child-abusing parents learn constructive parenting practices, does so largely through providing social supports to families. Its local chapters offer self-help group meetings, daily phone calls, and regular home visits to relieve social isolation and teach alternative child-rearing skills.

Besides these efforts, changes are needed in American culture. Many experts believe that child maltreatment cannot be eliminated as long as violence is widespread and corporal punishment regarded as an acceptable child-rearing alternative.

Although more cases reach the courts than in decades past, child maltreatment remains a crime that is difficult to prove. Most of the time, the only witnesses are the child victims or other loyal family members. Even in court cases in which the evidence is strong, judges hesitate to impose the ultimate safeguard against further harm: permanently removing the child from the family.

There are several reasons for this reluctant attitude. First, in American society, government intervention into family life is viewed as a last resort, to be used only when there is near certainty that a child will be denied basic care and protection. Second, despite destructive family relationships, maltreated children and their parents usually are attached to one another. Most of the time, neither desires separation. Finally, the American legal system tends to regard children as parental property rather than as human beings in their own right, and this also has stood in the way of court-ordered protection.

Even with intensive treatment, some adults persist in their abusive acts. An estimated 1,500 American children die from maltreatment each year (U.S. Department of Health and Human Services, 1997). When parents are unlikely to change their behavior, the drastic step of separating parent from child and legally terminating parental rights is the only reasonable course of action.

Child maltreatment is a distressing and horrifying topic—a sad note on which to end our discussion of a period of childhood that is so full of excitement, awakening, and discovery. But there is reason to be optimistic. Great strides have been made over the last several decades in understanding and preventing child maltreatment.

Summary

ERIKSON'S THEORY: INITIATIVE VERSUS GUILT

What personality changes take place during Erikson's stage of initiative versus guilt?

■ According to Erikson, preschoolers develop a new sense of purposefulness as they grapple with the psychological conflict of **initiative versus guilt.** A healthy sense of initiative depends on resolving the Freudian Oedipus and Electra conflicts, in which conscience is formed through **identification** with the same-sex parent.

■ Although Freud's ideas are no longer widely accepted, Erikson's image of initiative captures the emotional and social changes that take place during this phase of development.

SELF-DEVELOPMENT

Describe preschoolers' self-concepts, understanding of intentions, and self-esteem.

■ Preschoolers' **self-concepts** largely consist of observable characteristics and typical beliefs, emotions, and attitudes. Their increasing self-awareness underlies struggles over objects as well as first efforts to cooperate. Children become more skilled over the preschool years at distinguishing intentional from unintentional acts.

■ During early childhood, **self-esteem** is not yet well differentiated. Preschoolers' high self-esteem contributes to their mastery-oriented approach to the environment. However, even a little adult disapproval can undermine a young child's self-esteem and enthusiasm for learning.

EMOTIONAL DEVELOPMENT

Cite changes in understanding and expression of emotion during early childhood, along with factors that influence those changes.

■ Young children have an impressive understanding of the causes, consequences, and behavioral signs of basic emotional reactions. By age 3 to 4, they are also aware of a variety of strategies that assist with emotional self-regulation. Temperament, adult modeling, and conversations about feelings influence the development of effective techniques for handling negative emotion.

■ Preschoolers experience self-conscious emotions more often as their self-concepts become better developed and they become increasingly sensitive to the praise and criticism of others. Empathy becomes more common over the preschool years. As with emotional self-regulation, temperament and social experience also contribute to these aspects of emotional development.

PEER RELATIONS

Describe the development of peer sociability, the quality of preschoolers' friendships, and parental and sibling influences on early peer relations.

■ During early childhood, interactive play with peers increases. According to Parten, it begins with **nonsocial activity,** shifts to **parallel play,** and then moves to **associative** and **cooperative play.** However, preschoolers do not follow this straightforward developmental sequence. Solitary play and parallel play remain common throughout early childhood. Sociodramatic play becomes especially frequent and supports many aspects of emotional and social development.

■ Preschoolers view friendship in concrete, activity-based terms. Their interactions with friends are especially positive and cooperative.

■ Parents influence early peer relations by arranging informal peer play activities and offering advice, guidance, and examples of how to act toward others. Children with stressful home lives often generalize their negative sibling interaction patterns to peers.

FOUNDATIONS OF MORALITY

What are the central features of psychoanalytic, behaviorist and social learning, and cognitive-developmental approaches to moral development?

■ The psychoanalytic and behaviorist approaches to morality focus on how children acquire ready-made standards held by adults. In contrast to Freud's theory, discipline promoting fear of punishment and loss of parental love does not foster conscience development. Instead, **induction** is far more effective in encouraging self-control and **prosocial, or altruistic, behavior.**

■ Behaviorism and social learning theory regard reinforcement and modeling as the basis for moral action. Effective adult models of morality are warm, powerful, and practice what they preach. Harsh punishment does not promote moral internalization and socially desirable behavior. Alternatives, such as **time out** and withdrawal of privileges, can reduce the undesirable side effects of punishment.

■ The cognitive-developmental perspective views children as active thinkers about social rules. By age 4, preschoolers understand the distinction between truthfulness and lying and say that disobeying moral rules is more serious than violating social conventions. Peer interaction provides children with important opportunities to work out their first ideas about justice and fairness. Parents who discuss moral issues with their children help them reason about morality.

Describe the development of aggression in early childhood, including family and television as major influences.

■ All children display aggression from time to time. During early childhood, **instru-**

Summary (continued)

mental aggression declines while **hostile aggression** increases. Two types of hostile aggression appear: **overt aggression,** which is more common in boys, and **relational aggression,** which is more common in girls.

- Ineffective discipline and a conflict-ridden family atmosphere promote and sustain aggression in children. Televised violence also promotes childhood aggression. Young children's limited understanding of TV content increases their willingness to uncritically accept and imitate what they see.

- Teaching parents effective child-rearing practices, providing children with **social problem-solving training,** reducing hostility in family relationships, and shielding children from violent TV content are ways of reducing aggressive behavior.

GENDER TYPING

Discuss genetic and environmental influences on preschoolers' gender-stereotyped beliefs and behavior.

- **Gender typing** is well underway in the preschool years. Gender stereotyping in the environment and cognitive limitations lead young children to acquire a wide range of gender-stereotyped beliefs and behaviors. Gender stereotypes during the preschool years operate like blanket rules rather than flexible guidelines.

- Genetic factors are believed to play a role in boys' higher activity level and overt aggression and children's preference for same-sex playmates. At the same time, parents, teachers, peers, television, and the broader social environment encourage

many gender-typed responses.

Describe and evaluate the accuracy of major theories of the emergence of gender identity.

- **Gender identity** is measured by asking children and adults to rate themselves on gender-stereotyped personality traits. Although most people have traditional gender identities, some are **androgynous,** scoring high on both masculine and feminine characteristics.

- According to social learning theory, preschoolers first acquire gender-typed responses through modeling and reinforcement and then organize them into gender-linked ideas about themselves. Cognitive-developmental theory suggests that **gender constancy** must be mastered before children develop gender-typed behavior. In contrast to cognitive-developmental predictions, gender-role behavior is acquired long before gender constancy.

- **Gender schema theory** is an information-processing approach to gender typing that combines social learning and cognitive-developmental features. As children acquire gender-stereotyped preferences and behaviors, they form masculine and feminine categories, or gender schemas, that they apply to themselves and use to interpret their world.

CHILD REARING AND EMOTIONAL AND SOCIAL DEVELOPMENT

Describe the impact of child-rearing styles on children's development, and explain why authoritative parenting is effective.

- Two broad dimensions, demandingness and responsiveness, yield four styles of

child rearing. The **authoritative style,** which is both demanding and responsive, promotes cognitive, emotional, and social competence. Parental caring concern, explanations, and reasonable demands for mature behavior account for its effectiveness.

- The **authoritarian style,** which is high in demandingness but low in responsiveness, is associated with anxious, withdrawn behavior. The **permissive style** is responsive but undemanding; children who experience it typically show poor self-control and achievement. The **uninvolved style** is low in both demandingness and responsiveness. It disrupts virtually all aspects of development.

Discuss the multiple origins of child maltreatment, its consequences for development, and prevention strategies.

- Child maltreatment is related to factors within the family, community, and larger culture. Child and parent characteristics often feed on one another to produce abusive behavior. Unmanageable parental stress and social isolation greatly increase the chances that abuse and neglect will occur. When a society approves of force and violence as a means for solving problems, child abuse is promoted.

- Maltreated children are impaired in emotional self-regulation, self-concept, social skills, and learning in school. Over time they show a wide variety of serious adjustment problems. Successful prevention of child maltreatment requires efforts at the family, community, and societal levels.

*I*mportant terms and concepts

androgyny (p. 392)
associative play (p. 374)
authoritarian style (p. 397)
authoritative style (p. 396)
cooperative play (p. 374)
gender constancy (p. 392)
gender identity (p. 392)
gender schema theory (p. 393)
gender typing (p. 388)

hostile aggression (p. 383)
identification (p. 367)
induction (p. 379)
initiative versus guilt (p. 366)
instrumental aggression (p. 383)
nonsocial activity (p. 374)
overt aggression (p. 383)
parallel play (p. 374)
permissive style (p. 397)

prosocial, or altruistic, behavior
  (p. 379)
relational aggression (p. 383)
self-concept (p. 368)
self-esteem (p. 369)
social problem-solving training (p. 387)
time out (p. 381)
uninvolved style (p. 397)

*F*yi . . .   FOR FURTHER INFORMATION AND HELP

CHILDREN'S TELEVISION

Center for Media Education
(202) 628-2620
Website: www.tap.epn.org/cme/cktv.html

*An organization aimed at improving policies
in the area of electronic media. Serves as a
strong advocate for better TV programming
for children and industry-wide strategies that
protect children from televised violence. Also
works with education, library, and child
advocacy organizations to expand low-SES
and minority children's access to new educational technologies.*

CHILD ABUSE AND NEGLECT

Child Help USA, Inc.
(800) 422-4453
Website: www.childhelpusa.org

*Promotes public awareness of child abuse
through publications, media campaigns, and
a speakers' bureau. Supports the National
Child Abuse Hotline, (800) 4-A-CHILD.
Callers may request information about child
abuse or speak with a crisis counselor.*

Parents Anonymous
(602) 248-0428
Website: www.parentsanon.org

*Dedicated to prevention and treatment of
child abuse. Local groups provide support to
child-abusing parents and training in nonviolent child-rearing techniques.*

National Clearinghouse on Child Abuse
and Neglect Information
(800) 394-3366
Website: www.calib.com/nccanch

*Provides information to states and communi-
ties wishing to develop programs and activities that identify, prevent, and treat child
abuse and neglect.*

ℳilestones

AGE	PHYSICAL	COGNITIVE	LANGUAGE	EMOTIONAL/SOCIAL
2 years	■ Slower gains in height and weight than in toddlerhood. (294) ■ Appetite usually declines. (303–304) ■ Running, jumping, hopping, throwing, and catching develop. (312) ■ Puts on and removes some items of clothing. (314) ■ Uses spoon effectively. (314)	■ Make-believe becomes less dependent on realistic toys, less self-centered, and more complex. (325) ■ Can take the perspective of others in simple situations. (331) ■ Recognition memory well developed. (341) ■ Aware of the difference between inner mental and outer physical events. (343)	■ Vocabulary increases rapidly. (356) ■ Sentences follow word order of native language; adds grammatical markers. (357) ■ Displays effective conversational skills. (358)	■ Begins to develop self-concept and self-esteem. (368–369) ■ Distinguishes own intentional from unintentional acts. (368) ■ Cooperation and instrumental aggression are evident. (368, 383) ■ Understands causes, consequences, and behavioral signs of basic emotions. (371) ■ Empathy increases. (373) ■ Gender-stereotyped beliefs and behavior increase. (389)
3–4 years	■ May no longer need a daytime nap. (303) ■ Running, jumping, hopping, throwing, and catching become better coordinated. (312) ■ Galloping and one-foot skipping appear. (312) ■ Rides tricycle. (312) ■ Uses scissors. (314) ■ Scribbles become pictures; draws first picture of a person. (314) ■ Can tell the difference between writing and nonwriting. (318)	■ Notices transformations, reverses thinking, and understands causality in familiar situations. (333) ■ Classifies familiar objects hierarchically. (334) ■ Understands models and simple maps as symbols. (327) ■ Uses private speech to guide behavior in challenging tasks. (337) ■ Attention becomes more sustained and planful. (340) ■ Uses scripts to recall familiar experiences. (342) ■ Understands that both beliefs and desires determine behavior. (343) ■ Aware of some features of written language. (346) ■ Counts small numbers of objects and grasps cardinality. (348)	■ Masters increasingly complex grammatical structures. (357) ■ Occasionally overextends grammatical rules to exceptions. (357) ■ Understands many culturally accepted ways of adjusting speech to fit the age, sex, and social status of speakers and listeners. (358)	■ Begins to distinguish others' intentional from unintentional acts. (368) ■ Emotional self-regulation improves. (372) ■ Self-conscious emotions become more common. (373) ■ Nonsocial activity declines and interactive play increases. (375) ■ Instrumental aggression declines, hostile aggression increases. (383) ■ Forms first friendships. (376) ■ Distinguishes moral rules from social conventions. (382) ■ Preference for same-sex playmates strengthens. (389)

AGE	PHYSICAL	COGNITIVE	LANGUAGE	EMOTIONAL/SOCIAL
5–6 years	■ Body is streamlined and longer-legged with proportions similar to those of adults. (294) ■ First permanent tooth erupts. (296) ■ Gross motor skills increase in speed and endurance. (311) ■ Skipping appears. (312) ■ Ties shoes, draws more complex pictures, writes name. (314–316) ■ Can discriminate fine-grained visual forms, such as letters of the alphabet. (318)	■ Ability to distinguish appearance from reality improves. (334) ■ Attention continues to improve. (340) ■ Recall, scripted memory, and autobiographical memory improve. (341–342) ■ Understands that letters and sounds are linked in systematic ways. (347) ■ Counts on and counts down, engaging in simple addition and subtraction. (348)	■ Vocabulary reaches about 10,000 words. (356) ■ Uses many complex grammatical forms. (358)	■ Bases understanding of people's intentions on a wider range of social cues. (369) ■ Ability to interpret, predict, and influence others' emotional reactions improves. (371) ■ Relies on language to express empathy. (373) ■ Has acquired many morally relevant rules and behaviors. (378) ■ Gender-stereotyped beliefs and behavior continue to increase. (389) ■ Grasps the genital basis of sex differences and shows gender constancy. (392)

Note: Numbers in parenthesis indicate the page on which each milestone is discussed.

"Horse Trading"
G. Munkh-Evdene
7 years, Mongolia

Middle childhood brings great advances in motor coordination, and children strive to master athletic skills valued in their culture. Whereas a Western child may want to be an accomplished soccer player or gymnast, a Mongolian child may desire to conquer the art of horse training. Chapter 11 takes up the diverse physical attainments of the school years.

Reprinted by permission from The International Museum of Children's Art, Oslo, Norway.

PHYSICAL DEVELOPMENT
in Middle Childhood

I'm on my way,

Mom!" hollered 10-year-old Joey as he stuffed the last bite of toast into his mouth, slung his book bag over his shoulder, dashed out the door, jumped on his bike, and headed down the street for school. Joey's 8-year-old sister Lizzie followed, quickly kissing her mother good-bye and peddling furiously until she caught up with Joey. Rena, the children's mother and one of my colleagues at the university, watched from the front porch as her son and daughter disappeared in the distance.

"They're branching out," Rena remarked to me over lunch that day as she described the children's expanding activities and relationships. Homework, household chores, soccer teams, music lessons, scouting, friends at school and in the neighborhood, and Joey's new paper route were all part of the children's routine. "It seems as if the basics are all there; I don't have to monitor Joey and Lizzie so constantly anymore. But being a parent is still very challenging. Now it's more a matter of refinements—helping them become independent, competent, and productive individuals."

Joey and Lizzie have entered the phase of development called middle childhood, which spans the years from 6 to 11. Around the world, children of this age are assigned new responsibilities as they begin the process of entering the adult world. Joey and Lizzie, like other youngsters in industrialized nations, spend many long hours in school. Indeed, middle childhood is often called the "school years," since its onset is marked by the start of formal schooling. In village and tribal cultures, the school may be a field or a jungle rather than a classroom. But universally, mature members of society guide children of this age period toward more realistic tasks that increasingly resemble those they will perform as adults (Rogoff, 1996).

This chapter focuses on physical growth in middle childhood—changes that are less spectacular than those of the earlier years. By age 6, the brain has reached 95 percent of its adult size, and the body continues to grow slowly. In this way, nature grants school-age children the mental powers to master challenging tasks as well as added time to learn before reaching physical maturity.

We begin by reviewing typical growth trends as well as special health concerns of middle childhood. Then we turn to rapid gains in motor abilities, which support practical everyday activities, athletic skills, and participation in organized games. We will see that each of these achievements is affected by and contributes to cognitive and social development. Our discussion will echo a familiar theme—that all areas of development are interrelated.

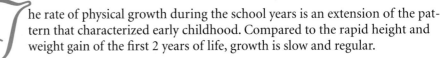

BODY GROWTH

The rate of physical growth during the school years is an extension of the pattern that characterized early childhood. Compared to the rapid height and weight gain of the first 2 years of life, growth is slow and regular.

CHANGES IN BODY SIZE AND PROPORTIONS

At age 6, the average North American child weighs about 45 pounds and is 3½ feet tall. As Figure 11.1 shows, children continue to add about 2 to 3 inches in height and 5 pounds in weight each year. However, when researchers carefully track individuals, growth is not quite as steady as these norms suggest. A longitudinal study of Scottish children, who were followed between ages 3 and 10, revealed slight spurts in height. Girls tended to forge ahead at ages 4½, 6½, 8½, and 10, boys slightly later, at 4½, 7, 9, and 10½. Between these spurts were lulls in which growth was slower (Butler, McKie, & Ratcliffe, 1990).

Look again at Figure 11.1, and you will see that girls are slightly shorter and lighter than boys at ages 6 to 8. By age 9, this trend reverses. Already, Rena noticed, Lizzie was starting to catch up with Joey in physical size. For many girls, the 10-year-old height spurt overlaps with the much more dramatic adolescent growth spurt, which takes place 2 years earlier in girls than boys.

Because the lower portion of the body is growing fastest at this age period, Joey and Lizzie appeared longer-legged than they had in early childhood. Rena discovered that they grew out of their jeans more quickly than their jackets and frequently needed larger shoes. As in early childhood, school-age girls have slightly more body fat and boys more muscle. After age 8, girls begin accumulating fat at a faster rate, and they will add even more during adolescence (Tanner, 1990).

During middle childhood, the lower portion of the body is growing fastest. These 8-year-old girls are taller and longer-legged than they were as preschoolers. *(Arnie Katz/ Stock South)*

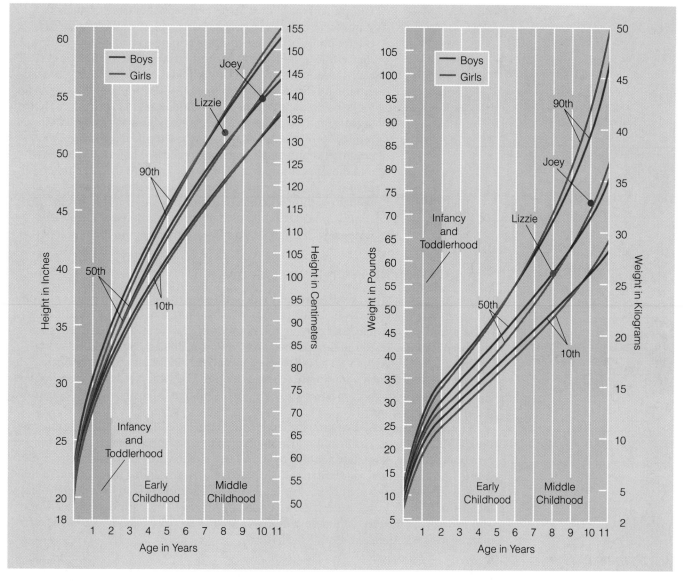

FIGURE 11.1

Gains in height and weight during middle childhood among North American children. The slow rate of growth established in early childhood extends into the school years. Girls are slightly shorter and lighter than boys until age 9, when this trend reverses as girls approach the adolescent growth spurt. Eight-year-old Lizzie is beginning to catch up with 10-year-old Joey in physical size. Wide individual differences in body size continue to exist, as the percentiles on these charts reveal.

WORLDWIDE VARIATIONS IN BODY SIZE

A glance into any elementary school classroom reveals that individual differences in body growth remain great in middle childhood. Diversity in physical size is especially apparent when we travel to different nations. Measurements of 8-year-olds living in many parts of the world reveal a 9-inch gap between the smallest and the largest youngsters. The shortest children tend to be found in South America, Asia, the Pacific Islands, and parts of Africa and include such ethnic groups as Colombian, Burmese, Thai, Vietnamese, Ethiopian, and Bantu. The tallest children reside in Australia, northern and central

Body size is sometimes the result of evolutionary adaptations to a particular climate. These nomadic boys of Niger in west-central Africa, who live in a hot, tropical region of the world, have long, lean physiques, which permit the body to cool easily. *(Victor Englebert/ Photo Researchers, Inc.)*

Europe, and the United States and consist of Czech, Dutch, Latvian, Norwegian, Swiss, and American black and white children (Meredith, 1978). These findings remind us that growth norms, such as those in Figure 11.1, must be interpreted cautiously, especially in countries like the United States, where so many ethnic groups are represented.

What accounts for these vast differences in physical size? Both heredity and environment are involved. Body size is sometimes the result of evolutionary adaptations to a particular climate. For example, long, lean physiques are typical in hot, tropical regions and short, stocky ones in cold, Arctic areas. At the same time, children who grow tallest usually reside in developed countries where food is plentiful and infectious diseases are largely controlled. In contrast, small children tend to live in less developed regions, where poverty, hunger, and disease are common (Tanner, 1990).

SECULAR TRENDS IN PHYSICAL GROWTH

Over the past century, **secular trends in physical growth**—changes in body size from one generation to the next—have taken place in industrialized nations. Joey and Lizzie are taller and heavier than their parents and grandparents were as children. These trends have been found in nearly all European nations, in Japan, and among black and white children in the United States. The difference appears early in life and becomes greater over childhood and early adolescence. Then, as mature body size is reached, it declines. This pattern suggests that the larger size of modern children is mostly due to a faster rate of physical maturation.

Why are so many children growing larger and maturing earlier than their ancestors? Once again, improved health and nutrition play major roles. Orphaned children from developing countries who are adopted by American parents often show faster physical growth and reach greater mature stature than do children remaining in their land of origin. Also, secular trends are not as large for low-income children, who have poorer diets and are more likely to suffer from growth-stunting illnesses. And in regions of the world with widespread poverty, famine, and disease, a secular decrease in body size has occurred (Barnes-Josiah & Augustin, 1995; Proos, 1993).

SKELETAL GROWTH

During middle childhood, the bones of the body lengthen and broaden. However, ligaments are not yet firmly attached to bones. This, combined with increasing muscle strength, grants children unusual flexibility of movement. School-age youngsters often seem like "physical contortionists," turning cartwheels and doing handstands. As their bodies become stronger, many children experience a greater desire for physical exercise. About 13 to 18 percent complain of evening "growing pains"—stiffness and aches in the legs—as muscles adapt to an enlarging skeleton (Walco, 1997).

One of the most striking aspects of skeletal growth in middle childhood is replacement of primary or "baby" teeth with permanent teeth. Recall from Chapter 8 that children lose their first tooth at the end of early childhood. Between ages 6 and 12, all 20 primary teeth are replaced by permanent ones, with girls losing their teeth slightly earlier than boys. The first teeth to go are the central incisors (lower and then upper front teeth), giving many first and second graders a "toothless" smile. For a while, permanent teeth seem much too large. Growth of facial bones, especially the jaw and chin, gradually causes the child's face to lengthen and mouth to widen, accommodating the newly erupting teeth.

secular trends in physical growth
Changes in body size from one generation to the next.

Care of the teeth is essential during the school years, since dental health affects the child's appearance, speech, and ability to chew properly. Children often neglect to brush thoroughly, and they usually cannot floss by themselves until about 9 years of age. Parents need to remind and help them with these tasks.

About 50 percent of American school-age children have at least some tooth decay. As in the preschool years, poverty-stricken, ethnic minority children have especially high levels (Edelstein & Douglass, 1995). Regular trips to the dentist, avoiding sugary foods, and water fluoridation continue to be effective in preventing cavities (see Chapter 8). *Plastic sealants* brushed onto the biting surfaces of back teeth can protect against decay. Unfortunately, since sealants usually are applied in private dental offices, children from low-income homes rarely receive them. Some state and local health departments have provided hard-to-reach children with sealants through school-based dental programs (Siegal, Farquhar, & Bouchard, 1997).

One-third of school-age youngsters suffer from **malocclusion,** a condition in which the upper and lower teeth do not meet properly. In about 14 percent of cases, serious difficulties in biting and chewing result. Malocclusion can be caused by thumb and finger sucking after permanent teeth erupt (Johnson & Larson, 1993). Children who were eager thumb suckers during infancy and early childhood may require gentle but persistent encouragement to give up the habit by school entry. A second cause of malocclusion is crowding of permanent teeth. In some children, this problem clears up as the jaw grows. Others need braces, a common sight by the end of elementary school.

BRAIN DEVELOPMENT

Brain development in middle childhood largely involves more efficient functioning of various structures. The *frontal lobes* of the cerebral cortex (responsible for thought and consciousness) show a slight increase in surface area between ages 5 and 7 due to continuing myelinization. Brain-imaging research reveals that the *corpus callosum* thickens, leading to improved communication between the two cortical hemispheres (see Chapter 8, page 300). Synaptic connections between active neurons strengthen as neural fibers become more elaborate, and *synaptic pruning* continues (Giedd, 1997). In addition, *lateralization* of the cerebral hemispheres, already well established in early childhood, increases over the school years.

Little information is available on how the brain changes in other ways during this age period. One idea is that development occurs at the level of **neurotransmitters,** chemicals that permit neurons to communicate across synapses (see Chapter 5, page 172). Over time, neurons become increasingly selective, responding only to certain chemical messages. This change may contribute to more efficient and flexible thinking and behavior in school-age children. Secretions of particular neurotransmitters are related to cognitive performance, social and emotional adjustment, and ability to withstand stress in children and adults. Children may suffer serious developmental problems, such as inattention and overactivity, emotional disturbance, and epilepsy (an illness involving brain seizures and loss of motor control) when neurotransmitters are not present in appropriate balances (Shonkoff, 1984; Zametkin et al., 1990).

Researchers also believe that brain functioning may change in middle childhood because of the influence of hormones. Around age 7 to 8, an increase in *androgens* (male sex hormones), secreted by the adrenal glands located on top of the kidneys, occurs in children of both sexes. Androgens will rise further among boys at puberty, when the testes release them in large amounts. In many animal species, androgens affect brain organization and behavior, and they do so in humans as well (Hines & Green, 1991). Recall from Chapter 10 that androgens contribute to boys' higher activity level. They may also promote social dominance and play fighting, topics we will take up at the end of this chapter (Maccoby, 1990).

malocclusion
A condition in which the upper and lower teeth do not meet properly.

neurotransmitters
Chemicals that permit neurons to communicate across synapses.

ASK YOURSELF . . .

■ *How is body growth during the school years consistent with the cephalocaudal trend of development that you studied in Chapter 5?*

■ *Joey complained to his mother that it wasn't fair that his younger sister Lizzie was almost as tall as he was. He worried that he wasn't growing fast enough. How should Rena respond to Joey's concern?*

BRIEF REVIEW

Body growth takes place slowly in middle childhood, at a pace similar to that of the preschool years. Gains in height occur in slight spurts followed by lulls; growth of the legs accounts for most of the increase. Large individual and cultural differences in body size result from both genetic and environmental factors. Children in industrialized nations are growing larger and reaching physical maturity earlier than they did in past generations because of better nutrition and health care. Between ages 6 and 12, all primary teeth are replaced by permanent ones. Brain development in middle childhood may involve neurotransmitter and hormonal influences.

COMMON HEALTH PROBLEMS

Children like Joey and Lizzie, who come from economically advantaged homes, appear to be at their healthiest during middle childhood, full of energy and play. The cumulative effects of good nutrition, combined with rapid development of the body's immune system, offer greater protection against disease. Infections occur less often now. At the same time, growth in lung size permits more air to be exchanged with each breath, so children are better able to exercise vigorously without tiring.

Nevertheless, a variety of health problems do occur during the school years. We will see that many of them are more prevalent among low-SES youngsters. Return to Chapter 8, page 307, to review the status of children's health care in the United States. Because economically disadvantaged families often lack health insurance and cannot afford to pay for medical visits on their own, many youngsters continue to be deprived of regular access to a doctor. And a growing number also lack such basic necessities as a comfortable home and regular meals. Not surprisingly, poverty continues to be a powerful predictor of ill health during middle childhood.

VISION AND HEARING

The most common vision problem in middle childhood is **myopia,** or nearsightedness. By the end of the school years, nearly 25 percent of children are affected, a rate that rises to 60 percent by early adulthood (Sperduto et al., 1983, 1996).

Heredity contributes to myopia, since identical twins are more likely than fraternal twins to have the condition to a similar degree (Teikari et al., 1991). But myopia is also related to experience, as it has increased in recent generations (Sperduto et al., 1996). Parents often warn their youngsters not to read in dim light or sit too close to the TV or computer screen, exclaiming, "You'll ruin your eyes!" Their concern may be well founded. Myopia is one of the few health conditions that increase with family income and education, an association that is almost entirely explained by how people use their eyes. The more time people spend reading and doing other close-up work, the more likely they are to be myopic (Angle & Wissmann, 1980). Fortunately, for those youngsters who develop nearsightedness because they love reading, sewing, drawing, or model building, the condition can easily be corrected with glasses.

During middle childhood, the eustachian tube (canal that runs from the inner ear to the throat) becomes longer, narrower, and more slanted, preventing fluid and bacteria from traveling so easily from the mouth to the ear. As a result, *otitis media* (middle ear infection) becomes less frequent (see Chapter 8). Still, some children have chronic ear infections that, if left untreated, can lead to permanent hearing defects. About 3 to 4 percent of the school-age population, and as many as 18 to 20 percent of low-SES young-

myopia
Nearsightedness; inability to see distant objects clearly.

sters, develop some hearing loss for this reason (Mott, James, & Sperhac, 1990). Regular screening tests for both vision and hearing are important so that defects can be corrected before they lead to serious learning difficulties.

MALNUTRITION

School-age children need a well-balanced, plentiful diet to provide energy for successful learning in school and increased physical activity. Many youngsters are so focused on play, friendships, and new activities that they spend little time at the table. Joey's hurried breakfast, described at the beginning of this chapter, is a common event during middle childhood. Readily available, healthy between-meal snacks—cheese, fruit, raw vegetables, and peanut butter—help meet nutritional needs during the school years.

As long as parents encourage healthy eating, the mild nutritional deficits that result from the child's busy daily schedule have no impact on development. But as we have seen in earlier chapters, many poverty-stricken children in developing countries and in the United States suffer from serious and prolonged malnutrition. By middle childhood, the effects are apparent in retarded physical growth, low intelligence test scores, poor motor coordination, inattention, and distractibility. Animal evidence reveals that diet affects the operation of neurotransmitters in the brain (Zeisel, 1986). The negative impact of malnutrition on learning and behavior may be extended during middle childhood in just this way.

Unfortunately, when malnutrition persists for many years, permanent damage is done. Prevention through government-sponsored food programs beginning in the early years and continuing throughout childhood and adolescence is necessary. In studies carried out in Kenya and Egypt, total calorie and protein intakes of school-age children were positively related to mental test scores (Sigman et al., 1989; Wachs et al., 1995). In both nations, better-quality protein (from animal sources) was the strongest dietary predictor of cognitive development in middle childhood.

OBESITY

Mona, a very overweight child in Lizzie's class, often stood on the sidelines and watched during recess. When she did join in the children's games, she was slow and clumsy. On a daily basis, Mona was the target of unkind comments: "Move it, Tubs!" "Tree trunks for legs!" "No fatsoes allowed!" Although Mona was a good student, other children continued to reject her inside the classroom. When it was time to choose partners for a special activity, Mona was one of the last to be selected. On most afternoons, she walked home from school by herself while the other children gathered in groups, talking, laughing, and chasing. Once home and in the kitchen, Mona sought comfort in high-calorie snacks, which promoted further weight gain.

Mona is one of over 22 percent of American children who suffer from **obesity,** a greater-than-20-percent increase over average body weight, based on the child's age, sex, and physical build (Troiano et al., 1995). Overweight and obesity are growing problems in affluent nations such as the United States. And as the Biology and Environment box on page 416 reveals, obesity is also rising in some developing nations, where high rates of growth stunting due to early, severe malnutrition make children more vulnerable to later excessive weight gain.

Over 80 percent of youngsters like Mona remain overweight as adults (Serdula et al., 1993). Besides serious emotional and social difficulties, obese children are at risk for lifelong health problems. High blood pressure and cholesterol levels along with respiratory abnormalities begin to appear in the early school years. As obesity continues it becomes a powerful predictor of heart disease, adult-onset diabetes, certain forms of cancer, and early death (Figueroa-Colon et al., 1997; Unger, Kreeger, & Christoffel, 1990). As you can see from Table 11.1, childhood obesity is a complex physical disorder with multiple causes.

obesity
A greater-than-20-percent increase over average body weight, based on the child's age, sex, and physical build.

BIOLOGY & ENVIRONMENT

GROWTH STUNTING DUE TO EARLY MALNUTRITION: RISK FACTOR FOR CHILDHOOD OBESITY

In research on overweight children in four developing nations, a disheartening link between early growth stunting due to malnutrition and childhood obesity has emerged. Nationwide surveys in Brazil, China, Russia, and South Africa yielded information on height for age (a measure of poor diet and stunting) and weight for height (a measure of obesity) for thousands of children (Popkin, Richards, & Montiero, 1996). The proportion of children who were stunted (very short for their age) ranged from 15 percent in Brazil to 22 percent in China and 30 percent in South Africa. In Russia, stunting is a new problem. It has emerged only in the last 8 years, after poverty rose while government-sponsored maternal and child nutrition programs deteriorated. About 9 percent of Russian children are growth stunted.

As Figure 11.2 shows, in each country except Brazil, rate of overweight was far greater among stunted than nonstunted children. Short, growth-retarded children were twice as likely as their peers to be fat in South Africa, three times as likely in China, and seven times as likely in Russia. Family income seemed to account for the lack of association between stunting and fatness in Brazil; many overweight Brazilian children come from financially better-off homes. But in the other three countries, income had no impact on the stunting–overweight relationship.

What explains excessive weight gain among growth-stunted children? Researchers believe two physiological changes are involved:

■ To protect itself, a malnourished body establishes a low basal metabolism rate, stretching its energy resources as far as possible—a change that may endure after nutrition improves.

■ Early malnutrition may cause brain structures responsible for appetite control to be reset at a higher level. Consequently, stunted children are likely to overeat when food—especially high-fat products—becomes more widely available as developing nations gain economically and modernize (Barker, 1994; Popkin, 1994).

The growth stunting–obesity link is evident among certain low-income, ethnic minorities in the United States, including Mexican-American and Hmong (Laotian) groups (Himes et al., 1992; Valdez et al., 1994). As economic conditions improve worldwide, a high-quality diet from the earliest ages may be vital for shielding children everywhere from an epidemic of obesity.

FIGURE 11.2

Relationship of growth stunting to overweight among 3- to 9-year-olds in four developing nations. Children identified as growth stunted were below the second percentile in height for their age, based on World Health Organization standards. Children identified as overweight were above the ninety-eighth percentile in weight for their height. Stunted children were twice as likely as their peers to be fat in South Africa, three times as likely in China, and seven times as likely in Russia. Family income seems to account for the lack of association between stunting and overweight in Brazil. *(Adapted from Popkin et al., 1996.)*

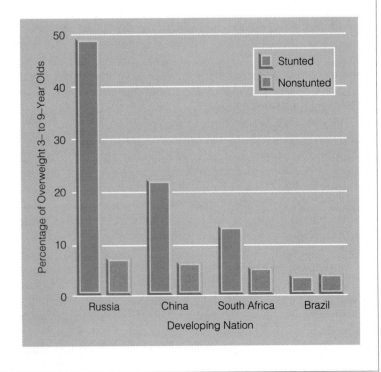

TABLE 11.1

Factors Associated with Childhood Obesity

FACTOR	DESCRIPTION
Heredity	Obese children are likely to have at least one obese parent, and concordance for obesity is greater in identical than fraternal twins.
Socioeconomic status	Obesity is more common in low-SES families.
Early growth pattern	Infants who gain weight rapidly during the first year are at slightly greater risk for obesity.
Family eating habits	When parents purchase high-calorie treats and junk food and use them to reward children and reduce anxiety, their youngsters are more likely to be obese.
Responsiveness to food cues	Obese children often decide when to eat on the basis of external cues, such as taste, smell, sight, and time of day, rather than hunger.
Physical activity	Obese children are less physically active than their normal-weight peers.
Television viewing	Children who spend many hours watching television are more likely to become obese.
Early malnutrition and growth stunting	Severe early malnutrition resulting in growth stunting increases the risk of later obesity.

■ **CAUSES OF OBESITY.**   Not all children are equally at risk for becoming overweight. Fat children tend to have fat parents, and concordance for obesity is greater in identical than fraternal twins. (Return to Chapter 2, page 87, to review the concept of concordance.) These findings suggest that heredity has some effect. But similarity among family members is not strong enough to imply that genetics accounts for any more than a tendency to gain weight (Bouchard, 1994; Dietz, Bandini, & Gortmaker, 1990).

One indication that environment is powerfully important is the consistent relation between low SES and obesity in industrialized nations (Stunkard & Sørenson, 1993). Among the factors responsible are lack of knowledge about healthy diet; a tendency to buy high-fat, low-cost foods; and family stress, which prompts overeating in some individuals. In addition, 6 percent of American low-SES children are growth stunted due to early malnutrition and are therefore at increased risk for obesity (consult the Biology and Environment box).

Recall from Chapter 5 that a slight relationship exists between very rapid weight gain in infancy and fatness in childhood. When early overweight persists, parental food choices and feeding practices seem to play important roles. In a recent study, fatter preschoolers were more likely to prefer and eat larger quantities of high-fat foods, perhaps because these foods were prominent in the diets offered by their parents, who also tended to be overweight (Fisher & Birch, 1995). Some parents anxiously overfeed their infants and young children, interpreting almost all their discomforts as a desire for food. Others are overly controlling, constantly monitoring what their children eat. In either case, they fail to help children learn to regulate their own energy intake appropriately. Furthermore, parents of obese children often use food to reinforce other behaviors—a practice that leads children to attach great value to the treat (Birch & Fisher, 1995).

Because of these feeding experiences, obese children soon develop maladaptive eating habits (Johnson & Birch, 1994). Research shows that they are more responsive to external stimuli associated with food—taste, sight, smell, and time of day—and less responsive to internal hunger cues than are normal-weight individuals. This difference is already present in middle childhood and may develop even earlier (Ballard et al., 1980; Constanzo & Woody, 1979). Overweight individuals also eat faster and chew their food less thoroughly, a behavior pattern that appears as early as 18 months of age (Drabman et al., 1979).

Fat children also are less physically active than their normal-weight peers. This inactivity is both cause and consequence of their overweight condition. Recent evidence indicates

Overweight children tend to have overweight parents. But genetics accounts for no more than a tendency to gain weight. A family environment where high-calorie, high-fat foods are readily available, food takes on powerful emotional meaning, and much time is spent in sedentary activities affects the health of both this father and his son. *(Dick Luria/FPG International)*

that the rise in childhood obesity in the United States over the past 30 years is in part due to television viewing. Next to already existing obesity, time spent in front of the TV set is the best predictor of future obesity among school-age children. The rate of obesity increases by 2 percent for each additional hour of TV watched per day (Gortmaker, Dietz, & Cheung, 1990). Television greatly reduces the time that children devote to physical exercise. At the same time, TV ads encourage them to eat fattening, unhealthy snacks—soft drinks, sweets, and salty chips and popcorn (Carruth, Goldberg, & Skinner, 1991).

■ **CONSEQUENCES OF OBESITY.** Unfortunately, physical attractiveness is a powerful predictor of social acceptance in our culture. Both children and adults rate obese youngsters as less likable than children with a wide range of physical disabilities (Brenner & Hinsdale, 1978; Lerner & Schroeder, 1971). By middle childhood, obese children report feeling more depressed and display more behavior problems than their peers. A vicious cycle emerges in which unhappiness and overeating contribute to one another, and the child remains overweight (Banis et al., 1988).

The psychological consequences of obesity combine with continuing discrimination to result in reduced life chances. By early adulthood, overweight individuals have completed fewer years of schooling, have lower incomes, and marry less often than do individuals with other chronic health problems. These outcomes are particularly strong for females (Gortmaker et al., 1993).

■ **TREATING OBESITY.** Childhood obesity is difficult to treat because it is a family disorder. In Mona's case, the school nurse suggested that Mona and her obese mother enter a weight loss program together. But Mona's mother, unhappily married for many years, had her own reasons for continuing to overeat. She rejected this idea, claiming that Mona would eventually decide to lose weight on her own.

Although many obese youngsters do try to slim down in adolescence, they often go on crash diets that deprive them of essential nutrients during a period of rapid growth. These efforts can make matters worse. Temporary starvation leads to physical stress, discomfort, and fatigue. Soon the child returns to old eating patterns, and weight rebounds to a higher level. Then, to protect itself, the body burns calories more slowly and becomes more resistant to future weight loss (Pinel, 1997).

When parents decide to seek treatment for an obese child, long-term changes in body weight do occur. A recent study found that the most effective interventions were family based and focused on changing behaviors. Both parent and child revised eating patterns, exercised daily, and reinforced each other with praise and points for progress, which they exchanged for special activities and times together. Follow-ups after 5 and 10 years showed that children maintained their weight loss more effectively than did adults—a finding that underscores the importance of intervening at an early age. Furthermore, weight loss was greater when treatments focused on both dietary and lifestyle changes, including regular vigorous exercise (Epstein et al., 1990, 1994).

Getting obese children to exercise, however, is challenging, since they find being sedentary so pleasurable. Positively reinforcing them for spending less time inactive is a successful technique. In two studies, researchers offered rewards (such as tickets to the zoo or a baseball game) for reducing sedentary time. Children receiving this treatment showed greater liking for and engagement in physical activity and lost more weight than did children reinforced for being physically active or punished (by loss of privileges) for inactivity (Epstein, Saelens, & O'Brien, 1995; Epstein et al., 1997). Rewarding children for giving up sedentary pursuits seems to increase their sense of personal control over exercise behavior—a factor linked to sustained physical activity.

BEDWETTING

One Friday afternoon, Terry called Joey to see if he could sleep over, but Joey refused. "I can't," said Joey anxiously, without giving an explanation.

"Why not? We can take our sleeping bags out in the backyard. Come on, it'll be super!"

"My mom won't let me," Joey responded, unconvincingly. "I mean, well, I think we're busy, we're doing something tonight."

"Gosh, Joey, this is the third time you've said no. See if I'll ask you again!" snapped Terry as he hung up the phone.

Joey is one of 8 percent of American school-age children who suffer from **nocturnal enuresis,** or bedwetting during the night (Rappaport, 1993). Enuresis evokes considerable distress in children and parents alike. For children, it restricts social activities and embarrasses them in front of family members. Most parents say that they worry about the problem and find the frequent night wakings and bedding changes annoying (Foxman, Valdez, & Brook, 1986). In one large-scale study, 36 percent admitted they punished their children for wetting (Haque et al., 1981).

Although enuretic children show a slightly higher rate of psychological distress than their peers, this may be an outcome of the bedwetting itself. In the overwhelming majority of cases, the problem has biological roots. Heredity is a major contributing factor. Parents with a history of bedwetting are far more likely to have a child with the problem, and concordance is greater among identical than fraternal twins (Christophersen & Edwards, 1992). Enuresis is unrelated to the depth of a child's sleep, and only rarely is it due to abnormalities in the urinary tract. Most often, it is caused by a failure of muscular responses that inhibit urination or by a hormonal imbalance that permits too much urine to accumulate during the night (Houts, 1991). Punishing a school-age child for wetting is only likely to make matters worse.

To treat enuresis, doctors often prescribe antidepressant drugs, which reduce the amount of urine produced. But once children stop taking the medication, they typically begin wetting again. Also, a small number of youngsters show side effects, such as anxiety, loss of sleep, and personality changes (Bath, Uing, & Williams, 1996; Moffatt et al., 1993). The most effective treatment for enuresis is a urine alarm that wakes the child at the first sign of dampness and works according to conditioning principles. Success rates of about 60 to 70 percent occur after 4 to 6 months of treatment. Most children who relapse achieve dryness after trying the alarm a second time (Houts, Berman, & Abramson, 1994; Rushton, 1989). Although many children outgrow enuresis without any form of intervention, it generally takes years for them to do so.

ILLNESSES

Children experience a somewhat higher rate of illness during the first 2 years of elementary school than they will later, due to exposure to sick children and the fact that their immune system is still developing. On the average, illness causes children to miss about 11 days of school per year, but most absences can be traced to a few students with chronic health problems. Among children without diagnosed health difficulties, girls are more likely to miss school than are boys, with intestinal and respiratory infections, allergies, and muscle sprains being the most frequently reported reasons (Kornguth, 1990). When a child shows symptoms of illness, gender stereotypes may cause parents to perceive their daughters as more vulnerable than their sons.

About 19 percent of American children have chronic diseases and conditions (including physical disabilities). By far the most common—and the most frequent cause of school absence and childhood hospitalization—is **asthma,** a condition in which the bronchial tubes (passages that connect the throat and lungs) are highly sensitive (Kliewer,

nocturnal enuresis
Repeated bedwetting during the night.

asthma
An illness in which highly sensitive bronchial tubes fill with mucus and contract, leading to episodes of coughing, wheezing, and serious breathing difficulties.

1997). In response to a variety of stimuli, such as cold weather, infection, exercise, allergies, and emotional stress, they fill with mucus and contract, leading to coughing, wheezing, and serious breathing difficulties.

The number of children with asthma has increased by 40 percent over the last decade. Today, 6 to 12 percent of American youngsters are affected, and asthma-related deaths have risen in recent years (Chadwick, 1996; Creer & Bender, 1995). Although heredity contributes to asthma, researchers believe that environmental factors are necessary to spark the illness. Boys, African-American children, and children who were born underweight, whose parents smoke, and who live in poverty are at greatest risk (Kay, Mortimer, & Jaron, 1995). Perhaps black and poverty-stricken youngsters experience a higher rate of asthma because of pollution in inner-city areas (which triggers allergic reactions), stressful home lives, and lack of access to good health care.

About 2 percent of American children have chronic illnesses that are more severe than asthma, such as sickle cell anemia, cystic fibrosis (see Table 2.3, pages 60–61 for a brief description of these conditions), diabetes, arthritis, cancer, and acquired immune deficiency syndrome (AIDS). Painful medical treatments, physical discomfort, and changes in appearance often disrupt the sick child's daily life, making it difficult to concentrate in school and causing withdrawal from peers. As the illness worsens, family stress increases. Mothers, who typically bear the burden of caring for a very ill child, report more health problems of their own. For these reasons, chronically ill youngsters are at risk for academic, emotional, and social difficulties (Drotar, 1997; Kliewer, 1997). Many interventions have been found to improve their adjustment, including

- Family and health education, in which parents and children learn about the illness and get training in how to manage it

- Home visits by health professionals, who offer counseling and social support to enhance children's strategies for coping with the stress of chronic illness

- Disease-specific summer camps, which teach children self-help skills and grant parents time off from the demands of caring for an ill youngster

- Parent and peer support groups

- Individual and family therapy

UNINTENTIONAL INJURIES

As we conclude our discussion of threats to children's health during the school years, let's return for a moment to the topic of unintentional injuries (discussed in detail in Chapter 8). As Figure 11.3 reveals, the frequency of injury fatalities increases from middle childhood into adolescence, with the rate for boys rising considerably above that for girls.

Motor vehicle accidents, involving children as passengers or pedestrians, continue to be the leading cause of injury during the school years, with bicycle accidents next in line (U.S. Department of Health and Human Services, 1997). Pedestrian injuries most often result from midblock dart-outs, bicycle accidents from disobeying traffic signals and rules. Young school-age children are not yet good at thinking before they act, especially when many stimuli impinge on them at once (Tuchfarber, Zins, & Jason, 1997). Whether on foot or bicycle, they need frequent reminders, supervision, and prohibitions against venturing into busy traffic conditions on their own.

As children spend more time away from parents and range farther from home, safety education becomes especially important, along with incentives for following safety rules. Programs that reward children with prizes for arriving at school properly restrained in car seat belts are effective, just as they were in early childhood (Roberts & Fanurik, 1986). However, when rewards are removed, behavior usually deteriorates.

School-based programs with longer-lasting effects use extensive modeling, role playing, and rehearsal of safety practices; give children feedback about their performance along with praise and tangible rewards for acquiring safety skills; and provide occasional booster sessions (Zins et al., 1994). An important part of injury prevention is educating parents about children's age-related safety capacities, since parents often overestimate their child's safety knowledge and behavior (Rivara, 1995).

Insisting that children wear protective helmets while bicycling, roller blading, or skateboarding is a vital safety intervention. This simple precaution leads to an 85 percent reduction in the risk of head injury, a leading cause of permanent physical disability and death during the school years (Peterson & Oliver, 1995). In Seattle, a community-wide publicity campaign to increase parent and child awareness of the benefits of helmet use resulted in a rise in compliance from 5 to 40 percent (Rivara et al., 1994). Some cities, counties, and states have passed laws that require children to wear bicycle helmets and issue tickets if they do not. In a few places, the cost of the ticket is waived if the child's family responds by purchasing a helmet.

Not all school-age children respond to efforts to increase their safety. By middle childhood, the greatest risk takers tend to be children whose parents do not act as safety-conscious models or who try to enforce rules by using punitive or inconsistent discipline (Tuchfarber, Zins, & Jason, 1997). These child-rearing techniques, as we saw in Chapter 10, spark defiance in children, reduce their willingness to comply, and may actually promote high-risk behavior. Highly active, impulsive boys remain particularly susceptible to injury in middle childhood. Although they have just as much safety knowledge as their peers, they are far less likely to implement it (Mori & Peterson, 1995). The greatest challenge for injury control programs is reaching these "more difficult to reach" youngsters, altering their family contexts, and reducing the dangers to which they are exposed.

Roller blading is a favorite pastime during the school years. Parents of these children insist that they wear protective helmets and knee guards. Taking these precautions dramatically reduces the chances of serious injury. *(Myrleen Ferguson/PhotoEdit)*

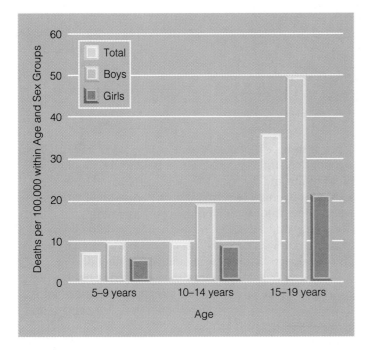

FIGURE 11.3

Rate of injury mortality in the United States from middle childhood to adolescence. Injury fatalities increase, and the gap between boys and girls expands. Motor vehicle (passenger and pedestrian) accidents are the leading cause, with bicycle injuries next in line. *(From U.S. Department of Health and Human Services, 1997)*

SOCIAL ISSUES

CHILDREN'S UNDERSTANDING OF HEALTH AND ILLNESS

Lizzie lay on the living room sofa with a stuffy nose and sore throat, disappointed that she was missing her soccer team's final game and pizza party. "How'd I get this dumb cold anyhow?" she wondered aloud to Joey. "I probably did it to myself by playing outside without a hat the other day when it was freezing cold."

"No, no," Joey contradicted. "You can't get sick that way. Some creepy little viruses got into your blood-stream and attacked, just like an army."

"What're viruses? I didn't eat any viruses," answered Lizzie, puzzled.

"You don't eat them, silly, you breathe them in. Somebody probably sneezed them all over you at school. That's how you got sick!"

Lizzie and Joey are at different developmental levels in their under-standing of health and illness—ideas that are influenced by cognitive devel-opment and exposure to biological knowledge. Researchers have asked preschool through high school stu-dents questions designed to tap what they know about the causes of health and certain illnesses, such as colds, AIDS, and cancer.

During the preschool and early school years, children do not have much biological knowledge to bring to bear on their understanding of health and illness. For example, if you ask 4- to 8-year-olds to tell you what is inside their bodies, you will find that they know little about their internal organs and how they work. As a result, young children fall back on their rich knowledge of people's behavior to account for health and illness (Carey, 1985; Parmelee, 1997). Children of this age regard health as a matter of engaging in specific practices (eating the right foods, getting enough exer-cise, and wearing warm clothing on cold days) and illness as a matter of failing to follow these rules or coming too close to a sick person (Bibace & Walsh, 1980).

Older school-age children acquire more knowledge about their bodies and are better able to make sense of it. By age 9 or 10, they name a wide variety of internal organs and view them as interconnected, working as a system (Carey, 1985). Around this time, children's concepts of health and ill-ness shift to biological explanations. Joey understands that illness can be caused by contagion—breathing in a harmful substance (a virus), which affects the operation of the body in some way.

By early adolescence, explanations become more elaborate and precise. Eleven- to 14-year-olds recognize health as a long-term condition that depends on the interaction of body, mind, and environmental influences (Hergenrather & Rabinowitz, 1991). And the adolescent's notions of illness involve clearly stated ideas about interference in normal body processes: "You get a cold when your sinuses fill up with mucus. Sometimes your lungs do, too, and you get a cough. Colds come from viruses. They get into the bloodstream and make your platelet count go down" (Bibace & Walsh, 1980).

HEALTH EDUCATION

Child development specialists have become intensely interested in finding ways to help school-age youngsters understand how their bodies work, acquire mature conceptions of health and illness, and develop patterns of behavior that foster good health throughout life. Successfully targeting children for intervention on any health issue requires information on their current health-related knowledge. What information can they understand? What reasoning processes do they use? What factors influence what they know? The Social Issues box above summarizes findings on children's concepts of health and illness during middle childhood.

The school-age period may be an especially important time for fostering healthy life-styles because of the child's growing independence, increasing cognitive capacities, and rapidly developing self-concept, which includes perceptions of physical well-being (Har-ter, 1998). During middle childhood, children can learn a wide variety of health-related information—about the structure and functioning of their bodies, about good nutrition,

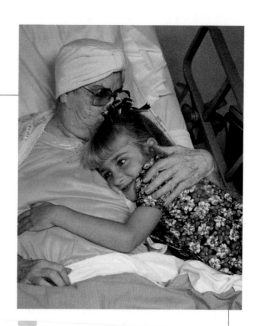

Children everywhere are capable of grasping basic biological ideas, but whether or not they do so depends on information in their everyday environments. Research reveals that children are likely to generalize their knowledge of familiar diseases to less familiar ones. As a result, they often conclude that risk factors for colds (sharing a Coke or sneezing on someone) can cause AIDS. And lacking much understanding of cancer, they assume that it (like colds and AIDS) is communicable (Sigelman et al., 1993). These incorrect ideas can lead to unnecessary anxiety about getting a serious disease. In one survey of fourth graders, 51 percent incorrectly believed that everyone is at risk for AIDS, and 59 percent said they "worry a lot" about getting it (Holcomb, 1990).

Although misconceptions decline with age, culturally transmitted attitudes can lead to gaps between knowledge and behavior. When certain diseases take on powerful symbolic meanings—for example, cancer as a malignant, destructive evil and

AIDS as a sign of moral decay—even adults with an accurate biological understanding irrationally expect bad things to happen from associating with affected people. These beliefs are quickly picked up by children, and they help explain the severe social rejection experienced by some youngsters with chronic diseases. As one school-age child admitted, "I'd be scared to even talk to them because they had AIDS, even though you can't get it that way" (Whalen et al., 1995, p. 434).

Education about the causes of various illnesses works best when it builds on current understandings. In the early grades, teachers can offer reassurance that children usually do not get seriously ill. Older children and adolescents can make use of more detailed information about disease transmission and prevention (Walsh & Bibace, 1991). And to combat irrational fears and prejudices, teachers need to encourage young people to examine their attitudes and feelings. Instruction that gives AIDS, cancer, and other debilitating and deadly ill-

This child comforts her grandmother, who is dying of cancer. Helping school-age children understand that cancer is not communicable can prevent them from developing negative attitudes toward its victims. *(Spencer Grant/The Picture Cube)*

nesses "a human face," such as bringing people with the disease into the classroom, may help older children and adolescents respond constructively and compassionately (Pryor & Reeder, 1993).

and about the causes and consequences of physical injuries and diseases (Perry, Story, & Lytle, 1997; Stewart et al., 1995).

Yet in most efforts to impart health concepts to school-age children, researchers have found that health habits show little change. Why is there such a gap between health knowledge and practice? There are several related reasons:

- Health is usually not an important goal for children, who feel good most of the time. They are far more concerned about schoolwork, friends, and play.

- Children do not yet have an adultlike time perspective, which relates past, present, and future. Engaging in preventive behaviors is difficult when so much time intervenes between what children do now and its health consequences.

- Much health information that children get is contradicted by other sources, such as television advertising (see Chapter 10) and the examples of adults and peers.

This does not mean that teaching school-age children health-related facts is unimportant. But information must be supplemented by other efforts. As we saw in earlier chap-

CAREGIVING CONCERNS

Strategies for Fostering Healthy Lifestyles in School-Age Children

STRATEGY	DESCRIPTION
Increase health-related knowledge and encourage healthy behaviors.	Provide health education through developmentally appropriate, enjoyable participatory activities that go beyond transmitting information to include modeling, role playing, rehearsal, and reinforcement of good health practices.
Involve parents in supporting health education.	Communicate with parents about health education in school, encouraging them to carry over these efforts to the home. Encourage proper parental supervision by providing information about the development of children's health-related skills.
Provide healthy environments in schools.	Breakfast and lunch services in schools should follow widely accepted dietary guidelines. Opportunities for pupils to voice food preferences in the context of those guidelines enhances food acceptance and healthy eating.
Make voluntary screening for risk factors available as part of health education.	Offer periodic measures of height, weight, body mass, blood pressure, and adequacy of diet while educating children about the meaning of each index and encouraging improvement.
Promote pleasurable physical activity.	Provide opportunities for regular moderate to vigorous physical exercise through activities that deemphasize competition and stress skill-building and personal and social enjoyment.
Teach children to be critical of media advertising.	Children are a targeted market for food manufacturers. More than half the ads on Saturday morning TV are for unhealthy foods. Besides teaching children to be skeptical of such ads, reduce advertising for non-nutritious foods in schools, where such messages are widespread.
Work for public policies that create safer community environments for children.	Form community action groups to improve child safety, school nutrition, and play environments and programs that foster healthy physical activity.

Sources: Perry, Story, & Lytle, 1997; Peterson & Oliver, 1995; Tuchfarber, Zins, & Jason, 1997.

ASK YOURSELF . . .

■ *Rena discovered that Joey had stopped drinking milk in the school cafeteria because several of his friends no longer drank it. Also, he often skipped the main dish in favor of an extra dessert. What can Joey's parents do to ensure that his diet supports healthy growth? What should Joey's school be doing to foster good nutrition?*

■ *Nine-year-old Talia is afraid to hug and kiss her grandmother, who has cancer. What explains Talia's mistaken belief that the same behaviors that cause colds to spread might lead her to catch cancer?*

ters, a powerful means of fostering children's health is to reduce hazards, such as pollution, inadequate medical care, and non-nutritious foods that are widely available in homes as well as school cafeterias (Perry, Story, & Lytle, 1997; Peterson & Oliver, 1995). At the same time, since environments will never be totally free of health risks, parents and teachers need to coach children in good health practices and model and reinforce these behaviors as much as possible. Refer to the Caregiving Concerns table above for ways to foster healthy lifestyles in school-age children.

BRIEF REVIEW

Although many children are at their healthiest in middle childhood, a variety of health problems do occur. Most are more common among low-SES youngsters, who are exposed to more health risks throughout development. Vision and hearing difficulties; malnutrition; overweight and obesity; nighttime bedwetting; intestinal and respiratory infections, allergies, and muscle sprains that result in school absences; and unintentional injuries are among the most frequent health concerns during the school years. Genetic and environmental factors combine to increase children's vulnerability to certain health problems, such as nearsightedness, obesity, and asthma. School-age children can learn a wide range of health information, but it has little impact on their everyday behavior. Interventions must also provide them with healthier environments and directly promote good health practices.

MOTOR DEVELOPMENT AND PLAY

Visit a city park on a pleasant weekend afternoon, watch several preschool and school-age children at play, and jot down their various physical activities. You will see that gains in body size and muscle strength support improved motor coordination during middle childhood. In addition, greater cognitive and social maturity permits older children to use their new motor skills in more complex ways. You are likely to notice a major change in children's play at this time.

GROSS MOTOR DEVELOPMENT

During middle childhood, running, jumping, hopping, and ball skills become more refined. At Joey and Lizzie's school one day, I watched during the third- to sixth-graders' recess. Children burst into sprints as they raced across the playground, jumped quickly over rotating ropes, engaged in intricate patterns of hopscotch, kicked and dribbled soccer balls, swung bats at balls pitched by their classmates, and balanced adeptly as they walked toe-to-toe across narrow ledges. Table 11.2 summarizes gross motor achievements between 6 and 12 years of age.

TABLE **11.2**

Changes in Gross Motor Skills During Middle Childhood

SKILL	DEVELOPMENTAL CHANGE
Running	Running speed increases from 12 feet per second at age 6 to over 18 feet per second at age 12.
Other gait variations	Skipping improves. Sideways stepping appears around age 6 and becomes more continuous and fluid with age.
Vertical jump	Height jumped increases from 4 inches at age 6 to 12 inches at age 12.
Standing broad jump	Distance jumped increases from 3 feet at age 6 to over 5 feet at age 12.
Precision jumping and hopping (on a mat divided into squares)	By age 7 children can accurately jump and hop from square to square, a performance that improves until age 9 and then levels off.
Throwing	Throwing speed, distance, and accuracy increase for both sexes, but much more for boys than girls. At age 6, a ball thrown by a boy travels 39 feet per second, one by a girl 29 feet per second. At age 12, a ball thrown by a boy travels 78 feet per second, one by a girl 56 feet per second.
Catching	Ability to catch small balls thrown over greater distances improves with age.
Kicking	Kicking speed and accuracy improve, with boys considerably ahead of girls. At age 6, a ball kicked by a boy travels 21 feet per second, one by a girl 13 feet per second. At age 12, a ball kicked by a boy travels 34 feet per second, one by a girl 26 feet per second.
Batting	Batting motions become more effective with age, increasing in speed and accuracy and involving the entire body.
Dribbling	Style of hand dribbling gradually changes, from awkward slapping of the ball to continuous, relaxed, even stroking.

Sources: Cratty, 1986; Malina & Bouchard, 1991; Roberton, 1984.

During middle childhood, gross motor skills become more refined. Gains in flexibility, balance, and agility permit these children to play a game of hopscotch with fancy footwork and to bend on one foot to retrieve an object. *(Bill Bachmann/The Image Works)*

The diverse motor skills that improve during the school years reflect gains in four basic motor capacities:

- *Flexibility.* Compared to the movements of preschoolers, those of school-age children are more pliable and elastic, a difference that can be seen as children swing a bat, kick a ball, jump over a hurdle, or execute tumbling routines.

- *Balance.* School-age children can walk a narrower balance beam than they could during early childhood, and their ability to remain in a one-foot stand increases. Improved balance supports advances in many athletic skills, including running, hopping, skipping, throwing, kicking, and the rapid changes of direction required in many team sports (Clark & Watkins, 1984).

- *Agility.* Greater quickness and accuracy of movement are evident in the fancy footwork of jump rope and hopscotch, as well as in the forward, backward, and sideways motions older children use as they dodge opponents in tag and soccer.

- *Force.* Older youngsters can throw and kick a ball harder and propel themselves further off the ground when running and jumping than they could at earlier ages (Cratty, 1986).

Although body growth contributes greatly to the improved motor performance of school-age children, more efficient information processing also plays an important role. Steady improvements in *reaction time* occur, with 14-year-olds responding almost twice as quickly as 6-year-olds (Kail, 1991; Southard, 1985). As a result, younger children often have difficulty with skills that require immediate responding. When they dribble a ball, they often lose control, and when up at bat, they usually swing too late.

Reaction time combines several cognitive skills that are crucial for effective motor performance—time to recognize a stimulus, time to formulate an appropriate response, and time for the plan of action to reach the muscles. That speed of reaction is not yet well developed in younger school-age children has practical implications for physical education (Seefeldt, 1996). Since 6- and 7-year-olds are seldom successful at batting a thrown ball, T-ball is more appropriate for them than baseball. And handball, four-square, and kickball should precede instruction in tennis, basketball, and football.

FINE MOTOR DEVELOPMENT

Fine motor development also improves steadily over the school years, a change that is apparent in the activities children of this age period enjoy. On rainy afternoons, Joey and Lizzie could be found experimenting with yo-yos, building model airplanes, weaving potholders on small looms, and working puzzles with hundreds of tiny pieces. Middle childhood is also the time when many children take up musical instruments, which demand considerable fine motor control.

Gains in fine motor skill are especially evident in children's writing and drawing. By age 6, most children can print the alphabet, their first and last names, and the numbers from 1 to 10 with reasonable clarity. However, as Figure 11.4 reveals, their writing tends to be quite large because they use the entire arm to make strokes rather than just the wrist and fingers. Children usually master uppercase letters first because horizontal and vertical motions are easier to control than the small curves of the lowercase alphabet. Legibility of writing gradually increases as children produce more accurate letters with uniform height and spacing. These improvements prepare children for mastering cursive writing by third grade.

Children's drawings show dramatic gains in organization, detail, and representation of depth during middle childhood. By the end of the preschool years, children can accurately copy many two-dimensional shapes, and they integrate these into their drawings. Some depth cues have also begun to appear, such as making distant objects smaller than

Ted's Picture with Label, Age 5

RETURN OF
THE LEDI

Ted's Space Trip Story, Age 7

The rokit is blasting of! Thay are going tho 100 galakses! Peple are climing a ladr to see them. it has a spashl sheld all a rond it. In cas there is a atak on the rokit. Becase you never no. thay are on TV allso.

The rocket is blasting off! They are going through 100 galaxies! People are climbing a ladder to see them. It has a special shield all around it. In case there is an attack on the rocket. Because you never know. They are on TV also.

Ted's War of 1812 Essay Age 9

There where sevral reasons the congress declared war with Britain. First British attacked American ships to keep France from obtaining supplies. Second Britain kidnapped American sailors. But Britain clamed the they were deserters and Britain forced sailors to serve British navy. Third settlers feared British in Canada becouse they wanted to claim land in Canada. Fourth all peaceful solutions failed. So thats what caused the War of 1812.

There were several reasons that Congress declared war with Britain. First, the British attacked American ships to keep France from obtaining supplies. Second, Britain kidnapped American sailors. But Britain claimed that there were deserters, and Britain forced sailors to serve the British Navy. Third, settlers feared the British in Canada because they wanted to claim land in Canada. Fourth, all peaceful solutions failed. So that's what caused the War of 1812.

FIGURE **11.4**

Fine motor coordination improves over middle childhood, as these writing samples reveal. At age 5, Ted printed in large, uppercase letters, asking for help in spelling the words. By age 7, he had mastered the lowercase alphabet, and his printing was small and evenly spaced. At age 9, he used cursive writing. Notice, also, how letter reversals and invented spellings decline with age. *(Ted's picture with label and space trip story from L. M. McGee & D. J. Richgels, 1990,* Literacy's Beginnings, *Boston: Allyn and Bacon, p. 312. Reprinted by permission of the authors. Ted's War of 1812 essay from D. J. Richgels, L. M. McGee, & E. A. Slaton, 1989, "Teaching Expository Text Structure in Reading and Writing," in K. D. Muth, Ed.,* Children's Comprehension of Text, *Newark, DE: International Reading Association, p. 180. Reprinted by permission.)*

near ones (Braine et al., 1993). Yet before age 9 or 10, most children have difficulty copying a three-dimensional form, such as a cube or cylinder. Around this time, the third dimension is clearly evident in children's drawings through overlapping objects, diagonal placement, and converging lines (see Figure 11.5).

All children do not follow precisely the same sequence in mastering representation of the third dimension (Nicholls & Kennedy, 1992). Furthermore, use of depth cues appears more advanced when children are asked to put stickers of objects on paper, a less demanding task than drawing. Clearly, children notice the way depth is depicted in pictures before they produce works that portray it (Braine et al., 1993; Cox & Littleton,

FIGURE 11.5

Integration of depth cues into children's drawings increases dramatically over the school years. Compare this 10-year-old's drawing to the one by a 6-year-old on page 315. Here, depth is indicated by overlapping objects, diagonal placement, and converging lines, as well as by making distant objects smaller than near ones. Although the young artist from Singapore who created this picture is highly talented, by the late elementary school years many children who attend school make good use of depth cues in their artwork. Experience with writing and instruction in artistic representation probably foster children's competence at depicting the third dimension. *(Laura Berk, left; International Museum of Children's Art, right)*

1995). Over the school years, they gradually solve the problem of how to include the third dimension in their artistic creations.

INDIVIDUAL AND GROUP DIFFERENCES

As was the case at younger ages, school-age children show marked individual differences in motor capacities that are influenced by both heredity and environment. Body build continues to affect gross motor performance, with taller, more muscular children excelling in many tasks. At the same time, parents who encourage physical exercise tend to have youngsters who enjoy it more and who are also more skilled. Family income affects children's opportunities to develop a variety of physical abilities. Economically advantaged children are far more likely to have ballet, tennis, gymnastics, and music lessons than are youngsters from low-income families.

Sex differences in motor skills that began to appear during the preschool years extend into middle childhood and, in some instances, become more pronounced. Girls remain ahead in the fine motor area, including handwriting and drawing. They also continue to have an edge in gross motor skills that depend on balance and precision of movement, such as skipping, jumping, and hopping. But on all other skills listed in Table 11.2, boys outperform girls, and in the case of throwing and kicking, the difference is large (Cratty, 1986).

What accounts for school-age boys' superiority in so many gross motor skills? Their genetic advantage in muscle mass is not great enough to explain it. Instead, environment plays a much larger role. Girl's sports participation has increased dramatically since the 1970s, but it does not equal that of boys (Coakley, 1990; Greendorfer, Lewko, & Rosengren, 1996). And despite improved media attention to women's athletics, most players in public sports events continue to be men. Although Lizzie played in the city soccer league, her parents believed that Joey was better at athletics and that it was more critical for his development that he do well at sports.

A study of over 800 elementary school pupils found that parents hold higher expectations for boys' athletic performance, and children absorb these social messages at an early age. Kindergartners through third graders of both sexes viewed sports in a gender-stereotyped fashion—as much more important for boys. Boys were also more likely to indicate that it was important to their parents that they participate in athletics. These attitudes affected children's physical self-images as well as behavior. Girls saw themselves as having less talent at sports, and by sixth grade they devoted less time to athletics than did their male classmates (Eccles & Harold, 1991; Eccles, Jacobs, & Harold, 1990).

These findings indicate that extra measures need to be taken to raise girls' confidence that they can do well at sports. Educating parents about the minimal differences in school-age boys' and girls' physical capacities and sensitizing them to unfair biases against girls' athletic ability may prove helpful. Parental enjoyment of physical activity is also important, since parents who like to engage in sports provide more encouragement to both sons and daughters (Brustad, 1993). In addition, greater emphasis on skill training for girls along with increased attention to their athletic achievements in schools and communities is likely to increase their involvement. Middle childhood may be a crucial time to take these steps, since during the school years children start to discover what they are good at and make some definite skill commitments.

ORGANIZED GAMES WITH RULES

The physical activities of school-age children reflect an important advance in the quality of their play: Organized games with rules become common. In cultures around the world, the variety of children's spontaneous rule-based games is enormous. Some are variants on popular sports, such as soccer, baseball, basketball, and football. Others are well-known childhood games, such as tag, jacks, and hopscotch. Children have also invented hundreds of less well-known games and passed them from one generation to the next (Sierra & Kaminski, 1995). You may remember some from your own childhood, such as red rover, statues, blind man's buff, leapfrog, one-o-cat, kick the can, and prisoner's base.

Gains in perspective taking—in particular, children's ability to understand the roles of several players in a game—permit this transition to rule-oriented games. The contribution of these play experiences to emotional and social development is great. Child-invented games usually rely on simple physical skills and a sizable element of luck. As a result, they rarely become contests of individual ability. Instead, they permit children to try out different styles of competing, winning, and losing with little personal risk (Devereux, 1976).

Western children devote more time to adult-organized sports and less time to gathering for spontaneous games than they did in generations past. Is this baseball coach careful to encourage rather than criticize? To what extent does he emphasize teamwork, fair play, courtesy, and skill development over winning? These factors determine whether or not adult-organized sports are pleasurable, constructive experiences for children. *(Lawrence Migdale/Photo Researchers)*

CAREGIVING CONCERNS

Pros and Cons of Adult-Organized Sports in Middle Childhood

PROS	CONS	RECOMMENDATIONS FOR COACHES AND PARENTS
Adult-structured athletics prepares children for realistic competition—the kind they may face as adults.	Adult involvement leads games to become overly competitive, placing too much pressure on children.	Permit children to select from among appropriate activities the ones that suit them best. Do not push children into sports they do not enjoy.
Regularly scheduled games and practices ensure that children get plenty of exercise and fill free time that might otherwise be devoted to less constructive pursuits.	When adults control the game, children learn little about leadership, followership, and fair play.	For children younger than age 9, emphasize basic skills, such as kicking, throwing, and batting, and simplified games that grant all participants adequate playing time.
Children get instruction in physical skills necessary for future success in athletics.	When adults assign children to specific roles (such as catcher, first base), children lose the opportunity to experiment with rules and strategies.	Permit children to progress at their own pace and to play for the fun of it, whether or not they become expert athletes.
Parents and children share an activity that both enjoy.	Highly structured, competitive sports are less fun than child-organized games; they resemble "work" more than "play."	Adjust practice time to children's attention spans and need for unstructured time with peers, with family, and for homework. Two practices a week, each no longer than 30 minutes for younger school-age children and 60 minutes for older school-age children, are sufficient.
		Emphasize effort, skill gains, and teamwork rather than winning. Avoid criticism for errors and defeat, which promote anxiety and avoidance of athletics.
		Involve children in decisions about team rules. To strengthen desirable responses, reinforce compliance rather than punishing noncompliance.

Sources: Kolata, 1992; Smith & Smoll, 1997.

Also, in their efforts to organize a game, children discover why rules are necessary and which ones work well. In fact, they often spend as much time working out the details of how a game should proceed as they do playing the game itself! As we will see in Chapter 13, these experiences help children form more mature concepts of fairness and justice.

Because of the value of child-organized games for children's development, some researchers are concerned about their recent decline. Today, school-age youngsters spend less time gathering on sidewalks and playgrounds than they did in generations past. Children's attraction to television and video games accounts for some of this change. But adult-organized sports, such as baseball, softball, basketball, and soccer leagues, also fill many hours that children used to devote to spontaneous play.

The past several decades have witnessed a tremendous expansion of youth sports programs. In the United States alone, about 50 percent of the youth population participates in some form of organized sports (Ewing & Seefeldt, 1996). Some researchers worry that adult-structured athletics, which mirror professional sports, are robbing children of crucial learning experiences and endangering their development. The Caregiving Concerns table above summarizes the pros and cons of adult-organized youth athletic leagues.

So far, research indicates that for most children, these experiences do not result in long-term psychological damage (Smoll & Smith, 1996). But the arguments of critics are valid in some cases. Children who join teams so early that the skills demanded are beyond their capabilities soon lose interest and want to drop out (Bailey & Rasmussen, 1996). And when parents and coaches criticize rather than encourage and do not let players who have lost a game forget about defeat, a few children react with intense anxiety. Eventually, they may avoid athletics entirely (Smith & Smoll, 1996). Finally, intense, frequent practice sessions can lead to serious "overuse" injuries. In extreme cases, physical stress fractures the soft cartilage in the epiphyses of the long bones, leading to premature closure and arrested growth (Lord & Kozar, 1996).

Refer again to the Caregiving Concerns table for ways to make adult-structured athletics positive experiences in the lives of children. When coaches are trained to emphasize effort, improvement, participation, and teamwork, young athletes enjoy their experience more, like their coach and teammates more, and gain in self-esteem. These effects are particularly strong for children whose self-confidence is low to begin with—and who are most in need of a rewarding sports experience (Smith & Smoll, 1997).

SHADOWS OF OUR EVOLUTIONARY PAST

Besides a new level of structure and organization, some additional qualities of physical play become common in middle childhood. While watching children at your city park, notice how they occasionally wrestle, roll, hit, and run after one another while smiling and laughing. This friendly chasing and play-fighting is called **rough-and-tumble play.** Research indicates that it is a good-natured, sociable activity that is quite distinct from aggressive fighting. Children in many cultures engage in it with peers whom they like especially well, and they continue interacting after a rough-and-tumble episode rather than separating, as they do at the end of an aggressive encounter.

Sometimes parents and teachers mistake rough-and-tumble for real fighting and try to intervene. In these instances, children often respond, "It's all right, we're only playing!" School-age youngsters are quite good at telling the difference between playful wrestling and a true aggressive attack (Costabile et al., 1991; Smith & Boulton, 1990). Only those who have poor peer relations sometimes confuse rough-and-tumble with hostility (Pellegrini, 1988).

Children's rough-and-tumble play is similar to the social behavior of young mammals of many species. Does it have some adaptive value? By age 11, children choose rough-and-tumble partners who are not only likable but similar in strength to themselves. In our evolutionary past, this form of interaction may have been important for the development of fighting skill (Humphreys & Smith, 1987). Rough-and-tumble play occurs more often among boys, but girls also display it. Girls' rough-and-tumble largely consists of running, chasing, and brief physical contact. Boys engage in more playful wrestling, restraining, and hitting (Boulton, 1996).

Rough-and-tumble tends to occur among children who are alike in physical capacity, but as we have seen, children of the same age vary greatly in size and strength. When children gather in groups for physical activity, social structures emerge on the basis of toughness and assertiveness. A **dominance hierarchy** is a stable ordering of individuals that predicts who will win when conflict arises between group members. Dominance hierarchies exist in the social organization of many animal species, and they are a basic feature of human group interaction as well. Observations of arguments, threats, and physical attacks between children reveal a consistent lineup of winners and losers as early as the preschool years. This hierarchy becomes increasingly stable during middle childhood and adolescence, especially among boys (Pettit et al., 1990; Savin-Williams, 1979).

Like dominance relations among animals, those among human children serve the adaptive function of limiting aggression among group members. Once a dominance hierarchy is clearly established, hostility is rare. When it occurs, it is very restrained, often taking the form of playful verbal insults that can be accepted cheerfully by a partner (Fine, 1980). For example, Joey rarely challenges Sean, a child much larger than he,

Rough-and-tumble play can be distinguished from aggression by its good-natured quality. In our evolutionary past, it may have been important for the development of fighting skill. *(Tony Freeman/PhotoEdit)*

rough-and-tumble play
A form of peer interaction involving friendly chasing and play-fighting that, in our evolutionary past, may have been important for the development of fighting skill.

dominance hierarchy
A stable ordering of group members that predicts who will win under conditions of conflict.

on the playground. But when he is unhappy about how things are going in a game, Joey is likely to tumble over humorously on the grass while saying something like "Hey, Sean, you've been up at bat so long you'll fall over dead if you swing at one more ball! Come on, give one of us a chance." This gradual replacement of direct hostility with friendly insults provides school-age children with an effective means of influencing their physically more powerful peers.

PHYSICAL EDUCATION

In the preceding sections, we have seen that physical activity supports many aspects of children's development—the health of their bodies, their sense of self-worth as physically active and capable beings, and the cognitive and social skills necessary for getting along well with others. Physical education classes that provide regularly scheduled opportunities for exercise and play help ensure that all children have access to these benefits.

Yet physical education is not taught often enough in American schools. Only one-third of elementary school pupils have a daily physical education class; the average school-age child gets only 20 minutes of physical education a week (Steinhardt, 1992; Wurtele, 1996). This means that children get most of their exercise outside school.

But on their own, American children often do not engage in enough vigorous physical activity. The growing fitness movement among adults has not yet filtered down to children, many of whom ride to and from school in buses and cars, sit in classrooms most of the day, and watch TV for 3 to 4 hours after they arrive home. The National Children and Youth Fitness Study, which tested thousands of schoolchildren on a variety of fitness items (such as pull-ups, sit-ups, and one-mile run), revealed that only two-thirds of 10- to 12-year-old boys and about half of 10- to 12-year-old girls met basic fitness standards for children their age (Looney & Plowman, 1990).

These findings indicate that American schools need to do a better job of providing physical education. Besides offering more frequent classes, many experts believe that schools should change the content of physical education programs. Training in competitive sports is often a high priority, but it is unlikely to reach the least physically fit youngsters, who draw back when an activity demands a high level of skill and they are criticized by peers for striking out at bat or missing a basket (Portman, 1995).

Instead, programs should emphasize informal games that most children can perform well and individual exercise—walking, running, jumping, tumbling, and climbing. These pursuits are the ones most likely to last into later years. Furthermore, children of widely varying skill levels tend to sustain physical activity when teachers focus on each child's personal progress and contribution to team accomplishment (Whitehead & Corbin, 1997). Then physical education fosters a healthy sense of self while satisfying school-age children's need for relatedness.

Physical fitness builds on itself. Children who are in good physical condition have more energy, and they take great pleasure in their rapidly developing motor skills and ability to control their own bodies. As a result, they seek out these activities in the future, developing rewarding interests in physical exercise that pave the way toward a lifelong commitment to an active and healthy lifestyle.

ASK YOURSELF . . .

■ *On Saturdays, 8-year-old Gina gathers with friends at a city park to play kickball. Besides improved ball skills, what is she learning?*

■ *Alex thinks he isn't good at sports and doesn't like physical education. Suggest some strategies his teacher can use to improve his enjoyment and involvement in physical activity.*

Summary

Body Growth

Describe changes in body size, proportions, and skeletal maturity during middle childhood.

- Gains in body size during middle childhood extend the pattern of growth established during the preschool period. On the average, children add about 5 pounds in weight and 2 to 3 inches in height each year. Growth is not steady; children show slight spurts in height followed by lulls. By age 9, girls overtake boys in physical size.

- Large individual and ethnic variations in body growth are influenced by evolutionary adaptations to a particular climate, food resources, and infectious disease. **Secular trends in physical growth** have occurred in industrialized nations. Because of improved health and nutrition, many children are growing larger and reaching physical maturity earlier than did their ancestors.

- During middle childhood, bones continue to lengthen and broaden, and all 20 primary teeth are replaced by permanent ones. Tooth decay affects half of American school-age children. Preventive measures, such as plastic sealants, are less accessible to low-income youngsters. About one-third of school-age children suffer from **malocclusion,** a condition in which the upper and lower teeth do not meet properly. Braces are common by the end of elementary school.

Describe brain development in middle childhood.

- Only a small increase in brain size occurs during middle childhood. Myelinization continues, the corpus callosum thickens, synaptic connections strengthen, and lateralization of the cerebral hemispheres increases. Brain development during the school years is believed to involve **neurotransmitter** and hormonal influences.

Common Health Problems

What vision and hearing problems are common during middle childhood?

- School-age children from economically advantaged homes are at their healthiest, due to the cumulative effects of good nutrition combined with rapid development of the body's immune system. At the same time, a variety of health problems do occur, many of which are more common among low-SES children.

- The most common vision problem in middle childhood is **myopia,** or nearsightedness. It is influenced by heredity as well as the way children use their eyes. Myopia is one of the few health conditions that increase with family education and income. Because of untreated ear infections, many low-income children experience some hearing loss during the school years.

Describe the causes and consequences of serious nutritional problems in middle childhood, granting special attention to obesity.

- Poverty-stricken children in developing countries and in the United States continue to suffer from malnutrition during middle childhood. When malnutrition is allowed to persist for many years, its negative impact on physical growth, intellectual development, and motor performance is permanent.

- Overweight and **obesity** are growing problems in affluent nations such as the United States. Although heredity contributes to obesity, parental feeding practices, maladaptive eating habits, and lack of exercise also play important roles. Obese children often are rejected by their classmates, report feeling more depressed, and display more behavior problems.

- Family-based interventions in which both parents and children revise eating patterns, engage in regular daily exercise, and reinforce one another's progress are the most effective approaches to treating childhood obesity. Rewarding obese children for reducing sedentary time is an effective approach to getting them to like and engage in more physical activity.

What factors contribute to nocturnal enuresis and asthma, and how can these health problems be reduced?

- **Nocturnal enuresis,** or bedwetting during the night, affects 8 percent of American school-age children. In the majority of cases, it has biological roots. The most effective treatment is a urine alarm that works according to conditioning principles.

- The most common cause of school absence and childhood hospitalization is **asthma.** It occurs more often among African-American and poverty-stricken children, perhaps because of pollution, stressful home lives, and lack of access to good health care. Children with severe chronic illnesses are at risk for academic, emotional, and social difficulties and benefit from a variety of interventions.

Describe changes in unintentional injuries during middle childhood and effective interventions.

- The rate of unintentional injury increases from middle childhood into adolescence. Motor vehicle collisions (with children as passengers or pedestrians) and bicycle accidents are the leading causes. Highly active, impulsive boys remain particularly susceptible to injury.

- Effective school-based safety education programs make use of modeling, role playing, and rehearsal of safety practices; reward children for good performance; and provide occasional booster sessions. In addition, parents need to be educated about children's age-related safety capacities.

Summary (continued)

HEALTH EDUCATION

What can parents and teachers do to encourage good health practices in school-age children?

■ School-age children can successfully acquire a wide range of health-related information, but it seldom changes their health-related behavior. Besides educating children about good health, adults need to reduce health hazards in children's environments and model and reinforce good health practices.

MOTOR DEVELOPMENT AND PLAY

Cite major changes in gross and fine motor development during middle childhood.

■ Gradual increases in body size and muscle strength support refinements in many gross motor skills in middle childhood. Gains in flexibility, balance, agility, and force occur. In addition, improvements in reaction time contribute to the athletic performance of school-age children.

■ Fine motor development also improves during the school years. Children's writing becomes more legible, and their drawings show dramatic increases in organization, detail, and representation of depth.

Describe individual and group differences in motor performance during middle childhood.

■ Children show wide individual differences in motor capacities that are influenced by both genetic and environmental factors. Body build, parental encouragement, and opportunities to take lessons support a variety of physical abilities. Gender stereotypes, which affect parental expectations for children's athletic performance, largely account for boys' superiority on a wide range of gross motor skills.

What qualities of children's play are evident in middle childhood?

■ Organized games with rules become common during the school years. Children's spontaneous games support many aspects of development. Expansion of youth sports programs has led to concerns about adult-structured athletics. Although most

players are not harmed, coaches and parents who emphasize competition and winning promote undue anxiety and avoidance of sports in some children.

■ Some features of children's physical activity reflect our evolutionary past. **Rough-and-tumble play** may have at one time been important for the development of fighting skill. **Dominance hierarchies** become increasingly stable in middle childhood and serve the adaptive function of limiting aggression among group members.

Why is high-quality physical education important during the school years?

■ Physical education classes help ensure that all children have access to the benefits of regular exercise and play. Yet physical education does not take place often enough in American schools. Many school-age youngsters do not meet basic physical fitness standards for children their age. Both the quantity and quality of physical education need to be improved.

Important terms and concepts

asthma (p. 419)
dominance hierarchy (p. 431)
malocclusion (p. 413)
myopia (p. 414)

neurotransmitters (p. 413)
nocturnal enuresis (p. 419)
obesity (p. 415)
rough-and-tumble play (p. 431)

secular trends in physical growth (p. 412)

Fyi...   FOR FURTHER INFORMATION AND HELP

INJURY PREVENTION

National SAFE KIDS Campaign
(202) 884-4993
Website: www.safekids.org

Dedicated to the prevention of unintentional injury in children and youths. Develops posters, stickers, brochures, and pamphlets about injury prevention designed in easy-to-read formats for children. Also produces materials to help parents protect children and minimize risks. State and local SAFE KIDS coalitions exist in all 50 U.S. States, the District of Columbia, and Puerto Rico.

CHRONIC ILLNESS IN CHILDHOOD

Asthma and Allergy Foundation
of America
(202) 466-7643
Website: www.aafa.com

Devoted to solving health problems posed by allergic diseases, including asthma. Supports research and medical training and provides information to health professionals and the public.

Candlelighters Childhood Cancer
Foundation
(301) 657-8401
Website: www:candlelighters.org

Increases public awareness of childhood cancer and provides information, guidance, and emotional support to parents with affected children. Has a crisis hotline: (800) 366-2223.

Cystic Fibrosis Foundation
(301) 951-4422
Website: www:cff.org

Supports research, education, and care centers to benefit children and young adults with cystic fibrosis.

ADULT-ORGANIZED SPORTS FOR CHILDREN

Little League Baseball
(717) 326-1921
Website: www.littleleague.org

Organizes baseball and softball programs for children 6 to 18 years of age. Operates a special division for children with disabilities and sponsors an annual world series.

United States Youth Soccer Association
(800) 4-SOCCER
Website: www.usysa.org

Supports soccer programs for children 6 to 18 years of age throughout the United States. Seeks to encourage widespread participation and offer equal opportunity regardless of ability or sex. Distributes supplies and support necessary to form teams.

"Dream"
Amit Saha
10 years, Bangladesh

A young dreamer sleeps soundly at the close of a busy day. His improved capacity to remember, reason, and solve problems makes middle childhood a time of rapidly expanding cognitive skills—the topic of Chapter 12.

Reprinted by permission from The International Museum of Children's Art, Oslo, Norway.

Cognitive Development

in Middle Childhood

"Finally!" Lizzie exclaimed the day she entered first grade. "Now I get to go to *real* school just like Joey!" Rena remembered how 6-year-old Lizzie had walked confidently into her classroom, pencils, crayons, and writing pad in hand, ready for a more disciplined approach to learning than she had experienced in early childhood. As a preschooler, Lizzie had loved playing school, giving assignments as the "teacher" and pretending to read and write as the "pupil." Now she was there in earnest, eager to master the tasks that had sparked her imagination as a 4- and 5-year-old.

Lizzie entered a whole new world of challenging mental activities. In a single morning, she and her classmates wrote in journals, met in reading groups, worked on addition and subtraction, and sorted leaves gathered on the playground for a special science project. As Lizzie and Joey moved through the elementary school grades, they tackled increasingly complex tasks and gradually became more accomplished at reading, writing, math skills, and general knowledge of the world.

Cognitive development had prepared Joey and Lizzie for this new phase. We begin by returning to Piaget's theory and the information-processing approach. Together, they provide an overview of cognitive change during the school years. Then we take an in-depth look at individual differences in mental development. We examine the genetic and environmental roots of IQ scores, which often enter into important educational decisions. Our discussion continues with language, which blossoms further during middle childhood. Finally, we consider the importance of schools in children's learning and development.

PIAGET'S THEORY: THE CONCRETE OPERATIONAL STAGE

When Lizzie visited my child development class as a 4-year-old, she was easily confused by Piaget's conservation problems (see Chapter 9, page 330). For example, she insisted that the amount of water was still the same after it had been poured from a tall, narrow container into a short, wide one. At age 8, when Lizzie returned, these tasks were easy. "Of course it's the same," she exclaimed. "The water's shorter but it's also wider. Pour it back," she instructed the college student who was interviewing her. "You'll see, it's the same amount!"

Lizzie's response indicates that she has entered Piaget's **concrete operational stage,** which spans the years from 7 to 11. Thought is now far more logical, flexible, and organized than it was during the preschool years. The older child is better at distinguishing fantasy from reality and reasons correctly about many changes in objects and events in the everyday world. Concrete operations are evident in school-age children's performance on a wide variety of Piagetian tasks.

CONSERVATION

The ability to pass *conservation tasks* provides clear evidence of *operations*—mental actions that obey logical rules (see Chapter 9, page 328, for examples). Notice how Lizzie coordinates several aspects of the task rather than *centering* on only one, as a preschooler would do. In other words, Lizzie is capable of **decentration;** she recognizes that a change in one aspect of the water (its height) is compensated for by a change in another aspect (its width). Lizzie also demonstrates **reversibility,** the capacity to mentally go through a series of steps and then reverse direction, returning to the starting point. Recall from Chapter 9 that reversibility is part of every logical operation. It is solidly achieved in middle childhood.

CLASSIFICATION

By the end of middle childhood, children pass Piaget's *class inclusion problem* (see page 331). They can group objects into hierarchies of classes and subclasses more effectively than they could at earlier ages (Achenbach & Weisz, 1975; Hodges & French, 1988). You can see this in children's play activities. Collections of all kinds of objects—stamps, coins, baseball cards, rocks, bottle caps, and more—become common in middle childhood. At age 10, Joey spent hours sorting and resorting his large box of baseball cards. At times he grouped them by league and team membership, at other times by playing position and batting average. He could separate the players into a variety of classes and subclasses and flexibly move back and forth between them. This understanding is beyond the grasp of preschoolers, who usually insist that a set of objects can be sorted in only one way.

concrete operational stage
Piaget's third stage, during which thought is logical, flexible, and organized in its application to concrete information. However, the capacity for abstract thinking is not yet present. Spans the years from 7 to 11.

decentration
The ability to focus on several aspects of a problem at once and relate them.

reversibility
The ability to mentally go through a series of steps in a problem and then reverse direction, returning to the starting point.

SERIATION

The ability to order items along a quantitative dimension, such as length or weight, is called **seriation**. To test for it, Piaget asked children to arrange sticks of different lengths from shortest to longest. Older preschoolers can create the series, but they do so haphazardly. They put the sticks in a row but make many errors and take a long time to correct them. In contrast, 6- to 7-year-olds are guided by an orderly plan. They create the series efficiently by beginning with the smallest stick, then moving to the next smallest, and so on, until the ordering is complete.

The concrete operational child's improved grasp of quantitative arrangements is also evident in a more challenging seriation problem—one that requires children to seriate mentally. This ability is called **transitive inference.** In a well-known transitive inference problem, Piaget showed children pairings of differently colored sticks. From observing that stick A is longer than stick B and stick B is longer than stick C, children must make the mental inference that A is longer than C. Not until age 9 or 10 do children perform well on this task (Chapman & Lindenberger, 1988; Piaget, 1967).

An improved ability to categorize underlies children's interest in collecting objects during middle childhood. These fourth graders can sort this shell collection into an elaborate structure of classes and subclasses. *(Brian Smith)*

SPATIAL REASONING

Piaget found that school-age youngsters have a more accurate understanding of space than they did in early childhood. Let's take two examples—children's understanding of distance and ability to give directions.

■ **DISTANCE.** Comprehension of distance improves in middle childhood, as a special conservation task reveals. To give this problem, make two small trees out of modeling clay and place them apart on a table. Next, put a block or thick piece of cardboard between the trees. Then ask the child whether the trees are nearer together, farther apart, or still the same distance apart.

Preschoolers say that the distance has become smaller. They do not understand that a filled-up space has the same value as an empty space (Piaget, Inhelder, & Szeminska, 1948/1960). By the early school years, children grasp this idea easily. Four-year-olds can conserve distance when questioned about objects that are very familiar to them or when a path is marked between two objects, which helps them represent the distance. However, their understanding is not as solid and complete as that of the school-age child (Fabricius & Wellman, 1993; Miller & Baillargeon, 1990).

■ **DIRECTIONS.** School-age children's more advanced understanding of space can also be seen in their ability to give directions. Stand facing a 5- or 6-year-old, and ask the child to name an object on your left and one on your right. Children of this age answer incorrectly; they apply their own frame of reference to that of others. Between 7 and 8 years, children start to perform *mental rotations,* in which they align the self's frame to match that of a person in a different orientation. As a result, they can identify left and right for positions they do not occupy (Roberts & Aman, 1993).

Around 8 to 10 years, children can give clear, well-organized directions for how to get from one place to another. Aided by their capacity for operational thinking, they use a "mental walk" strategy in which they imagine another person's movements along a route (Gauvain & Rogoff, 1989b). Six-year-olds give more organized directions after they walk the route themselves or are specially prompted. Otherwise, they focus on the end point without describing exactly how to get there (Plumert et al., 1994).

seriation
The ability to order items along a quantitative dimension, such as length or weight.

transitive inference
The ability to seriate—or order items along a quantitative dimension—mentally.

In tribal and village societies, conservation is often delayed. This boy, who is growing up in Belize, Central America, gathers firewood for his family. His everyday activities may not promote the kind of reasoning required to pass Piagetian conservation tasks. Compared to his agemates in Western industrialized nations, he may have fewer opportunities to see the same quantity arranged in different ways. *(Jeff Lawrence/ Stock Boston)*

horizontal décalage
Development within a Piagetian stage. Gradual mastery of logical concepts during the concrete operational stage is an example.

LIMITATIONS OF CONCRETE OPERATIONAL THOUGHT

Because of their improved ability to conserve, classify, seriate, and deal with spatial concepts, school-age children are far more capable problem solvers than they were during the preschool years. But concrete operational thinking suffers from one important limitation. Children think in an organized, logical fashion only when dealing with concrete information they can directly perceive. Their mental operations work poorly when applied to abstract ideas—ones not apparent in the real world.

Children's solutions to transitive inference problems provide a good illustration. When shown pairs of sticks of unequal length, Lizzie easily figured out that if stick A is longer than stick B and stick B is longer than stick C, then stick A is longer than stick C. But when given an entirely hypothetical version of this task, such as "Susan is taller than Sally and Sally is taller than Mary. Who is the tallest?" she had great difficulty. Not until age 11 or 12 can children solve this problem easily.

The fact that logical thought is at first tied to immediate situations helps account for a special feature of concrete operational reasoning. Perhaps you have already noticed that school-age children do not master all of Piaget's concrete operational tasks at once. Instead, they do so in a step-by-step fashion. For example, they usually grasp conservation problems in a certain order: first number; then length, mass, and liquid; and finally area and weight. Piaget used the term **horizontal décalage** (meaning development within a stage) to describe this gradual mastery of logical concepts.

The horizontal décalage is another indication of the concrete operational child's difficulty with abstractions. School-age children do not come up with the general principle of conservation and then apply it to all relevant situations. Rather, they seem to work out the logic of each problem they encounter separately.

RECENT RESEARCH ON CONCRETE OPERATIONAL THOUGHT

From researchers' attempts to verify Piaget's assumptions about concrete operations, two themes emerge. The first has to do with the impact of specific experiences on the attainment of the concrete operational stage. The second deals with how best to explain children's sequential mastery of logical problems during middle childhood. Some theorists believe that the horizontal décalage can best be understood within an information-processing framework.

■ **IMPACT OF CULTURE AND SCHOOLING.** According to Piaget, brain maturation combined with exposure to a rich and varied external world should lead children in every culture to reach the concrete operational stage. Yet recent evidence indicates that specific experiences have much to do with Piagetian task performance.

A large body of evidence shows that conservation is often delayed in non-Western societies. For example, among the Hausa of Nigeria, who live in small agricultural settlements and rarely send their children to school, even the most basic conservation tasks—number, length, and liquid—are not understood until age 11 or later (Fahrmeier, 1978). This suggests that for children to master conservation and other Piagetian concepts, they must take part in everyday activities that promote this way of thinking (Light & Perrett-Clermont, 1989). Joey and Lizzie, for example, have learned to think of fairness in terms of equal distribution—a value emphasized in their culture. They have many opportunities to divide materials, such as crayons, Halloween treats, and lemonade, equally among their friends. Because they often see the same quantity arranged in different ways, they grasp conservation early. In societies where equal sharing of goods is not common, conservation is unlikely to appear at the expected age.

The very experience of going to school seems to promote concrete operational reasoning. When children of the same age are tested, those who have been in school longer do better on transitive inference problems (Artman & Cahan, 1993). The many opportunities schooling affords for seriating objects, learning about order relations, and remembering the parts of a complex problem are probably responsible.

Yet certain nonschool, informal experiences can also foster operational thought. In one study, Brazilian 6- to 9-year-old street vendors, who seldom attend school, were given two class-inclusion problems: (1) the traditional Piagetian task, and (2) an informal version in which the researcher became a customer. After setting aside four units of mint and two units of strawberry chewing gum, the researcher asked, "For you to get more money, is it better to sell me the mint chewing gum or [all] the chewing gum? Why?" Street vendors did much better on the informal problem, which captured their interest and motivation. In contrast, Brazilian schoolchildren from economically advantaged homes were more successful on the Piagetian task than a version in which they were asked to role-play street vendors—an activity unfamiliar to them (Ceci & Roazzi, 1994).

These findings may remind you of a challenge to Piaget's theory we have mentioned several times before. Some investigators believe that the forms of logic required by Piagetian tasks do not emerge spontaneously in children but are socially generated—as outcomes of practical activities in particular cultures. This approach to cognitive development is much like Vygotsky's sociocultural theory, which we discussed in earlier chapters.

■ **AN INFORMATION-PROCESSING VIEW OF THE HORIZONTAL DÉCALAGE.** If you think carefully about the horizontal décalage, you will see that it too raises a familiar question about Piaget's theory: Is an abrupt stagewise transition to logical thought the best way to describe cognitive development in middle childhood? In Chapter 9, we showed that the beginnings of logical thinking are evident during the preschool years on simplified and familiar tasks. The horizontal décalage suggests that logical understanding continues to improve over the school years.

Some theorists argue that the development of operational thinking can best be understood in terms of gains in information-processing capacity rather than a sudden shift to a new stage (Case, 1992; Fischer & Farrar, 1987, Halford, 1993). For example, Robbie Case (1996, 1998) proposes that with practice, cognitive schemes demand less attention and become more automatic. This frees up space in *working memory* (see page 224) so children can focus on combining old schemes and generating new ones. For instance, the child confronted with water poured from one container to another recognizes that the height of the liquid changes. As this understanding becomes routine, the child notices that the width of the water changes as well. Soon the child coordinates both of these observations, and conservation of liquid is achieved. Then, as this logical idea becomes well practiced, the child transfers it to more demanding situations, such as area and weight.

Once the schemes of a Piagetian stage are sufficiently automatic, enough working memory is available to integrate them into an improved representational form. As a result, children acquire *central conceptual structures*, networks of concepts and relations that permit them to think about a wide range of situations in more advanced ways. The central conceptual structures that emerge from practice and integration of concrete operational schemes are highly efficient, abstract principles—the kind of change we will see when we discuss formal operational thought in Chapter 15.

Is there evidence to support Case's information-processing view of gains in operational thought? Case (1996) has successfully applied his ideas to a wide variety of tasks, including number, space, and scientific reasoning. In each

Some theorists explain the development of operational thinking in information-processing terms. As these children pour water from one container to another, their understanding of what happens to the height and width of the liquid becomes better coordinated, and conservation of liquid is achieved. Once this logical idea becomes automatic, enough space is available in working memory to form a more general representation of conservation that can be applied to a wider range of situations. *(Lawrence Migdale/Stock Boston)*

domain, young preschoolers first grasp schemes one by one, without relating them. Then, between 4 and 6 years of age, they merge two schemes into a unit. Around age 7 to 8, these two-scheme combinations begin to be coordinated. By 9 to 11 years, children start to form complex relationships that can be generalized to many problems.

Case and his collaborators have also shown that children not at the expected level of scheme integration for their age can usually be trained to reach it. And their improved understanding readily transfers to tasks in school (Griffin & Case, 1996). Consequently, this information-processing reformulation of Piaget's theory is proving to be practically useful. It is helping children who are behind their classmates in academic knowledge catch up and learn more effectively.

EVALUATION OF THE CONCRETE OPERATIONAL STAGE

Piaget was indeed correct that school-age youngsters approach a great many problems in systematic and rational ways that were not possible just a few years before. But whether it is best to regard this period in terms of *continuous* improvement in logical skills or *discontinuous* restructuring of children's thinking (as Piaget's stage idea assumes) is still an issue about which there is little agreement. Many researchers think that both types of change may be involved (Carey, 1985; Case, 1996, 1998; Fischer & Farrar, 1987; Sternberg & Okagaki, 1989). From early to middle childhood, children apply logical schemes to a much wider range of tasks. Yet in the process, their thought seems to undergo qualitative change—toward a more comprehensive grasp of the underlying principles of logical thought.

Piaget himself seems to have recognized this possibility in the very concept of the horizontal décalage. So perhaps some blend of Piagetian and information-processing ideas holds greatest promise for understanding cognitive development in middle childhood. With this in mind, let's take a closer look at the information-processing perspective on changes in thinking during the school years.

ASK YOURSELF . . .

■ *Mastery of conservation problems provides one illustration of Piaget's horizontal décalage. Review the preceding sections. Then list additional examples showing that operational reasoning develops gradually during middle childhood.*

■ *Nine-year-old Adrienne spends many hours helping her father build furniture in his woodworking shop. Explain how this experience may have contributed to her advanced performance on Piagetian seriation problems.*

BRIEF REVIEW

During the concrete operational stage, thought is more logical, flexible, and organized than it was during the preschool years. The ability to conserve indicates that children can decenter and reverse their thinking. School-age children also have an improved grasp of classification, seriation, and spatial concepts. However, they cannot yet think abstractly. Cross-cultural findings raise questions about Piaget's assumption that mastery of concrete operational tasks emerges spontaneously in all children. In addition, the gradual development of operational concepts challenges Piaget's notion of an abrupt stagewise transition to logical thought. A blend of Piagetian stage and information-processing views may be the best way to understand cognitive change in middle childhood.

INFORMATION PROCESSING

*I*n contrast to Piaget's focus on cognitive change, the information-processing perspective examines separate aspects of thinking. Attention and memory, which underlie every act of cognition, are central concerns in middle childhood, just as they were during infancy and the preschool years. In addition, researchers are interested in finding out how children's growing knowledge of the world and awareness of their own mental activities affect these basic components of thinking. Finally, increased understanding of how children process information is being applied to their academic learning in school—in particular, to reading and mathematics.

Researchers believe that brain development contributes to two basic changes in information processing that facilitate the diverse aspects of thinking we are about to consider:

- *An increase in information-processing capacity.* When children, adolescents, and young adults in three countries—Canada, Korea, and the United States—were given a variety of cognitive tasks and asked to react as quickly as possible, a consistent pattern emerged: fairly rapid decline in time needed to process information during middle childhood that trailed off around age 12 (Kail & Park, 1992, 1994). Similarity across many tasks in several cultures suggests a biologically based, age-related gain in speed of thinking, possibly due to myelinization and synaptic pruning in the brain (see Chapter 8, page 297) (Kail, 1993; Miller & Vernon, 1997). More efficient thinking leads to greater information-processing capacity, since a faster thinker can hold onto and operate on more information at once.

- *Gains in inhibition.* Although **inhibitory control**—the ability to resist interference from irrelevant information—improves from infancy on, great strides occur during middle childhood. EEG recordings reveal that brain waves involved in evaluating stimuli and preparing a response become more pronounced from 5 to 12 years of age (Ridderinkhof & Molen, 1997). Gains in inhibitory control, believed to be due to further maturation of the frontal lobes of the cerebral cortex, support a wide range of information-processing skills (Dempster, 1992, 1993; Shimamura, 1995).

Besides brain development, strategy use contributes to more effective information processing. As we will see, school-age children are much more strategic thinkers than are preschoolers. At the same time, neurological changes undoubtedly support gains in strategy use.

ATTENTION

During middle childhood, attention changes in three ways. It becomes more selective, adaptable, and planful.

■ **SELECTIVITY AND ADAPTABILITY.** As Joey and Lizzie moved through the elementary school years, they became better at deliberately attending to just those aspects of a situation that were relevant to their task goals, ignoring other sources of information. Researchers study this increasing selectivity of attention by introducing irrelevant stimuli into a task. Then they see how well children attend to its central elements. Findings of many studies show that this aspect of attention improves sharply between 6 and 9 years of age (Lane & Pearson, 1982).

Older children are also more adaptable, flexibly adjusting their attention to the momentary requirements of situations. For example, in judging whether pairs of stimuli are the same or different, sixth graders quickly shift their basis of judgment (from size to shape to color) when asked to do so. Second graders have trouble with this type of task (Pick & Frankel, 1974). Older children also adapt their attention to changes in their own learning. When studying for a spelling test, 10-year-old Joey devoted most attention to the words he knew least well. Lizzie was much less likely do so (Masur, McIntyre, & Flavell, 1973).

How do children acquire attentional strategies that focus on relevant information and adapt to task requirements? Children's performance on many tasks reveals that strategy development follows a predictable, four-step sequence:

1. **Production deficiency.** Preschoolers rarely engage in attentional strategies. In other words, they fail to *produce* strategies when they could be helpful.

2. **Control deficiency.** Young elementary school children sometimes produce strategies, but not consistently. They fail to *control*, or execute, strategies effectively.

3. **Utilization deficiency.** Slightly later, children apply strategies consistently, but their performance does not improve.

inhibitory control
The ability to resist interference from irrelevant information. A basic information-processing capacity that improves greatly during middle childhood.

production deficiency
The failure to produce a mental strategy when it could be helpful.

control deficiency
The inability to execute a mental strategy consistently.

utilization deficiency
The failure of performance to improve after consistently using a mental strategy.

FIGURE **12.1**

Play grocery store used to investigate children's planning. Five- to 9-year-olds were given "shopping lists," each consisting of five cards with a picture of a food item on it. Along the walls and on the shelves of the doll-sized store were pictures of food items that could be picked up by moving a figurine called the "shopper" down the aisles. Researchers recorded children's scanning of the store before starting on a shopping trip and along the way. The length of the route used to gather the items served as the measure of planning effectiveness. *(Adapted from Szepkouski, Gauvain, & Carberry, 1994.)*

4. **Effective strategy use.** By the mid-elementary school years, children use strategies consistently, and performance improves (Miller & Seier, 1994).

As we will see shortly, these phases also characterize the development of memory strategies. Why, when children first use a strategy, does it usually work poorly? A likely reason is that applying a new strategy takes so much effort and attention that children do not have enough left over to both execute the strategy and perform other parts of the task well (Miller et al., 1991; Miller, Woody-Ramsey, & Aloise, 1991).

■ **PLANNING.** School-age children's attentional strategies also become more planful. They scan detailed pictures and written materials for similarities and differences more thoroughly than do preschoolers (Vurpillot, 1968). And on complex tasks, school-age children make decisions about what to do first and what to do next in an orderly fashion. In one study, 5- to 9-year-olds were given lists of items to obtain from a play grocery store. Older children more often took time to scan the store before starting on a shopping trip. They also paused more often along the way to look for each item before moving to get it (see Figure 12.1). Consequently, they followed shorter routes through the aisles (Gauvain & Rogoff, 1989a; Szepkouski, Gauvain, & Carberry, 1994).

The development of planning illustrates how attention becomes coordinated with other cognitive processes. To solve problems involving multiple steps, children must postpone action in favor of weighing alternatives, organizing task materials (such as items on a grocery list), and remembering the steps of their plan so they can attend to each one in sequence. Along the way, they must monitor how well the plan is working and revise it if necessary. Practice in planning helps children understand its components and increases the likelihood that they will use this knowledge to guide future activities (Scholnick, 1995).

The attentional strategies we have considered are crucial for success in school, and the demands of school tasks undoubtedly contribute to their development. Unfortunately, some children have great difficulty paying attention during the school years. See the Biology and Environment box on pages 446–447 for a discussion of the serious learning and behavior problems of children with attention-deficit hyperactivity disorder.

effective strategy use
Consistent use of a mental strategy that leads to improvement in performance.

MEMORY STRATEGIES

As attention improves with age, so do *memory strategies,* the deliberate mental activities we use to store and retain information. During the school years, these techniques for holding information in working memory and transferring it to our long-term knowledge base take a giant leap forward (Schneider & Pressley, 1997).

■ **REHEARSAL AND ORGANIZATION.** When Lizzie had a list of things to learn, such as a phone number, the capitals of the United States, or the names of geometric shapes, she immediately used **rehearsal,** repeating the information to herself over and over again. This memory strategy first appears in the early grade school years. Soon after, a second strategy becomes common: **organization.** Children group together related items (for example, all capitals in the same part of the country), an approach that improves recall dramatically (Bjorklund & Muir, 1988).

Memory strategies require time and effort to perfect. At first, *control deficiencies* are evident (Bjorklund & Coyle, 1995). For example, at age 8, Lizzie rehearsed in a piecemeal fashion. After being given the word "cat" in a list of items, she said, "Cat, cat, cat." In contrast, 10-year-old Joey combined previous words with each new item, saying, "Desk, man, yard, cat, cat" (Kunzinger, 1985). Not surprisingly, Joey retained much more information. Joey also organized more skillfully, grouping items into fewer categories. And he used organization in a wide range of memory tasks, whereas Lizzie used it only when relations among items were very obvious. Experience with materials that form clear categories helps children organize more effectively and begin to apply the strategy to less related materials (Bjorklund et al., 1994).

Furthermore, both Joey and Lizzy often applied several memory strategies at once—rehearsing, organizing, and stating the category name of a group of items as they tried to learn them. With age, children use more strategies simultaneously, and the more they use, the better they remember (Coyle & Bjorklund, 1997).

Although younger school-age children's use of multiple strategies has little impact on performance (a *utilization deficiency*), their tendency to experiment is adaptive. By generating a variety of memory strategies, they discover which ones work best on different tasks. And with practice, strategies gradually become more effective. Indeed, children experiment with strategies in just this way when faced with many cognitive challenges—not just recalling information, but reading new words, acquiring basic math facts, and telling time (Siegler, 1996).

■ **ELABORATION.** Children start to use a third memory strategy, **elaboration,** by the end of middle childhood. It involves creating a relationship, or shared meaning, between two or more pieces of information that are not members of the same category. For example, suppose "fish" and "pipe" are among a list of words you need to learn. If, in trying to remember them, you generate a mental image of a fish smoking a pipe or recite a sentence expressing this relationship ("The fish puffed the pipe"), you are using elaboration. Once children discover this memory technique, they find it so effective that it tends to replace other strategies. The very reason elaboration is so successful helps explain why it is late to develop. To use elaboration, we must translate items into images and think of a relationship between them. Children's working memories must expand before they can carry out these activities at the same time. Elaboration becomes increasingly common during adolescence and young adulthood (Schneider & Pressley, 1997).

Because the strategies of organization and elaboration combine items into *meaningful chunks,* they permit children to hold on to much more information. As a result, the strategies contribute further to expansion of working memory. In addition, when children store a new item in long-term memory by linking it to information they already know, they can *retrieve* it easily by thinking of other items associated with it. As we will

rehearsal
The memory strategy of repeating information.

organization
The memory strategy of grouping together related items.

elaboration
The memory strategy of creating a relation between two or more items that are not members of the same category.

BIOLOGY & ENVIRONMENT

CHILDREN WITH ATTENTION-DEFICIT HYPERACTIVITY DISORDER

While the other fifth graders worked quietly at their desks, Calvin squirmed in his seat, dropped his pencil, looked out the window, fiddled with his shoelaces, and talked out. "Hey Joey," he yelled over the top of several desks, "wanna play ball after school?"

Joey and the other children weren't eager to play with Calvin. Out on the playground, Calvin was a poor listener and failed to follow the rules of the game. When up at bat, he had difficulty taking turns. In the outfield, he tossed his mitt up in the air and looked elsewhere when the ball came his way. Calvin's desk at school and his room at home were a chaotic mess. He often lost pencils, books, and other materials necessary for completing assignments. And very often, he had difficulty remembering his assignments and when they were due.

■ **SYMPTOMS OF ADHD.** Calvin is one of 3 to 5 percent of school-age children with **attention-deficit hyperactivity disorder (ADHD)** (American Psychiatric Association, 1994). Boys are diagnosed five to ten times more often than girls. However, many girls with ADHD may be overlooked because their symptoms usually are not as flagrant (Gaub & Carlson, 1997).

Children with ADHD have great difficulty staying on task for more than a few minutes. In addition, they often act impulsively, ignoring social rules and lashing out with hostility when frustrated. Many (but not all) are *hyperactive*. They charge through their days with excessive motor activity, leaving parents and teachers frazzled and other children annoyed. ADHD youngsters have few friends; they are soundly rejected by their classmates. According to one view that has amassed substantial research support, these diverse symptoms are unified by a common theme: an impairment in inhibitory control, which makes it hard to delay action in favor of thought (Barkley, 1997; Schachar et al., 1995).

The intelligence of ADHD children is normal, and they show no signs of serious emotional disturbance. Instead, because they have trouble thinking before they act, they do poorly on laboratory tasks requiring sustained attention and find it hard to ignore irrelevant information. Their distractibility results in forgetfulness and difficulties with planning, reasoning, and problem solving in academic and social situations (Barkley, 1997; Denckla, 1996). Although some children catch up in development, most continue to have problems concentrating and finding friends in adolescence and adulthood (Claude & Firestone, 1995).

■ **ORIGINS OF ADHD.** Heredity plays a major role in ADHD, since the disorder runs in families, and identical twins share it more often than do fraternal twins. Also, an adopted child who is inattentive and hyperactive is likely to have a biological parent (but not an adoptive parent) with similar symptoms (Faraone et al., 1995; Zametkin, 1995). Recent psychophysiological research, including EEG and fMRI studies, reveals differences between children with and without ADHD, particularly in the frontal lobes of the cerebral cortex and in other areas responsible for attention and inhibi-

see in the next section, this is one reason that memory improves steadily during the school years.

THE KNOWLEDGE BASE AND MEMORY PERFORMANCE

During middle childhood, the long-term knowledge base grows larger and becomes better organized. Children arrange the vast amount of information in their memories into increasingly elaborate, hierarchically structured networks. Many researchers believe that this rapid growth of knowledge helps children use strategies and remember. In other words, knowing more about a particular topic makes new information more meaningful and familiar so it is easier to store and retrieve (Schneider, 1993).

To test this idea, Michelene Chi (1978) looked at how well third- through eighth-grade chess experts could remember complex chessboard arrangements. The children recalled the configurations considerably better than did adults who knew how to play chess but were not especially knowledgeable (see Figure 12.2). Yet the adults did better than the children at recalling lists of numbers on a standard memory test. The children showed superior memory performance only in the domain of knowledge in which they were expert.

attention-deficit hyperactivity disorder (ADHD)
A childhood disorder involving inattentiveness, impulsivity, and excessive motor activity. Often leads to academic failure and social problems.

tion of behavior (Novak, Solanto, & Abikoff, 1995; Riccio et al., 1993).

At the same time, ADHD is associated with a variety of environmental factors. These children are somewhat more likely to come from homes in which marriages are unhappy and family stress is high (Bernier & Siegel, 1994). But researchers agree that a stressful home life rarely causes ADHD. Instead, the behaviors of these children can contribute to family problems, which (in turn) are likely to intensify the child's pre-existing difficulties. Furthermore, recall from earlier chapters that prenatal teratogens (including certain illegal drugs, alcohol, and cigarettes) are linked to inattention and hyperactivity. Dietary causes, such as food additives and sugar, have also been suggested, but there is little evidence that they play important roles (Hynd et al., 1991).

■ TREATING ADHD. Calvin's doctor eventually prescribed stimulant medication, the most common treatment for ADHD. As long as dosage is carefully regulated, these drugs reduce activity level and improve attention,

academic performance, and peer relations for 70 percent of children who take them (Barkley, DuPaul, & Costello, 1993; Rapport & Kelly, 1993). Researchers do not know precisely why stimulants are helpful. Some speculate that they change the chemical balance in brain regions that inhibit impulsiveness and hyperactivity, thereby decreasing the child's need to engage in off-task and self-stimulating behavior.

Although stimulant medication is relatively safe, its impact is only short term. Drugs cannot teach children ways of compensating for inattention and impulsivity. Combining medication with interventions that model and reinforce appropriate academic and social behavior seems to be the most effective approach to treatment (Barkley, 1995; Pelham & Hoza, 1996). Teachers can also create conditions in classrooms that support these pupils' special learning needs. Short work periods followed by a chance to get up and move around help them concentrate.

Finally, family intervention is particularly important. Inattentive, overactive children strain the patience of

While his classmates try to work, this boy constantly looks up from his assignment and fires paper airplanes across the room. Children with ADHD have great difficulty staying on task and often act impulsively, ignoring social rules. *(David Young-Wolff/PhotoEdit)*

parents, who are likely to react punitively and inconsistently in return—a child-rearing style that strengthens inappropriate behavior. Breaking this cycle is as important for ADHD children as it is for the defiant, aggressive youngsters we discussed in Chapter 10. In fact, at least 35 percent of the time, these two sets of behavior problems occur together (Nottelmann & Jensen, 1995).

Although knowledge clearly plays an important role in memory development, it may have to be quite broad and well structured before it can facilitate the use of strategies and recall. A brief series of lessons designed to increase knowledge in a particular area does not affect children's ability to remember new information in that domain (DeMarie-Dreblow, 1991).

Finally, knowledge is not the only important factor in children's strategic memory processing. Children who are expert in a particular area, whether it be chess, math, social studies, or spelling, are usually highly motivated. As a result, they not only acquire knowledge more

FIGURE 12.2

Performance of skilled child chess players and adults on two tasks: memory for complex chessboard arrangements and numerical digits. The child chess experts recalled more on the chess task, the adults on the digit task. These findings show that size of the knowledge base contributes to memory performance. *(Adapted from Chi, 1978)*

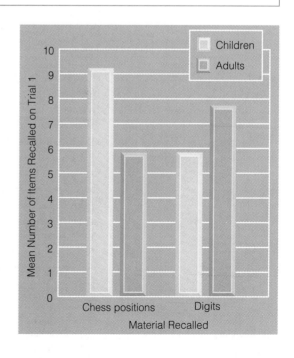

As these Guatemalan Mayan boys discuss the intricacies of effective kite-flying, they demonstrate a keen memory for information embedded in meaningful contexts. Yet when given a list-memory task of the kind American children often perform in school, they do poorly. *(Ulrike Welsch/Photo Researchers)*

quickly, but they *actively use what they know* to add more. In contrast, academically unsuccessful children fail to ask how previously stored information can clarify new material. This, in turn, interferes with the development of a broad knowledge base (Schneider & Bjorklund, 1998). So at least by the end of the school years, knowledge acquisition and use of memory strategies are intimately related and support one another.

CULTURE AND MEMORY STRATEGIES

Think, for a moment, about the kinds of situations in which the strategies of rehearsal, organization, and elaboration are useful. People usually employ these techniques when they need to remember information for its own sake. On many other occasions, they participate in daily activities that produce excellent memory as a natural by-product of the activity itself (Rogoff & Chavajay, 1995). For example, Joey can spout off a wealth of facts about baseball teams and players—information he picked up from watching the game, discussing it, and trading baseball cards with his friends. And without prior rehearsal, he can recount the story line of an exciting movie or novel—narrative material that is already meaningfully organized. (To review how children recall this kind of information, return to the discussion of scripts in Chapter 9, page 342.)

A repeated finding of cross-cultural research is that people in non-Western cultures who have no formal schooling do not use or benefit from instruction in memory strategies. Tasks that require children to recall isolated bits of information are common in classrooms, and they provide children with a great deal of motivation to use memory strategies. In fact, Western children get so much practice with this type of learning that they do not refine other techniques for remembering that rely on spatial location and arrangement of objects, cues that are readily available in everyday life. Australian Aboriginal and Guatemalan Mayan children are considerably better at these memory skills (Kearins, 1981; Rogoff, 1986).

Looked at in this way, the development of memory strategies is not just a matter of a more competent information-processing system. It is also a product of task demands and cultural circumstances.

THE SCHOOL-AGE CHILD'S THEORY OF MIND

During middle childhood, children's *theory of mind*, or set of beliefs about mental activities, becomes much more elaborate and refined. You may recall from Chapter 9 that this awareness of cognitive processes is called *metacognition*. School-age children's improved ability to reflect on their own mental life is another reason for their advances in thinking and problem solving. They become increasingly conscious of cognitive capacities and effective strategies.

■ **KNOWLEDGE OF COGNITIVE CAPACITIES.** Unlike preschoolers, who view the mind as a passive container of information, older children regard it as an active, constructive agent capable of selecting and transforming information (Chandler & Lalonde, 1996). Consequently, they have a much better understanding of the process of thinking and the impact of psychological factors on performance.

Six- and 7-year-olds, for example, realize that mental inferences can be a source of knowledge and that doing well on a task depends on focusing attention—concentrating on it, wanting to do it, and not being tempted by anything else (Carpendale & Chandler, 1996; Miller & Bigi, 1979). And by age 10, children distinguish mental activities on the basis of the certainty of their knowledge. They realize that if you "remember," "know," or "understand," then you are more certain than if you "guessed," "estimated," or "compared" (Schwanenflugel, Fabricius, & Noyes, 1996).

What promotes this more reflective, process-oriented view of the mind? Perhaps children become aware of mental activities through quiet-time observation of their own thinking and through exposure to talk about the mind in active terms, as when they hear people say, "I was thinking a lot" or "My mind wandered" (Wellman & Hickling, 1994). Schooling may contribute as well. Instructing children to keep their minds on what they are doing and to remember mental steps calls attention to the workings of the mind. And as children engage in reading, writing, and math, they often use private speech, at first speaking aloud and later silently to themselves. As they "hear themselves think," they probably detect many aspects of mental life (Astington, 1995; Flavell, Green, & Flavell, 1995).

■ **KNOWLEDGE OF STRATEGIES.** Consistent with their more active view of the mind, school-age children are far more conscious of mental strategies than are preschoolers. By third grade, they realize that in studying material for later recall, it is helpful to devote most effort to items that you know least well. And they know quite a bit about effective memory strategies. Witness this 8-year-old's response to the question of what she would do to remember a phone number:

> Say the number is 663-8854. Then what I'd do is—say that my number is 663, so I won't have to remember that, really. And then I would think now I've got to remember 88. Now I'm 8 years old, so I can remember, say, my age two times. Then I say how old my brother is, and how old he was last year. And that's how I'd usually remember that phone number. [Is that how you would most often remember a phone number?] Well, usually I write it down. (Kreutzer, Leonard, & Flavell, 1975, p. 11)

This child clearly understands the importance of establishing connections between new information and existing knowledge. And she also recognizes that she can use external aids to enhance memory—in this case, writing down the phone number.

Once children become conscious of the many factors that influence mental activity, they combine them into an integrated understanding. By the end of middle childhood, children take account of *interactions* among variables—how age and motivation of the learner, effective use of strategies, and nature and difficulty of the task work together to affect cognitive performance (Wellman, 1990). In this way, metacognition truly becomes a comprehensive theory.

COGNITIVE SELF-REGULATION

Although metacognition expands, school-age children often have difficulty putting what they know about thinking into action. They are not yet good at **cognitive self-regulation,** the process of continuously monitoring progress toward a goal, checking outcomes, and redirecting unsuccessful efforts. For example, Lizzie is aware that she should group items together in a memory task and that she should read a complicated paragraph more than once to make sure she understands it. But she does not always do these things when working on an assignment.

It is not surprising that the capacity for self-regulation develops slowly. Monitoring learning outcomes is a cognitively demanding activity, requiring constant evaluation of effort and progress. Self-regulation does not become well developed until adolescence. By then it is a strong predictor of academic success. Students who do well in school know when they possess a skill and when they do not. If they run up against obstacles, such as poor study conditions, a confusing text passage, or a class presentation that is unclear, they take steps to organize the learning environment, review the material, or seek other sources of support. This active, purposeful approach contrasts sharply with the passive orientation of students who do poorly (Zimmerman & Risemberg, 1997).

Parents and teachers can foster self-regulation by pointing out the special demands of tasks, indicating how strategies will improve performance, and emphasizing the value of self-correction. As adults ask children questions and help them monitor their own behavior in circumstances where they are likely to encounter difficulties, children internalize these procedures (Pressley, 1995).

School-age children have an improved ability to reflect on their own mental life. This child is aware that external aids to memory are often necessary to ensure that information will be retained. *(Will Faller)*

cognitive self-regulation
The process of continuously monitoring progress toward a goal, checking outcomes, and redirecting unsuccessful efforts.

Do these practical suggestions remind you of Vygotsky's theory of the social origins of higher cognitive processes? Many studies show that providing children with instructions to check and monitor their progress has a substantial impact on their learning. In addition, going beyond demonstrating a strategy to emphasizing why it is effective enhances children's use of it in new situations (Pressley & El-Dinary, 1993; Schunk & Zimmerman, 1994). When adults provide a rationale for future action, then children learn not just how to get a task done, but what to do when faced with new problems.

Children who acquire effective self-regulatory skills succeed at challenging tasks. As a result, they develop confidence in their own ability—a belief that supports the use of self-regulation in the future (Zimmerman, Bonner, & Kovach, 1996). Unfortunately, some children receive messages from parents and teachers that seriously undermine their academic self-esteem and self-regulatory skills. We will consider the special problems of these *learned helpless* youngsters, along with ways to help them, in Chapter 13.

APPLICATIONS OF INFORMATION PROCESSING TO ACADEMIC LEARNING

Joey entered first grade able to recognize only a handful of written words. By fifth grade, he was a proficient reader. His eyes moved quickly across the page, and his hand flew up when the teacher asked questions that probed how well the children understood an assignment. Similarly, at age 6, Joey had an informally acquired knowledge of number concepts. By age 10, he could add, subtract, multiply, and divide with ease, and he had begun to master fractions and percentages.

Over the past decade, fundamental discoveries about the development of information processing have been applied to children's learning of reading and mathematics. Researchers have begun to identify the cognitive ingredients of skilled performance, trace their development, and distinguish good from poor learners by pinpointing the cognitive skills in which they are deficient. They hope, as a result, to design teaching methods that will help children master these essential skills.

In this first-grade whole-language classroom, children acquire a sight vocabulary and learn to read through exposure to whole, meaningful text. Research indicates that kindergartners just starting to read benefit from an emphasis on whole language. In the early grades, combining the whole-language and basic-skills approaches seems most effective. *(Will Hart)*

■ **READING.** While reading, we use a large number of skills at once, taxing all aspects of our information-processing systems. We must perceive single letters and letter combinations, translate them into speech sounds, hold chunks of text in working memory while interpreting their meaning, and combine the meanings of various parts of a text passage into an understandable whole. In fact, reading is so demanding that most or all of these skills must be done automatically. If one or more are poorly developed, they will compete for space in our limited working memories, and reading performance will decline (Perfetti, 1988).

Researchers do not yet know how children manage to acquire and combine all these varied skills into fluent reading. Currently, psychologists and educators are engaged in a "great debate" about how to teach beginning reading. On one side are those who take a **whole-language approach** to reading instruction. They argue that reading should be taught in a way that parallels natural language learning. From the very beginning, children should be exposed to text in its complete form—stories, poems, letters, posters, and lists—so they can appreciate the communicative function of written language. According to these experts, as long as reading is kept whole and meaningful, children will be motivated to discover the specific skills they need as they gain experience with the printed word (Goodman, 1986; Watson, 1989). On the other side of the debate are those who advocate a **basic-skills approach.** According to this view, children should be given simplified text materials. At first, they should be coached on *phonics*—the basic rules for translating written symbols into sounds. Only later, after they have mastered these skills, should they get complex reading material (Rayner & Pollatsek, 1989; Samuels, 1985).

TABLE 12.1

Sequence of Reading Development

GRADE/AGE	DEVELOPMENT	METHOD OF LEARNING
Preschool and Kindergarten 2–6 years	"Pretends" to read; recognizes some familiar signs ("on," "off," "pizza"); "pretends" to write; prints own name and other words	Informal literacy experiences through literacy-rich physical environments, literacy-related play, and storybook reading (see Chapter 9, page 347)
Grades 1 and 2 6–7 years	Masters letter–sound correspondences; sounds out one-syllable words; reads simple stories; reads about 600 words	Direct teaching, through exposure to many types of texts and the basic rules of decoding written symbols into sounds
Grades 2 and 3 7–8 years	Reads simple stories more fluently; masters basic decoding rules; reads about 3,000 words	Same as above
Grades 4 to 9 9–14 years	Reads to learn new knowledge, usually from one perspective	Reading and studying; participating in classroom discussion; completing written assignments
Grades 10 to 12 15–17 years	Reads more widely, tapping materials with diverse viewpoints	Reading more widely; writing papers
College 18 years and older	Decoding and comprehension skills reach a high level of efficiency; reads with a self-defined purpose	Reading even more widely; writing more sophisticated papers

Source: Chall, 1983.

As yet, research does not show clear-cut superiority for either of these approaches (Stahl, McKenna, & Pagnucco, 1994). In fact, a third group of experts believes that children may learn best when they receive a mixture of both (Pressley, 1994; Stahl, 1992). Kindergartners just starting to read benefit from an emphasis on whole language, with gradual introduction of phonics as reading skills improve (Sacks & Mergendoller, 1997). In the early grades, balancing the two methods seems most effective. In one study, 7-year-old poor readers showed greater reading gains when assigned to a "phonics/meaningful reading" intervention than to either a "phonics alone" or a "reading alone" teaching condition (Hatcher, Hulme, & Ellis, 1994).

Why might combining phonics with whole language work best? Learning the basics—relations between letters and sounds—enables children to *decode,* or decipher, words they have never seen before. As this process becomes more automatic, it releases children's attention to the higher-level activities involved in comprehending the text's meaning (Adams, Treiman, & Pressley, 1998). Yet if practice in basic skills is overemphasized, children may lose sight of the goal of reading—understanding. Many teachers report cases of pupils who can read aloud fluently but who register little or no meaning. These children might have been spared serious reading problems if they had been exposed to rich early childhood literacy experiences (see Chapter 9) followed by meaning-based instruction with attention to basic skills.

Table 12.1 charts the general sequence of reading development. Notice how a major shift occurs around age 7 to 8, from "learning to read" to "reading to learn" (Ely, 1997). As decoding and comprehension skills reach a high level of efficiency, older readers can become actively engaged with the text. They adjust the way they read to fit their current purpose—at times seeking new facts and ideas, at other times questioning, agreeing, or disagreeing with the writer's viewpoint.

■ **MATHEMATICS.** In elementary school, children apply their rich informal knowledge of number concepts and counting to more complex mathematical skills (Resnick, 1989). For example, children first understand multiplication as a kind of repeated addition. When given the following problem, "Sue has 5 books. Joe has 3 times as many. How many books does Joe have?" Lizzie thought to herself, "What's 5 x 3?" When she had difficulty remembering the answer, she said, "Okay, it's got to be 5 books + 5 books + 5 books.

whole-language approach
An approach to beginning reading instruction that parallels children's natural language learning and keeps reading materials whole and meaningful.

basic-skills approach
An approach to beginning reading instruction that emphasizes training in phonics—the basic rules for translating written symbols into sounds—and simplified reading materials.

I know, it's 15!" Lizzie's use of addition strengthened her understanding of multiplication. It also helped her recall a multiplication fact that she had been trying to memorize.

Mathematics as taught in many classrooms, however, does not make good use of children's basic grasp of number concepts. Children are given procedures for solving problems without linking these to their informally acquired understandings. Consequently, they often apply a rule that is close to what they have been taught but that yields a wrong answer. Their mistakes indicate that they have tried to memorize a method, but they do not comprehend the basis for it. For example, look at the following subtraction errors made by two of Lizzie's classmates:

$$
\begin{array}{r}
4\,2\,7 \\
-\,1\,3\,8 \\
\hline
3\,1\,1
\end{array}
\qquad
\begin{array}{r}
{}^{6}7\,0\,0\,{}^{1}2 \\
5\,4\,4\,5 \\
\hline
1\,4\,4\,7
\end{array}
$$

In the first problem, the child consistently subtracts a smaller from a larger digit, regardless of which is on top. In the second, columns with zeros are skipped in a borrowing operation, and whenever there is a zero on top, the bottom digit is written as the answer. Researchers believe that drill-oriented math instruction that provides children with little information on the reasons behind procedures is at the heart of these difficulties (Fuson, 1990; Resnick, 1989).

Arguments about how to teach early mathematics closely resemble the positions we considered earlier in the area of reading. Drill in computational skills is pitted against "number sense," or understanding. Yet once again, a blend is probably best.

Research reveals that poor math students spend little time experimenting with strategies for acquiring basic math facts. Instead, they rush headlong toward the answer, trying to retrieve it from memory. By trying out strategies (as Lizzie did when she used repeated addition to solve 5 x 3), good students grapple with underlying concepts, develop effective math solution techniques, and build solid associations between problems and answers (Siegler, 1996). This suggests that teaching children how to apply strategies successfully and encouraging them to take time to do so is vital for solid mastery of basic math.

In Asian countries, pupils receive a variety of supports for acquiring mathematical knowledge that are not broadly available in the United States. For example, use of the metric system, which presents ones, tens, hundreds, and thousands values in all areas of measurement, helps Asian children think in ways that foster a grasp of place value. The consistent structure of number words in Asian languages ("ten two" for 12, "ten three" for 13) also makes this idea clear (Miller et al., 1995). Furthermore, Asian number words are shorter and more quickly pronounced. This eases verbal counting strategies, since more digits can be held in working memory. It also increases the speed with which children can retrieve math facts from long-term memory (Geary et al., 1996; Jensen & Whang, 1994). Finally, as we will see later in this chapter, in Asian classrooms, much more time is spent exploring underlying math concepts and much less on drill and repetition.

Culture and language-based factors contribute to Asian children's skill at mathematics. The abacus supports these Japanese pupils' understanding of place value. Ones, tens, hundreds, and thousands are each represented by a different column of beads, and calculations are performed by moving the beads to different positions. As children become skilled at using the abacus, they learn to think in ways that facilitate solving complex arithmetic problems. *(Fuji Fotos/The Image Works)*

BRIEF REVIEW

Over the school years, brain development contributes to gains in information-processing capacity and inhibitory control—factors that facilitate many aspects of thinking. Attention becomes more selective, adaptable, and planful, and memory strategies become more effective. An expanding knowledge base contributes to improved memory performance. However, children's willingness to use what they know when learning new information is also important. Metacognition moves from a passive to an active view of mental functioning during middle childhood. Self-regulation develops slowly; school-age children do not always apply their metacognitive understanding, but they can be taught to improve their self-regulatory skills. Information processing has been applied to children's academic learning in school. Instruction that provides balanced attention to basic skills and understanding seems to be most effective in reading and mathematics.

INDIVIDUAL DIFFERENCES IN MENTAL DEVELOPMENT

During middle childhood, intelligence tests become increasingly important for assessing individual differences in mental development. Around age 6, IQ becomes more stable than it was at earlier ages, and it correlates well with academic achievement, from .40 to .70 (Brody, 1992). Because IQ predicts school performance, it plays an important role in educational decisions. Do intelligence tests provide an accurate indication of the school-age child's ability to profit from academic instruction? Let's take a close look at this controversial issue.

DEFINING AND MEASURING INTELLIGENCE

Take a moment to jot down a list of behaviors that you regard as typical of a highly intelligent school-age child. Did you come up with just one or two or a great many? Virtually all intelligence tests provide an overall score (the IQ), which is taken to represent *general intelligence* or reasoning ability. Yet a diverse array of tasks appear on most tests for children. Today, there is widespread agreement that intelligence is a collection of many mental capacities, not all of which are included on currently available tests.

Test designers use a complicated statistical technique called *factor analysis* to identify the various abilities measured by intelligence tests. This procedure determines which sets of items on the test correlate strongly with one another. Those that do are assumed to measure a similar ability and therefore are designated as a separate factor. To understand the types of intellectual factors measured in middle childhood, let's look at some representative intelligence tests and how they are administered.

■ **REPRESENTATIVE INTELLIGENCE TESTS.**   The intelligence tests that Joey and Lizzie take every so often in school are *group-administered tests*. They permit large numbers of pupils to be tested at once and require very little training of teachers who give them. Group tests are useful for instructional planning and identifying children who require more extensive evaluation with *individually administered tests*. Unlike group tests, individually administered ones demand considerable training and experience to give well. The examiner not only considers the child's answers but carefully observes the child's behavior, noting such things as attentiveness to and interest in the tasks and wariness of the adult. These reactions provide insight into whether the test score is accurate or underestimates the child's abilities.

ASK YOURSELF . . .

■ One day, the children in Lizzie and Joey's school saw a slide show about endangered species. They were told to remember as many animal names as they could. Fifth and sixth graders recalled considerably more than did second and third graders. What factors might account for this difference?

■ Lizzie knows that if you have difficulty learning part of a task, you should devote most of your attention to that aspect. But she plays each of her piano pieces from beginning to end instead of picking out the hard parts for extra practice. What explains Lizzie's failure to apply what she knows?

Two individual tests—the Stanford-Binet and the Wechsler—are most often used to identify highly intelligent children and diagnose those with learning problems. As we look at each, refer to Figure 12.3, which shows some of the items that typically appear on intelligence tests for children.

The Stanford-Binet Intelligence Scale. The modern descendent of Alfred Binet's first successful intelligence test is the **Stanford-Binet Intelligence Scale,** for individuals between 2 years of age and adulthood. Its latest version measures both general intelligence and four intellectual factors: verbal reasoning, quantitative reasoning, abstract/visual reasoning, and short-term memory (Thorndike, Hagen, & Sattler, 1986). Within these factors are 15 subtests that permit a detailed analysis of each child's mental abilities. The verbal and quantitative factors emphasize culturally loaded, fact-oriented information, such as vocabulary and sentence comprehension. In contrast, the abstract/visual reasoning factor is believed to be less culturally biased because it demands little in the way of specific information. Instead, it tests children's ability to see complex relationships, as illustrated by the spatial visualization item shown in Figure 12.3.

Like many current tests, the Stanford-Binet is designed to be sensitive to minority children and children with disabilities and to reduce gender bias. Pictures of children from different ethnic groups, a child in a wheelchair, and "unisex" figures that can be interpreted as male or female are included.

The Wechsler Intelligence Scale for Children–III. The **Wechsler Intelligence Scale for Children–III (WISC–III)** is the third edition of a widely used test for 6- through 16-year-olds. A downward extension of it—the *Wechsler Preschool and Primary Scale of Intelligence-Revised (WPPSI–R)*—is appropriate for children 3 through 8 (Wechsler, 1989, 1991). The Wechsler tests offered both a measure of general intelligence and a variety of factor scores long before the Stanford-Binet. As a result, over the past two decades, many psychologists and educators have come to prefer the WISC and WPPSI.

Both the WISC–III and the WPPSI–R measure two broad intellectual factors: verbal and performance. Each contains six subtests, yielding 12 separate scores in all. Performance items (see examples in Figure 12.3) require the child to arrange materials rather than talk to the examiner. Consequently, these tests provided one of the first means through which non-English-speaking children and children with speech and language disorders could demonstrate their intellectual strengths.

The Wechsler tests were also the first to be standardized on samples representing the total population of the United States, including ethnic minorities. Their broadly representative standardization samples have served as models for many other tests, including the recent version of the Stanford-Binet.

■ **RECENT DEVELOPMENTS IN DEFINING INTELLIGENCE.** Researchers have begun to combine the factor analytic approach to defining intelligence with information processing. They believe that factors on intelligence tests are of limited usefulness unless we can identify the cognitive processes responsible for them. Once we understand the underlying basis of IQ, we will know much more about why a particular child does well or poorly and what skills must be worked on to improve performance. These researchers conduct *componential analyses* of children's mental test scores. This means that they look for relationships between aspects (or components) of information processing and children's IQs.

Many studies reveal that speed of processing, measured in terms of reaction time on diverse cognitive tasks, is moderately related to IQ scores as well as gains in mental test performance over time (Deary, 1995; Kranzler & Jensen, 1989; Vernon, 1993). These findings suggest that individuals whose nervous systems function more efficiently, permitting them to take in and manipulate information quickly, have an edge in intellectual skills. In support of this interpretation, fast, strong EEG waves in response to stimulation also predict speed of processing and mental test scores (Vernon, 1993).

Wechsler Intelligence Scale for Children–III (WISC–III)
An individually administered intelligence test that includes both a measure of general intelligence and a variety of verbal and performance scores.

Stanford-Binet Intelligence Scale
An individually administered intelligence test that is the modern descendent of Alfred Binet's first successful test for children. Measures general intelligence and four factors: verbal reasoning, quantitative reasoning, abstract/visual reasoning, and short-term memory.

Item Type	Typical Verbal Items
Vocabulary	Tell me what "carpet" means.
General Information	How many ounces make a pound? What day of the week comes right after Thursday?
Verbal Comprehension	Why are police officers needed?
Verbal Analogies	A rock is hard; a pillow is _____ .
Logical Reasoning	Five girls are sitting side by side on a bench. Jane is in the middle and Betty sits next to her on the right. Alice is beside Betty, and Dale is beside Ellen, who sits next to Jane. Who are sitting on the ends?
Number Series	Which number comes next in the series? **4 8 6 12 10 ___**

Typical Nonverbal Items

Picture Oddities	Which picture does not belong with the others? 

Spatial Visualization	Which of the boxes on the right can be made from the pattern shown on the left? 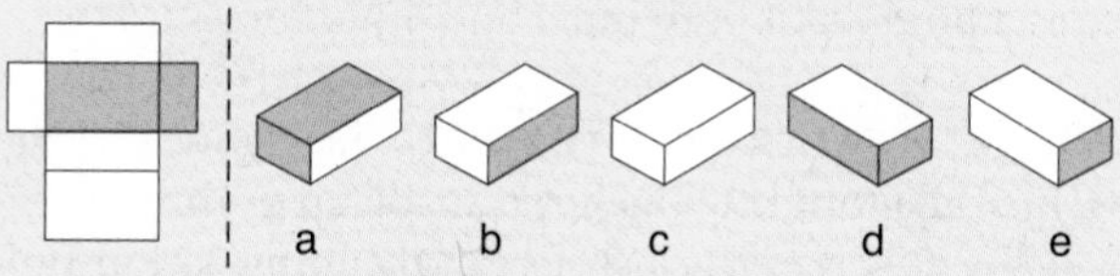

a   b   c   d   e

Typical Performance Items

Picture Series	Put the pictures in the right order so that what is happening makes sense. 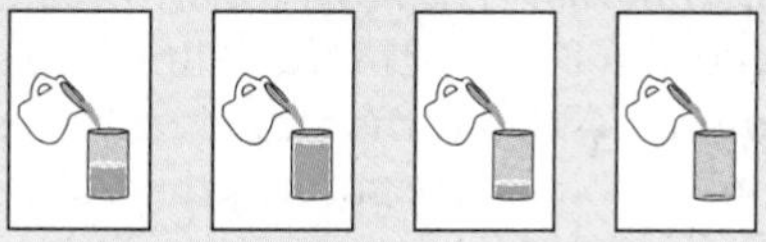

Puzzles	Put these pieces together so they make a wagon. 

FIGURE 12.3

Sample items similar to those that appear on common intelligence tests for children. In contrast to verbal items, nonverbal items do not require reading or direct use of language. Performance items are also nonverbal, but they require the child to draw or construct something rather than merely give a correct answer. As a result, they appear only on individually administered intelligence tests. *(Logical reasoning, picture oddities, and spatial visualization examples are adapted with permission of The Free Press, a Division of Macmillan, Inc., from A. R. Jensen, 1980,* Bias in Mental Testing, *New York: The Free Press, pp. 150, 154, 157)*

But rapid responding is not the only processing correlate of mental test performance. Strategy use also makes a difference, and it explains some of the association between speed of thinking and IQ (Miller & Vernon, 1992). Children who apply strategies effectively acquire more knowledge. As a result, they develop fast, accurate thinking, which seems to carry over to performance on intelligence test items.

FIGURE 12.4

Sternberg's triarchic theory of intelligence.

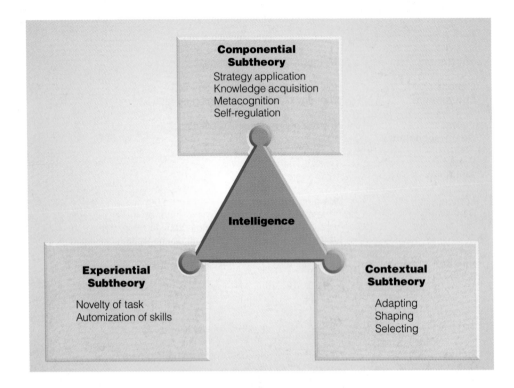

FIGURE 12.4

Sternberg's triarchic theory of intelligence.

The componential approach has one major shortcoming: It regards intelligence as entirely due to causes within the child. Yet throughout this book, we have seen how cultural and situational factors profoundly affect children's cognitive skills. Recently, Robert Sternberg expanded the componential approach into a comprehensive theory that regards intelligence as a product of both inner and outer forces.

■ **STERNBERG'S TRIARCHIC THEORY.** As Figure 12.4 shows, Sternberg's (1985, 1997) **triarchic theory of intelligence** is made up of three interacting subtheories. The first, the *componential subtheory,* spells out the information-processing skills that underlie intelligent behavior. You are already familiar with its main elements—strategy application, knowledge acquisition, metacognition, and self-regulation.

According to Sternberg, children's use of these components is not just a matter of internal capacity. It is also a function of the conditions under which intelligence is assessed. The *experiential subtheory* states that highly intelligent individuals, compared to less intelligent ones, process information more skillfully in novel situations. When given a relatively new task, the bright person learns rapidly, making strategies automatic so working memory is freed for more complex aspects of the situation.

Think, for a moment, about the implications of this idea for measuring children's intelligence. To accurately compare children in *brightness*—in ability to deal with novelty and learn efficiently—all children would need to be presented with equally unfamiliar test items. Otherwise, some children will appear more intelligent than others simply because of their past experiences, not because they are really more cognitively skilled. These children start with the unfair advantage of prior practice on the tasks.

This point brings us to the third part of Sternberg's model, the *contextual subtheory.* It proposes that intelligent people skillfully *adapt* their information-processing skills to fit their personal desires and the demands of their everyday worlds. When they cannot adapt to a situation, they try to *shape,* or change, it to meet their needs. If they cannot shape it, they *select* new contexts that are consistent with their goals. The contextual subtheory emphasizes that intelligent behavior is never culture free. Because of their backgrounds, some children come to value behaviors required for success on intelligence tests, and they easily adapt to the tasks and testing conditions. Others with different life histories misin-

triarchic theory of intelligence Sternberg's theory, which states that information-processing skills, ability to learn efficiently in novel situations, and contextual (or cultural) factors interact to determine intelligent behavior.

TABLE 12.2

Gardner's Multiple Intelligences

INTELLIGENCE	PROCESSING OPERATIONS	END-STATE PERFORMANCE POSSIBILITIES
Linguistic	Sensitivity to the sounds, rhythms, and meanings of words and the different functions of language	Poet, journalist
Logico-mathematical	Sensitivity to, and capacity to detect, logical or numerical patterns; ability to handle long chains of logical reasoning	Mathematician
Musical	Ability to produce and appreciate pitch, rhythm (or melody), and aesthetic-sounding tones; understanding of the forms of musical expressiveness	Violinist, composer
Spatial	Ability to perceive the visual-spatial world accurately, to perform transformations on those perceptions, and to re-create aspects of visual experience in the absence of relevant stimuli	Sculptor, navigator
Bodily-kinesthetic	Ability to use the body skillfully for expressive as well as goal-directed purposes; ability to handle objects skillfully	Dancer, athlete
Naturalist	Ability to recognize and classify all varieties of animals, minerals, and plants	Biologist
Interpersonal	Ability to detect and respond appropriately to the moods, temperaments, motivations, and intentions of others	Therapist, salesperson
Intrapersonal	Ability to discriminate complex inner feelings and to use them to guide one's own behavior; knowledge of one's own strengths, weaknesses, desires, and intelligences	Person with detailed, accurate self-knowledge

Sources: Gardner, 1983, 1993.

terpret the testing context or reject it entirely because it does not suit their needs. Yet such children may display very sophisticated abilities in daily life—for example, telling stories, engaging in complex artistic activities, or interacting skillfully with other people (Sternberg, 1996b).

Sternberg's theory emphasizes the complexity of intelligent behavior and the wide variety of human mental skills. As you can already see, his ideas are relevant to the controversy surrounding cultural bias in IQ testing, which we will address shortly.

■ **GARDNER'S THEORY OF MULTIPLE INTELLIGENCES.** Howard Gardner's (1983, 1993) **theory of multiple intelligences** provides yet another view of how information-processing skills underlie intelligent behavior. But unlike the componential approach, it does not begin with existing mental tests and try to isolate the processing elements required to succeed on them. Instead, Gardner believes that intelligence should be defined in terms of distinct sets of processing operations that permit individuals to engage in a wide range of culturally valued activities. Therefore, Gardner dismisses the idea of general intelligence and proposes eight independent intelligences, which are described in Table 12.2.

Gardner argues that each intelligence has a unique biological basis, a distinct course of development, and different expert, or "end-state," performances. At the same time, he emphasizes that a lengthy process of education is required to transform any raw potential into a mature social role. This means that cultural values and learning opportunities have a great deal to do with the extent to which a child's intellectual strengths are realized and the ways in which they are expressed.

Gardner's list of abilities has yet to be firmly grounded in research. For example, biological evidence for the independence of his abilities is weak. Similarly, there are exceptionally gifted individuals whose abilities are broad rather than limited to a particular domain (Feldman, 1991). Finally, current mental tests do tap several of Gardner's intelligences (linguistic, logico-mathematical, and spatial), and evidence suggests that they have

According to Gardner, humans are capable of at least eight distinct intelligences. As this child uses art materials creatively to sculpt a snowman, she enriches her spatial intelligence. *(Myrleen Ferguson Cate)*

theory of multiple intelligences
Gardner's theory, which identifies eight independent intelligences on the basis of distinct sets of processing operations that permit individuals to engage in a wide range of culturally valued activities.

at least some common features. Nevertheless, Gardner's theory has been especially helpful in efforts to understand and nurture children's special talents, a topic we will discuss at the end of this chapter.

EXPLAINING INDIVIDUAL AND GROUP DIFFERENCES IN IQ

When we compare individuals in terms of academic achievement, years of education, and occupational status, it quickly becomes clear that certain sectors of the population are advantaged over others. In trying to explain these differences, researchers have examined the intelligence test performance of children varying in ethnicity and SES. Many studies show that American black children score, on the average, 15 IQ points below American white children, although the difference has been shrinking (Nisbett, 1995; Suzuki & Valencia, 1997). SES differences in IQ also exist. In one large-scale study, low-SES children scored 9 points below children in the middle range of the SES distribution (Jensen & Figueroa, 1975). These figures are, of course, averages. There is considerable variation *within* each ethnic and SES group. Still, ethnic and SES differences in IQ are large enough and of serious enough consequence that they cannot be ignored.

In 1969, psychologist Arthur Jensen published a controversial article in the *Harvard Educational Review* entitled, "How Much Can We Boost IQ and Scholastic Achievement?" Jensen's answer to this question was "not much." He argued that heredity is largely responsible for individual, ethnic, and SES variations in intelligence (Jensen, 1980, 1985). Jensen's work received widespread public attention. It was followed by an outpouring of responses and research studies, leading to a heated nature–nurture debate on the origins of IQ. Recently, the controversy was rekindled in Richard Herrnstein and Charles Murray's (1994) *The Bell Curve*. Like Jensen, these authors concluded that the contribution of heredity to individual and SES differences in IQ is substantial. At the same time, they stated that the relative role of heredity and environment in the black–white IQ gap remains unresolved. Let's look closely at some important evidence.

■ **NATURE VERSUS NURTURE.** In Chapter 2, we introduced the *heritability estimate*. Recall that heritabilities are obtained from *kinship studies,* which compare family members. The most powerful evidence regarding heritability of IQ involves twin comparisons. Identical twins (who share all their genes) have more similar IQ scores than do fraternal twins (who are genetically no more alike than ordinary siblings). On the basis of this and other kinship evidence, current researchers estimate the heritability of IQ to be about .50 (Plomin, 1994a). This means that about half the differences in IQ among children can be traced to their genetic makeup.

However, in Chapter 2 (pages 87–88), we noted that heritabilities risk overestimating genetic influences and underestimating environmental influences. Although research offers convincing evidence that genetics contribute to IQ, disagreement persists over just how large the role of heredity really is (Sternberg & Grigorenko, 1997).

Furthermore, a widespread misconception exists that if a characteristic is heritable, then the environment can do little to affect it. A special type of kinship study, involving adopted children and their biological and adoptive relatives, shows that this assumption is incorrect. In one investigation of this kind, children of two extreme groups of biological mothers, those with IQs below 95 and those with IQs above 120, were chosen for special study. All the children were adopted at birth by parents who were well above average in income and education. During the school years, children of the low-IQ biological mothers scored above average in IQ, indicating that test performance can be greatly improved by an advantaged home life! At the same time, they did not do as well as children of high-IQ biological mothers placed in similar adoptive families (Horn, 1983). Adoption research confirms the balanced position that both heredity and environment affect IQ scores (Devlin et al., 1995).

Some intriguing adoption research also sheds light on the origins of the black–white IQ gap. African-American children placed in economically well-off white homes during the first year of life also score high on intelligence tests. In two such studies, adopted black children attained mean IQs of 110 and 117 by middle childhood, well above average and 20 to 30 points higher than the typical scores of children growing up in low-income black communities (Moore, 1986; Scarr & Weinberg, 1983). However, a follow-up in one investigation revealed that adoptees' IQs declined in adolescence. The drop may have been due to use of different tests at the two ages (Waldman, Weinberg, & Scarr, 1994; Weinberg, Scarr, & Waldman, 1992).

Adoption findings do not completely resolve questions about ethnic differences in IQ. Nevertheless, the IQ gains of black children "reared in the culture of the tests and schools" are consistent with a wealth of evidence indicating that poverty severely depresses the intelligence of large numbers of ethnic minority youngsters (Nisbett, 1995; Sternberg, 1996a). And in many other cases, unique cultural values and practices do not prepare these children for the kinds of tasks that are sampled by intelligence tests and valued in school.

■ **CULTURAL INFLUENCES.** Jermaine, a black child in Lizzie's third-grade class, participated actively in class discussion and wrote complex, imaginative stories. But he had not entered first grade feeling comfortable with classroom life. At the beginning, Jermaine responded, "I don't know," to the simplest of questions, including "What's your name?" Fortunately, Jermaine's teacher understood his uneasiness. Slowly and gently, she helped him build a bridge between the learning style fostered by his cultural background and the style necessary for academic success. A growing body of evidence reveals that IQ scores are affected by specific learning experiences, including exposure to certain language customs and knowledge.

Language Customs. Ethnic minority subcultures often foster unique language skills that do not fit the expectations of most classrooms and testing situations. Shirley Brice Heath (1982, 1989), an anthropologist who has spent many hours observing in low-income black homes in a southeastern American city, found that black adults asked children very different kinds of questions than is typical in white middle-income families. From an early age, white parents ask knowledge-training questions, such as "What color is it?" and "What's this story about?" that resemble the questioning style of tests and classrooms. In contrast, the black parents asked only "real" questions—ones they themselves could not answer. Often these were analogy questions ("What's that like?") or story-starter questions ("Didja hear Miss Sally this morning?") that called for elaborate responses about personal experiences and no single right answer.

Heath and other researchers report that these experiences lead low-income black children to develop complex verbal skills at home, such as storytelling and exchanging quick-witted remarks. But their language differs from that of white middle-income children in emphasizing emotional and social topics rather than facts about the world (Blake, 1994). Not surprisingly, black children may be confused by the "objective" questions they encounter in classrooms and withdraw into silence.

Other minority youngsters also develop distinct language customs. For example, children of Hispanic immigrants are taught to respect adult authority rather than express their own knowledge and opinions. Yet American teachers, who value self-assertive speaking, typically equate the silence of Hispanic children with having a negative attitude toward learning (Greenfield & Suzuki, 1998). As the child listens politely but does not answer out of deference to the adult, a culturally valued style of communicating quickly leads to unfair, negative evaluations in school and on mental tests.

When faced with the strangeness of the testing situation, the minority child may look to the examiner for cues about how to respond. Yet most intelligence tests permit tasks to

When black children grow up "in the culture of the tests and schools," they perform substantially above the population mean in IQ. Transracial adoption research supports the view that rearing environment underlies the black–white IQ gap. *(Tony Freeman/PhotoEdit)*

be presented in only one way, and they allow no feedback to children. Consequently, minority children may simply give the first answer that comes to mind, not one that truly represents what they know. For example, look at the following responses of a black child to a series of test questions:

Tester: "How are wood and coal alike? How are they the same?"

Child: "They're hard."

Tester: "An apple and a peach?"

Child: "They taste good."

Tester: "A ship and an automobile?"

Child: "They're hard."

Tester: "Iron and silver?"

Child: "They're hard." (Miller-Jones, 1989, p. 362)

Earlier in the testing session, this child asked whether she was doing all right but got no reply. She probably repeated her first answer because she had trouble figuring out the task's meaning, not because she was unable to classify objects. Had the tester prompted her to look at the questions in a different way, her performance might have been better.

Familiarity with Test Content. Many researchers argue that IQ scores are affected by specific information acquired as part of majority-culture upbringing. Unfortunately, attempts to change tests by eliminating fact-oriented verbal tasks and relying only on spatial reasoning and performance items (believed to be less culturally loaded) have not raised the scores of low-income minority children very much (Kaplan, 1985).

Nevertheless, even these test items depend on learning opportunities. In one study, children's performance on a spatial reasoning task was related to the extent to which they had played a popular but expensive game that (like the test items) required them to arrange blocks to duplicate a design as quickly as possible (Dirks, 1982). Low-income minority children, who often grow up in more "people-oriented" than "object-oriented" homes, may lack opportunities to use games and objects that promote certain intellectual skills. In line with this possibility, when ethnically diverse parents were asked for their idea of an intelligent first grader, Caucasian Americans valued cognitive traits over noncognitive ones. In contrast, ethnic minorities (Cambodian, Filipino, Vietnamese, and Mexican immigrants) saw noncognitive characteristics—motivation, self-management, and social skills—as equally or more important than cognitive skills (Okagaki & Sternberg, 1993).

That specific experiences affect performance on intelligence tests is also supported by evidence indicating that the amount of time a child spends in school is a strong predictor of IQ. When children of the same age who are in different grades are compared, those who have been in school longer score higher on intelligence tests. Similarly, dropping out of school leads to a decrease in IQ. The earlier young people leave school, the greater their loss of IQ points (Ceci 1991; Ceci & Williams, 1997).

Taken together, these findings indicate that a more intelligent child may come to school with a greater ability to profit from instruction. But teaching children the factual knowledge and ways of thinking valued in classrooms has a sizable impact on their intelligence test performance.

REDUCING CULTURAL BIAS IN INTELLIGENCE TESTING

Although not all experts agree, today there is greater acknowledgment than ever before that IQ scores can underestimate the intelligence of culturally different children.

Dynamic assessment introduces purposeful teaching into the testing situation to find out what the child can attain with social support. Many ethnic minority children perform more competently after adult assistance. And the approach helps identify the teaching style to which the child is most responsive. *(Bob Daemmrich/Stock Boston)*

A special concern exists about incorrectly labeling minority children as slow learners and assigning them to remedial classes, which are far less stimulating than regular school experiences. Because of this danger, test scores need to be combined with assessments of children's adaptive behavior—their ability to cope with the demands of their everyday environments (Landesman & Ramey, 1989). The child who does poorly on an IQ test yet plays a complex game on the playground, figures out how to rewire a broken TV, or cares for younger siblings responsibly is unlikely to be mentally deficient.

In addition, test designers are becoming more aware of the importance of using culturally relevant testing procedures. Minority children are often capable of the cognitive operations called for by test items. But because they are used to thinking in other ways in daily life, they may not access the required operation (Greenfield, 1997). **Dynamic assessment,** an innovative approach to testing consistent with Vygotsky's concept of the *zone of proximal development* (see Chapter 6, page 229), narrows this gap between actual and potential performance. Instead of emphasizing previously acquired knowledge, dynamic assessment introduces purposeful teaching into the testing situation to see what the child can do with social support.

Several dynamic assessment models exist, each of which uses a pretest–intervene–retest procedure with intelligence test items (Lidz, 1991). The best known of these is Reuben Feuerstein's (1979, 1980) *Learning Potential Assessment Device,* in which the adult tries to find the teaching style best suited to the child and communicates strategies that children can apply to new situations.

Research on dynamic assessment reveals that the IQs of ethnic minority children underestimate their ability to perform intellectual tasks after adult assistance. Instead, children's receptiveness to teaching and capacity to transfer what they have learned to novel problems add substantially to the prediction of future performance (Rand & Kaniel, 1987; Tzuriel, 1989). An added benefit is that dynamic assessment helps identify forms of intervention likely to help children achieving poorly in school.

Dynamic assessment is time consuming and requires extensive knowledge of minority children's cultural values and practices. Until we have the resources to implement these procedures broadly, should we suspend the use of intelligence testing in schools? Most experts regard this solution as unacceptable, since important educational decisions would be based only on subjective impressions—a policy that could increase discriminatory placement of minority children. Intelligence tests are useful as long as they are interpreted carefully by examiners who are sensitive to cultural influences on test performance. And despite their limitations, IQ scores continue to be valid measures of school learning potential for the majority of Western children.

dynamic assessment
An approach to testing consistent with Vygotsky's concept of the zone of proximal development, in which purposeful teaching is introduced into the testing situation to see what the child can do with social support.

■ *Desiree, an African-American child, was quiet and withdrawn while taking an intelligence test. Later she remarked to her mother, "I can't understand why that lady asked me all those questions, like what a ball and stove are for. She's a grownup. She must know what a ball and stove are for!" Using Sternberg's triarchic theory, explain Desiree's reaction to the testing situation. Why is Desiree's score likely to underestimate her intelligence?*

BRIEF REVIEW

Intelligence tests for children measure overall IQ as well as a variety of separate intellectual factors. Researchers have combined the factor analytic approach to defining intelligence with information processing in an effort to discover the cognitive processes underlying IQ scores. Sternberg has expanded this componential approach into a triarchic theory of intelligence. It states that information-processing skills, ability to learn efficiently in novel situations, and contextual factors (the child's cultural background and interpretation of the testing situation) interact to determine IQ. According to Gardner's theory of multiple intelligences, eight distinct abilities, each defined by unique processing operations, represent the diversity of human intelligence.

Heritability and adoption research shows that both genetic and environmental factors contribute to individual differences in intelligence. Because of different language customs and unfamiliar test content, the IQ scores of low-income minority children often do not reflect their true abilities. Supplementing IQ tests with measures of adaptive behavior and adjusting testing procedures to take cultural differences into account are ways of reducing test bias.

LANGUAGE DEVELOPMENT

Vocabulary, grammar, and pragmatics continue to develop in middle childhood, although less obviously than at earlier ages. In addition, children's attitude toward language undergoes a fundamental shift. Whereas preschoolers view language largely as a means of communicating, school-age children treat it as an object of thought. They develop **metalinguistic awareness,** the ability to think about language as a system.

Besides cognitive development, schooling contributes greatly to metalinguistic awareness. Talk about language is extremely common during literacy instruction but rare outside of classrooms (Gombert, 1992). In the following sections, we will see how an improved capacity to reflect on language supports a wide range of complex language skills.

VOCABULARY

Because the average 6-year-old's vocabulary is already quite large (about 10,000 words), parents and teachers usually do not notice rapid gains during the school years. Between the start of elementary school and its completion, vocabulary increases fourfold, eventually reaching about 40,000 words. On the average, about 20 new words are learned each day—a rate of growth that exceeds that of early childhood.

In addition to the fast-mapping process we discussed in Chapter 9, school-age children enlarge their vocabularies through an increasingly powerful ability to analyze the structure of complex words. From "happy," "wise," and "decide," they quickly derive the meanings of "happiness," "wisdom," and "decision" (Anglin, 1993). Many more words are picked up from context, especially while reading (Miller, 1991).

As their conceptual knowledge becomes better organized, school-age children think about and use words more precisely. Word definitions offer examples of this change. Five- and 6-year-olds give very concrete descriptions that refer to functions or appearance—for example, knife: "when you're cutting carrots"; bicycle: "it's got wheels, a chain, and handlebars." By the end of elementary school, synonyms and explanations of categorical relationships appear—for example, knife: "something you could cut with. A saw

metalinguistic awareness
The ability to think about language as a system.

is like a knife. It could also be a weapon" (Litowitz, 1977; Wehren, DeLisi, & Arnold, 1981). This advance reflects the ability to deal with word meanings on an entirely verbal plane. Older children no longer need to be shown what a word refers to in order to understand it. They can add new words to their vocabulary simply by being given a definition (Dickinson, 1984).

School-age children's more reflective and analytical approach to language permits them to appreciate the multiple meanings of words. For example, they recognize that many words, such as "cool" or "neat," have psychological as well as physical meanings: "What a cool shirt!" or "That movie was really neat!" This grasp of double meanings permits 8- to 10-year-olds to comprehend subtle, mental metaphors, such as "sharp as a tack," "spilling the beans," and "left high and dry" (Wellman & Hickling, 1994; Winner, 1988). It also leads to a change in children's humor. By the mid-elementary school years, riddles and puns are common:

"Hey, did you take a bath?" "No! Why, is one missing?"

"Order! Order in the court!" "Ham and cheese on rye, Your Honor?"

"Why did the old man tiptoe past the medicine cabinet?" "Because he didn't want to wake up the sleeping pills."

Six-year-olds may laugh at these statements because they are nonsensical. But most cannot tell a good riddle or pun, nor do they understand why these jokes are funny (Ely & McCabe, 1994).

GRAMMAR

Although children have mastered most of the grammar of their language by the time they enter school, use of complex grammatical constructions improves. The passive voice is an example. At all ages, children produce more abbreviated passives ("It got broken" or "They got lost") than full passives ("The glass was broken by Mary"). However, full passives are rarely used by 3- to 6-year-olds. They increase steadily over middle childhood (Horgan, 1978).

Older children also apply their understanding of the passive voice to a wider range of nouns and verbs. Preschoolers comprehend the passive best when the subject of the sentence is an animate being and the verb is an action word ("The *boy* is *kissed* by the girl"). During the school years, inanimate subjects, such as "drum" or "hat," and experiential verbs, such as "like" or "know," are included (Lempert, 1989; Pinker, Lebeaux, & Frost, 1987).

Another grammatical achievement of middle childhood is advanced understanding of infinitive phrases, such as the difference between "John is eager to please" and "John is easy to please" (Chomsky, 1969). Like gains in vocabulary, appreciation of these subtle grammatical distinctions is supported by metalinguisitic awareness. During middle childhood, children can judge the grammatical correctness of a sentence even if its meaning is false or senseless, whereas preschoolers cannot (Bialystok, 1986).

PRAGMATICS

Improvements in *pragmatics*, the communicative side of language, take place in middle childhood. School-age children become better at adapting to the needs of listeners in challenging communicative situations. In one study, 3- to 10-year-olds were asked which of eight similar objects they liked best as a birthday present for an imaginary friend. Preschoolers gave ambiguous descriptions, such as "the red one." In contrast, school-age youngsters referred to the objects in much more precise ways—for example, "the round red one with stripes on it" (Deutsch & Pechmann, 1982).

Conversational strategies also become more refined. For example, older children are better at phrasing things to get their way. When faced with an adult who refuses to hand over a desired object, 9-year-olds, but not 5-year-olds, state their second requests more politely (Axia & Baroni, 1985). School-age children are also more sensitive than preschoolers to distinctions between what people say and what they really mean. For example, Lizzie knew that when her mother said, "The garbage is beginning to smell," she really meant, "Take that garbage out!" (Ackerman, 1978).

Narratives are yet another aspect of communicative competence that improves. Most school-age children's narratives increasingly follow a *topic-focused* formula. They build toward a high point, describe a critical event, and then resolve and evaluate it. Yet each culture has its own way of telling stories. African-American children, for example, typically tell *topic-associating* stories, which involve several main characters and shifts in time and setting. When teachers criticize this approach as "disorganized," they devalue the child's culture (McCabe, 1998; Michaels, 1991). Accepting and nurturing the minority child's narrative style, while introducing others, can foster a positive attitude toward school and literacy. We will encounter this theme again as we turn to bilingualism in childhood.

LEARNING TWO LANGUAGES AT A TIME

Like most American children, Joey and Lizzie speak only one language, their native tongue of English. Yet throughout the United States and the world, many children grow up *bilingual.* They learn two languages, and sometimes more than two, during childhood. An estimated 6 million American school-age children speak a language other than English at home, a figure expected to increase steadily in the twenty-first century (U.S. Bureau of the Census, 1997).

Children can become bilingual in two ways: (1) by acquiring both languages at the same time in early childhood, or (2) by learning a second language after mastering the first. Children of bilingual parents who teach them both languages in early childhood show no special problems with language development. For a time, they appear to develop more slowly because they mix the two languages. But this is not a sign of confusion, since bilingual parents do not maintain strict language separation either (Baker, 1993). These bilingual children acquire normal native ability in the language of their surrounding community and good to native ability in the second language, depending on their exposure to it. When school-age children acquire a second language after they already speak another language, it generally takes them 3 to 5 years to become as competent in the second language as native-speaking agemates (Ramirez et al, 1991).

A large body of research shows that bilingualism has a positive impact on cognitive development. Children who are fluent in two languages do better than their single-language agemates on tests of analytical reasoning, concept formation, and cognitive flexibility (Hakuta, Ferdman, & Diaz, 1987). And their metalinguistic skills are particularly well developed. They are more aware that words are arbitrary symbols, more conscious of spoken and written language structure, and better at noticing errors of grammar and meaning—capacities that enhance their reading achievement (Bialystok, 1997; Campbell & Sais, 1995; Ricciardelli, 1992).

The advantages of bilingualism provide strong justification for bilingual education programs in schools. The Social Issues box on the following page describes the current controversy over bilingual education in the United States. As you will see, bilingual children rarely receive support for their native language in classrooms. Yet bilingualism provides one of the best examples of how language, once learned, becomes an important tool of the mind and fosters cognitive development. In fact, the goals of schooling could reasonably be broadened to include helping all children become bilingual, thereby fostering the cognitive, language, and cultural enrichment of the entire nation (Mohanty & Perregaux, 1997).

SOCIAL   ISSUES

BILINGUAL EDUCATION

incente, a 7-year-old boy who recently immigrated from Mexico to the United States, attends a bilingual education classroom in a large American city. His teacher, Serena, is fluent in both Spanish and English. At the beginning of the year, Serena instructed Vincente and his classmates in their native tongue. As the children mixed with English-speaking youngsters at school and in the community, they quickly picked up English phrases, such as "My name is …," "I wanna," and "Show me." Serena reinforced her pupil's first efforts to speak English, helping them feel confident about communicating in a second language. Gradually, she introduced more English into classroom learning experiences. At the same time, she continued to strengthen the children's native language and culture.

Vincente is enrolled in one of many bilingual education programs serving the growing number of American children with limited proficiency in English. Yet the question of how Vincente and his classmates should be taught continues to be hotly debated.

On one side of the controversy are those who believe that Vincente should be instructed only in English. According to this view, time spent communicating in the child's native tongue subtracts from English language achievement, which is vital for forging national unity and easing communication in education, business, and everyday life.

On the other side are educators like Serena, who are committed to truly *bilingual* education—developing Vincente's native language while fostering his mastery of English. Supporters of this view believe that providing instruction in the native tongue lets minority children know that their heritage is respected (McGroarty, 1992). In addition, by avoiding abrupt immersion in an English-speaking environment, bilingual education prevents *semilingualism,* or inadequate proficiency in both languages. When minority children experience a gradual loss of the first language as a result of being taught the second, they end up limited in both languages for a period of time, a circumstance that leads to serious academic difficulties. Semilingualism is one factor believed to contribute to the high rates of school failure and dropout among low-income Hispanic youngsters, who make up nearly 50 percent of the American language-minority population.

At present, public opinion sides with the first of these two viewpoints. Many states have passed laws declaring English to be their official language, creating conditions in which schools have no obligation to teach minority pupils in languages other than English. In 1998, California voters passed a law that eliminated bilingual education in favor of a one-year, English-only immersion course for non-English-speaking pupils, a move expected to spread to other states. Yet research underscores the value of instruction in the child's native tongue. In classrooms where both languages are integrated into the curriculum, minority children are more involved in learning, participate more actively in class discussions, and acquire the second language more easily. In contrast, when teachers speak only a language their pupils can barely understand, children display frustration, boredom, withdrawal, and academic failure (Crawford, 1995, 1997).

English-only supporters often point to Canada, which recognizes the linguistic rights of its French-speaking minority but where friction between English- and French-speaking groups is intense. Nevertheless, both English and French are official languages, and most Canadian children become fluent in both—ideal conditions for building greater ethnic harmony (Piatt, 1993).

When bilingual education programs provide instruction in both the child's native language and in English, children are more involved in learning and are advanced in language development. *(Will Faller)*

ASK YOURSELF . . .

- *Ten-year-old Shana arrived home from school after a long day, sank into the living room sofa, and commented, "I'm totally wiped out!" Megan, her 5-year-old sister, looked puzzled and asked, "What didya wipe out, Shana?" Explain Shana and Megan's different understanding of the meaning of this expression.*

BRIEF REVIEW

During the school years, development of metalinguistic awareness supports many complex language skills. Vocabulary increases rapidly, and children develop a more precise and flexible understanding of word meanings. Mastery of complex grammatical constructions becomes more refined. School-age children express themselves well in challenging communicative situations, acquire more subtle conversational strategies, and display better-organized narratives. Bilingualism has a positive impact on cognitive development and metalinguistic awareness.

CHILDREN'S LEARNING IN SCHOOL

Throughout this chapter, we have touched on evidence indicating that schools are vital forces in children's cognitive development, affecting their modes of remembering, reasoning, problem solving, and language skills. How do schools exert such a powerful impact? Research looking at schools as complex social systems—their class size, educational philosophies, teacher–pupil interaction patterns, and the larger cultural context in which they are embedded—provides important insights into this question.

CLASS SIZE

As each school year began, Rena telephoned the principal's office and asked, "How large will Joey and Lizzie's classes be?" Her concern is well founded. A large-scale field experiment revealed that class size influences children's learning.

Over 6,000 kindergartners in 76 Tennessee elementary schools were randomly assigned to three class types: small (13 to 17 pupils), regular (22 to 25 pupils), and regular with a full-time teacher's aide. These arrangements continued into third grade. Small-class pupils scored higher in reading and math achievement each year, an effect that was particularly strong for minority pupils. Placing teacher's aides in regular-size classes had no consistent impact. Finally, even after all pupils returned to regular-size classes in fourth and fifth grades, children who had experienced the small classes remained ahead in achievement (Mosteller, 1995).

Why is small class size beneficial? Teachers of fewer children spend less time disciplining and more time giving individual attention, and children's interactions with one another are more positive and cooperative. Also, when class size is small, teachers and pupils are more satisfied with school experiences. The learning advantages of small classes are greatest in the early years of schooling, when children require more adult assistance (Blatchford & Mortimore, 1994).

EDUCATIONAL PHILOSOPHIES

Each teacher brings to the classroom an educational philosophy that plays a major role in children's learning experiences. Two philosophical approaches have received the most research attention. They differ in what children are taught, the way they are believed to learn, and how their progress is evaluated.

■ **TRADITIONAL VERSUS OPEN CLASSROOMS.** In a **traditional classroom,** children are relatively passive in the learning process. The teacher is the sole authority for knowledge, rules, and decision making and does most of the talking. Pupils spend most of their time at their desks—listening, responding when called on, and completing teacher-

traditional classroom
An elementary school classroom based on the educational philosophy that children are passive learners who acquire information presented by teachers. Pupils are evaluated on the basis of how well they keep up with a uniform set of standards for all pupils in their grade.

assigned tasks. Their progress is evaluated by how well they keep pace with a uniform set of standards for all pupils in their grade.

In contrast, in an **open classroom,** children are viewed as active agents in their own development. The teacher assumes a flexible authority role, sharing decision making with pupils, who learn at their own pace. Pupils are evaluated by considering their progress in relation to their own prior development. How well they compare to other same-age pupils is of lesser importance. A glance inside the door of an open classroom reveals richly equipped learning centers, small groups of pupils working on tasks they choose themselves, and a teacher who moves from one area to another, guiding and supporting in response to children's individual needs.

Over the past few decades, the pendulum in American education has swung back and forth between these two views. In the 1960s and early 1970s, open education gained in popularity, inspired by Piaget's vision of the child as an active, motivated learner. Then, as concern over the academic progress of American children and youths became widespread, a "back to basics" movement arose. Classrooms returned to traditional, teacher-directed instruction, a style still prevalent today.

The combined results of many studies reveal that older school-age children in traditional classrooms have a slight edge in academic achievement. But open settings are associated with other benefits. Open-classroom pupils are more critical thinkers, and they value and respect individual differences in their classmates more. Pupils in open environments also like school better than those in traditional classrooms, and their attitude toward school becomes increasingly positive as they spend more time there (Walberg, 1986).

Recall from Chapter 9 that whole-class, teacher-directed instruction has filtered down to the preschool years (see page 351). It has increased in kindergarten and the early school grades as well. When kindergartners spend much time passively sitting and doing worksheets as opposed to being actively engaged in learning centers, they display more stress behaviors, such as wiggling and rocking, withdrawal, and talking out. Follow-ups reveal that traditional-classroom kindergartners show poorer study habits and achieve less well in grade school (Burts et al., 1992; Hart et al., 1998). These outcomes are strongest for low-SES children. Yet teachers tend to prefer a traditional approach for economically disadvantaged pupils—a disturbing trend in view of its negative impact on motivation and learning (Eccles et al., 1993b; Stipek & Byler, 1997).

■ **NEW VYGOTSKY-INSPIRED DIRECTIONS.** The philosophies of some teachers fall somewhere in between traditional and open. They want to foster high achievement as well as critical thinking, positive social relationships, and excitement about learning. New experiments in elementary education, grounded in Vygotsky's sociocultural theory, represent this point of view (Forman, Minick, & Stone, 1993). Vygotsky's emphasis on the social origins of higher cognitive processes has inspired the following educational themes:

■ *Teachers and children as partners in learning.* A classroom rich in dialogue—both teacher–child and child–child collaboration—fosters transfer of culturally valued ways of thinking to children.

■ *Experience with many types of symbolic communication in meaningful activities.* As children master reading, writing, and quantitative reasoning, they become aware of their culture's communication systems, reflect on their own thinking, and bring it under voluntary control. (Can you identify research presented earlier in this chapter that supports this theme?)

■ *Teaching adapted to each child's zone of proximal development.* Providing assistance that is responsive to current understandings but that encourages children to take the next step forward helps ensure that each pupil will make the best progress possible.

Let's look at two examples of a growing number of programs that have translated these ideas into action.

open classroom
An elementary school classroom based on the educational philosophy that children are active agents in their own development and learn at different rates. Teachers share decision making with pupils. Pupils are evaluated in relation to their own prior development.

Reciprocal teaching is a Vygotsky-inspired educational innovation in which a teacher and two to four pupils form a cooperative learning group and engage in dialogue about a text passage. Elementary and junior high school pupils who participate in reciprocal teaching show impressive gains in reading comprehension. *(Mark Pokempner/Impact Visuals)*

reciprocal teaching
A method of teaching based on Vygotsky's theory in which a teacher and two to four pupils form a cooperative learning group. Dialogues occur that create a zone of proximal development in which reading comprehension improves.

Kamehameha Elementary Education Program (KEEP)
The most well-known and extensive educational reform effort based on Vygotsky's theory. Instruction is organized around activity settings, designed to enhance teacher–child and child–child interaction and to be culturally responsive.

Reciprocal Teaching. Originally designed to improve reading comprehension in pupils achieving poorly, **reciprocal teaching** has been adapted to other subjects and is a useful model for all school-age children (Palincsar, 1992). A teacher and two to four pupils form a cooperative learning group and take turns leading dialogues on the content of a text passage. Within the dialogues, group members apply four cognitive strategies: questioning, summarizing, clarifying, and predicting.

The dialogue leader (at first a teacher, later a pupil) begins by *asking questions* about the content of the text passage. Pupils offer answers, raise additional questions, and in case of disagreement, reread the original text. Next, the leader *summarizes* the passage, and children discuss the summary and *clarify* ideas that are unfamiliar to any group members. Finally the leader encourages pupils to *predict* upcoming content based on clues in the passage (Palincsar & Klenk, 1992).

Elementary and junior high school pupils exposed to reciprocal teaching show impressive gains in reading comprehension compared to controls taught in other ways (Palincsar, Brown, & Campione, 1993; Rosenshine & Meister, 1994). Notice how reciprocal teaching creates a zone of proximal development in which children gradually assume more responsibility for comprehending complex text passages. By collaborating with others, they acquire skills vital for learning and success in everyday life.

The Kamehameha Elementary Education Program. The most well-known and extensive educational reform effort based on Vygotsky's theory is the **Kamehameha Elementary Education Program (KEEP)**. To foster development, KEEP instruction is organized around activity settings specially designed to enhance teacher–child and child–child interaction. In each setting, children work on a project that ensures that their learning will be active and directed toward a meaningful goal. For example, they might read a story and discuss its meaning or draw a map of the playground to promote an understanding of geography.

All children enter a focal activity setting, called "Center One," at least once each morning for scaffolding of challenging literacy skills. Text content is carefully selected to relate to children's experiences, and instruction builds on children's ideas. The precise organization of each KEEP classroom is adjusted to fit the unique learning styles of its pupils, creating culturally responsive environments (Au, 1997; Tharp, 1993, 1994).

Thousands of low-SES minority children have attended KEEP classrooms in the public schools of Hawaii, on a Navajo reservation in Arizona, and in Los Angeles. So far, research suggests that the approach is highly effective. In KEEP schools, minority pupils performed at their expected grade level in reading achievement, much better than children of the same background enrolled in traditional schools. Furthermore, KEEP pupils more often participated actively in class discussion, used elaborate language structures, and supported one another's learning than did non-KEEP controls (Tharp & Gallimore, 1988). As the KEEP model becomes more widely applied, perhaps it will prove successful with all types of children because of its comprehensive goals and effort to meet the learning needs of a wide range of pupils.

TEACHER–PUPIL INTERACTION

Teachers vary in their interactions with children—differences that affect academic achievement. Whereas Lizzie's teacher emphasized factual knowledge, Joey's teacher encouraged children to grapple with ideas and apply their knowledge to new situations. He asked, "Why is the main character in this story a hero?" and "Now that you are good at division, how many teams should we have at recess? How many children on each team?"

CAREGIVING CONCERNS

Encouraging Critical Thinking in School-Age Children

SUGGESTION	DESCRIPTION
Promote open-ended questioning and interaction.	Engaging in open-ended questioning ("why" and "how") and discussing answers to those questions encourage children to be adventurous and inquiring and to prompt each other's thinking.
Ask children to clarify and draw inferences.	Asking "What is the main point?" "What does it mean?" or "What might happen next?" encourages children to be active, precise thinkers and to consider the implications of their ideas.
Help children view situations from multiple perspectives.	Once children give their own opinion on an issue, ask them to state and try to support opposing perspectives. Seeing things from other viewpoints makes children more aware of their own thinking patterns and encourages them to be open-minded and flexible.
Use a precise "language of thinking."	When adults use a specific "thinking vocabulary" that includes such terms as *hypothesis, reasons, conclusions, evidence,* and *opinion,* their verbal cues evoke a richer variety of thought processes in children.
Explain thinking possibilities.	Explaining thinking possibilities makes children conscious of the ingredients of critical thinking and, therefore, more likely to apply this knowledge. For example, an adult might discuss with children what the word hypothesis means and how a hypothesis in science differs from one in history or everyday life.
Model critical thinking.	When children observe adults engaged in critical thinking, they are more likely to adopt it as a valued activity for themselves.
Give feedback that supports critical thinking.	Positive feedback and suggestions for how to do better rather than criticism establishes a safe haven for critical thinking that permits children to take risks.

Sources: Byrnes, 1993; Tishman, Perkins, & Jay, 1995.

In a study of fifth-grade social studies and math lessons, students were far more attentive when teachers encouraged high-level thinking (Stodolsky, 1988). The Caregiving Concerns table above suggests ways to encourage children to think critically—to consider the deeper meaning of problems by reflecting, evaluating, and expressing their ideas in clear and useful ways.

Teachers do not interact in the same way with all children. Some get more attention and praise than others. Well-behaved, high-achieving pupils typically experience positive interactions with teachers. In contrast, teachers may actively dislike children who achieve poorly and are also disruptive. These unruly pupils are often criticized and are rarely called on to contribute to class discussion. When they seek special help or permission, their requests are usually denied (Good & Brophy, 1994).

Unfortunately, once teachers' attitudes toward pupils are established, they are in danger of becoming more extreme than is warranted by children's behavior. A special concern is that an **educational self-fulfilling prophecy** can be set in motion: Children may adopt teachers' positive and negative views and start to live up to them. Many studies show that school-age pupils become increasingly aware of teacher opinion, and it can influence their motivation and performance (Skinner & Belmont, 1993). This effect is particularly strong in classrooms where teachers emphasize competition and public comparisons between children (Weinstein et al., 1987).

Teacher expectations have a greater impact on low achievers than high achievers (Madom, Jussim, & Eccles, 1997). High-achieving pupils have less room to improve when teachers think well of them, and they can fall back on their long history of success experiences when a teacher is critical. Low-achieving pupils' sensitivity to self-fulfilling prophecies can be beneficial when teachers believe in them. But they may only rarely have the chance to reap these benefits.

educational self-fulfilling prophecy
The idea that children may adopt teachers' positive or negative attitudes toward them and start to live up to these views.

GROUPING PRACTICES

Children can be grouped for instruction in many ways. Often pupils are assigned to *homogenous* groups or classes in which children of similar achievement levels are taught together. Some researchers believe that teachers' treatment of different ability groups may be an especially powerful source of self-fulfilling prophecies. In low-ability groups, pupils get more drill on basic facts and skills, a slower learning pace, and less time on academic work. Gradually, children in low-ability groups show a drop in self-esteem and are viewed by themselves and others as "not smart." Not surprisingly, ability grouping widens the performance gap between high and low achievers (Dornbusch, Glasgow, & Lin, 1996; Fuligni, Eccles, & Barber, 1995; Gamoran et al., 1995).

Yet another approach to grouping has been to increase the *heterogeneity* of pupils. In mixed-age classrooms, pupils who otherwise would be assigned to different grades are taught together. When academic performance differs between mixed-and single-age classrooms, it favors the mixed-age arrangement. Self-esteem and attitudes toward school are also more positive, perhaps because mixed-age grouping decreases competition and increases harmony in the classroom (Jensen & Green, 1993; Pratt, 1986).

The opportunity mixed-age grouping affords for peer tutoring may also contribute to its favorable outcomes. When older or more expert pupils teach younger or less expert pupils, both tutors and tutees benefit in academic achievement and self-esteem (Renninger, 1998). Perhaps peer tutoring helps make mixed-age classrooms particularly cooperative.

COMPUTERS IN THE CLASSROOM

Besides teachers and peers, another interactive aid to learning can be found in schools. In Joey and Lizzie's classrooms, a computer sat in a quiet corner. Children took turns working on special assignments, sometimes by themselves and at other times with their classmates. By 1995, over 98 percent of American public schools had integrated computers into their instructional programs, a trend also apparent in other industrialized nations (Collis et al., 1996; U.S. Bureau of the Census, 1997). A growing research literature reveals that computers can have rich educational benefits.

■ **ADVANTAGES OF COMPUTERS.** Computers in classrooms are used in a variety of ways. In *computer-assisted instruction,* specially designed educational software permits children to practice basic skills and acquire new knowledge. Gains in achievement occur when computer-assisted instruction is a regular part of children's school experiences. Benefits are greatest for younger pupils and those who are achieving poorly in school (Clements & Nastasi, 1992).

As soon as children begin to read and write, they can use the computer for *word processing.* It permits them to write freely and experiment with letters and words without having to struggle with handwriting at the same time. In addition, children can plan and revise the text's meaning and style as well as check their spelling. As a result, they worry less about making mistakes, and their written products tend to be longer and of higher quality (Clements, 1995). However, computers by themselves do not help children master the mechanics of writing (such as spelling and grammar). So it is best to use computers to build on and enhance, not replace, other classroom writing experiences.

Programming offers children the highest degree of control over the computer, since they must tell it what to do. Specially designed computer languages are available to introduce children to programming skills. As long as teachers encourage and support children's efforts, computer programming leads to improvements in concept formation, problem solving, and creativity (Clements, 1995; Clements & Nastasi, 1992). Also, since children must detect errors in their programs to get them to work, programming helps them reflect on their thought processes, leading to gains in metacognition and self-regulation (Clements, 1990).

Finally, *new communications technology* is available through electronic mail (e-mail), the World Wide Web, and other computer-based services. As a result, teachers are developing website-based learning activities, and children can access information and interact with people around the world (Windschitl, 1998). Although little research exists on the impact of these innovations, one study highlights their power to enhance understanding of other cultures. Groups of six to nine classrooms, from the United States and foreign countries, formed "learning circles." Each class planned a project and consulted with their learning circle to complete it. E-mail messages revealed a broadening of horizons about other people and places. For example, pupils in Persian Gulf nations wrote candidly about their fears as one circle discussed world security and peace (Reil, 1992).

Special steps are needed to ensure that girls have equal access to computers during the school years. When classrooms emphasize cooperative learning and software is designed with the interests of girls in mind, they become enthusiastic users. *(Stephen Marks)*

■ **CONCERNS ABOUT COMPUTERS.** Although computers provide children with many learning advantages, they raise serious concerns as well. Computers appear most often in the schools and homes of economically well-off pupils (Rocheleau, 1995). As a result, some experts believe that computers are widening the intellectual performance gap between low- and higher-SES children.

Furthermore, by the end of elementary school, boys spend much more time with computers than do girls, both in and out of school. Parents of sons are more likely than parents of daughters to install a computer in the home. Even when girls have ready access to computers, much software is unappealing to them because it emphasizes themes of war, violence, and male-dominated sports (Collis et al., 1996; Griffiths, 1997). Girls' reduced involvement with computers may contribute to sex differences in mathematical achievement and interest in scientific careers that emerge by adolescence (see Chapter 15). Yet girls' tendency to retreat from computers can be overcome, since the gender gap is declining (Rocheleau, 1995). When teachers present computers in the context of cooperative rather than competitive learning activities and software is designed with the interests of girls in mind, they become enthusiastic users (Hawkins & Sheingold, 1986).

Finally, video games account for most out-of-school, recreational computer use, especially by boys. Many parents are concerned that their children will become overly involved as well as more aggressive because of these fast-paced amusements with highly violent content. The limited evidence available suggests that about 5 percent of children become "passionate," or excessive, players. And violent video games do seem to contribute to aggressive behavior (Goldstein, 1994; Irwin & Gross, 1995; Phillips et al., 1995).

TEACHING CHILDREN WITH SPECIAL NEEDS

So far, we have seen that effective teachers flexibly adjust their teaching strategies to accommodate pupils with a wide range of abilities and characteristics. But such adjustments are increasingly difficult at the very low and high ends of the ability distribution. How do schools serve children with special learning needs?

■ **CHILDREN WITH LEARNING DIFFICULTIES.** The Individuals with Disabilities Education Act (Public Law 101-475), first passed by Congress in 1975 and revised in 1990, mandates that schools place children who require special supports for learning in the "least restrictive" environments that meet their educational needs. The law led to a rapid increase in **mainstreaming,** or placement of pupils with learning difficulties in regular classrooms for part of the school day, a practice designed to better prepare them

mainstreaming
Placement of pupils with learning difficulties in regular classrooms for part of the school day.

for participation in society. Largely due to parental pressures, in some schools main-streaming has been extended to **full inclusion**—placement in regular classrooms full time (Siegel, 1996). Most mainstreamed or fully included pupils are mildly retarded or learning disabled.

Children with Mild Retardation. About 1.5 percent of the child population suffers from **mental retardation,** or substantially below-average intellectual functioning and adaptive behavior (social and self-help skills in everyday life). Approximately 85 percent of these children are *mildly mentally retarded*—the highest functioning category. Typically, a mildly mentally retarded child has an IQ between 55 and 70 and can be educated to the level of an average sixth grader. In adulthood, most can live independently and hold routine jobs, although they require extra guidance and support during times of stress (American Psychiatric Association, 1994).

As you know from earlier chapters, the depressed intellectual functioning that characterizes mentally retarded children can develop in many ways. Hereditary defects, a faulty prenatal environment, birth complications, childhood injuries, a severely impoverished home life, or some combination of these factors are common causes.

Children with Learning Disabilities. The largest number of mainstreamed children have **learning disabilities.** About 5 to 10 percent of school-age children are affected. These youngsters obtain average or above-average IQ scores. Nevertheless, they have great difficulty with one or more aspects of learning. As a result, their achievement is considerably behind what would be expected on the basis of their IQ. Their problems cannot be traced to any obvious physical or emotional difficulty or to environmental disadvantage. Instead, faulty brain functioning is believed to be responsible (Bender, 1996; Polloway et al., 1997). Some of the disorders run in families, suggesting that they are at least partly genetic. In most instances, the cause is unknown.

Learning-disabled children display a wide variety of cognitive processing deficits. Most have *dyslexia,* or a problem with reading. Others have *dyscalculia,* a problem with arithmetic, or *dysgraphia,* a problem with writing. But impairments are more varied than these categories suggest. For example, one dyslexic child might have difficulty interpreting visual stimuli, confusing the letters *d, b, p, q,* and *g* and reading "dog" as "god" and "ball" as "gall." Another might have trouble tracking from left to right and read the same line twice, jump over words, or skip lines. Serious memory problems can contribute to poor recall of events in a story as well as spelling and math difficulties. Finally, sometimes the muscles of the hand fail to work together, resulting in extremely slow, unclear handwriting.

The learning problems of these children are so frustrating that they can lead to serious emotional, social, and family difficulties (Bender & Wall, 1994). Yet those who are treated with patience and understanding and who receive appropriate educational intervention have a good chance of making a satisfactory adjustment and becoming economically self-sufficient in adulthood.

How Effective Are Mainstreaming and Full Inclusion? Does placement of pupils with disabilities in regular classes accomplish its two goals—providing more appropriate academic experiences and integrated participation in classroom life? At present, research findings are not positive on either of these points.

Achievement differences between mainstreamed pupils and those taught in self-contained classrooms are not great (Buysse & Bailey, 1993; MacMillan, Keogh, & Jones, 1986). Furthermore, children with disabilities in regular classrooms are often rejected by peers. Those who are mentally retarded are overwhelmed by the social skills of their classmates; they cannot interact adeptly in a conversation or game. And the processing deficits of some learning-disabled children lead to problems in social awareness and responsiveness (Gresham & MacMillan, 1997; Vaughn, Elbaum, & Schumm, 1996).

full inclusion
Placement of pupils with learning difficulties in regular classrooms for the entire school day.

mental retardation
Substantially below-average intellectual functioning.

learning disabilities
Specific learning disorders that lead children to achieve poorly in school, despite an average or above-average IQ. Believed to be due to faulty brain functioning.

The pupil on the left, who has a learning disability, has been mainstreamed into a regular classroom. Because his teacher takes special steps to encourage peer acceptance, individualizes instruction, minimizes comparisons with classmates, and promotes cooperative learning, this boy looks forward to school and is doing well. *(Will Hart)*

Does this mean that special-needs children cannot be served in regular classrooms? This extreme conclusion is not warranted. Often these children do best when they receive instruction in a *resource room* for part of the day and in the regular classroom for the remainder. In the resource room, a special education teacher works with pupils on an individual and small-group basis. Then, depending on their abilities, children are mainstreamed for different subjects and amounts of time. This flexible approach makes it more likely that the unique academic needs of each child will be served (Hocutt, 1996; Keogh, 1998).

Once children enter the regular classroom, special steps must be taken to promote peer acceptance. Cooperative learning and peer-tutoring experiences in which mainstreamed children and their classmates work together on the same task lead to friendly interaction and more favorable attitudes (Scruggs & Mastropieri, 1994; Siegel, 1996). Teachers also can prepare children for the arrival of a special-needs pupil. Under these conditions, mainstreaming may foster gains in emotional sensitivity and prosocial behavior among regular classmates.

■ **GIFTED CHILDREN.** In Joey and Lizzie's school, some children were **gifted.** They displayed exceptional intellectual strengths. Like mainstreamed pupils, their characteristics were diverse. In every grade were one or two pupils with IQ scores above 130, the standard definition of giftedness based on intelligence test performance (Gardner, 1998). High-IQ children, as we have seen, are particularly quick at academic work. They have keen memories and an exceptional capacity to solve challenging problems rapidly and accurately.

Yet earlier in this chapter, we noted that intelligence tests do not sample the entire range of human mental skills. Over the past two decades, recognition of this fact has led to an expanded conception of giftedness in schools.

Creativity and Talent. High *creativity* can result in a child being designated as gifted. Tests of creativity tap **divergent thinking**—the generation of multiple and unusual possibilities when faced with a task or problem. Divergent thinking contrasts sharply with **convergent thinking,** which involves arriving at a single correct answer and is emphasized on intelligence tests (Guilford, 1985).

Recognizing that highly creative children (like high-IQ children) are often better at some types of tasks than others, researchers have devised verbal, figural, and "real-world-problem" tests of divergent thinking (Runco, 1992; Torrance, 1988). A verbal measure might ask children to name as many uses for common objects (such as a newspaper) as they can. A figural measure might ask them to come up with as many drawings based on a circular motif as possible (see Figure 12.5). A "real-world" measure either gives children everyday

giftedness
Exceptional intellectual ability. Includes high IQ, creativity, and specialized talent.

divergent thinking
The generation of multiple and unusual possibilities when faced with a task or problem. Associated with creativity.

convergent thinking
The generation of a single correct answer to a problem. The type of cognition emphasized on intelligence tests.

FIGURE **12.5**

Responses of an 8-year-old who scored high on a figural measure of divergent thinking. This child was asked to make as many pictures as she could from the circles on the page. The titles she gave her drawings, from left to right, are as follows: "Dracula," "one-eyed monster," "pumpkin," "Hula-Hoop," "poster," "wheelchair," "earth," "moon," "planet," "movie camera," "sad face," "picture," "stoplight," "beach ball," "the letter O," "car," "glasses." Tests of divergent thinking tap only one of the complex, cognitive contributions to creativity. *(Test form copyright © 1980 by Scholastic Testing Service, Inc. Reprinted by permission of Scholastic Testing Service, Inc., from* The Torrance Tests of Creative Thinking *by E. P. Torrance)*

problems or requires them to think of such problems and then suggest solutions. Responses to all these tests can be scored for the number of ideas generated and their originality.

Yet critics of these measures point out that at best, they are imperfect predictors of creative accomplishment in everyday life, since they tap only one of the complex cognitive contributions to creativity (Cramond, 1994). Also involved are the ability to define a new and important problem, to evaluate divergent ideas and choose the most promising, and to call on relevant knowledge to understand and solve the problem (Sternberg & Lubart, 1995).

Consider these additional ingredients, and you will see why both children and adults usually demonstrate creativity in only one or a few related areas. Partly for this reason, definitions of giftedness have been extended to include *specialized talent*. There is clear evidence that outstanding performance in particular fields, such as mathematics, science, music, art, athletics, and leadership, have roots in specialized skills that first appear at an early age. Highly talented children seem biologically prepared to master their domain of interest. And they usually display a passion—a burning drive—to do so (Gardner, 1998; Winner, 1996).

At the same time, talent must be nurtured in a favorable environment. Studies of the backgrounds of talented children and highly accomplished adults often reveal homes rich in stimulating activities and parents who emphasize curiosity and are highly accepting of their youngster's unique characteristics (Albert, 1994; Perleth & Heller, 1994). In addition, such parents recognize their child's creative potential and (as the talent develops) arrange for apprenticeship under inspiring teachers (Bloom, 1985; Feldman, 1991). Classrooms in which children can take risks, challenge the teacher, and reflect on ideas without being rushed to the next assignment are also important (Sternberg & Lubart, 1991).

Educating the Gifted. Although programs for the gifted exist in many schools, debate about their effectiveness usually focuses on factors irrelevant to giftedness—whether to offer enrichment in regular classrooms, to pull children out for special instruction (the most common practice), or to advance brighter pupils to a higher grade. Children of all ages fare well academically and socially within each of these models (Moon & Feldhusen, 1994; Southern, Jones, & Stanley, 1994). Yet the extent to which they foster creativity and talent depends on opportunities to acquire relevant skills.

Recently, Gardner's theory of multiple intelligences has inspired several model programs that provide enrichment to all pupils. A wide variety of meaningful activities, each tapping a specific intelligence or set of intelligences, serve as contexts for assessing strengths and weaknesses and, on that basis, teaching new knowledge and original thinking. For example, linguistic intelligence might be fostered through storytelling or playwriting; spatial intelligence through drawing, sculpting, or taking apart and reassembling objects; and kinesthetic intelligence through dance or pantomime (Gardner, 1993).

Evidence is still needed on how effectively these programs nurture children's talents. But so far, they have succeeded in one way—by highlighting the strengths of some pupils who previously had been considered ordinary or even at risk for school failure. Consequently, they may be especially useful in identifying talented minority children who are underrepresented in school programs for the gifted (Frazier, 1994).

HOW WELL EDUCATED ARE AMERICA'S CHILDREN?

Our discussion of schooling has largely focused on what teachers can do to support the education of children. Yet a great many factors, both within and outside schools, affect children's learning. Societal values, school resources, quality of teaching, and parental encouragement all play important roles. Nowhere are these multiple influences more apparent than when schooling is examined in cross-cultural perspective.

Perhaps you are aware from news reports that American children fare poorly when their achievement is compared with that of children in other industrialized nations. In international studies of mathematics and science achievement, young people from Hong Kong, Japan, Korea, and Taiwan have consistently been among the top performers, whereas Americans have scored no better than at the mean and often below it (Lapointe, Askew, & Mead, 1992; Lapointe, Mead, & Askew, 1992; U. S. Department of Education, 1998).

These trends emerge early in development. In a comparison of elementary school children in Japan, Taiwan, and the United States, large differences in mathematics achievement were present in kindergarten and became greater with increasing grade. Although less extreme gaps occurred in reading, by high school both Asian groups scored better in this area as well (Stevenson, 1992; Stevenson & Lee, 1990).

Why do American children fall behind in academic accomplishments? To find out, researchers have looked closely at learning environments in top-performing Asian nations. A common assumption is that Asian children are high achievers because they are "smarter," but this is not true. Except for the influence of language on early counting skills (see page 452), they do not start school with cognitive advantages over their American peers (Geary, 1996). Instead, as the Cultural Influences box on page 476 indicates, a variety of social forces combine to foster a much stronger commitment to learning in Asian families and schools.

The Japanese and Taiwanese examples underscore that families, schools, and the larger society must work together to upgrade education. The current educational reform movement in the United States is an encouraging sign. Throughout the country, academic standards and teacher certification requirements are being strengthened. In addition, many schools are working to increase parent involvement in children's education. Parents who create stimulating learning environments at home, monitor their child's academic progress, help with homework, and communicate often with teachers have children who consistently show superior academic progress (Connors & Epstein, 1996).

The returns of these efforts can be seen in recent national assessments of educational progress (Campbell, Voelkl, & Donahue, 1997). After two decades of decline, American children's overall achievement in reading, mathematics, and science seems to be on the rise. And elementary school pupils report reading more as part of school assignments and doing more homework than they did a decade ago.

ASK YOURSELF . . .

■ *Ray is convinced that his 5-year-old son Tripper would do better in school if only Tripper's kindergarten would provide more teacher-directed lessons and worksheets and reduce the time devoted to learning-center activities. Is Ray correct? Explain.*

■ *Sandy, a parent of a third grader, wonders whether she should support her school board's decision to teach first, second, and third graders together, in mixed-age classrooms. How would you advise Sandy, and why?*

CULTURAL INFLUENCES

EDUCATION IN JAPAN, TAIWAN, AND THE UNITED STATES

Why do Asian children perform so well academically? Research examining societal, school, and family conditions in Japan, Taiwan, and the United States provides some answers.

CULTURAL VALUING OF ACADEMIC ACHIEVEMENT.

In Japan and Taiwan, natural resources are limited. Progress in science and technology is essential for economic well-being. Since a well-educated work force is necessary to meet this goal, children's mastery of academic skills is vital. In the United States, attitudes toward academic achievement are far less unified. Many Americans believe it is more important to encourage children to feel good about themselves and to explore various areas of knowledge than to perform well in school.

Japanese children achieve considerably better than their American counterparts for a variety of reasons. Their culture stresses the importance of working hard to master academic skills. Their parents help more with homework and communicate more often with teachers. And a longer school day permits frequent alternation of academic instruction with pleasurable activity. This approach makes learning easier and more enjoyable. *(Eiji Miyazawa/Black Star)*

EMPHASIS ON EFFORT.

Japanese and Taiwanese parents and teachers believe that all children have the potential to master challenging academic tasks if they work hard enough. In contrast, many more of their American counterparts regard native ability as the key to academic success (Stevenson, 1992). These differences in attitude may contribute to the fact that American parents are less inclined to encourage activities at home that might enhance school performance. Japanese and Taiwanese children spend more free time studying, reading, and playing academic-related games than do children in the United States (Stevenson & Lee, 1990). In high school, Asian students continue to devote more time to academic pursuits, whereas American students spend more time working and socializing (Fuligni & Stevenson, 1995).

INVOLVEMENT OF PARENTS IN EDUCATION.

Asian parents devote many hours to helping their children with homework. American parents spend very little time and, at least while their children are in elementary school, do not regard homework as especially important. Overall, American parents are far more satisfied with the quality of their children's education, hold lower standards for their children's academic performance, and are less concerned about how well their youngsters are doing in school (Stevenson, Chen, & Lee, 1993; Stevenson & Lee, 1990).

HIGH-QUALITY EDUCATION FOR ALL.

Unlike American teachers, Japanese and Taiwanese teachers do not make early educational decisions on the basis of achievement. There are no separate ability groups or tracks in elementary school. Instead, all pupils receive the same high-quality instruction. Academic lessons are particularly well orga-

nized and presented in ways that capture children's attention. Topics in mathematics are addressed in greater depth, and there is less repetition of material taught the previous year.

MORE TIME DEVOTED TO INSTRUCTION.

In Japan and Taiwan, the school year is over 50 days longer than in the United States. Much more of the school day is devoted to academic pursuits, especially mathematics. However, Asian schools are not regimented places, as many Americans believe. An 8-hour school day permits extra recesses and a longer lunch period, with plenty of time for play, social interaction, field trips, and extracurricular activities (Stevenson, 1992, 1994).

COMMUNICATION BETWEEN TEACHERS AND PARENTS.

Japanese and Taiwanese teachers get to know their pupils especially well. They teach the same children for 2 or 3 years and make visits to the home once or twice a year. Continuous communication between teachers and parents takes place with the aid of small notebooks that children carry back and forth every day and in which messages about assignments, academic performance, and behavior are written. No such formalized system of frequent teacher–parent communication exists in the United States (Stevenson & Lee, 1990).

Do Japanese and Taiwanese children pay a price for the pressure placed on them to succeed? By high school, academic work often displaces other experiences, since Asian adolescents must pass a highly competitive entrance exam to gain admission to college. Yet the highest performing Asian students are very well adjusted (Crystal et al., 1994). Awareness of the ingredients of Asian success has prompted Americans to rethink current educational practices.

Summary

PIAGET'S THEORY: THE CONCRETE OPERATIONAL STAGE

What are the major characteristics of concrete operational thought?

■ During the **concrete operational stage,** thought is far more logical and organized than it was during the preschool years. Mastery of conservation tasks indicates that children can **decenter** and **reverse** their thinking. In addition, they are better at hierarchical classification, **seriation,** and **transitive inference.** School-age youngsters' spatial reasoning improves, as their understanding of distance and ability to give directions reveals.

■ Concrete operational thought is limited in that children can reason logically only about concrete, tangible information; they have difficulty with abstractions. Piaget used the term **horizontal décalage** to describe the school-age child's gradual mastery of logical concepts such as conservation.

Discuss recent research on concrete operational thought.

■ Recent evidence indicates that specific cultural practices, especially those associated with schooling, affect children's mastery of Piagetian tasks. The phrasing of questions also has a profound effect on children's operational reasoning. Some theorists believe that the horizontal décalage can best be understood within an information-processing framework.

INFORMATION PROCESSING

Cite two basic changes in information processing, and describe the development of attention and memory in middle childhood.

■ Brain development contributes to gains in information-processing capacity and **inhibitory control** during the school years. These changes facilitate many aspects of information processing.

■ During middle childhood, attention becomes much more selective and adapt-

able. Attention (and memory) strategies develop in a four-step sequence; (1) **production deficiency** (failure to use the strategy); (2) **control deficiency** (failure to execute the strategy consistently); (3) **utilization deficiency** (consistent use of the strategy, but no improvement in performance); and (4) **effective strategy use.**

■ School-age children also become better at planning. On tasks requiring systematic visual search or the coordination of many acts, they are more likely to decide ahead of time how to proceed and allocate their attention accordingly.

■ Memory strategies also improve. **Rehearsal** appears first, followed by **organization** and then **elaboration.** Development of the long-term knowledge base facilitates strategic memory processing. At the same time, children's motivation to use what they know contributes to memory development. Memory strategies are promoted by learning activities in school.

Describe the school-age child's theory of mind and capacity to engage in self-regulation.

■ Metacognition expands over middle childhood. School-age children regard the mind as an active, constructive agent, and they combine their metacognitive knowledge into an integrated theory of mind.

■ School-age children are not yet good at **cognitive self-regulation**—putting what they know about thinking into action. Providing children with instructions to monitor their cognitive activity improves self-regulatory skills and task performance.

Discuss current controversies in teaching reading and mathematics to elementary school children.

■ Skilled reading draws on all aspects of the information-processing system. Experts disagree on whether a **whole-language approach** or **basic-skills approach** should be used to teach beginning reading. A mixture of both is probably most effective.

■ As with reading, instruction that combines practice in basic skills with conceptual understanding seems best in mathematics. Compared to poor math

students, good students spend more time experimenting with strategies for acquiring basic math facts. In this way, which they grapple with underlying concepts and discover which solution techniques are most effective.

INDIVIDUAL DIFFERENCES IN MENTAL DEVELOPMENT

Cite commonly used intelligence tests in middle childhood, and describe major approaches to defining intelligence.

■ During the school years, IQ becomes more stable, and it correlates well with academic achievement. Most intelligence tests yield an overall score representing general intelligence as well as scores for separate intellectual factors. Current widely used intelligence tests for children are the **Stanford-Binet Intelligence Scale** and the **Wechsler Intelligence Scale for Children–III (WISC–III).**

■ To search for the precise mental processes underlying mental ability factors, researchers have combined the factor analytic approach to defining intelligence with information processing. Findings reveal that speed of thinking and effective strategy use are related to IQ. Sternberg's **triarchic theory of intelligence** extends these efforts. It views intelligence as a complex interaction of information-processing skills, specific experiences, and contextual (or cultural) influences.

■ According to Gardner's **theory of multiple intelligences,** mental abilities should be defined in terms of distinct sets of processing operations applied in culturally valued activities. His eight independent intelligences have been helpful in efforts to understand and nurture children's special talents.

Describe evidence indicating that both heredity and environment contribute to intelligence.

■ Heritability estimates and adoption research reveal that intelligence is a product of heredity and environment. Studies of African-American children adopted

Summary (continued)

into economically well-off white homes indicate that the black–white IQ gap is substantially determined by environment.

- IQ scores are affected by specific learning experiences, including exposure to certain language customs and familiarity with the kind of knowledge sampled by the test. Cultural bias in intelligence testing can lead test scores to underestimate minority children's intelligence. By introducing purposeful teaching into the testing situation, **dynamic assessment** narrows the gap between a child's actual and potential performance.

LANGUAGE DEVELOPMENT

Describe changes in metalinguistic awareness, vocabulary, grammar, and pragmatics during middle childhood.

- During middle childhood, children develop **metalinguistic awareness,** which supports a wide range of complex language skills. Vocabulary continues to grow rapidly, and children have a more precise and flexible understanding of word meanings. Grasp of complex grammatical constructions also improves. School-age children can adapt to listeners' needs in challenging communicative situations, and their conversational strategies and narratives become more refined.

What are the advantages of bilingualism in childhood?

- Research shows that bilingual children are advanced in cognitive development. They score higher on tests of analytical reasoning, concept formation, cognitive flexibility, and metalinguistic awareness.

CHILDREN'S LEARNING IN SCHOOL

Describe the impact of class size and educational philosophies on children's motivation and academic achievement.

- Schools exert powerful influences on children's cognitive development. As class size

drops to 13 to 17 pupils, academic achievement improves. Older pupils in **traditional classrooms** have a slight edge in academic achievement. Those in **open classrooms** tend to be critical thinkers who respect individual differences and have more positive attitudes toward school. Kindergartners in traditional classrooms display more stress behaviors, followed by poorer study habits and achievement in grade school.

- Vygotsky's sociocultural theory has inspired new experiments in elementary education, including **reciprocal teaching** and the **Kamehameha Elementary Education Program (KEEP).** In each, learning experiences are rich in teacher–child and child–child collaboration, children acquire literacy skills in meaningful activities, and teaching is adapted to each child's zone of proximal development.

Discuss the role of teacher–pupil interaction and grouping practices in academic achievement.

- Patterns of teacher–pupil interaction affect children's academic progress. Instruction that encourages high-level thinking fosters children's interest and involvement.

- **Educational self-fulfilling prophecies,** in which children start to live up to the positive or negative opinions of their teachers, are most likely to occur in classrooms that emphasize competition and public evaluation, and they have a greater impact on low achievers.

- Ability grouping is linked to poorer quality instruction and a drop in self-esteem and achievement for children in low-ability groups. In contrast, mixed-age classrooms promote self-esteem and positive school attitudes, perhaps because of greater classroom harmony and opportunity for peer tutoring.

Describe learning advantages of and concerns about computers.

- Computers can have rich educational benefits. Gains in academic performance

result from computer-assisted instruction and word processing. Programming promotes a variety of complex cognitive skills. New communications technology can broaden understanding of other cultures. However, computers may be widening intellectual gaps between SES groups and the sexes.

Under what conditions is placement of mildly retarded and learning disabled children in regular classrooms successful?

- Pupils with mild **mental retardation** and **learning disabilities** are often placed in regular classrooms, usually through **mainstreaming** but also through **full inclusion.** The success of regular classroom placement depends on tailoring learning experiences to children's needs and promoting positive peer relations.

Describe the characteristics of gifted children and current efforts to meet their educational needs.

- **Giftedness** includes high IQ, creativity, and specialized talent. Tests of creativity that tap **divergent** rather than **convergent thinking** focus on only one of the complex cognitive ingredients of creativity. People usually demonstrate creativity in one or a few related areas. Highly talented children seem biologically prepared to master their domain of interest, but they also have parents and teachers who nurture their creative potential. Gifted children are best served by educational programs that build on their special strengths.

Why do American children fall behind children in other industrialized nations in academic accomplishments?

- American children fare poorly when their achievement is compared to that of children in other industrialized nations. In contrast, children from Asian nations are consistently among the top performers. A stronger commitment to learning in families and schools underlies the greater academic success of Asian pupils.

Important terms and concepts

attention-deficit hyperactivity disorder (ADHD) (p. 446)
basic-skills approach (p. 451)
cognitive self-regulation (p. 449)
concrete operational stage (p. 438)
control deficiency (p. 443)
convergent thinking (p. 473)
decentration (p. 438)
divergent thinking (p. 473)
dynamic assessment (p. 461)
educational self-fulfilling prophecy (p. 469)
effective strategy use (p. 444)
elaboration (p. 445)
full inclusion (p. 472)

giftedness (p. 473)
horizontal décalage (p. 440)
inhibitory control (p. 443)
Kamehameha Elementary Education Program (KEEP) (p. 468)
learning disabilities (p. 472)
mainstreaming (p. 471)
mental retardation (p. 472)
metalinguistic awareness (p. 462)
open classroom (p. 467)
organization (p. 445)
production deficiency (p. 443)
reciprocal teaching (p. 468)
rehearsal (p. 445)
reversibility (p. 438)

seriation (p. 439)
Stanford-Binet Intelligence Scale (p. 454)
theory of multiple intelligences (p. 457)
traditional classroom (p. 466)
transitive inference (p. 439)
triarchic theory of intelligence (p. 456)
utilization deficiency (p. 443)
Wechsler Intelligence Scale for Children–III (WISC–III) (p. 454)
whole-language approach (p. 451)

Fyi... FOR FURTHER INFORMATION AND HELP

ATTENTION-DEFICIT HYPERACTIVITY DISORDER

Children with Attention Deficit Disorders
(954) 587-3700
Website: www.chadd.org

Provides support and education to families of children with attention-deficit hyperactivity disorder. Encourages schools and health care professionals to be responsive to their needs.

BILINGUAL EDUCATION

National Association for
Bilingual Education
(202) 898-1829
Website: www.nabe.org

An organization of educators, public citizens, and students aimed at increasing public understanding of the importance of bilingual education.

MENTAL RETARDATION

Division on Mental Retardation and
Developmental Disabilities
of the Council for Exceptional Children
(404) 546-6132
Website: www.cec.sped.org

An organization of teachers of the mentally retarded aimed at advancing education, research, and public education. Publishes the journal Education and Training in Mental Retardation.

LEARNING DISABILITIES

Learning Disabilities Association
of America
(412) 341-1515
Website: www.ldanatl.org

A 60,000-member organization of parents of learning-disabled children and interested professionals. Local groups provide parent support and education and sponsor recreational programs and summer camps for children.

GIFTEDNESS

The Association for the Gifted of the
Council for Exceptional Children
(703) 620-3660
Website: www.cec.sped.org

An organization of educators and parents aimed at stimulating interest in program development for gifted children. Publishes Journal for the Education of the Gifted.

National Association for Gifted Children
(202) 785-4268
Website: www.nagc.org

Association of scholars, educators, and librarians devoted to advancing education for gifted children. Distributes information and sponsors institutes. Publishes the journal Gifted Child Quarterly.

"My Friends"
Sapan Sarad
8 years, India

As Chapter 13 reveals,
children's relationships
include a much wider social
network during middle childhood than at younger ages.
This powerful portrait conveys the vital role of friends
in school-age children's lives.

EMOTIONAL AND SOCIAL DEVELOPMENT
IN MIDDLE CHILDHOOD

ne late afternoon

Rena heard Joey dash through the front door, run upstairs, and call up his best friend Terry. "Terry, gotta talk to you," pleaded Joey, out of breath from running home. "Everything was going great until that word I got—*porcupine*," remarked Joey, referring to the fifth-grade spelling bee at school that day. "Just my luck! *P-o-r-k*, that's how I spelled it! I can't believe it. Maybe I'm not so good at social studies," Joey confided, "but I *know* I'm better at spelling than that stuck-up Belinda Brown. Gosh, I knocked myself out studying those spelling lists. Then *she* got all the easy words. Did'ya see how snooty she acted after she won? If I *had* to lose, why couldn't it be to a nice person, anyhow!"

Joey's conversation reflects a whole new constellation of emotional and social capacities. First, Joey shows evidence of *industriousness*. By entering

When Joey and Belinda Brown competed in the spelling bee, they showed evidence of industriousness by pursuing meaningful achievement in their culture. According to Erikson, developing a sense of industry is the critical psychosocial task of middle childhood. *(Charles Gupton/Stock Boston)*

industry versus inferiority
In Erikson's theory, the psychological conflict of middle childhood, which is resolved positively when experiences lead children to develop a sense of competence at useful skills and tasks.

the spelling bee, he energetically pursued meaningful achievement in his culture—a major change of the middle childhood years. At the same time, Joey's social understanding has greatly expanded. He can size up himself and others in terms of strengths, weaknesses, and personality characteristics—a capacity that was beyond him during the preschool years. Furthermore, friendship means something quite different to Joey than it did at younger ages. Terry is not just a convenient playmate; he is a best friend whom Joey counts on for understanding and emotional support.

We begin this chapter by returning to Erikson's theory for an overview of the personality changes of middle childhood. Then we take a close look at emotional and social development. We will see how, as children reason more effectively and spend more time in school and with peers, their views of themselves, of others, and of social relationships become more complex.

Although school-age children spend less time with parents than they did at earlier ages, the family remains powerfully influential. Joey and Lizzie, along with many children of their generation, are growing up in homes profoundly affected by social change. Rena, unlike her own mother, has been employed since her children were preschoolers. In addition, Joey and Lizzie's home life has been disrupted by family discord; Rena is divorced. Although family lifestyles are more diverse than ever before, Joey and Lizzie's experiences will help us appreciate that family functioning is far more important than family structure in ensuring children's well-being.

Finally, when stress is overwhelming and social support lacking, school-age children experience serious adjustment difficulties. Our chapter concludes with a discussion of some common emotional problems of middle childhood.

ERIKSON'S THEORY: INDUSTRY VERSUS INFERIORITY

According to Erikson (1950), the personality changes of the school years build on Freud's *latency stage* (see Chapter 1, page 16). Although Freud's theory is no longer widely accepted, children whose experiences with caregivers have been positive enter middle childhood with the calm confidence Freud intended by the term *latency*. Their energies are redirected from the make-believe of early childhood into realistic accomplishment.

Erikson believed that the combination of adult expectations and children's drive toward mastery sets the stage for the psychological conflict of middle childhood: **industry versus inferiority.** Industry means developing competence at useful skills and tasks. In cultures everywhere, improved physical and cognitive capacities mean that adults impose new demands. Children, in turn, are ready to meet these challenges and benefit from them:

- Among the Baka hunters and gatherers of Cameroon, 5- to 7-year-olds begin to fetch and carry water, bathe and mind younger siblings, and accompany adults on food-gathering missions. Behind the main camp stands a miniature village. In this "school" of the Baka society, children practice the arts of hut building, spear shaping, and fire making (Avis & Harris, 1991).

- The Ngoni of Malawi, Central Africa, believe that when children shed their first teeth, they are ready for a different kind of life. Between ages 6 and 7, they stop their childish games and start skill training. Boys move out of the huts of family members into dormitories, where they enter a system of male domination and instruction. At that time, children are expected to show independence and are held personally accountable for irresponsible and disrespectful behavior (Read, 1968; Rogoff, 1996).

In industrialized nations, the transition to middle childhood is marked by the beginning of formal schooling. With it comes literacy training, which provides the widest possible preparation for the vast array of specialized careers in complex societies. In school, children engage in productive work beside and with other children. They become aware of their own and others' unique capacities, learn the value of division of labor, and develop a sense of moral commitment and responsibility. The danger at this stage is *inferiority,* reflected in the sad pessimism of some children who have little confidence in their ability to do things well. This sense of inadequacy can develop when family life has not prepared children for school life or when experiences with teachers and peers are so negative that they undermine children's feelings of competence and mastery.

Erikson's sense of industry combines several developments of middle childhood: a positive but realistic self-concept, pride in accomplishment, moral responsibility, and cooperative participation with agemates. Let's look at how these aspects of self and social relationships change over the school years.

SELF-DEVELOPMENT

*I*n middle childhood, several transformations in self-understanding take place. First, children can describe themselves in terms of psychological traits. Second, they start to compare their own characteristics to those of their peers. Finally, they speculate about the causes of their strengths and weaknesses. These ways of thinking about the self have a major impact on children's self-esteem.

CHANGES IN SELF-CONCEPT

During the school years, children develop a much more refined *me-self,* or self-concept, organizing their observations of behaviors and internal states into general dispositions, with a major change taking place between ages 8 and 11. The following responses of two children, who were asked to tell about themselves, reflect this change:

A boy age 7: I am 7 and I have hazel brown hair and my hobby is stamp collecting. I am good at football and I am quite good at sums and my favorite game is football and I love school and I like reading books and my favorite car is an Austin. (Livesley & Bromley, 1973, p. 237)

A girl age 11½: My name is A. I'm a human being. I'm a girl. I'm a truthful person. I'm not pretty. I do so-so in my studies. I'm a very good cellist. I'm a very good pianist. I'm a little bit tall for my age. I like several boys. I like several girls. I'm old-fashioned. I play tennis. I am a very good swimmer. I try to be helpful. I'm always ready to be friends with anybody. Mostly I'm good, but I lose my temper. I'm not well liked by some girls and boys. I don't know if I'm liked by boys or not. (Montemayor & Eisen, 1977, pp. 317–318)

Notice that instead of specific behaviors, school-age children emphasize competencies, as in "I am quite good at sums" or "I'm a very good cellist" (Damon & Hart, 1988). In addition, the younger of the two children does not refer to any psychological traits, whereas the older one clearly describes her personality, noting that she is truthful, old-fashioned, helpful, friendly, and short-tempered. And she acknowledges the existence of both positive and negative attributes—"truthful" but "not pretty," a "good cellist [and] pianist" but only "so-so in my studies." Unlike their younger counterparts, older school-age children are far less likely to describe themselves in all-or-none ways (Harter, 1996).

Another change in self-concept takes place in middle childhood: Children begin to make **social comparisons.** They judge their appearance, abilities, and behavior in relation to those of others. In his comments about the spelling bee, Joey expressed some thoughts about how good he was compared to Belinda Brown—better at spelling but not so great

social comparisons
Judgments of appearance, abilities, behavior, and other characteristics in relation to those of others.

at social studies. Children younger than 7 practically never include social comparisons in their self-descriptions (Ruble & Frey, 1991).

COGNITIVE, SOCIAL, AND CULTURAL INFLUENCES ON SELF-CONCEPT

What factors are responsible for these revisions in self-concept? Cognitive development certainly affects the changing *structure* of the self. School-age children, as we saw in Chapter 12, are better at coordinating several aspects of a situation in reasoning about their physical world. They show an improved ability to relate separate observations in the social realm as well. Consequently, they combine typical experiences and behaviors into stable psychological dispositions and blend positive and negative characteristics into a consistent picture (Harter, 1996, 1998).

The changing *content* of self-concept is a product of both cognitive capacities and feedback from others. Early in this century, sociologist George Herbert Mead (1934) described the self as a blend of what important people in our lives think of us. He believed that a well-organized psychological self emerges when the child's *I-self* adopts a view of the *me-self* that resembles the attitude of significant others. In other words, *perspective-taking* skills emerging during middle childhood—in particular, the ability to imagine what other people are thinking—play a crucial role in the development of a psychological self. Indeed, as we will see later in this chapter, perspective taking improves greatly over the school years. Children become better at "reading" messages they receive from others and incorporating these into their self-definitions.

During middle childhood, children look to more people for information about themselves as they enter a wider range of settings in school and community. This is reflected in children's frequent reference to social groups in their self-descriptions (Livesley & Bromley, 1973). "I'm a Boy Scout, a paper boy, and a Prairie City soccer player," Joey remarked when asked to describe himself. Gradually, as children move toward adolescence, their sources of self-definition become more selective. Although parents remain influential, between ages 8 and 15 peers become more important. And over time, self-concept becomes increasingly vested in feedback from close friends (Rosenberg, 1979).

Keep in mind, however, that the changes just described are based on interviews with North American and Western European children. Other evidence indicates that development of self-concept does not follow the same path in all societies. In collectivist cultures, the self and social group are not differentiated so completely. Recall from earlier chapters that Asian parents stress harmonious interdependence, whereas Western parents emphasize the person's separateness and uniqueness. Consequently, in China and Japan, the self is defined in relation to the social group. In the United States, the self usually becomes the "property" of a self-contained individual (Markus & Kitayama, 1991).

A strong collectivist theme is also reflected in the values of many subcultures in Western nations. In one study, the self-descriptions of children in a Puerto Rican fishing village were compared with those of children in an American town. The Puerto Rican children more often described themselves as "polite," "nice," "respectful," and "obedient" and justified these social traits by noting the positive reactions they evoke from others. In contrast, the small-town children more often mentioned individualistic traits, such as interests, preferences, and skills (Damon & Hart, 1988).

DEVELOPMENT OF SELF-ESTEEM

Self-esteem, the judgments children make about their own worth, is also reorganized in middle childhood. Recall from Chapter 10 that most preschoolers have extremely high self-esteem. As children enter school, they get much more feedback about their performance in different activities compared with that of their peers. Grades on papers and tests, report cards, and the comments of adults and other children are integrated into self-

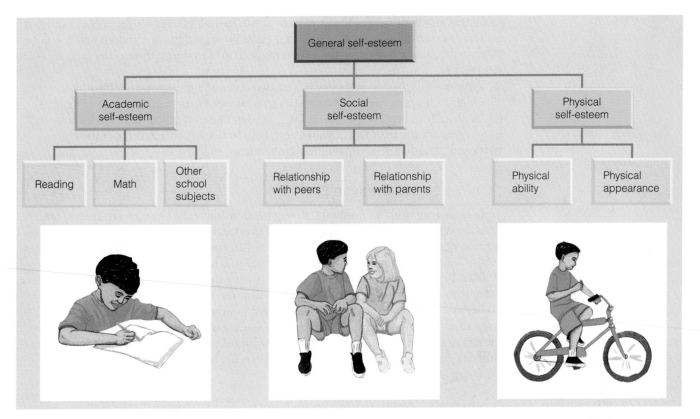

FIGURE **13.1**

Hierarchical structure of self-esteem in the mid-elementary school years. From their experiences in different settings, children form at least three separate self-esteems—academic, social, and physical. These differentiate into additional self-evaluations and combine to form an overall sense of self-worth.

evaluations. As a result, self-esteem differentiates, and it also adjusts to a more realistic level (Stipek & Mac Iver, 1989).

■ **A HIERARCHICALLY STRUCTURED SELF-ESTEEM.** Susan Harter (1982, 1986) asked children to indicate the extent to which a variety of statements, such as "I am good at homework," "I'm usually the one chosen for games," and "Most kids like me," are true of themselves. Her findings, and those of other researchers, reveal that classrooms, playgrounds, and peer groups are key contexts in which children evaluate their own competence. By age 7 to 8, children have formed at least three separate self-esteems—academic, social, and physical—that become more refined with age. For example, academic self-worth divides into performance in different school subjects, social self-worth into peer and parental relationships (Marsh, 1990).

Furthermore, school-age children's newfound ability to view themselves in terms of stable dispositions permits them to combine their separate self-evaluations into a general psychological image of themselves—an overall sense of self-esteem (Harter, 1990, 1998). Consequently, by the mid-elementary school years, self-esteem takes on the hierarchical structure shown in Figure 13.1. Separate self-evaluations, however, do not contribute equally to general self-esteem. Instead, as children attach greater importance to some aspects, those self-judgments are weighted more heavily in the total picture.

■ **CHANGES IN LEVEL OF SELF-ESTEEM.** As children evaluate themselves in various areas, they lose the sunny optimism of early childhood. Self-esteem drops during the first few years of elementary school (Stipek & Mac Iver, 1989). This decline can be explained by the fact that children gradually adjust their self-judgments to fit the opinions of others as well as their performance in relation to agemates. In one study, kindergartners through third graders were asked to rate their own and each of their classmates' "smartness" at school. Even the youngest children were able to judge their peers fairly accurately. But their own self-ratings were overly favorable; most kindergartners and first graders placed themselves at the top of the class! By second grade, children had begun to make social comparisons, and their self-esteem tended to match these observations (Stipek, 1981).

Typically, this drop in self-esteem is not great enough to be harmful. Most (but not all) children appraise their characteristics and competencies realistically while maintaining an attitude of self-acceptance and self-respect. Then, from fourth to sixth grade, self-esteem rises for the majority of youngsters, who feel especially good about their peer relationships and athletic capabilities (Nottelmann, 1987).

INFLUENCES ON SELF-ESTEEM

Beginning in middle childhood, strong relationships exist between self-esteem and everyday behavior. For example, academic self-esteem predicts children's school achievement as well as their willingness to try hard at challenging tasks (Marsh, Smith, & Barnes, 1985). Children with high social self-esteem are consistently better liked by their peers (Harter, 1982). And as we saw in Chapter 11, boys come to believe they have more athletic talent than do girls, and they are also more advanced in a variety of physical skills.

Because self-esteem is so powerfully related to individual differences in behavior, researchers have been intensely interested in finding out exactly which social influences cause it to be high for some children and low for others. If ways can be found to improve children's sense of self-worth, then many aspects of child development might be enhanced as well.

The collectivist orientation of these Puerto Rican fishing-village children leads them to define themselves and their self-worth in terms of connectedness to others. Consequently, they almost never mention social comparisons in their self-evaluations. *(Will Faller)*

■ **CULTURE.** As with self-concept, cultural forces profoundly affect self-esteem. For example, the strong role of social comparison in self-evaluation does not characterize children everywhere. Puerto Rican fishing-village children, mentioned earlier, almost never make social comparisons, either in their self-descriptions or everyday conversations. Yet among American children, such comments as "I'm better at kickball than he is" and "How many math problems did you get right?" are common (Damon & Hart, 1988).

An even stronger emphasis on social comparison in school may underlie the finding that Japanese and Taiwanese children score lower in self-esteem than do American children, despite their higher academic achievement (Chiu, 1992–1993; Hawkins, 1994). In Asian classrooms, competition is tough and achievement pressure is high. At the same time, Asian children less often call on social comparisons to bolster their own self-esteem. Because their culture places a high value on modesty and social harmony, they tend to be reserved about judging themselves positively but generous in their praise of others (Heine & Lehman, 1995; Falbo et al., 1997).

■ **CHILD-REARING PRACTICES.** School-age children whose parents are warm and responsive and who provide firm but reasonable expectations for behavior—that is, who use an *authoritative* child-rearing style (see Chapter 10)—feel especially good about themselves (Bishop & Ingersoll, 1989; Lord, Eccles, & McCarthy, 1994). If you think carefully about this finding, you will see that it makes perfect sense. Warm, positive parenting lets children know that they are accepted as competent, worthwhile human beings. And firm but appropriate expectations, backed up with explanations, seem to help children make sensible choices and evaluate their own behavior against reasonable standards.

In contrast, highly coercive parenting communicates a sense of inadequacy to children. It tells them that their behavior needs to be controlled by adults because they cannot manage it themselves. And indulgent parenting that promotes a "feel good" attitude no matter how children behave creates a false sense of self-esteem. Sooner or later, such children begin to doubt their self-worth (Damon, 1995).

Although parental warmth and maturity demands are undoubtedly important ingredients of high self-esteem, we must keep in mind that these findings are correlational. We cannot really tell the extent to which child-rearing styles are causes of or reactions to children's characteristics and behavior. Research on the precise content of adults' messages to children has been far more successful at isolating factors that affect children's sense of self-worth. Let's see how these messages mold children's evaluations of themselves in achievement contexts.

■ **MAKING ACHIEVEMENT-RELATED ATTRIBUTIONS.** **Attributions** are our common, everyday explanations for the causes of behavior—the answers we provide to the question, "Why did I (or another person) do that?" Look back at Joey's conversation about the spelling bee at the beginning of this chapter. Notice how he attributes his second-place performance to *luck* (Belinda got all the easy words) and his usual success at spelling to *ability* (he knows he's a better speller than Belinda). Joey also appreciates that *effort* makes a difference; he "knocked himself out studying those spelling words."

This second grader works on a paper maché globe with effort and determination. Adult communication—specifically, the extent to which his parents and teachers implicate effort when he fails and express confidence in his ability to overcome obstacles and succeed—contribute to his mastery-oriented approach to learning. *(Charles Thatcher/ Tony Stone Images)*

Cognitive development permits school-age children to recognize and separate all these variables in explaining performance (Skinner, 1995). Yet they differ greatly in how they account for their successes and failures. Children who are high in academic self-esteem develop **mastery-oriented attributions**. They believe their successes are due to ability—a characteristic they can improve through trying hard and can count on in the future when faced with new challenges. And they attribute failure to factors that can be changed and controlled, such as insufficient effort or a very difficult task. So regardless of whether these children succeed or fail, they take an industrious, persistent, and enthusiastic approach to learning (Dweck & Leggett, 1988).

Unfortunately, children who develop **learned helplessness** hold very discouraging explanations for their performance. They attribute their failures, not their successes, to ability. When they succeed, they are likely to conclude that external factors, such as luck, are responsible. Furthermore, unlike their mastery-oriented counterparts, learned-helpless children have come to believe that ability is fixed and cannot be changed (Cain & Dweck, 1995). They do not think that competence can be improved by trying hard. So when a task is difficult, these children experience an anxious loss of control—in Erikson's terms, a pervasive sense of inferiority. They quickly give up, saying "I can't do this," before they have really tried.

Over time, the ability of learned-helpless children no longer predicts their performance. Many are very bright pupils who have concluded that they are incompetent (Wagner & Phillips, 1992). Because they fail to make the connection between effort and success, learned-helpless children do not develop the metacognitive and self-regulatory skills that are necessary for high achievement (see Chapter 12). Lack of effective learning strategies, reduced persistence, and a sense of being controlled by external forces sustain one another in a vicious cycle (Heyman & Dweck, 1992).

■ **INFLUENCES ON ACHIEVEMENT-RELATED ATTRIBUTIONS.** What accounts for the very different attributions of mastery-oriented and learned-helpless children? Adult communication plays a key role. Children with a learned-helpless style tend to have parents who set unusually high standards yet believe their child is not very capable and has to work much harder than others to succeed (Parsons, Adler, & Kaczala, 1982; Phillips, 1987). When these children fail, the adult might say, "You can't do that, can you? It's okay if you quit" (Hokoda & Fincham, 1995). And when the child succeeds, the adult might respond, "Gee, I'm surprised you got that A."

attributions
Common, everyday explanations for the causes of behavior.

mastery-oriented attributions
Attributions that credit success to high ability and failure to insufficient effort. Leads to high self-esteem and a willingness to approach challenging tasks.

learned helplessness
Attributions that credit success to luck and failure to low ability. Leads to anxious loss of control in the face of challenging tasks.

Because their classrooms emphasize mastery and cooperation rather than ability and competition, Israeli children growing up on kibbutzim are shielded from learned helplessness. *(Wolf/Monkmeyer Press)*

In one study, researchers manipulated the feedback that fourth and fifth graders received after they failed at a task. Those receiving negative messages about their competence more often attributed failure to lack of ability than did children who were told that they had not tried hard enough (Dweck et al., 1978).

Some children are especially likely to have their performance undermined by adult feedback. Girls more often than boys blame their ability for poor performance. Girls also tend to receive messages from teachers and parents that their ability is at fault when they do not do well (Ruble & Martin, 1998). Low-income ethnic minority children are also vulnerable to learned helplessness. In several studies, African-American and Mexican-American children received less favorable teacher feedback than did other children (Aaron & Powell, 1982; Irvine, 1986; Losey, 1995). Furthermore, when ethnic minority children observe that adults in their own family are not rewarded by society for their achievement efforts, they may give up themselves. Many African-American children may come to believe that even if they do try in school, social prejudice will prevent them from succeeding in the end (Ogbu, 1988).

Finally, cultural values for achievement affect the likelihood that children will develop learned helplessness. Recall from Chapter 12 that compared to Americans, Japanese and Taiwanese parents and teachers believe that success in school depends much more on effort than ability—a message they transmit to children (Tuss, Zimmer, & Ho, 1995). And Israeli children growing up on cooperative agricultural settlements called kibbutzim are shielded from learned helplessness by classrooms that emphasize mastery and cooperation rather than ability and competition. When asked why children look at each other's work at school, kibbutz third graders more often give a mastery-related reason ("You need to be sure what you're supposed to do, so you might check"). In contrast, urban Israeli third graders are likely to make a social comparison assessing ability ("You'd want to see if someone else's picture is better than yours") (Butler & Ruzany, 1993).

■ **SUPPORTING CHILDREN'S SELF-ESTEEM.** Attribution research suggests that even adults who are, on the whole, warm and supportive may send subtle messages to children that undermine their competence. **Attribution retraining** is an approach to intervention that encourages learned-helpless children to believe that they can overcome failure by exerting more effort. Most often, children are asked to work on tasks that are hard enough that they will experience some failure. Then they get repeated feedback that helps them revise their attributions, such as "You can do it if you try harder." Children are also taught to view their successes as due to both ability and effort rather than chance factors, by giving them additional feedback after they succeed, such as "You're really good at this" or "You really tried hard on that one" (Schunk, 1983).

Another approach is to encourage low-effort children to focus less on grades and more on mastery for its own sake. A large-scale study showed that classrooms emphasizing the intrinsic value of acquiring new knowledge led to impressive gains in failing pupils' academic self-esteem and motivation (Ames, 1992). Learned-helpless children also need instruction in metacognition and self-regulation to make up for development lost in this area and to ensure that renewed effort will pay off (Borkowski & Methukrisna, 1995).

To work well, attribution retraining is best begun in middle childhood, before children's views of themselves become hard to change (Eccles, Wigfield, & Schiefele, 1998).

attribution retraining
An approach to intervention in which attributions of learned-helpless children are modified through feedback that encourages them to believe in themselves and persist in the face of task difficulty.

CAREGIVING CONCERNS

Fostering a Mastery-Oriented Approach to Learning and Preventing Learned Helplessness

Provision of tasks	Select tasks that are meaningful, responsive to a diversity of pupil interests, and appropriately matched to current competence so the child is challenged but not overwhelmed.
Parent and teacher encouragement	Communicate warmth, confidence in the child's abilities, the value of achievement, and the importance of effort in success.
	Model high effort in overcoming failure.
	(For teachers) Communicate often with parents, suggesting ways to foster children's effort and progress.
	(For parents) Monitor schoolwork; provide scaffolded assistance that promotes knowledge of effective strategies and and self-regulation.
Performance evaluations	Make evaluations private; avoid publicizing success or failure through wall posters, stars, privileges to "smart" children, and prizes for "best" performance.
	Stress individual progress and self-improvement.
School environment	Offer small classes, which permit teachers to provide individualized support for mastery.
	Provide for cooperative learning and peer tutoring, in which children assist each other; avoid ability grouping, which makes evaluations of children's progress public.
	Accommodate individual and cultural differences in styles of learning.
	Create an atmosphere that values academics and sends a clear message to teachers, parents, and children that all pupils can learn.

Sources: Ames, 1992; Eccles, Wigfield, & Schiefele, 1998.

An even better approach is to prevent low self-esteem before it happens. The Caregiving Concerns table above lists ways to foster a mastery-oriented approach to learning and prevent learned helplessness in middle childhood.

BRIEF REVIEW

Erikson's stage of industry versus inferiority indicates that when family, school, and peer experiences are positive, school-age children develop an industrious approach to productive work and feelings of competence and mastery. During middle childhood, psychological traits and social comparisons appear in children's self-descriptions. A differentiated, hierarchically organized self-esteem emerges, and children's sense of self-worth declines as they adjust their self-judgments to fit the opinions of others and objective performance. Parental warmth and reasonable maturity demands are related to high self-esteem. In contrast, coercive and indulgent parenting practices undermine children's sense of self-worth. Attribution research has identified adult messages that affect children's explanations for success and failure and, in turn, their academic self-esteem, motivation, and task performance.

ASK YOURSELF . . .

■ *Asked to describe herself, 9-year-old Diane responded, "I'm pretty friendly and nice. Also, mostly I'm smart. I do well in language and science, but I feel pretty dumb in social studies, particularly when I see how well the other kids are doing. I still like myself as a person, though." How does Diane's self-description illustrate changes in self-concept during middle childhood?*

■ *In view of Joey's attributions for his spelling bee performance, is he likely to enter the next spelling bee and try hard to do well? Why or why not?*

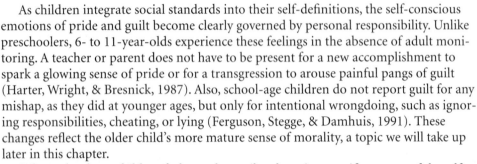

EMOTIONAL DEVELOPMENT

Greater self-awareness and social sensitivity support emotional development in middle childhood. Gains take place in children's experiencing of self-conscious emotions, understanding of emotional states, and emotional self-regulation.

SELF-CONSCIOUS EMOTIONS

As children integrate social standards into their self-definitions, the self-conscious emotions of pride and guilt become clearly governed by personal responsibility. Unlike preschoolers, 6- to 11-year-olds experience these feelings in the absence of adult monitoring. A teacher or parent does not have to be present for a new accomplishment to spark a glowing sense of pride or for a transgression to arouse painful pangs of guilt (Harter, Wright, & Bresnick, 1987). Also, school-age children do not report guilt for any mishap, as they did at younger ages, but only for intentional wrongdoing, such as ignoring responsibilities, cheating, or lying (Ferguson, Stegge, & Damhuis, 1991). These changes reflect the older child's more mature sense of morality, a topic we will take up later in this chapter.

When school-age children feel proud or guilty, they view specific aspects of the self as leading to success or failure, as in "I tried hard on that difficult task, and it paid off" (pride) or "I made a mistake, and now I have to deal with it" (guilt). Shame is often felt when violating a standard is not under one's control. For example, Lizzie felt ashamed when she dropped a spoonful of spaghetti at lunch time and had a large spot on her shirt for the rest of the school day. But as children develop an overall sense of self-esteem, they may experience shame after a controllable breach of standards if the self-as-a-whole is blamed for it. For example, the child who does poorly on a test and whose teacher or parent reprimands him ("Everyone else can do it! Why can't you?") may hang his head in shame while repeating to himself, "I'm stupid!" (Mascolo & Fischer, 1995).

Pride motivates children to take on further challenges. And guilt prompts them to make amends and strive for self-improvement as well. Of course, excessive guilt (as we saw in Chapter 10) undermines children's well-being. But profound feelings of shame are particularly destructive. They involve taking a single unworthy act to be the whole of self-worth, setting up maladaptive responses of passive retreat or intense anger at others who participated in the shame-evoking situation (Lindsay-Hartz, de Rivera, & Mascolo, 1995; Reimer, 1996).

EMOTIONAL UNDERSTANDING

School-age children's understanding of psychological dispositions means that they are likely to explain emotion by making reference to internal states rather than physical events, as they did at younger ages (Strayer, 1993). They are also more aware of the diversity of emotional experiences. By age 8, children realize that they can experience more than one emotion at a time, each of which may be positive or negative and may differ in intensity (Harter & Buddin, 1987; Wintre & Vallance, 1994). For example, recalling the birthday present he received from his grandmother, Joey reflected, "I was very happy I got something but a little sad that I didn't get just what I wanted."

Similarly, Joey appreciates that emotional reactions need not reflect a person's true feelings. Consequently, he is much better at hiding his emotions when it is socially appropriate to do so (Saarni, 1997). "I got all excited and told Grandma I liked that dumb plastic toy train," Joey said to Rena one day, "but I really don't. It's too babyish for a 10-year-old."

School-age children may experience shame that weakens their overall sense of self-esteem. After failing a test and being reprimanded by his teacher, this boy hangs his head and is probably saying to himself, "I'm no good and stupid" —thoughts and feelings that are destructive to his development. (MacDonald Photography/Envision)

Along with a more complex understanding of one's own feelings comes the ability to take more information into account in detecting the emotions of others. School-age children can reconcile contradictory facial and situational cues in figuring out another's feelings. Recall that preschoolers rely only on the emotional expression (see Chapter 10, page 371). Furthermore, older children can use information about a person's past experiences to predict how he or she will feel in a new situation. They realize, for example, that a child rejected by her best friend will probably feel sad at later meeting the friend. Younger children rely only on the current situation, saying, "She'll be happy to see her friend" (Gnepp, 1989).

As with self-understanding, gains in emotional understanding are supported by cognitive development and social experiences, especially adults' sensitivity to children's feelings and willingness to discuss emotions. Together, these factors contribute to a rise in empathy as well (Ricard & Kamberk-Kilicci, 1995). The greater school-age children's perspective-taking skill and recognition and acceptance of their own feelings, the more likely they are to respond empathically. Empathy, in turn, continues to predict prosocial behavior in middle childhood (Roberts & Strayer, 1996).

As children move closer to adolescence, advances in perspective taking permit an empathic response not just to people's immediate distress, but also to their general life condition (Hoffman, 1991). As Joey and Lizzie imagined how people who are chronically ill or hungry feel and evoked those emotions in themselves, their prosocial acts expanded further. They gave part of their allowance to charity and joined in fundraising projects through school, church, and scouting organizations.

EMOTIONAL SELF-REGULATION

Rapid gains in emotional self-regulation occur in middle childhood. As children engage in social comparison, they more often encounter distressing circumstances in which they must manage negative emotion that threatens their sense of self.

By age 10, most children have an adaptive set of techniques for regulating emotion (Kliewer, Fearnow, & Miller, 1996). In situations where they have some control over an outcome (an anxiety-provoking test at the end of the week or a friend who is angry at them), they view problem solving and seeking social support as the best strategies. When outcomes are beyond their control (having received a bad grade or awaiting a painful injection at the doctor's office), they opt for distraction or redefining the situation in ways that help them accept current conditions ("Things could be worse. There'll be another test"). And older children seem to know that complete avoidance of negative feelings— by leaving the scene or going to sleep—is usually counterproductive (Aldwin, 1994; Compas, Phares, & Ledoux, 1989).

Cognitive development and a wider range of social experiences contribute to flexible coping strategies. When the development of emotional self-regulation has gone along well, school-age children acquire a sense of *emotional self-efficacy*—a feeling of being in control of their emotional experience (Saarni, 1997). This fosters a favorable self-image and an optimistic outlook, which assists them further in the face of emotional challenges.

Emotionally well-regulated children are generally upbeat in mood, more empathic and prosocial, and better liked by their peers. In contrast, poorly regulated children are overwhelmed by negative emotion, a response that interferes with prosocial behavior and peer acceptance. Girls with weak self-regulatory skills tend to freeze with anxiety, whereas boys more often lash out with hostility (Eisenberg, Fabes, & Losoya, 1997). Recall from previous chapters that temperament and quality of parenting influence emotional self-regulation. We will revisit these

During the school years, children show gains in empathy as they become better at detecting the thoughts and feelings of others and imagining themselves in another's place. Empathy continues to predict prosocial behavior. *(Susan Johns/Photo Researchers)*

themes later in this chapter when we take up peer acceptance and children's ability to cope with stressful family circumstances.

UNDERSTANDING OTHERS

Already we have seen that middle childhood brings major advances in **perspective taking**—the capacity to imagine what other people may be thinking and feeling. Now let's take a close look at these changes, which support self-development, understanding of others, and a wide variety of social skills.

SELMAN'S STAGES OF PERSPECTIVE TAKING

Robert Selman developed a five-stage model of children's perspective-taking skill by asking preschool through adolescent youngsters to respond to social dilemmas in which characters have differing information and opinions about an event. Here is an example:

> Holly is an 8-year-old girl who likes to climb trees. She is the best tree climber in the neighborhood. One day while climbing down from a tall tree she falls off the bottom branch but does not hurt herself. Her father sees her fall. He is upset and asks her to promise not to climb the trees anymore. Holly promises.
>
> Later that day, Holly and her friends meet Sean. Sean's kitten is caught up in a tree and cannot get down. Something has to be done right away or the kitten may fall. Holly is the only one who climbs trees well enough to reach the kitten and get it down, but she remembers her promise to her father. (Selman & Byrne, 1974, p. 805)

After the dilemma is presented, children answer questions that highlight their ability to interpret the story from varying points of view, such as

> Does Sean know why Holly cannot decide whether or not to climb the tree?
>
> What will Holly's father think? Will he understand if she climbs the tree?
>
> Does Holly think she will be punished for climbing the tree? Should she be punished for doing so?

Table 13.1 summarizes Selman's five stages of perspective taking. As you can see, children gradually include a wider range of information in their understanding of others' viewpoints. At first, they have only a limited idea of what other people might be thinking and feeling. Over time, they become more conscious of the fact that people can interpret the same event in quite different ways. Soon they can "step in another person's shoes" and reflect on how that person might regard their own thoughts, feelings, and behavior. Finally, they can examine the relationship between two people's perspectives simultaneously, at first from the vantage point of a disinterested spectator and later by making reference to societal values.

Both cross-sectional and longitudinal research provides support for Selman's stages (Gurucharri & Selman, 1982; Selman, 1980). Even so, perspective-taking skill differs greatly among children of the same age. These individual differences are due to variations in cognitive maturity as well as everyday experiences in which adults and peers clarify their viewpoints, encouraging children to look at situations from another's perspective (Dixon & Moore, 1990; Krebs & Gillmore, 1982).

perspective taking
The capacity to imagine what other people may be thinking and feeling.

TABLE 13.1

Selman's Stages of Perspective Taking

STAGE	APPROXIMATE AGE RANGE	DESCRIPTION	TYPICAL RESPONSE TO "HOLLY" DILEMMA
Level 0: Undifferentiated perspective taking	3–6	Children recognize that self and other can have different thoughts and feelings, but they frequently confuse the two.	The child predicts that Holly will save the kitten because she does not want it to get hurt and believes that Holly's father will feel just as she does about her climbing the tree: "Happy, he likes kittens."
Level 1: Social-informational perspective taking	4–9	Children understand that different perspectives may result because people have access to different information.	When asked how Holly's father will react when he finds out that she climbed the tree, the child responds, "If he didn't know anything about the kitten, he would be angry. But if Holly shows him the kitten, he might change his mind."
Level 2: Self-reflective perspective taking	7–12	Children can "step into another person's shoes" and view their own thoughts, feelings, and behavior from the other person's perspective. They also recognize that others can do the same.	When asked whether Holly thinks she will be punished, the child says, "No. Holly knows that her father will understand why she climbed the tree." This response assumes that Holly's point of view is influenced by her father being able to "step in her shoes" and understand why she saved the kitten.
Level 3: Third-party perspective taking	10–15	Children can step outside a two-person situation and imagine how the self and other are viewed from the viewpoint of a third, impartial party.	When asked whether Holly should be punished, the child says, "No, because Holly thought it was important to save the kitten. But she also knows that her father told her not to climb the tree. So she'd think she shouldn't be punished only if she could get her father to understand why she had to climb the tree." This response steps outside the immediate situation to view both Holly's and her father's perspectives simultaneously.
Level 4: Societal perspective taking	14–adult	Individuals understand that third-party perspective taking can be influenced by one or more systems of larger societal values.	When asked if Holly should be punished, the individual responds, "No. The value of humane treatment of animals justifies Holly's action. Her father's appreciation of this value will lead him not to punish her."

Sources: Selman, 1976; Selman & Byrne, 1974.

PERSPECTIVE TAKING AND SOCIAL BEHAVIOR

Perspective taking is related to a wide variety of social skills in middle childhood. Good perspective takers are more likely to display empathy, and they are better at *social problem solving*, or thinking of effective ways to handle difficult social situations (Marsh, Serafica, & Barenboim, 1981). In fact, once children are capable of self-reflective perspective taking (see Table 13.1), they often rely on it to clear up everyday misunderstandings. For example, one day when Joey teased Terry in a friendly way, Terry took offense. Joey made use of advanced perspective taking to patch things up. "Terry, I didn't mean it," he explained, "I *thought you would think* I was just kidding when I said that."

Children with very poor social skills—in particular, the angry, aggressive styles that we discussed in Chapter 10—have great difficulty imagining the thoughts and feelings of others. They often mistreat adults and peers without feeling the guilt and remorse engendered by awareness of another's viewpoint. Interventions that provide these children with coaching and practice in perspective taking are helpful in reducing antisocial behavior and increasing empathy and prosocial responding (Chalmers & Townsend, 1990; Chandler, 1973).

MORAL DEVELOPMENT

Recall from Chapter 10 that preschoolers pick up a great many morally relevant behaviors through modeling and reinforcement. By middle childhood, they have had time to reflect on these experiences, putting them together into rules for good conduct, such as "It's good to help others in trouble" or "It's wrong to take something that doesn't belong to you." Consequently, school-age children are not as dependent on modeling and reinforcement as they were at younger ages. They can follow internalized standards.

These changes lead children to become considerably more independent and trustworthy. During middle childhood, they can take on many more responsibilities, including household chores, running errands in the neighborhood, and watching over younger siblings (Weisner, 1996). Of course, these advances take place only when children have had much time to profit from the consistent guidance and example of caring adults in their lives.

In Chapter 10, we also saw that children do not just copy their morality from those around them. As the cognitive-developmental approach emphasizes, from an early age they actively think about right and wrong. Children's expanding social world and perspective-taking skill lead moral understanding to improve greatly in middle childhood.

These five school-age children have figured out how to divide up two pizzas fairly among themselves. Already, they have a well-developed sense of distributive justice. *(Will Faller)*

LEARNING ABOUT JUSTICE THROUGH SHARING

In everyday life, children frequently experience situations that involve **distributive justice**—beliefs about how to divide up material goods fairly. Heated discussions often take place over how much weekly allowance is to be given to siblings of different ages, who has to sit where in the family car on a long trip, and in what way an eight-slice pizza is to be shared by six hungry playmates. William Damon (1977, 1988) has studied children's changing concepts of distributive justice over early and middle childhood.

Preschoolers recognize the importance of sharing, but their reasons for doing so often seem contradictory and self-serving: "I shared because if I didn't, she wouldn't play with me" or "I let her have some, but most are for me because I'm older." As children enter middle childhood, they start to express more mature notions of distributive justice (see Table 13.2). At first, their ideas of fairness are based on *equality*. Children in the early school grades are intent on making sure that each person gets the same amount of a treasured resource, such as money, turns in a game, or a delicious treat.[1]

distributive justice
Beliefs about how to divide up material goods fairly.

---

[1]Recall from Chapter 12 that in some cultures, equal sharing of goods among children is not common, and conservation is greatly delayed (see page 440). It is possible that Damon's sequence of distributive justice reasoning does not represent children's concepts of fairness in all societies.

TABLE 13.2

Damon's Sequence of Distributive Justice Reasoning

BASIS OF REASONING	AGE	DESCRIPTION
Equality	5–6	Fairness involves strictly equal distribution of goods. Special considerations, such as merit and need, are not taken into account.
Merit	6–7	Fairness is based on deservingness. Children recognize that some people should get more because they have worked harder.
Benevolence	8	Fairness includes giving special consideration to those who are disadvantaged. More should be given to those who are in need.

Sources: Damon, 1977, 1988.

A short time later, children start to view fairness in terms of *merit*. Extra rewards should be given to someone who has worked especially hard or otherwise performed in an exceptional way. Finally, around 8 years, children can reason on the basis of *benevolence*. They recognize that special consideration should be given to those who are at a disadvantage, like the needy or the disabled. Older children indicate that an extra amount might be given to a child who cannot produce as much or who does not get any allowance from his parents. They also adapt their basis of fairness to the situation—for example, relying more on merit when interacting with strangers and more on benevolence when interacting with friends (McGillicuddy-De Lisi, Watkins, & Vinchur, 1994).

According to Damon (1988), parental advice and encouragement support these developing standards of justice, but the give-and-take of peer interaction is especially important. Peer disagreements, along with efforts to resolve them, make children more sensitive to others' perspectives, and this supports their developing ideas of fairness (Kruger, 1993). Advanced distributive justice reasoning, in turn, is associated with more effective social problem solving and a greater willingness to help and share with others (Blotner & Bearison, 1984; McNamee & Peterson, 1986).

CHANGES IN MORAL AND SOCIAL-CONVENTIONAL UNDERSTANDING

As their ideas about justice advance, children clarify and create linkages between moral rules and social conventions. During middle childhood, they realize that the two can overlap. Sometimes violations of social conventions are moral matters! For example, saying "thank you" after receiving a present is an arbitrary practice arrived at by social agreement. Yet not doing so can injure others by hurting their feelings (Turiel, 1983). School-age children are also aware that people whose knowledge differs may not be equally responsible for moral transgressions. They say that a parent who spanks a child in a country where everyone believes that corporal punishment scares away evil spirits that make children misbehave is less to blame than a parent who has not been taught this superstition (Wainryb, 1993).

As children think in more complex ways about social situations, they realize that certain conventions, such as gender stereotypes, are far more arbitrary than they formerly believed. We will see later that school-age children have a more flexible appreciation of activities and occupations possible for males and females—a development that parallels their improved understanding of moral rules and social conventions (Carter & Patterson, 1982; Serbin, Powlishta, & Gulko, 1993).

Children in non-Western cultures also separate morality from social convention (Wainryb & Turiel, 1995). But the boundary between the two domains may differ. For example, 8- to 12-year-old Indian Hindu children agree with their American counterparts that breaking promises, destroying another person's property, and kicking harmless animals are morally wrong. Yet they regard food and politeness transgressions, such as

This Hindu Indian girl is likely to say that eating forbidden foods and calling parents by their first names are very serious moral transgressions. Like American children, she grasps the distinction between moral rules and social conventions. But the dividing line between them differs in her culture. *(Renato Rotolo/The Gamma Liason Network)*

eating chicken the day after a father's death or calling parents by their first names, as far more serious than selfish behavior or even family violence (Haidt, Koller, & Diaz, 1993; Shweder, Mahapatra, & Miller, 1990). In India, as in many developing countries, culturally specific practices that strike Western outsiders as arbitrary often have profound moral and religious significance.

ASK YOURSELF . . .

■ *Return to Joey's description of Belinda Brown at the beginning of this chapter. Explain how it reflects changes in children's understanding of others in middle childhood.*

■ *When given the Holly dilemma and asked, "Does Holly think she will be punished for climbing the tree?" Lizzie responded, "No, Holly knows that her father will understand how sad she would feel if she let that kitten fall out of the tree." Which of Selman's perspective-taking stages is Lizzie in? Explain.*

BRIEF REVIEW

In middle childhood, self-conscious emotions of pride and guilt become clearly linked to personal responsibility. Emotional understanding expands as children realize that people can experience more than one emotion at a time and consider a wider array of cues in detecting others' feelings. In addition, older children come up with adaptive strategies for regulating emotion that vary with their control over a situation. Perspective taking also undergoes major advances and is related to a wide variety of positive social skills. In the realm of morality, children construct more complex notions of distributive justice, and they clarify the distinction between moral rules and social conventions.

PEER RELATIONS

In middle childhood, the society of peers becomes an increasingly important context for development. Formal schooling exposes children to agemates who differ in many ways, including achievement, ethnicity, religion, interests, and personality. Peer contact, as we have seen, plays a major role in the school-age child's perspective taking and understanding of self and others. These developments, in turn, contribute to the quality of peer interaction, which becomes more prosocial over the school years. In line with this change, aggression declines, but the drop is greatest for physical attacks (Rubin, Bukowski, & Parker, 1998). As we will see, other types of aggression continue as school-age children form peer groups and distinguish "insiders" from "outsiders."

PEER GROUPS

Watch children in the school yard or neighborhood, and notice how groups of three to a dozen or more often gather. The organization of these collectives changes greatly with age. By the end of middle childhood, children display a strong desire for group belonging. Together, they generate unique values and standards for behavior. They also create a social structure of leaders and followers that ensures group goals will be met. When these characteristics are present, a **peer group** is formed.

The practices of these informal groups lead to a "peer culture" that typically consists of a specialized vocabulary, dress code, and place to "hang out" during leisure hours. For example, Joey formed a club with three other boys. The children met in the treehouse in Joey's backyard, called each other by nicknames, and wore a "uniform" consisting of T-shirts, jeans, and tennis shoes. Calling themselves "the pack," the boys developed a secret handshake and chose Joey as their leader. Their activities included improving the clubhouse, trading baseball cards, making trips to the video arcade, and—just as important—keeping girls and adults out!

As children develop these exclusive associations, the codes of dress and behavior that grow out of them become more broadly influential. At school, children who deviate are often rebuffed by their peers. "Kissing up" to teachers, wearing the wrong kind of shirt or

peer group
Peers who form a social unit by generating shared values and standards of behavior and a social structure of leaders and followers.

shoes, tattling on classmates, or carrying a strange-looking lunchbox are grounds for critical glances and comments until a child's behavior is brought in line with group expectations.

These special customs bind peers together, creating a sense of group identity. In addition, by participating in peer groups, children acquire many valuable social skills. The group provides a context in which children practice cooperation, leadership, and followership and develop a sense of loyalty to collective goals. Through these experiences, children experiment with and learn much about social organizations.

The beginning of peer group ties is also a time in which some of the "nicest children begin to behave in the most awful way" (Redl, 1966, p. 395). During their 10-year-old daughter's slumber party, two parents I know listened in on a stream of petty, malicious remarks about several uninvited classmates. The parents vowed to never permit their daughter to have friends sleep over again! Relational aggression—gossip, rumor spreading, and exclusion—remains common among girls (Crick & Grotpeter, 1995). Boys are more straightforward in their hostility toward the "outgroup." Overt aggression, in the form of verbal insults and pranks—toilet-papering a front yard or ringing a doorbell and running away—occurs often among small groups of boys, who provide one another with temporary social support for these mildly antisocial behaviors (Fine, 1980).

The school-age child's desire for group belonging can also be satisfied through formal group ties—Girl Scouts, Boy Scouts, 4-H, church groups, and other associations. Adult involvement holds in check the negative behaviors associated with children's informal peer groups. In addition, children gain in social and moral understanding as they work on joint projects and help in their communities (Harris, Mussen, & Rutherford, 1976; Keasey, 1971).

Peer groups first form in middle childhood. These boys have probably established a social structure of leaders and followers as they gather often for joint activities, such as bike riding and basketball. Their body language suggests that they feel a strong sense of group belonging. (R. Sidney/The Image Works)

FRIENDSHIPS

Whereas peer groups provide children with insight into larger social structures, close, one-to-one friendships contribute to the development of trust and sensitivity. During the school years, children's concepts of friendship become more complex and psychologically based. Compare the following answers of a 5-year-old and an 8-year-old to questions about what makes a best friend:

(five-year-old). Why is Amy your best friend? *I like her. I knew her in . . . [preschool] and I knew her before I came to school.* How did you meet Amy? *We sat on the bus, we played together. . . .* Would you let Amy ride your bike? *Yes, if she came over to my house.* Why would Amy come over to your house? *Because I want her to. . . .* How do you make a friend? *You say, "Hi, what's your name," and that's all.*

(eight-year-old). Who's your best friend? *Shelly.* Why is Shelly your best friend? Because she helps me when I'm sad, and she shares. . . . What makes Shelly so special? *I've known her longer, I sit next to her and got to know her better. . . .* How come you like Shelly better than anyone else? *She's done the most for me. She never disagrees, she never eats in front of me, she never walks away when I'm crying, and she helps me on my homework. . . .* How do you get someone to like you? *. . . If you're nice to [your friends], they'll be nice to you.* (Damon, 1988, pp. 80–81)

As these statements show, friendship in middle childhood is no longer just a matter of engaging in the same activities. Instead, it is a mutually agreed-on relationship in which children like each other's personal qualities and respond to one another's needs and desires. Since friendship involves both children wanting to be together, getting it started

In integrated schools and neighborhoods, many children form close other-race friendships. *(Carol Palmer/The Picture Cube)*

takes more time and effort than before. Once a friendship forms, *trust* becomes its defining feature. School-age children state that a good friendship is based on acts of kindness that signify each person can be counted on to support the other. Consequently, events that break up a friendship are quite different than they were during the preschool years. Older children regard violations of trust, such as not helping when others need help, breaking promises, and gossiping behind the other's back, as serious breaches of friendship (Damon, 1977; Selman, 1980).

Because of these features, school-age children are more selective about their friendships. Preschoolers say they have lots of friends—sometimes, everyone in their class! By age 8 or 9, children have only a handful of people they call friends and, very often, only one best friend. Girls, especially, are exclusive in their friendships because they demand greater closeness than do boys (Parker & Asher, 1993).

Otherwise, children tend to select friends like themselves in sex, race, ethnicity, and SES. Friends also resemble one another in personality (shyness, sociability, aggression), peer popularity, and academic achievement (Hartup, 1996; Kupersmidt, DeRosier, & Patterson, 1995). Note, however, that school and neighborhood characteristics affect friendship choices. For example, in integrated schools, as many as 50 percent of pupils report at least one close other-race friend (DuBois & Hirsch, 1990).

Friendships remain fairly stable over middle childhood; most last for several years. Through them, children learn the importance of emotional commitment. They come to realize that close relationships can survive disagreements if both parties are secure in their liking for one another (Laursen, Hartup, & Koplas, 1996). Yet the extent to which children's friendships support their development depends on the company they keep (Hartup, 1996).

Children who bring kindness and compassion to their friendships strengthen their prosocial tendencies; they behave in a more caring way toward others in general (McGuire & Weisz, 1982). When aggressive children make friends, the relationship often becomes a context for magnifying antisocial acts. The friendships of relationally aggressive girls are high in self-disclosure (exchange of private feelings) but full of jealousy, conflict, and betrayal. These girls frequently elicit personal information from their friends and then use it to gain control over the relationship by threatening to betray confidences. In contrast, overtly aggressive boys are seldom hostile toward their friends. Instead, they expect their friends to join them in aggressive acts against peers *outside* the relationship (Grotpeter & Crick, 1996).

These findings reveal that the social problems of aggressive children operate within their closest peer ties. As we will see next, these children are also at risk for rejection in the wider world of peers.

PEER ACCEPTANCE

Peer acceptance refers to likability—the extent to which a child is viewed by agemates as a worthy social partner. In Chapters 11 and 12, we saw that obese children and children with serious learning problems often have difficulty with peer acceptance. Yet there are other children whose appearance and intellectual abilities are quite normal; still, their classmates despise them.

Researchers usually assess peer acceptance with self-report measures called **sociometric techniques.** For example, children may be asked to nominate several peers in their class whom they especially like or dislike, to indicate for all possible pairs of classmates which one they prefer to play with, or to rate each peer on a scale from "like very much" to "like very little" (Rubin, Bukowski, & Parker, 1998).

sociometric techniques
Self-report measures that ask peers to evaluate one another's likability.

Sociometric techniques yield four different categories of peer acceptance: **popular children,** who get many positive votes; **rejected children,** who are actively disliked; **controversial children,** who get a large number of positive and negative votes; and **neglected children,** who are seldom chosen, either positively or negatively. About two-thirds of pupils in a typical elementary school classroom fit one of these categories. The remaining one-third are *average* in peer acceptance; they do not receive extreme scores (Coie, Dodge, & Coppotelli, 1982).

Peer acceptance is a powerful predictor of current as well as later psychological adjustment. Rejected children, especially, are unhappy, alienated, poorly achieving children with a low sense of self-esteem. Both teachers and parents rate them as having a wide range of emotional and social problems. Peer rejection in middle childhood is also strongly associated with poor school performance, absenteeism, dropping out, antisocial behavior, and delinquency in adolescence and criminality in young adulthood (Coie et al., 1995; DeRosier, Kupersmidt, & Patterson, 1994; Parker & Asher, 1987).

■ **DETERMINANTS OF PEER ACCEPTANCE.**   What causes one child to be liked and another to be rejected? A wealth of research reveals that social behavior plays a powerful role.

Popular children have very positive social skills. They communicate with peers in sensitive, friendly, and cooperative ways and are appropriately assertive; they rarely behave in ways that interfere with others' goals. When they do not understand another child's reaction, they ask for an explanation. If they disagree with a play partner in a game, they go beyond voicing their displeasure; they suggest what the other child could do instead. When they want to enter an ongoing play group, they adapt their behavior to the flow of the activity (Dodge, McClaskey, & Feldman, 1985; Newcomb, Bukowski, & Pattee, 1993).

Rejected children, in contrast, display a wide range of negative social behaviors. But not all these disliked children look the same. At least two subtypes exist:

- **Rejected-aggressive children,** the largest subgroup, show severe conduct problems—high rates of conflict, hostility, and hyperactive, inattentive, and impulsive behavior. They are also deficient in social understanding. For example, they are more likely than others to be poor perspective takers, to misinterpret the innocent behaviors of peers as hostile, and to blame others for their social difficulties (Crick & Ladd, 1993; Dekovic & Gerris, 1994). Furthermore, girls' relational aggression is just as good a predictor of peer rejection as is boys' overt aggression (Crick, 1996).

- **Rejected-withdrawn children,** a smaller subgroup, are passive and socially awkward. These children, especially, feel lonely, hold negative expectations for how peers will treat them, and are very concerned about being scorned and attacked (Bierman, Smoot, & Aumiller, 1993; Rabiner, Keane, & MacKinnon-Lewis, 1993; Stewart & Rubin, 1995). Because of their inept, submissive style of interaction, rejected-withdrawn children are at risk for abuse by bullies (see the Biology and Environment box on page 500).

Consistent with the mixed peer opinion they engender, controversial children display a blend of positive and negative social behaviors. Like rejected-aggressive children, they are hostile and disruptive, but they also engage in high rates of positive, prosocial acts. Even though they are disliked by some peers, controversial children have some qualities that protect them from social exclusion. As a result they are relatively happy and comfortable with their peer relationships (Newcomb, Bukowski, & Pattee, 1993; Parkhurst & Asher, 1992).

Finally, perhaps the most surprising finding on peer acceptance is that neglected children, once thought to be in need of treatment, are usually well adjusted. Although they engage in low rates of interaction and are considered shy by their classmates, they are not less socially skilled than average children. They do not report feeling especially lonely or

popular children
Children who get many positive votes on sociometric measures of peer acceptance.

rejected children
Children who are actively disliked and get many negative votes on sociometric measures of peer acceptance.

controversial children
Children who get a large number of positive and negative votes on sociometric measures of peer acceptance.

neglected children
Children who are seldom chosen, either positively or negatively, on sociometric measures of peer acceptance.

rejected-aggressive children
A subgroup of rejected children who engage in high rates of conflict, hostility, and hyperactive, inattentive, and impulsive behavior.

rejected-withdrawn children
A subgroup of rejected children who are passive and socially awkward.

BIOLOGY & ENVIRONMENT   BULLIES AND THEIR VICTIMS

Follow the activities of aggressive children over a school day, and you will see that they reserve their hostilities for a small number of peers. A particularly destructive form of interaction that emerges during middle childhood is bullying and victimization. What sustains repeated assault–retreat cycles between certain pairs of children, leading one member to become an attacker and the other a target of abuse?

In one of the most comprehensive studies of the aggressor–victim relationship, Dan Olweus (1978, 1984) asked Swedish teachers to nominate adolescent male bullies, their "whipping boys," and well-adjusted classmates. Then judgments of each group's characteristics were obtained from teachers, mothers, peers, and the boys themselves. Compared to bullies and well-adjusted adolescents, whipping boys were chronically anxious (at home and at school), low in self-esteem, ostracized by peers, physically weak, and afraid to defend themselves.

These findings suggest that victimized children are attacked more than others because they are perceived as weak and likely to provide their aggressors with rewarding conse-

quences. Indeed, frequently victimized children often reinforce bullies by giving in to their demands, crying, assuming defensive postures, and failing to fight back. Biologically based, temperamental traits of inhibition and fearfulness probably contribute to their behavior. But they also have histories of resistant attachment and maternal overprotectiveness. These child-rearing experiences undermine effective emotional self-regulation, resulting in a demeanor that radiates anxious vulnerability (Olweus, 1993; Troy & Sroufe, 1987).

By elementary school, 10 percent of children are harassed by aggressive agemates, and peers view these targets differently. They expect victims to give up desirable objects, show signs of distress, and fail to retaliate far more often than nonvictims. In addition, children (especially those who are aggressive) report less discomfort at the thought of causing pain and suffering to victims than nonvictims, thereby minimizing in their own minds the possibility of harmful consequences (Perry, Williard, & Perry, 1990). Although bullies and victims are most often boys, at times girls harass a vulnerable classmate with relational hostility (Crick & Grotpeter, 1996).

Aggression and victimization are not polar opposites. Some of the most extreme victims are also aggressive, picking arguments and fights (Boulton & Smith, 1994). Perhaps these children foolishly provoke stronger agemates, who then prevail over them. Although both aggressive and victimized children are rejected by peers, these highly aggressive–highly abused youngsters are the most despised, placing them at severe risk for maladjustment.

Interventions that change victimized children's negative opinions of themselves and that teach them to respond in nonreinforcing ways to their attackers are vital. Nevertheless, victimized children's behavior should not be taken to mean they are to blame for their abuse. Instead, the responsibility lies with bullies who brutally attack and adults who supervise children's interactions. Developing a school code against bullying, enlisting parents' assistance in changing both bullies' and victims' behavior, and moving aggressive children to another class or school can greatly reduce bully–victim problems, which account for a substantial portion of peer aggression in middle childhood (Olweus, 1995).

Children who are bullied by agemates have characteristics that make them easy targets. They are highly anxious, physically weak, rejected by peers, and afraid to defend themselves. Both temperamental traits and child-rearing experiences underlie their cowering behavior, which reinforces their attackers' abusive acts. (Aloma/ Monkmeyer Press)

unhappy about their social life, and when they want to, they can break away from their usual pattern of playing by themselves (Crick & Ladd, 1993; Wentzel & Asher, 1995). Neglected children remind us that there are other paths to emotional well-being besides the outgoing, gregarious personality style so highly valued in our culture. In China, cautious, inhibited children are actually viewed as advanced in social maturity! In accord with this standard, shyness and sensitivity are associated with peer acceptance and teacher-rated social competence and leadership among Chinese 8- to 10-year-olds (Chen, Rubin, & Li, 1995).

■ **HELPING REJECTED CHILDREN.** A variety of interventions exist to improve the peer relations and psychological adjustment of rejected children. Most involve coaching, modeling, and reinforcing positive social skills, such as how to begin interacting with a peer, cooperate in play, and respond to another child with friendly emotion and approval. Several of these programs have produced gains in social competence and peer acceptance still present from several weeks to a year later (Bierman, 1986; Lochman et al., 1993; Mize & Ladd, 1990).

Some researchers believe that these interventions might be even more effective when combined with other treatments. Often rejected children are poor students, and their low academic self-esteem magnifies their negative reactions to teachers and classmates. Intensive academic tutoring improves both their school achievement and their social acceptance (Coie & Krehbiel, 1984). Other interventions focus on training in perspective taking and social problem solving (Ladd & Mize, 1983). Still another approach is to increase rejected children's expectations for social success. Many conclude, after repeated rebuffs from peers, that no matter how hard they try, they will never be liked. Rejected youngsters make better use of social skills when they believe peers will accept them (Rabiner & Coie, 1989).

Finally, we have seen in previous chapters that children's socially incompetent behaviors often originate in a poor fit between the child's temperament and parenting practices. Therefore, interventions that focus on the child alone are unlikely to be sufficient. If the quality of parent–child interaction is not changed, rejected children may soon return to their old behavior patterns.

GENDER TYPING

Children's understanding of gender roles broadens in middle childhood, and their gender identities (views of themselves as relatively masculine or feminine) change as well. We will see that the direction of development is different for boys and girls, and it can vary considerably across cultures.

GENDER-STEREOTYPED BELIEFS

During the school years, children extend gender-stereotyped beliefs acquired in early childhood. As children think more about people as personalities, they label some traits as more typical of one sex than the other—for example, "tough," "aggressive," "rational," and "dominant" as masculine and "gentle," "sympathetic," "excitable," and "affectionate" as feminine. Research in many countries reveals that stereotyping of personality traits increases steadily in middle childhood, becoming adultlike around age 11 (Best et al., 1977; Serbin, Powlishta, & Gulko, 1993).

Shortly after entering elementary school, children figure out which academic subjects and skill areas are "masculine" and which are "feminine." They regard reading, art, and music as more for girls and mathematics, athletics, and mechanical skills as more for boys (Eccles, Jacobs, & Harold, 1990; Huston, 1983). Children acquire these biases from parents and teachers, who also harbor them, as well as from observing what people do in their everyday lives (Jacobs & Weisz, 1994). Achievement stereotypes, in turn, affect children's liking for subjects, self-concepts of ability at them, and how well they perform. For example, boys feel more competent than girls at math, whereas girls feel more competent than boys at reading—even when children of equal skill level are compared (Eccles et al., 1993b). As we will see in Chapter 15, gender stereotypes of achievement become realities for many young people by adolescence.

Although school-age children are aware of more gender stereotypes, they have a more flexible view of what males and females *can do*. As they develop the capacity to integrate conflicting social cues, children realize that a person's sex is not a certain predictor of his or her personality traits, activities, and behaviors (Biernat, 1991a; Bigler, 1995). However, acknowledging that people *can* cross gender lines does not mean that children always *approve* of doing so. In one study, 4- and 8-year-olds and adults were asked how much they would like being friends with an agemate who violated gender-role expectations (such as a male wearing a dress or a female playing football) and how bad they thought such "transgressions" were. Children and adults expressed tolerance of females violating gender-role expectations. But they judged violations by males quite harshly—a finding that reflects greater social pressure on boys and men to conform to gender roles (Levy, Taylor, & Gelman, 1995).

GENDER IDENTITY AND BEHAVIOR

Boys' and girls' gender identities follow different paths of development in middle childhood. Self-ratings on personality traits reveal that from third to sixth grade, boys strengthen their identification with the "masculine" role. In contrast, girls' identification with "feminine" attributes declines. Although girls still lean toward the "feminine" side, they begin to describe themselves as having some "other-gender" characteristics (Boldizar, 1991; Serbin, Powlishta, & Gulko, 1993). This difference is also evident in the activities children choose in middle childhood. Whereas boys usually stick to "masculine" pursuits, girls experiment with a wider range of options. Besides cooking, sewing, and baby-sitting, they join organized sports teams, take up science projects, and build forts in the backyard.

In Chapter 10, we saw that parents are far less tolerant when sons as opposed to daughters cross gender lines. These child-rearing influences play important roles in the developmental trends just described. Peers are also influential. A tomboyish girl can make her way into boys' activities without losing status with her female peers, but a boy who hangs out with girls is likely to be ridiculed and rejected. Finally, older school-age children realize that society attaches greater prestige to "masculine" characteristics (Thorne, 1993). As a result, girls may want to try some of the activities and behaviors associated with the more highly valued gender role.

CULTURAL INFLUENCES ON GENDER TYPING

Although the sex differences just described are typical in Western nations, they do not apply to children everywhere. Girls are less likely to experiment with "masculine" activities in cultures and subcultures in which the gap between male and female roles is especially wide. And when social and economic conditions make it necessary for boys to take over "feminine" tasks, their personalities and behaviors become less stereotyped.

To clarify how cultures shape gender-typed behavior, Beatrice Whiting and Carolyn Edwards (1988a, 1988b) collected detailed information on the daily activities of children in 12 communities around the world. Their findings revealed that in most societies, boys were dominant and aggressive and girls were dependent, compliant, and nurturant. But striking exceptions emerged in communities in which children were given "cross-gender" assignments as part of their daily responsibilities.

This third grader demonstrates a science experiment for her teacher and classmates. Whereas boys usually stick to "masculine" pursuits, school-age girls explore a wider range of options. They want to try some of the activities and behaviors associated with the more valued gender role.

For example, in Nyansongo, a small agricultural settlement in Kenya, mothers work 4 to 5 hours a day in the gardens. They assign the care of young children, the tending of the cooking fire, and the washing of dishes to older siblings. Since children of both sexes perform these duties, girls are relieved of total responsibility for "feminine" tasks and have more time to interact with agemates. Their greater freedom and independence lead them to score higher than girls of other village and tribal cultures in dominance, assertiveness, and playful roughhousing. In contrast, boys' caregiving responsibilities mean that they often display help-giving and emotional support.

Should these findings be taken to suggest that boys in Western cultures be assigned more "cross-gender" tasks? The consequences of doing so are not straightforward. Research shows that when fathers hold traditional gender-role beliefs and their sons engage in "feminine" housework, boys experience strain in the father–child relationship, feel stressed by their responsibilities, and judge themselves as less competent (McHale et al., 1990). So parental values may need to be consistent with task assignments for children to benefit from them.

BRIEF REVIEW

During middle childhood, children become members of peer groups, through which they learn much about the functioning of larger social structures. Friendships change, emphasizing mutual trust and assistance. Peer acceptance is a powerful predictor of current and future psychological adjustment. Popular children interact in a cooperative, friendly fashion; rejected children behave antisocially and ineptly; and controversial children display a mixture of positive and negative social behaviors. Although neglected children engage in low rates of peer interaction, they are usually competent and well adjusted. Interventions that train social skills, improve academic performance, and increase social understanding lead to improved peer acceptance of rejected children.

Over the school years, children extend their gender-typed beliefs to personality characteristics and achievement areas. Boys' "masculine" gender identities strengthen, whereas girls' identities become more flexible. However, cultural values and practices can modify these trends.

ASK YOURSELF . . .

■ *Apply your understanding of attributions to rejected children's social self-esteem. How are rejected children likely to explain their failure to gain peer acceptance? What impact on future efforts to get along with agemates will those attributions have?*

■ *Return to Chapter 10, page 392, and review the concept of androgyny. Which of the two sexes is more androgynous in middle childhood, and why?*

FAMILY INFLUENCES

Children's growing competence and entry into school, peer, and community contexts mean that the parent–child relationship changes. We will see that a gradual lessening of direct control supports development, as long as it is built on continuing parental warmth and involvement.

Our discussion will also reveal that families in industrialized nations have become more pluralistic than ever before. For example, today there are fewer births per family unit. In addition, rapid transitions over the past several decades—a dramatic rise in marital breakup, single-parent households, remarried parents, gay and lesbian parents who are open about their sexual orientation, and mothers entering the labor force—have resulted in a diverse array of family forms.

As you read about each of these shifts in family life, think back to Bronfenbrenner's ecological systems theory. Notice how children's well-being continues to depend on the quality of family interaction, which is sustained by supportive ties to kin and community and favorable policies at the level of the larger culture.

PARENT–CHILD RELATIONSHIPS

In middle childhood, the amount of time children spend with parents declines dramatically. The child's growing independence means that parents must deal with new issues. "I've struggled with how many chores to assign, how much allowance to give, and whether their friends are good influences," noted Rena. "And then there's the problem of how to keep track of them when they're out of the house or even when they're home and I'm not there to see what's going on."

Although parents face a new set of concerns, child rearing actually becomes easier for those who established an authoritative style during the early years. Reasoning works more effectively with school-age children because of their capacity for logical thinking and increased respect for parents' expert knowledge and skill (Braine et al., 1991). Of course, older children sometimes use their cognitive powers to bargain and negotiate. "Mom," Joey pleaded for the third time, "if you let Terry and me go to the mall tonight, I'll rake all the leaves in the yard, I promise."

Fortunately, parents can appeal to the child's better developed sense of self-esteem, humor, and morality to resolve these difficulties. "Joey, you know it's a school night, and you have a test tomorrow," Rena responded. "You'll be unhappy at the results if you stay out late and don't study. Come on, no more wheeler-dealering!" Perhaps because parents and children have, over time, learned how to resolve conflicts, coercive discipline declines over the school years (Collins, Harris, & Susman, 1996).

As children demonstrate that they can manage daily activities and responsibilities, effective parents gradually shift control from adult to child. This does not mean that they let go entirely. Instead, they engage in **coregulation,** a transitional form of supervision in which they exercise general oversight, while permitting children to be in charge of moment-by-moment decision making. Coregulation supports and protects children, who are not yet ready for total independence. At the same time, it prepares them for adolescence, when they will need to make many important decisions themselves.

Coregulation grows out of a cooperative relationship between parent and child—one based on give-and-take and mutual respect. Here is a summary of its ingredients:

> First, [parents] must monitor, guide, and support their children at a distance—that is, when their children are out of their presence; second, they must effectively use the times when direct contact does occur; and third, they must strengthen in their children the abilities that will allow them to monitor their own behavior, to adopt acceptable standards of good [conduct], to avoid undue risks, and to know when they need parental support and guidance. Children must be willing to inform parents of their whereabouts, activities, and problems so that parents can mediate and guide when necessary. (Maccoby, 1984, pp. 191–192)

Although school-age children often press for greater independence, they also know how much they need their parents' continuing support. In one study, fifth and sixth graders described parents as the most influential people in their lives. They often turned to mothers and fathers for affection, advice, enhancement of self-worth, and assistance with everyday problems (Furman & Buhrmester, 1992).

SIBLINGS

In addition to parents and friends, siblings are important sources of support to school-age youngsters. Siblings provide one another with companionship, help with difficult tasks, and comfort during times of emotional stress.

Yet sibling rivalry tends to increase in middle childhood. At times, it is evoked by one child making new friends, sparking jealousy in a sibling who feels left out (Dunn, 1996). Also, as children participate in a wider range of activities, parents often compare siblings'

coregulation
A transitional form of supervision in which parents exercise general oversight while permitting children to be in charge of moment-by-moment decision making.

traits and accomplishments. The child who gets less parental attention, more disapproval, and fewer material resources is likely to resent a sibling who receives more favorable treatment (Brody, Stoneman, & McCoy, 1994).

When siblings are close in age and the same sex, parental comparisons are more frequent, resulting in more quarreling and antagonism. This effect is particularly strong when fathers prefer one child. Perhaps because fathers usually spend less time with children, their favoritism is more noticeable and triggers greater anger (Brody, Stoneman, & McCoy, 1992; Brody et al., 1992).

Siblings often take steps to reduce this rivalry by striving to be different from one another (Huston, 1983). For example, two brothers I know deliberately selected different school subjects, athletic pursuits, and music lessons. If the older one did especially well at an activity, the younger one did not want to try it. Of course, parents can reduce these effects by making an effort not to compare children. But some feedback about their competencies is inevitable, and as siblings strive to win recognition for their own uniqueness, they shape important aspects of each other's development.

Birth order plays an important role in sibling experiences. For a time, oldest children have their parents' attention all to themselves. Even after brothers and sisters are born, they receive greater pressure for mature behavior from parents. For this reason, the oldest child is slightly advantaged in IQ and school achievement (Zajonc & Mullally, 1997). Younger siblings, in contrast, tend to be more popular with agemates, perhaps as a result of becoming skilled at negotiating and compromising from interacting with more powerful brothers and sisters (Miller & Maruyama, 1976).

ONLY CHILDREN

Sibling relationships bring many benefits, but they are not essential for normal development. Contrary to popular belief, only children are not spoiled and selfish. Instead, they are just as well adjusted as other children and advantaged in some respects. Children growing up in one-child families score higher in self-esteem and achievement motivation. Consequently, they do better in school and attain higher levels of education (Falbo, 1992). A major reason may be that only children have somewhat closer relationships with parents, who exert more pressure for mastery and accomplishment (Falbo & Polit, 1986).

Favorable development also characterizes only children in China, where a one-child family policy is strictly enforced to control overpopulation. Compared to agemates with siblings, Chinese only children are advanced in performance on a variety of cognitive tasks and in academic achievement (Falbo & Poston, 1993; Jiao, Ji, & Jing, 1996). They also feel more emotionally secure, perhaps because government disapproval promotes tension and unhappiness in families with more than one child (Falbo & Poston, 1993; Yang et al., 1995). Although many Chinese adults remain convinced that the one-child family policy breeds self-centered "little emperors," Chinese only children do not differ from children with siblings in social skills and peer acceptance (Chen, Rubin, & Li, 1994).

DIVORCE

Children's interactions with parents and siblings are affected by other aspects of family life. Joey and Lizzie's relationship, Rena told me, had been particularly negative only a few years before. Joey pushed, hit, taunted, and called Lizzie names. Although she tried to retaliate, she was little match for Joey's larger size. The arguments usually ended with Lizzie running in tears to her mother. Joey and Lizzie's fighting coincided with Rena and her husband's growing marital unhappiness. When Joey was 8 and Lizzie 5, their father, Drake, moved out.

The children were not alone in having to weather this traumatic event. Between 1960 and 1985, the divorce rate in the United States doubled and then stabilized. Currently, it is the highest in the world (see Figure 13.2). About half of American marriages end in

This mural reminds citizens that limiting family size to one child is a basic national policy in the People's Republic of China. As in the United States, only children in China develop favorably—cognitively, emotionally, and socially. *(Owen Franken/Stock Boston)*

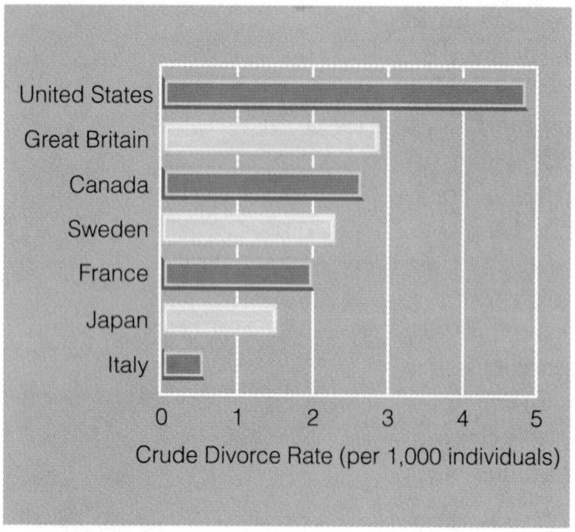

FIGURE 13.2

Divorce rate in seven industrialized nations. The divorce rate in the United States is the highest in the world. *(Adapted from McKenry & Price, 1995.)*

divorce, three-fourths of which involve children. This means that at any given time, about 1 in 4 American children live in single-parent households. Although the large majority (85 percent) reside with their mothers, the number in father-headed households has increased over the past decade, from 9 to 14 percent (Hetherington & Stanley-Hagan, 1997).

Children spend an average of 5 years in a single-parent home, or almost a third of their total childhood. For many, divorce eventually leads to new family relationships. About two-thirds of divorced parents marry a second time. Half of these children eventually experience a third major change—the end of their parent's second marriage (Hetherington & Henderson, 1997).

These figures reveal that divorce is not a single event in the lives of parents and children. Instead, it is a transition that leads to a variety of new living arrangements, accompanied by changes in housing, income, and family roles and responsibilities. Since the 1960s, many studies have reported that marital breakup is quite stressful for children—more so when it is repeated (Hetherington, Bridges, & Insabella, 1998). But the research also reveals wide individual differences in how children respond. The custodial parent's psychological health, the child's characteristics, and social supports within the family and surrounding community contribute to children's adjustment.

■ **IMMEDIATE CONSEQUENCES.** "Things were worst during the period in which Drake and I decided to separate," Rena reflected. "We fought over everything—from custody of the children to the living room furniture, and the kids really suffered. Once, sobbing, Lizzie told me she was 'sorry she made Daddy go away.' Joey kicked and threw things at home. At school, his teacher complained that he was distracted and often didn't do his work. In the midst of everything, I could hardly deal with their problems. We had to sell the house; I couldn't afford it alone. And I needed a better-paying job. I had to change from teaching part-time to full-time at the university or start looking."

Rena's description captures conditions in many newly divorced households. Family conflict often rises for a time as parents try to settle disputes over children and personal belongings. Once one parent moves out, additional events threaten supportive interactions between parents and children. Mother-headed households typically experience a sharp drop in income. Three-fourths of divorced mothers in the United States get less than the full amount of child support from the absent father or none at all (Children's Defense Fund, 1998). They often have to move to new housing for economic reasons, reducing supportive ties to neighbors and friends.

These life circumstances often lead to high maternal stress, depression, and anxiety and to a disorganized family situation called "minimal parenting" (Hetherington, 1989; Wallerstein & Kelly, 1980). "Meals and bedtimes were at all hours, the house didn't get cleaned, and I stopped taking Joey and Lizzie on weekend outings," said Rena. As children react with distress and anger to their less secure home lives, discipline may become harsh and inconsistent as mothers try to recapture control of their upset youngsters. Noncustodial fathers usually spend more time with children immediately after divorce, but often this contact decreases over time. About 20 percent of American children of divorce have little or no paternal contact. When fathers see their children only occasionally, they are inclined to be permissive and indulgent. This often conflicts with the mother's style of parenting and makes her task of managing the child on a day-to-day basis even more difficult (Furstenberg & Nord, 1985).

In view of these changes, it is not surprising that children experience painful emotional reactions. But the intensity of their feelings and the way these are expressed varies with the child's age, temperament, and sex.

Children's Age. Five-year-old Lizzie's fear that she had caused her father to leave home is not unusual. The cognitive immaturity of preschool and early school-age children makes it difficult for them to grasp the reasons behind their parent's separation. Younger children often blame themselves and take the marital breakup as a sign that they could be abandoned by both parents. They may whine and cling, displaying intense separation anxiety. Preschoolers are especially likely to fantasize that their parents will get back together (Wallerstein, 1983; Wallerstein, Corbin, & Lewis, 1988).

Older children are better able to understand the reasons behind their parents' divorce. They recognize that strong differences of opinion, incompatible personalities, and lack of caring for one another are responsible (Mazur, 1993). The ability to accurately assign blame may reduce some of the pain that children feel. Still, many school-age and adolescent youngsters react strongly to the end of their parents' marriage, particularly when family conflict is high (Forehand et al., 1991). Some escape into undesirable peer activities, such as running away, truancy, and delinquent behavior (Doherty & Needle, 1991; Dornbusch et al., 1985).

However, not all older children react this way. For some—especially daughters—divorce can trigger more mature behavior. These youngsters may willingly take on extra burdens, such as household tasks, care and protection of younger siblings, and emotional support of a depressed, anxious mother. But if these demands are too great, older children may eventually become resentful and withdraw into some of the destructive behavior patterns just described (Hetherington, 1995).

Children's Temperament and Sex. When temperamentally difficult children are exposed to stressful life events and inadequate parenting, their problems are magnified. In contrast, easy children are less often targets of parental anger and are also better at coping with adversity when it hits. After a moderately stressful divorce, some easy children (usually girls) actually emerge with enhanced coping skills (Hetherington, 1995).

These findings help us understand sex differences in children's response to divorce. Girls sometimes respond as Lizzie did, with crying, self-criticism, and withdrawal. At other times, they show demanding, attention-getting behavior. But in mother-custody families, boys typically experience more serious adjustment problems. Recall from Chapter 10 that boys are more active and noncompliant—behaviors that increase with exposure to parental conflict and inconsistent discipline. Studies in Great Britain and the United States reveal that long before the marital breakup, many sons of divorcing couples were impulsive and defiant—behaviors that may have contributed to as well as been caused by their parents' problems. As a result, these boys entered the period of turmoil surrounding divorce with a reduced capacity to cope with family stress (Cherlin et al., 1991; Hetherington, 1991).

Perhaps because their behavior is so unruly, boys of divorcing parents receive less emotional support from mothers, teachers, and peers. And as Joey's behavior toward Lizzie illustrates, the coercive cycles of interaction between boys and their divorced mothers soon spread to sibling relations (MacKinnon, 1989). These outcomes compound boys' difficulties. Children of both sexes show declines in school achievement during the aftermath of divorce, but school problems are greater for boys (Guidubaldi & Cleminshaw, 1985).

■ **LONG-TERM CONSEQUENCES.** Rena eventually found full-time work at the university and gained control over the daily operation of the household. Her own feelings of anger and rejection over the divorce also declined. And after several meetings with a counselor, Rena and Drake realized the harmful impact of their quarreling on Joey and Lizzie. They resolved to keep the children out of future disagreements. Drake visited regularly and handled Joey's unruliness with firmness and consistency. Soon Joey's school performance improved, his behavior problems subsided, and both children seemed calmer and happier.

Like Joey and Lizzie, the majority of children show improved adjustment by 2 years after divorce. Yet a few continue to have serious difficulties into adulthood (Chase-Lansdale, Cherlin, & Kiernan, 1995). Boys and children with difficult temperaments are especially likely to drop out of school and display antisocial behavior in adolescence, but some girls also show these lasting problems (Hetherington, 1993; McLanahan & Sandefur, 1994). The most consistent long-term effects for girls involve heterosexual behavior—a rise in sexual activity at adolescence, in teenage childbearing, and in risk of divorce in their adult lives (Cherlin, Kiernan, & Chase-Lansdale, 1995; Hetherington, 1997).

The overriding factor in positive adjustment following divorce is effective parenting—in particular, how well the custodial parent handles stress, shields the child from family conflict, and engages in authoritative parenting (Hetherington, 1991). Contact with fathers is also important. For girls, a good father–child relationship appears to contribute to heterosexual development. For boys, it seems to affect overall psychological well-being. In fact, several studies indicate that outcomes for sons are better when the father is the custodial parent (Camara & Resnick, 1988; Clarke-Stewart & Hayward, 1996). Fathers are more likely to praise a boy's good behavior and less likely to ignore his disruptiveness. The father's image of greater power and authority may also help him obtain more compliance from a son.

Although divorce is painful for children, there is clear evidence that remaining in a high-conflict intact family is much worse than making the transition to a low-conflict, single-parent household (Amato, Loomis, & Booth, 1995). When divorcing parents put aside their disagreements and support one another in their child-rearing roles, children have the best chance of growing up competent, stable, and happy. Caring extended-family members, teachers, and friends are also important in reducing the likelihood that divorce will result in long-term disruption (Grych & Fincham, 1997).

■ **DIVORCE MEDIATION, JOINT CUSTODY, AND CHILD SUPPORT.** Awareness that divorce is highly stressful for children and families has led to community-based services aimed at helping them through this difficult time. One is **divorce mediation.** It consists of a series of meetings between divorcing adults and a trained professional, who tries to help them settle disputes, such as property division and child custody. Its purpose is to avoid legal battles that intensify family conflict. Research reveals that it increases out-of-court settlements, compliance with these agreements, and feelings of well-being among divorcing parents. By reducing family hostilities, it probably has great benefits for children (Emery, Mathews, & Kitzmann, 1994).

A relatively new child custody option tries to keep both parents involved with children. In **joint custody,** the court grants the mother and father equal say in important decisions about the child's upbringing. Yet many experts have raised questions about the practice. Joint custody results in a variety of living arrangements. In most instances, children reside with one parent and see the other on a fixed schedule, much like the typical sole-custody situation. But in other cases, parents share physical custody, and children must move between homes and sometimes schools and peer groups. These transitions introduce a new kind of instability that is especially hard on some children (Johnston, Kline, & Tschann, 1989). The success of joint custody requires a cooperative relationship between divorcing parents. If they continue to quarrel, it prolongs children's exposure to a hostile family atmosphere (Furstenberg & Cherlin, 1991).

Finally, many single-parent families depend on child support from the absent parent to relieve financial strain. In response to a recent federal law, all states have established procedures for withholding wages from parents who fail to make these court-ordered payments. Although child support is usually not enough to lift a single-parent family out of poverty, it can ease the burden substantially. An added benefit is that children are more likely to maintain contact with a noncustodial father if he pays child support (Garfinkel & McLanahan, 1995). The Caregiving Concerns table on the following page summarizes ways to help children adjust to their parents' divorce.

divorce mediation
A series of meetings between divorcing adults and a trained professional, who tries to help them settle disputes. Aimed at avoiding legal battles that intensify family conflict.

joint custody
A child custody arrangement following divorce in which the court grants both parents equal say in important decisions about the child's upbringing.

CAREGIVING CONCERNS

Helping Children Adjust to Their Parents' Divorce

SUGGESTION	EXPLANATION
Shield children from conflict.	Witnessing intense parental conflict is very damaging to children. If one parent insists on expressing hostility, children fare better if the other parent does not respond in kind.
Provide children with as much continuity, familiarity, and predictability as possible.	Children adjust better during the period surrounding divorce when their lives have some stability—for example, the same school, bedroom, baby-sitter, and playmates and a dependable daily schedule.
Explain the divorce and tell children what to expect.	Children are more likely to develop fears of abandonment if they are not prepared for their parents' separation. They should be told that their mother and father will not be living together anymore, which parent will be moving out, and when they will be able to see that parent. If possible, mother and father should explain the divorce together. Parents should provide a reason for the divorce that the child can understand and assure the child that he or she is not to blame.
Emphasize the permanence of the divorce.	Fantasies of parents getting back together can prevent children from accepting the reality of their current life. Children should be told that the divorce is final and that there is nothing they can do to change that fact.
Respond sympathetically to children's feelings.	Children need a supportive and understanding response to their feelings of sadness, fear, and anger. For children to adjust well, their painful emotions must be acknowledged, not denied or avoided.
Promote a continuing relationship with both parents.	When parents disentangle their lingering hostility toward the former spouse from the child's need for a continuing relationship with the other parent, children adjust well. Grandparents and other extended-family members can help by not taking sides.

Source: Teyber, 1992.

BLENDED FAMILIES

"If you get married to Wendell and Daddy gets married to Carol," Lizzie wondered aloud to Rena, "then I'll have two sisters and one more brother. And let's see, how many grandmothers and grandfathers? Gosh, a lot!" exclaimed Lizzie. "But what will I call them all?" she asked, looking worried.

For many children, life in a single-parent family is temporary. Their parents remarry within a few years. Others cohabit, or share an intimate sexual relationship and residence with a partner outside of marriage. As Lizzie's comments indicate, entry into these **blended,** or **reconstituted, families** leads to a complex set of new relationships. For some children, this expanded family network is a positive turn of events that brings with it greater adult attention. But for most, it presents difficult adjustments. Stepparents often use different child-rearing practices than the child was used to, and having to switch to new rules and expectations can be stressful. In addition, children often regard steprelatives as "intruders" into the family. But how well children adapt is, once again, related to the overall quality of family functioning. This often depends on which parent remarries as well as the age and sex of the child. As we will see, older children and girls seem to have the hardest time.

■ **MOTHER–STEPFATHER FAMILIES.** The most frequent form of blended family is a mother–stepfather arrangement, since mothers generally retain custody of the child. Boys often adjust quickly. They welcome a stepfather who is warm and responsive and who offers relief from the coercive cycles of interaction that tend to build with their divorced mothers. Mothers' friction with sons also declines due to greater economic security, another adult to share household tasks, and an end to loneliness (Stevenson & Black,

blended, or reconstituted, family
A family structure resulting from cohabitation or remarriage that includes parent, child, and steprelatives.

1995). In contrast, girls adapt less favorably when custodial mothers remarry. Stepfathers disrupt the close ties many girls established with their mother in the single-parent family, and girls often react to the new arrangement with sulky, resistant behavior (Vuchinich et al., 1991).

Note, however, that age affects these findings. Older school-age and adolescent youngsters of both sexes find it harder to adjust to blended families (Hetherington, 1993). Perhaps because they are more aware of the impact of remarriage on their own lives, they challenge some aspects of it that younger children simply accept, creating more relationship issues with their steprelatives.

■ **FATHER–STEPMOTHER FAMILIES.** Research reveals more confusion for children in father–stepmother families. In the case of noncustodial fathers, remarriage often leads to reduced contact. They tend to withdraw from their "previous" families, more so if they have daughters than sons (Hetherington & Henderson, 1997). When fathers have custody, children typically react negatively to remarriage. One reason is that children living with fathers often start out with more problems. Perhaps the biological mother could no longer handle the unruly child (usually a boy), so the father and his new wife are faced with a youngster who has serious behavior problems. In other instances, the father is granted custody because of a very close relationship with the child, and his remarriage disrupts this bond (Brand, Clingempeel, & Bowen-Woodward, 1988).

Girls, especially, have a hard time getting along with their stepmothers (Hobart & Brown, 1988). Sometimes (as just mentioned) this occurs because the girl's relationship with her father is threatened by the remarriage. In addition, girls often become entangled in loyalty conflicts between their two mother figures. But the longer girls live in father–stepmother households, the more positive their interaction with stepmothers becomes. With time and patience they do adjust, and eventually girls benefit from the support of a second mother figure (Hetherington & Jodl, 1994).

■ **SUPPORT FOR BLENDED FAMILIES.** In blended families, as in divorce, there are multiple pathways leading to diverse outcomes. Family life education and therapy can help parents and children adapt to the complexities of their new circumstances. Effective approaches encourage stepparents to move into their new roles gradually rather than abruptly. Only when a warm bond has formed between stepparents and stepchildren is more active parenting possible. In addition, couples often need help in forming a "parenting coalition"—cooperation and consistency in child rearing (Visher, 1994). By limiting loyalty conflicts, this allows children to benefit from stepparent relationships and increased diversity in their lives.

GAY AND LESBIAN FAMILIES

Several million American gay men and lesbians are parents, most through heterosexual marriages that ended in divorce, a few through adoption or reproductive technologies (Patterson, 1996). In the past, laws assuming that homosexuals could not be adequate parents led those who divorced a heterosexual partner to lose custody of their children. Today, several states hold that sexual orientation is irrelevant to custody. In others, fierce prejudice against homosexual parents still prevails.

Families headed by a homosexual parent or a gay or lesbian couple are very similar to those of heterosexuals. Gay and lesbian parents are as committed to and effective at the parental role, and sometimes more so. Indeed, some research indicates that gay fathers are more consistent in setting limits and more responsive to their children's needs than are heterosexual fathers, perhaps because gay men's less traditional gender identity fosters involvement with children (Bigner & Jacobsen,

These adopted children spend a quiet hour watching television with their two fathers. Homosexual parents are as committed to and effective at child rearing as are heterosexual parents. Their children are well adjusted, and the large majority develop a heterosexual orientation. *(S. Grazin/The Image Works)*

1989). Children of gay and lesbian parents are as well adjusted as other children, and the large majority are heterosexual (Bailey et al., 1995; Golombok & Tasker, 1996).

Partners of homosexual parents usually take on some caregiving responsibilities and are attached to the children. But their involvement varies with the way children were brought into the relationship. When children were adopted or conceived through reproductive technologies, partners tend to be more involved than when children resulted from a previous heterosexual relationship (Hare & Richards, 1993).

Overall, children of homosexuals can be distinguished from other children only by issues related to living in a nonsupportive society. The greatest concern of gay and lesbian parents is that their children will be stigmatized by their parents' sexual orientation (Hare, 1994).

MATERNAL EMPLOYMENT AND DUAL-EARNER FAMILIES

Today, single and married mothers are in the labor market in nearly equal proportions, and over 70 percent of those with school-age children are employed (U.S. Bureau of the Census, 1997). Indeed, the dominant family form today is the dual-earner family, in which both parents work. In Chapter 7, we saw that the impact of maternal employment on infant development depends on the quality of substitute care and the continuing parent–child relationship. This same conclusion applies during later years. In addition, a host of factors—the mother's work satisfaction, the support she receives from her husband, and the child's sex—have a bearing on how well children fare.

■ **MATERNAL EMPLOYMENT AND CHILD DEVELOPMENT.** Children of mothers who enjoy their work and remain committed to parenting show especially positive adjustment—a higher sense of self-esteem, more positive family and peer relations, less gender-stereotyped beliefs, and better grades in school. Girls, especially, profit from the image of female competence. Daughters of employed mothers perceive the woman's role as involving more freedom of choice and satisfaction and are more achievement and career oriented (Hoffman, 1989; Williams & Radin, 1993).

These benefits undoubtedly result from parenting practices. Employed mothers who value their parenting role are more likely to use authoritative child rearing (Greenberger & Goldberg, 1989). They schedule special times to devote to their children and also encourage greater responsibility and independence. A modest increase in fathers' involvement in child care and household duties also accompanies maternal employment (Coltrane, 1996). More contact with the father is related to intelligence, achievement, mature social behavior, and flexible gender-role attitudes (Gottfried, 1991; Radin, 1994).

However, when employment places heavy demands on the mother's schedule, children are at risk for ineffective parenting. Working long hours and spending little time with school-age children are associated with less favorable adjustment (Moorehouse, 1991). In contrast, part-time employment seems to have benefits for children of all ages, probably because it permits mothers to meet the needs of children with a wide range of characteristics (Lerner & Abrams, 1994; Williams & Radin, 1993).

■ **SUPPORT FOR EMPLOYED PARENTS AND THEIR FAMILIES.** As long as mothers have the necessary supports to engage in effective child rearing, maternal employment offers children many advantages. In dual-earner families, the husband's willingness to share responsibilities is crucial. If the father helps very little or not at all, the mother carries a double load, at home and at work, leading to fatigue, distress, and reduced time and energy for children.

Employed mothers and dual-earner parents need assistance from work settings and communities in their child-rearing roles. Part-time employment and time off when children are ill would help them juggle the demands of work and child rearing. Although these workplace supports are available in Canada and Western Europe, at present only

CAREGIVING CONCERNS

Signs of Readiness for Self-Care and Ways to Help Children Manage on Their Own

SIGNS OF CHILD'S READINESS	HELPING CHILDREN MANAGE
At least 9 or 10 years old[a]	Establish a telephone check-in procedure with the parent, a relative, or a friend.
Can follow important rules and directions	Leave emergency numbers, as well as the numbers of friends and neighbors, by the telephone.
Can recognize dangerous situations and respond appropriately	
Can make phone calls and take messages in an emergency	Teach safety skills, including a fire escape plan and basic first aid.
Can use household appliances safely	Structure the child's after-school time by assigning regular responsibilities.
Can respond to strangers properly (not opening the door, not saying he or she is alone)	Establish rules about having friends over, going out, how much television, and which appliances can be used.
Can keep track of keys and lock and unlock doors	Select a safe, well-traveled route home from school, and do not let the child wear a house key on a chain that advertises his or her self-care status.
Can resolve sibling conflicts independently	
Does not feel frightened or unhappy	

Sources: Galambos & Maggs, 1991; Peterson, 1989.
[a]Before age 9 or 10, children should not be left unsupervised because they do not yet have the cognitive and social skills to deal with emergencies.

Child care for school-age children is widely available in Australia but rare in the United States. These Australian children have access to special lessons as part of a government-supported out-of-school-hours program. Low-income children, who otherwise would have few opportunities for such enrichment activities, benefit greatly—in school performance, peer relations, and psychological adjustment.
(Carly Wolinsky/Stock Boston)

unpaid employment leave is mandated by U.S. federal law. Equal pay and equal employment opportunities for women are also important. Because these policies enhance financial status and morale, they improve the way mothers feel and behave when they arrive home at the end of the working day.

■ **CHILD CARE FOR SCHOOL-AGE CHILDREN.** High-quality child care is vital for parents' peace of mind and children's well-being, even during middle childhood. In recent years, much public concern has been voiced about the estimated 2.4 million 5- to 13-year-olds in the United States who regularly look after themselves during after-school hours.

Research on these **self-care children** reveals inconsistent findings. Some studies report that they suffer from low self-esteem, antisocial behavior, poor academic achievement, and fearfulness, whereas others show no such effects (Padilla & Landreth, 1989). What explains these contradictions? The way self-care children spend their time seems to be the crucial factor. Children who have a history of authoritative child rearing, are monitored from a distance by telephone calls, and have regular after-school chores appear responsible and well adjusted. In contrast, those left to their own devices are more likely to bend to peer pressures and engage in antisocial behavior (Steinberg, 1986).

The Caregiving Concerns table above lists signs of readiness for self-care along with ways to help children manage on their own. Unfortunately, when children are not mature enough to handle the self-care arrangement, many employed parents have no alternative. After-school programs for 6- to 13-year-olds are rare in American communities. Where high-quality programs do exist, low-income children who otherwise would have few opportunities for enrichment activities (scouting, music lessons, and organized sports) show improved school performance, peer relations, and psychological adjustment (Posner & Vandell, 1994).

BRIEF REVIEW

During the school years, child rearing shifts toward coregulation, in which parents exercise general oversight while granting children more decision-making power. Sibling rivalry tends to increase, and children often take steps to reduce it by striving to be different from one another. Only children are just as well adjusted as children with siblings, and they are advantaged in academic achievement and educational attainment. Large numbers of American children experience the divorce of their parents. Although many adjust well by 2 years after the divorce, boys and temperamentally difficult children are likely to experience more severe and lasting problems. Effective parenting is the most important factor in helping children adapt to life in a single-parent family. When parents cohabit or remarry, children living in father–stepmother families, daughters especially, have a harder time.

Children of gay and lesbian parents develop as favorably as other children, and most are heterosexual. Maternal employment is related to high self-esteem, reduced gender stereotyping, and mature social behavior. However, outcomes depend on the demands of the mother's job and the father's participation in child rearing. The impact of self-care on school-age children varies with parenting practices and how children spend their time.

ASK YOURSELF . . .

■ *"How come you don't study hard and get good grades like your sister?" a mother exclaimed in exasperation after seeing her son's poor report card. What impact do remarks like this have on sibling interaction, and why?*

■ *What advice would you give divorcing parents of two school-age sons about how to help their children adapt to life in a single-parent family?*

■ *Eight-year-old Bobby's mother has just found employment, so Bobby takes care of himself after school. What factors are likely to affect Bobby's adjustment to this arrangement?*

SOME COMMON PROBLEMS OF DEVELOPMENT

Throughout our discussion, we have considered a variety of stressful experiences that place children at risk for future problems. In the following sections, we touch on two more areas of concern: school-age children's fears and anxieties and the devastating consequences of child sexual abuse. Finally, we review factors that help school-age children cope effectively with stress and those that predispose them to long-term psychological dysfunction.

FEARS AND ANXIETIES

Although fears of the dark, thunder and lightning, and supernatural beings (often stimulated by movies and television) persist into middle childhood, children's anxieties are also directed toward new concerns. As children begin to understand the realities of the wider world, the possibility of personal harm (being robbed, stabbed, or shot) and media events (war and disasters) often trouble them. Other common worries include academic performance, parents' health, physical injuries, and rejection by classmates (Silverman, La Greca, & Wasserstein, 1995).

Children's fears are shaped in part by their culture. For example, in China, where self-restraint and complying with social standards are highly valued, more children mention failure and adult criticism as salient fears than in Australia or the United States. Chinese children, however, are not more fearful overall. The number and intensity of fears they report resemble those of Western children (Ollendick et al., 1996).

Most children handle their fears constructively, by talking about them with parents, teachers, and friends and relying on the more sophisticated emotional self-regulation strategies that develop in middle childhood. Consequently, fears decline steadily with age, especially for girls, who express more fears than do boys throughout childhood and adolescence (Gullone & King, 1997).

About 20 percent of school-age children develop an intense, unmanageable anxiety of some kind (Beidel, 1991). **School phobia** is an example. Typically, children with this

self-care children
Children who look after themselves while their parents are at work.

school phobia
Severe apprehension about attending school, often accompanied by physical complaints that disappear once the child is allowed to remain home.

disorder are middle-SES youngsters whose achievement is average or above. Still, they feel severe apprehension about attending school, often accompanied by physical complaints (dizziness, nausea, stomachaches, and vomiting) that disappear once they are allowed to remain home. About one-third are 5- to 7-year-olds, most of whom do not fear school so much as separation from their mother. The difficulty often can be traced to a troubled parent–child relationship in which the mother encourages dependency. Intensive family therapy is necessary to help these children (Pilkington & Piersel, 1991).

Most cases of school phobia appear later, around 11 to 13, during the transition from middle childhood to adolescence. These youngsters usually find a particular aspect of school experience frightening—an overcritical teacher, a school bully, the jeering remarks of insensitive peers, or too much parental pressure for school success. Treating this form of school phobia may require a change in school environment or parenting practices. Firm insistence that the child return to school along with training in how to cope with difficult situations is also helpful (Blagg & Yule, 1996).

Severe childhood anxieties may also arise from harsh living conditions. A great many children live in the midst of constant violence. In inner-city ghettos and in war-torn areas of the world, they learn to drop to the floor at the sound of gunfire, and they witness the wounding and killing of friends and relatives. As the Cultural Influences box on the following page reveals, these youngsters often suffer from long-term emotional distress. Finally, as we saw in our discussion of child abuse in Chapter 10, too often violence and other destructive acts become part of adult–child relationships. During middle childhood, child sexual abuse increases.

CHILD SEXUAL ABUSE

Until recently, child sexual abuse was viewed as a rare occurrence. When children came forward with it, adults often thought they had fantasized the experience and did not take their claims seriously. In the 1970s, efforts by professionals along with media attention caused child sexual abuse to be recognized as a serious and widespread problem. Several hundred thousand cases are reported in the United States each year (see Chapter 10).

■ **CHARACTERISTICS OF ABUSERS AND VICTIMS.** Sexual abuse is committed against children of both sexes, but more often against girls than boys. Reported cases are highest in middle childhood, but sexual abuse also occurs at younger and older ages. Few children experience only a single episode. For some, the abuse begins early in life and continues for many years (Burkhardt & Rotatori, 1995).

Generally, the abuser is a male—a parent or someone whom the parent knows well. Often it is a father, stepfather, or live-in boyfriend; somewhat less often an uncle or older brother. In a few instances, mothers are the offenders, more often with sons than daughters. If the abuser is a nonrelative, it is usually someone the child has come to know and trust (Kolvin & Trowell, 1996).

In the overwhelming majority of cases, the abuse is serious—vaginal or anal intercourse, oral genital contact, fondling, and forced stimulation of the adult. Abusers make the child comply in a variety of distasteful ways, including deception, bribery, verbal intimidation, and physical force (Gomez-Schwartz, Horowitz, & Cardarelli, 1990).

You may be wondering how any adult—especially a parent or close relative—could possibly violate a child sexually. Many offenders deny their own responsibility. They blame the abuse on the willing participation of a seductive youngster. Yet children are not capable of making a deliberate, informed decision to enter into a sexual relationship! Even at older ages, they are not free to say yes or no. Instead, abusers tend to have characteristics that predispose them toward sexual exploitation of children. As Table 13.3 shows, they have great difficulty controlling their impulses, may suffer from psychological disorders, and often are addicted to alcohol or drugs. Often they pick out children who are

CULTURAL INFLUENCES

THE IMPACT OF ETHNIC AND POLITICAL VIOLENCE ON CHILDREN

On May 27, 1992, Zlata Filipovic, a 10-year-old Bosnian girl, recorded in her diary the following reactions to the intensifying Serb attack on the city of Sarajevo:

SLAUGHTER! MASSACRE! HORROR! CRIME! BLOOD! SCREAMS! TEARS! DESPAIR!

That's what Vaso Miskin Street looks like today. Two shells exploded in the street and one in the market. Mommy was nearby at the time.... Daddy and I were beside ourselves because she hadn't come home. I saw some of it on TV but I still can't believe what I actually saw.... I've got a lump in my throat and a knot in my tummy. HORRIBLE. They're taking the wounded to the hospital. It's a madhouse. We kept going to the window hoping to see Mommy, but she wasn't back.... Daddy and I were tearing our hair out.... I looked out the window one more time and ... I SAW MOMMY RUNNING ACROSS THE BRIDGE. As she came into the house she started shaking and crying. Through her tears she told us how she had seen dismembered bodies.... Thank God, Mommy is with us. Thank God. (Filipovic, 1994, p. 55)

Violence stemming from ethnic and political tensions is being felt increasingly around the world. Today, virtually all armed conflicts are internal civil wars in which well-established ways of life are threatened or destroyed and children are frequently victims (Ressler, 1993).

Children's experiences under conditions of armed conflict are diverse. Some may participate in the fighting, either because they are forced or because they want to please adults. Others are kidnapped, terrorized, or tortured. Those who are bystanders often come under direct fire and may be killed or physically maimed for life. And as Zlata's diary entry illustrates, many children of war watch in horror as family members, friends, and neighbors flee, are wounded, or die (Ladd & Cairns, 1996).

When war and social crises are temporary, most children are comforted by caregivers' reassuring messages and do not show long-term emotional difficulties. But chronic danger requires children to make substantial adjustments, and their psychological functioning can be seriously impaired. Many children of war lose their sense of safety, become desensitized to violence, are haunted by terrifying memories, and build a pessimistic view of the future (Cairns, 1996).

The extent to which children are negatively affected by war depends on mediating factors. Closeness to wartime events increases the chances of maladjustment. For example, an estimated 50 percent of traumatized 6- to 12-year-old Cambodian war refugees continued to show intense stress reactions when they reached young adulthood (Kinzie et al., 1989). The support and affection of parents is the best safeguard against lasting problems. Unfortunately, many children of war are separated from family members. Sometimes, the child's community can offer protection. For example, Israeli children who lost a parent in battle fared best when they lived in kibbutzim, where many adults knew the child well and felt responsible for his or her welfare (Lifschitz et al., 1977).

When wartime drains families and communities of resources, international organizations need to step in and help children. Until we know how to prevent war, efforts to preserve children's physical, psychological, and educational well-being may be the best way to stop transmission of violence to the next generation in many parts of the world.

This Rwandan refugee child has experienced the trauma of civil war. Here he watches as his home burns, and he has probably witnessed the wounding and death of family members, friends, and neighbors. If he survives, he is likely to show lasting emotional problems without special support from caring adults. *(Michael Simpson/The Picture Cube)*

TABLE 13.3

Factors Related to Child Sexual Abuse

FACTOR	DESCRIPTION
Abuser	Usually a male and a member of the child's family. Finds children sexually arousing, has difficulty controlling impulses, rationalizes that the victim wants sex and will enjoy it, and has learned to believe that sexual abuse of others is appropriate. May have a history of alcohol or drug addiction, serious psychological disturbance, or sexual abuse as a child.
Victim	More often female than male. Abusers tend to select children that seem like easy targets—ones who are physically weak, compliant in personality, emotionally needy, and socially isolated.
Family	Often associated with poverty and repeated marital breakup. However, also occurs in relatively stable, middle-SES families.

Sources: Faller, 1990; Kolvin & Trowell, 1996.

So there really was a monster in her bedroom.

For many kids, there's a real reason to be afraid of the dark.

Last year in Indiana, there were 6,912 substantiated cases of sexual abuse. The trauma can be devastating for the child and for the family. So listen closely to the children around you.

If you hear something you don't want to believe, perhaps you should. For helpful information on child abuse prevention, contact the LaPorte County Child Abuse Prevention Council, 7451 Johnson Road, Michigan City, IN 46360. (219) 874-0007

LaPorte County Child Abuse Prevention Council

This public service announcement reminds adults that child sexual abuse, until recently regarded as a product of children's vivid imaginations, is a devastating reality. Victims are in urgent need of protection and treatment. *(La Porte County Child Abuse Protection Council)*

unlikely to defend themselves—those who are physically weak, emotionally deprived, and socially isolated (Faller, 1990).

Reported cases of child sexual abuse are strongly linked to poverty, marital instability, and resulting weakening of family ties. Children who live in homes with a history of constantly changing characters—repeated marriages, separations, and new partners—are especially vulnerable. But community surveys reveal that children in economically advantaged, stable families are also victims; they are simply more likely to escape detection. Intense pressure toward secrecy and feelings of confusion and guilt prevent most children from seeking help (Gomez-Schwartz, Horowitz, & Cardarelli, 1990).

■ **CONSEQUENCES OF SEXUAL ABUSE.** Virtually all children are emotionally distressed at the time sexual abuse occurs. Long-term consequences can be prevented if the abuse is stopped after only a few instances and children are assured that caring, nonabusive adults will support and protect them (Goodman et al., 1992). Unfortunately, the outcomes for many youngsters are not so favorable. Sexually abused children often become known to authorities only after they have developed extreme behavioral symptoms. Perhaps a school official suspects abuse, or a parent observes the child's emotional difficulties and seeks professional help (Faller, 1990).

The adjustment problems of child sexual abuse victims are often severe. Depression, low self-esteem, mistrust of adults, and anger and hostility can persist for years after the abusive episodes. Younger children react with sleep difficulties, loss of appetite, and generalized fearfulness and anxiety. Adolescents may run away or show suicidal reactions, substance abuse, and delinquency (Kendall-Tackett, Williams, & Finkelhor, 1993; Tebbutt et al., 1997).

Sexually abused children frequently display sexual knowledge and behavior beyond their years. They have learned from their abusers that sexual overtures are acceptable ways to get attention and rewards. As they move toward young adulthood, abused girls often enter into unhealthy relationships. Many become promiscuous, believing that their bodies are for the use of others. When they marry, they are likely to choose husbands who are abusive toward them and their children (Faller, 1990). And as mothers, they often show poor parenting skills, abusing and neglecting their youngsters (Pianta, Egeland, & Erickson, 1989). In these ways, the harmful impact of sexual abuse is transmitted to the next generation.

■ **PREVENTION AND TREATMENT.** Treating child sexual abuse is difficult. The reactions of family members—anxiety about harm to the child, anger toward the abuser, and sometimes hostility toward the victim for telling—can increase children's distress. Sensitive work with parents is essential for helping the abused child. Since sexual abuse typically appears in the midst of other serious family problems, long-term therapy with children and families is usually necessary (Briere, 1992; Gomez-Schwartz, Horowitz, & Cardarelli, 1990).

The best way to reduce the suffering of child sexual abuse victims is to prevent it from continuing. Today, courts are prosecuting abusers (especially nonrelatives) more rigorously. And, as the Social Issues box on the following page indicates, children's testimony is

SOCIAL ISSUES

CHILDREN'S EYEWITNESS TESTIMONY

*R*enata, a physically abused and neglected 8-year-old, was taken from her parents and placed in foster care. There, she was seen engaging in sexually aggressive behavior toward other children, including grabbing their sex organs and using obscene language. Renata's foster mother suspected that sexual abuse had taken place in her natural home. She informed the child protective service worker, who met with Renata to gather information. But Renata seemed anxious and uncomfortable. She did not want to answer any questions.

Increasingly, children are being called on to testify in court cases involving child abuse and neglect, child custody, and other matters. Having to provide such information can be difficult and traumatic. Almost always, children must report on highly stressful events. In doing so, they may have to speak against a parent or other relative to whom they feel a strong sense of loyalty. In some family disputes, they may fear punishment for telling the truth. In addition, child witnesses are faced with a strange and unfamiliar situation—at the very least, an interview in the judge's chambers, and at most, an open courtroom with judge, jury, spectators, and the possibility of unsympathetic cross-examination. Not surprisingly, there is considerable debate about the accuracy of children's recall under these conditions.

In most states, it is rare for children younger than age 5 to be asked to testify, whereas those age 6 and older often are. Children between ages 10 and 14 are generally assumed competent to testify. These guidelines make good sense in terms of what we know about memory development. Compared to preschoolers, school-age children are better able to give detailed

descriptions of past experiences and make accurate inferences about others' motives and intentions. Also, older children are more resistant to misleading questions of the sort asked by attorneys when they probe for more information or, in cross-examination, try to influence the content of the child's response (Ceci & Bruck, 1993; Goodman & Tobey, 1994).

Nevertheless, when properly questioned, even 3-year-olds can recall recent events accurately—including ones that were highly stressful (Baker-Ward et al., 1993; Goodman et al., 1991). But court testimony often involves repeated interviews. When adults lead children by suggesting incorrect facts ("He touched you there, didn't he?"), they increase the likelihood of incorrect reporting—even among school-age children, whose descriptions are usually elaborate and dependable (Ornstein et al., 1997). By the time children come to court, it is weeks, months, or even years after the occurrence of the target events. When a long delay is combined with suggestions about what happened and stereotyping of the accused ("He's in jail because he's been bad"), children can easily be misled into giving false information. Younger children are more likely to treat suggested memories as actually witnessed events (Ceci, Leichtman, & Bruck, 1994; Leichtman & Ceci, 1995).

When children are interviewed in a frightening legal setting, their ability to report past events completely and accurately is reduced further (Saywitz & Nathanson, 1993). To ease the task of providing testimony, special interviewing methods have been devised for children. In Renata's case, a professional used puppets to ask questions and had Renata respond through them. In many child sexual abuse cases, anatomically correct dolls have been used to prompt children's recall.

However, serious concerns have been raised about this method. Research indicates that it does not improve the accuracy of young children's answers. And it can encourage them to report physical and sexual contact that, in fact, never happened (Ceci & Bruck, 1998).

Child witnesses need to be prepared so that they understand the courtroom process and know what to expect. Before age 8, children have little grasp of the differing roles of judge, attorney, and police officer. Many regard the court negatively, as "a room you pass through on your way to jail" (Saywitz, 1989, p. 149). In some places, "court schools" exist in which children are taken through the setting and given an opportunity to role-play court activities. As part of this process, children can be encouraged to admit not knowing an answer rather than guessing or going along with what an adult expects of them. At the same time, legal professionals need to take steps to lessen the risk of suggestibility—by limiting the number of times children are interviewed, asking questions in nonleading ways, and being warm and patient (Ceci & Bruck, 1993).

If a child is likely to experience emotional trauma or later punishment (in a family dispute), then courtroom procedures can be adapted to protect them. For example, Renata eventually testified over closed circuit TV so she would not have to face her abusive father. When it is not wise for a child to participate directly, expert witnesses can provide testimony that reports on the child's psychological condition and includes important elements of the child's story. But for such testimony to be worthwhile, witnesses need to be impartial and carefully trained in how to question children in ways that minimize false reporting (Ceci & Bruck, 1995).

being taken more seriously. New ways have been devised to enable children to tell about their experiences without suffering additional emotional harm.

Educational programs can help children recognize inappropriate sexual advances and show them where to go for help. Yet because of controversies over teaching children about sexual abuse, few schools offer these interventions. New Zealand is the only country in the world with a national, school-based prevention program targeting sexual abuse. In *Keeping Ourselves Safe*, 5- to 13-year-olds learn that when abuse occurs, someone close to them, not a stranger, is usually responsible. Parent involvement ensures that home and school work together in teaching children self-protection skills (Sanders, 1997). Evaluations reveal that virtually all New Zealand parents and children support the program and that it has helped many children avoid or report abuse (Briggs & Hawkins, 1996, 1999).

FOSTERING RESILIENCE IN MIDDLE CHILDHOOD

Throughout middle childhood—and other phases of development as well—children are confronted with challenging and sometimes threatening situations that require them to cope with psychological stress. In this trio of chapters, we have considered such topics as chronic illness, learning disabilities, achievement expectations, divorce, and child sexual abuse. Each taxes children's coping resources, creating serious risks for development.

At the same time, many studies indicate only a modest relationship between stressful life experiences and psychological disturbance in childhood (Garmezy, 1993; Rutter, 1979). Think back to our discussion in Chapter 4 of the long-term consequences of birth complications. We noted that some children manage to overcome the combined effects of birth trauma, poverty, and a deeply troubled family life. The same is true when we look at findings on school difficulties, family transitions, and child maltreatment.

Recall from Chapter 1 that research highlights three broad factors that protect against maladjustment:

- personal characteristics of children—an easy temperament, high self-esteem, and a mastery-oriented approach to new situations

- a family environment that provides warmth, closeness, and order and organization to the child's life

- a person outside the immediate family—perhaps a grandparent, teacher, or close friend—who develops a special relationship with the child, offering a support system and a positive coping model

Return to pages 10–11 to review these ingredients of resilience. Any one of them can account for why one child fares well and another poorly when exposed to hardship. Yet most of the time, personal and environmental resources are interconnected (Smith & Prior, 1995; Sorenson, 1993). Throughout this book, we have seen many examples of how unfavorable life experiences increase the chances that parents and children will act in ways that expose them to further hardship. Children can usually handle one stressor in their lives, even if it is chronic. But when negative conditions pile up, such as marital discord, poverty, crowded living conditions, parental psychological disorder, and abuse, the rate of maladjustment is multiplied (Capaldi & Patterson, 1991; Sameroff et al., 1993).

Social supports are especially important during periods of developmental transition—when children are more vulnerable because they are faced with many new tasks (Rutter, 1987). One such turning point is the beginning of middle childhood, a time of new challenges in academic work and peer relations. We have seen how families, schools, communities, and society as a whole can enhance or undermine the school-age child's developing sense of competence. Another major turning point is the transition to adolescence. As the next three chapters will reveal, young people whose experiences have helped them learn how to overcome obstacles and strive for self-direction meet the challenges of this new phase quite well.

ASK YOURSELF . . .

- *Explain how the three factors that foster resilience, listed in the previous section, help account for variations in children's adjustment after marital breakup.*

- *How does each level of Bronfenbrenner's ecological systems theory—microsystem, mesosystem, exosystem, and macrosystem—contribute to the effects of maternal employment on children's development?*

Summary

ERIKSON'S THEORY: INDUSTRY VERSUS INFERIORITY

What personality changes take place during Erikson's stage of industry versus inferiority?

■ According to Erikson, children who successfully resolve the critical psychological conflict of **industry versus inferiority** develop the capacity to engage in productive work, learn the value of division of labor, and develop a sense of moral commitment and responsibility.

SELF-DEVELOPMENT

Describe school-age children's self-concept and self-esteem, and discuss factors that affect their achievement-related attributions.

■ During middle childhood, children's self-concepts include personality traits and **social comparisons.** Self-esteem becomes hierarchically organized and declines over the early school years as children adjust their self-judgments to feedback from the environment. Child-rearing practices that are warm and responsive and that provide firm but reasonable expectations for behavior are consistently related to high self-esteem.

■ Research on achievement-related **attributions** has identified adult messages that affect children's academic self-esteem. Children with **mastery-oriented attributions** credit their successes to high ability and their failures to insufficient effort. In contrast, those with **learned helplessness** attribute their successes to luck and failures to low ability. Children who receive negative feedback about their ability develop the learned-helpless pattern. **Attribution retraining** encourages learned helpless children to revise their failure-related attributions, thereby improving self-esteem.

EMOTIONAL DEVELOPMENT

Cite changes in understanding and expression of emotion in middle childhood.

■ In middle childhood, self-conscious emotions of pride and guilt become clearly integrated with personal responsibility. When children experience intense shame, their overall sense of self-worth can be profoundly shattered.

■ School-age children recognize that people can experience more than one emotion at a time. They also attend to more cues—facial, situational, and past experiences—in interpreting another's feelings. Gains in perspective taking and emotional understanding lead empathy to increase in middle childhood.

■ By the end of middle childhood, most children have an adaptive set of techniques for regulating emotion. Emotionally well-regulated children are optimistic, prosocial, and well liked by peers.

UNDERSTANDING OTHERS

How does perspective taking change in middle childhood?

■ Perspective taking improves greatly over middle childhood, as Selman's five-stage sequence indicates. Cognitive maturity and experiences in which adults and peers encourage children to take note of another's viewpoint support school-age children's perspective-taking skill. Good perspective takers show more positive social skills.

MORAL DEVELOPMENT

Describe changes in moral understanding during middle childhood.

■ By middle childhood, children have internalized a wide variety of moral rules. Consequently, they are less dependent on modeling and reinforcement for morally relevant behavior than they were at younger ages.

■ Children's concepts of **distributive justice** change over middle childhood, from equality to merit to benevolence. School-age children also begin to grasp the linkage between moral rules and social conventions.

PEER RELATIONS

How do peer sociability and friendship change in middle childhood?

■ In middle childhood, peer interaction becomes more positive and prosocial, and physical aggression declines. By the end of the school years, children organize themselves into **peer groups.**

■ Friendships develop into mutual relationships based on trust. Children tend to select friends like themselves in sex, race, ethnicity, SES, personality, popularity, and academic achievement.

Describe major categories of peer acceptance and ways to help rejected children.

■ **Sociometric techniques** are used to distinguish four types of peer acceptance: (1) **popular children,** who are liked by many agemates; (2) **rejected children,** who are actively disliked; (3) **controversial children,** who are both liked and disliked; and (4) **neglected children,** who are seldom chosen, either positively or negatively.

■ At least two subtypes of peer rejection exist: **rejected-aggressive children,** who show severe conduct problems, and **rejected-withdrawn children,** who are passive and socially awkward. Both subgroups often experience lasting adjustment difficulties.

■ Coaching in social skills, academic tutoring, and training in social understanding have been used to help rejected youngsters. To produce lasting change, intervening in parent–child interaction is probably necessary.

GENDER TYPING

What changes in gender-stereotyped beliefs and gender-role identity take place during middle childhood?

Summary (continued)

■ School-age children extend their awareness of gender stereotypes to personality characteristics and academic subjects. Although they develop a more open-minded view of what males and females can do, they often do not approve of males who violate gender-role expectations.

■ Boys strengthen their identification with the masculine role, whereas girls feel free to experiment with "opposite gender" activities. Cultures shape gender-typed behavior through the daily activities assigned to children.

FAMILY INFLUENCES

How do parent–child communication and sibling relationships change in middle childhood?

■ Effective parents of school-age youngsters engage in **coregulation,** exerting general oversight while permitting children to be in charge of moment-by-moment decision making. Coregulation depends on a cooperative relationship between parent and child.

■ During middle childhood, sibling rivalry tends to increase as children participate in a wider range of activities and parents compare their traits and accomplishments. Siblings often try to reduce this rivalry by striving to be different from one another. Older siblings are slightly advantaged in IQ and school achievement. Younger siblings are more popular.

■ Only children are as well adjusted as are children with siblings. In addition, they do better in school and attain higher levels of education, probably because of their closer relationships with parents, who exert more pressure for mastery and accomplishment.

What factors influence children's adjustment to divorce and blended family arrangements, and how do children fare in gay and lesbian families?

■ Divorce is common in the lives of American children. Although painful emotional reactions usually accompany the period surrounding divorce, children with difficult temperaments and boys in mother-custody homes are more likely to show lasting adjustment problems.

■ The overriding factor in positive adjustment following divorce is good parenting. Contact with noncustodial fathers is also important. Because **divorce mediation** helps parents resolve their disputes, it can reduce children's exposure to conflict. **Joint custody** is a controversial practice that may create additional strains for children.

■ When divorced parents enter new relationships through cohabitation or remarriage, children must adapt to a **blended, or reconstituted, family.** How well they fare depends on which parent remarries and the age and sex of the child. Girls, older children, and children in father–stepmother families display the greatest adjustment problems.

How do maternal employment and life in dual-earner families affect children's development?

■ As long as mothers enjoy their work and remain committed to parenting, maternal employment is associated with favorable consequences for children, including a higher sense of self-esteem, more positive family and peer relations, less gender-stereotyped beliefs, and better grades in school. In dual earner families, the father's willingness to share responsibilities is vital. The availability of workplace supports, such as part-time employment and generous parental leave, assists parents in balancing the demands of work and child rearing.

■ **Self-care children** who are monitored from a distance and experience authoritative parenting appear responsible and well adjusted. In contrast, children left to their own devices are at risk for antisocial behavior. High-quality day care for school-age children is not widely available in the United States.

SOME COMMON PROBLEMS OF DEVELOPMENT

Cite common fears and anxieties in middle childhood.

■ During middle childhood, children's fears are directed toward new concerns having to do with physical safety, media events, achievement, parents' health, and peer relations. Some children develop intense, unmanageable fears, such as **school phobia.** Severe anxiety can also result from harsh living conditions.

Discuss factors related to child sexual abuse and its consequences for children's development.

■ Child sexual abuse is generally committed by male family members, more often against girls than boys. Abusers have characteristics that predispose them toward sexual exploitation of children. Reported cases are strongly associated with poverty and marital instability. Adjustment problems of abused children are often severe. Common reactions are depression, low self-esteem, mistrust of adults, anger and hostility, and inappropriate sexual behavior.

Cite factors that foster resilience in middle childhood.

■ Overall, a modest relationship exists between stressful life experiences and psychological disturbance in childhood. Personal characteristics of children, a warm, well-organized home life, and social supports outside the family are related to resilience in the face of stress.

ℐmportant terms and concepts

attribution retraining (p. 488)
attributions (p. 487)
blended, or reconstituted, families
    (p. 509)
coregulation (p. 504)
controversial children (p. 499)
distributive justice (p. 494)
divorce mediation (p. 508)
industry versus inferiority (p. 482)

joint custody (p. 508)
learned helplessness (p. 487)
mastery-oriented attributions
    (p. 487)
neglected children (p. 499)
peer group (p. 496)
perspective taking (p. 492)
popular children (p. 499)
rejected-aggressive children (p. 499)

rejected children (p. 499)
rejected-withdrawn children (p. 499)
school phobia (p. 513)
self-care children (p. 513)
social comparisons (p. 483)
sociometric techniques (p. 498)

ℱyi...   FOR FURTHER INFORMATION AND HELP

DIVORCE

Parents Without Partners
(800) 637-7974
Website: www.parentswithout partners.org

Organization of custodial and noncustodial single parents that provides support in the upbringing of children. Many local groups exist throughout the United States.

BLENDED FAMILIES

Stepfamily Association of America
(800) 735-0329
Website: www.stepfam.org

Association of families interested in stepfamily relationships. Organizes support groups and offers education and children's services.

Stepfamily Foundation
(212) 877-3244
Website: www.stepfamily.org

Organization of remarried parents, interested professionals, and divorced individuals. Arranges group counseling sessions for stepfamilies and provides training for professionals.

CHILD SEXUAL ABUSE

Parents United International
(408) 453-7616

Organization of individuals who have experienced child sexual abuse. Assists families affected by incest and other types of sexual abuse by providing information and arranging for medical and legal counseling.

Society's League Against Molestation
(609) 858-7800

A 100,000-member organization that works to prevent child sexual abuse through public education. Offers counseling and assistance to victims and their families.

$\mathcal{M}$ilestones

OF DEVELOPMENT IN MIDDLE CHILDHOOD

AGE	PHYSICAL	COGNITIVE	LANGUAGE	EMOTIONAL/SOCIAL
6–8 years	■ Slow gains in height and weight continue until adolescent growth spurt. (410) ■ Gradual replacement of primary teeth by permanent teeth throughout middle childhood. (412) ■ Writing becomes smaller and more legible. Letter reversals decline. (426–427) ■ Drawings become more organized and detailed and start to include some depth cues. (426) ■ Organized games with rules and rough-and-tumble play become common. (429–431) ■ Dominance hierarchies become more stable, especially among boys. (431)	■ Thought becomes more logical, as shown by the ability to pass Piagetian conservation, class inclusion, and seriation problems. (438–439) ■ Understanding of spatial concepts improves, as illustrated by conservation of distance and ability to give clear, well-organized directions. (439) ■ Attention becomes more selective and adaptable. (443) ■ Uses memory strategies of rehearsal and organization. (445) ■ Regards the mind as an active, constructive agent, capable of transforming information. (448) ■ Awareness of the importance of memory strategies and the impact of psychological factors (attention, motivation) in task performance improves. (448–449) ■ By the end of this period, makes the transition from "learning to read" to "reading to learn." (451) ■ Uses informal knowledge of number concepts and counting to master more complex mathematical skills. (451–452)	■ Vocabulary increases rapidly throughout middle childhood. (462) ■ Word definitions are concrete, referring to functions and appearance. (462) ■ Metalinguistic awareness improves. (462)	■ Self-concept begins to include personality traits and social comparisons. (483) ■ Self-esteem differentiates, becomes hierarchically organized, and declines to a more realistic level. (485) ■ Self-conscious emotions of pride and guilt are governed by personal responsibility. (490) ■ Recognizes that individuals can experience more than one emotion at a time. (490) ■ Attends to more cues—facial, situational, and past experiences—in interpreting another's feelings. (491) ■ Understands that access to different information often causes people to have different perspectives. (492–493) ■ Becomes more responsible and independent. (494) ■ Distributive justice reasoning changes from equality to merit to benevolence. (494–495) ■ Peer interaction becomes more prosocial, and physical aggression declines. (496)

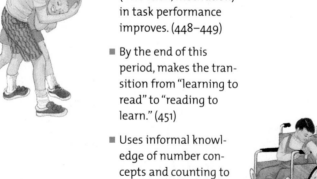

AGE	PHYSICAL	COGNITIVE	LANGUAGE	EMOTIONAL/SOCIAL
9–11 years	■ Adolescent growth spurt begins 2 years earlier for girls than boys. (410) ■ Gross motor skills of running, jumping, throwing, catching, kicking, batting, and dribbling are executed more quickly and with better coordination. (425) ■ Reaction time improves, contributing to motor skill development. (426) ■ Depth cues evident in drawings through overlapping objects, diagonal placement, and converging lines. (427-428) 	■ Logical thought remains tied to concrete situations until the end of middle childhood. (440) ■ Piagetian tasks continue to be mastered in a step-by-step fashion. (440) ■ Planning improves. (444) ■ Memory strategies of rehearsal and organization become more effective. (445) ■ Applies several memory strategies at once. (445) ■ Memory strategy of elaboration appears. (445) ■ Long-term knowledge base grows larger and becomes better organized. (446) ■ Cognitive self-regulation improves. (449)	■ Word definitions emphasize synonyms and categorical relations. (462) ■ Grasps double meanings of words, as reflected in comprehension of metaphors and humor. (463) ■ Understanding of complex grammatical constructions improves. (463) ■ Adapts messages to the needs of listeners in complex communicative situations. (463) ■ Conversational strategies become more refined. (464) 	■ Self-esteem tends to rise. (486) ■ Distinguishes ability, effort, and luck in attributions for success and failure. (487) ■ Has an adaptive set of strategies for regulating emotion. (491) ■ Can "step into another's shoes" and view the self from that person's perspective. (492–493) ■ Later, can view the relationship between self and other from the perspective of a third, impartial party. (492–493) ■ Appreciates the linkage between moral rules and social conventions. (495) ■ Peer groups emerge. (496) ■ Friendships are based on mutual trust. (498) ■ Becomes aware of more gender stereotypes, including personality traits and school subjects, but has a more flexible appreciation of what males and females can do. (501–502) ■ Sibling rivalry tends to increase. (504)

Note: Numbers in parenthesis indicate the page on which each milestone is discussed.

"Happiness in the Wilderness"
Satyen D. Joshi
15 years, Kenya

The dramatic physical and cognitive changes of adolescence enable teenagers to see themselves and their surroundings from new vantage points. As Chapter 14 indicates, puberty is both an exhilarating and an apprehensive phase. In all societies, young people are expected to give up childish ways in favor of greater responsibility.

Reprinted by permission from The International Museum of Children's Art, Oslo, Norway.

PHYSICAL DEVELOPMENT

IN ADOLESCENCE

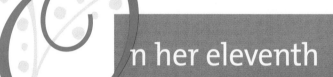

n her eleventh

birthday, Sabrina's friend Joyce gave a
surprise party, but Sabrina seemed
somber and withdrawn during the celebration. Although Sabrina and Joyce
had been close friends since third
grade, their relationship was faltering.
Sabrina was a head taller and some 20
pounds heavier than most of the other
girls in her sixth-grade class. Her
breasts were already well developed,
her hips and thighs had broadened,
and she had begun to menstruate. In
contrast, Joyce still had the short, lean,
angular, flat-chested body of a school-
age child.

Sabrina hadn't told Joyce about her
menstrual periods or talked about how
she felt about her developing body.
Since Joyce wasn't "there" yet, Sabrina
was convinced she wouldn't understand. Ducking into the bathroom
while Joyce and the other girls set the
table for cake and ice cream, Sabrina
looked herself over in the mirror,
straightened her blouse, smoothed her

skirt, and whispered, "Gosh, I feel so big and heavy." At church youth group on Sunday evenings, Sabrina broke away from Joyce and spent time with the eighth-grade girls, around whom she didn't feel so large and awkward.

Once every 2 weeks, parents gathered at Sabrina and Joyce's school for discussions about child-rearing concerns. Sabrina's Italian-American parents, Franca and Antonio, came whenever they could. "How you know they are becoming teenagers is this," volunteered Antonio. "The bedroom door is closed, and they want to be alone. Also, they contradict and disagree. I tell Sabrina, 'Only three minutes in the shower—there has to be water for the rest of us.' Or I say, 'You have to go to Aunt Gina's on Saturday for dinner with the family.' The next thing I know, she is arguing with me."

"All our four children were early developers," Franca added. "The three boys, too, were tall by age 12 or 13, but it was easier for them. They felt big and important. Sabrina is moody and doesn't want to be with her old friends. She was skinny as a little girl, but now she says she is too fat and wants to diet. She thinks about boys and doesn't concentrate on her studies. I try to be patient and listen to her," reflected Franca sympathetically. "It's not so easy for her to adjust."

Sabrina has entered adolescence, a period of development in which she will cross the dividing line between childhood and adulthood. In modern societies, the skills young people must master are so complex and the choices confronting them so diverse that adolescence lasts for nearly a decade. But around the world, the basic tasks of this phase are much the same. Sabrina must accept her full-grown body, acquire adult ways of thinking, attain emotional and economic independence, develop more mature ways of relating to peers of both sexes, and construct an identity—a secure sense of who she is, sexually, morally, politically, and vocationally.

The beginning of adolescence is marked by **puberty,** a flood of biological events leading to an adult-size body and sexual maturity. As Sabrina's reactions suggest, entry into adolescence can be a trying time, more so for some youngsters than for others. In this chapter, we trace the events of puberty and take up a variety of health concerns—nutrition, sexual activity, and serious health problems affecting teenagers who encounter difficulties on the path to maturity. We conclude with a discussion of adolescent motor development, which highlights the large sex differences that appear at this time. But before we delve into these specifics, let's begin with an overview of changing views of adolescence during this century.

CONCEPTIONS OF ADOLESCENCE

hat explains Sabrina's self-consciousness, argumentativeness, and retreat from family activities? Historically, theorists explained the impact of puberty on psychological development by resorting to extremes—either a biological or environmental explanation. Today, researchers realize that biological, social, and cultural forces jointly determine adolescent psychological change.

THE BIOLOGICAL PERSPECTIVE

Ask several parents of young children what they expect their sons and daughters to be like as teenagers. You will probably get some answers like these: "Rebellious and uncontrollable," "Full of rages and tempers." This view, widespread in contemporary American society, dates back to the writings of eighteenth-century philosopher Jean-Jacques Rousseau, whom we introduced in Chapter 1. Rousseau believed that a natural outgrowth of the biological upheaval of puberty was heightened emotionality, conflict, and defiance of adults.

puberty
Biological changes at adolescence that lead to an adult-size body and sexual maturity.

In the twentieth century, this storm-and-stress perspective was picked up by major theorists. The most influential was G. Stanley Hall, whose view of development was grounded in Darwin's theory of evolution (see Chapter 1, page 12). Hall (1904) described adolescence as a cascade of instinctual passions, a phase of growth so turbulent that it resembled the period in which human beings evolved from savages into civilized beings.

Sigmund Freud, as well, emphasized the emotional storminess of the teenage years. He called adolescence the *genital stage,* a period in which instinctual drives reawaken and shift to the genital region of the body. The struggle of the earlier phallic period is renewed, resulting in psychological conflict and volatile, unpredictable behavior. But unlike preschool children, adolescents can find romantic partners outside the family. As they do so, inner forces gradually achieve a new, more mature harmony, and the stage concludes with marriage, birth, and the rearing of children. In this way, young people fulfill their biological destiny: sexual reproduction and the survival of the species.

THE ENVIRONMENTAL PERSPECTIVE

Recent research on large numbers of teenagers suggests that Rousseau, Hall, and Freud's image of adolescence as a biologically determined, inevitable period of storm and stress is greatly exaggerated. A number of problems, such as eating disorders, depression, suicide, and law breaking, occur more often in adolescence than earlier. But the overall rate of serious psychological disturbance rises only slightly from childhood to adolescence, when it is the same as in the adult population—about 20 percent (Costello & Angold, 1995; Powers, Hauser, & Kilner, 1989). Although some teenagers encounter serious difficulties, emotional turbulence is not a routine feature of this phase of development.

The first researcher to point out the wide variability in adolescent adjustment was anthropologist Margaret Mead. In 1926, she traveled to the Pacific Islands of Samoa and returned with a startling conclusion: Samoan adolescence was free of all those characteristics that made it hazardous for young people and dreaded by adults in more complex societies. Because of the culture's relaxed social relationships and openness toward sexuality, adolescence, Mead (1928) reported, "is perhaps the pleasantest time the Samoan girl (or boy) will ever know" (p. 308).

Mead offered an alternative view in which the social environment is entirely responsible for the range of teenage experiences, from erratic and agitated to calm and stress free. Yet this conclusion is just as extreme as the biological perspective it tried to replace! Later researchers found that Samoan adolescence was not as untroubled as Mead had assumed (Freeman, 1983). Still, Mead convinced researchers that greater attention must be paid to social and cultural influences for adolescent development to be understood.

A BALANCED POINT OF VIEW

Today, we know that adolescence is a product of *both* biological and social forces. Biological changes are universal—found in all primates and all cultures. These internal stresses and the social expectations accompanying them—that the young person move away from childish ways of behaving, develop new interpersonal relationships, and take on greater responsibility—are likely to prompt moments of uncertainty, self-doubt, and disappointment in all teenagers.

At the same time, the length of adolescence and the number of hurdles a young person must overcome vary greatly from one culture to the next. Although simpler societies have a shorter transition to adulthood, adolescence is not absent (Weisfield, 1997). A study of 186 tribal and village cultures revealed that almost all had an intervening phase, however brief, between childhood and full assumption of adult roles (Schlegel & Barry, 1991).

In industrialized nations, successful participation in economic life requires many years of education. Young people face extra years of dependence on parents and postponement of sexual gratification while they prepare for a productive work life. As a result, adolescence is greatly extended, and researchers commonly divide it into three phases:

1. *Early adolescence,* from 11 or 12 to 14 years of age, a period of rapid pubertal change

2. *Middle adolescence,* from 14 to 18 years, when pubertal changes are nearly complete

3. *Late adolescence,* from 18 to 21 years, when the young person achieves full adult appearance and faces more complete assumption of adult roles

These divisions correspond to the way industrialized societies commonly group adolescents—into middle or junior high school, high school, and college (Steinberg, 1993).

Throughout our discussion, we will see that the extent to which the social environment supports young people in achieving adult responsibilities has much to do with how well they fare. For all the biological tensions and uncertainties about the future that modern teenagers feel, most are surprisingly good at negotiating the twists and turns of this period of life. With this idea in mind, let's look closely at puberty, the dawning of adolescent development.

PUBERTY: THE PHYSICAL TRANSITION TO ADULTHOOD

*T*he changes of puberty are dramatic and momentous. Within a few years, the body of the school-age child is transformed into that of a full-grown adult. The various aspects of pubertal growth are regulated by genetically influenced hormonal processes. Girls, who have been advanced in physical maturity since the prenatal period, reach puberty, on the average, 2 years earlier than boys.

HORMONAL CHANGES

To young adolescents and their parents, major signs of puberty often seem to appear quite suddenly. But the complex hormonal changes that underlie them are actually very gradual, already under way by age 8 or 9 (see Figure 14.1). Recall from Chapter 8 that the *pituitary gland,* located at the base of the brain, plays a vital role in physical growth. It releases *growth hormone (GH)* and stimulates other glands to produce hormones that act on body tissues, causing them to mature. GH and *thyroxine* (a hormone released by the thyroid gland) contribute to the tremendous gains in body size and completion of skeletal maturation during puberty.

Sexual maturation is controlled by the sex hormones. Although *estrogens* are thought of as female hormones and *androgens* as male hormones, both types are present in each sex, but in different amounts. The boy's testes release large quantities of the androgen *testosterone,* which leads to muscle growth, body and facial hair, and other male sex characteristics. Testosterone also contributes to gains in body size. The testes secrete small amounts of estrogen as well—the reason that 50 percent of boys experience temporary breast enlargement during the early phase of puberty (Larson, 1996).

Estrogens released by the girl's ovaries cause the breasts, uterus, and vagina to mature, the body to take on feminine proportions, and fat to accumulate. In addition, estrogens contribute to regulation of the menstrual cycle. Girls' changing bodies are also affected by the release of androgens from the adrenal glands, located on top of each kidney. *Adrenal androgens* influence the

The pubertal growth spurt takes place, on the average, 2 years earlier for girls than boys. Although the boy and girl standing next to each other are both sixth graders, the girl is much taller and more mature looking. *(Will Hart)*

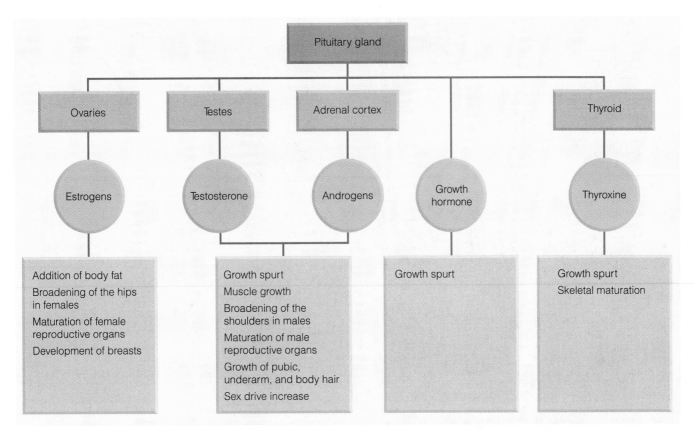

FIGURE **14.1**

Hormonal influences on the body at puberty.

girl's height spurt and stimulate growth of underarm and pubic hair. They have little impact on boys, whose physical characteristics are mainly influenced by androgen secretions from the testes.

As you can already tell, pubertal changes can be divided into two types: (1) overall body growth, including size, proportion, and muscle–fat makeup, and (2) maturation of sexual characteristics (Malina, 1990). Although we will discuss these changes separately, they are interrelated. We have already seen that the hormones responsible for sexual maturity also affect body growth; boys and girls differ in both aspects. In fact, puberty is the time of greatest sexual differentiation since prenatal life.

CHANGES IN BODY SIZE AND PROPORTIONS

The first outward sign of puberty is the rapid gain in height and weight known as the **growth spurt.** On the average, it is under way for North American and European girls shortly after age 10, for boys around age 12½ (Malina, 1990). The girl is taller and heavier during early adolescence, but this advantage is shortlived. At age 14, she is surpassed by the typical boy, whose adolescent growth spurt has started, whereas hers is almost finished. Growth in body size is complete for most girls by age 16 and for boys by age 17½, when the epiphyses at the ends of the long bones close completely (see Chapter 8, page 296).

Altogether, adolescents add almost 10 inches in height and about 40 pounds in weight during puberty. But even more striking is how fast these changes take place. When growing at their peak, boys add more than 4 inches and 26 pounds in a single year, girls about 3.5 inches and as much as 20 pounds. Figure 14.2 provides an overview of general body growth from infancy through adolescence.

During puberty, the cephalocaudal trend of infancy and childhood reverses. At first, the hands, legs, and feet accelerate, and then the torso, which accounts for most of the

growth spurt
Rapid gain in height and weight during adolescence.

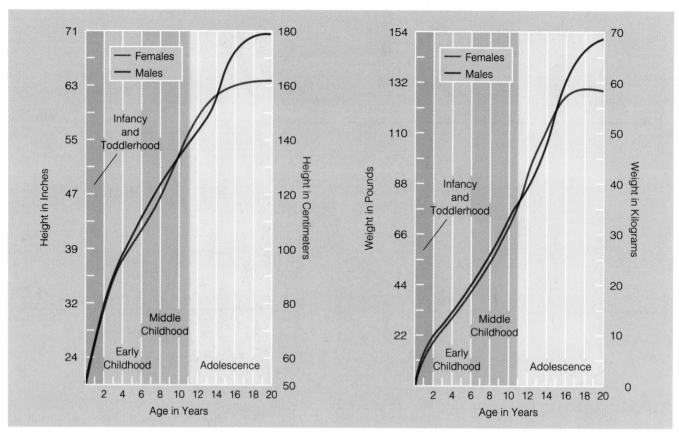

FIGURE 14.2

Average gains in height and weight from infancy through adolescence among North American children. Note that the adolescent growth spurt takes place earlier for girls than boys. *(From R. M. Malina, 1975, Growth and Development: The First Twenty Years in Man, Minneapolis: Burgess Publishing Company, p. 19. Adapted by permission.)*

adolescent height gain (Wheeler, 1991). This pattern of development helps us understand why early adolescents often appear awkward and out of proportion—long-legged and with giant feet and hands (Malina, 1990; Tanner, 1990).

Large differences in boys' and girls' body proportions also appear, caused by the action of sex hormones on the skeleton. Boys' shoulders broaden relative to the hips, whereas girls' hips broaden relative to the shoulders and waist. Of course, boys also end up considerably larger than girls, and their legs are longer in relation to the rest of the body. The major reason is that boys have 2 extra years of preadolescent growth, when the legs are growing the fastest (Graber, Petersen, & Brooks-Gunn, 1996).

MUSCLE–FAT MAKEUP AND OTHER INTERNAL CHANGES

One reason that 11-year-old Sabrina became very concerned about her weight is that compared to her later-developing girlfriends, her more mature body had accumulated much more fat. Around age 8, girls start to add more fat than do boys on their arms, legs, and trunk, and they continue to do so throughout puberty. In contrast, the arm and leg fat of adolescent boys decreases. Although both sexes gain in muscle, this increase is much greater for boys, who develop larger skeletal muscles, hearts, and lung capacity. Also, the number of red blood cells, and therefore the ability to carry oxygen from the lungs to the muscles, increases in boys but not in girls. Altogether, boys gain far more muscle strength than do girls, a difference that contributes to boys' superior athletic performance during the teenage years (Beunen & Malina, 1996).

During puberty, the sex hormones stimulate glandular secretions. Consequently, perspiration, body odor, and oiliness of the skin and hair increase. Greater activity of the sebaceous glands of the skin leads to the most common medical disorder of adolescence—acne. About 80 to 90 percent of teenage boys and girls are affected. Usually acne is mild and clears up on its own by the end of puberty. In the few severe cases, it can be

TABLE 14.1

Average Age and Age Range of Major Pubertal Changes in North American Boys and Girls

GIRLS	AVERAGE	RANGE	BOYS	AVERAGE	RANGE
Breasts begin to "bud"	10	(8–13)	Testes begin to enlarge	11.5	(9.5–13.5)
Height spurt begins	10	(8–13)	Pubic hair appears	12	(10–15)
Pubic hair appears	10.5	(8–14)	Penis begins to enlarge	12	(10.5–14.5)
Peak of strength spurt	11.6	(9.5–14)	Height spurt begins	12.5	(10.5–16)
Peak of height spurt	11.7	(10–13.5)	Spermarche (first ejaculation) occurs	13	(12–16)
Menarche (first menstruation) occurs	12.8	(10.5–15.5)	Peak of height spurt	14	(12.5–15.5)
Adult stature reached	13	(10–16)	Facial hair begins to grow	14	(12.5–15.5)
Breast growth completed	14	(10–16)	Voice begins to deepen	14	(12.5–15.5)
Pubic hair growth completed	14.5	(14–15)	Penis growth completed	14.5	(12.5–16)
			Peak of strength spurt	15.3	(13–17)
			Adult stature reached	15.5	(13.5–17.5)
			Pubic hair growth completed	15.5	(14–17)

Sources: Malina and Bouchard, 1991; Tanner, 1990.

physically disfiguring and psychologically damaging. Fortunately, medical treatments are highly successful in controlling it (Sykes, 1994).

SEXUAL MATURATION

Accompanying the rapid increase in body size are changes in physical features related to sexual functioning. Some, called **primary sexual characteristics,** involve the reproductive organs directly (ovaries, uterus, and vagina in females; penis, scrotum, and testes in males). Others, called **secondary sexual characteristics,** are visible on the outside of the body and serve as additional signs of sexual maturity (for example, breast development in females, appearance of underarm and pubic hair in both sexes). As you can see in Table 14.1, these characteristics develop in a fairly standard sequence, although the age at which each begins and is completed varies greatly.

■ **SEXUAL MATURATION IN GIRLS.** **Menarche** (from the Greek word *arche,* meaning "beginning") is the scientific name for first menstruation. Because most people view it as the major sign that puberty has arrived in girls, you may be surprised to learn that menarche actually occurs late in the sequence of pubertal events. Female puberty usually begins with the budding of the breasts and the growth spurt. (For about 15 percent of girls, pubic hair is present before breast development.) Menarche typically happens around 12½ years for North American girls, around 13 for Europeans. But the age range is wide, extending from 10½ to 15½ years. Following menarche, pubic hair and breast development are completed, and underarm hair appears. Most girls take 3 to 4 years to complete this sequence. Some mature more rapidly, in as little as a year and a half. Others take longer, perhaps as much as 5 years (Tanner, 1990; Wheeler, 1991).

Table 14.1 shows that all girls experience menarche after the peak of the height spurt, once they have nearly reached their mature body size. This sequence has clear adaptive value. Nature delays menstruation until the girl's body is large enough for successful childbearing. As an extra measure of security, for 12 to 18 months following menarche, the menstrual cycle often takes place without an ovum being released from the ovaries. However, this temporary period of sterility does not apply to all girls, and it cannot be counted on for protection against pregnancy (Tanner, 1990).

primary sexual characteristics
Physical features that involve the reproductive organs directly (ovaries, uterus, and vagina in females; penis, scrotum, and testes in males).

secondary sexual characteristics
Features visible on the outside of the body that serve as signs of sexual maturity but do not involve the reproductive organs (for example, breast development in females, appearance of underarm and pubic hair in both sexes).

menarche
First menstruation.

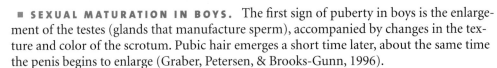

■ **SEXUAL MATURATION IN BOYS.** The first sign of puberty in boys is the enlargement of the testes (glands that manufacture sperm), accompanied by changes in the texture and color of the scrotum. Pubic hair emerges a short time later, about the same time the penis begins to enlarge (Graber, Petersen, & Brooks-Gunn, 1996).

Refer again to Table 14.1, and you will see that the growth spurt occurs much later in the sequence of pubertal events for boys than for girls. When it reaches its peak (at about age 14), enlargement of the testes and penis is nearly complete, and underarm hair appears soon after. Facial and body hair also emerges just after the peak in body growth, but it increases slowly, continuing to develop for several years after puberty. Another landmark of male physical maturity is the deepening of the voice as the larynx enlarges and the vocal cords lengthen. (Girls' voices also deepen slightly.) Voice change usually takes place at the peak of the male growth spurt and often is not complete until puberty is over. When it first occurs, many boys have difficulty with voice control. Occasionally their newly acquired baritone breaks into a high-pitched sound (Katchadourian, 1977).

While the penis is growing, the prostate gland and seminal vesicles (which together produce semen, the fluid in which sperm are bathed) enlarge. (To see where these organs are located, return to Chapter 3, page 102.) Then, around age 13, **spermarche,** or first ejaculation, occurs (Jorgensen & Keiding, 1991). For a while, the semen contains few living sperm. So, like girls, boys have an initial period of reduced fertility.

INDIVIDUAL AND GROUP DIFFERENCES IN PUBERTAL GROWTH

Heredity is partly responsible for the timing of puberty, since identical twins generally reach menarche within a month or two of each other, whereas fraternal twins differ by about 12 months (Tanner, 1990). Nutrition and exercise also contribute. In females, a sharp rise in body weight and fat may trigger sexual maturation. Girls who begin serious athletic training at young ages or who eat very little (both of which reduce the percentage of body fat) often show delayed menarche. In contrast, overweight girls typically start menstruating early (Rees, 1993).

Variations in pubertal growth also exist between regions of the world and SES groups. Heredity probably plays little role, since adolescents with very different genetic origins living under similarly advantaged conditions resemble one another in pubertal timing. For example, in Japan, the United States, and Western Europe, menarche occurs at approximately the same age—between 12½ and 13½ years (Eveleth & Tanner, 1976). Instead, physical health is largely responsible. In poverty-stricken regions where malnutrition and infectious disease are widespread, menarche is greatly delayed. In many parts of Africa, it does not occur until age 14 to 17. And within countries, girls from higher-income families consistently reach menarche 6 to 18 months earlier than do those living in economically disadvantaged homes.

Because of improved health and nutrition, secular trends in physical growth have taken place in industrialized nations. The adolescent girl on the left is taller than her grandmother, mother, and aunt, and she probably reached menarche at an earlier age. Improved nutrition and health are responsible for gains in body size and faster physical maturation from one generation to the next. *(Bob Daemmrich/The Image Works)*

THE SECULAR TREND

In Chapter 11, we saw that children in industrialized nations are growing faster and larger than in generations past. Similarly, age of menarche has declined steadily from 1860 to 1970, by about 3 to 4 months per decade (see Figure 14.3). This *secular trend* in pubertal timing lends added support to the role of physical well-being in adolescent growth. Nutrition, health care, sanitation, and control of infectious disease have improved greatly during this time.

Of course, humans cannot keep growing larger and maturing earlier indefinitely, since we cannot exceed the genetic limitations of our species. Secular gains have slowed or

spermarche
First ejaculation of seminal fluid.

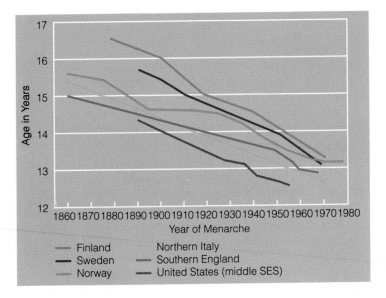

stopped entirely in some developed countries, such as Canada, Great Britain, Sweden, Norway, Japan, and the United States (McAnarney et al., 1992; Roche, 1979). Consequently, modern young people reared under good nutritional and social conditions are likely to resemble their parents in physical growth more than at any time during the previous 130 years.

BRIEF REVIEW

Adolescence is the transitional period between childhood and adulthood, a time of dramatic physical change leading to an adult-size body and sexual maturity. Early biologically oriented theories viewed puberty as an inevitable period of storm and stress. This perspective was challenged by evidence that serious psychological disturbance is not a common feature of the teenage years. Modern researchers recognize that adolescent development and adjustment are a product of both biological and social forces. Adolescence is greatly extended in complex societies that require a long period of education for a productive work life.

Puberty is the time of greatest sexual differentiation since the prenatal period—in body size, proportions, muscle–fat makeup, and primary and secondary sexual characteristics. The physical changes of adolescence are regulated by growth and sex hormones. On the average, girls experience puberty 2 years earlier than do boys. However, wide individual differences exist, to which both heredity and environment contribute. Nutrition and health account for regional and SES differences in pubertal timing and the secular trend in industrialized nations.

ASK YOURSELF . . .

■ *Millie, mother of an 11-year-old son, is convinced that the rising sexual passions of puberty cause rebelliousness in all adolescents. Where did this belief originate? Explain why it is incorrect.*

■ *Sabrina, who reached menarche before age 11, was already much taller and heavier than her classmates. She worried that she was going to keep on growing larger and larger. How would you respond to Sabrina's concern?*

THE PSYCHOLOGICAL IMPACT OF PUBERTAL EVENTS

Think back to your late elementary school and junior high school days. Were you early, late, or about on time in physical maturation with respect to your peers? How did your feelings about yourself and your relationships with others change? A large body of research reveals that puberty affects the adolescent's self-image, mood, and interaction with parents and peers. Some of these outcomes are a response to dramatic physical change, regardless of when it occurs. Others have to do with the timing of pubertal maturation.

REACTIONS TO PUBERTAL CHANGES

How do girls and boys react to the massive physical changes of puberty? Most research aimed at answering this question has focused on girls' feelings about menarche.

■ **GIRLS' REACTIONS TO MENARCHE.** Research of a generation or two ago indicated that menarche was often traumatic. Today, girls commonly react with "surprise," undoubtedly due to the sudden nature of the event. Otherwise, they typically report a mixture of positive and negative emotions—"excited and pleased" as well as "scared and upset" (Brooks-Gunn, 1988b). Yet wide individual differences exist that depend on prior knowledge and support from family members. Both are influenced by cultural attitudes toward puberty and sexuality.

For girls who have no advance information, menarche can be shocking and disturbing. In the 1950s, up to 50 percent were given no prior warning (Shainess, 1961). Today, no more than 10 to 15 percent are uninformed (Brooks-Gunn, 1988b). This shift is probably due to modern parents' greater willingness to discuss sexual matters with their youngsters. Almost all girls get some information from their mothers (Brooks-Gunn & Ruble, 1983). And girls whose fathers are told about pubertal changes adjust especially well. Perhaps a father's involvement reflects a family atmosphere that is highly understanding and accepting of physical and sexual matters (Brooks-Gunn & Ruble, 1980, 1983).

■ **BOYS' REACTIONS TO SPERMARCHE.** Like girls' reactions to menarche, boys' responses to spermarche reflect mixed feelings. Virtually all boys know about ejaculation ahead of time, but few get any information from parents. Usually they obtain it from reading material (Gaddis & Brooks-Gunn, 1985). Despite advance information, many boys say that their first ejaculation occurred earlier than they expected and that they were unprepared for it. As with girls, the better prepared boys feel, the more positively they react (Stein & Reiser, 1994).

In addition, although at first girls keep menarche secret from their peers, within 6 months almost all tell a friend that they are menstruating. In contrast, far fewer boys ever tell anyone about spermarche (Brooks-Gunn et al., 1986; Downs & Fuller, 1991). Overall, boys seem to get much less social support for the physical changes of puberty than do girls. This suggests that boys, especially, might benefit from opportunities to ask questions and discuss feelings with a sympathetic parent or health professional.

■ **CULTURAL INFLUENCES.** The experience of puberty is affected by the larger cultural context in which boys and girls live. Many tribal and village societies celebrate puberty with a *rite of passage*—a community-wide event that marks an important change in privilege and responsibility. Consequently, all young people know that pubertal changes are honored and valued in their culture (see the Cultural Influences box on pages 536–537). In contrast, Western societies grant little formal recognition to movement from childhood to adolescence or from adolescence to adulthood. Certain religious ceremonies, such as confirmation and the Jewish bar or bat mitzvah, do resemble a rite of passage. But not all young people take part in these rituals, and they usually do not lead to any meaningful change in social status.

Instead, Western adolescents are confronted with many ages at which they are granted partial adult status—for example, an age for starting employment, for driving, for leaving high school, for voting, and for drinking. In some contexts (on the highway and at work), they may be treated like adults. In others (at school and at home), they may still be regarded as children. The absence of a widely accepted marker of physical and social maturity makes the process of becoming an adult especially confusing.

PUBERTAL CHANGE, EMOTION, AND SOCIAL BEHAVIOR

In the preceding sections, we considered adolescents' reactions to their sexually maturing bodies. Puberty can also affect the young person's emotional state and social behavior. A common belief is that pubertal change has something to do with adolescent moodiness and the desire for greater physical and psychological separation from parents.

■ **ADOLESCENT MOODINESS.**   Recently, researchers have explored the role of sex hormones in adolescents' emotional reactions. Indeed, higher hormone levels are related to greater moodiness, in the form of anger and irritability for males and anger and depression for females, between 9 and 14 years of age (Brooks-Gunn & Warren, 1989; Nottelmann et al., 1990). But these links are not strong and are less consistent for boys than girls (Buchanan, Eccles, & Becker, 1992). We cannot really be sure that a rise in pubertal hormones causes adolescent moodiness.

What else might contribute to the common observation that adolescents are moody? In several studies, the mood fluctuations of children, adolescents, and adults were tracked over a week by having them carry electronic pagers. At random intervals, they were beeped and asked to write down what they were doing, whom they were with, and how they felt.

As expected, adolescents reported somewhat lower moods than did school-age children or adults (Csikszentmihalyi & Larson, 1984; Larson & Lampman-Petraitis, 1989). But young people whose moods were especially negative were experiencing a greater number of negative life events, such as difficulties in getting along with parents, disciplinary actions at school, and breaking up with a boyfriend or girlfriend. Negative events increased steadily from childhood to adolescence, and teenagers also seemed to react to them with greater emotion than did children (Larson & Ham, 1993).

Furthermore, compared to the moods of adults, adolescents' feelings were less stable. They often varied from cheerful to sad and back again. But teenagers also moved from one situation to another more often, and their mood swings were strongly related to these changes. High points of their days were times spent with friends and in self-chosen leisure and hobby activities. Low points tended to occur in adult-structured settings—class, job, school halls, school library, and church. Taken together, these findings suggest that situational factors may combine with hormonal influences to affect teenagers' moodiness—an explanation consistent with the balanced view of biological and social forces described earlier in this chapter.

Compared to children and adults, adolescents often seem moody. But young people whose moods are especially negative experience more negative life events. This dispirited boy may have had an argument with his parents, received a detention at school, or broken up with his girlfriend. Events like these increase in adolescence. *(David Young Wolff/Tony Stone Images)*

■ **PARENT–CHILD RELATIONSHIPS.**   Sabrina's father noticed that as his children entered adolescence, their bedroom doors started to close, they resisted spending time with the family, and they became more argumentative. Within a 2-day period, Sabrina and her mother squabbled over Sabrina's messy room ("Mom, it's *my* room. You don't have to live in it!") and her clothing purchases ("Sabrina, if you *buy* it, then *wear* it. Otherwise, you are wasting money!"). And Sabrina resisted the family's regular weekend visit to Aunt Gina's ("Why do I have to go *every* week?"). Many studies show that puberty is related to a rise in parent–child conflict. Bickering and standoffs increase as adolescents move toward the peak of pubertal growth. During this time, both parents and teenagers report feeling less close to one another (Holmbeck, 1996; Holmbeck & Hill, 1991).

Why should a youngster's more adultlike appearance trigger these petty disputes between parent and child? Researchers believe the association may have some adaptive value. Among nonhuman primates, the young typically leave the family group around the time of puberty. The same is true in many nonindustrialized cultures (Caine, 1986; Schlegel & Barry, 1991). Departure of young people from the family discourages sexual relations among close blood relatives. But because children in industrialized societies

CULTURAL INFLUENCES

ADOLESCENT INITIATION CEREMONIES

An **adolescent initiation ceremony** is a ritualized announcement to the community that a young person is ready to make the transition from childhood into adolescence or full adulthood. These special rites of passage reach their fullest expression in small tribal and village societies. Besides celebration, they often include such features as separation from parents and members of the other sex; instruction in cultural customs and work roles; and fertility rituals that incorporate the young person into the sexual and childbearing world of adults. According to anthropologists, each of these ceremonial features is a cultural expression of the adaptive value of biological puberty.

■ **SEPARATION.** The beginning of an initiation ceremony is usually marked by separation from parents and members of the other sex, and sometimes by seclusion from the entire settlement. Among the !Kung hunters and gatherers of Botswana, Africa, a girl menstruating for the first time is carried to a special shelter by an old woman, who cares for her until the menstrual flow stops. Some Native American boys must start a lonely pil-

grimage to seek their vision. The Tiwi, an Aboriginal group of northern Australia, greet male puberty by arranging to have a group of strange men take boys to a special campsite in the bush. Initiates are expected to shed their childish ways abruptly in favor of adultlike reverence and self-restraint (Spindler, 1970).

A same-sex nonparent usually oversees the initiation, since puberty is accompanied by a rise in conflict and psychological distancing between parent and child, which reduces parents' power to teach the adolescent (Eibl-Eibesfeldt, 1989). Gender segregation fosters the young person's assumption of adult gender roles, which are sharply divided in most tribal and village societies (Weisfeld, 1986).

Boys are typically initiated in large peer groups, a custom that promotes social solidarity. When agemates undergo challenging and painful experiences together, they bond with one another, an outcome that enhances cooperation in hunting, defending the group, and other adult tasks (Schlegel & Barry, 1991). Girls, in contrast, are generally initiated singly. In adulthood, they will spend more time with their family and in small groups. Consequently, large-group

unity is deemed less important (Schlegel, 1995).

■ **INSTRUCTION.** During initiation rights, years of childhood teachings are supplemented with information on ceremonial matters, courtship, sexual techniques, duties to one's spouse and in-laws, and subsistence skills. Elders often convey tribal secrets and stress cultural values. Among the Mano of Liberia, older men take young boys off into the forest, where they are taught secret folklore along with farming and other skills they will need to earn a living. They return with a new name, signifying their adult identity, and an even stronger allegiance to their culture. !Kung women teach the newly menstruating girl not to shame her husband or touch his hunting gear and about birth and infant care (Fried & Fried, 1980).

■ **ENTRY INTO ADULT SOCIETY.** The training period culminates in a formal celebration, which usually grants young people permission to engage in sex and to marry. Most of the time, the appearance of initiates is changed so all members of the community can identify and treat them differently. Sometimes physical markers of

remain economically dependent on parents long after they reach puberty, they cannot leave the family. Consequently, a modern substitute for physical departure seems to have emerged—psychological distancing between parents and children (Steinberg, 1987).

In later chapters, we will see that adolescents' new powers of reasoning may also contribute to a rise in family tensions. Also, the need for families to redefine relationships as children become physically mature and demand to be treated in adultlike ways can induce a temporary period of conflict. The greater the gap between parents' and adolescents' views of teenagers' readiness to take on developmental tasks (such as handling their own money, getting involved in a sexual relationship, or choosing a philosophy of life), the more quarreling there tends to be (Deković, Noom, & Meeus, 1997).

The conflict that does take place is generally mild. Only a small minority of families experience a serious break in parent–child relationships. In reality, parents and children display both conflict and affection toward one another throughout adolescence. This also makes sense from an evolutionary perspective. Although separation from parents is adap-

adolescent initiation ceremony
A ritual, or rite of passage, announcing to the community that a young person is making the transition into adolescence or full adulthood.

In this adolescent initiation ceremony, N'Jembe women of Gabon in west-central Africa celebrate the arrival of puberty in two young girls (located just behind the leader, wearing elaborate headdresses) with a special ritual. *(Sylvain Grandadam/Photo Researchers, Inc.)*

increased status involve temporary body decorations, such as painting and jewelry. At other times, the changes are permanent, consisting of new types of clothing or scars engraved on some part of the body—usually the face, back, chest, or penis.

Many ceremonies include an ordeal, typically more severe for males than for females. A boy might need to kill game or endure cold and hunger, a girl might grind grain or remain secluded for several days. These rites stress responsibility, wisdom, and bravery. They also subject adolescents with a rebellious streak to the authority of their elders (Weisfield, 1997).

Male genital operations (usually circumcision) occur in about one-third of cultures with puberty rites and usually are followed by sexual activity. Female surgery (removal of part or all of the clitoris and sometimes the labia) takes place in only 8 percent of initiation ceremonies, to ensure the girl's continued virginity and therefore her value as a bride (Weisfield, 1990).[1]

■ **CULTURAL VARIATIONS.** Adolescent initiation ceremonies for girls are more common than those for boys in the simplest societies. In small bands

of hunters and gatherers, females are in short supply. The loss of any woman of childbearing age can threaten the survival of the group. In these cultures, female rites typically last for several weeks and are especially elaborate, designed to provide the girl with both social recognition and magical protection. As cultures move from simple

foraging to farming communities, rituals for boys increase in frequency. Initiation rites in farming villages typically recognize young people of both sexes for their distinct reproductive and economic roles. In more complex cultures, adolescent initiation ceremonies recede in importance and disappear (Schlegel & Barry, 1980).

[1]*Female genital mutilation*, widespread in Africa, Indonesia, Malaysia, and the Middle East, as a means of guaranteeing chastity and therefore a good marriage partner, is usually inflicted on girls early (at an average age of 3), before they know enough to resist (Weisfield, 1997). Although illegal in many countries, the practice is difficult for governments to control. Today, there are millions of genitally mutilated girls and women in the developing world. International organizations are sending social scientists and health professionals into villages to work within each culture's belief system to bring an end to this violation of human rights (Bashir, 1997).

tive, both generations benefit from warm, protective family bonds that last for many years to come (Steinberg, 1990).

EARLY VERSUS LATE MATURATION

Recall that Sabrina's mother reported that all her children matured early, but her daughter had difficulty adjusting whereas her sons reacted with confidence. Maturational timing influences adolescent adjustment, in opposite directions for girls than for boys.

■ **EFFECTS OF MATURATIONAL TIMING.** Sabrina was self-conscious about her well-developed body, felt awkward and unsure of herself, and withdrew from her peers. In contrast, her brothers were confident and proud of their large, muscular physiques.

Findings of many studies match the experiences of Sabrina and her brothers. Early maturing boys appeared advantaged in many aspects of emotional and social functioning.

Both adults and peers viewed them as relaxed, independent, self-confident, and physically attractive. Popular with agemates, they held many leadership positions in school and tended to be athletic stars. In contrast, late maturing boys were not well liked. Peers and adults viewed them as anxious, overly talkative, and attention seeking in behavior (Brooks-Gunn, 1988a; Clausen, 1975; Jones, 1965; Jones & Bayley, 1950).

Among girls, the impact of maturational timing was just the reverse. Early maturing girls had emotional and social difficulties. They were below average in popularity, appeared withdrawn, lacking in self-confidence, and psychologically stressed; and held few positions of leadership (Ge, Conger, & Elder, 1996; Jones & Mussen, 1958). In addition, they were more involved in deviant behavior (getting drunk, staying out late, participating in early sexual activity) and achieved less well in school (Caspi et al., 1993; Stattin & Magnusson, 1990). In contrast, their late maturing counterparts were well adjusted—regarded as physically attractive, lively, sociable, and leaders at school.

Two factors seem to account for these trends: (1) how closely the adolescent's body matches cultural ideals of physical attractiveness, and (2) how well young people "fit in" physically with their agemates.

■ **THE ROLE OF PHYSICAL ATTRACTIVENESS.** Flip through the pages of your favorite popular magazine, and look at the figures of men and women in the ads. You will see evidence for our society's view of an attractive female as thin and long-legged and a good-looking male as tall, broad-shouldered, and muscular. The female image is a girlish shape that favors the late developer. The male image fits the early maturing boy.

As their bodies change, adolescents become preoccupied with their physical selves. Girls are especially likely to analyze all their body features—whether their eyebrows and lips are too thick or too thin, their breasts and hips too large or too small, and their arms and legs sufficiently graceful and shapely. In addition, adolescents get a great deal of feedback from others—both directly, through remarks about their appearance, and indirectly, through the tendency of children and adults to treat physically attractive people more positively. The conclusions young people draw about their appearance strongly affect their satisfaction with their bodies and, ultimately, their self-esteem and psychological well-being (Harter, 1993; Mendelson, White, & Mendelson, 1996).

In several studies, early maturing girls reported a less positive **body image**—conception of and attitude toward their physical appearance—than did their on-time and late maturing agemates. Among boys, the opposite occurred: early maturation was linked to a positive body image, whereas late maturation predicted dissatisfaction with the physical self (Duncan et al., 1985; Petersen, 1984; Simmons & Blyth, 1987). The difference in body image between early and late maturing boys was short lived; it disappeared as the late maturers reached puberty. Early maturing girls' less favorable body image not only persisted but became more extreme. In sum, the adoption of society's "beauty is best" stereotype appears to be a factor in pubertal timing effects, particularly for girls.

■ **THE IMPORTANCE OF FITTING IN WITH PEERS.** A second way of explaining differences in adjustment between early and late maturers is in terms of their physical status in relation to peers. From this perspective, early maturing girls and late maturing boys have difficulty because they fall at the extremes of physical development. Recall that Sabrina felt "out of place" and embarrassed when with her agemates. She was not just larger than the girls; she also towered over the boys. Late maturing boys are self-conscious about their childish appearance, and many harbor doubts and fears about whether they will grow larger. Not surprisingly, adolescents feel most comfortable with peers who match their own level of biological maturity (Brooks-Gunn et al., 1986; Stattin & Magnusson, 1990).

Because few agemates of the same physical status are available, early maturing adolescents of both sexes seek out older companions—at times with unfavorable consequences. Older peers often encourage early maturing youngsters into activities that they find difficult to resist and are not yet ready to handle emotionally, including drug and alcohol use,

body image
Conception of and attitude toward one's physical appearance.

sexual activity, and minor delinquent acts. For example, the eighth graders that Sabrina met at church introduced her to several high school boys, who were quite unconcerned that she was just a sixth grader! Sabrina welcomed their attentions, which gratified her desire to feel socially accepted and physically attractive. Perhaps because of involvements like these, the academic performance of early maturers tends to suffer (Duncan et al., 1985; Stattin & Magnusson, 1990).

Interestingly, school contexts can modify these maturational timing effects. In one study, early maturing sixth-grade girls felt better about themselves when they attended kindergarten through sixth grade (K–6) rather than kindergarten through eighth grade (K–8) schools, where they could mix with older adolescents. In the K–6 settings, they were relieved of pressures to adopt behaviors for which they were not ready (Blyth, Simmons, & Zakin, 1985). Similarly, a New Zealand study found that delinquency among early maturing girls was greatly reduced in all-girl schools, which limit opportunities to associate with norm-violating peers (most of whom are older boys) (Caspi et al., 1993).

■ **LONG-TERM CONSEQUENCES.** Do the effects of early and late maturation persist into adulthood? Long-term follow-ups show some striking turnabouts in overall well-being. Many early maturing boys and late maturing girls, who had been the focus of admiration in adolescence, became rigid, inflexible, conforming, and somewhat discontented adults. In contrast, late maturing boys and early maturing girls, who were stress-ridden as teenagers, often developed into adults who were independent, flexible, cognitively competent, and satisfied with the direction of their lives (Livson & Peshkin, 1980; Macfarlane, 1971). How can we explain these remarkable reversals? Perhaps the confidence-inducing adolescence of early maturing boys and late maturing girls does not promote the coping skills needed to solve life's later problems. In contrast, the painful experiences associated with off-time pubertal growth may, in time, contribute to sharpened awareness, clarified goals, and greater stability.

Finally, it is important to note that these long-term outcomes may not hold completely in all cultures. In a Swedish study, achievement difficulties of early maturing girls persisted into young adulthood. They were twice as likely to leave high school after completing the minimum years of compulsory education as their on-time and later maturing counterparts (Stattin & Magnusson, 1990). In countries with highly selective college entrance systems, perhaps it is harder for early maturers to recover from declines in school performance. Clearly, the effects of maturational timing involve a complex blend of biological, immediate social setting, and cultural factors.

When early maturing girls seek out older companions, they may become involved in unfavorable activities, such as alcohol use, sexual activity, and delinquency. In all-girl schools, however, delinquency among early maturers is greatly reduced, since there are few opportunities to associate with norm-violating boys. *(B. Daemmrich/The Image Works)*

ASK YOURSELF . . .

■ *Sasha remembers menarche as a traumatic experience. When she discovered she was bleeding, she thought she had a deadly illness and didn't tell anyone for 2 days. What is the likely cause of Sasha's negative reaction?*

■ *How might adolescent moodiness contribute to the psychological distancing between parents and children that accompanies puberty? (Hint: Think about bidirectional influences in parent-child relationships discussed in previous chapters.)*

■ *Return to the beginning of this chapter and review Sabrina's feelings about her well-developed body and her behavior toward peers. How are they typical of an early maturing girl?*

BRIEF REVIEW

Puberty has important psychological and social consequences. Typically, girls' reactions to menarche and boys' reactions to spermarche are mixed, although prior knowledge and social support affect their responses. Adolescent moodiness is related to both sex hormones and changes in the social environment. Puberty prompts increased conflict and psychological distancing between parent and child. These reactions appear to be modern substitutes for physical departure from the family in our evolutionary history. Standards and expectations of the culture and peer group lead early maturing boys and late maturing girls to be advantaged in emotional and social adjustment. In contrast, late maturing boys and early maturing girls have adjustment difficulties. The stresses associated with off-time pubertal growth may eventually spark more effective coping skills.

HEALTH ISSUES

As young people move into adolescence, they begin to view physical health in a broader way—as more than just the absence of illness. To teenagers, being healthy means functioning physically, mentally, and socially at their best (Millstein & Litt, 1990). Consistent with this new view, the arrival of puberty is accompanied by new health concerns related to the young person's striving to meet physical and psychological needs. As the body grows and takes on mature proportions, eating disturbances appear in many young people who worry about falling short of their idealized image of attractiveness and fitness. Sexual activity brings with it the risk of early pregnancy and sexually transmitted disease. Substance abuse and certain unintentional injuries also increase. (We will take up suicide—another serious adolescent health problem—in Chapter 16.)

Perhaps you can already tell from this list of health issues that the young person's own behavior, or lifestyle, plays a much larger role than it did at earlier ages. As adolescents are granted greater autonomy, personal decision making becomes important, in health as well as other areas (Bearison, 1998). Yet none of the health difficulties we are about to discuss can be traced to a single cause within the individual. Throughout development, biological, psychological, family, and cultural factors jointly contribute to health and well-being.

NUTRITIONAL NEEDS

When their sons reached puberty, Franca and Antonio reported a "vacuum cleaner effect" in the kitchen as the boys routinely emptied the refrigerator. Rapid body growth during adolescence leads to a dramatic rise in food intake. During the growth spurt, boys require about 2,700 calories a day and much more protein, girls about 2,200 calories and somewhat less protein than boys because of their smaller size and muscle mass. Calcium is especially important for skeletal growth. Extra iron is needed to support gains in muscle mass and blood volume in boys and to make up for the loss of blood in the menstrual flow of girls (Larson, 1996).

This increase in nutritional requirements comes at a time when the eating habits of many young people are the poorest. Of all age groups, adolescents are the most likely to consume empty calories and eat on the run. Fast-food restaurants, which are favorite teenage gathering places, have started to offer more healthful menu options. But adolescents need to know how to select these alternatives—baked foods and salads instead of fried foods, milk and fruit juice instead of soft drinks and high-calorie shakes. The eating habits of teenagers are particularly harmful if they extend a lifelong pattern of poor nutrition, less serious if they are just a temporary response to peer influences and a busy schedule.

The most common nutritional problem of adolescence is iron deficiency. A tired, listless, irritable adolescent may be suffering from anemia rather than unhappiness and should have a medical checkup. Most adolescents do not get enough calcium, and they are also deficient in riboflavin (vitamin B_2) and magnesium, both of which support metabolism. And contrary to what many parents believe, obese children rarely outgrow their weight problem when they become teenagers (Serdula et al., 1993).

Adolescents, especially girls who are concerned about their weight, tend to be attracted to the latest fad diets. Unfortunately, most are too limited in nutrients and calories to be healthful for fast-growing, active teenagers. The adolescent years are also a time when many young people choose to become vegetarians. As they begin to formulate a philosophy of life, some find the killing of animals distasteful. Others claim that meats are sources of impurities and toxins. Still others cannot yet explain their reasons. A properly planned vegetarian diet can be very healthy, but one that is not well chosen can be dangerous (Donatelle & Davis, 1997). When a youngster insists on trying a special diet, parents should, in turn, insist that they first consult with a doctor or dietitian.

SERIOUS EATING DISTURBANCES

Franca worried about Sabrina's desire to lose weight at such an early age, explained to her that she was really quite average in build for an adolescent girl, and reminded Sabrina that her Italian ancestors thought a plump female body was more beautiful than a thin one. Girls who reach puberty early, who are very dissatisfied with their body image, and who grow up in homes where a cultural concern with weight and thinness is especially strong are at risk for eating problems. The two most serious eating disorders with adolescent onset are anorexia nervosa and bulimia.

■ **ANOREXIA NERVOSA.**   **Anorexia nervosa** is a tragic eating disturbance in which young people starve themselves because of a compulsive fear of getting fat. About 1 in every 500 teenage girls in the United States is affected. Occasionally, boys are diagnosed, although little is known about their development (Garner, 1993; Seligmann, 1994). Caucasian-American girls are at greater risk than African-American girls, who are more satisfied with their size and shape (Abood & Chandler, 1997; Story et al., 1995). Hispanic and Asian Americans, who report as much dissatisfaction with their body image as do their Caucasian agemates, are at considerable risk as well (Robinson et al., 1996). Whereas obesity is more prevalent in low-SES families (see Chapter 11), recent evidence suggests that the unhealthy behaviors involved in anorexia nervosa are unrelated to SES (Rogers et al., 1997).

Anorexics have an extremely distorted body image. Even after they have become severely underweight, they conclude that they are fat. Most lose weight by going on a self-imposed diet so strict that they struggle to avoid eating in response to hunger. To enhance weight loss, they exercise strenuously.

The physical consequences of this attempt to reach "perfect" slimness are severe. Anorexics lose between 25 and 50 percent of their body weight and appear painfully thin. Because a normal menstrual cycle requires about 15 percent body fat, either menarche does not occur or menstrual periods stop. Malnutrition causes additional physical symptoms—pale skin; brittle, discolored nails; fine dark hairs all over the body; and extreme sensitivity to cold. If allowed to continue, anorexia nervosa can result in shrinking of the heart muscle and kidney failure. As many as 10 percent die of the disorder (Wilson, Heffernan, & Black, 1996).

Anorexia nervosa is the combined result of forces within the individual, the family, and the larger culture. We have already seen that the societal image of "thin is beautiful" contributes to the poorer body image of early maturing girls, who are at greatest risk for anorexia (Graber et al., 1994). But though almost all adolescent girls go on diets at one time or another, anorexics persist in weight loss to an extreme. Many are perfectionists who have high standards for their own behavior and performance. Typically, these girls are excellent students who are responsible and well behaved—ideal daughters in many respects.

Yet interactions between parents and anorexic daughters reveal problems related to adolescent autonomy that may trigger the compulsive dieting. Often their mothers have high expectations for achievement and social acceptance, are overprotective and controlling, and have eating problems themselves (Pike & Rodin, 1991). Although the daughter tries to meet these demands, inside she is angry at not being recognized as an individual in her own right. Instead of rebelling openly, the anorexic girl indirectly tells her parents, "I am a separate person, and I can do what I want with my own body!" At the same time, this youngster, who has been so used to having parents make decisions for her, meets the challenges of adolescence with depression and lack of self-confidence. Starving herself is

This anorexic girl's strict, self-imposed diet and obsession with strenuous physical exercise has led her to become painfully thin. Even so, her body image is so distorted that she probably regards herself as fat. *(Wm. Thompson/The Picture Cube)*

anorexia nervosa
An eating disorder in which individuals (usually females) starve themselves because of a compulsive fear of getting fat.

also a way of avoiding new expectations by returning to a much younger, preadolescent image (Halmi, 1987; Maloney & Kranz, 1991).

Because anorexic girls typically deny that any problem exists, treating the disorder is difficult. Hospitalization is often necessary to prevent life-threatening malnutrition. Family therapy, aimed at changing parent–child interaction and expectations, is the most successful treatment. As a supplementary approach, applied behavior analysis—in which hospitalized anorexics are rewarded for gaining weight with praise, social contact, and opportunities for exercise—is helpful. Still, only 50 percent of anorexics fully recover. For many others, eating problems continue in less extreme form. One-fifth show signs of a less severe disorder—bulimia—that is still physically and psychologically damaging (Fichter & Quadflieg, 1996).

■ **BULIMIA.** When Sabrina's 16-year-old brother Louis brought his girlfriend Cassie to the house, Sabrina admired her good figure. "What willpower! Cassie hardly touches food," Sabrina thought to herself. "But what in the world is wrong with Cassie's teeth?"

Willpower was not the secret of Cassie's slender shape. When it came to food, she actually had great difficulty controlling herself. Cassie suffered from **bulimia,** an eating disorder in which young people (again, mainly girls, but gay adolescent boys are also vulnerable) engage in binge eating followed by deliberate vomiting, purging with laxatives, and strict dieting (Heffernan, 1994). When by herself, Cassie had periods of feeling lonely, unhappy, and anxious. She responded with eating rampages, consuming thousands of calories in an hour or two. The vomiting that followed eroded the enamel on Cassie's teeth. In some cases, life-threatening damage to the throat and stomach occurs (Halmi, 1987).

Bulimia is much more common than anorexia nervosa. About 1 to 3 percent of teenage girls are affected; only 5 percent have previously been anorexic (Fairburn & Belgin, 1990). Although bulimics share with anorexics a pathological fear of getting fat and a family background with high expectations, they may have experienced their parents as disengaged and emotionally unavailable rather than overcontrolling. One conjecture is that bulimics turn to food to compensate for a feeling of emptiness resulting from lack of parental involvement (Attie & Brooks-Gunn, 1996; Johnson & Connors, 1987).

Typically, bulimics are not just impulsive eaters; they also lack self-control in other areas of their lives. Although they tend to be good students and liked by peers, many engage in petty shoplifting and alcohol abuse. Bulimics also differ from anorexics in that they are aware of their abnormal eating habits, feel depressed and guilty about them, and usually are desperate to get help. As a result, bulimia is usually easier to treat through individual and family therapy, support groups, and nutrition education (Harris, 1991; Thackwray et al., 1993).

SEXUAL ACTIVITY

Louis and Cassie hadn't planned to have intercourse after taking a ride in Louis's car one Friday night. It "just happened." But before and after, a lot of things passed through Cassie and Louis's minds. Cassie had been dating Louis for 3 months, and she began to think, "Will he think I'm normal if I don't have sex with him? If he wants to and I say no, will I lose him?"

Both young people knew their parents wouldn't approve. In fact, when Franca and Antonio noticed how attached Louis was to Cassie, they talked to him about the importance of waiting and the dangers of pregnancy. Still, Louis was sure he loved Cassie, and that Friday evening, his feelings for her seemed overwhelming. As things went farther and farther, Louis thought, "If I don't make a move, will she think I'm a wimp?" And Cassie had heard from one of her girlfriends that you couldn't get pregnant the first time.

Virtually all theorists agree that adolescence is an especially important time for the development of sexuality. With the arrival of puberty, hormonal changes—in particular,

bulimia
An eating disorder in which individuals (mainly females) go on eating binges followed by deliberate vomiting, other purging techniques such as heavy doses of laxatives, and strict dieting.

the production of androgens in young people of both sexes—lead to an increase in sex drive (Halpern, Udry, & Suchindran, 1997; Udry, 1990). As Louis and Cassie's inner thoughts reveal, adolescents become very concerned about how to manage sexuality in social relationships. New cognitive capacities involving perspective taking and self-reflection affect their efforts to do so. Yet like the eating behaviors we have just discussed, adolescent sexuality is heavily influenced by the social context in which the young person is growing up.

■ **THE IMPACT OF CULTURE.**   Think, for a moment, about when you first learned about the facts of life and how you found out about them. In your family, was sex discussed openly or treated with secrecy? Cross-cultural research reveals that exposure to sex, education about it, and efforts to restrict the sexual curiosity of children and adolescents vary widely around the world. At one extreme are a number of Middle Eastern peoples, who are known to kill girls who dishonor their families by losing their virginity before marriage. At the other extreme are several Asian and Pacific Island groups with very permissive sexual attitudes and practices. For example, among the Trobriand Islanders of Melanesia, older companions provide children with explicit instruction in sexual practices. Bachelor houses are maintained, where adolescents are expected to engage in sexual experimentation with a variety of partners (Benedict, 1934a; Ford & Beach, 1951).

Despite the publicity granted to the image of a sexually free and sophisticated modern adolescent, sexual attitudes in the United States are relatively restrictive. Typically, American parents give children little information about sex, discourage sex play, and rarely talk about sex in their presence. When young people become interested in sex, they seek information from friends, books, magazines, movies, and television. On prime-time TV shows, which adolescents watch the most, sex between partners with little commitment to each other occurs often and is spontaneous and passionate. Characters are rarely shown taking steps to avoid pregnancy and sexually transmitted disease (Braverman & Strasburger, 1994; Ward, 1995).

Consider the contradictory and confusing messages delivered by these two sets of sources. On the one hand, adults emphasize that sex at a young age and outside of marriage is wrong. On the other hand, adolescents encounter much in the broader social environment that extols the excitement and romanticism of sex. These mixed messages leave many American teenagers bewildered, poorly informed about sexual facts, and with little sound advice on how to conduct their sex lives responsibly.

■ **ADOLESCENT SEXUAL ATTITUDES AND BEHAVIOR.**   Although differences between subcultural groups exist, over the past 30 years the sexual attitudes of American adolescents and adults have become more liberal. Compared to a generation ago, more people believe that sexual intercourse before marriage is all right, as long as two people are emotionally committed to each other (Michael et al., 1994). Recently, a slight swing back in the direction of conservative sexual beliefs has occurred, largely due to the risk of sexually transmitted disease, especially AIDS (Glassman, 1996).

Trends in the sexual behavior of adolescents are quite consistent with their attitudes. The rate of premarital sex among young people rose over several decades but recently declined slightly. For example, among unmarried 15- to 19-year-olds, females claiming to have had sexual intercourse grew from 28 percent in 1971 to 55 percent in 1990 and then dropped to 52 percent in 1995 (U.S. Department of Health and Human Services, 1997b). Nevertheless, as Table 14.2 reveals, a substantial minority of boys and girls are sexually active quite early, by ninth grade. Males tend to have their first intercourse earlier than do females, and sexual activity is especially high among African-American adolescents—particularly boys.

Yet timing of first intercourse provides only a limited picture of adolescent sexual behavior. Most teenagers engage in relatively low levels of sexual activity. The typical

TABLE 14.2

Teenage Sexual Activity Rates by Sex, Ethnic Group, and Grade

SEX	ETHNIC GROUP			GRADE				TOTAL
	WHITE	BLACK	HISPANIC	9	10	11	12	
Male	48.9	81.0	62.0	40.6	50.0	57.1	67.1	54.0
Female	49.0	67.0	53.3	32.1	46.0	60.2	66.0	52.1
Total	48.9	74.4	57.6	36.9	48.0	58.6	66.4	53.1

Note: Data reflect the percentage of high school students who report ever having had sexual intercourse.
Source: U.S. Department of Health and Human Services, 1997b.

15- to 19-year-old sexually active male—white, black, or Hispanic—has relations with only one girl at a time and spends half the year with no partner at all (Sonenstein, Pleck, & Ku, 1991). Contrary to popular belief, a runaway sexual revolution does not characterize American young people. In fact, the rate of teenage sexual activity in the United States is about the same as in Western European nations (Creatsas et al., 1995).

■ **CHARACTERISTICS OF SEXUALLY ACTIVE ADOLESCENTS.** Early and frequent teenage sexual activity is linked to a wide range of personal, family, peer, and educational variables. These include early physical maturation, parental divorce, large family size, sexually active friends and older siblings, poor school performance, lower educational aspirations, and tendency to engage in norm-violating acts, including alcohol and drug use and delinquency (Braverman & Strasburger, 1994; Cooper & Orcutt, 1997; Costa et al., 1995). Since many of these factors are associated with growing up in a low-SES family, it is not surprising that early sexual activity is more common among young people from economically disadvantaged homes. In fact, the high rate of premarital intercourse among black teenagers can largely be accounted for by widespread poverty in the black population (Sullivan, 1993).

At one time, researchers thought that all sexually active adolescents suffered from serious adjustment difficulties (Dreyer, 1982). Recent evidence shows that this is true only for some of them. Teenagers who feel inadequate and inferior, who are without the rewards of meaningful education and work, and who feel compelled to prove something to themselves or others through sex are especially likely to engage in irresponsible sexual behavior. Often they have several casual partners, and their sex acts tend to be exploitative, as when boys misrepresent their feelings to persuade a girl to have sex or force her to do so. Girls who become involved in these unhealthy relationships generally have serious family, peer, and school difficulties (Moore, Morrison, & Glei, 1995).

■ **CONTRACEPTIVE USE.** Contraceptive use among American teenagers has risen sharply in the last few years—a trend believed to be partly due to improved sex education in many schools and public dissemination of information about safe sex practices (Cooksey, Rindfuss, & Guilkey, 1996). Still, about one-half of sexually active adolescents are at risk for unplanned pregnancy because they do not use contraception at all or use it only occasionally (Furstenberg et al., 1997; U.S. Department of Health and Human Services, 1997b).

Why do so many teenagers fail to take precautions? In Chapter 15, we will see that compared to school-age children, adolescents can consider many more possibilities when faced with a problem. But at first, they fail to apply this reasoning to everyday situations. As a result, they do not do the kind of planning and decision making necessary to protect themselves from harmful outcomes. In several studies, teenagers were asked to explain why they did not use birth control. Here are some typical answers:

> You don't say, "Well, I'm going to his house, and he's probably going to try to get to bed with me, so I better make sure I'm prepared." I mean, you don't know it's coming, so how are you to be prepared?

I wouldn't [use contraception] if I was going . . . to have sex casually, you know, like once a month or once every two months. It's more for somebody who has a steady boyfriend. (Kisker, 1985, p. 84)

One reason for responses like these is that advances in perspective taking lead teenagers, for a time, to be extremely concerned about others' opinion of them. Recall how Cassie and Louis each worried about what the other would think if they decided not to have sex. Another reason for lack of planning before sex is that intense self-reflection leads many adolescents to believe they are unique and invulnerable to danger. Recent evidence indicates that teenagers and adults differ very little on questionnaires asking about consequences of engaging in risky behaviors; both report similar levels of vulnerability (Beyth-Marom et al., 1993; Quadrel, Fischhoff, & Davis, 1993). Still, in the midst of everyday social pressures, adolescents often seem to conclude that pregnancy happens to others, not to themselves (Jaskiewicz & McAnarney, 1994).

Although adolescent cognition may have something to do with teenagers' reluctance to use contraception, the social environment also contributes to it. Adolescents who talk openly with their parents about sex are not less sexually active, but they are more likely to use birth control (Brooks-Gunn, 1988b). Unfortunately, many adolescents say they are too scared or embarrassed to ask parents questions about sex or contraception. And too many leave sex education classes with incomplete or factually incorrect knowledge. Some do not know where to get birth control counseling and devices. When they do, they tend to be just as uncomfortable about going to a doctor or family planning clinic as they are about seeking advice from parents (Alan Guttmacher Institute, 1994; Winn, Roker, & Coleman, 1995).

■ **SEXUAL ORIENTATION.** Up to this point, our discussion has focused only on heterosexual behavior. About 3 to 6 percent of young people discover they are lesbian or gay (see the Biology and Environment box on pages 546–547). An as-yet-unknown but significant number are bisexual (Michael et al., 1994; Patterson, 1995). Adolescence is an equally crucial time for the sexual development of these individuals, and societal attitudes, once again, loom large in how well they fare.

Although the extent to which homosexuality is due to genetic versus environmental forces remains highly controversial, recent evidence indicates that heredity makes an important contribution. Identical twins of both sexes are much more likely than fraternal twins to share a homosexual orientation; the same is true for biological as opposed to adoptive relatives (Bailey & Pillard, 1991; Bailey et al., 1993). Furthermore, male homosexuality tends to be more common on the maternal than paternal side of families. This suggests that it might be X-linked (see Chapter 2). Indeed, one gene-mapping study found that among 40 pairs of homosexual brothers, 33 (82 percent) had an identical segment of DNA on the X chromosome. One or several genes in that region might predispose males to become homosexual (Hamer et al., 1993).

How might heredity lead to homosexuality? According to some researchers, certain genes affect the level or impact of prenatal sex hormones, which modify brain structures in ways that induce homosexual feelings and behavior (Bailey et al., 1995; LeVay, 1993). Keep in mind, however, that both genetic and environmental factors can alter prenatal hormones. Girls exposed in utero to abnormal levels of androgens or estrogens—either because of a genetic defect or drugs given to the mother to prevent miscarriage—are more likely to become homosexual or bisexual (Meyer-Bahlburg et al., 1995). Furthermore, homosexual men tend to have a later birth order and a higher than average number of older brothers (Blanchard et al., 1995, 1996; Blanchard & Bogaert, 1996). One controversial speculation is that mothers with several male children sometimes produce antibodies to androgens, which reduce the prenatal impact of male sex hormones on the brains of later-born boys.

Family factors are also associated with homosexuality. Looking back at their childhoods, both male and female homosexuals tend to view their same-sex parent as cold and distant (Bell, Weinberg, & Hammersmith, 1981). This does not mean that parents cause

HOMOSEXUALITY: COMING OUT TO ONESELF AND OTHERS

Cultures vary as much in their acceptance of homosexuality as they do in their approval of premarital sex. In the United States, homosexuals are stigmatized, as shown by the degrading language often used to describe them. This makes forming a sexual identity a much greater challenge for gay and lesbian youths than for their heterosexual counterparts, who appreciate from an early age that people like themselves fall in love with members of the other sex (Rotheram-Borus & Fernandez, 1995).

Wide variations in homosexual identity formation exist, depending on personal, family, and community factors. Yet interviews with homosexual adolescents and adults reveal that many (but not all) move through a three-phase sequence in coming out to themselves and others:

■ **FEELING DIFFERENT.** Gay men and lesbians often say that they felt different from other children when they were young. Typically, this first sense of their biologically determined sexual orientation appears between age 6 and 12 and results from play interests more like those of the other gender (Mondimore, 1996; Troiden, 1989). Boys may find that they are less interested in sports, drawn to quieter activities, and more emotionally sensitive than other boys, girls that they are more athletic and active than other girls.

In Chapter 10, we noted that children who do not conform to traditional gender roles (especially boys) are often ridiculed—an early experience of many homosexuals. In addition, when children hear derogatory labels for homosexuality, they absorb a bias against their own sexual orientation at an early age.

■ **CONFUSION.** With the arrival of puberty, feeling different begins to include feeling sexually different. In one study of 200 ethnically diverse gay, lesbian, and bisexual youths, awareness of a same-sex attraction occurred, on the average, between ages 11 and 12 (Herdt & Boxer, 1993). Realizing that homosexuality has personal relevance generally sparks confusion, largely because most young people had assumed they were heterosexual like everyone else.

A few adolescents resolve their discomfort by crystallizing a gay or lesbian identity quickly, with a flash of insight into their sense of being different. Most experience an inner struggle and deep sense of isolation—outcomes intensified by lack of role models and social support. Some throw themselves into activities they have come to associate with heterosexuality. Boys may go out for athletic teams, girls may drop softball and basketball in favor of dance. And they may try heterosexual dating. Others are so bewildered, uncomfortable, guilt ridden, and lonely that they escape into alcohol and drug abuse and suicidal thinking (Mondimore, 1996).

■ **ACCEPTANCE.** The majority of gay and lesbian teenagers reach a point of accepting their homosexuality. Then they face another crossroad: whether to tell others. The most difficult disclosure is to parents, but many fear rejec-

their youngsters to become homosexual. Rather, for some children, a biological bias away from traditional gender-role behavior may lead them to feel alienated from same-sex parents and peers. A strong desire for affection from people of their own sex may join with biology to strengthen their homosexual orientation (Green, 1987). However, homosexuality does not always develop in this way, since some homosexuals are very comfortable with their gender role and have warm relationships with their parents. Homosexuality probably results from a variety of biological and environmental combinations that are not well understood.

Stereotypes and misconceptions about homosexuality continue to be widespread. For example, contrary to common belief, most homosexual adolescents are not "gender deviant" in dress or behavior. Furthermore, attraction to members of the same sex is not limited to gay and lesbian teenagers. Among heterosexual adolescents, about 18 percent of boys and 6 percent of girls report participating in at least one homosexual act (Braverman & Strasburger, 1993).

Sexually active adolescents, both heterosexual and homosexual, face serious health risks. In the following sections, we examine the high rates of pregnancy, childbirth, and sexually transmitted disease among American teenagers.

This gay couple enjoys an evening at a high school prom. As long as friends and family members react with acceptance, coming out strengthens the young person's view of homosexuality as a valid, meaningful, and fulfilling identity. *(Donnie Binder/Impact Visuals)*

tion by peers as well (Cohen & Savin-Williams, 1996). Powerful stigma against their sexual orientation at home and school lead some to decide that no disclosure is possible. As a result, they self-define but otherwise "pass" as heterosexual. In one interview study of gay adolescents, 85 percent said they tried concealment for a time (Newman & Muzzonigro, 1993).

Many homosexuals eventually acknowledge their sexual orientation publicly, usually by telling trusted friends first, then family members and acquaintances. When people whose love and acceptance is strongly desired react positively, coming out strengthens the young person's view of homosexuality as a valid, meaningful, and fulfilling identity. Contact with other gays and lesbians seems to be important for reaching this phase, and changes in society permit many adolescents in urban areas to attain it earlier than they did a decade or two ago (Anderson, 1994; Edwards, 1996). Gay and lesbian communities exist in large cities, along with specialized interest groups, social clubs, religious groups, newspapers, and periodicals. Increasing numbers of favorable media images are also helpful. In small towns and rural areas, it remains difficult to meet other homosexuals and to find a supportive environment. Teenagers in these locales have a special need for caring adults and peers who can help them find self and social acceptance (Sturdevant & Ramafedi, 1992).

Gay and lesbian youths who succeed in coming out to themselves and others integrate their sexual orientation into a broader sense of identity, a process we will address in Chapter 16. As a result, they no longer need to focus so heavily on their homosexual self, and energy is freed for other aspects of psychological growth. In sum, coming out has the potential to foster many aspects of adolescent development, including self-esteem, psychological well-being, and relationships with family, friends, and co-workers.

TEENAGE PREGNANCY AND CHILDBEARING

Cassie was lucky not to get pregnant after having sex with Louis, but some of her high school classmates weren't so fortunate. She'd heard about Veronica, who missed several periods, pretended nothing was wrong, and didn't go to a doctor until a month before she gave birth. Veronica lived at home until she became pregnant a second time. At that point, her parents told her there wasn't room in the house for a second baby. So Veronica dropped out of school and moved in with her 17-year-old boyfriend, Todd, who worked in a fast-food restaurant. A few months later, Todd left Veronica because he couldn't stand being tied down with the babies. Veronica had to apply for public aid to support herself and the two infants.

Each year, approximately a million American teenagers become pregnant, 30,000 under age 15. As Figure 14.4 shows, the adolescent pregnancy rate in the United States is twice that of Great Britain, Canada, France, and Australia, three times that of Sweden, and six times that of the Netherlands. The United States differs from these nations in three important ways: (1) effective sex education reaches fewer teenagers; (2) convenient,

FIGURE **14.4**

Teenage pregnancy rate in seven industrialized nations. *(Adapted from United Nations, 1991.)*

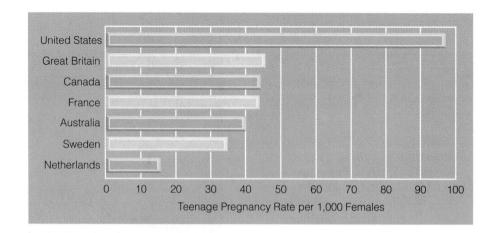

low-cost contraceptive services for adolescents are scarce; and (3) many more families live in poverty, which encourages young people to take risks without considering the future implications of their behavior.

About 40 percent of teenage pregnancies end in abortion, 13 percent in miscarriage (Chase-Lansdale & Brooks-Gunn, 1994; Henshaw, 1997). Because the United States has one of the highest adolescent abortion rates of any developed country, the total number of teenage births is actually lower than it was 30 years ago (Ventura et al., 1997). But teenage parenthood is a much greater problem today because modern adolescents are far less likely to marry before childbirth. In 1960 only 15 percent of teenage births were to unmarried females, whereas today 75 percent are (Coley & Chase-Lansdale, 1998).

Increased social acceptance of single motherhood, along with the belief of many teenage girls that a baby might fill a void in their lives, means that only a small number give up their infants for adoption. Each year, about 350,000 unmarried adolescent girls take on the responsibilities of parenthood before they are psychologically mature.

■ **CORRELATES AND CONSEQUENCES OF TEENAGE PARENTHOOD.** Becoming a parent is challenging and stressful for any person, but it is especially difficult for adolescents. Teenage parents have not yet established a clear sense of direction for their own lives. And most face stressful life circumstances that are compounded after the baby is born.

As we have seen, adolescent sexual activity is linked to economic disadvantage. Teenage mothers are many times more likely to come from poor families than are agemates who postpone childbearing. Their life experiences often include poor school performance; alcohol and drug use; and adult models of unmarried parenthood, limited education, and unemployment—and residence in neighborhoods where other adolescents also display these risks. A high percentage of out-of-wedlock births are to members of low-income minorities, especially Hispanic, African-American, and Native-American teenagers (see Figure 14.5). Many of these young people seem to turn to early parenthood as a way to move into adulthood when educational and career avenues are unavailable (Caldas, 1993; Luker, 1996).

Think about these characteristics of teenage parents, and you will quickly see why early childbirth imposes lasting hardships on two generations—adolescent and newborn baby. The lives of pregnant teenagers are troubled in many ways, and after the baby is born, their circumstances tend to worsen in at least three respects:

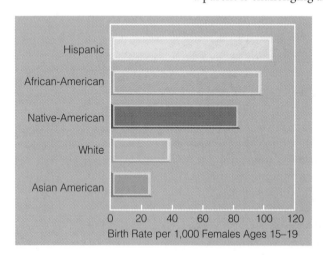

FIGURE **14.5**

Births per 1,000 females ages 15 to 19 by ethnic group. Poverty, weak academic skills, and resulting narrowing of life options are key reasons birth rates are much higher among Hispanic, African-American, and Native-American teenagers than among whites and Asian Americans. *(From Ventura, 1997.)*

challenges. At the end of the school year, pregnancy, school failure, and school suspension were substantially lower in the group enrolled in Teen Outreach, which fostered social skills, connectedness to the community, and self-respect (Allen et al., 1997),

Finally, teenagers who look forward to a promising future are far less likely to engage in early and irresponsible sex. Society can provide young people with good reasons to postpone early childbearing by expanding their educational, vocational, and employment opportunities. We will take up these issues in Chapter 15.

■ **INTERVENING WITH TEENAGE PARENTS.** The most difficult and costly way to deal with adolescent parenthood is to wait until it has happened. Young single mothers need health care for themselves and their children, encouragement to stay in school, job training, instruction in parenting and life management techniques, and high-quality, affordable day care.

Adolescent mothers also benefit from family relationships that are sensitive to their developmental needs. In our discussion of the African-American extended family in Chapter 2, we noted that older teenage mothers display more effective parenting when they establish their own residence with the help of relatives—an arrangement that grants the teenager a balance of autonomy and support. Similarly, teenage mothers of other ethnic backgrounds who live apart from grandmothers but receive high levels of assistance from them have warmer extended-family ties and children who are developing more favorably (East & Felice, 1996). These findings raise questions about a new U.S. welfare policy that requires teenage mothers to live at home to receive benefits.

Programs focusing on fathers are attempting to increase their emotional and financial commitment to the baby (Coley & Chase-Lansdale, 1998). Although almost half of young fathers visit their children during the first few years after birth, contact usually diminishes. By school age, fewer than one-fourth are still involved (Lerman, 1993). But new laws that encourage mothers to help establish paternity and that enforce child support payments may lead to a turnabout in paternal responsibility and interaction. Children of teenage parents with warm, lasting ties to their fathers show better long-term adjustment (Furstenberg & Harris, 1993).

SEXUALLY TRANSMITTED DISEASE

Early sexual activity combined with inconsistent contraceptive use leads to another health problem that is widespread among teenagers: sexually transmitted disease (STD) (see Table 14.3). Adolescents have the highest incidence of STD of any age group. Despite a recent decline in STD in the United States, one out of six sexually active teenagers—3 million young people—contract an STD each year, a rate 50 to 100 times higher than that of other industrialized nations (U.S. Centers for Disease Control, 1997). If left untreated, sterility and life-threatening complications can result. Teenagers in greatest danger of STD are the same ones who tend to engage in irresponsible sexual behavior—poverty-stricken young people who feel a sense of inferiority and hopelessness about their lives (Holmbeck, Waters, & Brookman, 1990).

By far the most serious STD is AIDS. Although not many adolescents have AIDS, over one-fifth of cases in the United States occur between ages 20 and 29. Nearly all of these originate in adolescence, since AIDS symptoms typically take 8 to 10 years to emerge in a person infected with HIV. Drug-abusing and homosexual teenagers account for most cases, but heterosexual spread has increased, especially among females (U.S. Centers for Disease Control, 1997).

Besides helping teenagers understand sex, pregnancy, and contraception, another important goal of sex education is to help them avoid STD. As the result of school courses and media campaigns, over 90 percent of high school students are aware of basic facts about AIDS. But some hold false beliefs that put them at risk—for example, that birth control pills provide some protection or that it is possible to tell whether people have

This teenager is a member of City Year Corps, an organization of young volunteers who represent a cross-section of their communities and who serve as teachers' aides in public schools. Building competence through community service reduces teenage pregnancy and school failure among at-risk high school students. *(Robert Harbison)*

TABLE 14.3

Most Common Sexually Transmitted Diseases of Adolescence

DISEASE	INCIDENCE AMONG 15 TO 19-YEAR-OLDS (RATE PER 100,000)	CAUSE	SYMPTOMS AND CONSEQUENCES	TREATMENT
AIDS	20[a]	Virus	Fever, weight loss, severe fatigue, swollen glands, and diarrhea. As the immune system weakens, severe pneumonias and cancers, especially on the skin, appear. Death due to other diseases usually occurs.	No cure; experimental drugs prolong life
Chlamydia	1,132	Bacteria	Discharge from the penis in males; painful itching, burning vaginal discharge, and dull pelvic pain in females. Often no symptoms. If left untreated, can lead to inflammation of the pelvic region, infertility, and sterility.	Antibiotic drugs
Cytomegalovirus	Unknown[b]	Virus of the herpes family	No symptoms in most cases. Sometimes, a mild flu-like reaction. In a pregnant woman, can spread to the embryo or fetus and cause miscarriage or serious birth defects (see page 116).	None, usually disappears on its own
Genital warts	451	Virus	Warts that grow near the vaginal opening in females, on the penis or scrotum in males. Can cause severe itching. Related to cancer of the cervix.	Removal of warts
Gonorrhea	570	Bacteria	Discharge from the penis or vagina, painful urination. Sometimes no symptoms. If left untreated, can spread to other regions of the body, resulting in such complications as infertility, sterility, blood poisoning, arthritis, and inflammation of the heart.	Antibiotic drugs
Herpes simplex 2 (genital herpes)	167	Virus	Fluid-filled blisters on the genitals, high fever, severe headache, and muscle aches and tenderness. No symptoms in a few people. In a pregnant woman, can spread to the embryo or fetus and cause birth defects (see page 116).	No cure, can be controlled with drug treatment
Syphilis	6.4	Bacteria	Painless chancre (sore) at site of entry of germ and swollen glands, followed by rash, patchy hair loss, and sore throat within 1 week to 6 months. These symptoms disappear without treatment. Latent syphilis varies from no symptoms to damage to the brain, heart, and other organs after 5 to 20 years. In pregnant women, can spread to the embryo and fetus and cause birth defects (see page 116).	Antibiotic drugs

[a] This figure includes both adolescents and young adults. For most of these cases, the virus is contracted in adolescence, and symptoms appear in early adulthood.

[b] Cytomegalovirus is the most common STD. Because there are no symptoms in most cases, its precise rate of occurrence is unknown. Half of the population or more may have had the virus sometime during their lives.

Source: U.S. Center for Disease Control, 1997.

AIDS by looking at them (DiClemente, 1993). Almost all parents favor AIDS education in the public schools, and most states now require it. The Caregiving Concerns table on the following page lists strategies for preventing STD.

SUBSTANCE USE AND ABUSE

Just as they experimented with sex, so Louis and Cassie tried several forbidden substances during their teenage years. When he was 14, Louis took a couple of cigarettes out of his uncle's pack, waited until he was alone in the house, and smoked them. At an unchaperoned party, he and Cassie drank several cans of beer, largely because everyone

CAREGIVING CONCERNS

Preventing Sexually Transmitted Disease

STRATEGY	DESCRIPTION
Know your partner well.	Take time to get to get to know your partner. Find out whether your partner has had sex with many people or has used injectable drugs.
Maintain mutual faithfulness.	For this strategy to work, neither partner can have an STD at the start of the relationship.
Do not use drugs.	Using a needle, syringe, or drug liquid previously used by others can spread STD. Alcohol, marijuana, or other illegal substances impair judgment, reducing your capacity to think clearly about the consequences of behavior.
Always use a latex condom and vaginal contraceptive when having sex with a nonmarital partner.	Latex condoms give good (but not perfect) protection against STD by reducing the passage of bacteria and viruses. Vaginal contraceptives containing nonoxynol-9 can kill several kinds of STD microbes. They increase protection when combined with condom use.
Do not have sex with a person you know has an STD.	Even if you are protected by a condom, your risk of contracting the disease is still there. In the case of the AIDS virus, you are risking your life. If either partner has engaged in behavior that might have risked HIV infection, a blood test must be administered and repeated at least 6 months after that behavior, since it takes time for the body to develop antibodies.
If you get an STD, inform all recent sexual partners.	Notifying people you may have exposed to STD permits them to get treatment before spreading the disease to others.

Source: Daugirdas, 1992.

else was doing it. One summer at a beach gathering, someone pulled out a handful of marijuana joints, and Louis and his friends lit up. Louis got little physical charge out of these experiences. He was a good student, was well liked by peers, and got along well with his parents. He had no need for drugs as an escape valve from daily life. But he knew of others at his school for whom things were different—students who started with alcohol and cigarettes, increased their consumption, moved to harder substances, and eventually were hooked.

In the United States, teenage alcohol and drug use is pervasive—higher than in any other industrialized nation. By age 14, 56 percent of young people have tried smoking, 81 percent drinking, and 39 percent at least one illegal drug (usually marijuana). By the end of high school, 16 percent are regular cigarette users, 30 percent have engaged in heavy drinking at least once, and over 45 percent have experimented with illegal drugs. Of these, about one-third have tried at least one highly addictive and toxic substance, such as amphetamines, cocaine, phencyclidine (PCP), inhalants, or heroin (U.S. Department of Health and Human Services, 1997a).

These high figures represent a steady increase in alcohol and drug use over the past few years, after a decade of decline (see Figure 14.6). Why do so many young people subject themselves to the health risks of these substances? Part of the reason is cultural. Modern adolescents live in a drug-dependent society. They see adults using caffeine to wake up in the morning, cigarettes to cope with daily hassles, a drink to calm down in the evening, and other remedies to relieve stress, headaches, depression, and physical illness. Reduced parental, school, and media attention to the hazards of drugs as the epidemic of the 1980s subsided may explain the recent upsurge in adolescent drug taking (U.S. Department of Health and Human Services, 1997a).

For most young people, drug use simply reflects their intense curiosity about "adult-like" behaviors. Research reveals that the majority of teenagers dabble in alcohol as well as tobacco and marijuana. These minimal *experimenters* are not headed for a life of decadence and addiction. Instead, they are psychologically healthy, sociable, curious young people (Shedler & Block, 1990). In a society in which substance use is commonplace, some involvement with drugs is normal and to be expected.

FIGURE 14.6

Percentage of high school seniors reporting use of alcohol, cigarettes, and illegal drugs in the past month, 1976–1995. Substance use continues to be widespread among adolescents. Although it declined from 1982 to 1992, a sharp increase during the past few years—largely accounted for by marijuana and cigarette smoking—has sounded a note of alarm. *(From U.S. Department of Health and Human Services, 1997a.)*

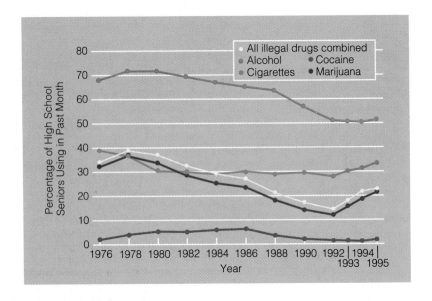

Yet adolescent drug experimentation should not be taken lightly. Because most drugs impair perception and thought processes, a single heavy dose can lead to permanent injury or death. And a worrisome minority of high-risk teenagers move from substance *use* to *abuse*—first experimenting, then taking drugs regularly, requiring increasing amounts to achieve the same effect, and finding themselves unable to stop (Luthar, Cushing, & McMahon, 1997). Four percent of high school seniors are daily drinkers, and almost as many indicate that they took an illegal drug on a daily basis over the past month (U.S. Department of Health and Human Services, 1997a).

Of all teenage drug habits, cigarette smoking has received the least attention because its short-term effects are minimal. Yet in the long run, it may be the deadliest substance, since it is an established cause of heart and lung disease and cancer. Cigarette use usually begins in early adolescence; 20 percent of American eighth graders say they smoked in the last month. Of high school students who smoke half a pack or more a day, 53 percent indicate that they tried to quit but could not (U.S. Department of Health and Human Services, 1997a).

■ **CORRELATES AND CONSEQUENCES OF ADOLESCENT SUBSTANCE ABUSE.** In contrast to experimenters, drug abusers are seriously troubled adolescents who are inclined to express their unhappiness through antisocial acts. Longitudinal evidence reveals that their impulsive, disruptive style is often evident in early childhood and seems to be perpetuated by a variety of other interrelated factors, including a low-SES background, family mental health problems, parental and older sibling drug abuse, lack of parent involvement and support, and poor school performance. By early adolescence, peer encouragement—friends who use drugs, urge the young person to do so, and provide access to illegal substances—is a strong predictor of substance abuse as at-risk teenagers seek out deviant agemates. Once an adolescent associates with drug-using peers, his or her own substance use approaches their level (Chassin et al., 1996; Dishion et al., 1995; Wills et al., 1996).

Teenage substance abuse is a devastating turn of events that often has lifelong consequences. When adolescents depend on alcohol and hard drugs to deal with daily stresses, they fail to learn responsible decision-making skills and alternative coping techniques—crucial lessons during this time of transition to adulthood. These young people show serious adjustment problems, including depression and antisocial behavior (Luthar & Cushing, 1997). They often enter into marriage, childbearing, and the work world prematurely and fail at them readily. Adolescent drug addiction is associated with high rates of divorce and job loss—painful outcomes that encourage further addictive behavior (Newcomb & Bentler, 1988).

■ **PREVENTION STRATEGIES.** School-based programs that promote effective parenting (including monitoring of teenagers' activities) and that teach adolescents skills for resisting peer pressure reduce drug experimentation to some degree (Steinberg, Fletcher, & Darling, 1994). But this approach is effective only if adults do not "pathologize" adolescents' tendency to try drugs from time to time. When teenagers are labeled as sick, screwed up, or "druggies" for having taken a sip or puff of an illegal substance, they are likely to rebel against the source of these alarmist and insulting messages. Under these conditions, the frequency of drug use often rises. Scare tactics, such as showing graphic films of the dire consequences of addiction, also work poorly (Newcomb & Bentler, 1989; Shedler & Block, 1990).

Modern adolescents observe adults using drugs to help themselves through their daily lives and relieve many common symptoms. So it is not surprising that most teenagers experiment with drugs at one time or another. Those who make the transition from use to abuse are seriously troubled young people who are inclined to express their unhappiness through impulsive, antisocial behavior. *(Michaud/Photo Researchers)*

Since some drug-taking seems to be inevitable, interventions that prevent adolescents from endangering themselves and others when they do experiment are essential. Many communities offer weekend on-call transportation services that any young person can contact for a safe ride home, with no questions asked. Providing appealing substitute activities, such as drug-free video arcades, dances, and sports activities, is also helpful. And educating teenagers about the dangers of drugs and alcohol is vital, since an increase in perceived risk closely paralleled the gradual decline in substance use in the 1980s and early 1990s (O'Malley, Johnston, & Bachman, 1995).

Drug abuse, as we have seen, occurs for quite different reasons than does occasional use. Therefore, different prevention strategies are required. One approach is to work with parents early, reducing family adversity and improving parenting skills, before children are old enough to become involved with drugs. Addicted mothers may be especially responsive to such interventions, since many seek treatment out of concern for the well-being of their children (Luthar, Cushing, & McMahon, 1997). Programs that teach at-risk teenagers effective strategies for handling life stressors and that build competence through community service have been found to reduce alcohol and drug use, just as they reduce teenage pregnancy (Richards-Colocino, McKenzie, & Newton, 1996).

When an adolescent becomes a drug abuser, hospitalization is often a necessary and even life-saving first step. Once the young person is weaned from the drug, long-term therapy to treat low self-esteem, anxiety, and impulsivity and academic and vocational training to improve life success and satisfaction are generally needed. Not much is known about the best way to treat adolescent drug abuse. Even the most comprehensive programs have alarmingly high relapse rates—from 35 to 70 percent (Newcomb & Bentler, 1989).

INJURIES

Adolescent risk taking, fueled by sensation seeking and a tendency to act without forethought, results in a rise in certain kinds of unintentional injuries. As we saw in Chapter 11, the total rate of unintentional injuries increases during adolescence (see pages 420–421). Automobile accidents are largely responsible. They are the leading killer of American teenagers, accounting for 42 percent of deaths between ages 15 and 19. Many result from driving at high speeds, using alcohol, and not wearing seatbelts (U.S. Department of Health and Human Services, 1997b). Parents need to set firm limits on their teenager's car use, particularly with respect to drinking and seatbelt use. These efforts are most likely to be successful when there is a history of good parent–child communication—a powerful preventive of adolescent injury (Millstein & Irwin, 1988).

Other injuries account for an additional 11 percent of adolescent deaths. The majority are caused by firearms. In a recent survey, 22 percent of American high school students reported carrying a weapon within the last month—8 percent, a gun (U.S. Centers for Disease Control, 1995). The rate of disability and death caused by firearms—mostly homicidal but occasionally accidental—is especially high in inner-city ghettos (Weissberg & Greenberg, 1998). In response, many American secondary schools have installed metal detectors, visitor sign-ins, and security guards. Unfortunately, these environmental changes increase teenagers' fear of crime but have little impact on violent victimizations (Duncan, 1996). In countries where gun sales are banned, such as Canada, all of Western Europe, and Japan, firearm injuries almost never happen.

A third form of adolescent injury—less prevalent but still serious and largely avoidable—is sports related. By high school, 15 percent of students involved in athletics experience injuries that require medical treatment. Most are mild, involving muscle strains and bruises, but an occasional serious injury (generally from playing football) does occur (Nelson, 1996).

Errors by coaches are an important source of athletic injuries. In their drive to win, they sometimes make unreasonable demands of players. Young adolescents are especially vulnerable. Many coaches match competitors on the basis of age and weight without considering physical maturity. Too often, this allows "[120 pounds] of mature muscle and mustache to compete against [120 pounds] of peach fuzz and baby fat" (Malina & Beunen, 1996; Malina & Stanitski, 1989, p. 35). The safest athletic activities during the period of rapid pubertal growth are limited-contact team sports, such as basketball, softball, and volleyball, and individual sports, such as track, swimming, and tennis.

BRIEF REVIEW

The arrival of puberty is accompanied by new health concerns. Greater nutritional requirements of a rapidly growing body come at a time when the eating habits of many young people are the poorest. For some teenagers, the cultural ideal of thinness combines with family and psychological problems to produce the serious eating disturbances of anorexia nervosa and bulimia.

The hormonal changes of puberty lead to an increase in sex drive, but how young people manage their sexuality is affected by social contexts. American adolescents receive mixed messages from adults and the larger culture about sexual activity. The percentage of sexually active teenagers increased over several decades and recently dropped slightly. Recent evidence indicates that genetic and environmental influences on prenatal sex hormones contribute to homosexuality.

Stressful life circumstances, adolescent cognitive processes, and lack of social supports for responsible sexual behavior contribute to high rates of teenage pregnancy, abortion, and childbirth in the United States. Adolescent parenthood is linked to low education, reduced chances of marriage, greater likelihood of divorce, and poverty—conditions that risk the development of mothers and their children. Sexually transmitted disease is an additional danger of early sexual activity and lack of contraceptive use.

Although most adolescents experiment with alcohol and drugs, a worrisome minority make the transition from use to abuse. Teenage substance abuse is linked to a variety of personal, family, peer, and school problems, and treatment is difficult. Motor vehicle, firearm, and sports-related injuries increase during adolescence.

ASK YOURSELF . . .

■ *Fourteen-year-old Lindsay says she's pretty certain she couldn't get pregnant from having sex with her boyfriend, since he told her he'd never do anything to "mess her up." What factors might account for Lindsay's unrealistic reasoning?*

■ *Return to page 547 to review Veronica's life circumstances after becoming a teenage mother. Why is it likely that Veronica and her children will experience long-term hardships?*

■ *Return to Chapter 1, page 10–11, and Chapter 13, page 518, to review factors that promote resilience in the face of high life stress. Then list characteristics common to effective pregnancy and substance abuse prevention programs. Are these components well suited to fostering resilience in at-risk adolescents? Explain.*

MOTOR DEVELOPMENT, SPORTS PARTICIPATION, AND PHYSICAL ACTIVITY

*P*uberty is accompanied by steady improvement in motor performance, but the pattern of change is quite different for boys and girls. Girls' gains are slow and gradual, leveling off by age 14. In contrast, boys show a dramatic spurt in strength, speed, and endurance that continues through the teenage years. The gender gap in physical skill widens over time. By mid-adolescence, very few girls perform as well as the average boy in such skills as running speed, broad jump, and throwing distance. And practically no boys score as low as the average girl (Malina & Bouchard, 1991).

Because girls and boys are no longer well matched physically, sex-segregated physical education usually begins in junior high school. At the same time, athletic options for both sexes expand. Many new sports are added to the curriculum—track and field, wrestling, tackle football, weight lifting, floor hockey, archery, tennis, and golf, to name just a few.

Since competence at sports is strongly related to peer admiration among adolescent boys, it becomes even more important in boys' self-esteem than it was at earlier ages. Some adolescents—about twice as many boys as girls—become so obsessed with physical prowess that they try to increase their skill artificially through the use of anabolic steroids. In the United States, about 5 percent of adolescent males and 2 percent of females take these illegal drugs to boost muscle size and strength, ignoring their serious side effects (Yesalis et al., 1997). These include damage to the liver, circulatory system, and reproductive organs as well as an increase in mood swings and aggressive behavior. Coaches and health professionals need to inform teenagers of the dangers of steroids and the importance of avoiding them.

In 1972, the federal government required schools receiving public funds to provide equal opportunities for males and females in all educational programs, including athletics. As Figure 14.7 shows, high school girls' sports participation quadrupled during the following decade and has continued to increase, although it still falls far short of boys'. In Chapter 11, we saw that beginning at an early age, girls get less encouragement and recognition for athletic achievement, a pattern that persists into the teenage years. Look in your

This high school cross-country team practices for an upcoming meet. After the U.S. government required schools receiving public funds to provide equal opportunities for males and females in athletics, girls' sports participation increased substantially. Still, throughout childhood and adolescence, girls get less encouragement and recognition for athletic achievement than do boys. *(Peter Cade/Tony Stone Images)*

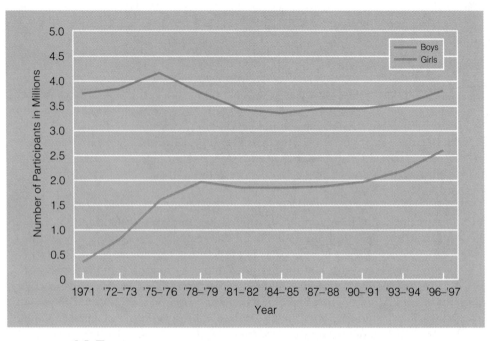

FIGURE 14.7

High school sports participation trends in the United States, 1971–1997. A legal mandate for equality of opportunity in school athletic participation led girls' involvement in sports to increase dramatically from the early 1970s to 1980. Since then, girls' participation has continued to rise gradually, although it still falls far short of boys. *(From National Federation of State High School Associations, 1997.)*

local newspaper and note the much greater attention given to boys' school sports than girls'. Girls' athletic events usually attract only a handful of spectators.

The sex differences just described also characterize physical activity rates of American adolescents. Overall, 74 percent of high school boys but only 52 percent of girls report regular vigorous physical activity (at least 20 minutes 3 days a week). The number of boys engaging in regular exercise increases from ninth to twelfth grade. In contrast, about 15 percent of girls who were physically active in ninth grade are no longer exercising regularly by grade 12 (U.S. Department of Health and Human Services, 1997b).

Besides improving motor performance, sports and exercise influence cognitive and social development. Interschool and intramural athletics provide important lessons in competition, assertiveness, problem solving, and teamwork. And regular physical activity is associated with enhanced functioning of the immune system and improved psychological well-being (Newcombe & Boyle, 1995; Nieman, 1994). Yet only 60 percent of American secondary school students are enrolled in physical education, and only 25 percent attend a class daily. Attendance drops off with each grade, especially for girls (U.S. Department of Health and Human Services, 1997b).

Required daily physical education, aimed at helping all teenagers find pleasure in sports and exercise, is a vital means of promoting adolescent health (Allensworth, 1996). A positive sign is that the sex difference in high school team sports participation is gradually shrinking. Although we still have a long way to go, we are closer today than ever before to equality of opportunity for the sexes in sports as well as other areas of human skill.

Summary

CONCEPTIONS OF ADOLESCENCE

How have conceptions of adolescence changed over the twentieth century?

■ Early biologically oriented theories viewed **puberty** as an inevitable period of storm and stress. An alternative perspective regarded the social environment as entirely responsible for the wide variability in adolescent adjustment.

■ Modern research shows that adolescence is neither biologically nor socially determined, but a product of the two. In cultures where many years of education are required for successful participation in the work life of the community, adolescence is greatly extended.

PUBERTY: THE PHYSICAL TRANSITION TO ADULTHOOD

Describe pubertal changes in body size, proportions, and sexual maturity.

■ Hormonal changes beginning in middle childhood initiate puberty, which begins, on the average, 2 years earlier for girls than for boys. The first outward sign of puberty is the rapid gain in height and weight known as the **growth spurt.** In early adolescence, the cephalocaudal trend of body growth reverses. Lengthening of the torso accounts for most of the adolescent height gain. As the body enlarges, girls' hips and boys' shoulders broaden. Girls add more fat, boys more muscle.

■ Sex hormones regulate changes in **primary** and **secondary sexual characteristics. Menarche** occurs relatively late in the girl's sequence of pubertal events, following the rapid increase in body size. After menarche, growth of the breasts and pubic and underarm hair are completed. Among boys, as the sex organs and body enlarge and pubic and underarm hair appear, **spermarche** (first ejaculation) takes place. This is followed by growth of facial and body hair and deepening of the voice.

What factors influence the timing of puberty?

■ In addition to heredity, nutrition and overall physical health contribute to the timing of puberty. Menarche is delayed in poverty-stricken regions of the world and among girls from economically disadvantaged homes. A secular trend toward an earlier age of puberty has occurred in industrialized nations.

THE PSYCHOLOGICAL IMPACT OF PUBERTAL EVENTS

What factors influence adolescents' reactions to the physical changes of puberty?

■ Girls generally react to menarche with surprise and mixed emotions, but whether their feelings lean in a positive or negative direction depends on advance information and support from family members. Boys usually know ahead of time about spermarche, but they receive less support for the physical changes of puberty than do girls.

■ Tribal and village societies often celebrate puberty with an **adolescent initiation ceremony.** The absence of a widely accepted marker for physical and social maturity in contemporary society makes the process of becoming an adult especially confusing.

■ Besides higher hormone levels, negative life events and situational changes are associated with adolescent moodiness. Puberty is accompanied by psychological distancing between parent and child. The reaction may be a modern substitute for physical departure from the family, which typically occurs at sexual maturity in primate species.

Describe the impact of maturational timing on adolescent adjustment, noting sex differences.

■ Timing of puberty influences adolescent psychological adjustment. Early maturing boys and late maturing girls, whose appearance closely matches cultural standards of physical attractiveness, have a

more positive **body image,** feel more self-confident, and hold more positions of leadership. In contrast, early maturing girls and late maturing boys, who fit in least well physically with peers, experience emotional and social difficulties.

■ School contexts can modify maturational timing effects. Although long-term follow-ups show some striking turnabouts in adjustment, the consequences of early and late maturation may persist in some cultures.

HEALTH ISSUES

Describe nutritional needs, and cite factors related to serious eating disturbances during adolescence.

■ As the body grows, nutritional requirements increase, at a time when the eating habits of young people are the poorest. Many adolescents suffer from iron, vitamin, and mineral deficiencies.

■ Girls who reach puberty early, who are very dissatisfied with their body images, and who grow up in homes where a concern with thinness is especially strong are at risk for eating disorders. **Anorexia nervosa** tends to appear in girls who have perfectionist personalities and overprotective and controlling mothers. The impulsive eating and purging of **bulimia** is associated with disengaged parenting and lack of self-control in other areas of life.

Discuss social and cultural influences on adolescent sexual attitudes and behavior.

■ The hormonal changes of puberty lead to an increase in sex drive, but social factors affect how teenagers manage their sexuality. Compared to most other cultures, the United States is fairly restrictive in its attitude toward adolescent sex. Young people receive contradictory messages from the larger social environment. Sexual attitudes and behavior of adolescents have become more liberal, with a slight swing back in recent years, largely due to the risk of sexually transmitted disease.

Summary (continued)

■ Early sexual activity is linked to a variety of factors associated with economic disadvantage. About half of sexually active American teenagers do not practice contraception regularly. Adolescent cognitive processes and a lack of social support for responsible sexual behavior underlie the failure of so many young people to protect themselves against pregnancy. Teenagers who talk openly with their parents about sex are more likely to use birth control.

Describe factors involved in the development of homosexuality.

■ About 3 to 6 percent of young people discover that they are lesbian or gay. Although heredity makes an important contribution, homosexuality probably results from a variety of biological and environmental combinations that are not yet well understood. Gay and lesbian teenagers face special challenges in establishing a positive sexual identity.

Discuss factors related to teenage pregnancy, childbearing, and sexually transmitted disease.

■ Teenage pregnancy, abortion, and childbearing are more prevalent in the United States than in many industrialized nations. Adolescent parenthood is associated with dropping out of school, reduced chances of marriage, greater likelihood of divorce, and poverty—circumstances that risk the well-being of both adolescent and newborn child.

■ Adolescent mothers benefit from extended-family support that is sensitive to their developmental needs. When teenage fathers stay involved, their children develop more favorably. Improved sex education, access to contraceptives, and programs that build social competence help prevent early pregnancy.

■ Early sexual activity combined with inconsistent contraceptive use results in high rates of sexually transmitted disease (STD) among American teenagers. A substantial proportion of AIDS victims contract the virus as adolescents. An important goal of sex education is prevention of STD.

What personal and social factors are related to adolescent substance use and abuse?

■ Teenage alcohol and drug use is widespread in the United States. For most young people, drug experimentation reflects curiosity about these forbidden substances. Those who move from use to abuse have serious personal, family, school, and peer problems. Programs that work with parents early to reduce family adversity and improve parenting skills and that build teenagers' competence help prevent substance abuse.

Cite common unintentional injuries in adolescence.

■ Motor vehicle collisions are the leading cause of adolescent injury and death. The rate of disability and death caused by firearms is also high. A third, less prevalent type of injury is sports related.

MOTOR DEVELOPMENT, SPORTS PARTICIPATION, AND PHYSICAL ACTIVITY

Describe sex differences in motor development during adolescence.

■ Pubertal changes lead both sexes to improve in gross motor performance during adolescence, although boys show much larger gains than girls. Although their involvement in high school sports has increased, girls continue to receive less encouragement and recognition for developing athletic skill than do boys.

■ Overall, the number of boys engaging in regular physical activity increases from ninth to twelfth grade, whereas the number of physically active girls declines. Required daily physical education that helps all teenagers find pleasure in sports and exercise is vital for promoting adolescent health.

Important terms and concepts

adolescent initiation ceremony
   (p. 536)
anorexia nervosa (p. 541)
body image (p. 538)
bulimia (p. 542)

growth spurt (p. 529)
menarche (p. 531)
puberty (p. 526)
primary sexual characteristics
   (p. 531)

secondary sexual characteristics
   (p. 531)
spermarche (p. 532)

Fyi...   FOR FURTHER INFORMATION AND HELP

EATING DISORDERS

Anorexia Nervosa and Related
Eating Disorders, Inc.
(541) 344-1144
Website: www.anred.com

An association of anorexics and bulimics, their families and friends, and concerned professionals that provides information about the disorders.

SEXUAL BEHAVIOR, PREGNANCY, AND CHILDBEARING

Alan Guttmacher Institute
(212) 248-1111
Website: www.agi-usa.org

Compiles information on sexual behavior, contraception, abortion, childbearing, and sexually transmitted disease and promotes public policy related to birth control. Publishes the journal Family Planning Perspectives, *which includes articles on adolescents.*

SEXUALLY TRANSMITTED DISEASE (STD)

American Social Health Association
(919) 361-8400
Website: www.sunsite.unc.edu/asha

A national health agency that works to expand research, provide information to communities, and improve public health policy related to STD. Operates the Herpes Resource Center, a support program for sufferers of incurable genital herpes.

   U.S. Centers for Disease Control
   Website: www.cdc.gov

A government agency devoted to promoting health and quality of life by preventing and controlling disease, injury, and disability. Compiles statistics on disease incidence and disseminates health information. Sponsors the National AIDS Hotline, (800)342-AIDS, and the National STD Hotline, (800)227-8922.

SUBSTANCE ABUSE

Cocaine Anonymous
(310) 559-5833
Website: www.ca.org

An organization devoted to helping adolescents and adults recover from addiction to cocaine and other mood-altering drugs that follows the methods used by Alcoholics Anonymous.

   Do It Now Foundation
   (602) 491-0393

Works to provide factual information to adolescents and adults about alcohol, drugs, and related health issues. Assists organizations engaged in drug education.

(See page 129 for additional organizations related to substance abuse.)

"Two Families"
John Ketchum
14 years, United States

During adolescence, cognition moves from the real to the possible. This 14-year-old's vision of the interdependence between human and animal life is a product of new, abstract reasoning powers discussed in Chapter 15.

Reprinted by permission from The International Museum of Children's Art, Oslo, Norway.

COGNITIVE DEVELOPMENT

IN ADOLESCENCE

One mid-December

evening, a knock at the front door
announced the arrival of Franca and
Antonio's oldest son, Jules, home for
vacation after the fall semester of his
sophomore year at college. Moments
later, the family gathered around the
kitchen table. "How did it all go, Jules?"
inquired Antonio while passing out
pieces of apple pie.

"Well, math was only so-so. But
physics and philosophy were awesome.
The last few weeks, our physics prof
introduced us to Einstein's theory of
relativity. Boggles my mind, it's so
incredibly counterintuitive."

"Counter-what?" asked 11-year-old
Sabrina, trying hard to follow the conversation.

"Counterintuitive. Unlike what
you'd normally expect," explained Jules.
"Imagine this. You're on a train, going
unbelievably fast, like 160,000 miles a
second. The faster you go approaching
the speed of light, the slower time

passes and the denser and heavier things get relative to on the ground. The theory revolutionized the way we think about time, space, matter—the entire universe."

Sabrina wrinkled her forehead in a puzzled expression, unable to comprehend Jules's other-worldly reasoning. "Time slows down when I'm bored, like right now, not on a train when I'm going somewhere exciting. No speeding train ever made me denser and heavier, but this apple pie will if I eat any more of it," Sabrina announced with finality, getting up and leaving the table.

Sixteen-year-old Louis reacted differently. "Totally cool, Jules. So what'd you do in philosophy?"

"It was a course in philosophy of technology. One of the things we studied was the ethics of futuristic methods in human reproduction. For example, we argued the pros and cons of a world in which all embryos develop in artificial wombs."

"What do you mean?" asked Louis. "You order your kid at the lab?"

"That's right. I wrote my term paper on it. I had to evaluate it in terms of principles of justice and freedom. I can see some advantages but also lots of dangers. . . ."

As this conversation illustrates, adolescence brings with it vastly expanded powers of reasoning. At age 11, Sabrina's logic is still concrete, tied to the here-and-now. She finds it difficult to move beyond her own firsthand experiences into a world of possibilities. Over the next few years, her thinking will take on the abstract qualities of her older brother's thought. Jules juggles variables in complex combinations and thinks about situations not easily detected in the real world or that do not exist at all—cognitive capacities that open up whole new realms of learning. Adolescents can grasp complex scientific and mathematical principles, grapple with puzzling social and political issues, and detect the hidden meaning of a poem or story. Compared to school-age children's thinking, adolescent thought is more enlightened, imaginative, and rational.

The first part of this chapter traces these extraordinary changes, from both Piaget's and the information-processing points of view. Next, we take a close look at research findings that have attracted a great deal of public attention: sex differences in mental abilities. We also discuss important gains in language that reflect as well as contribute to the advanced thinking of the teenage years. The middle portion of this chapter is devoted to the primary setting in which adolescent thought takes shape: the school. We conclude with a consideration of vocational development during the teenage years.

PIAGET'S THEORY: THE FORMAL OPERATIONAL STAGE

formal operational stage
Piaget's final stage, in which adolescents develop the capacity for abstract, scientific thinking. Begins around 11 years of age.

hypothetico-deductive reasoning
A formal operational problem-solving strategy in which adolescents begin with a general theory of all possible factors that could affect an outcome in a problem and deduce specific hypotheses, which they test in an orderly fashion.

propositional thought
A type of formal operational reasoning in which adolescents evaluate the logic of verbal statements without referring to real-world circumstances.

According to Piaget, the capacity for abstract thinking begins around age 11. At the **formal operational stage,** the adolescent reasons much like a scientist searching for solutions in the laboratory. Concrete operational children can only "operate on reality," but formal operational adolescents can "operate on operations." In other words, concrete things and events are no longer required as objects of thought. Instead, adolescents can come up with new, more general logical rules through internal reflection (Brainerd, 1978; Inhelder & Piaget, 1955/1958). Table 15.1 summarizes two major features of formal operational reasoning.

HYPOTHETICO-DEDUCTIVE REASONING

At adolescence, young people first become capable of **hypothetico-deductive reasoning.** When faced with a problem, they start with a *general theory* of all possible factors that might affect the outcome and *deduce* from it specific *hypotheses* (or predictions) about what might happen. Then they test these hypotheses in an orderly fashion to see which ones work in the real world. Notice how this form of problem solving begins with possibility and proceeds to reality. In contrast, concrete operational children start with real-

TABLE 15.1

Major Characteristics of Formal Operational Thought

CHARACTERISTIC	DESCRIPTION	EXAMPLE
Hypothetico-deductive reasoning	When faced with a problem, formal operational adolescents think of all possible factors that could affect the outcome, even those not immediately suggested by concrete features of the situation. Then they try them out in a step-by-step fashion to find out which ones work in the real world.	In biology class, Louis had to determine which of two fertilizers was best for growing African violets. Louis thought, "The kind of fertilizer might not be the only factor that's important. Its concentration and how often the plant is fed might also make a difference." So Louis planned an experiment in which each fertilizer would be applied in several strengths and according to different feeding schedules. He made sure to design the experiment so he could determine the separate effects of each factor, and their combined effects, on plant growth.
Propositional thought	Formal operational adolescents can evaluate the logic of statements by reflecting on the statements themselves. They do not need to consider them against real-world circumstances.	Louis was given the following propositional task and asked to indicate whether the conclusion was true, false, or uncertain: Premise 1: All animals are purple. Premise 2: A frobe is purple. Conclusion: A frobe is an animal. Louis concluded, correctly, that whether a frobe is an animal is uncertain. "A frobe might be an animal," he answered, "but it might also be a purple thing that is not an animal."

ity—with the most obvious predictions about a situation. When these are not confirmed, they cannot think of alternatives and fail to solve the problem.

Adolescents' performance on Piaget's famous *pendulum problem* illustrates this new hypothetico-deductive approach. Suppose we present several school-age children and adolescents with strings of different lengths, objects of different weights to attach to the strings, and a bar from which to hang the strings. Then we ask each of them to figure out what influences the speed with which a pendulum swings through its arc.

Formal operational adolescents come up with four hypotheses: (1) the length of the string; (2) the weight of the object hung on it; (3) how high the object is raised before it is released; and (4) how forcefully the object is pushed. Then, by varying one factor at a time while holding all the others constant, they try out each of these possibilities. Eventually they discover that only string length makes a difference.

In contrast, concrete operational children's experimentation is unsystematic. They cannot separate out the effects of each variable. For example, they may test for the effect of string length without holding weight constant by comparing a short, light pendulum with a long, heavy one. Also, school-age youngsters fail to notice variables that are not immediately suggested by the concrete materials of the task—the height and forcefulness with which the pendulum is released.

PROPOSITIONAL THOUGHT

A second important characteristic of the formal operational stage is **propositional thought.** Adolescents can evaluate the logic of propositions (verbal statements) without referring to real-world circumstances. In contrast, concrete operational children can evaluate the logic of statements only by considering them against concrete evidence in the real world.

In one study of propositional reasoning, an experimenter showed children and adolescents a pile of poker chips and indicated that some

In Piaget's formal operational stage, adolescents engage in propositional thought. As these students discuss problems in a precalculus class, they show that they can reason with symbols that do not necessarily represent objects in the real world. (Will Hart)

statements would be made about them. Each participant was asked to tell whether each statement was true, false, or uncertain. In one condition, the experimenter hid a chip in her hand and then asked the young person to evaluate the following propositions:

"*Either* the chip in my hand is green *or* it is not green."

"The chip in my hand is green *and* it is not green."

In another condition, the experimenter held either a red or a green chip in full view and made the same statements.

School-age children focused on the concrete properties of the poker chips rather than on the logic of the statements. As a result, they replied that they were uncertain to both statements when the chip was hidden from view. When it was visible, they judged both statements to be true if the chip was green and false if it was red. In contrast, adolescents analyzed the logic of the statements as propositions. They understood that the "either–or" statement is always true and the "and" statement is always false, regardless of the poker chip's color (Osherson & Markman, 1975).

Although Piaget believed that language does not play a central role in cognitive development (see Chapter 9), he acknowledged that it is more important during adolescence. Abstract thought requires language-based systems of representation that do not stand for real things, such as those that exist in higher mathematics. Junior high and high school students use these systems in algebra and geometry. Formal operational thought also involves verbal reasoning about abstract concepts. Jules showed that he could think in this way when he pondered the relationships between time, space, and matter in physics and wondered about justice and freedom in philosophy.

RECENT RESEARCH ON FORMAL OPERATIONAL THOUGHT

Recent research on formal operational thought poses questions similar to those we discussed with respect to Piaget's earlier stages: Is there evidence that abstract reasoning appears earlier than Piaget expected? Do all individuals reach formal operations during their teenage years?

■ **ARE YOUNG CHILDREN CAPABLE OF ABSTRACT THINKING?** School-age children show the glimmerings of hypothetico-deductive reasoning, but they are not as competent as adolescents and adults. For example, in simplified situations—ones involving no more than two possible causal variables—6-year-olds understand that hypotheses must be confirmed by appropriate evidence. They also realize that once supported, a hypothesis shapes predictions about what might happen in the future (Ruffman et al., 1993). But unlike adolescents, children cannot sort out evidence that bears on three or more variables at once. And as we will see when we take up information-processing research on scientific reasoning in a later section, children have difficulty explaining why a pattern of observations supports a hypothesis, even when they recognize the connection between the two.

School-age children's capacity for propositional thought is also limited. For example, they have great difficulty reasoning from premises that contradict reality or their own beliefs. Consider the following set of statements: "If dogs are bigger than elephants and elephants are bigger than mice, then dogs are bigger than mice." Children younger than 10 judge this reasoning to be false, since all the relations specified do not occur in real life (Moshman & Franks, 1986).

Furthermore, in instances in which school-age children respond correctly to propositional tasks, their success seems to be due to an "atmosphere effect." Positive statements are always answered yes and negative statements are always answered no, even though this strategy often violates the most basic rules of logic (Markovits, Schleifer, & Fortier, 1989).

For example, when given the following premises (one of which is negative), school-age children usually draw an incorrect conclusion:

Premise 1: If there is a knife, then there is a fork.

Premise 2: There is not a knife.

Question: Is there a fork?

Wrong Conclusion: No, there is not a fork. (Kodroff & Roberge, 1975)

Around age 11, young people can analyze the logic of a series of propositions, regardless of whether statements are positive, negative, or consistent with reality or their own values. As Piaget's theory indicates, propositional thought improves steadily over the adolescent years (Markovits & Bouffard-Bouchard, 1992; Markovits & Vachon, 1989, 1990).

■ **DO ALL INDIVIDUALS REACH THE FORMAL OPERATIONAL STAGE?** Try giving the knife-and-fork task to some of your friends and see how well they do. You are likely to find that even well-educated adults have difficulty with abstract thinking! About 40 to 60 percent of college students fail Piaget's formal operational problems (Keating, 1979).

Why is it that so many college students, and adults in general, are not fully formal operational? The reason is that people are most likely to think abstractly in situations in which they have had extensive experience. This is supported by the finding that adolescents and adults can be trained to a high level of performance on formal operational tasks (Kuhn, Ho, & Adams, 1979). Other evidence indicates that taking college courses leads to improvements in formal operational reasoning related to course content (Lehman & Nisbett, 1990). The physics student grasps Piaget's pendulum problem with ease. The English enthusiast excels at analyzing the themes of a Shakespeare play, whereas the history buff skillfully evaluates the causes and consequences of the Vietnam War. Because of differences in training and interest, the person who does well at one of these tasks may not be especially good at the others.

Consider these findings carefully, and you will see that formal operations, like the concrete reasoning that preceded it, does not emerge in all contexts at once. Rather, it is specific to situation and task (Keating, 1990). Adolescents and adults are likely to demonstrate it only in areas in which they have achieved considerable mastery.

Furthermore, you may recall from Chapter 13 that the development of concrete operations is greatly delayed in some village and tribal societies. In many of these cultures, formal operational tasks are not mastered at all (Cole, 1990; Gellatly, 1987). For example, when asked to engage in propositional thought, many people in nonliterate societies refuse, explaining that they must see an event to discern its logical implications. Consider this Central Asian peasant's response to a hypothetical proposition:

> [Interviewer]: In the far North, where there is snow, all bears are white. Novaya Zemlya is in the Far North and there is always snow there. What color are the bears there?
>
> [Peasant]: . . . We always speak only of what we see; we don't talk about what we haven't seen.
>
> [Interviewer]: . . . But on the basis of my words—in the North, where there is always snow, the bears are white, can you gather what kind of bears there are in Novaya Zemlya?

If asked, these nonliterate Mongolian nomads would probably refuse to engage in propositional thought, explaining that an event must be seen to discern its logical implications. Because of lack of opportunity to solve hypothetical problems, formal operational reasoning is not evident in all societies. *(Noburu Komine/ Photo Researchers, Inc.)*

[Peasant]: If a man was sixty or eighty and had seen a white bear and had told about it, he could be believed, but I've never seen one and hence I can't say. That's my last word. Those who saw can tell, and those who didn't see can't say anything! (Luria, 1976, pp. 108–109)

Notice that the peasant and the interviewer disagree on the definition of truth. The first insists on first-hand knowledge, whereas the second states that truth can be based on ideas alone. Yet the peasant uses propositions to defend his point of view: "*If* a man . . . had seen a white bear and had told about it, *[then]* he could be believed, *but* I've never seen one and *hence* I can't say." Although he rarely displays it in everyday life, clearly the peasant is capable of formal operational thought!

Piaget acknowledged that because of lack of opportunity to solve hypothetical problems, formal operations might not be evident in some societies. Still, these findings raise further questions about Piaget's stage sequence. Is the formal operational stage largely an outgrowth of children and adolescents' independent efforts to make sense of their world? Or is it a culturally transmitted way of reasoning that is particularly useful in literate societies and fostered by experiences encountered in school?

Finally, critics claim that just how individuals make the transition from concrete to formal operational thought is not made clear by Piaget's theory. They state that Piaget's explanation of cognitive change—in particular, the processes of *adaptation* and *organization* (see page 213)—is too vague and imprecise. This issue, especially, has prompted many investigators to turn toward an information-processing view.

AN INFORMATION-PROCESSING VIEW OF ADOLESCENT COGNITIVE DEVELOPMENT

*I*nformation-processing theorists agree with the broad outlines of Piaget's description of adolescent cognition (Case, 1992, 1998; Demetriou et al., 1993). However, they refer to a variety of specific mechanisms of cognitive change, each of which was discussed in previous chapters. Now let's draw them together:

- *Attention* becomes more thorough and better adapted to the demands of tasks (see page 443).

- *Strategies* become more effective, improving storage, representation, and retrieval of information (see pages 443–445).

- *Knowledge* increases, easing strategy use (see page 446).

- *Metacognition* (awareness of thought) expands, leading to new insights into effective strategies for acquiring information and solving problems (see page 448).

- *Processing capacity* increases due to the joint effects of brain development and the factors just mentioned. Consequently, space in working memory is freed so more information can be held at once and combined into highly efficient, abstract representations (see page 441).

As we look at some influential findings from an information-processing perspective, we will see some of these mechanisms of change in action. And we will discover that researchers regard one of them—*metacognition*—as central to the development of abstract thought.

SCIENTIFIC REASONING: COORDINATING THEORY WITH EVIDENCE

During a free moment in physical education class, Sabrina wondered why more of her tennis serves and returns seemed to pass the net and drop in her opponent's court when

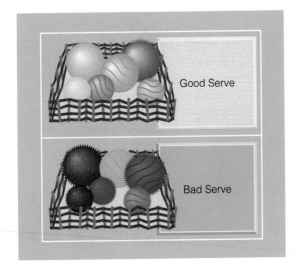

FIGURE **15.1**

Example of evidence in the sports ball problem. Participants were asked to tell which of four features of sports balls—size, color, surface texture, or presence or absence of ridges—influences the quality of a player's serve. This set of evidence suggests that color might be important, since light-colored balls are largely in the good-serve basket and dark-colored balls in the bad-serve basket. But the same is true for texture! The good-serve basket has mostly smooth balls, the bad-serve basket rough balls. Since all light-colored balls are smooth and all dark-colored balls are rough, we cannot tell whether color or texture makes a difference. However, we can deduce that size and presence or absence of ridges are not important, since these variables are equally represented in the good-serve and bad-serve baskets. *(From D. Kuhn, E. Amsel, & M. O'Loughlin, 1988, The development of scientific thinking skills, Orlando, FL: Academic Press, p. 140. Reprinted by permission.)*

she used a particular brand of balls. "Maybe it's something about their color or size? Hmm, more likely it's their surface texture, which might affect their bounce," she thought to herself as she carefully inspected several balls.

The heart of scientific reasoning is coordinating theories with evidence. A scientist can clearly describe the theory that he or she favors, knows what evidence is needed to support it and what would refute it, and can explain how pitting evidence against available theories led to the acceptance of one theory as opposed to others. What evidence would Sabrina need to confirm her theory about the tennis balls?

Deanna Kuhn has conducted extensive research into the development of scientific reasoning, giving children and adolescents problems that resemble those used by Piaget in that they involve several variables that might affect an outcome. In one series of studies, third, sixth, and ninth graders; adults of mixed educational backgrounds; and professional scientists were provided with evidence, sometimes consistent and sometimes conflicting with theories. Then they were asked questions about the accuracy of each theory.

For example, participants were given a problem much like the one Sabrina posed. They were asked to theorize about which of four features of sports balls—size (large or small), color (light or dark), surface texture (rough or smooth), or presence or absence of ridges—influences the quality of a player's serve. Next, they were told about the theory of Mr. (or Ms.) S, who believes that size of the ball is important, and the theory of Mr. (or Ms.) C, who thinks that color makes a difference. Finally, the interviewer presented evidence by placing balls with certain characteristics in two baskets labeled "good serve" and "bad serve" (see Figure 15.1).

Kuhn and her collaborators (1988) found that the capacity to reason like a scientist improved with age. The youngest participants often ignored conflicting evidence or distorted it in ways consistent with their theory. When one third grader, who judged that size was causal (with large balls producing good serves and small balls, bad serves), was shown incomplete evidence (a single, large, light-colored ball in the "good serve" basket and no balls in the "bad serve" basket), he insisted on the accuracy of Mr. S's theory (which was also his own). Asked to explain, he stated flatly, "Because this ball is big . . . the color doesn't really matter" (Kuhn, 1989, p. 677).

These findings, and others like them, reveal that instead of viewing evidence as separate from and bearing on a theory, children often blend the two into a single representation of "the way things are." The ability to distinguish theory from evidence and use logical rules to examine their relationship in complex, multi-variable situations improves from childhood into adolescence and adulthood (Foltz, Overton, & Ricco, 1995; Kuhn et al., 1995; Schauble, 1996).

HOW DOES SCIENTIFIC REASONING DEVELOP?

What factors support adolescents' skill at coordinating theory with evidence? Greater information-processing capacity, permitting a theory and the effects of several variables to be compared at once, is vital. In addition, adolescents benefit from exposure to increasingly complex problems and instruction that highlights critical features of tasks and effective strategies. It is not surprising that scientific reasoning is strongly influenced by years of schooling, whether individuals grapple with traditional scientific tasks (like the sports ball problem or Piaget's pendulum task) or engage in informal reasoning—for example, justify a theory about what causes children to fail in school (Kuhn, 1993).

Many investigators believe that increasingly sophisticated *metacognitive understanding* is at the heart of advanced cognitive development. When children receive continuous opportunities to pit theory against evidence, eventually they *reflect* on their current strategies, revise them, and become aware of the nature of logic. Then they apply their abstract appreciation of logical necessity to a wide variety of situations. Although children can distinguish a hypothesis from data and test it in simplified situations, the ability to *think about* theories, *deliberately* isolate variables, and *actively seek* disconfirming evidence is rarely present before adolescence (Moshman, 1990, 1998).

Research reveals that adolescents develop formal operational abilities in a similar, step-by-step fashion on different kinds of tasks. In a series of studies, 10- to 20-year olds were given sets of problems graded in difficulty. For example, one set consisted of quantitative-relational tasks like the pendulum problem on page 565. Another set contained verbal propositional tasks like the poker chip problem on page 566. And in still another set were causal-experimental tasks, such as the sports ball problem described in the previous section and the fertilizer problem in Table 15.1.

In each task domain, adolescents mastered component skills in sequential order by expanding their metacognitive awareness. For example, on causal-experimental tasks, they first became aware of the many variables—separately and in combination—that could influence an outcome. This enabled them to formulate and test hypotheses. Over time, adolescents combined separate skills into a smoothly functioning system. They constructed a general model that could be applied to many instances of a given type of problem. In the researchers' words, young people seem to form a "hypercognitive system," or supersystem, that understands, organizes, and influences other aspects of cognition (Demetriou, Efklides, & Platsidou, 1993; Demetriou et al., 1993, 1996).

Return to Chapter 12, page 441, and review Robbie Case's information-processing view of development during Piaget's concrete operational stage. Does Case's concept of *central conceptual structures* remind you of the metacognitive advances just described? Piaget also underscored the role of metacognition in formal operational thought when he spoke of "operating on operations" (see page 564). However, information-processing findings reveal that scientific reasoning is not the result of an abrupt, stagewise change, as Piaget believed. Instead, it develops gradually out of many specific experiences that require children and adolescents to match theory against evidence and reflect on and evaluate their thinking.

A RATIONAL APPROACH TO THINKING

How can we sum up the cognitive advances we have just considered? Ideally, adolescence opens the door to truly rational thought—a "critical spirit" in which the person seeks relevant evidence and alternative views and is willing to alter his or her beliefs in accord with them. Teenagers, as we have seen, make great strides toward becoming rational thinkers. Yet researchers who study **postformal thought** have shown that cognitive development is not complete at adolescence.

Piaget (1967) acknowledged the possibility that important advances in cognition follow the attainment of formal operations. He observed that many adolescents place

postformal thought
Cognitive development beyond Piaget's formal operational stage.

excessive faith in abstract systems, preferring a logical, internally consistent perspective on the world to one that is vague, contradictory, and constantly open to revision. Their theories often take on the status of right or wrong, good or bad. College-educated young people are much more aware of a diversity of opinions on almost any topic. They move toward **relativistic reasoning**, viewing all knowledge as embedded in a framework of thought (Perry, 1970, 1981). As a result, they give up the possibility of absolute truth in favor of multiple truths. Then they seek good reasons for choosing a belief or course of action, recognizing that in certain instances, one option may be better justified than others.

Research reveals that most adolescents can think relativistically about hypothetical situations related to their personal experiences. For example, they realize that a group of parents who favor a later driving age and a group of high school students who want the driving age to stay the same each have legitimate claims (Chandler, Boyes, & Ball, 1990). But exposure to the multiple viewpoints typical of a college education greatly enhances relativistic thinking, permitting it to be applied in a much wider range of situations (King & Kitchener, 1994).

In sum, over time abstract thinking becomes increasingly flexible—less constrained by the need to find one answer and more responsive to its context. As we turn now to adolescents' reasoning in everyday life, we will see additional examples of this change.

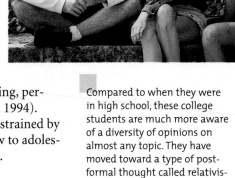

Compared to when they were in high school, these college students are much more aware of a diversity of opinions on almost any topic. They have moved toward a type of postformal thought called relativistic reasoning, which accepts the existence of multiple truths. *(B. Daemmrich/The Image Works)*

CONSEQUENCES OF ABSTRACT THOUGHT

The development of formal operations results in dramatic revisions in the way adolescents see themselves, others, and the world in general. Adjusting to thinking on a higher plane presents as many challenges as coming to terms with the physical changes of puberty. Just as adolescents are occasionally awkward in the use of their transformed bodies, they are initially faltering and clumsy in the use of abstract thought.

Parents and teachers must be careful not to mistake the many typical reactions of the teenage years—argumentativeness, self-concern, insensitive remarks, and indecisiveness—for anything other than inexperience with new reasoning powers. Although these behaviors often prompt concern in adults, they are usually beneficial in the long run. The Caregiving Concerns table on page 572 suggests ways to handle the everyday consequences of teenagers' newfound capacity for abstraction.

ARGUMENTATIVENESS

As adolescents acquire formal operations, they are motivated to use them. The once pliable school-age child becomes a feisty, argumentative teenager who can marshal facts and ideas to build a case (Elkind, 1994). "A simple, straightforward explanation used to be good enough to get Louis to obey," complained Antonio. "Now, he wants a thousand reasons. And worse yet, he finds a way to contradict them all!" Antonio was reflecting on the previous evening, when he had taken a strong stand in forbidding Louis to go to a movie with Cassie. Here is what happened:

Antonio: "Louis, no going out tonight. It's a school night, and you have homework."

Louis: "Dad, I've done most of my homework. I can do the rest before class in the morning. Besides, I fell asleep this afternoon. There's no way I'll be able to go to bed early."

Antonio: "You fell asleep because you didn't get enough rest the night before. You've been out several evenings in a row. You need to stay home."

relativistic reasoning
A type of postformal thought that views all knowledge as embedded in a framework of thought and that accepts the existence of multiple truths.

CAREGIVING CONCERNS

Ways to Handle the Consequences of Teenagers' New Capacity for Abstraction

CONSEQUENCE	SUGGESTION
Argumentativeness	During disagreements, remain calm, rational, and focused on principles. Express your point of view and the reasons behind it. Although adolescents may continue to challenge, explanations permit them to consider the validity of your beliefs at a later time.
Sensitivity to public criticism	Refrain from finding fault with the adolescent in front of others. If the matter is important, wait until you can speak to the teenager alone.
Exaggerated sense of personal uniqueness	Acknowledge the adolescent's unique characteristics. At opportune times, point out how you felt similarly as a young teenager, encouraging a more balanced perspective.
Idealism and criticism	Respond patiently to the adolescent's grand expectations and critical remarks. Point out positive features of targets, helping them see that all worlds and people are blends of virtues and imperfections.
Difficulty making everyday decisions	Refrain from deciding for the adolescent. Offer patient reminders and diplomatic suggestions until he or she can make choices more confidently.

Louis: "You never made Jules stay in on school nights when he was my age. How come you don't treat me equally?"

Antonio: "I did just the same thing with Jules. Homework is one of your responsibilities. It comes before going out on school nights."

Louis: "If it's my responsibility, then I'll take care of it. It's my personal business, so don't worry about it."

Antonio: "But you're not taking care of it unless you stay home and do it."

Louis: "Dad, you're unfair! You treat Jules like an adult. You treat me like a child!"

Parents often comment that teenagers "argue for the sake of arguing." As long as parent–child disagreements remain focused on principles and do not deteriorate into meaningless battles, they can promote development. Through discussions of family rules and practices, adolescents become more aware of their parents' values and the reasons behind them. Gradually, they come to see the validity of parental beliefs and adopt many as their own (Alessandri & Wozniak, 1987).

Teenagers' capacity for effective argument opens the door to intellectually stimulating pastimes, such as debate teams and endless bull sessions with friends over ethical and political concerns. By proposing, justifying, criticizing, and defending a variety of solutions, adolescents often move to a higher level of understanding than they attain in individual reasoning—on challenging scientific tasks as well as social and moral problems (Moshman, 1998).

SELF-CONSCIOUSNESS AND SELF-FOCUSING

Adolescents' ability to reflect on their own thoughts, combined with the physical and psychological changes they are undergoing, means that they start to think more about themselves. Piaget believed that the arrival of formal operations is accompanied by a new form of egocentrism: the inability to distinguish the abstract perspectives of self and others (Inhelder & Piaget, 1955/1958). For a time, teenagers become very wrapped up in the importance of their own thoughts, appearance, and behavior. As they imagine what others must be thinking, two distorted images of the relation between self and other appear.

The first is called the **imaginary audience.** Young teenagers regard themselves as always on stage. They are convinced that they are the focus of everyone else's attention

imaginary audience
Adolescents' belief that they are the focus of everyone else's attention and concern.

and concern (Elkind & Bowen, 1979). As a result, they become extremely self-conscious, often going to great lengths to avoid embarrassment. Sabrina, for example, woke up one Sunday morning with a large pimple on her chin. "I can't possibly go to church!" she cried. "*Everyone* will notice how ugly I look." The imaginary audience helps us understand the long hours adolescents spend in the bathroom inspecting every detail of their appearance as they envision the response of the rest of the world. It also accounts for their extreme sensitivity to public criticism. To teenagers, who believe that everyone is monitoring their performance, a critical remark from a parent or teacher can be mortifying.

These seventh- and eighth-grade drama students really are on stage. But the imaginary audience leads them to think that everyone is monitoring their performance at other times as well. Consequently, young teenagers are extremely self-conscious and go to great lengths to avoid embarrassment. *(Will Hart)*

A second cognitive distortion is the **personal fable.** Because teenagers are so sure that others are observing and thinking about them, they develop an inflated opinion of their own importance. They start to feel that they are special and unique. Many adolescents view themselves as reaching great heights of glory as well as sinking to unusual depths of despair—experiences that others could not possibly understand (Elkind, 1994). On one occasion, for example, Sabrina had a crush on a boy who failed to return her affections. As she lay on the sofa feeling depressed, Franca tried to assure her that there would be other boys. "Mom," Sabrina snapped. "You don't know what it's like to be in love!" The personal fable may also contribute to adolescent risk taking. Teenagers who have sex without contraceptives or weave in and out of traffic at 80 miles an hour seem, at least for the moment, to be convinced of their uniqueness and invulnerability (see Chapter 14, page 545).

The imaginary audience and personal fable are strongest during the transition from concrete to formal operations. They gradually decline as abstract thinking becomes better established (Enright, Lapsley, & Shukla, 1979; Lapsley et al., 1988). Yet these distorted visions of the self are probably not due to egocentrism, as Piaget suggested. Instead, they seem to be an outgrowth of advances in perspective taking, which cause young teenagers to be very concerned with what others think (Lapsley, 1985; Lapsley et al., 1986).

Take a moment to look back at Selman's stages of perspective taking on page 493 of Chapter 13. Recent evidence indicates that the *self-reflective* approach of late childhood and early adolescence contributes to the imaginary audience and personal fable (Vartanian & Powlishta, 1996). Adolescents also may have emotional reasons for clinging to the idea that others are preoccupied with their thoughts and feelings. Doing so helps them maintain a hold on important relationships as they struggle to separate from parents and establish an independent sense of self (Lapsley, 1993).

IDEALISM AND CRITICISM

Because abstract thinking permits adolescents to go beyond the real to the possible, it opens up the world of the ideal and of perfection. Teenagers can imagine alternative family, religious, political, and moral systems, and they want to explore them. Doing so is part of investigating new realms of experience, developing larger social commitments, and defining their own values and preferences.

The idealism of teenagers leads them to construct grand visions of a perfect world—with no injustice, discrimination, or tasteless behavior. They do not make room for the shortcomings of everyday life. Adults, with their longer life experience, have a more realistic outlook. The disparity between adults' and teenagers' world views is often called the "generation gap," and it creates tension between parent and child. Aware of the perfect family against which their real parents and siblings do not measure up, adolescents become fault-finding critics.

Yet overall, teenage idealism and criticism are advantageous. Once adolescents learn to see other people as having both strengths and weaknesses, they have a much greater capacity to work constructively for social change and to form positive and lasting relationships (Elkind, 1994). Parents can help teenagers forge a better balance between the ideal and the

personal fable
Adolescents' belief that they are special and unique. Leads them to conclude that others cannot possibly understand their thoughts and feelings. May promote a sense of invulnerability to danger.

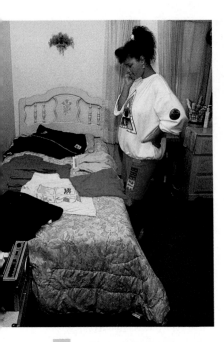

Young teenagers often have difficulty with planning and decision making in everyday life. Overwhelmed by possibilities, this 13-year-old can't decide what to wear. *(M. Siluk/ The Image Works)*

ASK YOURSELF . . .

■ *Louis suggested that Franca and Antonio vote for a certain candidate in the upcoming election, offering many good reasons. Franca and Antonio countered with reasons that Louis's favored candidate might not be best, but Louis insisted that his view was right and perfectly justified. What limitations of formal operational thought may have prevented Louis from seeing beyond his own perspective?*

■ *Cassie insisted that she had to have high heels to go with her prom dress. "No way I can wear those low heels, Mom. They'll make me look way too short next to Louis, and the whole evening will be ruined!" Why is Cassie so concerned about a detail of her appearance that most people would be unlikely to notice?*

real by being tolerant of their criticism while reminding the young person that all people, including adolescents themselves, are blends of virtues and imperfections.

PLANNING AND DECISION MAKING

Adolescents, who think more analytically, handle cognitive tasks more effectively than they did at younger ages. Given a homework assignment, they are far better at *self-regulation*—planning what to do first and what to do next, monitoring progress toward a goal, and redirecting actions that prove unsuccessful. For this reason, study skills improve from middle childhood into adolescence.

In addition, adolescents are better at a form of self-regulation called **comprehension monitoring.** While reading or listening, they continually evaluate how well they understand. Compared to younger pupils, 12- and 13-year-olds more often notice when a passage does not make sense. Rather than just moving ahead, they slow down and look back to see if they missed some important information (Garner, 1990). Their greater sensitivity to text errors means that they are more likely to revise their written work (Beal, 1990).

But when it comes to planning and decision making in everyday life, teenagers (especially young ones) often feel overwhelmed by the possibilities before them. As a result, their efforts to choose among alternatives frequently break down, and they may resort to habit, act on impulse, or not make a decision at all (Elkind, 1994). On many mornings, for example, Sabrina tried on five or six outfits before leaving for school. Often she shouted from the bedroom, "Mom, what shall I wear?" Then, when Franca made a suggestion, Sabrina rejected it, opting for one of the two or three sweaters she had worn for weeks. Similarly, Louis procrastinated about registering for college entrance tests. When Franca mentioned that he was about to miss the deadline, Louis sat over the forms, unable to decide when or where he wanted to take the test.

Everyday planning and decision making are challenging for teenagers because they have many more opportunities to create options for themselves. Consequently, they ask, "What behaviors could I perform?" before choosing a course of action. When they were younger, adults usually specified their options, reducing the number of decisions that had to be made. As adolescents gather more experience, they make choices with greater confidence and certainty.

BRIEF REVIEW

In Piaget's formal operational stage, adolescents become capable of abstraction, as indicated by hypothetico-deductive reasoning and propositional thought. Recent research shows that abstract reasoning is not well developed until after age 11. Adolescents and adults are most likely to think abstractly in areas in which they have had extensive experience. In many village and tribal cultures, adults do not master formal operational tasks. These findings challenge Piaget's view of formal operations as resulting from independent discovery.

Information-processing research reveals that abstract reasoning develops gradually, is strongly influenced by schooling, and is fostered by increasingly sophisticated metacognition. Investigators studying postformal thought have found that cognitive development continues beyond Piaget's formal operational stage. Over time, young people become better at relativistic reasoning.

The dramatic cognitive changes of adolescence are reflected in many aspects of teenagers' everyday behavior. The ability to think abstractly leads teenagers to become more argumentative, self-conscious and self-focused, and idealistic and critical. Because of gains in self-regulation, study skills improve. Yet in everyday life, adolescents are often overwhelmed by the options before them, and planning and decision making may break down.

SEX DIFFERENCES IN MENTAL ABILITIES

Sex differences in intellectual performance have been studied since the beginning of this century, and they have sparked almost as much controversy as the ethnic and SES differences in IQ considered in Chapter 12. Although boys and girls do not differ in general intelligence, they do vary in specific mental abilities. Girls, as we saw in Chapter 6, are ahead in early language development. Throughout the school years, girls attain higher scores in reading and writing and account for a lower percentage of children referred for remedial reading instruction (Campbell, Voelkl, & Donahue, 1997; Halpern, 1992). Girls' advantage on tests of general verbal ability is still present in adolescence. However, it is so slight that it is not really meaningful (Hyde & Linn, 1988).

Sex differences in mathematics do not exist in the early years, but by adolescence boys do better than girls (Hedges & Nowell, 1995; Linn & Hyde, 1989). The gender gap is largest among gifted youngsters. In some widely publicized research on bright seventh and eighth graders who were invited to take the Scholastic Aptitude Test (SAT) long before they needed to do so for college admission, boys outscored girls on the mathematics subtest year after year. Twice as many boys as girls had scores above 500; 13 times as many scored over 700 (Benbow & Stanley, 1983; Lubinski & Benbow, 1994). Sex differences are not present on all test items. Boys and girls do equally well on tests of basic math knowledge, and girls do better in computational skills. The difference appears on tests of mathematical reasoning, primarily in solving complex word problems (Hyde, Fenema, & Lamon, 1990).

Some researchers believe that the gender gap in mathematics—especially the tendency for many more boys to be extremely talented in math—is genetic. One common assumption is that sex differences in mathematical ability are rooted in boys' biologically based superior spatial reasoning. See the Biology and Environment box on pages 576–577 for a discussion of this issue.

Although heredity is involved, social pressures also contribute to girls' underrepresentation among the mathematically talented. The mathematics gender gap is related to pupil attitudes and self-esteem. Long before sex differences in math achievement are present, elementary school boys and girls view math as a "male domain" (see Chapter 13, page 501). In addition, girls regard math as less useful for their future lives, perceive themselves as having to work harder at it to do well, and more often blame their errors on lack of ability. These beliefs, in turn, lead girls to become less interested in math, to be less likely to consider math- or science-related careers, and to enroll in fewer math and science courses in high school and college (Byrnes & Takahira, 1993; Catsambis, 1994). The result of this chain of events is that girls—even those who are highly talented academically—are less likely to develop abstract mathematical concepts and effective problem-solving strategies.

A positive sign is that sex differences in cognitive abilities of all kinds have declined steadily over the past several decades. Today, boys are ahead of girls in mathematical reasoning by a much smaller margin than in the 1960s. Paralleling this change is an increase in girls' enrollment in advanced high school math and science courses, a critical factor in reducing sex differences in knowledge and skill (Campbell, Voelkl, & Donahue, 1997).

Still, extra steps must be taken to promote girls' interest in and confidence at math and science. By the end of high school, sex differences in attitudes are much larger than the

This girl is probably the only female enrolled in her high school metal shop class. Experience with manipulative activities, including model building and carpentry, contribute to sex differences in spatial abilities. Superior spatial skills and confidence at doing math, in turn, contribute to the ease with which young people solve complex math problems. *(Bob Daemmrich/ Stock Boston)*

comprehension monitoring
Sensitivity to how well one understands a spoken or written message.

BIOLOGY & ENVIRONMENT

SEX DIFFERENCES IN SPATIAL ABILITIES

Spatial skills have become a key focus of researchers' efforts to explain sex differences in mathematics performance. Clear sex differences in spatial reasoning exist, but they occur only on certain types of tasks (see Figure 15.2). The gender gap favoring males is large for *mental rotation tasks,* in which individuals must rotate a three-dimensional figure rapidly and accurately inside their heads. In addition, males do considerably better on *spatial perception tasks,* in which people must determine spatial relationships by considering the orientation of the surrounding environment. Sex differences on *spatial visualization tasks,* involving analysis of complex visual forms, are weak or nonexistent, perhaps because many strategies can be used to solve them. Both sexes may come up with effective procedures (Linn & Petersen, 1985; Voyer, Voyer, & Bryden, 1995).

Sex differences in spatial abilities emerge by middle childhood and per-

sist throughout the lifespan (Kerns & Berenbaum, 1991). The pattern is consistent enough to suggest a biological explanation. One hypothesis is that heredity, perhaps through prenatal exposure to androgen hormones, enhances right hemispheric functioning, granting males a spatial advantage. (Recall that for most people, spatial skills are housed in the right hemisphere of the cerebral cortex.) Consistent with this idea, girls and women whose prenatal androgen levels were abnormally high show superior performance on spatial rotation tasks (Collaer & Hines, 1995). And people with severe prenatal deficits in either male or female hormones have difficulty with spatial reasoning (Hier & Crowley, 1982; Temple & Carney, 1995).

However, research on hormone variations within normal range is less clear. Two studies report a link between prenatal androgens and spatial abilities during the preschool years, but only for girls and in the opposite direction expected: The

greater the hormone exposure, the lower the spatial score (Finegan, Niccols, & Sitarenios, 1992; Jacklin, Wilcox, & Maccoby, 1988). Prenatal hormones seem to affect spatial skills, but not in a straightforward fashion.

Although biology is involved in sex differences in spatial performance, experience also makes a difference. Children who engage in manipulative activities, such as block play, model building, and carpentry, do better on spatial tasks (Baenninger & Newcombe, 1995). Furthermore, playing video games that require rapid mental rotation of visual images enhances spatial scores of boys and girls alike (Okagaki & Frensch, 1996; Subrahmanyam & Greenfield, 1996). Yet boys spend far more time at all these pursuits than do girls.

Do superior spatial skills contribute to the greater ease with which males solve complex math problems? Research indicates that they do (Casey et al., 1995). Yet in a recent study of high-ability college-bound

gap in test performance. Clearly, many more girls have the capacity to study advanced math and science than choose to do so. When parents hold nonstereotyped gender-role values, daughters are less likely to show declines in math and science achievement at adolescence (Updegraff, McHale, & Crouter, 1996). In schools, teachers need to do a better job of demonstrating the relevance of math and science to everyday life. Girls, especially, respond positively to math and science instruction taught from an applied, hands-on perspective rather than a purely book-learning approach (Eccles, 1994) And all students benefit from encouragement and constructive feedback rather than criticism when engaged in problem solving.

Finally, a common assumption is that girls show better math and science achievement in single-sex secondary schools, where they may encounter fewer gender-biased messages and more same-sex role models. Although past research supported this belief, new evidence indicates that gender-segregated schools do not enhance boys' or girls' learning or self-esteem (Bryk, Lee, & Holland, 1993; LePore & Warren, 1997). Recently, both single-sex and coeducational schools have sharpened their focus on reducing gender discrimination. Consequently, the gender makeup of the student body seems to be far less relevant than it once was for girls' academic development.

adolescents, *both* mental rotation ability and self-confidence at doing math predicted higher scores on the math subtest of the SAT (Casey, Nuttall, & Pezaris, 1997). Boys are advantaged not only in mental rotation but in math self-confidence. Even when their grades are poorer than girls', boys judge themselves to be better at math (Eccles et al., 1993b). In sum, biology and environment *jointly* determine variations in spatial and math performance—within and between the sexes.

FIGURE 15.2

Types of spatial tasks. Large sex differences favoring males appear on spatial rotation, and males do considerably better than females on spatial perception. In contrast, sex differences on spatial visualization are weak or nonexistent. *(From M. C. Linn & A. C. Petersen, 1985, "Emergence and Characterization of Sex Differences in Spatial Ability: A Meta-Analysis,"* Child Development, *56, pp. 1482, 1483, 1485. © The Society for Research in Child Development, Inc. Reprinted by permission.)*

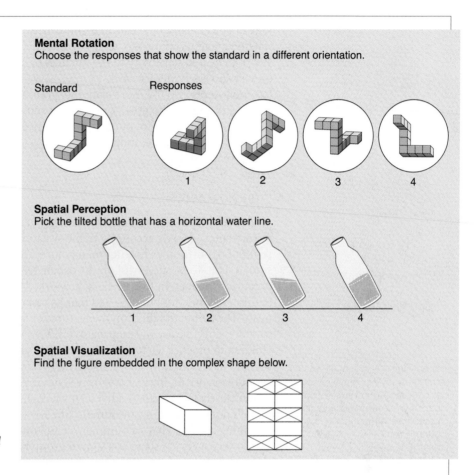

Mental Rotation
Choose the responses that show the standard in a different orientation.

Standard   Responses

1   2   3   4

Spatial Perception
Pick the tilted bottle that has a horizontal water line.

1   2   3   4

Spatial Visualization
Find the figure embedded in the complex shape below.

LANGUAGE DEVELOPMENT

Although language development is largely complete by the end of childhood, subtle but important changes take place during adolescence. These gains are largely influenced by adolescents' improved capacity for reflective thought and abstraction, which enhance their *metalinguistic awareness,* or ability to think about language as a system.

VOCABULARY AND GRAMMAR

Adolescents add a wide variety of abstract words to their vocabularies and can define them easily and accurately. In the conversation at the beginning of this chapter, note Jules's use of "counterintuitive," "incredible," "revolutionized," "philosophy," "reproduction," and "justice." As a 9- or 10-year-old, he rarely used such words, and he had difficulty grasping their meaning.

Formal operations permits adolescents to become masters of irony and sarcasm (Winner, 1988). "Don't have a major brain explosion," Louis commented to Sabrina when she complained about having to work on an essay for school. And when Franca fixed a dish for dinner that Louis disliked, he quipped, "Oh boy, my favorite!" Young children sometimes realize that a sarcastic remark is insincere if it is said in a very exaggerated, mocking tone of voice. But adolescents and adults need only notice the discrepancy between the statement and its context to grasp the intended meaning (Capelli, Nakagawa, & Madden, 1990). Increased sensitivity to the nuances of language enables teenagers to read and understand adult literary works.

Adolescents also use more elaborate grammatical constructions. Their sentences are longer and consist of a greater number of subordinate clauses than do those of children. In addition, teenagers are much more effective at analyzing and reflecting on grammar. Not surprisingly, diagramming sentences is a skill reserved for the junior high and high school years.

PRAGMATICS

Perhaps the most obvious change in language at adolescence is an improved capacity to vary language style according to the situation (Obler, 1997). This change is partly the result of opportunities to enter many more situations in which there is pressure to adjust speech style. To be successful on the debate team, Louis had to speak in a rapid-fire, well-organized manner. In theater class, he worked on reciting memorized lines as if they were natural. At work, his boss insisted that he respond to customers cheerfully and courteously. The ability to reflect on the features of language and engage in self-regulation also supports effective use of language styles. Teenagers are far more likely than school-age children to practice what they want to say in an expected situation, review what they did say, and figure out how they could say it better (Romaine, 1984).

Adolescents' mastery of language styles is particularly apparent in their use of slang. Listen closely to a group of adolescents talk, and you will hear expressions like this: "That's dope!" (meaning awesome). "She's a real airhead." "That music's really bad" (meaning good). "That's a bummer." "Chill out!" (meaning relax) (Eble, 1996; Lighter, 1997). Teenagers use slang as a sign of group belonging and as a way of distinguishing themselves from adults. Doing so is part of separating from parents and seeking a temporary self-definition in the peer group. We will discuss these developments in Chapter 16.

SECOND-LANGUAGE LEARNING

Many people assume that the best time to become bilingual is in childhood—that picking up a second language is harder during adolescence and adulthood. Research supports this widely held idea. In a study of Chinese and Korean adults who had immigrated to the United States at varying ages, those who began mastering English between ages 3 and 7 scored as well as native speakers on a test of grammatical knowledge. Figure 15.3 shows that as age of arrival in the United States increased through adolescence, test scores gradually declined (Johnson & Newport, 1989). The ability to pronounce a second language without an accent also declines with age—gradually during childhood and sharply at adolescence (Anderson & Graham, 1994; Flege & Fletcher, 1992).

Research on children deprived of early language stimulation shows that there is a *sensitive period* for first-language development. That is, mastery of a native tongue must begin sometime in childhood for full development to occur (Mayberry, 1993). This

These high school seniors started studying French in adolescence, after the sensitive period for acquiring language has passed. Although they can become competent speakers, they are unlikely reach the level of skill they would have attained had they begun second-language learning in childhood. *(Le Duc/Monkmeyer Press)*

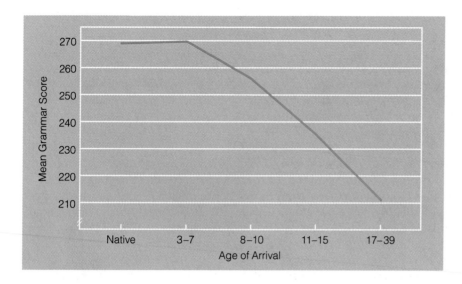

FIGURE **15.3**

Relationship between age of arrival of Chinese and Korean immigrants in the United States and performance on a test of English grammar. Individuals who began learning English in child-hood attained the competence of native speakers. With increasing age through adolescence, scores declined. *(From J. S. Johnson & E. L. Newport, 1989, "Critical Period Effects in Second Language Learning: The Influence of Maturational State on the Acquisition of English as a Second Language,"* Cognitive Psychology, *21, p. 79. Copyright © 1989 by Academic Press. Reprinted by permission.)*

same principle applies to second-language learning. Although adolescents can become competent speakers, biological readiness for acquiring a second language is greatest in childhood. Consequently bilingual development is best begun at an early age. In contrast to European nations, where children learn foreign languages in elementary school, American schools usually wait too long—until junior high or high school, after the sensitive period has passed.

BRIEF REVIEW

Although girls score better than boys on tests of general verbal ability, the difference is so slight that it is not meaningful. By adolescence, boys are ahead of girls in mathematical performance, a difference related to attitudes toward math, self-perceptions of ability, enrollment in advanced mathematics courses, and use of effective problem-solving strategies. Sex differences in mathematical reasoning have declined over the past several decades, while girls' enrollment in advanced high school math and science courses has increased.

During adolescence, language continues to develop in subtle but important ways. Teenagers add many abstract words to their vocabularies. The ability to move beyond the literal meaning of words improves, and the grammatical structure of speech becomes more complex. Adolescents are better than children at modifying their language style to fit different situations. They also make faster initial progress in learning a second language, although their ultimate attainment is not as high.

LEARNING IN SCHOOL

In complex societies, adolescence coincides with entry into secondary school. Most young people move into either a middle or junior high school and then into a high school. With each change, academic achievement becomes more serious business, affecting college choices and job opportunities. In the following sections, we take up a variety of aspects of secondary school life. We also consider the serious problem of high school dropout, and how well prepared American high school graduates are for life in a technologically advanced, rapidly changing world.

ASK YOURSELF . . .

■ *Research shows that girls perform more poorly on certain formal operational tasks such as the pendulum problem (Meehan, 1984). On the basis of what you know about the development of formal operational thought and sex differences in mental abilities, how would you account for this finding?*

■ *At home, Louis often created humorous parodies of the way his teachers spoke at school. Sabrina tried to do the same, but her imitations were less accurate and effective. What accounts for the skill of older adolescents in mimicking the speech mannerisms of the people they know?*

SCHOOL TRANSITIONS

When Sabrina started junior high, she left a small, intimate, self-contained sixth-grade classroom for a much larger, impersonal school. "I don't know most of the kids in my classes," Sabrina complained to her mother at the end of the first week. Besides, there's too much homework. I get assignments in all my classes at once. I can't do all this!" she shouted, bursting into tears.

■ **IMPACT OF SCHOOL TRANSITIONS.** As Sabrina's reactions suggest, school transitions can drastically alter academic and social experiences, creating new adjustment problems. With each school change—from elementary to middle or junior high and then to high school—adolescents' course grades decline. The drop is partly due to tighter academic standards. At the same time, the transition to junior high school often brings with it less personal attention, more whole-class instruction, and fewer opportunities to participate in classroom decision making (Eccles, Lord, & Buchanan, 1996).

In view of these changes, it is not surprising that students rate their junior-high learning experiences less favorably than their elementary school experiences (Wigfield & Eccles, 1994). They also report that their junior high teachers care less about them, are less friendly, grade less fairly, and stress competition more and mastery and improvement less. Consequently, many young people feel less academically competent and show a drop in motivation (Anderman & Midgley, 1997; Eccles et al., 1993c).

Inevitably, the transition to junior high and then to high school requires students to readjust their feelings of self-confidence and self-worth as academic expectations are revised and students enter a more complex social world. A comprehensive study revealed that the timing of school transition is important, especially for girls (Simmons & Blyth, 1987). Over 300 adolescents living in a large Midwestern city were followed from sixth to tenth grade. Some were enrolled in school districts with a 6–3–3 grade organization (a K–6 elementary school, a 3-year junior high, and a 3-year high school). These students made two school changes, one to junior high and one to high school. A comparison group attended schools with an 8–4 grade organization. They made only one school transition, from a K–8 elementary school to high school.

For the sample as a whole, grade-point average dropped and feelings of anonymity increased after each transition. Participation in extracurricular activities declined more in the 6–3–3 than in the 8–4 arrangement, although the drop was greater for girls. Sex differences in self-esteem were even more striking. As Figure 15.4 shows, boys' self-esteem increased throughout junior high and high school, except in 6–3–3 schools, where it leveled off after entering high school. Girls in the 6–3–3 arrangement fared especially poorly. Their self-esteem declined with each school change. In contrast, their 8–4 counterparts gained steadily in feelings of self-worth throughout the secondary school years.

These findings show that any school transition is likely to temporarily depress adolescents' psychological well-being, but the earlier it occurs, the more dramatic and long lasting its impact. Girls in 6–3–3 schools fared poorest, the researchers argued, because movement to junior high tended to coincide with other life changes—namely, the onset of puberty and dating. Adolescents who must cope with added transitions, such as family disruption, parental unemployment, or a shift in residence around the time they change schools, are at greatest risk for academic and emotional difficulties (Flanagan & Eccles, 1993).

Poorly achieving and poverty-stricken young people show an especially sharp drop in school performance after the transition to junior high school. These students are likely to turn to peers, whose values they describe as becoming increasingly antisocial, for the support they lack in other spheres of school life (Seidman et al., 1994). For some, school transition initiates a downward spiral in academic performance and school involvement that eventually leads to failure and dropping out (Simmons, Black, & Zhou, 1991).

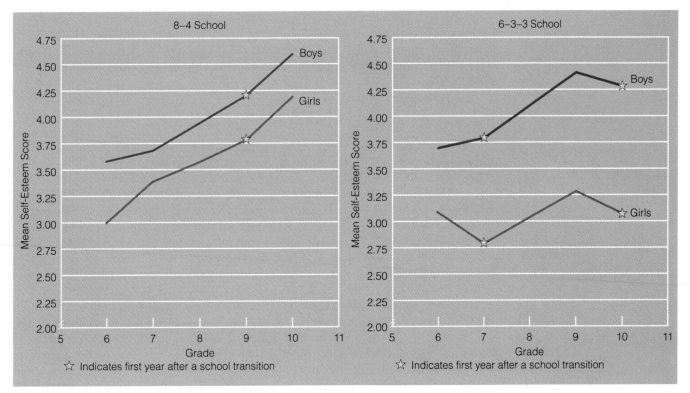

FIGURE **15.4**

Self-esteem from sixth to tenth grade by school type for boys and girls. In this longitudinal study of more than 300 adolescents, self-esteem increased steadily for both sexes in the 8–4 school arrangement. Girls in 6–3–3 schools fared especially poorly. Their self-esteem dropped sharply after each school change. *(Adapted from Simmons & Blyth, 1987.)*

■ **HELPING ADOLESCENTS ADJUST TO SCHOOL TRANSITIONS.** Consider the findings we have just reviewed, and you will see that school transitions often lead to environmental changes that fit poorly with adolescents' developmental needs. They disrupt close relationships with teachers at a time when adolescents need adult support. They emphasize competition during a period of heightened self-focusing. They reduce decision making and choice as the desire for autonomy is increasing. And they interfere with peer networks at a time of increased concern with peer acceptance.

Fortunately, there are ways to ease the strain of going from elementary to secondary school. Since most students do better in an 8–4 school arrangement, school districts thinking about reorganization might give serious thought to this plan.[1] When early school transitions cannot be avoided, smaller social units can be formed within large schools to relieve students' feelings of anonymity. Some schools use a "team" or "house" approach that reduces the size of the young person's reference group, permitting closer relations with teachers and peers and greater extracurricular involvement (Berk, 1992b; Seidman & French, 1997).

Other, less extensive changes are also helpful. During the first year after a school transition, homerooms can be provided in which teachers offer academic and personal counseling and work closely with parents to promote favorable school adjustment. Students can also be assigned to classes with several familiar peers or a constant group of new peers—arrangements that promote emotional security and social support. In one study, high school freshmen experiencing these interventions showed much better academic performance and psychological adjustment at the end of the school year than did controls. A follow-up after 4 years revealed that only half as many students in the intervention group had dropped out of school (Felner & Adan, 1988).

[1]Recall from Chapter 14 (page 539) that girls who reach puberty early fare better in K–6 schools, where they are relieved of pressures from older adolescents to become involved in dating, sexual activity, and drug experimentation before they are ready. Although the 8–4 organization is best for the majority of adolescents, early maturing girls require special support under these conditions.

Finally, successful transitions are most likely to occur in schools that foster adolescents' growing capacity for autonomy and responsibility. Rigid school rules that strike young people as unfair and punitive frustrate their developmental needs, contributing to long-term dissatisfaction with school life (Eccles et al., 1993a; Fenzel, Blyth, & Simmons, 1990).

ACADEMIC ACHIEVEMENT

Adolescent achievement is the result of a long history of cumulative effects. Early on, positive educational environments, both family and school, lead to personal traits that support achievement—intelligence, confidence in one's own abilities, the desire to succeed, and high educational aspirations (Masten & Coatsworth, 1998). In contrast, living in an environment that provides little encouragement or opportunity for success results in a decline in ability and the belief that trying hard is futile. Yet improving an unfavorable environment can help a poorly performing young person bounce back and open the door to a more satisfying adult life. The Caregiving Concerns table below summarizes environmental factors that enhance achievement during the teenage years.

■ **CHILD-REARING PRACTICES.** Authoritative parenting (which combines warmth with firm, reasonable demands for maturity) is linked to achievement in adolescence, just as it predicts mastery-oriented behavior during the childhood years. Research involving thousands of adolescents reveals that the authoritative style is related to higher grades for both boys and girls varying widely in SES. In contrast, authoritarian and permissive styles are often associated with lower grades (Dornbusch et al., 1987; Steinberg et al., 1995). Of all parenting approaches, a neglectful style (low in both warmth and maturity demands) predicts the poorest grades along with worsening school performance over time (Baumrind, 1991; Glasgow et al., 1997; Lamborn et al., 1991; Steinberg et al., 1994).

The child rearing–school performance relationships just described vary somewhat with ethnicity. Recall from Chapter 10 that some Asian and African-American parents are more demanding of their children than are Caucasian-American parents (see pages 398–399). For Asian parents, high control represents deep parental concern and commitment, stemming from Confucian values. For African-American parents, dangerous inner-city neighborhoods may require greater strictness to foster children's competence. Consistent with these trends, parenting especially high in control is linked to better grades among Asian and African-American teenagers (Florsheim, Tolan, & Gorman-Smith, 1996; Glasgow et al., 1997; Steinberg et al., 1994).

CAREGIVING CONCERNS
Factors that Support High Achievement During Adolescence

FACTOR	DESCRIPTION
Child-rearing practices	Authoritative parenting (warmth with moderate to high demandingness, in accord with the young person's ethnic background)
	Joint parent–adolescent decision making
	Parent involvement in the adolescent's education
Peer influences	Peer valuing of and support for high achievement
School characteristics	Teachers who are warm and supportive, develop personal relationships with parents, and show them how to support their child's learning
	Learning activities that encourage high-level thinking
	Active student participation in learning activities and classroom decision making
Employment schedule (see pages 594–595)	Job commitment limited to less than 15 to 20 hours per week
	High-quality vocational education for non-college-bound adolescents

Why does combining warmth with moderate to high demandingness promote intellectual persistence during adolescence? In Chapter 10, we noted that authoritative parents adjust their expectations to children's capacity to take responsibility for their own behavior. Parents who engage in joint decision making with adolescents, gradually permitting more autonomy with age, have youngsters who achieve especially well (Dornbusch et al., 1990). Open discussion accompanied by warmth and firmness makes adolescents feel competent and valued, encourages constructive thinking and self-regulation, and increases awareness of the importance of doing well in school. These factors, in turn, are related to independent effort and achievement among high school students (Baumrind, 1991; Carlson, Hsu, & Cooper, 1990; Wentzel & Feldman, 1993).

■ **PARENT–SCHOOL INVOLVEMENT.** High-achieving young people typically have parents who keep tabs on their child's progress, communicate with teachers, and make sure their child is enrolled in challenging, well-taught classes. Although many parents reduce their school involvement as their children get older, it is just as important during junior and senior high school as it was earlier. Parents who are in frequent contact with the school send a message to their child about the value of education, promote wise educational decisions, and model constructive solutions to academic problems. Involved parents can also prevent school personnel from placing a bright student not working up to potential in unstimulating learning situations (Grolnick & Slowiaczek, 1994).

Secondary schools need to do a better job of increasing parent involvement during adolescence. They can do so by fostering personal relationships between parents and teachers, by showing parents how to support their adolescent's education at home, and by developing assignments that give parents a meaningful role to play (such as finding out about cultural heritage, parents' experiences while growing up, or community history). Schools can also include parents in basic planning and governance to ensure that they are invested in school goals (Eccles & Harold, 1993).

Community characteristics affect the ease with which schools attain these goals. Parents living in high-risk neighborhoods are often more preoccupied with protecting their youngsters from danger than developing their talents. And since these parents face many daily stresses that reduce the time and energy they have for school involvement, they are harder for schools to reach. Yet schools could relieve some of this stress by forging stronger home–school links. There are parents highly involved in their adolescent's education living in every type of neighborhood (Eccles & Harold, 1996).

■ **PEER INFLUENCES.** Peers also play an important role in achievement during adolescence, in a way that is related to both family and school. Adolescents whose parents

This parent is involved with her adolescent's school career. Besides keeping tabs on his progress, she is probably in frequent contact with the school. She sends a message to her son about the importance of education and teaches him how to solve academic problems and make wise educational decisions. *(Erika Stone)*

value achievement are likely to choose friends who share those values (Berndt & Keefe, 1995; Kinderman, 1993). For example, when Sabrina began to make new friends in junior high, she often studied with her girlfriends and called them to check answers to homework assignments. Each girl wanted to do well in school and reinforced the same desire in the others.

Peer support for high achievement also depends on the overall climate of the peer culture. Many low-income ethnic minority students react against working hard, convinced that getting good grades will have little payoff in the future and regarding it as a threat to their ethnic identity (Ogbu, 1997). In one case study of an inner-city high school, African-American students who did achieve were labeled as "brainiacs" and had to cope with the "burden of acting white." Many capable adolescents felt caught between achievement and peer approval and resolved the dilemma by "putting the brakes" on academic effort (Fordham & Ogbu, 1986).

Yet not all economically disadvantaged minority students react this way. A case study of six inner-city, poverty-stricken African-American adolescents who were high-achieving and optimistic about their future revealed that they were intensely aware of oppression but believed in striving to alter their social position. How did they develop this sense of agency? Parents, relatives, and teachers had convinced them through discussion and example that injustice should not be tolerated and that together, blacks could overcome it. David, whose family was on welfare and lived in rundown housing, illustrates the experiences of these achievement-oriented students:

> My 20 year brother, he talks about it a lot. The way that Blacks have been treated as time went on. And he stress a lot that it [racism] still goes on—is alive and well. And he talks about it. He says you always have to give back and maintain. Never forget where you came from. *Make our selves one—make Whites stand up and take notice*—'cause that's the only way we [Blacks] going to get out of the situation we always been in. They [Whites] don't plan on just giving us nothing. (O'Connor, 1997, p. 618)

Dispositions toward collective struggle seemed to facilitate academic motivation in the face of peer pressures against doing well in school.

■ **SCHOOL CHARACTERISTICS.** Adolescents need school environments that are responsive to their expanding powers of reasoning and emotional and social needs. Without appropriate learning experiences, the potential for abstract thought is unlikely to be realized.

Classroom Learning Experiences. As we discussed earlier, the transition to junior high school often brings impersonal schools and classrooms that offer few opportunities for active participation. In a study focusing on math classes, researchers found that students moving from an elementary school classroom perceived high in support (in terms of teacher friendliness, fairness, and student involvement) to a junior high classroom low in support showed a sharp decline in their liking for and personal sense of competence in the subject. When the direction of change was reversed—that is, when students moved from classrooms low in support to ones high in support—their evaluations of themselves and attitudes toward the subject improved (Midgley, Feldlaufer, & Eccles, 1989).

The perception of many adolescents that their classes lack warmth and supportiveness is the result of a large, departmentalized school organization that makes it difficult for teachers and students to get to know each other well. Adolescents, like children, need opportunities to form close relationships with teachers. As they begin to develop an identity beyond the family, they seek adult models other than their parents (Eccles & Harold, 1996).

Of course, an important reason for separate classes in each subject is that adolescents can be taught by experts, who are more likely to expect students to perform well and encourage high-level thinking—factors that promote school attendance and achievement

(Phillips, 1997). But the classroom experiences of many junior and senior high school students do not work out this way. In a study of seventh- through tenth-grade English, social studies, and science teachers with reputations for excellence, students were not equally or consistently given assignments that stimulated abstract thought (Sanford, 1985).

Because of the uneven quality of instruction in American schools, a great many seniors graduate from high school poorly equipped with basic academic skills. Although the achievement gap separating African-American and Hispanic students from white students has declined since the 1970s, mastery of reading, writing, mathematics, and science by low-SES ethnic minority students remains disappointing (Campbell, Voelkl, & Donahue, 1997; Ogbu, 1997). Many attend underfunded schools with run-down buildings, outdated equipment, and textbook shortages. In some, crime and discipline have become so overwhelming that attention to these problems has taken the lead over learning and instruction. By junior high, large numbers of poverty-stricken minority students have been placed in low academic tracks, compounding their learning difficulties.

Tracking. Ability grouping, as we saw in Chapter 12, is detrimental during the elementary school years. Students in low groups generally get poor-quality instruction. Soon they view themselves as failures, and their peers label them this way as well. Students in the same ability groups typically stick together, forming separate subcultures. High-group students often feel superior, and low-group students respond with hostility and resentment. These influences severely undermine the motivation and academic progress of low-group students. At least into the early years of secondary school, mixed-ability classes are desirable. Research suggests that they do not stifle the more able students, and they have intellectual and social benefits for poorly performing youngsters (see Chapter 12, page 470).

By high school, some grouping is unavoidable because certain aspects of education must dovetail with the young person's future educational and career plans. In the United States, high school students are counseled into college preparatory, vocational, or general education tracks. Unfortunately, this sorting tends to perpetuate educational inequalities of earlier years.

Low-income minority students are assigned in large numbers to noncollege tracks. One study found that a good student from an economically disadvantaged family had only half as much chance of ending up in an academically oriented program as a student of equal ability from a middle-SES background (Vanfossen, Jones, & Spade, 1987). When high-ability students (as indicated by eighth grade math score) end up in low tracks, they "sink" to the achievement level of their trackmates. Furthermore, teachers of noncollege-track classes tend to view the parental role in education as passive. They are less likely to communicate with parents about what they can do to support their child's learning. Indeed, these parents often are unaware of their child's track placement (Dornbusch & Glasgow, 1997).

High school students are separated into academic and vocational tracks in virtually all industrialized nations. But the American system differs from those of Western Europe, Japan, and China in important respects. In most of those countries, students take a national examination to determine their placement in high school. The outcome usually fixes future possibilities for the young person. In the United States, educational decisions are more fluid. Students who are not assigned to a college preparatory track or who do poorly in high school can still get a college education. But by the adolescent years, SES differences in quality of education and academic achievement have already sorted American students more drastically than is the case in other countries. In the end, many young people do not benefit from this more open system.

Compared with other developed nations, the United States has a higher percentage of high school dropouts and adolescents with very limited academic skills. To create equality of educational opportunity, many aspects of school organization and teaching practices need to be addressed. And as the Social Issues box on page 586 indicates, school desegregation is yet another vital means for countering minority students' reduced educational and life chances.

SOCIAL ISSUES

SCHOOL DESEGREGATION AND LIFE CHANCES OF AFRICAN-AMERICAN ADOLESCENTS

In 1954, a historic U.S. Supreme Court decision proclaimed the injustice of separate schools for racially and ethnically different students. The law gradually led to desegregation of many American schools, but not without community polarization in many areas of the country. Prejudice, fierce defense of the neighborhood school, and strong objections to busing led many parents to oppose the practice. Where desegregation did take place, teachers had to take steps to promote cross-race contact and interracial acceptance. Only then did gains in black students' self-esteem and achievement appear (Johnson, Johnson, & Maruyama, 1984). School desegregation efforts began to decline in the 1970s because many studies reported little or no impact on intergroup relations and test scores.

Yet research reveals that although short-term benefits of desegregation are mixed, long-term effects are striking. Attending desegregated schools is related to higher occupational aspirations among African-American students (Dawkins, 1983; Gable, Thompson, & Iwanicki, 1983). Desegregation also increases the likelihood that black young people will make educational and employment decisions appropriate to their goals. Black graduates of ethnically diverse high schools are more likely to enroll in desegregated colleges and to enter careers in which African Americans have been underrepresented (Braddock & McPartland, 1982, 1987). And once in the work world, they can more often be found in professional jobs and in ethnically mixed settings, where they report feeling more comfortable than do their counterparts with a segregated education (Trent, 1991).

How does school desegregation achieve these effects? According to several theorists, attending a mixed high school grants all groups equal access to information about educational and occupational opportunities and methods of taking advantage of them. College fairs, teacher and peer reminders about college options and application deadlines, assistance with the college application process, and counselors with strong ties to college admissions offices are far more abundant in racially mixed schools (Wells, Crain, & Uchetelle, 1995). Furthermore, black graduates of interracial high schools are more likely to use desegregated networks to find jobs, including informal referrals and unsolicited approaches to white employers. These are popular techniques for securing entry-level positions that lead to higher occupational status and income in later life (Braddock & McPartland, 1987).

In sum, desegregated schools grant black students access to better educational and occupational opportunities, which help break the cycle of perpetual segregation by contributing to success in the labor market. An even more extended outcome could be improved academic achievement for future generations of African-American students (Wells & Crain, 1994).

Desegregated schools grant African-American students access to better educational and occupational opportunities. Through such supports as college fairs and reminders about college possibilities and application deadlines, ethnically diverse high schools help break the cycle of perpetual segregation by contributing to success in the labor market. *(R. Sidney/The Image Works)*

DROPPING OUT

Across the aisle from Louis in math class sat Norman, who daydreamed, crumpled his notes into his pocket, and rarely did his homework. On test days, he twirled a rabbit's foot for good luck but left most of the questions blank. Louis had been in school with Norman since fourth grade, but the two boys had little to do with one another. To Louis, who was quick at schoolwork, Norman seemed to live in another world.

Once or twice each week, Norman cut class, and one spring day, he stopped coming altogether. Several months later, Louis ran into Norman at the supermarket, where he had a part-time job stocking shelves.

"Norm, where ya' been? Haven't seen you at school lately," remarked Louis.

"Come on, Louis, you oughta know. There wasn't nothin' for me there. Got to the point where I just couldn't go back. I'd go to those classes, and the minute I got there I'd wanna get out. My mind just turned off, I felt so ashamed and stupid."

Norman is one of 13 percent of American young people who, by 18 years of age, leave high school without a diploma (U.S. Department of Education, 1997). The dropout rate is particularly high among low-income ethnic minority youths, especially Hispanic teenagers (see Figure 15.5). The decision to leave school has dire consequences. As Figure 15.6 reveals, dropouts are far less likely to be employed than are high school graduates who do not go to college. And even when they are employed, they have

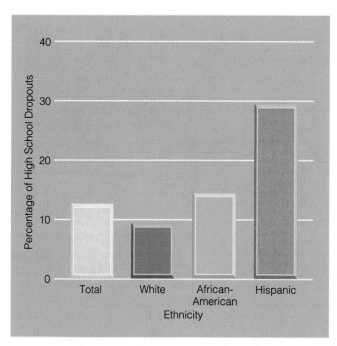

FIGURE 15.5

Percentage of high school dropouts in the United States by ethnicity. Because African-American and Hispanic teenagers are more likely to come from low-income and poverty-stricken families, their dropout rates are above the national average. The rate for Hispanic young people is especially high. *(From U.S. Department of Education, 1997)*

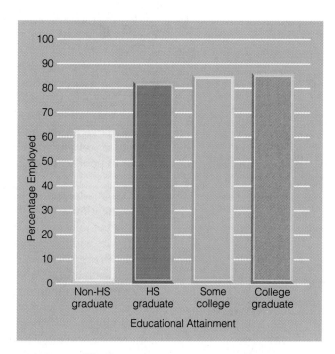

FIGURE 15.6

Employment rates of 20- to 24-year-olds by educational attainment in the United States. Those who do not graduate from high school are much less likely to get jobs than are their counterparts with high school diplomas. Employment rates increase with years of schooling completed. *(From U.S. Department of Education, 1997)*

TABLE 15.2

Factors Related to Dropping Out of High School

STUDENT CHARACTERISTICS	FAMILY CHARACTERISTICS	SCHOOL CHARACTERISTICS
Poor school attendance	Parents who do not support or emphasize achievement	Unstimulating classes
Inattentiveness in class		Lack of opportunity to form personal relationships with teachers
School discipline problems, especially aggressive behavior	Parents who were high school dropouts	Curriculum irrelevant to student interests and needs
Inability to get along with teachers	Parents who are uninvolved in the adolescent's education	
1 to 2 years behind in grade level	Parents who react with anger and punishment to the adolescent's low grades	School authority structure that emphasizes the teacher; student input is discouraged
Low academic achievement		
A sharp drop in achievement after school transition		Large student body
Dislike of school	Single-parent household	
Enrollment in a general education or vocational track	Low income	
Low educational aspirations		
Low self-esteem, especially academic self-esteem		
Friendships with peers who have left school		
Low involvement in extracurricular activities		
Drug use		
Law-breaking behavior		
Teenage childbearing		

Sources: Garnier, Stein, & Jacobs, 1997; Roderick, 1994; Rumberger, 1990; West, 1991.

a much greater chance of remaining in menial, low-paying jobs and of being out of work from time to time.

■ **FACTORS RELATED TO DROPPING OUT.** Table 15.2 lists the many factors related to leaving school early. The more that are present at once, the greater the risk that an adolescent will drop out. Norman showed many of these signs. Because of a long history of poor school performance, his perception of his own ability was extremely low. He gave up on tasks that presented the least bit of challenge and counted on luck—his rabbit's foot—to get him by. As Norman got older, he attended class less regularly, failed to pay attention when he was there, rarely did his homework, and was a discipline problem. He didn't join any school clubs or participate in athletics. Because he was uninvolved in activities within and outside the classroom, few teachers or students got to know him well. The day Norman left, he felt alienated from all aspects of school life.

As with other dropouts, Norman's family background contributed to his problems. Compared to other students, even those with the same grade profile, dropouts are more likely to have parents who are less involved in their youngster's education. Many did not finish high school themselves and are unemployed, on welfare, or coping with the aftermath of divorce. When their youngsters bring home poor report cards, these parents are more likely to respond with punishment and anger—reactions that cause adolescents to rebel further against academic work (Melby & Conger, 1996). Sometimes suspension or expulsion for serious misbehavior prompts the teenager to leave altogether. And more often in ethnic minority families, a daughter has to care for adult relatives or children (her own or those of family members) and cannot handle school at the same time (Jordan, Lara, & McPartland, 1996).

Academically marginal students who drop out often have school experiences that undermine their chances for success. Recent reports indicate that over 60 percent of adolescents enrolled in some inner-city high schools do not graduate. These institutions are unresponsive, crime ridden, and rejecting. Students in general education and vocational tracks, where teaching tends to be the least stimulating, are three times more likely to drop out as those in a college preparatory track (Office of Educational Research and Improvement, 1997). Some young people leave with a powerful critique of their school experiences, claiming that what happens in the classroom is unrelated to their cultural background and everyday lives. As one African-American student who dropped out of school reflected,

"I'm not smart, but I'm wise. I understand people and situations. Don't take much for me to know what's going on. I know what people be thinkin'. But I don't know what they be talkin' about in history class" (Fine, 1986, p. 402).

■ **PREVENTION STRATEGIES.** Many programs have been developed to help teenagers who are at risk for leaving school early. The strategies used are diverse, but several common themes are related to success:

■ *High-quality vocational training.* At-risk young people often benefit from special school programs that emphasize high-quality vocational training. For many marginal students, the real-life nature of vocational education is more comfortable and effective than purely academic work. But to work well, it must carefully integrate academic and job-related instruction so students can see the relevance of what happens in the classroom to their future goals (Ianni & Orr, 1996).

■ *Remedial instruction and counseling that offer personalized attention.* Most potential dropouts need intensive remedial instruction in small classes that permit warm, caring teacher–student relationships to form. To overcome the negative psychological effects of repeated school failure, good academic assistance must be combined with social support and special counseling (Rumberger, 1990).

■ *Efforts to address the many factors in students' lives related to leaving school early.* Programs that strengthen parent involvement, offer flexible work–study arrangements, and provide on-site child care for teenage mothers can make staying in school easier for at-risk adolescents (Jordan, Lara, & McPartland, 1996).

■ *Participation in extracurricular activities.* Another way of helping marginal students is to draw them into the community life of the school (Mahoney & Cairns, 1997). The most powerful influence on extracurricular involvement is small school size. In smaller high schools (500 to 700 students or fewer), a greater proportion of the student body is needed to staff and operate activities. As a result, potential dropouts are far more likely to participate, gain recognition for their abilities, feel a sense of competence and efficacy, and remain until graduation. Note that "house" plans, which create smaller units within large schools, can have the same effect (Berk, 1992b).

As we conclude our discussion of academic achievement, let's place the school dropout problem in historical perspective. Over the last half century, the percentage of American adolescents completing high school has risen dramatically—from 39 percent in 1940 to 87 percent in the 1990s (U.S. Department of Education, 1997). During that same period, college attendance also increased. Today, nearly 40 percent of 18- to 24-year-old high school graduates are working toward college degrees—the highest rate in the world. Finally, about one-third of all high school dropouts return on their own to finish their education within a few years, and some extend their schooling further (Children's Defense Fund, 1998). Although leaving school early is still a very serious problem, as the end of adolescence approaches, many young people realize how essential education is for a rewarding job and career.

ASK YOURSELF . . .

■ *Tanisha is finishing sixth grade. She could either continue in her current school through eighth grade or switch to a much larger junior high school in town. What would you suggest she do, and why?*

■ *In a workshop for parents of adolescents, one father asks what he might do to encourage his teenage children to do well in school. Provide a list of suggestions, along with the reasons they are effective.*

BRIEF REVIEW

School transitions create new adjustment problems for adolescents, especially when they coincide with other life stresses. With the transition to junior high and then to high school, learning environments become more impersonal and competitive and permit less student decision making. As a result, sense of academic competence, motivation, and grades tend to decline, especially for poorly achieving and poverty-stricken young people.

Academic achievement is the result of a complex blend of personal and environmental forces. Authoritative child rearing, joint parent–child decision making, and parent involvement in the young person's secondary school career support achievement during adolescence. Peers who value achievement and classroom environments that encourage warm teacher–student relations and high-level thinking also promote academic success. Quality of instruction is often poorest in general education and vocational tracks, which enroll a large number of low-SES, ethnic minority students. Disengagement from school and dropping out are particularly high among these adolescents. For many teenagers, family background and school experiences combine to either promote or undermine academic success.

VOCATIONAL DEVELOPMENT

During late adolescence, young people face a major life decision: the choice of a suitable work role. As we will see in Chapter 16, the selection of a vocation is a central part of identity development for modern adolescents. This is not surprising, since paid employment and economic independence are hallmarks of adulthood in industrialized societies.

Being a productive worker calls for many of the same qualities needed to be an active citizen and nurturant family member—good judgment, responsibility, dedication, and cooperation. An adolescent well prepared for work is better able to fulfill other adult roles. How do young people make decisions about careers, and what influences their choices? What is the transition from school to work like, and what factors make it easy or difficult?

SELECTING A VOCATION

In societies with an abundance of career possibilities, occupational choice is a gradual process, beginning long before adolescence. Major theorists view the young person as moving through several phases of vocational development (Ginzberg, 1988; Super, 1980, 1984).

■ **PHASES OF VOCATIONAL DEVELOPMENT.** Sabrina, Louis, and Jules are each at different points in the development of occupational plans. All three began to toy with career possibilities during early and middle childhood. Louis is further along than Sabrina in selecting a vocational direction. Jules is close to crystallizing his career choice.

1. The **fantasy period** (early and middle childhood). As we saw in Chapter 10, young children gain insight into career options by fantasizing about them. However, their preferences bear little relation to the decisions they will eventually make. When Sabrina announced at age 8 that she wanted to be an astronaut, a dancer, or a news reporter, her choices were determined by familiarity, glamour, and excitement. They did not include a realistic appraisal of her strengths, weaknesses, and special talents.

fantasy period
The period of vocational development in which young children fantasize about career options through make-believe play. Spans early and middle childhood.

2. The **tentative period** (early and middle adolescence). Between ages 11 and 17, adolescents start to think about careers in more complex ways. During early adolescence, they evaluate vocational options in terms of their *interests*. For example, Sabrina wrote a paper on the pyramids of Egypt and was fascinated by what she learned. For a time, she wanted to be an archeologist. One summer, she visited a national park, learned to ride a horse, and thought it would be fun to be a forest ranger.

By mid-adolescence, young people become more aware of personal and educational requirements for different vocations. Louis weighed possibilities not just against his interests, but also against his *abilities* and *values*. "I like business and selling things," he said one day to Jules. "I won a prize for raising the most money for our class trip. Trouble is, I'm not a very exacting person. I'm good with people, though, and I'd like to do something to help others. So maybe counseling or social work would fit my needs."

3. The **realistic period** (late adolescence and young adulthood). By the end of the teenage years, the economic and practical realities of adulthood are just around the corner, and adolescents start to narrow their options. At first, many do so through further *exploration*, gathering more information about a set of possibilities that blends with their personal characteristics. Then they enter a final phase of *crystallization* in which they focus on a general vocational category. Within it, they experiment for a time before settling on a single occupation. As a college sophomore, Jules plans to enter a scientific field, but he is not sure whether he prefers chemistry, math, or physics. Within the next few months, he will decide on a major. Then he will consider whether he wants to work for a company following graduation or study further to become a doctor or research scientist.

■ **FACTORS INFLUENCING VOCATIONAL CHOICE.** Although most adolescents follow this general pattern of vocational development, there are exceptions in both timing and sequence. A few know from an early age just what they want to be and follow a direct path to a career goal. Others keep their options open for an extended period. College students are granted added time to explore and decide. In contrast, the life conditions of low-income and minority youths restrict their range of choices.

Consider for a moment how an occupational choice is made, and you will see that it is not just a rational process in which young people match abilities, interests, and values against career options. Like other developmental milestones, it is the result of a dynamic interaction between person and environment. A great many influences feed into the adolescent's decision.

Personality. People are attracted to occupations that complement their personalities. John Holland (1966, 1985) has identified six personality types that affect vocational choice:

■ The *investigative person*, who enjoys working with ideas and is likely to select a scientific occupation (for example, anthropologist, physicist, or engineer).

■ The *social person*, who likes interacting with people and gravitates toward human services (counseling, social work, or teaching).

■ The *realistic person*, who prefers real-world problems and work with objects and tends to choose a mechanical occupation (construction, plumbing, or surveying).

■ The *artistic person*, who is emotional and high in need for individual expression and looks toward an artistic field (writing, music, or the visual arts).

■ The *conventional person*, who likes well-structured tasks and values material possessions and social status—traits well suited to certain business fields (accounting, banking, or quality control).

tentative period
The period of vocational development in which adolescents weigh vocational options against their interests, abilities, and values. Spans early and middle adolescence.

realistic period
The period of vocational development in which adolescents focus on a general career category and, slightly later, settle on a single occupation. Spans late adolescence and young adulthood.

- ■ The *enterprising person,* who is adventurous, persuasive, and a strong leader and is drawn to sales and supervisory positions.

Research reveals a clear relationship between personality and vocational choice, but it is only moderate. Personality is not a stronger predictor because many people are blends of several personality types and can do well at more than one kind of occupation. Louis, for example, is both enterprising and social—dispositions that led him to consider both business and a human services career. Furthermore, as ecological systems theory reminds us, career decisions are the joint result of individual and contextual factors, including family background, educational opportunities, and societal conditions.

Family Influences. Adolescents' vocational aspirations are strongly correlated with the jobs of their parents. Teenagers from higher-SES homes are more likely to select high-status, white-collar occupations, such as doctor, lawyer, scientist, and engineer. In contrast, those with lower-SES backgrounds tend to choose less prestigious, blue-collar careers—for example, plumber, construction worker, food service employee, and secretary. Parent–child similarity is partly a function of educational attainment. The single best predictor of occupational status is number of years of schooling completed (Featherman, 1980).

Family resemblance in occupational choice also comes about for other reasons. Higher-SES parents are more likely to give their children important information about the world of work and to have connections with people who can help the young person obtain a high-status position (Grotevant & Cooper, 1988). Parenting practices also shape work-related values. Recall from Chapter 2 (page 76) that higher-SES parents tend to promote independence and curiosity, which are required in many high-status careers. Lower-SES parents, in contrast, emphasize conformity and obedience. At work, they are used to following the directives of others. Eventually, young people are likely to choose careers that are compatible with these values. The jobs that appeal to them are often like those of their parents (Mortimer & Borman, 1988).

Although consistency between parent and child vocational choice is considerable, it is far from perfect. Parental pressure to do well in school and encouragement toward high-status occupations predict vocational attainment beyond SES (Bell et al., 1996). Although parental values and goals frequently lead adolescents to seek occupations similar to their parents', parents can also foster higher aspirations.

Teachers. Teachers play a powerful role in adolescents' career decisions. Jules regards his high school chemistry teacher as the most important influence on his choice of a scientific vocation. "Mr. Garvin showed me how to think about chemistry—and science in general. If I hadn't taken his class my junior year, I probably wouldn't have considered a career in science."

In one study, college freshmen were asked who had the greatest impact on their choice of a field of study. The people most often mentioned (by 39 percent of the sample) were high school teachers (Johnson, 1967, as cited by Rice, 1996). College-bound adolescents are likely to have closer relations with teachers than are other students, whose parents are more influential. These findings provide yet another reason for promoting positive teacher–student relations, especially for low-income adolescents. The power of teachers as role models could serve as an important source of upward mobility for these young people.

Gender Stereotypes. Over the past two decades, high school boys' career preferences have remained strongly gender stereotyped, whereas girls have expressed increasing interest in occupations largely held by men (Gottfredson, 1996). Changes in gender-role attitudes along with the dramatic rise in employed mothers, who serve as career-oriented models for their daughters (see Chapter 13), are common explanations for girls' interest in nontraditional careers.

Adolescents benefit when schools encourage warm, supportive teacher–student relationships. Under these conditions, teachers serve as influential models of character and accomplishment. *(© Will Faller 1994)*

At the same time, women's progress in entering and excelling at male-dominated professions has been slow. As Table 15.3 shows, the percentage of women engineers, lawyers, and doctors increased between 1972 and 1996 in the United States, but it falls far short of equal representation. Women remain heavily concentrated in the less well-paid, traditionally feminine professions of literature, social work, education, and nursing (U.S. Bureau of the Census, 1997). In virtually all fields, their achievements lag behind those of men, who write more books, make more discoveries, hold more positions of leadership, and produce more works of art.

Ability cannot account for these dramatic sex differences. As we have seen, the gender gap in cognitive performance of all kinds is declining. Instead, gender-stereotyped messages from the social environment play a key role. Although girls' grades are higher than boys', girls reach secondary school less confident of their ability and more likely to underestimate their achievement (Bornholt, Goodnow, & Cooney, 1994). Over time, the proportion of girls in gifted programs decreases. Girls make up about half the population in

TABLE 15.3

Percentage of Females in Various Professions, 1972, 1983, 1996

PROFESSION	1972	1983	1996
Engineering	0.8	5.8	8.5
Law	3.8	15.8	21.4
Medicine	9.3	15.8	20.4
Business—executive and managerial	17.6	32.4	43.0[a]
Writing, art, entertainment	31.7	42.7	47.2
Social work	55.1	64.3	68.9
Elementary and secondary education	70.0	70.9	74.8
Higher education	28.0	36.3	40.9
Library, museum curatorship	81.6	84.4	83.6
Nursing	92.6	95.8	94.3

Source: U.S. Bureau of the Census, 1997.

[a]This percentage includes executives and managers at all levels. Women make up only 9 percent of senior management at big firms, although that figure represents a three-fold increase in the past decade.

these programs in elementary school. By secondary school, they account for less than 30 percent, and their presence continues to drop during high school. Those who remain do not develop their talents to the same degree as do boys, either educationally or vocationally (Winner, 1996). When asked what discouraged them from continuing in gifted classes, parental and peer pressures and attitudes of teachers and counselors ranked high on girls' lists (Read, 1991).

During college, the career aspirations of academically talented females decline further. In one longitudinal study, high school valedictorians were followed over a 10-year period—through college and into the work world. By their sophomore year, young women shifted their expectations toward less demanding careers because of concerns about combining work with child rearing and unresolved questions about their ability. Even though female valedictorians outperformed their male counterparts in college courses, they achieved at lower levels after career entry (Arnold, 1994). Another study reported similar results. Educational aspirations of mathematically talented females declined considerably during college, as did the number majoring in the sciences (Benbow & Arjmand, 1990).

These findings reveal a pressing need for programs that sensitize parents, teachers, and school counselors to the special problems girls face in developing and maintaining high career aspirations. Research shows that academically talented girls' aspirations rise in response to career guidance that encourages them to set goals that match their abilities, interests, and values (Kerr, 1983). Models of accomplished women who have successfully dealt with family–career role conflict are also important (Schroeder, Blood, & Maluso, 1993).

Access to Vocational Information. Finally, all adolescents could profit from greater access to career information. Like many high school students, Louis had little notion of just what he would have to do to enter a career in business, teaching, or social work. In one study of over 6,000 high school seniors, more than one-third had only sketchy knowledge of their preferred vocation. Only about half planned to get the appropriate amount of education to reach their goals, and many selected occupations that were not compatible with their interests (Grotevant & Durrett, 1980). The limited work knowledge and experience of American adolescents—especially those who terminate their education with a high school diploma—complicates the transition from school to work life.

MAKING THE TRANSITION FROM SCHOOL TO WORK

Franca and Antonio's middle son, 18-year-old Martin, graduated from high school in a vocational track. Like 25 percent of young people with a high school diploma, he had no plans to go to college. He hoped to work in data processing after graduation, but 6 months later he was still a part-time sales clerk at the candy store where he had worked during high school. Although Martin had filled out many job applications, he got no interviews or offers.

Martin's inability to find a job other than the one he held as a student is typical for American non-college-bound high school graduates. As a college student, his brother, Jules, will have a much easier time. Jules will emerge from school as a young adult, having profited from the advice of faculty in his major field of study, access to a wide variety of career services, and perhaps an internship in his chosen vocation.

Although high school graduates are more likely to find employment than those who drop out, they have fewer work opportunities than they did several decades ago. More than one-fifth of high school graduates younger than 20 who do not continue their education are unemployed (U.S. Department of Education, 1997). When they do find work, most are limited to low-paid, unskilled jobs. In addition, they have few alternatives to turn to for vocational counseling and job placement as they make the transition from school to work (Bailey, 1993; Hamilton, 1990).

American employers prefer to hire young adults, regarding the recent high school graduate as poorly prepared for a demanding, skilled occupation. Indeed, there is some truth to this conclusion. During high school, almost half of American adolescents are employed—a greater percentage than in any other developed country. But most of these are middle-SES students in pursuit of spending money rather than vocational exploration and training. Low-income teenagers who need to contribute to family income find it harder to get jobs (Children's Defense Fund, 1998).

Furthermore, the jobs adolescents hold largely involve low-level repetitive tasks that provide little contact with adult supervisors and that do not prepare them for well-paid careers. A heavy commitment to such jobs is actually harmful. High school students who work more than 15 to 20 hours per week have poorer school attendance, lower grades, and less time for extracurricular activities. They also report more drug and alcohol use and feel more distant from their parents. Although young people whose school performance is already compromised are more likely to work long hours, doing so makes a bad situation worse. And perhaps because of the menial nature of their jobs, employed teenagers tend to become cynical about work life. Many admit to having stolen from their employers (Barling, Rogers, & Kelloway, 1995; Steinberg & Dornbusch, 1991; Steinberg, Fegley & Dornbusch, 1993).

When work experiences are specially designed to meet educational and vocational goals and involve responsibility and challenge, outcomes are very different. Work–study programs are related to positive school and work attitudes, improved achievement, and lower dropout rates among teenagers whose low-income backgrounds and weak academic skills make them especially vulnerable to unemployment (Owens, 1982; Steinberg, 1984). Yet high-quality vocational preparation for American adolescents who do not go to college is scarce. Unlike European nations, the United States has no widespread training system to prepare its youths for skilled business and industrial occupations and manual trades (Hamilton & Hurrelmann, 1994). The federal government does support some job-training programs, and funding for them has recently increased. But most are too short to make a difference in the lives of poorly skilled adolescents, who need intensive training and academic remediation before they are ready to enter the job market. And at present, these programs serve only a small minority of young people who need assistance (Children's Defense Fund, 1998).

Inspired by successful programs in Europe, youth apprenticeship strategies that coordinate on-the-job training with classroom instruction are being considered as an important dimension of educational reform in the United States. The Cultural Influences box on page 596 describes Germany's highly successful apprenticeship system. Bringing together the worlds of schooling and work offers many benefits. These include helping non-college-bound adolescents establish productive lives right after graduation, motivating at-risk youths to stay in school, and contributing to the nation's economic growth (Hamilton, 1993; Safyer, Leahy, & Colan, 1995).

Although vocational development is a lifelong process, adolescence is a crucial period for defining occupational goals and launching a career. Young people well prepared for an economically and personally satisfying vocation are much more likely to become productive citizens, devoted family members, and contented adults. The support of families, schools, communities, and society as a whole can contribute greatly to a positive outcome.

ASK YOURSELF . . .

■ *In high school, Valerie wanted to become an astronomer. By her second year in college, she continued to excel in physics classes, but she gave up her dream of becoming a research scientist. What factors might have led Valerie to change her mind?*

■ *What steps can schools take to help ensure that adolescents' occupational choices match their interests, personality dispositions, and abilities?*

CULTURAL INFLUENCES

WORK–STUDY APPRENTICESHIPS IN GERMANY

Rolf, an 18-year-old German vocational student, is an apprentice at Brandt, a large industrial firm known worldwide for its high-quality products. Like many German companies, Brandt has a well-developed apprenticeship program that includes a full-time professional training staff, a suite of classrooms, and a lab equipped with the latest learning aids. Apprentices move through more than 10 major company divisions that are carefully selected to meet their learning needs. Rolf has worked in purchasing, inventory, production, personnel, marketing, sales,

High-quality vocational training combined with apprenticeship enables German youths who do not go to college to enter well-paid careers. This electronics trainee works at a hydraulics system factory. His education involves integrating academic skills with on-the-job experience to ensure that he becomes competent at both.
(M. Granitsas/The Image Works)

and finance. Now in cost accounting, he assists Herr Stein, his supervisor, in designing a computerized inventory control system. Rolf draws a flow chart of the new system under the direction of Herr Stein, who explains that each part of the diagram will contain a set of procedures to be built into a computer program.

Rolf is involved in complex and challenging projects, guided by caring mentors who love their work and want to teach it to others. Two days a week, he attends the *Berufsschule*, a part-time vocational school. On the job, Rolf applies a wide range of academic skills, including reading, writing, problem solving, and logical thinking. His classroom learning is directly relevant to his daily life (Hamilton, 1990).

Germany has one of the most successful apprenticeship systems in the world for preparing young people to enter modern business and industry. More than 60 percent of adolescents participate in it, making it the most common form of secondary education. German adolescents who do not go to the *Gymnasium* (college preparatory high school) usually complete full-time schooling by age 15 or 16, but education remains compulsory until age 18. They fill the 2-year gap with part-time vocational schooling combined with apprenticeship. Students are trained for a wide range of occupations—more than 400, leading to over 20,000 specialized careers. Each apprenticeship is jointly planned by educators and employers. Apprentices who complete training and pass a qualifying examination are certified as skilled workers and earn union-set wages for that occupation. Businesses provide financial support for the program because they know it guarantees a competent, dedicated work

force (Hamilton, 1990, 1994).

The German apprenticeship system offers a smooth and rewarding path from school to career for young people who do not enter higher education. Many apprentices are hired by the firms in which they were trained. Most others find jobs in the same occupation. For those who change careers, the apprentice certificate is a powerful credential. Employers view successful apprentices as responsible and capable workers. They are willing to invest in further training to adapt the individual's skills to other occupations. As a result, German young people establish themselves in well-paid careers with security and advancement possibilities between the ages of 18 and 20 (Hamilton, 1990).

The success of the German system—and of similar systems in Austria, Denmark, Switzerland, and several East European countries—suggests that some kind of national apprenticeship program would improve the transition from school to work for young people in the United States. Nevertheless, implementing an American apprenticeship system poses major challenges. Among these are overcoming the reluctance of employers to assume part of the responsibility for vocational training; creating institutional structures that ensure cooperation between schools and businesses; and finding ways to prevent low-income youths from being concentrated in the lowest skilled apprenticeship placements, which would perpetuate current social inequalities (Bailey, 1993; Hamilton, 1994). Pilot apprenticeship projects are currently under way, in an effort to solve these problems and build bridges between learning and working in the United States.

Summary

PIAGET'S THEORY: THE FORMAL OPERATIONAL STAGE

What are the major characteristics of formal operational thought?

■ During Piaget's **formal operational stage,** abstract thinking appears. Adolescents engage in **hypothetico-deductive reasoning.** When faced with a problem, they think of all possibilities, including ones that are not obvious, and test them against reality in an orderly fashion. **Propositional thought** also develops. Young people can evaluate the logic of verbal statements without considering them against real-world circumstances.

Discuss recent research on formal operational thought and its implications for the accuracy of Piaget's formal operational stage.

■ Recent research reveals that school-age children display the beginnings of abstract reasoning, but they are not as cognitively competent as adolescents and adults. In addition, many college students and adults think abstractly only in situations in which they have had extensive experience, and formal operational tasks are not mastered in many village and tribal societies. These findings indicate that Piaget's highest stage is affected by specific learning opportunities.

AN INFORMATION-PROCESSING VIEW OF ADOLESCENT COGNITIVE DEVELOPMENT

How do information-processing researchers account for the development of abstract thought?

■ Information-processing researchers believe that a variety of specific mechanisms of change foster abstract thought, including improved attention; more effective strategies; greater knowledge; gains in information-processing capacity; and, especially, advances in metacognition.

■ Research on scientific reasoning reveals that the ability to coordinate theory with evidence improves from childhood to adolescence as young people solve increasingly complex problems and reflect on their thinking, acquiring more sophisticated metacognitive understanding.

■ Adolescents develop formal operational abilities in a similar, step-by-step fashion on different types of tasks, constructing general models that can be applied to many instances of a given type of problem. Formal operational thought is not the result of an abrupt, stagewise change. Rather, it develops gradually.

■ Researchers who study **postformal thought** have shown that cognitive development is not complete at adolescence. It becomes increasingly rational as young people move toward **relativistic reasoning,** or awareness of multiple truths.

CONSEQUENCES OF ABSTRACT THOUGHT

Describe typical reactions of adolescents that result from new abstract reasoning powers.

■ Adolescents' new cognitive powers are reflected in many aspects of their daily behavior. Teenagers become more argumentative, idealistic, and critical. As they think more about themselves, two distorted images of the relation between self and other appear—the **imaginary audience** and the **personal fable.**

■ Adolescents show gains in self-regulation and **comprehension monitoring** on cognitive tasks. However, they often have difficulty making decisions in everyday life.

SEX DIFFERENCES IN MENTAL ABILITIES

Describe sex differences in mental abilities at adolescence, along with factors that influence them.

■ Although boys and girls do not differ in general intelligence, they do vary in specific mental abilities. During adolescence, the female advantage in general verbal ability is very slight. Boys do better in mathematical reasoning, especially in solving complex word problems.

■ Sex differences in mathematics stem, in part, from boys' biologically based advantage in spatial reasoning. At the same time, a variety of environmental factors, including childhood play activities, young people's self-confidence and interest in doing math, and math and science course taking, contribute to the gender gap. Girls' environmental disadvantage stems from gender stereotyping of math as a "male domain."

LANGUAGE DEVELOPMENT

Describe changes in vocabulary, grammar, and pragmatics during adolescence.

■ Teenagers add many abstract words to their vocabulary and use more elaborate grammatical constructions. The capacity to think flexibly about word meanings permits adolescents to understand irony and sarcasm and interpret adult literary works. The most obvious change in language at adolescence is the ability to make subtle adjustments in language style, depending on the situation.

Compare adolescents' capacity for second-language learning to that of children.

■ Biological readiness for language learning is greatest in childhood. As with first-lan-

Summary (continued)

guage learning, the ability to master a second language to the level of a native speaker declines with age, dropping sharply at adolescence.

LEARNING IN SCHOOL

Discuss the impact of school transitions on adolescent adjustment.

■ School transitions in adolescence can be stressful. As school environments become larger and more impersonal, grades and feelings of competence decline. Girls experience more adjustment difficulties after the elementary to junior high transition, since other life changes (puberty and the beginning of dating) tend to occur at the same time. Adolescents who have to cope with added stresses—especially poorly achieving and poverty-stricken young people—are at greatest risk for academic and emotional difficulties.

Discuss family, peer, and school influences on academic achievement during adolescence.

■ A variety of interrelated environmental factors affect academic performance during adolescence. Authoritative parenting, joint parent–child decision making, and parents' involvement in the adolescent's secondary school career promote high achievement. Teenagers with parents who encourage high achievement are likely to choose friends who do the same. Warm, supportive learning environments with activities that emphasize high-level thinking enable adolescents to reach their cognitive potential.

■ By high school, separate educational tracks that dovetail with adolescents' future plans are necessary. Unfortunately,

high school tracking in the United States usually extends the educational inequalities of earlier years. High-ability, low-SES students are at risk for unfair placement in noncollege tracks and reduced parental involvement in their education.

What factors are related to dropping out of school?

■ Thirteen percent of American young people leave high school without a diploma, many of them low-income, ethnic minority youths. Dropping out is the result of a slow, cumulative process of disengagement from school. A variety of family and school influences combine to undermine the young person's chances for success.

VOCATIONAL DEVELOPMENT

Trace the development of vocational choice.

■ During late adolescence, young people face a major life decision: the choice of a suitable work role. Vocational development moves through three phases: a **fantasy period,** in which children explore career options through play; a **tentative period,** in which teenagers weigh different careers against their interests, abilities, and values; and a **realistic period,** in which older adolescents and young adults settle on a vocational category and, finally, a specific career.

What factors influence adolescents' vocational decisions?

■ People are attracted to occupations that compliment their personalities. However, personality is only moderately related to vocational choice, since individual and contextual factors combine to influence adolescents' decisions.

■ Teenagers' career aspirations are strongly correlated with the jobs of their parents. The resemblance is due to educational opportunities, available information about the world of work, and teaching of work-related values. Teachers often have a powerful impact on adolescents' vocational choice.

■ Today, more girls express interest in male-dominated occupations. However, gender-stereotyped messages prevent many girls from reaching their career potential. Girls' vocational aspirations decline from high school into college.

What problems do American non-college-bound youths face in making the transition from school to work?

■ The United States needs to help its non-college-bound high school graduates make an effective transition from school to work. Unlike Western European young people, American adolescents have no widespread vocational training system to assist them in preparing for challenging, well-paid careers in business, industry, and manual trades.

■ Most teenagers who work part time are limited to low-paid, unskilled jobs. Too many hours spent in these work settings undermines school performance and work-related attitudes. In contrast, work–study programs designed to meet educational and vocational goals foster a positive orientation toward academic achievement and work.

*I*mportant terms and concepts

comprehension monitoring (p. 575)
fantasy period (p. 590)
formal operational stage (p. 564)
hypothetico-deductive reasoning
   (p. 564)

imaginary audience (p. 572)
personal fable (p. 573)
postformal thought (p. 570)
propositional thought (p. 564)
realistic period (p. 591)

relativistic reasoning (p. 571)
tentative period (p. 591)

*F*yi . . . **FOR FURTHER INFORMATION AND HELP**

ACADEMIC ACHIEVEMENT

National Assessment of Educational
Progress
National Center for Education Statistics
United States Department of Education
(800) 233-0267
Website: nces.ed.gov/NAEP/indextxt.html

*A nationally representative and continuing
assessment of the achievement of American
students in various subject areas. Distributes
reports of recent findings.*

Pursuing Excellence: The Third International Mathematics and Science Study
National Center for Education Statistics
United States Department of Education
(800) 233-0267
Website: nces.ed.gov/timss

*Presents findings of the largest, most comprehensive international comparison of mathematics and science achievement. A
half-million students at five grade levels from
41 nations participated.*

DROPOUT PREVENTION

National Dropout Prevention Center
Clemson University
(803) 656-2599
Website: www.dropoutprevention.org

*A center offering information on school
dropout prevention and identifying high-risk
youth. Provides consultation and referral services to school systems, agencies, and associations dealing with the dropout problem.*

YOUTH EMPLOYMENT

National School-to-Work Learning and
Information Center
Employment and Training Administration
(800) 251-7236
Website: www.stw.ed.gov

*Provides information on the U.S. School-to-
Work Opportunities Act, which provides seed
money to the states for stimulating school-to-
work partnerships between local businesses,
schools, community organizations, and government. Although there is no single model,
each local program must combine relevant
education with job training that meets industry standards.*

"Sorrow"
Valentina Guljqueva
11 years, Byelorussia

As adolescents search for a set of values to have faith in, they bring a sense of idealism and hopefulness to society. Yet as this young artist's painting conveys, their dreams can easily be shattered by a world in which destruction and hatred are permitted to triumph over human caring and love.

Reprinted by permission from The International Museum of Children's Art, Oslo, Norway.

EMOTIONAL AND SOCIAL DEVELOPMENT IN ADOLESCENCE

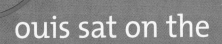

ouis sat on the grassy hillside overlooking the high school, waiting for his best friend Darryl to arrive from his fourth-period class. The two boys often met at noontime and then crossed the street to have lunch together at a nearby hamburger stand.

Watching as hundreds of students poured onto the school grounds, Louis reflected on what Mrs. Kemp had said in government class that day. "Suppose by chance I had been born in the People's Republic of China. I'd be sitting here, speaking a different language, being called by a different name, going home to different parents, and thinking about the world in different ways. Gosh, I am who I am through some quirk of fate," Louis pondered, looking around as the crowd of students picnicking on the grass grew denser.

Louis awoke from his thoughts with a start. Darryl was standing in front of him. "Hey, dreamer! I've been shouting and waving from the bottom of the hill for 5 minutes."

"Sorry," Louis responded, jumping up and joining his friend.

As they walked off, Darryl asked, "How come you're so spaced out lately, Louis?"

"Oh, just wondering about stuff—like what I want, what I believe in. My older brother Jules—I envy him. He seems to know just where he's going. Most of the time, I'm up in the air about it. You ever feel that way?"

"Yeah, a lot," admitted Darryl, looking at Louis seriously as they approached the hamburger stand. "I often think—What am I really like? Who will I become?"

Louis and Darryl's introspective remarks are signs of a major reorganization of the self at adolescence: the development of identity. Both young people are attempting to formulate who they are—their personal values and the directions they will pursue in life. As you know from earlier chapters, important changes in self-concept take place throughout childhood. But the restructuring of the self that happens at adolescence is profound. The rapid physical changes of puberty taking place on the outside prompt teenagers to reconsider what they are like as persons on the inside. And for the first time, adolescents have the capacity to think hypothetically and, therefore, to project themselves into the distant future. They start to realize how important their choice of values and goals is for their later lives.

We begin this chapter with Erikson's account of identity development and the research it has stimulated on teenagers' thoughts and feelings about themselves. The quest for identity extends to many aspects of development. We will see how sense of cultural belonging, moral understanding, and masculine and feminine self-images are refined during the teenage years. And as parent–child relationships are revised and young people become increasingly independent of the family, friendships and peer networks become crucial contexts for bridging the gap between childhood and adulthood. Our chapter concludes with a discussion of several serious adjustment problems of adolescence—depression, suicide, and delinquency.

ERIKSON'S THEORY: IDENTITY VERSUS IDENTITY CONFUSION

Erikson (1950, 1968) was the first to recognize **identity** as the major personality achievement of adolescence and as a crucial step toward becoming a productive, happy adult. Constructing an identity involves defining who you are, what you value, and the directions you choose to pursue in life. This search for self is the driving force behind many commitments—to a sexual orientation (see Chapter 14); to a vocation (see Chapter 15); to interpersonal relationships and community involvement; to ethnic group membership; and to moral, political, religious, and cultural ideals.

Identity formation actually begins long before the teenage years. Erikson regarded successful outcomes of earlier stages as paving the way toward a positive resolution of the adolescent psychological conflict, which he called **identity versus identity confusion.** Young people who reach adolescence with a weak sense of *trust* have trouble finding ideals to have faith in. Those with little *autonomy* or *initiative* do not engage in the active exploration required to choose among alternatives. And those who lack a sense of *industry* fail to select a vocation that matches their interests and skills.

Although the seeds of identity formation are planted early, not until adolescence do young people become absorbed in this task. According to Erikson, in complex societies, teenagers experience an *identity crisis*—a temporary period of confusion and distress as they experiment with alternatives before settling on a set of values and goals. During this period, what adolescents once took for granted they question. "I've gone to church every Sunday morning since I was a little kid," Louis confided in Darryl. "Now I'm not so sure I can accept my parents' way of thinking about God." Teenagers who go through a process of inner soul-searching eventually arrive at a mature identity. They sift through characteristics that defined the self in childhood and combine them with new commitments. Then

identity
A well-organized conception of the self made up of values, beliefs, and goals to which the individual is solidly committed.

identity versus identity confusion
In Erikson's theory, the psychological conflict of adolescence, which is resolved positively when adolescents attain an identity after a period of exploration and inner soul-searching.

they mold these into a solid inner core that provides a sense of sameness as they move through different roles in daily life. Once formed, identity continues to be refined in adulthood as individuals re-evaluate earlier commitments and choices.

Current theorists agree with Erikson that questioning of values, plans, and priorities is necessary for a mature identity, but they no longer refer to this process as a "crisis" (Grotevant, 1998). The term suggests a sudden, intense upheaval of the self. For some young people, identity development is traumatic and disturbing, but for most it is not. "Exploration" better describes the typical adolescent's experience. Identity formation usually proceeds in a very gradual, uneventful way. The many daily choices that teenagers make—"whom to date, whether or not to break up, having intercourse, taking drugs, going to college or working, which college, what major, studying or playing, being politically active"—and the reasons for them are gradually put together into an organized self-structure (Marcia, 1980, p. 161).

The negative outcome of this stage is *identity confusion.* Some adolescents appear shallow and directionless, either because earlier conflicts have been resolved negatively or society restricts their choices to ones that do not match their abilities and desires. As a result, they are unprepared for the psychological challenges of adulthood. For example, Erikson's young adult stage centers on the development of *intimacy* (see Chapter 1, page 17). Individuals find it difficult to risk the self-sharing involved in intimacy if they are not certain that there is a firm sense of self (an identity) to which they can return.

Is there research to support Erikson's ideas about identity development? In the following sections, we will see that adolescents go about the task of defining the self in ways that closely match Erikson's description.

"Exploration" describes the typical adolescent's gradual, uneventful approach to identity formation. This teenager's eager experimentation with photography in his high school journalism class may help crystallize a vocational path or lead to an absorbing, long-term hobby. *(Bob Daemmrich/The Image Works)*

SELF-DEVELOPMENT

During adolescence, cognitive changes transform the young person's vision of the self into a more complex, well-organized, and consistent picture. Changes in self-concept and self-esteem set the stage for development of a unified personal identity.

CHANGES IN SELF-CONCEPT

Recall from Chapter 13 that by the end of middle childhood, children describe themselves in terms of personality traits, such as "I'm smart," "I'm shy," or "I'm honest." This change permits young people to establish links between their past, present, and future selves.

In early adolescence, self-statements are not interconnected, and often they include contradictory descriptions. For example, 12- to 14-year-olds might mention such opposing traits as "smart" and "dumb" or "shy" and "outgoing." These disparities result from social pressures to display different selves in different relationships—with parents, classmates, close friends, and romantic partners. As adolescents' social world expands, contradictory self-descriptions increase, and teenagers frequently agonize over "which is the real me." Although young teenagers are disturbed by these inconsistencies, they usually cannot explain or resolve them (Harter, 1998; Harter & Monsour, 1992).

By middle to late adolescence, the capacity for abstract thinking permits teenagers to combine their various traits into an organized system. They unify separate traits, such as "smart" and "creative," into higher-order, abstract descriptors, such as "intelligent." And they begin to use qualifiers ("I have a *fairly* quick temper," "I'm not *thoroughly* honest"), which reveal their awareness that psychological qualities often change from one situation to the next. Older adolescents also add integrating principles, which make sense out of formerly troublesome contradictions. For example, one young person remarked, "I'm very adaptable. When I'm around my friends, who think that what I say is important, I'm very talkative; but around my family I'm quiet because they're never interested enough to really listen to me" (Damon, 1990, p. 88).

Compared to school-age children, teenagers also place more emphasis on social virtues, such as being friendly, considerate, kind, and cooperative. Adolescents, as we have seen, are very preoccupied with being liked and viewed positively by others, and their statements about themselves reflect this concern (Damon & Hart, 1988). In addition, personal and moral values appear as key themes in older adolescents' self-concepts. For example, here is how one 16-year-old boy named Ben described himself in terms of honesty to himself and others:

> I like being honest like with yourself and with everyone. . . . [A person] could be, in the eyes of everyone else the best person in the world, but if I knew they were lying or cheating, in my eyes they wouldn't be. . . . When I'm friendly, it's more to tell people that it's all right to be yourself. Not necessarily don't conform, but just whatever you are, you know, be happy with that. . . . So I'm not an overly bubbly person that goes around, "Hi, how are you?" . . . But if someone wants to talk to me, you know, sure. I wouldn't like, not talk to someone. (pp. 120–121)

Ben's well-integrated account of his personal traits and values is quite different from the fragmented, listlike self-descriptions of children. As adolescents revise their views of themselves to include enduring beliefs and plans, they move toward the kind of unity of self that Erikson described in his theory of identity development.

CHANGES IN SELF-ESTEEM

Self-esteem, the evaluative side of self-concept, continues to differentiate during the teenage years. To the self-evaluations of middle childhood—academic competence, physical ability, and social self-worth—are added several new dimensions: close friendship, romantic appeal, and job competence. These reflect important concerns of this new period (Harter, 1990).

Level of self-esteem changes as well. Turn back to Figure 15.4 on page 581, and you will see that except for a temporary decline associated with school transition, self-esteem is on the rise for most adolescents (Nottelmann, 1987). This steady increase is yet another reason that modern researchers question the assumption that adolescence is a time of emotional turmoil. To the contrary, the rise in self-worth suggests that for most young people, becoming an adolescent leads to feelings of pride and self-confidence (Powers, Hauser, & Kilner, 1989). This is true not just in the United States but elsewhere in the world. A study of self-esteem in 10 industrialized countries showed that the majority of teenagers had an optimistic outlook on life, a positive attitude toward school and work, and faith in their ability to cope with life's problems (Offer, 1988).

 INFLUENCES ON SELF-ESTEEM

Of course, as we already saw in Chapters 14 and 15, adolescents vary widely in self-esteem. Those who are off time in pubertal development, who are heavy drug users, and who fail in school feel poorly about themselves. Look again at Figure 15.4, and you will see that girls score lower than boys in overall sense of self-worth. In addition, of those young people whose self-esteem drops during adolescence, most are girls (Block & Robins, 1994; Zimmerman et al., 1997). Recall that teenage girls worry more about their physical appearance and feel more insecure about their abilities.

At the same time, the contexts in which young people find themselves can modify these group differences, since self-esteem continues to be profoundly affected by feedback from significant adults and peers. Parental warmth, approval, and appropriate expectations for maturity (authoritative parenting) predict high self-esteem in adolescence, just as they did in childhood (Steinberg et al., 1995). In contrast, when support from adults or peers is *conditional* (withheld unless the young person meets very high standards), teenagers frequently engage in behaviors they consider "false"—not representative of their true self. Although most adolescents report acting "phony" from time to time, they usually do so to win temporary approval or experiment with new roles. Those who display false-self behavior because others (and therefore they) devalue their true self suffer from low self-esteem, depression, and pessimism about the future (Harter et al., 1996).

Adolescents' sense of self-worth is also influenced by the larger social environment. Teenagers who attend schools or live in neighborhoods where their SES or ethnic group is well represented have fewer self-esteem problems. For example, the self-esteem of African-American, Jewish, and Catholic teenagers is higher in schools where there are many students of the same background than where there are just a few (Rosenberg, 1988). Schools and communities that are accepting of the young person's cultural heritage support a positive sense of self-worth. And as we will see shortly, they foster the development of a solid and secure personal identity as well.

These Hispanic teenagers congregate in a city neighborhood where their ethnicity is well represented. Schools and communities that are accepting of the young person's cultural heritage promote high self-esteem. *(Don Smetzer/Tony Stone Images)*

PATHS TO IDENTITY

Adolescents' well-organized self-descriptions and expanded sense of self-esteem provide the cognitive foundation for forming an identity. Using a clinical interviewing procedure devised by James Marcia (1966, 1980), researchers group adolescents into four *identity statuses,* which show the progress they have made toward formulating a mature identity. Table 16.1 summarizes these identity statuses: **identity achievement, moratorium, identity foreclosure,** and **identity diffusion.**

Adolescents often shift from one status to another until identity is achieved. For example, in junior high school, Louis accepted his parents' religious beliefs (foreclosure) and gave only passing thought to a vocational direction (diffusion). In high school, he started to actively explore these identity issues. Many young people start out as identity foreclosed and diffused, but by late adolescence they have moved toward moratorium and identity achievement (Archer, 1982; Meilman, 1979). College triggers increased exploration as young people are exposed to new career options and lifestyles. Most teenagers who go to work after high school graduation settle on a self-definition earlier than do college-bound youths (Munro & Adams, 1977). But those who find it difficult to realize their occupational goals because of lack of training or vocational choices (see Chapter 15) are at risk for identity foreclosure or diffusion (Archer, 1989b; Kroger, 1993).

At one time, researchers thought that adolescent girls postponed the task of establishing an identity and, instead, focused their energies on Erikson's next stage, intimacy development. We now know that this is not so. Girls do show more sophisticated reasoning in identity areas related to intimacy, such as sexuality and family–career priorities. In this respect, they are actually ahead of boys in identity development. Otherwise, the process and timing of identity formation is the same for boys and girls (Archer, 1989a; Archer & Waterman, 1994; Streitmatter, 1993).

IDENTITY STATUS AND PSYCHOLOGICAL WELL-BEING

Identity achievement and moratorium are viewed as psychologically healthy routes to a mature self-definition, whereas foreclosure and diffusion are maladaptive. Research

identity achievement
The identity status of individuals who have explored and committed themselves to self-chosen values and occupational goals.

moratorium
The identity status of individuals who are exploring alternatives in an effort to find values and goals to guide their life.

identity foreclosure
The identity status of individuals who have accepted ready-made values and goals that authority figures have chosen for them.

identity diffusion
The identity status of individuals who do not have firm commitments to values and goals and are not actively trying to reach them.

The Four Identity Statuses

IDENTITY STATUS	DESCRIPTION	EXAMPLE
Identity achievement	Having already explored alternatives, identity-achieved individuals are committed to a clearly formulated set of self-chosen values and goals. They feel a sense of psychological well-being, of sameness through time, and of knowing where they are going.	When asked how willing she would be to give up going into her chosen occupation if something better came along, Darla responded, "Well, I might, but I doubt it. I've thought long and hard about law as a career. I'm pretty certain it's for me."
Moratorium	The word moratorium means "delay or holding pattern." These individuals have not yet made definite commitments. They are in the process of exploration—gathering information and trying out activities, with the desire to find values and goals to guide their life.	When asked if he had ever had doubts about his religious beliefs, Ramon said, "Yes, I guess I'm going through that right now. I just don't see how there can be a god and yet so much evil in the world."
Identity foreclosure	Identity-foreclosed individuals have committed themselves to values and goals without taking time to explore alternatives. Instead, they accept a ready-made identity that authority figures (usually parents but sometimes teachers, religious leaders, or romantic partners) have chosen for them.	When asked if she had ever reconsidered her political beliefs, Hillary answered, "No, not really, our family is pretty much in agreement on these things."
Identity diffusion	Identity-diffused individuals lack clear direction. They are not committed to values and goals, nor are they actively trying to reach them. They may have never explored alternatives, or they may have tried to do so but found the task too threatening and overwhelming.	When asked about his attitude toward nontraditional gender roles, Joel responded, "Oh, I don't know. It doesn't make much difference to me. I can take it or leave it."

supports this conclusion. Young people who are identity achieved or actively exploring have a higher sense of self-esteem, are more likely to engage in abstract and critical thinking, report greater similarity between their ideal self (what they hoped to become) and their real self, and are more advanced in moral reasoning (Josselson, 1994; Marcia et al., 1993). Although they spend more time thinking about themselves than do adolescents who lag behind in identity development, they are also more secure about revealing their true selves to others (O'Connor, 1995).

Adolescents who get stuck in either foreclosure or diffusion have adjustment difficulties. Foreclosed individuals tend to be dogmatic, inflexible, and intolerant. Some use their commitments in a defensive way, regarding any difference of opinion as a threat. Most are afraid of rejection by people on whom they depend for affection and self-esteem (Frank, Pirsch, & Wright, 1990; Kroger, 1995). A few foreclosed teenagers who are alienated from their families and society may join cults or other extremist groups, uncritically adopting a way of life that is different from their past.

Long-term diffused teenagers are the least mature in identity development. They typically entrust themselves to luck or fate, have an "I don't care" attitude, and tend to go along with whatever the "crowd" is doing at the moment. As a result, they are most likely to use and abuse drugs. At the heart of their apathy and impulsiveness is often a sense of hopelessness about the future (Archer & Waterman, 1990). Ethnic and religious prejudices are typical of both foreclosed and diffused young people. The foreclosed teenager tends to pick them up from authority figures, the diffused young person from peers (Streitmatter & Pate, 1989).

FACTORS THAT AFFECT IDENTITY DEVELOPMENT

Adolescent identity is the beginning of a lifelong process of refinement in commitments that reflect a dynamic blend of personality with situational context. Whenever the individual or the context changes, the possibility for reformulating identity exists (Grotevant, 1998). A wide variety of factors influence identity development.

■ **PERSONALITY.**   In the previous section, we showed that identity status is linked to personality characteristics. The attributes considered are both *cause and consequence* of identity development. In particular, a flexible, open-minded approach to grappling with competing beliefs and values is important. Adolescents who assume that absolute truth is always attainable tend to be foreclosed, whereas those who lack confidence in the prospect of ever knowing anything with certainty are more often identity diffused or in a state of moratorium. Adolescents who appreciate that rational criteria can be used to choose among alternative visions are likely to be identity achieved (Boyes & Chandler, 1992).

■ **FAMILY.**   Recall from Chapter 7 that toddlers with a healthy sense of self have mothers who provide both emotional support and freedom to explore. A similar link between parenting and identity exists at adolescence. When the family serves as a "secure base" from which teenagers can confidently move out into the wider world, identity development is enhanced. Adolescents who feel attached to their parents but who are also free to voice their own opinions tend to be identity achieved or in a state of moratorium (Grotevant & Cooper, 1985, 1998; Hauser, Powers, & Noam, 1991). Foreclosed teenagers usually have close bonds with parents, but they lack opportunities for healthy separation. And diffused young people report the lowest levels of warm, open communication at home (Papini, 1994).

As these adolescents exchange opinions about a recent news event, they become more aware of a diversity of viewpoints. A flexible, open-minded approach to grappling with competing beliefs and values fosters identity development. *(Tony Freeman/PhotoEdit)*

■ **SCHOOL AND COMMUNITY.**   Identity development also depends on schools and communities offering rich and varied opportunities for exploration. Erikson (1968, p. 132) noted that it is "the inability to settle on an occupational identity which most disturbs young people." Classrooms that promote high-level thinking; extracurricular and community activities that permit teenagers to take on responsible roles; teachers and counselors who encourage low-SES and ethnic minority students to go to college; and vocational training programs that immerse adolescents in the real world of adult work foster identity achievement (Cooper, 1998).

Variations in opportunity can lead to regional differences in identity development. For example, between ages 13 and 17, exploration increases among Australian adolescents living in urban environments, whereas it decreases among youths in rural areas. Lack of educational and vocational options in Australian rural regions is undoubtedly responsible (Nurmi, Poole, & Kalakoski, 1996). Regardless of where young people live, a chance to talk with adults and older peers who have worked through identity questions can be helpful (Waterman, 1989).

■ **LARGER SOCIETY.**   The larger cultural context and historical time period affect identity development. Among modern adolescents, exploration and commitment take place earlier in the identity domains of gender-role preference and vocational choice than in religious and political values. Yet a generation ago, when the Vietnam War divided Americans and disrupted the lives of thousands of young people, the political beliefs of American youths took shape sooner (Archer, 1989b). Societal forces are also responsible for the special problems that gay and lesbian youths (see Chapter 14) and ethnic minority adolescents face in forming a secure identity, as the Cultural Influences box on the following page describes. The Caregiving Concerns table on page 609 summarizes ways that adults can support identity development in adolescence.

CULTURAL INFLUENCES

IDENTITY DEVELOPMENT AMONG ETHNIC MINORITY ADOLESCENTS

Most Caucasian-American adolescents are aware of their cultural ancestry, but it is not a matter of intense concern for them. Since the values of their home life were consistent with those of mainstream American culture, ethnicity does not prompt intense identity exploration (Phinney, 1993).

But for teenagers who are members of minority groups, ethnicity is central to the quest for identity, and it presents difficult, sometimes overwhelming challenges. As they develop cognitively and become more sensitive to feedback from the social environment, minority youths become painfully aware that they are targets of discrimination and inequality. The discovery complicates their efforts to develop a sense of cultural belonging and a set of personally meaningful life goals. One African-American journalist, looking back on his own adolescence, remarked, "If you were black, you didn't quite measure up . . . . you didn't see any black people doing certain things, and you couldn't rationalize it. I mean, you don't think it out but you say, 'Well, it must mean that white people are better than we are. Smarter, brighter—whatever'" (Monroe, Goldman, & Smith, 1988, pp. 98–99).

Minority youths often feel caught between the standards of the larger society and the traditions of their culture of origin. Some respond by rejecting aspects of their ethnic background. In one study, Asian-American 15- to 17-year-olds were more likely than blacks and Hispanics to hold negative attitudes toward their subcultural group. Perhaps the absence of a social movement stressing ethnic pride of the kind available to black and Hispanic teenagers underlies this finding. (Phinney, 1989). Some parents are overly restrictive of their teenagers out of fear that assimilation into the larger society will undermine their cultural traditions, and their youngsters rebel. One Southeast-Asian refugee described his daughter's behavior, "She complains about going to the Lao temple on the weekend and instead joined a youth group in a neighborhood Christian Church. She refused to wear traditional dress on the Lao New Year. The girl is setting a very bad example for her younger sisters and brothers" (Nidorf, 1985, pp. 422-423).

Other minority teenagers react to years of shattered self-esteem, school failure, and barriers to success in the American mainstream by defining themselves in contrast to majority values. A Mexican-American teenager who had given up on school commented, "Mexicans don't have a chance to go on to college and make something of themselves." Another, responding to the question of what it takes to be a successful adult, pointed to his uncle, leader of a local gang, as an example (Matute-Bianche, 1986, p. 250-251).

Because it is painful and confusing, minority high school students often dodge the task of forming an ethnic-identity. Many are diffused or foreclosed on ethnic identity issues (Markstrom-Adams & Adams, 1995). How can society help them resolve identity conflicts constructively? A variety of efforts are relevant, including

- reducing poverty;

- promoting effective parenting, in which children and adolescents benefit from family ethnic pride yet are encouraged to explore the meaning of ethnicity in their own lives;

- ensuring that schools respect minority youths' native language and unique learning styles; and

- fostering multicultural knowledge, contact, and respect between ethnic groups in integrated schools and neighborhoods (García Coll & Magnuson, 1997).

Minority adolescents who have constructed a **bicultural identity**—by exploring and adopting values from both their subculture and the dominant culture—tend to be achieved in other areas of identity as well. They also have a higher sense of self-esteem, a greater sense of mastery over the environment, and more positive family and peer relations (Phinney, 1993; Phinney & Alipuria, 1990). In sum, ethnic-identity achievement enhances many aspects of emotional and social development.

These Native-American adolescents dress in traditional costume in preparation for demonstrating a ceremonial dance to citizens of a small Wyoming town. When minority youths encounter respect for their cultural heritage in schools and communities, they are more likely to retain ethnic values and customs as an important part of their identities. *(John Eastcott/Yva Momatiuk/The Image Works)*

CAREGIVING CONCERNS

Ways that Adults can Support Healthy Identity Development in Adolescence

STRATEGY	RATIONALE
Warm, open communication	Provides both emotional support and freedom to explore values and goals.
Discussions at home and school that promote high-level thinking	Encourages rational and deliberate selection among competing beliefs and values.
Opportunities to participate in extracurricular activities and vocational training programs	Permits young people to explore the real world of adult work.
Opportunities to talk with adults and peers who have worked through identity questions	Offers models of identity achievement and advice on how to resolve identity concerns.
Opportunities to explore ethnic heritage and learn about other cultures in an atmosphere of respect	Fosters identity achievement in all areas and ethnic tolerance, which supports the identity explorations of others.

BRIEF REVIEW

Erikson's stage of identity versus identity confusion recognizes the formation of a coherent set of values and life plans as the major personality achievement of adolescence. An organized self-concept and more differentiated sense of self-esteem prepare the young person for constructing an identity. For most teenagers, self-worth rises over the adolescent years, and the identity task does not spark a serious emotional crisis. Four identity statuses describe progress toward forming a mature identity. Identity achievement and moratorium are adaptive statuses associated with psychological well-being. Teenagers in a long-term state of identity foreclosure or diffusion tend to have adjustment difficulties. Identity development is fostered by a rational approach to choosing among competing beliefs and values, by parents who provide emotional support and freedom to explore, by schools and communities that are rich in opportunities, and by societies that permit young people from all backgrounds to realize their personal goals.

MORAL DEVELOPMENT

Sabrina sat at the kitchen table reading the Sunday newspaper, her face wide-eyed with interest. "You gotta see this," she said to Louis, who sat munching cereal across from her. Sabrina held up a page of large photos, which showed a 70-year-old woman standing in the center of her home. The floor and furniture were piled with belongings, including stacks of newspapers, cardboard boxes, tin cans, glass containers, food, clothing, and other items. A bare lightbulb with exposed wiring hung from the ceiling. The plaster on the walls was crumbling, the pipes in the house were frozen, and the sinks, toilet, and furnace no longer worked. The headline read: "Loretta Perry: My Life Is None of Their Business."

"Look what they're trying to do to this poor lady," exclaimed Sabrina. "They wanna throw her out of her house and tear it down! Those city inspectors must not care about anyone. Here it says, 'Mrs. Perry has devoted much of her life to helping veterans and doing favors for people.' Why doesn't someone help her?"

ASK YOURSELF . . .

■ At age 13, Jeremy described himself as both "cheerful" and "glum." At age 16, he said, "Sometimes I'm cheerful, at other times I'm glum, so I guess I'm kind of moody." What accounts for this change in Jeremy's self-concept?

■ Return to the opening of this chapter and review the conversation between Louis and Darryl. What identity status best characterizes the two boys? Explain your answer.

■ Jules is an identity-achieved young person, secure in his self-chosen values and future goals. What have you learned about Franca and Antonio's parenting style in previous chapters that helps explain Jules's adaptive approach to identity formation?

bicultural identity
The identity constructed by adolescents who explore and adopt values from both their subculture and the dominant culture.

"Sabrina, you missed the point," Louis responded. "Mrs. Perry is in violation of 30 building code standards. The law says you're supposed to keep your house clean and in good repair."

"But Louis, she's old and she needs help. She says her life will be over if they destroy her home."

"The building inspectors aren't being mean, Sabrina. Mrs. Perry is stubborn. She refuses to obey the law. By not taking care of her house, she's not just a threat to herself. She's a danger to her neighbors, too. Suppose her house caught on fire. You can't live around other people and say your life is nobody's business."

"You don't just knock someone's home down," Sabrina replied angrily. "Where're her friends and neighbors in all this? Why aren't they over there fixing up that house? You're like those building inspectors, Louis. You've got no feeling!"

Louis and Sabrina's disagreement over Mrs. Perry's plight illustrates the tremendous advances in moral understanding during adolescence. Changes in cognition and social experience permit young people to better understand larger social structures—societal institutions and lawmaking systems—that govern moral responsibilities in complex cultures. As their grasp of social arrangements expands, adolescents' ideas about what ought to be done when the needs and desires of people are in conflict also change, toward increasingly just and fair solutions to moral problems (Gibbs, 1991).

PIAGET'S THEORY OF MORAL DEVELOPMENT

The most influential approach to moral development is Lawrence Kohlberg's cognitive-developmental perspective, which was inspired by Piaget's early work on the moral judgment of the child. Piaget (1932/1965) saw children as moving through two broad stages of moral understanding.

The first stage **is heteronomous morality**, which extends from about 5 to 10 years of age. The word *heteronomous* means under the authority of another. As the term suggests, children of this stage view rules as handed down by authorities (God, parents, and teachers), as having a permanent existence, as unchangeable, and as requiring strict obedience. Also, in judging an act's wrongness, they focus on objective consequences rather than intent to do harm. When asked to decide which child is naughtier—John, who accidentally breaks 15 cups while on his way to dinner or Henry, who breaks 1 cup while stealing some jam—a 6- or 7-year-old chooses John.

According to Piaget, around age 10 children make the transition to the stage of **autonomous morality.** They realize that people can have different perspectives on moral matters and that intentions, not just outcomes, should serve as the basis for judging behavior. Piaget believed that improvements in perspective taking, which result from cognitive development and opportunities to interact with peers, are responsible for this change. Autonomous individuals no longer view rules as fixed. Instead, they regard them as socially agreed-on principles that can be revised when there is a need to do so. In creating and changing rules, older children and adolescents use a standard of fairness called *reciprocity.* They express the same concern for the welfare of others as they do for themselves. Most of us are familiar with reciprocity in the form of the Golden Rule: "Do unto others as you would have them do unto you."

Take a moment to consider Piaget's theory in light of what you learned about moral development in earlier chapters (return to pages 382–383 and 494–496). You will see that his account of young children as rigid, external, and focused on physical consequences underestimates their moral capacities. Nevertheless, Piaget's account of morality, like his cognitive theory, does describe the general direction of moral development. Although children are less rigid moral thinkers than Piaget made them out to be, they are not as advanced as adolescents and adults. Over the past two decades, Piaget's groundbreaking work has been replaced by Kohlberg's more comprehensive theory, which regards moral development as extending beyond childhood into adolescence and adulthood in a six-stage sequence.

heteronomous morality
Piaget's first stage of moral development, in which children view moral rules as permanent features of the external world that are handed down by authorities and cannot be changed. Extends from about 5 to 10 years of age.

autonomous morality
Piaget's second stage of moral development, in which children view rules as flexible, socially agreed-on principles that can be revised when there is a need to do so. Begins around age 10.

KOHLBERG'S EXTENSION OF PIAGET'S THEORY

Kohlberg used a clinical interviewing procedure to study the development of moral understanding. He gave children, adolescents, and adults **moral dilemmas**—stories that present a genuine conflict between two moral values. Participants were asked to indicate what the main actor should do and why. The best known of these is the "Heinz dilemma," which presents a choice between the value of obeying the law (not stealing) and the value of human life (saving a dying person):

> In Europe a woman was near death from cancer. There was one drug that the doctors thought might save her. A druggist in the same town had discovered it, but he was charging ten times what the drug cost him to make. The sick woman's husband, Heinz, went to everyone he knew to borrow the money, but he could only get together half of what it cost. The druggist refused to sell it cheaper or let Heinz pay later. So Heinz got desperate and broke into the man's store to steal the drug for his wife. Should Heinz have done that? Why? (paraphrased from Colby et al., 1983, p. 77)

Kohlberg emphasized that it is *the way an individual reasons* about the dilemma, not *the content of the response* (whether to steal or not to steal), that determines moral maturity. Individuals who believe Heinz should take the drug and those who think he should not can be found at each of Kohlberg's first four stages. At the highest two stages, moral reasoning and content come together. Individuals do not just agree on why certain actions are justified; they also agree on what people ought to do when faced with a moral dilemma. Given a choice between obeying the law and preserving individual rights, the most advanced moral thinkers support individual rights (in the Heinz dilemma, stealing the drug to save a life).

As we look at development in Kohlberg's scheme, we will see that moral reasoning and content are at first independent, but eventually they are integrated into a coherent ethical system (Kohlberg, Levine, & Hewer, 1983). Does this remind you of adolescents' effort to formulate a sound, well-organized set of personal values in identity development? According to some theorists, the development of identity and moral understanding are part of the same process (Davidson & Youniss, 1991; Marcia, 1988).

■ KOHLBERG'S STAGES OF MORAL UNDERSTANDING.

Kohlberg organized his six stages into three general levels of moral development. He believed that moral understanding is promoted by the same factors that Piaget thought were important for cognitive growth: (1) actively grappling with moral issues and noticing weaknesses in one's current thinking, and (2) advances in perspective taking, which permit individuals to resolve moral conflicts in more complex and effective ways. As Table 16.2 shows, Kohlberg's moral stages are related to Piaget's cognitive and Selman's perspective-taking stages. As we examine Kohlberg's developmental sequence and illustrate it with responses to the Heinz dilemma, look for changes in perspective taking that each stage assumes.

The Preconventional Level.

At the **preconventional level**, morality is externally controlled. As in Piaget's heteronomous stage, children accept the rules of authority figures and judge actions by their consequences. Behaviors that result in punishment are viewed as bad, and those that lead to rewards are seen as good.

■ **Stage 1: The punishment and obedience orientation.** Children at this stage find it difficult to consider two points of view in a moral dilemma. As a result, they ignore peoples' intentions and, instead, focus on fear of authority and avoidance of punishment as reasons for behaving morally.

Prostealing: "If you let your wife die, you will get in trouble. You'll be blamed for not spending the money to help her and there'll be an investigation of you and the druggist for your wife's death." (Kohlberg, 1969, p. 381)

moral dilemma
A conflict situation presented to individuals who are asked to decide both what the main actor should do and why. Used to assess the development of moral reasoning.

preconventional level
Kohlberg's first level of moral development, in which moral understanding is based on rewards, punishments, and the power of authority figures.

TABLE **16.2**

The Relation Between Kohlberg's Moral, Piaget's Cognitive, and Selman's Perspective-Taking Stages

KOHLBERG'S MORAL STAGE	DESCRIPTION	PIAGET'S COGNITIVE STAGE	SELMAN'S PERSPECTIVE-TAKING STAGE[a]
Punishment and obedience orientation	Fear of authority and avoidance of punishment are reasons for behaving morally.	Preoperational, early concrete operational	Social-informational
Instrumental purpose orientation	Satisfying personal needs determines moral choice.	Concrete operational	Self-reflective
"Good boy–good girl" orientation	Maintaining the affection and approval of friends and relatives motivates good behavior.	Early formal operational	Third-party
Social-order-maintaining orientation	A duty to uphold laws and rules for their own sake justifies moral conformity.	Formal operational	Societal
Social contract orientation	Fair procedures for changing laws to protect individual rights and the needs of the majority are emphasized.		
Universal ethical principle orientation	Abstract universal principles that are valid for all humanity guide moral decision making.		

[a]To review these stages, return to Chapter 13, page 493.

Antistealing: "You shouldn't steal the drug because you'll be caught and sent to jail if you do. If you do get away, your conscience would bother you thinking how the police would catch up with you any minute." (Kohlberg, 1969, p. 381)

- **Stage 2: The instrumental purpose orientation.** Children become aware that people can have different perspectives in a moral dilemma, but this understanding is, at first, very concrete. Individuals view right action as what satisfies their personal needs, and they believe others also act out of self-interest. Reciprocity is understood as equal exchange of favors—"You do this for me and I'll do that for you."

Prostealing: "The druggist can do what he wants and Heinz can do what he wants to do. . . . But if Heinz decides to risk jail to save his wife, it's his life he's risking; he can do what he wants with it. And the same goes for the druggist; it's up to him to decide what he wants to do." (Rest, 1979, p. 26)

Antistealing: "[Heinz] is running more risk than it's worth unless he's so crazy about her he can't live without her. Neither of them will enjoy life if she's an invalid." (Rest, 1979, p. 27)

The Conventional Level. At the **conventional level,** individuals continue to regard conformity to social rules as necessary, but not for reasons of self-interest. They believe that actively maintaining the current social system is important for ensuring positive human relationships and societal order.

- **Stage 3: The "good boy–good girl" orientation, or the morality of interpersonal cooperation.** The desire to obey rules because they promote social harmony first appears in the context of close personal ties. Stage 3 individuals want to maintain the affection and approval of friends and relatives by being a "good person"—trustworthy, loyal, respectful, helpful, and nice. The capacity to view a two-person relationship from the vantage point of an impartial, outside observer supports this new approach to morality. At this stage, the individual understands reciprocity in terms of the Golden Rule.

Prostealing: "No one will think you're bad if you steal the drug, but your family will think you're an inhuman husband if you don't. If you let your wife die, you'll never be able to look anyone in the face again." (Kohlberg, 1969, p. 381)

conventional level
Kohlberg's second level of moral development, in which moral understanding is based on conforming to social rules to ensure positive human relationships and societal order.

Antistealing: "It isn't just the druggist who will think you're a criminal, everyone else will too. After you steal it, you'll feel bad thinking how you've brought dishonor on your family and yourself; you won't be able to face anyone again." (Kohlberg, 1969, p. 381)

■ **Stage 4: The social-order-maintaining orientation.** At this stage, the individual takes into account a larger perspective—that of societal laws. Moral choices no longer depend on close ties to others. Instead, rules must be enforced in the same even-handed fashion for everyone, and each member of society has a personal duty to uphold them. The Stage 4 individual believes that laws cannot be disobeyed under any circumstances because they are vital for ensuring societal order.

Prostealing: "He should steal it. Heinz has a duty to protect his wife's life; it's a vow he took in marriage. But it's wrong to steal, so he would have to take the drug with the idea of paying the druggist for it and accepting the penalty for breaking the law later."

Antistealing: "It's a natural thing for Heinz to want to save his wife, but it's still always wrong to steal. You have to follow the rules regardless of how you feel or regardless of the special circumstances. Even if his wife is dying, it's still his duty as a citizen to obey the law. No one else is allowed to steal, why should he be? If everyone starts breaking the law in a jam, there'd be no civilization, just crime and violence." (Rest, 1979, p. 30)

The Postconventional or Principled Level. Individuals at the **postconventional level** move beyond unquestioning support for the laws and rules of their own society. They define morality in terms of abstract principles and values that apply to all situations and societies.

■ **Stage 5: The social contract orientation.** At Stage 5, individuals regard laws and rules as flexible instruments for furthering human purposes. They can imagine alternatives to their social order, and they emphasize fair procedures for interpreting and changing the law when there is a good reason to do so. When laws are consistent with individual rights and the interests of the majority, each person follows them because of a *social contract orientation*—free and willing participation in the system because it brings about more good for people than if it did not exist.

Prostealing: "Although there is a law against stealing, the law wasn't meant to violate a person's right to life. Taking the drug does violate the law, but Heinz is justified in stealing in this instance. If Heinz is prosecuted for stealing, the law needs to be reinterpreted to take into account situations in which it goes against people's natural right to keep on living."

■ **Stage 6: The universal ethical principle orientation.** At this highest stage, right action is defined by self-chosen ethical principles of conscience that are valid for all humanity, regardless of law and social agreement. These values are abstract, not concrete moral rules like the Ten Commandments. Stage 6 individuals typically mention such principles as equal consideration of the claims of all human beings and respect for the worth and dignity of each person.

Prostealing: "If Heinz does not do everything he can to save his wife, then he is putting some value higher than the value of life. It doesn't make sense to put respect for property above respect for life itself. [People] could live together without private property at all. Respect for human life and personality is absolute and accordingly [people] have a mutual duty to save one another from dying." (Rest, 1979, p. 37)

■ **RESEARCH ON KOHLBERG'S STAGE SEQUENCE.** Is there support for Kohlberg's stage sequence? Longitudinal studies provide the most convincing evidence. With few exceptions, individuals move through the stages in the order that Kohlberg expected (Colby et al., 1983; Walker, 1989; Walker & Taylor, 1991b). A striking finding is that moral development is very slow and gradual. Stages 1 and 2 decrease in early adoles-

postconventional level
Kohlberg's highest level of moral development, in which individuals define morality in terms of abstract principles and values that apply to all situations and societies.

Will the 14-year-old girls on the left decide to accept a peer's offer of a cigarette? How will they justify their decision? Real-life moral dilemmas bring out the motivational and emotional side of moral judgment along with a variety of strategies for resolving conflicts. These teenagers may talk the matter through with each other or call on intuition, since they must make an on-the-spot decision. *(Elizabeth Zuckerman/ PhotoEdit)*

cence, whereas Stage 3 increases through mid-adolescence and then declines. Stage 4 rises over the teenage years until, by early adulthood, it is the typical response. Few people move beyond it to Stage 5. In fact, postconventional morality is so rare that there is no clear evidence that Kohlberg's Stage 6 actually follows Stage 5. The highest stage of moral development is still a matter of speculation.

■ **HYPOTHETICAL VERSUS REAL-LIFE MORAL DILEMMAS.** As you read the Heinz dilemma, you probably came up with your own solution to it. Now try to think of a moral dilemma you recently faced in everyday life. How did you solve it, and what factors influenced your choice? Did your reasoning fall at the same stage as your thinking about Heinz and his dying wife?

Kohlberg's theory has contributed greatly to our understanding of moral development. Yet in focusing on hypothetical dilemmas, it emphasizes rationally weighing alternatives to the neglect of other influences on moral judgment. When researchers had adolescents and adults recall and discuss a real-life moral dilemma, the most frequent strategy advocated for resolving it *was* reasoning it out. But participants also posed other strategies, such as talking through issues with others and relying on intuition that their decision was right. Especially striking was the expression of anguish in working through everyday dilemmas. People mentioned feeling drained, confused, and torn by temptation—a motivational and emotional side of moral judgment not tapped by hypothetical situations (Walker et al., 1995).

Although everyday moral reasoning corresponds to Kohlberg's scheme, it typically falls at a lower stage than do responses to hypothetical dilemmas (Walker & Moran, 1991). Real-life problems seem to elicit reasoning below a person's actual capacity because they bring out the many practical considerations involved in an actual moral conflict. The influence of situational factors on moral reasoning suggests that Kohlberg's account of moral development is best viewed in terms of a loose rather than strict concept of stage. Rather than developing in a neat stepwise fashion, each individual draws on a range of moral responses that vary with context. With age, this range shifts upward as less mature moral reasoning is gradually replaced by more advanced moral thought.

ENVIRONMENTAL INFLUENCES ON MORAL REASONING

Many environmental factors promote moral stage change, including child-rearing practices, schooling, peer interaction, and aspects of culture. Growing evidence suggests that these experiences present young people with cognitive challenges, which stimulate them to think about moral problems in more complex ways.

■ **CHILD-REARING PRACTICES.** In Chapter 10, we saw that in childhood, parents who are warm and consistent and who discuss moral concerns have children who are advanced in moral understanding. The same is true in adolescence. Teenagers who gain most in moral development have parents who encourage moral discussions and who create a supportive atmosphere by listening sensitively, asking clarifying questions, presenting higher-level reasoning, and using praise and humor. In contrast, parents who lecture, use threats, or make sarcastic remarks have youngsters who change little or not at all (Walker & Taylor, 1991a). In sum, the kind of parent who facilitates moral reasoning uses an authoritative approach that is verbal, rational, and affectionate and that promotes a cooperative style of family life.

■ **SCHOOLING.**   Years of schooling completed is one of the most powerful predictors of moral development. Research indicates that moral reasoning advances in late adolescence and young adulthood only as long as a person remains in school (Rest & Narvaez, 1991; Speicher, 1994). Perhaps higher education has a strong impact on moral development because it introduces young people to social issues that extend beyond personal relationships to entire political and cultural groups. Consistent with this idea, college students who report more academic perspective-taking opportunities (for example, classes that emphasize open discussion of opinions) and who indicate that they have become more aware of social diversity tend to be advanced in moral reasoning (Mason & Gibbs, 1993a, 1993b).

■ **PEER INTERACTION.**   Many studies confirm Piaget's belief that interaction among peers, who confront one another with differing viewpoints, promotes moral understanding. But peer interaction must have certain features to be effective. Look back at Sabrina and Louis's argument over the plight of Loretta Perry on pages 609–610. Each teenager directly confronts and criticizes the other's statements, and emotionally intense expressions of disagreement occur. Peer discussions like this lead to much greater stage change than those in which adolescents state their opinions in a disorganized, uninvolved way (Berkowitz & Gibbs, 1983; Haan, Aerts, & Cooper, 1985). Also, note that Sabrina and Louis do not revise their ways of thinking after just one discussion. Because moral development is a gradual process, it takes many peer interaction sessions over weeks or months to produce moral change.

■ **CULTURE.**   Cross-cultural research reveals that individuals in industrialized nations move through Kohlberg's stages more quickly and advance to higher levels than do individuals in simpler societies, who rarely move beyond Stage 3. In tribal and village societies, moral cooperation is based on direct relations between people. Laws and governmental institutions do not exist to regulate it. Yet reasoning at Stages 4 and above depends on an understanding of the role of larger societal structures in resolving moral conflict (Snarey, 1995).

In cultures where young people begin to participate in the institutions of their society at early ages, moral development is advanced. For example, on *kibbutzim*, small but technologically complex agricultural settlements in Israel, children receive training in the governance of their community in middle childhood. By third grade, they mention more concerns about societal laws and rules when discussing moral conflicts than do Israeli city-reared or American children (Fuchs et al., 1986). During adolescence and young adulthood, a greater percentage of kibbutz than American individuals reach Kohlberg's Stages 4 and 5 (Snarey, Reimer, & Kohlberg, 1985).

Young people growing up on Israeli kibbutzim receive training in the governance of their community at an early age. As a result, they understand the role of societal laws in resolving moral conflict and are advanced in moral reasoning. *(Louis Goldman/Photo Researchers)*

Other cultural variations in moral understanding cannot be accounted for by Kohlberg's stages. Recall from Chapter 13 that self-concepts in collectivist cultures (including village societies) are more other-directed than in Western Europe and North America. This very difference seems to characterize moral reasoning as well (Miller, 1994). In these cultures, moral statements that portray the individual as vitally connected to the social group through a deep sense of community responsibility are common. For example, one New Guinea village leader placed the blame for the Heinz dilemma on the entire social group, stating, "If I were the judge, I would give him only light punishment because he asked everybody for help but nobody helped him" (Tietjen & Walker, 1985, p. 990).

Similarly, in some Eastern nations, well-educated adults often think in ways that differ from typical postconventional reasoning. In a study conducted in India, the most morally mature individuals rarely appealed to personal ethical principles in discussing the Heinz dilemma. Instead, they resisted choosing a course of action, explaining that a moral solution should not be the burden of a single individual but of the entire society (Vasudev & Hummel, 1987). These findings raise the question of whether Kohlberg's highest stages represent a culturally specific rather than universal way of thinking—one limited to Western societies that emphasize individual rights and an appeal to an inner, private conscience.

ARE THERE SEX DIFFERENCES IN MORAL REASONING?

The debate over the universality of Kohlberg's stages has been extended to gender. In Sabrina and Louis's moral discussion, Sabrina's argument focuses on caring and commitment to others. Louis's approach is more impersonal. He looks at the dilemma of Loretta Perry in terms of competing rights and justice. Do Sabrina and Louis's moral approaches reflect a sex difference in moral understanding?

Carol Gilligan (1982) is the most well-known figure among those who have argued that Kohlberg's theory does not adequately represent the morality of girls and women. She believes that feminine morality emphasizes an "ethic of care," but Kohlberg's system devalues it. Notice how Sabrina's reasoning falls at Stage 3, which focuses on the importance of mutual trust and affection between people. Louis, who emphasizes the value of obeying the law to ensure societal order, is at Stage 4. According to Gilligan, a concern for others is a *different*, not less valid, basis for moral judgment than a focus on impersonal rights.

Many studies have tested Gilligan's claim that Kohlberg's approach underestimates the moral maturity of females, and most do not support it (Walker, 1991). On hypothetical dilemmas as well as everyday moral problems, adolescent and adult females do not fall behind males in development. To the contrary, in some studies girls are ahead of boys in moral maturity! Also, themes of justice and caring appear in the responses of both sexes, and when girls do raise interpersonal concerns, they are not downscored in Kohlberg's system (Jadack et al., 1995; Kahn, 1992; Walker, 1995). These findings suggest that although Kohlberg emphasized justice rather than caring as the highest of moral ideals, his theory does include both sets of values.

Still, Gilligan's claim that research on moral development has been limited by too much attention to rights and justice (a "masculine" ideal) and too little attention to care and responsiveness (a "feminine" ideal) is a powerful one. Some evidence shows that although the morality of males and females taps both orientations, females do tend to stress care, or empathic perspective taking, whereas males either stress justice or use justice and care equally (Galotti, Kozberg, & Farmer, 1991; Garmon et al., 1996; Wark & Krebs, 1996). The difference in emphasis appears most often on real-life rather than hypothetical dilemmas. Consequently, it may be largely a function of women's greater involvement in daily activities involving care and concern for others.

These findings suggest that like her older brother Louis, Sabrina will one day reason at Stage 4 or higher, but her justifications for moral action will continue to include concern for others. Although current evidence indicates that justice and caring are not gender-specific moralities, Gilligan's work has had the effect of broadening conceptions of the highly moral person. When Gilligan's and Kohlberg's theories are considered together,

> the moral person is seen as one whose moral choices reflect reasoned and deliberate judgments that ensure justice be accorded each person while maintaining a passionate concern for the well-being and care of each individual. Justice and care are then joined . . . in an enlarged and more adequate conception of morality. (Brabeck, 1983, p. 289)

MORAL REASONING AND BEHAVIOR

According to Kohlberg, moral thought and action should come together at the higher levels of moral understanding. Mature moral thinkers realize that behaving in line with their beliefs is an important part of creating and maintaining a just social world (Blasi, 1990; Gibbs, 1995). Consistent with this idea, advanced moral reasoning is related to many aspects of social behavior. Higher-stage adolescents more often engage in prosocial acts, such as helping, sharing, and defending victims of injustice (Gibbs et al., 1986). They are also more honest. For example, they are less likely to cheat in school (Harris, Mussen, & Rutherford, 1976). In contrast, lower-stage adolescents are likely to be less honest and to engage in antisocial behavior (Gregg, Gibbs, & Fuller, 1994).

Yet even though a clear connection between moral thought and action exists, it is only moderate. As we saw in earlier chapters, moral behavior is influenced by a great many factors besides cognition, including self-conscious emotions and a long history of experiences that affect moral choice and decision making. Researchers have yet to discover how all these complex facets of morality work together.

GENDER TYPING

As Sabrina entered adolescence, some aspects of her thinking and behavior became more gender typed. For example, she began to place more emphasis on excelling in the traditionally feminine subjects of language, art, and music than in math and science. And when with peers, Sabrina worried a great deal about how she should walk, talk, eat, dress, laugh, and compete, judged according to accepted social standards for maleness and femaleness.

Research suggests that early adolescence is period of **gender intensification**—increased gender stereotyping of attitudes and behavior (Galambos, Almeida, & Petersen, 1990). Although it occurs in both sexes, gender intensification is stronger for girls. Recall from earlier chapters that girls are less gender typed than boys during childhood, a difference that extends into the teenage years. But early adolescent girls feel less free to experiment with "other-gender" activities and behavior than they did in middle childhood (Huston & Alvarez, 1990).

What accounts for gender intensification? Biological, social, and cognitive factors are involved. Puberty magnifies sex differences in appearance, causing teenagers to spend more time thinking about themselves in gender-linked ways. Pubertal changes also prompt gender-typed pressures from others. Parents—especially those with traditional gender-role beliefs—may encourage "gender-appropriate" activities and behavior to a greater extent than they did in middle childhood (Crouter, Manke, & McHale, 1995). And when adolescents start to date, they often become more gender typed as a way of increasing their attractiveness to other-sex peers (Crockett, 1990). Finally, cognitive changes—in particular, greater concern with what others think—make young teenagers more responsive to gender-role expectations.

Gender intensification seems to decline by middle to late adolescence, but not all young people move beyond it to the same degree. The social environment is a primary force in promoting gender-role flexibility, just as it was at earlier ages. Teenagers who are encouraged to explore non-gender-typed options and to question the value of gender stereotypes for themselves and society are more likely to build an androgynous gender identity, selecting "masculine" and "feminine" traits that suit their personally chosen goals (Eccles, 1987). Overall, androgynous adolescents tend to be psychologically healthier—more self-confident, more willing to speak their own mind, better liked by peers, and identity achieved (Dusek, 1987; Harter, 1998).

Early adolescence is a period of gender intensification. Puberty magnifies gender differences in appearance, causing teenagers to begin thinking about themselves in gender-linked ways. And when adolescents start to date, they often become more gender typed as a way of increasing their attractiveness to the other sex. *(Bob Daemmrich/Stock Boston)*

gender intensification
Increased gender stereotyping of attitudes and behavior. Occurs in early adolescence.

ASK YOURSELF . . .

■ *In our discussion of Kohlberg's theory, why were examples of both prostealing and anti-stealing responses to the Heinz dilemma presented for Stages 1 through 4 but only prostealing responses for Stages 5 and 6?*

■ *Tam grew up in a small village culture, Lydia in a large industrial city. At age 15, Tam reasons at Kohlberg's Stage 2, Lydia at Stage 4. What factors might account for the difference?*

BRIEF REVIEW

According to Piaget, children move from an authority-focused, heteronomous morality to an autonomous morality based on reciprocity by the end of childhood. Lawrence Kohlberg's three-level, six-stage theory was inspired by Piaget's work. From late childhood into adulthood, morality changes from concrete, externally controlled reasoning to more abstract, principled justifications for moral choices. However, Kohlberg's account of moral development fits a loose rather than strict concept of stage. A broad range of experiences fosters moral development, including moral discussions with parents and peers, years of schooling, and contact with larger social structures in complex societies. Although Kohlberg's theory emphasizes a "masculine" morality of justice rather than a "feminine" morality of care, it does not underestimate the moral maturity of females. As moral reasoning advances, it becomes better related to behavior.

Biological, social, and cognitive factors combine to make early adolescence a period of gender intensification. Teenagers who are encouraged to explore non-gender-typed options typically display greater gender-role flexibility by middle to late adolescence.

THE FAMILY

Franca and Antonio remember Louis's freshman year of high school as a difficult time. Because of a demanding project at work, Franca was away from home many evenings and weekends. Antonio took over in her absence, but when business declined at his hardware store, he, too, had less energy to devote to family life. Franca and Antonio began to argue over household responsibilities and expenses and to devote less attention to their children.

That year, Louis and two friends became involved in some unfavorable activities. They used their computer know-how to crack the code of a long-distance telephone service. From the family basement, they made calls around the country. Louis's grades fell, and he often left the house without saying where he was going. Franca and Antonio began to feel uncomfortable about the long hours Louis spent in the basement and their lack of contact with him. Finally, when the telephone company traced the illegally made calls to the family's phone number, Franca and Antonio knew they had cause for concern.

Development at adolescence involves striving for **autonomy** on a much higher plane than during the second year of life, when independence first became a major issue for the child. Teenagers seek to establish themselves as separate, self-governing individuals. This means relying more on oneself and less on parents for direction and guidance. It also means making decisions by carefully weighing one's own judgment and the suggestions of others to arrive at a well-reasoned course of action (Hill & Holmbeck, 1986; Steinberg & Silverberg, 1986). A major way that teenagers seek greater self-directedness is to shift away from family to peers, with whom they explore courses of action that depart from earlier, more secure and stable patterns.

Nevertheless, parent–child relationships remain vital for assisting adolescents in becoming autonomous, responsible individuals. And in line with ecological systems theory, effective family functioning during this period, like others, remains greatly influenced by contextual factors, including the *chronosystem*, or changes in each family member's development (see Chapter 1, page 28), and family stresses and supports.

autonomy
At adolescence, a sense of oneself as a separate, self-governing individual. Involves relying more on oneself and less on parents for direction and guidance and engaging in careful, well-reasoned decision making.

PARENT–CHILD RELATIONSHIPS

Throughout our discussion, we have emphasized that adolescents require freedom to experiment. Yet, as Franca and Antonio's episode with Louis reveals, they also need parental involvement and, at times, protection from situations that are dangerous. Think back to what we said earlier about parent–child relationships that foster academic achievement (Chapter 15), identity formation, and moral maturity. You will find a common thread. Effective parenting of adolescents strikes a *balance between connection and separation.*

Research consistently reveals that parental warmth and acceptance combined with firm (but not overly restrictive) monitoring of teenagers' activities is related to many aspects of competence—in adolescents of diverse SES and ethnic backgrounds and family structures (single-parent, two-parent, and stepparent) (Eccles et al., 1997; Herman et al., 1997; Steinberg et al., 1994). Note that these features make up the authoritative style that was adaptive in childhood as well (Holmbeck, Paikoff, & Brooks-Gunn, 1995). The Caregiving Concerns table below summarizes practices emanating from authoritative parenting that foster adolescent cognitive and social development.

Yet maintaining an authoritative style with adolescents involves special challenges and adjustments. In Chapters 14 and 15, we showed that puberty brings increased parent–child conflict, for both biological and cognitive reasons. Teenagers' improved ability to reason about social relationships adds to family tensions. Perhaps you can recall a time during your own adolescence when you stopped viewing your parents as all-knowing and perfect and saw them as "just people" (Steinberg & Silverberg, 1986). Once teenagers *de-idealize* their parents, they no longer bend as easily to parental authority as they did at earlier ages. One outcome of this shift is that adolescents regard many more matters, such as cleaning their rooms and coming and going from the household, as their own personal business. Parents continue to think of these as important social conventions—as shared concerns that permit family members to live together in harmony (Smetana, 1995a). Disagreements are harder to settle when parents and teenagers approach situations from such different perspectives.

CAREGIVING CONCERNS
Parenting Practices that Foster Adolescent Competence

PARENTING PRACTICE	ADOLESCENT OUTCOMES
Warmth and acceptance	Promotes high self-esteem, identity exploration and achievement, prosocial behavior, more positive parent–adolescent communication.
Supervision and involvement	Promotes high self-esteem and reduced likelihood of engaging in antisocial behavior. Most effective when parents modify their supervision to fit adolescents' increasing competence.
Democratic decision making, verbal give-and-take	Promotes self-esteem and self-reliant, responsible behavior.
Firm control and consistent discipline	When accompanied by explanations and verbal give-and-take, promotes self-reliant, responsible behavior. (Firm control without explanations that lead adolescents to view parents' rules as legitimate can undermine self-reliance and responsibility.)
Information provision and skill modeling	Promotes competencies as diverse as academic achievement and effective negotiation and conflict resolution; protects against high-risk behaviors, such as sex without contraception and substance use.

Source: Holmbeck, Paikoff, & Brooks-Gunn, 1995.

In Chapter 2, we described the family as a *system* that must adapt to changes in its members. But when development is very rapid, the process of adjustment is harder. Adolescents may not be the only family members undergoing a major life transition. Many parents who have reached their forties are changing as well. While teenagers face a boundless future and a wide array of choices, their parents must come to terms with the fact that half their life is over and possibilities are narrowing. In addition, parents of adolescents are often caught in a "middle-generation squeeze"—faced with competing demands of children, aging parents, and employment. As a result, they have a harder time caring for themselves.

The pressures experienced by each generation act in opposition to one another (Holmbeck & Hill, 1991). Parents often can't understand why the adolescent wants to skip family activities to be with peers. And teenagers fail to appreciate that parents want the family to be together as often as possible because an important stage in adult life—parenthood—will soon be over. In addition, parents and adolescents—especially early adolescents—differ sharply on the appropriate time the young person should be granted certain responsibilities and privileges, such as control over clothing, school courses, and going out with friends (Collins et al., 1997). Parents typically say the young person is not yet ready for these signs of independence, whereas teenagers think they should have been granted long ago!

As adolescents move closer to adulthood, the task for parents and children is not one of just separating. They must establish a blend of togetherness and independence—a relationship in which parental control gradually relaxes without breaking the parent–child bond. When teenagers remain attached to parents and continue to listen to their thoughts, feelings, and advice but do so in a context of greater freedom, they display a wide variety of positive outcomes—higher self-esteem, assertiveness, and dating competence; more advanced identity development; and greater ease of separation at the transition to college (Allen et al., 1994; Allen, Moore, & Kuperminc, 1996).

By middle to late adolescence, most parents and children achieve this more mature, mutual relationship. The mild conflict that occurs along the way facilitates the development of adolescent identity and autonomy by helping family members learn to express and tolerate disagreement (Steinberg, 1990). Conflicts also inform parents of adolescents' changing needs and expectations, signaling them that adjustments in the parent–child relationship are necessary. The diminishing time teenagers spend with their family actually has less to do with conflict than with expanding opportunities—being able to drive, having a part-time job, and being allowed to stay out later. After a decline in early adolescence, positive parent-child interaction is on the rise (Larson et al., 1996).

FAMILY CIRCUMSTANCES

As Franca and Antonio's experience with Louis reminds us, difficulties at work as well as other life stresses can interfere with parental happiness; with nurturant, involved child rearing; and (in turn) with children's adjustment at any phase of development (Conger et al., 1993, 1994). However, we must keep in mind that maternal employment or a dual-earner family does not by itself reduce parental time spent with teenagers, nor is it harmful to adolescent development (Richards & Duckett, 1994). To the contrary, parents who are financially secure, invested in their work, and content with their marriages usually have fewer mid-life difficulties and find it easier to grant teenagers appropriate autonomy (Seltzer & Ryff, 1994). When Franca and Antonio's work and financial stresses eased and they realized Louis's need for more support and guidance, his problems subsided.

Less than 10 percent of families with adolescents have seriously troubled relationships—chronic and escalating levels of conflict and repeated arguments over serious issues. Of these, most have difficulties that began in childhood—before the transition to adolescence (Paikoff & Brooks-Gunn, 1991). Table 16.3 summarizes family circumstances considered in earlier chapters that pose challenges for adolescents. Teenagers who develop well despite family stresses continue to benefit from personal and contextual factors that fostered resilience in earlier years: an appealing, easygoing disposition; high self-esteem; a caring parent who combines warmth with high expectations; and (especially if parental supports are lacking) bonds to prosocial adults outside the family who care deeply about the young person's well-being (Masten & Coatsworth, 1998).

SIBLINGS

Like parent–child relationships, sibling interactions adapt to change at adolescence. As younger siblings mature and become more self-sufficient, they are no longer willing to accept as much direction from their older brothers and sisters (Stocker & Dunn, 1990). Consequently, teenage siblings relate to one another on a more equal footing than they did earlier. Furthermore, as teenagers become more involved in friendships and romantic relationships, they invest less time and energy in their siblings. Also, adolescents may not want to interact as much with siblings, who are part of the family from which they are trying to establish autonomy (Furman & Buhrmester, 1992; Stocker & Dunn, 1994). As a result, sibling relationships often become less intense in adoloescence, in both positive and negative feelings.

Despite a drop in companionship, attachment between siblings, like closeness to parents, remains strong for most young people. Quality of sibling relationships is quite stable over time. Brothers and sisters who established a positive bond in early childhood are more likely to display affection and caring during the teenage years (Dunn, Slomkowski, & Beardsall, 1994). In addition, sibling interaction at adolescence continues to be affected by other relationships, both within and outside the family. Teenagers whose parents are warm and supportive have more positive sibling ties (Brody et al., 1992). And for those who have difficulty making friends at school, siblings can provide compensating emotional supports (East & Rook, 1992).

PEER RELATIONS

As adolescents spend less time with family members, peers become increasingly important. Contact among adolescents is common in all cultures, but it is especially high in industrialized societies, where young people spend most of each weekday with agemates in school. Teenagers also spend much out-of-class time together, especially in the United States. American teenagers average 18 nonschool hours a week with peers, compared to 12 hours for Japanese and 9 hours for Taiwanese adolescents (Fuligni & Stevenson, 1995). Higher rates of maternal employment and less demanding academic standards probably account for this difference.

Is the large amount of time American teenagers spend together beneficial or harmful? We will see that adolescent peer relations can be both positive and negative. At their best, peers serve as crucial bridges between the family and adult social roles.

TABLE 16.3

Family Circumstances with Implications for Adolescent Adjustment

FAMILY CIRCUMSTANCE	TO REVIEW, TURN TO . . .
Type of Family	
Adoptive	Chapter 2, page 70; Chapter 12, pages 458–459
Divorced and single-parent	Chapter 13, pages 505–509
Blended	Chapter 13, pages 509–510
Employed mother and dual-earner	Chapter 13, page 511
Gay and lesbian	Chapter 13, pages 510–511
Family conditions	
Child maltreatment	Chapter 10, pages 399–402; Chapter 13, pages 514–518
Economic hardship	Chapter 2, pages 77–78
Teenage childbearing	Chapter 14, pages 547–551

FRIENDSHIPS

When together, best friends Louis and Darryl relaxed, joked, watched TV, listened to tapes, or just talked about themselves, their classmates, and events in the wider world. During these times, the two boys felt they were understood and could fully be themselves. It is not surprising that adolescents report their most favorable moods when in the company of friends (Larson & Richards, 1991).

■ **CHARACTERISTICS OF ADOLESCENT FRIENDSHIPS.** The number of individuals young people call best friends declines from about four to six in early adolescence to one or two in adulthood. At the same time, the nature of the relationship changes. When asked to comment on the meaning of friendship, teenagers stress two characteristics. The first, and most important, is *intimacy.* Adolescents seek psychological closeness, trust, and mutual understanding from their friends—the reason that self-disclosure to friends increases steadily over the adolescent years (see Figure 16.1). Second, more than younger children, teenagers want their friends to be *loyal*—to stick up for them and not to leave them for somebody else (Berndt & Perry, 1990; Buhrmester, 1996).

As frankness and faithfulness increase in friendships, teenagers get to know each other better as personalities. With age, best friends can describe one another's psychological traits with greater accuracy and completeness (Diaz & Berndt, 1982). Cooperation and mutual affirmation between friends also rise at adolescence. This change may reflect greater effort and skill at preserving the relationship as well as increased sensitivity to a friend's needs and desires (Windle, 1994). Teenagers are also less possessive of their friends than they were in childhood. They recognize that friends need a certain degree of autonomy, which they also desire for themselves (Rubin, Bukowski, & Parker, 1998).

With whom do adolescents share their innermost thoughts and feelings? Like school-age friends, adolescent friends are similar in sex, race, ethnicity, SES, personality, peer popularity, and school achievement. They are also alike in educational aspirations, political beliefs, and willingness to try drugs and engage in minor lawbreaking acts. Friendship similarity is partly due to the way the social world of adolescents is organized. Most teenagers live in neighborhoods that are segregated by income, ethnicity, and belief systems. And schools sort them through tracking. Teenagers may also choose companions like themselves to increase the supportiveness of friendship. Once they do so, friends influence each other. Adolescent friends become more alike in attitudes, values, school grades, and social behavior over time (Berndt & Keefe, 1995; Savin-Williams & Berndt, 1990).

During adolescence, intimacy and loyalty become defining features of friendship. Yet girls place a higher value on emotional closeness than do boys. Girls more often get together to "just talk," and they rate their friendships as higher in self-disclosure and emotional support. *(Robert Harbison)*

■ **SEX DIFFERENCES IN FRIENDSHIPS.** Ask several adolescent girls and boys to describe their close friendships. You are likely to find a consistent sex difference. Emotional closeness and trust are more common in girls' talk about friends than in boys' (Buhrmester & Prager, 1995). Whereas girls frequently get together to "just talk," boys more often gather for an activity—usually sports and competitive games that foster control, power, and excitement. When boys talk, their discussions often focus on recognition and mastery issues, such as the accomplishments of sports figures or their own attainments in sports and school (Buhrmester, 1996).

In a study illustrating this difference, 12- to 15-year-olds were telephoned each evening over 5 days and asked to report social experiences of the previous 24 hours. For each interaction lasting 10 minutes or longer, participants judged the extent of self-disclosure and emotional support. Girls reported more frequent interaction

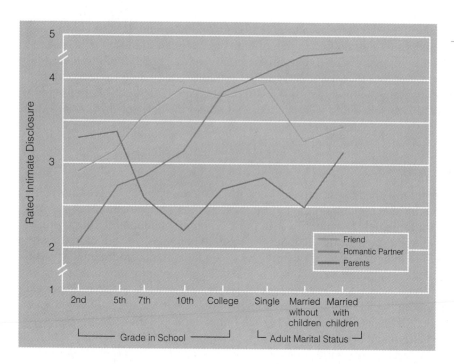

FIGURE **16.1**

Age changes in reported self-disclosure to parents and peers, based on data from several studies. Self-disclosure to friends increases steadily during adolescence, reflecting intimacy as a major basis of friendship. Self-disclosure to romantic partners also rises. However, not until the college years does it surpass intimacy with friends. Self-disclosure to parents declines in early adolescence, a time of mild parent–child conflict. As family relationships readjust to the young person's increasing autonomy, self-disclosure to parents rises. (*From D. Buhrmester, 1996, "Need Fulfillment, Interpersonal Competence, and the Developmental Contexts of Early Adolescent Friendship," in W. M. Bukowski, A. F. Newcomb, & W. W. Hartup, Eds.,* The Company They Keep: Friendship during Childhood and Adolescence, *New York: Cambridge University Press, p. 168. Reprinted by permission.*)

with friends, and they rated their friendship interactions substantially higher on these qualities (Buhrmester & Carbery, 1992).

Because of gender-role expectations, boys and girls seem to enter friendships with different social needs. Then their friendships nurture those needs further—girls toward communal concerns, boys toward achievement and status concerns. This does not mean that boys rarely form close friendship ties. They often do, but the quality of their friendships is more variable. The intimacy of boys' friendships is related to gender identity. Androgynous boys are just as likely as girls to form intimate same-sex ties, whereas boys who identify strongly with the traditional masculine role are less likely to do so (Jones & Dembo, 1989).

■ **BENEFITS OF ADOLESCENT FRIENDSHIPS.**   What benefits do adolescents derive from their friends? Close friendship ties during the teenage years are related to many aspects of psychological health and competence (Buhrmester, 1996). Although teenagers who are well adjusted to begin with are better able to form and sustain close peer ties, friendships further their emotional and social development. The reasons are several:

■ *Close friendships provide opportunities to explore the self and develop a deep understanding of another.* Through open, honest communication, adolescent friends become sensitive to each other's strengths and weaknesses, needs and desires. They get to know themselves and their friend especially well, a process that supports the development of self-concept, perspective taking, identity, and intimate ties beyond the family. Look again at Figure 16.1, and you will see that self-disclosure to friends precedes disclosure to romantic partners. The lengthy, often emotionally laden psychological discussions between adolescent friends appear to prepare the young person for love relationships (Savin-Williams & Berndt, 1990; Sullivan, 1953).

■ *Close friendships help young people deal with the stresses of adolescence.* Because friendship enhances sensitivity to and concern for another, it increases the likelihood of empathy and prosocial behavior. Teenagers with supportive friendships report fewer daily hassles and more "uplifts" than do others (Kanner et al., 1987). As a result, anxiety and loneliness are reduced while self-esteem and sense of well-being are fostered.

■ *Close friendships can improve adolescents' attitudes toward school.* Teenagers with satisfying friendships tend to do well in school. The link between friendship and academic performance depends, of course, on the extent to which each friend values achievement. But overall, close friendship ties promote good school adjustment in both middle- and low-SES students. When teenagers enjoy interacting with friends at school, perhaps they begin to view all aspects of school life more positively (Berndt & Keefe, 1995: Vandell & Hembree, 1994).

CLIQUES AND CROWDS

Friends do not just spend time in pairs. They also gather in *peer groups* (see Chapter 13), which become increasingly common during adolescence. The peer groups of the early teenage years are more tightly structured than those of middle childhood. They are organized around **cliques,** small groups of about five to seven members who are good friends and, therefore, resemble one another in family background, attitudes, and values. In early adolescence, cliques are limited to same-sex members, but by the mid-adolescent years, mixed groups become common. The cliques within a typical high school can be identified by their interests and social status, as the well-known "popular" and "unpopular" groups reveal (Cairns et al., 1995; Gillmore et al., 1997). Cliques develop dress codes, ways of speaking, and behaviors that separate them from one another and from the adult world.

Sometimes several cliques with similar values form a larger, more loosely organized group called a **crowd.** Unlike the more intimate clique, membership in a crowd is based on reputation and stereotype. Whereas the clique serves as the main context for direct interaction, the crowd grants the adolescent an identity within the larger social structure of the school. For example, Louis and Darryl hung out with the debate team, who wore identical sweatshirts to practices, tournaments, and informal weekend gatherings. Other crowds included the "jocks," who were very involved in athletics; the "brains," who worried about their grades; and the "workers," who had part-time jobs and lots of spending money. The "druggies" used drugs on more than a one-time basis, while the "greasers" wore leather jackets, crossed the street to smoke cigarettes, and felt alienated from most aspects of school life (Urberg et al., 1995).

What influences the assortment of teenagers into cliques and crowds? In addition to adolescent personality and interests, family factors seem to be important. In a study of 8,000 ninth to twelfth graders, adolescents who described their parents as authoritative tended to be members of "brain," "jock," and "popular" groups that accepted both the adult and peer reward systems of the school. In contrast, boys with permissive parents valued interpersonal relationships and aligned themselves with the "fun culture" or "partyer" crowd. And teenagers who viewed their parents as uninvolved more often affiliated with the "partyer" and "druggie" crowds, suggesting lack of identification with adult reward systems (Durbin et al., 1993).

These findings indicate that many peer group values are extensions of ones acquired at home. But once adolescents join a clique or crowd, it can modify their beliefs and behaviors. For example, when adolescents associate with peers who have authoritative parents, their friends' competence "rubs off" on them in terms of better academic performance and lower levels of delinquency and substance abuse (Fletcher et al., 1995). However, the positive impact of having academically and socially skilled peers is greatest for teenagers whose own parents are authoritative. And the negative impact of having antisocial, drug-using friends is strongest for teenagers whose parents use less effective child-rearing styles (Mounts & Steinberg, 1995). In sum, family experiences affect the extent to which adolescents become like their peer associates over time.

In early adolescence, as interest in dating increases, boys' and girls' cliques come together. The merger takes place slowly. At junior high school dances and parties, clusters of boys and girls can be seen standing on opposite sides of the room, watching but sel-

clique
A small group of about five to seven members who are either close or good friends.

crowd
A large, loosely organized group consisting of several cliques. Membership is based on reputation and stereotype.

dom interacting. As mixed-sex cliques form and "hang out" together, they provide a supportive context for boys and girls to get to know each other. Cliques offer models for how to interact with the opposite sex and a chance to do so without having to be intimate. In addition, members can check with one another to find out if their attraction to someone is likely to be returned. Gradually, the larger group divides into couples, several of whom spend time together, going to parties and movies. By late adolescence, boys and girls feel comfortable enough about approaching each other directly that the mixed-sex clique is no longer needed and disappears (Padgham & Blyth, 1990).

Crowds also decline in importance. As adolescents formulate their own personal values and goals, they no longer feel a strong need to broadcast, through dress, language, and preferred activities, who they are. Nevertheless, both cliques and crowds serve vital functions. The clique provides a context for acquiring new social skills and for experimenting with values and roles in the absence of adult monitoring. The crowd offers adolescents the security of a temporary identity as they separate from the family and begin to construct a coherent sense of self (Brown, 1990).

These high school international club members form a crowd. Unlike the more intimate clique, the larger, more loosely organized crowd grants adolescents an identity within the larger social structure of the school. *(Will Faller)*

DATING

Although sexual interest is affected by the hormonal changes of puberty (see Chapter 14), the beginning of dating is regulated by social expectations of the peer group (Dornbusch et al., 1981). In one study, early, middle, and late adolescents were asked about their reasons for dating. Younger teenagers were more likely to say that they dated for recreation and to achieve status with agemates. In choosing a partner, they often focused on the person's external characteristics and approval by peers. By late adolescence, these factors were less important. As young people become ready for greater psychological intimacy in a dating relationship, they look for someone who shares their interests, who has clear goals for the future, and who is likely to make a good permanent partner (Roscoe, Diana, & Brooks, 1987).

Adolescent friendships, as mentioned earlier, prepare the young person for romantic relationships. Consequently, it is not surprising that the achievement of intimacy in dating typically lags behind that of friendships. (Buhrmester & Furman, 1987). Perhaps because communication between boys and girls remains stereotyped and shallow through mid-adolescence, early dating does not foster social maturity (Zani, 1993). And whereas early-adolescent boys involved in dating gain in status among their same-sex peers, girls often experience more conflicts due to competition and jealousy from other girls (Miller, 1990). Sticking with group activities, such as parties and dances, before becoming involved with a steady boyfriend or girlfriend is best for young teenagers.

Homosexual youths face special challenges in initiating and maintaining visible romances. Their first dating relationships seem to be short-lived and to involve little emotional commitment for different reasons than those of heterosexuals: They fear peer harassment and rejection (Sears, 1991). Recall from Chapter 14 that because of intense prejudice, homosexual adolescents often retreat into heterosexual dating. In addition, many have difficulty finding a same-sex partner because their homosexual peers have not yet come out—a circumstance that prompts profound feelings of loneliness. Homosexuals with a high proportion of same-sex romances are usually "out" to peers. Yet a deep sense of isolation from the larger peer world frequently means that early dating partners place unreasonable demands on each other—for fulfilling all social needs (Savin-Williams, 1996).

As long as it does not begin too soon, dating provides adolescents with lessons in cooperation, etiquette, and how to deal with people in a wider range of situations. As teenagers form an emotional tie with someone whose needs differ from their own, sensitivity, empathy, and identity development are enhanced (Furman & Wehner, 1994). First romances usually serve as practice for later, more mature bonds. About half of heterosexual romances do not survive high school graduation and entry into college, and those that do become less satisfying (Shaver, Furman, & Buhrmester, 1985). Because young people are still forming their identities, those who like each other at one point in time often find that they do not have much in common later.

PEER PRESSURE AND CONFORMITY

When Franca and Antonio discovered Louis's lawbreaking during his freshman year of high school, they began to worry (as many parents do) about the negative side of adolescent peer networks. Conformity to peer pressure is greater during adolescence than in childhood or young adulthood—a finding that is not surprising, when we consider how much time teenagers spend together. But contrary to popular belief, adolescence is not a period in which young people blindly do what their peers ask. Peer conformity is actually a complex process that varies with the adolescent's age and need for social approval and with the situation.

In one study of nearly 400 junior and senior high school students, adolescents felt greatest pressure to conform to the most obvious aspects of the peer culture—dressing and grooming like everyone else and participating in social activities, such as dating and going to parties and school dances (see Figure 16.2). Peer pressure to engage in proadult behavior, such as getting good grades and cooperating with parents, was also strong. Although pressure toward misconduct rose in early adolescence, compared to other areas it was low. Many teenagers said that their friends actively discouraged antisocial acts. These findings show that peers and parents often act in concert, toward desirable ends! Finally, peer pressures were only modestly related to teenagers' actual values and behaviors. Clearly, these young people did not always follow the dictates of peers (Brown, Lohr, & McClenahan, 1986).

Perhaps because of their greater concern with what their friends think of them, early adolescents are more likely than younger or older individuals to give in to peer pressure (Brown, Clasen, & Eicher, 1986). Yet when parents and peers disagree, even young teenagers do not consistently rebel against the family. Instead, parents and peers differ in their spheres of greatest influence. Parents have more impact on teenagers' basic life values and educational plans (Sebald, 1986). Peers are more influential in short-term, day-to-day matters, such as dress, music, and choice of friends. Adolescents' personal

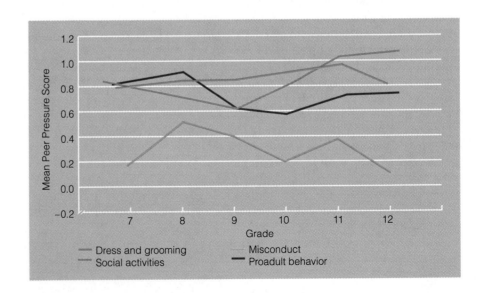

FIGURE 16.2

Grade changes in perceived peer pressure for four areas of behavior in a cross-sectional study of junior and senior high school students. Overall, teenagers felt greatest pressure to conform to dress and grooming styles and social activities. Pressure to engage in proadult behavior was also high. Although peer pressure toward misconduct peaked in early adolescence, it was relatively low. *(From B. B. Brown, M. J. Lohr, & E. L. McClenahan, 1986, "Early Adolescents' Perceptions of Peer Pressure," Journal of Early Adolescence, 6, p. 147. Reprinted by permission.)*

characteristics also make a difference. Young people who feel competent and worthwhile are less likely to fall in line behind peers.

Finally, authoritative parenting is consistently related to resistance to unfavorable peer pressure (Fletcher et al., 1995; Mason et al., 1996). In contrast, adolescents who experience extremes of parental behavior—either too much restrictiveness or too little monitoring—tend to be highly peer oriented. They more often rely on friends for advice about their personal lives and future and are more willing to break their parents' rules, ignore their school work, and hide their talents to be popular with agemates (Fuligni & Eccles, 1993).

BRIEF REVIEW

Within the family, parents who strike a balance between connection and separation through authoritative child rearing assist teenagers in achieving autonomy. Sibling relationships become less intense as adolescents increase their independence from the family and spend more time with peers.

Intimacy and loyalty are central features of friendship during the teenage years. Close friendship ties are related to many aspects of psychological health and competence. Adolescent peer groups are organized around cliques (small groups of good friends) and crowds (large, loosely organized groups based on reputation and stereotype). The clique provides a setting in which adolescents learn social skills and try out new values and roles. The crowd offers a temporary identity as teenagers work on constructing their own. As adolescents become interested in dating, mixed-sex cliques form, which divide into couples. Although dating relationships increase in intimacy with age, they lag behind same-sex friendships.

Peer conformity rises in early adolescence, but teenagers do not mindlessly "follow the crowd." Peers are more influential on dress, music, and social activities, parents on life values and educational plans. Authoritative parenting protects against unfavorable peer pressure.

ASK YOURSELF . . .

- *How does Louis and Darryl's lunchtime conversation at the beginning of this chapter reflect the special characteristics of adolescent friendship?*

- *Phyllis likes her 14-year-old daughter Farrah's friends, but she wonders what Farrah gets out of hanging out at Jake's Pizza Parlor with them on Friday and Saturday evenings. Explain to Phyllis what Farrah is learning.*

- *How might gender intensification contribute to the shallow quality of early adolescent dating relationships?*

PROBLEMS OF DEVELOPMENT

Although most young people move through adolescence without serious difficulty, we have seen in previous chapters that some encounter major disruptions in development, such as premature parenthood, substance abuse, and school failure. Our discussion has also shown that psychological and behavior problems cannot be accounted for by any single factor. Instead, an ecological systems view reveals that healthy as well as problematic development is the combined result of several levels of influence. Biological and psychological change, families, schools, peers, communities, and society act together to produce a particular outcome. This theme is apparent in three additional problems of the teenage years: depression, suicide, and delinquency.

DEPRESSION

Depression—feeling sad, frustrated, and hopeless about life, accompanied by loss of pleasure in most activities and disturbances in sleep, appetite, concentration, and energy—is the most common psychological problem of adolescence. Depression is not absent in the first decade of life; about 1 to 2 percent of children are seriously depressed, 70 to 75 percent of whom continue to display severe depression in adolescence (Kovacs et

Depression in teenagers should not be dismissed as a temporary side effect of puberty. Because adolescent depression can lead to long-term emotional problems, it deserves to be taken seriously. Without treatment, depressed teenagers have a high likelihood of becoming depressed adults. *(Nancy Richmond/The Image Works)*

al., 1994). Yet depressive symptoms increase dramatically around the time of puberty.

This change is understandable, if we stop and think about the many challenges adolescents face and their greater capacity for focusing on themselves. About 20 to 35 percent of American teenagers experience mild to moderate feelings of depression, bouncing back after a short time. Others display a more worrisome picture. About 15 to 20 percent have had one or more major depressive episodes (a rate comparable to that of adults). From 2 to 8 percent are chronically depressed—gloomy and self-critical for many months and sometimes years (Birmaher et al., 1996; Kessler et al., 1994).

Depression prevents young people from mastering important developmental tasks. Without treatment, depressed teenagers have a high likelihood of becoming depressed adults. Adolescent depression is also associated with persistent anxiety, drug abuse, lawbreaking, and auto accidents, and it predicts future problems in school performance, employment, marriage, and child rearing (Harrington, Rutter, & Fombonne, 1996; Kovacs, 1996).

Unfortunately, depressive symptoms tend to be overlooked by parents and teachers alike; 70 to 80 percent of depressed teenagers do not receive any treatment. Because of the popular stereotype of adolescence as a period of storm and stress, many adults interpret depressive reactions as normal and just a passing phase (Strober, McCracken, & Hanna, 1990). Depression is also hard to recognize in teenagers because they manifest it in such a wide variety of ways. Some translate their pessimistic outlook into excessive brooding, worries about their health, and restless, undirected behavior. Others act it out by running away or behaving rebelliously. The first of these patterns is more typical of girls, the second more characteristic of boys (Gjerde, 1995).

■ **FACTORS RELATED TO ADOLESCENT DEPRESSION.** Researchers believe that diverse combinations of biological and environmental factors lead to depression; the precise blend differs from one individual to another (see Table 16.4). As we saw in Chapter 2, kinship studies reveal that heredity plays an important role. Genes can promote depression by affecting the balance of neurotransmitters in the brain, the development of brain regions involved in inhibiting negative emotion, or the body's hormonal response to stress (Cicchetti & Toth, 1998b).

But experience can also activate depression, promoting any of the biological changes just described. Parents of depressed children and adolescents have a high incidence of depression and other psychological disorders. Although a genetic risk may be passed from parent to child, in earlier chapters we saw that depressed or otherwise stressed parents often engage in maladaptive caregiving. As a result, their child's emotional self-regulation, attachment, and self-esteem may be impaired, with serious consequences for many cognitive and social skills (Garber, Braafladt, & Weiss, 1995; Garber et al., 1991). Depressed youths usually display a learned-helpless attributional style (see Chapter 13) in which they view positive outcomes in school performance and peer relations as beyond their control. Their inability to imagine a worthwhile future for themselves seriously disrupts identity development (Chandler, 1994).

By adolescence, myriad events can spark depression in a vulnerable young person. The arrival of puberty can prompt it in early maturing girls, especially if they face school transition at the same time (see Chapter 14). Sometimes depression follows a profound loss, such as parental divorce or the end of a close friendship or dating relationship. At other times, failing at something important sets it off. Because of its association with stressful life events, low-SES places teenagers at higher risk for depressive episodes (Sadler, 1991).

■ **SEX DIFFERENCES.** Although no sex differences in childhood depression exist, by early adolescence severe depression occurs twice as often in girls as in boys—a difference

TABLE 16.4

Factors Related to Adolescent Depression

FACTOR	DESCRIPTION
Heredity	The concordance rate for depression is higher among identical than fraternal twins. Depressed children and adolescents show a stronger resemblance to biological than adoptive relatives; their biological parents have a high incidence of depression and other psychological disorders.
Stress	Depression is higher among teenagers who experience high levels of stress due to low SES. It is also higher among adolescent girls who experience puberty and school transition at the same time.
Sex	In industrialized nations, the rate of depression is twice as high in girls as in boys.
Gender identity	Adolescents with a feminine gender identity are more likely to experience depression than those with a masculine or androgynous identity.
Thoughts about the self	Learned helplessness, the belief that trying hard will not improve negative life conditions, is related to depression. Identity development is often impaired, due to an inability to imagine a worthwhile future.

that is sustained throughout the lifespan. Biological changes associated with puberty cannot account for the gender gap, since it is limited to industrialized nations. In developing countries, rates of depression are similar for males and females, and occasionally higher for males (Culbertson, 1997).

Instead, gender-typed coping styles seem to be responsible. The gender intensification girls experience in early adolescence often strengthens passivity, dependency, and selflessness—maladaptive approaches to the many challenges teenagers encounter in complex cultures (Nolen-Hoeksema & Girgus, 1994). Consistent with this explanation, one study found that adolescents who identified strongly with "feminine" traits were more depressed, regardless of their sex (Hart & Thompson, 1996). And in another study, girls with either an androgynous or masculine gender identity showed a much lower rate of depressive symptoms—one no different from that of masculine-identified boys (Wilson & Cairns, 1988).

Profound depression often leads to suicidal thoughts, which all too often are translated into action. When a teenager tries to take, or succeeds at taking, his or her own life, depression is one of the factors that precedes it.

SUICIDE

Compared to his sister, who was an outstanding student, 17-year-old Brad just couldn't measure up. Brad's parents had been critical of his school performance for years. Now, with adulthood just around the corner, they berated him for being so undirected. "At your age, you oughta know where you're going!" Brad's father shouted one day. "Pick a college or get a trade. But for heaven's sake, stop sitting around."

Throughout high school, Brad had been a loner. Although he excelled in art class, his parents never showed much interest in his drawings, which were piled in a corner of his room. There, Brad spent hours by himself sketching. It bothered Brad's parents that he seemed unhappy and didn't have many friends. But at least he wasn't getting into much trouble like some other kids.

One day, Brad got up enough nerve to ask out a girl. His father, encouraged by Brad's interest in dating, gave him permission to use the family car. But when Brad arrived to pick the girl up, she wasn't home. Several hours later, Brad's parents got a call from the police. He had been picked up for speeding, "driving under the influence," and evading the police. The chase through city streets finally ended when Brad drove off the road into a ditch. Although he wasn't injured, the car was totaled. A terrible argument followed between Brad and his parents.

FIGURE 16.3

Suicide rates over the lifespan in the United States. Although teenagers do not commit suicide as often as adults and the aged, the suicide rate rises sharply from childhood to adolescence. Rates are greater for males than females and for white majority than nonwhite ethnic minority individuals. *(From U.S. Bureau of the Census, 1997.)*

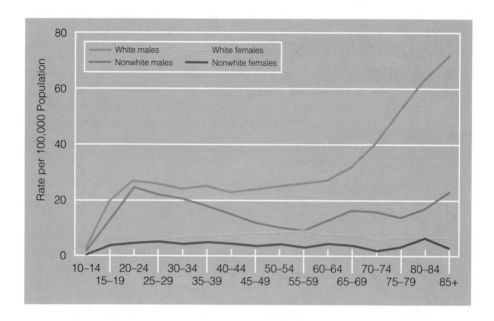

TABLE 16.5

Warning Signs of Suicide

Efforts to put personal affairs in order—smoothing over troubled relationships, giving away treasured possessions

Verbal cues—saying goodbye to family members and friends, making direct or indirect references to suicide ("I won't have to worry about these problems much longer"; "I wish I were dead"; "I wonder what dying is like")

Feelings of sadness, despondency, "not caring" anymore

Extreme fatigue, lack of energy, and boredom

No desire to socialize; withdrawal from friends

Easily frustrated

Emotional outbursts—spells of crying or laughing, bursts of energy

Inability to concentrate, distractible

Decline in grades, absence from school, discipline problems

Neglect of personal appearance

Sleep change—loss of sleep or excessive sleepiness

Appetite change—eating more or less than usual

Physical complaints—stomachaches, backaches, headaches

Source: Capuzzi, 1989.

Over the next 2 days, Brad was somber and withdrawn. Then, after dinner one night, he seemed resolved to make things better. "I've taken care of things, I won't be any more trouble to you," he remarked to his parents. Handing several of his favorite drawings to his sister, he said, "Here, I want you to have these—for keeps, to think of me." Early the next morning, Brad's parents found him hanging from a rope in his room.

■ **FACTORS RELATED TO ADOLESCENT SUICIDE.** The suicide rate increases over the lifespan. As Figure 16.3 shows, it is lowest in childhood and highest in old age, but it jumps sharply at adolescence. Currently, suicide is the third leading cause of death among young people, after motor vehicle collisions and homicides. It is a growing national problem, having tripled over the past 30 years, perhaps because modern teenagers face more stresses and have fewer supports than they did in past decades (U.S. Department of Health and Human Services, 1997).

Striking sex differences in suicidal behavior exist. The number of boys who kill themselves exceeds the number of girls by 4 or 5 to 1. This may seem surprising, since girls show a higher rate of depression. Yet the findings are not inconsistent. Girls make more unsuccessful suicide attempts and use methods with a greater likelihood of revival, such as a sleeping pill overdose. In contrast, boys tend to select more active techniques that lead to instant death, such as firearms or hanging. Once again, gender-role expectations may be responsible. There is less tolerance for feelings of helplessness and failed efforts in males than females (Garland & Zigler, 1993).

Compared to the white majority, nonwhite ethnic minority teenagers (including African Americans, Hispanics, and Native Americans) have slightly lower suicide rates—a difference that increases in adulthood. Higher levels of support through extended families may be responsible.

Suicide tends to occur in two types of young people. In the first group are adolescents much like Brad—highly intelligent but solitary, withdrawn, and unable to meet their own standards or those of important people in their lives. A second, larger group shows antisocial tendencies. These young people express their despondency through bullying, fighting, stealing, and increased risk taking and drug use (Lehnert, Overholser, & Spirito, 1994). Besides turning their anger and disappointment inward, they are hostile and destructive toward others. The fragile self-esteem of these teenagers quickly disintegrates in the face of stressful life events. Common circumstances just before a suicide include the breakup of an important peer relationship or the humiliation of having been caught engaging in irresponsible, antisocial acts (King, 1997).

Why is suicide rare in childhood but on the rise in adolescence? Teenagers' improved ability to plan ahead seems to be involved. Few successful suicides are sudden and impulsive. Instead, young people at risk usually take purposeful steps toward killing themselves. Warning signs, some of which are intended as calls for help, are listed in Table 16.5. Other cognitive changes also contribute to the age-related increase in suicide. Belief in the personal fable leads many depressed young people to conclude that no one could possibly understand the intense pain they feel. As a result, their despair, hopelessness, and isolation deepen. Loss of identity in depressed teenagers, accompanied by absence of a sense of personal continuity, can spark suicide attempts as well.

■ **PREVENTION AND TREATMENT.**   Picking up on the signals that a troubled teenager sends is a crucial first step in preventing suicide. Parents and teachers need to be trained in warning signs. Schools can help by providing sympathetic counselors, peer support groups, and information about telephone hot lines. Once a teenager takes steps toward suicide, staying with the young person, listening, and expressing sympathy and concern until professional help can be obtained is essential. The Caregiving Concerns table below suggests specific ways to respond to a young person who might be suicidal.

Intervention with depressed and suicidal adolescents takes many forms, from antidepressant medication to individual, family, and group therapy. Sometimes hospitalization is necessary to ensure the teenager's safety and swift entry into treatment. Until the adolescent improves, parents are usually advised to remove weapons, knives, razors, scissors, and drugs from the home. On a broader scale, gun control legislation that limits adolescents' access to the most frequent and deadly suicide method would greatly reduce both the number of suicides and the high teenage homicide rate (Clark & Mokros, 1993).

CAREGIVING CONCERNS

Ways to Respond to a Young Person Who Might be Suicidal

STRATEGY	DESCRIPTION
Be psychologically and physically available.	Grant the young person your full attention; indicate when and where you can be located, and emphasize that you are always willing to talk.
Communicate a caring, capable attitude.	Such statements as "I'm concerned. I care about you" encourage the adolescent to discuss feelings of despair. Conveying a capable attitude helps redirect the young person's world of confusion toward psychological order.
Assess the immediacy of risk.	Gently inquire into the young person's motives with such questions as "Do you want to harm yourself? Do you want to die or kill yourself?" If the answer is yes, ask about the adolescent's plan. If it is specific (involves a method and a time), the risk of suicide is very high.
Empathize with the young person's feelings.	Empathy, through such statements as "I understand your confusion and pain," increases your persuasive power and defuses the adolescent's negative emotion.
Oppose the suicidal intent.	Communicate sensitively but firmly that suicide is not an acceptable solution and that you want to help the adolescent explore other options.
Offer a plan for help.	Offer to assist the young person in finding professional help and in telling others, such as parents and school officials, who need to know about the problem.
Obtain a commitment.	Ask the adolescent to agree to the plan. If he or she refuses, negotiate a promise to contact you or another supportive person if and when suicidal thoughts return.

Source: Kirk, 1993.

BIOLOGY & ENVIRONMENT

TWO ROUTES TO ADOLESCENT DELINQUENCY

Persistent adolescent delinquency follows two paths of development, one with an onset of conduct problems in childhood, the second with an onset in adolescence. Longitudinal research reveals that the early-onset type is far more likely to lead to a life-course pattern of aggression and criminality. The late-onset type usually does not persist beyond the transition to young adulthood (Loeber & Stouthamer-Loeber, 1998; Patterson, 1993).

Childhood-onset and adolescent-onset youths look very similar during the teenage years. They both show comparable levels of serious offenses, involvement with deviant peers, substance abuse, unsafe sex, dangerous driving, and time spent in correctional facilities. Why does antisocial activity more often persist and escalate into violence in the first group than in the second? Longitudinal research extending from childhood into early adulthood sheds light on this question. So far, investigators have focused only on boys because of their greater involvement in delinquent activity.

■ **EARLY-ONSET TYPE.** A difficult temperament distinguishes these boys; they are emotionally negative, restless, and willful as early as age 3. In addition, they show subtle deficits in cognitive functioning that seem to contribute to disruptions in the development of language, memory, and self-regulation (Moffitt et al., 1994, 1996). Some have attention-deficit hyperactivity disorder (ADHD), which compounds their learning and self-control problems (see Chapter 12, page 446) (Moffitt, 1990; White et al., 1996).

Yet these biological risks are not sufficient to sustain antisocial behavior, since about half of early-onset boys do not display serious delinquency followed by adult criminality. Among those who follow the life-course path, inept parenting transforms their undercontrolled style into hostility and defiance. As they fail academically and are rejected by peers, they befriend other deviant youths, who provide the attitudes and motivations for violent behavior (see Figure 16.4) (Simons et al., 1994). Compared to their adolescent-onset counterparts, early-onset teenagers feel distant from their families and leave school early (Moffitt et al., 1996). Their limited cognitive and social skills result in high rates of unemployment, contributing further to their antisocial involvements.

■ **LATE-ONSET TYPE.** A larger number of youths begin to display antisocial behavior around the time of puberty, gradually increasing their involvement. Their conduct problems arise from the peer context of early adolescence, not from biological deficits and a history of unfavorable development (Moffitt, Lynam, & Silva, 1994). For some, quality of parenting may decline for a time, perhaps due to family stresses or the challenges of disciplining an unruly teenager. When age brings gratifying adult privileges, they draw on prosocial skills mastered before adolescence

---

After a suicide, family and peer survivors need support to assist them in coping with grief, anger, and guilt over not having been able to help the victim. Teenage suicides often take place in clusters. When one occurs, it increases the likelihood of others among peers who knew the young person or heard about the death through the media (Lewinsohn, Rohde, & Seeley, 1994). In view of this trend, adults should keep an especially watchful eye on vulnerable adolescents after a suicide happens. Restraint by journalists in reporting teenage suicides on television or in newspapers can also aid in prevention (Diekstra, Kienhorst, & de Wilde, 1995).

DELINQUENCY

Juvenile delinquents are children or adolescents who engage in illegal acts. Young people under the age of 21 account for a large proportion of police arrests in the United States—about 30 percent (U.S. Department of Justice, 1997). Yet when teenagers are asked directly, and confidentially, about lawbreaking, almost all admit that they are guilty of an offense of one sort or another (Farrington, 1987). Most of the time, they do not commit major crimes. Instead, they engage in petty stealing, disorderly conduct, and acts that are illegal only for minors, such as underage drinking, violating curfews, and running away from home.

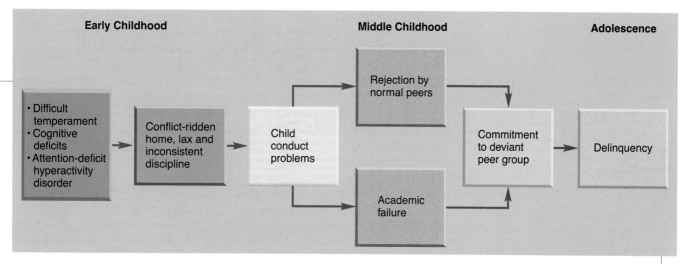

FIGURE 16.4

Developmental path to chronic delinquency for adolescents with childhood-onset antisocial behavior. Difficult temperament and deficits in cognitive functioning characterize many of these youths in early childhood; some have attention-deficit hyperactivity disorder. But these risks are not sufficient to sustain antisocial behavior. Instead, inept parenting transforms biologically based self-control difficulties into hostility and defiance. *(Adapted from Patterson, DeBaryshe, & Ramsey, 1989.)*

and give up their antisocial ways (Moffitt et al., 1996).

A few late-onset youths, however, continue to engage in antisocial acts. The seriousness of their adolescent offenses seems to act as a "snare," trapping them in situations that rule out opportunities for responsible behavior. In one study, finding a steady, well-paying job and entering a happy marriage led to a large reduction in repeat offending. One former delinquent commented, "I worked steadily to support [my family] and take care of my responsibilities. I never had any time to get into trouble." In contrast, the more time antisocial young people spent in prison, the more likely they were to sustain a life of crime (Sampson & Laub, 1993).

These findings suggest a need for a fresh look at policies aimed at stopping youth crime. Keeping adolescent and young adult offenders locked up for many years disrupts their vocational and marital lives during a crucial period of development, committing them to a future that is bleak.

Both police arrests and self-reports show that delinquency rises over the early teenage years, remains high during middle adolescence, and then declines into young adulthood. What is responsible for this trend? Recall that the desire for peer approval increases antisocial behavior among young teenagers. Over time, peers become less influential, moral reasoning matures, and young people enter social contexts (such as marriage, work, and career) that are less conducive to lawbreaking.

For most adolescents, a brush with the law does not forecast long-term antisocial behavior. But repeated arrests are cause for concern. Teenagers are responsible for 27 percent of violent crimes (homicide, rape, robbery, and assault) and 42 percent of property crimes (burglary and theft) (U.S. Department of Justice, 1997). A small percentage commit most of them, developing into recurrent offenders. Some enter a life of crime. As the Biology and Environment box above reveals, childhood- onset conduct problems are far more likely to persist than are conduct problems that emerge during the teenage years.

■ **FACTORS RELATED TO DELINQUENCY.** Many factors are related to chronic delinquency. Depending on the estimate, about three to eight times as many boys as girls commit major crimes. Although SES and ethnicity are strong predictors of arrests, they are only mildly related to teenagers' self-reports of antisocial acts. The difference is due to biases in the juvenile justice system—in particular, the tendency to arrest, charge, and punish low-SES, ethnic minority youths more often than their higher-SES white and Asian counterparts (Elliott, 1994).

Difficult temperament, low intelligence, poor school performance, peer rejection in childhood, and association with antisocial peers are also linked to delinquency. How do these factors fit together? Think back to what you learned about the development of cognitive and social competence in earlier chapters. One of the most consistent findings about delinquent youths is that their family environments are low in warmth, high in conflict, and characterized by lax and inconsistent discipline (Feldman & Weinberger, 1994; Miller et al., 1993).

Return for a moment to our discussion of the development of aggression on page 384 in Chapter 10. It explains how ineffective parenting can promote and sustain hostile responding in all family members. Boys are more likely than girls to be targets of angry, inconsistent discipline because they are more active and impulsive and therefore harder to control. When children extreme in these characteristics are exposed to inept parenting, aggression rises during childhood, is transformed into criminality by adolescence, and persists into adulthood (refer again to the Biology and Environment box on the previous page).

Factors beyond the family and peer group also contribute to delinquency. Students enrolled in schools that fail to meet their developmental needs—those with large classes, poor-quality instruction, and rigid rules—show higher rates of lawbreaking, even after other influences are controlled (Hawkins & Lam, 1987). And in poverty-stricken neighborhoods with fragmented community ties and adult criminal subcultures, teenagers have few constructive alternatives to antisocial behavior (Staub, 1996). Youth gangs often originate in these environments (see the Social Issues box on the following page).

■ **PREVENTION AND TREATMENT.** Because delinquency often has roots in childhood and results from events in several contexts, prevention must start early and take place at multiple levels. Helping parents to use authoritative parenting, schools to teach children more effectively, and communities to provide the economic and social conditions necessary for healthy development would go a long way toward reducing adolescent criminality.

Treating serious offenders also requires an approach that recognizes the multiple determinants of delinquency. When interventions address only one aspect, they are generally ineffective. So far as possible, adolescents are best kept in their own homes and communities to increase the possibility that treatment changes will transfer to their daily lives. Many treatment models exist, including halfway houses, day treatment centers, special classrooms, work experience programs, and summer camps. Delinquents who engage in serious, violent crimes usually must be removed from the community and placed in a correctional facility. Regardless of where treatment takes place, approaches that work best are lengthy and intensive and use problem-focused methods that teach cognitive and social skills needed to overcome family, peer, and school difficulties (Guerra, Tolan, & Hammond, 1994).

In one program, called EQUIP, *positive peer culture*—an adult-guided but youth-conducted small-group approach designed to create a climate in which prosocial acts replace antisocial behavior—served as the basis for treatment. It was supplemented with social skills training, anger management training, training to correct cognitive distortions (such as misperceiving others' intent as hostile and blaming the victim), and moral discussions to promote "catch-up" to age-appropriate moral reasoning (Gibbs, Potter, & Goldstein, 1995). In a recent evaluation, delinquents in a medium-security correctional facility who participated in EQUIP displayed improved social skills and conduct within the institution relative to controls who received motivational messages or no treatment. One year after

SOCIAL ISSUES

YOUTH GANGS

National surveys report a steady increase in youth gangs in the United States over the past two decades. Serious gang problems exist in the 115 largest American cities, where an estimated 8,600 gangs with more than 375,000 members commit nearly 450,000 crimes annually (Curry, Ball, & Decker, 1996). Although most gangs operate in inner-city areas, a growing number are springing up in places where once there was little or no trouble—in working-class neighborhoods, well-to-do suburbs, medium-size cities, and even small towns. Consequently, the figures just given underestimate that national gang problem. Most members are males, ranging in age from preteen to the mid-twenties. Girls are usually attracted to gangs through their friendships with boys. However, the number of independent female gangs is on the rise (Fagan, 1996). Adolescents in the same gang are generally alike in ethnic and low-income background.

Why have gangs increased in number? Experts offer two explanations. First, the gang problem, although spreading, is concentrated in poverty-stricken areas. Today, there are many more poor urban youths who face a life of hopelessness. Second, young

people with stressful home lives are particularly likely to join gangs. Gang members want what all adolescents desire—friendship, pride, identity, self-esteem, excitement, and access to resources. Their disorganized homes and communities offer few avenues for attaining these goals in other ways (Goldstein & Soriano, 1994).

Besides being more widespread, gangs are far more violent than they used to be. Their illegal activities include everything from vandalism and muggings to auto theft, armed robbery, drug trafficking, and murder. They are responsible for the majority of weapon-related crimes in schools (Huff, 1996). What explains this increased criminality? Many of today's gangs are led by young adults who did not leave the group for employment in late adolescence. Some could not find jobs; others chose to remain with the gang instead of risking a return to their former unhappy life. Instead, they became hardened criminals (Covey, Menard, & Franzese, 1997). Often gang violence seems undirected, aimed at anyone and anything. It appears to stem from intense anger, sparked by personal problems or unrelenting poverty. In addition, many gang members believe that the only way to avoid being victims themselves is to commit acts of brutality that dis-

play their power and "guts" (Decker & Lauritsen, 1996). When used against other gangs, these hostilities become part of a vicious cycle.

How can gang activity be reduced and controlled? Redirecting the energies of members and potential members is crucial. New educational, employment, and leisure-time opportunities need to be created in fragmented neighborhoods that breed gang violence. Until these are in place, caring and committed streetworkers can provide counseling for troubled youths and discourage young people from joining. Social agencies can help parents of difficult youths understand teenagers' needs and teach them how to monitor and set limits on their children's activities (Goldstein & Huff, 1993).

Curbing the gang problem is especially challenging. Members have established strong emotional bonds and are accustomed to an exciting life in which illegal activities pay off more quickly and at a higher rate than going to school or engaging in routine, regular work. Gangs are not so much *the* problem as a symptom of a more pervasive problem—the failure of society to provide poverty-stricken and troubled youths with supportive contexts for development (Huff, 1996).

Youth gangs are a growing problem in the United States. These teenagers probably joined a gang to escape from stressful homelives and a future that looks bleak. In the gang, they satisfy their desire for recognition and belonging. *(Robert Harbison)*

their release, EQUIP youths were far less likely to have committed another crime (Leeman, Gibbs, & Fuller, 1993).

Yet even multidimensional treatments can fall short if adolescents remain embedded in hostile home lives, antisocial peer groups, and violent neighborhood settings. Intensive efforts to create nonaggressive environments—at the family, community, and cultural levels—are needed to support interventions for delinquent youths and to foster healthy development for all young people.

AT THE THRESHOLD

Because some of the most complex and rapid changes of development take place during adolescence, teenagers are vulnerable to certain problems, but most do not show serious depression, suicidal tendencies, or persistent antisocial behavior. As we look back on the demands and expectations, the dangers and temptations of the adolescent period, the strength and vitality of young people are all the more remarkable.

We have seen that teenagers in industrialized nations confront challenges that are far more numerous and complex than those of adolescents in other cultures and at previous times during history. On a daily basis, young people must decide how vigorously to apply themselves in school, what kinds of friends to make, and whether to adopt risky behaviors, such as premarital sex and drug experimentation. These short-term choices can have a major impact on long-term options—length and type of formal education, vocational direction, and values and moral ideals. Yet as influential as the teenage years are, they occur within the context of an overall life course. Children enter adolescence having been shaped by heredity and a multitude of prior experiences. The paths adolescents choose and the contexts that affect their choices, in turn, shape many aspects of their future lives.

Society has good reason to treasure its youth as a rich national resource. Adolescents' ability to think seriously and deeply about possibilities, to commit themselves to idealistic causes, to be loyal to one another, and to experiment and take risks, while sometimes hazardous to themselves, energizes progress. Each new generation arrives at the threshold of adulthood with the capacity to benefit from the past while charting new, more fruitful directions. As individuals, as communities, and as a nation, we can do much to enhance adolescence as a final period of preparation for adulthood and a gateway to a better life for all. As we invest in the next generation, we invest in ourselves and the future of humankind. To our youth will be entrusted the task of taking care of us and our world.

ASK YOURSELF . . .

■ *Return to Chapter 14 and reread the sections on teenage pregnancy and substance abuse. What factors do these problems have in common with adolescent suicide and delinquency? How would you explain the finding that teenagers who experience one of these difficulties are likely to display others?*

■ *Throughout his school years, Mac had difficulty learning, was disobedient, and picked fights with peers. At age 16, he was arrested for burglary. Zeke had been a well-behaved child in elementary school, but around age 13 he started spending time with the "wrong crowd." At age 16, he was arrested for property damage. Which boy is more likely to become a long-term offender, and why?*

ummary

ERIKSON'S THEORY: IDENTITY VERSUS IDENTITY CONFUSION

According to Erikson, what is the major personality achievement of adolescence?

■ Erikson's theory emphasizes **identity** as the major personality achievement of adolescence. Young people who successfully resolve the psychological conflict of **identity versus identity confusion** construct a solid self-definition consisting of self-chosen values and goals.

SELF-DEVELOPMENT

Describe changes in self-concept and self-esteem during adolescence.

■ Changes in self-concept and self-esteem set the stage for identity formation. Adolescents' capacity for abstract thinking leads their self-descriptions to become more organized and consistent, and personal and moral values appear as key themes. New dimensions of self-esteem are also added.

■ For most adolescents, self-esteem rises, although it continues to be profoundly affected by feedback from others. Parental warmth, approval, and appropriate expectations and schools and neighborhoods where the young person's SES or ethnic group is well represented support self-esteem.

Describe the four identity statuses, along with factors that promote identity development.

■ In complex societies, a period of exploration is necessary to form a personally meaningful identity. **Identity achievement** and **moratorium** are psychologically healthy identity statuses. Long-term **identity foreclosure** (commitment without exploration) and **identity diffusion** (absence of clear direction) are related to adjustment difficulties.

■ Adolescents who have a flexible, open-minded approach to grappling with competing beliefs and values and who feel attached to parents but free to disagree are likely to be advanced in identity development. Schools and communities that provide young people of all backgrounds with rich and varied options for exploration support the search for identity. Ethnic minority youths who construct a **bicultural identity** are advantaged in many aspects of emotional and social development.

MORAL DEVELOPMENT

Describe Piaget's theory of moral development, and evaluate its accuracy.

■ Piaget identified two broad stages of moral understanding: (1) **heteronomous morality,** in which moral rules are viewed as fixed dictates of authority figures; and (2) **autonomous morality,** in which rules are seen as flexible, socially agreed-on principles that can be changed when there is a need to do so. Although Piaget's theory describes the general direction of moral development, it underestimates young children's moral capacities.

Describe Kohlberg's extension of Piaget's theory, and evaluate its accuracy.

■ According to Kohlberg, moral development is a gradual process that extends beyond childhood into adolescence and adulthood. By examining responses to **moral dilemmas,** Kohlberg found that moral reasoning advances through three levels, each of which contains two stages: (1) the **preconventional level,** in which morality is viewed as controlled by rewards, punishments, and the power of authority figures; (2) the **conventional level,** in which conformity to laws and rules is regarded as necessary to preserve positive human relationships and societal order; and (3) the **postconventional level,** in which individuals define morality in terms of abstract, universal principles of justice.

■ In focusing on hypothetical moral dilemmas, Kohlberg's theory overlooks other strategies, besides rationally weighing alternatives, that affect moral judgment. Because situational factors affect moral reasoning, Kohlberg's moral stages are best viewed in terms of a loose rather than strict concept of stage.

What environmental factors affect moral reasoning?

■ Many experiences contribute to moral maturity, including warm, rational child-rearing practices, years of schooling, and peer discussion of moral issues. Young people in industrialized nations advance to higher levels of moral understanding than do those in simpler societies.

■ Kohlberg's theory does not fully capture moral understanding in collectivist cultures. This finding raises the question of whether his highest stages represent a culturally specific rather than universal way of thinking.

Evaluate claims that Kohlberg's theory does not adequately represent the morality of females, and describe the relationship of moral reasoning to behavior.

■ Although Kohlberg's theory does not underestimate the moral maturity of females, it emphasizes justice rather than caring as a moral ideal. As individuals advance to higher stages, moral reasoning and behavior come closer together.

GENDER TYPING IN ADOLESCENCE

Why is early adolescence a period of gender intensification?

■ **Gender intensification** occurs in early adolescence for several reasons. Physical and cognitive changes prompt young teenagers to view themselves in gender-linked ways, and gender-typed pressures from parents and peers increase. Teenagers who eventually build an androgynous

*S*ummary (continued)

gender identity show better psychological adjustment.

THE FAMILY

Discuss changes in parent–child relationships during adolescence.

- Effective parenting of adolescents strikes a balance between connection and separation. Adapting family interaction to meet adolescents' need for **autonomy** is especially challenging. As teenagers de-idealize their parents, they often question parental authority. Furthermore, parents of adolescents are often caught in a "middle-generation squeeze" and are undergoing major life transitions themselves. As a result, each generation approaches situations from very different perspectives.

- Family circumstances continue to influence parent–child relationships during adolescence. Parents who are financially secure, invested in their work, and content with their marriages usually find it easier to grant teenagers support, guidance, and appropriate autonomy. When parents and adolescents have seriously troubled relationships, the difficulties usually began in childhood.

How do sibling relationships change during adolescence?

- Sibling relationships become less intense as adolescents separate from the family and turn toward peers. Still, attachment to siblings remains strong for most young people.

PEER RELATIONS

Describe adolescent friendships and their consequences for development.

- Teenagers in industrialized nations spend many hours in the company of agemates. The nature of friendship changes, toward greater intimacy and loyalty. Girls' friendships place greater emphasis on intimate

sharing, boys' on joint activities that foster control, power, and excitement.

- Close friendship ties promote self-concept, perspective taking, identity, and the capacity for romantic involvements. They also help young people deal with the stresses of adolescence and can foster improved academic performance.

Describe peer groups and dating relationships in adolescence.

- Adolescent peer groups are organized around **cliques,** small groups of friends with common interests, dress styles, and behavior. Sometimes several cliques form a larger, more loosely organized group called a **crowd** that grants the adolescent an identity within the larger social structure of the school. Parenting practices affect teenagers' choice of peer groups and the impact of group membership on their beliefs and behavior.

- Mixed-sex cliques provide a supportive context for boys and girls to acquire social skills and get to know one another. Intimacy in dating relationships lags behind that of same-sex friendships. Because of intense prejudice, initiating and maintaining visible romances is especially challenging for homosexual youths. First romances serve as practice for later, more mature bonds. They generally dissolve or become less satisfying after graduation from high school.

Discuss conformity to peer pressure in adolescence.

- Peer conformity is greater during adolescence than at younger or older ages. Young teenagers are more likely than older teenagers to give in to peer pressure for antisocial behavior. At the same time, most peer pressures are not in conflict with important adult values. Peers have the greatest influence on short-term, day-to-day matters. Adults have more impact on long-term values and educational plans. Authoritative parenting is related to resistance to unfavorable peer pressure.

PROBLEMS OF DEVELOPMENT

What factors are related to adolescent depression and suicide?

- Depression is the most common psychological problem of the teenage years. Adolescents who are severely depressed are likely to remain so as adults. Diverse combinations of biological and environmental factors lead to depression. Heredity contributes to depression, but maladaptive parenting and stressful life events of the teenage years may trigger it. Severe depression occurs twice as often in teenage girls as boys—a difference believed to be due to girls' greater passivity, dependency, and selflessness.

- Profound depression often leads to suicidal thoughts. The suicide rate increases dramatically at adolescence. Boys account for most suicides because their efforts usually succeed. Girls make more unsuccessful attempts. Teenagers at risk for suicide are sometimes solitary and withdrawn; more often, they are antisocial youths who react intensely to loss, failure, or humiliation.

Discuss factors related to delinquency.

- Almost all teenagers become involved in some delinquent activity, but only a few are serious repeat offenders. Childhood-onset conduct problems are linked to difficult temperament, cognitive deficits, and inept parenting—a pattern likely to result in persistent delinquency and criminality. Adolescent-onset antisocial behavior typically arises from peer pressures of the teenage years. It usually subsides by young adulthood.

- Factors beyond the family and peer group contribute to delinquency. Schools that fail to meet adolescents' developmental needs and poverty-stricken neighborhoods with high crime rates and few constructive alternatives to antisocial activity promote adolescent lawbreaking.

Important terms and concepts

autonomous morality (p. 610)
autonomy (p. 618)
bicultural identity (p. 609)
clique (p. 624)
conventional level (p. 612)
crowd (p. 624)
gender intensification (p. 617)

heteronomous morality (p. 610)
identity (p. 602)
identity achievement (p. 605)
identity diffusion (p. 605)
identity foreclosure (p. 605)
identity versus identity confusion
(p. 602)

moratorium (p. 605)
moral dilemma (p. 611)
preconventional level (p. 611)
postconventional level (p. 613)

Fyi... FOR FURTHER INFORMATION AND HELP

SUICIDE

Youth Suicide Prevention
(617) 738-0700

A volunteer network of parents and professionals that works to increase public awareness of youth suicide, publicize warning signs, and develop prevention programs in schools and communities.

DELINQUENCY

National Council on Crime
and Delinquency
(415) 896-6223
Website: www.cascomm/users/nccd

An organization of 11,000 professionals and other concerned individuals interested in the development of programs that prevent and treat crime and delinquency. Publishes the journal Crime and Delinquency.

$\mathcal{M}$ilestones

OF DEVELOPMENT IN ADOLESCENCE

AGE	PHYSICAL	COGNITIVE	LANGUAGE	EMOTIONAL/SOCIAL
11–14 years	■ If a girl, reaches peak of growth spurt. (529) ■ If a girl, adds more body fat than muscle. (530) ■ If a girl, starts to menstruate. (531) ■ If a boy, begins growth spurt. (529) ■ If a boy, starts to ejaculate seminal fluid. (532) ■ Likely to become aware of sexual orientation. (546) ■ If a girl, motor performance gradually increases and then levels off. (557)	■ Becomes capable of formal operational reasoning. (564) ■ Becomes better at coordinating theory with evidence. (569) ■ Can argue more effectively. (571) ■ Becomes more self-conscious and self-focused. (572) ■ Becomes more idealistic and critical. (573) ■ Metacognition and cognitive self-regulation continue to improve. (570, 574) ■ Evaluates vocational options in terms of interests. (591)	■ Vocabulary continues to increase as abstract words are added. (577) ■ Grasps irony and sarcasm. (578) ■ Understanding and use of complex grammatical constructions continue to improve. (578) ■ Can make subtle adjustments in speech style, depending on the situation. (578)	■ Moodiness and parent–child conflict increase. (535) ■ Is likely to show increased gender stereotyping of attitudes and behavior. (617) ■ As strives for autonomy, spends less time with parents and siblings. (618, 621) ■ Spends more time with peers. (621) ■ Friendships are based on intimacy and loyalty. (622) ■ Peer groups become organized around cliques. (624) ■ Cliques with similar values come together, forming crowds. (624) ■ Conformity to peer pressure increases. (626)

AGE	PHYSICAL	COGNITIVE	LANGUAGE	EMOTIONAL/SOCIAL
Middle adolescence 14–18 years	■ If a girl, completes growth spurt. (529) ■ If a boy, reaches peak and then completes growth spurt. (529) ■ If a boy, voice deepens. (532) ■ If a boy, adds muscle while body fat declines. (530) ■ May have had sexual intercourse. (543) ■ If a boy, motor performance increases dramatically. (557) 	■ Is likely to show formal operational reasoning on familiar tasks. (567) ■ Displays relativistic reasoning in familiar situations. (571) ■ Masters the components of formal operational reasoning in sequential order on different types of tasks. (570) ■ Becomes less self-conscious and self-focused. (573) ■ Becomes better at everyday planning and decision making. (574) ■ Evaluates vocational options in terms of interests, abilities, and values. (591)	■ Can read and interpret adult literary works. (578) 	■ Combines features of the self into an organized self-concept. (603) ■ Self-esteem differentiates further. (604) ■ Self-esteem tends to rise. (604) ■ Is likely to be searching for an identity. (605) ■ Is likely to engage in societal perspective taking. (493, 612) ■ Is likely to have a conventional moral orientation. (612) ■ Gender stereotyping may decline. (617) ■ Has probably started dating.(625) ■ Conformity to peer pressure may decline. (626)
Late adolescence 18–21 years	■ If a boy, gains in motor performance continue. (557) 	■ If goes to college, develops relativistic reasoning in a wide range of situations. (571) ■ Narrows vocational options and settles on a specific occupation. (591)		■ Is likely to be identity achieved. (605) ■ May develop a postconventional moral orientation. (613) ■ Cliques and crowds decline in importance. (624) ■ Is likely to move away from home.

Note: Numbers in parenthesis indicate the page on which each milestone is discussed.

GLOSSARY

AB search error The error made by 8- to 12-month-olds after an object is moved from hiding place A to hiding place B. Infants in Piaget's Substage 4 search for it only in the first hiding place (A).

academic preschools Preschools in which teachers structure the program, training children in academic skills through repetition and drill. Distinguished from *child-centered preschools*.

accommodation That part of adaptation in which new schemes are created and old ones adjusted to produce a better fit with the environment. Distinguished from *assimilation*.

acquired immune deficiency syndrome (AIDS) A relatively new viral infection that destroys the immune system and is spread through transfer of body fluids from one person to another. It can be transmitted prenatally.

adaptation In Piaget's theory, the process of building schemes through direct interaction with the environment. Made up of two complementary processes: *assimilation* and *accommodation*.

adolescent initiation ceremony A ritual, or rite of passage, announcing to the community that a young person is making the transition into adolescence or full adulthood.

age of viability The age at which the fetus can first survive if born early. Occurs sometime between 22 and 26 weeks.

allele Each of two forms of a gene located at the same place on the autosomes.

amnion The inner membrane that forms a protective covering around the prenatal organism.

amniotic fluid The fluid that fills the amnion, helping to keep temperature constant and to provide a cushion against jolts caused by the mother's movement.

analgesic A mild pain-relieving drug.

androgyny A type of gender identity in which the person scores high on both traditionally masculine and traditionally feminine personality characteristics.

anesthetic A strong pain-killing drug that blocks sensation.

animistic thinking The belief that inanimate objects have lifelike qualities, such as thoughts, wishes, feelings, and intentions.

anorexia nervosa An eating disorder in which individuals (usually females) starve themselves because of a compulsive fear of getting fat.

anoxia Inadequate oxygen supply.

Apgar Scale A rating used to assess the newborn baby's physical condition immediately after birth.

applied behavior analysis A set of practical procedures that combine reinforcement, modeling, and the manipulation of situational cues to change behavior.

assimilation That part of adaptation in which the external world is interpreted in terms of current schemes. Distinguished from *accommodation*.

associative play A form of true social participation, in which children are engaged in separate activities, but they interact by exchanging toys and commenting on one another's behavior. Distinguished from *nonsocial activity, parallel play,* and *cooperative play.*

asthma An illness in which highly sensitive bronchial tubes fill with mucus and contract, leading to episodes of coughing, wheezing, and serious breathing difficulties.

attachment The strong, affectional tie that humans feel toward special people in their lives.

Attachment Q-Sort An efficient method for assessing the quality of the attachment bond in which a parent or an expert informant sorts a set of 90 descriptors of attachment-related behaviors on the basis of how descriptive they are of the child. A score is then computed that permits children to be assigned to securely or insecurely attached groups.

attention-deficit hyperactivity disorder (ADHD) A childhood disorder involving inattentiveness, impulsivity, and excessive motor activity. Often leads to academic failure and social problems.

attribution retraining An approach to intervention in which attributions of learned-helpless children are modified through feedback that encourages them to believe in themselves and persist in the face of task difficulty.

attributions Common, everyday explanations for the causes of behavior.

authoritarian style A child-rearing style that is demanding but low in responsiveness to children's rights and needs. Conformity and obedience are valued over open communication with the child. Distinguished from *authoritative, permissive,* and *uninvolved styles.*

authoritative style A child-rearing style that is demanding and responsive. A rational, democratic approach in which parents' and children's rights are respected. Distinguished from *authoritarian, permissive,* and *uninvolved styles.*

autobiographical memory Representations of special, one-time events that are long lasting because they are imbued with personal meaning.

autonomous morality Piaget's second stage of moral development, in which children view rules as flexible, socially agreed-on principles that can be revised when there is a need to do so. Begins around age 10.

autonomy At adolescence, a sense of oneself as a separate, self-governing individual. Involves relying more on oneself and less on parents for direction and guidance and engaging in careful, well-reasoned decision making.

autonomy versus shame and doubt In Erikson's theory, the psychological conflict of toddlerhood, which is resolved positively if parents provide young children with suitable guidance and appropriate choices.

autosomes The 22 matching chromosome pairs in each human cell.

avoidant attachment The quality of insecure attachment characterizing infants who are usually not distressed by parental separation and who avoid the parent when she returns. Distinguished from *secure, resistant,* and *disorganized/disoriented attachment.*

babbling Repetition of consonant–vowel combinations in long strings, beginning around 6 months of age.

basic emotions Emotions that can be directly inferred from facial expressions, such as happiness, interest, surprise, fear, anger, sadness, and disgust.

basic trust versus mistrust In Erikson's theory, the psychological conflict of infancy, which is resolved positively if caregiving, especially during feeding, is sympathetic and loving.

basic-skills approach An approach to beginning reading instruction that emphasizes training in phonics—the basic rules for translating written symbols into sounds—and simplified reading materials. Distinguished from *whole-language approach.*

behaviorism An approach that views directly observable events—stimuli and responses—as the appropriate focus of study and the development of behavior as taking place through classical and operant conditioning.

bicultural identity The identity constructed by adolescents who explore and adopt values from both their subculture and the dominant culture.

blastocyst The zygote 4 days after fertilization, when the tiny mass of cells forms a hollow, fluid-filled ball.

blended, or reconstituted, family A family structure resulting from cohabitation or remarriage that includes parent, child, and step-relatives.

body image Conception of and attitude toward one's physical appearance.

bonding Parents' feelings of affection and concern for the newborn baby.

brain plasticity The ability of other parts of the brain to take over functions of damaged regions. Disappears when hemispheres of the cortex lateralize.

breech position A position of the baby in the uterus that would cause the buttocks or feet to be delivered first.

Broca's area A language structure located in the frontal lobe of the cerebral cortex that controls language production.

bulimia An eating disorder in which individuals (mainly females) go on eating binges followed by deliberate vomiting, other purging techniques such as heavy doses of laxatives, and strict dieting.

canalization The tendency of heredity to restrict the development of some characteristics to just one or a few outcomes.

cardinality A principle stating that the last number in a counting sequence indicates the quantity of items in the set.

carrier A heterozygous individual who can pass a recessive trait to his or her children.

centration The tendency to focus on one aspect of a situation and neglect other important features. Distinguished from *decentration.*

cephalocaudal trend An organized pattern of physical growth and motor control that proceeds from head to tail.

cerebellum A brain structure that aids in balance and control of body movements.

cerebral cortex The largest structure of the human brain that accounts for the highly developed intelligence of the human species. Surrounds the rest of the brain, much like a half-shelled walnut.

cerebral palsy A general term for a variety of problems, all of which involve muscle coordination, that result from brain damage before, during, or just after birth.

cesarean delivery A surgical delivery in which the doctor makes an incision in the mother's abdomen and lifts the baby out of the uterus.

child development A field of study devoted to understanding all aspects of human growth and change from conception through adolescence.

child-centered preschools Preschools in which teachers provide a wide variety of activities from which children select, and most of the day is devoted to free play. Distinguished from *academic preschools.*

child-directed speech (CDS) A form of language adults use to speak to infants and toddlers that consists of short sentences with high-pitched, exaggerated expression, clear pronunciation, and distinct pauses between speech segments.

chorion The outer membrane that forms a protective covering around the prenatal organism. It sends out tiny, fingerlike villi, from which the placenta begins to emerge.

chromosomes Rodlike structures in the cell nucleus that store and transmit genetic information.

chronosystem In ecological systems theory, temporal changes in children's environments, which produce new conditions that affect development. These changes can be imposed externally or arise from within the child.

circular reaction In Piaget's theory, a means of building schemes in which infants try to repeat a chance event caused by their own motor activity.

classical conditioning A form of learning that involves associating a neutral stimulus with a stimulus that leads to a reflexive response.

clinical interview A method in which the researcher uses a flexible, conversational style to probe for the participant's point of view.

clinical method A method in which the researcher attempts to understand the unique individual child by combining interview data, observations, test scores, and sometimes psychophysiological measures.

clique A small group of about five to seven members who are either close or good friends.

codominance A pattern of inheritance in which both alleles in a heterozygous combination are expressed.

cognitive self-regulation The process of continuously monitoring progress toward a goal, checking outcomes, and redirecting unsuccessful efforts.

cognitive-developmental theory An approach introduced by Piaget that views the child as actively building psychological structures and cognitive development as taking place in stages.

cohort effects The effects of cultural-historical change on the accuracy of findings: Children born in one period of time are influenced by a particular set of cultural and historical conditions.

collectivist societies Societies in which people define themselves as part of a group and stress group over individual goals. Distinguished from *individualistic societies.*

compliance Voluntary obedience to adult requests and commands.

comprehension In language development, the words and word combinations that children understand. Distinguished from *production.*

comprehension monitoring Sensitivity to how well one understands a spoken or written message.

concordance rate The percentage of instances in which both members of a twin pair show a trait when it is present in one pair member. Used to study the role of heredity in emotional and behavioral disorders, which can be judged as either present or absent.

concrete operational stage Piaget's third stage, during which thought is logical, flexible, and organized in its application to concrete information. However, the capacity for abstract thinking is not yet present. Spans the years from 7 to 11.

conditioned response (CR) In classical conditioning, an originally reflexive response that is produced by a conditioned stimulus (CS).

conditioned stimulus (CS) In classical conditioning, a neutral stimulus that through pairing with an unconditioned stimulus (UCS) leads to a new response (CR).

conservation The understanding that certain physical characteristics of objects remain the same, even when their outward appearance changes.

continuous development A view that regards development as a cumulative process of adding on more of the same types of skills that were there to begin with. Distinguished from *discontinuous development.*

contrast sensitivity A general principle accounting for early pattern preferences, which states that if babies can detect a difference in contrast between two or more patterns, they will prefer the one with more contrast.

control deficiency The inability to execute a mental strategy consistently. Distinguished from *production deficiency, utilization deficiency,* and *effective strategy use.*

controversial children Children who get a large number of positive and negative votes on sociometric measures of peer acceptance. Distinguished from *popular, neglected,* and *rejected children.*

conventional level Kohlberg's second level of moral development, in which moral understanding is based on conforming to social rules to ensure positive human relationships and societal order.

convergent thinking The generation of a single correct answer to a problem. The type of cognition emphasized on intelligence tests. Distinguished from *divergent thinking.*

cooing Pleasant vowel-like noises made by infants, beginning around 2 months of age.

cooperative play A form of true social participation, in which children's actions are directed toward a common goal. Distinguished from *nonsocial activity, parallel play,* and *associative play.*

coregulation A transitional form of supervision in which parents exercise general oversight while permitting children to be in charge of moment-by-moment decision making.

corpus callosum The large bundle of fibers that connects the two hemispheres of the brain.

correlation coefficient A number, ranging from +1.00 to −1.00, that describes the strength and direction of the relationship between two variables.

correlational design A research design in which the researcher gathers information without altering participants' experiences and examines relationships between variables. Does not permit inferences about cause and effect.

cross-sectional design A research design in which groups of participants of different ages are studied at the same point in time. Distinguished from *longitudinal design.*

crossing over Exchange of genes between chromosomes next to each other during meiosis.

crowd A large, loosely organized group consisting of several cliques. Membership is based on reputation and stereotype.

decentration The ability to focus on several aspects of a problem at once and relate them. Distinguished from *centration.*

deferred imitation The ability to remember and copy the behavior of models who are not immediately present.

deoxyribonucleic acid (DNA) Long, double-stranded molecules that make up chromosomes.

dependent variable The variable the researcher expects to be influenced by the independent variable in an experiment.

deprivation dwarfism A growth disorder observed between 2 and 15 years of age. Characterized by very short stature, weight that is usually appropriate for height, immature skeletal age, and decreased GH secretion. Caused by emotional deprivation.

developmental quotient, or DQ A score on an infant intelligence test, based primarily on perceptual and motor responses. Computed in the same manner as an IQ.

developmentally appropriate practice A set of standards devised by the National Association for the Education of Young Children that specify program characteristics that meet the developmental and individual needs of young children of varying ages, based on current research and the consensus of experts.

diethylstilbestrol (DES) A synthetic hormone widely used between 1945 and 1970 to prevent miscarriage. Children whose mothers took the hormone during pregnancy had an increased chance of developing genital tract abnormalities and cancer of the vagina and testes in adolescence and young adulthood.

differentiation theory The view that perceptual development involves the detection of increasingly fine-grained, invariant features in the environment.

difficult child A child whose temperament is such that he or she is irregular in daily routines, is slow to accept new experiences, and tends to react negatively and intensely. Distinguished from *easy child* and *slow-to-warm-up child.*

dilation and effacement of the cervix Widening and thinning of the cervix during the first stage of labor.

discontinuous development A view in which new and different ways of interpreting and responding to the world emerge at specific time periods. Distinguished from *continuous development.*

dishabituation Increase in responsiveness after stimulation changes.

disorganized/disoriented attachment The quality of insecure attachment characterizing infants who respond in a confused, contradictory fashion when reunited with the parent.

distributive justice Beliefs about how to divide up material goods fairly.

divergent thinking The generation of multiple and unusual possibilities when faced with a task or problem. Associated with creativity. Distinguished from *convergent thinking.*

divorce mediation A series of meetings between divorcing adults and a trained professional, who tries to help them settle disputes. Aimed at avoiding legal battles that intensify family conflict.

dominance hierarchy A stable ordering of group members that predicts who will win under conditions of conflict.

dominant cerebral hemisphere The hemisphere of the brain responsible for skilled motor action. The left hemisphere is dominant in right-handed individuals. In left-handed individuals, the right hemisphere may be dominant, or motor and language skills may be shared between the hemispheres.

dominant–recessive inheritance A pattern of inheritance in which, under heterozygous conditions, the influence of only one allele is apparent.

dynamic assessment An approach to testing consistent with Vygotsky's concept of the zone of proximal development, in which purposeful teaching is introduced into the testing situation to see what the child can do with social support.

dynamic systems perspective A view that regards the child's mind, body, and physical and social worlds as a dynamic, integrated system. A change in any part of the system leads the child to reorganize his or her behavior so the system operates in a more complex and effective way.

dynamic systems theory of motor development A theory that views new motor skills as reorganizations of previously mastered skills that lead to more effective ways of exploring and controlling the environment. Each new skill is a product of central nervous system development, movement possibilities of the body, the task the child has in mind, and environmental supports.

easy child A child whose temperament is such that he or she quickly establishes regular routines in infancy, is generally cheerful, and adapts easily to new experiences. Distinguished from *difficult child* and *slow-to-warm-up child.*

ecological systems theory Bronfenbrenner's approach, which views the child as developing within a complex system of relationships affected by multiple levels of the environment, from immediate settings of family and school to broad cultural values and programs.

educational self-fulfilling prophecy The idea that children may adopt teachers' positive or negative attitudes toward them and start to live up to these views.

effective strategy use Consistent use of a mental strategy that leads to improvement in performance. Distinguished from *production deficiency, control deficiency,* and *utilization deficiency.*

egocentrism The inability to distinguish the symbolic viewpoints of others from one's own.

elaboration The memory strategy of creating a relation between two or more items that are not members of the same category.

embryo The prenatal organism from 2 to 8 weeks after conception, during which time the foundations of all body structures and internal organs are laid down.

embryonic disk A small cluster of cells on the inside of the blastocyst, from which the embryo will develop.

emergent literacy Young children's active efforts to construct literacy knowledge through informal experiences.

emotional self-regulation Strategies for adjusting our emotional state to a comfortable level of intensity.

empathy The ability to understand another's emotional state and *feel for* that person, or respond emotionally in a similar way.

epiphyses Growth centers in the bones where new cartilage cells are produced and gradually harden.

episiotomy A small incision made during childbirth to increase the size of the vaginal opening.

episodic memory Memory for everyday experiences.

ethnography A method in which the researcher attempts to understand the unique values and social processes of a culture or a distinct social group by living with its members and taking field notes for an extended period of time.

ethological theory of attachment A theory formulated by Bowlby, which views the infant's emotional tie to the caregiver as an evolved response that promotes survival.

ethology An approach concerned with the adaptive, or survival, value of behavior and its evolutionary history.

exosystem In ecological systems theory, settings that do not contain children but that affect their experiences in immediate settings. Examples are parents' workplace and health and welfare services in the community.

expansions Adult responses that elaborate on a child's utterance, increasing its complexity.

experimental design A research design in which the investigator randomly assigns participants to treatment conditions. Since the researcher directly manipulates changes in an independent variable and observes their effects on a dependent variable, the design permits inferences about cause and effect.

expressive style A style of early language learning in which toddlers use language mainly to talk about the feelings and needs of themselves and other people. Initial vocabulary emphasizes pronouns and social formulas. Distinguished from *referential style.*

extended-family household A household in which parent and child live with one or more adult relatives.

extinction In classical conditioning, decline of the conditioned response (CR) as a result of presenting the conditioned stimulus (CS) enough times without the unconditioned stimulus (UCS).

fast mapping Connecting a new word with an underlying concept after only a brief encounter.

fetal alcohol effects (FAE) The condition of children who display some but not all the defects of fetal alcohol syndrome. Usually their mothers drank alcohol in smaller quantities during pregnancy.

fetal alcohol syndrome (FAS) A set of defects that results when women consume large amounts of alcohol during most or all of pregnancy. Includes mental retardation, slow physical growth, and facial abnormalities.

fetal monitors Electronic instruments that track the baby's heart rate during labor.

fetus The prenatal organism from the beginning of the third month to the end of pregnancy, during which time completion of body structures and dramatic growth in size takes place.

fontanels Six soft spots that separate the bones of the skull at birth.

forceps Metal clamps placed around the baby's head, used to pull the infant from the birth canal.

formal operational stage Piaget's final stage, in which adolescents develop the capacity for abstract, scientific thinking. Begins around 11 years of age.

fraternal, or dizygotic, twins Twins resulting from the release and fertilization of two ova. They are genetically no more alike than ordinary siblings. Distinguished from *identical, or monozygotic, twins.*

full inclusion Placement of pupils with learning difficulties in regular classrooms for the entire school day. Distinguished from *mainstreaming.*

functional play A type of play involving pleasurable motor activity with or without objects. Enables infants and toddlers to practice sensorimotor schemes.

gametes Human sperm and ova, which contain half as many chromosomes as a regular body cell.

gender constancy The understanding that sex remains the same even if clothing, hairstyle, and play activities change.

gender identity An image of oneself as relatively masculine or feminine in characteristics.

gender intensification Increased gender stereotyping of attitudes and behavior. Occurs in early adolescence.

gender schema theory An information-processing approach to gender typing that combines social learning and cognitive-developmental features to explain how environmental pressures and children's cognitions work together to shape gender-role development.

gender typing The process of developing gender roles, or gender-linked preferences and behaviors valued by the larger society.

gene A segment of a DNA molecule that contains hereditary instructions.

general growth curve A curve that represents overall changes in body size—rapid growth during infancy, slower gains in early and middle childhood, and rapid growth once more during adolescence.

genetic counseling A communication process designed to help couples assess their chances of giving birth to a baby with a hereditary disorder and choose the best course of action in view of risks and family goals.

genetic imprinting A pattern of inheritance in which alleles are imprinted, or chemically marked, in such a way that one pair member is activated, regardless of its makeup.

genetic–environmental correlation The idea that heredity influences the environments to which individuals are exposed.

genotype The genetic makeup of an individual.

giftedness Exceptional intellectual ability. Includes high IQ, creativity, and specialized talent.

glial cells Cells that serve the function of myelinization.

goodness-of-fit model Thomas and Chess's model, which states that an effective match, or "good fit," between child-rearing practices and a child's temperament leads to favorable development and psychological adjustment. A "poor fit" leads to adjustment problems.

growth hormone (GH) A pituitary hormone that affects the development of all body tissues except the central nervous system and the genitals.

growth spurt Rapid gain in height and weight during adolescence.

habituation A gradual reduction in the strength of a response as the result of repetitive stimulation.

heritability estimate A statistic that measures the extent to which individual differences in complex traits, such as intelligence or personality, are due to genetic factors.

heteronomous morality Piaget's first stage of moral development, in which children view moral rules as permanent features of the external world that are handed down by authorities and cannot be changed. Extends from about 5 to 10 years of age.

heterozygous Having two different alleles at the same place on a pair of chromosomes. Distinguished from *homozygous.*

hierarchical classification The organization of objects into classes and subclasses on the basis of similarities and differences between the groups.

Home Observation for Measurement of the Environment (HOME) A checklist for gathering information about the quality of children's home lives through observation and parental interview.

homozygous Having two identical alleles at the same place on a pair of chromosomes. Distinguished from *heterozygous.*

horizontal décalage Development within a Piagetian stage. Gradual mastery of logical concepts during the concrete operational stage is an example.

hostile aggression Aggression intended to harm another person. Distinguished from *instrumental aggression.*

hypothetico-deductive reasoning A formal operational problem-solving strategy in which adolescents begin with a general theory of all possible factors that could affect an outcome in a problem and deduce specific hypotheses, which they test in an orderly fashion.

I-self A sense of self as subject, or agent, who is separate from but attends to and acts on objects and other people. Distinguished from *me-self.*

identical, or monozygotic, twins Twins that result when a zygote, during the early stages of cell duplication, divides in two. They have the same genetic makeup. Distinguished from *fraternal,* or *dizygotic, twins.*

identification In psychoanalytic theory, the process leading to the formation of conscience, in which children take the same-sex parent's characteristics into their personality, thereby adopting the moral and gender-role standards of their society.

identity A well-organized conception of the self made up of values, beliefs, and goals to which the individual is solidly committed.

identity achievement The identity status of individuals who have explored and committed themselves to self-chosen values and occupational goals. Distinguished from *moratorium, identity foreclosure,* and *identity diffusion.*

identity diffusion The identity status of individuals who do not have firm commitments to values and goals and are not actively trying to reach them. Distinguished from *identity achievement, moratorium,* and *identity foreclosure.*

identity foreclosure The identity status of individuals who have accepted ready-made values and goals that authority figures have chosen for them. Distinguished from *identity achievement, moratorium,* and *identity diffusion.*

identity versus identity confusion In Erikson's theory, the psychological conflict of adolescence, which is resolved positively when adolescents attain an identity after a period of exploration and inner soul-searching.

imaginary audience Adolescents' belief that they are the focus of everyone else's attention and concern.

imitation Learning by copying the behavior of another person. Also called *modeling* or *observational learning.*

implantation Attachment of the blastocyst to the uterine lining 7 to 9 days after fertilization.

independent variable The variable manipulated by the researcher in an experiment.

individualistic societies Societies in which people think of themselves as separate entities and are largely concerned with their own personal needs.

induced labor A labor started artificially by breaking the amnion and giving the mother a hormone that stimulates contractions.

induction A type of discipline in which the effects of the child's misbehavior on others are communicated to the child.

industry versus inferiority In Erikson's theory, the psychological conflict of middle childhood, which is resolved positively when experiences lead children to develop a sense of competence at useful skills and tasks.

infant mortality The number of deaths in the first year of life per 1,000 live births.

information processing An approach that views the human mind as a symbol-manipulating system through which information flows and regards cognitive development as a continuous process.

inhibited, or shy, child A child whose temperament is such that he or she reacts negatively to and withdraws from novel stimuli. Resembles slow-to-warm-up child. Distinguished from *uninhibited,* or *sociable, child.*

inhibitory control The ability to resist interference from irrelevant information. A basic information-processing capacity that improves greatly during middle childhood.

initiative versus guilt In Erikson's theory, the psychological conflict of early childhood, which is resolved positively through play experiences that foster a healthy sense of initiative and through development of a superego, or conscience, that is not overly strict and guilt ridden.

instrumental aggression Aggression aimed at obtaining an object, privilege, or space with no deliberate intent to harm another person. Distinguished from *hostile aggression.*

intelligence quotient, or IQ A score that permits an individual's performance on an intelligence test to be compared to the performances of other individuals of the same age.

intentional, or goal-directed, behavior A sequence of actions in which schemes are deliberately combined to solve a problem.

interactional synchrony A sensitively tuned "emotional dance," in which the caregiver responds to infant signals in a well-timed, appropriate fashion and both partners match emotional states, especially the positive ones.

intermodal perception Perception that combines information from more than one sensory system.

internal working model A set of expectations derived from early caregiving experiences concerning the availability of attachment figures and their likelihood of providing support during times of stress. Becomes a model, or guide, for all future close relationships.

intersubjectivity The process whereby two participants who begin a task with different understandings arrive at a shared understanding.

invariant features In differentiation theory of perceptual development, features that remain stable in a constantly changing perceptual world.

irreversibility The inability to mentally go through a series of steps in a problem and then reverse direction, returning to the starting point. Distinguished from *reversibility*.

joint custody A child custody arrangement following divorce in which the court grants both parents equal say in important decisions about the child's upbringing.

Kamehameha Elementary Education Program (KEEP) The most well-known and extensive educational reform effort based on Vygotsky's theory. Instruction is organized around activity settings, designed to enhance teacher–child and child–child interaction and to be culturally responsive.

kinship studies Studies comparing the characteristics of family members to determine the importance of heredity in complex human characteristics.

kwashiorkor A disease usually appearing between 1 and 3 years of age that is caused by a diet low in protein. Symptoms include an enlarged belly, swollen feet, hair loss, skin rash, and irritable, listless behavior.

language acquisition device (LAD) In Chomsky's theory, a biologically based innate system for picking up language that permits children, as soon as they have learned enough words, to combine them into grammatically consistent expressions and to understand the meaning of sentences they hear.

language-making capacity A built-in set of procedures for analyzing language that supports the discovery of grammatical regularities.

lanugo A white, downy hair that covers the entire body of the fetus, helping the vernix stick to the skin.

lateralization Specialization of functions of the two hemispheres of the cortex.

learned helplessness Attributions that credit success to luck and failure to low ability. Leads to anxious loss of control in the face of challenging

tasks. Distinguished from *mastery-oriented attributions*.

learning disabilities Specific learning disorders that lead children to achieve poorly in school, despite an average or above-average IQ. A problem with reading is called *dyslexia*, one with arithmetic *dyscalculia*, and one with writing *dysgraphia*. Believed to be due to faulty brain functioning.

long-term memory In information processing, the part of the mental system that contains our permanent knowledge base.

longitudinal design A research design in which one group of participants is studied repeatedly at different ages. Distinguished from *cross-sectional design*.

longitudinal-sequential design A research design with both longitudinal and cross-sectional components in which groups of participants born in different years are followed over time.

macrosystem In ecological systems theory, cultural values, laws, customs, and resources that influence experiences and interactions at inner levels of the environment.

mainstreaming Placement of pupils with learning difficulties in regular classrooms for part of the school day. Distinguished from *full inclusion*.

make-believe play A type of play in which children pretend, acting out everyday and imaginary activities.

malocclusion A condition in which the upper and lower teeth do not meet properly.

marasmus A disease usually appearing in the first year of life that is caused by a diet low in all essential nutrients. Leads to a wasted condition of the body.

mastery-oriented attributions Attributions that credit success to high ability and failure to insufficient

effort. Leads to high self-esteem and a willingness to approach challenging tasks. Distinguished from *learned helplessness*.

maturation A genetically determined, naturally unfolding course of growth.

me-self A reflective observer that treats the self as an object of knowledge and evaluation. Distinguished from *I-self*.

mechanistic theories Theories that regard the child as a passive reactor to environmental inputs. Distinguished from *organismic theories*.

meiosis The process of cell division through which gametes are formed and in which the number of chromosomes in each cell is halved.

memory strategies Deliberate mental activities that improve the likelihood of remembering.

menarche First menstruation.

mental representation An internal image of an absent object or a past event.

mental retardation Substantially below-average intellectual functioning.

mental strategies In information processing, procedures that operate on and transform information, thereby increasing the efficiency and flexibility of thinking and the chances that information will be retained.

mesosystem In ecological systems theory, connections between children's immediate settings.

metacognition Thinking about thought; awareness of mental activities.

metalinguistic awareness The ability to think about language as a system.

microsystem In ecological systems theory, the activities and interaction patterns in the child's immediate surroundings.

mitosis The process of cell duplication, in which each new cell receives an exact copy of the original chromosomes.

modular view of the mind A nativist view that regards the mind as a collection of separate modules, or genetically prewired neural systems in the brain, each equipped with structures for making sense of a certain type of knowledge.

moral dilemma A conflict situation presented to individuals who are asked to decide both what the main actor should do and why. Used to assess the development of moral reasoning.

moratorium The identity status of individuals who are exploring alternatives in an effort to find values and goals to guide their life. Distinguished from *identity achievement, identity foreclosure,* and *identity diffusion.*

mutation A sudden but permanent change in a segment of DNA.

myelinization A process in which neural fibers are coated with an insulating fatty sheath (called myelin) that improves the efficiency of message transfer.

myopia Nearsightedness; inability to see distant objects clearly.

natural, or prepared, childbirth An approach designed to reduce pain and medical intervention and to make childbirth a rewarding experience for parents.

naturalistic observation A method in which the researcher goes into the natural environment to observe the behavior of interest. Distinguished from *structured observation.*

nature–nurture controversy Disagreement among theorists about whether genetic or environmental factors are the most important determinants of development and behavior.

neglected children Children who are seldom chosen, either positively or negatively, on sociometric measures of peer acceptance. Distinguished

from *popular, rejected,* and *controversial children.*

Neonatal Behavioral Assessment Scale (NBAS) A test developed to assess the behavior of the infant during the newborn period. Considers reflexes, state changes, responsiveness to physical and social stimuli, motor abilities, and other reactions.

neonatal mortality The number of deaths in the first month of life per 1,000 live births.

neural tube The primitive spinal cord that develops from the ectoderm, the top of which swells to form the brain.

neurons Nerve cells that store and transmit information.

neurotransmitters Chemicals that permit neurons to communicate across synapses.

niche-picking A type of genetic–environmental correlation in which individuals actively choose environments that complement their heredity.

noble savage Rousseau's view of the child as naturally endowed with an innate plan for orderly, healthy growth.

nocturnal enuresis Repeated bedwetting during the night.

non-rapid-eye movement (NREM) sleep A "regular" sleep state in which the body is quiet and heart rate, breathing, and brain wave activity are slow and regular.

nonorganic failure to thrive A growth disorder usually present by 18 months of age that is caused by lack of affection and stimulation.

nonsocial activity Unoccupied, onlooker behavior and solitary play. Distinguished from *parallel, associative,* and *cooperative play.*

normative approach An approach in which age-related averages are computed to represent typical development.

obesity A greater-than-20-percent increase over average body weight, based on the child's age, sex, and physical build.

object permanence The understanding that objects continue to exist when they are out of sight.

operant conditioning A form of learning in which a spontaneous behavior is followed by a stimulus that changes the probability that the behavior will occur again.

operations Mental representations of actions that obey logical rules.

oral rehydration therapy (ORT) A treatment for diarrhea in which sick children are given a glucose, salt, and water solution that quickly replaces fluids the body loses.

ordinality A principle specifying order (more-than and less-than) relationships between quantities.

organismic theories Theories that assume the existence of psychological structures inside the child that underlie and control development. Distinguished from *mechanistic theories.*

organization In Piaget's theory, the internal rearrangement and linking together of schemes so that they form a strongly interconnected cognitive system. In information processing, the memory strategy of grouping together related items.

otitis media Middle ear infection.

overextension An early vocabulary error in which a word is applied too broadly, to a wider collection of objects and events than is appropriate. Distinguished from *underextension.*

overregularization Application of regular grammatical rules to words that are exceptions.

overt aggression A form of hostile aggression that harms others through physical injury or the threat of such injury—for example, hitting, kicking, or threatening to beat up a peer. Distinguished from *relational aggression.*

parallel play A form of limited social participation in which the child plays near other children with similar materials but does not interact with them. Distinguished from *nonsocial, associative,* and *cooperative play.*

peer group Peers who form a social unit by generating shared values and standards of behavior and a social structure of leaders and followers.

perception bound Being easily distracted by the concrete, perceptual appearance of objects. A characteristic of Piaget's preoperational stage

permissive style A child-rearing style that is responsive but undemanding. An overly tolerant approach to child rearing. Distinguished from *authoritative* and *authoritarian styles.*

personal fable Adolescents' belief that they are special and unique. Leads them to conclude that others cannot possibly understand their thoughts and feelings. May promote a sense of invulnerability to danger.

perspective taking The capacity to imagine what other people may be thinking and feeling.

phenotype The individual's physical and behavioral characteristics, which are determined by both genetic and environmental factors.

physical causality The causal action one object exerts on another through contact.

pincer grasp The well-coordinated grasp emerging at the end of the first year, involving thumb and forefinger opposition.

pituitary gland A gland located near the base of the brain that releases hormones affecting physical growth.

placenta The organ that separates the mother's bloodstream from the embryo or fetal bloodstream but permits exchange of nutrients and waste products.

polygenic inheritance A pattern of inheritance in which many genes determine a characteristic.

popular children Children who get many positive votes on sociometric measures of peer acceptance. Distinguished from *rejected, controversial,* and *neglected children.*

postconventional level Kohlberg's highest level of moral development, in which individuals define morality in terms of abstract principles and values that apply to all situations and societies.

postformal thought Cognitive development beyond Piaget's formal operational stage.

postpartum depression Feelings of sadness and withdrawal that appear shortly after childbirth and that continue for weeks or months.

postterm Infants who spend a longer than average time in the uterus— more than 42 weeks.

pragmatics The practical, social side of language that is concerned with how to engage in effective and appropriate communication with others.

preconventional level Kohlberg's first level of moral development, in which moral understanding is based on rewards, punishments, and the power of authority figures.

preformationism Medieval view of the child as a miniature adult.

prenatal diagnostic methods Medical procedures that permit detection of developmental problems before birth.

preoperational stage Piaget's second stage, in which rapid growth in representation takes place. However, thought is not yet logical. Spans the years from 2 to 7.

prereaching The poorly coordinated, primitive reaching movements of newborn babies.

preterm Infants born several weeks or more before their due date. Although small in size, their weight may still be appropriate for the time they spent in the uterus.

primary sexual characteristics Physical features that involve the reproductive organs directly (ovaries, uterus, and vagina in females; penis, scrotum, and testes in males). Distinguished from *secondary sexual characteristics.*

principle of mutual exclusivity The assumption by children in the early stages of vocabulary growth that words mark entirely separate (nonoverlapping) categories.

private speech Self-directed speech that children use to plan and guide their own behavior.

production In language development, the words and word combinations that children use. Distinguished from *comprehension.*

production deficiency The failure to produce a mental strategy when it could be helpful. Distinguished from *control deficiency, utilization deficiency,* and *effective strategy use.*

Project Head Start A federal program that provides low-income children with a year or two of preschool education before school entry, along with nutritional and medical services, and that encourages parent involvement in children's development.

propositional thought A type of formal operational reasoning in which adolescents evaluate the logic of verbal statements without referring to real-world circumstances.

prosocial, or altruistic, behavior Actions that benefit another person without any expected reward for the self.

proximodistal trend An organized pattern of physical growth and motor control that proceeds from the center of the body outward.

psychoanalytic perspective An approach to personality development introduced by Freud that assumes children move through a series of stages in which they confront conflicts between biological drives and social expectations. The way these conflicts are resolved determines psychological adjustment.

psychophysiological methods Methods that measure the relation between physiological processes and behavior. Among the most common are measures of autonomic nervous system activity (such as heart rate and respiration) and brain functioning (such as the EEG and fMRI).

psychosexual theory Freud's theory, which emphasizes that how parents manage children's sexual and aggressive drives during the first few years is crucial for healthy personality development.

psychosocial theory Erikson's theory, which emphasizes that the demands of society at each Freudian stage not only promote the development of a unique personality but also ensure that individuals acquire attitudes and skills that help them become active, contributing members of their society.

puberty Biological changes at adolescence that lead to an adult-size body and sexual maturity.

public policies Laws and government programs designed to improve current conditions.

punishment In operant conditioning, removing a desirable stimulus or presenting an unpleasant one to decrease the occurrence of a response.

range of reaction Each person's unique, genetically determined response to a range of environmental conditions.

rapid-eye-movement (REM) sleep An "irregular" sleep state in which brain wave activity is similar to that of the waking state; eyes dart beneath the lids; heart rate, blood pressure, and breathing are uneven; and slight body movements occur. Distinguished from *non-rapid-eye-movement (NREM) sleep.*

recall A type of memory that involves remembering a stimulus that is not present.

recasts Adult responses that restructure children's incorrect speech into a more appropriate form.

reciprocal teaching A method of teaching based on Vygotsky's theory in which a teacher and two to four pupils form a cooperative learning group. Dialogues occur that create a zone of proximal development in which reading comprehension improves.

recognition A type of memory that involves noticing whether a stimulus is identical or similar to one previously experienced.

referential style A style of early language learning in which toddlers use language mainly to label objects.

reflex An inborn, automatic response to a particular form of stimulation.

rehearsal The memory strategy of repeating information.

reinforcer In operant conditioning, a stimulus that increases the occurrence of a response.

rejected children Children who are actively disliked and get many negative votes on sociometric measures of peer acceptance. Distinguished from *popular, controversial,* and *neglected children.*

rejected-aggressive children A subgroup of rejected children who engage in high rates of conflict, hostility, and hyperactive, inattentive, and impulsive behavior. Distinguished from *rejected-withdrawn children.*

rejected-withdrawn children A subgroup of rejected children who are passive and socially awkward. Distinguished from *rejected-withdrawn children.*

relational aggression A form of hostile aggression that does damage to another's peer relationships, as in social exclusion or rumor spreading. Distinguished from *overt aggression.*

relativistic reasoning A type of postformal thought that views all knowledge as embedded in a framework of thought and that accepts the existence of multiple truths.

resistant attachment The quality of insecure attachment characterizing infants who remain close to the parent before departure and display angry, resistive behavior when she returns. Distinguished from *secure, avoidant,* and *disorganized/disoriented attachment.*

respiratory distress syndrome A disorder of preterm infants in which the lungs are so immature that the air sacs collapse, causing serious breathing difficulties.

reticular formation A brain structure that maintains alertness and consciousness.

reversibility The ability to mentally go through a series of steps in a problem and then reverse direction, returning to the starting point. Distinguished from *irreversibility.*

Rh factor A protein that, when present in the fetus's blood but not in the mother's, can cause the mother to build up antibodies. If these return to the fetus's system, they destroy red blood cells, reducing the oxygen supply to organs and tissues.

rooming in An arrangement in which the newborn baby stays in the mother's hospital room all or most of the time.

rough-and-tumble play A form of peer interaction involving friendly chasing and play-fighting that, in our evolutionary past, may have been important for the development of fighting skill.

rubella Three-day German measles. Causes a wide variety of prenatal abnormalities, especially when it strikes during the embryonic period.

scaffolding A changing quality of support over the course of a teaching session in which the adult adjusts the assistance provided to fit the child's current level of performance. As competence increases, the adult permits the child to take over her guiding role and apply it to his own activity.

scheme In Piaget's theory, a specific structure, or organized way of making sense of experience, that changes with age.

school phobia Severe apprehension about attending school, often accompanied by physical complaints that disappear once the child is allowed to remain home.

scripts General descriptions of what occurs and when it occurs in a particular situation. A basic means through which children organize and interpret familiar everyday experiences.

secondary sexual characteristics Features visible on the outside of the body that serve as signs of sexual maturity but do not involve the reproductive organs (for example, breast development in females, appearance of underarm and pubic hair in both sexes). Distinguished from *primary sexual characteristics*.

secular trends in physical growth Changes in body size from one generation to the next.

secure attachment The quality of attachment characterizing infants who are distressed by parental separation and easily comforted by the parent when she returns. Distinguished from secure, avoidant, and *disorganized/disoriented attachment*.

secure base The use of the familiar caregiver as a base from which the infant confidently explores the environment and returns for emotional support.

self-care children Children who look after themselves while their parents are at work.

self-concept The set of attributes, abilities, attitudes, and values that an individual believes defines who he or she is.

self-conscious emotions Emotions that involve injury to or enhancement of the sense of self. Examples are shame, embarrassment, guilt, envy, and pride.

self-control The capacity to resist an impulse to engage in socially disapproved behavior.

self-esteem The aspect of self-concept that involves judgments about one's own worth and the feelings associated with those judgments.

semantic bootstrapping Figuring out grammatical rules by relying on word meanings.

sensitive caregiving Caregiving involving prompt, consistent, and appropriate responding to infant signals.

sensitive period A time span that is optimal for certain capacities to emerge and in which the individual is especially responsive to environmental influences.

sensorimotor stage Piaget's first stage, during which infants and toddlers "think" with their eyes, ears, hands, and other sensorimotor equipment. Spans the first 2 years of life.

sensory register In information processing, that part of the mental system in which sights and sounds are held briefly before they decay or are transferred to working, or short-term, memory.

separation anxiety An infant's distressed reaction to the departure of the familiar caregiver.

separation–individuation In Mahler's theory, the process of separating from the mother and becoming aware of the self, which is triggered by crawling and walking.

seriation The ability to order items along a quantitative dimension, such as length or weight.

sex chromosomes The twenty-third pair of chromosomes, which determines the sex of the child. In females, called XX; in males, called XY.

shape constancy Perception of an object's shape as the same, despite changes in the shape of its retinal image.

Size constancy Perception of an object's size as the same, despite changes in the size of its retinal image.

skeletal age An estimate of physical maturity based on development of the bones of the body.

slow-to-warm-up child A child whose temperament is such that he or she is inactive, shows mild, low-key reactions to environmental stimuli, is negative in mood, and adjusts slowly when faced with new experiences. Distinguished from *easy child* and *difficult child*.

small for date Infants whose birth weight is below normal when length of pregnancy is taken into account.

social comparisons Judgments of appearance, abilities, behavior, and other characteristics in relation to those of others.

social learning theory An approach that emphasizes the role of modeling, or observational learning, in the development of behavior. Its most recent revision stresses the importance of thinking in social learning and is called *social-cognitive theory*.

social problem-solving training Training in which children are taught how to resolve social conflicts through discussing and trying out successful strategies.

social referencing Relying on a trusted person's emotional reaction to decide how to respond in an uncertain situation.

social smile The smile evoked by the stimulus of the human face. First appears between 6 and 10 weeks.

sociocultural theory Vygotsky's theory, in which children acquire the ways of thinking and behaving that make up a community's culture through cooperative dialogues with more knowledgeable members of society.

sociodramatic play The make-believe play with others that is under way by age 2½.

socioeconomic status (SES) A measure of a family's social position and economic well-being that combines three interrelated, but not completely overlapping, variables: (1) years of education and (2) the prestige of and skill required by one's job, both of which measure social status; and (3) income, which measures economic status.

sociometric techniques Self-report measures that ask peers to evaluate one another's likability.

spermarche First ejaculation of seminal fluid.

stage A qualitative change in thinking, feeling, and behaving that characterizes a specific time period of development.

Stanford-Binet Intelligence Scale An individually administered intelligence test that is the modern descendent of Alfred Binet's first successful test for children. Measures general intelligence and four factors: verbal reasoning, quantitative reasoning, abstract/visual reasoning, and short-term memory.

states of arousal Different degrees of sleep and wakefulness.

states rather than transformations The tendency to treat the initial and final states in a problem as completely unrelated.

Strange Situation A procedure involving short separations from and reunions with the parent that assesses the quality of the attachment bond.

stranger anxiety The infant's expression of fear in response to unfamiliar adults. Appears in many babies after 6 months of age.

structured interview A method in which each participant is asked the same questions in the same way.

structured observation A method in which the investigator sets up a situation that evokes the behavior of interest and observes it in a labora-

tory. Distinguished from *naturalistic observation.*

subculture A group of people with beliefs and customs that differ from those of the larger culture.

sudden infant death syndrome (SIDS) The unexpected death, usually during the night, of an infant under 1 year of age that remains unexplained after thorough investigation.

symbiosis In Mahler's theory, the baby's intimate sense of oneness with the mother, encouraged by warm, physical closeness and gentle handling.

synapses The gaps between neurons, across which chemical messages are sent.

synaptic pruning Loss of connective fibers by seldom-stimulated neurons, thereby returning them to an uncommitted state so they can support the development of future skills.

syntactic bootstrapping Figuring out word meanings by observing how words are used in the structure of sentences.

tabula rasa Locke's view of the child as a blank slate whose character is shaped by experience.

telegraphic speech Toddlers' two-word utterances that, like a telegram, leave out smaller and less important words.

temperament Stable individual differences in quality and intensity of emotional reaction, activity level, attention, and emotional self-regulation.

teratogen Any environmental agent that causes damage during the prenatal period.

thalidomide A sedative widely available in Europe, Canada, and South America in the early 1960s. When taken by mothers between the fourth and sixth weeks after conception, it produced gross deformities of the embryo's arms and legs.

theory An orderly, integrated set of statements that describes, explains, and predicts behavior.

theory of multiple intelligences Gardner's theory, which identifies eight independent intelligences on the basis of distinct sets of processing operations that permit individuals to engage in a wide range of culturally valued activities.

thyroid-stimulating hormone (TSH) A pituitary hormone that stimulates the thyroid gland to release thyroxine, which is necessary for normal brain development and body growth.

time out A form of mild punishment in which children are removed from the immediate setting until they are ready to act appropriately.

toxemia An illness of the last half of pregnancy in which the mother's blood pressure increases sharply and her face, hands, and feet swell. If untreated, it can cause convulsions in the mother and death of the fetus.

toxoplasmosis A parasitic disease caused by eating raw or undercooked meat or coming in contact with the feces of infected cats. During the first trimester, it leads to eye and brain damage.

traditional classroom An elementary school classroom based on the educational philosophy that children are passive learners who acquire information presented by teachers. Pupils are evaluated on the basis of how well they keep up with a uniform set of standards for all pupils in their grade. Distinguished from *open classroom.*

transductive reasoning Reasoning from one particular event to another particular event, instead of from general to particular or particular to general. A characteristic of Piaget's preoperational stage.

transition Climax of the first stage of labor, in which the frequency and strength of contractions are at their peak and the cervix opens completely.

transitive inference The ability to seriate—or order items along a quantitative dimension—mentally.

triarchic theory of intelligence Sternberg's theory, which states that information-processing skills, ability to learn efficiently in novel situations, and contextual (or cultural) factors interact to determine intelligent behavior.

trimesters Three equal time periods in prenatal development, each of which lasts 3 months.

ulnar grasp The clumsy grasp of the young infant, in which the fingers close against the palm.

umbilical cord The long cord connecting the prenatal organism to the placenta that delivers nutrients and removes waste products.

unconditioned response (UCR) In classical conditioning, a reflexive response that is produced by an unconditioned stimulus (UCS).

unconditioned stimulus (UCS) In classical conditioning, a stimulus that leads to a reflexive response.

underextension An early vocabulary error in which a word is applied too narrowly, to a smaller number of objects and events than is appropriate. Distinguished from *overextension*.

uninhibited, or sociable, child A child whose temperament is such that he or she displays positive emotion to and approaches novel stimuli. Distinguished from *inhibited*, or *shy, child*.

uninvolved style A child-rearing style that is both undemanding and unresponsive. Reflects minimal commitment to parenting. Distinguished from *authoritative, authoritarian,* and *permissive style*.

utilization deficiency The failure of performance to improve after consistently using a mental strategy. Distinguished from *production deficiency, control deficiency,* and *effective strategy use*.

vacuum extractor A plastic cup attached to a suction tube, used to deliver the baby.

vernix A white, cheeselike substance that covers the fetus and prevents the skin from chapping due to constant exposure to amniotic fluid.

visual acuity Fineness of visual discrimination.

Wechsler Intelligence Scale for Children–III (WISC–III) An individually administered intelligence test that includes both a measure of general intelligence and a variety of verbal and performance scores.

Wernicke's area A language structure located in the temporal lobe of the cerebral cortex that is responsible for interpreting language.

whole-language approach An approach to beginning reading instruction that parallels children's natural language learning and keeps reading materials whole and meaningful. Distinguished from *basic-skills approach*.

working, or short-term, memory In information processing, the conscious part of the mental system, where we actively "work" on a limited amount of information to ensure that it will be retained.

X-linked inheritance A pattern of inheritance in which a recessive gene is carried on the X chromosome. Males are more likely to be affected.

zone of proximal development In Vygotsky's theory, a range of tasks that the child cannot yet handle alone but can do with the help of more skilled partners.

zygote The newly fertilized cell formed by the union of sperm and ovum at conception.

REFERENCES

AARON, R., & POWELL, G. (1982). Feedback practices as a function of teacher and pupil race during reading groups instruction. *Journal of Negro Education, 51,* 50–59.

ABBOTT, S. (1992). Holding on and pushing away: Comparative perspectives on an eastern Kentucky child-rearing practice. *Ethos, 20,* 33–65.

ABBOTTS, B., & OSBORN, L. M. (1993). Immunization status and reasons for immunization delay among children using public health immunization clinics. *American Journal of Diseases of Children, 147,* 965–968.

ABOOD, D. A., & CHANDLER, S. B. (1997). Race and the role of weight, weight change, and body dissatisfaction in eating disorders. *American Journal of Health Behavior, 21,* 21–25.

ABRAMOVITCH, R., FREEDMAN, J. L., HENRY, K., & VAN BRUNSCHOT, M. (1995). Children's capacity to consent to participation in psychological research: Some empirical findings. *Child Development, 62,* 1100–1109.

ABRAMOVITCH, R., FREEDMAN, J. L., THODEN, K., & NIKOLICH, C. (1991). Children's capacity to consent to participation in psychological research: Some empirical findings. *Child Development, 62,* 1100–1109.

ACHENBACH, T. M., PHARES, V., HOWELL, C. T., RAUH, V. A., & NURCOMBE, B. (1990). Seven-year outcome of the Vermont program for low-birthweight infants. *Child Development, 61,* 1672–1681.

ACHENBACH, T. M., & WEISZ, J. R. (1975). A longitudinal study of developmental synchrony between conceptual identity, seriation, and transitivity of color, number, and length. *Child Development, 46,* 840–848.

ACKERMAN, B. P. (1978). Children's understanding of speech acts in unconventional frames. *Child Development, 49,* 311–318.

ADAMS, M. J., TREIMAN, R., & PRESSLEY, M. (1998). Reading, writing, and literacy. In D. Kuhn & R. S. Siegler (Eds.), *Handbook of child psychology: Vol. 2. Cognition, perception, and language* (5th ed., pp. 275–355). New York: Wiley.

ADAMS, R. J. (1987). An evaluation of color preference in early infancy. *Infant Behavior and Development, 10,* 143–150.

ADAMS, R. J., COURAGE, M. L., & MERCER, M. E. (1994). Systematic measurement of human neonatal color vision. *Vision Research, 34,* 1691–1701.

ADOLPH, K. E. (1997). Learning in the development of infant locomotion. *Monographs of the Society for Research in Child Development, 62* (3, Serial No. 251).

ADOLPH, K. E., EPPLER, M. A., & GIBSON, E. J. (1993). Crawling versus walking infants' perception of affordances for locomotion over sloping surfaces. *Child Development, 64,* 1158–1174.

AHAJA, K. K., EMERSON, G., SEATON, A., MAMISO, J., & SIMONS, E. G. (1997). Widow's attempt to use her dead husband's sperm. *British Medical Journal, 314,* 143.

AHLSTEN, G., CNATTINGIUS, S., & LINDMARK, G. (1993). Cessation of smoking during pregnancy improves fetal growth and reduces infant morbidity in the neonatal period: A population-based prospective study. *Acta Paediatrica, 82,* 177–181.

AINSWORTH, M. D. S., BLEHAR, M. C., WATERS, E., & WALL, S. (1978). *Patterns of attachment.* Hillsdale, NJ: Erlbaum.

ALAN GUTTMACHER INSTITUTE. (1994). *Sex and America's teenagers.* New York: Author.

ALBERT, R. S. (1994). The achievement of eminence: A longitudinal study of exceptionally gifted boys and their families. In R. F. Sobotnik & K. D. Arnold (Eds.), *Beyond Terman: Contemporary studies of giftedness and talent* (pp. 282–315). Norwood, NJ: Ablex.

ALBRIGHT, A. (1993). Postpartum depression: An overview. *Journal of Counseling & Development, 71,* 316–319.

ALDWIN, C. (1994). *Stress, coping, and development.* New York: Guilford.

ALES, K. L., DRUZIN, M. L., & SANTINI, D. L. (1990). Impact of advanced maternal age on the outcome of pregnancy. *Surgery, Gynecology & Obstetrics, 171,* 209–216.

ALESSANDRI, S. M., & WOZNIAK, R. H. (1987). The child's awareness of parental beliefs concerning the child: A developmental study. *Child Development, 58,* 316–323.

ALLAN, K., & COLTRANE, S. (1996). Gender displaying television commercials: A comparative study of television commercials in the 1950s and 1980s. *Sex Roles, 35,* 185–203.

ALLEN, J. P., HAUSER, S. T., BELL, K. L., & O'CONNOR, T. G. (1994). Longitudinal assessment of autonomy and relatedness in adolescent—family interactions as predictors of adolescent ego development and self-esteem. *Child Development, 65,* 179–194.

ALLEN, J. P., MOORE, C. M., & KUPERMINC, G. P. (1996). Developmental approaches to understanding adolescent deviance. In S. S. Luthar, J. A. Burack, D. Cicchetti, & J. R. Weisz (Eds.), *Developmental psychopathology: Perspectives on adjustment, risk, and disorder* (pp. 548–567). New York: Cambridge University Press.

ALLEN, J. P., PHILLIBER, S., HERRLING, S., & KUPERMINC, G. P. (1997). Preventing teen pregnancy and academic failure: Experimental evaluation of a developmentally based approach. *Child Development, 64,* 729–742.

ALLEN, L. F., PALOMARES, R. S., DEFOREST, P., SPRINKLE, B., & REYNOLDS, C. R. (1991). The effects of intrauterine cocaine exposure: Transient or teratogenic? *Archives of Clinical Neurospsychology, 6,* 133–146.

ALLENSWORTH, D. (1996). Cardiovascular objectives for youth in Healthy People 2000: Update on the status of risk factors. *Journal of Health Education, 27,* S17–S23.

ALPERT-GILLIS, L. J., & CONNELL, J. P. (1989). Gender and sex-role influences on children's self-esteem. *Journal of Personality, 57,* 97–114.

AMATO, P. R., LOOMIS, L. S., & BOOTH, A. (1995). Parental divorce, marital conflict, and offspring well-being during early adulthood. *Social Forces, 73,* 895-915.

AMERICAN ACADEMY OF FAMILY PHYSICIANS. (1997). Decline in SIDS rates. *American Family Physician, 55,* 358–359.

AMERICAN ACADEMY OF PEDIATRICS. (1993). *Caring for your baby and young child: Birth to age 5.* New York: Bantam.

AMERICAN ACADEMY OF PEDIATRICS. (1995). Injuries associated with infant walkers. *Pediatrics, 95,* 778–780.

AMERICAN ACADEMY OF PEDIATRICS, Committee on Infectious Diseases. (1998). Recommended childhood immunization schedule—United States, January–December 1998. *Pediatrics, 101,* 154–157.

AMERICAN PSYCHIATRIC ASSOCIATION. (1994). *Diagnostic and statistical manual of mental disorders* (4th ed.). Washington, DC: Author.

AMERICAN PSYCHOLOGICAL ASSOCIATION. (1992). Ethical principles of psychologists and code of conduct. *American Psychologist, 44,* 1597–1611.

AMES, C. (1992). Classrooms: Goals, structures, and student motivation. *Journal of*

Educational Psychology, 84, 261–271.

ANAND, K. (1990). The biology of pain perception in newborn infants. In D. Tyler & E. Krane (Eds.), *Advances in pain research therapy* (pp. 113–155). New York: Raven Press.

ANDERMAN, E. M., & MIDGLEY, C. (1997). Changes in achievement goal orientations, perceived academic competence, and grades across the transition to middle-level schools. *Contemporary Educational Psychology, 22,* 269–298.

ANDERSON, D. A. (1994). Lesbian and gay adolescents: Social and developmental considerations. *High School Journal, 77,* 13–19.

ANDERSON, E. S. (1984). The acquisition of sociolinguistic knowledge: Some evidence from children's verbal role play. *Western Journal of Speech Communication, 48,* 125–144.

ANDERSON, G. C. (1991). Current knowledge about skin-to-skin (kangaroo) care for preterm infants. *Journal of Perinatology, 11,* 216–226.

ANDERSON, P. J., & GRAHAM, S. M. (1994). Issues in second-language phonological acquisition among children and adults. *Topics in Language Disorders, 14,* 84–100.

ANDERSSON, B-E. (1989). Effects of public day care—A longitudinal study. *Child Development, 60,* 857–866.

ANDERSSON, B-E. (1992). Effects of day care on cognitive and socioemotional competence of thirteen-year-old Swedish schoolchildren. *Child Development, 63,* 20–36.

ANDRACCHIO, B., & WEISBERG, P. (1996). Children's understanding of equality–inequality relationships for liquid quantities: The role of minimal-difference concept examples. *Journal of Genetic Psychology, 157,* 477–488.

ANGLE, J., & WISSMANN, D. A. (1980). The epidemiology of myopia. *American Journal of Epidemiology, 111,* 220–228.

ANGLIN, J. M. (1993). Vocabulary development: A morphological analysis. *Monographs of the Society for Research in Child Development, 58* (10, Serial No. 238).

ANTONARAKIS, S. E. (1992). The meiotic stage of nondisjunction in trisomy 21: Determination by using DNA polymorphisms. *American Journal of Human Genetics, 50,* 544–550.

APGAR, V. (1953). A proposal for a new method of evaluation in the newborn infant. *Current Research in Anesthesia and Analgesia, 32,* 260–267.

ARCHER, S. L. (1982). The lower age boundaries of identity development. *Child Development, 53,* 1551–1556.

ARCHER, S. L. (1989a). Gender differences in identity development: Issues of process, domain, and timing. *Journal of Adolescence, 2,* 117–138.

ARCHER, S. L. (1989b). The status of identity: Reflections on the need for intervention. *Journal of Adolescence, 12,* 345–359.

ARCHER, S. L., & WATERMAN, A. S. (1990). Varieties of identity diffusions and foreclosures: An exploration of subcategories of the identity statuses. *Journal of Adolescent Research, 5,* 96–111.

ARCHER, S. L., & WATERMAN, A. S. (1994). Adolescent identity development: Contextual perspectives. In C. B. Fisher & R. M. Lerner (Eds.), *Applied developmental psychology* (pp. 76–100). New York: McGraw-Hill.

ARCUS, D., & KAGAN, J. (1995). Temperament and craniofacial variation in the first two years. *Child Development, 66,* 1529–1540.

ARIÈS, P. (1962). *Centuries of childhood.* New York: Random House.

ARNOLD, K. (1994). The Illinois Valedictorian Project: Early adult careers of academically talented male and female high school students. In R. F. Subotnik & K. D. Arnold (Eds.), *Beyond Terman: Contemporary longitudinal studies of giftedness and talent* (pp. 24–51). Norwood, NJ: Ablex.

ARTERBERRY, M. E., CRATON, L. G., & YONAS, A. (1993). Infants' sensitivity to motion-carried information for depth and object properties. In C. E. Granrud (Ed.), *Visual perception and cognition in infancy* (pp. 215–234). Hillsdale, NJ: Erlbaum.

ARTMAN, L., & CAHAN, S. (1993). Schooling and the development of transitive inference. *Developmental Psychology, 29,* 753–759.

ASENDORPF, J. B., WARKENTIN, V., & BAUDONNIERE, P. (1996). Self-awareness and other-awareness II: Mirror self-recognition, social contingency awareness, and synchronic imi-

tation. *Developmental Psychology, 32,* 313–321.

ASHMEAD, D. H., DAVIS, D. L., WHALEN, T., & ODOM, R. D. (1991). Sound localization and sensitivity to interaural time differences in human infants. *Child Development, 62,* 1211–1226.

ASHMEAD, D. H., & PERLMUTTER, M. (1980). Infant memory in everyday life. In M. Perlmutter (Ed.), *New directions for child development* (Vol. 10, pp. 1–16). San Francisco: Jossey-Bass.

ASLIN, R. N. (1993). Perception of visual direction in human infants. In C. E. Granrud (Ed.), *Visual perception and cognition in infancy* (pp. 91–119). Hillsdale, NJ: Erlbaum.

ASLIN, R. N., JUSCZYK, P. W., & PISONI, D. B. (1997). Speech and auditory processing during infancy: Constraints on and precursors to language. In D. K. Kuhn & R. S. Siegler (Eds.), *Handbook of child psychology: Vol. 2. Cognition, perception, and language* (5th ed., pp. 147–198). New York: Wiley.

ASTINGTON, J. W. (1991). Intention in the child's theory of mind. In C. Moore & D. Frye (Eds.), *Children's theories of mind* (pp. 157–172). Hillsdale, NJ: Erlbaum.

ASTINGTON, J. W. (1993). *The child's discovery of the mind.* Cambridge, MA: Harvard University Press.

ASTINGTON, J. W. (1995). Commentary: Talking it over with my brain. In J. H. Flavell, F. L. Green, & E. R. Flavell. Young children's knowledge about thinking. *Monographs of the Society for Research in Child Development, 60* (1, Serial No. 243).

ASTINGTON, J. W., & JENKINS, J. M. (1995). Theory of mind development and social understanding. *Cognition & Emotion, 9,* 151–165.

ASTLEY, S. J., CLARREN, S. K., LITTLE, R. E., SAMPSON, P. D., & DALING, J. R. (1992). Analysis of facial shape in children gestationally exposed to marijuana, alcohol, and/or cocaine. *Pediatrics, 89,* 67–77.

ATKINSON, R. C., & SHIFFRIN, R. M. (1968). Human memory: A proposed system and its control processes. In K. W. Spence & J. T. Spence (Eds.), *Advances in the psychology of learning and motivation* (Vol. 2, pp. 90–195). New York: Academic Press.

ATTIE, I., & BROOKS-GUNN, J. (1996). The development of eating regulation across the life span. In D. Cicchetti & D. J. Cohen (Eds.), *Developmental psychology: Vol. 2. Risk, disorder, and adaptation* (pp. 332–368). New York: Wiley.

AU, K. H. (1997). A sociocultural model of reading instruction: The Kamehameha Elementary Education Program. In S. A. Stahl & D. A. Hayes (Eds.), *Instructional models in reading* (pp. 181–202). Mahwah, NJ: Erlbaum.

AU, T. K., SIDLE, A. L., & ROLLINS, K. B. (1993). Developing an intuitive understanding of conservation and contamination: Invisible particles as a plausible mechanism. *Developmental Psychology, 29,* 286–299.

AVIS, J., & HARRIS, P. L. (1991). Belief–desire reasoning among Baka children: Evidence for a universal conception of mind. *Child Development, 62,* 460–467.

AXIA, G., & BARONI, R. (1985). Linguistic politeness at different age levels. *Child Development, 56,* 918–927.

AZMITIA, M. (1988). Peer interaction and problem solving: When are two heads better than one? *Child Development, 59,* 87–96.

BADER, A. P. (1995). Engrossment revisited: Fathers are still falling in love with their newborn babies. In J. L. Shapiro, M. J. Diamond, & M. Greenberg (Eds.), *Becoming a father* (pp 224–233). New York: Springer.

BAENNINGER, M., & NEWCOMBE, N. (1995). Environmental input to the development of sex-related differences in spatial and mathematical ability. *Learning and Individual Differences, 7,* 363–379.

BAHRICK, L. E. (1992). Infants' perception of substance and temporal synchrony in multimodal events. *Infant Behavior and Development, 6,* 429–451.

BAHRICK, L. E., MOSS, L., & FADIL, C. (1996). Development of visual self-recognition in infancy. *Ecological Psychology, 8,* 189–208.

BAI, D. L., & BERTENTHAL, B. I. (1992). Locomotor status and the development of spatial search skills. *Child Development, 63,* 215–226.

BAILEY, A., LE COUTEUR, A., GOTTESMAN, I., BOLTON, P.,

SIMONOFF, E., YUZDA, E., & RUTTER, M. (1995). Autism as a strongly genetic disorder. *Psychological Medicine, 25,* 63–77.

BAILEY, D. A., & RASMUSSEN, R. L. (1996). Sport and the child: Physiological and skeletal issues. In F. L. Smoll & R. E. Smith (Eds.), *Children and youth in sport: A biopsychological perspective* (pp. 187–199). Dubuque, IA: Brown & Benchmark.

BAILEY, J. M., BOBROW, D., WOLFE, M., & MIKACH, S. (1995). Sexual orientation of adult sons of gay fathers. *Developmental Psychology, 31,* 124–129.

BAILEY, J. M., & PILLARD, R. C. (1991). A genetic study of male sexual orientation. *Archives of General Psychology, 43,* 808–812.

BAILEY, J. M., PILLARD, R. C., NEALE, M. C., & AGYEI, Y. (1993). Heritable factors influence sexual orientation in women. *Archives of General Psychiatry, 50,* 217–223.

BAILEY, R. C. (1990). Growth of African pygmies in early childhood. *New England Journal of Medicine, 323,* 1146.

BAILEY, T. (1993). Can youth apprenticeship thrive in the United States? *Educational Researcher, 22* (3), 4–10.

BAILLARGEON, R. (1987). Object permanence in 3½- and 4½-month-old infants. *Developmental Psychology, 23,* 655–664.

BAILLARGEON, R. (1994a). How do infants learn about the physical world? *Current Directions in Psychological Science, 3,* 133–140.

BAILLARGEON, R. (1994b). Physical reasoning in infancy. In M. S. Gazzaniga (Ed.), *The cognitive neurosciences* (pp. 181–204). Cambridge, MA: MIT Press.

BAILLARGEON, R. (1995). A model of physical reasoning in infancy. In C. Rovee-Collier & L. P. Lipsitt (Eds.), *Advances in infancy research* (Vol. 9, pp. 305–371). Norwood, NJ: Ablex.

BAILLARGEON, R., & DEVOS, J. (1991). Object permanence in young infants: Further evidence. *Child Development, 62,* 1227–1246.

BAILLARGEON, R., GRABER, M., DEVOS, J., & BLACK, J. (1990). Why do young infants fail to search for hidden objects? *Cognition, 36,* 255–284.

BAILLARGEON, R., NEEDHAM, A., & DEVOS, J. (1992). The development of young infants' intuitions about support. *Early Development and Parenting, 1,* 68–78.

BAIRD, P. A., & SADOVNICK, A. D. (1987). Maternal age-specific rates for Down syndrome: Changes over time. *American Journal of Medical Genetics, 29,* 917–927.

BAKER, C. (1993). Foundations of bilingual education and bilingualism. Clevedon, England: Multilingual Matters.

BAKER-WARD, L., GORDON, B. N., ORNSTEIN, P. A., LARUS, D. M., & CLUBB, P. A. (1993). Young children's long-term retention of a pediatric examination. *Child Development, 64,* 1519–1533.

BALDWIN, A., BALDWIN, C., & COLE, R. E. (1990). Stress-resistant families and stress-resistant children. In J. E. Rolf, A. S. Masten, D. Cicchetti, K. N. Wechterlein, & S. Weintraub (Eds.), *Risk and protective factors in the development of psychopathology* (pp. 257–280). New York: Cambridge University Press.

BALLARD, B. D., GIPSON, M. T., GUTTENBERG, W., & RAMSEY, K. (1980). Palatability of food as a factor influencing obese and normal-weight children's eating habits. *Behavior Research and Therapy, 18,* 598–600.

BANDURA, A. (1977). *Social learning theory.* Englewood Cliffs, NJ: Prentice-Hall.

BANDURA, A. (1986). *Social foundations of thought and action: A social cognitive theory.* Englewood Cliffs, NJ: Prentice-Hall.

BANDURA, A. (1989). Social cognitive theory. In R. Vasta (Ed.), *Annals of child development* (Vol. 6, pp. 1–60). Greenwich, CT: JAI Press.

BANDURA, A. (1997). *Self-efficacy: The exercise of control.* New York: Freeman.

BANIS, H. T., VARNI, J. W., WALLANDER, J. L., KORSCH, B. M., JAY, S. M., ADLER, R., GARCIA-TEMPLE, E., & NEGRETE, V. (1988). Psychological and social adjustment of obese children and their families: *Child: Care, Health, and Development, 14,* 157–173.

BANKS, M. S. (1980). The development of visual accommodation during early infancy. *Child Development, 51,* 157–173.

BANKS, M. S., & BENNETT, P. J. (1988). Optical and photoreceptor immaturities limit the spatial and chromatic vision of human neonates. *Journal of the Optical Society of America, 5,* 2059–2079.

BANKS, M. S., & GINSBURG, A. P. (1985). Early visual preferences: A review and new theoretical treatment. In H. W. Reese (Ed.), *Advances in child development and behavior* (Vol. 19, pp. 207–246). New York: Academic Press.

BANKS, M. S., & SALAPATEK, P. (1983). Infant visual perception. In M. M. Haith & J. J. Campos (Eds.), *Handbook of child psychology: Vol. 2. Infancy and developmental psychobiology* 4th ed., (pp. 435–571). New York: Wiley.

BARKER, D. J. P. (1994). *Mothers, babies, and disease in later life.* London: British Medical Journal Publishing.

BARKER, D. J. P., GLUCKMAN, P. D., GODFREY, K. M., HARDING, J. E., OWENS, J. A., & ROBINSON, J. S. (1993). Fetal nutrition and cardiovascular disease in adult life. *Lancet, 341,* 938–941.

BARKER, R. G. (1955). *Midwest and its children.* Stanford, CA: Stanford University Press.

BARKLEY, R. A. (1995). *Taking charge of ADHD.* New York: Guilford.

BARKLEY, R. A. (1997). Behavioral inhibition, sustained attention, and executive functions: Constructing a unifying theory of ADHD. *Psychological Bulletin, 121,* 65–94.

BARKLEY, R. A., DUPAUL, G. J., & COSTELLO, A. J. (1993). Stimulant medications. In J. Werry & M. Aman (Eds.), *Disruptive behavior disorders in childhood* (pp. 11–57). New York: Plenum.

BARLING, J., ROGERS, K., & KELLOWAY, K. (1995). Some effects of teenagers' part-time employment: The quantity and quality of work make the differences. *Journal of Organizational Behavior, 16,* 143–154.

BARNAS, M. V., & CUMMINGS, E. M. (1994). Caregiver stability and toddlers' attachment-related behavior toward caregivers in day care. *Infant Behavior and Development, 17,* 141–147.

BARNES-JOSIAH, D., & AUGUSTIN, A. (1995). Secular trend in the age at menarche in Haiti. *American Journal of Human Biology, 7,* 357–362.

BARNETT, D., MANLY, J., & CICCHETTI, D. (1993). Defining child maltreatment: The interface between policy and research. In D. Cicchetti & S. Toth (Eds.), *Child abuse, child development, and social policy* (pp. 7–73). Norwood, NJ: Ablex.

BARNETT, W. S. (1993). New wine in old bottles: Increasing the coherence of early childhood care and educational policy. *Early Childhood Research Quarterly, 8,* 519–558.

BARNETT, W. S. (1995). Long-term effects of early childhood programs on cognitive and school outcomes. *Future Child, 5,* 25–50.

BAROL, B. (1986, July 28). Cocaine babies: Hooked at birth. *Newsweek,* pp. 56–57.

BARON-COHEN, S. (1993). From attention–goal psychology to belief–desire psychology: The development of a theory of mind and its dysfunction. In S. Baron-Cohen, H. Tager-Flusberg, & D. Cohen (Eds.), *Understanding other minds: Perspectives from autism* (pp. 59–82). Oxford, England: Oxford University Press.

BARON-COHEN, S., BALDWIN, D. A., & CROWSON, M. (1997). Do children with autism use the speaker's direction of gaze strategy to crack the code of language? *Child Development, 68,* 48–57.

BARR, H. M., STREISSGUTH, A. P., DARBY, B. L., & SAMPSON, P. D. (1990). Prenatal exposure to alcohol, caffeine, tobacco, and aspirin: Effects on fine and gross motor performance in 4-year-old children. *Developmental Psychology, 26,* 339–348.

BARTH, R. P., PETRO, J. V., & LELAND, N. (1992). Preventing adolescent pregnancy with social and cognitive skills. *Journal of Adolescent Research, 7,* 208–222.

BARTON, M. E., & TOMASELLO, M. (1991). Joint attention and conversation in mother–infant–sibling triads. *Child Development, 62,* 517–529.

BARTON, S. J., HARRIGAN, R., & TSE, A. M. (1995). Prenatal cocaine exposure: Implications for practice, policy development, and needs for future research. *Journal of Perinatology, 15,* 10–22.

BARTSCH, K., & WELLMAN, H. M. (1995). *Children talk about the mind.* New York: Oxford University Press.

BASHIR, L. M. (1997). Female genital mutilation—balancing

intolerance of the practice with tolerance of culture. *Journal of Women's Health, 6,* 11–14.

BASTIAN, H. (1993). Personal beliefs and alternative childbirth choices: A survey of 552 women who planned to give birth at home. *Birth, 20,* 186–192.

BATES, E. (1979). *The emergence of symbols: Cognition and communication in infancy.* New York: Academic Press.

BATES, E. (1995). *Modularity, domain specificity, and the development of language.* Unpublished manuscript, University of California, San Diego.

BATES, E., BRETHERTON, I., & SNYDER, L. (1988). *From first words to grammar.* Cambridge, England: Cambridge University Press.

BATES, E., MARCHMAN, V., THAL, D., FENSON, L., DALE, P., REZNICK, J. S., REILLY, J., & HARTUNG, J. (1994). Developmental and stylistic variation in the composition of early vocabulary. *Journal of Child Language, 21,* 85–123.

BATES, E., & MACWHINNEY, B. (1987). Competition, variation, and language learning. In B. MacWhinney (Ed.), *Mechanisms of language acquisition* (pp. 157–193). Hillsdale, NJ: Erlbaum.

BATES, J. E., BAYLES, K., BENNETT, D. S., RIDGE, B., & BROWN, M. M. (1991). Origins of externalizing behavior problems at eight years of age. In E. J. Pepler & K. H. Rubin (Eds.), *The development and treatment of childhood aggression* (pp. 93–120). Hillsdale, NJ: Erlbaum.

BATH, R., UING, A., & WILLIAMS, C. (1996). Nocturnal enuresis and the use of desmopressin: Is it helpful? *Child: Care, Health and Development, 22,* 73–84.

BAUER, P. J. (1996). What do infants recall of their lives? Memory for specific events by one- to two-year-olds. *American Psychologist, 51,* 29–41.

BAUER, P. J., & DOW, G. A. A. (1994). Episodic memory in 16- and 20-month-old children: Specifics are generalized, but not forgotten. *Developmental Psychology, 30,* 403–417.

BAUER, P. J., & MANDLER, J. M. (1992). Putting the horse before the cart: The use of temporal order in recall of events by one-year-old children. *Developmental Psychology, 28,* 441–452.

BAUMRIND, D. (1967). Child are practices anteceding three patterns of preschool behavior. *Genetic Psychology Monographs, 75,* 43–88.

BAUMRIND, D. (1971). Current patterns of parental authority. *Developmental Psychology Monograph, 4* (No. 1, Pt. 2).

BAUMRIND, D. (1983). Rejoinder to Lewis's reinterpretation of parental firm control effects: Are authoritative families really harmonious? *Psychological Bulletin, 94,* 132–142.

BAUMRIND, D. (1991). The influence of parenting style on adolescent competence and substance use. *Journal of Early Adolescence, 11,* 56–95.

BAUMRIND, D., & BLACK, A. E. (1967). Socialization practices associated with dimension of competence in preschool boys and girls. *Child Development, 38,* 291–327.

BAYLEY, N. (1969). *Bayley Scales of Infant Development.* New York: Psychological Corporation.

BAYLEY, N. (1993). *Bayley Scales of Infant Development* (2nd ed.). New York: Psychological Corporation.

BEAL, C. R. (1990). The development of text evaluation and revision skills. *Child Development, 61,* 247–258.

BEARISON, D. J. (1998). Pediatric psychology and children's medical problems. In I. G. Sigel & K. A. Renninger (Eds.), *Handbook of child psychology: Vol. 4. Child psychology in practice* (5th ed., pp. 635–711). New York: Wiley.

BEATTY, W. W. (1992). Gonadal hormones and sex differences in nonreproductive behaviors. In A. A. Gerall, H. Moltz, & I. L. Ward (Eds.), *Handbook of behavioral neurobiology: Vol. 11. Sexual differentiation* (pp. 85–128). New York: Plenum.

BEAUTRAIS, A. L., FERGUSSON, D. M., & SHANNON, F. T. (1982). Life events and childhood morbidity: A prospective study. *Pediatrics, 70,* 935–940.

BECK, M. (1994, January 17). How far should we push mother nature? *Newsweek,* pp. 54–57.

BECKWITH, L., & SIGMAN, M. D. (1995). Preventive interventions in infancy. *Child and Adolescent Psychiatric Clinics of North America, 4,* 683–700.

BEHREND, D. (1988). Overextensions in early language comprehension: Evidence from a signal detection approach. *Journal of Child Language, 15,* 63–75.

BEHREND, D. A., ROSENGREN, K. S., & PERLMUTTER, M. (1992). The relation between private speech and parental interactive style. In R. M. Diaz & L. E. Berk (Eds.), *Private speech: From social interaction to self-regulation* (pp. 85–100). Hillsdale, NJ: Erlbaum.

BEHRMAN, R. E., & VAUGHAN, V. C. (1987). *Nelson textbook of pediatrics* (13th ed.). Philadelphia: Saunders.

BEIDEL, D. (1991). Social phobia and overanxious disorder in school-age children. *Journal of the American Academy of Child and Adolescent Psychiatry, 30,* 545–552.

BEILIN, H. (1978). Inducing conservation through training. In G. Steiner (Ed.), *Psychology of the twentieth century* (Vol. 7, pp. 260–289). Munich: Kindler.

BEILIN, H. (1992). Piaget's enduring contribution to developmental psychology. *Developmental Psychology, 28,* 191–204.

BELL, A., Weinberg, M., & Hammersmith, S. (1981). *Sexual preference: Its development in men and women.* Bloomington, IN: Indiana University Press.

BELL, K. L., ALLEN, J. P., HAUSER, S. T., & O'CONNOR, T. G. (1996). Family factors and young adult transitions: Educational attainment and occupational prestige. In J. A. Graber, J. Brooks-Gunn, & A. C. Petersen (Eds.), *Transitions through adolescence: Interpersonal domains and context* (pp. 345–366). Mahwah, NJ: Erlbaum.

BELL, M. A., & FOX, N. A. (1992). The relations between frontal brain electrical activity and cognitive development during infancy. *Child Development, 63,* 1142–1163.

BELL, M. A., & FOX, N. A. (1994). Brain development over the first year of life: Relations between EEG frequency and coherence and cognitive and affective behaviors. In G. Dawson & K. W. Fischer (Eds.), *Human behavior and the developing brain* (pp. 314–345). New York: Guilford.

BELL, M. A., & FOX, N. A. (1998). Crawling experience is related to changes in cortical organization during infancy: Evidence from EEG coherence. *Developmental Psychology.*

BELL, R. J., PALMA, S. M., & LUMLEY, J. M. (1995). The effect of vigorous exercise during pregnancy on birth-weight. *Australian and New Zealand Journal of Obstetrics and Gynaecology, 35,* 46–51.

BELLAMY, C. (1997). *The state of the world's children 1997.* New York: Oxford University Press (in cooperation with UNICEF).

BELLINGER, D., LEVITON, A., WATERNAUX, C., NEEDLEMAN, H., & RABINOWITZ, M. (1987). Longitudinal analysis of prenatal and postnatal lead exposure and early cognitive development. *New England Journal of Medicine, 316,* 1037–1043.

BELSKY, J. (1989). Infant–parent attachment and day care: In defense of the Strange Situation. In J. Lande, S. Scarr, & N. Gunzenhauser (Eds.), *Caring for children: Challenge to America* (pp. 23–48). Hillsdale, NJ: Erlbaum.

BELSKY, J. (1992). Consequences of child care for children's development: A deconstructionist view. In A. Booth (Ed.), *Child care in the 1990s: Trends and consequences* (pp. 83–85). Hillsdale, NJ: Erlbaum.

BELSKY, J. (1993). Etiology of child maltreatment: A developmental-ecological analysis. *Psychological Bulletin, 114,* 413–434.

BELSKY, J. (1996). Parent, infant, and social-contextual antecedents of father–son attachment security. *Developmental Psychology, 32,* 905–913.

BELSKY, J., & CASSIDY, J. (1994). Attachment: Theory and evidence. In M. Rutter & D. Hay (Eds.), *Development through life* (pp. 373–402). Oxford, England: Blackwell.

BELSKY, J., FISH, M., & ISABELLA, R. (1991). Continuity and discontinuity in infant negative and positive emotionality: Family antecedents and attachment consequences. *Developmental Psychology, 27,* 421–431.

BELSKY, J., & KELLY, J. (1994). *The transition to parenthood.* New York: Delacorte Press.

BELSKY, J., ROVINE, M., & TAYLOR, D. G. (1984). The Pennsylvania Infant and Family Development Project: III. The origins of individual differences in infant–mother attachment: Maternal and infant contributions. *Child Development, 55,* 718–728.

BELTRAMINI, A. U., & HERTZIG, M. E. (1983). Sleep and bedtime behavior in preschool-aged children. *Pediatrics, 71,* 153–158.

BEM, S. L. (1984). Androgyny and gender schema theory: A conceptual and empirical integration. In R. A. Dienstbier & T. B. Sondregger (Eds.), *Nebraska Symposia on Motivation* (Vol. 34, pp. 179–226). Lincoln: University of Nebraska Press.

BEM, S. L. (1989). Genital knowledge and gender constancy in preschool children. *Child Development, 60,* 649–662.

BEM, S. L. (1993). *The lenses of gender: Transforming the debate on sexual inequality.* New Haven, CT: Yale University Press.

BENACERRAF, B. R., GREEN, M. F., SALTZMAN, D. H., BARSS, V. A., PENSO, C. A., NADEL, A. S., HEFFNER, L. J., STRYKER, J. M., SANDSTROM, M. M., & FRIGOLETTO, F. D., JR. (1988). Early amniocentesis for prenatal cytogenetic evaluation. *Radiology, 169,* 709–710.

BENBOW, C. P., & ARJMAND, O. (1990). Predictors of high academic achievement in mathematics and science by mathematically talented students: A longitudinal study. *Journal of Educational Psychology, 82,* 430–441.

BENBOW, C. P., & STANLEY, J. C. (1983). Sex differences in mathematical reasoning: More facts. *Science, 222,* 1029–1031.

BENDER, W. N. (1996). Learning disabilities. In P. J. McLaughlin & P. Wehman (Eds.), *Mental retardation and developmental disabilities* (2nd ed., pp. 259–279). Austin, TX: PRO-ED.

BENDER, W. N., & WALL, M. E. (1994). Social-emotional development of students with learning disabilities. *Learning Disability Quarterly, 17,* 323–341.

BENEDICT, R. (1934a). Anthropology and the abnormal. *Journal of Genetic Psychology, 10,* 59–82.

BENEDICT, R. (1934b). *Patterns of culture.* Boston: Houghton Mifflin.

BENENSON, J. F. (1993). Greater preference among females than males for dyadic interaction in early childhood. *Child Development, 64,* 544–555.

BENNETTO, L., PENNINGTON, B. F., & ROGERS, S. J. (1996). Intact and impaired memory functions in autism. *Child Development, 67,* 1816–1835.

BERCU, B. B. (1996). Use of growth hormone for non-growth hormone deficient children [letter]. *Journal of the American Medical Association, 276,* 1878.

BERG, M., & MEDRICH, E. A. (1980). Children in four neighborhoods: The physical environment and its effects on play and play patterns. *Environment and Behavior, 12,* 320–348.

BERK, L. E. (1985). Relationship of caregiver education to child-oriented attitudes, job satisfaction, and behaviors toward children. *Child Care Quarterly, 14,* 103–129.

BERK, L. E. (1992a). Children's private speech: An overview of theory and the status of research. In R. M. Diaz & L. E. Berk (Eds.), *Private speech: From social interaction to self-regulation* (pp. 17–53). Hillsdale, NJ: Erlbaum.

BERK, L. E. (1992b). The extracurriculum. In P. W. Jackson (Ed.), *Handbook of research on curriculum* (pp. 1002–1043). New York: Macmillan.

BERK, L. E. (1994a). Vygotsky's theory: The importance of make-believe play. *Young Children, 50*(1), 30–39.

BERK, L. E. (1994b, November). Why children talk to themselves. *Scientific American, 271*(5), 78–83.

BERK, L. E., & LANDAU, S. (1993). Private speech of learning disabled and normally achieving children in classroom academic and laboratory contexts. *Child Development, 64,* 556–571.

BERK, L. E., & SPUHL, S. T. (1995). Maternal interaction, private speech, and task performance in preschool children. *Early Childhood Research Quarterly, 10,* 145–169.

BERKO GLEASON, J. (1997). Language development: An overview and a preview. In J. Berko Gleason (Ed.), *The development of language* (4th ed., pp. 1–39). Boston: Allyn and Bacon.

BERKOWITZ, M. W., & GIBBS, J. C. (1983). Measuring the developmental features of moral discussion. *Merrill-Palmer Quarterly, 29,* 399–410.

BERLIN, JR., C. M. (1997). Lead poisoning in children. *Current Opinion in Pediatrics, 9,* 173–177.

BERMAN, P. W. (1980). Are women more responsive than men to the young? A review of developmental and situational variables. *Psychological Bulletin, 88,* 668–695.

BERMEJO, V. (1996). Cardinality development and counting. *Developmental Psychology, 32,* 263-268.

BERNDT, T. J. (1988). The nature and significance of children's friendships. In R. Vasta (Ed.), *Annals of child development* (Vol. 5, pp. 155–186). Greenwich, CT: JAI Press.

BERNDT, T. J., CHEUNG, P. C., LAU, S., HAU, K-T., & LEW, W. J. F. (1993). Perceptions of parenting in mainland China, Taiwan, and Hong Kong: Sex differences and societal differences. *Developmental Psychology, 29,* 156–164.

BERNDT, T. J., & KEEFE, K. (1995). Friends' influence on adolescents' adjustment to school. *Child Development, 66,* 1312–1329.

BERNDT, T. J., & PERRY, T. B. (1990). Distinctive features and effects of early adolescent friendships. In R. Montemayor, G. R. Adams, & T. P. Gullotta (Eds.), *From childhood to adolescence: A transitional period?* (pp. 269–287). Newbury Park, CA: Sage.

BERNIER, J. C., & SIEGEL, D. H. (1994). Attention-deficit hyperactivity disorder: A family ecological systems perspective. *Families in Society, 75,* 142–150.

BERRUETA-CLEMENT, J. R., SCHWEINHART, L. J., BARNETT, W. S., EPSTEIN, A. S., & WEIKART, D. P. (1984). Changed lives: The effects of the Perry Preschool Program on youths through age 19. *Monographs of the High/Scope Research Foundation, 8.*

BERTENTHAL, B. I. (1993). Infants' perception of biomechanical motions: Intrinsic image and knowledge-based constraints. In C. Granrud (Ed.), *Visual percpetion and cognition in infancy* (pp. 175–214). Hillsdale, NJ: Erlbaum.

BERTENTHAL, B. I., & CAMPOS, J. J. (1987). New directions in the study of early experience. *Child Development, 58,* 560–567.

BERTENTHAL, B. I., CAMPOS, J. J., & BARRETT, K. (1984). Self-produced locomotion: An organizer of emotional, cognitive, and social development in infancy. In R. Emde & R. Harmon (Eds.), *Continuities and discontinuities in development* (pp. 174–210). New York: Plenum.

BERTENTHAL, B. I., & CLIFTON, R. K. (1998). Perception and action. In D. Kuhn & R. S. Siegler (Eds.), *Handbook of child psychology: Vol. 2. Cognition, perception, and language* (pp. 51–102). New York: Wiley.

BERTENTHAL, B. I., PROFFITT, D. R., KRAMER, S. J., & SPETNER, N. B. (1987). Infants' encoding of kinetic displays varying in relative coherence. *Developmental Psychology, 23,* 171–178.

BERTENTHAL, B. I., PROFFITT, D. R., SPETNER, N. B., & THOMAS, M. A. (1985). The development of infant sensitivity to biomechanical motions. *Child Development, 56,* 531–543.

BEST, D. L., WILLIAMS, J. E., CLOUD, J. M., DAVIS, S. W., ROBERTSON, L. S., EDWARDS, J. R., GILES, H., & FOWLES, J. (1977). Development of sex-trait stereotypes among young children in the United States, England, and Ireland. *Child Development, 48,* 1375–1384.

BETZ, C. (1994, March). Beyond time-out: Tips from a teacher. *Young Children, 49*(3), 10–14.

BEUNEN, G., & MALINA, R. M. (1996). Growth and biological maturation: Relevance to athletic performance. In O. Bar-Or (Ed.), *The child and adolescent athlete* (pp. 2–24). Oxford: Blackwell Science.

BEYTH-MAROM, R., AUSTIN, L., FISCHHOFF, B., PALMGREN, C., & JACOBS-QUADREL, M. (1993). Perceived consequences of risky behaviors: Adults and adolescents. *Developmental Psychology, 29,* 549–563.

BHATT, R. S., ROVEE-COLLIER, C. K., & WEINER, S. (1994). Developmental changes in the interface between perception and memory retrieval. *Developmental Psychology, 30,* 151–162.

BIALYSTOK, E. (1986). Factors in the growth of linguistic awareness. *Child Development, 57,* 498–510.

BIALYSTOK, E. (1997). Effects of bilingualism and biliteracy on children's emerging concepts of print. *Developmental Psychology, 33,* 429–440.

BIBACE, R., & WALSH, M. E. (1980). Development of children's concepts of illness. *Pediatrics, 66,* 912–917.

BIERMAN, K. L. (1986). Process of change during social skills training with preadolescents and its relation to treatment outcome. *Child Development, 57,* 230–240.

BIERMAN, K. L., SMOOT, D. L., & AUMILLER, K. (1993). Characteristics of aggressive-rejected, aggressive (nonrejected), and rejected (nonaggressive) boys. *Child Development, 64,* 139–151.

BIERNAT, M. (1991). Gender stereotypes and the relationship between masculinity and femininity: A developmental analysis. *Journal of Personality and Social Psychology, 61,* 351–365.

BIGLER, R. S. (1995). The role of classification skill in moderating environmental influences on children's gender stereotyping: A study of the functional use of gender in the classroom. *Child Development, 66,* 1072–1087.

BIGLER, R. S., & LIBEN, L. S. (1990). The role of attitudes and interventions in gender-schematic processing. *Child Development, 61,* 1440–1452.

BIGLER, R. S., & LIBEN, L. S. (1992). Cognitive mechanisms in children's gender stereotyping: Theoretical and educational implications of a cognitive-based intervention. *Child Development, 63,* 1351–1363.

BIGNER, J. J., & JACOBSEN, R. B. (1989). Parenting behaviors of homosexual and heterosexual fathers. *Journal of Homosexuality, 18,* 173–186.

BIJELJAC-BABIC, R., BERTON-CINI, J., & MEHLER, J. (1993). How do 4-day-old infants categorize multisyllable utterances? *Developmental Psychology, 29,* 711–721.

BIRCH, E. E. (1993). Stereopsis in infants and its developmental relation to visual acuity. In K. Simons (Ed.), *Early visual development: Normal and abnormal* (pp. 224–236). New York: Oxford University Press.

BIRCH, L. L. (1990). Development of food acceptance patterns. *Developmental Psychology, 26,* 515–519.

BIRCH, L. L., & FISHER, J. A. (1995). Appetite and eating behavior in children. *Pediatric Clinics of North America, 42,* 931–953.

BIRCH, L. L., JOHNSON, S. L., ANDRESEN, G., PETERS, J. C., & SCHULTE, M. C. (1991). The variability of young children's energy intake. *New England Journal of Medicine, 324,* 232–235.

BIRCH, L. L., JOHNSON, S. L., & FISHER, J. A. (1995, January). Children's eating: The development of food acceptance patterns. *Young Children, 50*(2), 71–78.

BIRCH, L. L., ZIMMERMAN, S., & HIND, H. (1980). The influence of social-affective context on preschool children's food preferences. *Child Development, 51,* 856–861.

BIRENBAUM-CARMELI, D. (1995). Maternal smoking during pregnancy: Social, medical, and legal perspectives on the conception of a human being. *Health Care for Women International, 16,* 57–73.

BIRINGEN, Z., EMBDE, R. N., CAMPOS, J. J., & APPELBAUM, M. I. (1995). Affective reorganization in the infant, the mother, and the dyad: The role of upright locomotion and its timing. *Child Development, 66,* 499–514.

BIRMAHER, B., RYAN, N., WILLIAMSON, D., BRENT, D., & KAUFMAN, J. (1996). Childhood and adolescent depression: A review of the past 10 years. Part II. *Journal of the American Academy of Child and Adolescent Psychiatry, 35,* 1575–1583.

BIRNHOLZ, J. C., & BENACERRAF, B. R. (1983). The development of human fetal hearing. *Science, 222,* 516–518.

BISCHOF–KÖHLER, D. (1991). The development of empathy in infants. In M. E. Lamb & H. Keller (Eds.), *Infant development: Perspectives from German-speaking countries* (pp. 1–33). Hillsdale, NJ: Erlbaum.

BISHOP, S. M., & INGERSOLL, G. M. (1989). Effects of marital conflict and family structure on the self-concepts of pre- and early adolescents. *Journal of Youth and Adolescence, 18,* 25–38.

BIVENS, J. A., & BERK, L. E. (1990). A longitudinal study of the development of elementary school children's private speech. *Merrill-Palmer Quarterly, 36,* 443–463.

BJORKLUND, D. F. (1997). In search of a metatheory for cognitive development (or, Piaget is dead and I don't feel so good myself). *Child Development, 68,* 144–148.

BJORKLUND, D. F., & COYLE, T. R. (1995). Utilization deficiencies in the development of memory strategies. In F. E. Weinert & W. Schneider (Eds.), *Research on memory development: State of the art and future directions* (pp. 161–180). Hillsdale, NJ: Erlbaum.

BJORKLUND, D. F., & MUIR, J. E. (1988). Children's development of free recall: Remembering on their own. In R. Vasta (Ed.), *Annals of child development* (Vol. 5, pp. 79–123). Greenwich, CT: JAI Press.

BLACK, M. (1993). *Girls and women: A UNICEF development priority.* New York: United Nations Children's Fund.

BLACK, M. M., HUTCHESON, J. J., DUBOWITZ, H., & BERENSON-HOWARD, J. (1994). Parenting style and developmental status among children with nonorganic failure to thrive. *Journal of Pediatric Psychology, 19,* 689–707.

BLAGG, N., & YULE, W. (1996). School phobia. In T. H. Ollendick, N. J. King, & W. Yule (Eds.), *International handbook of phobic and anxiety disorders in children and adolescents* (pp. 169–186). New York: Plenum.

BLAKE, I. K. (1994). Language development and socialization in young African-American children. In P. M. Greenfield & R. R. Cocking (Eds.), *Cross-cultural roots of minority child development* (pp. 167–195). Hillsdale, NJ: Erlbaum.

BLAKE, J. (1989). *Family size and achievement.* Berkeley: University of California Press.

BLAKE, J., & BOYSSON-BARDIES, B. DE (1992). Patterns in babbling: A cross-linguistic study. *Journal of Child Language, 19,* 51–74.

BLANCHARD, M., & MAIN, M. (1979). Avoidance of the attachment figure and social-emotional adjustment in day-care infants. *Developmental Psychology, 15,* 445–446.

BLANCHARD, R., & BOGAERT, A. F. (1996). Homosexuality in men and number of older brothers. *American Journal of Psychiatry, 153,* 27–31.

BLANCHARD, R., ZUCKER, K. J., BRADLEY, S. J., & HUME, C. S. (1995). Birth order and sibling sex ratio in homosexual male adolescents and probably prehomosexual feminine boys. *Developmental Psychology, 31,* 22–30.

BLANCHARD, R., ZUCKER, K. J., COHEN-KETTENIS, P. T., GOOREN, L. J. G., & BAILEY, J. M. (1996). Birth order and sibling sex ratio in two samples of Dutch gender-dysphoric homosexual males. *Archives of Sexual Behavior, 25,* 495–512.

BLASI, A. (1990). Kohlberg's theory and moral motivation. In D. Schrader (Ed.), *New directions for child development* (No. 47, pp. 51–57). San Francisco: Jossey-Bass.

BLASS, E. M., GANCHROW, J. R., & STEINER, J. E. (1984). Classical conditioning in newborn humans 2–48 hours of age. *Infant Behavior and Development, 7,* 223–235.

BLATCHFORD, P., & MORTIMORE, P. (1994). The issue of class size for young children in schools: What can we learn from research? *Oxford Review of Education, 20,* 411–428.

BLOCK, G., & ABRAMS, B. (1993). Vitamin and mineral status of women of childbearing potential. *Annals of the New York Academy of Sciences, 678,* 255–265.

BLOCK, G., & KELLY, J. (1994). *The transition to parenthood.* New York: Delacorte Press.

BLOCK, J., BLOCK, J. H., & GJERDE, P. F. (1988). Parental functioning and home environment in families of divorce: Prospective and concurrent analyses. *Journal of the American Academy of Child and Adolescent Psychiatry, 27,* 207–213.

BLOCK, J., & ROBINS, R. W. (1994). A longitudinal study of consistency and change in self-esteem from early adolescence to early adulthood. *Child Development, 64,* 909–923.

BLOOM, B. S. (Ed.). (1985). *Developing talent in young people.* New York: Ballantine Books.

BLOOM, L. (1990). Developments in expression: Affect and speech. In N. Stein & T. Trabasso (Eds.), *Psychological and biological approaches to emotion* (pp. 215–245). Hillsdale, NJ: Erlbaum.

BLOOM, L. (1998). Language acquisition in its developmental context. In D. Kuhn & R. S. Siegler (Eds.), *Handbook of child psychology: Vol. 2. Cognition, perception, and language* (5th ed., pp. 309–370). New York: Wiley.

BLOOM, L., MARGULIS, C., TINKER, E., & FUJITA, N. (1996). Early conversations and word learning: Contributions from child and adult. *Child Development, 67,* 3154–3175.

BLOOM, L., TINKER, E., & MARGULIS, C. (1993). The words children learn: Evidence against a noun bias in early vocabularies. *Cognitive Development, 8,* 431–450.

BLOTNER, R., & BEARISON, D. J. (1984). Developmental consistencies in socio-moral knowledge: Justice reasoning and altruistic behavior. *Merrill-Palmer Quarterly, 30,* 349–367.

BLUM, N. J., & CAREY, W. B. (1996). Sleep problems among infants and young children. *Pediatrics in Review, 17,* 87–93.

BLYTH, D. A., SIMMONS, R. G., & ZAKIN, D. F. (1985). Satisfaction with body image for early adolescent females: The impact of pubertal timing within different school environments. *Journal of Youth and Adolescence, 14,* 207–225.

BOBAK, I. M., JENSEN, M. D., & ZALAR, M. K. (1989). *Maternity and gynecologic care.* St. Louis: Mosby.

BODMER, W., & MCKIE, R. (1997). *The book of man: The human genome project and the quest to discover our genetic heritage.* New York: Oxford University Press.

BOHANNON, J. N., III, & BONVILLIAN, J. D. (1997). Theoretical approaches to language acquisition. In J. Berko Gleason (Ed.), *The development of language* (4th ed., pp. 259–316). Boston: Allyn and Bacon.

BOHANNON, J. N., III, & STANOWICZ, L. (1988). The issue of negative evidence: Adult responses to children's language errors. *Developmental Psychology, 24,* 684–689.

BOLDIZAR, J. P. (1991). Assessing sex typing and androgyny in children: The children's sex role inventory. *Developmental Psychology, 27,* 505–515.

BORJA-ALVAREZ, T., ZARBATANY, L., & PEPPER, S. (1991). Contributions of male and female guests and hosts to peer group entry. *Child Development, 62,* 1079–1090.

BORKE, H. (1975). Piaget's mountains revisited: Changes in the egocentric landscape. *Developmental Psychology, 11,* 240–243.

BORKOWSKI, J. G., & MUTHUKRISNA, N. (1995). Learning environments and skill generalization: How contexts facilitate regulatory processes and efficacy beliefs. In F. Weinert & W. Schneider (Eds.), *Memory performances and competence: Issues in growth and development* (pp. 283-300). Hillsdale, NJ: Erlbaum.

BORNHOLT, L. J., GOODNOW, J. J., & COONEY, G. H. (1994). Influences of gender stereotypes on adolescents' perceptions of their own achievement. *American Educational Research Journal, 31,* 675–692.

BORNSTEIN, M. H. (1989). Sensitive periods in development: Structural characteristics and causal interpretations. *Psychological Bulletin, 105,* 179–197.

BORNSTEIN, M. H. (1992). Perception across the life cycle. In M. H. Bornstein & M. E. Lamb (Eds.), *Developmental psychology: An advanced textbook* (3rd ed., pp. 155–209). Hillsdale, NJ: Erlbaum.

BORNSTEIN, M. H., & LAMB, M. E. (1992). *Development in infancy: An introduction* (3rd ed.). New York: McGraw-Hill.

BORNSTEIN, M. H., TAL, J., RAHN, C., GALPERÍN, C. Z., PÊCHEUX, M., LAMOUR, M., TODA, S., AZUMA, H., OGINO, M., & TAMIS-LEMONDA, C. S. (1992a). Functional analysis of the contents of maternal speech to infants of 5 and 13 months in four cultures: Argentina, France, Japan, and the United States. *Developmental Psychology, 28,* 593–603.

BORNSTEIN, M. H., VIBBERT, M., TAL, J., & O'DONNELL, K. (1992b). Toddler language and play in the second year: Stability, covariation, and influences of parenting. *First Language, 12,* 323–338.

BORST, C. G. (1995). *Catching babies: The professionalization of childbirth, 1870–1920.* Cambridge, MA: Harvard University Press.

BORSTELMANN, L. J. (1983). Children before psychology: Ideas about children from antiquity to the late 1800s. In W. Kessen (Ed.), *Handbook of child psychology: Vol. 1. History, theory, and methods* (pp. 1–40). New York: Wiley.

BOUCHARD, C. (1994). *The genetics of obesity.* Boca Raton, FL: CRC Press.

BOUCHARD, T. J., JR., LYKKEN, D. T., MCGUE, M., SEGAL, N. L., & TELLEGEN, A. (1990). Sources of human psychological differences: The Minnesota Study of Twins Reared Apart. *Science, 250,* 223–228.

BOUCHARD, T. J., JR., & MCGUE, M. (1981). Familial studies of intelligence: A review. *Science, 212,* 1055–1058.

BOUKYDIS, C. F. Z., & BURGESS, R. L. (1982). Adult physiological response to infant cries: Effects of temperament of infant, parental status and gender. *Child Development, 53,* 1291–1298.

BOULTON, M. J. (1996). A comparison of 8- and 11-year-old girls' and boys' participation in specific types of rough-and-tumble play and aggressive fighting: Implications for functional hypotheses. *Aggressive Behavior, 22,* 271–287.

BOULTON, M. J., & SMITH, P. K. (1994). Bully/victim problems in middle-school children: Stability, self-perceived competence, peer perceptions and peer acceptance. *British Journal of Developmental Psychology, 12,* 315–329.

BOWLBY, J. (1969). *Attachment and loss: Vol. 1. Attachment.* New York: Basic Books.

BOWLBY, J. (1980). *Attachment and loss: Vol. 3. Loss.* New York: Basic Books.

BOWMAN, M. C., & SAUNDERS, D. M. (1994). Community attitudes to maternal age and pregnancy after assisted reproductive technology: Too old at 50 years? *Human Reproduction, 9,* 167–171.

BOYER, K., & DIAMOND, A. (1992). Development of memory for temporal order in infants and young children. In A. Diamond (Ed.), *Development and neural bases of higher cognitive function* (pp. 267–317). New York: New York Academy of Sciences.

BOYES, M. C., & CHANDLER, M. (1992). Cognitive development, epistemic doubt, and identity formation in adolescence. *Journal of Youth and Adolescence, 21,* 277–304.

BOYSSON-BARDIES, B. DE, & VIHMAN, M. M. (1991). Adaptation to language: Evidence from babbling and first words in four languages. *Language, 67,* 297–319.

BRABECK, M. (1983). Moral judgment: Theory and research on differences between males and females. *Developmental Review, 3,* 274–291.

BRACKBILL, Y., MCMANUS, K., & WOODWARD, L. (1985). *Medication in maternity: Infant exposure and maternal information.* Ann Arbor: University of Michigan Press.

BRADDOCK, J. H., & MCPARTLAND, J. M. (1982). Assessing school desegregation effects: New directions in research. *Research in Sociology of Education and Socialization, 3,* 259–282.

BRADDOCK, J. H., & MCPARTLAND, J. M. (1987). How minorities continue to be excluded from equal employment opportunities: Research on labor market and institutional barriers. *Journal of Social Issues, 43,* 5–39.

BRADLEY, R. H., & CALDWELL, B. M. (1979). Home Observation for Measurement of the Environment: A revision of the preschool scale. *American Journal of Mental Deficiency, 84,* 235–244.

BRADLEY, R. H., & CALDWELL, B. M. (1981). The HOME Inventory: A validation of the preschool scale for black children. *Child Development, 52,* 708–710.

BRADLEY, R. H., & CALDWELL, B. M. (1982). The consistency of the home environment and its relation to child development. *International Journal of Behavioral Development, 5,* 445–465.

BRADLEY, R. H., CALDWELL, B. M., ROCK, S. L., RAMEY, C. T., BARNARD, D. E., GRAY, C., HAMMOND, M. A., MITCHELL, S., GOTTFRIED, A., SIEGEL, L., & JOHNSON, D. L. (1989). Home environment and cognitive development in the first 3 years of life: A collaborative study involving six sites and three ethnic groups in North America. *Developmental Psychology, 25,* 217–235.

BRADLEY, R. H., WHITESIDE, L., MUNDFROM, D. J., CASEY, P. H., KELLEHER, K. J., & POPE, S. K. (1994). Contribution of early intervention and early caregiving experiences to resilience in low-birthweight, premature children living in poverty. *Journal of Clinical Child Psychology, 23,* 425–434.

BRAINE, L. G., POMERANTZ, E., LORBER, D., & KRANTZ, D. H. (1991). Conflicts with authority: Children's feelings, actions, and justifications. *Developmental Psychology, 27,* 829–840.

BRAINE, L. G., SCHAUBLE, L., KUGELMASS, S., & WINTER, A. (1993). Representation of depth by children: Spatial strategies and lateral biases. *Developmental Psychology, 29,* 466–479.

BRAINE, M. D. S. (1994). Is nativism sufficient? *Journal of Child Language, 21,* 1–23.

BRAINERD, C. J. (1978). *Piaget's theory of intelligence.* Englewood Cliffs, NJ: Prentice-Hall.

BRAND, E., CLINGEMPEEL, W. G., & BOWEN-WOODWARD, K. (1988). Family relationships and children's psychological adjustment in stepmother and stepfather families: Findings and conclusions from the Philadelphia Stepfamily Research Project. In E. M. Hetherington & J. D. Arasteh (Eds.), *Impact of divorce, single-parenting, and stepparenting on children* (pp. 299–324). Hillsdale, NJ: Erlbaum.

BRAUNGART, J. M., PLOMIN, R., DeFRIES, J. C., & FULKER, D. W. (1992). Genetic influence on tester-rated infant temperament as assessed by Bayley's Infant Behavior Record: Nonadoptive and adoptive siblings and twins. *Developmental Psychology, 28,* 40–47.

BRAVERMAN, P. K., & STRASBURGER, V. C. (1993). Adolescent sexual activity. *Clinical Pediatrics, 32,* 658–668.

BRAVERMAN, P. K., & STRASBURGER, V. C. (1994). Sexually transmitted diseases. *Clinical Pediatrics, 33,* 26–37.

BRAZELTON, T. B. (1997). *Toilet training your child*. New York: Consumer Visions.

BRAZELTON, T. B., KOSLOWSKI, B., & TRONICK, E. (1976). Neonatal behavior among urban Zambians and Americans. *Journal of the American Academy of Child Psychiatry, 15,* 97–107.

BRAZELTON, T. B., & NUGENT, J. K. (1995). *Neonatal Behavioral Assessment Scale.* London: Mac Keith Press.

BRAZELTON, T. B., NUGENT, J. K., & LESTER, B. M. (1987). Neonatal Behavioral Assessment Scale. In J. D. Osofsky (Ed.), *Handbook of infant development* (2nd ed., pp. 780–817). New York: Wiley.

BREAD FOR THE WORLD INSTITUTE. (1994). *Hunger 1994.* Silver Spring, MD: Author.

BREDEKAMP, S., & COPPLE, C. (Eds.). (1997). *Developmentally appropriate practice in early childhood programs* (rev. ed.). Washington, DC: National Association for the Education of Young Children.

BRENNAN, W. M., AMES, E. W., & MOORE, R. W. (1966). Age differences in infants' attention to patterns of different complexities. *Science, 151,* 354–356.

BRENNER, D., & HINSDALE, G. (1978). Body build stereotypes and self-identification in three age groups of females. *Adolescence, 13,* 551–562.

BRETHERTON, I. (1992). The origins of attachment theory: John Bowlby and Mary Ainsworth. *Developmental Psychology, 28,* 759–775.

BRETHERTON, I., FRITZ, J., ZAHN-WAXLER, C., & RIDGEWAY, D. (1986). Learning to talk about emotions: A functionalist perspective. *Child Development, 57,* 529–548.

BRIEN, M. J., & WILLIS, R. J. (1997). Costs and consequences for the fathers. In R. A. Maynard (Ed.), *Kids having kids* (pp. 95–144). Washington, DC: Urban Institute.

BRIERE, J. N. (1992). *Child abuse trauma.* Newbury Park, CA: Sage.

BRIGGS, F., & HAWKINS, R. (1996). *Keeping ourselves safe: Who benefits?* Wellington, NZ: New Zealand Council for Educational Research.

BRIGGS, F., & HAWKINS, R. (1998). The importance of parent involvement in child protection curricula. In L. E. Berk (Ed.), *Landscapes of development* (pp. 321–335). Belmont, CA: Wadsworth.

BRINDLEY, B. A., & SOKOL, R. J. (1988). Induction and augmentation of labor: Basis and methods for current practice. *Obstetrics and Gynecology Survey, 43,* 730–743.

BROBERG, A. G., WESSELS, H., LAMB, M. E., & HWANG, C. P. (1997). Effects of day care on the development of cognitive abilities in 8-year-olds: A longitudinal study. *Developmental Psychology, 33,* 62–69.

BRODY, G. H., STONEMAN, Z., & McCOY, J. K. (1992). Associations of maternal and paternal direct and differential behavior with sibling relationships: Contemporaneous and longitudinal analyses. *Child Development, 63,* 82–92.

BRODY, G. H., STONEMAN, Z., & McCOY, J. K. (1994). Forecasting sibling relationships in early adolescence from child temperament and family processes in middle childhood. *Child Development, 65,* 771–784.

BRODY, G. H., STONEMAN, Z., McCOY, J. K., & FOREHAND, R. (1992). Contemporaneous and longitudinal associations of sibling conflict with family relationship assessments and family discussions about sibling problems. *Child Development, 63,* 391–400.

BRODY, L. R., & HALL, J. A. (1993). Gender and emotion. In M. Lewis & J. M. Haviland (Eds.), *Handbook of emotions* (pp. 447–460). New York: Guilford.

BRODY, N. (1992). *Intelligence* (2nd ed.). San Diego: Academic Press.

BRODY, N. (1997). Intelligence, schooling, and society. *American Psychologist, 52,* 1046–1050.

BRODZINSKY, D. M. (1990). A stress and coping model of adoption adjustment. In D. M. Brodzinsky & M. D. Schechter (Eds.), *The psychology of adoption* (pp. 3–24). New York: Oxford University Press.

BROMAN, S. H. (1983). Obstetric medications. In C. C. Brown (Ed.), *Childhood learning disabilities and prenatal risk* (pp. 56–64). New York: Johnson & Johnson.

BRONFENBRENNER, U. (1979). *The ecology of human development: Experiments by nature and design.* Cambridge, MA: Harvard University Press.

BRONFENBRENNER, U. (1989). Ecological systems theory. In R. Vasta (Ed.), *Annals of child development* (Vol. 6, pp. 187–251). Greenwich, CT: JAI Press.

BRONFENBRENNER, U. (1993). The ecology of cognitive development: Research models and fugitive findings. In R. H. Wozniak & K. W. Fischer (Eds.), *Development in context* (pp. 3–44). Hillsdale, NJ: Erlbaum.

BRONFENBRENNER, U. (1995). The bioecological model from a life course perspective: Reflections of a participant observer. In P. Moen, G. H. Elder, Jr., & K. Lüscher (Eds.), *Examining lives in context* (pp. 599–618). Washington, DC: American Psychological Association.

BRONFENBRENNER, U., & CECI, S. J. (1994). Nature–nurture reconceptualized in developmental perspective: A bioecological model. *Psychological Review, 101,* 568–586.

BRONSON, G. W. (1991). Infant differences in rate of visual encoding. *Child Development, 62,* 44–54.

BRONSON, M. B. (1995). *The right stuff for children birth to 8.* Washington, DC: National Association for the Education of Young Children.

BROOKS-GUNN, J. (1986). The relationship of maternal beliefs about sex typing to maternal and young children's behavior. *Sex Roles, 14,* 21–35.

BROOKS-GUNN, J. (1988a). Antecedents and consequences of variations in girls' maturational timing. *Journal of Adolescent Health Care, 9,* 365–373.

BROOKS-GUNN, J. (1988b). The impact of puberty and sexual activity upon the health and education of adolescent girls and boys. *Peabody Journal of Education, 64,* 88–113.

BROOKS-GUNN, J., & CHASE-LANSDALE, P. L. (1995). Adolescent parenthood. In M. H. Bornstein (Ed.), *Handbook of parenting: Vol. 3. Status and social conditions of parenting* (pp. 113–149). Mahwah, NJ: Erlbaum.

BROOKS-GUNN, J., McCARTON, C. M., CASEY, P. H., McCORMICK, M. C., BAUER, C. R., BERNBAUM, J. C., TYSON, J., SWANSON, M., BENNETT, F. C., SCOTT, D. T., TONASCIA, J., & MEINERT, C. L. (1994). Early intervention in low-birth-weight premature infants. *Journal of the American Medical Association, 272,* 1257–1262.

BROOKS-GUNN, J., & RUBLE, D. N. (1980). Menarche: The interaction of physiology, cultural, and social factors. In A. J. Dan, E. A. Graham, & C. P. Beecher (Eds.), *The menstrual cycle: A synthesis of interdisciplinary research* (pp. 141–159). New York: Springer-Verlag.

BROOKS-GUNN, J., & RUBLE, D. N. (1983). The experience of menarche from a developmental perspective. In J. Brooks-Gunn & A. C. Peterson (Eds.), *Girls at puberty* (pp. 155–177). New York: Plenum.

BROOKS-GUNN, J., & WARREN, M. P. (1989). Biological and social contributions to negative affect in young adolescent girls. *Child Development, 60,* 40–55.

BROOKS-GUNN, J., WARREN, M. P., SAMELSON, M., & FOX, R. (1986). Physical similarity of and disclosure of menarcheal status to friends: Effects of grade and pubertal status. *Journal of Early Adolescence, 6,* 3–14.

BROWN, B., CLASEN, D., & EICHER, S. (1986). Perceptions of peer pressure, peer conformity dispositions, and self-reported behavior among adolescents. *Developmental Psychology, 22,* 521–530.

BROWN, B. B. (1990). Peer groups. In S. Feldman & G. Elliott (Eds.), *At the threshold: The developing adolescent* (pp. 171–196). Cambridge, England: Cambridge University Press.

BROWN, B. B., LOHR, M. J., & McCLENAHAN, E. L. (1986). Early adolescents' perceptions of peer pressure. *Journal of Early Adolescence, 6,* 139–154.

BROWN, R. W. (1973). *A first language: The early stages.* Cambridge, MA: Harvard University Press.

BROWNELL, C. A., & CARRIGER, M. S. (1990). Changes in cooperation and self–other differentiation during the second year. *Child Development, 61,* 1164–1174.

BRUERD, B., & JONES, C. (1996). Preventing baby bottle tooth decay: Eight-year results. *Public Health Reports, 111,* 63–65.

BRUNER, J. S. (1983). *Child's talk: Learning to use language.* Oxford: Oxford University Press.

BRUSTAD, R. J. (1993). Who will go out and play? Parental and psychological influences on children's attraction to physical activity. *Pediatric Exercise Science, 5,* 210–223.

BRYANT, B. K. (1985). The neighborhood walk: Sources of support in middle childhood. *Monographs of the Society for Research in Child Development, 50* (3, Serial No. 210).

BRYK, A. S., LEE, V. E., & HOLLAND, P. B. (1993). *Catholic schools and the common good.* Cambridge, MA: Harvard University Press.

BUCHANAN, C. M., ECCLES, J. S., & BECKER, J. B. (1992). Are adolescents the victims of raging hormones? Evidence for activational effects of hormones on moods and behaviors at adolescence. *Psychological Bulletin, 111,* 62–107.

BUEKENS, P., KOTELCHUCK, M., BLONDEL, B., KRISTENSEN, F. B., CHEN, J-H., & MASUY-STROOBANT, G. (1993). A comparison of prenatal care use in the United States and Europe. *American Journal of Public Health, 83,* 31–36.

BUGENTAL, D. B., BLUE, J., & CRUZCOSA, M. (1989). Perceived control over caregiving outcomes: Implications for child abuse. *Developmental Psychology, 25,* 532–539.

BUHRMESTER, D. (1996). Need fulfillment, interpersonal competence, and the developmental contexts of early adolescent friendship. In W. M. Bukowski, A. F. Newcomb, & W. W. Hartup (Eds.), *The company they keep: Friendship during childhood and adolescence* (pp. 158–185). New York: Cambridge University Press.

BUHRMESTER, D., & CARBERY, J. (1992, March). *Daily patterns of self-disclosure and adolescent adjustment.* Paper presented at the biennial meeting of the Society for Research on Adolescence, Washington, DC.

BUHRMESTER, D., & FURMAN, W. (1987). The development of companionship and intimacy. *Child Development, 58,* 1101–1115.

BUHRMESTER, D., & FURMAN, W. (1990). Perceptions of sibling relationships during middle childhood and adolescence. *Child Development, 61,* 1387–1398.

BUHRMESTER, D., & PRAGER, K. (1995). Patterns and functions of self-disclosure during childhood and adolescence. In K. J. Rotenberg (Ed.), *Disclosure processes in children and adolescents* (pp. 10–56). New York: Cambridge University Press.

BULLOCK, M., & LUTKENHAUS, P. (1990). Who am I? The development of self-understanding in toddlers. *Merrill-Palmer Quarterly, 36,* 217–238.

BURCHINAL, M. R., ROBERTS, J. E., NABORS, L. A., & BRYANT, D. M. (1996). Quality of center child care and infant cognitive and language development. *Child Development, 67,* 606–620.

BURHANS, K. K., & DWECK, C. S. (1995). Helplessness in early childhood: The role of contingent worth. *Child Development, 66,* 1719–1738.

BURKETT, G., YASIN, S. Y., PALOW, D., LaVOIE, L., & MARTINEZ, M. (1994). Patterns of cocaine binging: Effect on pregnancy. *American Journal of Obstetrics and Gynecology, 171,* 373–379.

BURKHARDT, S. A., & ROTATORI, A. F. (1995). *Treatment and prevention of childhood sexual abuse.* Washington, DC: Taylor & Francis.

BURNS, S. M., & BRAINERD, C. J. (1979). Effects of constructive and dramatic play on perspective taking in very young children. *Developmental Psychology, 15,* 512–521.

BURTON, B. K. (1992). Limb anomalies associated with chorionic villus sampling. *Obstetrics and Gynecology, 79* (Pt. 1), 726–730.

BURTS, D. C., HART, C. H., CHARLESWORTH, R., FLEEGE, P. O., MOSLEY, J., & THOMASSON, R. H. (1992). Observed activities and stress behaviors of children in developmentally appropriate and inappropriate kindergarten classrooms. *Early Childhood Research Quarterly, 7,* 297–318.

BUSHNELL, E. W. (1985). The decline of visually guided reaching during infancy. *Infant Behavior and Development, 8,* 139–155.

BUSHNELL, E. W., & BOUDREAU, J. P. (1993). Motor development and the mind: The potential role of motor abilities as a determinant of aspects of perceptual development. *Child Development, 64,* 1005–1021.

BUSS, A. H., & PLOMIN, R. (1984). *Temperament: Early developing personality traits.* Hillsdale, NJ: Erlbaum.

BUSSEY, K. (1992). Lying and truthfulness: Children's definitions, standards, and evaluative reactions. *Child Development, 63,* 129–137.

BUSSEY, K., & BANDURA, A. (1992). Self-regulatory mechanisms governing gender development. *Child Development, 63,* 1236–1250.

BUTLER, G. E., McKIE, M., & RATCLIFFE, S. G. (1990). The cyclical nature of prepubertal growth. *Annals of Human Biology, 17,* 177–198.

BUTLER, R., & RUZANY, N. (1993). Age and socialization effects on the development of social comparison motives and normative ability assessment in kibbutz and urban children. *Child Development, 64,* 532–543.

BUYSSE, U., & BAILEY, D. B. (1993). Behavioral and developmental outcomes in young children with disabilities in integrated and segregated settings: A review of comparative studies. *Journal of Special Education, 26,* 434–461.

BYRNES, J. P. (1993). Analyzing perspectives on rationality and critical thinking: A commentary on the *Merrill-Palmer Quarterly* invitational issue. *Merrill-Palmer Quarterly, 39,* 159–171.

BYRNES, J. P., & TAKAHIRA, S. (1993). Explaining gender differences on SAT-math items. *Developmental Psychology, 29,* 805–810.

CADOFF, J. (1995, March). Can we prevent SIDS? *Parents,* pp. 30–31, 35.

CAIN, K. M., & DWECK, C. S. (1995). The relation between motivational patterns and achievement cognitions through the elementary school years. *Merrill-Palmer Quarterly, 41,* 25–52.

CAINE, N. (1986). Behavior during puberty and adolescence. In G. Mitchell & J. Erwin (Eds.), *Comparative primate biology: Vol. 2A. Behavior, conservation, and ecology* (pp. 327–361). New York: Liss.

CAIRNS, E. (1996). *Children and political violence.* Cambridge: Blackwell.

CAIRNS, R. B. (1983). The emergence of developmental psychology. In W. Kessen (Ed.), *Handbook of child psychology: Vol. 1. History, theory, and methods* (4th ed., pp. 41–102). New York: Wiley.

CAIRNS, R. B. (1998). The making of developmental psychology. In R. M. Lerner (Ed.), *Handbook of child psychology: Vol. 1. Theoretical models of human development* (5th ed., pp. 25–105). New York: Wiley.

CAIRNS, R. B., LEUNG, M., BUCHANAN, L., & CAIRNS, B. D. (1995). Friendships and social networks in childhood and adolescence: Fluidity, reliability, and interrelations. *Child Development, 66,* 1330–1345.

CALDAS, S. J. (1993). Current theoretical perspectives on adolescent pregnancy and childbearing in the United States. *Journal of Adolescent Research, 8,* 4–20.

CALDWELL, B. M., & BRADLEY, R. H. (1994). Environmental issues in developmental follow-up research. In S. L. Friedman & H. C. Haywood (Eds.), *Developmental follow-up* (pp. 235–256). San Diego: Academic Press.

CALISO, J., & MILNER, J. (1992). Childhood history of abuse and child abuse screening. *Child Abuse and Neglect, 16,* 647–659.

CALKINS, S. D., FOX, N. A., & MARSHALL, T. R. (1996). Behavioral and physiological antecedents of inhibited and uninhibited behavior. *Child Development, 67,* 523–540.

CAMARA, K. A., & RESNICK, G. (1988). Interparental conflict and cooperation: Factors moderating children's post-divorce adjustment. In E. M. Hetherington & J. D. Arasteh (Eds.), *Impact of divorce, single parenting, and stepparenting on children* (pp. 169–195). Hillsdale, NJ: Erlbaum.

CAMPBELL, F. A., & RAMEY, C. T. (1991). *The Carolina Abecedarian Project.* Paper presented at the biennial meeting of the Society for Research in Child Development, Seattle, WA.

CAMPBELL, F. A., & RAMEY, C. T. (1994). Effects of early intervention on intellectual and academic achievement: A follow-up study of children from low-income families. *Child Development, 65,* 684–698.

CAMPBELL, F. A., & RAMEY, C. T. (1995). Cognitive and school outcomes for high-risk African-American students at middle adolescence: Positive effects of early intervention. *American Educational Research Journal, 32,* 743–772.

CAMPBELL, J. R., VOELKL, K. E., & DONAHUE, P. L. (1997). *NAEP 1996 trends in academic progress.* Washington, DC: U.S. Government Printing Office.

CAMPBELL, R., & SAIS, E. (1995). Accelerated metalinguistic (phonological) awareness in bilingual children. *British Journal of Developmental Psychology, 13,* 61–68.

CAMPBELL, S. B., COHEN, J. F., & MEYERS, T. (1995). Depression in first-time mothers: Mother–infant interaction and depression chronicity. *Developmental Psychology, 31,* 349–357.

CAMPOS, J. J., & BERTENTHAL, B. I. (1989). Locomotion and psychological development. In F. Morrison, K. Lord, & D. Keating (Eds.), *Applied developmental psychology* (Vol. 3, pp. 229–258). New York: Academic Press.

CAMPOS, J. J., CAPLOVITZ, K. B., LAMB, M. E., GOLDSMITH, H. H., & STENBERG, C. (1983). Socioemotional development. In M. M. Haith & J. J. Campos (Eds.), *Handbook of child psychology: Vol. 2. Infancy and developmental psychobiology* (4th ed., pp. 783–915). New York: Wiley.

CAMPOS, J. J., KERMOIAN, R., & ZUMBAHLEN, M. R. (1992). Socioemotional transformation in the family system following infant crawling onset. In N. Eisenberg & R. A. Fabes (Eds.), *New directions for child development* (No. 55, pp. 25–40). San Francisco: Jossey-Bass.

CAMPOS, R., RAFFAELLI, M., UDE, W., GRECO, M., RUFF, A., ROLF, J., ANTUNES, C. M., HALSEY, N., GRECO, D., & STREET YOUTH STUDY GROUP. (1994). Social networks and daily activities of street youth in Belo Horitzonte, Brazil. *Child Development, 65,* 319–330.

CAMPOS, R. G. (1989). Soothing pain-elicited distress in infants with swaddling and pacifiers. *Child Development, 60,* 781–792.

CAMRAS, L. A., OSTER, H., CAMPOS, J. J., MIYAKE, K., & BRADSHAW, D. (1992). Japanese and American infants' responses to arm restraint. *Developmental Psychology, 28,* 578–583.

CANDY-GIBBS, S., SHARP, K., & PETRUN, C. (1985). The effects of age, object, and cultural/reli-

gious background on children's concepts of death. *Omega, 15,* 329–345.

CANICK, J. A., & SALLER, D. N., JR. (1993). Maternal serum screening for aneuploidy and open fetal defects. *Obstetrics and Gynecology Clinics of North America, 20,* 443–454.

CANNELLA, G. S. (1993). Learning through social interaction: Shared cognitive experience, negotiation strategies, and joint concept construction for young children. *Early Childhood Research Quarterly, 8,* 427–444.

CANTOR, J., & HARRISON, K. (1996). Ratings and advisories for television programming: University of Wisconsin, Madison study. In Mediascope (Ed.), *National Television Violence Study: Scientific Papers 1994–1995.* Studio City, CA: Author.

CAPALDI, D. M., & PATTERSON, G. R. (1991). Relation of parental transitions to boys' adjustment problems: I. A linear hypothesis. II. Mothers at risk for transitions and unskilled parenting. *Developmental Psychology, 27,* 489–504.

CAPELLI, C. A., NAKAGAWA, N., & MADDEN, C. M. (1990). How children understand sarcasm: The role of context and intonation. *Child Development, 61,* 1824–1841.

CAPLAN, M., VESPO, J., PEDERSEN, J., & HAY, D. F. (1991). Conflict and its resolution in small groups of one- and two-year-olds. *Child Development, 62,* 1513–1524.

CAPUZZI, D. (1989). *Adolescent suicide prevention.* Ann Arbor, MI: ERIC Counseling and Personnel Services Clearinghouse.

CAREY, S. (1985). *Conceptual change in childhood.* Cambridge, MA: MIT Press.

CARLE, E. (1969). *The very hungry caterpillar.* New York: Philomel.

CARLSON, C., HSU, J., & COOPER, C. R. (1990, March). *Predicting school achievement in early adolescence: The role of family process.* Paper presented at the Conference on Human Development, Atlanta, GA.

CARLSON, K. J., EISENSTAT, S. A., & ZIPORYN, T. (1996). *The Harvard guide to women's health.* Cambridge, MA: Harvard University Press.

CARPENDALE, J. I., & CHANDLER, M. J. (1996). On the distinction between false belief understanding and subscribing

to an interpretive theory of mind. *Child Development, 67,* 1686–1706.

CARPENTER, C. J. (1983). Activity structure and play: Implications for socialization. In M. Liss (Eds.), *Social and cognitive skills: Sex roles and children's play* (pp. 117–145). New York: Academic Press.

CARRUTH, B. R., GOLDBERG, D. L., & SKINNER, J. D. (1991). Do parents and peers mediate the influence of television advertising on food-related purchases? *Journal of Adolescent Research, 6,* 253–271.

CARTER, D. B., & MCCLOSKEY, L. A. (1984). Peers and the maintenance of sex-typed behavior: The development of children's conceptions of cross-gender behavior in their peers. *Social Cognition, 2,* 294–314.

CARTER, D. B., & PATTERSON, C. J. (1982). Sex roles as social conventions: The development of children's conceptions of sex-role stereotypes. *Developmental Psychology, 18,* 812–824.

CASAER, P. (1993). Old and new facts about perinatal brain development. *Journal of Child Psychology and Psychiatry, 34,* 101–109.

CASE, R. (1985). *Intellectual development: A systematic reinterpretation.* New York: Academic Press.

CASE, R. (1991). Stages in the development of the young child's first sense of self. *Developmental Review, 11,* 210–230.

CASE, R. (1992). *The mind's staircase: Exploring the conceptual underpinnings of children's thought and knowledge.* Hillsdale, NJ: Erlbaum.

CASE, R. (1996). Introduction: Reconceptualizing the nature of children's conceptual structures and their development in middle childhood. In R. Case & Y. Okamoto (Eds.), The role of central conceptual structures in the development of children's thought. *Monographs of the Society for Research in Child Development, 246* (61, Serial No. 246), pp. 1–26.

CASE, R. (1998). The development of conceptual structures. In D. Kuhn & R. S. Siegler (Eds.), *Handbook of child psychology: Vol. 2. Cognition, perception, and language* (pp. 745–800). New York: Wiley.

CASE, R., GRIFFIN, S., MCKEOUGH, A., & OKAMOTO, Y. (1992). Parallels in the development of children's social, numerical,

and spatial thought. In R. Case (Ed.), *The mind's staircase* (pp. 269–284). Hillsdale, NJ: Erlbaum.

CASEY, M. B. (1986). Individual differences in selective attention among preaders: A key to mirror-image confusions. *Developmental Psychology, 22,* 824–831.

CASEY, M. B., NUTTALL, R., PEZARIS, E., & BENBOW, C. P. (1995). The influence of spatial ability on gender differences in mathematics college entrance test scores across diverse samples. *Developmental Psychology, 31,* 697–705.

CASEY, M. B., NUTTALL, R. L., & PEZARIS, E. (1997). Mediators of gender differences in mathematics college entrance test scores: A comparison of spatial skills with internalized beliefs and anxieties. *Developmental Psychology, 33,* 669–680.

CASPI, A. (1998). Personality development across the life course. In N. Eisenberg (Ed.), *Handbook of child psychology: Vol. 3. Social, emotional, and personality development* (5th ed., pp. 311–388). New York: Wiley.

CASPI, A., ELDER, G. H., JR., & BEM, D. J. (1987). Moving against the world: Life-course patterns of explosive children. *Developmental Psychology, 23,* 308–313.

CASPI, A., ELDER, G. H., JR., & BEM, D. J. (1988). Moving away from the world: Life-course patterns of shy children. *Developmental Psychology, 24,* 824–831.

CASPI, A., LYNAM, D., MOFFITT, T. E., & SILVA, P. A. (1993). Unraveling girls' delinquency: Biological, dispositional, and contextual contributions to adolescent misbehavior. *Developmental Psychology, 29,* 19–30.

CASPI, A., & SILVA, P. A. (1995). Temperamental qualities at age three predict personality traits in young adulthood: Longitudinal evidence from a birth cohort. *Child Development, 66,* 486–498.

CASSIDY, J., & BERLIN, L. J. (1994). The insecure/ambivalent pattern of attachment: Theory and research. *Child Development, 65,* 971–991.

CASSIDY, J., PARKE, R. D., BUTKOVSKY, L., & BRAUNGART, J. M. (1992). Family-peer connections: The roles of emotional expressiveness within the family and children's understanding of emotions. *Child Development, 63,* 603–618.

CASSIDY, S. B. (1995). Uniparental disomy and genomic imprinting as causes of human genetic disease. *Environmental and Molecular Mutagenesis, 25,* 13–20.

CATANZARITE, V., DEUTCHMAN, M., JOHNSON, C. A., & SCHERGER, J. E. (1995). Pregnancy after 35: What's the real risk? *Patient Care, 29,* 41–49.

CATSAMBIS, S. (1994). The path to math: Gender and racial-ethnic differences in mathematics participation from middle school to high school. *Sociology of Education, 67,* 199–215.

CECI, S. J. (1991). How much does schooling influence general intelligence and its cognitive components? A reassessment of the evidence. *Developmental Psychology, 27,* 703–722.

CECI, S. J., & BRUCK, M. (1993). Suggestibility of the child witness: A historical review and synthesis. *Psychological Bulletin, 113,* 403–439.

CECI, S. J., & BRUCK, M. (1995). *Jeopardy in the courtroom: A scientific analysis of children's testimony.* Washington, DC: American Psychological Association.

CECI, S. J., & BRUCK, M. (1998). Children's testimony: Applied and basic issues. In I. Sigel & K. A. Renninger (Eds.), *Handbook of child psychology: Vol. 4. Child psychology in practice* (5th ed., pp. 713–774). New York: Wiley.

CECI, S. J., LEICHTMAN, M. D., & BRUCK, M. (1994). The suggestibility of children's eyewitness reports: Methodological issues. In F. Weinert & W. Schneider (Eds.), *Memory development: State of the art and future directions.* Hillsdale, NJ: Erlbaum.

CECI, S. J., & ROAZZI, A. (1994). The effects of context on cognition: Postcards from Brazil. In R. J. Sternberg (Ed.), *Mind in context* (pp. 74–101). New York: Cambridge University Press.

CECI, S. J., & WILLIAMS, W. M. (1997). Schooling, intelligence, and income. *American Psychologist, 52,* 1051–1058.

CENTRAL INTELLIGENCE AGENCY. (1996). *The world fact book.* Washington, DC: U.S. Government Printing Office.

CERNOCH, J. M., & PORTER, R. H. (1985). Recognition of maternal axillary odors by infants. *Child Development, 56,* 1593–1598.

CHADWICK, E. G., & YOGEV, R. (1995). Pediatric AIDS. In G. E. Gaull (Ed.), *Pediatric Clinics of Normal America* (Vol. 42, No. 4, pp. 969–992). Philadelphia: Saunders.

CHADWICK, S. (1996). The impact of asthma in an inner city general practice. *Child: Care, Health, and Development, 22,* 175–186.

CHALL, J. S. (1983). *Stages of reading development.* New York: McGraw-Hill.

CHALMERS, J. B., & TOWNSEND, M. A. R. (1990). The effects of training in social perspective taking on socially maladjusted girls. *Child Development, 61,* 178–190.

CHAMBERLAIN, M. C., NICHOLS, S. L., & CHASE, C. H. (1991). Pediatric AIDS: Comparative cranial MRI and CT scans. *Pediatric Neurology, 7,* 357–362.

CHANDLER, M. (1994). Adolescent suicide and the loss of personal continuity. In D. Cicchetti & S. L. Toth (Eds.), *Rochester Symposium on Developmental Psychopathology: Vol. 5. Disorders and dysfunctions of the self* (pp. 371–390). Rochester, NY: University of Rochester Press.

CHANDLER, M., BOYES, M., & BALL, L. (1990). Relativism and stations of epistemic doubt. *Journal of Experimental Child Psychology, 50,* 370–395.

CHANDLER, M., & LALONDE, C. (1996). Shifting to an interpretive theory of mind: 5- to 7-year-olds' changing conceptions of mental life. In A. J. Sameroff & M. M. Haith (Eds.), *The five to seven year shift* (pp. 111–139). Chicago: University of Chicago Press.

CHANDLER, M. J. (1973). Egocentrism and antisocial behavior: The assessment and training of social perspective-taking skills. *Developmental Psychology, 9,* 326–332.

CHANDRA, R. K. (1991). Interactions between early nutrition and the immune system. In *Ciba Foundation Symposium No. 156* (pp. 77–92). Chichester, England: Wiley.

CHANG, H. (1992). *Adolescent life and ethos: An ethnography of a U.S. high school.* Washington, DC: Falmer.

CHAO, R. K. (1994). Beyond parental control and authoritarian parenting style: Understanding Chinese parenting through the cultural notion of training. *Child Development, 65,* 1111–1119.

CHAPMAN, M., & LINDENBERGER, U. (1988). Functions, operations, and décalage in the development of transitivity. *Developmental Psychology, 24,* 542–551.

CHARMAN, T., SWETTENHAM, J., BARON-COHEN, S., COX, A., BAIRD, G., & DREW, A. (1997). Infants with autism: An investigation of empathy, pretend play, joint attention, and imitation. *Developmental Psychology, 33,* 781–789.

CHASE-LANSDALE, P. L., & BROOKS-GUNN, J. (1994). Correlates of adolescent pregnancy and parenthood. In C. B. Fisher & R. M. Lerner (Eds.), *Applied developmental psychology* (pp. 207–236). New York: McGraw-Hill.

CHASE-LANSDALE, P. L., & BROOKS-GUNN, J. (Eds.). (1994). *Escape from poverty: What makes a difference for children?* New York: Cambridge University Press.

CHASE-LANSDALE, P. L., BROOKS-GUNN, J., & ZAMSKY, E. S. (1994). Young African-American multigenerational families in poverty: Quality of mothering and grandmothering. *Child Development, 65,* 373–393.

CHASE-LANSDALE, P. L., CHERLIN, A. J., & KIERNAN, K. E. (1995). The long-term effects of parental divorce on the mental health of young children. *Child Development, 66,* 1614–1634.

CHASE-LANSDALE, P. L., & VINOVSKIS, M. A. (1995). *Escape from poverty: What makes a difference for children?* New York: Cambridge University Press.

CHASSIN, L., CURRAN, P. J., HUSSONG, A. M., & COLDER, C. R. (1996). The relation of parent alcoholism to adolescent substance use: A longitudinal follow-up study. *Journal of Abnormal Psychology, 105,* 70–80.

CHATKUPT, S., MINTZ, M., EPSTEIN, L. G., BHANSALI, D., & KOENIGSBERGER, M. R. (1989). Neuroimaging studies in children with human immunodeficiency virus type 1 infection. *Annals of Neurology, 26,* 453.

CHEN, X., RUBIN, K. H., & LI, B. (1994). Only children and sibling children in urban China: A re-examination. *International Journal of Behavioral Development, 17,* 413–421.

CHEN, X., RUBIN, K. H., & LI, Z. (1995). Social functioning and adjustment in Chinese children: A longitudinal study. *Developmental Psychology, 31,* 531–539.

CHENG, M., & HANNAH, M. (1993). Breech delivery at term: A critical review of the literature. *Obstetrics & Gynecology, 82,* 605–618.

CHERLIN, A. J., & FURSTENBERG, F. F., JR. (1986). *The new American grandparent.* New York: Basic Books.

CHERLIN, A. J., FURSTENBERG, F. F., JR., CHASE-LANSDALE, P. L., KIERNAN, K. E., ROBINS, P. K., MORRISON, D. R., & TEITLER, J. O. (1991). Longitudinal studies of effects of divorce on children in Great Britain and the United States. *Science, 252,* 1386-1389.

CHERLIN, A. J., KIERNAN, K. E., & CHASE-LANSDALE, P. L. (1995). Parental divorce in childhood and demographic outcomes in young adulthood. *Demography, 32,* 299–318.

CHERNY, S. S. (1994). Home environmental influences on general cognitive ability. In J. C. DeFries, R. Plomin, & D. W. Fulker (Eds.), *Nature and nurture during middle childhood* (pp. 262–280). Cambridge, MA: Blackwell.

CHESS, S., & THOMAS, A. (1984). *Origins and evolution of behavior disorders.* New York: Brunner/Mazel.

CHEZ, B. F. (1997). Electronic fetal monitoring then and now. *Journal of Perinatal and Neonatal Nursing, 10,* 1–4.

CHI, M. T. H. (1978). Knowledge structures and memory development. In R. S. Siegler (Ed.), *Children's thinking: What develops?* (pp. 73–96). Hillsdale, NJ: Erlbaum.

CHILDREN'S DEFENSE FUND. (1992). *The health of America's children.* Washington, DC: Author.

CHILDREN'S DEFENSE FUND. (1998). *The state of America's children: Yearbook 1998.* Washington, DC: Author.

CHILDS, C. P., & GREENFIELD, P. M. (1982). Informal modes of learning and teaching: The case of Zinacanteco weaving. In N. Warren (Ed.), *Advances in cross-cultural psychology* (Vol. 2, pp. 269–316). London: Academic Press.

CHISHOLM, J. S. (1989). Biology, culture, and the development of temperament: A Navajo example. In J. K. Nugent, B. M. Lester, & T. B. Brazelton (Eds.), *Biology, culture, and development* (Vol. 1, pp. 341–364). Norwood, NJ: Ablex.

CHIU, L-H. (1992-1993). Self-esteem in American and Chinese (Taiwanese) children. *Current Psychology: Research and Reviews, 11,* 309–313.

CHOI, S., & GOPNIK, A. (1995). Early acquisition of verbs in Korean: A cross-linguistic study. *Journal of Child Language, 22,* 497–529.

CHOMSKY, C. (1969). *The acquisition of syntax in children from five to ten.* Cambridge, MA: MIT Press.

CHOMSKY, N. (1957). *Syntactic structures.* The Hague: Mouton.

CHRISTOPHERSEN, E. R., & EDWARDS, K. J. (1992). Treatment of elimination disorders: State of the art 1991. *Applied and Preventive Psychology, 1,* 15–22.

CHUGANI, H. T. (1994). Development of regional brain glucose metabolism in relation to behavior and plasticity. In G. Dawson & K. W. Fischer (Eds.), *Human behavior and the developing brain* (pp. 153–175). New York: Guilford.

CHURCHILL, S. R. (1984). Disruption: A risk in adoption. In P. Sachdev (Ed.), *Adoption: Current issues and trends* (pp. 115–127). Toronto: Butterworth.

CICCHETTI, D., & ABER, J. L. (1986). Early precursors of later depression: An organizational perspective. In L. P. Lipsitt & C. Rovee-Collier (Eds.), *Advances in infancy research* (Vol. 4, pp. 87–137). Norwood, NJ: Ablex.

CICCHETTI, D., & GARMEZY, N. (1993). Prospects and promises in the study of resilience. *Development and Psychopathology, 5,* 497–502.

CICCHETTI, D., & TOTH, S. L. (1998a). Perspectives on research and practice in developmental psychology. In I. E. Sigel & K. A. Renninger (Eds.), *Handbook of child psychology: Vol. 4. Child psychology in practice* (5th ed., pp. 479–582). New York: Wiley.

CICCHETTI, D., & TOTH, S. L. (1998b). The development of depression in children and adolescents. *American Psychologist, 53,* 221–241.

CLARK, D. C., & MOKROS, H. R. (1993). Depression and suicidal behavior. In P. H. Tolan & B. J. Cohler (Eds.), *Handbook of*

clinical research and practice with adolescents (pp. 333–358). New York: Wiley.

CLARK, E. V. (1983). Meanings and concepts. In J. H. Flavell & E. M. Markman (Eds.), *Handbook of child psychology: Vol. 3. Cognitive development* (pp. 787–840). New York: Wiley.

CLARK, E. V. (1995). The lexicon and syntax. In J. L. Miller & P. D. Eimas (Eds.), *Speech, language, and communication* (pp. 303–337). San Diego: Academic Press.

CLARK, J. E., PHILLIPS, S., & PETERSEN, R. (1989). Developmental stability in jumping. *Developmental Psychology, 25,* 929–935.

CLARK, J. E., & WATKINS, D. L. (1984). Static balance in young children. *Child Development, 55,* 133–139.

CLARK, R., HYDE, J. S., ESSEX, M. J. & KLEIN, M. H. (1997). Length of maternity leave and quality of mother-infant interaction. *Child Development, 68,* 364–383.

CLARKE-STEWART, K. A. (1992). Consequences of child care for children's development. In A. Booth (Ed.), *Child care in the 1990s: Trends and consequences* (pp. 63–83). Hillsdale, NJ: Erlbaum.

CLARKE-STEWART, K. A., & HAYWARD, C. (1996). Advantages of father custody and contact for the psychological well-being of school-age children. *Journal of Applied Developmental Psychology, 17,* 239–270.

CLAUDE, E., & FIRESTONE, P. (1995). The development of ADHD boys: A 12-year follow-up. *Canadian Journal of Behavioural Science, 27,* 226–249.

CLAUSEN, J. A. (1975). The social meaning of differential physical and sexual maturation. In S. E. Dragastin & G. H. Elder (Eds.), *Adolescence in the life cycle: Psychological change and the social context* (pp. 25–47). New York: Halsted.

CLEMENTS, D. H. (1990). Metacomponential development in a Logo programming environment. *Journal of Educational Psychology, 82,* 141–149.

CLEMENTS, D. H. (1995). Teaching creativity with computers. *Educational Psychology Review, 7,* 141–161.

CLEMENTS, D. H., & NASTASI, B. K. (1992). Computers and early childhood education. In M. Gettinger, S. N. Elliott, &

T. R. Kratochwill (Eds.), *Advances in school psychology: Preschool and early childhood treatment directions* (pp. 187–246). Hillsdale, NJ: Erlbaum.

CLIFTON, R. K., ROCHAT, P., ROBIN, D. J., & BERTHIER, N. E. (1994). Multimodal perception in the control of infant reaching. *Journal of Experimental Psychology: Human Perception and Performance, 20,* 876–886.

COAKLEY, J. (1990). *Sport and society: Issues and controversies* (4th ed.). St. Louis: Mosby.

COHEN, F. L. (1984). *Clinical genetics in nursing practice.* Philadelphia: Lippincott.

COHEN, F. L. (1993). Epidemiology of HIV infection and AIDS in children. In F. L. Cohen & J. D. Durham (Eds.), *Women, children, and HIV/ AIDS* (pp. 137–155). New York: Springer.

COHEN, K. M., & SAVIN-WILLIAMS, R. C. (1996). Developmental perspectives on coming out to self and others. *The lives of lesbians, gays, and bisexuals: Children to adults* (pp. 113–151). Ft. Worth, TX: Harcourt Brace.

COIE, J. D., & DODGE, K. A. (1998). Aggression and antisocial behavior. In N. Eisenberg (Ed.), *Handbook of child psychology: Vol. 3. Social, emotional, and personality development* (5th ed., pp. 779–862). New York: Wiley.

COIE, J. D., DODGE, K. A., & COPPOTELLI, H. (1982). Dimensions and types of social status: A cross-age perspective. *Developmental Psychology, 18,* 557–570.

COIE, J. D., & KREHBIEL, G. (1984). Effects of academic tutoring on the social status of low-achieving, socially rejected children. *Child Development, 55,* 1465–1478.

COIE, J. D., TERRY, R., LENOX, K., LOCHMAN, J., & HYMAN, C. (1995). Childhood peer rejection and aggression as predictors of stable patterns of adolescent disorder. *Development and Psychopathology, 7,* 697–714.

COLBY, A., KOHLBERG, L., GIBBS, J., & LIEBERMAN, M. (1983). A longitudinal study of moral judgment. *Monographs of the Society for Research in Child Development, 48*(1–2, Serial No. 200).

COLE, M. (1990). Cognitive development and formal schooling: The evidence from

cross-cultural research. In L. C. Moll (Ed.), *Vygotsky and education* (pp. 89–110). New York: Cambridge University Press.

COLEY, R. L., & CHASE-LANS-DALE, P. L. (1998). Adolescent pregnancy and parenthood: Recent evidence and future directions. *American Psychologist, 53,* 152–166.

COLLAER, M. L., & HINES, M. (1995). Human behavioral sex differences: A role for gonadal hormones during early development? *Psychological Bulletin, 118,* 55–107.

COLLINS, J. A. (1994). Reproductive technology—the price of progress. *New England Journal of Medicine, 331,* 270–271.

COLLINS, W. A. (1997). Relationships and development during adolescence: Interpersonal adaptation to individual change. *Personal Relationships, 4,* 1–14.

COLLINS, W. A., HARRIS, M. L., & SUSMAN, A. (1996). Parenting during middle childhood. In M. H. Bornstein (Ed.), *Handbook of parenting: Vol. 1. Children and parenting* (pp. 65–90). Mahwah, NJ: Erlbaum.

COLLINS, W. A., LAURSEN, B., MORTENSEN, N., LUEBKER, C., & FERREIRA, M. (1997). Conflict processes and transitions in parent and peer relationships: Implications for autonomy and regulation. *Journal of Adolescent Research, 12,* 178–198.

COLLINS, W. A., WELLMAN, H., KENISTON, A. H., & WESTBY, S. D. (1978). Age-related aspects of comprehension and inference from a televised dramatic narrative. *Child Development, 49,* 389–399.

COLLIS, B. A., KNEZEK, G. A., LAI, K-W., MIYASHITA, K. T., PELGRUM, W. J., PLOMP, T., & SAKAMOTO, T. (1996). *Children and computers in school.* Mahwah, NJ: Erlbaum.

COLMAN, L. L., & COLMAN, A. D. (1991). *Pregnancy: The psychological experience.* Noonday Press.

COLOMBO, J. (1993). *Infant cognition: Predicting later intellectual functioning.* Newbury Park, CA: Sage.

COLOMBO, J. (1995). On the neural mechanisms underlying developmental and individual differences in visual fixation in infancy. *Developmental Review, 15,* 97–135.

COLTRANE, S. (1990). Birth timing and the division of labor in dual-earner families. *Journal of Family Issues, 11,* 157–181.

COLTRANE, S. (1996). *Family man.* New York: Oxford University Press.

COMPAS, B., PHARES, V., & LEDOUX, N. (1989). Stress and coping: Preventive interventions for children and adolescents. In L. Bond & B. Compas (Eds.), *Primary prevention and promotion in the schools* (pp. 319–340). London: Sage.

COMSTOCK, G. A. (1993). The medium and society: The role of television in American life. In G. L. Berry & J. K. Asamen (Eds.), *Children and television* (pp. 117–131). Newbury Park, CA: Sage.

COMSTOCK, G. A., & PAIK, H. (1994). The effects of television violence on antisocial behavior: A meta-analysis. *Communication Research, 21,* 269–277.

CONDRY, J., & ROSS, D. F. (1985). Sex and aggression: The influence of gender label on the perceptions of aggression in children. *Child Development, 56,* 225–233.

CONEL, J. L. (1959). *The postnatal development of the human cerebral cortex.* Cambridge, MA: Harvard University Press.

CONGER, R. D., CONGER, K. J., ELDER, G. H., JR., LORENZ, F. O., SIMONS, R. L., & WHITBECK, L. B. (1992). A family process model of economic hardship and adjustment of early adolescent boys. *Child Development, 63,* 527–541.

CONGER, R. D., CONGER, K. J., ELDER, G. H., JR., LORENZ, F. O., SIMONS, R. L., & WHITBECK, L. B. (1993). Family economic stress and adjustment of early adolescent girls. *Developmental Psychology, 29,* 206–219.

CONGER, R. D., GE, X., ELDER, G. H., JR., LORENZ, F. O., & SIMONS, R. L. (1994). Economic stress, coercive family process, and developmental problems of adolescents. *Child Development, 65,* 541–561.

CONGER, R., PATTERSON, G. R., & GE, X. (1995). It takes two to replicate: A mediational model for the impact of parents' stress on adolescent adjustment. *Child Development, 66,* 80–97.

CONNOLLY, J. A., & DOYLE, A. B. (1984). Relations of social fantasy play to social competence in preschoolers.

Developmental Psychology, 20, 797–806.

CONNORS, L. J., & EPSTEIN, J. L. (1996). Parent and school partnerships. In M. H. Bornstein (Ed.), *Handbook of parenting: Vol. 4. Applied and practical parenting* (pp. 437–458). Mahwah, NJ: Erlbaum.

CONSTANZO, P. R., & WOODY, E. Z. (1979). Externality as a function of obesity in children: Pervasive style or eating-specific attribute? *Journal of Personality and Social Psychology, 37,* 2286–2296.

COOK, R., GOLOMBOK, S., BISH, A., & MURRAY, C. (1995). Disclosure of donor insemination: Parental attitudes. *American Orthopsychiatric Association, 65,* 549–559.

COOKE, R. A. (1982). The ethics and regulation of research involving children. In B. B. Wolman (Ed.), *Handbook of developmental psychology* (pp. 149–172). Englewood Cliffs, NJ: Prentice-Hall.

COOKSEY, E. C., RINDFUSS, R. R., & GUILKEY, D. K. (1996). The initiation of adolescent sexual and contraceptive behavior during changing times. *Journal of Health and Social Behavior, 37,* 59–74.

COOPER, C. R. (1998). *The weaving of maturity: Cultural perspectives on adolescent development.* New York: Oxford University Press.

COOPER, M. L., & ORCUTT, H. K. (1997). Drinking and sexual experience on first dates among adolescents. *Journal of Abnormal Psychology, 106,* 191–202.

COOPER, P., & MURRAY, L. (1997). Prediction, detection, and treatment of postnatal depression. *Archives of Diseases of Children, 77,* 97–99.

COOPER, R. P., & ASLIN, R. N. (1994). Developmental differences in infant attention to the spectral properties of infant-directed speech. *Child Development, 65,* 1663–1677.

COPLAN, R. J., RUBIN, K. H., FOX, N. A., CALKINS, S. D., & STEWART, S. L. (1994). Being alone, playing alone, and acting alone: Distinguishing among reticence and passive and active solitude in young children. *Child Development, 65,* 129–137.

COPPER, R. L., GOLDENBERG, R. L., CREASY, R. K., DUBARD, M. B., DAVIS, R. O., ENTMAN, S. S., IAMS, J. D., & CLIVER, S. P. (1993). A multicenter

study of preterm birth weight and gestational age-specific neonatal mortality. *American Journal of Obstetrics and Gynecology, 168,* 78–84.

CORAH, N. L., ANTHONY, E. J., PAINTER, P., STERN, J. A., & THURSTON, D. L. (1965). Effects of perinatal anoxia after seven years. *Psychological Monographs 79* (3, Whole No. 596).

COREN, S., & HALPERN, D. F. (1991). Left-handedness: A marker for decreased survival fitness. *Psychological Bulletin, 109,* 90–106.

CORRIGAN, R. (1987). A developmental sequence of actor–object pretend play in young children. *Merrill-Palmer Quarterly, 33,* 87–106.

CORWIN, M. J., LESTER, B. M., SEPKOSKI, C., PEUCKER, M., KAYNE, H., & GOLUB, H. L. (1995). Newborn acoustic cry characteristics of infants subsequently dying of sudden infant death syndrome. *Pediatrics, 96,* 73–77.

COST, QUALITY, AND OUTCOMES STUDY TEAM. (1995). Cost, quality, and child outcomes in child care centers: Key findings and recommendations. *Young Children, 50*(4), 40–44.

COSTA, F. M., JESSOR, R., DONOVAN, J. E., & FORTENBERRY, J. D. (1995). Early initiation of sexual intercourse: The influence of psychosocial unconventionality. *Journal of Research on Adolescence, 5,* 93–121.

COSTABILE, A., SMITH, P. K., MATHESON, L., ASTON, J., HUNTER, T., & BOULTON, M. (1991). Cross-national comparison of how children distinguish serious and playful fighting. *Developmental Psychology, 27,* 881–887.

COSTELLO, E. J., & ANGOLD, A. (1995). Developmental epidemiology. In D. Cicchetti & D. Cohen (Eds.), *Developmental psychopathology: Vol. 1. Theory and method* (pp. 23–56). New York: Wiley.

COTTON, P. (1990). Sudden infant death syndrome: Another hypothesis offered but doubts remain. *Journal of the American Medical Association, 263,* 2865, 2869.

COTTON, P. (1994). Smoking cigarettes may do the developing fetus more harm than ingesting cocaine, some experts say. *Journal of the American Medical Association, 271,* 576–577.

COULTON, C., KORBIN, J., SU, M., & CHOW, J. (1995).

Community level factors and child maltreatment rates. *Child Development, 66,* 1262–1276.

COURAGE, M. L., & ADAMS, R. J. (1990). Visual acuity assessment from birth to three years using the acuity card procedures: Cross-sectional and longitudinal samples. *Optometry and Vision Science, 67,* 713–718.

COVEY, H. C., MENARD, C., & FRANZESE, R. J. (1997). *Juvenile gangs* (2nd ed.). Springfield, IL: Charles C. Thomas.

COWAN, C. P., & COWAN, P. A. (1992). *When partners become parents: The big life change for couples.* New York: Basic Books.

COWAN, C. P., & COWAN, P. A. (1995). Interventions to ease the transition to parenthood: Why they are needed and what they can do. *Family Relations, 44,* 412–423.

COWAN, P. A. (1997). Beyond meta-analysis: A plea for a family systems view of attachment. *Child Development, 68,* 601–603.

COWAN, P. A., COWAN, C. P., SCHULZ, M., & HEMING, G. (1994). Prebirth to preschool family factors predicting children's adaptation to kindergarten. In R. D. Parke & S. Kellam (Eds.) *Exploring family relationships with other social contexts: Advances in family research* (Vol. 4, pp. 75–114). Hillsdale, NJ: Erlbaum.

COX, K., & SCHWARTZ, J. D. (1990). *The well-informed patient's guide to caesarean births.* New York: Dell.

COX, M. (1993). *Children's drawings of the human figure.* Hillsdale, NJ: Erlbaum.

COX, M., & LITTLETON, K. (1995). Children's use of converging obliques in their perspective drawings. *Educational Psychology, 15,* 127–139.

COX, M. J., OWEN, M., LEWIS, J. M., & HENDERSON, V. K. (1989). Marriage, adult adjustment, and early parenting. *Child Development, 60,* 1015–1024.

COX, M. J., OWEN, M. T., HENDERSON, V. K., & MARGAND, N. A. (1992). Prediction of infant–father and infant–mother attachment. *Developmental Psychology, 28,* 474–483.

COYLE, T. R., & BJORKLUND, D. F. (1997). Age differences in, and consequences of, multiple- and variable-strategy use on a multitrial sort-recall task. *Developmental Psychology, 33,* 372–380.

CRAIK, F. I. M., & LOCKHART, R. S. (1972). Levels of processing: A framework for memory research. *Journal of Verbal Learning and Verbal Behavior, 11*, 671–684.

CRAIN-THORESON, C., & DALE, P. S. (1992). Do early talkers become early readers? Linguistic precocity, preschool language, and emergent literacy. *Developmental Psychology, 28*, 421–429.

CRAMOND, B. (1994). The Torrance Tests of Creative Thinking: From design through establishment of predictive validity. In R. F. Subotnik & K. D. Arnold (Eds.), *Beyond Terman: Contemporary longitudinal studies of giftedness and talent* (pp. 229–254). Norwood, NJ: Ablex.

CRATTY, B. J. (1986). *Perceptual and motor development in infants and children* (3rd ed.). Englewood Cliffs, NJ: Prentice-Hall.

CRAWFORD, J. (1995). *Bilingual education: History, politics, theory, and practice.* Los Angeles: Bilingual Education Services.

CRAWFORD, J. (1997). *Best evidence: Research foundations of the bilingual education act.* Washington, DC: National Clearinghouse for Bilingual Education.

CREASEY, G. L., JARVIS, P. A., & BERK, L. E. (1998). Play and social competence. In O. N. Saracho & B. Spodek (Eds.), *Multiple perspectives on play in early childhood education* (pp. 116–143). Albany: State University of New York Press.

CREATSAS, G. K., VEKEMANS, M., HOREJSI, J., UZEL, R., LAURITZEN, C., & OSLER, M. (1995). Adolescent sexuality in Europe: A multicentric study. *Adolescent and Pediatric Gynecology, 8*, 59–63.

CREER, T. L., & BENDER, B. G. (1995). Pediatric asthma. In M. C. Roberts (Ed.), *Handbook of pediatric psychology* (2nd ed., pp. 219–240). New York: Guilford.

CRICK, N. R. (1996). The role of overt aggression, relational aggression, and prosocial behavior in the prediction of children's future social adjustment. *Child Development, 67*, 2317–2327.

CRICK, N. R., CASAS, J. F., & MOSHER, M. (1997). Relational and overt aggression in preschool. *Developmental Psychology, 33*, 579–588.

CRICK, N. R., & GROTPETER, J. K. (1995). Relational aggression, gender, and social-psychological adjustment. *Child Development, 66*, 710–722.

CRICK, N. R., & GROTPETER, J. K. (1996). Children's treatment by peers: Victims of relational and overt aggression. *Development and Psychopathology, 8*, 367–380.

CRICK, N. R., & LADD, G. W. (1993). Children's perceptions of their peer experiences: Attributions, loneliness, social anxiety, and social avoidance. *Developmental Psychology, 29*, 244–254.

CROCKETT, L. J. (1990). Sex role and sex-typing in adolescence. In R. M. Lerner, A. C. Petersen, & J. Brooks-Gunn (Eds.), *The encyclopedia of adolescence* (Vol. 2, pp. 1007–1017). New York: Garland.

CROOK, C. K. (1978). Taste perception in the newborn infant. *Infant Behavior and Development, 1*, 52–69.

CROOK, C. K., & LIPSITT, L. P. (1976). Neonatal nutritive sucking: Effects of taste stimulation upon sucking rhythm and heart rate. *Child Development, 47*, 518–522.

CROUTER, A. C., MANKE, B. A., & MCHALE, S. M. (1995). The family context of gender intensification in early adolescence. *Child Development, 66*, 317–329.

CRYSTAL, D. S., CHEN, C., FULIGNI, A. J., STEVENSON, H. W., HSU, C-C., KO, H-J., KITAMURA, S., & KIMURA, S. (1994). Psychological maladjustment and academic achievement: A cross-cultural study of Japanese, Chinese, and American high school students. *Child Development, 65*, 738–753.

CSIKSZENTMIHALYI, M., & LARSON, R. (1984). *Being adolescent. Conflict and growth in the teenage years.* New York: Basic Books.

CUDDY-CASEY, M., & ORVASCHEL, H. (1997). Children's understanding of death in relation to child suicidality and homicidality. *Clinical Psychology Review, 17*, 33–45.

CULBERTSON, F. M. (1997). Depression and gender: An international review. *American Psychologist, 52*, 25–51.

CUMMINGS, E. M., & DAVIES, P. (1994a). *Children and marital conflict.* New York: Guilford.

CUMMINGS, E. M., & DAVIES, P. T. (1994b). Maternal depression and child development. *Journal of Child Psychology and Psychiatry, 35*, 73–112.

CURRIE, J., & THOMAS, D. (1995). Does Head Start make a difference? *American Economic Review, 85*, 341–364.

CURRIE, J., & THOMAS, D. (1997, Spring). Can Head Start lead to long term gains in cognition after all? *SRCD Newsletter, 40*(2), 3–5.

CURRY, G. D., BALL, R. A., & DECKER, S. H. (1996). Estimating the national scope of gang crime from law enforcement data. In C. R. Huff (Ed.), *Gangs in America* (2nd ed., pp. 21–36). Thousand Oaks, CA: Sage.

CUTTLER, L., SILVERS, J. B., SINGH, J., MARRERO, U., FINKELSTEIN, B., TANNIN, G., & NEUHAUSER, D. (1996). Short stature and growth hormone therapy. *Journal of the American Medical Association, 276*, 531–537.

DAHL, R. E., SCHER, M. S., WILLIAMSON, D. E., ROBLES, N., & DAY, N. (1995). A longitudinal study of prenatal marijuana use: Effects on sleep and arousal at age 3 years. *Archives of Pediatric and Adolescent Medicine, 149*, 145–150.

DAMON, W. (1977). *The social world of the child.* San Francisco: Jossey-Bass.

DAMON, W. (1988). *The moral child.* New York: Free Press.

DAMON, W. (1990). Self-concept, adolescent. In R. M. Lerner, A. C. Petersen, & J. Brooks-Gunn (Eds.), *The encyclopedia of adolescence* (Vol. 2, pp. 87–91). New York: Garland.

DAMON, W. (1995). *Greater expectations: Overcoming the culture of indulgence in America's homes and schools.* New York: Free Press.

DAMON, W., & HART, D. (1988). *Self-understanding in childhood and adolescence.* New York: Cambridge University Press.

DANFORTH, J. S., BARKLEY, R. A., & STOKES, T. F. (1990). Observations of parent–child interactions with hyperactive children: Research and clinical applications. *Clinical Psychology Review, 11*, 703–727.

DANIELS, K., & LEWIS, G. M. (1996). Openness of information in the use of donor gametes: Developments in New Zealand. *Journal of Reproductive and Infant Psychology, 14*, 57–68.

DANNEMILLER, J. L., & STEPHENS, B. R. (1988). A critical test of infant pattern preference models. *Child Development, 59*, 210–216.

DARWIN, C. (1877). Biographical sketch of an infant. *Mind, 2*, 285–294.

DARWIN, C. (1936). *On the origin of species by means of natural selection.* New York: Modern Library. (Original work published 1859)

DAUGIRDAS, J. T. (1992). *Sexually transmitted diseases.* Hinsdale, IL: Medtext.

DAVIDSON, E., LEVINE, M., MALVERN, J., NIEBYL, J., & TOBIN, M. (1993, May). A rebirth of obstetrical care. *Medical World News, 34* (5), 42–47.

DAVIDSON, P., & YOUNISS, J. (1991). Which comes first, morality or identity? In W. M. Kurtines & J. L. Gewirtz (Eds.), *Handbook of moral behavior and development* (Vol. 1, pp. 105–121). Hillsdale, NJ: Erlbaum.

DAVIDSON, R. J. (1994). Asymmetric brain function, affective style, and psychopathology: The role of early experience and plasticity. *Development and Psychopathology, 6*, 741–758.

DAVIES, P. T., & CUMMINGS, M. T. (1994). Marital conflict and child adjustment: An emotional security hypothesis. *Psychological Bulletin, 116*, 387–411.

DAWKINS, M. P. (1983). Black students' occupational expectations: A national study of the impact of school desegregation. *Urban Education, 18*, 98–113.

DAY, S. (1993, May). Why genes have a gender. *New Scientist, 138* (1874), 34–38.

DE LISI, R., & GALLAGHER, A. M. (1991). Understanding gender stability and constancy in Argentinean children. *Merrill-Palmer Quarterly, 37*, 483–502.

DE VILLIERS, J. G., & DE VILLIERS, P. A. (1973). A cross-sectional study of the acquisition of grammatical morphemes in child speech. *Journal of Psycholinguistic Research, 2*, 267–278.

DE VILLIERS, P. A., & DE VILLIERS, J. G. (1992). Language development. In M. H. Bornstein & M. E. Lamb (Eds.), *Developmental psychology: An advanced textbook* (3rd ed., pp. 337–418). Hillsdale, NJ: Erlbaum.

DE WINTER, M., BALLEDUZ, M., & DE MARE, J. (1997). A

critical evaluation of Dutch preventive child health care. *Child: Care, Health and Development, 23,* 437–446.

DE WOLFF, M. S., & VAN IJZENDOORN, M. H. (1997). Sensitivity and attachment: A meta-analysis on parental atnecedents of infant attachment. *Child Development, 68,* 571–591.

DEARY, I. J. (1995). Auditory inspection time and intelligence: What is the direction of causation? *Developmental Psychology, 31,* 237–250.

DEATER-DECKARD, K., & DODGE, K. A. (1997). Externalizing behavior problems and discipline revisited: Nonlinear effects and variation by culture, context, and gender. *Psychological Inquiry, 8,* 161–175.

DEATER-DECKARD, K., & DODGE, K. A., BATES, J.E., & PETIT, G.S. (1996). Physical discipline among African American and European American mothers: Links to children's externalizing behaviors. *Developmental Psychology, 32,* 1065-1072.

DEATER-DECKARD, K., SCARR, S., MCCARTNEY, K., & EISENBERG, M. (1994). Paternal separation anxiety: Relationships with parenting stress, child-rearing attitudes, and maternal anxieties. *Psychological Science, 5,* 341–346.

DEBERRY, K. M., SCARR, S., & WEINBERG, R. (1996). Family racial socialization and ecological competence: Longitudinal assessments of African-American transracial adoptees. *Child Development, 67,* 2375–2399.

DECASPER, A. J., & SPENCE, M. J. (1986). Prenatal maternal speech influences newborns' perception of speech sounds. *Infant Behavior and Development, 9,* 133–150.

DECKER, S. H., & LAURITSEN, J. L. (1996). Breaking the bonds of membership. In C. R. Huff (Ed.), *Gangs in America* (2nd ed., pp. 103–122). Thousand Oaks, CA: Sage.

DEKOVIC, M., & GERRIS, J. R. M. (1994). Developmental analysis of social cognitive and behavioral differences between popular and rejected children. *Journal of Applied Developmental Psychology, 15,* 367–386.

DEKOVIC, M., NOOM, M. J., & MEEUS, W. (1997). Expectations regarding development during adolescence: Parent and adolescent perceptions. *Journal of Youth and Adolescence, 26,* 253–271.

DELANEY-BLACK, V., COVINGTON, C., OSTREA, JR., E. ROMERO, A., BAKER, D., TAGLE, M., & NORDSTROM-KLEE, B. (1996). Prenatal cocaine and neonatal outcome: Evaluation of dose-response relationship. *Pediatrics, 98,* 735-740.

DELGADO-GAITAN, C. (1992). School matters in the Mexican-American home: Socializing children to education. *American Educational Research Journal, 29,* 495–515.

DELGADO-GAITAN, C. (1994). Socializing young children in Mexican-American families: An intergenerational perspective. In P. M. Greenfield & R. R. Cocking (Eds.), *Cross-cultural roots of minority child development* (pp. 55–86). Hillsdale, NJ: Erlbaum.

DELLAS, M., & JERNIGAN, L. P. (1990). Affective personality characteristics associated with undergraduate ego identity formation. *Journal of Adolescent Research, 5,* 306–324.

DELOACHE, J. S. (1987). Rapid change in symbolic functioning of very young children. *Science, 238,* 1556–1557.

DELOACHE, J. S. (1991). Symbolic functioning in very young children: Understanding of pictures and models. *Child Development, 62,* 736–752.

DELOACHE, J. S. (1995). Early symbolic understanding and use. In D. Medin (Ed.), *The psychology of learning and motivation* (Vol. 33, pp. 65–114). New York: Academic Press.

DELOACHE, J. S., & TODD, C. M. (1988). Young children's use of spatial categorization as a mnemonic strategy. *Journal of Experimental Child Psychology, 46,* 1–20.

DEMARIE-DREBLOW, D. (1991). Relation between knowledge and memory: A reminder that correlation does not imply causality. *Child Development, 62,* 484–498.

DEMETRIOU, A., EFKLIDES, A., PAPADAKI, M., PAPANTONIOU, G., & ECONOMOU, A. (1993). Structure and development of causal–experimental thought: From early adolescence to youth. *Developmental Psychology, 29,* 480–497.

DEMETRIOU, A., EFKLIDES, A., & PLATSIDOU, M. (1993). The architecture and dynamics of developing mind. *Monographs of the Society for Research in Child Development, 58*(No. 5–6, Serial No. 234).

DEMETRIOU, A., PACHAURY, A., METALLIDOU, Y., & KAZI, S. (1996). Universals and specificities in the structure and development of quantitative-relational thought: A cross-cultural study in Greece and India. *International Journal of Behavioral Development, 19,* 255–290.

DEMPSTER, F. N. (1992). The rise and fall of the inhibitory mechanism: Toward a unified theory of cognitive development and aging. *Developmental Review, 12,* 45–75.

DEMPSTER, F. N. (1993). Resistance to interference: Developmental changes in a basic processing mechanism. In M. L. Howe & R. Pasnak (Eds.), *Emerging themes in cognitive development: Vol. 1* (pp. 3–27). New York: Springer-Verlag.

DENCKLA, M. B. (1996). Biological correlates of learning and attention: What is relevant to learning disability and attention-deficit hyperactivity disorder? *Developmental and Behavioral Pediatrics, 17,* 114–119.

DENHAM, S., ZOLLER, D., & COUCHOUD, E. (1994). Socialization of preschoolers' emotion understanding. *Developmental Psychology, 30,* 928–936.

DENHAM, S. A., RENWICK, S. M., & HOLT, R. W. (1991). Working and playing together: Prediction of preschool social-emotional competence from mother–child interaction. *Child Development, 62,* 242–249.

DENNIS, W. (1960). Causes of retardation among institutionalized children: Iran. *Journal of Genetic Psychology, 96,* 47–59.

DEROM, C., THIERY, E., VLIETINCK, R., LOOS, R., & DEROM, R. (1996). Handedness in twins according to zygosity and chorion type: A preliminary report. *Behavior Genetics, 26,* 407–408.

DEROSIER, M. E., KUPERSMIDT, J. B., & PATTERSON, C. J. (1994). Children's academic and behavioral adjustment as a function of the chronicity and proximity of peer rejection. *Child Development, 65,* 1799–1813.

DEUTSCH, F. M., RUBLE, D. N., FLEMING, A., BROOKS-GUNN, J., & STANGOR, C. (1988). Information-seeking and maternal self-definition during the transition to motherhood. *Journal of Personality and Social Psychology, 55,* 420–431.

DEUTSCH, W., & PECHMANN, T. (1982). Social interaction and the development of definite descriptions. *Cognition, 11,* 159–184.

DEVEREUX, E. C. (1976). Backyard versus Little League Baseball: The impoverishment of children's games. In D. M. Landers (Ed.), *Social problems in athletics* (pp. 37–56). Urbana: University of Illinois Press.

DEVLIN, B., FIENBERG, S. E., RESNICK, D. P., & ROEDER, K. (1995). Galton redux: Intelligence, race and society: A review of *The Bell Curve: Intelligence and Class Structure in American Life. American Statistician, 90,* 1483–1488.

DEVRIES, M. W. (1984). Temperament and infant mortality among the Masai of East Africa. *American Journal of Psychiatry, 141,* 1189–1194.

DEWSBURY, D. A. (1992). Comparative psychology and ethology: A reassessment. *American Psychologist, 47,* 208–215.

DIAMOND, A. (1991). Neuropsychological insights into the meaning of object concept development. In S. Carey & R. Gelman (Eds.), *The epigenesis of mind: Essays on biology and knowledge* (pp. 67–110). Hillsdale, NJ: Erlbaum.

DIAMOND, A., PREVOR, M. B., CALLENDER, G., & DRUIN, D. P. (1997). Prefrontal cortex cognitive deficits in children treated early and continuously for PKU. *Monographs of the Society for Research in Child Development, 62* (4, Serial No. 252).

DIAS, M. G., & HARRIS, P. L. (1990). The influence of imagination on reasoning by young children. *British Journal of Developmental Psychology, 8,* 305–318.

DIAZ, R. M., & BERNDT, T. J. (1982). Children's knowledge of a best friend: Fact or fancy. *Developmental Psychology, 18,* 787–794.

DIBIASE, R., & WADDELL, S. (1995). Some effects of homelessness on the psychological functioning of preschoolers. *Journal of Abnormal Child Psychology, 23,* 783–792.

DICK-READ, G. (1959). *Childbirth without fear.* New York: Harper & Brothers.

DICKENSON, G. (1975). Dating behavior of black and white

adolescents before and after desegregation. *Journal of Marriage and the Family, 37,* 602–608.

DICKINSON, D. K. (1984). First impressions: Children's knowledge of words gained from a single exposure. *Applied Psycholinguistics, 5,* 359–373.

DICLEMENTE, R. J. (1993). Preventing HIV/AIDS among adolescents. *Journal of the American Medical Association, 270,* 760–762.

DIEKSTRA, R. F. W., KIENHORST, C. W. M., & DE WILDE, E. J. (1995). Suicide and suicidal behaviour among adolescents. In M. Rutter & D. J. Smith (Eds.), *Psychosocial disorders in young people* (pp. 686–761). Chichester, England: Wiley.

DIENER, M. L., GOLDSTEIN, L. H., & MANGELSDORF, S. C. (1995). The role of prenatal expectations in parents' reports of infant temperament. *Merrill-Palmer Quarterly, 41,* 172–190.

DIETZ, W. H., JR., BANDINI, L. G., & GORTMAKER, S. L. (1990). Epidemiologic and metabolic risk factors for childhood obesity. *Klinische Pädiatrie, 202,* 69–72.

DILALLA, L. F., KAGAN, J., & REZNICK, J. S. (1994). Genetic etiology of behavioral inhibition among 2-year-old children. *Infant Behavior and Development, 17,* 405–412.

DILDY, G. A., JACKSON, G. M., FOWERS, G. K., OSHIRO, B. T., VARNER, M. W., & CLARK, S. L. (1996). Very advanced maternal age. Pregnancy after age 45. *American Journal of Obstetrics and Gynecology, 175,* 668–674.

DILLER, L. (1996). Use of growth hormone for non-growth hormone deficient children [letter]. *Journal of the American Medical Association, 276,* 1877–1878.

DION, K. K. (1995). Delayed parenthood and women's expectations about the transition to parenthood. *International Journal of Behavioral Development, 18,* 315–333.

DIPIETRO, J. A., HODGSON, D. M., COSTIGAN, K. A., & HILTON, S. C. (1996a). Fetal neurobehavioral development. *Child Development, 67,* 2553–2567.

DIPIETRO, J. A., HODGSON, D. M., COSTIGAN, K. A., & JOHNSON, T. R. B. (1996b). Fetal antecedents of infant

temperament. *Child Development, 67,* 2568–2583.

DIRKS, J. (1982). The effect of a commercial game on children's Block Design scores on the WISC–R test. *Intelligence, 6,* 109–123.

DISHION, T. J., CAPALDI, D., SPRACKLEN, K. M., & LI, F. (1995). Peer ecology of male adolescent drug use. *Development and Psychopathology, 7,* 803–824.

DITTRICHOVA, J., BRICHACEK, V., PAUL, K., & TAUTER-MANNOVA, M. (1982). The structure of infant behavior: An analysis of sleep and waking in the first months of life. In W. W. Hartup (Ed.), *Review of child development research* (Vol. 6, pp. 73–100). Chicago: University of Chicago Press.

DIXON, J. A., & MOORE, C. F. (1990). The development of perspective taking: Understanding differences in information and weighting. *Child Development, 61,* 1502–1513.

DIXON, R. A., & LERNER, R. M. (1992). A history of systems in developmental psychology. In M. H. Bornstein & M. E. Lamb (Eds.), *Developmental psychology: An advanced textbook* (3rd ed., pp. 3–58). Hillsdale, NJ: Erlbaum.

DLUGOSZ, L., & BRACKEN, M. B. (1992). Reproductive effects of caffeine: A review and theoretical analysis. *Epidemiological Review, 14,* 83–100.

DODGE, K. A., MCCLASKEY, C. L., & FELDMAN, E. (1985). A situational approach to the assessment of social competence in children. *Journal of Consulting and Clinical Psychology, 53,* 344–353.

DODGE, K. A., PETTIT, G. S., & BATES, J. E. (1994). Socialization mediators of the relation between socioeconomic status and child conduct problems. *Child Development, 65,* 649–665.

DODGE, K. A., & SOMBERG, D. R. (1987). Hostile attributional biases among aggressive boys are exacerbated under conditions of threats to the self. *Child Development, 58,* 213–224.

DODWELL, P. C., HUMPHREY, G. K., & MUIR, D. W. (1987). Shape and pattern perception. In P. Salapatek & L. Cohen (Eds.), *Handbook of infant perception* (Vol. 2, pp. 1–77). Orlando, FL: Academic Press.

DOHERTY, W. J., & NEEDLE, R. H. (1991). Psychological adjustment and substance use among adolescents before and after parental divorce. *Child Development, 62,* 328–337.

DOLLAGHAN, C. (1985). Child meets word: "Fast mapping" in preschool children. *Journal of Speech and Hearing Research, 28,* 449–454.

DONATELLE, R. J., & DAVIS, L. G. (1997). *Health: The basics* (2nd ed.). Englewood Cliffs, NJ: Prentice-Hall.

DONNERSTEIN, E., SLABY, R. G., & ERON, L. D. (1994). The mass media and youth aggression. In L. D. Eron, J. H. Gentry, & P. Schlegel (Eds.), *Reason to hope: A psychosocial perspective on violence and youth* (pp. 219–250). Washington, DC: American Psychological Association.

DONTAS, C., MARATSOS, O., FAFOUTIS, M., & KARANGELIS, A. (1985). Early social development in institutionally reared Greek infants: Attachment and peer interaction. In I. Bretherton & E. Waters (Eds.), Growing points of attachment theory and research. *Monographs of the Society for Research in Child Development, 50* (1–2, Serial No. 209).

DORNBUSCH, S. M., CARLSMITH, J., GROSS, R., MARTIN, J., JENNINGS, D., ROSENBERG, A., & DUKE, P. (1981). Sexual development, age, and dating: A comparison of biological and social influences upon one set of behaviors. *Child Development, 52,* 179–185.

DORNBUSCH, S. M., CARLSMITH, J. M., BUSHWALL, S. J., RITTER, P. L., LEIDERMAN, H., HASTORF, A. H., & GROSS, R. T. (1985). Single parents, extended households, and the control of adolescents. *Child Development, 56,* 326–341.

DORNBUSCH, S. M., & GLASGOW, K. L. (1997). The structural context of family–school relations. In A. Booth & J. F. Dunn (Eds.), *Family–school links: How do they affect educational outcomes?* (pp. 35–55). Mahwah, NJ: Erlbaum.

DORNBUSCH, S. M., GLASGOW, K. L., & LIN, I-C. (1996). The social structure of schooling. *Annual Review of Psychology, 47,* 401–429.

DORNBUSCH, S. M., RITTER, P. L., LIEDERMAN, P. H., ROBERTS, D. F., & FRALEIGH,

M. J. (1987). The relation of parenting style to adolescent school performance. *Child Development, 58,* 1244–1257.

DORNBUSCH, S. M., RITTER, P. L., MONT-REYNAUD, R., & CHEN, Z. (1990). Family decision making and academic performance in a diverse high school population. *Journal of Adolescent Research, 5,* 143–160.

DORRIS, M. (1989). *The broken cord.* New York: Harper & Row.

DOW-EDWARDS, D. L. (1995). Developmental toxicity of cocaine: Mechanisms of action. In M. Lewis & M. Bendersky (Eds.), *Mothers, babies, and cocaine* (pp. 5–17). Hillsdale, NJ: Erlbaum.

DOWNEY, G., & WALKER, E. (1989). Social cognition and adjustment in children at risk for psychopathology. *Developmental Psychology, 25,* 835–845.

DOWNS, A. C., & FULLER, M. J. (1991). Recollections of spermarche: An exploratory investigation. *Current Psychology: Research and Reviews, 10,* 93–102.

DRABMAN, R. S., CORDUA, G. D., HAMMER, D., JARVIE, G. J., & HORTON, W. (1979). Developmental trends in eating rates of normal and overweight preschool children. *Child Development, 50,* 211–216.

DREYER, P. (1982). Sexuality during adolescence. In B. Wolman (Ed.), *Handbook of developmental psychology* (pp. 559–601). Englewood Cliffs, NJ: Prentice-Hall.

DROTAR, D. (1997). Relating parent and family functioning to the psychological adjustment of children with chronic health conditions: What have we learned? What do we need to know? *Journal of Pediatric Psychology, 22,* 149–165.

DROTAR, D., PALLOTTA, J., & ECKERLE, D. (1994). A prospective study of family environments of children hospitalized for nonorganic failure-to-thrive. *Developmental and Behavioral Pediatrics, 15,* 78–85.

DUBOIS, D. L., & HIRSCH, B. J. (1990). School and neighborhood friendship patterns of black and whites in early adolescence. *Child Development, 61,* 524–536.

DUBOW, E. F., & LUSTER, T. (1990). Adjustment of children born to teenage mothers: The contribution of risk and protective factors. *Journal of Marriage and the Family, 52,* 393–404.

DUBOW, E. F., & MILLER, L. S. (1996). Television violence viewing and aggressive behavior. In T. M. MacBeth (Eds.), *Tuning into young viewers* (pp. 117–147). Thousand Oaks, CA: Sage.

DUNCAN, D. F. (1996). Growing up under the gun: Children and adolescents coping with violent neighborhoods. *Journal of Primary Prevention, 16,* 343–356.

DUNCAN, G. J., BROOKS-GUNN, J., & KLEBANOV, P. K. (1994). Economic deprivation and early childhood development. *Child Development, 65,* 296–318.

DUNCAN, P., RITTER, P., DORNBUSCH, S., GROSS, R., & CARLSMITH, J. (1985). The effects of pubertal timing on body image, school behavior, and deviance. *Journal of Youth and Adolescence, 14,* 227–236.

DUNCAN, S. W., & MARKMAN, H. J. (1988). Intervention programs: Prevention perspective. In G. Y. Michaels & W. A. Goldberg (Eds.), *The transition to parenthood* (pp. 270–310). New York: Cambridge University Press.

DUNHAM, P. J., & DUNHAM, F. (1992). Lexical development during middle infancy: A mutually driven infant–caregiver process. *Developmental Psychology, 28,* 414–420.

DUNHAM, P. J., DUNHAM, F., & CURWIN, A. (1993). Joint-attentional states and lexical acquisition at 18 months. *Developmental Psychology, 29,* 827–831.

DUNIZ, M., SCHEER, P. J., TROJOVSKY, A., KASCHNITZ, W., KVAS, E., & MACARI, S. (1996). *European Child & Adolescent Psychiatry, 5,* 93–100.

DUNN, J. (1989). Siblings and the development of social understanding in early childhood. In P. G. Zukow (Ed.), *Sibling interaction across cultures* (pp. 106–116). New York: Springer-Verlag.

DUNN, J. (1992). Sisters and brothers: Current issues in developmental research. In F. Boer & J. Dunn (Eds.), *Children's sibling relationships* (pp. 1–17). Hillsdale, NJ: Erlbaum.

DUNN, J. (1993). *Young children's close relationships.* Newbury Park, CA: Sage.

DUNN, J. (1994). Temperament, siblings, and the development

of relationships. In W. B. Carey & S. C. McDevitt (Eds.), *Prevention and early intervention* (pp. 50–58). New York: Brunner/Mazel.

DUNN, J. (1996). Sibling relationships and perceived self-competence: Patterns of stability between childhood and early adolescence. In A. J. Sameroff & M. M. Haith (Eds.), *The five to seven year shift* (pp. 253–270). Chicago: University of Chicago Press.

DUNN, J., BRETHERTON, I., & MUNN, P. (1987). Conversations about feeling states between mothers and their young children. *Developmental Psychology, 23,* 132–139.

DUNN, J., BROWN, J., SLOMKOWSKI, C. T., & YOUNGBLADE, L. (1991). Young children's understanding of other people's feelings and beliefs: Individual differences and their antecedents. *Child Development, 62,* 1352–1366.

DUNN, J., BROWN, J. R., & MAGUIRE, M. (1995). The development of children's moral sensibility: Individual differences and emotion understanding. *Developmental Psychology, 31,* 649–659.

DUNN, J., & KENDRICK, C. (1982). *Siblings: Love, envy and understanding.* Cambridge, MA: Harvard University Press.

DUNN, J., SLOMKOWSKI, C., & BEARDSALL, L. (1994). Sibling relationships from the preschool period through middle childhood and early adolescence. *Developmental Psychology, 30,* 315–324.

DURBIN, D. L., DARLING, N., STEINBERG, L., & BROWN, B. B. (1993). Parenting style and peer group membership among European-American adolescents. *Journal of Research on Adolescence, 3,* 87–100.

DUSEK, J. B. (1987). Sex roles and adjustment. In D. B. Carter (Ed.), *Current conceptions of sex roles and sex typing* (pp. 211–222). New York: Praeger.

DWECK, C. S., DAVIDSON, W., NELSON, S., & ENNA, B. (1978). Sex differences in learned helplessness: III. An experimental analysis. *Developmental Psychology, 14,* 268–276.

DWECK, C. S., & LEGGETT, E. L. (1988). A social-cognitive approach to motivation and personality. *Psychological Review, 95,* 256–273.

DYE-WHITE, E. (1986). Environmental hazards in the work setting: Their effect on women of

child-bearing age. *American Association of Occupational Health and Nursing Journal, 34,* 76–78.

DYSON, A. H. (1984). Emerging alphabetic literacy in school contexts: Toward defining the gap between school curriculum and child mind. *Written Communication, 1,* 5–55.

EAST, P. L., & FELICE, M. E. (1996). *Adolescent pregnancy and parenting: Findings from a racially diverse sample.* Mahwah, NJ: Erlbaum.

EAST, P. L., & ROOK, K. S. (1992). Compensatory patterns of support among children's peer relationships: A test using school friends, nonschool friends, and siblings. *Developmental Psychology, 28,* 168–172.

EBELING, K. S., & GELMAN, S. A. (1994). Children's use of context in interpreting "big" and "little." *Child Development, 65,* 1178–1192.

EBERHART-PHILLIPS, J. E., FREDERICK, P. D., & BARON, R. C. (1993). Measles in pregnancy: A descriptive study of 58 cases. *Obstetrics and Gynecology, 82,* 797–801.

EBLE, C. (1996). *Slang and sociability: In-group language among college students.* Chapel Hill, NC: University of North Carolina Press.

ECCLES, J. S. (1987). Adolescence: Gateway to gender-role transcendence. In D. B. Carter (Ed.), *Current conceptions of sex roles and sex typing: Theory and research* (pp. 225–241). New York: Praeger.

ECCLES, J. S. (1994). Understanding women's educational and occupational choices: Applying the Eccles et al. model of achievement-related choices. *Psychology of Women Quarterly, 18,* 585–609.

ECCLES, J. S., EARLY, D., FRASIER, K., BELANSKY, E., & MCCARTHY, K. (1997). The relation of connection, regulation, and support for autonomy to adolescents' functioning. *Journal of Adolescent Research, 12,* 263–286.

ECCLES, J. S., & HAROLD, R. D. (1991). Gender differences in sport involvement: Applying the Eccles' expectancy-value model. *Journal of Applied Sport Psychology, 3,* 7–35.

ECCLES, J. S., & HAROLD, R. D. (1993). Parent–school involvement during the early adolescent years. *Teachers College Record, 94,* 568–587.

ECCLES, J. S., & HAROLD, R. D. (1996). Family involvement in children's and adolescents' schooling. In A. Booth & J. F. Dunn (Eds.), *Family–school links: How do they affect educational outcomes?* (pp. 3–34). Mahwah, NJ: Erlbaum.

ECCLES, J. S., JACOBS, J., & HAROLD, R. D. (1990). Gender-role stereotypes, expectancy effects, and parents' role in the socialization of gender differences in self-perceptions and skill acquisition. *Journal of Social Issues, 46,* 183–201.

ECCLES, J. S., LORD, S., & BUCHANAN, C. M. (1996). School transitions in early adolescence: What are we doing to our young people? In J. A. Graber, J. Brooks-Gunn, & A. C. Petersen (Eds.), *Transitions through adolescence* (pp. 251–284). Mahwah, NJ: Erlbaum.

ECCLES, J. S., MIDGLEY, C., WIGFIELD, A., BUCHANAN, C. M., REUMAN, D., FLANAGAN, C., & MAC IVER, D. (1993a). Development during adolescence: The impact of stage–environment fit on young adolescents' experiences in schools and in families. *American Psychologist, 48,* 90–101.

ECCLES, J. S., WIGFIELD, A., HAROLD, R., & BLUMENFELD, P. B. (1993b). Age and gender differences in children's self- and task perceptions during elementary school. *Child Development, 64,* 830–847.

ECCLES, J. S., WIGFIELD, A., MIDGLEY, C., REUMAN, D., MAC IVER, D., & FELDLAUFER, H. (1993c). Negative effects of traditional middle schools on students' motivation. *Elementary School Journal, 93,* 553–574.

ECCLES, J. S., WIGFIELD, A., & SCHIEFELE, U. (1998). Motivation to succeed. In N. Eisenberg (Ed.), *Handbook of child psychology: Vol. 3. Social, emotional, and personality development* (5th ed., pp. 1017–1095). New York: Wiley.

ECKENRODE, J., LAIRD, M., & DORIS, J. (1993). School performance and disciplinary problems among abused and neglected children. *Developmental Psychology, 29,* 53–62.

ECKERMAN, C. O., & DIDOW, S. M. (1996). Nonverbal imitation and toddlers' mastery of verbal means of achieving coordinated action.

Developmental Psychology, 32, 141–152.

EDELSTEIN, B. L., & DOUGLASS, C. W. (1995). Dispelling the myth that 50 percent of U.S. schoolchildren have never had a cavity. *Public Health Reports, 110,* 522–533.

EDER, R. A. (1989). The emergent personologist: The structure and content of 3½-, 5½-, and 7½-year-olds' concepts of themselves and other persons. *Child Development, 60,* 1218–1228.

EDER, R. A. (1990). Uncovering young children's psychological selves: Individual and developmental differences. *Child Development, 61,* 849–863.

EDWARDS, W. J. (1996). A sociological analysis of an invisible minority group: Male adolescent homosexuals. *Youth & Society, 27,* 334–353.

EGELAND, B., & HIESTER, M. (1995). The long-term consequences of infant daycare and mother–infant attachment. *Child Development, 66,* 474–485.

EGELAND, B., JACOBVITZ, D., & SROUFE, L. A. (1988). Breaking the cycle of abuse. *Child Development, 59,* 1080–1088.

EGELAND, B., KALKOSKE, M., GOTTESMAN, N., & ERICKSON, M. F. (1990). Preschool behavior problems: Stability and factors accounting for change. *Journal of Child Psychology and Psychiatry, 31,* 891–909.

EIBL-EIBESFELDT, I. (1989). *Human ethology.* Hawthorne, NY: Aldine.

EILERS, R., & OLLER, D. K. (1994). Infant vocalizations and the early diagnosis of severe hearing impairment. *Journal of Pediatrics, 124,* 199–203.

EISENBERG, N. (1997). Introduction. In N. Eisenberg (Ed.), *Handbook of child psychology: Vol. 3. Social, emotional, and personality development* (pp. 1–24). New York: Wiley.

EISENBERG, N., FABES, R., MURPHY, B., KARBON, M., SMITH, M., & MASZK, P. (1996). The relations of children's dispositional empathy-related responding to their emotionality, regulation, and social functioning. *Developmental Psychology, 32,* 195–209.

EISENBERG, N., & FABES, R. A. (1998). Prosocial development. In N. Eisenberg (Ed.), *Handbook of child psychology:*

Vol. 3. Social, emotional, and personality development (5th ed., pp. 701–778). New York: Wiley.

EISENBERG, N., FABES, R. A., BERNZWEIG, J., KARBON, M., POULIN, R., & HANISH, L. (1993). The relations of emotionality and regulation to preschoolers' social skills and sociometric status. *Child Development, 64,* 1418–1438.

EISENBERG, N., FABES, R. A., CARLO, G., & KARBON, M. (1992). Emotional responsivity to others: Behavioral correlates and socialization antecedents. In N. Eisenberg & R. A. Fabes (Eds.), *New directions in child development* (No. 55, pp. 57–73). San Francisco: Jossey-Bass.

EISENBERG, N., FABES, R. A., & LOSOYA, S. (1997). Emotional responding: Regulation, social correlates, and socialization. In P. Salovey & D. J. Sluyter (Eds.), *Emotional development and emotional intelligence* (pp. 129–162). New York: Basic Books.

EISENBERG, N., FABES, R. A., MURPHY, B., MASZK, P., SMITH, M., & KARBON, M. (1995). The role of emotionality and regulation in children's social functioning: A longitudinal study. *Child Development, 66,* 1360–1384.

EISENBERG, N., FABES, R. A., SHEPARD, S. A., MURPHY, B. C., GUTHRIE, I. K., JONES, S., FRIEDMAN, J., POULIN, R., & MASZK, P. (1997a). Contemporaneous and longitudinal prediction of children's social functioning from regulation and emotionality. *Child Development, 68,* 642–664.

EISENBERG, N., GUTHRIE, I. K., FABES, R. A., REISER, M., MURPHY, B. C., HOLGREN, R., MASZK, P., & LOSOYA, S. (1997b). The relations of regulation and emotionality to resiliency and competent social functioning in elementary school children. *Child Development, 68,* 295–311.

EKMAN, P., & FRIESEN, W. (1972). Constants across culture in the face and emotion. *Journal of Personality and Social Psychology, 17,* 124–129.

EL-SHEIKH, M., CUMMINGS, E. M., & REITER, S. (1996). Preschoolers' responses to ongoing interadult conflict: The role of prior exposure to resolved versus unresolved arguments. *Journal of Abnormal Child Psychology, 24,* 665–679.

ELARDO, R., & BRADLEY, R. H. (1981). The Home Observation

for Measurement of the Environment (HOME) Scale: A review of research. *Developmental Review, 1,* 113–145.

ELICKER, J., ENGLUND, M., & SROUFE, L. A. (1992). Predicting peer competence and peer relationships in childhood from early parent–child relationships. In R. D. Parke & G. W. Ladd (Eds.), *Family–peer relationships: Modes of linkage* (pp. 77–106). Hillsdale, NJ: Erlbaum.

ELKIND, D. (1985). Egocentrism redux. *Developmental Review, 5,* 218–226.

ELKIND, D. (1994). *A sympathetic understanding of the child: Birth to sixteen* (3rd ed.). Boston: Allyn and Bacon.

ELKIND, D., & BOWEN, R. (1979). Imaginary audience behavior in children and adolescents. *Developmental Psychology, 15,* 33–44.

ELLIOTT, D. S. (1994). Serious violent offenders: Onset, developmental course, and termination. *Criminology, 32,* 1–21.

ELLIOTT, D. S., WILSON, W. J., HUIZINGA, D., SAMPSON, R. J., ELLIOTT, A., & RANKIN, B. (1996). The effects of neighborhood disadvantage on adolescent development. *Journal of Research in Crime and Delinquency, 33,* 389–426.

ELLSWORTH, C. P., MUIR, D. W., & HAINS, S. M. J. (1993). Social competence and person–object differentiation: An analysis of the still-face effect. *Developmental Psychology, 29,* 63–73.

ELSEN, H. (1994). Phonological constraints and overextensions. *First Language, 14,* 305–315.

ELY, R. (1997). Language and literacy in the school years. In J. Berko Gleason (Ed.), *The development of language* (4th ed., pp. 398–439). Boston: Allyn and Bacon.

ELY, R., & MCCABE, A. (1994). The language play of kindergarten children. *First Language, 14,* 19–35.

EMDE, R. N. (1992). Individual meaning and increasing complexity: Contributions of Sigmund Freud and René Spitz to developmental psychology. *Developmental Psychology, 28,* 347–359.

EMDE, R. N., & BUCHSBAUM, H. K. (1990). "Didn't you hear my mommy?" Autonomy with connectedness in moral self-emergence. In D. Cicchetti & M. Beeghly (Eds.), *Development of the self through transi-*

tion (pp. 35–60). Chicago: University of Chicago Press.

EMDE, R. N., PLOMIN, R., ROBINSON, J., CORLEY, R., DEFRIES, J., FULKER, D. W., REZNICK, J. S., CAMPOS, J., KAGAN, J., & ZAHN-WAXLER, C. (1992). Temperament, emotion, and cognition at fourteen months: The MacArthur Longitudinal Twin Study. *Child Development, 63,* 1437–1455.

EMERY, R. E., MATHEWS, S. G., & KITZMANN, K. M. (1994). Child custody mediation and litigation: Parents' satisfaction and functioning a year after settlement. *Journal of Consulting and Clinical Psychology, 62,* 124–129.

EMORY, E. K., & TOOMEY, K. A. (1988). Environmental stimulation and human fetal responsibility in late pregnancy. In W. P. Smotherman & S. R. Robinson (Eds.), *Behavior of the fetus* (pp. 141–161). Caldwell, NJ: Telford.

ENGEL, N. (1989). An American experience of pregnancy and childbirth in Japan. *Birth, 16,* 81–86.

ENNS, J. T. (Ed.). (1990). *The development of attention: Research and theory.* Amsterdam: North-Holland.

ENRIGHT, R. D., LAPSLEY, D. K., & SHUKLA, D. (1979). Adolescent egocentrism in early and late adolescence. *Adolescence, 14,* 687–695.

EPSTEIN, C. J. (Ed.). (1993). *The phenotypic mapping of Down syndrome and other aneuploid conditions.* New York: Wiley-Liss.

EPSTEIN, H. T. (1980). EEG developmental stages. *Developmental Psychobiology, 13,* 629–631.

EPSTEIN, L. H., MCCURLEY, J., WING, R. R., & VALOSKI, A. (1990). Five-year follow-up of family-based treatments for childhood obesity. *Journal of Consulting and Clinical Psychology, 58,* 661–664.

EPSTEIN, L. H., MCKENZIE, S. J., VALOSKI, A., KLEIN, K. R., & WING, R. R. (1994). Effects of mastery criteria and contingent reinforcement for family-based child weight control. *Addictive Behaviors, 19,* 135–145.

EPSTEIN, L. H., SAELENS, B. E., MYERS, M. D., & VITO, D. (1997). Effects of decreasing sedentary behaviors on activity choice in obese children. *Health Psychology, 16,* 107–113.

EPSTEIN, L. H., SAELENS, B. E., & O'BRIEN, J. G. (1995). Effects of reinforcing increases in active versus decreases in sedentary behavior for obese children. *International Journal of Behavioral Medicine, 2,* 41–50.

ERIKSON, E. H. (1950). *Childhood and society.* New York: Norton.

ERIKSON, E. H. (1968). *Identity, youth, and crisis.* New York: Norton.

ERVIN-TRIPP, S. (1991). Play in language development. In B. Scales, M. Almy, A. Nicolopoulou, & S. Ervin-Tripp (Eds.), *Play and the social context of development in early care and education* (pp. 84–97). New York: Teachers College Press.

ESSA, E. L., & MURRAY, C. I. (1994, May). Young children's understanding and experience with death. *Young Children, 49* (4), 74–81.

EVELETH, P. B., & TANNER, J. M. (1976). *Worldwide variation in human growth.* Cambridge, England: Cambridge University Press.

EWING, M. E., & SEEFELDT, V. (1996). Patterns of participation and attrition in American agency-sponsored youth sports. In F. L. Smoll & R. E. Smith (Eds.), *Children and youth in sport: A biopsychological perspective* (pp. 31–45). Dubuque, IA: Brown & Benchmark.

EYER, D. E. (1992). *Mother–infant bonding: A scientific fiction.* New Haven, CT: Yale University Press.

FABES, R. A., EISENBERG, N., MCCORMICK, S. E., & WILSON, M. S. (1988). Preschoolers' attributions of the situational determinants of others' naturally occurring emotions. *Developmental Psychology, 24,* 376–385.

FABES, R. A., EISENBERG, N., NYMAN, M., & MICHEALIEU, Q. (1991). Young children's appraisals of others' spontaneous emotional reactions. *Developmental Psychology, 27,* 858–866.

FABRICIUS, W. V., & WELLMAN, H. M. (1993). Two roads diverged: Young children's ability to judge distance. *Child Development, 64,* 399–414.

FACCHINETTI, F., BATTAGLIA, C., BENATTI, R., BORELLA, P., & GENAZZANI, A. R. (1992). Oral magnesium supplementation improves fetal circulation. *Magnesium Research, 3,* 179–181.

FACKELMANN, K. A. (1992, November 28). Finding Marfan syndrome in the womb. *Science News, 142*(22), 382.

FAGAN, J. (1996). Gangs, drugs, and neighborhood change. In C. R. Huff (Ed.), *Gangs in America* (2nd ed., pp. 39–74). Thousand Oaks, CA: Sage.

FAGAN, J. F., & DETTERMAN, D. K. (1992). The Fagan Test of Infant Intelligence: A technical summary. *Journal of Applied Developmental Psychology, 13,* 173–193.

FAGAN, J. F., III. (1973). Infants' delayed recognition memory and forgetting. *Journal of Experimental Child Psychology, 16,* 424–450.

FAGOT, B. I. (1978). The influence of sex of child on parental reactions to toddler children. *Child Development, 49,* 459–465.

FAGOT, B. I. (1984). The child's expectations of differences in adult male and female interactions. *Sex Roles, 11,* 593–600.

FAGOT, B. I., & HAGAN, R. I. (1991). Observations of parent reactions to sex-stereotyped behaviors: Age and sex effects. *Child Development, 62,* 617–628.

FAGOT, B. I., & LEINBACH, M. D. (1989). The young child's gender schema: Environmental input, internal organization. *Child Development, 60,* 663–672.

FAGOT, B. I., LEINBACH, M. D., & O'BOYLE, C. (1992). Gender labeling, gender stereotyping, and parenting behaviors. *Developmental Psychology, 28,* 225–230.

FAHRMEIER, E. D. (1978). The development of concrete operations among the Hausa. *Journal of Cross-Cultural Psychology, 9,* 23–44.

FAIRBURN, C. G., & BELGIN, S. J. (1990). Studies of the epidemiology of bulimia nervosa. *American Journal of Psychiatry, 147,* 401–408.

FALBO, T. (1992). Social norms and the one-child family: Clinical and policy implications. In F. Boer & J. Dunn (Eds.), *Children's sibling relationships* (pp. 71–82). Hillsdale, NJ: Erlbaum.

FALBO, T., & POLIT, D. (1986). A quantitative review of the only child literature: Research evidence and theory development. *Psychological Bulletin, 100,* 176–189.

FALBO, T., & POSTON, D. L., JR. (1993). The academic, personality, and physical outcomes of only children in China. *Child Development, 64,* 18–35.

FALLER, K. C. (1990). *Understanding child sexual maltreatment.* Newbury Park, CA: Sage.

FANTZ, R. L. (1961, May). The origin of form perception. *Scientific American, 204*(5), 66–72.

FANTZ, R. L. (1963). Pattern vision in newborn infants. *Science, 140,* 296–297.

FARAONE, S. V., BIEDERMAN, J., CHEN, W. J., MILBERGER, S., WARBURTON, R., & TSUANG, M. T. (1995). Genetic heterogeneity in attention-deficit hyperactivity disorder (ADHD): Gender, psychiatric comorbidity, and maternal ADHD. *Journal of Abnormal Psychology, 104,* 334–345.

FARRAR, M. J. (1990). Discourse and the acquisition of grammatical morphemes. *Journal of Child Language, 17,* 607–624.

FARRAR, M. J., & GOODMAN, G. S. (1992). Developmental changes in event memory. *Child Development, 63,* 173–187.

FARRINGTON, D. P. (1987). Epidemiology. In H. C. Quay (Ed.), *Handbook of juvenile delinquency* (pp. 33–61). New York: Wiley.

FARVER, J. M. (1993). Cultural differences in scaffolding pretend play: A comparison of American and Mexican mother–child and sibling–child pairs. In K. MacDonald (Ed.), *Parent–child play* (pp. 349–366). Albany, NY: SUNY Press.

FARVER, J. M., & KIM, Y. K., & LEE, Y. (1995). Cultural differences in Korean- and Anglo-American preschoolers' social interaction and play behaviors. *Child Development, 66,* 1099–1099.

FARVER, J. M., & BRANSTETTER, W. H. (1994). Preschoolers' prosocial responses to their peers' distress. *Developmental Psychology, 30,* 334–341.

FARVER, J. M., & WIMBARTI, S. (1995). Indonesian children's play with their mothers and older siblings. *Child Development, 66,* 1493–1503.

FEAGANS, L. V., KIPP. E., & BLOOD, I. (1994). The effects of otitis media on the attention skills of day-care-attending toddlers. *Developmental Psychology, 30,* 701–708.

FEAGANS, L. V., & PROCTOR, A. (1994). The effects of mild illness in infancy on later development: The sample case of the effects of otitis media (middle ear effusion). In C. B. Fisher & R. M. Lerner (Eds.), *Applied developmental psychology* (pp. 139–173). New York: McGraw-Hill.

FEATHERMAN, D. (1980). Schooling and occupational careers: Constancy and change in worldly success. In O. Brim, Jr., & J. Kagan (Eds.), *Constancy and change in human development* (pp. 675–738). Cambridge, MA: Harvard University Press.

FEIN, G. G., GARIBOLDI, A., & BONI, R. (1993). The adjustment of infants and toddlers to group care: The first six months. *Early Childhood Research Quarterly, 8,* 1–14.

FEINGOLD, A. (1994). Gender differences in personality: A meta-analysis. *Psychological Bulletin, 116,* 429–456.

FEIS, C. L., & SIMONS, C. (1985). Training preschool children in interpersonal cognitive problem-solving skills: A replication. *Prevention in Human Services, 3,* 59–70.

FELDMAN, D. H. (1991). *Nature's gambit.* New York: Teacher's College Press.

FELDMAN, S. S., & WEINBERGER, D. A. (1994). Self-restraint as a mediator of family influences on boys' delinquent behavior: A longitudinal study. *Child Development, 65,* 195–211.

FELNER, R. D., & ADAN, A. M. (1988). The School Transitional Environment Project: An ecological intervention and evaluation. In R. H. Price, E. L. Cowan, R. P. Lorion, & J. Ramos-McKay (Eds.), *14 ounces of prevention: A casebook for practitioners* (pp. 111–122). Washington, DC: American Psychological Association.

FENSON, L., DALE, P. S., REZNICK, J. S., BATES, E., THAL, D. J., & PETHICK, S. J. (1994). Variability in early communicative development. *Monographs of the Society for Research in Child Development, 59* (5, Serial No. 242).

FENZEL, L. M., BLYTH, D. A., & SIMMONS, R. G. (1990). School transitions: Secondary. In R. M. Lerner, A. C. Petersen, & J. Brooks-Gunn (Eds.), *The encyclopedia of adolescence* (pp. 970–973). New York: Garland.

FERGUSON, T. J., STEGGE, H., & DAMHUIS, I. (1991). Children's understanding of guilt and shame. *Child Development, 62,* 827–839.

FERGUSSON, D. M., HORWOOD, L. J., & LYNSKEY, M. T. (1993). Maternal smoking before and after pregnancy: Effects on behavioral outcomes in middle childhood. *Pediatrics, 92,* 815–822.

FERGUSSON, D. M., HORWOOD, L. J., & SHANON, F. T. (1987). Breast-feeding and subsequent social adjustment in six- to eight-year-old children. *Journal of Child Psychology and Psychiatry, 28,* 378–386.

FERNALD, A., & MORIKAWA, H. (1993). Common themes and cultural variations in Japanese and American mothers' speech to infants. *Child Development, 64,* 637–656.

FERNALD, A., TAESCHNER, T., DUNN, J., PAPOUSEK, M., BOYSSEN-BARDIES, B., & FUKUI, I. (1989). A cross-language study of prosodic modifications in mothers' and fathers' speech to preverbal infants. *Journal of Child Language, 16,* 477–502.

FERREIRO, E. (1986). The interplay between information and assimilation in beginning literacy. In W. H. Teale & E. Sulzby (Eds.), *Emergent literacy: Writing and reading* (pp. 15–49). Norwood, NJ: Ablex.

FESHBACH, N. D., & FESHBACH, S. (1982). Empathy training and the regulation of aggression: Potentialities and limitations. *Academic Psychology Bulletin, 4,* 399–413.

FEUERSTEIN, R. (1979). *Dynamic assessment of retarded performers: The learning potential assessment device: Theory, instruments, and techniques.* Baltimore: University Park Press.

FEUERSTEIN, R. (1980). *Instrumental enrichment.* Baltimore: University Park Press.

FICHTER, M. M., & QUADFLIEG, N. (1996). Course and two-year outcome in anorexic and bulimic adolescents. *Journal of Youth and Adolescence, 25,* 545–562.

FIELD, T. (1994). The effects of mother's physical and emotional unavailability on emotion regulation. In N. A. Fox (Ed.), The development of emotion regulation: Biological and behavioral considerations. *Monographs of the Society for Research in Child Development, 59*(2–3, Serial No. 240).

FIELD, T. M., SCHANBERG, S. M., SCAFIDI, F., BAUER, C. R., VEGA-LAHR, N., GARCIA, R., NYSTROM, J., & KUHN, C. M.

(1986). Effects of tactile/kinesthetic stimulation on preterm neonates. *Pediatrics, 77,* 654–658.

FIELD, T. M., WOODSON, R., GREENBERG, R., & COHEN, D. (1982). Discrimination and imitation of facial expressions by neonates. *Science, 218,* 179–181.

FIESE, B. (1990). Playful relationships: A contextual analysis of mother–toddler interaction and symbolic play. *Child Development, 61,* 1648–1656.

FIGUEROA-COLON, R., FRANKLIN, F. A., LEE, J. Y., ALDRIDGE, R., & ALEXANDER, L. (1997). Prevalence of obesity with increased blood pressure in elementary school-aged children. *Southern Medical Journal, 90,* 806–813.

FILE, N. (1993). The teacher as guide of children's competence with peers. *Child & Youth Care Forum, 22,* 351–360.

FILIPOVIC, Z. (1994). *Zlata's diary: A child's life in Sarajevo.* New York: Penguin.

FINE, G. A. (1980). The natural history of preadolescent male friendship groups. In H. C. Foot, A. J. Chapman, & J. R. Smith (Eds.), *Friendship and social relations in children* (pp. 293–320). Chichester, England: Wiley.

FINE, M. (1986). Why urban adolescents drop into and out of public high school. *Teacher's College Record, 87,* 393–409.

FINEGAN, J. K., NICCOLS, G. A., & SITARENIOS, G. (1992). Relations between prenatal testosterone levels and cognitive abilities at 4 years. *Developmental Psychology, 28,* 1075–1089.

FISCHER, K. W., & BIDELL, T. R. (1997). Dynamic development of psychological structures in action and thought. In R. M. Lerner (Ed.), *Handbook of child psychology: Vol. 1. Theoretical models of human development* (5th ed., pp. 467–561). New York: Wiley.

FISCHER, K. W., & BIDELL, T. R. (1998). Dynamic development of psychological structures in action and thought. In R. M. Lerner (Ed.), *Handbook of child psychology: Vol. 1. Theoretical models of human development* (5th ed., pp. 467–562). New York: Wiley.

FISCHER, K. W., & FARRAR, M. J. (1987). Generalizations about generalizations: How a theory of skill development explains both generality and specificity.

International Journal of Psychology, 22, 643–677.

FISCHER, K. W., & PIPP, S. L. (1984). Processes of cognitive development: Optimal level and skill acquisition. In R. J. Sternberg (Ed.), *Mechanisms of cognitive development* (pp. 45–80). New York: Freeman.

FISCHER, K. W., & ROSE, S. P. (1994). Dynamic development of coordination of components in brain and behavior: A framework for theory. In G. Dawson & K. W. Fischer (Eds.), *Human behavior and the developing brain* (pp. 3–66). New York: Guilford.

FISCHER, K. W., & ROSE, S. P. (1995, Fall). Concurrent cycles in the dynamic development of brain and behavior. *SRCD Newsletter,* pp. 3–4, 15–16.

FISHER, C. B. (1993, Winter). Integrating science and ethics in research with high-risk children and youth. *Social Policy Report of the Society for Research in Child Development, 4*(4).

FISHER, C. B., BORNSTEIN, M. H., & GROSS, G. G. (1985). Left–right coding skills related to beginning reading. *Journal of Developmental and Behavioral Pediatrics, 6,* 279–283.

FISHER, E. A., VAN HORN, L., & MCGILL, JR., H. C. (1997). Nutrition and children: A statement for healthcare professionals from the Nutrition Committee, American Heart Association. *Circulation, 95,* 2332–2333.

FISHER, J. A., & BIRCH, L. L. (1995). 3–5 year-old children's fat preferences and fat consumption are related to parental adiposity. *Journal of the American Dietetic Association, 95,* 759–764.

FISHLER, K., & KOCH, R. (1991). Mental development in Down syndrome mosaicism. *American Journal of Mental Retardation, 96,* 345–351.

FIVUSH, R. (1991). The social construction of personal narratives. *Merrill-Palmer Quarterly, 37,* 59–81.

FIVUSH, R. (1995). Language, narrative, and autobiography. *Consciousness and Cognition, 4,* 100–103.

FIVUSH, R., HADEN, C., & ADAM, S. (1995). Structure and coherence of preschoolers' personal narratives over time: Implications for childhood amnesia. *Journal of Experimental Child Psychology, 60,* 32–56.

FIVUSH, R., KUEBLI, J., & CLUBB, P. A. (1992). The

structure of events and event representations: A developmental analysis. *Child Development, 63,* 188–201.

FLAKE, A., RONCAROLO, M., PUCK, J. M., ALMEIDAPORADA, G., EVINS, M. I., JOHNSON, M. P., ABELLA, E. M., HARRISON, D. D., & ZANJANI, E. D. (1996). Treatment of X-linked severe combined immunodeficiency by in utero transplantation of paternal bone marrow. *New England Journal of Medicine, 335,* 1806–1810.

FLAMM, B. L., & QUILLIGAN, E. J. (Eds.). (1995). *Cesarean section: Guidelines for appropriate utilization.* New York: Springer-Verlag.

FLANAGAN, C. A., & ECCLES, J. S. (1993). Changes in parents' work status and adolescents' adjustment at school. *Child Development, 64,* 247–257.

FLANNERY, K. A., & LIEDERMAN, J. (1995). Is there really a syndrome involving the co-occurrence of neurodevelopmental disorder, talent, nonright handedness and immune disorder among children? *Cortex, 31,* 503–515.

FLAVELL, J. H. (1963). *The developmental psychology of Jean Piaget.* New York: Van Nostrand.

FLAVELL, J. H. (1985). *Cognitive development* (2nd ed.). Englewood Cliffs, NJ: Prentice-Hall.

FLAVELL, J. H., GREEN, F. L., & FLAVELL, E. R. (1987). Development of knowledge about the appearance–reality distinction. *Monographs of the Society for Research in Child Development, 51* (1, Serial No. 212).

FLAVELL, J. H., GREEN, F. L., & FLAVELL, E. R. (1989). Young children's ability to differentiate appearance–reality and level 2 perspectives in the tactile modality. *Child Development, 60,* 201–213.

FLAVELL, J. H., GREEN, F. L., & FLAVELL, E. R. (1993). Children's understanding of the stream of consciousness. *Child Development, 64,* 387–398.

FLAVELL, J. H., GREEN, F. L., & FLAVELL, E. R. (1995). Young children's knowledge about thinking. *Monographs of the Society for Research in Child Development, 60* (1, Serial No. 243).

FLAVELL, J. H., GREEN, F. L., FLAVELL, E. R., & GROSSMAN,

J. B. (1997). The development of children's knowledge about inner speech. *Child Development, 68,* 39–47.

FLAVELL, J. H., & MILLER, P. H. (1998). Social cognition. In D. Kuhn & R. S. Siegler (Eds.), *Handbook of child psychology: Vol. 2. Cognition, perception, and language* (4th ed., pp. 851–898). New York: Wiley.

FLEGE, J. E., & FLETCHER, K. L. (1992). Talker and listener effects on the perception of degree of foreign accent. *Journal of the Acoustical Society of America, 91,* 370–389.

FLEMING, P. J., BLAIR, P. S., BACON, C., BENSLEY, D., SMITH, I., TAYLOR, E., BERRY, J., GOLDING, J., & TRIPP, J. (1996). Environment of infants during sleep and risk of the sudden infant death syndrome: Results of 1993-5 case-control study for confidential inquiry into stillbirths and deaths in infancy. *British Medical Journal, 313,* 191–195.

FLETCHER, A. C., DARLING, N. E., STEINBERG, L., & DORN-BUSCH, S. M. (1995). The company they keep: Relation of adolescents' adjustment and behavior to their friends' perceptions of authoritative parenting in the social network. *Developmental Psychology, 31,* 300–310.

FLORIAN, V., & KRAVETZ, S. (1985). Children's concepts of death: A cross-cultural comparison among Muslims, Druze, Christians, and Jews in Israel. *Journal of Cross-Cultural Psychology, 16,* 174–179.

FLORSHEIM, P., TOLAN, P. H., & GORMAN-SMITH, D. (1996). Family processes and risk for externalizing behavior problems among African American and Hispanic boys. *Journal of Consulting and Clinical Psychology, 64,* 1222–1230.

FLYNN, J. R. (1996). What environmental factors affect intelligence: The relevance of IQ gains over time. In D. K. Detterman (Ed.), *The environment: Current topics in human intelligence* (Vol. 5, pp. 17–29). Norwood, NJ: Ablex.

FOGEL, A., TODA, S., & KAWAI, M. (1988). Mother–infant face-to-face interaction in Japan and the United States: A laboratory comparison using 3-month-old infants. *Developmental Psychology, 24,* 398–406.

FOLTZ, C., OVERTON, W. F., & RICCO, R. B. (1995). Proof construction: Adolescent development from inductive to

deductive problem-solving strategies. *Journal of Experimental Child Psychology, 59,* 179–195.

FONAGY, P., STEELE, H., & STEELE, M. (1991). Maternal representations of attachment during pregnancy predict the organization of infant–mother attachment at one year of age. *Child Development, 62,* 891–905.

FORD, C., & BEACH, F. (1951). *Patterns of sexual behavior.* New York: Harper & Row.

FORDHAM, S., & OGBU, J. U. (1986). Black students' school success: Coping with the "burden of 'acting white.'" *Urban Review, 18,* 176–206.

FOREHAND, R., WIERSON, M., THOMAS, A. M., FAUBER, R., ARMISTEAD, L., KEMPTON, T., & LONG, N. (1991). A short-term longitudinal examination of young adolescent functioning following divorce: The role of family factors. *Journal of Abnormal Child Psychology, 19,* 97–111.

FORMAN, E. A., & McPHAIL, J. (1993). A Vygotskian perspective on children's collaborative problem-solving activities. In E. A. Forman, N. Minick, & C. A. Stone (Eds.), *Contexts for learning* (pp. 323–347). New York: Cambridge University Press.

FORMAN, E. A., MINICK, N., & STONE, C. A. (Eds.). (1993). *Contexts for learning.* New York: Oxford University Press.

FORTIER, I., MARCOUX, S., & BEAULAC-BAILLARGEON, L. (1993). Relation of caffeine intake during pregnancy to intrauterine growth retardation and preterm birth. *American Journal of Epidemiology, 137,* 931–940.

FORTIER, I., MARCOUX, S., & BRISSON, J. (1994). Passive smoking during pregnancy and the risk of delivering a small-for-gestational-age infant. *American Journal of Epidemiology, 139,* 294–301.

FOX, N. A. (1991). If it's not left, it's right: Electroencephalograph asymmetry and the development of emotion. *American Psychologist, 46,* 863–872.

FOX, N. A., BELL, M. A., & JONES, N. A. (1992). Individual differences in response to stress and cerebral asymmetry. *Developmental Neuropsychology, 8,* 161–184.

FOX, N. A., CALKINS, S. D., & BELL, M. A. (1994). Neural plasticity and development in

the first two years of life: Evidence from cognitive and socioemotional domains of research. *Development and Psychopathology, 6,* 677–696.

FOX, N. A., & DAVIDSON, R. J. (1986). Taste-elicited changes in facial signs of emotion and the asymmetry of brain electrical activity in newborn infants. *Neuropsychologia, 24,* 417–422.

FOX, N. A., & FITZGERALD, H. E. (1990). Autonomic functioning in infancy. *Merrill-Palmer Quarterly, 36,* 27–51.

FOX, N. A., KIMMERLY, N. L., & SCHAFER, W. D. (1991). Attachment to mother/attachment to father: A meta-analysis. *Child Development, 62,* 210–225.

FOXMAN, B., VALDEZ, R. B., & BROOK, R. H. (1986). Childhood enuresis: Prevalence, perceived impact, and prescribed treatments. *Pediatrics, 77,* 482–487.

FRACASSO, M. P., & BUSCH-ROSSNAGEL, N. A. (1992). Parents and children of Hispanic origin. In M. E. Procidano & C. B. Fisher (Eds.), *Contemporary families* (pp. 83–98). New York: Teachers College Press.

FRANCIS, P. L., & McCROY, G. (1983). *Bimodal recognition of human stimulus configurations.* Paper presented at the biennial meeting of the Society for Research in Child Development, Detroit.

FRANK, S. J., PIRSCH, L. A., & WRIGHT, V. C. (1990). Late adolescents' perceptions of their relationships with their parents: Relationships among deidealization, autonomy, relatedness, and insecurity and implications for adolescent adjustment and ego identity status. *Journal of Youth and Adolescence, 19,* 571–588.

FRANKEL, K. A., & BATES, J. E. (1990). Mother–toddler problem solving: Antecedents in attachment, home behavior, and temperament. *Child Development, 61,* 810–819.

FRAZIER, M. M. (1994). Issues, problems and programs in nurturing the disadvantaged and culturally different talented. In K. A. Heller, F. J. Jonks, & H. A. Passow (Eds.), *International handbook of research and development of giftedness and talent* (pp. 685–692). Oxford, England: Pergamon Press.

FREEDMAN, D. G., & FREEDMAN, N. (1969). Behavioral differences between Chinese-

American and European-American newborns. *Nature, 224,* 1227.

FREEMAN, D. (1983). *Margaret Mead and Samoa: The making and unmaking of an anthropological myth.* Cambridge, MA: Harvard University Press.

FREUD, S. (1973). *An outline of psychoanalysis.* London: Hogarth. (Original work published 1938)

FREUD, S. (1974). *The ego and the id.* London: Hogarth. (Original work published 1923)

FRIED, M. N., & FRIED, M. H. (1980). *Transitions: Four rituals in eight cultures.* New York: Norton.

FRIED, P. A., & MAKIN, J. E. (1987). Neonatal behavioral correlates of prenatal exposure to marijuana, cigarettes, and alcohol in a low risk population. *Neurobehavioral Toxicology and Teratology, 9,* 1–7.

FRIED, P. A., & WATKINSON, B. (1990). 36- and 48-month neurobehavioral follow-up of children prenatally exposed to marijuana, cigarettes, and alcohol. *Journal of Developmental and Behavioral Pediatrics, 11,* 49–58.

FRODI, A. (1985). When empathy fails: Aversive infant crying and child abuse. In B. M. Lester & C. F. Z. Boukydis (Eds.), *Infant crying: Theoretical and research perspectives* (pp. 263–277). New York: Plenum.

FROOM, J., & CULPEPPER, L. (1991). Otitis media in daycare children: A report from the International Primary Care Network. *Journal of Family Practice, 32,* 289–294.

FROST, J. J., & FORREST, J. D. (1995). Understanding the impact of effective teenage pregnancy prevention programs. *Family Planning Perspectives, 27,* 188–195.

FROST, J. L., SHIN, D., & JACOBS, P. J. (1998). Physical environments and children's play. In O. N. Saracho & B. Spodek (Eds.), *Multiple perspectives on play in early childhood education* (pp. 255–294). Albany: State University of New York Press.

FUCHS, I., EISENBERG, N., HERTZ-LAZAROWITZ, R., & SHARABANY, R. (1986). Kibbutz, Israeli city, and American children's moral reasoning about prosocial moral conflicts. *Merrill-Palmer Quarterly, 32,* 37–50.

FULIGNI, A. J., & ECCLES, J. S. (1993). Perceived parent–child relationships and early adolescents' orientation toward peers. *Developmental Psychology, 29,* 622–632.

FULIGNI, A. J., ECCLES, J. S., & BARBER, B. L. (1995). The long-term effects of seventh-grade ability grouping in mathematics. *Journal of Early Adolescence, 15,* 58–89.

FULIGNI, A. J., & STEVENSON, H. W. (1995). Time use and mathematics achievement among American, Chinese, and Japanese high school students. *Child Development, 66,* 830–842.

FURMAN, E. (1990, November). Plant a potato—learn about life (and death). *Young Children, 46*(1), 15–20.

FURMAN, W., & BUHRMESTER, D. (1992). Age and sex differences in perceptions of networks of personal relationships. *Child Development, 63,* 103–115.

FURMAN, W., & WEHNER, E. A. (1994). Romantic views: Toward a theory of adolescent romantic relationships. In R. Montemayor, G. R. Adams, & T. P. Gullotta (Eds.), *Advances in adolescent development: Vol. 3. Relationships in adolescence* (pp. 168–195). Beverly Hills, CA: Sage.

FURSTENBERG, F. F., JR., BROOKS-GUNN, J., & MORGAN, S. P. (1987). *Adolescent mothers and their children in later life.* Cambridge, England: Cambridge University Press.

FURSTENBERG, F. F., JR., & CHERLIN, A. J. (1991). *Divided families.* Cambridge, MA: Harvard University Press.

FURSTENBERG, F. F., JR., GEITZ, L. M., TEITLER, J. O., & WEISS, C. C. (1997). Does condom availability make a difference? An evaluation of Philadelphia's health resource centers. *Family Planning Perspectives, 29,* 123–127.

FURSTENBERG, F. F., JR., & HARRIS, K. M. (1993). When and why fathers matter: Impact of father involvement on children of adolescent mothers. In R. I. Lerman & T. J. Ooms (Eds.), *Young unwed fathers* (pp. 117–138). Philadelphia: Temple University Press.

FURSTENBERG, F. F., JR., HUGHES, M. E., & BROOKS-GUNN, J. (1992). The next generation: Children of teenage mothers grow up. In M. K. Rosenheim & M. F. Testa (Eds.), *Early parenthood* (pp. 113–135). New Brunswick, NJ: Rutgers University Press.

FURSTENBERG, F. F., JR., & NORD, C. W. (1985).

Parenting apart: Patterns of childrearing after marital disruption. *Journal of Marriage and the Family, 47,* 893–904.

FURUNO, S., O'REILLY, K., INATSUKA, T., HOSAKA, C., ALLMAN, T., & ZEISLOFT-FALBEY, B. (1987). *Hawaii Early Learning Profile.* Palo Alto, CA: VORT Corporation.

FUSON, K. C. (1988). *Children's counting and concepts of number.* New York: Springer-Verlag.

FUSON, K. C. (1990). Issues in place-value and multidigit addition and subtraction learning and teaching. *Journal for Research in Mathematics Education, 21,* 273–280.

GABLE, R. K., THOMPSON, D. L., & IWANICKI, E. F. (1983). The effects of voluntary desegregation on occupational outcomes. *Vocational Guidance Quarterly, 31,* 230–239.

GADDIS, A., & BROOKS-GUNN, J. (1985). The male experience of pubertal change. *Journal of Youth and Adolescence, 14,* 61–69.

GALAMBOS, N. L., ALMEIDA, D. M., & PETERSEN, A. C. (1990). Masculinity, femininity, and sex role attitudes in early adolescence: Exploring gender intensification. *Child Development, 61,* 1905–1914.

GALAMBOS, S. J., & MAGGS, J. L. (1991). Children in self-care: Figures, facts and fiction. In J. V. Lerner & N. L. Galambos (Eds.), *Employed mothers and their children* (pp. 131–157). New York: Garland.

GALINSKY, E., HOWES, C., KONTOS, S., & SHINN, M. (1994). *The study of children in family child care and relative care: Highlights of findings.* New York: Families and Work Institute.

GALLER, J. R., RAMSEY, C. F., MORLEY, D. S., ARCHER, E., & SALT, P. (1990). The long-term effects of early kwashiorkor compared with marasmus. IV. Performance on the National High School Entrance Examination. *Pediatric Research, 28,* 235–239.

GALLER, J. R., RAMSEY, F., & SOLIMANO, G. (1985a). A follow-up study of the effects of early malnutrition on subsequent development: I. Physical growth and sexual maturation during adolescence. *Pediatric Research, 19,* 518–523.

GALLER, J. R., RAMSEY, F., & SOLIMANO, G. (1985b). A follow-up study of the effects of early malnutrition on subse-

quent development: II. Fine motor skills in adolescence. *Pediatric Research, 19,* 524–527.

GALLER, J. R., RAMSEY, F., SOLIMANO, G., KUCHARSKI, L. T., & HARRISON, R. (1984). The influence of early malnutrition on subsequent behavioral development: IV. Soft neurological signs. *Pediatric Research, 18,* 826–832.

GALLISTEL, C. R., & GELMAN, R. (1992). Preverbal and verbal counting and computation. *Cognition, 44,* 43–74.

GALOTTI, K. M., KOZBERG, S. F., & FARMER, M. C. (1991). Gender and developmental differences in adolescents' conceptions of moral reasoning. *Journal of Youth and Adolescence, 20,* 13–30.

GAMORAN, A., NYSTRAND, M., BERENDS, M., & LePORE, P. C. (1995) An organizational analysis of the effects of ability grouping. *American Educational Research Journal, 32,* 687-715.

GANDOUR, M. J. (1989). Activity level as a dimension of temperament in toddlers: Its relevance for the organismic specificity hypothesis. *Child Development, 60,* 1092–1098.

GANNON, S., & KORN, S. J. (1983). Temperament, cultural variation, and behavior disorder in preschool children. *Child Psychiatry and Human Development, 13,* 203–212.

GARBARINO, J., & KOSTELNY, K. (1992). Child maltreatment as a community problem. *Child Abuse and Neglect, 16,* 455–464.

GARBARINO, J., & KOSTELNY, K. (1993). Neighborhood and community influences on parenting. In T. Luster & L. Okagaki (1993), *Parenting: An ecological perspective* (pp. 203–226). Hillsdale, NJ: Erlbaum.

GARBER, J., BRAAFLADT, N., & WEISS, B. (1995). Affect regulation in depressed and nondepressed children and young adolescents. *Developmental and Psychopathology, 7,* 93–115.

GARBER, J., QUIGGLE, N., PANAK, W., & DODGE, K. (1991). Aggression and depression in children: Comorbidity, specificity, and social cognitive processing. In D. Cicchetti & S. L. Toth (Eds.), *Rochester Symposium on Developmental Psychopathology: Vol. 2. Internalizing and externalizing expressions of dysfunction* (pp. 225–264). Hillsdale, NJ: Erlbaum.

GARCÍA COLL, C., & MAGNUSON, K. (1997). The psychological experience of immigration: A developmental perspective. In A. Booth, A. C. Crouter, & N. Landale (Eds.), *Immigration and the family* (pp. 91–131). Mahwah, NJ: Erlbaum.

GARDNER, H. (1980). *Artful scribbles: The significance of children's drawings.* New York: Basic Books.

GARDNER, H. (1983). *Frames of mind: The theory of multiple intelligences.* New York: Basic Books.

GARDNER, H. (1993). *Multiple intelligences: The theory in practice.* New York: Basic Books.

GARDNER, H., & HATCH, T. (1989, November). Multiple intelligences go to school. *Educational Researcher, 18*(8), 4–10.

GARDNER, H. E. (1998). Extraordinary cognitive achievements (ECA): A symbol systems approach. In R. M. Lerner (Ed.), *Handbook of child psychology: Vol. 1. Theoretical models of human development* (5th ed., pp. 415–466). New York: Wiley.

GARDNER, M. J., SNEE, M. P., HALL, A. J., POWELL, C. A., DOWNES, S., & TERRELL, J. D. (1990). Leukemia cases linked to fathers' radiation dose. *Nature, 343,* 423–429.

GARFINKEL, I., & McLANAHAN, S. (1995). The effects of child support reform on child well-being. In P. L. Chase-Lansdale & J. Brooks-Gunn (Eds.), *Escape from poverty: What makes a difference for children?* (pp. 211–238). New York: Cambridge University Press.

GARLAND, A. F., & ZIGLER, E. (1993). Adolescent suicide prevention: Current research and social policy implications. *American Psychologist, 48,* 169–182.

GARMEZY, N. (1993). Children in poverty: Resilience despite risk. *Psychiatry, 56,* 127–136.

GARMON, L. C., BASINGER, K. S., GREGG, V. R., & GIBBS, J. C. (1996). Gender differences in stage and expression of moral judgment. *Merrill-Palmer Quarterly, 42,* 418–437.

GARNER, D. M. (1993). Pathogenesis of anorexia nervosa. *Lancet, 341,* 1631–1635.

GARNER, P. W., JONES, D. C., & MINER, J. L. (1994). Social competence among low-income preschoolers: Emotion socialization practices and social cognitive correlates. *Child Development, 65,* 622–637.

GARNER, R. (1990). Children's use of strategies in reading. In D. F. Bjorklund (Ed.), *Children's strategies: Contemporary views of cognitive development* (pp. 245–268). Hillsdale, NJ: Erlbaum.

GARNIER, H. E., STEIN, J. A., & JACOBS, J. K. (1997). The process of dropping out of high school: A 19-year perspective. *American Educational Research Journal, 34,* 395–419.

GARRETT, P., NG'ANDU, N., & FERRON, J. (1994). Poverty experiences of young children and the quality of their home environments. *Child Development, 65,* 331–345.

GARVEY, C. (1990). *Play.* Cambridge, MA: Harvard University Press.

GASKINS, S. (1994). Symbolic play in a Mayan village. *Merrill-Palmer Quarterly, 40,* 344–359.

GATHERCOLE, S. E., ADAMS, A-M., & HITCH, G. (1994). Do young children rehearse? An individual-differences analysis. *Memory & Cognition, 22,* 201–207.

GATHERCOLE, S. E., WILLIS, C. S., EMSLIE, H., & BADDELEY, A. D. (1992). Phonological memory and vocabulary development during the early school years: A longitudinal study. *Developmental Psychology, 28,* 887–898.

GAUB, M., & CARLSON, C. L. (1997). Gender differences in ADHD: A meta-analysis and critical review. *Journal of the American Academy of Child and Adolescent Psychiatry, 36,* 1036–1045.

GAUVAIN, M., & ROGOFF, B. (1989a). Collaborative problem solving and children's planning skills. *Developmental Psychology, 25,* 139–151.

GAUVAIN, M., & ROGOFF, B. (1989b). Ways of speaking about space: The development of children's skill in communicating spatial knowledge. *Cognitive Development, 4,* 295–307.

GE, X., CONGER, R. D., & ELDER, G. H., JR. (1996). Coming of age too early: Pubertal influences on girls' vulnerability to psychological distress. *Child Development, 67,* 3386–3400.

GEARY, D. C. (1994). *Children's mathematical development.* Washington, DC: American Psychological Association.

GEARY, D. C. (1996). International differences in mathematics achievement: The nature, causes, and consequences. *Current Directions in Psychological Science, 5,* 133–137.

GEARY, D. C., BOW-THOMAS, C. C., LIU, F., & SIEGLER, R. S. (1996). Development of arithmetical competencies in Chinese and American children: Influence of age, language, and schooling. *Child Development, 67,* 2022–2044.

GELLATLY, A. R. H. (1987). Acquisition of a concept of logical necessity. *Human Development, 30,* 32–47.

GELLES, R. J., & CORNELL, C. P. (1983). International perspectives on child abuse. *Child Abuse & Neglect, 7,* 375–386.

GELMAN, R. (1972). Logical capacity of very young children: Number invariance rules. *Child Development, 43,* 75–90.

GELMAN, R., & SHATZ, M. (1978). Appropriate speech adjustments: The operation of conversational constraints on talk to two-year-olds. In M. Lewis & L. A. Rosenblum (Eds.), *Interaction, conversation, and the development of language* (pp. 27–61). New York: Wiley.

GENTRY, J. R. (1981, January). Learning to spell developmentally. *The Reading Teacher, 35*(2), 378–381.

GERSHKOFF-STOWE, L., & SMITH, L. B. (1997). A curvilinear trend in naming errors as a function of early vocabulary growth. *Cognitive Psychology 34,* 37–71.

GERVAI, J., TURNER, P. J., & HINDE, R. A. (1995). Gender-related behaviour, attitudes, and personality in parents of young children in England and Hungary. *International Journal of Behavioral Development, 18,* 105–126.

GESELL, A. (1933). Maturation and patterning of behavior. In C. Murchison (Ed.), *A handbook of child psychology.* Worcester, MA: Clark University Press.

GESELL, A., & ILG, F. L. (1949). The child from five to ten. In A. Gesell & F. L. Ilg (Eds.), *Child development* (pp. 394–454). New York: Harper & Row. (Original work published 1946)

GESELL, A., & ILG, F. L. (1949). The infant and child in the culture of today. In A. Gesell & F. L. Ilg (Eds.), *Child development* (pp. 1–393). New York: Harper & Row. (Original work published 1943)

GETCHELL, N., & ROBERTON, M. A. (1989). Whole body stiffness as a function of developmental level in children's hopping. *Developmental Psychology, 25,* 920–928.

GETZELS, J. W., & JACKSON, P. W. (1962). *Creativity and intelligence.* New York: Wiley.

GHIM, H.R. (1990). Evidence for perceptual organization in infants: Perception of subjective contours by young infants. *Infant Behavior and Development, 13,* 221–248.

GIBBS, J. C. (1991). Toward an integration of Kohlberg's and Hoffman's theories of morality. In W. M. Kurtines & J. L. Gewirtz (Eds.), *Handbook of moral behavior and development* (Vol. 1, pp. 183–222). Hillsdale, NJ: Erlbaum.

GIBBS, J. C. (1995). The cognitive developmental perspective. In W. M. Kurtines & J. L. Gewirtz (Eds.), *Moral development: An introduction* (pp. 27–48). Boston: Allyn and Bacon.

GIBBS, J. C., CLARK, P. M., JOSEPH, J. A., GREEN, J. L., GOODRICK, T. S., & MAKOWSKI, D. G. (1986). Relations between moral judgment, moral courage, and field independence. *Child Development, 57,* 185–193.

GIBBS, J. C., POTTER, G. B., & GOLDSTEIN, A. P. (1995). *The EQUIP program: Teaching youth to think and act responsibly through a peer-helping approach.* Champaign, IL: Research Press.

GIBSON, E. J. (1970). The development of perception as an adaptive process. *American Scientist, 58,* 98–107.

GIBSON, E. J. (1988). Exploratory behavior in the development of perceiving, acting, and the acquiring of knowledge. *Annual Review of Psychology, 39,* 1–41.

GIBSON, E. J., & WALK, R. D. (1960). The "visual cliff." *Scientific American, 202,* 64–71.

GIBSON, J. J. (1979). *The ecological approach to visual perception.* Boston: Houghton Mifflin.

GIEBINK, G. S. (1993). Care of the ill child in day-care settings. *Pediatrics, 91,* 229–233.

GIEDD, J. N. (1997). Normal development. *Child and Adolescent Psychiatric Clinics of North America, 6,* 265–282.

GILFILLAN, M. C., CURTIS, L., LISTON, W. A., PULLEN, I., WHYTE, D. A., & BROCK, J. J. H. (1992). Prenatal screening for cystic fibrosis. *Lancet, 340,* 214–216.

GILLIGAN, C., & ATTANUCCI, J. (1989). Two moral orientations: Gender differences and similarities. *Merrill-Palmer Quarterly, 34,* 223–237.

GILLIGAN, C. F. (1982). *In a different voice.* Cambridge, MA: Harvard University Press.

GILLMORE, M. R., HAWKINS, J. D., DAY, L. E., & CATALANO, R. F. (1997). Friendship and deviance: New evidence on an old controversy. *Journal of Early Adolescence, 16,* 80–95.

GINSBURG, H. P., & OPPER, S. (1988). *Piaget's theory of intellectual development* (3rd ed.). Englewood Cliffs, NJ: Prentice-Hall.

GINZBERG, E. (1988). Toward a theory of occupational choice. *Career Development Quarterly, 36,* 358–363.

GJERDE, P. F. (1995). Alternative pathways to chronic depressive symptoms in young adults: Gender differences in developmental trajectories. *Child Development, 66,* 1277–1300.

GLASGOW, K. L., DORNBUSCH, S. M., TROYER, L., STEINBERG, L., & RITTER, P. L. (1997). Parenting styles, adolescents' attributions, and educational outcomes in nine heterogeneous high schools. *Child Development, 68,* 507–523.

GLASSMAN, B. S. (Ed.). (1996). *The new view almanac.* Woodbridge, CT: Blackbirch Press.

GLEITMAN, L. R. (1990). The structural sources of verb meanings. *Language Acquisition, 1,* 3–55.

GLEITMAN, L. R., & NEWPORT, E. (1996). The invention of language by children. Cambridge, MA: MIT Press.

GLIDDEN, L. M., & PURSLEY, J. T. (1989). Longitudinal comparisons of families who have adopted children with mental retardation. *American Journal on Mental Retardation, 94,* 272–277.

GNEPP, J. (1983). Children's social sensitivity: Inferring emotions from conflicting cues. *Developmental Psychology, 19,* 805–814.

GNEPP, J. (1989). Children's use of personal information to understand other people's feelings. In C. Saarni & P. Harris (Eds.), *Children's understanding of emotion* (pp. 151–180). Cambridge, England: Cambridge University Press.

GOLDFIELD, B. A. (1987). Contributions of child and

caregiver to referential and expressive language. *Applied Psycholinguistics, 8,* 267–280.

GOLDIN-MEADOW, S., & MORFORD, M. (1985). Gesture in early language: Studies of deaf and hearing children. *Merrill-Palmer Quarterly, 31,* 145–176.

GOLDSMITH, H. H., BUSS, K. A., & LEMERY, K. S. (1997). Toddler and childhood temperament: Expanded content, stronger genetic evidence, new evidence for the importance of the environment. *Developmental Psychology, 33,* 891–905.

GOLDSMITH, H. H., & GOTTESMAN, I. I. (1981). Origins of variation in behavioral style: A longitudinal study of temperament in young twins. *Child Development, 52,* 91–103.

GOLDSTEIN, A. P., & HUFF, C. R. (Eds.). (1993). *The gang intervention handbook.* Champaign, IL: Research Press.

GOLDSTEIN, A. P., & SORIANO, F. I. (1994). Juvenile gangs. In L. D. Eron, J. H. Gentry, & P. Schlegel (Eds.), *Reason to hope: A psychosocial perspective on violence and youth* (pp. 315–333). Washington, DC: American Psychological Association.

GOLDSTEIN, J. H. (1994). Sex differences in toy play and use of video games. In J. H. Goldstein (Ed.), *Toys, play, and child development* (pp. 110–129). New York: Cambridge University Press.

GOLOMB, C. (1992). *The child's creation of a pictorial world.* Berkeley: University of California Press.

GOLOMB, C., & GALASSO, L. (1995). Make believe and reality: Explorations of the imaginary realm. *Developmental Psychology, 31,* 800–810.

GOLOMBOK, S., COOK, R., BISH, A., & MURRAY, C. (1995). Families created by the new reproductive technologies: Quality of parenting and social and emotional development of the children. *Child Development, 66,* 285–298.

GOLOMBOK, S., & TASKER, F. (1996). Do parents influence the sexual orientation of their children? Findings from a longitudinal study of lesbian families. *Developmental Psychology, 32,* 3–11.

GOMBERT, J. E. (1992). *Metalinguistic development.* Chicago: University of Chicago Press.

GOMEZ-SCHWARTZ, B., HOROWITZ, J. M., & CARDARELLI, A. P. (1990). *Child sexual abuse: Initial effects.* Newbury Park, CA: Sage.

GÖNCÜ, A. (1993). Development of intersubjectivity in the dyadic play of preschoolers. *Early Childhood Research Quarterly, 8,* 99–116.

GONZALES, N. A., CAUCE, A. M., FRIEDMAN, R. J., & MASON, C. A. (1996). Family, peer, and neighborhood influences on academic achievement among African-American adolescents: One-year prospective effects. *American Journal of Community Psychology, 24,* 365–387.

GOOD, T. L., & BROPHY, J. E. (1994). *Looking in classrooms* (6th ed.). New York: HarperCollins.

GOODFELLOW, P. N., & LOVELL, B. R. (1993). SRY and sex determination in mammals. *Annual Review of Genetics, 27,* 71–92.

GOODMAN, G. S., HIRSCHMAN, J. E., HEPPS, D., & RUDY, L. (1991). Children's memory for stressful events. *Merrill-Palmer Quarterly, 37,* 109–158.

GOODMAN, G. S., TAUB, E. P., JONES, D. P. H., ENGLAND, P., PORT, L. K., RUDY, L., & PRADO, L. (1992). Testifying in criminal court: Emotional effects on child sexual assault victims. *Monographs of the Society for Research in Child Development, 57* (No. 5, Serial No. 229).

GOODMAN, G. S., & TOBEY, A. E. (1994). Memory development within the context of child sexual abuse investigations. In C. B. Fisher & R. M. Lerner (Eds.), *Applied developmental psychology* (pp. 46–75). New York: McGraw-Hill.

GOODMAN, K. S. (1986). *What's whole in whole language?* Portsmouth, NH: Heinemann.

GOODMAN, S. H., GRAVITT, G. W., JR., & KASLOW, N. J. (1995). Social problem solving: A moderator of the relation between negative life stress and depression symptoms in children. *Journal of Abnormal Child Psychology, 23,* 473–485.

GOODWYN, S. W., & ACREDOLO, L. P. (1993). Symbolic gesture versus word: Is there a modality advantage for onset of symbol use? *Child Development, 64,* 688–701.

GOOSSENS, F. A., & VAN IJZENDOORN, M. H. (1990). Quality of infants' attachments to professional caregivers: Relation to infant–parent attachment and day-care characteristics. *Child Development, 61,* 832–837.

GOPNIK, A., & CHOI, S. (1990). Do linguistic differences lead to cognitive differences? A cross-linguistic study of semantic and cognitive development. *First Language, 11,* 199–215.

GOPNIK, A., & MELTZOFF, A. N. (1986). Relations between semantic and cognitive development in the one-word stage: The specificity hypothesis. *Child Development, 57,* 1040–1053.

GOPNIK, A., & MELTZOFF, A. N. (1987). The development of categorization in the second year and its relation to other cognitive and linguistic developments. *Child Development, 58,* 1523–1531.

GOPNIK, A., & MELTZOFF, A. N. (1992). Categorization and naming: Basic-level sorting in eighteen-month-olds and its relation to language. *Child Development, 63,* 1091–1103.

GORTMAKER, S. L., DIETZ, W. H., JR., & CHEUNG, L. W. Y. (1990). Inactivity, diet, and the fattening of America. *Journal of the American Dietetic Association, 90,* 1247–1252.

GORTMAKER, S. L., MUST, A., PERRIN, J. M., SOBOL, A. M., & DIETZ, W. H., JR. (1993). Social and economic consequences of overweight in adolescence and young adulthood. *New England Journal of Medicine, 329,* 1008–1012.

GOTTESMAN, I. I. (1963). Genetic aspects of intelligent behavior. In N. Ellis (Ed.), *Handbook of mental deficiency* (pp. 253–296). New York: McGraw-Hill.

GOTTESMAN, I. I. (1991). *Schizophrenia genetics: The origins of madness.* New York: Freeman.

GOTTESMAN, I. I., CAREY, G., & HANSON, D. R. (1983). Pearls and perils in epigenetic psychopathology. In S. B. Guze, E. J. Earls, & J. E. Barrett (Eds.), *Childhood psychopathology and development* (pp. 287–300). New York: Raven Press.

GOTTFREDSON, L. S. (1996). Gottfredson's theory of circumscription and compromise. In D. Brown & L. Brooks (Eds.), *Career choice and development* (3rd ed.). San Francisco: Jossey-Bass.

GOTTFRIED, A. E. (1991). Maternal employment in the family setting: Developmental and environmental issues. In J. V. Lerner & N. L. Galambos (Eds.), *Employed mothers and their children* (pp. 63–84). New York: Garland.

GOTTFRIED, A. E., GOTTFRIED, A. W., & BATHURST, K. (1988). Maternal employment, family environment, and children's development: Infancy through the school years. In A. E. Gottfried & A. W. Gottfried (Eds.), *Maternal employment and children's development: Longitudinal research* (pp. 11–58). New York: Plenum.

GOTTLIEB, G. (1991). Experiential canalization of behavioral development: Theory. *Developmental Psychology, 27,* 4–13.

GOTTMAN, J. M., KATZ, L. F., & HOOVEN, C. (1996). Meta-emotion: How families communicate emotionally. Mahwah, NJ: Erlbaum.

GOULD, J. L., & KEETON, W. T. (1996). *Biological science* (6th ed.). New York: Norton.

GRABER, J. A., BROOKS-GUNN, J., PAIKOFF, R. L., & WARREN, M. P. (1994). Prediction of eating problems: An 8-year study of adolescent girls. *Developmental Psychology, 30,* 823–834.

GRABER, J. A., PETERSEN, A. C., & BROOKS-GUNN, J. (1996). Pubertal processes: Methods, measures, and models. In J. A. Graber, J. Brooks-Gunn, & A. C. Petersen (Eds.), *Transitions through adolescence* (pp. 23–53). Mahwah, NJ: Erlbaum.

GRAHAM, F. K., ERNHART, C. B., THURSTON, D. L., & CRAFT, M. (1962). Development three years after perinatal anoxia and other potentially damaging newborn experiences. *Psychological Monographs, 76* (3, Whole No. 522).

GRAHAM, S., DOUBLEDAY, C., & GUARINO, P. A. (1984). The development of relations between perceived controllability and the emotions of pity, anger, and guilt. *Child Development, 55,* 561–565.

GRALINSKI, J. H., & KOPP, C. B. (1993). Everyday rules for behavior: Mothers' requests to young children. *Developmental Psychology, 29,* 573–584.

GRANT, J. P. (1994). *The state of the world's children.* New York: Oxford University Press (in cooperation with UNICEF).

GRANT, J. P. (1995). *The state of the world's children.* New York: Oxford University Press (in cooperation with UNICEF).

GRANTHAM-MCGREGOR, S., POWELL, C., WALKER, S., CHANG, S., & FLETCHER, P. (1994). The long-term follow-up of severely malnourished children who participated in an intervention program. *Child Development, 65,* 428–439.

GRATTAN, M. P., DE VOS, E., LEVY, J., & MCCLINTOCK, M. K. (1992). Asymmetric action in the human newborn: Sex differences in patterns of organization. *Child Development, 63,* 273–289.

GRAVES, S. B. (1993). Television, the portrayal of African Americans, and the development of children's attitudes. In G. L. Erry & J. K. Asamen (Eds.), *Children and television* (pp. 179–190). Newbury Park, CA: Sage.

GREEN, J., COUPLAND, V., & KITZINGER, J. (1990). Expectations, experiences, and psychological outcomes of childbirth: A prospective study of 825 women. *Birth, 17,* 15–24.

GREEN, R. (1987). *The "sissy boy" syndrome and the development of homosexuality.* New Haven, CT: Yale University Press.

GREENBERG, P. (1990, February). Why not academic preschool? *Young Children, 45(2),* 70–80.

GREENBERGER, E., & GOLDBERG, W. A. (1989). Work, parenting, and the socialization of children. *Developmental Psychology, 25,* 22–35.

GREENBERGER, E., O'NEIL, R., & NAGEL, S. K. (1994). Linking workplace and homeplace: Relations between the nature of adults' work and their parenting behaviors. *Developmental Psychology, 30,* 990–1002.

GREENDORFER, S. L., LEWKO, J. H., & ROSENGREN, K. S. (1996). Family and gender-based socialization of children and adolescents. In F. L. Smoll & R. E. Smith (Eds.), *Children and youth in sport: A biopsychological perspective* (pp. 89–111). Dubuque, IA: Brown & Benchmark.

GREENFIELD, P. M. (1992, June). *Notes and references for developmental psychology.* Conference on Making Basic Texts in Psychology More Culture-Inclusive and Culture-Sensitive, Western Washington University, Bellingham, WA.

GREENFIELD, P. M. (1994). Independence and interdependence as developmental scripts: Implications for theory, research, and practice. In P. M. Greenfield & R. R. Cocking (Eds.), *Cross-cultural roots of minority child development* (pp. 1–37). Hillsdale, NJ: Erlbaum.

GREENFIELD, P. M. (1997). You can't take it with you: Why ability assessments don't cross cultures. *American Psychologist, 52,* 1115–1124.

GREENFIELD, P. M., & SUZUKI, L. (1998). Culture and human development: Implications for parenting education, pediatrics, and mental health. In I. E. Sigel & K. A. Renninger (Eds.), *Handbook of child psychology: Vol. 4. Child psychology in practice* (5th ed., pp. 1059–1109). New York: Wiley.

GREENO, J. G. (1989). A perspective on thinking. *American Psychologist, 44,* 134–141.

GREENOUGH, W. T., & BLACK, J. E. (1992). Induction of brain structure by experience: Substrates for cognitive development. In M. R. Gunnar & C. A. Nelson (Eds.), *Minnesota Symposia on Child Psychology* (Vol. 25, pp. 155–200). Hillsdale, NJ: Erlbaum.

GREENOUGH, W. T., WALLACE, C. S., ALCANTARA, A. A., ANDERSON, B. J., HAWRY-LAK, N., SIREVAAG, A. M., WEILER, I. J., & WITHERS, G. S. (1993). Development of the brain: Experience affects the structure of neurons, glia, and blood vessels. In N. J. Anastasiow & S. Harel (Eds.), *At-risk infants: Interventions, families, and research* (pp. 173–185). Baltimore: Paul H. Brookes.

GREGG, V., GIBBS, J. C., & FULLER, D. (1994). Patterns of developmental delay in moral judgment by male and female delinquents. *Merrill-Palmer Quarterly, 40,* 538–553.

GRESHAM, F. M., & MACMILLAN, D. L. (1997). Social competence and affective characteristics of students with mild disabilities. *Review of Educational Research, 67,* 377–415..

GRIBBLE, P. A., COWEN, E. L., WYMAN, P. A., WORK, W. C., WANNON, M., & RAOOF, A. (1993). Parent and child views of parent–child relationship qualities and resilient outcomes among urban children. *Journal of Child Psychology and Psychiatry, 34,* 507–519.

GRIFFIN, S. (1992). Structural analysis of the development of their inner world: A neo-structural analysis of the development of intrapersonal intelligence. In R. Case (Ed.), *The mind's staircase* (pp. 123–146). Hillsdale, NJ: Erlbaum.

GRIFFIN, S., & CASE, R. (1996). Evaluating the breadth and depth of training effects when central conceptual structures are taught. *Monographs of the Society for Research in Child Development, 246* (61, Serial No. 246), pp. 83–102.

GRIFFITHS, M. (1997). Computer game playing in early adolescence. *Youth & Society, 29,* 223–237.

GROLNICK, W. S., BRIDGES, L. J., & CONNELL, J. P. (1996). Emotion regulation in two-year-olds: Strategies and emotional expression in four contexts. *Child Development, 67,* 928–941.

GROLNICK, W. S., & SLOWIAC-ZEK, M. L. (1994). Parents' involvement in children's schooling: A multidimensional conceptualization and motivational model. *Child Development, 65,* 237–252.

GROSS, S. J., GELLER, J., & TOMARELLI, R. M. (1981). Composition of breast milk from mothers of preterm infants. *Pediatrics, 68,* 480–493.

GROSSMANN, K., GROSSMANN, K. E., SPANGLER, G., SUESS, G., & UNZNER, L. (1985). Maternal sensitivity and newborns' orientation responses as related to quality of attachment in Northern Germany. In I. Bretherton & E. Waters (Eds.), Growing points of attachment theory and research. *Monographs of the Society for Research in Child Development, 50* (1–2, Serial No. 209).

GROTEVANT, H. D. (1997). Adolescent development in family contexts. In N. Eisenberg (Ed.), *Handbook of child psychology: Vol. 3. Social, emotional, and personality development* (pp. 1097–1149). New York: Wiley.

GROTEVANT, H. D. (1998). Adolescent development in family contexts. In N. Eisenberg (Ed.), *Handbook of child psychology: Vol. 3. Social, emotional, and personality development* (5th ed., pp. 1097–1149). New York: Wiley.

GROTEVANT, H. D., & COOPER, C. R. (1985). Patterns of interaction in family relationships and the development of identity exploration in adolescence. *Child Development, 56,* 415–428.

GROTEVANT, H. D., & COOPER, C. R. (1988). The role of family experience in career exploration during adolescence. In P. Baltes, D. Featherman, & R. Lerner (Eds.), *Life-span development and behavior* (Vol. 8, pp. 231–258). Hillsdale, NJ: Erlbaum.

GROTEVANT, H. D., & COOPER, C. R. (1998). Individuality and connectedness in adolescent development: Review and prospects for research on identity, relationships, and context. In E. Skoe & A. von der Lippe (Eds.), *Personality development in adolescence.* London: Routledge & Kegan Paul.

GROTEVANT, H. D., & DUR-RETT, M. (1980). Occupational knowledge and career development in adolescence. *Journal of Vocational Behavior, 17,* 171–182.

GROTPETER, J. K., & CRICK, N. R. (1996). Relational aggression, overt aggression, and friendship. *Child Development, 67,* 2328–2338.

GRUSEC, J. E. (1988). *Social development: History, theory, and research.* New York: Springer-Verlag.

GRYCH, J. H., & FINCHAM, F. D. (1997). Children's adaptation to divorce: From description to explanation. In S. A. Wolchik & I. N. Sandler (Eds.), *Handbook of children's coping: Linking theory to intervention* (pp. 159–193). New York: Plenum.

GUERRA, N. G., TOLAN, P. H., & HAMMOND, W. R. (1994). prevention and treatment of adolescent violence. In L. D. Eron, J. H. Gentry, & P. Schlegel (Eds.), *Reason to hope: A psychosocial perspective on violence and youth* (pp. 383–403). Washington, DC: American Psychological Association.

GUIDUBALDI, J., & CLEMIN-SHAW, H. K. (1985). Divorce, family health and child adjustment. *Family Relations, 34,* 35–41.

GUILFORD, J. P. (1985). The structure-of-intellect model. In B. B. Wolman (Ed.), *Handbook of intelligence* (pp. 225–266). New York: Wiley.

GULLONE, E., & KING, N. J. (1997). Three-year follow-up of normal fear in children and adolescents aged 7 to 18 years. *British Journal of Developmental Psychology, 15,* 97–111.

GUNNAR, M. R., & NELSON, C. A. (1994). Event-related potentials in year-old infants: Relations with emotionality and cortisol. *Child Development, 65,* 80–94.

GURUCHARRI, C., & SELMAN, F. L. (1982). The development of interpersonal understanding during childhood, preadolescence, and adolescence: A longitudinal follow-up study. *Child Development, 53,* 924–927.

GUSTAFSON, G. E., GREEN, J. A., & CLELAND, J. W. (1994). Robustness of individual identity in the cries of human infants. *Developmental Psychobiology, 27*, 1–9.

GUSTAFSON, G. E., & HARRIS, K. L. (1990). Women's responses to young infants' cries. *Developmental Psychology, 26*, 144–152.

HAAN, N., AERTS, E., & COOPER, B. (1985). *On moral grounds: The search for practical morality.* New York: New York University Press.

HACK, M., WRIGHT, L. L., SHANKARAN, S., & TYSON, J. E. (1995). Very low birth weight outcomes of the National Institute of Child Health and Human Development Neonatal Network, November 1989 to October 1990. *American Journal of Obstetrics and Gynecology, 172*, 457–464.

HACK, M. B., TAYLOR, H. G., KLEIN, N., EIBEN, R., SCHATSCHNEIDER, C., & MERCURI-MINICH, N. (1994). School-age outcomes in children with birth weights under 750 g. *New England Journal of Medicine, 331*, 753–759.

HACKEL, L. S., & RUBLE, D. N. (1992). Changes in the marital relationship after the first baby is born: Predicting the impact of expectancy disconfirmation. *Journal of Personality and Social Psychology, 62*, 944–957.

HADJISTAVROPOULOS, H. D., CRAIG, K. D., GRUNAU, R. V. E., & JOHNSTON, C. C. (1994). Judging pain in newborns: Facial and cry determinants. *Journal of Pediatric Psychology, 19*, 485–491.

HAGERMAN, R. J. (1996). Biomedical advances in developmental psychology. *Developmental Psychology, 32*, 416–424.

HAHN, W. K. (1987). Cerebral lateralization of function: From infancy through childhood. *Psychological Bulletin, 101*, 376–392.

HAIDT, J., KOLLER, S. H., & DIAZ, M. G. (1993). Affect, culture, and morality, or is it wrong to eat your dog? *Journal of Personality and Social Psychology, 65*, 613–628.

HAIGHT, W. L., & MILLER, P. J. (1993). *Pretending at home: Early development in a sociocultural context.* Albany: State University of New York Press.

HAINLINE, L. (1993). Conjugate eye movements of infants. In K. Simons (Ed.), *Early visual development: Normal and abnormal* (pp. 47–55). New York: Oxford University Press.

HAITH, M. M., & BENSON, J. B. (1998). Infant cognition. In D. Kuhn & R. S. Siegler (Eds.), *Handbook of child psychology: Vol. 2 Cognition, perception, and language* (pp. 199–254). New York: Wiley.

HAKUTA, K., FERDMAN, B. M., & DIAZ, R. M. (1987). Bilingualism and cognitive development: Three perspectives. In S. Rosenberg (Ed.), *Advances in applied psycholinguistics: Vol. 2. Reading, writing, and language learning* (pp. 284–319). New York: Cambridge University Press.

HALFORD, G. S. (1993). *Children's understanding: The development of mental models.* Hillsdale, NJ: Erlbaum.

HALL, D. G. (1996). Preschoolers' default assumptions about word meaning: Proper names designate unique individuals. *Developmental Psychology, 32*, 177–186.

HALL, G. S. (1904). *Adolescence.* New York: Appleton-Century-Crofts.

HALL, S. S. (1996, January/February). Short like me. *Health*, pp. 98–106.

HALLIDAY, J. L., WATSON, L. F., LUMLEY, J., DANKS, D. M., & SHEFFIELD, L. S. (1995). New estimates of Down syndrome risks at chorionic villus sampling, amniocentesis, and live birth in women of advanced maternal age from a uniquely defined population. *Prenatal Diagnosis, 15*, 455–465.

HALMI, K. A. (1987). Anorexia nervosa and bulimia. In V. B. Van Hasselt & M. Hersen (Eds.), *Handbook of adolescent psychology* (pp. 265–287). New York: Pergamon.

HALPERN, C. T., UDRY, J. R., & SUCHINDRAN, C. (1997). Testosterone predicts initiation of coitus in adolescent females. *Psychosomatic Medicine, 59*, 161–171.

HALPERN, D. F. (1992). *Sex differences in cognitive abilities* (2nd ed.). Hillsdale, NJ: Erlbaum.

HALPERN, D. F. (1997). Sex differences in intelligence. *American Psychologist, 52*, 1091–1102.

HALVERSON, H. M. (1931). An experimental study of prehension in infants by means of systematic cinema records. *Genetic Psychology Monographs, 10*, 107–286.

HAMELIN, K., & RAMACHANDRAN, C. (1993, June). Kangaroo care. *Canadian Nurse, 89*(6), 15–17.

HAMER, D. H., HU, S., MAGNUSON, V. L., HU, N., & PATTA-TUCCI, A. M. L. (1993). A linkage between DNA markers on the X chromosome and male sexual orientation. *Science, 261*, 321–327.

HAMILTON, S. F. (1990). *Apprenticeship for adulthood: Preparing youth for the future.* New York: Free Press.

HAMILTON, S. F. (1993). Prospects for an American-style youth apprenticeship system. *Educational Researcher, 22*(3), 11–16.

HAMILTON, S. F. (1994). Social roles for youths: Interventions in unemployment. In A. C. Petersen & J. T. Mortimer (Eds.), *Youth employment and society* (pp. 248–269). New York: Cambridge University Press.

HAMILTON, S. F., & HURRELMANN, K. (1994). The school-to-career transition in Germany and the United States. *Teachers College Record, 96*, 329–344.

HAMMERSLEY, M. (1992). *What's wrong with ethnography?* New York: Routledge.

HANDLER, A. S., MASON, E. D., ROSENBERG, D. L., & DAVIS, F. G. (1994). The relationship between exposure during pregnancy to cigarette smoking and cocaine use and placenta previa. *American Journal of Obstetrics and Gynecology, 170*, 884–889.

HANIGAN, W. C., MORGAN, A. M., STAHLBERG, L. K., & HILLER, J. L. (1990). Tentorial hemorrhage associated with vacuum extraction. *Pediatrics, 85*, 534–539.

HANNA, E., & MELTZOFF, A. N. (1993). Peer imitation by toddlers in laboratory, home, and day-care contexts: Implications for social learning and memory. *Developmental Psychology, 29*, 701–710.

HAPPÉ, F. G. E. (1995). The role of age and verbal ability in the theory of mind task performance of subjects with autism. *Child Development, 66*, 843–855.

HAQUE, M., ELLERSTEIN, N. S., GUNDY, J. H., SHELOV, S. P., WEISS, J. C., MCINTIRE, M. S., OLNESS, K. N., JONES, D. J., HEAGARTY, M. C., & STARFIELD, B. H. (1981). Parental perceptions of enuresis. *American Journal of Diseases of Children, 135*, 809–811.

HARE, J. (1994). Concerns and issues faced by families headed by a lesbian couple. *Families in Society, 43*, 27–35.

HARE, J., & RICHARDS, L. (1993). Children raised by lesbian couples: Does context of birth affect father and partner involvement? *Family Relations, 42*, 249–255.

HARLOW, H. F., & ZIMMERMAN, R. (1959). Affectional responses in the infant monkey. *Science, 130*, 421–432.

HARRINGTON, R., RUTTER, M., & FOMBONNE, E. (1996). Developmental pathways in depression: Multiple meanings, antecedents, and endpoints. *Development and Psychopathology, 8*, 601–616.

HARRIS, I. B. (1996). *Children in jeopardy.* New Haven, CT: Yale University Press.

HARRIS, R. T. (1991, March–April). Anorexia nervosa and bulimia nervosa in female adolescents. *Nutrition Today, 26* (2), 30–34.

HARRIS, S., MUSSEN, P. H., & RUTHERFORD, E. (1976). Some cognitive, behavioral, and personality correlates of maturity of moral judgment. *Journal of Genetic Psychology, 128*, 123–135.

HARRISON, A. O., WILSON, M. N., PINE, C. J., CHAN, S. Q., & BURIEL, R. (1994). Family ecologies of ethnic minority children. In G. Handel & G. G. Whitchurch (Eds.), *The psychosocial interior of the family* (pp. 187–210). New York: Aldine De Gruyter.

HARRISON, M. R. (1993). Fetal surgery. *Western Journal of Medicine, 159*, 341–349.

HARRIST, A. W., PETTIT, G. S., DODGE, K. A., & BATES, J. E. (1994). Dyadic synchrony in mother–child interaction—relation with children's subsequent kindergarten adjustment. *Family Relations, 43*, 417–424.

HART, B. (1991). Input frequency and children's first words. *First Language, 11*, 289–300.

HART, B., & RISLEY, T. R. (1995). *Meaningful differences in the everyday experience of young American children.* Baltimore: Paul H. Brookes.

HART, B. I., & THOMPSON, J. M. (1996). Gender role characteristics and depressive symptomatology among adolescents. *Journal of Early Adolescence, 16*, 407–426.

HART, C. H., BURTS, D. C., DURLAND, M. A., CHARLESWORTH, R., DEWOLF, M., & FLEEGE, P. O. (1998). Stress behaviors and activity type participation of preschoolers in more and less developmentally appropriate classrooms: SES and sex differences. *Journal of Research in Childhood Education, 13.*

HART, J., GUNNAR, M., & CICCHETTI, D. (1995). Salivary cortisol in maltreated children: Evidence of relations between neuroendocrine activity and social competence. *Development and Psychopathology, 7,* 11–26.

HARTER, S. (1982). The perceived competence scale for children. *Child Development, 53,* 87–97.

HARTER, S. (1986). Processes underlying the construction, maintenance, and enhancement of self-concept in children. In S. Suhls & A. Greenwald (Eds.), *Psychological perspectives of the self* (Vol. 3, pp. 136–182). Hillsdale, NJ: Erlbaum.

HARTER, S. (1990). Issues in the assessment of the self-concept of children and adolescents. In A. LaGreca (Ed.), *Through the eyes of a child* (pp. 292–325). Boston: Allyn and Bacon.

HARTER, S. (1993). Causes and consequences of low self-esteem in children and adolescents. In R. F. Baumeister (Ed.), *Self-esteem: The puzzle of low self-regard* (pp. 87–116). New York: Plenum.

HARTER, S. (1996). Developmental changes in self-understanding across the 5 to 7 shift. In A. J. Sameroff & M. M. Haith (Eds.), *The five to seven year shift* (pp. 207–236). Chicago: University of Chicago Press.

HARTER, S. (1998). The development of self-representations. In N. Eisenberg (Ed.), *Handbook of child psychology: Vol. 3. Social, emotional, and personality development* (5th ed., pp. 553–618). New York: Wiley.

HARTER, S., & BUDDIN, B. J. (1987). Children's understanding of the simultaneity of two emotions: A five-stage developmental acquisition sequence. *Developmental Psychology, 23,* 388–399.

HARTER, S., MAROLD, D. B., WHITESELL, N. R., & COBBS, G. (1996). A model of the effects of parent and peer support on adolescent false self-behavior. *Child Development, 67,* 360–374.

HARTER, S., & MONSOUR, A. (1992). Developmental analysis of conflict caused by opposing attributes in the adolescent self-portrait. *Developmental Psychology, 28,* 251–260.

HARTER, S., & WHITESELL, N. (1989). Developmental changes in children's understanding of simple, multiple, and blended emotion concepts. In C. Saarni & P. Harris (Eds.), *Children's understanding of emotion* (pp. 81–116). Cambridge, England: Cambridge University Press.

HARTER, S., WRIGHT, K., & BRESNICK, S. (1987). A developmental sequence of the emergence of self affects. Paper presented at the biennial meeting of the Society for Research in Child Development, Baltimore.

HARTUP, W. W. (1983). Peer relations. In E. M. Hetherington (Ed.), *Handbook of child psychology: Vol. 4. Socialization, personality, and social development* (4th ed., pp. 103–196). New York: Wiley.

HARTUP, W. W. (1996). The company they keep: Friendships and their developmental significance. *Child Development, 67,* 1–13.

HARTUP, W. W., & LAURSEN, B. (1991). Relationships as developmental contexts. In R. Cohen & A. W. Siegel (Eds.), *Context and development* (pp. 253–279). Hillsdale, NJ: Erlbaum.

HASHIMOTO, K., NOGUCHI, M., & NAKATSUJI, N. (1992). Mouse offspring derived from fetal ovaries or reaggregates which were cultured and transplanted into adult females. *Development: Growth & Differentiation, 34,* 233–238.

HATCH, M. C., SHU, X-O., MCLEAN, D. E., LEVIN, B., BEGG, M., REUSS, L., & SUSSER, M. (1993). Maternal exercise during pregnancy, physical fitness, and fetal growth. *American Journal of Epidemiology, 137,* 1105–1114.

HATCHER, P. J., HULME, C., & ELLIS, A. W. (1994). Ameliorating early reading failure by integrating the teaching of reading and phonological skills: The phonological linkage hypothesis. *Child Development, 65,* 41–57.

HAUSER, S. T., POWERS, S. I., & NOAM, G. G. (1991). *Adolescents and their families: Paths of ego development.* New York: Free Press.

HAUTH, J. C., GOLDENBERG, R. L., PARKER, C. R., CUTTER, G. R., & CLIVER, S. P. (1995). Low-dose aspirin—lack of association with an increase in abruptio placentae or perinatal mortality. *Obstetrics and Gynecology, 85,* 1055–1058.

HAWKE, S., & KNOX, D. (1978). The one-child family: A new life-style. *The Family Coordinator, 27,* 215–219.

HAWKINS, A. J., CHRISTIANSEN, S. L., SARGENT, K. P., & HILLS, E. J. (1993). Rethinking fathers' involvement in child care: A developmental perspective. *Journal of Family Issues, 14,* 531–549.

HAWKINS, D. J., & LAM, T. (1987). Teacher practices, social development, and delinquency. In J. D. Burchard & S. N. Burchard (Eds.), *Prevention of delinquent behavior* (pp. 241–274). Newbury Park, CA: Sage.

HAWKINS, J., & SHEINGOLD, K. (1986). The beginnings of a story: Computers and the organization of learning in classrooms. In J. A. Culbertson & L. L. Cunningham (Eds.), *Microcomputers and education* (85th Yearbook of the National Society for the Study of Education, pp. 40–58). Chicago: University of Chicago Press.

HAWKINS, J. N. (1994). Issues of motivation in Asian education. In H. F. O'Neil, Jr., & M. Drillings (Eds.), *Motivation: Theory and research* (pp. 101–115). Hillsdale, NJ: Erlbaum.

HAWORTH, K., & STROSNIDER, K. (1997, March 14). Controversy grows over cloning research as scientists report new breakthoughs. *Chronicle of Higher Education,* p. A14.

HAYGHE, H. V. (1990, March). Family members in the work force. *Monthly Labor Review.* Washington, DC: U.S. Government Printing Office.

HAYNE, H., ROVEE-COLLIER, C., & PERRIS, E. E. (1987). Categorization and memory retrieval by three-month-olds. *Child Development, 58,* 750–767.

HAYNES, S. N. (1991). Clinical applications of psychophysiological assessment: An introduction and overview. *Psychological Assessment, 3,* 307–308.

HAYSLIP, B., JR. (1994). Stability of intelligence. In R. J. Sternberg (Ed.), *Encyclopedia of human intelligence* (Vol. 2, pp. 1019–1026). New York: Macmillan.

HEATH, S. B. (1982). Questioning at home and at school: A comparative study. In G. Spindler (Ed.), *Doing the ethnography of schooling: Educational anthropology in action* (pp. 102–127). New York: Holt.

HEATH, S. B. (1989). Oral and literate traditions among black Americans living in poverty. *American Psychologist, 44,* 367–373.

HEATH, S. B. (1990). The children of Trackton's children: Spoken and written language in social change. In J. Stigler, G. Herdt, & R. A. Shweder (Eds.), *Cultural psychology: Essays on comparative human development* (pp. 496–519). New York: Cambridge University Press.

HEDGES, L. V., & NOWELL, A. (1995). Sex differences in mental scores, variability, and numbers of high-scoring individuals. *Science, 269,* 41–45.

HEFFERNAN, K. (1994). Sexual orientation as a factor in risk for binge eating and bulimia nervosa: A review. *International Journal of Eating Disorders, 16,* 335–348.

HEFFNER, R. W., & KELLEY, M. L. (1994). Nonorganic failure to thrive: Developmental outcomes and psychosocial assessment and intervention issues. *Research in Developmental Disabilities, 15,* 247–268.

HEINE, S. J., & LEHMAN, D. R. (1995). Cultural variation in unrealistic optimism: Does the West feel more invulnerable than the East? *Journal of Personality and Social Psychology, 68,* 595–607.

HEINL, T. (1983). *The baby massage book.* London: Coventure.

HEINONEN, O. P., SLONE, D., & SHAPIRO, S. (1977). *Birth defects and drugs in pregnancy.* Littleton, MA: PSG Publishing.

HELBURN, S. W. (Ed.). (1995). *Cost, quality and child outcomes in child care centers.* Denver: University of Colorado.

HELD, R. (1993). What can rates of development tell us about underlying mechanisms? In C. E. Granrud (Ed.), *Visual perception and cognition in infancy* (pp. 75–89). Hillsdale, NJ: Erlbaum.

HENSHAW, S. K. (1997). Teenager abortion and pregnancy statistics by state, 1992. *Family Planning Perspectives, 29,* 115–122.

HEPPER, P. G. (1997). Fetal habituation: Another Pandora's box? *Developmental Medicine and Child Neurology, 39,* 274–278.

HERDT, G., & BOXER, A. M. (1993). *Children of horizons: How gay and lesbian teens are leading a new way out of the closet.* Boston: Beacon Press.

HERGENRATHER, J. R., & RABINOWITZ, M. (1991). Age-related differences in the organization of children's knowledge of illness. *Developmental Psychology, 27,* 952–959.

HERMAN, M. R., DORNBUSCH, S. M., HERRON, M. C., & HERTING, J. R. (1997). The influence of family regulation, connection, and psychological autonomy on six measures of adolescent functioning. *Journal of Adolescent Research, 12,* 34–67.

HERNANDEZ, D. J. (1994, Spring). Children's changing access to resources: A historical perspective. *Social Policy Report of the Society for Research in Child Development, 8* (1).

HERRNSTEIN, R. J., & MURRAY, C. (1994). *The bell curve.* New York: Free Press.

HETHERINGTON, E. M. (1989). Coping with family transitions: Winners, losers and survivors. *Child Development, 60,* 1–14.

HETHERINGTON, E. M. (1991). The role of individual differences and family relationships in children's coping with divorce and remarriage. In P. A. Cowan & E. M. Hetherington (Eds.), *Family transitions* (pp. 165–194). Hillsdale, NJ: Erlbaum.

HETHERINGTON, E. M. (1993). An overview of the Virginia Longitudinal Study of Divorce and Remarriage: A focus on early adolescence. *Journal of Family Psychology, 7,* 39–56.

HETHERINGTON, E. M. (1997). Teenaged childbearing and divorce. In S. Luthar, J. A. Burack, D. Cicchetti, & J. Weisz (Eds.), *Developmental psychopathology: Perspectives on adjustment, risk, and disorders* (pp. 350-373). Cambridge: Cambridge University Press.

HETHERINGTON, E. M., BRIDGES, M., & INSABELLA, G. M. (1998). What matters? What does not? Five perspectives on the association between marital transitions and children's adjustment. *American Psychologist, 53,* 167-184.

HETHERINGTON, E. M., & CLINGEMPEEL, W. G. (1992). Coping with marital transitions: A family systems perspective. *Monographs of the Society for Research in Child Development, 57* (2–3, Serial No. 227).

HETHERINGTON, E. M., & HENDERSON, S. H. (1997). Fathers in stepfamilies. In M. E. Lamb (Ed.), *The role of the father in child development* (pp. 212–226). New York: Wiley.

HETHERINGTON, E. M., & JODL, K. M. (1994). Stepfamilies as settings for child development.

In A. Booth & J. Dunn (Eds.) *Stepfamilies: Who benefits? Who does not?* (pp. 55-79). Hillsdale, NJ: Erlbaum.

HETHERINGTON, E. M., & STANLEY-HAGAN, M. M. (1997). The effects of divorce on fathers and their children. In M. E. Lamb (Ed.), *The role of the father in child development* (pp. 191–211). New York: Wiley.

HETHERINGTON, P. (1995, March). *The changing American family and the well-being of children.* Master lecture presented at the biennial meeting of the Society for Research in Child Development, Indianapolis.

HETHERINGTON, S. E. (1990). A controlled study of the effect of prepared childbirth classes on obstetric outcomes. *Birth, 17,* 86–90.

HEWLETT, B. S. (1992). Husband–wife reciprocity and the father–infant relationship among Aka pygmies. In B. S. Hewlett (Ed.), *Father–child relations: Cultural and biosocial contexts* (pp. 153–176). New York: Aldine De Gruyter.

HEYMAN, G. D., & DWECK, C. S. (1992). Achievement goals and intrinsic motivation: Their relation and their role in adaptive motivation. *Motivation and Emotion, 16,* 231–247.

HEYMAN, G. D., DWECK, C. S., & CAIN, K. M. (1992). Young children's vulnerability to self-blame and helplessness: Relationship to beliefs about goodness. *Child Development, 63,* 401–415.

HICKEY, T. L., & PEDUZZI, J. D. (1987). Structure and development of the visual system. In P. Salapatek & L. Cohen (Eds.), *Handbook of infant perception: Vol. 1. From sensation to perception* (pp. 1–42). New York: Academic Press.

HIER, D. B., & CROWLEY, W. F. (1982). Spatial ability in androgen-deficient men. *New England Journal of Medicine, 302,* 1202–1205.

HILL, J. P., & HOLMBECK, G. N. (1986). Attachment and autonomy during adolescence. In G. Whitehurst (Ed.), *Annals of child development* (Vol. 3, pp. 145–189). Greenwich, CT: JAI Press.

HILL, J. P., & HOLMBECK, G. N. (1987). Family adaptation to biological change during adolescence. In R. M. Lerner & T. T. Foch (Eds.), *Biological-psychosocial interactions in early adolescence* (pp. 207–224). Hillsdale, NJ: Erlbaum.

HILL, P. M., & HUMPHREY, P. (1982). *Human growth and development throughout life: A nursing perspective.* New York: Delmar.

HILLIER, L., HEWITT, K. L., & MORRONGIELLO, B. A. (1992). Infants' perception of illusions in sound localization: Reaching to sounds in the dark. *Journal of Experimental Child Psychology, 53,* 159–179.

HILLS-BANCZYK, S. G., AVERY, M. D., SAVIK, K., POTTER, S., & DUCKETT, L. J. (1993). Women's experiences with combining breast-feeding and employment. *Journal of Nurse-Midwifery, 38,* 257–266.

HIMES, J. H., STORY, M., CZAPLINSKI, K., & DAHLBERG-LUBY, E. (1992). Indications of early obesity in low-income Hmong children. *American Journal of Diseases of Children, 146,* 67–69.

HINDE, R. A. (1989). Ethological and relationships approaches. In R. Vasta (Ed.), *Annals of child development* (Vol. 6, pp. 251– 285). Greenwich, CT: JAI Press.

HINES, M., & GREEN, R. (1991). Human hormonal and neural correlates of sex-typed behaviors. *Review of Psychiatry, 10,* 536–555.

HIRSH-PASEK, K., KEMLER NELSON, D. G., JUSCZYK, P. W., CASSIDY, K. W., DRUSS, B., & KENNEDY, L. (1987). Clauses are perceptual units for young infants. *Cognition, 26,* 269–286.

HISCOCK, M., & KINSBOURNE, M. (1987). Specialization of the cerebral hemispheres: Implications for learning. *Journal of Learning Disabilities, 20,* 130–143.

HOBART, C., & BROWN, D. (1988). Effects of prior marriage children on adjustment in remarriages: A Canadian study. *Journal of Comparative Family Studies, 19,* 381–396.

HOBSON, R. P. (1993). *Autism and the development of mind.* London: Erlbaum.

HOCK, E., SCHIRTZINGER, M. B., LUTZ, W. J., & WIDAMAN, K. (1995). Maternal depressive symptomatology over the transition to parenthood: Assessing the influence of marital satisfaction and marital sex role traditionalism. *Journal of Family Psychology, 9,* 79–88.

HOCUTT, A. M. (1996). Effectiveness of special education: Is placement the critical factor? *Future of Children, 6,* 77–102.

HODGES, J., & TIZARD, B. (1989). Social and family relationships of ex-institutional adolescents. *Journal of Child Psychology and Psychiatry, 30,* 77–97.

HODGES, R. M., & FRENCH, L. A. (1988). The effect of class and collection labels on cardinality, class-inclusion, and number conservation tasks. *Child Development, 59,* 1387–1396.

HOFF-GINSBERG, E. (1986). Function and structure in maternal speech: Their relation to the child's development of syntax. *Developmental Psychology, 22,* 155–163.

HOFF-GINSBERG, E., & TARDIFF, T. (1995). Socioeconomic status and parenting. In M. Bornstein (Ed.), *Handbook of parenting* (Vol. 2, pp. 161–188). Hillsdale, NJ: Erlbaum.

HOFFMAN, L. W. (1989). Effects of maternal employment in the two-parent family. *American Psychologist, 44,* 283–292.

HOFFMAN, L. W. (1994). Commentary on Plomin, R. (1994). A proof and disproof questioned. *Social Development, 3,* 60–63.

HOFFMAN, M. L. (1988). Moral development. In M. H. Bornstein & M. E. Lamb (Eds.), *Developmental psychology: An advanced textbook* (2nd ed., pp. 497–548). Hillsdale, NJ: Erlbaum.

HOFFMAN, M. L. (1991). Empathy, cognition, and social action. In W. M. Kurtines & J. L. Gewirtz (Eds.), *Handbook of moral behavior and development* (Vol. 1, pp. 275–303). Hillsdale, NJ: Erlbaum.

HOFFMAN, S., & HATCH, M. C. (1996). Stress, social support and pregnancy outcome: A reassessment based on research. *Paediatric and Perinatal Epidemiology, 10,* 380–405.

HOFSTADTER, M., & REZNICK, J. S. (1996). Response modality affects human infant delayed-response performance. *Child Development, 67,* 646–658.

HOFSTEN, C. VON (1984). Developmental changes in the organization of prereaching movements. *Developmental Psychology, 20,* 378–388.

HOFSTEN, C. VON (1989). Motor development as the development of systems: Comments on the special section. *Developmental Psychology, 25,* 950–953.

HOFSTEN, C. VON, & SPELKE, E. S. (1985). Object perception and object-directed reaching in infancy. *Journal of Experimental Psychology: General, 114,* 198–212.

HOKODA, A., & FINCHAM, F. D. (1995). Origins of children's helpless and mastery achievement patterns in the family. *Journal of Educational Psychology, 87,* 375–385.

HOLCOMB, T. F. (1990). Fourth graders' attitudes toward AIDS issues: A concern for the elementary school counselor. *Elementary School Guidance & Counseling, 25,* 83–90.

HOLDEN, G. W. (1983). Avoiding conflict: Mothers as tacticians in the supermarket. *Child Development, 54,* 233–240.

HOLDEN, G. W., COLEMAN, S. M., & SCHMIDT, K. L. (1995). Why 3-year-old children get spanked: Determinants as reported by college-educated mothers. *Merrill-Palmer Quarterly, 41,* 431–452.

HOLDEN, G. W., & WEST, M. J. (1989). Proximate regulation by mothers: A demonstration of how differing styles affect young children's behavior. *Child Development, 60,* 64–69.

HOLLAND, J. L. (1966). *The psychology of vocational choice.* Waltham, MA: Blaisdell.

HOLLAND, J. L. (1985). *Making vocational choices: A theory of vocational personalities and work environments.* Englewood Cliffs, NJ; Prentice-Hall.

HOLMBECK, G. N. (1996). A model of family relational transformations during the transition to adolescence: Parent–adolescent conflict and adaptation. In J. A. Graber, J. Brooks-Gunn, & A. C. Petersen (Eds.), *Transitions through adolescence* (pp. 167–199). Mahwah, NJ: Erlbaum.

HOLMBECK, G. N., & HILL, J. P. (1991). Conflictive engagement, positive affect, and menarche in families with seventh-grade girls. *Child Development, 62,* 1030–1048.

HOLMBECK, G. N., PAIKOFF, R. L., & BROOKS-GUNN, J. (1995). Parenting adolescents. In M. H. Bornstein (Ed.), *Handbook of parenting: Vol. 1. Children and parenting* (pp. 91–118). Mahwah, NJ: Erlbaum.

HOLMBECK, G. N., WATERS, K. A., & BROOKMAN, R. R. (1990). Psychosocial correlates of sexually transmitted diseases and sexual activity in black adolescent females. *Journal of Adolescent Research, 5,* 431–448.

HOLMES, L. B. (1993). Report on the National Institute of Child Health and Human Development workshop on chorionic villus sampling and limb and other defects. *Teratology, 48,* 7–13.

HOLZMAN, C., & PANETH, N. (1994). Maternal cocaine use during pregnancy and perinatal outcomes. *Epidemiologic Reviews, 16,* 315–334.

HOOD, B. M., MURRAY, L., KING, F., HOOPER, R., ATKINSON, J., & BRADDICK, O. (1996). Habituation changes in early infancy: Longitudinal measures from birth to 6 months. *Journal of Reproductive and Infant Psychology, 14,* 177–185.

HOOK, E. B. (1988). Evaluation and projection of rates of chromosome abnormalities in chorionic villus studies (c.v.s.). *American Journal of Human Genetics Supplement, 43,* A108.

HOPKINS, B., & WESTRA, T. (1988). Maternal handling and motor development: An intracultural study. *Genetic, Social and General Psychology Monographs, 14,* 377–420.

HOPKINS-TANNE, J. (1994). U.S. campaign for women to take folic acid to prevent birth defects. *British Medical Journal, 308,* 223.

HORGAN, D. (1978). The development of the full passive. *Journal of Child Language, 5,* 65–80.

HORN, J. M. (1983). The Texas Adoption Project: Adopted children and their intellectual resemblance to biological and adoptive parents. *Child Development, 54,* 268–275.

HORNER, T. M. (1980). Two methods of studying stranger reactivity in infants: A review. *Journal of Child Psychology and Psychiatry, 21,* 203–219.

HOROWITZ, F. D. (1987). *Exploring developmental theories: Toward a structural/behavioral model of child development.* Hillsdale, NJ: Erlbaum.

HOROWITZ, F. D. (1992). John B. Watson's legacy: Learning and environment. *Developmental Psychology, 28,* 360–367.

HOTZ, V. J., McELROY, S. W., & SANDERS, S. G. (1997). The costs and consequences of teenage childbearing for mothers. In R. A. Maynard (Ed.), *Kids having kids* (pp. 55–94). Washington, DC: Urban Institute.

HOUTS, A. C. (1991). Nocturnal enuresis as a biobehavioral problem. *Behavior Therapy, 22,* 133–151.

HOUTS, A. C., BERMAN, J. S., & ABRAMSON, H. (1994). Effectiveness of psychological and pharmacological treatments for noctural enuresis. *Journal of Consulting and Clinical Psychology, 62,* 737–745.

HOWARD, M., & McCABE, J. B. (1990). Helping teenagers postpone sexual involvement. *Family Planning Perspectives, 22,* 21–26.

HOWARD, M., & McCABE, J. B. (1992). An information and skills approach for younger teens: Postponing Sexual Involvement Program. In B. C. Miller (Ed.), *Preventing adolescent pregnancy* (pp. 83–109). Newbury Park, CA: Sage.

HOWE, M. L., & COURAGE, M. L. (1993). On resolving the enigma of infantile amnesia. *Psychological Bulletin, 113,* 305–326.

HOWE, M. L., & COURAGE, M. L. (1997). The emergence and early development of autobiographical memory. *Psychological Review, 104,* 499–523.

HOWE, N., & ROSS, H. S. (1990). Socialization, perspective-taking, and the sibling relationship. *Developmental Psychology, 26,* 160–165.

HOWES, C. (1988). Relations between early child care and schooling. *Developmental Psychology, 24,* 53–57.

HOWES, C. (1990). Can the age of entry into child care and the quality of child care predict adjustment in kindergarten? *Developmental Psychology, 26,* 292–303.

HOWES, C. (1992). *The collaborative construction of pretend.* Albany: State University of New York Press.

HOWES, C., & HAMILTON, C. E. (1993). The changing experience of child care: Changes in teachers and in teacher–child relationships and children's social competence with peers. *Early Childhood Research Quarterly, 8,* 15–32.

HOWES, C., & MATHESON, C. C. (1992). Sequences in the development of competent play with peers: Social and social pretend play. *Developmental Psychology, 28,* 961–974.

HOWES, C., PHILLIPS, D. A., & WHITEBOOK, M. (1992). Thresholds of quality: Implications for the social development of children in center-based child care. *Child Development, 63,* 449–460.

HOWES, P., & CICCHETTI, D. (1993). A family/relational perspective on maltreating families: Parallel processes across systems and social policy implications. In D. Cicchetti & S. L. Toth (Eds.), *Child abuse, child development and social policy* (pp. 249–300). Norwood, NJ: Ablex.

HOWES, P., & MARKMAN, H. J. (1989). Marital quality and child functioning: A longitudinal investigation. *Child Development, 60,* 1044–1051.

HUDSON, J. A. (1990). The emergence of autobiographic memory in mother–child conversations. In R. Fivush & J. A. Hudson (Eds.), *Knowing and remembering in young children* (pp. 166–196). New York: Cambridge University Press.

HUDSON, J. A., FIVUSH, R., & KUEBLI, J. (1992). Scripts and episodes: The development of event memory. *Applied Cognitive Psychology, 6,* 483–505.

HUDSON, J. A., & NELSON, K. (1983). Effects of script structure on children's story recall. *Developmental Psychology, 19,* 625–635.

HUDSPETH, W. J., & PRIBRAM, K. H. (1992). Psychophysiological indices of cerebral maturation. *International Journal of Psychophysiology, 12,* 19–29.

HUESMANN, L. R. (1986). Psychological processes promoting the relation between exposure to media violence and aggressive behavior by the viewer. *Journal of Social Issues, 42,* 125–139.

HUESMANN, L. R., & MILLER, L. S. (1994). Long-term effects of repeated exposure to media violence in childhood. In L. R. Huesmann (Ed.), *Aggressive behavior: Current perspectives* (pp. 153–186). New York: Plenum.

HUFF, C. R. (1996). The criminal behavior of gang members and nongang at-risk youth. In C. R. Huff (Ed.), *Gangs in America* (2nd ed., pp. 75–102). Thousand Oaks, CA: Sage.

HUGHES, F. P. (1998). Play in special populations. In O. N. Saracho & B. Spodek (Eds.), *Multiple perspectives on play in early childhood education* (pp. 171–193). Albany: State University of New York Press.

HUMAN GENOME PROGRAM. (1998). *Count of mapped genes by chromosome.* Washington, DC: U.S. Department of Energy, Office of Biological and Environmental Research.

HUMPHREY, T. (1978). Function of the nervous system during

prenatal life. In U. Stave (Ed.), *Perinatal physiology* (pp. 651–683). New York: Plenum.

HUMPHREYS, A. P., & SMITH, P. K. (1987). Rough and tumble, friendship, and dominance in schoolchildren: Evidence for continuity and change with age. *Child Development, 58,* 201–212.

HUNT, E., STREISSGUTH, A. P., KERR, B., & OLSON, H. C. (1995). Mothers' alcohol consumption during pregnancy: Effects on spatial-visual reasoning in 14-year-old children. *Psychological Science, 6,* 339–342.

HUNTINGTON, L., HANS, S. L., & ZESKIND, P. S. (1990). The relations among cry characteristics, demographic variables, and developmental test scores in infants prenatally exposed to methadone. *Infant Behavior and Development, 13,* 533–538.

HUSTON, A. C. (1983). Sex-typing. In E. M. Hetherington (Ed.), *Handbook of child psychology: Vol. 4. Socialization, personality, and social development* (4th ed., pp. 387–467). New York: Wiley.

HUSTON, A. C. (Ed.). (1991). *Children in poverty: Child development and public policy.* Cambridge: Cambridge University Press.

HUSTON, A. C., & ALVAREZ, M. M. (1990). The socialization context of gender role development in early adolescence. In R. Montemayor, G. R. Adams, & T. P. Gullotta (Eds.), *From childhood to adolescence: A transitional period?* (pp. 156–179). Newbury Park, CA: Sage.

HUSTON, A. C., DONNERSTEIN, E., FAIRCHILD, H., FESH-BACH, N. D., KATZ, P. A., MURRAY, J. P., RUBINSTEIN, E. A., WILCOX, B. L., & ZUCKERMAN, D. (1992). *Big world, small screen: The role of television in American society.* Lincoln: University of Nebraska Press.

HUSTON, A. C., & WRIGHT, J. C. (1998). Mass media and children's development. In I. E. Sigel & K. A. Renninger (Eds.), *Handbook of child psychology: Vol. 4. Child psychology in practice* (5th ed., pp. 999–1058). New York: Wiley.

HUSTON, T. L., & VANGELISTI, A. L. (1995). How parenthood affects marriage. In M. A. Fitzpatrick & A. L. Vangelisti (Eds.), *Explaining family interactions* (pp. 147–176). Thousand Oaks, CA: Sage.

HUSTON-STEIN, A., FOX, S., GREER, D., WATKINS, B. A., & WHITAKER, J. (1981). The effects of TV action and violence on children's social behavior. *Journal of Genetic Psychology, 138,* 183–191.

HUTTENLOCHER, J., HAIGHT, W., BRYK, A., SELTZER, M., & LYONS, T. (1991). Early vocabulary growth: Relation to language input and gender. *Developmental Psychology, 27,* 236–248.

HUTTENLOCHER, P. R. (1994). Synaptogenesis in the human cerebral cortex. In G. Dawson & K. W. Fischer (Eds.), *Human behavior and the developing brain* (pp. 137–152). New York: Guilford.

HYDE, J. S. (1995). Women and maternity leave: Empirical data and public policy. *Psychology of Women Quarterly, 19,* 299–313.

HYDE, J. S., FENEMA, E., & LAMON, S. J. (1990). Gender differences in mathematics performance: A meta-analysis. *Psychological Bulletin, 107,* 139–155.

HYDE, J. S., KLEIN, M. H., ESSEX, M. J., & CLARK, R. (1995). Maternity leave and women's mental health. *Psychology of Women Quarterly, 19,* 257–285.

HYDE, J. S., & LINN, M. C. (1988). Gender differences in verbal ability: A meta-analysis. *Psychological Bulletin, 104,* 53–69.

HYND, G. W., HORN, K. L., VOELLER, K. K., & MAR-SHALL, R. M. (1991). Neurobiological basis of attention-deficit hyperactivity disorder (ADHD). *School Psychology Review, 20,* 174–186.

IANNI, F. A. J., & ORR, M. T. (1996). Dropping out. In J. A. Graber, J. Brooks-Gunn, & A. C. Petersen (Eds.), *Transitions through adolescence: Interpersonal domains and context* (pp. 285–322). Mahwah, NJ: Erlbaum.

INFANTE-RIVARD, C., FERNÁN-DEZ, A., GAUTHIER, R., & RIVARD, G. E. (1993). Fetal loss associated with caffeine intake before and during pregnancy. *Journal of the American Medical Association, 270,* 2940–2943.

INHELDER, B., & PIAGET, J. (1958). *The growth of logical thinking from childhood to adolescence: An essay on the construction of formal operational structures.* New York: Basic Books. (Original work published 1955)

INTERNATIONAL EDUCATION ASSOCIATION. (1988). *Science achievement in seventeen countries: A preliminary report.* Oxford, England: Pergamon Press.

INTONS-PETERSON, M. J. (1988). *Gender concepts of Swedish and American youth.* Hillsdale, NJ: Erlbaum.

IRGENS, L. M., MARKESTAD, T., BASTE, V., SCHREUDER, P., SKJAERVEN, R., & OYEN, N. (1995). Sleeping position and sudden infant death syndrome in Norway 1967–1991. *Archives of Disease in Childhood, 72,* 478–482.

IRVINE, J. J. (1986). Teacher-student interactions: Effects of student race, sex, and grade level. *Journal of Educational Psychology, 78,* 14–21.

IRWIN, A. R., & GROSS, A. M. (1995). Cognitive tempo, violent video games, and aggressive behavior in young boys. *Journal of Family Violence, 10,* 337–350.

ISABELLA, R. (1993). Origins of attachment: Maternal interactive behavior across the first year. *Child Development, 64,* 605–621.

ISABELLA, R., & BELSKY, J. (1991). Interactional synchrony and the origins of infant– mother attachment: A replication study. *Child Development, 62,* 373–384.

ISABELLA, R. A., BELSKY, J., & VON EYE, A. (1989). Origins of infant–mother attachment: An examination of interactional synchrony during the infant's first year. *Developmental Psychology, 25,* 12–21.

IZARD, C. E. (1979). *The maximally discriminative facial movement scoring system.* Unpublished manuscript, University of Delware.

IZARD, C. E. (1991). *The psychology of emotions.* New York: Plenum.

IZARD, C. E., FANTAUZZO, C. A., CASTLE, J. M., HAYNES, O. M., RAYIAS, M. F., & PUTNAM, P. H. (1995). The ontogeny and significance of infants' facial expressions in the first 9 months of life. *Developmental Psychology, 31,* 997–1013.

IZARD, C. E., HAYNES, O. M., CHISHOLM, G., & BAAK, K. (1991). Emotional determinants of infant–mother attachment. *Child Development, 62,* 906–917.

JACKLIN, C. N., & MACCOBY, E. E. (1978). Issues of gender differentiation in normal develop-

ment. In M. D. Levine, W. B. Carey, A. C. Crocker, & R. T. Gross (Eds.), *Developmental-behavioral pediatrics* (pp. 174–184). Philadelphia: Saunders.

JACKLIN, C. N., WILCOX, K. T., & MACCOBY, E. E. (1988). Neonatal sex-steroid hormones and cognitive abilities at six years. *Developmental Psychology, 21,* 567–574.

JACOBS, J. E., & WEISZ, V. (1994). Gender stereotypes: Implications for gifted education. *Roeper Review, 16,* 152–155.

JACOBSON, J. L., JACOBSON, S. W., & HUMPHREY, H. E. B. (1990). Effects of in utero exposure to polychlorinated biphenyls on cognitive functioning in young children. *Journal of Pediatrics, 116,* 38–45.

JACOBSON, J. L., JACOBSON, S. W., FEIN, G., SCHWARTZ, P. M., & DOWLER, J. (1984). Prenatal exposure to an environmental toxin: A test of the multiple effects model. *Developmental Psychology, 20,* 523–532.

JACOBSON, J. L., JACOBSON, S. W., PADGETT, R. J., BRUMITT, G. A., & BILLINGS, R. L. (1992). Effects of prenatal PCB exposure on cognitive processing efficiency and sustained attention. *Developmental Psychology, 28,* 297–306.

JACOBSON, S. W., FEIN, G. G., JACOBSON, J. L., SCHWARTZ, P. M., & DOWLER, J. (1985). The effect of intrauterine PCB exposure on visual recognition memory. *Child Development, 56,* 853–860.

JACOBSON, S. W., JACOBSON, J. L., SOKOL, R. J., MARTIER, S. S., & AGER, J. W. (1993). Prenatal alcohol exposure and infant information processing ability. *Child Development, 64,* 1706–1721.

JADACK, R. A., HYDE, J. S., MOORE, C. F., & KELLER, M. L. (1995). Moral reasoning about sexually transmitted diseases. *Child Development, 66,* 167–177.

JAMESON, S. (1993). Zinc status in pregnancy: The effect of zinc therapy on perinatal mortality, prematurity, and placental ablation. *Annals of the New York Academy of Sciences, 678,* 178–192.

JAMIN, J. R. (1994). Language and socialization of the child in African families living in France. In P. M. Greenfield & R. R. Cocking (Eds.), *Cross-*

cultural roots of minority child development (pp. 147–166). Hillsdale, NJ: Erlbaum.

JANSSENS, J. M. A. M., & DEKOVIC, M. (1997). Child rearing, prosocial moral reasoning, and prosocial behavior. *International Journal of Behavioral Development, 20,* 509–527.

JARROLD, C., CARRUTHERS, P., SMITH, P. K., & BOUCHER, J. (1994). Pretend play: Is it metarepresentational? *Mind & Language, 9,* 445–468.

JASKIEWICZ, J. A., & MCANARNEY, E. R. (1994). Pregnancy during adolescence. *Pediatrics in Review, 15,* 32–38.

JENKINS, J. M., & ASTINGTON, J. W. (1996). Cognitive factors and family structure associated with theory of mind development in young children. *Developmental Psychology, 32,* 70–78.

JENSEN, A. R. (1969). How much can we boost IQ and scholastic achievement? *Harvard Educational Review, 39,* 1–123.

JENSEN, A. R. (1980). *Bias in mental testing.* New York: Free Press.

JENSEN, A. R. (1985). The nature of the black–white difference on various psychometric tests: Spearman's hypothesis. *Behavioral and Brain Sciences, 8,* 193–219.

JENSEN, A. R., & FIGUEROA, R. A. (1975). Forward and backward digit-span interaction with race and IQ: Predictions from Jensen's theory. *Journal of Educational Psychology, 67,* 882–893.

JENSEN, A. R., & WHANG, P. A. (1994). Speed of accessing arithmetic facts in long-term memory: A comparison of Chinese-American and Anglo-American children. *Contemporary Educational Psychology, 19,* 1–12.

JENSEN, M. K., & GREEN, V. P. (1993). The effects of multi-age grouping on young children and teacher preparation. *Early Child Development and Care, 91,* 25–31.

JIAO, S., JI, G., & JING, Q. (1996). Cognitive development of Chinese urban only children and children with siblings. *Child Development, 67,* 387–395.

JOHANSON, R. B., RICE, C., COYLE, M., ARTHUR, J., ANYANWU, L., IBRAHIM, J., WARWICK, A., REDMAN, C. W. E., & O'BRIEN, P. M. S. (1993). A randomised prospective study comparing the new vacuum extractor policy with forceps delivery. *British Journal of Obstetrics and Gynaecology, 100,* 524–530.

JOHNSON, C., & CONNORS, M. E. (1987). *The etiology and treatment of bulimia nervosa: A biopsychosocial perspective.* New York: Basic Books.

JOHNSON, D. W., JOHNSON, R. T., & MARUYAMA, G. (1984). Goal interdependence and interpersonal attraction in heterogeneous classrooms: A meta-analysis. In N. Miller & M. B. Brewer (Eds.), *Groups in contact: The psychology of desegregation* (pp. 187–212). New York: Academic Press.

JOHNSON, E. D., & LARSON, B. E. (1993). Thumb-sucking—literature review. *Journal of Dentistry for Children, 60,* 385–391.

JOHNSON, J. E., & HOOPER, F. E. (1982). Piagetian structuralism and learning: Two decades of educational application. *Contemporary Educational Psychology, 7,* 217–237.

JOHNSON, J. S., & NEWPORT, E. L. (1989). Critical period effects in second language learning: The influence of maturational state on the acquisition of English as a second language. *Cognitive Psychology, 21,* 60–99.

JOHNSON, M. (1991). Infant and toddler sleep: A telephone survey of parents in one community. *Developmental and Behavioral Pediatrics, 12,* 108–114.

JOHNSON, M. H. (1998). The neural basis of cognitive development. In D. Kuhn & R. S. Siegler (Eds.), *Handbook of child psychology: Vol. 2. Cognition, perception, and language* (pp. 1–49). New York: Wiley.

JOHNSON, S. L., & BIRCH, L. L. (1994). Parents' and children's adiposity and eating style. *Pediatrics, 94,* 653–661.

JOHNSON, S. P. (1996). Habituation patterns and object perception in young infants. *Journal of Reproductive and Infant Psychology, 14,* 207–218.

JOHNSON, S. P. (1997). Young infants' perception of object unity: Implications for development of attentional and cognitive skills. *Current Directions in Psychological Science, 6,* 5–11.

JOHNSTON, J. R., KLINE, M., & TSCHANN, J. M. (1989). Ongoing post-divorce conflict. *American Journal of Orthopsychiatry, 57,* 587–600.

JONES, G. P., & DEMBO, M. H. (1989). Age and sex role differences in intimate friend-ships during childhood and adolescence. *Merrill-Palmer Quarterly, 35,* 445–462.

JONES, M. C. (1965). Psychological correlates of somatic development. *Child Development, 36,* 899–911.

JONES, M. C., & BAYLEY, N. (1950). Physical maturing among boys as related to behavior. *Journal of Educational Psychology, 41,* 129–148.

JONES, M. C., & MUSSEN, P. H. (1958). Self-conceptions, motivations, and interpersonal attitudes of early- and late-maturing girls. *Child Development, 29,* 491–501.

JONES, S. S., & RAAG, T. (1989). Smile production in older infants: The importance of a social recipient for the facial signal. *Child Development, 60,* 811–818.

JORDAN, B. (1993). *Birth in four cultures.* Prospect Heights, IL: Waveland.

JORDAN, P. (1990). Laboring for relevance: The male experience of expectant and new parenthood. *Nursing Research, 39,* 15–19.

JORDAN, W. J., LARA, J., & MCPARTLAND, J. M. (1996). Exploring the causes of early dropout among race-ethnic and gender groups. *Youth & Society, 28,* 62–94.

JORGENSEN, M., & KEIDING, N. (1991). Estimation of spermarche from longitudinal spermaturia data. *Biometrics, 47,* 177–193.

JOSSELSON, R. (1994). The theory of identity development and the question of intervention. In S. L. Archer (Ed.), *Interventions for adolescent identity development* (pp. 12–25). Thousand Oaks, CA: Sage.

JUSCZYK, P. W. (1995). Language acquisition: Speech sounds and phonological development. In J. L. Miller & P. D. Eimas (Eds.), *Handbook of perception and cognition: Vol. 11. Speech, language, and communication* (pp. 263–301). Orlando, FL: Academic Press.

JUSCZYK, P. W., & ASLIN, R. N. (1995). Infants' detection of the sound patterns of words in fluent speech. *Cognitive Psychology, 29,* 1–23.

JUSCZYK, P. W., CUTLER, A., & REDANZ, N. J. (1993). Infants' preference for the predominant stress patterns of English words. *Child Development, 64,* 675–687.

JUSCZYK, P. W., & HOHNE, E. A. (1997). Infants' memory for spoken words. *Science, 277,* 1984–1986.

KAGAN, J. (1989). *Unstable ideas: Temperament, cognition, and self.* Cambridge, MA: Harvard University Press.

KAGAN, J. (1992). Behavior, biology, and the meanings of temperamental constructs. *Pediatrics, 90,* 510–513.

KAGAN, J. (1994). *Galen's prophecy.* New York: Basic Books.

KAGAN, J. (1998). Biology and the child. In N. Eisenberg (Ed.), *Handbook of child psychology: Vol. 3. Social, emotional, and personality development* (5th ed., pp. 177–236). New York: Wiley.

KAGAN, J., ARCUS, D., SNIDMAN, N., FENG, W. Y., HENDLER, J., & GREENE, S. (1994). Reactivity in infants: A cross-national comparison. *Developmental Psychology, 30,* 342–345.

KAGAN, J., KEARSLEY, R. B., & ZELAZO, P. R. (1978). *Infancy: Its place in human development.* Cambridge, MA; Harvard University Press.

KAGAN, J., REZNICK, J. S., & SNIDMAN, N. (1988). Biological bases of childhood shyness. *Science, 240,* 167–171.

KAGAN, J., & SNIDMAN, N. (1991). Temperamental factors in human development. *American Psychologist, 46,* 856–862.

KAHN, P. H., JR. (1992). Children's obligatory and discretionary moral judgments. *Child Development, 63,* 416–430.

KAIL, R. (1990). *The development of memory in children* (3rd ed.). New York: Freeman.

KAIL, R. (1991). Processing time declines exponentially during childhood and adolescence. *Developmental Psychology, 27,* 259–266.

KAIL, R. (1993). The role of a global mechanism in developmental change in speed of processing. In M. L. Howe & R. Pasnak (Eds.), *Emerging themes in cognitive development: Vol. 1. Foundations.* New York: Springer-Verlag.

KAIL, R., & PARK, Y. (1992). Global developmental change in processing time. *Merrill-Palmer Quarterly, 38,* 525–541.

KAIL, R., & PARK, Y. (1994). Processing time, articulation time, and memory span. *Journal of Experimental Child Psychology, 57,* 281–291.

KAITZ, M., GOOD, A., ROKEM, A. M., & EIDELMAN, A. I. (1987). Mothers' recognition of their newborns by olfactory cues. *Developmental Psychobiology, 20,* 587–591.

KAITZ, M., GOOD, A., ROKEM, A. M., & EIDELMAN, A. I. (1988). Mothers' and fathers' recognition of their newborns' photographs during the postpartum period. *Journal of Developmental and Behavioral Pediatrics, 9,* 223–226.

KAITZ, M., MEIROV, H., LANDMAN, I., & EIDELMAN, A. I. (1993a). Infant recognition by tactile cues. *Infant Behavior and Development, 16,* 333–341.

KAITZ, M., SHIRI, S., DANZIGER, S., HERSHKO, Z., & EIDELMAN, A. I. (1993b). Fathers can also recognize their newborns by touch. *Infant Behavior and Development, 17,* 205–207.

KALB, C. (1997, May 5). How old is too old? *Newsweek,* p. 64.

KALER, S. R., & KOPP, C. B. (1990). Compliance and comprehension in very young toddlers. *Child Development, 61,* 1997–2003.

KALLÓS, D., & BROMAN, I. T. (1997). Swedish child care and early childhood education in transition. *Early Education & Development, 8,* 265–284.

KAMERMAN, S. B. (1993). International perspectives on child care policies and programs. *Pediatrics, 91,* 248–252.

KANDALL, S. R., GAINES, J., HABEL, L., DAVIDSON, G., & JESSOP, D. (1993). Relationship of maternal substance abuse to subsequent sudden infant death syndrome in offspring. *Journal of Pediatrics, 123,* 120–126.

KANNER, A. D., FELDMAN, S. S., WEINBERGER, D. A., & FORD, M. E. (1987). Uplifts, hassles, and adaptational outcomes in early adolescents. *Journal of Early Adolescence, 7,* 371–394.

KAPLAN, R. M. (1985). The controversy related to the use of psychological tests. In B. B. Wolman (Ed.), *Handbook of intelligence* (pp. 465–504). New York: Wiley.

KAPLOWITZ, P. B. (1995). Effect of growth hormone therapy on final versus predicted height in short twelve- to sixteen-year-old boys without growth hormone deficiency. *Journal of Pediatrics, 126,* 478–480.

KARADSHEH, R. (1991). *This room is a junkyard!: Children's comprehension of metaphorical language.* Paper presented at the biennial meeting of the Society for Research in Child Development, Seattle, WA.

KARMILOFF-SMITH, A. (1992). *Beyond modularity: A developmental perspective on cognitive science.* Cambridge, MA: MIT Press.

KATCHADOURIAN, H. (1977). *The biology of adolescence.* San Francisco: Freeman.

KATCHADOURIAN, H. (1990). Sexuality. In S. S. Feldman & G. R. Elliott (Eds.), *At the threshold: The developing adolescent* (pp. 330–351). Cambridge, MA: Harvard University Press.

KAVALE, K. (1982). Meta-analysis of the relationship between visual perceptual skills and reading achievement. *Journal of Learning Disabilities, 15,* 42–51.

KAVANAUGH, R. D., & ENGEL, S. (1998). The development of pretense and narrative in early childhood. In O. N. Saracho & B. Spodek (Eds.), *Multiple perspectives on play in early childhood education* (pp. 80–99). Albany: State University of New York Press.

KAWASAKI, C., NUGENT, J. K., MIYASHITA, H., MIYAHARA, H., & BRAZELTON, T. B. (1994). The cultural organization of infants' sleep. *Children's Environments, 11,* 135–141.

KAY, J., MORTIMER, M. J., & JARON, A. G. (1995). Do both paternal and maternal smoking influence the prevalence of childhood asthma? A study into the prevalence of asthma in children and the effects of parental smoking. *Journal of Asthma, 32,* 47–55.

KAYE, K., & MARCUS, J. (1981). Infant imitation: The sensory-motor agenda. *Developmental Psychology, 17,* 258–265.

KAYE, K., & WELLS, A. J. (1980). Mothers' jiggling and the burst–pause pattern in neonatal feeding. *Infant Behavior and Development, 3,* 29–46.

KEARINS, J. M. (1981). Visual spatial memory in Australian aboriginal children of desert regions. *Cognitive Psychology, 13,* 434–460.

KEASEY, C. B. (1971). Social participation as a factor in the moral development of preadolescents. *Developmental Psychology, 5,* 216–220.

KEATING, D. (1979). Adolescent thinking. In J. Adelson (Ed.), *Handbook of adolescent psychology* (pp. 211–246). New York: Wiley.

KEATING, D. (1990). Adolescent thinking. In S. S. Feldman & G. R. Elliott (Eds.), *At the threshold* (pp. 54–89). Cambridge, MA: Harvard University Press.

KEEN, C. L., & ZIDENBERG-CHERR, S. (1994). Should vitamin-mineral supplements be recommended for all women with childbearing potential? *American Journal of Clinical Nutrition, 59,* 532S–539S.

KEIL, F. C. (1986). Conceptual domains and the acquisition of metaphor. *Cognitive Development, 1,* 73–96.

KELLEY, M. L., POWER, T. G., & WIMBUSH, D. D. (1992). Determinants of disciplinary practices in low-income black mothers. *Child Development, 63,* 573–582.

KELLMAN, P. J. (1993). Kinematic foundations of infant visual perception. In C. E. Granrud (Ed.), *Visual perception and cognition in infancy* (pp. 121–173). Hillsdale, NJ: Erlbaum.

KELLY, M. L., SANCHEZ-HUCLES, J., & WALKER, R. (1993). Correlates of disciplinary practices in working- to middle-class African-American mothers. *Merrill-Palmer Quarterly, 39,* 252–264.

KEMP, J. S., & THACH, B. T. (1993). A sleep position-dependent mechanism for infant death on sheepskins. *American Journal of Diseases of Children, 147,* 642–646.

KEMPE, C. H., SILVERMAN, B. F., STEELE, P. W., DROEGE-MUELLER, P. W., & SILVER, H. K. (1962). The battered-child syndrome. *Journal of the American Medical Association, 181,* 17–24.

KENDALL-TACKETT, K. A., WILLIAMS, L. M., & FINKEL-HOR, D. (1993). Impact of sexual abuse on children: A review and synthesis of recent empirical studies. *Psychological Bulletin, 113,* 164–180.

KENDRICK, A. S., KAUFMAN, R., & MESSENGER, K. P. (1991). *Healthy young children: A manual for programs.* Washington, DC: National Association for the Education of Young Children.

KENNELL, J. H., KLAUS, M., MCGRATH, S., ROBERTSON, S., & HINKLEY, C. (1991). Continuous emotional support during labor in a U.S. hospital. *Journal of the American Medical Association, 265,* 2197–2201.

KEOGH, B. K. (1988). Improving services for problem learners. *Journal of Learning Disabilities, 21,* 6–11.

KERMOIAN, R., & CAMPOS, J. J. (1988). Locomotor experience: A facilitator of spatial cognitive development. *Child Development, 59,* 908–917.

KERNS, K. A., & BERENBAUM, S. A. (1991). Sex differences in spatial ability in children. *Behavior Genetics, 21,* 383–396.

KERR, B. A. (1983). Raising the career aspirations of gifted girls. *Vocational Guidance Quarterly, 32,* 37–43.

KERR, M., LAMBERT, W. W., STATTIN, H., & KLACKENBERG-LARSSON, I. (1994). Stability of inhibition in a Swedish longitudinal sample. *Child Development, 65,* 138–146.

KERR, S., & JOWETT, S. (1994). Sleep problems in pre-school children: A review of the literature. *Child: Care, Health and Development, 20,* 379–391.

KESSEN, W. (1967). Sucking and looking: Two organized congenital patterns of behavior in the human newborn. In H. W. Stevenson, E. H. Hess, & H. L. Rheingold (Eds.), *Early behavior: Comparative and developmental approaches* (pp. 147–179). New York: Wiley.

KESSLER, R., MCGONAGLE, K., ZHAO, S., NELSON, C., HUGHES, M., ESHLEMAN, S., WITTCHEN, H., & KENDLER, K. (1994). Lifetime and 12-month prevalence of DSM-III-R psychiatric disorders in the United States: Results from the national comorbidity survey. *Archives of General Psychiatry, 51,* 8–19.

KILLEN, M., & NUCCI, L. P. (1995). Morality, autonomy, and social conflict. In M. Killen & D. Hart (Eds.), *Morality in everyday life: Developmental perspectives* (pp. 52–86). Cambridge, England: Cambridge University Press.

KINDERMAN, T. A. (1993). Natural peer groups as contexts for individual development: The case of children's motivation in school. *Developmental Psychology, 29,* 970–977.

KING, C. A. (1997). Suicidal behavior in adolescence. In R. W. Maris, M. M. Silverman, & S. S. Canetto (Eds.), *Review of suicidology, 1997* (pp. 61–95). New York: Guilford.

KING, P. M., & KITCHENER, K. S. (1994). *Developing reflective judgment: Understanding and promoting intellectual growth and critical thinking in adolescents and adults.* San Francisco: Jossey-Bass.

KINZIE, J. D., SACK, W., ANGELL, R., CLARKE, G., & BEN, R. (1989). A three-year follow-up of Cambodian young people traumatized as children. *Journal of the American Academy of Child and Adolescent Psychiatry, 28,* 501–504.

KIRBY, D., SHORT, L., COLLINS, J., RUGG, D., KOLBE, L., HOWARD, M., MILLER, B., SONENSTEIN, F., & ZABIN, L. S. (1994). School-based programs to reduce sexual behaviors: A review of effectiveness. *Public Health Reports, 109*(3), 339–360.

KIRK, W. G. (1993). *Adolescent suicide.* Champaign, IL: Research Press.

KISKER, E. E. (1985). Teenagers talk about sex, pregnancy, and contraception. *Family Planning Perspectives, 17,* 83–90.

KITCHENER, K. S., LYNCH, C. L., FISCHER, K. W., & WOOD, P. K. (1993). Developmental range of reflective judgment: The effect of contextual support and practice on developmental stage. *Developmental Psychology, 29,* 893–906.

KLAHR, D., & MACWHINNEY, B. (1998). Information processing. In D. Kuhn & R. S. Siegler (Eds.), *Handbook of child psychology: Vol. 2. Cognition, perception, and language* (5th ed., pp. 631–678). New York: Wiley.

KLAUS, M. H., & KENNELL, J. H. (1982). *Parent–infant bonding.* St. Louis: Mosby.

KLIEWER, W. (1997). Children's coping with chronic illness. In S. A. Wolchik & I. N. Sandler (Eds.), *Handbook of children's coping* (pp. 275–300). New York: Plenum.

KLIEWER, W., FEARNOW, M. D., & MILLER, P. A. (1996). Coping socialization in middle childhood: Tests of maternal and paternal influences. *Child Development, 67,* 2339–2357.

KLIMES-DOUGAN, B., & KISTNER, J. (1990). Physically abused preschoolers' responses to peers' distress. *Developmental Psychology, 26,* 599–602.

KLONOFF-COHEN, H. S., EDELSTEIN, S. L., LEFKOWITZ, E. S., SRINIVASAN, I. P., KAEGI, D., CHANG, J. C., & WILEY, K. J. (1995). The effect of passive smoking and tobacco exposure through breast milk on sudden infant death syndrome. *Journal of the American Medical Association, 273,* 795–798.

KNOBLOCH, H., & PASAMANICK, B. (Eds.). (1974). *Gesell and Amatruda's Developmental Diagnosis.* Hagerstown, MD: Harper & Row.

KNOBLOCH, H., STEVENS, F., & MALONE, A. F. (1980). *Manual of developmental diagnosis.* Hagerstown, MD: Harper & Row.

KOCHANSKA, G. (1991). Socialization and temperament in the development of guilt and conscience. *Child Development, 62,* 1379–1392.

KOCHANSKA, G. (1992). Children's interpersonal influence with mothers and peers. *Developmental Psychology, 28,* 491–499.

KOCHANSKA, G. (1993). Toward a synthesis of parental socialization and child temperament in early development of conscience. *Child Development, 64,* 325–347.

KOCHANSKA, G. (1995). Children's temperament, mothers' discipline, and security of attachment: Multiple pathways to emerging internalization. *Child Development, 66,* 597–615.

KOCHANSKA, G. (1997). Multiple pathways to conscience for children with different temperaments: From toddlerhood to age 5. *Developmental Psychology, 33,* 228–240.

KOCHANSKA, G., AKSAN, N., & KOENIG, A. L. (1959). A longitudinal study of the roots of preschoolers' conscience: Committed compliance and emerging internalization. *Child Development, 66,* 643–656.

KOCHANSKA, G., CASEY, R. J., & FUKUMOTO, A. (1995). Toddlers' sensitivity to standard violations. *Child Development, 66,* 643–656.

KOCHANSKA, G., & RADKE-YARROW, M. (1992). Inhibition in toddlerhood and the dynamics of the child's interaction with an unfamiliar peer at age five. *Child Development, 63,* 325–335.

KODROFF, J. K., & ROBERGE, J. J. (1975). Developmental analysis of the conditional reasoning abilities of primary-grade children. *Developmental Psychology, 11,* 21–28.

KOHLBERG, L. (1966). A cognitive-developmental analysis of children's sex-role concepts and attitudes. In E. E. Maccoby (Ed.), *The development of sex differences* (pp. 82–173). Stanford, CA: Stanford University Press.

KOHLBERG, L. (1969). Stage and sequence: The cognitive-developmental approach to socialization. In D. A. Goslin (Ed.), *Handbook of socialization theory and research* (pp. 347–480). Chicago: Rand McNally.

KOHLBERG, L. (1984). *Essays on moral development. Vol. 2: The psychology of moral development.* San Francisco: Harper & Row.

KOHLBERG, L., LEVINE, C., & HEWER, A. (1983). *Moral stages: A current formulation and a response to critics.* Basel, Switzerland: Karger.

KOJIMA, H. (1986). Childrearing concepts as a belief–value system of the society and the individual. In H. Stevenson, H. Azuma, & K. Hakuta (Eds.), *Child development and education in Japan* (pp. 39–54). New York: Freeman.

KOLATA, G. (1992, April 26). A parents' guide to kids' sports. *New York Times Magazine,* pp. 12–15, 40, 44, 46.

KOLBERG, R. (1993). Human embryo cloning reported. *Science, 262,* 652–653.

KOLVIN, I., & TROWELL, J. (1996). Child sexual abuse. In I. Rosen (Ed.), *Sexual deviation* (3rd ed., pp. 337–360). Oxford, England: Oxford University Press.

KOPP, C. B. (1987). The growth of self-regulation: Caregivers and children. In N. Eisenberg (Ed.), *Contemporary topics in developmental psychology* (pp. 34–55). New York: Wiley.

KOPP, C. B. (1994). Infant assessment. In C. B. Fisher & R. M. Lerner (Eds.), *Applied developmental psychology* (pp. 265–293). New York: McGraw-Hill.

KORNER, A. F. (1996). Reliable individual differences in preterm infants' excitation management. *Child Development, 67,* 1793–1805.

KORNGUTH, M. L. (1990). School illnesses: Who's absent and why? *Pediatric Nursing, 16,* 95–99.

KORTE, D. (1997). *The VBAC companion: The expectant mother's guide to vaginal birth after cesarean.* Cambridge, MA: Harvard Common Press.

KORTE, D., & SCAER, R. (1992). *A good birth, a safe birth.* Cambridge, MA: Harvard Common Press.

KOVACS, M. (1996). Presentation and course of major depressive disorder during childhood and later years of the lifespan. *Journal of the American Academy of Child and Adolescent Psychiatry, 35,* 705–715.

KOVACS, M., AKISKAL, H., GATSONIS, C., & PARRONE, P. (1994). Childhood-onset dysthymic disorder: Clinical features and prospective naturalistic outcome. *Archives of General Psychiatry, 51,* 365–374.

KRANZLER, J. H., & JENSEN, A. R. (1989). Inspection time and intelligence: A meta-analysis. *Intelligence, 13,* 329–347.

KREBS, D., & GILLMORE, J. (1982). The relationship among the first stages of cognitive development, role-taking abilities, and moral development. *Child Development, 53,* 877–886.

KREUTZER, M. A., LEONARD, C., & FLAVELL, J. H. (1975). An interview study of children's knowledge about memory. *Monographs of the Society for Research in Child Development, 40* (1, Serial No. 159).

KREVANS, J., & GIBBS, J. C. (1996). Parents' use of inductive discipline: Relations to children's empathy and prosocial behavior. *Child Development, 67,* 3263–3277.

KROGER, J. (1993). Identity and context: How the identity statuses choose their match. In R. Josselson & A. Lieblich (Eds.), *The narrative study of lives* (Vol. 1, pp. 130–162). Newbury Park, CA: Sage.

KROGER, J. (1995). The differentiation of "firm" and "developmental" foreclosure identity statuses: A longitudinal study. *Journal of Adolescent Research, 10,* 317–337.

KRONENFELD, J. J., & GLIK, D. C. (1995). Unintentional injury: A major health problem for young children and youth. *Journal of Family and Economic Issues, 16,* 365–393.

KRUGER, A. C. (1993). Peer collaboration: Conflict, cooperation, or both? *Social Development, 2,* 165–182.

KUCZAJ, S. A., II. (1986). Thoughts on the intentional basis of early object word extension: Evidence from comprehension and production. In S. A. Kuczaj, II, & M. D. Barrett (Eds.), *The development of word meaning* (pp. 99–120). New York: Springer-Verlag.

KUCZYNSKI, L. (1984). Socialization goals and mother–child interaction: Strategies for long-term and short-term compliance. *Developmental Psychology, 20,* 1061–1073.

KUCZYNSKI, L., KOCHANSKA, G., RADKE-YARROW, M., & GIRNIUS-BROWN, O. (1987). A developmental interpretation of young children's noncompliance. *Developmental Psychology, 23,* 799–806.

Kuebli, J., Butler, S., & Fivush, R. (1995). Mother–child talk about past emotions: Relations of maternal language and gender over time. *Cognition and Emotion, 9,* 265–283.

Kuebli, J., & Fivush, R. (1992). Gender differences in parent–child conversations about past emotions. *Sex Roles, 27,* 683–698.

Kuhl, P. K., Williams, K. A., Lacerda, F., Stevens, K. N., & Lindblom, B. (1992). Linguistic experience alters phonetic perception in infants by 6 months of age. *Science, 255,* 606–608.

Kuhn, D. (1989). Children and adults as intuitive scientists. *Psychological Review, 96,* 674–689.

Kuhn, D. (1992). Cognitive development. In M. H. Bornstein & M. E. Lamb (Eds.), *Developmental psychology: An advanced textbook* (3rd ed., pp. 211–272). Hillsdale, NJ: Erlbaum.

Kuhn, D., (1993). Connecting scientific and informal reasoning. *Merrill-Palmer Quarterly, 39,* 74–103.

Kuhn, D. (1995). Microgenetic study of change: What has it told us? *Psychological Science, 6,* 133–139.

Kuhn, D., Amsel, E., & O'Loughlin, M. (1988). *The development of scientific thinking skills.* Orlando, FL: Academic Press.

Kuhn, D., Garcia-Mila, M., Zohar, A., & Andersen, C. (1995). Strategies of knowledge acquisition. *Monographs of the Society for Research in Child Development, 60* (245, Serial No. 4).

Kuhn, D., Ho, V., & Adams, C. (1979). Formal reasoning among pre- and late adolescents. *Child Development, 50,* 1128–1135.

Kuhn, L., & Stein, Z. (1997). Infant survival, HIV infection, and feeding alternatives in less-developed countries. *American Journal of Public Health, 87,* 926–931.

Kunkel, D. (1993). Policy and the future of children's television. In G. L. Berry & J. K. Asamen (Eds.), *Children & television* (pp. 273–290). Newbury Park, CA: Sage.

Kunzinger, E. L., III. (1985). A short-term longitudinal study of memorial development during early grade school. *Developmental Psychology, 21,* 642–646.

Kupersmidt, J. B., DeRosier, M. E., & Patterson, C. P. (1995). Similarity as the basis for children's friendships: The roles of sociometric status, aggressive and withdrawn behavior, academic achievement, and demographic characteristics. *Journal of Social and Personal Relationships, 12,* 439–452.

Kurdek, L. A., & Fine, M. A. (1994). Family acceptance and family control as predictors of adjustment in young adolescents: Linear, curvilinear, or interactive effects? *Child Development, 65,* 1137–1146.

Kutner, L. (1993, June). Getting physical. *Parents,* Vol. 68, N. 6, pp. 96–98.

Ladd, G. W., & Cairns, E. (1996). Children: Ethnic and political violence. *Child Development, 67,* 14–18.

Ladd, G. W., LeSieur, K., & Profilet, S. M. (1993). Direct parental influences on young children's peer relations. In S. Duck (Ed.), *Learning about relationships* (Vol. 2, pp. 152–183). London: Sage.

Ladd, G. W., & Mize, J. (1983). A cognitive-social learning model of social skill training. *Psychological Review, 90,* 127–157.

Lagercrantz, H., & Slotkin, T. A. (1986). The "stress" of being born. *Scientific American, 254,* 100–107.

Lamaze, F. (1958). *Painless childbirth.* London: Burke.

Lamb, M. (1994). Infant care practices and the application of knowledge. In C. B. Fisher & R. M. Lerner (Eds.), *Applied developmental psychology* (pp. 23–45). New York: McGraw-Hill.

Lamb, M. E. (1987). *The father's role: Cross-cultural perspectives.* Hillsdale, NJ: Erlbaum.

Lamb, M. E. (1997). The development of father–infant relationships. In M. E. Lamb (Ed.), *The role of the father in child development* (3rd ed., pp. 104–120). New York: Wiley.

Lamb, M. E. (1998). Nonparental child care: Context, quality, correlates, and consequences. In I. E. Sigel & K. A. Renninger (Eds.), *Handbook of child psychology: Vol. 4. Child psychology in practice* (5th ed., pp. 73–133). New York: Wiley.

Lamb, M. E., & Oppenheim, D. (1989). Fatherhood and father–child relationships: Five years of research. In S. H. Cath, A. Gurwitt, & L. Gunsberg (Eds.), *Fathers and their families* (pp. 11–26). Hillsdale, NJ: Erlbaum.

Lamb, M. E., Sternberg, K. J., & Prodromidis, M. (1992). Nonmaternal care and the security of infant–mother attachment: A reanalysis of the data. *Infant Behavior and Development, 15,* 71–83.

Lamb, M. E., Thompson, R. A., Gardner, W., Charnov, E. L., & Connell, J. P. (1985). Infant–mother attachment: The origins and developmental significance of individual differences in the Strange Situation: Its study and biological interpretation. *Behavioral and Brain Sciences, 7,* 127–147.

Lamb, S. (1991). First moral sense: Aspects of and contributors to a beginning morality in the second year of life. In W. M. Kurtines & J. L. Gewirtz (Eds.), *Handbook of moral behavior and development* (Vol. 2, pp. 171–189). Hillsdale, NJ: Erlbaum.

Lamborn, S. D., Mounts, N. S., Steinberg, L., & Dornbusch, S. M. (1991). Patterns of competence and adjustment among adolescents from authoritative, authoritarian, indulgent, and neglectful families. *Child Development, 62,* 1049–1065.

Lampl, M. (1993). Evidence of saltatory growth in infancy. *American Journal of Human Biology, 5,* 641–652.

Lampl, M., Veldhuis, J. D., & Johnson, M. L. (1992). Saltation and stasis: A model of human growth. *Science, 258,* 801–803.

Lander, E. S. (1996). The new genomics: Global views of biology. *Science, 274,* 536–539.

Landesman, S., & Ramey, C. (1989). Developmental psychology and mental retardation: Integrating scientific principles with treatment practices. *American Psychologist, 44,* 409–415.

Landry, S. H., & Whitney, J. A. (1996). The impact of prenatal cocaine exposure: Studies of the developing infant. *Seminars in Perinatology, 20,* 99–106.

Lane, D. M., & Pearson, D. A. (1982). The development of selective attention. *Merrill-Palmer Quarterly, 28,* 317–337.

Lange, G., & Pierce, S. H. (1992). Memory-strategy learning and maintenance in preschool children. *Developmental Psychology, 28,* 453–462.

Lansky, V. (1991). *Getting your child to sleep . . . and back to sleep: Tips for parents of infants, toddlers, and preschoolers.* New York: Book Peddlers.

Lapointe, A. E., Askew, J. M., & Mead, N. A. (1992). *Learning mathematics.* Princeton, NJ: Educational Testing Service.

Lapointe, A. E., Mead, N. A., & Askew, J. M. (1992). *Learning science.* Princeton, NJ: Educational Testing Service.

Lapsley, D. K. (1985). Elkind on egocentrism. *Developmental Review, 5,* 227–236.

Lapsley, D. K. (1993). Toward an integrated theory of adolescent ego development: The "new look" at adolescent egocentrism. *American Journal of Orthopsychiatry, 63,* 562–571.

Lapsley, D. K., Jackson, S., Rice, K., & Shadid, G. (1988). Self-monitoring and the "new look" at the imaginary audience and personal fable: An ego-developmental analysis. *Journal of Adolescent Research, 3,* 17–31.

Lapsley, D. K., Milstead, M., Quintana, S., Flannery, D., & Buss, R. (1986). Adolescent egocentrism and formal operations: Tests of a theoretical assumption. *Developmental Psychology, 22,* 800–807.

Larson, D. E. (1996). *Mayo Clinic family health book.* New York: Morrow.

Larson, R., & Ham, M. (1993). Stress and "storm and stress" in early adolescence: The relationship of negative events with dysphoric affect. *Developmental Psychology, 29,* 130–140.

Larson, R., & Lampman-Petraitis, C. (1989). Daily emotional states as reported by children and adolescents. *Child Development, 60,* 1250–1260.

Larson, R. W., & Richards, M. H. (1991). Daily companionship in late childhood and early adolescence: Changing developmental contexts. *Child Development, 62,* 284–300.

Larson, R. W., Richards, M. H., Moneta, G., Holmbeck, G., & Duckett, E. (1996). Changes in adolescents' daily interactions with their families from ages 10 to 18: Disengagement and transformation. *Developmental Psychology, 32,* 744-754.

Laursen, B., Hartup, W. W., & Koplas, A. L. (1996). Toward understanding peer conflict.

Merrill-Palmer Quarterly, 42, 76–102.

LAZAR, A., & TORNEY-PURTA, J. (1991). The development of the subconcepts of death in young children: A short-term longitudinal study. *Child Development, 62,* 1321–1333.

LAZAR, I., & DARLINGTON, R. (1982). Lasting effects of early education: a report from the Consortium for Longitudinal Studies. *Monographs of the Society for Research in Child Development, 47*(2–3, Serial No. 195).

LEAPER, C. (1991). Influence and involvement in children's discourse. *Child Development, 62,* 797–811.

LEAPER, C., ANDERSON, K. J., & SANDERS, P. (1998). Moderators of gender effects on parents' talk to their children: A meta-analysis. *Developmental Psychology, 34,* 3–27.

LEAPER, C., LEVE, L., STRASSER, T., & SCHWARTZ, R. (1995). Mother–child communication sequences: Play activity, child gender, and marital status effects. *Merrill-Palmer Quarterly, 41,* 307–327.

LEE, A. M. (1980). Child-rearing practices and motor performance of black and white children. *Research Quarterly for Exercise and Sport, 51,* 494–500.

LEE, C. L., & BATES, J. E. (1985). Mother–child interaction at age two years and perceived difficult temperament. *Child Development, 56,* 1314–1325.

LEE, S. H., EWERT, D. P., FREDERICK, P. D., & MASCOLA, L. (1992). Resurgence of congenital rubella syndrome in the 1990s. *Journal of the American Medical Association, 267,* 2616–2620.

LEE, V. E., BROOKS-GUNN, J., & SCHNUR, E. (1988). Does Head Start work? A 1-year follow-up of disadvantaged children attending Head Start, no preschool. *Developmental Psychology, 24,* 210–222.

LEE, V. E., BROOKS-GUNN, J., SCHNUR, E., & LIAW, F. (1990). Are Head Start effects sustained? A longitudinal follow-up comparison of disadvantaged children attending Head Start, no preschool, and other preschool programs. *Child Development, 61,* 495–507.

LEE, V. E., & LOEB, S. (1995). Where do Head Start attendees end up? One reason why preschool effects fade out.

Educational Evaluation & Policy Analysis, 17, 62–82.

LEEMAN, L. W., GIBBS, J. C., & FULLER, D. (1993). Evaluation of a multi-component group treatment program for juvenile delinquents. *Aggressive Behavior, 19,* 281–292.

LEHMAN, D. R., & NISBETT, R. E. (1990). A longitudinal study of the effects of undergraduate training on reasoning. *Developmental Psychology, 26,* 952–960.

LEHNERT, K. L., OVERHOLSER, J. C., & SPIRITO, A. (1994). Internalized and externalized anger in adolescent suicide attempters. *Journal of Adolescent Research, 9,* 105–119.

LEICHTMAN, M. D., & CECI, S. J. (1995). The effect of stereotypes and suggestions on preschoolers' reports. *Developmental Psychology, 31.*

LEMPERT, H. (1989). Animacy constraints on preschoolers' acquisition of syntax. *Child Development, 60,* 237–245.

LENNEBERG, E. H. (1967). *Biological foundations of language.* New York: Wiley.

LEONARD, M. F., RHYMES, J. P., & SOLNIT, A. J. (1986). Failure to thrive in infants: A family problem. *American Journal of Diseases of Children, 111,* 600–612.

LEPORE, P. C., & WARREN, J. R. (1997). A comparison of single-sex and coeducational Catholic secondary schooling: Evidence from the National Educational Longitudinal Study of 1988. *American Educational Research Journal, 34,* 485–511.

LERMAN, R. I. (1993). A national profile of young unwed fathers. In R. I. Lerman & T. J. Ooms (Eds.), *Young unwed fathers* (pp. 27–51). Philadelphia: Temple University Press.

LERNER, J. V., & ABRAMS, A. (1994). Developmental correlates of maternal employment influences on children. In C. B. Fisher & R. M. Lerner (Eds.), *Applied developmental psychology* (pp. 174–206). New York: McGraw-Hill.

LERNER, R. M., & SCHROEDER, C. (1971). Physique identification, preference, and aversion in kindergarten children. *Developmental Psychology, 5,* 538.

LESTER, B. M. (1985). Introduction: There's more to crying than meets the ear. In B. M. Lester & C. F. Z. Boukydis (Eds.), *Infant crying* (pp. 1–27). New York: Plenum.

LESTER, B. M. (1987). Developmental outcome prediction from acoustic cry analysis in term and preterm infants. *Pediatrics, 80,* 529–534.

LESTER, B. M., & DREHER, M. (1989). Effects of marijuana use during pregnancy on newborn cry. *Child Development, 60,* 765–771.

LESTER, B. M., FREIER, B. M., & LaGASSE, L. (1995). Prenatal cocaine exposure and child outcome. In M. Lewis & M. Bendersky (Eds.), *Mothers, babies, and cocaine* (pp. 19–29). Hillsdale, NJ: Erlbaum.

LESTER, B. M., KOTELCHUCK, M., SPELKE, E., SELLERS, M. J., & KLEIN, R. E. (1974). Separation protest in Guatemalan infants: Cross-cultural and cognitive findings. *Developmental Psychology, 10,* 79–85.

LeVAY, S. (1993). *The sexual brain.* Cambridge, MA: MIT Press.

LEVESQUE, R. J. R. (1996). International children's rights: Can they make a difference in American family policy? *American Psychologist, 51,* 1251–1256.

LEVINE, L. E. (1983). Mine: Self-definition in 2-year-old boys. *Developmental Psychology, 19,* 544–549.

LEVINE, L. J. (1995). Young children's understanding of the causes of anger and sadness. *Child Development, 66,* 697–709.

LeVINE, R. A., DIXON, S., LeVINE, S., RICHMAN, A., LEIDERMAN, P. H., KEEFER, C. H., & BRAZELTON, T. B. (1994). *Child care and culture: Lessons from Africa.* New York: Cambridge University Press.

LEVY, G. D., TAYLOR, M. G., & GELMAN, S. A. (1995). Traditional and evaluative aspects of flexibility in gender roles, social conventions, moral rules, and physical laws. *Child Development, 66,* 515–531.

LEVY-SHIFF, R. (1994). Individual and contextual correlates of marital change across the transition to parenthood. *Developmental Psychology, 30,* 591–601.

LEVY-SHIFF, R., & ISRAELASHVILI, R. (1988). Antecedents of fathering: Some further exploration. *Developmental Psychology, 24,* 434–440.

LEWINSOHN, P. M., ROHDE, P., & SEELEY, J. R. (1994). Psychosocial risk factors for future suicide attempts. *Journal of Consulting and Clinical Psychology, 62,* 297–305.

LEWIS, C., FREEMAN, N. H., KYRIADIDOU, C., MARIDA-

KIKASSOTAKI, K., & BERRIDGE, D. M. (1996). Social influences on false belief access—specific sibling influences or general apprenticeship? *Child Development, 67,* 2930–2947.

LEWIS, C. C. (1981). The effects of parental firm control: A reinterpretation of findings. *Psychological Bulletin, 90,* 547–563.

LEWIS, M. (1991). Ways of knowing: Objective self-awareness or consciousness. *Developmental Review, 11,* 231–243.

LEWIS, M. (1992). *Shame: The exposed self.* New York: Free Press.

LEWIS, M. (1994). Myself and me. In S. T. Parker, R. W. Mitchell, & M. L. Boccia (Eds.), *Self-awareness in animals and humans: Developmental perspectives* (pp. 20–34). New York: Cambridge University Press.

LEWIS, M. (1995). Embarrassment: The emotion of self-exposure and evaluation. In J. P. Tangney & K. W. Fischer (Eds.), *Self-conscious emotions* (pp. 198–218). New York: Guilford Press.

LEWIS, M., ALESSANDRI, S. M., & SULLIVAN, M. W. (1992). Differences in shame and pride as a function of children's gender and task difficulty. *Child Development, 63,* 630–638.

LEWIS, M., & BROOKS-GUNN, J. (1979). *Social cognition and the acquisition of self.* New York: Plenum.

LEWIS, M., RAMSAY, D. S., & KAWAKAMI, K. (1993). Differences between Japanese infants and Caucasian American infants in behavioral and cortisol response to inoculation. *Child Development, 64,* 1722–1731.

LEWIS, M., SULLIVAN, M. W., STANGER, C., & WEISS, M. (1989). Self development and self-conscious emotions. *Child Development, 60,* 146–156.

LEWIS, M., SULLIVAN, M. W., & VASEN, A. (1987). Making faces: Age and emotion differences in the posing of emotional expressions. *Developmental Psychology, 23,* 690–697.

LI, C. Q., WINDSOR, R. A., & PERKINS, L. (1993). The impact on infant birth weight and gestational age of cotinine-validated smoking reduction during pregnancy. *Journal of the American Medical Association, 269,* 1519–1524.

LIAW, F., & BROOKS-GUNN, J. (1993). Patterns of low-birthweight children's cognitive development. *Developmental Psychology, 29,* 1024–1035.

LIBEN, L. S., & SIGNORELLA, M. L. (1993). Gender-schematic processing in children: The role of initial interpretations of stimuli. *Developmental Psychology, 29,* 141–149.

LIDZ, C. S. (1991). *Practitioner's guide to dynamic assessment.* New York: Guilford.

LIE, S. O. (1990). Children in the Norwegian health care system. *Pediatrics, 86* (6, Pt. 2), 1048–1052.

LIFSCHITZ, M., BERMAN, D., GALILI, A., & GILAD, D. (1977). Bereaved children: The effects of mother's perception and social system organization on their short range adjustment. *Journal of Child Psychiatry, 16,* 272–284.

LIGHT, P., & PERRET-CLERMONT, A-N. (1989). Social context effects in learning and testing. In A. Gellatly, D. Rogers, & J. Sloboda (Eds.), *Cognition and social worlds* (pp. 99–112). Oxford, England: Clarendon Press.

LIGHTER, J. E. (1997). *Random House historical dictionary of American slang.* New York: Random House.

LILLARD, A. S. (1993). Pretend play skills and the child's theory of mind. *Child Development, 64,* 348–371.

LILLARD, A. S. (1998). Playing with a theory of mind. In O. N. Saracho & B. Spodek (Eds.), *Multiple perspectives on play in early childhood education* (pp. 11–33). Albany: State University of New York Press.

LILLIS, K. A., & JAFFE, D. M. (1997). Playground injuries in children. *Pediatric Emergency Care, 13,* 149–153.

LIMBER, S. P., & FLEKKØY, M. G. (1995). The U.N. Convention on the Rights of the Child: Its relevance for social scientists. *Social Policy Report of the Society for Research in Child Development, 9* (2).

LIMBER, S. P., & WILCOX, B. L. (1996). Application of the U.N. Convention on the Rights of the Child to the United States. *American Psychologist, 51,* 1246–1250.

LIN, C. C., & FU, V. R. (1990). A comparison of child-rearing practices among Chinese, immigrant Chinese, and Caucasian-American parents. *Child Development, 61,* 429–433.

LINDSAY-HARTZ, J., DE RIVERA, J., & MASCOLO, M. F. (1995).

Differentiating guilt and shame and their effects on motivation. In J. P. Tangney & K. W. Fischer (Eds.), *Self-conscious emotions* (pp. 274–300). New York: Guilford.

LINN, M. C., & HYDE, J. S. (1989). Gender, mathematics, and science. *Educational Researcher, 18,* 17–27.

LINN, M. C., & PETERSEN, A. C. (1985). Emergence and characterization of sex differences in spatial ability: A meta-analysis. *Child Development, 56,* 1479–1498.

LINN, S., LIEBERMAN, E., SCHOENBAUM, S. C., MONSON, R. R., STUBBLEFIELD, P. G., & RYAN, K. J. (1988). Adverse outcomes of pregnancy in women exposed to diethylstilbestrol in utero. *Journal of Reproductive Medicine, 33,* 3–7.

LIPSITT, L. P. (1990). Learning and memory in infants. *Merrill-Palmer Quarterly, 36,* 53–66.

LISSENS, W., & SERMON, K. (1997). Preimplantation genetic diagnosis—current status and new developments. *Human Reproduction, 12,* 1756–1761.

LITOWITZ, B. (1977). Learning to make definitions. *Journal of Child Language, 8,* 165–175.

LIVESLEY, W. J., & BROMLEY, D. B. (1973). *Person perception in childhood and adolescence.* London: Wiley.

LIVSON, N., & PESKIN, H. (1980). Perspectives on adolescence from longitudinal research. In J. Adelson (Ed.), *Handbook of adolescent psychology* (pp. 47–98). New York: Wiley.

LOCHE, S., CAMBIASO, P., CARTA, D., MARINI, R., BORELLI, P., & CAPPS, M. (1994). Final height after growth hormone therapy in non-growth-hormone-deficient children with short stature. *Journal of Pediatrics, 125,* 196–200.

LOCHMAN, J. E., COIE, J. D., UNDERWOOD, M. K., & TERRY, R. (1993). Effectiveness of a social relations intervention program for aggressive and nonaggressive, rejected children. *Journal of Consulting and Clinical Psychology, 61,* 1053–1058.

LOCKE, J. (1892). Some thoughts concerning education. In R. H. Quick (Ed.), *Locke on education* (pp. 1–236). Cambridge, England: Cambridge University Press. (Original work published 1690)

LOEBER, R., & STOUTHAMER-LOEBER, M. (1998). Development of juvenile aggression and violence: Some common misconceptions and controversies. *American Psychologist, 53,* 242–259.

LOEHLIN, J. C. (1992). *Genes and environment in personality development.* Newbury Park, CA: Sage.

LOEHLIN, J. C., WILLERMAN, L., & HORN, J. M. (1988). Human behavior genetics. *Annual Review of Psychology, 38,* 101–133.

LOONEY, M. A., & PLOWMAN, S. A. (1990). Passing rates of American children and youth on the FITNESSGRAM criterion-referenced physical fitness standards. *Research Quarterly of Exercise and Sport, 61,* 215–223.

LORD, R. H., & KOZAR, B. (1996). Overuse injuries in young athletes. In F. L. Smoll & R. E. Smith (Eds.), *Children and youth in sport: A biopsychological perspective* (pp. 281–294). Dubuque, IA: Brown & Benchmark.

LORD, S., ECCLES, J. S., & MCCARTHY, K. (1994). Risk and protective factors in the transition to junior high school. *Journal of Early Adolescence, 14,* 162–199.

LORENZ, K. Z. (1943). Die angeborenen Formen möglicher Erfahrung. *Zeitschrift für Tierpsychologie, 5,* 235–409.

LORENZ, K. Z. (1952). *King Solomon's ring.* New York: Crowell.

LOSEY, K. M. (1995). Mexican-American students and classroom interaction: An overview and critique. *Review of Educational Research, 65,* 283–318.

LOZOFF, B. (1989). Nutrition and behavior. *American Psychologist, 44,* 231–236.

LOZOFF, B., WOLF, A., LATZ, S., & PALUDETTO, R. (1995, March). *Cosleeping in Japan, Italy, and the U.S.: Autonomy versus interpersonal relatedness.* Paper presented at the biennial meeting of the Society for Research in Child Development, Indianapolis.

LUBINSKI, D., & BENBOW, C. P. (1994). The study of mathematically precocious youth: The first three decades of a planned 50-year study of intellectual talent. In R. F. Subotnik & K. D. Arnold (Eds.), *Beyond Terman: Contemporary longitudinal studies of giftedness and talent* (pp. 255–281). Norwood, NJ: Ablex.

LUDEMANN, P. M. (1991). Generalized discrimination of positive facial expressions by seven- and ten-month-old infants. *Child Development, 62,* 55–67.

LUKER, K. (1996). *Dubious conceptions: The politics of teenage pregnancy.* Cambridge, MA: Harvard University Press.

LURIA, A. R. (1976). *Cognitive development: Its cultural and social foundations.* Cambridge, MA: Harvard University Press.

LUSTER, T., & DUBOW, E. (1992). Home environment and maternal intelligence as predictors of verbal intelligence: A comparison of preschool and school-age children. *Merrill-Palmer Quarterly, 38,* 151–175.

LUSTER, T., RHOADES, K., & HAAS, B. (1989). The relation between parental values and parenting behavior. *Journal of Marriage and the Family, 51,* 139–147.

LUTHAR, S. S., & CUSHING, G. (1997). Substance use and personal adjustment among disadvantaged teenagers: A six-month prospective study. *Journal of Youth and Adolescence, 26,* 353–372.

LUTHAR, S. S., CUSHING, T. J., & MCMAHON, T. J. (1997). Interdisciplinary interface: Developmental principles brought to substance abuse research. In S. S. Luthar, J. A. Burack, D. Cicchetti, & Weisz, J. R. (1997). *Developmental psychopathology* (pp. 437–456). Cambridge: Cambridge University Press.

LUTHAR, S. S., & ZIGLER, E. (1991). Vulnerability and competence: A review of research on resilience in childhood. *American Journal of Orthopsychiatry, 6,* 6–22.

LUTZ, S. E., & RUBLE, D. N. (1995). Children and gender prejudice: Context, motivation, and the development of gender conception. In R. Vasta (Ed.), *Annals of child development* (Vol. 10, pp. 131–166). Greenwich, CT: JAI Press.

LYON, T. D., & FLAVELL, J. H. (1994). Young children's understanding of "remember" and "forget." *Child Development, 65,* 1357–1371.

LYONS-RUTH, K., & BLOCK, D. (1996). The disturbed caregiving system: Relations among childhood trauma, maternal caregiving, and infant affect and attachment. *Infant Mental Health Journal, 17,* 257–275.

LYONS-RUTH, K., CONNELL, D. B., GRUNEBAUM, H. U., &

BOTEIN, S. (1990). Infants at social risk: Maternal depression and family support services as mediators of infant development and security of attachment. *Child Development, 61,* 85–98.

LYTTON, H., & ROMNEY, D. M. (1991). Parents' sex-related differential socialization of boys and girls: A meta-analysis. *Psychological Bulletin, 109,* 267–296.

MACCOBY, E. E. (1984). Middle childhood in the context of the family. In W. A. Collins (Ed.), *Development during middle childhood* (pp. 184–239). Washington, DC: National Academy Press.

MACCOBY, E. E. (1990). Gender and relationships. *American Psychologist, 45,* 513–520.

MACCOBY, E. E., & JACKLIN, C. N. (1987). Gender segregation in childhood. In E. H. Reese (Ed.), *Advances in child development and behavior* (Vol. 20, pp. 239–287). New York: Academic Press.

MACCOBY, E. E., & MARTIN, J. A. (1983). Socialization in the context of the family: Parent–child interaction. In E. M. Hetherington (Ed.), *Handbook of child psychology: Vol. 4. Socialization, personality, and social development* (4th ed., pp. 1–101). New York: Wiley.

MACFARLANE, J., SMITH, D. M., & GARROW, D. H. (1978). The relationship between mother and neonate. In S. Kitzinger (Ed.), *The place of birth* (pp. 185–200). New York: Oxford University Press.

MACFARLANE, J. W. (1971). From infancy to adulthood. In M. C. Jones, N. Bayley, J. W. Macfarlane, & M. P. Honzik (Eds.), *The course of human development* (pp. 406–410). Waltham, MA: Xerox College Publishing.

MACKEY, M. C. (1995). Women's evaluation of their childbirth performance. *Maternal–Child Nursing Journal, 23,* 57–72.

MACKINNON, C. E. (1989). An observational investigation of sibling interactions in married and divorced families. *Developmental Psychology, 25,* 36–44.

MACMILLAN, D. L., KEOGH, B. K., & JONES, R. L. (1986). Special educational research on mildly handicapped learners. In M. C. Wittrock (Ed.), *Handbook of research on teaching* (3rd ed., pp. 686–724). New York: Macmillan.

MACWHINNEY, B. (1996). Lexical connectionism. In P. Broeder & J. M. J. Murre (Eds.), *Models of language acquisition: Inductive and deductive approaches.* Cambridge, MA: MIT Press.

MADOM, S., JUSSIM, L., & ECCLES, J. (1997). In search of the powerful self-fulfilling prophecy. *Journal of Personality and Social Psychology, 72,* 791–809.

MAHLER, M. S., PINE, F., & BERGMAN, A. (1975). *The psychological birth of the human infant.* New York: Basic Books.

MAHONEY, J. L., & CAIRNS, R. B. (1997). Do extracurricular activities protect against early school dropout? *Developmental Psychology, 33,* 241–253.

MAIN, M., & CASSIDY, J. (1988). Categories of response to reunion with the parent at age 6: Predictable from infant attachment classifications and stable over a 1-month period. *Developmental Psychology, 24,* 415–426.

MAIN, M., & SOLOMON, J. (1990). Procedures for identifying infants as disorganized/-disoriented during the Ainsworth Strange Situation. In M. Greenberg, D. Cicchetti, & M. Cummings (Eds.), *Attachment in the preschool years: Theory, research, and intervention* (pp. 121–160). Chicago: University of Chicago Press.

MAKIN, J. E., FRIED, P. A., & WATKINSON, B. (1991). A comparison of active and passive smoking during pregnancy: Long-term effects. *Neurotoxicology and Teratology, 13,* 5–12.

MAKIN, J. W., & PORTER, R. H. (1989). Attractiveness of lactating females' breast odors to neonates. *Child Development, 60,* 803–810.

MALATESTA, C. Z., GRIGORYEV, P., LAMB, C., ALBIN, M., & CULVER, C. (1986). Emotion socialization and expressive development in preterm and full-term infants. *Child Development, 57,* 316–330.

MALATESTA, C. Z., & HAVILAND, J. M. (1982). Learning display rules: The socialization of emotion expression in infancy. *Child Development, 53,* 991–1003.

MALATESTA-MAGAI, C. Z., IZARD, C. E., & CAMRAS, L. A. (1991). Conceptualizing early infant affect: Emotions as fact, fiction or artifact? In K. Strongman (Ed.), *International review of studies on emotion* (pp. 1–36). New York: Wiley.

MALINA, R. M. (1975). *Growth and development: The first twenty years in man.* Minneapolis: Burgess.

MALINA, R. M. (1990). Physical growth and performance during the transitional years (9–16). In R. Montemayor, G. R. Adams, & T. P. Gullotta (Eds.), *From childhood to adolescence: A transitional period?* (pp. 41–62). Newbury Park, CA: Sage.

MALINA, R. M., & BEUNEN, G. (1996). Matching of opponents in youth sports. In O. Bar-Or (Ed.), *The child and adolescent athlete* (pp. 202–213). Oxford: Blackwell.

MALINA, R. M., & BOUCHARD, C. (1991). *Growth, maturation, and physical activity.* Champaign, IL: Human Kinetics.

MALINA, R. M., & STANITSKI, C.L. (1989). Common injuries in preadolescent and adolescent athletes. *Sports Medicine, I,* 32–41.

MALLOY, M. H., & HOFFMAN, H. J. (1995). Prematurity, sudden infant death syndrome, and age of death. *Pediatrics, 96,* 464–471.

MALONEY, M., & KRANZ, R. (1991). *Straight talk about eating disorders.* New York: Facts on File.

MANDLER, J. M. (1998). Representation. In D. Kuhn & R. S. Siegler (Eds.), *Handbook of child psychology: Vol. 1. Theoretical models of human development* (5th ed., pp. 255–308). New York: Wiley.

MANDLER, J. M., BAUER, P. J., & MCDONOUGH, L. (1991). Separating the sheep from the goats: Differentiating global categories. *Cognitive Psychology, 23,* 263–298.

MANDLER, J. M., & MCDONOUGH, L. (1993). Concept formation in infancy. *Cognitive Development, 8,* 291–318.

MANGE, E. J., & MANGE, A. P. (1994). *Basic human genetics.* Sunderland, MA: Sinauer Associates.

MANGELSDORF, S., GUNNAR, M., KESTENBAUM, R., LANG, S., & ANDREAS, D. (1990). Infant proneness-to-distress temperament, maternal personality, and mother–infant attachment: Associations and goodness of fit. *Child Development, 61,* 820–831.

MARATSOS, M. (1998). The acquisition of grammar. In D. Kuhn & S. R. Siegler (Eds.), *Handbook of child psychology: Vol. 2. Cognition, perception, and language* (4th ed., pp. 21–466). New York: Wiley.

MARATSOS, M. (1998). The acquisition of grammar. In D. Kuhn & R. S. Siegler (Eds.), *Handbook of child psychology: Vol. 1. Theoretical models of human development* (5th ed., pp. 255–308). New York: Wiley.

MARATSOS, M. P., & CHALKLEY, M. A. (1980). The internal language of children's syntax: The ontogenesis and representation of syntactic categories. In K. Nelson (Ed.), *Children's language* (Vol. 2, pp. 127–214). New York: Gardner Press.

MARCIA, J. E. (1966). Development and validation of ego identity status. *Journal of Personality and Social Psychology, 3,* 551–558.

MARCIA, J. E. (1980). Identity in adolescence. In J. Adelson (Ed.), *Handbook of adolescent psychology* (pp. 159–187). New York: Wiley.

MARCIA, J. E. (1988). Common processes underlying ego identity, cognitive/moral development, and individuation. In D. K. Lapsley & F. P. Clark (Eds.), *Self, ego, and identity* (pp. 211–225). New York: Springer-Verlag.

MARCIA, J. E., WATERMAN, A. S., MATTESON, D., ARCHER, S. L., & ORLOFSKY, J. L. (1993). *Ego identity: A handbook for psychosocial research.* New York: Springer-Verlag.

MARCUS, G. F. (1993). Negative evidence in language acquisition. *Cognition, 46,* 53–85.

MARCUS, G. F. (1995). Children's overregularization of English plurals: A quantitative analysis. *Journal of Child Language, 22,* 447–459.

MARCUS, G. F., PINKER, S., ULLMAN, M., HOLLANDER, M., ROSEN, T. J., & XU, F. (1992). Overregularization in language acquisition. *Monographs of the Society for Research in Child Development, 57*(4, Serial No. 228).

MARINI, Z., & CASE, R. (1989). Parallels in the development of preschoolers' knowledge about their physical and social worlds. *Merrill-Palmer Quarterly, 35,* 63–87.

MARINI, Z., & CASE, R. (1994). The development of abstract reasoning about the physical and social world. *Child Development, 65,* 147–159.

MARKMAN, E. M. (1989). *Categorization and naming in children.* Cambridge, MA: MIT Press.

MARKMAN, E. M. (1992). Constraints on word learning:

Speculations about their nature, origins, and domain specificity. In M. R. Gunnar & M. P. Maratsos (Eds.), *Minnesota Symposia on Child Psychology* (Vol. 25, pp. 59–101). Hillsdale, NJ: Erlbaum.

MARKOVITS, H., & BOUFFARD-BOUCHARD, T. (1992). The belief-bias effect in reasoning: The development and activation of competence. *British Journal of Developmental Psychology, 10,* 269–284.

MARKOVITS, H., SCHLEIFER, M., & FORTIER, L. (1989). Development of elementary deductive reasoning in young children. *Developmental Psychology, 25,* 787–793.

MARKOVITS, H., & VACHON, R. (1989). Reasoning with contrary-to-fact propositions. *Journal of Experimental Child Psychology, 47,* 398–412.

MARKOVITS, H., & VACHON, R. (1990). Conditional reasoning, representation, and level of abstraction. *Developmental Psychology, 26,* 942–951.

MARKSTROM-ADAMS, C., & ADAMS, G. R. (1995). Gender, ethnic group, and grade differences in psychosocial functioning during middle adolescence? *Journal of Youth and Adolescence, 24,* 397–414.

MARKUS, H. R., & KITAYAMA, S. (1991). Culture and the self: Implications for cognition, emotion, and motivation. *Psychological Review, 98,* 224–253.

MARSH, D. T., SERAFICA, F. C., & BARENBOIM, C. (1981). Interrelationships among perspective taking, interpersonal problem solving, and interpersonal functioning. *Journal of Genetic Psychology, 138,* 37–48.

MARSH, H. W. (1990). The structure of academic self-concept: The Marsh/Shavelson model. *Journal of Educational Psychology, 82,* 623–636.

MARSH, H. W., SMITH, I. D., & BARNES, J. (1985). Multidimensional self-concepts: Relations with sex and academic achievement. *Journal of Educational Psychology, 77,* 581–596.

MARSHALL, E. (1996). The genome program's conscience. *Science, 274,* 488–491.

MARTIN, C. L. (1989). Children's use of gender-related information in making social judgments. *Developmental Psychology, 25,* 80–88.

MARTIN, C. L. (1993). New directions for investigating children's gender knowledge. *Developmental Review, 13,* 184–204.

MARTIN, C. L., EISENBUD, L., & ROSE, H. (1995). Children's gender-based reasoning about toys. *Child Development, 66,* 1453–1471.

MARTIN, C. L., & HALVERSON, C. F. (1981). A schematic processing model of sex typing and stereotyping in children. *Child Development, 52,* 1119–1134.

MARTIN, C. L., & HALVERSON, C. F. (1987). The role of cognition in sex role acquisition. In D. B. Carter (Ed.), *Current conceptions of sex roles and sex typing: Theory and research* (pp. 123–137). New York: Praeger.

MARTIN, G. B., & CLARK, R. D., III (1982). Distress crying in neonates: Species and peer specificity. *Developmental Psychology, 18,* 3–9.

MARTIN, J. A. (1981). A longitudinal study of the consequences of early mother–infant interaction: A microanalytic approach. *Monographs of the Society for Research in Child Development, 46*(3, Serial No. 190).

MARTIN, J. B. (1987). Molecular genetics: Applications to the clinical neurosciences. *Science, 298,* 765–772.

MARTIN, J. C., BARR, H. M., MARTIN, D. C., & STREISSGUTH, A. P. (1996). Neonatal exposure to cocaine. *Neurotoxicology and Teratology, 18,* 617–625.

MARTIN, R. M. (1975). Effects of familiar and complex stimuli on infant attention. *Developmental Psychology, 11,* 178–185.

MARTLEW, M., & CONNOLLY, K. J. (1996). Human figure drawings by schooled and unschooled children in Papua New Guinea. *Child Development, 67,* 2743–2762.

MARTORELL, R. (1980). Interrelationships between diet, infectious disease, and nutritional status. In L. S. Greene & F. E. Johnston (Eds.), *Social and biological predictors of nutritional status, physical growth, and neurological development* (pp. 81–106). New York: Academic Press.

MARZOLF, D. P., & DELOACHE, J. S. (1994). Transfer in young children's understanding of spatial representations. *Child Development, 65,* 1–15.

MASATAKA, N. (1992). Motherese in a signed language. *Infant Behavior and Development, 15,* 453–460.

MASCOLO, M. F., & FISCHER, K. W. (1995). Developmental transformations in appraisals for pride, shame, and guilt. In J. P. Tangney & K. W. Fischer (Eds.), *Self-conscious emotions* (pp. 114–139). New York: Guilford.

MASON, C. A., CAUCE, A. M., CONZALES, N., & HIRAGA, Y. (1996). Neither too sweet nor too sour: Problem peers, maternal control, and problem behavior in African American adolescents. *Child Development, 67,* 2115–2130.

MASON, M. G., & GIBBS, J. C. (1993a). Role-taking opportunities and the transition to advanced moral judgment. *Moral Education Forum, 18,* 1–12.

MASON, M. G., & GIBBS, J. C. (1993b). Social perspective taking and moral judgment among college students. *Journal of Adolescent Research, 8,* 109–123.

MASSAD, C. M. (1981). Sex role identity and adjustment during adolescence. *Child Development, 52,* 1290–1298.

MASTEN, A. S., & COATSWORTH, J. D. (1998). The development of competence in favorable and unfavorable environments: Lessons from research on successful children. *American Psychologist, 53,* 205–220.

MASUR, E. F. (1995). Infants' early verbal imitation and their later lexical development. *Merrill-Palmer Quarterly, 41,* 286–306.

MASUR, E. F., MCINTYRE, C. W., & FLAVELL, J. H. (1973). Developmental changes in apportionment of study time among items in a multi-trial free recall task. *Journal of Experimental Child Psychology, 15,* 237–246.

MATAS, L., AREND, R., & SROUFE, L. A. (1978). Continuity of adaptation in the second year: The relationship between quality of attachment and later competence. *Child Development, 49,* 547–556.

MATHENY, A. P., JR. (1987). Psychological characteristics of childhood accidents. *Journal of Social Issues, 43,* 45–60.

MATHENY, A. P., JR. (1991). Children's unintentional injuries and gender: Differentiation and psychosocial aspects. *Children's Environment Quarterly, 8,* 51–61.

MATTSON, S. N., & RILEY, E. P. (1995). Prenatal exposure to alcohol: What the images reveal. *Alcohol Health and World Research, 19,* 273–278.

MATUTE-BIANCHI, M. E. (1986). Ethnic identities and patterns of school success and failure among Mexican-descent and Japanese-American students in a California high school: An ethnographic analysis. *American Journal of Education, 95,* 233–255.

MAYBERRY, R. I. (1993). First-language acquisition after childhood differs from second-language acquisition: The case of American Sign Language. *Journal of Speech and Hearing Research, 36,* 1258–1270.

MAYES, L. C., & ZIGLER, E. (1992). An observational study of the affective concomitants of mastery in infants. *Journal of Child Psychology and Psychiatry, 33,* 659–667.

MAZUR, E. (1993). Developmental differences in children's understanding of marriage, divorce, and remarriage. *Journal of Applied Developmental Psychology, 14,* 191–212.

MAZZOCCO, M. M. M., NORD, A. M., VAN DOORNINCK, W., GREEN, C. L., DOVAR, C. G., & PENNINGTON, B. F. (1994). Cognitive development among children with early-treated phenylketonuria. *Developmental Neuropsychology, 10,* 133–151.

MCADOO, H. P. (1993). Ethnic families: Strengths that are found in diversity. In H. P. McAdoo (Ed.), *Family ethnicity* (pp. 3–14). Newbury Park, CA: Sage.

MCANARNEY, E. R., KREIPE, R. E., ORR, D. P., & COMERCI, G. D. (1992). *Textbook of adolescent development.* Philadelphia: Saunders.

MCCABE, A. (1998). *Chameleon readers: Teaching children to appreciate all kinds of good stories.* New York: McGraw-Hill.

MCCABE, A. E., & PETERSON, C. (1988). A comparison of adults' versus children's spontaneous use of *because* and *so. Journal of Genetic Psychology, 149,* 257–268.

MCCALL, R. B., APPELBAUM, M. I., & HOGARTY, P. S. (1973). Developmental changes in mental performance. *Monographs of the Society for Research in Child Development, 42*(3, Serial No. 171).

MCCALL, R. B., & CARRIGER, M. S. (1993). A meta-analysis

of infant habituation and recognition memory performance as predictors of later IQ. *Child Development, 64,* 57–79.

McCARTNEY, K. (1984). The effect of quality of day care environment upon children's language development. *Developmental Psychology, 20,* 244–260.

McCARTON, C. M., BROOKS-GUNN, J., WALLACE, I. F., BAUER, C. R., BENNETT, F. C., BERNBAUM, J. C., BROYLES, R. S., CASEY, P. H., McCORMICK, M. C., SCOTT, D. T., TYSON, J., TONASCIA, J., & MEINERT, C. L. (1997). Results at age 8 years of early intervention for low-birth-weight premature infants: The infant health and development program. *Journal of the American Medical Association, 277,* 126–132.

McCLOSKEY, L. A., FIGUEREDO, A. J., & KOSS, M. P. (1995). The effects of systemic family violence on children's mental health. *Child Development, 66,* 1239–1261.

McCONAGHY, M. J. (1979). Gender permanence and the genital basis of gender: Stages in the development of constancy of gender identity. *Child Development, 50,* 1223–1226.

McCORMICK, M. C., GORTMAKER, S. L., & SOBOL, A. M. (1990). Very low birth weight children: Behavior problems and school difficulty in a national sample. *Journal of Pediatrics, 117,* 687–693.

McCUNE, L. (1993). The development of play as the development of consciousness. In M. H. Bornstein & A. O'Reilly (Eds.), *New directions for child development* (No. 59, pp. 67–79). San Francisco: Jossey-Bass.

McDONALD, J. A., & POTTER, N. U. (1996). Lead's legacy? Early and late mortality of 454 lead-poisoned children. *Achives of Environmental Health, 51,* 116–121.

McFALLS, J. A., JR. (1990). The risk of reproductive impairment in the later years of childbearing. *Annual Review of Sociology, 16,* 491–519.

McGEE, G. (1997). Legislating gestation. *Human Reproduction, 12,* 407–408.

McGEE, L. M., & RICHGELS, D. J. (1990). *Literacy's beginnings: Supporting young readers and writers.* Boston: Allyn and Bacon.

McGEE, L. M., & RICHGELS, D. J. (1996). *Literacy's beginnings* (2nd ed.). Boston: Allyn and Bacon.

McGILLICUDDY-DE LISI, A. V., WATKINS, C., & VINCHUR, A. J. (1994). The effect of relationship on children's distributive justice reasoning. *Child Development, 65,* 1694–1700.

McGROARTY, M. (1992, March). The societal context of bilingual education. *Educational Researcher, 21*(2), 7–9.

McGUFFIN, P., & SARGEANT, M. P. (1991). Major affective disorder. In P. McGuffin & R. Murray (Eds.), *The new genetics of mental illness* (pp. 165–181). London: Butterworth-Heinemann.

McGUINNESS, D., & PRIBRAM, K. H. (1980). The neuropsychology of attention: Emotional and motivational controls. In M. C. Wittcock (Ed.), *The brain and psychology* (pp. 95–139). New York: Academic Press.

McGUIRE, J. (1988). Gender stereotypes of parents with two-year-olds and beliefs about gender differences in behavior. *Sex Roles, 19,* 233–240.

McGUIRE, K. D., & WEISZ, J. R. (1982). Social cognition and behavior correlates of preadolescent chumship. *Child Development, 53,* 1483–1484.

McHALE, S. M., BARTKO, W. T., CROUTER, A. C., & PERRY-JENKINS, M. (1990). Children's housework and psychosocial functioning: The mediating effects of parents' sex-role behaviors and attitudes. *Child Development, 61,* 1413–1426.

McKENRY, P. C., & PRICE, S. J. (1995). Divorce: A comparative perspective. In B. B. Ingoldsby & S. Smith (Eds.), *Families in multicultural perspective* (pp. 187–212). New York: Guilford.

McKUSICK, V. A. (1995). *Mendelian inheritance in man: Catalogs of autosomal dominant, autosomal recessive, and X-linked phenotypes* (10th ed.). Baltimore: Johns Hopkins University Press.

McLANAHAN, S., & SANDEFUR, G. (1994). *Growing up with a single parent.* Cambridge, MA: Harvard University Press.

McLEOD, J. D., & SHANAHAN, M. J. (1996). Trajectories of poverty and children's mental health. *Journal of Health and Social Behavior, 37,* 207–220.

McLOYD, V. C. (1998). Children in poverty: Development, public policy, and practice. In I. Sigel & A. Renninger (Eds.), *Handbook of child psychology: Vol. 4. Child psychology in practice* (5th ed., pp. 135–208). New York: Wiley.

McLOYD, V. C., JAYARATNE, T. E., CEBALLO, R., & BORQUEZ, J. (1994). Unemployment and work interruption among African American single mothers: Effects on parenting and adolescent socioemotional functioning. *Child Development, 65,* 562–589.

McMAHON, C. A., UNGERER, J. A., BEAUREPAIRE, J., TENNANT, C., & SAUNDERS, D. (1995). Psychosocial outcomes for parents and children after in vitro fertilization: A review. *Journal of Reproductive and Infant Psychology, 13,* 1–6.

McMANUS, I. C., SIK, G., COLE, D. R., MELLON, A. F., WONG, J., & KLOSS, J. (1988). The development of handedness in children. *British Journal of Developmental Psychology, 6,* 257–273.

McNAMEE, M. J., BARTEK, J. K., & LYNES, D. (1994). Health problems of sheltered homeless children using mobile health services. *Issues in Comprehensive Pediatric Nursing, 17,* 233–242.

McNAMEE, S., & PETERSON, J. (1986). Young children's distributive justice reasoning, behavior, and role taking: Their consistency and relationship. *Journal of Genetic Psychology, 146,* 399–404.

MEAD, G. H. (1934). *Mind, self, and society.* Chicago: University of Chicago Press.

MEAD, M. (1928). *Coming of age in Samoa.* Ann Arbor, MI: Morrow.

MEAD, M., & NEWTON, N. (1967). Cultural patterning of perinatal behavior. In S. Richardson & A. Guttmacher (Eds.), *Childbearing: Its social and psychological aspects* (pp. 142–244). Baltimore: Williams & Wilkins.

MEBERT, C. J. (1991). Dimensions of subjectivity in parents' ratings of infant temperament. *Child Development, 62,* 352–361.

MECHAM, M. J. (1996). *Cerebral palsy.* Austin, TX: PRO-ED.

MEDIASCOPE. (1996). *National television violence study: Executive summary 1994–1995.* Studio City, CA: Author.

MEEHAN, A. M. (1984). A meta-analysis of sex differences in formal operational thought. *Child Development, 55,* 1110–1124.

MEHLMADRONA, L., & MADRONA, M. M. (1997). Physician- and midwife-attended home births —effects of breech, twin, and post-dates outcome data on mortality rates. *Journal of Nurse-Midwifery, 42,* 91–98.

MEILMAN, P. W. (1979). Cross-sectional age changes in ego identity status during adolescence. *Developmental Psychology, 15,* 230–231.

MEISELS, S. J., DICHTELMILLER, M., & LIAW, F. R. (1993). A multidimensional analysis of early childhood intervention programs. In C. H. Zeanah (Ed.), *Handbook of infant mental health* (pp. 361–385). New York: Guilford.

MELBY, J. N., & CONGER, R. D. (1996). Parental behaviors and adolescent academic performance: A longitudinal analysis. *Journal of Research on Adolescence, 6,* 113–137.

MELNIKOW, J., & ALEMAGNO, S. (1993). Adequacy of prenatal care among inner-city women. *Journal of Family Practice, 37,* 575–582.

MELTZOFF, A., & GOPNIK, A. (1993). The role of imitation in understanding persons and developing a theory of mind. In S. Baron-Cohen & H. Tager-Flusberg (Eds.), *Understanding other minds* (pp. 335–366). Oxford: Oxford University Press.

MELTZOFF, A. N. (1988). Infant imitation and memory: Nine-month-olds in immediate and deferred tests. *Child Development, 59,* 217–255.

MELTZOFF, A. N. (1990). Towards a developmental cognitive science. *Annals of the New York Academy of Sciences, 608,* 1–37.

MELTZOFF, A. N. (1994). What infant memory tells us about infantile amnesia: Long-term recall and deferred imitation. *Journal of Experimental Child Psychology, 59,* 497–515.

MELTZOFF, A. N. (1995). Understanding the intentions of others: Re-enactment of intended acts by 18-month-old children. *Developmental Psychology, 31,* 838–850.

MELTZOFF, A. N., & BORTON, R. W. (1979). Intermodal matching by human neonates. *Nature, 282,* 403–404.

MELTZOFF, A. N., & KUHL, P. K. (1994). Faces and speech: Intermodal processing of biologically relevant signals in infants and adults. In D. J. Lewkowicz & R. Lickliter (Eds.), *The development of intersensory perception: Comparative perspectives* (pp. 335–369). Hillsdale, NJ: Erlbaum.

MELTZOFF, A. N., & MOORE, M. K. (1977). Imitation of

facial and manual gestures by human neonates. *Science, 198,* 75–78.

MELTZOFF, A. N., & MOORE, M. K. (1992). Early imitation within a functional framework: The importance of person identity, movement, and development. *Infant Behavior and Development, 15,* 479–505.

MELTZOFF, A. N., & MOORE, M. K. (1994). Imitation, memory, and the representation of persons. *Infant Behavior and Development, 17,* 83–99.

MENDELSON, B. K., WHITE, D. R., & MENDELSON, M. J. (1996). Self-esteem and body esteem: Effects of gender, age, and weight. *Journal of Applied Developmental Psychology, 17,* 321–346.

MENIG-PETERSON, C. L. (1975). The modification of communicative behavior in preschool-aged children as a function of the listener's perspective. *Child Development, 46,* 1015–1018.

MENYUK, P., LIEBERGOTT, J. W., & SCHULTZ, M. C. (1995). *Early language development in full-term and premature infants.* Hillsdale, NJ: Erlbaum.

MEREDITH, N. V. (1978). *Human body growth in the first ten years of life.* Columbia, SC: State Printing.

MERVIS, C. B. (1987). Child-basic object categories and early lexical development. In U. Neisser (Ed.), *Concepts and conceptual development: Ecological and intellectual factors in categorization* (pp. 201–233). Cambridge, England: Cambridge University Press.

MERVIS, C. B., GOLINKOFF, R. M., & BERTRAND, J. (1994). Two-year-olds readily learn multiple labels for the same basic-level category. *Child Development, 65,* 1163–1177.

MERVIS, C. B., JOHNSON, K. E., & MERVIS, C. (1994). Acquisition of subordinate categories by 3-year-olds: The roles of attribute salience, linguistic input, and child characteristics. *Cognitive Development, 9,* 211–234.

MEYER-BAHLBURG, H. F. L. (1990). Short stature: Psychological issues. In F. Lifshitz (Ed.), *Pediatric endocrinology: A clinical guide* (2nd ed., pp. 173–196). New York: Marcel Dekker.

MEYER-BAHLBURG, H. F. L., EHRHARDT, A. A., ROSEN, L. R., GRUEN, R. S., VERIDIANO, N. P., VANN, F. H., & NEUWALDER, H. F. (1995).

Prenatal estrogens and the development of homosexual orientation. *Developmental Psychology, 31,* 12–21.

MEYERS, C., ADAM, R., DUNGAN, J., & PRENGER, V. (1997). Aneuploidy in twin gestations: When is maternal age advanced? *Obstetrics & Gynecology, 89,* 248–251.

MICHAEL, R. T., GAGNON, J. H., LAUMANN, E. O., & KOLATA, G. (1994). *Sex in America.* Boston: Little, Brown.

MICHAELS, G. Y. (1988). Motivational factors in the decision and timing of pregnancy. In G. Y. Michaels & W. A. Goldberg (Eds.), *The transition to parenthood: Current theory and research* (pp. 23–61). New York: Cambridge University Press.

MICHAELS, S. (1991). The dismantling of narrative. In A. McCabe & C. Peterson (Eds.), *Developing narrative structure* (pp. 303–351). Hillsdale, NJ: Erlbaum.

MICHEL, C. (1989). Radiation embryology. *Experientia, 45,* 69–77.

MIDGLEY, C., FELDLAUFER, H., & ECCLES, J. S. (1989). Student/teacher relations and attitudes toward mathematics before and after the transition to junior high school. *Child Development, 60,* 981–992.

MILGRAM, N. A., & PALTI, G. (1993). Psychosocial characteristics of resilient children. *Journal of Research in Personality, 27,* 207–221.

MILLER, G. A. (1991). *The science of words.* New York: Scientific American Library.

MILLER, J. G. (1994). Cultural diversity in the morality of caring: Individually oriented versus duty-based interpersonal moral codes. *Cross-cultural Research: The Journal of Comparative Social Science, 28,* 3–39.

MILLER, J. M., BOUDREAUS, M. C., & REGAN, F. A. (1995). A case-control study of cocaine use in pregnancy. *American Journal of Obstetrics and Gynecology, 172,* 180–185.

MILLER, K. E. (1990). Adolescents' same-sex and opposite-sex peer relations: Sex differences in popularity, perceived social competence and social cognitive skills. *Journal of Adolescent Research, 5,* 222–241.

MILLER, K. F., & BAILLARGEON, R. (1990). Length and distance: Do preschoolers think that occlusion brings things togeth-

er? *Developmental Psychology, 26,* 103–114.

MILLER, K. F., SMITH, C. M., ZHU, J., & ZHANG, H. (1995). Preschool origins of cross-national differences in mathematical competence: The role of number-naming systems. *Psychological Science, 6,* 56–60.

MILLER, L. T., & VERNON, P. A. (1992). The general factor in short-term memory, intelligence, and reaction time. *Intelligence, 16,* 5–29.

MILLER, L. T., & VERNON, P. A. (1997). Developmental changes in speed of information processing in young children. *Developmental Psychology, 33,* 549–554.

MILLER, N., & MARUYAMA, G. (1976). Ordinal position and peer popularity. *Journal of Personality and Social Psychology, 33,* 123–131.

MILLER, N. B., COWAN, P. A., COWAN, C. P., HETHERINGTON, E. M., & CLINGEMPEEL, W. G. (1993). Externalizing in preschoolers and early adolescents: A cross-study replication of a family model. *Developmental Psychology, 29,* 3–16.

MILLER, P. H. (1993). *Theories of developmental psychology* (3rd ed.). New York: Freeman.

MILLER, P. H., & BIGI, L. (1979). The development of children's understanding of attention. *Merrill-Palmer Quarterly, 25,* 235–250.

MILLER, P. H., & SEIER, W. L. (1994). Strategy utilization deficiencies in children: When, where, and why. In H. W. Reese (Ed.), *Advances in child development and behavior* (Vol. 25, pp. 107–156). New York: Academic Press.

MILLER, P. H., SEIER, W. L., PROBERT, J. S., & ALOISE, P. A. (1991). Age differences in the capacity demands of a strategy among spontaneously strategic children. *Journal of Experimental Child Psychology, 52,* 149–165.

MILLER, P. H., WOODY-RAMSEY, J., & ALOISE, P. A. (1991). The role of strategy effortfulness in strategy effectiveness. *Developmental Psychology, 27,* 738–745.

MILLER, S. A. (1998). *Developmental research methods* (2nd ed.). Englewood Cliffs, NJ: Prentice-Hall.

MILLER-JONES, D. (1989). Culture and testing. *American Psychologist, 44,* 360–366.

MILLS, D. L., COFFEY-CORINA, S. A., & NEVILLE, H. J.

(1993). Language acquisition and cerebral specialization in 20-month-old infants. *Journal of Cognitive Neuroscience, 5,* 317–334.

MILLS, D. L., COFFEY-CORINA, S. A., & NEVILLE, H. J. (1994). Variability in cerebral organization during primary language acquisition. In G. Dawson & K. W. Fischer (Eds.), *Human behavior and the developing brain* (pp. 427–455). New York: Guilford.

MILLS, R., & GRUSEC, J. E. (1989). Cognitive, affective, and behavioral consequences of praising altruism. *Merrill-Palmer Quarterly, 35,* 299–326.

MILLSTEIN, S. G., & IRWIN, C. E. (1988). Accident-related behaviors in adolescents: A biosocial view. *Alcohol, Drugs, and Driving, 4,* 21–29.

MILLSTEIN, S. G., & LITT, I. F. (1990). Adolescent health. In S. S. Feldman & G. R. Elliott (Eds.), *At the threshold: The developing adolescent* (pp. 431–456). Cambridge, MA: Harvard University Press.

MISCHEL, W., & LIEBERT, R. M. (1966). Effects of discrepancies between observed and imposed reward criteria on their acquisition and transmission. *Journal of Personality and Social Psychology, 3,* 45–53.

MIYAKE, K., CHEN, S., & CAMPOS, J. J. (1985). Infant temperament, mother's mode of interaction, and attachment in Japan: An interim report. In I. Bretherton & E. Waters (Eds.), Growing points of attachment theory and research. *Monographs of the Society for Research in Child Development, 50*(1–2, Serial No. 209).

MIZE, J., & LADD, G. W. (1990). A cognitive–social learning approach to social skill training with low-status preschool children. *Developmental Psychology, 26,* 388–397.

MOFFATT, M. E. K., HARLOS, S., KIRSHEN, A. J., BURD, L. (1993). DDAVP and nocturnal enuresis: How much do we know? *Pediatrics, 92,* 420–425.

MOFFITT, T. E. (1990). Juvenile delinquency and attention deficit disorder: Boys' developmental trajectories from age 3 to age 15. *Child Development, 61,* 893–910.

MOFFITT, T. E., CASPI, A., DICKSON, N., SILVA, P., & STANTON, W. (1996). Childhood-onset versus adolescent-onset antisocial conduct problems in males: Natural history from ages 3 to 18 years. *Development and Psychopathology, 8,* 399–424.

MOFFITT, T. E., LYNAM, D. R., & SILVA, P. A. (1994). Neuropsychological tests predicting persistent male delinquency. *Criminology, 32,* 277–300.

MOHANTY, A. K., & PERREGAUX, C. (1997). Language acquisition and bilingualism. In J. W. Berry, P. R. Dasen, & T. S. Saraswathi (Eds.), *Handbook of cross-cultural psychology: Vol. 2. Basic processes and human development* (2nd ed., pp. 217–254). Boston: Allyn and Bacon.

MOILANEN, I. (1989). The growth, development, and education of Finnish twins: A longitudinal follow-up study in a birth cohort from pregnancy to nineteen years of age. *Growth, Development and Aging, 18,* 302–306.

MONDIMORE, F. M. (1996). *A natural history of homosexuality.* Baltimore: Johns Hopkins University Press.

MONEY, J. (1993). Specific neurocognitional impairments associated with Turner (45,X) and Klinefelter (47,XXY) syndromes: A review. *Social Biology, 40,* 147–151.

MONROE, S., GOLDMAN, P., & SMITH, V. E. (1988). *Brothers: Black and poor—a true story of courage and survival.* New York: Morrow.

MONTEMAYOR, R., & EISEN, M. (1977). The development of self-conceptions from childhood to adolescence. *Developmental Psychology, 13,* 314–319.

MOON, C., COOPER, R. P., & FIFER, W. P. (1993). Two-day-old infants prefer their native language. *Infant Behavior and Development, 16,* 495–500.

MOON, S. M., & FELDHUSEN, J. F. (1994). The Program for Academic and Creative Enrichment (PACE): A follow-up study ten years later. In R. F. Subotnik & K. D. Arnold (Eds.), *Beyond Terman: Contemporary longitudinal studies of giftedness and talent* (pp. 375–400). Norwood, NJ: Ablex.

MOORE, D. S., SPENCE, M. J., & KATZ, G. S. (1997). Six-month-olds' categorization of natural infant-directed utterances. *Developmental Psychology, 33,* 980–989.

MOORE, E. G. J. (1986). Family socialization and the IQ test performance of traditionally and transracially adopted black children. *Developmental Psychology, 22,* 317–326.

MOORE, K. A., MORRISON, D. R., & GLEI, D. A. (1995). Welfare and adolescent sex: The effects of family history, benefit levels, and community context. *Journal of Family and Economic Issues, 16,* 207–237.

MOORE, K. A., MORRISON, D. R., & GREEN, A. D. (1997). Effects on the children born to adolescent mothers. In R. A. Maynard (Ed.), *Kids having kids* (pp. 145–180). Washington, DC: Urban Institute.

MOORE, K. A., MYERS, D. E., MORRISON, D. R., NORD, C. W., BROWN, B., & EDMONSTON, B. (1993). Age at first childbirth and later poverty. *Journal of Research on Adolescence, 3,* 393–422.

MOORE, K. L., & PERSAUD, T. V. N. (1993). *Before we are born* (4th ed.). Philadelphia: Saunders.

MOORE, K. L., PERSAUD, T. V. N., & SHIOTA, K. (1994). *Color atlas of clinical embryology.* Philadelphia: Saunders.

MOOREHOUSE, M. J. (1991). Linking maternal employment patterns to mother–child activities and children's school competence. *Developmental Psychology, 27,* 295–303.

MORAN, G. F., & VINOVSKIS, M. A. (1986). The great care of godly parents: Early childhood in Puritan New England. *Monographs of the Society for Research in Child Development, 50*(4–5, Serial No. 211).

MORELLI, G., ROGOFF, B., OPPENHEIM, D., & GOLDSMITH, D. (1992). Cultural variation in infants' sleeping arrangements: Questions of independence. *Developmental Psychology, 28,* 604–613.

MORGAN, J. L., BONAMA, K. M., & TRAVIS, L. L. (1995). Negative evidence on negative evidence. *Developmental Psychology, 31,* 180–197.

MORGAN, J. L., & SAFFRAN, J. R. (1995). Emerging integration of sequential and suprasegmental information in preverbal speech segmentation. *Child Development, 66,* 911–936.

MORGANE, P. J., AUSTIN-LAFRANCE, R., BRONZINO, J., TONKISS, J., DIAZ-CINTRA, S., CINTRA, L., KEMPER, T., & GALLER, J. R. (1993). Prenatal malnutrition and development of the brain. *Neuroscience and Biobehavioral Reviews, 17,* 91–128.

MORI, L., & PETERSON, L. (1995). Knowledge of safety of high and low active–impulsive boys: Implications for child injury prevention. *Journal of Clinical Child Psychology, 24,* 370–376.

MORONEY, J. T., & ALLEN, M. H. (1994). Cocaine and alcohol use in pregnancy. In O. Devinsky, F. Feldmann, & B. Hainline (Eds.), *Neurological complications of pregnancy* (pp. 231–242). New York: Raven Press.

MORRONGIELLO, B. A. (1986). Infants' perception of multiple-group auditory patterns. *Infant Behavior and Development, 9,* 307–319.

MORTIMER, J. T., & BORMAN, K. M. (Eds.). (1988). *Work experience and psychological development throughout the lifespan.* Boulder, CO: Westview Press.

MORTON, J. (1993). Mechanisms in infant face processing. In B. de Boysson-Bardies, S. de Schonen, P. Jusczyk, P. McNeilage, & J. Morton (Eds.), *Developmental neurocognition: Speech and face processing in the first year of life* (pp. 93–102). London: Kluwer.

MORTON, J., & JOHNSON, M. H. (1991). CONSPEC and CONLERN: A two-process theory of infant face recognition. *Psychological Review, 98,* 164–181.

MOSHMAN, D. (1990). The development of metalogical understanding. In W. F. Overton (Ed.), *Reasoning, necessity, and logic: Developmental perspectives* (pp. 205–225). Hillsdale, NJ: Erlbaum.

MOSHMAN, D. (1998). Cognitive development beyond childhood. In D. Kuhn & R. S. Siegler (Eds.), *Handbook of child psychology: Vol. 2. Cognition, perception, and language* (5th ed., pp. 947–978). New York: Wiley.

MOSHMAN, D., & FRANKS, B. A. (1986). Development of the concept of inferential validity. *Child Development, 57,* 153–165.

MOSS, M., COLOMBO, J., MITCHELL, D. W., & HOROWITZ, F. D. (1988). Neonatal behavioral organization and visual processing at three months. *Child Development, 59,* 1211–1220.

MOSTELLER, F. (1995). The Tennessee Study of Class Size in the Early School Grades. *Future of Children, 5* (2), 113–127.

MOTT, S. R., JAMES, S. R., & SPERHAC, A. M. (1990). *Nursing care of children and families.* Redwood City, CA: Addison-Wesley.

MOUNTS, N. S., & STEINBERG, L. (1995). An ecological analysis of peer influence on adolescent grade point average and drug use. *Developmental Psychology, 31,* 915–922.

MUMME, D. L., FERNALD, A., & HERRERA, C. (1996). Infants' responses to facial and vocal emotional signals in a social referencing paradigm. *Child Development, 67,* 3219–3237.

MUNRO, G., & ADAMS, G. R. (1977). Ego identity formation in college students and working youth. *Developmental Psychology, 13,* 523–524.

MURPHY-BERMAN, V., & WEISZ, V. (1996). U.N. Convention on the Rights of the Child: Current challenges. *American Psychologist, 51,* 1231–1233.

MURRAY, A. D. (1985). Aversiveness is in the mind of the beholder. In B. M. Lester & C. F. Z. Boukydis (Eds.), *Infant crying* (pp. 217–239). New York: Plenum.

MURRAY, L., & COOPER, P. J. (1997). Postpartum depression and child development. *Psychological Medicine, 27,* 253–260.

MURRAY, M. J., & MEACHAM, R. B. (1993). The effect of age on male reproductive function. *World Journal of Urology, 11,* 137–140.

MURRETT-WAGSTAFF, S., & MOORE, S. G. (1989). The Hmong in America: Infant behavior and rearing practices. In J. K. Nugent, B. M. Lester, & T. B. Brazelton (Eds.), *Biology, culture, and development* (Vol. 1, pp. 319–339). Norwood, NJ: Ablex.

MUSSEN, P., & EISENBERG-BERG, N. (1977). *Roots of caring, sharing, and helping.* San Francisco: Freeman.

NACHTIGALL, R. D. (1993). Secrecy: An unresolved issue in the practice of donor insemination. *American Journal of Obstetrics and Gynecology, 168,* 1846–1851.

NAIGLES, L. G., & GELMAN, S. A. (1995). Overextensions in comprehension and production revisited: Preferential-looking in a study of dog, cat, and cow. *Journal of Child Language, 22,* 19–46.

NAIGLES, L. R., & HOFF-GINSBERG, E. (1995). Input to verb learning: Evidence for the plausibility of syntactic bootstrapping. *Developmental Psychology, 31,* 827–837.

NANEZ, J. (1987). Perception of impending collision in 3- to 6-week-old infants. *Infant Behavior and Development, 11,* 447–463.

NANEZ, J., SR., & YONAS, A. (1994). Effects of luminance and texture motion on infant defensive reactions to optical collision. *Infant Behavior and Development, 17,* 165–174.

NATIONAL ASSOCIATION FOR THE EDUCATION OF YOUNG CHILDREN. (1991). *Accreditation criteria and procedures of the National Academy of Early Childhood Programs* (rev. ed.). Washington, DC: Author.

NATIONAL CENTER FOR HEALTH STATISTICS, U.S. DEPARTMENT OF HEALTH AND HUMAN SERVICES. (1997). *Vital statistics of the United States, 1993.* Washington, DC: U.S. Government Printing Office.

NATIONAL CENTER FOR HEALTH STATISTICS. (1997). *Advance Report of Final Natality Statistics* (Vol. 45). Washington, DC: U.S. Government Printing Office.

NATIONAL FEDERATION OF STATE HIGH SCHOOL ASSOCIATIONS (1997). *High school athletic participation survey.* Kansas City, MO: Author.

NATIONAL INSTITUTE FOR CHILD HEALTH AND DEVELOPMENT, EARLY CHILD CARE RESEARCH NETWORK. (1996). Characteristics of infant care: Factors contributing to positive caregiving. *Early Childhood Research Quarterly, 11,* 269–306.

NATIONAL INSTITUTE FOR CHILD HEALTH AND DEVELOPMENT, EARLY CHILD CARE RESEARCH NETWORK. (1997). The effects of infant child care on infant–mother attachment security: Results of the NICHD Study of Early Child Care. *Child Development, 68,* 860–879.

NEEDLEMAN, H. L., SCHELL, A., BELLINGER, D., LEVITON, A., & ALLRED, E. N. (1990). The long-term effects of exposure to low doses of lead in childhood. *New England Journal of Medicine, 322,* 83–88.

NEISSER, U., BOODOO, G., BOUCHARD, T. J., JR., BOYKIN, A. W., BRODY, N., CECI, S. J., HALPERN, D. F., LOEHLIN, J. C., PERLOFF, R., STERNBERG, R. J., & URBINA, S. (1996). Intelligence: Knowns and unknowns. *American Psychologist, 51,* 77–101.

NELSON, C. A. (1995). The ontogeny of human memory: A cognitive neuroscience perspective. *Developmental Psychology, 31,* 723–738.

NELSON, G. (1993). Risk, resistance, and self-esteem: A longitudinal study of elementary school-aged children from mother-custody and two-parent families. *Journal of Divorce and Remarriage, 19,* 99–119.

NELSON, K. (1973). Structure and strategy in learning to talk. *Monographs of the Society for Research in Child Development, 38*(1–2, Serial No. 149).

NELSON, K. (1993). The psychological and social origins of autobiographical memory. *Psychological Science, 1,* 1–8.

NELSON, M. A. (1996). Protective equipment. In O. Bar-Or (Ed.), *The child and adolescent athlete* (pp. 214–223). Oxford: Blackwell.

NETLEY, C. T. (1986). Summary overview of behavioural development in individuals with neonatally identified X and Y aneuploidy. *Birth Defects, 22,* 293–306.

NEVILLE, H. J. (1991). Neurobiology of cognitive and language processing: Effects on early experience. In K. R. Gibson & A. C. Petersen (Eds.), *Brain maturation and cognitive development: Comparative and cross-cultural perspectives* (pp. 355–380). New York: Aldine De Gruyter.

NEWACHECK, P. W., HUGHES, D. C., & STODDARD, J. J. (1996). Children's access to primary care: Differences by race, income, and insurance status. *Pediatrics, 97,* 26–32.

NEWBORG, J., STOCK, J. R., & WNEK, L. (1984). *Battelle Developmental Inventory.* Allen, TX: LINC Associates.

NEWCOMB, A. F., BUKOWSKI, W. M., & PATTEE, L. (1993). Children's peer relations: A meta-analytic review of popular, rejected, neglected, controversial, and average sociometric status. *Psychological Bulletin, 113,* 99–128.

NEWCOMB, M. D., & BENTLER, P. M. (1988). Consequences of adolescent substance use on young adult health status and utilization of health services: A structural equation model over four years. *Social Science and Medicine, 24,* 71–82.

NEWCOMB, M. D., & BENTLER, P. M. (1989). Substance use and abuse among children and teenagers. *American Psychologist, 44,* 242–248.

NEWCOMBE, N. & FOX, N. A. (1994). Infantile amnesia: Through a glass darkly. *Child Development, 65,* 31–40.

NEWCOMBE, N., & HUTTENLOCHER, J. (1992). Children's early ability to solve perspective-taking problems. *Developmental Psychology, 28,* 635–643.

NEWCOMBE, P. A., & BOYLE, G. J. (1995). High school students' sports personalities: Variations across participation level, gender, type of sport, and success. *International Journal of Sports Psychology, 26,* 277–294.

NEWMAN, B. S., MUZZONIGRO, P. G. (1993). The effects of traditional family values on the coming out process of gay male adolescents. *Adolescence, 28,* 213–226.

NEWMAN, L. S. (1990). Intentional versus unintentional memory in young children: Remembering versus playing. *Journal of Experimental Child Psychology, 50,* 243–258.

NEWNHAM, J. P., EVANS, S. F., MICHAEL, C. A., STANLEY, F. J., & LANDAU, L. I. (1993). Effects of frequent ultrasound during pregnancy: A randomized controlled trial. *Lancet, 342,* 887–890.

NEWSON, J., & NEWSON, E. (1975). Intersubjectivity and the transmission of culture: On the social origins of symbolic functioning. *Bulletin of the British Psychological Society, 28,* 437–446.

NICHOLLS, A. L., & KENNEDY, J. M. (1992). Drawing development: From similarity of features to direction. *Child Development, 63,* 227–241.

NICOLOPOULOU, A. (1993). Play, cognitive development, and the social world: Piaget, Vygotsky, and beyond. *Human Development, 36,* 1–12.

NIDORF, J. F. (1985). Mental health and refugee youths: A model for diagnostic training. In T. C. Owen (Ed.), *Southeast Asian mental health: Treatment, prevention, services, training, and research* (pp. 391–427). Washington, DC: National Institute of Mental Health.

NIEMAN, D. (1994). Exercise: Immunity from respiratory infections. *Swimming Technique, 31*(2), 38–43.

NILSSON, L., & HAMBERGER, L. (1990). *A child is born.* New York: Delacorte.

NISBETT, R. (1995). Race, IQ, and scientism. In S. Fraser (Ed.), *The bell curve wars: Race, intelligence and the future of America* (pp. 36–57). New York: Basic Books.

NOLEN-HOEKSEMA, S., & GIRGUS, J. S. (1994). The emergence of gender differences in depression in adolescence. *Psychological Bulletin, 115,* 424–443.

NOTTELMANN, E. D. (1987). Competence and self-esteem during transition from childhood to adolescence. *Developmental Psychology, 23,* 441–450.

NOTTELMANN, E. D., INOFF-GERMAIN, G., SUSMAN, E. J., & CHROUSOS, G. P. (1990). Hormones and behavior at puberty. In J. Bancroft & J. M. Reinisch (Eds.), *Adolescence and puberty* (pp. 88–123). New York: Oxford University Press.

NOTTELMANN, E. D., & JENSEN, P. S. (1995). Comorbidity of disorders in children and adolescents. In T. H. Ollendick & R. J. Prinz (Eds.), *Advances in clinical child psychology* (pp. 109–155). New York: Plenum.

NOTZON, F. C. (1990). International differences in the use of obstetric interventions. *Journal of the American Medical Association, 263,* 3286–3291.

NOVAK, G. P., SOLANTO, M., & ABIKOFF, H. (1995). Spatial orienting and focused attention in attention deficit hyperactivity disorder. *Journal of Psychophysiology, 32,* 546–559.

NOVY, M. J., McGREGOR, J. A., & IAMS, J. D. (1995). New perspectives on the prevention of extreme prematurity. *Clinical Obstetrics and Gynecology, 38,* 790–808.

NOWAKOWSKI, R. S. (1987). Basic concepts of CNS development. *Child Development, 58,* 568–595.

NUCKOLLS, K., CASSEL, J., & KAPLAN, B. (1972). Psychosocial assets, life crisis, and the prognosis of pregnancy. *American Journal of Epidemiology, 95,* 431–441.

NURMI, J., POOLE, M. E., & KALAKOSKI, V. (1996). Age differences in adolescent identity exploration and commitment in urban and rural environments. *Journal of Adolescence, 19,* 443–452.

O'CONNOR, B. P. (1995). Identity development and perceived parental behavior as sources of adolescent egocentrism. *Journal of Youth and Adolescence, 24,* 205–227.

O'CONNOR, C. (1997). Dispositions toward (collective) struggle and educational resilience in the inner city: A case analysis of six African-American high school students. *American Educational Research Journal, 34,* 593–629.

O'MALLEY, P. M., JOHNSTON, L. D., & BACHMAN, J. G. (1995). Adolescent substance use: Epidemiology and implications for public policy. *Pediatric Clinics of North America, 42,* 241–260.

O'NEIL, R., & PARKE, R. D. (1997, March). *Objective and subjective features of children's neighborhoods: Relations to parental regulatory strategies and children's social competence.* Paper presented at the biennial meeting of the Society for Research in Child Development, Washington, DC.

O'REILLY, A. W. (1995). Using representations: Comprehension and production of actions with imagined objects. *Child Development, 66,* 999–1010.

O'REILLY, A. W., & BORNSTEIN, M. H. (1993). Caregiver–child interaction in play. In M. H. Bornstein & A. W. O'Reilly (Eds.), *New directions for child development* (No. 59, pp. 55–66). San Francisco: Jossey-Bass.

OAKES, J., GAMORAN, A., & PAGE, R. N. (1992). Curriculum differentiation: Opportunities, outcomes, and meanings. In P. W. Jackson (Ed.), *Handbook of research on curriculum* (pp. 570–608). New York: Macmillan.

OAKES, L. M. (1994). Development of infants' use of continuity cues in their perception of causality. *Developmental Psychology, 30,* 869–879.

OAKES, L. M., & COHEN, L. B. (1995). Infant causal perception. In C. Rovee-Collier & L. P. Lipsitt (Eds.), *Advances in infancy research* (Vol. 9, pp. 1–54). Norwood, NJ: Ablex.

OAKES, L. M., COPPAGE, D. J., & DINGEL, A. (1997). By land or by sea: The role of perceptual similarity in infants' categorization of animals. *Developmental Psychology, 33,* 396–407.

OATES, R. K., PEACOCK, A., & FORREST, D. (1985). Long-term effects of nonorganic failure to thrive. *Pediatrics, 75,* 36–40.

OBERG, C. N., BRYANT, N., & BACH, M. L. (1995). A portrait of America's children: The impact of poverty and a call to action. *Journal of Social Distress and the Homeless, 4,* 43–57.

OBLER, L. K. (1997). Development and loss: Changes in the adult years. In J. Berko Gleason (Ed.), *The development of language* (4th ed., pp. 440–472). Boston: Allyn and Bacon.

OFFER, D. (1988). *The teenage world: Adolescents' self-image in ten countries.* New York: Plenum.

OFFICE OF EDUCATIONAL RESEARCH AND IMPROVEMENT. (1997). *Youth indicators 1997: Trends in the well-being of American youth.* Washington, DC: U.S. Government Printing Office.

OGBU, J. U. (1988). Black education: A cultural-ecological perspective. In H. P. McAdoo (ed.), *Black families* (pp. 169–186). Beverly Hills, CA: Sage.

OGBU, J. U. (1997). Understanding the school performance of urban blacks: Some essential background knowledge. In H. J. Walberg, O. Reyes, & R. P. Weissberg (Ed.), *Children and youth: Interdisciplinary perspectives* (pp. 190– 222). Thousand Oaks, CA: Sage.

OKAGAKI, L., & FRENSCH, P. A. (1996). Effects of video game playing on measures of spatial performance: Gender effects in late adolescence. In P. M. Greenfield & R. R. Cocking (Eds.), *Interacting with video* (pp. 115–140). Norwood, NJ: Ablex.

OKAGAKI, L., & STERNBERG, R. J. (1993). Parental beliefs and children's school performance. *Child Development, 64,* 36–56.

OLLENDICK, T. H., YANG, B., KING, N. J., DONG, Q., & AKANDE, A. (1996). Fears in American, Australian, Chinese, and Nigerian children and adolescents: A cross-cultural study. *Journal of Child Psychology and Psychiatry, 37,* 213–220.

OLLER, D. K., & EILERS, R. E. (1988). The role of audition in infant babbling. *Child Development, 59,* 441–449.

OLSEN, O. (1997). Meta-analysis of the safety of home birth. *Birth–Issues in Perinatal Care, 24,* 4–13.

OLWEUS, D. (1978). *Aggression in the schools: Bullies and whipping boys.* Washington, DC: Hemisphere.

OLWEUS, D. (1984). Aggressors and their victims: Bullying at school. In N. Frude & H. Gault (Eds.), *Disruptive behaviors in schools* (pp. 57–76). New York: Wiley.

OLWEUS, D. (1993). *Bullying at school.* Oxford: Blackwell.

OLWEUS, D. (1995). Bullying or peer abuse at school: Facts and intervention. *Current Directions in Psychological Science, 4,* 196–200.

OMER, H., & EVERLY, G. S. (1988). Psychological factors in preterm labor: Critical review and theoretical synthesis. *American Journal of Psychiatry, 145,* 1507–1513.

ORNSTEIN, P. A., SHAPIRO, L. R., CLUBB, P. A., & FOLLMER, A. (1997). The influence of prior knowledge on children's memory for salient medical experiences. In N. Stein, P. A. Ornstein, C. J. Brainerd, & B. Tversky (Eds.), *Memory for everyday and emotional events* (pp. 83–112). Hillsdale, NJ: Erlbaum.

OSHERSON, D. N., & MARKMAN, E. M. (1975). Language and the ability to evaluate contradictions and tautologies. *Cognition, 2,* 213–226.

OTAKI, M., DURRETT, M., RICHARDS, P., NYQUIST, L., & PENNEBAKER, J. (1986). Maternal and infant behavior in Japan and America: A partial replication. *Journal of Cross-Cultural Psychology, 17,* 251–268.

OWEN, M. T., & COX, M. J. (1997). Marital conflict and the development of infant–parent attachment relationships. *Journal of Family Psychology, 11,* 152–164.

OWENS, R. (1996). *Language development: An introduction* (4th ed.). Boston: Allyn and Bacon.

OWENS, T. (1982). Experience-based career education: Summary and implications of research and evaluation findings. *Child and Youth Services Journal, 4,* 77–91.

PADGHAM, J. J., & BLYTH, D. A. (1990). Dating during adolescence. In R. M. Lerner, A. C. Petersen, & J. Brooks-Gunn (Eds.), *The encyclopedia of adolescence* (Vol. 1, pp. 196–198). New York: Garland.

PADILLA, M. L., & LANDRETH, G. L. (1989). Latchkey children: A review of the literature. *Child Welfare, 68,* 445–454.

PAIKOFF, R. L., & BROOKS-GUNN, J. (1991). Do parent–child relationships change during puberty? *Psychological Bulletin, 110,* 47–66.

PALINCSAR, A. S. (1992, April). *Beyond reciprocal teaching: A retrospective and prospective view.* Raymond B. Cattell Early Career Award Address at the annual meeting of the American Educational Research Association, San Francisco.

PALINCSAR, A. S., BROWN, A. L., & CAMPIONE, J. C. (1993). First-grade dialogues for knowledge-acquisition and use. In E. A. Forman, N. Minick, & C. A. Stone (Eds.), *Contexts for learning* (pp. 43–57). New York: Oxford University Press.

PALINCSAR, A. S., & KLENK, L. (1992). Fostering literacy learning in supportive contexts. *Journal of Learning Disabilities, 25,* 211–225.

PAN, H. W. (1994). Children's play in Taiwan. In J. L. Roopnarine, J. E. Johnson, & F. H. Hooper (Eds.), *Children's play in diverse cultures* (pp. 31–50). Albany, NY: SUNY Press.

PAPINI, D. R. (1994). Family interventions. In S. L. Archer (Ed.), *Interventions for adolescent identity development* (pp. 47–61). Thousand Oaks, CA: Sage.

PARK, S-Y., BELSKY, J., PUTNAM, S., & CRNIC, K. (1997). Infant emotionality, parenting, and 3-year inhibition: Exploring stability and lawful discontinuity in a male sample. *Developmental Psychology, 33,* 218–227.

PARKE, R. D., & BURIEL, R. (1998). Socialization in the family: Ethnic and ecological perspectives. In N. Eisenberg (Ed.), *Handbook of child psychology: Vol. 3. Social, emotional, and personality development* (5th ed., pp. 463–552). New York: Wiley.

PARKE, R. D., & TINSLEY, B. R. (1981). The father's role in infancy: Determinants of involvement in caregiving and play. In M. E. Lamb (Ed.), *The role of the father in child development* (pp. 429–458). New York: Wiley.

PARKER, J. G., & ASHER, S. R. (1987). Peer relations and later personal adjustment: Are low-accepted children at risk? *Psychological Bulletin, 102,* 357–389.

PARKER, J. G., & ASHER, S. R. (1993). Friendship and friendship quality in middle childhood: Links with peer group acceptance and feelings of loneliness and social dissatisfaction. *Developmental Psychology, 29,* 611–621.

PARKHURST, J. T., & ASHER, S. R. (1992). Peer relations and later personal adjustment: Are low-accepted children at risk?

Psychological Bulletin, 102, 357–389.

PARMELEE, A. H. (1997). Illness and the development of social competence. *Developmental and Behavioral Pediatrics, 18,* 120–124.

PARMELEE, A., WENNER, W., AKIYAMA, Y., STERN, E., & FLESCHER, J. (1967). Electroencephalography and brain maturation. In A. Minkowski (Ed.), *Symposium on regional development of the brain in early life.* Philadelphia: Davis.

PARSONS, J. E., ADLER, T. F., & KACZALA, C. M. (1982). Socialization of achievement attitudes and beliefs: Parental influences. *Child Development, 53,* 310–321.

PARTEN, M. (1932). Social participation among preschool children. *Journal of Abnormal and Social Psychology, 27,* 243–269.

PASSMAN, R. H. (1987). Attachment to inanimate objects: Are children who have security blankets insecure? *Journal of Consulting and Clinical Psychology, 55,* 825–830.

PATTERSON, C. J. (1995). Sexual orientation and human development: An overview. *Developmental Psychology, 31,* 3–11.

PATTERSON, C. J. (1996). Lesbian and gay parenthood. In M. H. Bornstein (Ed.), *Handbook of parenting* (Vol. 3, pp. 255–274). Mahwah, NJ: Erlbaum.

PATTERSON, G. R. (1982). *Coercive family processes.* Eugene, OR: Castilia Press.

PATTERSON, G. R. (1993). Orderly change in a stable world: The antisocial trait as a chimera. *Journal of Consulting and Clinical Psychology, 61,* 911–919.

PATTERSON, G. R. (1995). Coercion—A basis for early age of onset for arrest. In J. McCord (Ed.), *Coercion and punishment in long-term perspective* (pp. 81–105). New York: Cambridge University Press.

PATTERSON, G. R., DEBARYSHE, B. D., & RAMSEY, E. (1989). A developmental perspective on antisocial behavior. *American Psychologist, 44,* 329–335.

PATTERSON, G. R., REID, J. B., & DISHION, T. J. (1992). *Antisocial boys.* Eugene, OR: Castalia.

PATTESON, D. M., & BARNARD, K. E. (1990). Parenting of low birth weight infants: A review of issues and interventions. *Infant Mental Health Journal, 11,* 37–56.

PEARSON, J. L., HUNTER, A. G. ENSMINGER, M. E., & KELLAM, S. G. (1990). Black grandmothers in multigenerational households: Diversity in family structure and parenting involvement in the Woodlawn community. *Child Development, 61,* 434–442.

PECKHAM, C. S., & LOGAN, S. (1993). Screening for toxoplasmosis during pregnancy. *Archives of Disease in Childhood, 68,* 3–5.

PEDERSON, D. R., & MORAN, G. (1995). A categorical description of infant–mother relationships in the home and its relation to Q-sort measures of infant–mother interaction. In E. Waters, B. E. Vaughn, G. Posada, & K. Kondo-Ikemura K. (Eds.), Caregiving, cultural, and cognitive perspectives on secure-base behavior and working models: New growing points of attachment theory and research. *Monographs of the Society for Research in Child Development, 60* (2–3, Serial No. 244).

PEDERSON, D. R., & MORAN, G. (1996). Expressions of the attachment relationship outside of the Strange Situation. *Child Development, 67,* 915–927.

PEDLOW, R., SANSON, A., PRIOR, M., & OBERKLAID, F. (1993). Stability of maternally reported temperament from infancy to 8 years. *Developmental Psychology, 29,* 998–1007.

PELHAM, W. E., JR., & HOZA, B. (1996). Intensive treatment: A summer treatment program for children with ADHD. In E. D. Hibbs & P. S. Jensen (Eds.), *Psychosocial treatments for child and adolescent disorders: Empirically based strategies for clinical practice* (pp. 311–340). Washington, DC: American Psychological Association.

PELLEGRINI, A. D. (1988). Elementary-school children's rough-and-tumble play and social competence. *Developmental Psychology, 24,* 802–806.

PENNINGTON, B. F., BENDER, B., PUCK, M., SALBENBLATT, J., & ROBINSON, A. (1982). Learning disabilities in children with sex chromosome abnormalities. *Child Development, 53,* 1182–1192.

PERELLE, I. B., & EHRMAN, L. (1994). An international study of human handedness: The data. *Behavior Genetics, 24,* 217–227.

PERFETTI, C. A. (1988). Verbal efficiency in reading ability. In M. Daneman, G. E. MacKinnon, & T. G. Waller (Eds.), *Reading research: Advances in theory and practice* (Vol. 6, pp. 109–143). San Diego, CA: Academic Press.

PERLETH, C., & HELLER, K. A. (1994). The Munich Longitudinal Study of Giftedness. In R. F. Subotnik & K. D. Arnold (Eds.), *Beyond Terman: Contemporary studies of giftedness and talent* (pp. 77–114). Norwood, NJ: Ablex.

PERLMUTTER, M. (1984). Continuities and discontinuities in early human memory: Paradigms, processes, and performances. In R. V. Kail, Jr., & N. R. Spear (Eds.), *Comparative perspectives on the development of memory* (pp. 253–287). Hillsdale, NJ: Erlbaum.

PERNER, J. (1991). *Understanding the representational mind.* Cambridge, MA: Bradford/MIT Press.

PERRY, C. L., STORY, M., & LYTLE, L. A. (1997). Promoting healthy dietary behaviors. In R. P. Weissberg, T. P. Gullotta, R. L. Hampton, B. A. Ryan, & G. R. Adams (Eds.), *Enhancing children's wellness* (pp. 214–249). Thousand Oaks, CA: Sage.

PERRY, D. G., PERRY, L. C., & WEISS, R. J. (1989). Sex differences in the consequences that children anticipate for aggression. *Developmental Psychology, 25,* 312–319.

PERRY, D. G., WILLIARD, J. C., & PERRY, L. C. (1990). Peers' perceptions of the consequences that victimized children provide aggressors. *Child Development, 61,* 1310–1325.

PERRY, W. G., JR. (1970). *Forms of intellectual and ethical development in the college years.* New York: Holt, Rinehart & Winston.

PERRY, W. G., JR. (1981). Cognitive and ethical growth. In A. Chickering (Ed.), *The modern American college* (pp. 76–116). San Francisco: Jossey-Bass.

PESHKIN, A. (1978). *Growing up American: Schooling and the survival of the community.* Chicago: University of Chicago Press.

PESHKIN, A. (1994). *Growing up American: Schooling and the survival of community.* Prospect Heights, IL: Waveland Press.

PETERSEN, A. C. (1984). The Early Adolescence Study: An overview. *Journal of Early Adolescence, 4,* 103–106.

PETERSON, L. (1989). Latchkey children's preparation for self-care: Overestimated, underrehearsed, and unsafe. *Journal of Clinical Child Psychology, 18,* 36–43.

PETERSON, L., & BROWN, D. (1994). Integrating child injury and abuse–neglect research: Common histories, etiologies, and solutions. *Psychological Bulletin, 116,* 293–315.

PETERSON, L., & MORI, L. (1985). Prevention of child injury: An overview of targets, methods, and tactics for psychologists. *Journal of Consulting and Clinical Psychology, 14,* 98–104.

PETERSON, L., & OLIVER, K. K. (1995). Prevention of injuries and disease. In M. C. Roberts (Ed.), *Handbook of pediatric psychology* (2nd ed., pp. 185–199). New York: Guilford.

PETITTO, L. A., & MARENTETTE, P. F. (1991). Babbling in the manual mode: Evidence for the ontogeny of language. *Science, 251,* 1493–1496.

PETTIT, G. S., BAKSHI, A., DODGE, K. A., & COIE, J. D. (1990). The emergence of social dominance in young boys' play groups: Developmental differences and behavioral correlates. *Developmental Psychology, 26,* 1017–1025.

PHELPS, K. E., & WOOLLEY, J. D. (1994). The form and function of young children's magical beliefs. *Developmental Psychology, 30,* 385–394.

PHILLIPS, C. A., ROLLS, S., ROUSE, A., & GRIFFITHS, M. D. (1995). Home video game playing in schoolchildren—A study of incidence and patterns of play. *Journal of Adolescence, 18,* 687–691.

PHILLIPS, D. A. (1987). Socialization of perceived academic competence among highly competent children. *Child Development, 58,* 1308–1320.

PHILLIPS, D. A., VORAN, M., KISKER, E., HOWES, C., & WHITEBOOK, M. (1994). Child care for children in poverty: Opportunity or inequity? *Child Development, 65,* 472–492.

PHILLIPS, M. (1997). What makes schools effective? A comparison of the relationships of communitarian climate and academic climate to mathematics achievement and attendance during middle school. *American Educational Research Journal, 34,* 633–662.

PHILLIPS, O. P., & ELIAS, S. (1993). Prenatal genetic counseling issues in women of advanced reproductive age. *Journal of Women's Health, 2,* 1–5.

PHINNEY, J. S. (1989). Stages of ethnic identity development in minority group adolescents. *Journal of Early Adolescence, 9,* 34–49.

PHINNEY, J. S. (1993). A three stage model of ethnic identity development in adolescents. In M. E. Bernal & G. P. Knight (Eds.), *Ethnic identity: Formation and transmission among Hispanic and other minorities* (pp. 61–80). Albany, NY: State University of New York Press.

PHINNEY, J. S. (1993). Multiple group identities: Differentiation, conflict, and integration. In J. Kroger (Ed.), *Discussions on ego identity* (pp. 47–73). Hillsdale, NJ: Erlbaum.

PHINNEY, J., & ALIPURIA, L. (1990). Ethnic identity in college students from four ethnic groups. *Journal of Adolescence, 13,* 171–183.

PIAGET, J. (1926). *The language and thought of the child.* New York: Harcourt, Brace & World. (Original work published 1923)

PIAGET, J. (1929). *The child's conception of physical causality.* New York: Harcourt, Brace & World. (Original work published 1926)

PIAGET, J. (1930). *The child's conception of the world.* New York: Harcourt, Brace, & World. (Original work published 1926)

PIAGET, J. (1950). *The psychology of intelligence.* New York: International Universities Press.

PIAGET, J. (1951). *Play, dreams, and imitation in childhood.* New York: Norton. (Original work published 1945)

PIAGET, J. (1952). *The origins of intelligence in children.* New York: International Universities Press. (Original work published 1936)

PIAGET, J. (1965). *The moral judgment of the child.* New York: Free Press. (Original work published 1932)

PIAGET, J. (1967). *Six psychological studies.* New York: Vintage.

PIAGET, J. (1971). *Biology and knowledge.* Chicago: University of Chicago Press.

PIAGET, J. (1985). *The equilibration of cognitive structures: The central problem of intellectual development.* Chicago: University of Chicago Press.

PIAGET, J., & INHELDER, B. (1956). *The child's conception of space.* London: Routledge & Kegan Paul. (Original work published 1948)

PIAGET, J., INHELDER, B., & SZEMINSKA, A. (1960). *The child's conception of geometry.* New York: Basic Books. (Original work published 1948)

PIANTA, R., EGELAND, B., & ERICKSON, M. F. (1989). The antecedents of maltreatment: Results of the Mother–Child Interaction Research Project. In D. Cicchetti & V. Carlson (Eds.), *Child maltreatment* (pp. 203–253). New York: Cambridge University Press.

PIATT, B. (1993). *Only English? Law and language policy in the United States.* Albuquerque: University of New Mexico Press.

PICK, A. D., & FRANKEL, G. W. (1974). A developmental study of strategies of visual selectivity. *Child Development, 45,* 1162–1165.

PICK, H. L., JR. (1989). Motor development: The control of action. *Developmental Psychology, 25,* 867–870.

PICKENS, J., FIELD, T., NAWROCKI, T. L., MARTINEZ, A., SOUTULLO, D., & GONZALEZ, J. (1994). Full-term and preterm infants' perception of face–voice synchrony. *Infant Behavior and Development, 17,* 447–455.

PICKERING, L. K., GRANOFF, D. M., ERICKSON, J. R., MASON, M. L., & CORDLE, C. T. (1998). Modulation of the immune system by human milk and infant formula containing nucleotides. *Pediatrics, 101,* 242–249.

PIERCE, W. D., & EPLING, W. F. (1995). *Behavior analysis and learning.* Englewood Cliffs, NJ: Prentice-Hall.

PIKE, K. M., & RODIN, J. (1991). Mothers, daughters, and disordered eating. *Journal of Abnormal Psychology, 100,* 198–204.

PILKINGTON, C. L., & PIERSEL, W. C. (1991). School phobia: A critical analysis of the separation anxiety theory and an alternative conceptualization. *Psychology in the Schools, 28,* 290–303.

PILLOW, B. H. (1988). The development of children's beliefs about the mental world. *Merrill-Palmer Quarterly, 34,* 1–32.

PINE, J. M. (1995). Variation in vocabulary development as a function of birth order. *Child Development, 66,* 272–281.

PINEL, J. P. J. (1997). *Biopsychology* (3rd ed.). Boston: Allyn and Bacon.

PINKER, S. (1984). *Language learnability and language development.* Cambridge, MA: Harvard University Press.

PINKER, S., LEBEAUX, D. S., & FROST, L. A. (1987). Productivity and constraints in the acquisition of the passive. *Cognition, 26,* 195–267.

PIPES, P. L. (1996). *Nutrition in infancy and childhood* (6th ed.). St. Louis: Mosby.

PIPP, S., EASTERBROOKS, M. A., & BROWN, S. R. (1993). Attachment status and complexity of infants' self- and other-knowledge when tested with mother and father. *Social Development, 2,* 1–14.

PLOMIN, R. (1994a). Nature, nurture, and social development. *Social Development, 3,* 37–53.

PLOMIN, R. (1994b). The Emanuel Miller Memorial Lecture 1993: Genetic research and identification of environmental influences. *Journal of Child Psychology and Psychiatry, 35,* 817–834.

PLOMIN, R., REISS, D., HETHERINGTON, E. M., & HOWE, G. W. (1994). Nature and nurture: Genetic contributions to measures of the family environment. *Developmental Psychology, 30,* 32–43.

PLUMERT, J. M., PICK, H. L., JR., MARKS, R. A., KINTSCH, A. S., & WEGESIN, D. (1994). Locating objects and communicating about locations: Organizational differences in children's searching and direction-giving. *Developmental Psychology, 30,* 443–453.

PODROUZEK, W., & FURROW, D. (1988). Preschoolers' use of eye contact while speaking: The influence of sex, age, and conversational partner. *Journal of Psycholinguistic Research, 17,* 89–93.

POETS, C. F., SCHLAUD, M., KEEMANN, W. J., RUDOLPH, A., DIEKMANN, U., & SENS, B. (1995). Sudden infant death and maternal cigarette smoking—results from the Lower Saxony Perinatal Working Group. *European Journal of Pediatrics, 154,* 326–329.

POINDRON, P., & LE NEINDRE, P. (1980). Endocrine and sensory regulation of maternal behavior in the ewe. In J. S. Rosenblatt , R. A. Hinde, C. Beer, & M. Busnel (Eds.), *Advances in the study of behavior* (pp. 76–119). New York: Academic Press.

POLANSKY, N. A., GAUDIN, J. M., AMMONS, P. W., & DAVIS, K. B. (1985). The psychological ecology of the neglectful mother. *Child Abuse & Neglect, 9,* 265–275.

POLIT, D. F., QUINT, J. C., & RICCIO, J. A. (1988). *The challenge of serving teenage mothers: Lessons from Project Redirection.* New York: Manpower Demonstration Research Corporation.

POLKA, L., & WERKER, J. F. (1994). Developmental changes in perception of non-native vowel contrasts. *Journal of Experimental Psychology: Human Perception and Performance, 20,* 421–435.

POLLACK, S., CICCHETTI, D., KLORMAN, R., & BRUMAGHIM, J. (1997). Cognitive brain event-related potentials and emotion processing in maltreated children. *Child Development, 68,* 773–787.

POLLITT, E., GORMAN, K. S., ENGLE, P. L., MARTORELL, R., & RIVERA, J. (1993). Early supplementary feeding and cognition. *Monographs of the Society for Research in Child Development, 58*(7, Serial No. 235).

POLLOCK, L. (1987). *A lasting relationship: Parents and children over three centuries.* Hanover, NH: University Press of New England.

POLLOWAY, E. A., PATTON, J. R., SMITH, T. E. C., & BUCK, G. H. (1997). Mental retardation and learning disabilities: Conceptual and applied issues. *Journal of Learning Disabilities, 30,* 297–308.

POPKIN, B. M. (1994). The nutrition transition in low-income countries: An emerging crisis. *Nutrition Review, 52,* 285–298.

POPKIN, B. M., RICHARDS, M. K., & MONTIERO, C. A. (1996). Stunting is associated with overweight in children of four nations that are undergoing the nutrition transition. *Journal of Nutrition, 126,* 3009–3016.

PORGES, S. W. (1991). Autonomic regulation and attention. In B. A. Campbell, H. Hayne, & R. Richardson (Eds.), *Attention and information processing in infants and adults* (pp. 201–223). Hillsdale, NJ: Erlbaum.

PORTER, R. H., MAKIN, J. W., DAVIS, L. B., & CHRISTENSEN, K. M. (1992). An assessment of the salient olfactory environment of formula-fed infants. *Physiology & Behavior, 50*, 907–911.

PORTMAN, P. A. (1995). Who is having fun in physical education classes? Experiences of sixth-grade students in elementary and middle schools. *Journal of Teaching in Physical Education, 14*, 445–453.

POSADA, G., GAO, Y., WU, F., POSADA, R., TASCON, M., SCHÖELMERICH, A., SAGI, A., KONDO-IKEMURA, K., HAALAND, W., & SYNNEVAAG, B. (1995). The secure-base phenomenon across cultures: Children's behavior, mothers' preferences, and experts' concepts. In E. Waters, B. E. Vaughn, G. Posada, & K. Kondo-Ikemura K. (Eds.), Caregiving, cultural, and cognitive perspectives on secure-base behavior and working models: New growing points of attachment theory and research. *Monographs of the Society for Research in Child Development, 60* (2–3, Serial No. 244).

POSNER, J. K., & VANDELL, D. L. (1994). Low-income children's after-school care: Are there beneficial effects of after-school programs? *Child Development, 64*, 440–456.

POSNER, M. I., ROTHBART, M. K., GERARDI, G., & THOMAS-THRAPP, L. (1997). Functions of orienting in early infancy. In P. Lange, M. Balaban, & R. F. Simmons (Eds.), *The study of attention: Cognitive perspectives from psychophysiology, reflexology, and neuroscience* (pp. 327–345). Hillsdale, NJ: Erlbaum.

POULIN-DUBOIS, D., & HÉROUX, G. (1994). Movement and children's attributions of life properties. *International Journal of Behavioral Development, 17*, 329–347.

POULIN-DUBOIS, D., SERBIN, L. A., KENYON, B., & DERBYSHIRE, A. (1994). Infants' intermodal knowledge about gender. *Developmental Psychology, 30*, 436–442.

POWELL, B., & STEELMAN, L. C. (1993). The educational benefits of being spaced out: Sibship density and educational progress. *American Sociological Review, 58*, 367–381.

POWERS, S. I., HAUSER, S. T., & KILNER, L. A. (1989). Adolescent mental health. *American Psychologist, 44*, 200–208.

POWERS, W. F., & WAMPLER, N. S. (1996). Further defining

risks confronting twins. *American Journal of Obstetrics and Gynecology, 175*, 1522–1528.

POWLS, A., BOTTING, N., COOKE, R. W. I., & MARLOW, N. (1996). Handedness in very-low-birthweight (VLBW) children at 12 years of age: Relation to perinatal and outcome variables. *Developmental Medicine and Child Neurology, 38*, 594–602.

PRATT, D. (1986). On the merits of multiage classrooms: Their work life. *Research in Rural Education, 3*, 111–116.

PRECHTL, H. F. R. (1958). Problems of behavioral studies in the newborn infant. In D. S. Lehrmann, R. A. Hinde, & E. Shaw (Eds.), *Advances in the study of behavior* (Vol. 1, pp. 75–98). New York: Academic Press.

PRECHTL, H. F. R., & BEINTEMA, D. (1965). *The neurological examination of the full-term newborn infant.* London: Heinemann Medical.

PRESSLEY, M. (1994). State-of-the-science primary-grades reading instruction or whole language? *Educational Psychologist, 29*, 211–215.

PRESSLEY, M. (1995). More about the development of self-regulation: Complex, long-term, and thoroughly social. *Educational Psychologist, 30*, 207–212.

PRESSLEY, M., & EL-DINARY, P. B. (Eds.). (1993). Strategies instruction [special issue]. *Elementary School Journal, 94* (2).

PREVIC, F. H. (1991). A general theory concerning the prenatal origins of cerebral lateralization. *Psychological Review, 98*, 299–334.

PREVOST, R. A., BRONSON, M. B., & CASEY, M. B. (1995). Planning processes in preschool children. *Journal of Applied Developmental Psychology, 16*, 505–527.

PREYER, W. (1888). *The mind of the child* (2 vols.). New York: Appleton. (Original work published 1882)

PROOS, L. A. (1993). Anthropometry in adolescence—secular trends, adoption, ethnic and environmental differences. *Hormone Research, 39*, 18–24.

PRYOR, J. B., & REEDER, G. D. (1993). Collective and individual representations of HIV/AIDS stigma. In J. B. Pryor & G. D. Reeder (Eds.), *The social psychology of HIV infection* (pp. 263–286). Hillsdale, NJ: Erlbaum.

QAZI, Q. H., SHEIKH, T. M., FIKRIG, S., & MENIKOFF, H. (1988). Lack of evidence for craniofacial dysmorphism in perinatal human immunodeficiency virus infection. *Journal of Pediatrics, 11*, 7–11.

QUADREL, M. J., FISCHHOFF, B., & DAVIS, W. (1993). Adolescent (in)vulnerability. *American Psychologist, 48*, 102–116.

QUIGGLE, N. L., GARBER, J., PANAK, W. F., & DODGE, K. A. (1992). Social information processing in aggressive and depressed children. *Child Development, 63*, 1305–1320.

QUINN, P. C., & EIMAS, P. D. (1996). Perceptual organization and categorization in young infants. In C. Rovee-Collier & P. P. Lipsitt (Eds.), *Advances in infancy research* (Vol. 10, pp. 1–36). Norwood, NJ: Ablex.

QUINN, T. M., & ADZICK, N. S. (1997). Fetal surgery. *Obstetrics and Gynecology Clinics of North America, 24*, 143–157.

QUINTERO, R. A., PUDER, K. S., & COTTON, D. B. (1993). Embryoscopy and fetoscopy. *Obstetrics and Gynecology Clinics of North America, 20*, 563–581.

RABINER, D. L., & COIE, J. D. (1989). Effect of expectancy inductions on rejected children's acceptance by unfamiliar peers. *Developmental Psychology, 25*, 450–457.

RABINER, D. L., KEANE, S. P., & MACKINNON-LEWIS, C. (1993). Children's beliefs about familiar and unfamiliar peers in relation to their sociometric status. *Developmental Psychology, 29*, 236–243.

RADIN, N. (1994). Primary caregiving fathers in intact families. In A. E. Gottfried & A. W. Gottfried (Eds.), *Redefining families: Implications for children's development* (pp. 11–54). New York: Plenum.

RADZISZEWSKA, B., & ROGOFF, B. (1988). Influence of adult and peer collaboration on the development of children's planning skills. *Developmental Psychology, 24*, 840–848.

RAFFERTY, Y. (1995). The legal rights and educational problems of homeless children and youth. *Educational Evaluation and Policy Analysis, 17*, 39–61.

RAFFERTY, Y., & SHINN, M. (1991). The impact of homelessness on children. *American Psychologist, 46*, 1170–1179.

RÄIHÄ. N. C. R., & AXELSSON, I. E. (1995). Protein nutrition

during infancy. *Pediatric Clinics of North America, 42*, 745–763.

RALOFF, J. (1995). More ways mother's milk fights disease. *Science News, 147*, 231.

RAMIREZ, J. D., YUEN, S. D., RAMEY, D. R., & PASTA, D. (1991). *Longitudinal study of structured English immersion strategy, early-exist and late-exist transitional bilingual education programs for language minority: Final Report* (Vols. 1 & 2). San Mateo, CA: Aguirre International.

RAMSAY, M., GISEL, E. G., & BOUTRY, M. (1993). Nonorganic failure to thrive: Growth failure secondary to feeding-skills disorder. *Developmental Medicine and Child Neurology, 35*, 285–297.

RAND, Y., & KANIEL, S. (1987). Group administration of the LPAD. In C. S. Lidz (Ed.), *Dynamic assessment: An interactional approach to evaluating learning potential* (pp. 196–214). New York: Guilford.

RAPPAPORT, L. (1993). The treatment of nocturnal enuresis—where are we now? *Pediatrics, 92*, 465–466.

RAPPORT, M. D., & KELLY, K. L. (1993). Psychostimulant effects on learning and cognitive function in children with attention deficit hyperactivity disorder: Findings and implications. In J. L. Matson (Ed.), *Hyperactivity in children: A handbook* (pp. 97–136). Boston: Allyn and Bacon.

RAST, M., & MELTZOFF, A. N. (1995). Memory and representation in young children with Down syndrome: Exploring deferred imitation and object permanence. *Development and Psychopathology, 7*, 393–407.

RATCLIFFE, S. G., PAN, H., & MCKIE, M. (1992). Growth during puberty in the XYY boy. *Annals of Human Biology, 19*, 579–587.

RATNER, N., & BRUNER, J. S. (1978). Social exchange and the acquisition of language. *Journal of Child Language, 5*, 391–402.

RATNER, N. B. (1997). Atypical language development. In J. Berko Gleason (Ed.), *The development of language* (4th ed., pp. 348–397). Boston: Allyn and Bacon.

RAYNER, K., & POLLATSEK, A. (1989). *The psychology of reading.* Englewood Cliffs, NJ: Prentice-Hall.

READ, C. R. (1991). Achievement and career choices: Comparisons of males and females. *Roeper Review, 13,* 188–193.

READ, M. (1968). *Children of their fathers: Growing up among the Ngoni of Malawi.* New York: Holt, Rinehart & Winston.

REDL, F. (1966). *When we deal with children.* New York: Free Press.

REES, M. (1993). Menarche: When and why? *Lancet, 342,* 1375–1376.

REICH, P. A. (1986). *Language development.* Englewood Cliffs, NJ: Prentice-Hall.

REIL, M. (1992). Making connections from urban schools. *Education and Urban Society, 24,* 477–488.

REIMER, M. (1996). "Sinking into the ground": The development and consequences of shame in adolescence. *Developmental Review, 16,* 321–363.

REISER, J., YONAS, A., & WIKNER, K. (1976). Radial localization of odors by human neonates. *Child Development, 47,* 856–859.

REISMAN, J. E. (1987). Touch, motion, and proprioception. In P. Salapatek & L. Cohen (Eds.), *Handbook of infant perception: Vol. 1. From sensation to perception* (pp. 265–303). Orlando, FL: Academic Press.

REMEZ, L. (1997). Planned home birth can be as safe as hospital delivery for women with low-risk pregnancies. *Family Planning Perspectives, 29,* 141–143.

RENNINGER, K. A. (1998). Developmental psychology and instruction: Issues from and for practice. In I. Sigel & K. A. Renninger (Eds.), *Handbook of child psychology: Vol. 4. Child psychology and practice* (pp. 211–274). New York: Wiley.

REPACHOLI, B. M., & GOPNIK, A. (1997). Early reasoning about desires: Evidence from 14- and 18-month-olds. *Developmental Psychology, 33,* 12–21.

REPKE, J. T. (1992). Drug supplementation in pregnancy. *Current Opinion in Obstetrics and Gynecology, 4,* 802–806.

RESNICK, L. B. (1989). Developing mathematical knowledge. *American Psychologist, 44,* 162–169.

RESNICK, R. (1988). Introduction to Postterm Gestation: A symposium. *Journal of Reproductive Medicine, 33,* 249–251.

RESSLER, E. M. (1993). *Children in war.* New York: United Nations Children's Fund.

REST, J. R. (1979). *Development in judging moral issues.* Minnea-

polis: University of Minnesota Press.

REST, J. R., & NARVAEZ, D. (1991). The college experience and moral development. In W. M. Kurtines & J. L. Gewirtz (Eds.), *Handbook of moral behavior and development* (Vol. 2, pp. 229–245). Hillsdale, NJ: Erlbaum.

REYNOLDS, A. (1992). Comparing measures of parental involvement and their effects on academic achievement. *Early Childhood Research Quarterly, 7,* 441–462.

REZNICK, J. S., & GOLDFIELD, B. A. (1992). Rapid change in lexical development in comprehension and production. *Developmental Psychology, 28,* 406–413.

RICARD, M., & KAMBERK-KILICCI, M. (1995). Children's empathic responses to emotional complexity. *International Journal of Behavioral Development, 18,* 211–225.

RICCIARDELLI, L. A. (1992). Bilingualism and cognitive development: Relation to threshold theory. *Journal of Psycholinguistic Research, 21,* 301–316.

RICCIO, C. A., HYND, G. W., COHEN, M. J., & GONZALEZ, J. J. (1993). Neurological basis of attention deficit hyperactivity disorder. *Exceptional Children, 60,* 118–124.

RICCIUTI, H. N. (1993). Nutrition and mental development. *Current Directions in Psychological Science, 2,* 43–46.

RICCO, R. B. (1989). Operational thought and the acquisition of taxonomic relations involving figurative dissimilarity. *Developmental Psychology, 25,* 996–1003.

RICE, F. P. (1996). *The adolescent: Development, relationships, and culture* (8th ed.). Boston: Allyn and Bacon.

RICE, M. L., HUSTON, A. C., TRUGLIO, R., & WRIGHT, J. (1990). Words from "Sesame Street": Learning vocabulary while viewing. *Developmental Psychology, 26,* 421–428.

RICHARDS, D. D., & SIEGLER, R. S. (1986). Children's understandings of the attributes of life. *Journal of Experimental Child Psychology, 42,* 1–22.

RICHARDS, M. H., & DUCKETT, E. (1994). The relationship of maternal employment to early adolescent daily experience with and without parents. *Child Development, 65,* 225–236.

RICHARDS-COLOCINO, N., MCKENZIE, P., & NEWTON, R. R. (1996). Project Success:

Comprehensive intervention services for middle school high-risk youth. *Journal of Adolescent Research, 11,* 130–163.

RICHARDSON, G. A., HAMEL, S. C., GOLDSCHMIDT, L., & DAY, N. L. (1996). The effects of prenatal cocaine use on neonatal neurobehavioral status. *Neurotoxicology and Teratology, 18,* 519–528.

RICHARDSON, S. A., KOLLER, H., & KATZ, M. (1986). Factors leading to differences in the school performance of boys and girls. *Developmental and Behavioral Pediatrics, 7,* 49–55.

RICHGELS, D. J., MCGEE, L. M., & SLATON, E. A. (1989). Teaching expository text structure in reading and writing. In K. D. Muth (Ed.), *Children's comprehension of text* (pp. 167–184). Newark, DE: International Reading Association.

RICHMAN, A. L., MILLER, P. M., & LEVINE, R. A. (1992). Cultural and educational variations in maternal responsiveness. *Developmental Psychology, 28,* 614–621.

RICHMOND, J., & AYOUB, C. C. (1993). Evolution of early intervention philosophy. In D. M. Bryant & M. A. Graham (Eds.), *Implementing early intervention* (pp. 1–17). New York: Guilford.

RICKEL, A. U., & BECKER, E. (1997). *Keeping children from harm's way.* Washington, DC: American Psychological Association.

RIDDERINKHOF, K. R., & MOLEN, M. W. VAN DER (1997). Mental resources, processing speed, and inhibitory control: A developmental perspective. *Biological Psychology, 45,* 241–261.

RIESE, M. L. (1987). Temperament stability between the neonatal period and 24 months. *Developmental Psychology, 23,* 216–222.

RIVARA, F. P. (1995). Developmental and behavioral issues in childhood injury prevention. *Developmental and Behavioral Pediatrics, 16,* 362–370.

RIVARA, F. P., THOMPSON, D. C., THOMPSON, R. S., ROGERS, L. W., ALEXANDER, B., FELIX, D., & BERGMAN, A. B. (1994). The Seattle children's bike helmet campaign: Changes in helmet use and head injury admissions. *Pediatrics, 93,* 467–469.

ROAZZI, A., & BRYANT, P. (1997). Explicitness and conservation:

Social class differences. *International Journal of Behavioral Development, 21,* 51–70.

ROBERTON, M. A. (1984). Changing motor patterns during childhood. In J. R. Thomas (Ed.), *Motor development during childhood and adolescence* (pp. 48–90). Minneapolis, MN: Burgess.

ROBERTON, M. A., & HALVERSON, L. E. (1988). The development of locomotor coordination: Longitudinal change and invariance. *Journal of Motor Behavior, 20,* 197–241.

ROBERTS, J. E., BURCHINAL, M. R., & CAMPBELL, F. (1994). Otitis media in early childhood and patterns of intellectual development and later academic performance. *Journal of Pediatric Psychology, 19,* 347–367.

ROBERTS, M. C., ALEXANDER, K., & KNAPP, L. G. (1990). Motivating children to use safety belts: A program combining rewards and "flash for life." *Journal of Community Psychology, 18,* 110–119.

ROBERTS, M. C., & FANURIK, D. (1986). Rewarding elementary schoolchildren for their use of safety belts. *Health Psychology, 5,* 185–196.

ROBERTS, M. C., FANURIK, D., & WILSON, D. R. (1988). A community program to reward children's use of seat belts. *American Journal of Community Psychology, 16,* 395–407.

ROBERTS, M. C., & TURNER, D. S. (1986). Rewarding parents for their children's use of safety seats. *Journal of Pediatric Psychology, 11,* 25–36.

ROBERTS, R. J., JR., & AMAN, C. J. (1993). Developmental differences in giving directions: Spatial frames of reference and mental rotation. *Child Development, 64,* 1258–1270.

ROBERTS, W., & STRAYER, J. (1996). Empathy, emotional expressiveness, and prosocial behavior. *Child Development, 67,* 449–470.

ROBINSON, E. J. (1981). The child's understanding of inadequate messages and communication failure: A problem of ignorance or egocentrism? In W. P. Dickson (Ed.), *Children's oral communication skills* (pp. 167–188). New York: Academic Press.

ROBINSON, J. L., KAGAN, J., REZNICK, J. S., & CORLEY, R. (1992). The heritability of inhibited and uninhibited behavior: A twin study.

Developmental Psychology, 28, 1030–1037.

ROBINSON, T. N., KILLEN, J. D., LITT, I. F., HAMMER, L. D., WILSON, D. M., HAYDEL, K. F., HAYWARD, C., & TAYLOR, C. B. (1996). Ethnicity and body dissatisfaction: Are Hispanic and Asian girls at increased risk for eating disorders? *Journal of Adolescent Health, 19,* 384–393.

ROCHAT, P. (1989). Object manipulation and exploration in 2- to 5-month-old infants. *Developmental Psychology, 25,* 871–884.

ROCHAT, P. (1992). Self-sitting and reaching in 5- to 8-month-old infants: The impact of posture and its development on early eye–hand coordination. *Journal of Motor Behavior, 24,* 210–220.

ROCHAT, P., & GOUBET, N. (1995). Development of sitting and reaching in 5- to 6-month-old infants. *Infant Behavior and Development, 18,* 53–68.

ROCHE, A. F. (1979). Secular trends in stature, weight, and maturation. In A. F. Roche (Ed.), Secular trends in human growth, maturation, and development. *Monographs of the Society for Research in Child Development, 44*(3–4, Serial No. 179).

ROCHE, A. F. (1981). The adipocyte-number hypothesis. *Child Development, 52,* 31–43.

ROCHELEAU, B. (1995). Computer use by school-age children: Trends, patterns, and predictors. *Journal of Educational Computing Research, 12,* 1–17.

RODERICK, M. (1994). Grade retention and school dropout: Investigating the association. *American Educational Research Journal, 31,* 729–759.

ROFFWARG, H. P., MUZIO, J. N., & DEMENT, W. C. (1966). Ontogenetic development of the human sleep–dream cycle. *Science, 152,* 604–619.

ROGERS, L., RESNICK, M. D., MITCHELL, J. E., & BLUM, R. W. (1997). The relationship between socioeconomic status and eating disordered behaviors in a community sample of adolescent girls. *International Journal of Eating Disorders, 22,* 15–23.

ROGGMAN, L. A., LANGLOIS, J. H., HUBBS-TAIT, L., & RIESER-DANNER, L. A. (1994). Infant day-care, attachment, and the "file drawer problem." *Child Development, 65,* 1429–1443.

ROGOFF, B. (1986). The development of strategic use of context in spatial memory. In M. Perlmutter (Ed.), *Perspectives on intellectual development* (pp. 107–123). Hillsdale, NJ: Erlbaum.

ROGOFF, B. (1990). *Apprenticeship in thinking.* New York: Oxford University Press.

ROGOFF, B. (1996). Developmental transitions in children's participation in sociocultural activities. In A. J. Sameroff & M. M.. Haith (Eds.), *The five to seven year shift: The age of reason and responsibility,* (pp. 273–294). Chicago: University of Chicago Press.

ROGOFF, B. (1998). Cognition as a collaborative process. In D. Kuhn & R. S. Siegler (Eds.), *Handbook of child psychology: Vol. 1. Theoretical models of human development* (5th ed., pp. 679–744). New York: Wiley.

ROGOFF, B., & CHAVAJAY, P. (1995). What's become of research on the cultural basis of cognitive development? *American Psychologist, 50,* 859–877.

ROGOFF, B., MALKIN, C., & GILBRIDE, K. (1984). Interaction with babies as guidance in development. In B. Rogoff & J. V. Wertsch (Eds.), *New directions for child development* (No. 23, pp. 31–44). San Francisco: Jossey-Bass.

ROGOFF, B., & MORELLI, G. (1989). Culture and American children: Section introduction. *American Psychologist, 44,* 341–342.

ROGOFF, B., MOSIER, C., MISTRY, J., & GÖNCÜ, A. (1993). Toddlers' guided participation with their caregivers in cultural activity. In E. A. Forman, N. Minick, & C. A. Stone (Eds.), *Contexts for learning* (pp. 230–253). New York: Oxford University Press.

ROHNER, R. P., & ROHNER, E. C. (1981). Parental acceptance–rejection and parental control: Cross-cultural codes. *Ethnology, 20,* 245–260.

ROMAINE, S. (1984). *The language of children and adolescents: The acquisition of communicative competence.* Oxford, England: Blackwell.

ROMANS, S. M., ROELTGEN, D. P., KUSHNER, H., & ROSS, J. L. (1997). Executive function in girls with Turner's syndrome. *Developmental Neuropsychology, 13,* 23–40.

ROOPNARINE, J. L., HOSSAIN, Z., GILL, P., & BROPHY, H.

(1994). Play in the East Indian context. In J. L. Roopnarine, J. E. Johnson, & F. H. Hooper (Eds.), *Children's play in diverse cultures* (pp. 9-30). Albany, NY: SUNY Press.

ROOPNARINE, J. L., TALUKDER, E., JAIN, D., JOSHI, P., & SRIVASTAV, P. (1990). Characteristics of holding, patterns of play, and social behaviors between parents and infants in New Delhi, India. *Developmental Psychology, 26,* 667–673.

ROSA, R. W. (1993). Retinoid embryopathy in humans. In G. Koren (Ed.), *Retinoids in clinical practice* (pp. 77–109). New York: Marcel Dekker.

ROSCOE, B., DIANA, M. S., & BROOKS, R. H. (1987). Early, middle, and late adolescents' views on dating and factors influencing partner selection. *Adolescence, 22,* 59–68.

ROSE, R. J. (1995). Genes and human behavior. *Annual Review of Psychology, 46,* 625–654.

ROSE, S. A., & FELDMAN, J. F. (1995). Prediction of IQ and specific cognitive abilities at 11 years from infancy measures. *Developmental Psychology, 31,* 685–696.

ROSE, S. A., & FELDMAN, J. F. (1997). Memory and speed: Their role in the relation of infant information processing to later IQ. *Child Development, 68,* 610–620.

ROSEN, A. B., & ROZIN, P. (1993). Now you see it, now you don't: The preschool child's conception of invisible particles in the context of dissolving. *Developmental Psychology, 29,* 300–311.

ROSEN, K. S., & ROTHBAUM, F. (1993). Quality of parental caregiving and security of attachment. *Developmental Psychology, 29,* 358–376.

ROSEN, M. G., & DICKINSON, J. C. (1992). Management of post-term pregnancy. *New England Journal of Medicine, 326,* 1628–1629.

ROSEN, W. D., ADAMSON, L. B., & BAKEMAN, R. (1992). An experimental investigation of infant social referencing: Mothers' messages and gender differences. *Developmental Psychology, 28,* 1172–1178.

ROSENBERG, M. (1979). *Conceiving the self.* New York: Basic Books.

ROSENBERG, S. (1988). Self and others: Studies in social personality and autobiography. In L. Berkowitz (Ed.), *Advances in experimental social psychology*

(Vol. 21, pp. 56–96). New York: Academic Press.

ROSENBLATT, J. S., & LEHRMAN, D. (1963). Maternal behavior of the laboratory rat. In H. R. Rheingold (Ed.). *Maternal behavior in mammals* (pp. 8–57). New York: Wiley.

ROSENGREN, K. S., & HICKLING, A. K. (1994). Seeing is believing: Children's explanations of commonplace, magical, and extraordinary transformations. *Child Development, 65,* 1605–1626.

ROSENSHINE, B., & MEISTER, C. (1994). Reciprocal teaching: A review of nineteen experimental studies. *Review of Educational Research, 64,* 479–530.

ROSKOS, K., & NEUMAN, S. B. (1998). Play as an opportunity for literacy. In In O. N. Saracho & B. Spodek (Eds.), *Multiple perspectives on play in early childhood education* (pp. 100–115). Albany: State University of New York Press.

ROSS, H. S., CONANT, C., CHEYNE, J. A., & ALEVIZOS, E. (1992). Relationships and alliances in the social interactions of kibbutz toddlers. *Social Development, 1,* 1–17.

ROTHBART, M. K., & BATES, J. E. (1998). Temperament. In N. Eisenberg (Ed.), *Handbook of child psychology: Vol. 3. Social, emotional, and personality development* (5th ed., pp. 105–176). New York: Wiley.

ROTHBART, M. K., & MAURO, J. A. (1990). Quesionnaire approaches to the study of infant temperament. In J. W. Fagen & J. Colombo (Eds.), *Individual differences in infancy: Reliability, stability and prediction* (pp. 411–429). Hillsdale, NJ: Erlbaum.

ROTHERAM-BORUS, M. J., & FERNANDEZ, I. (1995). Sexual orientation and developmental challenges experienced by gay and lesbian youths. *Suicide & Life-Threatening Behavior, 25,* 26–34.

ROTHMAN, K. J., MOORE, L. L., SINGER, M. R., NGUYEN, U. S., MANNENO, S., & MILUNSKY, A. (1995). Teratogenicity of high vitamin A intake. *New England Journal of Medicine, 333,* 1369–1373.

ROURKE, B. P. (1988). Socioemotional disturbances of learning disabled children. *Journal of Consulting and Clinical Psychology, 56,* 801–810.

ROUSSEAU, J. J. (1955). *Emile.* New York: Dutton. (Original work published 1762)

ROVEE-COLLIER, C. K. (1987). Learning and memory. In J. D. Osofsky (Ed.), *Handbook of infant development* (2nd ed., pp. 98–148). New York: Wiley.

ROVEE-COLLIER, C. K., & BHATT, R. S. (1993). Evidence of long-term memory in infancy. *Annals of Child Development, 9,* 1–45.

ROVEE-COLLIER, C. K., & HAYNE, H. (1987). Reactivation of infant memory: Implications for cognitive development. In H. W. Reese (Ed.), *Advances in child development and behavior* (Vol. 20, pp. 185–238). New York: Academic Press.

ROVEE-COLLIER, C. K., & SHYI, G. (1992). A functional and cognitive analysis of infant long-term retention. In C. J. Brainerd, M. L. Howe, & V. Reyna (Eds.), *Development of long-term retention* (pp. 3–55). New York: Springer-Verlag.

ROVET, J., NETLEY, C., KEENAN, M., BAILEY, J., & STEWART, D. (1996). The psychoeducational profile of boys with Klinefelter syndrome. *Journal of Learning Disabilities, 29,* 180–196.

ROYCE, J. M., DARLINGTON, R. B., & MURRAY, H. W. (1983). Pooled analyses: Findings across studies. In Consortium for Longitudinal Studies (Ed.), *As the twig is bent: Lasting effects of preschool programs* (pp. 411–459). Hillsdale, NJ: Erlbaum.

RUBIN, K., BUKOWSKI, W., & PARKER, J. G. (1998). Peer interactions, relationships, and groups. In N. Eisenberg (Ed.), *Handbook of child psychology: Vol. 3. Social, emotional, and personality development* (5th ed., pp. 619–700). New York: Wiley.

RUBIN, K. H., & COPLAN, R. J. (1998). Social and nonsocial play in childhood: An individual differences perspective. In O. N. Saracho & B. Spodek (Eds.), *Multiple perspectives on play in early childhood education* (pp. 144–170). Albany, NY: State University of New York Press.

RUBIN, K. H., FEIN, G. G., & VANDENBERG, B. (1983). Play. In E. M. Hetherington (Ed.), *Handbook of child psychology: Vol. 4. Socialization, personality, and social development* (4th ed., pp. 693–744). New York: Wiley.

RUBIN, K. H., HASTINGS, P. D., STEWART, S. L., HENDERSON, H. A., & CHEN, X. (1997). The consistency and concomitants of inhibition: Some of the children, all of the time. *Child Development, 68,* 467–483.

RUBIN, K. H., STEWART, S. L., & COPLAN, R. J. (1995). Social withdrawal in childhood: Conceptual and empirical perspectives. In T. H. Ollendick & R. J. Prinz (Eds.), *Advances in clinical child psychology* (Vol. 17, pp. 157–196). New York: Plenum.

RUBIN, K. H., WATSON, K. S., & JAMBOR, T. W. (1978). Free-play behaviors in preschool and kindergarten children. *Child Development, 49,* 539–536.

RUBLE, D. N., & FREY, K. S. (1991). Changing patterns of comparative behavior as skills are acquired: A functional model of self-evaluation. In J. Suls & T. A. Wills (Eds.), *Social comparison: Contemporary theory and research* (pp. 70–112). Hillsdale, NJ: Erlbaum.

RUBLE, D. N., & MARTIN, C. L. (1998). Gender development. In N. Eisenberg (Ed.), *Handbook of child psychology: Vol. 3. Social, emotional, and personality development* (pp. 933–1016). New York: Wiley.

RUFF, H. A., & LAWSON, K. R. (1990). Development of sustained, focused attention in young children during free play. *Developmental Psychology, 26,* 85–93.

RUFF, H. A., LAWSON, K. R., PARRINELLO, R., & WEISSBERG, R. (1990). Long-term stability of individual differences in sustained attention in the early years. *Child Development, 61,* 60–75.

RUFF, H. A., & ROTHBART, M. K. (1996). *Attention in early development.* New York: Oxford University Press.

RUFFMAN, T., PERNER, J., NAITO, M., PARKIN, L., & CLEMENTS, W. A. (1998). Older (but not younger) siblings facilitate false belief understanding. *Developmental Psychology, 34,* (161-174).

RUFFMAN, T., PERNER, J., OLSON, D. R., & DOHERTY, M. (1993). Reflecting on scientific thinking: Children's understanding of the hypothesis–evidence relation. *Child Development, 64,* 1617–1636.

RUMBERGER, R. W. (1990). Second chance for high school dropouts: Dropout recovery programs in the United States. In D. Inbar (Ed.), *Second chance in education: An interdisciplinary and international perspective* (pp. 227–250). Philadelphia: Falmer.

RUNCO, M. A. (1992). Children's divergent thinking and creative ideation. *Developmental Review, 12,* 233–264.

RUSHTON, H. G. (1989). Nocturnal enuresis: Epidemiology, evaluation, and currently available treatment options. *Journal of Pediatrics, 114,* 691–696.

RUSSELL, J. A. (1990). The preschooler's understanding of the causes and consequences of emotion. *Child Development, 61,* 1872–1881.

RUTTER, M. (1979). Protective factors in children's responses to stress and disadvantage. In M. W. Kent & J. Rolf (Eds.), *Primary prevention of psychopathology: Vol 3. Social competence in children* (pp. 49–74). Hanover, NH: University Press of New England.

RUTTER, M. (1985). Resilience in the face of adversity: Protective factors and resistance to psychiatric disorder. *British Journal of Psychiatry, 147,* 598–611.

RUTTER, M. (1987). Psychosocial resilience and protective mechanisms. *American Journal of Orthopsychiatry, 57,* 316–331.

RUTTER, M. (1996). Maternal deprivation. In M. H. Bornstein (Ed.), *Handbook of parenting: Vol. 4. Applied and practical parenting* (pp. 3–31). Mahwah, NJ: Erlbaum.

RYYNÄNEN, M., KIRKINEN, P., MANNERMAA, A., & SAARIKOSKI, S. (1995). Carrier diagnosis of the fragile X syndrome —a challenge in antenatal clinics. *American Journal of Obstetrics and Gynecology, 172,* 1236–1239.

SAARNI, C. (1993). Socialization of emotion. In M. Lewis & J. M. Haviland (Eds.), *Handbook of emotions* (pp. 435–446). New York: Guilford.

SAARNI, C. (1997). Emotional competence and self-regulation in childhood. In P. Salovey & D. J. Sluyter (Eds.), *Emotional development and emotional intelligence* (pp. 35–66). New York: Basic Books.

SAARNI, C., MUMME, D. L., & CAMPOS, J. J. (1998). Emotional development: Action, communication, and understanding. In N. Eisenberg (Ed.), *Handbook of child psychology: Vol. 3. Social, emotional, and personality development* (5th ed., pp. 237–309). New York: Wiley.

SACKS, C. H., & MERGENDOLLER, J. R. (1997). The relationship between teachers' theoretical orientation toward reading and student outcomes in kindergarten children with different initial reading abilities. *American Educational Research Journal, 34,* 721–739.

SADEH, A. (1997). Sleep and melatonin in infants: A preliminary study. *Sleep, 20,* 185–191.

SADLER, L. S. (1991). Depression in adolescents: Context, manifestations, and clinical management. *Nursing Clinics of North America, 26,* 559–572.

SADLER, T. W. (1995). *Langman's medical embryology* (7th ed.). Baltimore: Williams & Wilkins.

SAFYER, A. W., LEAHY, B. H., & COLAN, N. B. (1995). The impact of work on adolescent development. *Families in Society, 76,* 38–45.

SALAPATEK, P. (1975). Pattern perception in early infancy. In L. B. Cohen & P. Salapatek (Eds.), *Infant perception: From sensation to cognition* (pp. 133–248). New York: Academic Press.

SAMEROFF, A. J., SEIFER, R., BALDWIN, A., & BALDWIN, C. (1993). Stability of intelligence from preschool to adolescence: The influence of social and family risk factors. *Child Development, 64,* 80–97.

SAMPSON, R. J., & LAUB, J. H. (1993). *Crime in the making: Pathways and turning points through life.* Cambridge, MA: Harvard University Press.

SAMSON, L. F. (1988). Perinatal viral infections and neonates. *Journal of Perinatal Neonatal Nursing, 1,* 56–65.

SAMUELS, M., & SAMUELS, N. (1986). *The well pregnancy book.* New York: Summit.

SAMUELS, M., & SAMUELS, N. (1996). *The new well pregnancy book.* New York: Fireside.

SAMUELS, S. J. (1985). Toward a theory of automatic information processing in reading: Updated. In H. Singer & R. B. Ruddell (Eds.), *Theoretical models and processes of reading* (3rd ed., pp. 719–721). Newark, DE: International Reading Association.

SANDBERG, D. E., BROOK, A. E., & CAMPOS, S. P. (1994). Short stature: A psychosocial burden requiring growth hormone therapy? *Pediatrics, 94,* 832–840.

SANDERS, O. (1997, August). *Keeping ourselves safe.* Public lecture, Illinois State University, Normal, IL.

SANDERSON, J. A., & SIEGAL, M. (1988). Conceptions of moral and social rules in rejected and nonrejected preschoolers. *Journal of Clinical Child Psychology, 17,* 66–72.

SANDQVIST, K. (1992). Sweden's sex-role scheme and commitment to gender equality. In S. Lewis, D. N. Izraeli, & H. Hottsmans (Eds.), *Dual-earner families: International perspectives.* London: Sage.

SANFORD, J. P. (1985). *Comprehension-level tasks in secondary classrooms.* Austin: Research and Development Center for Teacher Education, University of Texas at Austin.

SANSAVINI, A., BERTONCINI, J., & GIOVANELLI, G. (1997). Newborns discriminate the rhythm of multisyllabic stressed words. *Developmental Psychology, 33,* 3–11.

SAUDINO, K., & EATON, W. O. (1991). Infant temperament and genetics: An objective twin study. *Child Development, 62,* 1167–1174.

SAVAGE-RUMBAUGH, E. S., MURPHY, J., SEVCIK, R. A., BRAKKE, K. E., WILLIAMS, S. L., & RUMBAUGH, D. M. (1993). Language comprehension in ape and child. *Monographs of the Society for Research in Child Development, 58* (3–4, Serial No. 233).

SAVIN-WILLIAMS, R. C. (1979). Dominance hierarchies in groups of early adolescents. *Child Development, 50,* 923–935.

SAVIN-WILLIAMS, R. C. (1996). Dating and romantic relationships among gay, lesbian, and bisexual youths. In R. C. Savin-Williams & K. M. Cohen (Eds.), *The lives of lesbians, gays, and bisexuals* (pp. 166–180). Fort Worth, TX: Harcourt Brace.

SAVIN-WILLIAMS, R. C., & BERNDT, T. J. (1990). Friendship and peer relations. In S. S. Feldman & G. R. Elliott (Eds.), *At the threshold: The developing adolescent* (pp. 277–307). Cambridge, MA: Harvard University Press.

SAXE, G. B. (1985). Effects of schooling on arithmetical understandings: Studies with Oksapmin children in Papua New Guinea. *Journal of Educational Psychology, 77,* 503–513.

SAXE, G. B. (1988, August–September). Candy selling and math learning. *Educational Researcher, 17*(6), 14–21.

SAYWITZ, K. J. (1989). Children's conceptions of the legal system: "Court is a place to play basketball." In M. P. Toglia (Eds.),

Perspectives on children's testimony (pp. 131–157). New York: Springer-Verlag.

SAYWITZ, K. J., & NATHANSON, R. (1993). Children's testimony and their perceptions of stress in and out of the courtroom. *Child Abuse & Neglect, 17,* 613–622.

SCARR, S. (1985). Constructing psychology: Making facts and fables for our times. *American Psychologist, 40,* 499–512.

SCARR, S. (1996). Individuality and community: The contrasting role of the state in family life in the United States and Sweden. *Scandinavian Journal of Psychology, 37,* 93–102.

SCARR, S., & MCCARTNEY, K. (1983). How people make their own environments: A theory of genotype → environment effects. *Child Development, 54,* 424–435.

SCARR, S., PHILLIPS, D., MCCARTNEY, K., & ABBOTT-SHIM, M. (1993). Quality of child care as an aspect of family and child care policy in the United States. *Pediatrics, 91,* 182–188.

SCARR, S., PHILLIPS, D. A., & MCCARTNEY, K. (1990). Facts, fantasies, and the future of child care in America. *Psychological Science, 1,* 26–35.

SCARR, S., & WEINBERG, R. A. (1983). The Minnesota adoption studies: Genetic differences and malleability. *Child Development, 54,* 260–267.

SCHACHAR, R., TANNOCK, R., MARRIOTT, M., & LOGAN, G. (1995). Deficient inhibitory control in attention deficit hyperactivity disorder. *Journal of Abnormal Child Psychology, 23,* 411–437.

SCHACHTER, F. F., & STONE, R. K. (1985). Difficult sibling–easy sibling: Temperament and the within-family environment. *Child Development, 56,* 1335–1344.

SCHAFFER, H. R., & EMERSON, P. E. (1964). The development of social attachments in infancy. *Monographs of the Society for Research in Child Development, 29* (3, Serial No. 94).

SCHANBERG, S., & FIELD, T. M. (1987). Sensory deprivation stress and supplemental stimulation in the rat pup and preterm human neonate. *Child Development, 58,* 1431–1447.

SCHAUBLE, L. (1996). The development of scientific reasoning in knowledge-rich contexts. *Developmental Psychology, 32,* 102–119.

SCHEIDT, P. C., HAREL, Y., TRUMBLE, A. C., JONES, D. H., OVERPECK, M. D., & BIJUR, P. E. (1995). The epidemiology of nonfatal injuries among U.S. children and youth. *American Journal of Public Health, 85,* 932–938.

SCHER, A., TIROSH, E., JAFFE, M., RUBIN, L., SADEH, A., & LAVIE, P. (1995). Sleep patterns of infants and young children in Israel. *International Journal of Behavioral Development, 18,* 701–711.

SCHIAVI, R. C., THEILGAARD, A., OWEN, D., & WHITE, D. (1984). Sex chromosome anomalies, hormones, and aggressivity. *Archives of General Psychiatry, 41,* 93–99.

SCHIFTER, T., HOFFMAN, J. M., HATTEN, H. P., & HANSON, M. W. (1994). Neuroimaging in infantile autism. *Journal of Child Neurology, 9,* 155–161.

SCHLEGEL, A. (1995). A cross-cultural approach to adolescence. *Ethos, 23,* 5–32.

SCHLEGEL, A., & BARRY, H., III. (1980). The evolutionary significance of adolescent initiation ceremonies. *American Ethnologist, 7,* 696–715.

SCHLEGEL, A., & BARRY, H., III. (1991). *Adolescence: An anthropological inquiry.* New York: Free Press.

SCHNEIDER, W. (1993). Domain-specific knowledge and memory performance in children. *Educational Psychology Review, 5,* 257–274.

SCHNEIDER, W., & BJORKLUND, D. F. (1998). Memory. In D. Kuhn & R. S. Siegler (Eds.), *Handbook of child psychology: Vol. 2. Cognition, perception, and language* (5th ed., pp. 467–521). New York: Wiley.

SCHNEIDER, W., & PRESSLEY, M. (1989). *Memory development between 2 and 20.* New York: Springer-Verlag.

SCHNEIDER, W., & PRESSLEY, M. (1997). *Memory development between two and twenty* (2nd ed.). Mahwah, NJ: Erlbaum.

SCHNEIRLA, T. C., ROSENBLATT, J. S., & TOBACH, E. (1963). Maternal behavior in the cat. In H. R. Rheingold (Ed.), *Maternal behavior in mammals* (pp. 122–168). New York: Wiley.

SCHOLL, T. O., HEIDIGER, M. L., & BELSKY, D. (1996). Prenatal care and maternal health during adolescent pregnancy: A review and meta-analysis. *Journal of Adolescent Health, 15,* 444–456.

SCHOLNICK, E. K. (1995, Fall). Knowing and constructing plans. *SRCD Newsletter,* pp. 1–2, 17.

SCHONFELD, D. J., & SMILANSKY, S. (1989). A cross-cultural comparison of Israeli and American children's death concepts. *Death Studies, 13,* 593–604.

SCHOTHORST, P. F., & VAN ENGELAND, H. (1996). Long-term behavioral sequelae of prematurity. *Journal of the American Academy of Child and Adolescent Psychiatry, 35,* 175–183.

SCHROEDER, K. A., BLOOD, L. L., & MALUSO, D. (1993). Gender differences and similarities between male and female undergraduate students regarding expectations for career and family roles. *College Student Journal, 27,* 237–249.

SCHULTZ, R. T., CHO, N. K., STAIB, L. H., & KIER, L. E. (1994). Brain morphology in normal and dyslexic children: The influence of sex and age. *Annals of Neurology, 35,* 732–742.

SCHUNK, D. H. (1983). Ability versus effort attributional feedback: Differential effects on self-efficacy and achievement. *Journal of Educational Psychology, 75,* 848–856.

SCHUNK, D. H., & ZIMMERMAN, B. J. (Eds.). (1994). *Self-regulation of learning and performance.* Englewood Cliffs, NJ: Erlbaum.

SCHWANENFLUGEL, P. J., FABRICIUS, W. V., & NOYES, C. R. (1996). Developing organization of mental verbs: Evidence for the development of a constructivist theory of mind in middle childhood. *Cognitive Development, 11,* 265–294.

SCRUGGS, T. E., & MASTROPIERI, M. A. (1994). Successful mainstreaming in elementary science classes: A qualitative study of three reputational cases. *American Educational Research Journal, 31,* 785–811.

SEARS, J. T. (1991). *Growing up gay in the South: Race, gender, and journeys of the spirit.* New York: Harrington Park Press.

SEARS, R. R., MACCOBY, E. E., & LEVIN, H. (1957). *Patterns of child rearing.* New York: Harper & Row.

SEBALD, H. (1986). Adolescents' shifting orientation toward parents and peers: A curvilinear trend over recent decades. *Journal of Marriage and the Family, 48,* 5–13.

SEEFELDT, V. (1996). The concept of readiness applied to the acquisition of motor skills. In F. L. Smoll & R. E. Smith (Eds.), *Children and youth in sport: A biopsychological perspective* (pp. 49–56). Dubuque, IA: Brown & Benchmark.

SEIDMAN, D. S., LAOR, A., GALE, R., STEVENSON, D. K., MASHIACH, S., & DANON, Y. L. (1991). Long-term effects of vacuum and forceps deliveries. *Epidemiology, 337,* 1583–1585.

SEIDMAN, E., ALLEN, L., ABER, J. L., MITCHELL, C., & FEINMAN, J. (1994). The impact of school transitions in early adolescence on the self-system and perceived social context of poor urban youth. *Child Development, 65,* 507–522.

SEIDMAN, E., & FRENCH, S. E. (1997). Normative school transitions among urban adolescents: When, where, and how to intervene. In H. J. Walberg, O. Reyes, & R. P. Weissberg (Eds.), *Children and youth: Interdisciplinary perspectives* (pp. 166–189). Thousand Oaks, CA: Sage.

SEIFER, R., & SCHILLER, M. (1995). The role of parenting sensitivity, infant temperament, and dyadic interaction in attachment theory and assessment. In E. Waters, B. E. Vaughn, G. Posada, & K. Kondo-Ikemura K. (Eds.), *Caregiving, cultural, and cognitive perspectives on secure-base behavior and working models: New growing points of attachment theory and research. Monographs of the Society for Research in Child Development, 60* (2–3, Serial No. 244).

SEIFER, R., SCHILLER, M., SAMEROFF, A. J., RESNICK, S., & RIORDAN, K. (1996). Attachment, maternal sensitivity, and infant temperament during the first year of life. *Developmental Psychology, 32,* 12–25.

SELIGMANN, J. (1994, May 2). The pressure to lose. *Newsweek,* pp. 60–61.

SELIGMAN, M. E. P. (1975). *Helplessness: On depression, development, and death.* San Francisco: Freeman.

SELMAN, R. L. (1976). Social-cognitive understanding: A guide to educational and clinical practice. In T. Lickona (Ed.), *Moral development and behavior: Theory, research, and social issues* (pp. 299–316). New York: Holt, Rinehart, & Winston.

SELMAN, R. L. (1980). *The growth of interpersonal understanding.* New York: Academic Press.

SELMAN, R. L., & BYRNE, D. F. (1974). A structural-developmental analysis of levels of role taking in middle childhood. *Child Development, 45,* 803–806.

SELTZER, M. M., & RYFF, C. D. (1994). Parenting across the life span: The normative and non-normative cases. In D. L. Featherman, R. M. Lerner, & M. Perlmutter (Eds.), *Life-span development and behavior* (pp. 1–40). Hillsdale, NJ: Erlbaum.

SERBIN, L. A., POWLISHTA, K. K., & GULKO, J. (1993). The development of sex typing in middle childhood. *Monographs of the Society for Research in Child Development, 58*(2, Serial No. 232).

SERDULA, M. K., IVERY, D., COATES, R. J., FREEDMAN, D. S., WILLIAMSON, D. F., & BYERS, T. (1993). Do obese children become obese adults? A review of the literature. *Preventive Medicine, 22,* 167–177.

SEVER, J. L. (1983). Maternal infections. In C. C. Brown (Ed.), *Childhood learning disabilities and prenatal risk* (pp. 31–38). New York: Johnson & Johnson.

SHAHAR, S. (1990). *Childhood in the Middle Ages.* London: Routledge & Kegan Paul.

SHAINESS, N. (1961). A re-evaluation of some aspects of femininity through a study of menstruation: A preliminary report. *Comparative Psychiatry, 2,* 20–26.

SHALALA, D. E. (1993). Giving pediatric immunizations the priority they deserve. *Journal of the American Medical Association, 269,* 1844–1845.

SHANTZ, C. U. (1987). Conflicts between children. *Child Development, 58,* 283–305.

SHAVER, P., FURMAN, W., & BUHRMESTER, D. (1985). Transition to college: Network changes, social skills, and loneliness. In S. Duck & D. Perlman (Eds.), *Understanding personal relationships: An interdisciplinary approach* (pp. 193–219). London: Sage.

SHEDLER, J., & BLOCK, J. (1990). Adolescent drug use and psychological health: A longitudinal inquiry. *American Psychologist, 45,* 612–630.

SHELOV, S. P. (1993). *Caring for your baby and young child: Birth to age 5.* New York: Bantam.

SHETH, S. S., & MALPANI, A. N. (1997). Inappropriate use of new technology—impact on women's health. *International Journal of Gynecology and Obstetrics, 58,* 159–165.

SHETTLES, L. B., & RORVIK, D. M. (1984). *How to choose the sex of your baby.* New York: Doubleday.

SHIELDS, P. J., & ROVEE-COLLIER, C. K. (1992). Long-term memory for context-specific category information at six months. *Child Development, 63,* 245–259.

SHILOH, S. (1996). Genetic counseling: A developing area of interest for psychologists. *Professional Psychology: Research and Practice, 27,* 475–486.

SHIMAMURA, A. P. (1995). Memory and frontal lobe function. In M. S. Gazzaniga (Ed.), *The cognitive neurosciences* (pp. 803–813). Cambridge, MA: MIT Press.

SHIME, J. (1988). Influence of prolonged pregnancy on infant development. *Journal of Reproductive Medicine, 33,* 277–284.

SHINN, M. W. (1900). *The biography of a baby.* Boston: Houghton Mifflin.

SHONKOFF, J. P. (1984). The biological substrate and physical health in middle childhood. In W. A. Collins (Ed.), *Development during middle childhood* (pp. 24–69). Washington, DC: National Academy Press.

SHURTLEFF, D. B., & LEMIRE, R. J. (1995). Epidemiology, etiologic factors, and prenatal diagnosis of open spinal dysraphism. *Neurosurgery Clinics of North America, 6,* 183–193.

SHWEDER, R. A., & HAIDT, J. (1993). The future of moral psychology: Truth, intuition, and the pluralistic way. *Psychological Science, 6,* 360–365.

SHWEDER, R. A., MAHAPATRA, M., & MILLER, J. G. (1990). Culture and moral development. In J. Stigler, R. A. Shweder, & G. Herdt (Eds.), *Cultural psychology: Essays on comparative human development* (pp. 130–204). New York: Cambridge University Press.

SIEGEL, B. (1996, Spring). Is the emperor wearing clothes? Social policy and the empirical support for full inclusion of children with disabilities in the preschool and early elementary school grades. *Social Policy Report of the Society for Research in Child Development, 10* (2–3), 2–17.

SIEGEL, M. D., FARQUHAR, C. L., & BOUCHARD, J. M. (1997). Dental sealants—who needs them? *Public Health Reports, 112,* 98–106.

SIEGLER, R. S. (1992). The other Alfred Binet. *Developmental Psychology, 28,* 179–190.

SIEGLER, R. S. (1995). How does change occur? A microgenetic study of number conservation. *Cognitive Psychology, 28,* 225–273.

SIEGLER, R. S. (1996). *Children's thinking.* (3rd ed.) Upper Saddle River, NJ: Prentice-Hall.

SIEGLER, R. S. (1996). *Emerging minds: The process of change in children's thinking.* New York: Oxford University Press.

SIEGLER, R. S. (1998). *Children's thinking* (3rd ed.). Upper Saddle River, NJ: Prentice-Hall.

SIEGLER, R. S., & CROWLEY, K. (1991). The microgenetic method: A direct means for studying cognitive development. *American Psychologist, 46,* 606–620.

SIEGLER, R. S., & CROWLEY, K. (1992). Microgenetic methods revisited. *American Psychologist, 47,* 1241–1243.

SIEGLER, R. S., & ROBINSON, M. (1982). The development of numerical understandings. In H. W. Reese & L. P. Lipsitt (Eds.), *Advances in child development and behavior* (Vol. 16, pp. 241–312). New York: Academic Press.

SIERRA, J., & KAMINSKI, R. (1995). *Children's traditional games.* Phoenix, AZ: Oryx.

SIGELMAN, C. K., MADDOCK, A., EPSTEIN, J., & CARPENTER, W. (1993). Age differences in understandings of disease causality: AIDS, colds, and cancer. *Child Development, 64,* 272–284.

SIGMAN, M. (1995). Nutrition and child development: More food for thought. *Current Directions in Psychological Science, 4,* 52–55.

SIGMAN, M., & KASARI, C. (1995). Joint attention across contexts in normal and autistic children. In C. Moore & P. J. Dunham (Eds.), *Joint attention: Its origins and role in development* (pp. 189–203). Hillsdale, NJ: Erlbaum.

SIGMAN, M., NEUMANN, C., JANSEN, A. A. J., & BWIBO, N. (1989). Cognitive abilities of Kenyan children in relation to nutrition, family characteristics, and education. *Child Development, 60,* 1462–1474.

SIGNORIELLI, N. (1993). Television, the portrayal of women, and children's attitudes. In G. L. Berry & J. K. Asamen (Eds.), *Children and television: Images in a changing sociocultural world* (pp. 229–242). Newbury Park, CA: Sage.

SILVERMAN, W. K., LA GRECA, A. M., & WASSERSTEIN, S. (1995). What do children worry about? Worries and their relation to anxiety. *Child Development, 66,* 671-686.

SIMMONS, R. G., BLACK, A., & ZHOU, Y. (1991). African-American versus white children and the transition to junior high school. *American Journal of Education, 99,* 481–520.

SIMMONS, R. G., & BLYTH, D. A. (1987). *Moving into adolescence.* New York: Aldine de Gruyter.

SIMON, R., ALTSTEIN, H., & MELLI, M. S. (1994). *The case for transracial adoption.* Washington, DC: American University Press.

SIMONS, R. L., LORENZ, R. O., CONGER, R. D., & WU, C–I. (1992). Support from spouse as a mediator and moderator of the disruptive influence of economic strain on parenting. *Child Development, 63,* 1282–1301.

SIMONS, R. L., WHITBECK, L. B., CONGER, R. D., & CHYI-IN, W. (1991). Intergenerational transmission of harsh parenting. *Developmental Psychology, 27,* 159–171.

SIMONS, R. L., WU, C., CONGER, R. D., & LORENZ, F. O. (1994). Two routes to delinquency: Differences between early and late starters in the impact of parenting and deviant peers. *Criminology, 32,* 247–274.

SIMPSON, S. A., & HARDING, A. E. (1993). Predictive testing for Huntington's disease after the gene. *Journal of Medical Genetics, 30,* 1036–1038.

SINGER, D. G., & SINGER, J. L. (1990). *The house of make-believe.* Cambridge, MA: Harvard University Press.

SITSKOORN, M. M., & SMITSMAN, A. W. (1995). Infants' perception of dynamic relations between objects: Passing through or support? *Developmental Psychology, 31,* 437–447.

SIVARD, R. L. (1996). *World military and social expenditures* (16th ed.). Leesburg, VA: WMSE.

SKINNER, B. F. (1957). *Verbal behavior.* New York: Appleton-Century-Crofts.

SKINNER, E. A. (1995). *Perceived control, motivation, and coping.* Thousand Oaks, CA: Sage.

SKINNER, E. A., & BELMONT, M. J. (1993). Motivation in the classroom: Reciprocal effects of teacher behavior and student engagement across the school year. *Journal of Educational Psychology, 85,* 571–581.

SLABY, R. G., & FREY, K. S. (1975). Development of gender constancy and selective attention to same-sex models. *Child Development, 46,* 849–856.

SLABY, R. G., ROEDELL, W. C., AREZZO, D., & HENDRIX, K. (1995). *Early violence prevention.* Washington, DC: National Association for the Education of Young Children.

SLATER, A. (1996). The organization of visual perception in early infancy. In F. Vital-Durand, J. Atkinson, & O. J. Braddick (Eds.), *Infant vision* (pp. 309–325). Oxford, England: Oxford University Press.

SLATER, A., BROWN, E., MATTOCK, A., & BORNSTEIN, M. H. (1996). Continuity and change in habituation in the first 4 months from birth. *Journal of Reproductive and Infant Psychology, 14,* 187–194.

SLATER, A. M., MATTOCK, A., & BROWN, E. (1990). Size constancy at birth: Newborn infants' responses to retinal and real size. *Journal of Experimental Child Psychology, 49,* 314–322.

SLOBIN, D. (1985). Crosslinguistic evidence for the language-making capacity. In D. Slobin (Ed.), *The cross-linguistic study of language acquisition* (Vol. 2, pp. 1157–1256). Hillsdale, NJ: Erlbaum.

SLOBIN, D. I. (1985). Cross-linguistic evidence for language-making capacity. In D. I. Slobin (Ed.), *The crosslinguistic study of language acquisition: Vol. 2. Theoretical issues* (pp. 1157–1256). Hillsdale, NJ: Erlbaum.

SMETANA, J. G. (1995a). Context, conflict, and constraint in adolescent–parent authority relationships. In M. Killen & D. Hart (Eds.), *Morality in everyday life* (pp. 225–255). New York: Cambridge University Press.

SMETANA, J. G. (1995b). Morality in context: Abstractions, ambiguities, and applications. In R. Vasta (Ed.), *Annals of child development* (Vol. 10, pp. 83–130). Greenwich, CT: JAI Press.

SMETANA, J. G., & BRAEGES, J. L. (1990). The development of toddlers' moral and conventional judgments. *Merrill-Palmer Quarterly, 36,* 329–346.

SMILEY, P. A., & DWECK, C. S. (1994). Individual differences in achievement goals among young children. *Child Development, 65,* 1723–1743.

SMITH, B. A., & BLASS, E. M. (1996). Taste-mediated calming in premature, preterm, and full-term human infants. *Developmental Psychology, 32,* 1084–1089.

SMITH, H. (1992). The detrimental health effects of ionizing radiation. *Nuclear Medicine Communications, 13,* 4–10.

SMITH, J., & PRIOR, M. (1995). Temperament and stress resilience in school-age children: A within-families study. *Journal of the American Academy of Child and Adolescent Psychiatry, 34,* 168–179.

SMITH, L. B., & KATZ, D. B. (1996). Activity-dependent processes in perceptual and cognitive development. In R. Gelman & T. K. Au (Eds.), *Perceptual and cognitive development* (pp. 414–445). San Diego: Academic Press.

SMITH, M. C. (1978). Cognizing the behavior stream: The recognition of intentional action. *Child Development, 49,* 736–743.

SMITH, P. K., & BOULTON, M. (1990). Rough-and-tumble play, aggression and dominance: Perception and behavior in children's encounters. *Human Development, 33,* 271–282.

SMITH, R. E., & SMOLL, F. L. (1996). The coach as a focus of research and intervention in youth sports. In F. L. Smoll & R. E. Smith (Eds.), *Children and youth in sport: A biopsychological perspective* (pp. 125–141). Dubuque, IA: Brown & Benchmark.

SMITH, R. E., & SMOLL, F. L. (1997). Coaching the coaches: Youth sports as a scientific and applied behavior setting. *Current Directions in Psychological Science, 6,* 16–21.

SMITH, S. (Ed.). (1995). Two-generation programs for families in poverty: A new intervention strategy. *Advances in applied developmental psychology* (Vol. 9). Norwood, NJ: Ablex.

SMOLL, F. L., & SMITH, R. E. (Eds.). (1996). *Children and youth in sport: A biopsychological perspective.* Dubuque, IA: Brown & Benchmark.

SMOLUCHA, L., & SMOLUCHA, F. (1998). The social origins of mind: Post-Piagetian perspectives on pretend play. In O. N. Saracho & B. Spodek (Eds.), *Multiple perspectives on play in early childhood education* (pp. 34–58). Albany: State University of New York Press.

SNAREY, J. (1995). In a communitarian voice: The sociological expansion of Kohlbergian theory, research, and practice. In W. M. Kurtines & J. L. Gewirtz (Eds.), *Moral development: An introduction* (pp. 109–134). Boston: Allyn and Bacon.

SNAREY, J. R., REIMER, J., & KOHLBERG, L. (1985). The development of social–moral reasoning among kibbutz adolescents: A longitudinal cross-cultural study. *Developmental Psychology, 21,* 3–17.

SNIDMAN, N., KAGAN, J., RIORDAN, L., & SHANNON, D. C. (1995). Cardiac function and behavioral reactivity. *Psychophysiology, 32,* 199–207.

SNOW, C. E. (1993). Families as social contexts for literacy development. In C. Daiute (Ed.), *New directions for child development* (No. 61, pp. 11–24). San Francisco: Jossey-Bass.

SOCIETY FOR RESEARCH IN CHILD DEVELOPMENT. (1993). Ethical standards for research with children. In *Directory of Members* (pp. 337–339). Ann Arbor, MI: Author.

SODIAN, B., TAYLOR, C., HARRIS, P. L., & PERNER, J. (1991). Early deception and the child's theory of mind: False trails and genuine markers. *Child Development, 62,* 468–483.

SOKEN, H. H., & PICK, A. D. (1992). Intermodal perception of happy and angry expressive behaviors by seven-month-old infants. *Child Development, 63,* 787–795.

SOMMERS-FLANAGAN, R., SOMMERS-FLANAGAN, J., & DAVIS, B. (1993). What's happening on music television? A gender-role content analysis. *Sex Roles, 28,* 745–753.

SOMMERVILLE, J. (1982). *The rise and fall of childhood.* Beverly Hills, CA: Sage.

SONENSTEIN, F. L., PLECK, J. H., & KU, L. C. (1991). Levels of sexual activity among adolescent males in the United States.

Family Planning Perspectives, 23, 162–167.

SONG, M., & GINSBURG, H. P. (1987). The development of informal and formal mathematical thinking in Korean and U.S. children. *Child Development, 58*, 1286–1296.

SOPHIAN, C. (1995). Representation and reasoning in early numerical development: Counting, conservation, and comparisons between sets. *Child Development, 66*, 559–577.

SORCE, J., EMDE, R., CAMPOS, J., & KLINNERT, M. (1985). Maternal emotional signaling: Its effect on the visual cliff behavior of 1-year-olds. *Developmental Psychology, 21*, 195–200.

SORENSON, E. S. (1993). *Children's stress and coping*. New York: Guilford.

SOSA, R., KENNELL, J., KLAUS, M., ROBERTSON, S., & URRUTIA, J. (1980). The effect of a supportive companion on perinatal problems, length of labor, and mother–infant interaction. *New England Journal of Medicine, 303*, 597–600.

SOSTEK, A. M., SMITH, Y. F., KATZ, K. S., & GRANT, E. G. (1987). Developmental outcome of preterm infants with intraventricular hemorrhage at one and two years of age. *Child Development, 58*, 779–786.

SOUTHARD, B. (1985). Interlimb movement control and coordination in children. In J. E. Clark & J. E. Humphrey (Eds.), *Motor development* (Vol. 1, pp. 55–66). Princeton, NJ: Princeton Books.

SOUTHERN, W. T., JONES, E. D., & STANLEY, J. C. (1994). Acceleration and enrichment: The context and development of program options. In K. A. Heller, F. J. Jonks, & H. A. Passow (Eds.), *International handbook of research and development of giftedness and talent* (pp. 387–409). Oxford: Pergamon Press.

SPÄTLING, L., & SPÄTLING, G. (1988). Magnesium supplementation in pregnancy: A double-blind study. *British Journal of Obstetrics and Gynecology, 95*, 120–125.

SPEECE, M. W., & BRENT, S. B. (1992). The acquisition of a mature understanding of three components of the concept of death. *Death Studies, 16*, 211–229.

SPEECE, M. W., & BRENT, S. B. (1996). The development of children's understanding of death. In C. A. Corr & D. M. Corr (Eds.), *Handbook of childhood death and bereavement* (pp. 29–50). New York: Springer.

SPEICHER, B. (1994). Family patterns of moral judgment during adolescence and early adulthood. *Developmental Psychology, 30*, 624–632.

SPELKE, E. S. (1987). The development of intermodal perception. In P. Salapatek & L. Cohen (Eds.), *Handbook of infant perception: Vol. 2. From perception to cognition* (pp. 233–273). Orlando, FL: Academic Press.

SPELKE, E. S. (1994). Initial knowledge: Six suggestions. *Cognition, 50*, 431–445.

SPELKE, E. S., BREINLINGER, K., MACOMBER, J., & JACOBSON, K. (1992). Origins of knowledge. *Psychological Review, 99*, 605–632.

SPELKE, E. S., GUTHEIL, G., & VAN DE WALLE, G. (1995). The development of object perception. In S. M. Kosslyn & D. N. Osherson (Eds.), Visual cognition (pp. 297–330). Cambridge, MA: MIT Press.

SPELKE, E. S., HOFSTEN, C. VON, & KESTENBAUM, R. (1989). Object perception in infancy: Interaction of spatial and kinetic information for object boundaries. *Developmental Psychology, 25*, 185–196.

SPELKE, E. S., & NEWPORT, E. L. (1998). Nativism, empiricism, and the development of knowledge. In R. M. Lerner (Ed.), *Handbook of child psychology: Vol. 1. Theoretical models of human development* (5th ed., pp. 199–254). New York: Wiley.

SPELLACY, W. N., MILLER, S. J., & WINEGAR, A. (1986). Pregnancy after 40 years of age. *Obstetrics and Gynecology, 68*, 452–454.

SPENCE, M. J., & DECASPER, A. J. (1987). Prenatal experience with low-frequency maternal voice sounds influences neonatal perception of maternal voice samples. *Infant Behavior and Development, 10*, 133–142.

SPERDUTO, R. D., HILLER, R., PODGOR, M. J., FREIDLIN, V., MILTON, R. C., WOLF, P. A., MYERS, R. H., DAGOSTINE, R. B., ROSEMAN, M. J., STOCKMAN, M. E., & WILSON, P. W. (1996). Familial aggregation and prevalence of myopia in the Framingham Offspring Eye Study. *Archives of Ophthalmology, 114*, 326–333.

SPERDUTO, R. D., SEIGEL, D., ROBERTS, J., & ROWLAND, M. (1983). Prevalence of myopia in the United States. *Archives of Ophthalmology, 101*, 405–407.

SPINDLER, G. D. (1970). The education of adolescents: An anthropological perspective. In D. Ellis (Ed.), *Adolescents: Readings in behavior and development* (pp. 152–161). Hinsdale, IL: Dryden.

SPITZ, R. A. (1945). Hospitalism: An inquiry into the genesis of psychiatric conditions in early childhood. *Psychoanalytic Study of the Child, 1*, 113–117.

SPITZ, R. A. (1946). Anaclitic depression. *Psychoanalytic Study of the Child, 2*, 313–342.

SPIVACK, G., & SHURE, M. B. (1974). *Social adjustment of young children: A cognitive approach to solving real life problems*. San Francisco: Jossey-Bass.

SPOCK, B., & PARKER, S. J. (1998). *Dr. Spock's baby and child care.* (7th ed.). New York: Pocket.

SPREADBURY, C. L. (1982). First date. *Journal of Early Adolescence, 2*, 83–89.

SPRINGER, N. P., & VAN WEEL, C. (1996). Home birth: Safe in selected women, and with adequate infrastructure and support. *British Medical Journal, 313*, 1276–1277.

SROUFE, L. A. (1979). Socioemotional development. In J. D. Osofsky (Ed.), *Handbook of infant development* (pp. 462–516). New York: Wiley.

SROUFE, L. A. (1985). Attachment classification from the perspective of infant–caregiver relationships and infant temperament. *Child Development, 56*, 1–14.

SROUFE, L. A. (1988). A developmental perspective on day care. *Early Childhood Research Quarterly, 3*, 283–292.

SROUFE, L. A., EGELAND, B., & KREUTZER, T. (1990). The fate of early experience following developmental change: Longitudinal approaches to individual adaptation. *Child Development, 61*, 1363–1373.

SROUFE, L. A., & WATERS, E. (1976). The ontogenesis of smiling and laughter: A perspective on the organization of development in infancy. *Psychological Review, 83*, 173–189.

SROUFE, L. A., & WUNSCH, J. P. (1972). The development of laughter in the first year of life. *Child Development, 43*, 1324–1344.

STAHL, S. A., (1992). Saying the "P" word: Nine guidelines for effective phonics instruction. *The Reading Teacher, 45*, 618–625.

STAHL, S. A., MCKENNA, M. C., & PAGNUCCO, J. R. (1994). The effects of whole-language instruction: An update and a reappraisal. *Educational Psychologist, 29*, 175–185.

STARK, L. J., ALLEN, K. D., HURST, M., NASH, D. A., RIGNEY, B., & STOKES, T. F. (1989). Distraction: Its utilization and efficacy with children undergoing dental treatment. *Journal of Applied Behavior Analysis, 22*, 297–307.

STARKEY, P., SPELKE, E. S., & GELMAN, R. (1990). Numerical abstraction by human infants. *Cognition, 36*, 97–128.

STATTIN, H., & MAGNUSSON, D. (1990). *Pubertal maturation in female development*. Hillsdale, NJ: Erlbaum.

STAUB, E. (1996). Cultural–societal roots of violence. *American Psychologist, 51*, 117–132.

STECHLER, G., & HALTON, A. (1982). Prenatal influences on human development. In B. B. Wolman (Ed.), *Handbook of developmental psychology* (pp. 175–189). Englewood Cliffs, NJ: Prentice-Hall.

STEELE, C. D., WAPNER, R. J., SMITH, J. B., HAYNES, M. K., & JACKSON, L. G. (1996). Prenatal diagnosis using fetal cells isolated from maternal blood: A review. *Clinical Obstetrics and Gynecology, 39*, 801–813.

STEELE, H., STEELE, M., & FONAGY, P. (1996). Associations among attachment classifications of mothers, fathers, and their infants. *Child Development, 67*, 541–555.

STEIN, J. H., & REISER, L. W. (1994). A study of white middle-class adolescent boys' responses to "semenarche" (the first ejaculation). *Journal of Youth and Adolescence, 23*, 373–384.

STEIN, Z., SUSSER, M., SAENGER, G., & MAROLLA, F. (1975). *Famine and human development: The Dutch hunger winter of 1944–1945.* New York: Oxford.

STEINBERG, L. (1984). The varieties and effects of work during adolescence. In M. Lamb, A. Brown, & B. Rogoff (Eds.), *Advances in developmental psychology* (pp. 1–37). Hillsdale, NJ: Erlbaum.

STEINBERG, L. (1986). Latchkey

children and susceptibility to peer pressure: An ecological analysis. *Developmental Psychology, 22,* 433–439.

STEINBERG, L. (1987). The impact of puberty on family relations: Effects of pubertal status and pubertal timing. *Developmental Psychology, 23,* 451–460.

STEINBERG, L. (1990). Interdependence in the family: Autonomy, conflict, and harmony in the parent–adolescent relationship. In S. S. Feldman & G. R. Elliott (Eds.), *At the threshold: The developing adolescent* (pp. 255–276). Cambridge, MA: Harvard University Press.

STEINBERG, L. (1993). *Adolescence* (3rd ed.). New York: McGraw-Hill.

STEINBERG, L., DARLING, N. E., & FLETCHER, A. C. (1995). Authoritative parenting and adolescent development: An ecological journey. In P. Moen, G. H. Elder, & K. Luscher (Eds.), *Examining lives in context* (pp. 423–466). Washington, DC: American Psychological Association.

STEINBERG, L., & DORNBUSCH, S. M. (1991). Negative correlates of part-time employment during adolescence: Replication and elaboration. *Developmental Psychology, 27,* 304–313.

STEINBERG, L., LAMBORN, S. D., DARLING, N., MOUNTS, N. S., & DORNBUSCH, S. M. (1994). Over-time changes in adjustment and competence among adolescents from authoritative, authoritarian, indulgent, and neglectful families. *Child Development, 65,* 754–770.

STEINBERG, L., & SILVERBERG, S. B. (1986). The vicissitudes of autonomy in early adolescence. *Child Development, 57,* 841–851.

STEINBERG, L. D., FEGLEY, S., & DORNBUSCH, S. (1993). Negative impact of part-time work on adolescent adjustment: Evidence from a longitudinal study. *Developmental Psychology, 29,* 171–180.

STEINBERG, L. D., FLETCHER, A., & DARLING, N. (1994). Parental monitoring and peer influences on adolescent substance use. *Pediatrics, 93,* 1060–1064.

STEINER, J. E. (1979). Human facial expression in response to taste and smell stimulation. In H. W. Reese & L. P. Lipsitt (Eds.), *Advances in child development and behavior* (Vol. 13, pp. 257–295). New York: Academic Press.

STEINHARDT, M. A. (1992). Physical education. In P. W. Jackson (Ed.), *Handbook of research on curriculum* (pp. 964–1001). New York: Macmillan.

STENBERG, C., & CAMPOS, J. (1990). The development of anger expressions in infancy. In N. Stein, B. Leventhal, & T. Trabasso (Eds.), *Psychological and biological approaches to emotion* (pp. 247–282). Hillsdale, NJ: Erlbaum.

STERN, M., & KARRAKER, K. H. (1989). Sex stereotyping of infants: A review of gender labeling studies. *Sex Roles, 20,* 501–522.

STERNBERG, K. J., LAMB, M. E., GREENBAUM, C., CICCHETTI, D., DAWAUD, S., CORTES, R. M., KRISPIN, O., & LOREY, F. (1993). Effects of domestic violence on children's behavior problems and depression. *Developmental Psychology, 29,* 44–52.

STERNBERG, R. J. (1985). *Beyond IQ: A triarchic theory of human intelligence.* New York: Cambridge University Press.

STERNBERG, R. J. (1996a). Myths, countermyths, and truths about intelligence. *Educational Researcher, 25,* 11–16.

STERNBERG, R. J. (1996b). *Successful intelligence: How practical and creative intelligence determine success in life.* New York: Simon & Schuster.

STERNBERG, R. J. (1997). *Successful intelligence.* New York: Plume.

STERNBERG, R. J., & GRIGORENKO, E. L. (Eds.). (1997). *Intelligence, heredity, and environment.* New York: Cambridge University Press.

STERNBERG, R. J., & LUBART, T. I. (1991). An investment theory of creativity and its development. *Human Development, 34,* 1–31.

STERNBERG, R. J., & LUBART, T. I. (1995). *Defying the crowd.* New York: Basic Books.

STERNBERG, R. J., & ODAGAKI, L. (1989). Continuity and discontinuity in intellectual development are not a matter of "either–or." *Human Development, 32,* 159–166.

STEVENS, J. H. (1984). Black grandmothers' and black adolescent mothers' knowledge about parenting. *Developmental Psychology, 20,* 1017–1025.

STEVENSON, D. L., & BAKER, D. P. (1987). The family-school relation and the child's school performance. *Child Development, 58,* 1348–1357.

STEVENSON, H. W. (1992, December). Learning from Asian schools. *Scientific American, 267*(6), 32–38.

STEVENSON, H. W. (1994). Extracurricular programs in East Asian schools. *Teachers College Record, 95,* 389–407.

STEVENSON, H. W., CHEN, C., & LEE, S-Y. (1993). Mathematics achievement of Chinese, Japanese, and American children: Ten years later. *Science, 259,* 53–58.

STEVENSON, H. W., & LEE, S-Y. (1990). Contexts of achievement: A study of American, Chinese, and Japanese children. *Monographs of the Society for Research in Child Development, 55* (1–2, Serial No. 221).

STEVENSON, M. R., & BLACK, K. N. (1995). *How divorce affects offspring: A research approach.* Dubuque, IA: Brown & Benchmark.

STEVENSON, R., & POLLITT, C. (1987). The acquisition of temporal terms. *Journal of Child Language, 14,* 533–545.

STEWART, D. A. (1982). *Children with sex chromosome aneuploidy: Follow-up studies.* New York: Liss.

STEWART, K. J., LIPIS, P. H., SEEMANS, C. M., MCFARLAND, L. D., WEINHOFER, J. J., & BROWN, C. S. (1995). Heart-healthy knowledge, food patterns, fatness, and cardiac risk factors in children receiving nutrition edition. *Journal of Health Education, 26,* 381–387.

STEWART, R. B. (1983). Sibling attachment relationships: Child–infant interactions in the Strange Situation. *Developmental Psychology, 19,* 192–199.

STEWART, S. L., & RUBIN, K. H. (1995). The social problem-solving skills of anxious withdrawn children. *Development and Psychopathology, 7,* 323–336.

STIFTER, C. A., COULEHAN, C. M., & FISH, M. (1993). Linking employment to attachment: The mediating effects of maternal separation anxiety and interactive behavior. *Child Development, 64,* 1451–1460.

STILLMAN, R. J. (1982). In utero exposure to diethylstilbestrol: Adverse effects on the reproductive tract and reproductive performance in male and female offspring. *American Journal of Obstetrics and Gynecology, 142,* 905–921.

STIPEK, D. (1995). The development of pride and shame in toddlers. In J. P. Tangney & K. W. Fischer (Eds.), *Self-conscious emotions* (pp. 237–252). New York: Guilford.

STIPEK, D. J. (1981). Children's perceptions of their own and their classmates' ability. *Journal of Educational Psychology, 73,* 404–410.

STIPEK, D. J., & BYLER, P. (1997). Early childhood education teachers: Do they practice what they preach? *Early Childhood Research Quarterly, 12,* 305–326.

STIPEK, D. J., FEILER, R., DANIELS, D., & MILBURN, S. (1995). Effects of different instructional approaches on young children's achievement and motivation. *Child Development, 66,* 209–223.

STIPEK, D. J., GRALINSKI, J. H., & KOPP, C. B. (1990). Self-concept development in the toddler years. *Developmental Psychology, 26,* 972–977.

STIPEK, D. J., & MAC IVER, D. (1989). Developmental change in children's assessment of intellectual competence. *Child Development, 60,* 531–538.

STIPEK, D. J., RECCHIA, S., & MCCLINTIC, S. (1992). Self-evaluation in young children. *Monographs of the Society for Research in Child Development, 57* (Serial No. 226, No. 1).

STOCH, M. B., SMYTHE, P. M., MOODIE, A. D., & BRADSHAW, D. (1982). Psychosocial outcome and CT findings after growth undernourishment during infancy: A 20-year developmental study. *Developmental Medicine and Child Neurology, 24,* 419–436.

STOCKER, C., & DUNN, J. (1990). Sibling relationships in adolescence. In R. M. Lerner, A. C. Petersen, & J. Brooks-Gunn (Eds.), *The encyclopedia of adolescence* (Vol. 2, pp. 1046–1048). New York: Garland.

STOCKER, C. M., & DUNN, J. (1994). Sibling relationships in childhood and adolescence. In J. C. DeFries, R. Plomin, & D. W. Fulker (Eds.), *Nature and nurture in middle childhood* (pp. 214–232). Cambridge: Blackwell.

STODOLSKY, S. S. (1988). *The subject matters.* Chicago: University of Chicago Press.

STOEL-GAMMON, C., & OTOMO, K. (1986). Babbling development of hearing-impaired and normal hearing subjects. *Journal of Speech and Hearing Disorders, 51,* 33–41.

STONE, L. (1977). *The family, sex, and marriage in England, 1500–1800*. New York: Harper & Row.

STONEMAN, Z., BRODY, G. H., & MACKINNON, C. E. (1986). Same-sex and cross-sex siblings: Activity choices, roles, behavior, and gender stereotypes. *Sex Roles, 15*, 495–511.

STORY, M., FRENCH, S. A., RESNICK, M. D., & BLUM, R. W. (1995). Ethnic/racial and socioeconomic differences in dieting behaviors and body image perceptions in adolescents. *International Journal of Eating Disorders, 18*, 173–179.

STRASSBERG, Z. (1995). Social information processing in compliance situations by mothers of behavior-problem boys. *Child Development, 66*, 376–389.

STRASSBERG, Z., DODGE, K., PETTIT, G. S., & BATES, J. E. (1994). Spanking in the home and children's subsequent aggression toward kindergarten peers. *Development and Psychopathology, 6*, 445–461.

STRAUSS, M. S., & CURTIS, L. E. (1984). Development of numerical concepts in infancy. In C. Sophian (Ed.), *Origins of cognitive skills: The Eighteenth Carnegie Symposium on Cognition* (pp. 131–155). Hillsdale, NJ: Erlbaum.

STRAYER, J. (1993). Children's concordant emotions and cognitions in response to observed emotions. *Child Development, 64*, 188–201.

STREISSGUTH, A., BOOKSTEIN, F. L., & BARR, H. M. (1996). A dose-response study of the enduring effects of prenatal alcohol exposure: Birth to 14 years. In H-L. Spohr & H-C. Steinhausen (Eds.), *Alcohol, pregnancy and the developing child* (pp. 141–168). New York: Cambridge University Press.

STREISSGUTH, A. P., BARR, H. M., SAMPSON, P. D., DARBY, B. L., & MARTIN, D. C. (1989). IQ at age 4 in relation to maternal alcohol use and smoking during pregnancy. *Developmental Psychology, 25*, 3–11.

STREISSGUTH, A. P., TREDER, R., BARR, H. M., SHEPARD, T., BLEYER, W. A., SAMPSON, P. D., & MARTIN, D. (1987). Aspirin and acetaminophen use by pregnant women and subsequent child IQ and attention decrements. *Teratology, 35*, 211–219.

STREITMATTER, J. L. (1993). Gender differences in identity development: An examination of longitudinal data. *Adolescence, 28*, 55–66.

STREITMATTER, J. L., & PATE, G. S. (1989). Identity status development and cognitive prejudice in early adolescents. *Journal of Early Adolescence, 9*, 142–152.

STROBER, M., MCCRACKEN, J., & HANNA, G. (1990). Affective disorders. In R. M. Lerner, A. C. Petersen, & J. Brooks-Gunn (Eds.), *The encyclopedia of adolescence* (Vol. 1, pp. 18–25). New York: Garland.

STROMSWOLD, K. (1995). The acquisition of subject and object wh- questions. *Language Acquisition, 4*, 5–48.

STUNKARD, A. J., & SØRENSON, T. I. A. (1993). Obesity and socioeconomic status—a complex relation. *New England Journal of Medicine, 329*, 1036–1037.

STUNKARD, A. J., SØRENSON, T. I. A., HANIS, C., TEASDALE, T. W., CHAKRABORTY, R., SCHULL, W. J., & SCHULSINGER, F. (1986). An adoption study of human obesity. *New England Journal of Medicine, 314*, 193–198.

STURDEVANT, M. S., & RAMAFEDI, G. (1992). Special health needs of homosexual youth. *Adolescent Medicine State of the Art Reviews, 3*, 359–372.

SUBBOTSKY, E. V. (1994). Early rationality and magical thinking in preschoolers: Space and time. *British Journal of Developmental Psychology, 12*, 97–108.

SUBRAHMANYAM, K., & GREENFIELD, P. M. (1996). Effect of video game practice on spatial skills in girls and boys. In P. M. Greenfield & R. R. Cocking (Eds.), *Interacting with video* (pp. 95–114). Norwood, NJ: Ablex.

SULLIVAN, H. S. (1953). *The interpersonal theory of psychiatry*. New York: Norton.

SULLIVAN, L. W. (1987). The risks of the sickle-cell trait: Caution and common sense. *New England Journal of Medicine, 317*, 830–831.

SULLIVAN, M. L. (1993). Culture and class as determinants of out-of-wedlock childbearing and poverty during late adolescence. *Journal of Research on Adolescence, 3*, 295–316.

SULLIVAN, S. A., & BIRCH, L. L. (1990). Pass the sugar, pass the salt: Experience dictates preference. *Developmental Psychology, 26*, 546–551.

SULLIVAN, S. A., & BIRCH, L. L. (1994). Infant dietary experience and acceptance of solid foods. *Pediatrics, 93*, 271–277.

SULZBY, E. (1985). Children's emergent reading of favorite books: A developmental study. *Reading Research Quarterly, 20*, 458–481.

SUPER, C. M. (1981). Behavioral development in infancy. In R. H. Monroe, R. L. Monroe, & B. B. Whiting (Eds.), *Handbook of cross-cultural human development* (pp. 181–270). New York: Garland.

SUPER, C. M., & HARKNESS, S. (1982). The infant's niche in rural Kenya and metropolitan America. In L. L. Adler (Ed.), *Cross-cultural research at issue* (pp. 247–255). New York: Academic Press.

SUPER, D. (1980). A life-span, life-space approach to career development. *Journal of Vocational Behavior, 16*, 282–298.

SUPER, D. (1984). Career and life development. In D. Brown & L. Brooks (Eds.), *Career choice and development* (pp. 192–234). San Francisco: Jossey-Bass.

SUREAU, C. (1997). Trials and tribulations of surrogacy: From surrogacy to parenthood. *Human Reproduction, 12*, 410–411.

SUZUKI, L. A., & VALENCIA, R. R. (1997). Race–ethnicity and measured intelligence: Educational implications. *American Psychologist, 52*, 1103–1114.

SWANSON, H. S. W. (1993). Donor anonymity in artificial insemination: Is it still necessary? *Columbia Journal of Law and Social Problems, 27*, 151–190.

SWAYZE, V. W., JOHNSON, V. P., HANSON, J. W., PIVEN, J., SATO, Y., GIEDD, J. N., MOSNIK, D., & ANDREASEN, N. C. (1997). Magnetic resonance imaging of brain anomalies in fetal alcohol syndrome. *Pediatrics, 99*, 232–240.

SYKES, N. L., JR. (1994). Acne: A review of optimum treatment drugs. *Drugs, 48*, 59–70.

SZEPKOUSKI, G. M., GAUVAIN, M., & CARBERRY, M. (1994). The development of planning skills in children with and without mental retardation. *Journal of Applied Developmental Psychology, 15*, 187–206.

TAGER-FLUSBERG, H. (1997). Putting words together: Morphology and syntax in the preschool years. In J. Berko Gleason (Ed.), *The development of language* (4th ed., pp. 159–209). Boston: Allyn and Bacon.

TAGER-FLUSBERG, H., & SULLIVAN, K. (1994). Predicting and explaining behavior: A comparison of autistic, mentally retarded, and normal children. *Journal of Child Psychology and Psychiatry, 35*, 1059–1079.

TAKAHASHI, K. (1990). Are the key assumptions of the "Strange Situation" procedure universal? A view from Japanese research. *Human Development, 33*, 23–30.

TAMIS-LEMONDA, C. S., & BORNSTEIN, M. H. (1989). Habituation and maternal encouragement of attention in infancy as predictors of toddler language, play, and representational competence. *Child Development, 60*, 738–751.

TAMIS-LEMONDA, C. S., & BORNSTEIN, M. H. (1994). Specificity in mother–toddler language–play relations across the second year. *Developmental Psychology, 30*, 283–292.

TANNER, J. M. (1990). *Foetus into man* (2nd ed.). Cambridge, MA: Harvard University Press.

TANNER, J. M., WHITEHOUSE, R. H., CAMERON, N., MARSHALL, W. A., HEALEY, M. J. R., & GOLDSTEIN, H. (1983). *Assessment of skeletal maturity and prediction of adult height* (TW2 method) (2nd ed.). New York: Academic Press.

TARDIF, T. (1996). Nouns are not always learned before verbs: Evidence from Mandarin speakers' early vocabularies. *Developmental Psychology, 32*, 492–504.

TAYLOR, B. J. (1991). A review of epidemiological studies of sudden infant death syndrome in southern New Zealand. *Journal of Paediatric Child Health, 27*, 344–348.

TAYLOR, J. A., & SANDERSON, M. (1995). A reexamination of the risk factors for the sudden infant death syndrome. *Journal of Pediatrics, 126*, 887–891.

TAYLOR, M., & CARLSON, S. M. (1997). The relation between individual differences in fantasy and theory of mind. *Child Development, 68*, 436–455.

TAYLOR, M., CARTWRIGHT, B. S., & CARLSON, S. M. (1993). A developmental investigation of children's imaginary companions. *Developmental Psychology, 29*, 276–285.

TAYLOR, M., ESBENSEN, B. M., & BENNETT, R. T. (1994).

Children's understanding of knowledge acquisition: The tendency for children to report that they have always known what they have just learned. *Child Development, 65,* 1581–1604.

TAYLOR, M. C., & HALL, J. A. (1982). Psychological androgyny: Theories, methods, and conclusions. *Psychological Bulletin, 92,* 347–366.

TAYLOR, R. D., & ROBERTS, D. (1995). Kinship support and maternal and adolescent well-being in economically disadvantaged African-American families. *Child Development, 66,* 1585–1597.

TEBBUTT, J., SWANSTON, H., OATES, R. K., & O'TOOLE, B. I. (1997). Five years after child sexual abuse: Persisting dysfunction and problems of prediction. *Journal of the American Academy of Child and Adolescent Psychiatry, 36,* 330–339.

TEDDER, J. L. (1991). Using the Brazelton Neonatal Assessment Scale to facilitate the parent–infant relationship in a primary care setting. *Nurse Practitioner, 16,* 27–36.

TEELE, D. W., KLEIN, J. O., CHASE, C., MENYUK, P., ROSNER, B. A., & THE GREATER BOSTON OTITIS MEDIA STUDY GROUP. (1990). Otitis media in infancy and intellectual ability, school achievement, speech, and language at age 7 years. *Journal of Infectious Diseases, 162,* 685–694.

TEIKARI, J. M., O'DONNELL, J. O., KAPRIO, J., & KOSKEN-VUO, M. (1991). Impact of heredity in myopia. *Human Heredity, 41,* 151–156.

TEMPLE, C. M., & CARNEY, R. A. (1995). Patterns of spatial functioning in Turner's syndrome. *Cortex, 31,* 109–118.

TERTINGER, D. A., GREENE, B. F., & LUTZKER, J. R. (1984). Home safety: Development and validation of one component of an ecobehavioral treatment program for abused and neglected children. *Journal of Applied Behavior Analysis, 17,* 159–174.

TETI, D. M., GELFAND, D. M., MESSINGER, D. S., & ISABELLA, R. (1995). Maternal depression and the quality of early attachment: An examination of infants, preschoolers, and their mothers. *Developmental Psychology, 31,* 364–376.

TETI, D. M., & McGOURTY, S. (1996). Using mothers versus trained observers in assessing children's secure base behavior: Theoretical and methodological considerations. *Child Development, 67,* 597–605.

TETI, D. M., SAKEN, J. W., KUCERA, E., & CORNS, K. M. (1996). And baby makes four: Predictors of attachment security among preschool-age firstborns during the transition to siblinghood. *Child Development, 67,* 579–596.

TEYBER, E. (1992). *Helping children cope with divorce.* New York: Lexington Books.

THACKER, S. B., ADDISS, D. G., GOODMAN, R. A., HOLLOWAY, B. R., & SPENCER, H. C. (1992). Infectious diseases and injuries in child day care. *Journal of the American Medical Association, 268,* 1720–1726.

THACKWRAY, D. E., SMITH, M. C., BODFISH, J. W., & MEYERS, A. W. (1993). A comparison of behavioral and cognitive-behavioral interventions for bulimia nervosa. *Journal of Consulting and Clinical Psychology, 61,* 639–645.

THAPAR, A., GOTTESMAN, I. I., OWEN, M. J., O'DONOVAN, M. C., & McGUFFIN, P. (1994). The genetics of mental retardation. *British Journal of Psychiatry, 164,* 747–758.

THARP, R. G. (1993). Institutional and social context of educational practice and reform. In E. A. Forman, N. Minick, & C. A. Stone (Eds.), *Contexts for learning* (pp. 269–282). New York: Oxford University Press.

THARP, R. G. (1994). Intergroup differences among Native Americans in socialization and child cognition: An ethnogenetic analysis. In P. M. Greenfield & R. Cocking (Eds.), *Cross-cultural roots of minority child development* (pp. 87–105). Hillsdale, NJ: Erlbaum.

THARP, R. G., & GALLIMORE, R. (1988). *Rousing minds to life: Teaching, learning, and schooling in social context.* Cambridge, England: Cambridge University Press.

THATCHER, R. W. (1991). Maturation of human frontal lobes: Physiological evidence for staging. *Developmental Neuropsychology, 7,* 397–419.

THATCHER, R. W. (1994). Cyclic cortical reorganization: Origins of human cognitive development. In G. Dawson & K. W. Fischer (Eds.), *Human behavior and the developing brain* (pp. 232–266). New York: Guilford.

THATCHER, R. W., WALKER, R. A., & GIUDICE, S. (1987). Human cerebral hemispheres develop at different rates and ages. *Science, 236,* 1110–1113.

THELEN, E. (1989). The (re)discovery of motor development: Learning new things from an old field. *Developmental Psychology, 25,* 946–949.

THELEN, E. (1994). Three-month-old infants can learn task-specific patterns of inter-limb coordination. *Psychological Science, 5,* 280–285.

THELEN, E., & ADOLPH, K. E. (1992). Arnold Gesell: The paradox of nature and nurture. *Developmental Psychology, 28,* 368–380.

THELEN, E., CORBETTA, D., KAMM, K., SPENCER, J. P., SCHNEIDER, K., & ZERNICKE, R. F. (1993). The transition to reaching: Mapping intention and intrinsic dynamics. *Child Development, 64,* 1058–1098.

THELEN, E., CORBETTA, D., & SPENCER, J. (1996). The development of reaching during the first year: The role of movement speed. *Journal of Experimental Psychology: Human Perception and Performance, 22,* 1059–1076.

THELEN, E., FISHER, D. M., & RIDLEY-JOHNSON, R. (1984). The relationship between physical growth and a newborn reflex. *Infant Behavior and Development, 7,* 479–493.

THELEN, E., & SMITH, L. B. (1994). *A dynamic systems approach to the development of cognition and action.* Cambridge, MA: MIT Press.

THELEN, E., & SMITH, L. B. (1998). Dynamic systems theories. In R. M. Lerner (Ed.), *Handbook of child psychology: Vol. 1. Theoretical models of human development* (5th ed., pp. 563–634). New York: Wiley.

THOMAN, E., & INGERSOLL, E. W. (1993). Learning in premature infants. *Developmental Psychology, 29,* 692–700.

THOMAS, A., & CHESS, S. (1977). *Temperament and development.* New York: Brunner/Mazel.

THOMAS, A., CHESS, S., & BIRCH, H. G. (1970, August). The origins of personality. *Scientific American, 223*(2), 102–109.

THOMAS, A., CHESS, S., & KORN, S. J. (1982). The reality of difficult temperament. *Merrill-Palmer Quarterly, 28,* 1–20.

THOMAS, J. R., & FRENCH, K. E. (1985). Gender differences across age in motor performance: A meta-analysis. *Psychological Bulletin, 98,* 260–282.

THOMPSON, R. A. (1990a). On emotion and self-regulation. In R. A. Thompson (Ed.), *Nebraska Symposia on Motivation* (Vol. 36, pp. 383–483). Lincoln: University of Nebraska Press.

THOMPSON, R. A. (1990b). Vulnerability in research: A developmental perspective on research risk. *Child Development, 61,* 1–16.

THOMPSON, R. A. (1994). Emotion regulation: A theme in search of definition. In N. A. Fox (Ed.), The development of emotion regulation. *Monographs of the Society for Research in Child Development, 59* (2–3, Serial No. 240).

THOMPSON, R. A. (1997). Sensitivity and security: New questions to ponder. *Child Development, 68,* 595–597.

THOMPSON, R. A. (1998). Early sociopersonality development. In N. Eisenberg (Ed.), *Handbook of child psychology: Vol. 3. Social, emotional, and personality development* (5th ed., pp. 25–104). New York: Wiley.

THOMPSON, R. A., & LEGER, D. W. (1998). From squalls to calls: The cry as a developing socioemotional signal. In B. Lester, J. Newman, & F. Pedersen (Eds.), *Biological and social aspects of infant crying.* New York: Plenum Press.

THOMPSON, R. A., & LIMBER, S. (1991). "Social anxiety" in infancy: Stranger wariness and separation distress. In H. Leitenberg (Ed.), *Handbook of social and evaluation anxiety* (pp. 85–137). New York: Plenum.

THORNDIKE, R. L., HAGEN, E. P., & SATTLER, J. M. (1986). *The Stanford-Binet Intelligence Scale.* Chicago: Riverside Publishing.

THORNTON, M., & TAYLOR, R. (1988). Black American perceptions of black Africans. *Ethnic and Racial Studies, 11,* 139–150.

THRONE, B. (1993). *Gender and play: Girls and boys in school.* New Brunswick, NJ: Rutgers University Press.

TIETJEN, A., & WALKER, L. (1985). Moral reasoning and leadership among men in a Papua New Guinea village. *Developmental Psychology, 21,* 982–992.

TISHMAN, S., PERKINS, D. N., & JAY, E. (1995). *The thinking classroom*. Boston: Allyn and Bacon.

TIZARD, B., & HODGES, J. (1978). The effect of early institutional rearing on the development of eight-year-old children. *Journal of Child Psychology and Psychiatry, 19,* 99–118.

TIZARD, B., & REES, J. (1975). The effect of early institutional rearing on the behaviour problems and affectional relationships of four-year-old children. *Journal of Child Psychology and Psychiatry, 16,* 61–73.

TOBIN, J. J., WU, D. Y. H., & DAVIDSON, D. H. (1989). *Preschool in three cultures*. New Haven, CT: Yale University Press.

TOLAROVA, M. (1986). Cleft lip and palate and isolated cleft palate in Czechoslovakia. *Advances in Bioscience, 61,* 251–268.

TOLSON, T. F. J., & WILSON, M. N. (1990). The impact of two- and three-generational black family structure on perceived family climate. *Child Development, 61,* 416–428.

TOMASELLO, M. (1995). Language is not an instinct. *Cognitive Development, 10,* 131–156.

TOMASELLO, M., & BARTON, M. (1994). Learning words in nonostensive contexts. *Developmental Psychology, 30,* 639–650.

TONG, S., CADDY, D., & SHORT, R. V. (1997). Use of dizygotic to monozygotic twinning ratio as a measure of fertility. *Lancet, 349,* 843–845.

TORFS, C. P., BERG, B. VAN DEN, OECHSLI, F. W., & CUMMINS, S. (1990). Prenatal and perinatal factors in the etiology of cerebral palsy. *Journal of Pediatrics, 116,* 615–619.

TORRANCE, E. P. (1980). *Torrance Tests of Creative Thinking*. New York: Scholastic Testing Service.

TORRANCE, E. P. (1988). The nature of creativity as manifest in its testing. In R. J. Sternberg (Ed.), *The nature of creativity: Contemporary psychological perspectives* (pp. 43–75). New York: Cambridge University Press.

TOTH, S. L., & CICCHETTI, D. (1996). Patterns of relatedness, depressive symptomatology, and perceived competence in maltreated children. *Journal of Consulting and Clinical Psychology, 64,* 32–41.

TOUWEN, B. C. L. (1984). Primitive reflexes—conceptual or semantic problem? In H. F. R. Prechtl (Ed.), *Continuity of neural functions from prenatal to postnatal life* (Clinics in Developmental Medicine No. 94, pp. 115–125). Philadelphia: Lippincott.

TOWER, R. B., SINGER, D. G., SINGER, J. L., & BIGGS, A. (1979). Differential effects of television programming on preschoolers' cognition, imagination, and social play. *American Journal of Orthopsychiatry, 49,* 265–281.

TRENT, K., & HARLAN, S. L. (1994). Teenage mothers in nuclear and extended households. *Journal of Family Issues, 15,* 309–337.

TRENT, W. (1991). *Desegregation analysis report*. New York: Legal Defense and Educational Fund.

TRIANDIS, H. C. (1989). The self and social behavior in differing cultural contexts. *Psychological Review, 96,* 506–520.

TRIANDIS, H. C., BONTEMPO, R., VILLAREAL, M. J., ASAI, M., & LUCCA, N. (1988). Individualism and collectivism: Cross-cultural perspectives on self–ingroup relationships. *Journal of Personality and Social Psychology, 54,* 323–338.

TRICKETT, P. K., ABER, J. L., CARLSON, V., & CICCHETTI, D. (1991). Relationship of socioeconomic status to the etiology and developmental sequelae of physical child abuse. *Developmental Psychology, 27,* 148–158.

TROIANO, R. P., FLEGAL, K. M., KUZMARSKI, R. J., CAMPBELL, S. M., & JOHNSON, C. L. (1995). Overweight prevalence and trends for children and adolescents. *Archives of Pediatric and Adolescent Medicine, 149,* 1085–1091.

TROIDEN, R. R. (1989). The formation of homosexual identities. *Journal of Homosexuality, 17,* 43–73.

TRONICK, E., MORELLI, G., & IVEY, P. (1992). The Efe forager infant and toddler's pattern of social relationships: Multiple and simultaneous. *Developmental Psychology, 28,* 568–577.

TRONICK, E. Z. (1989). Emotions and emotional communication in infants. *American Psychologist, 44,* 112–119.

TRONICK, E. Z., THOMAS, R. B., & DALTABUIT, M. (1994). The Quechua manta pouch: A caretaking practice for buffering the Peruvian infant against the multiple stressors of high altitude. *Child Development, 65,* 1005–1013.

TROY, M., & SROUFE, L. A. (1987). Victimization among preschoolers: Role of attachment relationship history. *Journal of the American Academy of Child and Adolescent Psychiatry, 26,* 166–172.

TUCHFARBER, B. S., ZINS, J. E., & JASON, L. A. (1997). Prevention and control of injuries. In R. Weissberg, T. P. Gullotta, R. L. Hampton, B. A. Ryan, & G. R. Adams (Eds.), *Enhancing children's wellness* (pp. 250–277). Thousand Oaks, CA: Sage.

TUDGE, J. R. H. (1992). Processes and consequences of peer collaboration: A Vygotskian analysis. *Child Development, 63,* 1364–1397.

TURIEL, E. (1983). *The development of social knowledge: Morality and convention*. New York: Cambridge University Press.

TURIEL, E., SMETANA, J. G., & KILLEN, M. (1991). Social contexts in social cognitive development. In W. M. Kurtines & J. L. Gewirtz (Eds.), *Handbook of moral behavior and development* (Vol. 2, pp. 307–332). Hillsdale, NJ: Erlbaum.

TURIEL, J. (1991a, February 3). At the survival borderline. *San Francisco Examiner,* pp. D13–D14.

TURIEL, J. (1991b, February 10). Life-and-death battle. *San Francisco Examiner,* pp. D13–D14.

TURK, J. (1995). Fragile X syndrome. *Archives of Diseases of Children, 72,* 3–5.

TURKHEIMER, E., & GOTTESMAN, I. I. (1991). Individual differences and the canalization of human behavior. *Developmental Psychology, 27,* 18–22.

TURNER, P. J., & GERVAI, J. (1995). A multidimensional study of gender typing in preschool children and their parents: Personality, attitudes, preferences, behavior, and cultural differences. *Developmental Psychology, 31,* 759–772.

TUSS, P., ZIMMER, J., & HO. H-Z. (1995). Causal attributions of underachieving fourth-grade students in China, Japan, and the United States. *Journal of Cross-Cultural Psychology, 26,* 408–425.

TYACK, D., & INGRAM, D. (1977). Children's production and comprehension of questions. *Journal of Child Language, 4,* 211–224.

TYC, V. L., FAIRCLOUGH, D., FLETCHER, B., & LEIGH, L. (1995). Children's distress during magnetic resonance imaging procedures. *Children's Health Care, 24,* 5–19.

TZURIEL, D. (1989). Inferential thinking modifiability in young socially disadvantaged and advantaged children. *International Journal of Dynamic Assessment and Instruction, 1,* 65–80.

U.S. BUREAU OF THE CENSUS. (1997). *Statistical abstract of the United States* (117th ed.). Washington, DC: U.S. Government Printing Office.

U.S. CENTERS FOR DISEASE CONTROL. (1995, March 24). CDC Surveillance Summaries. *MMWR, 44*(No. SS-1).

U.S. CENTERS FOR DISEASE CONTROL. (1997). *Sexually transmitted disease surveillance, 1996*. Atlanta: Author.

U.S. DEPARTMENT OF EDUCATION, NATIONAL CENTER FOR EDUCATION STATISTICS. (1996). *Digest of education statistics 1994*. Washington, DC: U.S. Government Printing Office.

U.S. DEPARTMENT OF EDUCATION. (1994). *Digest of educational statistics* (31st ed.). Washington, DC: U.S. Government Printing Office.

U.S. DEPARTMENT OF EDUCATION. (1997). *Digest of education statistics 1997*. Washington, DC: U.S. Government Printing Office.

U.S. DEPARTMENT OF EDUCATION. (1998). *Pursuing excellence: A study of U.S. twelfth-grade mathematics and science achievement in international context*. Washington, DC: U.S. Government Printing Office.

U.S. DEPARTMENT OF HEALTH AND HUMAN SERVICES, NATIONAL INSTITUTE ON DRUG ABUSE (1994b). *National survey results on drug use from Monitoring the Future study: Vol. 1. Secondary school students*. Washington, DC: U.S. Government Printing Office.

U.S. DEPARTMENT OF HEALTH AND HUMAN SERVICES. (1997). *Health United States 1996–1997 and injury chartbook*. Washington, DC: U.S. Bureau of the Census.

U.S. DEPARTMENT OF HEALTH AND HUMAN SERVICES. (1997). *Vital statistics of the United States, 1994*.

Washington, DC: U.S. Government Printing Office.

U.S. DEPARTMENT OF HEALTH AND HUMAN SERVICES. (1997a). *National survey results on drug use from the Monitoring the Future Study, 1975–1995: Vol. 1. Secondary School Students.* Washington, DC: U.S. Government Printing Office.

U.S. DEPARTMENT OF HEALTH AND HUMAN SERVICES. (1997b). Youth risk behavior surveillance—U.S., 1995. *MMWR, 45* (No. SS–4).

U.S. DEPARTMENT OF JUSTICE. (1997). *Crime in the United States.* Washington, DC: U.S. Government Printing Office.

U.S. PUBLIC HEALTH SERVICE. (1995). Screening for lead exposure in children. *American Family Physician, 51,* 139–143.

UDRY, J. R. (1990). Hormonal and social determinants of adolescent sexual initiation. In J. Bancroft & J. M. Reinisch (Eds.), *Adolescence and puberty* (pp. 70–87). New York: Oxford University Press.

ULRICH, B. D., & ULRICH, D. A. (1985). The role of balancing in performance of fundamental motor skills in 3-, 4-, and 5-year-old children. In J. E. Clark & J. H. Humphrey (Eds.), *Motor development* (Vol. 1, pp. 87–98). Princeton, NJ: Princeton Books.

UNGER, R., KREEGER, L., & CHRISTOFFEL, K. K. (1990). Childhood obesity: Medical and familial correlates and age of onset. *Clinical Pediatrics, 29,* 368–372.

UNITED NATIONS. (1991). *World population trends and policies.* New York: Author.

UPDEGRAFF, K. A., MCHALE, S. M., & CROUTER, A. C. (1996). Gender roles in marriage: What do they mean for girls' and boys' school achievement? *Journal of Youth and Adolescence, 25,* 73–88.

URBERG, K. A., DEGIRMENCIO-GLUE, S. M., TOLSON, J. M., & HALLIDAY-SCHER, K. (1995). The structure of adolescent peer networks. *Developmental Psychology, 31,* 540–547.

URIBE, F. M. T., LEVINE, R. A., & LEVINE, S. E. (1994). Maternal behavior in a Mexican community: The changing environments of children. In P. M. Greenfield & R. R. Cocking (Eds.), *Cross-cultural roots of minority child development* (pp. 41–54). Hillsdale, NJ: Erlbaum.

UTTAL, D. H., MARZOLF, D. P., PIERROUTSAKOS, S. L., SMITH, C. M., TROSETH, G. L., SCUDDER, K. V., & DELOACHE, J. S. (1998). Seeing through symbols: The development of children's understanding of symbol relations. In O. N. Saracho & B. Spodek (Eds.), *Multiple perspectives on play in early childhood education* (pp. 59–79). Albany: State University of New York Press.

UZGIRIS, I. C., & HUNT, J. McV. (1975). *Assessment in infancy: Ordinal scales of psychological development.* Urbana: University of Illinois Press.

VALDEZ, R., ATHENS, M. A., THOMPSON, G. H., BRADSHAW, G. H., & STERN, M. P. (1994). Birthweight and adult health outcomes in a biethnic population in the U.S.A. *Diabetologia, 37,* 624.

VALDEZ-MENCHACA, M. C., & WHITEHURST, G. J. (1992). Accelerating language development through picture book reading: A systematic extension to Mexican day care. *Developmental Psychology, 28,* 1106–1114.

VALIAN, V. V. (1993). *Parental replies: Linguistic status and didactic role.* Cambridge, MA: MIT Press.

VAN DEN BOOM, D. C. (1995). Do first-year intervention effects endure? Follow-up during toddlerhood of a sample of Dutch irritable infants. *Child Development, 66,* 1798–1816.

VAN DEN BOOM, D. C., & HOEKSMA, J. B. (1994). The effect of infant irritability on mother–infant interaction: A growth-curve analysis. *Developmental Psychology, 30,* 581–590.

VAN IJZENDOORN, M. H. (1995a). Adult attachment representations, parental responsiveness, and infant attachment: A meta-analysis on the predictive validity of the Adult Attachment Interview. *Psychological Bulletin, 117,* 387–403.

VAN IJZENDOORN, M. H. (1995b). Of the way we are: On temperament, attachment, and the transmission gap: A rejoinder to Fox (1995). *Psychological Bulletin, 117,* 411–415.

VAN IJZENDOORN, M. H., & DE WOLFF, M. S. (1997). In search of the absent father—meta-analyses of infant–father attachment: A rejoinder to our discussants. *Child Development, 68,* 604–609.

VAN IJZENDOORN, M. H., GOLDBERG, S., KROONENBERG, P. M. & FRENKEL, O. J. (1992). The relative effects of maternal and child problems on the quality of attachment: A meta-analysis of attachment in clinical samples. *Child Development, 63,* 840–858.

VAN IJZENDOORN, M. H., KRANENBURG, M. J., ZWART-WOUDSTRA, A., VAN BUSSCHBACH, A. M., & LAMBERMON, M. W. E. (1991). Parental attachment and children's socioemotional development: Some findings on the validity of the adult attachment interview in the Netherlands. *International Journal of Behavioral Development, 14,* 375–394.

VAN IJZENDOORN, M. H., & KROONENBERG, P. M. (1988). Cross-cultural patterns of attachment: A meta-analysis of the Strange Situation. *Child Development, 59,* 147–156.

VANCE, M. D. (1994, April). *Short stature and psychosocial risks in a nonclinical sample.* Proceedings of the Fourth North Coast Conference of the Society for Pediatric Psychology, Amherst, NY.

VANDELL, D. L., & HEMBREE, S. E. (1994). Peer social status and friendship: Independent contributors to children's social and academic adjustment. *Merrill-Palmer Quarterly, 40,* 461–477.

VANDELL, D. L., & MUELLER, E. C. (1995). Peer play and friendships during the first two years. In H. C. Foot, A. J. Chapman, & J. R. Smith (Eds.), *Friendship and social relations in children* (pp. 181–208). New Brunswick, NJ: Transaction.

VANDELL, D. L., & WILSON, K. S. (1987). Infants' interactions with mother, sibling, and peer: Contrasts and relations between interaction systems. *Child Development, 58,* 176–186.

VANDELL, D. L., WILSON, K. S., & BUCHANAN, N. R. (1980). Peer interaction in the first year of life: An examination of its structure, content, and sensitivity to toys. *Child Development, 51,* 481–488.

VANDENBERG, B. (1998). Real and not real: A vital developmental dichotomy. In O. N. Saracho & B. Spodek (Eds.), *Multiple perspectives on play in early childhood education* (pp. 295–305). Albany: State University of New York Press.

VANFOSSEN, B., JONES, J., & SPADE, J. (1987). Curriculum tracking and status maintenance. *Sociology of Education, 60,* 104–122.

VARTANIAN, L. R., & POWLISHTA, K. K. (1996). A longitudinal examination of the social-cognitive foundations of adolescent egocentrism. *Journal of Early Adolescence, 16,* 157–178.

VASUDEV, J., & HUMMEL, R. C. (1987). Moral stage sequence and principled reasoning in an Indian sample. *Human Development, 30,* 103–118.

VAUGHN, B. E., BRADLEY, C. F., JOFFE, L. S., SEIFER, R., & BARGLOW, P. (1987). Maternal characteristics measured prenatally are predictive of ratings of temperamental "difficulty" on the Carey Infant Temperament Questionnaire. *Developmental Psychology, 23,* 152–161.

VAUGHN, B. E., KOPP, C. B., & KRAKOW, J. B. (1984). The emergence and consolidation of self-control from eighteen to thirty months of age: Normative trends and individual differences. *Child Development, 55,* 990–1004.

VAUGHN, B. E., STEVENSON-HINDE, J., WATERS, E., KOTSAFTIS, A., LEFEVER, G. B., SHOULDICE, A., TRUDEL, M., & BELSKY, J. (1992). Attachment security and temperament in infancy and early childhood: Some conceptual clarifications. *Developmental Psychology, 28,* 463–473.

VAUGHN, S., ELBAUM, B. E., & SCHUMM, J. S. (1996). The effects of inclusion on the social functioning of students with learning disabilities. *Journal of Learning Disabilities, 29,* 598–608.

VENTURA, S. J. (1989). Trends and variations in first births to older women in the United States, 1970–86. *Vital and Health Statistics* (Series 21). Hyattsville, MD: U.S. Department of Health and Human Services.

VENTURA, S. J., MARTIN, J. A., CURTIN, S. C., & MATHEWS, T. J. (1997). *Report of final natality statistics, 1995. Monthly Vital Statistics Report, 45* (11, Suppl. 2). Hyattsville, MD: National Center for Health Statistics.

VERBRUGGE, H. P. (1990a). The national immunization program of the Netherlands. *Pediatrics, 86* (6, Pt. 2), 1060–1063.

VERBRUGGE, H. P. (1990b). Youth health care in the Netherlands:

A bird's eye view. *Pediatrics, 86* (6, Pt. 2), 1044–1047.

VERHULST, F. C., & VERSLUIS-DEN BIEMAN, H. J. M. (1995). Developmental course of problem behaviors in adolescent adoptees. *Journal of the American Academy of Child and Adolescent Psychiatry, 34,* 151–159.

VERNON, P. A. (1993). Intelligence and neural efficiency. In D. K. Detterman (Ed.), *Current topics in human intelligence* (Vol. 3, pp. 171–187). Norwood, NJ: Ablex.

VERNON-FEAGANS, L., MANLOVE, E. E., & VOLLING, B. L. (1996). Otitis media and the social behavior of day-care-attending children. *Child Development, 67,* 1528–1539.

VINDEN, P. G. (1996). Junín Quechua children's understanding of mind. *Child Development, 67,* 1707–1716.

VISHER, J. S. (1994). Stepfamilies: A work in progress. *American Journal of Family Therapy, 22,* 337–344.

VISNESS, C. M., & KENNEDY, K. I. (1997). Maternal employment and breast-feeding: Findings from the 1988 National Maternal and Infant Health Survey. *American Journal of Public Health, 87,* 945–950.

VOGEL, D. A., LAKE, M. A., EVANS, S., & KARRAKER, H. (1991). Children's and adults' sex-stereotyped perceptions of infants. *Sex Roles, 24,* 605–616.

VOHR, B. R., & GARCIA-COLL, C. T. (1988). Follow-up studies of high-risk low-birth-weight infants: Changing trends. In H. E. Fitzgerald, B. M. Lester, & M. W. Yogman (Eds.), *Theory and research in behavioral pediatrics* (pp. 1–65). New York: Plenum.

VOLLING, B. L., & BELSKY, J. (1992). Contribution of mother–child and father–child relationships to the quality of sibling interaction: A longitudinal study. *Child Development, 63,* 1209–1222.

VORHEES, C. V. (1986). Principles of behavioral teratology. In E. P. Riley & C. V. Vorhees (Eds.), *Handbook of behavioral teratology* (pp. 23–48). New York: Plenum.

VORHEES, C. V., & MOLLNOW, E. (1987). Behavioral teratogenesis: Long-term influences on behavior from early exposure to environmental agents. In J. D. Osofsky (Ed.), *Handbook of infant development* (2nd ed., pp. 913–971). New York: Wiley.

VOSTANIS, P., GRATTAN, E., & CUMELLA, S. (1997). Psychosocial functioning of homeless children. *Journal of the American Academy of Child and Adolescent Psychiatry, 36,* 881–889.

VOYER, D., VOYER, S., & BRYDEN, M. P. (1995). Magnitude of sex differences in spatial abilities: A meta-analysis and consideration of critical variables. *Psychological Bulletin, 117,* 250–270.

VUCHINICH, S., HETHERINGTON, E. M., VUCHINICH, R. A., & CLINGEMPEEL, W. G. (1991). Parent–child interaction and gender differences in early adolescents' adaptation to stepfamilies. *Developmental Psychology, 27,* 618–626.

VURPILLOT, E. (1968). The development of scanning strategies and their relation to visual differentiation. *Journal of Experimental Psychology, 6,* 632–650.

VYGOTSKY, L. S. (1978). *Mind in society: The development of higher psychological processes.* Cambridge, MA: Harvard University Press. (Original works published 1930, 1933, and 1935)

VYGOTSKY, L. S. (1987). Thinking and speech. In R. W. Rieber, A. S. Carton (Eds.), & N. Minick (Trans.), *The collected works of L. S. Vygotsky: Vol. 1. Problems of general psychology* (pp. 37–285). New York: Plenum. (Original work published 1934)

WACHS, T. D. (1975). Relation of infants' performance on Piagetian scales between twelve and twenty-four months and their Stanford-Binet performance at thirty-one months. *Child Development, 46,* 929–935.

WACHS, T. D. (1994). Commentary on Plomin, R. (1994). Genetics, nurture and social development: An alternative viewpoint. *Social Development, 3,* 66–70.

WACHS, T. D. (1995). Relation of mild-to-moderate malnutrition to human development: Correlational studies. *Journal of Nutrition Supplement, 125,* 2245S–2254S.

WACHS, T. D., BISHRY, Z., MOUSSA, W., YUNIS, F., MCCABE, G., HARRISON, G., SWEFI, I., KIRKSEY, A., GALAL, O., JEROME, N., & SHAHEEN, F. (1995). Nutritional intake and context as predictors of cognition and adaptive behavior of Egyptian school-age children. *International Journal of Behavioral Development, 18,* 425–450.

WACHS, T. D., SIGMAN, M., BISHRY, Z., MOUSSA, W., NEUMANN, C., BUIBO, N., & MCDONALD, M. A. (1992). Caregiver–child interaction patterns in two cultures in relation to nutritional intake. *International Journal of Behavioral Development, 15,* 1–8.

WADDINGTON, C. H. (1957). *The strategy of the genes.* London: Allen & Unwin.

WAGNER, B. M., & PHILLIPS, D. A. (1992). Beyond beliefs: Parent and child behaviors and children's perceived academic competence. *Child Development, 63,* 1380–1391.

WAHLSTEN, D. (1994). The intelligence of heritability. *Canadian Psychology, 35,* 244–259.

WAINRYB, C. (1993). The application of moral judgments to other cultures: Relativism and universality. *Child Development, 64,* 924–933.

WAINRYB, C., & TURIEL, E. (1995). Diversity in social development: Between or within cultures? In M. Killen & D. Hart (Eds.), *Morality in everyday life* (pp. 283–313). New York: Cambridge University Press.

WAKAT, D. K. (1978). Physiological factors of race and sex in sport. In L. K. Bunker & R. J. Rotella (Eds.), *Sport psychology: From theory to practice* (pp. 194–209). Charlotte, VA: University of Virginia. (Proceedings of the 1978 Sport Psychology Institute)

WALBERG, H. J. (1986). Synthesis of research on teaching. In M. C. Wittrock (Ed.), *Handbook of research on teaching* (3rd ed., pp. 214–229). New York: Macmillan.

WALCO, G. A. (1997). Growing pains. *Developmental and Behavioral Pediatrics, 18,* 107–108.

WALDMAN, I. D., WEINBERG, R. A., & SCARR, S. (1994). Racial-group differences in IQ in the Minnesota Transracial Adoption Study: A reply to Levin and Lynn. *Intelligence, 19,* 29–44.

WALES, R. (1990). Children's pictures. In R. Grieve & M. Hughes (Eds.), *Understanding children* (pp. 140–155). Oxford: Blackwell.

WALKER, D., GREENWOOD, C., HART, B., & CARTA, J. (1994). Prediction of school outcomes based on early language production and socioeconomic factors. *Child Development, 65,* 606–621.

WALKER, L. (1995). Sexism in Kohlberg's moral psychology? In W. M. Kurtines & J. L. Gewirtz (Eds.), *Moral development: An introduction* (pp. 83–107). Boston: Allyn and Bacon.

WALKER, L. J. (1989). A longitudinal study of moral reasoning. *Child Development, 60,* 157–166.

WALKER, L. J. (1991). Sex differences in moral reasoning. In W. M. Kurtines & J. L. Gewirtz (Eds.), *Handbook of moral behavior and development* (Vol. 2, pp. 333–364). Hillsdale, NJ: Erlbaum.

WALKER, L. J., & MORAN, T. J. (1991). Moral reasoning in a communist Chinese society. *Journal of Moral Education, 20,* 139–155.

WALKER, L. J., PITTS, R. C., HENNIG, K. H., & MATSUBA, M. K. (1995). Reasoning about morality and real-life moral problems. In M. Killen & D. Hart (Eds.), *Morality in everyday life* (pp. 371–407). New York: Cambridge University Press.

WALKER, L. J., & TAYLOR, J. H. (1991a). Family interactions and the development of moral reasoning. *Child Development, 62,* 264–283.

WALKER, L. J., & TAYLOR, J. H. (1991b). Stage transitions in moral reasoning: A longitudinal study of developmental processes. *Developmental Psychology, 27,* 330–337.

WALLERSTEIN, J. S. (1983). Children of divorce: The psychological tasks of the child. *American Journal of Orthopsychiatry, 53,* 230–243.

WALLERSTEIN, J. S., CORBIN, S. B., & LEWIS, J. M. (1988). Children of divorce: A ten-year study. In E. M. Hetherington & J. Arasteh (Eds.), *Impact of divorce, single parenting, and stepparenting on children* (pp. 198–214). Hillsdale, NJ: Erlbaum.

WALLERSTEIN, J. S., & KELLY, J. B. (1980). *Surviving the break-up: How children and parents cope with divorce.* New York: Basic Books.

WALSH, M. E., & BIBACE, R. (1991). Children's conceptions of AIDS: A developmental analysis. *Journal of Pediatric Psychology, 16,* 273–285.

WARD, L. M. (1995). Talking about sex: Common themes about sexuality in the prime-time television programs children and adolescents view most. *Journal of Youth and Adolescence, 24,* 595–616.

WARK, G. R., & KREBS, D. L. (1996). Gender and dilemma differences in real-life moral judgment. *Developmental Psychology, 32,* 220–230.

WARREN, A. R., & TATE, C. S. (1992). Egocentrism in children's telephone conversations. In R. M. Diaz & L. E. Berk (Eds.), *Private speech: From social interaction to self-regulation* (pp. 245–264). Hillsdale, NJ: Erlbaum.

WARTNER, U. G., GROSSMANN, K., FREMMER-BOMBIK, E., & SUESS, G. (1994). Attachment patterns at age six in south Germany: Predictability from infancy and implications for preschool behavior. *Child Development, 65,* 1014–1027.

WATERMAN, A. S. (1989). Curricula interventions for identity change: Substantive and ethical considerations. *Journal of Adolescence, 12,* 389–400.

WATERS, E., VAUGHN, B. E., POSADA, G., & KONDO-IKEMURA, K. (Eds.). (1995). Caregiving, cultural, and cognitive perspectives on secure-base behavior and working models: New growing points of attachment theory and research. *Monographs of the Society for Research in Child Development, 60* (2–3, Serial No. 244).

WATSON, D. J. (1989). Defining and describing whole language. *Elementary School Journal, 90,* 129–141.

WATSON, J. B., & RAYNOR, R. (1920). Conditioned emotional reactions. *Journal of Experimental Psychology, 3,* 1–14.

WATSON, M. (1990). Aspects of self development as reflected in children's role playing. In D. Cicchetti & M. Beeghly (Eds.), *The self in transition: Infancy to childhood* (pp. 281–307). Chicago: University of Chicago Press.

WAXMAN, S. R. (1995). Words as invitations to form categories: Evidence from 12- to 13-month-old infants. *Cognitive Psychology, 29,* 254–302.

WAXMAN, S. R., & HATCH, T. (1992). Beyond the basics: Preschool children label objects flexibly at multiple hierarchical levels. *Journal of Child Language, 19,* 153–166.

WAXMAN, S. R., & SENGHAS, A. (1992). Relations among word meanings in early lexical development. *Developmental Psychology, 28,* 862–873.

WECHSLER, D. (1989). *Manual for the Wechsler Preschool and Primary Scale of Intelligence–Revised.* New York: Psychological Corporation.

WECHSLER, D. (1991). *Manual for the Wechsler Intelligence Test for Children—III.* New York: Psychological Corporation.

WEHREN, A., DELISI, R., & ARNOLD, M. (1981). The development of noun definition. *Journal of Child Language, 8,* 165–175.

WEINBERG, M. K., & TRONICK, E. Z. (1994). Beyond the face: An empirical study of infant affective configurations of facial, vocal, gestural, and regulatory behaviors. *Child Development, 65,* 1503–1515.

WEINBERG, M. K., & TRONICK, E. Z. (1996). Infant affective reactions to the resumption of maternal interaction after the still face. *Child Development, 67,* 905–914.

WEINBERG, R. A., SCARR, S., & WALDMAN, I. D. (1992). The Minnesota transracial adoption study: A follow-up of IQ test performance at adolescence. *Intelligence, 16,* 117–135.

WEINSTEIN, R. S., MARSHALL, H. H., SHARP, L., & BOTKIN, M. (1987). Pygmalion and the student: Age and classroom differences in children's awareness of teacher expectations. *Child Development, 58,* 1079–1093.

WEISFIELD, G. (1997). Puberty rites as clues to the nature of human adolescence. *Cross-Cultural Research, 31,* 27–54.

WEISFIELD, G. E. (1986). Teaching about sex differences in human behavior and the biological approach in general. *Politics and the Life Sciences, 5,* 36–43.

WEISFIELD, G. E. (1990). Socio-biological patterns of Arab culture. *Ethology and Sociobiology, 11,* 23–49.

WEISNER, T. S. (1996). The 5 to 7 transition as an ecocultural project. In A. J. Sameroff & M. M. Haith (Eds.), *The five to seven year shift* (pp. 295–326). Chicago: University of Chicago Press.

WEISNER, T. S., & WILSON-MITCHELL, J. E. (1990). Nonconventional family lifestyles and sex typing in six-year-olds. *Child Development, 61,* 1915–1933.

WEISSBERG, R. P., & GREENBERG, M. T. (1998). School and community competence-enhancement and prevention programs. In I. E. Sigel & K. A. Renninger (Eds.), *Handbook of child psychology: Vol. 4. Child psychology in practice* (5th ed., 877–954). New York: Wiley.

WEISZ, J. R., CHAIYASIT, W., WEISS, B., EASTMAN, K. L., & JACKSON, E. W. (1995). A multimethod study of problem behavior among Thai and American children in school: Teacher reports versus direct observations. *Child Development, 66,* 402–415.

WELLMAN, H. M. (1988). The early development of memory strategies. In F. F. Weinert & M. Perlmutter (Eds.), *Memory development: Universal changes and individual differences* (pp. 3–29). Hillsdale, NJ: Erlbaum.

WELLMAN, H. M. (1990). *The child's theory of mind.* Cambridge, MA: MIT Press.

WELLMAN, H. M., & HICKLING, A. K. (1994). The mind's "I": Children's conception of the mind as an active agent. *Child Development, 65,* 1564–1580.

WELLMAN, H. M., SOMERVILLE, S. C., & HAAKE, R. J. (1979). Development of search procedures in real-life spatial environments. *Developmental Psychology, 15,* 530–542.

WELLMAN, H. M., & WOOLLEY, J. (1990). From simple desires to ordinary beliefs: The early development of everyday psychology. *Cognition, 35,* 245–275.

WELLS, A. S., & CRAIN, R. L. (1994). Perpetuation theory and the long-term effects of school desegregation. *Review of Educational Research, 64,* 531–555.

WELLS, A. S., CRAIN, R. L., & UCHETELLE, S. (1995). *Stepping over the color line: Black inner-city students in suburban schools.* New Haven: Yale University Press.

WENTZEL, K., & FELDMAN, S. S. (1993). Parental predictors of boys' self-restraint and motivation to achieve at school: A longitudinal study. *Journal of Early Adolescence, 13,* 183–203.

WENTZEL, K. R., & ASHER, S. R. (1995). The academic lives of neglected, rejected, popular, and controversial children. *Child Development, 66,* 754–763.

WERKER, J. F., PEGG, J. E., & MCLEOD, P. J. (1994). A cross-language investigation of infant preference for infant-directed communication. *Infant Behavior and Development, 17,* 323–333.

WERNER, E. E. (1989, April). Children of the garden island. *Scientific American, 260(4),* 106–111.

WERNER, E. E., & SMITH, R. S. (1982). *Vulnerable but invincible: A study of resilient children.* New York: McGraw-Hill.

WERNER, E. E., & SMITH, R. S. (1992). *Overcoming the odds: High risk children from birth to adulthood.* Ithaca, NY: Cornell University Press.

WERTSCH, J. V., & TULVISTE, P. (1992). L. S. Vygotsky and contemporary developmental psychology. *Developmental Psychology, 28,* 548–557.

WESLEY, B. D., VAN DEN BERG, B. J., & REECE, E. A. (1993). The effect of forceps delivery on cognitive development. *American Journal of Obstetrics and Gynecology, 169,* 1091–1095.

WEST, L. L. (1991). Introduction. In L. L. West (Ed.), *Effective strategies for dropout prevention of at-risk youth* (pp. 1–42). Gaithersburg, MD: Aspen.

WHALEN, C. K., HENKER, B., BURGESS, S., & O'NEIL, R. (1995). Young people talk about AIDS: "When you get sick, you stay sick." *Journal of Clinical Child Psychology, 24,* 338–345.

WHEELER, M. D. (1991). Physical changes of puberty. *Endocrinology and Metabolism Clinics of North America, 20,* 1–14.

WHITE, B., & HELD, R. (1966). Plasticity of sensorimotor development in the human infant. In J. F. Rosenblith & W. Allinsmith (Eds.), *The causes of behavior* (pp. 60–70). Boston: Allyn and Bacon.

WHITE, J. L., MOFFITT, T. E., CASPI, A., BARTUSCH, D. J., NEEDLES, D. J., & STOUTHAMER-LOEBER, M. (1996). Measuring impulsivity and examining its relationship to delinquency. *Journal of Abnormal Psychology, 103,* 192–205.

WHITE, S. H. (1976). The active organism in theoretical behaviorism. *Human Development 19,* 99–107.

WHITE, S. H. (1992). G. Stanley Hall: From philosophy to developmental psychology. *Developmental Psychology, 28,* 25–34.

WHITEHEAD, J. R., & CORBIN, C. B. (1997). Self-esteem in children and youth: The role of sport and physical education. In K. R. Fox (Ed.), *The physical self: From motivation to well-being* (pp. 175–204). Champaign, IL: Human Kinetics.

WHITEHURST, G. J., ARNOLD, D. S., EPSTEIN, J. N., ANGELL, A. L., SMITH, M., & FISCHEL, J. E. (1994). A picture book reading intervention in day care and home for children from low-income families. *Developmental Psychology, 30,* 679–689.

WHITEHURST, G. J., & VASTA, R. (1975). Is language acquired through imitation? *Journal of Psycholinguistic Research, 4,* 37–59.

WHITING, B., & EDWARDS, C. P. (1988a). *Children in different worlds.* Cambridge, MA: Harvard University Press.

WHITING, B., & EDWARDS, C. P. (1988b). A cross-cultural analysis of sex differences in the behavior of children aged 3 through 11. In G. Handel (Ed.), *Childhood socialization* (pp. 281–297). New York: Aldine de Gruyter.

WHITNEY, M. P., & THOMAN, E. B. (1993). Early sleep patterns of premature infants are differentially related to later developmental disabilities. *Journal of Developmental and Behavioral Pediatrics, 14,* 71–80.

WHITNEY, M. P., & THOMAN, E. B. (1994). Sleep in premature and full-term infants from 24-hour home recordings. *Infant Behavior and Development, 17,* 223–234.

WHYTE, J., & SCHAEFER, C. (1995). Introduction to sleep and its disorders. In C. E. Schaefer (Ed.), *Clinical handbook of sleep disorders in children* (pp. 1–14). Northvale, NJ: Aronson.

WIGFIELD, A., & ECCLES, J. S. (1994). Children's competence beliefs, achievement values, and genderal self-esteem change across elementary and middle school. *Journal of Early Adolescence, 14,* 107–138.

WIGFIELD, R. E., FLEMING, P. J., BERRY, P. J., RUDD, P. T., & GOLDING, J. (1992). Can the fall in Avon's sudden infant death rate be explained by changes in sleeping position? *British Medical Journal, 304,* 282–283.

WILCOX, A. J., WEINBERG, C. R., & BAIRD, D. D. (1995). Timing of sexual intercourse in relation to ovulation: Effects on the probability of conception, survival of the pregnancy, and sex of the baby. *New England Journal of Medicine, 333,* 1517–1519.

WILENSKY, H. L. (1983). Evaluating research and politics: Political legitimacy and consensus as missing variables in the assessment of social policy. In E. Spiro & E. Yuchtman-Yaar (Eds.), *Evaluating the welfare state: Social and political perspectives* (pp. 51–74). New York: Academic Press.

WILLE, D. E. (1991). Relation of preterm birth with quality of infant–mother attachment at one year. *Infant Behavior and Development, 14,* 227–240.

WILLER, B., HOFFERTH, S. L., KISKER, E. E., DIVINE-HAWKINS, P., FARQUHAR, E., & GLANTZ, F. B. (1991). *The demand and supply of child care in 1990: Joint findings from the National Child Care Survey 1990 and A Profile of Child Care Settings.* Washington, DC: National Association for the Education of Young Children.

WILLIAMS, B. C., & KOTCH, J. B. (1990). Excess injury mortality among children in the United States: Comparison of recent international statistics. *Pediatrics, 86* (6, Pt. 2), 1067–1073.

WILLIAMS, E., & RADIN, N. (1993). Paternal involvement, maternal employment, and adolescents' academic achievement: An 11-year follow-up. *American Journal of Orthopsychiatry, 63,* 306–312.

WILLS, T. A., MCNAMARA, G., VACCARO, D., & HIRKY, A. E. (1996). Escalated substance use: A longitudinal grouping analysis from early to middle adolescence. *Journal of Abnormal Psychology, 105,* 166–180.

WILSON, G. T., HEFFERNAN, K., & BLACK, C. M. D. (1996). Eating disorders. In E. J. Mash & R. A. Barkley (Eds.), *Child psychopathology* (pp. 541–571). New York: Guilford.

WILSON, M. N., GREENE-BATES, C., MCKIM, L., SIMMONS, T. A., CURRY-EL, J., & HINTON, I. D. (1995). African American family life: The dynamics of interactions, relationships, and roles. In M. N. Wilson (Ed.), *African American family life: Its structural and ecological aspects* (pp. 5–21). San Francisco: Jossey-Bass.

WILSON, R., & CAIRNS, E. (1988). Sex-role attributes, perceived competence and the development of depression in adolescence. *Journal of Child Psychology and Psychiatry, 29,* 635–650.

WILSON, R. S. (1983). The Louisville Twin Study: Developmental synchronies in behavior. *Child Development, 54,* 298–316.

WILSON, W. J. (1991). Studying inner-city social dislocations: The challenge of public agenda research. *American Sociological Review, 56,* 1–14.

WINDLE, M. A. (1994). A study of friendship characteristics and problem behaviors among middle adolescents. *Child Development, 65,* 1764–1777.

WINDSCHITL, M. (1998). The WWW and classroom research: What path should we take? *Educational Researcher, 27*(1), 28–33..

WINN, S., ROKER, D., & COLEMAN, J. (1995). Knowledge about puberty and sexual development in 11–16 year-olds: Implications for health and sex education in schools. *Educational Studies, 21,* 187–201.

WINNER, E. (1986, August). Where pelicans kiss seals. *Psychology Today, 20*(8), 25–35.

WINNER, E. (1988). *The point of words: Children's understanding of metaphor and irony.* Cambridge, MA: Harvard University Press.

WINNER, E. (1996). *Gifted children: Myths and realities.* New York: Basic Books.

WINTHROP, R. H. (1991). *Dictionary of concepts in cultural anthropology.* New York: Greenwood Press.

WINTRE, M. G., & VALLANCE, D. D. (1994). A developmental sequence in the comprehension of emotions: Intensity, multiple emotions, and valence. *Developmental Psychology, 30,* 509–514.

WITELSON, S. F., & KIGAR, D. L. (1988). Anatomical development of the corpus callosum in humans: A review with reference to sex and cognition. In D. L. Molfese & S. J. Segalowitz (Eds.), *Brain lateralization in children* (pp. 35–57). New York: Guilford Press.

WOLF, A., & LOZOFF, B. (1989). Object attachment, thumb-sucking, and the passage to sleep. *Journal of the American Academy of Child and Adolescent Psychiatry, 28,* 287–292.

WOLF, A. W., JIMENEZ, E., & LOZOFF, B. (1994). No evidence of developmental ill effects of low-level lead exposure in a developing country. *Developmental and Behavioral Pediatrics, 15,* 224–231.

WOLFF, P. H. (1966). The causes, controls and organization of behavior in the neonate. *Psychological Issues, 5*(1, Serial No. 17).

WOLPE, J., & PLAUD, J. J. (1997). Pavlov's contributions to behavior therapy: The obvious and not so obvious. *American Psychologist, 52,* 966–972.

WOOD, D. J. (1989). Social interaction as tutoring. In M. H. Bornstein & J. S. Bruner (Eds.), *Interaction in human development* (pp. 59–80). Hillsdale, NJ: Erlbaum.

WOODWARD, A. L., MARKMAN, E. M., & FITZSIMMONS, C. M. (1994). Rapid word learning in 13- and 18-month-olds. *Developmental Psychology, 30,* 553–566.

WRIGHT, J. C., & HUSTON, A. C. (1995, June). *Effects of educational TV viewing of lower income preschoolers on academic skills, school readiness, and school adjustment one to three years later.* Report to Children's Television Workshop, Center for Research on the Influences of Television on Children, University of Kansas, Lawrence.

WRIGHT, J. C., HUSTON, A. C., REITZ, A. L., & PIEMYAT, S. (1994). Young children's perceptions of television reality: Determinants and developmental differences. *Developmental Psychology, 30,* 229–239.

WRIGHT, J. W. (Ed.). (1997). *The universal almanac 1997.* Kansas City: Andrews and McMeel.

WURTELE, S. K. (1996). Health promotion. In M. C. Roberts (Ed.), *Handbook of pediatric psychology* (2nd ed., pp. 200–216). New York: Guilford.

WYMAN, P. A., COWEN, E. L., WORK, W. C., RAOOF, A., GRIBBLE, P. A., PARKER, G. R., & WANNON, M. (1992). Interviews with children who experienced major life stress: Family and child attributes that predict resilient outcomes. *Journal of the American Academy of Child and Adolescent Psychiatry, 31,* 904–910.

XENAKIS, E. M. J., PIPER, J. M., CONWAY, D. L., & LANGER, O. (1997). Induction of labor in the nineties—conquering the unfavorable cervix. *Obstetrics and Gynecology, 90,* 235–239.

YANG, B., OLLENDICK, T. H., DONG, Q., XIA, Y., & LIN, L. (1995). Only children and children with siblings in the People's Republic of China: Levels of fear, anxiety, and depression. *Child Development, 66,* 1301–1311.

YARROW, A. L. (1991). *Latecomers: Children of parents over 35.* New York: Free Press.

YARROW, M. R., SCOTT, P. M., & WAXLER, C. Z. (1973). Learning concern for others. *Developmental Psychology, 8,* 240–260.

YAZIGI, R. A., ODEM, R. R., & POLAKOSKI, K. L. (1991). Demonstration of specific binding of cocaine to human spermatozoa. *Journal of the American Medical Association, 266,* 1956–1959.

YESALIS, C.E., BARSUKIEWICZ, C.K., KOPSTEIN, A.N., & BAHRKE, M.S. (1997). Trends in anabolic–androgenic steroid use among adolescents. *Archives of Pediatrics & Adolescent Medicine, 151,* 1197–1206.

YIP, R., SCANLON, K., & TROW-BRIDGE, F. (1993). Trends and patterns in height and weight status of low-income U.S. children. *Critical Reviews in Food Science and Nutrition, 33,* 409–421.

YIRMIYA, N., & SHULMAN, C. (1996). Seriation, conservation, and theory of mind abilities in individuals with autism, individuals with mental retardation, and normally developing children. *Child Development, 67,* 2045–2059.

YIRMIYA, N., SOLOMONICA-LEVI, D., & SHULMAN, C. (1996). The ability to manipulate behavior and to understand manipulation of beliefs: A comparison of individuals with autism, mental retardation, and normal development. *Developmental Psychology, 32,* 62–69.

YOGMAN, M. W. (1981). Development of the father–infant relationship. In H. Fitzgerald, B. Lester, & M. W. Yogman (Eds.), *Theory and research in behavioral pediatrics* (Vol. 1, pp. 221–279). New York: Plenum.

YONAS, A., GRANRUD, E. C., ARTERBERRY, M. E., & HANSON, B. L. (1986). Infants' distance perception from linear perspective and texture gradients. *Infant Behavior and Development, 9,* 247–256.

YOUNG, D. (1997). A new push to reduce cesareans in the United States. *Birth, 24,* 1–3.

YOUNGBLADE, L. M., & DUNN, J. (1995). Individual differences in young children's pretend play with mother and sibling: Links to relationships and understanding of other people's feelings and beliefs. *Child Development, 66,* 1472–1492.

YOUNGER, B. A. (1985). The segregation of items into categories by ten-month-old infants. *Child Development, 56,* 1574–1583.

YOUNGER, B. A. (1993). Understanding category members as "the same sort of thing": Explicit categorization in ten-month infants. *Child Development, 64,* 309–320.

YOUNISS, J. (1980). *Parents and peers in social development: A Piagetian-Sullivan perspective.* Chicago: University of Chicago Press.

YUILL, N., & PERNER, J. (1988). Intentionality and knowledge in children's judgments of actor's responsibility and recipient's emotional reaction. *Developmental Psychology, 24,* 358–365.

ZABIN, L. S., & HAYWARD, S. C. (1993). *Adolescent sexual behavior and childbearing.* Newbury Park, CA: Sage.

ZAHN-WAXLER, C., & RADKE-YARROW, M. (1990). The origins of empathic concern. *Motivation and Emotion, 14,* 107–130.

ZAHN-WAXLER, C., & ROBINSON, J. (1995). Empathy and guilt: Early origins of feelings of responsibility. In J. P. Tangney & K. W. Fischer (Eds.), *Self-conscious emotions* (pp. 143–173). New York: Guilford.

ZAHN-WAXLER, C., IANNOTTI, R. J., CUMMINGS, E. M., & DENHAM, S. (1990a). Antecedents of problem behaviors in children of depressed mothers. *Development and Psychopathology, 2,* 271–291.

ZAHN-WAXLER, C., KOCHANSKA, G., KRUPNICK, J., & McKNEW, D. (1990b). Patterns of guilt in children of depressed and well mothers. *Developmental Psychology, 26,* 51–59.

ZAHN-WAXLER, C., RADKE-YARROW, M., & KING, R. M. (1979). Child-rearing and children's prosocial initiations toward victims of distress. *Child Development, 50,* 319–330.

ZAHN-WAXLER, C., RADKE-YARROW, M., WAGNER, E., & CHAPMAN, M. (1992).

Development of concern for others. *Developmental Psychology, 28,* 126–136.

ZAJONC, R. B., & MULLALLY, P. R. (1997). Birth order: Reconciling conflicting effects. *American Psychologist, 52,* 685–699.

ZAMETKIN, A. J. (1995). Attention-deficit disorder: Born to be hyperactive? *Journal of the American Medical Association, 273,* 1871–1874.

ZAMETKIN, A. J., NORDAHL, T. E., GROSS, M., KING, A. C., SEMPLE, W. E., RUMSEY, J., HAMBURGER, S., & COHEN, R. M. (1990). Cerebral glucose metabolism in adults with hyperactivity of childhood onset. *New England Journal of Medicine, 323,* 1413–1415.

ZANI, B. (1993). Dating and interpersonal relationships in adolescence. In S. Jackson & H. Rodriguez-Tomé (Eds.), *Adolescence and its social worlds* (pp. 95–119). Hillsdale, NJ: Erlbaum.

ZEISEL, S. H. (1986). Dietary influences on neurotransmission. *Advances in Pediatrics, 33,* 23–48.

ZELAZO, N. A., ZELAZO, P. R., COHEN, K. M., & ZELAZO, P. D. (1993). Specificity of practice effects on elementary neuromotor patterns. *Developmental Psychology, 29,* 686–691.

ZELAZO, P. R. (1983). The development of walking: New findings on old assumptions. *Journal of Motor Behavior, 2,* 99–137.

ZESKIND, P. S., & RAMEY, C. T. (1978). Fetal malnutrition: An experimental study of its consequences on infant development in two caregiving environments. *Child Development, 49,* 1155–1162.

ZESKIND, P. S., & RAMEY, C. T. (1981). Preventing intellectual and interactional sequelae of fetal malnutrition: A longitudinal, transactional, and synergistic approach to development. *Child Development, 52,* 213–218.

ZHANG, J., CAI, W., & LEE, D. J. (1992). Occupational hazards and pregnancy outcomes. *American Journal of Industrial Medicine, 21,* 397–408.

ZIGLER, E., & HALL, N. W. (1989). Physical child abuse in America: Past, present, and future. In D. Cicchetti & V. Carlson (Eds.), *Child maltreat-*

ment (pp. 203–253). New York: Cambridge University Press.

ZIGLER, E., & STYFCO, S. J. (1994). Head Start: Criticisms in a constructive context. *American Psychologist, 49,* 127–132.

ZIGLER, E., & STYFCO, S. J. (1995). Is the Perry Preschool better than Head Start? Yes and no. *Early Childhood Research Quarterly, 9,* 269–287.

ZIGLER, E. F., & FINN-STEVENSON, M. E. (1992). Applied developmental psychology. In M. H. Bornstein & M. E. Lamb (Eds.), *Developmental psychology: An advanced textbook* (2nd ed., pp. 677–729). Hillsdale, NJ: Erlbaum.

ZILL, N., DAVIES, M., & DALY, M. (1994). *Viewing of Sesame Street by preschool children in the United States and its relationship to school readiness.* Rockville, MD: Westat.

ZILLMAN, D., BRYANT, J., & HUSTON, A. C. (1994). *Media, family, and children.* Hillsdale, NJ: Erlbaum.

ZIMMERMAN, B. J., BONNER, S., & KOVACH, R. (1996). *Developing self-regulated learners: Beyond achievement to self-efficacy.* Washington, DC: American Psychological Association.

ZIMMERMAN, B. J., & RISEMBERG, R. (1997). Self-regulatory dimensions of academic learning and motivation. In G. D. Phye (Ed.), *Handbook of academic learning: Construction of knowledge* (pp. 105–125). San Diego: Academic Press.

ZIMMERMAN, M. A., & ARUNKUMAR, R. (1994). Resiliency research: Implications for schools and policy. *Social Policy Report of the Society for Research in Child Development, 8(4).*

ZIMMERMAN, M. A., COPE-LAND, L. A., SHOPE, J. T., & DIELMAN, T. E. (1997). A longitudinal study of self-esteem: Implications for adolescent development. *Journal of Youth and Adolescence, 26,* 117–141.

ZINS, J. E., GARCIA, V. F., TUCHFARBER, B. S., CLARK, K. M., & LAURENCE, S. C. (1994). Preventing injury in children and adolescents. In R. J. Simeonsson (Ed.), *Risk, resilience, and prevention: Promoting the well-being of all children* (pp. 183–202). Baltimore: Paul H. Brookes.